# Lecture Notes in Computer Science 4563

*Commenced Publication in 1973*
Founding and Former Series Editors:
Gerhard Goos, Juris Hartmanis, and Jan van Leeuwen

Randall Shumaker (Ed.)

# Virtual Reality

Second International Conference, ICVR 2007
Held as part of HCI International 2007
Beijing, China, July 22-27, 2007
Proceedings

Springer

Volume Editor

Randall Shumaker
University of Central Florida
Institute for Simulation & Training
3100 Technology Parkway and 3280 Progress Dr.
Orlando, FL 32826, USA
E-mail: shumaker@ist.ucf.edu

Library of Congress Control Number: 2007929636

CR Subject Classification (1998): H.5, H.4, I.3, I.2, C.3, I.4, I.6

LNCS Sublibrary: SL 3 – Information Systems and Application, incl. Internet/Web and HCI

ISSN 0302-9743
ISBN-10 3-540-73334-5 Springer Berlin Heidelberg New York
ISBN-13 978-3-540-73334-8 Springer Berlin Heidelberg New York



Springer is a part of Springer Science+Business Media

springer.com


Printed in Germany

Typesetting: Camera-ready by author, data conversion by Scientific Publishing Services, Chennai, India
Printed on acid-free paper SPIN: 12083091 06/3180 5 4 3 2 1 0

# Foreword

The 12th International Conference on Human-Computer Interaction, HCI International 2007, was held in Beijing, P.R. China, 22-27 July 2007, jointly with the Symposium on Human Interface (Japan) 2007, the 7th International Conference on Engineering Psychology and Cognitive Ergonomics, the 4th International Conference on Universal Access in Human-Computer Interaction, the 2nd International Conference on Virtual Reality, the 2nd International Conference on Usability and Internationalization, the 2nd International Conference on Online Communities and Social Computing, the 3rd International Conference on Augmented Cognition, and the 1st International Conference on Digital Human Modeling.

A total of 3403 individuals from academia, research institutes, industry and governmental agencies from 76 countries submitted contributions, and 1681 papers, judged to be of high scientific quality, were included in the program. These papers address the latest research and development efforts and highlight the human aspects of design and use of computing systems. The papers accepted for presentation thoroughly cover the entire field of Human-Computer Interaction, addressing major advances in knowledge and effective use of computers in a variety of application areas.

This volume, edited by Randall Shumaker, contains papers in the thematic area of Virtual Reality, addressing the following major topics:

- 3D Rendering and Visualization
- Interacting and Navigating in Virtual and Augmented Environments
- Industrial Applications of Virtual Reality
- Health, Cultural, Educational and Entertainment Applications

The remaining volumes of the HCI International 2007 proceedings are:

- Volume 1, LNCS 4550, Interaction Design and Usability, edited by Julie A. Jacko
- Volume 2, LNCS 4551, Interaction Platforms and Techniques, edited by Julie A. Jacko
- Volume 3, LNCS 4552, HCI Intelligent Multimodal Interaction Environments, edited by Julie A. Jacko
- Volume 4, LNCS 4553, HCI Applications and Services, edited by Julie A. Jacko
- Volume 5, LNCS 4554, Coping with Diversity in Universal Access, edited by Constantine Stephanidis
- Volume 6, LNCS 4555, Universal Access to Ambient Interaction, edited by Constantine Stephanidis
- Volume 7, LNCS 4556, Universal Access to Applications and Services, edited by Constantine Stephanidis
- Volume 8, LNCS 4557, Methods, Techniques and Tools in Information Design, edited by Michael J. Smith and Gavriel Salvendy
- Volume 9, LNCS 4558, Interacting in Information Environments, edited by Michael J. Smith and Gavriel Salvendy

- Volume 10, LNCS 4559, HCI and Culture, edited by Nuray Aykin
- Volume 11, LNCS 4560, Global and Local User Interfaces, edited by Nuray Aykin
- Volume 12, LNCS 4561, Digital Human Modeling, edited by Vincent G. Duffy
- Volume 13, LNAI 4562, Engineering Psychology and Cognitive Ergonomics, edited by Don Harris
- Volume 15, LNCS 4564, Online Communities and Social Computing, edited by Douglas Schuler
- Volume 16, LNAI 4565, Foundations of Augmented Cognition 3rd Edition, edited by Dylan D. Schmorrow and Leah M. Reeves
- Volume 17, LNCS 4566, Ergonomics and Health Aspects of Work with Computers, edited by Marvin J. Dainoff

I would like to thank the Program Chairs and the members of the Program Boards of all Thematic Areas, listed below, for their contribution to the highest scientific quality and the overall success of the HCI International 2007 Conference.

## Ergonomics and Health Aspects of Work with Computers

**Program Chair: Marvin J. Dainoff**

Arne Aaras, Norway
Pascale Carayon, USA
Barbara G.F. Cohen, USA
Wolfgang Friesdorf, Germany
Martin Helander, Singapore
Ben-Tzion Karsh, USA
Waldemar Karwowski, USA
Peter Kern, Germany
Danuta Koradecka, Poland
Kari Lindstrom, Finland
Holger Luczak, Germany
Aura C. Matias, Philippines
Kyung (Ken) Park, Korea
Michelle Robertson, USA
Steven L. Sauter, USA
Dominique L. Scapin, France
Michael J. Smith, USA
Naomi Swanson, USA
Peter Vink, The Netherlands
John Wilson, UK

## Human Interface and the Management of Information

**Program Chair: Michael J. Smith**

Lajos Balint, Hungary
Gunilla Bradley, Sweden
Hans-Jörg Bullinger, Germany
Alan H.S. Chan, Hong Kong
Klaus-Peter Fähnrich, Germany
Michitaka Hirose, Japan
Yoshinori Horie, Japan
Richard Koubek, USA
Yasufumi Kume, Japan
Mark Lehto, USA
Jiye Mao, P.R. China
Robert Proctor, USA
Youngho Rhee, Korea
Anxo Cereijo Roibás, UK
Francois Sainfort, USA
Katsunori Shimohara, Japan
Tsutomu Tabe, Japan
Alvaro Taveira, USA
Kim-Phuong L. Vu, USA
Tomio Watanabe, Japan
Sakae Yamamoto, Japan
Hidekazu Yoshikawa, Japan

Jon Gunderson, USA
Andreas Holzinger, Austria
Arthur Karshmer, USA
Simeon Keates, USA
George Kouroupetroglou, Greece
Jonathan Lazar, USA
Seongil Lee, Korea
Gregg Vanderheiden, USA
Gerhard Weber, Germany
Harald Weber, Germany
Toshiki Yamaoka, Japan
Mary Zajicek, UK
Panayiotis Zaphiris, UK

## Virtual Reality

**Program Chair: Randall Shumaker**

Terry Allard, USA
Pat Banerjee, USA
Robert S. Kennedy, USA
Heidi Kroemker, Germany
Ben Lawson, USA
Ming Lin, USA
Bowen Loftin, USA
Holger Luczak, Germany
Annie Luciani, France
Gordon Mair, UK
Ulrich Neumann, USA
Albert "Skip" Rizzo, USA
Lawrence Rosenblum, USA
Dylan Schmorrow, USA
Kay Stanney, USA
Susumu Tachi, Japan
John Wilson, UK
Wei Zhang, P.R. China
Michael Zyda, USA

## Usability and Internationalization

**Program Chair: Nuray Aykin**

Genevieve Bell, USA
Alan Chan, Hong Kong
Apala Lahiri Chavan, India
Jori Clarke, USA
Pierre-Henri Dejean, France
Susan Dray, USA
Paul Fu, USA
Emilie Gould, Canada
Sung H. Han, South Korea
Veikko Ikonen, Finland
Richard Ishida, UK
Esin Kiris, USA
Tobias Komischke, Germany
Masaaki Kurosu, Japan
James R. Lewis, USA
Rungtai Lin, Taiwan
Aaron Marcus, USA
Allen E. Milewski, USA
Patrick O'Sullivan, Ireland
Girish V. Prabhu, India
Kerstin Röse, Germany
Eunice Ratna Sari, Indonesia
Supriya Singh, Australia
Serengul Smith, UK
Denise Spacinsky, USA
Christian Sturm, Mexico
Adi B. Tedjasaputra, Singapore
Myung Hwan Yun, South Korea
Chen Zhao, P.R. China

## Online Communities and Social Computing

**Program Chair: Douglas Schuler**

Chadia Abras, USA
Lecia Barker, USA
Amy Bruckman, USA
Peter van den Besselaar, The Netherlands
Peter Day, UK
Fiorella De Cindio, Italy
John Fung, P.R. China
Michael Gurstein, USA
Tom Horan, USA
Piet Kommers, The Netherlands
Jonathan Lazar, USA
Stefanie Lindstaedt, Austria
Diane Maloney-Krichmar, USA
Isaac Mao, P.R. China
Hideyuki Nakanishi, Japan
A. Ant Ozok, USA
Jennifer Preece, USA
Partha Pratim Sarker, Bangladesh
Gilson Schwartz, Brazil
Sergei Stafeev, Russia
F.F. Tusubira, Uganda
Cheng-Yen Wang, Taiwan

## Augmented Cognition

**Program Chair: Dylan D. Schmorrow**

Kenneth Boff, USA
Joseph Cohn, USA
Blair Dickson, UK
Henry Girolamo, USA
Gerald Edelman, USA
Eric Horvitz, USA
Wilhelm Kincses, Germany
Amy Kruse, USA
Lee Kollmorgen, USA
Dennis McBride, USA
Jeffrey Morrison, USA
Denise Nicholson, USA
Dennis Proffitt, USA
Harry Shum, P.R. China
Kay Stanney, USA
Roy Stripling, USA
Michael Swetnam, USA
Robert Taylor, UK
John Wagner, USA

## Digital Human Modeling

**Program Chair: Vincent G. Duffy**

Norm Badler, USA
Heiner Bubb, Germany
Don Chaffin, USA
Kathryn Cormican, Ireland
Andris Freivalds, USA
Ravindra Goonetilleke, Hong Kong
Anand Gramopadhye, USA
Sung H. Han, South Korea
Pheng Ann Heng, Hong Kong
Dewen Jin, P.R. China
Kang Li, USA
Zhizhong Li, P.R. China
Lizhuang Ma, P.R. China
Timo Maatta, Finland
J. Mark Porter, UK
Jim Potvin, Canada
Jean-Pierre Verriest, France
Zhaoqi Wang, P.R. China
Xiugan Yuan, P.R. China
Shao-Xiang Zhang, P.R. China
Xudong Zhang, USA

In addition to the members of the Program Boards above, I also wish to thank the following volunteer external reviewers: Kelly Hale, David Kobus, Amy Kruse, Cali Fidopiastis and Karl Van Orden from the USA, Mark Neerincx and Marc Grootjen from the Netherlands, Wilhelm Kincses from Germany, Ganesh Bhutkar and Mathura Prasad from India, Frederick Li from the UK, and Dimitris Grammenos, Angeliki Kastrinaki, Iosif Klironomos, Alexandros Mourouzis, and Stavroula Ntoa from Greece.

This conference could not have been possible without the continuous support and advise of the Conference Scientific Advisor, Prof. Gavriel Salvendy, as well as the dedicated work and outstanding efforts of the Communications Chair and Editor of HCI International News, Abbas Moallem, and of the members of the Organizational Board from P.R. China, Patrick Rau (Chair), Bo Chen, Xiaolan Fu, Zhibin Jiang, Congdong Li, Zhenjie Liu, Mowei Shen, Yuanchun Shi, Hui Su, Linyang Sun, Ming Po Tham, Ben Tsiang, Jian Wang, Guangyou Xu, Winnie Wanli Yang, Shuping Yi, Kan Zhang, and Wei Zho.

I would also like to thank for their contribution towards the organization of the HCI International 2007 Conference the members of the Human Computer Interaction Laboratory of ICS-FORTH, and in particular Margherita Antona, Maria Pitsoulaki, George Paparoulis, Maria Bouhli, Stavroula Ntoa and George Margetis.

Constantine Stephanidis
General Chair, HCI International 2007

# HCI International 2009

The 13th International Conference on Human-Computer Interaction, HCI International 2009, will be held jointly with the affiliated Conferences in San Diego, California, USA, in the Town and Country Resort & Convention Center, 19-24 July 2009. It will cover a broad spectrum of themes related to Human Computer Interaction, including theoretical issues, methods, tools, processes and case studies in HCI design, as well as novel interaction techniques, interfaces and applications. The proceedings will be published by Springer. For more information, please visit the Conference website: http://www.hcii2009.org/

General Chair
Professor Constantine Stephanidis
ICS-FORTH and University of Crete
Heraklion, Crete, Greece
Email: program@hcii2009.org

# Preface

I would like to thank all the reviewers and the contributors, who put so much effort into producing excellent papers from which to select. I would also like to particularly acknowledge Prof. Kay Stanney, Dr. Lawrence Rosenblum, Dr. Dylan Schmorrow and Dr. Bowen Loftin as long term colleagues and contributors to making this VR conference successful.

Randall Shumaker, Editor

# Table of Contents

## Part 1: 3D Rendering and Visualization

## Part 2: Interacting and Navigating in Virtual and Augmented Environments

## Part 3: Industrial Applications of Virtual Reality

# Part 1

# 3D Rendering and Visualization

# The Storage Independent Polygonal Mesh Simplification System

Hung-Kuang Chen[1], Chin-Shyurng Fahn[2], and Ming-Bo Lin[3]

[1] Dept. of Electronic Engineering, National Chin-Yi University of Technology, Taichung, Taiwan, ROC.
[2] Dept. of Computer Science and Information Engineering, National Taiwan University of Science and Technology, Taipei, Taiwan, R.O.C.
[3] Dept. of Electronic Engineering, National Taiwan University of Science and Technology, Taipei, Taiwan, R.O.C.
hankchentw@gmail.com, csfahn@ntust.edu.tw, mblin@et.ntust.edu.tw

**Abstract.** Traditional simplification algorithms operate either in the main memory or in the disk space. In this paper, we propose a novel storage independent polygonal mesh simplification system (SIPMSS). The new system offers an advanced memory utilization scheme and efficient storage-independent primitives that achieve constant main memory footprint and excellent runtime efficiency. It not only provides a very flexible platform for both in-core and out-of-core simplification algorithms but also permits very efficient integration of various types of simplification algorithms. The results presented in the section of experiments further approve its effectiveness and usefulness for both in-core and out-of-core of simplification.

## 1 Introduction

The polygonal mesh has been the de facto standard representation of 3D objects owing to its mathematical simplicity and the direct support of rendering hardware [1]. For this reason, the majority of graphics algorithms for manipulating surfaces are designed for polygonal meshes, and most contemporary methods for model acquisition start with the construction of polygonal meshes. However, the above representation has an inherent limitation to the realism of a rendered scene imposed by the maximum number of polygons that can be processed by the rendering hardware at an interactive rate.

To overcome such a limitation, one can either minimize the number of geometric/topological primitives of each object within an allowable range of approximation errors or maximize the use of limited rendering resources by adaptively adjusting the resolution of each object according to their contribution to the rendered image. The former can be achieved by applying polygonal mesh simplification to automatically generate an optimized approximation of an object. The latter is essentially the basic concept of the level of detail (LOD) scheme originally suggested by Clark [2], which usually requires the generation of LOD representations through the use of polygonal mesh simplification.

R. Shumaker (Ed.): Virtual Reality, HCII 2007, LNCS 4563, pp. 3–12, 2007.

Most traditional polygonal mesh simplification algorithms operate either in the main memory space or the disk space. Those who place their data inside the main memory space are called in-core algorithms; on the contrary, those who place their data in the external memory space such as disks are called out-of-core algorithms. In general, in-core algorithms featuring with high performance memory access efficiency mostly perform memory access intensive complex operations with a higher degree of optimization [3-6]. Hence, most of these algorithms are capable of producing very good quality outputs. However, owing to the limited main memory space, this type of algorithms is not able to deal with high-resolution scanned objects with a huge amount of polygons.

On the other hand, out-of-core algorithms mostly apply a spatial partitioning scheme to lower the memory access frequency [7,8]. Among these algorithms, the grid-based vertex re-sampling scheme has the best run-time efficiency. Nevertheless, it comes at the cost of inferior output quality when the input mesh is sampled with a low resolution grid. For high-resolution outputs using high-resolution grids, the runtime efficiency of such a method decreases radically. For instance, if an $n \times n \times n$ grid is used for re-sampling the mesh, both the time and space complexities are $O(n^3)$.

A compromise approach proposed by Garland et al. suggested a two-phase simplification that begins with a uniform-grid out-of-core vertex-clustering phase similar to the OoCS method proposed by Lindstrom et al. followed by an in-core iterative edge collapse phase [9]. In principle, the memory cost of their method is related to the grid resolution of the first phase that affects the quality of approximations in the first phase. Lower resolution may greatly reduce the quality of resulting approximations. However, higher resolution may require much more memory space. The increase of grid resolution may raise the memory cost by $O(n^3)$.

In this paper, we propose a novel storage independent polygonal mesh simplification system (SIPMSS). The new system offers an advanced memory utilization scheme and efficient storage-independent primitives that achieve constant main memory footprint and excellent runtime efficiency. It not only provides a very flexible platform for both in-core and out-of-core simplification algorithms, but also permits very efficient integration of various types of simplification algorithms.

## 2 System Overview

To provide a storage independent environment for various types of polygonal mesh simplification algorithms, we extend the idea from our cache-based approach [10] by

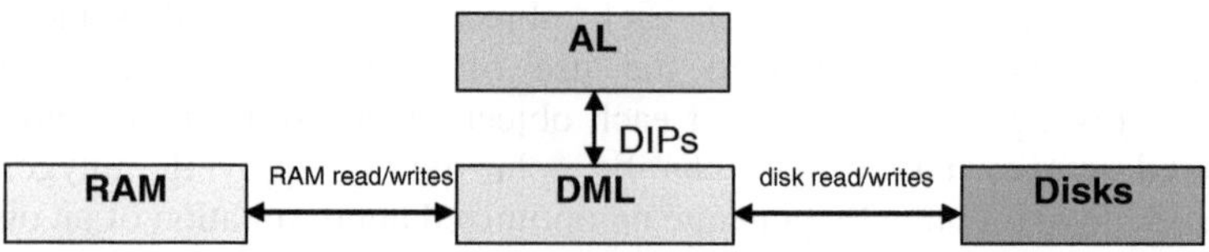


**Fig. 1.** The storage independent polygonal mesh simplification system

dividing the simplification system into two layers: the *algorithm layer* (AL) and *data management layer* (DML). A block diagram of this system is shown in Fig. 1.

The simplification algorithms are implemented in the AL where a set of *device independent primitives* (DIPs) is supported by the DML regardless of the physical location of the data. To enable device independent simplification, the DML has to manage the allocation of the storage space, accesses to different types of storage devices, and configures the operation mode according to the memory requirement of the simplification layer and the available system memory space. A detailed discussion of the two layers is given in the following two subsections.

## 2.1 The Initialization Flows

Prior to the start of the simplification, the AL begins with the requests sent to the DML through the DIPs describing the basic data structures, usable disk directories, and the amount of available system memory. On the basis of such a profile, the DML decides the operation mode by comparing the estimated main memory cost with the amount of allocated main memory space. If the allocated main memory space is larger than the estimated memory cost, the simplification is performed in core; conversely, it will be operated under the cache-based out-of-core mode.

## 2.2 The Operation Modes

The new system is able to operate under two operation modes: the in-core and out-of-core operation modes. The system operates under the in-core operation mode only when the memory requirement of the AL is lower than the available main memory space; otherwise, it runs under the out-of-core operation mode. During in-core operations, the DML puts all the data of the AL in the main memory buffer. Accesses to the data are re-directed to the main memory blocks.

By contrast, under the out-of-core mode, the DML allocates all the data to the available disks and uses the available system memory as cache blocks. During the simplification, the AL carries out the simplification using the read/write DIPs supported by the DML. To serve the requests, the DML first searches the required data from the cache blocks in the main memory space. If the search completes successfully, the required data is sent from the cache blocks in the main memory space; otherwise, the request is re-directed to the disks and the required data is read from the disk files. The two basic operation states are illustrated in Fig. 2.

Since the memory cost of the AL decreases as the mesh simplifies, it is possible to allow in-core simplification after a series of simplifications. Hence, the simplification can be performed in the combination of in-core and out-of-core modes where the simplification starts with the out-of-core mode then switches to the in-core operation mode when the memory cost of the AL is less than the size of available in-core buffers. Such combination is enabled by periodically issuing a request to reconfigure the operation mode by the AL, which may further improve the runtime efficiency.

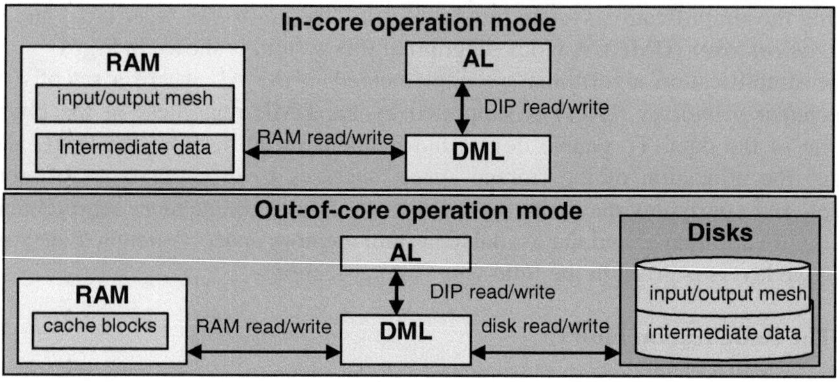


**Fig. 2.** The two operation modes: the in-core operation and out-of-core operation modes

## 3 The Data Management Layer

The data management layer (DML) provides a set of device-independent primitives to the algorithm layer (AL), which abstracts the allocation, de-allocation, and read/write accesses to all the data sets.

### 3.1 The Device Independent Primitives

We intend to provide three classes of primitives:

- *The operation mode configuration primitives*: they are employed to determine or reset the operation modes.
- **int Config**(ProfileT <profile>) : it calculates the maximum memory cost according to the table of data structures in the initial system profile and determines the operation mode according to the following rules: let the bound to the main memory cost be *B* and the memory cost is *C*. The DML operates under the in-core simplification mode if $C \le B$ ; otherwise, it operates under the out-of-core mode.
- *The storage allocation/de-allocation primitives*: they are employed to set up the buffers and files for the data structures used by the simplification layer.
- **int OpenBlock(int** <element size>, **int** <no of elements>): it allocates a file or a memory block of <element size>×<no of elements> bytes and returns the block ID.
- **void CloseBlock(int** <block ID>): it releases the memory and file of the block specified by the block ID.
- *The data read/*write *primitives*: they are used for accessing the content of these data structures either from the buffers or from the disks.
- **void read(int** <block ID>, **int** <element size>, **int** <element index>, **char** *<destination>): it reads an element from a file or a main memory block specified by the block ID.
- **void write(int** <blockid>, **int** <element size>, **int** <element *index*>, **char** *<source>): it writes an element to a file or a main memory block specified by the block ID.

# 4 The Algorithm Layer

The AL is essentially an implementation of the simplification algorithm using the DIPs supported by the data management layer. To show how the new system works, we have implemented two types of polygonal mesh simplification algorithms on this new system, namely Algorithm I and Algorithm II. The former, Algorithm I, is an implementation of a linear-time in-core iterative edge collapse algorithm proposed in our precious work [11]. The latter, Algorithm II, is a variation of the famous OoCS algorithm performing out-of-core uniform-grid vertex re-sampling [7].

The memory footprint of Algorithm I is large; hence, in its original implementation, the simplification of large meshes requires an enormous amount of system memory. Algorithm II is designed for efficient out-of-core simplification; however, it is output sensitive and assumed to accept the STL format rather than the common index-faced format. Both of them adopt the quadric error metrics proposed by [4].

With our new system, both Algorithms I and II are possible to perform simplification on large meshes with constant main memory footprint. Furthermore, with the automatic detection and adjustment of the operation modes, we do not need a precise estimate of the output size to allow the simplification in the second phase when the multiphase simplification approach is applied.

## 4.1 Algorithm I– A Linear-Time Iterative Edge Collapse Algorithm

Algorithm I is an in-core iterative full edge collapse polygonal mesh simplification algorithm. In the main, the algorithm is composed of three stages: the preprocessing stage, the simplification stage, and the output stage. In the preprocessing stage, the vertex rings are constructed through a single pass over the faces of the input mesh. Upon processing each face, the face index is inserted to the incident face lists of the three vertices. Following the preprocessing stage, the simplification stage and the output stage are repeatedly performed until the termination condition is satisfied. Every pass of the loop outputs a new level of approximation. Thus, if *k* iterations are executed, the algorithm may produce *k* LODs.

## 4.2 Algorithm II– A Uniform-Grid Vertex Clustering Algorithm

The second type of algorithms is designed for radical out-of-core simplification [7], which comprises three phases: vertex re-sampling, face re-sampling and grid quadric calculation, and the calculation of representative vertices. The first phase re-samples all the vertices with a uniform grid. This gives the mapping between a vertex and a grid ID.

After the re-sampling of vertices, the algorithm re-samples the faces by outputting only those faces whose three vertices are sampled to distinct grids. In the meantime, it also calculates grid quadrics by summing all the face quadrics sampled to each grid. In the finale phase, an optimal placement of the representative vertex of each grid is calculated by solving the linear system presented by the grid quadrics. In the original work, a set of rules is suggested to prevent from numerical errors. We do not employ those rules in this implementation. Rather, we simply use one of the sampled vertices of a grid if the solved position is out of the range of such a grid.

## 5 Experimental Results

The storage independent polygonal mesh simplification system (SIPMSS) has been implemented with C++ codes on a PC equipped with an Intel Pentium 4 2.2 GHz CPU, 1 GB RAM, and a RAID disk system of two IDE 7,200 rpm hard drives. The operating system and the compiler are the Microsoft Windows 2000 and Visual C++ 6.0, respectively. The test models are downloaded from the Stanford Scanning Repository. A summary of the test models is listed in Table 1.

**Table 1.** A summary of the test models

| Model | Dragon | David (2mm) | Lucy |
|---|---|---|---|
| **Number of vertices** | 437,645 | 3,614,098 | 14,027,872 |
| **Number of faces** | 871,414 | 7,227,031 | 28,055,742 |

To determine whether the system is successful, we may evaluate the new system from three perspectives. First, we have to verify if our new system indeed improves the performance of the out-of-core algorithm (OoCS) by comparing the running times of the OoCSx with those of Algorithm II. Second, we also have to prove that the implementation of the in-core algorithm, Algorithm I, is able to simplify large meshes with a constant amount of main memory footprint. Third, how does the multiphase approach work in the new system? To provide a basis of comparison, the running times of the HQMS [11] and OoCSx [8] for the simplification of the three meshes are shown in Table 2.

**Table 2.** The running times of the HQMS and OoCSx by seconds

| **Algorithm** | **Model** | | |
|---|---|---|---|
| | **Dragon** | **David (2mm)** | **Lucy** |
| **HQMS** | 7 | 66 | - |
| **OoCSx**[1] | 22 | 284 | 1,414 |
| [1]Our implementation of the OoCSx. | | | |

The performance of the new system under the in-core operation mode running the Algorithms I, II, and the two-stage approach are respectively presented in Table 3 where the results are compared with their original version and the QSLIM V2.0.

**Table 3.** The running times of Algorithms I, II, and their two-stage combination in the in-core mode by seconds

| Algorithm | | Model | | |
|---|---|---|---|---|
| | | Dragon | David (2mm) | Lucy |
| Algorithm I (o. s.=10K Δs)[1,2,3] | | 10 | 81 | 2,284[4] |
| Algorithm II (m. g. d. =50)[5] | | 5 | 38 | 148 |
| Two-stage | Stage 1: (m. g. d. =300)[5] | 6 | 33 | 125 |
| | Stage 2: (o. s.=10K Δs)[1,2,3] | 3 | 2 | 3 |
| [1]o. s. = output size.; [2]1K=1,000.; [3]Δs = triangles; [4]The system memory is not enough for in-core mode simplification; [5]m. g. d. = maximum grid dimension. | | | | |

The test of the out-of-core mode is conducted by restricting the main memory size to be below 8 MB, which is much less than the main memory size of a desktop PC that usually has more than 256 MB main memory space. Under such a strict condition, the simplification of all the three models is executed using the out-of-core operation mode. The test results are given in Table 4.

**Table 4.** The running times of Algorithms I, II, and their two-stage combination in the out-of-core modes by seconds

| Algorithm | | Model | | |
|---|---|---|---|---|
| | | Dragon | David (2mm) | Lucy |
| Algorithm I (o. s.=10K Δs)[1,2,3] | | 23 | 362 | 2,931 |
| Algorithm II (m. g. d. =50) | | 6 | 58 | 217 |
| Two-stage | Stage 1: (m. g. d. =300)[4] | 20 | 49 | 219 |
| | Stage 2: (o. s.=10K Δs)[1,2,3] | 8 | 5 | 10 |
| [1]o. s. = output size; [2]1K=1,000.; [3]Δs = triangles; [4]m. g. d. = maximum grid dimension. | | | | |

To show the integration of different types of algorithms is possible, an experiment is carried out to test the performance of applying a two-stage integration called Algorithm Two-Stage. The Algorithm Two-Stage adopts the idea from the multiphase approach proposed in [7] and is a two-stage method integrating Algorithm I and II by applying Algorithm II at the first stage followed by Algorithm I.

In addition to the running times, the rendered images of the simplified Lucy meshes are demonstrated in Fig. 3.

According to Tables 2-4, Algorithm II takes only 217 seconds to simplify the Lucy mesh with 8 MB RAM while its original memory insensitive version, OoCSx, takes 1,414 seconds. Hence, the running time of the out-of-core algorithm improves

Algorithm I, 10,000 triangles | Algorithm II, 11,506 triangles | Two-Stage, 10,000 triangles

**Fig. 3.** The simplified Lucy meshes generated by Algorithm I, II, and Two-Stage

significantly with our new system. Also from Tables 2-4, we may notice that Algorithm I, the implementation of the HQMS algorithm, is able to simplify the Lucy mesh with only 8 MB main memory, which approves our statements as expected.

Furthermore, simplification results shown in Tables 3 and 4 prove that the two-stage integration is not only possible but also successful. With 512 MB system memory, Algorithm Two-Stage is capable of simplifying the Lucy mesh in the in-core mode using 128 seconds. With 8 MB RAM, it successfully simplifies the Lucy mesh using only 229 seconds without manual intervention.

## 6 Discussions and Conclusions

In this paper, we have addressed the issue of high-performance large mesh simplification by presenting a storage independent platform for the implementation and integration of various types of in-core and out-of-core polygonal mesh simplification algorithms. The proposed approach successfully ensures a constant main memory cost, unbounded input mesh size, high external memory access efficiency, and permits tight integration of various types of polygonal mesh simplification algorithms. The results presented in the experiments section further approve both its effectiveness and usefulness for the two types of simplification.

In summary, the experimental results verify our statements with the following facts:

- The Algorithm I, or the implementation of an in-core iterative edge collapse method (HQMS) on the SIPMSS, is capable of simplifying large meshes with a constant main memory cost.

- The Algorithm II, or the implementation of an out-of-core grid-based re-sampling method (OoCS) on the SIPMSS, has significantly better runtime efficiency than its original version.
- The integration of Algorithms I and II, or the two-stage approach, having the advantages of high runtime efficiency and good output quality proves that the SIPMSS is a very good system for integrating various types of simplification algorithms.
- Despite the aforementioned achievements, a number of issues are to be studied in the future.
- For some data structures of variable lengths, they could not be supported by our system. Hence, it is not feasible to port these algorithms directly to our system.
- The policy for optimum allocation of buffers to each data structure has not been studied in this paper. The amount of allocation is decided by the weight of the data structure, which is simply given by the ratio of its file size to the average file size.

**Acknowledgments.** We would like to thank the Stanford 3D Scanning Repository for providing all the test models. This work was supported by the National Science Council of Republic of China under the contract number NSC-95-2218-E-046-003.

## References

1. Lubke, D., Reddy, M., Cohen, J.D., Varshney, A., Watson, B., Huebner, R.: Level-of-Detail for 3D Graphics. Morgan Kaufman, San Fransisco, California (2003)
2. Clark, J.H.: Hierarchical geometric models for visible surface algorithms. Communications of the ACM 19(10), 547–554 (1976)
3. Hoppe, H.: Progressive meshes. In: Proceedings of the SIGGRAPH '96, vol. 30, pp. 99–108 (1996)
4. Garland, M., Heckbert, P.S.: Surface simplification using quadric error metrics. In: Proceedings of the SIGGRAPH '96, vol. 30, pp. 209–216 (1996)
5. Lindstrom, P., Turk, G.: Evaluation of memoryless simplification. IEEE Transactions on Visualization and Computer Graphics 5(2), 98–115 (1999)
6. Wu, J., Kobbelt, L.: A stream algorithm for the decimation of massive meshes. In: Proceedings of the Graphics Interface '03, pp. 185–192 (2003)
7. Lindstrom, P.: Out-of-core simplification of large polygonal models. In: Proceedings of the SIGGRAPH '00, vol. 34, pp. 259–270 (2000)
8. Lindstrom, P., Silva, C.T.: A memory insensitive technique for large model simplification. In: Proceedings of the IEEE Visualization '01, pp. 121–126 (2001)
9. Garland, M., Shaffer, E.: A multiphase approach to efficient surface simplification. In: Proceedings of the IEEE Visualization '02, pp. 117–124 (2002)
10. Chen, H.K., Fahn, C.S., Tsai, J.P., Lin, M.B.: A novel cache-based approach to large polygonal mesh simplification. Journal of Information Science and Engineering 22(4), 843–861 (2006)
11. Chen, H.K., Fahn, C.S., Tsai, J.P., Chen, R.M., Lin, M.B.: A linear time algorithm for high quality mesh simplification. In: Proceeding of the IEEE 6th International Symposium on Multimedia Software Engineering, pp. 169–176 (2004)

12. Chen, H.K., Fahn, C.S., Tsai, J.P., Chen, R.M., Lin, M.B.: Generating high-quality discrete LOD meshes for 3D computer games in linear time. Multimedia Systems 11(5), 480–494 (2006)
13. Carr, R.W., Hennessy, J.L.: WSClock– A simple and effective algorithm for virtual memory management. In: Proceedings of the Symposium on Operating Systems Principles '81, pp. 87–95 (1981)

# A Wavelet-Based Image Enhancement Algorithm for Real Time Multi-resolution Texture Mapping

Hai-feng Cui[1] and Xin Zheng[1,2,*]

[1] Image Processing and Pattern Recognition Laboratory, Beijing Normal University, Beijing 100875, China

[2] State Key Laboratory of Computer Science, Institute of Software, Chinese Academy of Sciences, Beijing 100080, China

zhengxin@bnu.edu.cn

**Abstract.** In order to get better rendering effect, we proposed a wavelet transform based image enhancement algorithm for real time multi-resolution texture mapping in this paper. In this algorithm, we proposed a concept of weighted pyramid. Texture images to be synthesized are weighted enhanced by wavelet transform. Comparing with original ones, the edges in this image is much clearer and the contrast of this image is more evident. And when dealing with the maps with their particular characteristics, we also proposed some method for algorithm improvement. By using this method, current multi-resolution texture mapping method will be much more improved. It can give us a more realistic and efficient rendering effect by using lower resolution image to replace higher resolution one.

**Keywords:** wavelet, image enhancement, texture mapping, multi-resolution.

## 1 Introduction

Virtual reality techniques have been widely used in many areas such as entertainment, aeronautics and etc. They have changed the life of people in many aspects. Reality and real time are the two key attributes of Virtual reality techniques. Without them we have no felling of being as in a real world when we browse in a virtual environment. Texture mapping is one of the most widely used techniques for realistic rendering in virtual reality systems. In order to reduce the computation in texture mapping process, multi-resolution texture mapping techniques [1], [2], such as mip-map, has been proposed, which gave us a way for fast rendering. As Virtual reality techniques being used further more and the resolution of devices for data acquiring being much larger, the number of data to be rendered in virtual environment has enlarged more and more, not only including the polygons of virtual environment but also the size of texture images. For example, the size of one satellite texture image used in a terrain rendering system[3] is 30G bytes or some even much larger. It exceeds the loading ability of the RAM in PC and graphics cards. We have to piece the large image into smaller patches and load one patch each time. The rendering efficiency is much influenced by the

* Corresponding author.

R. Shumaker (Ed.): Virtual Reality, HCII 2007, LNCS 4563, pp. 13–21, 2007.

process of data IO. In order to debase the frequency of data IO process, many people have to use lower resolution texture image to replace higher resolution one for texture mapping. Consequently this method reduces the rendering quality. It not only blurs the final rendering image but also introduces some match artifacts between different layers of the multi-resolution texture image for the reason of detail lost. Our suggestion to resolve this problem is to use the technique of image enhancement [4], [5]. Facing the problem of how to debase the resolution of the texture image with the least loss of detail about the edges, we choose the wavelet transform [6] method at last after experimenting in many methods.

The organization of this paper is as follows: In the next section, we will give the process of constructing our multi-resolution texture pyramid by edge detection and also introduce a new concept named weighted pyramid. In Section 3, we will present a new method of constructing weighted pyramid by using wavelet transform. In last section, we will present the results of our experiments and give the conclusions.

## 2 The Real-Time Rendering and Weighted Pyramid

### 2.1 The Real-Time Rendering

When reviewing the history of computer graphics, we find it is the reality and high quality of the image that traditional algorithms focus on. However the virtual reality system nowadays requires limited rendering time. Because of the huger and huger amounts of data need to be rendered in complicated and veracious scenes, the way we mostly used for speeding is often to lose some quality. Here the “lose” mainly means the debasing of the image reality and the growing of the alias. For example, we adopt simply local lighting model [1] or multi-resolution texture mapping [1], [2] techniques to improve our rendering speed.

Based on the visual character of people, the object seems smaller when it is far away from our eyes. And just few pixels are covered when projected on the screen. So, we needn’t to render all the details for such object. The same thing occurs in texture mapping. Because the number of pixels projected on screen is often much smaller than number of pixels in texture images being mapped on object. We needn’t to use high resolution texture in such cases. Or it will be a waste of resource. For this, the multi-resolution texture mapping is feasible. It makes us create different levels of image with different resolution based on one texture image (if we pick up every four neighbor pixels on the first level to create a new one on the next level, then the scale is debased by 2 exponential ) . Then we get a pyramid constructed by the different sub levels of image. When mapping the texture, we can choose the corresponding one according to its distance from our eyes. And the farther the object goes, the smaller resolution we choose.

### 2.2 Weighted Pyramid

By comparing the two images in figure 1 and figure 2, we find that it becomes blurry while the resolution falling down. In fact, when this falling process goes on the loss of edge information will reach some degree and breaking will occur in lower resolution image. This will introduce some match artifacts between different layers of the multi-resolution texture mapped rendering image [3].

**Fig. 1.** The standard image called "house"

For keeping enough more detail information, we hope the new born pixel can contain more edge information when we construct the multi-level pyramid. Then we propose a concept of weighted pyramid by adding a weight to each pixel in the process of constructing pyramid. This can make some information outstanding and is useful for our rendering.

First we do the edge detection [7], [8] to the image. All pixels are marked with edge point and non-edge point based on the result of the detection. When building the pyramid, we add a weight to each four neighbor pixel--bigger weight to edge point, and smaller weight to non-edge point, which depend on the result of the edge detection. So the new born pixel on the next level by averaging the four weighted pixels will comparatively keep more edge information.

There are many existent edge detecting operators. Figure 3 gives the result of low resolution enhanced image by using Sobel operator. In this algorithm, all our behaviors take place in the space area and we deal with the pixels in image. For parting the two kinds of pixels, we need to set up a threshold of gray value. But the threshold value is often not accurate. And because of its inherent mathematics disadvantage, this method may bring more blur. Although those shortcomings, by comparing the histograms of the two images in figure 2 and figure 3, we can see that the result image in figure 3 not only keep higher pixel values but also distributes grey values more uniformly. This means that it contains more detail information and has better rendering effect. However, this result is still need to be improved for us.

After studying and analyzing many other existent techniques, we lead the wavelet technique into our weighted pyramid at last.

Fig. 2. The half-resolution image and its histogram

Fig. 3. The half-resolution image enhanced by Sobel detector and its histogram

# 3 Wavelet Decomposition Used for the Image Enhancement

## 3.1 Characteristics of the Wavelet Transform

Wavelet transform [6] is an analysis technique for non-stationary signal processing. By using this method we can use a set of functions to approximate one function wanted. The set of functions used are called wavelet functions. In real application we often chose dyadic wavelet transform. Give a function f (t) in space $L^2(R)$, its dyadic wavelet transform is

$$C_{m,n} = \int_{\infty}^{+\infty} f(t)\psi_{m,n}(t)dt \tag{1}$$

where $\psi_{m,n}(t) = 2^{\frac{m}{2}} \psi(2^{m}t \quad n)$, and $\int_{\infty}^{+\infty} \psi(t)dt = 0$. When we extend the transform to two-dimensional space, it can be used to process or analyze images. The image can be decomposed into four sub-bands which are horizontal, vertical, diagonal and low-frequency half resolution portions through different filters respectively. And the low-frequency part can still be decomposed.

Wavelet has the abilities of multi-resolution analysis about the images and reflecting the local characteristics of the signals. We can get the wavelet coefficient images by using discrete wavelet transform, and the level to be decomposed is depend on the actual effect you want. The coefficient images is composed of several sub-band coefficient images which describe the horizontal and vertical space frequency characteristics of the image. Sub-bands on different level can describe the characteristics in different space resolution of the image. Then through multi-level decomposing, the coefficient images we get can not only show the high-frequency information of the local areas in the image (ex. the edge) but also the low-frequency information (ex. the background). So that we can still keep more detail information about the image even though in the low-bit rate situation. The image described by coefficient of the second level is just half resolution of the first level. So, we can get image (clear or blurry) with any resolution we want.

### 3.2 Wavelet Enhancement

Through the wavelet transform decomposing, we have got four sub-band coefficient images. Each of them is one quarter of primary image in size. They are one low-frequency approximate image and three high-frequency approximate images of horizontal part, vertical part and the diagonal part. So information of the image is classified very well. Detail information on edge or in texture is mainly collected in the high-frequency sub-band images with higher values. From some existent research results we know that people are sensitive to the change on horizontal and vertical edges, which represent the main edge characteristics of image. On account of those advantages of wavelet transform, we can introduce it into weighted pyramid structure we mentioned in section 2. By adding weights to the horizontal and vertical high-frequency coefficient images on each level we make some adequate enhancements to multi-scale images decomposed by wavelet transform. And a new weighted texture pyramid with more detail information was achieved by reconstructing an enhanced image on each level with modified coefficients. Much different from method working in space area we used in section 2, this method works in the frequency area. In fact, the wavelet decomposition of image separates the whole signal into different sub-bands with different frequency scale. Then we can take different means with those sub-bands to achieve our different goals. Taking image enhancement for example, we will see that it is very flexible and convenient to strengthen the weight of details with different frequency scale and make it obvious visually. Then we can improve its holistic quality and get a better visual effect, as shown in figure 4.

We have three steps to make the enhancement of image f(x, y) by using wavelet transform. First, we decompose the image with wavelet. Then we make some adequate enhancement to the horizontal and vertical high-frequency images on each level. At last, we make the inverse-transform with those results and get a better enhanced image.

**Fig. 4.** The half-resolution image enhanced by wavelet algorithm and its histogram

### 3.3 Improved Wavelet Enhancement

The former wavelet enhancement method still needs to be improved for different images with their own characteristics. For example, if the image has excessive noise, we should set up a soft-threshold filter before wavelet transform. Cause the noises are mainly distributed on small scale wavelet coefficients in scope of wavelet transform, just as the most detail information of image (which is the key point considered in the enhancement) do. If we directly make the enhancement with equation (1), we will strengthen noises in image uniformly. Sometimes, this will lead to terrible rendering effect. To solve this problem, we set up a soft-threshold filter to eliminate most noise before our wavelet enhancement process begins. See equation (2) as below, we set up threshold $T_{ij}$ on each scale level, where i means different sub-band image and j represents the scale.

$$WT^{i}_{j}(x,y)=\begin{cases} WT^{i}_{j}(x,y)-T_{j,i} & WT^{i}_{j}(x,y)\geq T_{j,i} \\ 0 & -T_{j,i}<WT^{i}_{j}(x,y)<T_{j,i} \\ WT^{i}_{j}(x,y)+T_{j,i} & WT^{i}_{j}(x,y)\leq -T_{j,i} \end{cases} \tag{2}$$

As for the images which are gloomy or blurry, an optimized effect can be achieved through adjusting its lightness for the reason that according to people's visual characteristics people is much more sensitive to lightness than hue. So we can do the image enhancement under the HLS model. Firstly we transform the image from RGB model into HLS model. Then process the wavelet enhancement to L (lightness) component in the same way we do before. I have to say that this maybe acquire amazing effect.

## 4 Experiment Results and Conclusion

For assuring the universality of the result, we choose another different kind of texture image with Chinese ethical characteristics for the experiment, as shown in figure 5. In the figure 6, we cut it into two parts just in the middle.

**Fig. 5.** High resolution texture image

**Fig. 6.** Two parts separated in the middle

We draw two connected rectangles F1 and F2 in 3-D space, where F1 is near to us and F2 is far away. We mapped this texture to them. Left part is mapped to F1 and right part is mapped to F2. Because F2 covers much less pixels on screen than F1, we can use a lower resolution texture instead for speeding. This is very common for two connected faces in real application. Here, we map texture with highest resolution to F1 and map texture on the next level with half resolution to F2.

Figure 7-9 give different results by using different lower resolution images. They are separately normal lower resolution image without enhancement in figure 7, lower resolution image enhanced by Sobel edge detector in figure 8 and lower resolution image enhanced by wavelet transform in figure 9. We can see that our algorithm proposed in this paper gives the best visual effect. Result image in figure 9 is more perfect both at the detail display or lightness balance. And the two

**Fig. 7.** Texture mapping result using normal lower resolution image without enhancement

**Fig. 8.** Texture mapping result using lower resolution image enhanced by Sobel edge detector

**Fig. 9.** Texture mapping result using lower resolution image enhanced by wavelet transform

connected texture image with different resolutions are matched well and joined smoothly.

Based on the life experiences, it is completely feasible to use the low resolution texture image to replace the higher one so that we can improve the mapping efficiency. We finally choose the wavelet enhancement technique processed in the frequency area to improve the low resolution image after many experiments and comparisons. Additionally we propose some methods to improve the wavelet technique for better effect when we are facing images with their own characteristics. For assuring the universality of the result, we do experiments for real time multi-resolution texture mapping separately by using original multi-resolution texture mapping method currently used, Sobel edge enhancement method and wavelet transform based image enhancement method proposed in this paper. Under the condition of same efficiency, all results show that our method give a more realistic rendering image, not only visually but also by image analysis results using histogram. Comparing with other two methods, our method is more perfect both at the detail display and lightness contrast. And image synthesized from adjacent layers are matched more smoothly.

**Acknowledgements.** The research work described in this paper was supported by the Open Foundation of State Key Laboratory of Computer Science Grant No.SYSKF0506.

## References

1. Walter, G., Kropatsch., Montanvert, A.: Irregular Pyramids, Technical Report PRIP TR-5, Institute f. Automation 183/2, Dept. for Pattern Recognition and Image Processing, TU Wien, Austria (1991)
2. Tang, R., Wang, J., Peng, Q.: Computer graphics tutorial, edit version, Science Press (2000)
3. Losasso, F., Hoppe, H.: Geometry Clipmaps: Terrain Rendering Using Nested Regular Grids, ACM SIGGRAPH, 769–776 (2004)
4. Jongsan, L.: Digital Image Enhancement and Noise Filtering by Using of Local Statistic[J]. IEEE Trans on Pattern Analysis and Machine Intelligence 2(2), 165–168 (1980)
5. Zhang, Y.: Image processing and analyze, Tsinghua Press (1999)
6. Chen, W.: Wavelet analyze and its use in image processing, Science Press, pp. 167–173 (2000)
7. Fan, L.: Research on Edge Detection of Color Image Based on Multi-structuring Elements Morphology of HSI Space. Journal of Engineering Graphics 26(2) (2005)
8. Ji, H., Sun, J., Fang, X., Mao, L.: The Algorithm for Image Edge Detection and Prospect. Computer Engineering and Applications 14, 70–73 (2004)

# 3D-Image Visualization and Its Performance in Teleoperation

Manuel Ferre[1], Salvador Cobos[1], Rafael Aracil, and Miguel A. Sánchez Urán[1]

[1] Universidad Politécnica de Madrid, Robots and Intelligent Machines Group
28006 Madrid, Spain
{mferre,cobosalvador,aracil}@etsii.upm.es,
miguelangel.sanchezuran@upm.es

**Abstract.** In this paper, stereoscopic image visualization for teleoperated robots is studied. The use of stereo vision systems shows some difficulties: image disparity is the main problem. It affects the correct image fusion process by the brain. Disparity curve calculations are shown and a method to calibrate stereoscopic images for telerobotics is explained. Experiments have been carried out to obtain the limits for a proper image fusion. The use of stereoscopic image has been assessed to execute teleoperated robot guidance tasks. The performance of stereoscopic and monoscopic image is compared. Stereoscopic images have shown a guaranteed depth perception.

**Keywords:** 3D-vision, stereoscopic interfaces, binocular, disparity, teleoperation.

## 1 Introduction

There are two ways to improve a teleoperated system performance: the first consists of increasing the automation level, and the second is the increase of operator presence level. The first way implies a greater system complexity since more sensors are required to obtain information regarding the remote environment and more computers processing such information. The second option goals the human-machine interaction improvement in order to show a more accurate teleoperation environment. In this way the operator can carry out teleoperated tasks more skillfully. For this purpose, on the one side, spatial perception of the remote environment can be improved and, on the other side, the applied strength can be reflected during the manipulation.

The described work in this article focuses on the stereoscopic vision for teleoperation. The way to calculate the space required for a proper perception of blended stereoscopic images is described. This result has been proved to be very interesting for teleoperation since operator's tiredness is avoided.

According to the authors' opinion, achievements in teleoperation interfaces are of great interest. In this way, teleoperated task productivity can be considerably improved and, at the time, number of telerobotics applications. Nowadays, there are few new applications apart from the classical teleoperation areas.

R. Shumaker (Ed.): Virtual Reality, HCII 2007, LNCS 4563, pp. 22–31, 2007.

## 2 Binocular Disparity

Depth perception through binocular images requires that the received images by each eye have a natural aspect so that a proper blending of the images takes place in the brain. The main factor for a suitable image fusion is the disparity among the images. This depends on the camera convergence angle and on the distance between the objects and the camera. In this section the human binocular field and its disparity development is analysed. This will allow to later study the scene visual fields in remote environments for teleoperation.

### 2.1 Binocular Field of Vision

The binocular field is the area that both eyes reach to see objects (114º). A horizontal section of the human visual field is shown in Fig. 1. Within the stereoscopic visual field, points with positive, or crossed, disparity and points with negative, or uncrossed, disparity can be distinguished. Points indicating crossed disparity are those located beyond the place where the optical axes of our eyes intersect. Uncrossed disparity is shown by those located before such place.

Each point in the binocular field is represented only by a corresponding point on each retina. Images that fall on these points have zero binocular disparity. However, images that fall on noncorresponding points are disparity images. The locus of spatial points that project images to the corresponding points on both retinas is known as horopter. This depends, evidently, on the position of both eyes. More details are given in [1]. The study of the binocular visual field provides the required criteria for the display of stereoscopic video images. To begin with the stereoscopic visualization, the images should be placed in the binocular field. For this reason, wide-angle lenses are not recommended for stereoscopic images. Secondly, stereoscopic images must respect crossed and uncrossed disparity limits. A further requirement is the front placement of the display inside the binocular field, but usually this is the normal position of a screen.

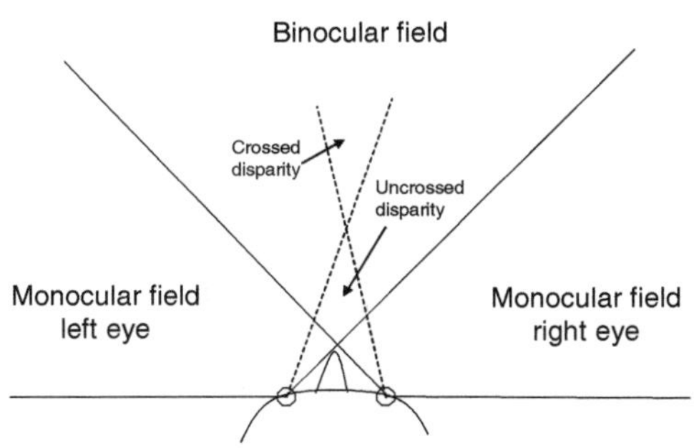


**Fig. 1.** Binocular visual field: crossed and uncrossed disparity regions

## 2.2 Binocular Disparity Evolution

Fig. 2 shows two points visualisation (A and B). In the case the eyes converge on point A at a distance d forming the angle α, and that point B is at a distance x under an angle β. Then point B does not have non-corresponding projections on each eye. In the right eye there will be a θ1 disparity, with a θ2 disparity in the left eye, with opposite values. The total angle disparity will result to be μ and corresponds to the addition of both disparities. If the distance between the eyes is o, then:

$$\mu = \alpha - \beta = \vartheta_1 - \vartheta_2 = 2\vartheta_1 \tag{1}$$

$$tg(\alpha/2) = \frac{o}{2d}, tg(\beta/2) = \frac{o}{2x} \tag{2}$$

$$\mu = 2\left(a\tan\left(\frac{o}{2d}\right) - a\tan\left(\frac{o}{2x}\right)\right) \tag{3}$$

$$p = \frac{o(x-d)}{x} \Rightarrow |disparity| = abs\left(\frac{o(x-d)}{x}\right) \tag{4}$$

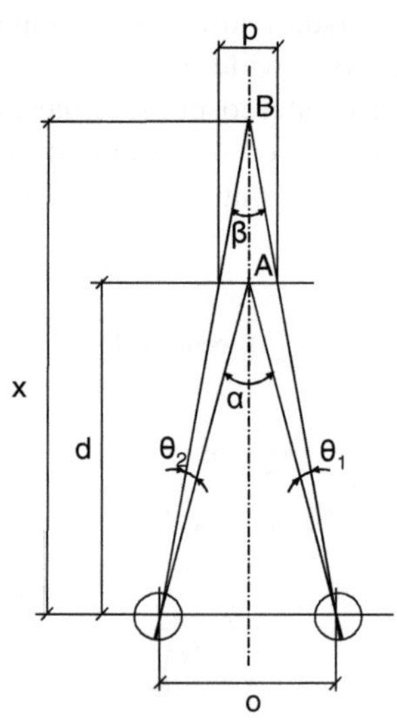


**Fig. 2.** Angular disparity from A and B

The graph appearing in Fig. 3 is obtained representing the disparity value according to the equation (4). The graph shows that uncrossed disparity increases faster than crossed disparity. It means that there is a greater variation for those objects which are nearer to the observer than for those which are further away. In the same way, it can be seen that the greater the value d is the slower the disparity variation results. This demonstrates the reduction in the disparity mechanism as distances increase.

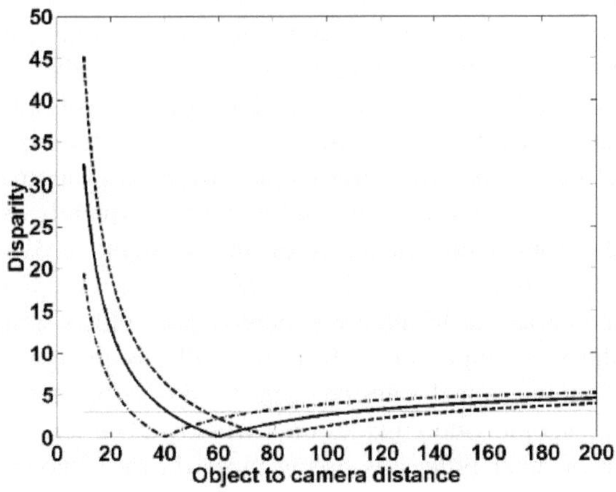


**Fig. 3.** Disparity evolution as to the object-to-camera distance, obtained from different convergence angles

## 2.3 Teleoperation Working Field

Fig. 3 shows disparity development of three different curves, being their focus axes at 40, 60 ad 80 cm. The horizontal line represents the maximum value of the accepted disparity. By looking at the curve intersections, the boundaries of the scene to be visualised can be calculated. For the central curve, that crosses the axes at 60 cm and its limits are set at 3 (as the marked lines show), it would be possible to view all objects at a distance ranging between 40 and 120 cm.

The teleoperation working field will be placed within the limits that allow a proper stereoscopic image blending. The calculation of the area where images blend requires knowing the maximum angular disparity limits. No consensus has been reached about where this limit might be in the different works. Most restrictive studies set the limit for crossed disparity around 27 min-arc and 24 min-arc for uncrossed disparity [2]. Lipton from SterooGraphics Corp., one of the main stereoscopic device manufacturers, suggests a maximum disparity of around 1.5° [3]. In other experiments carried out by Ian Howard [1] limits between 4° - 7° for crossed disparity and between 9 - 12° for uncrossed disparity are given. According to Howard, the variability of these findings result from the numerous factors affecting the correct image blending, like scene lighting conditions, contrast between objects and the time that images are exposed. In the fifth section, these results will be used to obtain an approximate value of the teleoperation working field.

## 3 M3D for Visualization of Stereoscopic Images

M3D is a system for stereoscopic image visualisation on a computer screen developed by the authors [4] and [5]. The objective of this system is to insert stereoscopic images into a window on a computer screen which displays all graphical interfaces. Stereoscopic systems are usually independent from the other computers in the teleoperated system interface. This task involves the use of numerous computer screens showing video, graphics, etc., which increases considerably the complexity of the operator's interface. A specific stereoscopic device with a smart and integrated teleoperation device was considered to be useful and consequently designed.

Fig. 4 shows the four main elements of this system: a 3D-video camera, a stereoscopic image processing device known as M3D, a computer to display the images, and shutter glasses. M3D receives stereoscopic video signals from the 3D-video camera and the VGA input signal from the CPU. Both signals are multiplexed so that the VGA output signal can be sent to the computer monitor showing sequentially the stereoscopic video images on a window. The screen space left is used for the visualisation of other processes taking place during teleoperation. To see the stereoscopic images properly the observer should use liquid crystal shutter glasses which are synchronised with the display refreshment of the screen.

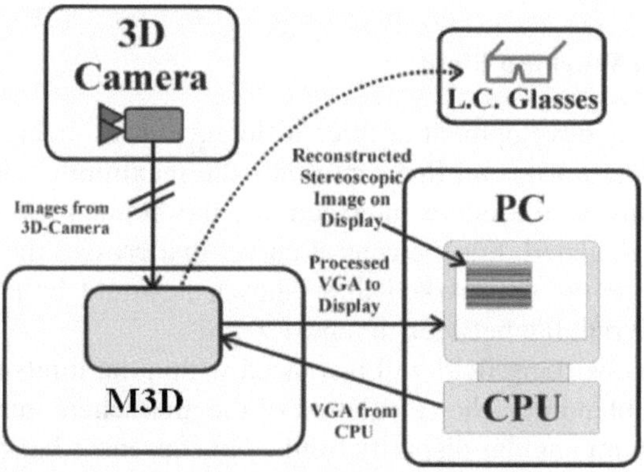


**Fig. 4.** Stereoscopic system for teleoperation interface

The 3D-Camera has two synchronised CCDs which are 6 cm horizontally separated, and have a variable convergence. In this way human sight mechanism is simulated. The device is designed as a computer peripheral, used to insert stereoscopic images on a computer screen window. It has two kinds of video inputs: on the one side, the VGA video signal coming from the computer; and on the other side, stereoscopic video signals coming from the 3D-Camera. The signal coming out of the DISTREC has the same VGA format as the one received by the computer. The stereoscopic video signal is reconstructed over the computer signal. The functioning is similar to a video image card but with this device stereoscopic images are processed.

The use of external equipment, apart from the computer, makes handling easier and also reduces the use of computer resources, such as the CPU or memory. Some integration costs are also eliminated because no driver is necessary to run the equipment. It is an external peripheral that blends images from the 3D-Camera and the VGA input, showing the stereoscopic image on a rectangular computer window, as shown in Fig. 5.

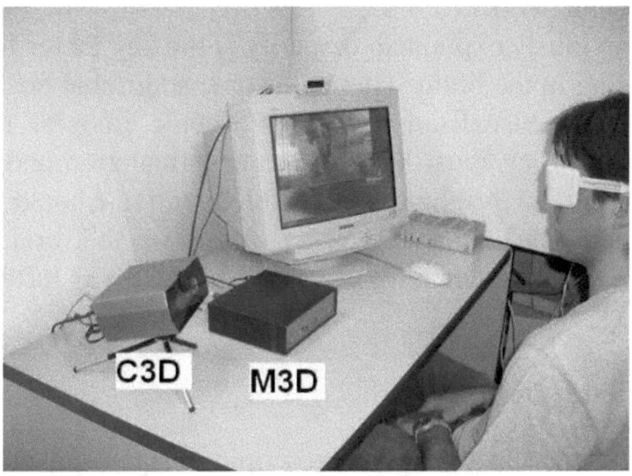


**Fig. 5.** M3D, shutter glasses and PC screen to visualize the stereoscopic images

The stereoscopic video signals are reconstructed and multiplexed in a synchronised manner according to the computer VGA frequencies. The VGA vertical frequency determines the reading memory. The left memory contains the images coming from the left CCD. It is read when the right eye is hidden by the shutter glasses and so on. The VGA horizontal frequency indicates the number of image lines. Using a pixel generator the column number is calculated. Information coming from the computer is shown on the remaining screen, which is very useful for the telerobotic system interface. The stereoscopic video window takes up from 30% to 70% of the screen depending on the monitor resolution. For the display of the corresponding image to each eye, the shutter glasses cover each one alternately, synchronised with the image reconstruction. When the monitor refreshment is lower than 70 Hz flicking problems may appear. Therefore, it is recommended to use monitor vertical frequencies higher than 75 Hz.

The M3D is made up by three modules connected to one another through independent buses and controlled by a CPLD. The modules are the following:

- Digitalisation
- Storage
- Reconstruction

A VHDL-programmed Xilinx CPLD is used for the control of the whole M3D system. This IC is the "system brain" and is in charge of programming and monitoring the remaining devices. The employed IC reaches working frequencies up to 80 MHz

## 4 Experiments for Stereoscopic Image Calibration

This section focuses on stereoscopic image visualization on a computer screen using shutter glasses, using the above mentioned M3D system. This kind of system is the most frequently used in teleoperation [6], and [7] and when a proper transmission speed is reached it will probably be also the most common system for future applications based on networks.

As it has been previously explained, disparity is the key factor for depth perception and for image blending in the brain. There are some additional factors to be taken into account for the correct visualisation of stereoscopic images. First of all, image similarity is necessary; they must have the same orientation and both images must have the same colour and brightness. Careful attention should be given to these factors so that the images can be easily fused in the brain. Possible colour discrepancies can hinder the matching process. This effect is further explained in [8] and [2].

### 4.1 Experiment Description

Depth perception when visualizing stereoscopic images depends highly on each person. It is thus necessary to give a test to users so that they can say how "natural" the stereoscopic images appear to them. The test has been given to 30 people and the results obtained are significant enough to be considered applicable to the general population.

The following test was developed to evaluate the limits of disparity. An object is placed at 14 different distances from the 3D-C and 10 seconds of images are recorded in each position. This process is repeated for different convergence angles of the 3D-C. The sequence of images has been repeated for angles of 12.5°, 7.5° and 5°, which correspond to intersections of the optical axes at a distance of 30, 50 and 70 cm respectively. Fig 6 shows a sequence of the captured and recorded stereoscopic images. The advantage of recording these images lies on the fact that all the participants used the same stereoscopic images under the same conditions, thus eliminating possible uncertainty regarding the experimental conditions.

30 participants can see then the recorded images. The test consists of showing the 14 images for each convergence angles. The user can state if the image visualized is perceived in a coherent way or if double images are perceived, i.e. the latter images correspond to those that cannot be fused in the brain. Participant's behavior is quite similar; some stop perceiving stereoscopic images before others do, but there is a region in which all participants perceive stereoscopic images and another region in which all of them perceive double images. When it comes to define disparity limits differences among participants arise. One interesting data is that in the transition area

some individuals say that they either do or do not perceive in stereo depending on where they focus. This suggests that disparity limits depend on the progressive accommodation of the eyes without an abrupt break. In order to assess the perception of stereoscopic images, a scale with three different values was developed, as follows:

- 10 points, if stereoscopy is perceived clearly
- 5 points, if it is necessary to re-focus the images, or if stereoscopy is perceived ith doubts
- 0 points, if double images are perceived.

The "stereoscopic assessment of each image" is the average number of points given to each image by the 30 participants. The point values given by all the individuals to each stereo image have been added up. The average is a measure of how easy or difficult it is to perceive the depth in the scene. The angular disparity of each image has also been calculated; i.e. the angle formed by corresponding points of each image seen from the viewer position, who is at a distance of 70 cm from the computer screen. Fig. 5.2 illustrates the angular disparity and the stereoscopic assessment of each image, with respect to the distance of the object visualized from the C3D. It shows that ordinate axis have the same scale, both for the angular disparity and for the stereoscopic image assessment.

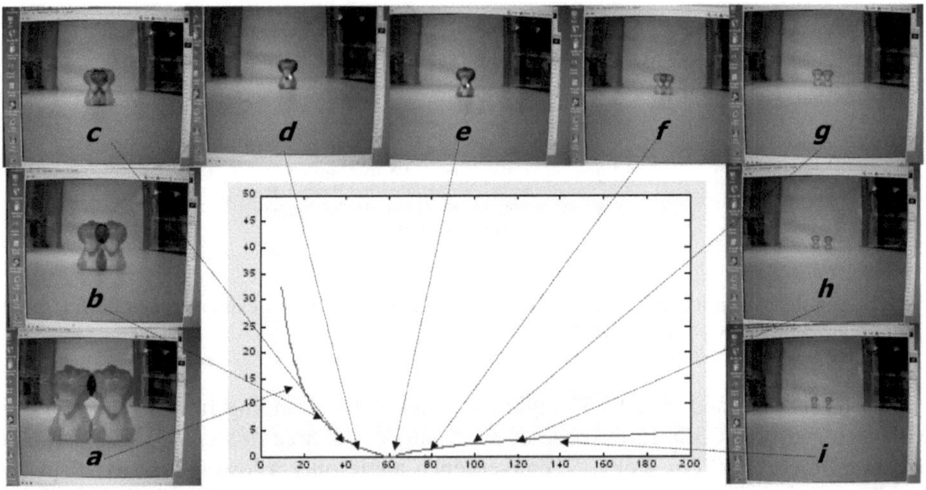


**Fig. 6.** Captured image sequence to detect visual disparity limits. Video camera axes intersect at 60 cm (picture e), pictures a to d reveal uncrossed disparity and crossed disparity in pictures f to i.

## 4.2 Analysis

It was taken 8 points as the minimum stereoscopic image assessment means that most individuals can see clearly the stereoscopic images. An analysis of the results shown in Fig. 7 reveals that if 8 are taken as the minimum stereoscopic image value, the limit for binocular disparity is 2° for the three graphs, while a minority may still have some doubts. Furthermore the limits of the scene can be significantly increased, which is realistic since work in the scene limits is not performed continuously, but only in particular moments. Taking 10 as an assessment value as a suitable work region would restrict the limits excessively, since when limits of perception are exceeded within the working field, the brain will admit images with a slightly higher disparity, at the cost of producing fatigue if the images persist for a long time.

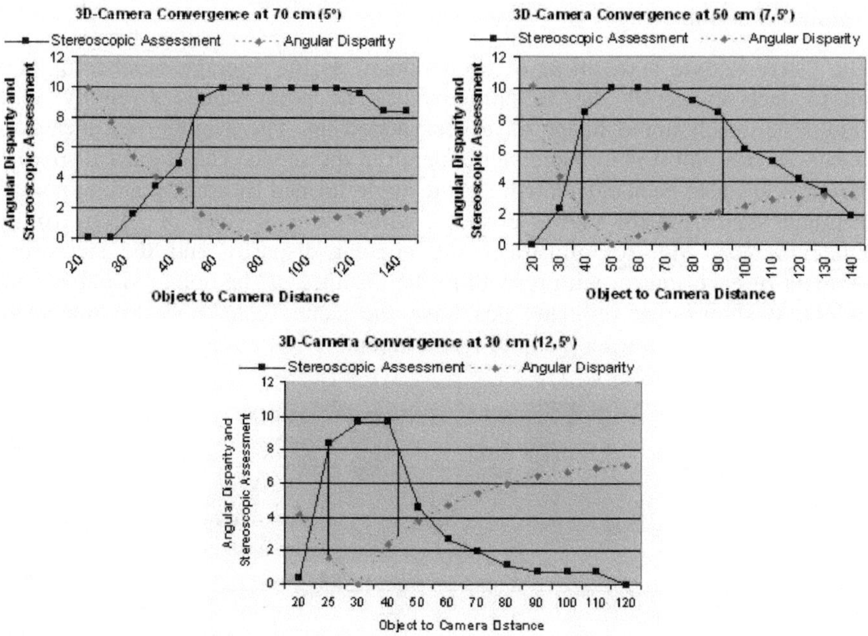


**Fig. 7.** Angular disparity and stereoscopic assessment vs. objet-to-camera distance for three convergence angles (5°, 7.5° and 12.5°)

The limits obtained in a 12.5º-angle are at a distance ranging from 25 and 50 cm with respect to the C3D. In the case of a 7.5º-angle, the area of stereoscopic vision is between 45 and 100 cm. For a 5º convergence angle only a lower limit exists at 55 cm. There is no upper limit because such a small angle means that disparity is not above 2º in the stereoscopic images. This result comes to be very valuable since it indicates that if a greater range of visualisation is desirable, it is necessary to work with small convergence angles. The disadvantage is that they have a lower limit which is relatively high. This means that the C3D must be placed relatively far from the scene. Consequently, the larger the convergence angle, the smaller the possible work space is. In the light of these test findings it can be concluded that the suitable working field will be one in which the disparity of the objects is less than 2º and that the greater the area is required the further away the camera must be from that field. The exact calculations must take into account the disparity graphs.

## 5 Conclusions

The need for suitable interface design for stereoscopic image visualisation has been analyzed. For this purpose, the key factors which are disparity and image quality have been studied. Disparity limits have been calculated in the stereoscopic image displayed on a computer screen. A method that calibrates stereoscopic image in remote environment teleoperations have been described. When monoscopic images are used, the degree of image quality provides spatial information about the location of the objects. Data such as shadows and reflections inform about 3D position. Such information could be sufficient in some cases but stereoscopic images always guarantee the proper depth perception.

The experiments have shown the proper performance of the developed 3D-Camera and M3D. The 3D-Camera determines convergence calibration. It has to be in accordance with the remote working environment in order to achieve an acceptable image disparity. Disparity limits for the proper calibration have been obtained around 2°. The M3D system allows stereoscopic image visualisation on a PC screen frame while the rest of the screen can be used for different processes involved in the teleoperated system. The integration of stereoscopic images on a computer screen has notably simplified the teleoperation interface. This fact improves performance of the teleoperated system and a seamless visual interface has been obtained, due to the use of a common screen for the visual interface.

## References

1. Howard, I.P., Rogers, B.J.: Binocular Vision and Stereopsis. Oxford University Press, Oxford (1995)
2. Yed, Y.Y., Silverstein, L.D.: Limits of fusion and depth judgement in stereoscopic color displays. Human factors 32(1), 45–60 (1990)
3. Lipton, L.: The Crystal Eyes Handbook, StereoGraphics Corporation, San Rafael, CA (1991)
4. Ferre, M., Aracil, R., Navas, M.: Stereoscopic video images for telerobotic applications. Int. Journal of Robotic Systems 22(3), 131–146 (2005)
5. Ferre, M., Aracil, R., Navas, M., Escalera, J.A.: Real Time Video Image Processing for Teleoperation: Image Blending and Stereoscopy. In: 9th IEEE Inter. Conf. on Emerging Technologies and Factory Automation. Lisbon, Portugal (2003)
6. Aracil, R., Ferre, M., Hernando, M., Pinto, E., Sebastián, J.M.: Telerobotics system for live-power line maintenance: ROBTET. Control Engineering Practice 10, 1271–1281 (2002)
7. Brunner, B., Hirzinger, G., Landzettel, K., Heindl, K.: Multisensory shared autonomy and tele-sensor-programming – Key issues in the space robot technology experiment ROTEX. In: Proc. IEEE/RSJ Int'l Conf. on Intelligent Robots and Systems, Yokohama (1993)
8. Hsu, E.J., Pizlo, J., Chelberg, Z., Babbs, D.M., Delp, C.F.: Isssues in the design of Studies to test the effectiveness of stereo imaging. IEEE Trans. on systems, man and cybernetics, Part A 26(6), 810–819 (1996)

# Manipulating Objects Behind Obstacles

Jan Flasar and Jiri Sochor

Faculty of Informatics, Masaryk University
Botanicka 68a, Brno, Czech Republic
{flasar,sochor}@fi.muni.cz

**Abstract.** This paper describes various techniques of accessing objects hidden behind obstacles in virtual environments. We show some of well known interaction techniques that are suitable for usage in this case. Next, we introduce new Head Manipulator method and several aids that allow a user to change the visibility of objects. We propose several combinations of interaction techniques and discuss their suitability for the given task. Finally, we describe our experiments when testing these methods and then we conclude with the results from the experiments and from users' observations.

## 1 Introduction

When users explore a virtual environment for the first time, they have no knowledge of the location and size of objects within a scene. They are able to interact directly only with objects which are visible. After some time, users gradually learn which objects are located in a given direction. Having this knowledge users may want to interact with the objects they know are occluded, but without the necessity to change the user's current position. Sometimes it may be even undesirable to walk around an obstacle because it is time consuming or it may not help anyway. For this type of interaction, a partial knowledge of the scene is required. This knowledge may be acquired with an appropriate exploration method.

In this study, we propose several combinations of well known interaction techniques and discuss their suitability for manipulating objects behind obstacles. We conclude with the results from the experiments and from users' observations.

## 2 Related Work

Applications for virtual reality are primarily designed for experts users. For new users, it might not always be clear how to manipulate with objects or travel in space, even in some small environments [1].

Manipulating the objects hidden behind obstacle requires users to change their position or expose a hidden part of the scene. Methods for travel and wayfinding were firstly categorized by Bowman et al. in [2,3]. A thorough study in [4] provides the taxonomy of travelling techniques based on translation and

R. Shumaker (Ed.): Virtual Reality, HCII 2007, LNCS 4563, pp. 32–41, 2007.

rotation components. Changing location in large and densely populated scenes necessitates a usage of more sophisticated navigation techniques. Stoakley et al. in [5] designed a *World In Miniature* (WIM) technique. A concept of closed world interactions (CWI) is described [6]. Using a wireframe and/or additional constraints, a user defines the closed world, which is then presented by a frame. All subsequent iterations are then restricted to the selected part of world.

Razzaque et al. [7] conducted a study of walking and exploring a large virtual room. To avoid the view at the missing back wall of the CAVE$^{TM}$, a technique called Redirected Walking in Place was used. The VE was slowly and imperceptibly rotated while the participant was walking in place. A participant could virtually walk in a full circle without turning towards the missing back wall.

In [8], Fukatsu et al. proposed the "bird's eye" view technique to improve navigation in an enormous virtual environment. Interlocking pairs of birds'eye and user's coordinate systems allows these systems to be manipulated intuitively. Navigation in densely populated VEs, such as a virtual city, was studied in [9]. This technique allows the modification of selected object properties which are tagged to indicate their constraints. Tagging helps to distinguish objects which cannot be modified, while other objects may change, for example, their position and size. The WIM technique is used to display copies of the objects to the user for a closer examination.

Annotated WIM-based aid [10] provides users an overview of their environs and allows to select and inquire about the objects contained. The WIM's position, scale and orientation is controlled by head-motion with non-linear mapping to emplacement.

LaViola and colleagues [11] investigated set of techniques for hands-free navigation through virtual environment. They experimented with a Step WIM, a miniature version of the world projected on the ground. The actual position of the user in the VE coincides with the approximate location of the user's feet in the miniature. The navigation is controlled by walking, toe and heel clicking, and leaning. Tools and actions are invoked using context-based gestures. The paper also addressed problems of WIM scaling.

## 3 Basic Interaction Techniques

In the following section, we shortly describe selected interaction techniques and tools that are related to a manipulation with objects behind obstacles.

For a local movement and an exploration of a scene we have selected techniques which use object manipulation metaphors. The virtual world or the user are represented by virtual objects which can be translated and rotated intuitively using e.g. hand or head. These techniques allow to observe different parts of a scene from different viewpoints and choose a new position of the user's viewpoint. The speed and range of the movement can be controlled using linear or non-linear mapping [12].

The *Scene In Hand* (SIH) tool described in [13], was originally designed for changing the user's view in a scene with the 3Space(bat). The technique maps translations and rotations of a tracked hand to translations and rotations of the scene. The user "takes" a virtual scene in his hand and explores it by turning, bringing it closer to his eyes etc. The usage is simple and intuitive.

With the *Eye In Hand* (EIH) tool [14] users control their view like using a camera attached to their hand. Moving and orienting the viewpoint is controlled by non-dominant hand, while the dominant hand is used for manipulating objects. The EIH technique is applicable both for immersive and non-immersive virtual reality. However, it is more natural to use it in non-immersive applications.

A *World In Miniature* (WIM) [5] technique uses a miniature of a scene as a tool. Users may interact not only with objects in the original scene but also with their proxies (small copies) in the WIM. The user can look at the scene from any viewpoint and solve local exploration and global navigation tasks easily. A small head model of an avatar displayed in the WIM is used to represent the user's viewpoint [15]. Later on, the WIM technique and its variations were used in many works in a different context (eg.[16], [17]).

Originally, the WIM was not suitable when users interact with virtual world at various levels of scale. To overcome this drawback, SSWIM [18] tool was created. It allows user to change the scale of the miniature according to the scale of the interaction context and scroll the miniaturized world like a map.

Mirroring techniques provide additional views which help to improve the insight and the comprehension of the scene. *The Magic Mirror* (MM) tool described in [19] is based on the metaphor of a mirror, which is used to explore the real world. The user manipulates the mirror tool the same way as any other object in the virtual environment. Using this method, users are able to explore the vicinity very fast. They can also swap viewpoints from their current position to the mirror's position and vice versa. It is possible to transfer the user to the mirror's location, let him/her interact with the virtual world from this viewpoint and return to the original place.

## 4 Additional Tools and Improvements

We tried to improve above mentioned approaches with additional tools. We have designed the Head Manipulator facilitating the control of a position only a slight movement of the user's head. We have also designed several aids that are based on changing the visibility of virtual objects and allow us to see occluded objects without a change of the user's viewpoint.

### 4.1 Head Manipulator

To look over and move around the obstacle, the *Head Manipulator* (HM) can be used. It maps the head motion in $x$, $z$ axes and pitch of the head to a virtual viewpoint motion in the following way. The deflections in $x$ axis from the original location are transferred to the motion on the surface of a sphere along its girth (Figure 1). The movement in the up direction on the surface is realized by mapping the head pitch. The deflection in the $z$ axis is used to draw the user closer to the place of interest or to distance him from this place. Basically, the radius of the sphere encompassing the local area changes with the deflection in the $z$ axis. The motion on the border is controlled either by a linear or a non-linear mapping.

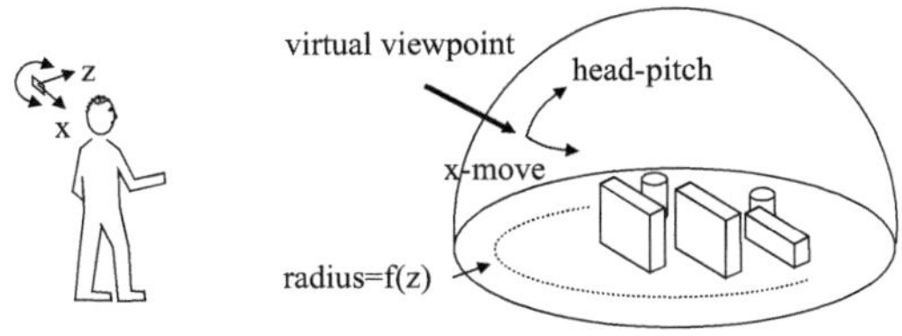


**Fig. 1.** HM tool maps slight movements of the user's head to the movements of the viewpoint on the sphere

To use this technique efficiently the user must determine an approximate center of the area explored. It can be done automatically or manually, depending on the application domain. Interactive choice of the center can be accomplished with some selection tool controlled e.g. by a user's hand. Additional aids such as the *Magic Mirror* tool may facilitate the exploration of a local space and finding an appropriate central point.

Scenario:

1. activation of HM tool positioned in an approximate center of the area explored
2. exploration of the neighbourhood of the obstacle with slight head and body movements
3. virtual move to the position convenient for interaction, (optional) deactivation of HM
4. interaction task
5. deactivation of HM
6. (optional) return to the original location

Controlling the viewpoint with this method is easy but it has several drawbacks. When moving on the sphere with the changing radius the user may get too close or even penetrate some objects occasionally. With such a confused view, the user is not able to interact with objects. This drawback shows up markedly in a densely populated virtual region. An automatically generated border can prevent the user from intervening with manually or automatically selected objects. However, this option can be disadvantageous because the user looses the control of the distance from the center of the working area. To overcome this limitation we designed a tool for changing transparencies of objects.

### 4.2 Changing the Visibility of Obstacles

To expose the space behind the obstacles the occluding objects can be temporarily removed or made transparent. Removing the obstacles may simplify the complex situations and may be convenient for many tasks. However, the position of the obstacle may be important for precise and/or restricted manipulation. In these cases it is better to leave the obstacle in the scene and to apply only such visibility changes which preserve the shape of the original object. We have designed tools which allow to control the visibility of a single object or a group of objects. The visibility changes may be applied to the whole occluder or only to a part of it. The first option can be realised by a *Change of Visibility* (COV) tool to selected objects (Figure 2(a)), while for the partial visibility we use a *Cutting plane* (CP) tool, see Figure 2.

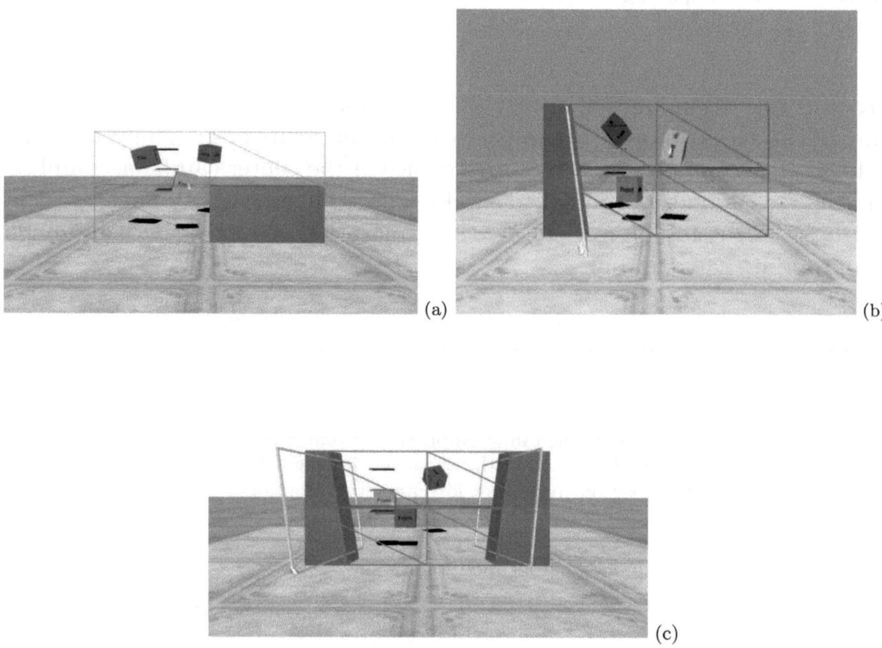


**Fig. 2.** (a) The change of occluder's visibility - individual or a multiple selection. (b) The partial change of occluder's visibility with the "cutting plane" tool. (c) Creating transparent corridors with CP tools.

The changes of visual attributes may also signal a contact between a manipulated object and other objects in the scene and thus help to consider an arrangement of nearby objects.

A *Cutting plane* (CP) tool (Figure2(b)) is visualized as the frame object. Its location is controlled by the user's hand. When the tool collides with some object, this object is split by an infinite cutting plane and according to the orientation of the tool the respective part of the object changes the visibility. Using CP tools users are able to gain the insight of the situation behind obstacles rapidly. Since visual feedback provides clear information of the CP tool's orientation, it is not necessary to indicate it by any mark.

For a work in a close environment the tool can posses a constant shape and size. Another option is adjusting parameters interactively, for example changing the length of the side nonlineary in a similar way as Go-Go technique.

Using these tools in a dense scene, it may be also difficult to change the visibility selectively, especially when the group of occluders surrounds the objects to be manipulated. Similar problems may arise when dealing with a non-convex obstacle. With multiple instances of CP tool, semi- or fully-transparent corridors to hidden parts of the scene can be created easily, as shown in Figure 2(c).

## 5 The Experiments

Interaction tools, virtual scenes and testing applications were implemented in the *VRECKO* system [20]. Users viewed scenes on a large stereoscopic wall with back projection. The modes and actions were controlled using FakeSpace PinchGloves to signal object grabbing or to change a state of an interaction technique. The Ascension Nest of Birds$^{TM}$was used for 6DOF tracking of hands and a head. All experiments were realized in a non-immersive virtual environment.

The eight subjects participated in this study. Each subject fulfilled 4 experimental tasks, each with 4 different tools (EIH, SIH, SSWIM, HM). In the tests 3 and 4 they could use also the COV tool. The fifth test was prepared to verify the usability of the mirror tool when offered to the user as the additional option.

The tools described above were tested in two virtual scenes. The scenes contained a floor and three cube-shaped objects hidden by obstacles, as can be seen in Figure 3. In the first scene, the obstacle blocked the front view only (test 1, 3 and 5). In the second scene, the obstacles formed a closed "room" surrounding completely the objects to be manipulated (test 2 and 4). The appointed task was to move the certain objects to the predefined positions denoted by markers. Typical training time for each method ranged from 2 to 10 minutes.

### 5.1 Results

The average time to complete all the tasks was approximately one hour. With the growing time users tried to find the shorter scenarios of interactions. Finally they commented their experiences using a simple questionnaire.

The results of the Head Manipulator technique and the Change of Visibility tool in the performance measures were positive, as depicted in Figure 4. All measurements showed that in all cases the average time to complete the task using the Head Manipulator was shorter in comparison to other methods.

The advantage of the Change of Visibility aid is markedly notable within some closed environment. In the less complex arrangements with a simple front obstacle, using this tool had rather negative effect and prolonged the time of completion.

**Fig. 3.** Testing scene 2: Room with objects, the change of visibility

### 5.2 Subjects' Comments

Each subject commented about experiences with the usage of mentioned techniques. For the Scene In Hand method most users gave their opinion that it is useful when objects are not very close and a suitable viewpoint can be found. But when the user entered into the enclosed area, objects were too close and their hands could be located outside the room (not visible to user). In such cases, the interaction with objects was painful. It was also difficult to orientate inside and they had to go out several times to find a suitable position. Some users did not search for a better position and tried to solve the respective task with tiny movements of their hands. The motion with SIH was preferred by users to the motion with EIH. Some users evaluated SIH as a very natural tool, while the rest had serious problems to use it in a limited space.

All users agreed, that using COV they were not forced to work in a close and limited space. They could manipulate objects from a more distant position. Moreover, the SIH was used less times as it was not necessary to walk around the obstacles.

Most users noted that using the EIH tool is far more difficult compared to other techniques. Using this method two users did not succeed to finish the task inside the room. But for the experienced users EIH provided finer adjustment of the user's location. Using EIH in combination with COV, every subject solved the tasks without problems. Surprisingly, all subjects rated this combination with the lowest grade. Especially for working in an open area, everybody preferred SIH+COV and HM+COV to this combination.

All subjects assessed HM tool as very intuitive and easy to use when avoiding obstacles. It is very natural to look over an obstacle with HM by bowing the head slightly. Bowing helped even to get a glimpse inside the closed room. Nevertheless, three users complained about tool's sensitivity which caused problems when moving on the surface of a sphere. The combination with COV was advantageous in situations when working area is partially occluded with more

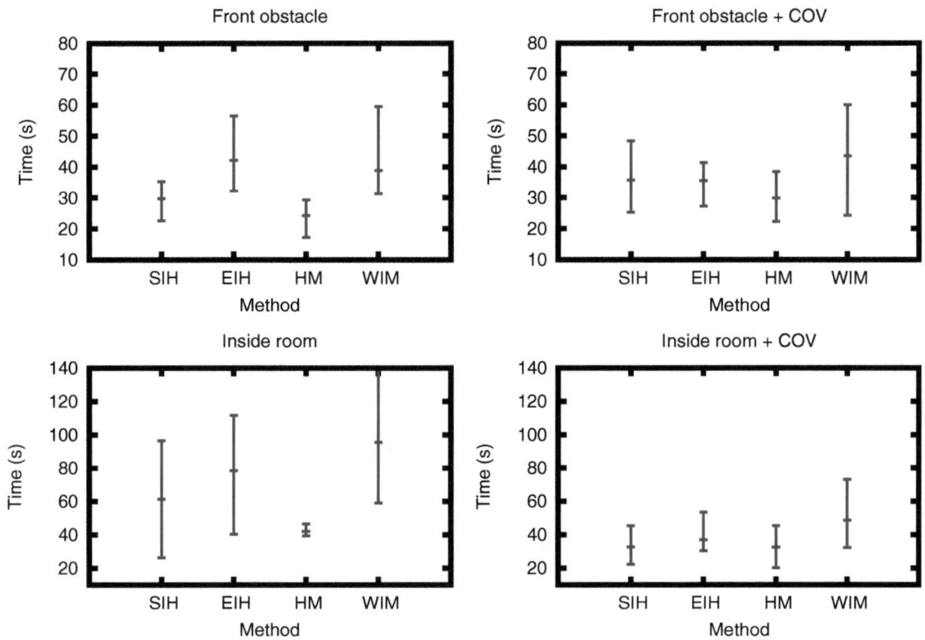


**Fig. 4.** Comparsion of the methods in experiments 1 – 4

obstacles. Most users preferred HM to SIH. Some users preferred single usage of SIH technique even though they admitted improvement with HM.

Assessing WIM, three users emphasized the easier control of scene's preview compared to SIH. Five users reported problems when manipulating with miniatures with scale $< 1/2$. All users reported serious problems using WIM for the manipulation in a closed room. They enlarged the WIM and preferred scale $> 1$. All users evaluated this method worse than SIH and HM. Using COV together with WIM users do not necessarily have to move very close to objects.

## 6 Conclusions and Future Work

In this paper we discussed the problem of manipulating objects behind obstacles. We have tested the usability of several well-known methods with respect to a movement and a manipulation in dense environments. Then we described our approach based on the Head Manipulator and the COV tools. We found out that HM and COV are intuitive and users can quickly reach the intended location to fulfil the interaction task.

This work has been supported by the Ministry of Education, Youth and Sports of the Czech Republic under the research program LC-06008 (Center for Computer Graphics).

## References


1. Bowman, D.A.: Principles for the design of performance-oriented interaction techniques. In: Stanney, K. (ed.) Handbook of virtual environments: Design, implementation, and applications, pp. 277–300. Lawrence Erlbaum Associates, Mahwah NJ (2002)
2. Bowman, D.A., Koller, D., Hodges, L.F.: Travel in immersive virtual environments: An evaluation of viewpoint motion control techniques. In: VRAIS '97. Proceedings of the 1997 Virtual Reality Annual International Symposium (VRAIS '97), IEEE Computer Society, Washington, DC, USA, p. 45 (1997)
3. Bowman, D.A., Johnson, D.B., Hodges, L.F.: Testbed evaluation of virtual environment interaction techniques. In: Proceedings of the ACM symposium on Virtual reality software and technology, pp. 26–33. ACM Press, New York, NY, USA (1999)
4. Arns, L.: A new taxonomy for locomotion in virtual environments. Phd thesis, Iowa State University, Ames, IA (2002)
5. Stoakley, R., Conway, M.J., Pausch, R.: Virtual reality on a WIM: Interactive worlds in miniature. In: Proceedings CHI'95 (1995)
6. Lin, C.R., Loftin, R.B.: Vr user interface: closed world interaction. In: VRST '00. Proceedings of the ACM symposium on Virtual reality software and technology, pp. 153–159. ACM Press, New York (2000)
7. Razzaque, S., Swapp, D., Slater, M., Whitton, M.C., Steed, A.: Redirected walking in place. In: EGVE '02: Proceedings of the workshop on Virtual environments 2002, Eurographics Association, pp. 123–130 (2002)
8. Fukatsu, S., Kitamura, Y., Masaki, T., Kishino, F.: Intuitive control of "bird's eye" overview images for navigation in an enormous virtual environment. In: Proceedings of the ACM symposium on Virtual reality software and technology, pp. 67–76. ACM Press, New York (1998)
9. Bell, B., Feiner, S., Höllerer, T.: View management for virtual and augmented reality. In: UIST '01. Proceedings of the 14th annual ACM symposium on User interface software and technology, pp. 101–110. ACM Press, New York (2001)
10. Bell, B., Höllerer, T., Feiner, S.: An annotated situation-awareness aid for augmented reality. In: UIST '02. Proceedings of the 15th annual ACM symposium on User interface software and technology, pp. 213–216. ACM Press, New York (2002)
11. Joseph, J., LaViola, J., Feliz, D.A., Keefe, D.F., Zeleznik, R.C.: Hands-free multiscale navigation in virtual environments. In: SI3D '01. Proceedings of the 2001 symposium on Interactive 3D graphics, pp. 9–15. ACM Press, New York, USA (2001)
12. Poupyrev, I., Billinghurst, M., Weghorst, S., Ichikawa, T.: The go-go interaction technique: non-linear mapping for direct manipulation in vr. In: UIST '96. Proceedings of the 9th annual ACM symposium on User interface software and technology, pp. 79–80. ACM Press, New York, USA (1996)
13. Ware, C., Jessome, D.R.: Using the bat: A six-dimensional mouse for object placement. IEEE Comput. Graph. Appl. 8(6), 65–70 (1988)
14. Ware, C., Osborne, S.: Exploration and virtual camera control in virtual three dimensional environments. In: SI3D '90. Proceedings of the 1990 symposium on Interactive 3D graphics, pp. 175–183. ACM Press, New York, USA (1990)
15. Pausch, R., Burnette, T., Brockway, D., Weiblen, M.E.: Navigation and locomotion in virtual worlds via flight into hand-held miniatures. In: SIGGRAPH '95. Proceedings of the 22nd annual conference on Computer graphics and interactive techniques, pp. 399–400. ACM Press, New York, USA (1995)

16. Billinghurst, M., Baldis, S., Matheson, L., Philips, M.: 3d palette: a virtual reality content creation tool. In: VRST '97. Proceedings of the ACM symposium on Virtual reality software and technology, pp. 155–156. ACM Press, New York (1997)
17. Tsang, M., Fitzmaurice, G.W., Kurtenbach, G., Khan, A., Buxton, B.: Boom chameleon: simultaneous capture of 3d viewpoint, voice and gesture annotations on a spatially-aware display. In: UIST '02. Proceedings of the 15th annual ACM symposium on User interface software and technology, pp. 111–120. ACM Press, New York (2002)
18. Wingrave, C.A., Haciahmetoglu, Y., Bowman, D.A.: Overcoming world in miniature limitations by a scaled and scrolling wim. 3dui, pp. 11–16 (2006)
19. Grosjean, J., Coquillart, S.: The magic mirror: A metaphor for assisting the exploration of virtual worlds. In: Proceedings Spring Conference on Computer Graphics, pp. 125–129 (1999)
20. Flasar, J., Pokluda, L., Oslejsek, R., Kolcarek, P., Sochor, J.: Vrecko: Virtual reality framework. In: Theory and Practice of Computer Graphics 2005, pp. 203–208. Eurographics Association, Canterbury (2005)

# Registration Based on Online Estimation of Trifocal Tensors Using Point and Line Correspondences

Tao Guan, Lijun Li, and Cheng Wang

Digital Engineering and Simulation Centre,
Huazhong University of Science and Technology,
No.1037 Luoyu Road,430074 Wuhan, China
qd_gt@126.com, lilijun@hust.edu.cn, wangcheng@hust.edu.cn

**Abstract.** This paper illustrates a novel registration method based on robust estimation of trifocal tensors using point and line correspondences synthetically. The proposed method distinguishes itself in following ways: Firstly, besides feature points, line segments are also used to calculate the needed trifocal tensors. The registration process can still be achieved even under poorly textured scenes. Secondly, to estimate trifocal tensors precisely, we use PROSAC instead of RANSAC algorithm to remove outliers. While improving the accuracy of our system, PROSAC also reduces the computation complexity to a large degree.

**Keywords:** Augmented Reality, Registration, Trifocal Tensors, Fundamental Matrix, PROSAC.

## 1 Introduction

Registration is one of the most pivotal problems currently limiting AR applications. It means that the virtual scenes generated by computers must be aligned with the real world seamlessly. Recently, many promising natural feature based registration approaches have been reported. However, most of them use local, viewpoint invariant regions [1],[2],[3]. These regions are extracted independently from reference images, characterized by a viewpoint invariant descriptor, and finally matched with online frames. Those methods are robust to large viewpoint and scale changes. However, the number of produced matches depends on the amount of visible distinctive texture contained in scenes. Images of poorly textured scenes provide only a few matches, and sometimes none at all. Despite lacking texture, these scenes often contain line segments which can be used as additional features. Line segments convey an important amount of geometrical information about the constitution of the scene, whereas regions capture the details of its local appearance. Using both types of features allows to exploiting their complementary information, making registration more reliable and generally applicable.

R. Shumaker (Ed.): Virtual Reality, HCII 2007, LNCS 4563, pp. 42–51, 2007.

In this paper, we propose a novel registration method based on online estimation of trifocal tensors using point and line correspondences, which distinguishes itself in following ways:

Firstly, we relax the restriction that the four specified points used to establish world coordinate system must form an approximate square. The only limitation of our approach is that these four coplanar points should not be collinear.

Secondly, besides feature points, line segments are also used to calculate the needed trifocal tensors. Using both types of features, the registration process can still be achieved even under poorly textured scenes.

Thirdly, benefiting from the tensor of previous frame and the normalized cross-correlation (NNC) operation, we propose a method to match features between current and reference images directly. By this method, not only do we fulfill the task of establishing points and lines correspondences respectively, but also constitute a NNC based criterion to evaluate the quality of points and lines matches in a uniform framework. In deed, this is an important precondition of the PROSAC algorithm we used to estimate the needed tensor.

Finally, to estimate trifocal tensors precisely, we use PROSAC to remove outliers. The matches with higher quality (normalized cross-correlation score) are tested prior to the others, by which the algorithm can arrive at termination criterion and stop sampling earlier. While improving the accuracy, the proposed method can also reduce sample times to a large degree.

## 2 Overview of Proposed Approach

Our method can be divided into two stages, namely, offline initialization and online registration. In initialization stage, a high quality set of point and line correspondences are obtained for two spatially separated reference images of the scenes in which we want to augment. The world coordinate system is established based on projective reconstruction technique and the four coplanar points specified by user in the two reference images respectively. In online stage, feature matches of the reference images are tracked in current frame benefiting from the tensor of previous frame. With the feature triplets, the trifocal tensor is calculated using PROSAC based algebraic minimization algorithm. Using this tensor, the four specified coplanar points are transferred into the living image, and the homographies between the world plane and the moving frame is recovered via the correspondence of these four points. Then the registration matrix is recovered using above homographies and the virtual objects is rendered on the real scenes using the graphics pipeline techniques, e.g., OpenGL.

## 3 Establishing World Coordinate System

Before establishing the world coordinate system, we should first recover the epipolar geometry between the two reference images. For a point $\mathbf{x}_i$ in the first reference image, its correspondence in the second image, $\mathbf{x}_i'$, must lie on the epipolar line in the second image, which is known as the epipolar constraint. Algebraically, in order for $\mathbf{x}_i$ and $\mathbf{x}_i'$ to be matched, the following equation must be satisfied [4]:

$$\mathbf{x}_i^{'} F \mathbf{x}_i = 0 \quad i = 1,\ldots,n \tag{1}$$

Where F, known as the fundamental matrix, is a 3×3 matrix of rank 2, defined up to a scale factor, which is also called the essential matrix in the case of two calibrated images. Let F be the fundamental matrix between two reference images. It can be factored as a product of an antisymmetric matrix $[e^{'}]_{\times}$ and a matrix T, i.e., $F = [e^{'}]_{\times} T$. In fact, *e'* is the epipole in the second image. Then, two projective camera matrices can be represented as follows:

$$P = [I \mid 0], P' = [T \mid e^{'}] \tag{2}$$

Given a pair of matched points in two reference images: $(\mathbf{x}_i, \mathbf{x}_i^{'})$, let $\mathbf{X}_i$ be the corresponding 3D point of real world. The following two equations can be obtained:

$$\mathbf{x}_i = \lambda P \mathbf{X}_i \tag{3}$$

$$\mathbf{x}_i^{'} = \lambda^{'} P^{'} \mathbf{X}_i \tag{4}$$

Where $\lambda$ and $\lambda^{'}$ are two arbitrary scalars. Let $p_i$ and $p_i^{'}$ be the vectors corresponding to the $i$-th row of $P$ and $P^{'}$ respectively. The above two scalars can be computed as follows:

$$\lambda = 1/p_3^T \mathbf{X}_i \tag{5}$$

$$\lambda^{'} = 1/p_3^{'T} \mathbf{X}_i \tag{6}$$

With equations (3) to (6), we can reconstruct $\mathbf{X}_i$ from its image matches $(\mathbf{x}_i, \mathbf{x}_i^{'})$ using the linear least square technique.

The next step is to specify four coplanar points $\mathbf{x}_i = (x_i, y_i, 1)^{\mathrm{T}}$, $(i = 1,\ldots,4)$ in each of the two reference images, respectively, to establish the world coordinate system. Previous work [4][5] has the restriction that these four points should form an approximate square, and the origin of the world coordinate system is set to the center of the square defined by the four known points, the X-axes and Y-axes are the direction of two different parallel sides respectively. However, this method still needs some special square planar structures to help to specify the planar points accurately in the control images.

From the study of [3], we know that the registration matrix can be computed from the homographies between current frame and the world plane, and to get this homographies, we need only four coplanar but non-collinear points of the world plane and their projections on the current image. Motivated by this property, we propose a new method to define world coordinate system without the needs of special square structures, and the only limitation of our approach is that the four specified coplanar points should not be collinear. Let $\mathbf{X}_i = (X_i, Y_i, Z_i, 1)^{\mathrm{T}}, (i = 1,\ldots,4)$ be the projective 3D coordinates of the four specified points, the origin of the world coordinate system will be the $\mathbf{X}_1$, the X-axes will be the direction of the vector $\overrightarrow{\mathbf{X}_1\mathbf{X}_2}$, the Z-axes will be the vertical direction of the plane defined by above four 3D points, and the Y-axes will be the cross product of Z-axes and X-axes. To improve accuracy, when one point has been specified in a reference image, its epipolar line in another image is drawn to limit the searching area of the correspondence in this image, because the correspondence is limited on this epipolar line according to the property of epipolar geometry.

## 4 Feature Tracking

We propose a normalized cross-correlation based method to match the features between current and reference images directly. We assume that the tensor of previous frame has been calculated accurately. With this tensor, the corresponding feature points detected from two reference images are transferred onto the live image, the correspondence is identified by searching in a small area surrounding the transferred point for a point that correlate well with one of the two reference matched points.

To match a line segment, following steps must be carried out. Firstly, the midpoint of the shorter one of the corresponding lines in reference images is extracted, and the correspondence of this midpoint on the longer segment in another image is also detected, in fact, this correspondence is the intersection of the longer segment and the epipolar line of the shorter segment's midpoint in this image. Secondly, with the previous tensor, the midpoint of the shorter segment and its correspondence is transferred onto the current image, and an appropriate searching window around the transferred point is fixed to limit the searching area of the correspondence. Finally, the operation similar to feature points is inflicted on the points belonging to the detected lines and within this searching window. The correspondence is the line with the point that has the maximal normalized cross-correlation score with one of the two extracted points in reference images.

In above steps, not only do we fulfill the task of establishing points and lines correspondences respectively, but also constitute a NNC based criterion to evaluate the quality of points and lines matches in a uniform framework. In deed, this is a very important precondition of the PROSAC algorithm we used to estimate trifocal tensor in section 5.

## 5 Estimating Trifocal Tensor Using PROSAC

We now turn to the problem of calculating trifocal tensor using point correspondences obtained from previous section. The trifocal tensor plays a similar role in three views to that played by the fundamental matrix in two. It encapsulates all the projective geometric relations between three views that are independent of scene structure [6]. For a triplet of images, the image of a 3D point $\mathbf{X}$ is $\mathbf{x}$, $\mathbf{x}'$ and $\mathbf{x}''$ in the first, second and third images respectively, where $\mathbf{x} = (x_1, x_2, x_3)^T$ is homogeneous three vectors. If the three camera matrices are in canonical form, where $P = [I \mid 0]$, $P' = [a_j^i]$, $P'' = [b_j^i]$, and the $a_j^i$ and $b_j^i$ denote the *ij*-th entry of the matrix $P'$ and $P''$ respectively, index *i* being the row index and *j* being the column index. Then the trifocal tensor can be computed by:

$$\mathrm{T}_i^{jk} = a_i^j b_4^k - a_4^j b_i^k \quad , j,k = 1,\ldots,3 \, , i = 1,\ldots,3 \tag{7}$$

Where the trifocal tensor $\mathrm{T} = [\mathrm{T}_1 , \mathrm{T}_2 , \mathrm{T}_3]^{\mathrm{T}}$ is a $3 \times 3 \times 3$ homogeneous tensor. Using the tensor a point can be transferred to a third image from correspondences in the first and second:

$$x_l^{''} = x_i^{'} \sum_{k=1}^{3} x_k \, \mathrm{T}_k^{jl} - x_j^{'} \sum_{k=1}^{3} x_k \, \mathrm{T}_k^{il} \, , i, j = 1,\ldots,3 , l = 1,\ldots,3 \tag{8}$$

Similarly, a line can be transferred as

$$l_i = \sum_{j=1}^{3} \sum_{k=1}^{3} l_j^{'} l_k^{''} \, \mathrm{T}_k^{ij} \tag{9}$$

The trifocal tensor has 27 elements, 26 equations are needed to calculate a tensor up to scale. Each triplet of point matches can give four independent linear equations for the entries of the tensor, and each triplet of line matches can provide two independent linear equations, accordingly, 7 points or 13 lines or something in the middle, if one uses both line and point matches are needed to compute the trifocal tensor linearly. The above method called linear algorithm or normalized linear algorithm when input data is pretreated. The drawback of these algorithms is that they do not take into account the internal constraints of the trifocal tensor and cannot necessarily yield a geometrically valid tensor. Algebraic minimization algorithm may be a good choice to obtain a valid tensor. However, due to using all available correspondences, this method is prone to being affected by the presence of mismatches (outliers). To overcome the disturbance of the mismatches, the 6-point RANSAC method has been brought forward. This method has the capability of generating a precise tensor even in the presence of a significant number of outliers. The shortcoming of RANSAC is that its computational complexity increases dramatically with the number of correspondences and proportion of mismatches. Moreover 6-point RANSAC approach does not take into consider the line matches, which is also an important clue to compute the need tensor. In our research, we propose a novel method to calculate trifocal tensor using point and line matches synthetically, which take full advantage of PROSAC and algebraic minimization algorithm.

### 5.1 Sampling with PROSAC

Unlike RANSAC, which treats all matches coequally and extracts random samples uniformly from the full set, PROSAC [7] samples are semi-randomly drawn from a subset of the data with the highest quality, and the size of the hypothesis generation set is gradually increased. The size of the set of potential matches has very small influence on its speed, since the solution is typically found early, when samples are taken from a smaller set. The improvement in efficiency relies on the presupposition that potential correspondences with high similarity are more likely to be inliers. In fact, PROSAC is designed to draw the same samples as RANSAC, but only in a different order. The matches that more likely to be inliers are tested prior to the others, thereby, the algorithm can arrive at termination criterion and stop sampling earlier.

In our method, the set of *K* potential matches is denoted as $U_K$. The data points in $U_K$ can be either point or line correspondence and are sorted in descending order with respect to the normalized cross-correlation score *s*.

$$u_i, u_j \in U_K : i < j \Rightarrow s(u_i) \geq s(u_j) \tag{10}$$

A set of *k* data points with the highest score is represented as $U_k$. Then, the initial subset contains the least top-ranked matches that can give 26 need equations. If all of the valid samples from the current subset $U_n = (u_1, u_2, ..., u_n)$ have been tested, then the next subset is $U_{n+1} = (u_1, u_2, ..., u_n, u_{n+1})$, and the following samples consist of $u_{n+1}$ and the data points drawn from $U_n$ at random. In above process, all the samples should contain the least matches (7 points or 13 lines or something in the middle) that can generate 26 equations needed in normalized linear algorithm.

### 5.2 Algebraic Minimization Algorithm

The standard algebraic minimization algorithm takes following steps [6]:

1. From the set of point and line correspondences construct the set of equations of the form. $\mathrm{At} = 0$, where $\mathrm{A}$ come from the equation (8) or (9), t is the vector of entries of tensor $\mathrm{T}_i^{jk}$.
2. Solve these equations using normalized linear algorithm to find an initial estimate of the trifocal tensor.
3. Find the two epipoles $e'(a_4)$ and $e''(b_4)$ from the initial tensor as the common perpendicular to the left null-vectors of the three $\mathrm{T}_i$.
4. According to Equation (7), construct the 27×18 matrix $\mathrm{E}$ such that $\mathrm{t} = \mathrm{Ea}$, where $\mathrm{a}$ is the vector representing entries of $a_i^j$ and $b_i^k$.
5. Compute the tensor by minimizing the algebraic error $\|\mathrm{AEa}\|$ subject to $\|\mathrm{Ea}\| = 1$.
6. Find an optimal solution by iteration over the two epipoles using an iterative method like Levenberg-Marquardt algorithm.

To get a fast non-iterative algorithm, we omit the last iteration step in our algorithm. It has been proved that the negative influence of this predigestion is very slightly and can be ignored.

### 5.3 Estimating Method

The following steps give the outline of our PROSAC based algebraic minimization algorithm.

1. Construct 26 equations from the sample given by PROSAC algorithm.
2. Solve these equations to get a candidate tensor using the method described in section 5.2.
3. Reproject all of the potential matches on to the current frame using above tensor and equation (8) or (9).
4. If the number of inliers is less than the predefined threshold T (varying with different environment), then generate a new sample using PROSAC and repeat the above steps.
5. If the number of inliers is greater than T, then re-estimate the tensor using these inliers and terminate.

The criterion to judge outliers is described as follows:

For points, we take a correspondence as outlier, if the distance between the reprojection and the detected point in current frame is greater than 3 pixels.

For line segments, if the orientation difference between the reprojection and the detected segment is larger than $5^{\circ}$ or the distance between the detected segment and the reprojection of the selected points of the lines on the references is greater than 3 pixels, we consider it as outlier.

## 6 Experimental Results

The proposed method has been implemented in C++ on a fast Graphics Workstation. On average, our system can run at 10fps with 320×240 pixel images. Some experiments have been carried out to demonstrate the validity of the proposed approach.

### 6.1 Tracking Accuracy

The first experiment is carried out to test the accuracy of our method. The reprojection errors between the original specified points and their reprojections are compared. Fig.1 shows the reprojection errors of our method. The average reprojection error of the first 500 frames is 3.2 pixels, which validates the accuracy of proposed method. Some images are also exhibited in Fig. 2.

### 6.2 Sample Times

Using the video sequence obtained from this experiment, we also compare the sample times between our modified RANSAC and standard RANSAC algorithm. The average and maximum sample times of the standard RANSAC is 36.7 and 194 respectively, which are 9.4 and 12.1 times of the values of our method. This experiment proves that our modified RANSAC is more stabile and can reduce sample times significantly, which makes our method suitable for online implementation.

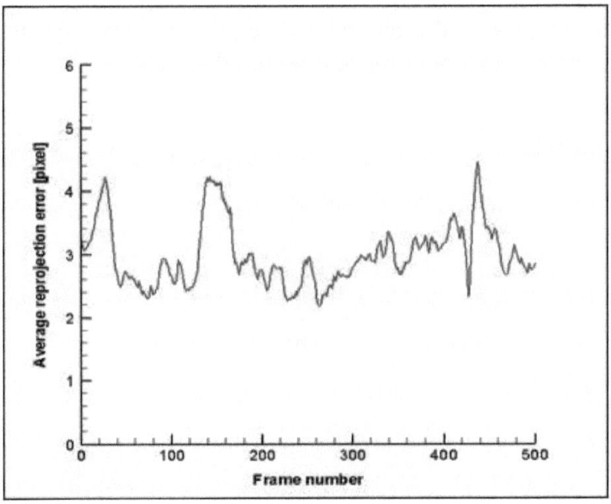


**Fig. 1.** Reprojection errors of the first 500 frames

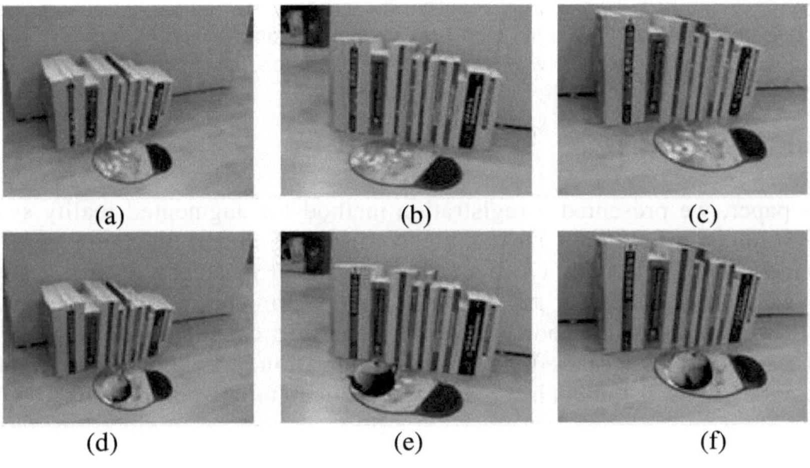


**Fig. 2.** Examples in first experiment. (a)-(c) are the 45th ,86th and 257th frames of the input video sequence with the inliers used to calculate the needed tensor, respectively. (d)-(f) are the corresponding registration images.

## 6.3 Registration with Line Segments

We also take an experiment to validate the usability of our method under the poorly textured scenes. In this experiment, 37 line correspondences (only lines of length 10 pixels or more are considered) are extracted from the two reference views. In online stage, only these line segments are tracked to compute the needed tensor. We have successfully augmented a 3D virtual word on the wall over 450 consecutive frames.

Fig.3 shows some images of the augmented sequence. This experiment proves that our method is effective even under the less textured scenes.

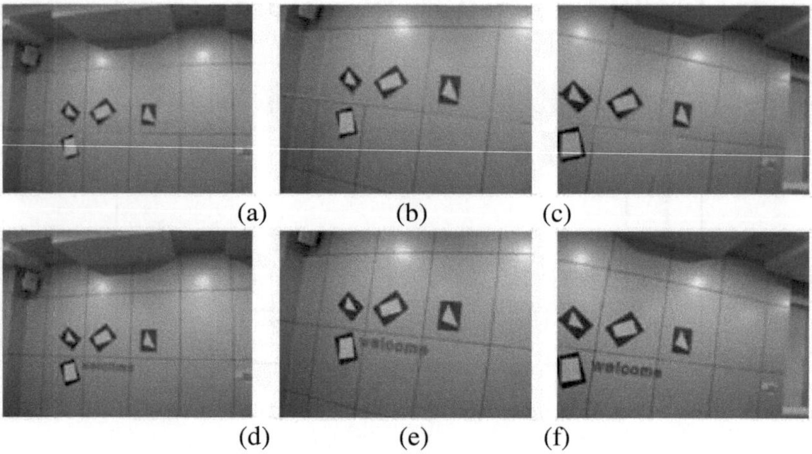


**Fig. 3.** Registration with Line Segments. (a)-(c) are the 23th, 56th and 233th frames of the input sequence with the inliers, respectively. (d)-(f) are the corresponding registration images.

## 7 Conclusion

In this paper, we presented a registration method for augmented reality systems based on robust estimation of trifocal tensor using point and line correspondences simultaneously. With both types of features, the robustness of the system is improved to a large degree. As shown in our experiments, the proposed method can still work even under poorly textured scenes. To calculate trifocal tensor, we put forward a PROSAC based algebraic minimization algorithm. While improves the accuracy, this method also reduces the computation complexity to a large degree.

## References

1. Simon, G., Fitzgibbon, A., Zisserman, A.: Markerless tracking using planar structures in the scene. In: Proc. of the ISAR, pp. 120–128 (2000)
2. Pang, Y., Yuan, M.L., Nee, A.Y.C., Ong, S.K.: A Markerless Registration Method for Augmented Reality based on Affine Properties. In: Proc. of the AUIC, pp. 25–32 (2006)
3. Simon, G., Berger, M.: Reconstructing while registering: a novel approach for markerless augmented reality. In: Proc. of the ISMAR, pp. 285–294 (2002)
4. Yuan, M.L., Ong, S.K., Nee, A.Y.C.: Registration Based on Projective Reconstruction Technique for Augmented Reality Systems. IEEE Trans. on Visualization and Computer Graphics 11(3), 254–264 (2005)

5. Yuan, M.L., Ong, S.K., Nee, A.Y.C.: Registration using natural features for augmented reality systems. IEEE Trans. on Visualization and Computer Graphics 12(4), 569–580 (2006)
6. Hartley, R., Zisserman, A.: Multiple View Geometry in Computer Vision. Cambridge University Press, Cambridge (2000)
7. Chum, O., Matas, J.: Matching with PROSAC - progressive sample consensus. In: Proc. of CVPR. 1(1), pp. 305–313 (2005)

# Non-commercial Object-Base Scene Description

S.R. Gulliver, G. Ghinea, and K. Kaur

School of Information System, Computing and Mathematics
Brunel University, United Kingdom
{Stephen.Gulliver,George.Ghinea,Kulveer.Kaur}@brunel.ac.uk

**Abstract.** This paper investigates methods of describing two-dimensional and three-dimensional scenes using eXtensible Mark-up Language (XML). It also investigates the initial development of a non-commercial object-based scene description language, for the effective capture of two- and three-dimensional scenes. Design science research techniques were applied to determine the ideal factors involved in effective scene capture. The solution facilitates the description of 2D and 3D environments via interpretation of object relationships; the implementation of the inheritance, functionality, interactions and behaviour.

**Keywords:** XML, Scene description, hierarchy, functionality, behaviour.

## 1 Introduction

The process of creating virtual environments is diverse, but is traditionally achieved by either describing object properties (coding / scripting), or by positioning predefined objects into a blank virtual space ('drag-and-drop', a metaphor that allows the user to pick up an object via the mouse pointer and move it to the desired location). There have been a number of languages developed to create 2D and 3D scenes and virtual environments. Sadly the languages possess problems of interoperability, reliability and performance; the inability to incorporate effectively dynamic or interactive scenes (Walczak, 2003); as well as limited or conflicting commercial support of rendering within web browsers (Macdonald, *et al., 2005*). Modifications to previous standards have been made, yet many of these problems still exist.

### 1.1 Scene Description Languages

Scene Description Languages aim to capture the physical world in a readable and convenient way. The advent of the XML based technologies has delivered a number of scene description languages with a range of advantages and disadvantages.

In 1994, first International Conference of the World Wide Web (WWW) was held in Geneva (Carson, *et, al.*, 1999). At this conference Mark Pesce, Tony Parisi, Tim Berners-Lee, and David Ragget presented the concept of VRML. In the same year a series of requirements was developed by the WWW and an open request for the proposal was issued. As a result Silicon Graphics introduced the Open Inventor format, which has been widely accepted. Silicon graphics engineer Gavin Bell developed the

R. Shumaker (Ed.): Virtual Reality, HCII 2007, LNCS 4563, pp. 52–61, 2007.

working document for a VRML 1.0 specification and the first draft was presented in October 1994 at the Second International World Wide Web Conference. The early VRML just was static world, allowing for no interaction between the objects. The extended version VRML 2.0 enhanced this with the support of JAVA, JavaScript, sound, animation. The main technique used by VRML files for describing 3D world is that of the hierarchical scene graph. Scene graph techniques were made popular by the OpenInventor programmer toolkit from silicon graphics (Nadeau, 1999). As its name suggests, a scene graph is a hierarchy of groups and shapes arranged in a tree structure. Each of the parents and children within a scene graph are called nodes. These nodes are used to construct 3D shapes, position the user's viewpoint, aim a light source, define animation paths, group shapes together and so forth. Scene graph parents manage groups of children that my have children of their own. To create a complex scene hierarchy, the children can be members of other scene graphs. The child node inherits the properties of the parent node, known as simple inheritance.

The Extensible 3D language (X3D), was proposed by the Web3D consortium in 2001. X3D defines a three-dimensional run time environment and a mechanism to deliver 3D content on the web; thus extending VRML with some new graphics features (Bullard, 2003). New features included: Non Uniform Rational B-splines (NURBs), Humanoid Animation, Multi-texturing, triangle primitives, 2D shapes inside 3D shapes, advanced application programming interfaces, additional data encoding formats, and a modular approach to implementation. Although adding graphical realism, such improvements do not consider either the issues of dynamic modelling and scene behaviour.

Walczak and Wojciech (2003) developed a high level language called X-VRML, an XML based language that adds dynamic modelling capabilities to virtual scene description standards such as VRML, X3D, MPEG-4. This language overcomes the limitations of passive virtual reality systems by providing access to databases, parameterisation, object-orientation and imperative programming techniques. Parameterised virtual scene models are used to build database driven Virtual Reality (VR) applications. The applications are able to generate virtual scene instances according to the models, user queries, data retrieved from database, user preferences and the current state of the application. X-VRML therefore allows a user to make changes in the models structure at runtime, which facilitates scene behaviour and interaction. The X-VRML language also permits designers to extend the language with new features without affecting the previous designed application.

Hulquist *et al.* (2006) proposed an interesting and effective technique for generating virtual environments *(VEs)* and describing scenes. Similar in nature to many computer game world simulators, this technique describes scenes by allowing the user to control the scene environment, for example: wet, sparse, tropical, cloudy, light, mountains and undulating. The main benefit of this technique, although not allowing description of object parameter, is that it allows large and complex virtual environments matching certain user requirements to be created relatively quickly.

### 1.2 Adding Behaviour to the Scene

In our opinion, the success of 3D applications on the web depends upon the degree of object behaviour and interactivity. Object behaviour could be the function, weight, gravity, kinematics, etc. For a number of decades, the use of visual representation in the process of building software has been studied and a number of high-level languages have been developed. Virtual environments are used for a number of applications including educational, industrial process, behavioural modifications and games. At present, many tools have been developed in order to generate static environments but a lot more could be done with respect to dynamic worlds.

Commonly behaviour is applied through short programs generally written in a script language and then connected to the 3D objects in the visual file. For example, Meyer and Conner (1995) have suggested language extensions that allow specifying new types of VRML nodes as well as behaviour descriptions, which can be reused and composite. They proposed a separator called prototyping nodes, which could allow defining something without actually using it. Another *behaviour system* has been described by Nadeau and Moreland (1995) that uses Perl scripts integrated with VRML worlds. In this system behaviour is defined using another set of objects. Example of this could be teapot, which includes a number of objects such as heating its content like tea, etc.

An intelligent behaviour system was also developed by Del Bimbo, *et al.* (1994), whereby an agent responds to events in a virtual environment using intelligent decision-making. Similarly, Arjomandy and Smedley (2004) described a method of adding behaviour to an object by using touch sensors and a scripting language. Messages are passed between objects in order to create behaviour. An example of this kind of behaviour was used in recent the film 'Lord of the Rings' to generate soldiers used in battle scenes.

In work closer to ours, Dachselt and Rukzio (2002) introduced an XML based framework for modelling 3D objects and developed a language called Behaviour3D. Furthermore, Burrows and England (2005) suggested a language called BDL (Behaviour Description Language). BDL proposed a view of behaviour and developed software architecture, which provides the basis for implementing behaviour at run time. The behaviour description language (BDL) described is based on VRML and adds a number of features to support behavioural specification for using it with their behaviour engine.

### 1.3 Interaction Added to the Objects in a Scene

Interactions are used to describe the dynamic operations of the user, objects and the environment. Interactions define how a user interacts with the environment, with the objects and shows how objects interact with each other.

Hendricks, *et al.* (2003) produced a Meta authoring tool, which allows both beginner and advanced users to create virtual reality applications. This allows the migration from non-programmer to experienced programmer. According to Hendricks, *et al.* (2003) there are two ways of implementing behaviour and interaction in the virtual application:

- *Behaviour Based Interaction*: The behaviour-based interactions of objects occur according to attributes of the objects themselves, providing them a level of autonomous behaviour. For example, the behaviour of a water toy is to float on the water. The interaction of this toy with any other liquid will be the same as it is with the water due to its floating nature.

- *Event-Based Interaction:* The event-based interaction takes place when the occurrence of an event is caused by user intervention or any change in the environment. For example, turning the light bulb on and off by pressing the switch. A user interacts with the object switch and it interacts with other object light bulb.

In addition, Walczak and Wojciechowski (2005) have suggested a method for creating interactive presentation dynamically for virtual environments. A non-programmer can create objects and their actual presentation employing a user-friendly content management application. The process of creating a presentation consists of (a) creating a presentation space, (b) selecting objects, (c) selecting a presentation template and (d) setting values of object and template parameters. The same presentation space can be presented differently by the use of multiple presentation template instances associated with different presentation domains.

The emphasis of our work is to consider both scene hierarchy, yet also the concepts of behaviour and interactivity. An office, for example, is defined by the effective placement of objects, such as a keyboard, a CPU, a mouse, a table, a desk and a chair. The table may be made up of other objects: drawers, legs, etc. This table is physically linked in some way to other objects in the environment, such as the floor, the keyboard, the monitor, etc. In addition, certain objects have definable functionality allowing interaction (both with the user, but also with other objects). Each object has a physical appearance, location and orientation, as well as possibly having considerable functional potential (often similar in nature to other instances of its type).

## 2 Initial Development

### 2.1 Examples and Assumptions

A design science approach was used in our work. Accordingly simple real world scene examples were used to establish the important factors involved in the effective capture of 2D and 3D scenes. Abduction processing was used to define the following design objectives:

1. The final solution should be able to define both 2- and 3-Dimensional scenes using a XML- based description.
2. A visual representation of hierarchy and interactivity is required to support non-technical users.
3. Each object should be able to inherit the properties of other objects.
4. The design should be able to add functionality to an object.
5. The design should be able to define behaviour on the basis of properties.
6. The concept of interaction should be clearly defined.

Assumptions that were made when undertaking this research include:

1. The physical properties of an object (such as shape, appearance, translation, etc) may be derived via the current X3D language.
2. There is a predefined, yet variable, set of relationship tags that will be used to describe the scene. For example, 'on the top', 'on the right hand side', 'touches', etc. Such tags could be defined by the user as required.

3. The concept of adding functionality will be described using UML flowcharts. Class diagrams are functionally implemented in object-orientated programming code.

Incorporation and collaboration of current visual object-based external standards facilitates acceptance, whilst limiting the need for technical programming skills.

## 2.2 Capturing Hierarchy Dependencies

In our solution, hierarchical dependencies is visually represented by relational dependencies of objects (see Figure 1). For example: the Table has two draws.

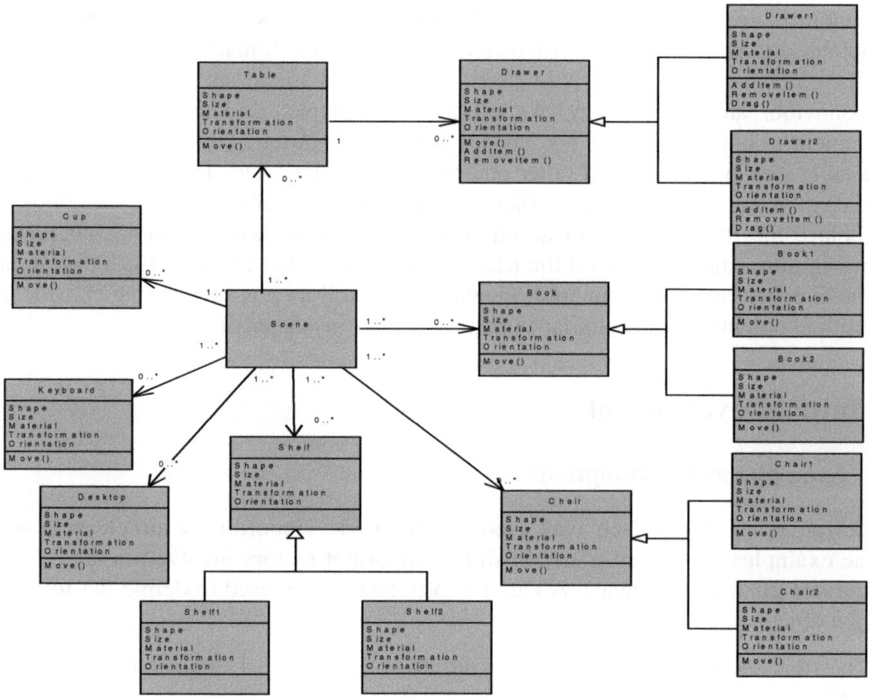


**Fig. 1.** Office objects defined within the scene hierarchy

## 2.3 Capturing Functional Dependencies

In our solution, function dependencies is visually represented by adding associated links between objects. For example: Drawer 1 On top of Drawer 2.

We made the assumption that there is a predefined, yet variable, set of relationship tags that will be used to describe the scene. Every relationship has a meaning that aids the description of interactivity. Although the list of link definitions is potentially unlimited, in our worked example interactions were restricted to: **On the top of** *(ObjA, ObjB)*; **Opposite to** *(ObjA, ObjB)*; **In the RHS** *(ObjA, ObjB)*; **In the LHS** *(ObjA, ObjB)*; **Next to the** *(ObjA, ObjB)*; **Touches** *(ObjA, ObjB)*. This is then visually represented using visual connections between object instances (see Figure 2).

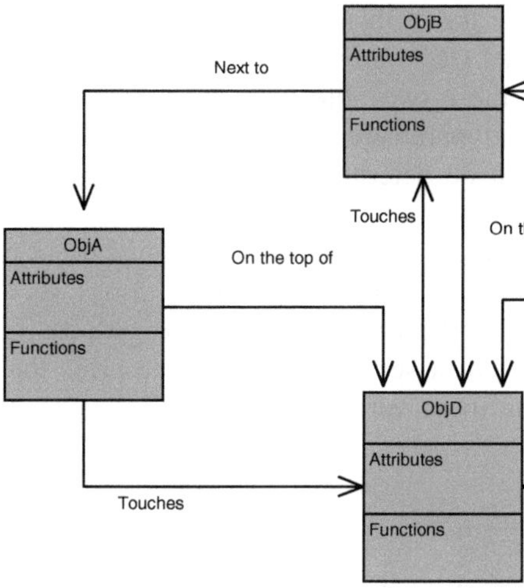


**Fig. 2.** Visual demonstration of object functional dependencies

Parameter information can be incorporated by manipulating the interactions. In our example, distance was added as the total length measured between two points (currently unit independent). Distance, as a parameter, can be used to calculate coordinates of the objects on the basis of the relationships that exist among objects. If

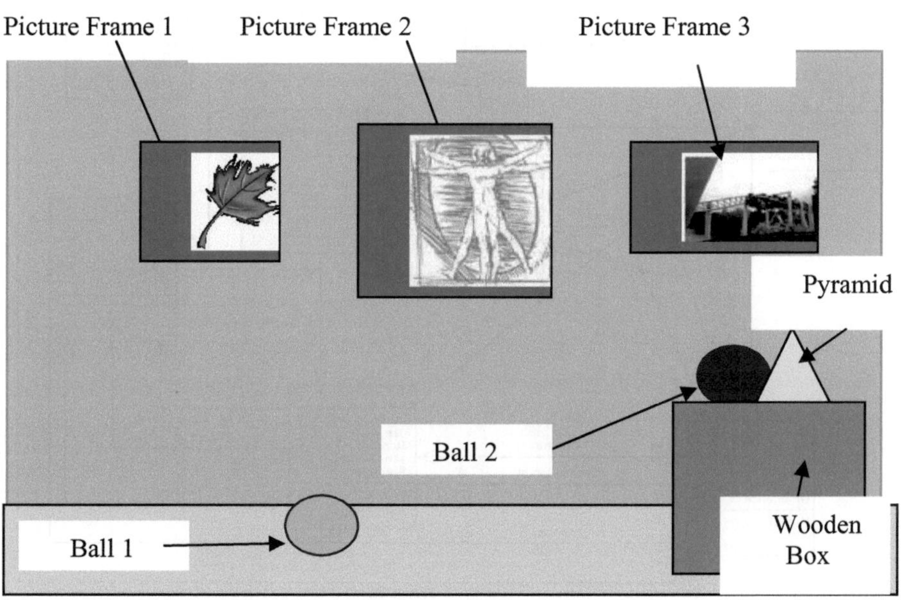


**Fig. 3.** Two-Dimensional Scene of a child's room

the objects used in the scene are cake (ObjA) and a party hat (ObjB). The relationships between these objects are "*ObjA may be to the RHS of ObjB*", "*ObjA is next to ObjB*" The distance between these two objects is given as 5. Interesting, as more interactions, both functional and parameter information, is defined between objects, more specific information can be determined concerning both the physical and functional dependencies in the model.

To explicate a scene, a simple layout has been chosen for description (see Figure 3). This scene is a room, which has got a number of things such as three picture frames, two balls, one pyramid and a wooden box (see Figure 3). The system requires coordinates for one of the object. User is supposed to describe the scene on the basis of relationship exists among these various objects. The scene is depicted using two dimensions of the objects

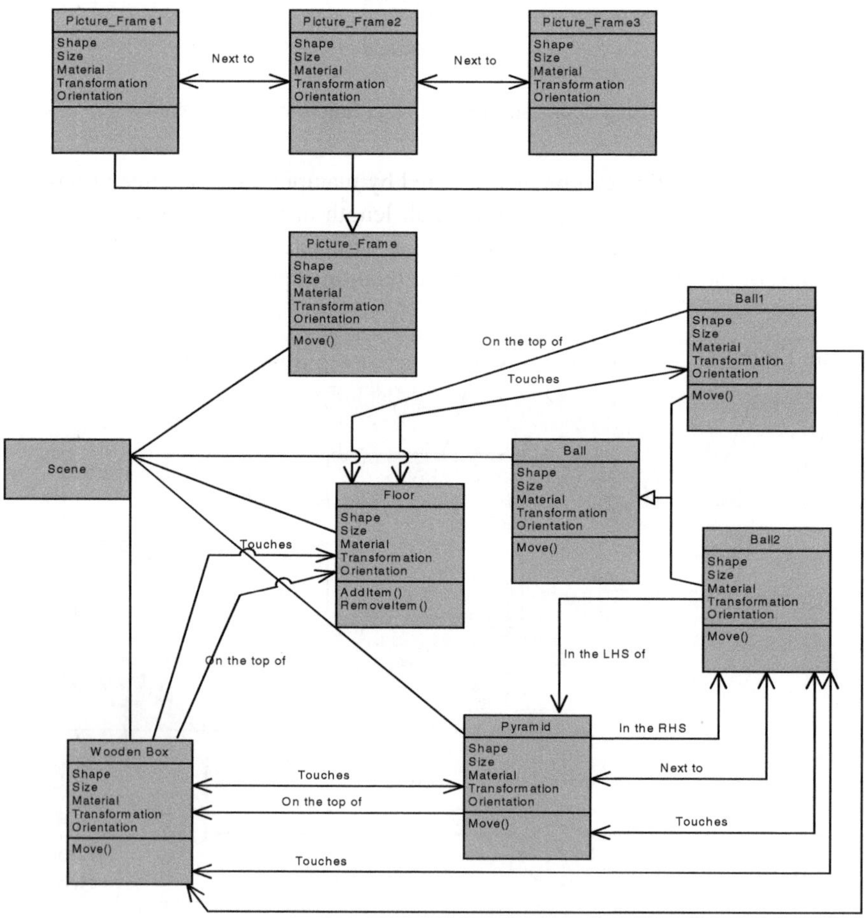


**Fig. 4.** Child's Room: objects and their functional relationships

In our example (Figure 3), there is a ball on the floor; it is also **touching** the floor. There is another ball, which looks similar to the ball on the floor but this ball is **on the top of** a wooden box. The bottom of ball **touches** the wooden box. A pyramid is **on the top** of box. It is placed **in the right hand side** of the second ball. The ball **touches** this pyramid. Both of the objects are **on the top of** wooden box and touch the box. There are three picture frames hanging on the wall. One of them is **in the right** corner of the room; second picture frame is **next to** it. The distance between these two frames is about 10m distances. The last picture frame is next to second picture frame and the distance is about 8m.

Visual description of functional relationships between objects allows a user to describe relationships in a scene in a natural form. Moreover, the user is not concerned with the co-ordinates of the object to describe the scene. The scene that is described above in Figure 16 can be explained using simple sentences i.e. in natural way. For instance the scene is described here in simple language as:

The relationship used for describing the scene is differentiated using bold fonts. The objects used in the scene are listed below: *Floor, Ball1, Ball2, Pyramid, Wooden Box, Picture Frame1, Picture Frame2, Picture Frame3*. The relationship include: **Next to** *(Picture1, Picture2)*; **Next to** *(Picture3, Picture2)*; **On the top of** *(Ball1, Floor)*; **Touches** *(Ball1, Floor)*; **On the top of** *(Pyramid, Wooden Box)*; **On the top of** *(Ball2, Wooden Box)*; **Touches** *(Ball2, Wooden Box)*; **Touches** *(Ball2, Pyramid)* **Part=** *"Right side";* **Next to** *(Ball2, Pyramid)*; **In the RHS** *(Pyramid, Ball2)*; **In the LHS** *(Ball2, Pyramid)*.

All the above relationships amongst objects was then represented in a visual way. Figure 4 clearly presents all the objects and the relationships that exist among these objects. All objects have a number of relationships with other objects. As shown in the diagram, classes for all three frames; thus *pictureframe1*, *pictureframe2* and *pictureframe3* are subclasses of the super class picture frame. According to the nature of child class, these three child classes inherit the properties and function of the parent class named picture frame. *Ball1* and *Ball2* also inherit the features of the parent class named *Ball.* This will help to reduce the complexity of the program as only one class will be needed to define and child classes will use inheritance methods in order to appear and perform the same functions. The next section will discuss the coding part for this scene.

## 3 XML File Structure

Each relationship is given an identity so that it can be used by each of the objects (see Figure 4). All information about relationships and locations of objects was described. A file link was used to describe the image appearance.

Shape / appearance of objects are described using current modelling languages; size / scale, orientation and object material / texture was dynamically manipulated in object parameters. Documentation of functionality and inheritance was achieved by launching a java-based programming environment and using java functional inheritance properties.

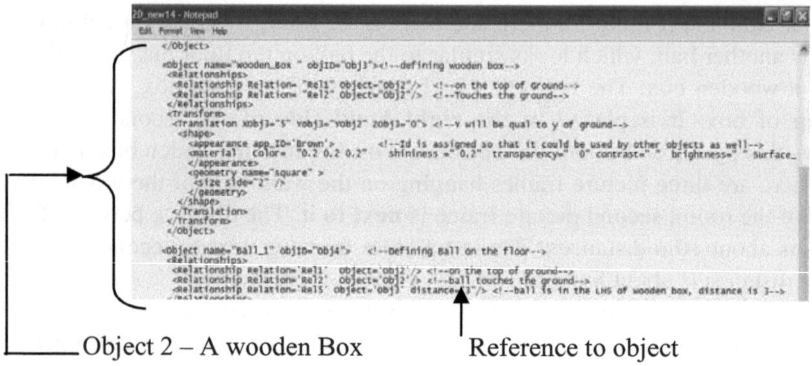


**Fig. 5.** 'A child's bedroom' - automatically generated from visual interactivity relationships

## 4 Conclusion

A XML- based description is described, that supports: a visual representation of hierarchy and interactivity; inheritance of properties from other objects; addition of object functionality and behaviour on the basis of properties. Previous scene description standards have been developed, yet they do not cover the multi-dimensional requirements that appear key to the capture of a dynamic scene. By incorporating multiple standards, external programming tools, we have taken positive steps towards a more eclectic implementation solution, for use in scene description.

## References

1. Arjomandy, S., Smedley, J.T.: Visual Specification of Behaviours in VRML Worlds. In: Proceedings of the ninth international conference on 3D Web technology, Monterey, California, USA, pp. 127–133 (2004)
2. Del Bimbo, A., Pala, P., Santini, S.: Visual image retrieval by elastic deformation of object sketches. In: Proceedings of IEEE Symposium on Visual Languages, pp. 216–223 (1994)
3. Carson, S.G., Pulk, F.R., Carey, R.: Developing the VRML 97 International Standard. IEEE Computer Graphics and Applications 19(2), 52–58 (1999)
4. Dachselt, R., Rukzio, E.: Behaviour3D: An XML based Framework for 3D Graphics Behaviour. In: Proceeding of the Eighth international Conference on 3D Web Technology, Saint Malo, France, 101–ff (2003)
5. Hendricks, Z., Marsden, G., Blake, E.: A Meta-Authoring Tool for Specifying Interactions in Virtual Reality Environments. In: Proceedings of the 2nd international Conference on Computer Graphics, Virtual Reality, Visualisation and interaction in Africa, Cape Town, South Africa, pp. 171–180 (2003)
6. Hultquist, C., Gain, J., Cairns, D.: Affective Scene Generation. In: Proceedings of the 4th international Conference on Computer Graphics, Virtual Reality, Visualisation and interaction in Africa, Cape Town, South Africa, pp. 59–63 (2006)
7. Macdonald, J.A., Brailsford, F.D., Bagley, R.S.: Encapsulating and manipulating Component object graphics (COGs) using SVG. In: Proceedings of the 2005 ACM Symposium on Document Engineering, Bristol, UK, pp. 61–63 (2005)

8. Meyer, T., Conner, B.: Adding Behaviour to VRML. In: Proceedings of the First Symposium on Virtual Reality Modeling Language, San Diego, California, USA, pp. 45–51 (1995)
9. Nadeau, R.D.: Building Virtual Worlds with VRML. IEEE Computer Graphics and Applications 19(2), 18–29 (1999)
10. Nadeau, R.D., Moreland, L.J.: The Virtual Behaviour System. A behaviour Language Protocol for VRML. In: Proceedings of the First Symposium on Virtual Reality Modeling Language, San Diego, California, USA, pp. 53–61 (1995)
11. Walczak, K., Cellary, W.: Building database Applications of Virtual Reality with X-VRML, Tempe, Arizona, USA, pp. 111–120 (2002)
12. Walczak, K., Wojceichowski, R.: Dynamic Creation of interactive mixed reality presentations. In: Proceedings of the ACM Symposium on Virtual Reality Software and Technology, Monterey, California, USA, pp. 167–176 (2005)

# Triangle Mesh Optimization for Improving Rendering Quality of 3D Virtual Environments

Qingwei Guo, Weining Yue, Qicheng Li, and Guoping Wang

Peking University, Beijing 100871, China
gqw@graphics.pku.edu.cn

**Abstract.** High-quality mesh provides good rendering effects of virtual reality systems. In this paper a solid technique for generating triangle meshes optimized for real-time rendering in virtual environments is proposed. Modified weighted Voronoi barycenter relaxation is used to improve the mesh geometry. A simulated annealing algorithm is presented for optimizing vertex connec tivity. The shape deviations are effectively prevented, and the boundaries and features are well preserved. The advantage and robustness of this technique are verified by many examples.

## 1 Introduction

In virtual environments, the rendering quality of 3D models and scenes directly affects the user evaluation. Currently the majority of virtual reality applications use triangle meshes as their fundamental modeling and rendering primitive. Such meshes can be the result of modeling software, or may come as an output of a scanning device, associated with reconstruction or computer vision algorithms. Their qualities are often not suited to high-quality real-time rendering. For instance, hardware accelerated rendering techniques, such as triangle strips and triangle fans, require fairly regular meshes. Additionally, subdivision has become a prevalent technique for multiresolution rendering and modeling. Therefore meshes should also have good vertex connectivity. That is, the valance of a boundary vertex should be four, and the valance of any other vertex should equal to six. In this paper a solid technique for triangular mesh model optimization is proposed. The face geometry will be improved, and the vertex connectivity will be optimized.

To improve the mesh quality, lots of previous algorithms [1]–[5] are based on global parameterization of the original mesh, and then a resampling of the parameter domain. Following this, the new triangulation is projected back into 3D space, resulting in an improved version of the original model. The main drawback of the global parameterization methods is the sensitivity of the result to the specific parameterization used, and to the cut used to force models that are not isomorphic to a disk to be so. The alternative to global parameterization is to work directly on the surface and perform a series of local modifications on the mesh. The distortion caused by mapping a 3D mesh to a 2D parametric domain can be considerably reduced. Gotsman et al. used area-equalization [6] and local Lloyd method [7] for remeshing. Similarly, Vorsatz et al. [8] employed local weighted 2D umbrella operator to relocate vertices.

R. Shumaker (Ed.): Virtual Reality, HCII 2007, LNCS 4563, pp. 62 – 70, 2007.

Inspired by these sophisticated algorithms, we give a solid technique of triangle model optimization, combining the advantages of previous works and improving their drawbacks.

## 2 Triangle Face Quality Improvements

### 2.1 Surface Energy

Denote the input mesh model as $M_0$, the output as $M$. To improve the triangle face geometry of $M_0$, we relocate vertices on the model. Since face geometry is closed related to surface energy, we first define the energy of model surface. For every vertex $v_i$ of $M$, we use the squared distance function $f_{v_i}(x)$ to define its energy:

$$E(M, v_i) = \int_{S_i} f_{v_i}(x)dx = \int_{S_i} \rho(x)\left|x - v_i\right|^2 dx \tag{1}$$

where $S_i$ is a region around $v_i$. $\rho(x)$ is the density function that will be defined in section 2.2. The surface energy of $M$ is then given by

$$E(M) = \sum_{i=1}^{n} E(M, v_i) = \sum_{i=1}^{n} \int_{Si} \rho(x)\left|x - v_i\right|^2 dx \tag{2}$$

### 2.2 Vertex Density

The density $\rho$ is defined by Gaussian and mean curvature. Let $v$ be any interior vertex, $v_1, v_2, \cdots, v_n$ be the ordered neighboring vertices (1-ring) of $v$, as shown in Fig.1.

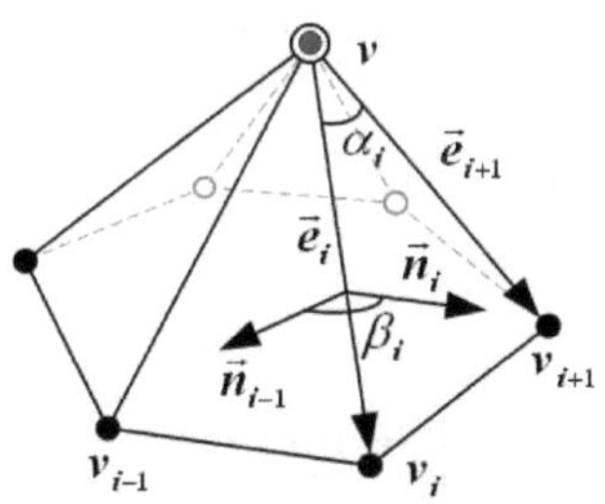


**Fig. 1.** Notations of vertex $v$ and its 1-ring

We denote the edge connecting $v$ and one of its neighbor $v_i$ as $\vec{e}_i = v_i - v$, $\alpha_i = ang(\vec{e}_i, \vec{e}_{i+1})$ as the angel between two successive edges $\vec{e}_i$ and $\vec{e}_{i+1}$, $\vec{n}_i = \frac{\vec{e}_i \times \vec{e}_{i+1}}{\left\|\vec{e}_i \times \vec{e}_{i+1}\right\|}$ as the unit normal of triangle face $(v, v_i, v_{i+1})$. The dihedral angle

$\beta_i = ang(\vec{n}_{i-1}, \vec{n}_i)$ at an edge $\vec{e}_i$ is the angle between the normals of the adjacent triangles. The Gaussian curvature $K$ and the mean curvature $H$ with respect to the region $S$ attributed to vertex $v$ are then given by:

$$K(v) = \frac{2\pi - \sum_{i=1}^{n} \alpha_i}{area(S)} \tag{3}$$

$$H(v) = \frac{\sum_{i=1}^{n} \|\vec{e}_i\| \cdot |\beta_i|}{4 \cdot area(S)} \tag{4}$$

where $S$ is defined using barycentric region which is one third of the area of the triangles adjacent to $v$.

The density of vertex $v$ is then given by:

$$\rho(v) = \mu |K(v)| + (1-\mu) H^2(v) \tag{5}$$

where $\mu$ is a positive weight factors less than unity.

### 2.3 Vertex Relocation

Improving the triangle geometry is to (1) relocation each vertex $v_i$ to a new position for a given region $S_i$ so that $E(M, v_i)$ is minimized; and (2) find an appropriate definition of $S_i$ for each vertex $v_i$ so that the global energy $E(M)$ is minimized.

For a certain region $S_i$, let $v^*$ be the desired vertex position where $E(M, v_i)$ is minimized. Since the second order differential of $E(M, v_i)$ is always positive, we have

$$\frac{dE(M, v_i)}{dv_i^*} = 2\int_{S_i} \rho(x)(x - v_i^*)dx = 2\int_{S_i} x\rho(x)dx - 2v_i^* \int_{S_i} \rho(x)dx = 0$$

Thus,

$$v^* = \frac{\int_{S_i} x\rho(x)dx}{\int_{S_i} \rho(x)dx} \tag{6}$$

That means $E(M, v_i)$ is minimized when $v_i$ is positioned to the centroid of $S_i$ with respect to the density function $\rho(x)$. As for the definition of $S_i$, it has been proven by [9] that $E(M)$ is minimized when $S_i$ is a Voronoi cell.

Thus what to do is relocating each vertex to its centroid of Voronoi region with respect to density function. First, a series of Delaunay edge swaps are applied on $M$ to ensure the local Delaunay property of the mesh. For each vertex $v$, the sub-mesh only containing $v$, its 1-ring neighboring vertices $v_1$, $v_2$,..., $v_n$, and the faces incident on $v$ is flatten onto a 2D parametric domain. Let $p, p_1, p_2, \ldots, p_n$ be the images of $v, v_1, v_2, \ldots, v_n$ on the parametric planar. $p$ is mapped to origin. $p_1, p_2, \ldots, p_n$ satisfy the conditions: the distance between $p$ and its neighbors are the same as the corresponding distance in $M$, namely, $\| p - p_i \| = \| v - v_i \|$. The angles of all triangles at $p$ are proportional to the corresponding angles in $M$ and sum to $2\pi$.

Then we construct the Voronoi cell of $p$ with respect to the circumcenters of the triangles built from $p$ and $p_1, p_2, \ldots, p_n$, and compute the centroid $p_{new}$ of this cell with respect to an approximation of the density function specified over the original mesh. Here a problem must be handled. Since the Voronoi cell of a vertex may be concave polygon, $p_{new}$ may be located outside of the polygon. In such situations, the illegal crossed edges will be produced. To avoid this problem, we calculate the "kernel" of this Voronoi cell, and compute the weighted mass barycenter of the kernel as $p_{new}$ (Fig.2). Finally vertex $v$ is updated by projecting $p_{new}$ back to $M$. When such relocation is done for all vertices of $M$, a series of Delaunay edge swaps are applied. The alternation between Delaunay edge swaps and vertex relocation is repeated until the convergence, being declared when $M$ does not change significantly, is achieved.

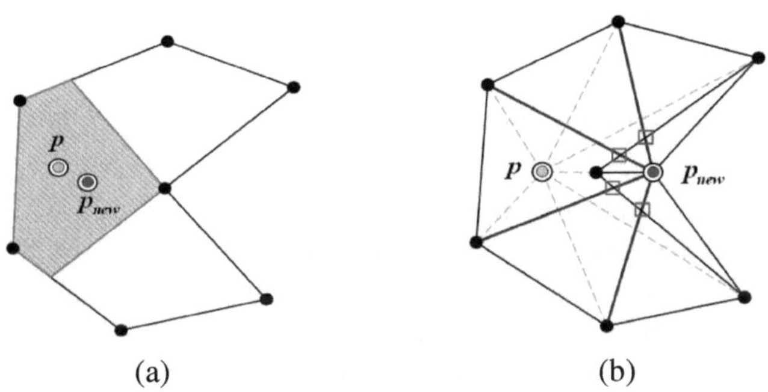


**Fig. 2.** Crossed edges caused by concave Voronoi region (a) can be prevented by using "kernel" region (b)

## 3 Connectivity Optimization

Regulating connectivity means minimizing the global valance covariance function,

$$D(M) = \sum_{v \in M} \left| d(v) - d_{opt}(v) \right|^2 \tag{7}$$

where $d(v)$ is the valance of vertex $v$, $d_{opt}(v)$ is six if $v$ is an interior vertex, and four on a boundary one. We propose a simulated annealing method to solve this optimization problem. The method introduced by [4] is first employed on $M$ to regularize the connectivity to be semi-regular. To every non-feature edge, an edge swap is performed only if it reduces the local valence dispersion. For instance, as shown in Fig.3, edge AB is swapped to CD if the squared sum of local valence $\sum_{v\in\{A,B,C,D\}} \left| d(v) - d_{opt}(v) \right|^2$ is reduced after the swap operation.

This newly processed mesh is used as the initial solution. With the objective function defined by (7) and a large enough control parameter (temperature) *T*, MonteCarlo iterations are applied to minimize *D*(*M*). Let *m* be the number of edges who have at least one irregular vertex as endpoint. We hold the value of *T* and randomly select *k* edges among them ($k < m$). Swap operations are then performed on these

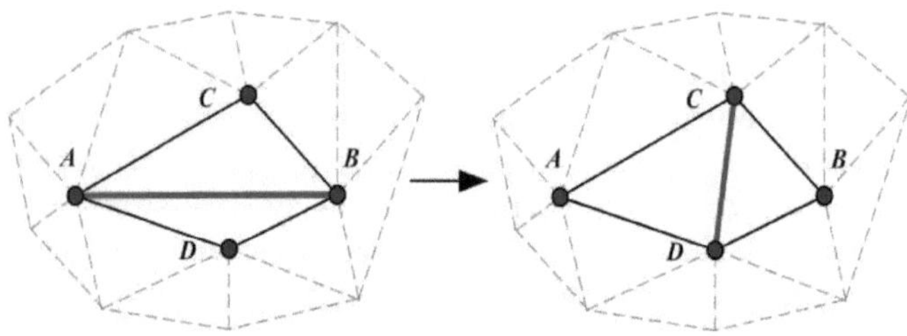


**Fig. 3.** Edge swap for local valence reduction

edges. After this is done, the global change in energy $\Delta D = D(M') - D(M)$ is computed. If the change in energy is negative, $M'$ is arbitrarily accepted as new solution. If the change in energy is positive, then $M'$ is accepted with the probability given by the Boltzmann factor $\exp(-\Delta D / kT)$, where *k* is the Boltzmann constant. This process is then repeated enough times until the reductions of *D*(*M*) become sufficiently discouraging with the current value of *T*. Then the control parameter *T* is decreased and the entire iterations are repeated. This repeats until a frozen state is achieved at $T = 0$, and the mesh *M* at this state is the final solution. The global minimum or at least a good local minimum of *D*(*M*) can be achieved by this method.

## 4 Shape Preservation

In the previous optimization, only *M* is processed, and $M_0$ is untouched as reference surface to preserve geometry shape. That is, in vertex relocation, each newly updated vertex will be projected back to $M_0$. In the applications requiring exact approximation error (e.g. CAD), the method used in [6] can be employed to realize the projection. However we notice that in most of virtual environments, slight shape deviations from the original models can be acceptable as long as such deformations do not weaken the visual effects. Thus every vertex can be directly projected back into the tangent plane of original vertex.

We also use a set of enabling criterions to evaluate and prevent the shape deviations caused by edge swaps. Let triangle *ABC* and *ABD*, denoted as $f_1$, $f_2$, respectively, be two faces sharing edge *AB*. The first intuitive criterion is the angle between the normal of $f_1$ and $f_2$:

$$\theta_1 = ang(\overrightarrow{n_1}, \overrightarrow{n_2}) \tag{8}$$

which measures the flatness of polygon *ABCD*. The second criterion, proposed by [10], evaluates the gap between the original and modified surface:

$$\theta_2 = \min_{1 \le i \le 2, 1 \le j \le 3} ang(\overrightarrow{n_i}, \overrightarrow{n_{ij}}) \tag{9}$$

where $n_{ij}$ is the normal of the *j*th vertex on face $f_i$. These two criterions are combined to control edge swap, namely, edge AB is swapped only if $\theta_1$, $\theta_2$ are below two predetermined thresholds $\theta_{T1}$, $\theta_{T2}$, respectively.

The boundaries and features of models are specifically handled. We define three primitives: (1) feature-edges are the edges on boundaries or creases, (2) feature-vertices are the endpoints of feature-edges, and (3) corner-vertices are those who have more than two adjacent feature-edges or explicitly selected by users. In optimization, feature-edges never get swapped; feature-vertices only move along the feature-edge directions; corner-vertices never get touched; and the Voronoi region of every vertex is truncated by feature-edges.

## 5 Examples

Some examples are shown in Fig.4-7. To measure the geometry quality of a mesh model, statistics are collected on the minimal and average angle of the triangles. For a high-quality mesh, the minimum of these values should be no less than 10°, and the average should be no less than 45°. As for the connectivity, the ratio of irregular vertices is of importance. The statistics of the examples, given in Table 1, verify the validity of our technique.

**Table 1.** Statistics of the optimized models

| Model | Vertices | Irreg | Min∠ | Avg∠ |
|---|---|---|---|---|
| fist(oringinal) | 4802 | 39.2% | 0.70° | 35.4° |
| fist(optimized) | 4923 | 5.45% | 17.2° | 51.8° |
| head(original) | 5989 | 24.9% | 1.4° | 30.1° |
| head(optimized) | 5892 | 3.57% | 13.0° | 46.3° |
| wolf(original) | 7228 | 64.7% | 0.20° | 29.6° |
| wolf(optimized) | 7123 | 15.2% | 9.3° | 49.6° |
| Aphrodite(original) | 32495 | 63.2% | 0.90° | 32.3° |
| Aphrodite(optimized) | 31248 | 14.4% | 10.2° | 50.1° |

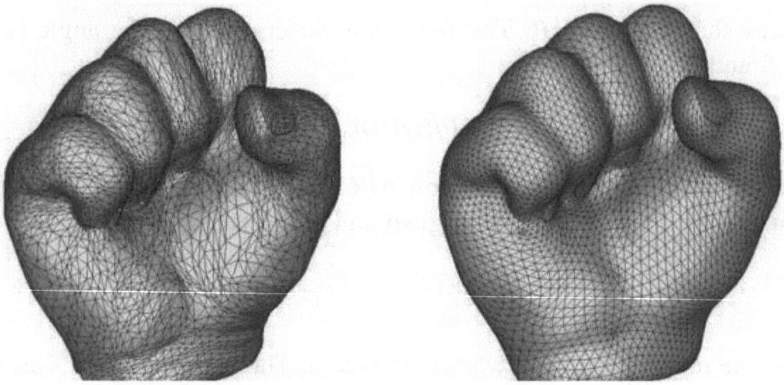

**Fig. 4.** Fist model optimization

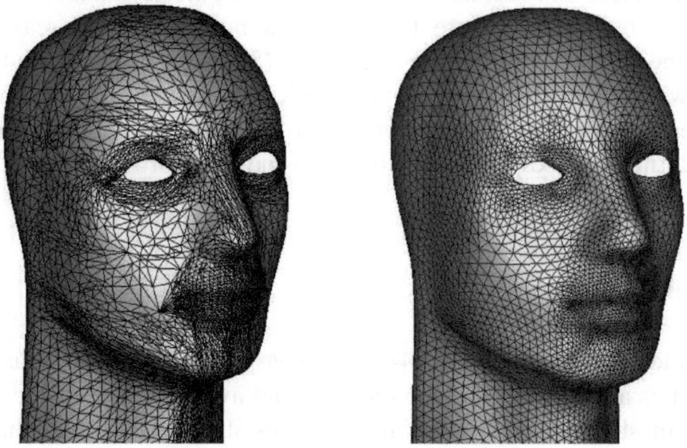

**Fig. 5.** Head model optimization

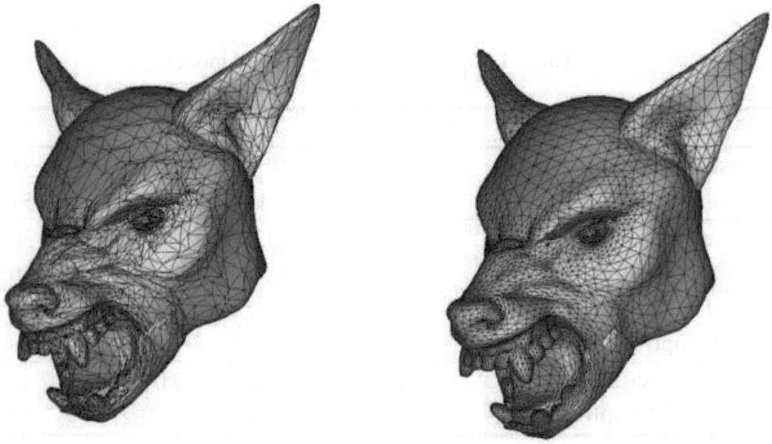

**Fig. 6.** Wolf model optimization

**Fig. 7.** Aphrodite model optimization

## 6 Conclusion

In this paper a solid technique for generating triangle meshes optimized for real-time rendering in virtual environments is proposed. The triangle face geometry is improved and the vertex connectivity is optimized, with the geometry shape and features well preserved. We prove the validity of this method by many examples.

**Acknowledgement.** This work was supported by China 973 Program granted No.2004CB719403, and National Science Foundation of China granted No.60473100 and 60573151.

## References

1. Hormann, K., Labsik, U., Greiner, G.: Remeshing triangulated surfaces with optimal parameterizations. Computer-Aided Design 33(11), 779–788 (2001)
2. Vorsatz, J., Rossl, C., Kobbelt, L., Seidel, H.: Feature sensitive remeshing. Computer Graphics Forum, pp. 393–401 (2001)
3. Alliez, P., Meyer, M., Desbrun, M.: Interactive geometry remeshing. In: Proceedings of ACM SIGGRAPH 2002, pp. 347–354 (2002)
4. Alliez, P., Cohen-Steiner, D., Devillers, O., Levy, B., Desbrun, M.: Anisotropic polygonal remeshing. ACM Transactions on Graphics 22, 485–493 (2003)
5. Alliez, P., Verdiere, E.C., Devillers, O., Isenburg, M.: Isotropic surface remeshing. In: Proceedings of Shape Modeling International 2003, pp. 49–58 (2003)
6. Surazhsky, V., Gotsman, C.: Explicit surface remeshing. In: Proceedings of the Eurographics/ACM SIGGRAPH Symposium on Geometry Processing, pp. 20–30 (2003)

7. Surazhsky, V., Alliez, P., Gotsman, C.: Isotropic remeshing of surfaces: a local parameterization approach. In: Proceedings of the 12th International meshing Roundtable, pp. 215–224 (2003)
8. Vorsatz, J., Rossl, C., Seidel, H.P.: Dynamic remeshing and applications. In: Proceedings of the 3th ACM Symposium on Solid Modeling and Applications, pp. 167–175 (2003)
9. Du, Q., Faber, V., Gunzburger, M.: Centroidal Voronoi tessellations: applications and algorithms. In: SIAM Review 41, 4, pp. 637–676 (1999)
10. Frey, P.J., Borouchaki, H.: Geometric surface mesh optimization. In: Computing and Visualization in Science 1, 113–121 (1998)

# Acceleration of Terrain Rendering Using Cube Mesh

Dong-Soo Kang and Byeong-Seok Shin

Department of Computer Science and Information Engineering, Inha University
253 Yonghyeon-Dong, Nam-Gu, Inchon, 402-751, Korea
kds@inhaian.net, bsshin@inha.ac.kr

**Abstract.** Terrain rendering is essential to represent virtual environment in interactive applications. We have explored voxel-based terrain rendering using ray casting method. Real-time applications such as computer games and simulations require interactive fly-through or walk-through on the terrain. However, since previous approaches usually require a tremendous amount of CPU computation for view-frustum culling and level-of-detail selection, they are not suitable for those applications. We propose an accelerated terrain rendering method using GPU, which exploits a novel data structure, named *Cube Mesh*, for the acceleration of the voxel-based terrain rendering. In addition, we expanded the conventional PARC (Polygon Assisted Ray Casing) algorithm by applying our method to accelerate rendering performance of GPU- based terrain rendering method.

## 1 Introduction

Terrain rendering is used in a variety of fields such as Geographic Information System (GIS), flight simulations and interactive computer games. Although triangular meshes or other polygonal models are used for terrain visualization, the height field data is mainly used to present a terrain. Ray casting method can directly render a scene without geometric modeling such as TIN (Triangle Irregular Network). Although ray casting can produce realistic images, it has a drawback of excessive processing time since the algorithm is inherently complex. Previous approaches for voxel-based terrain rendering usually have common demerits of requiring a tremendous amount of CPU computation, for instance, to perform view-frustum culling and detail level selection.

We present a GPU-based acceleration method that can be applied to interactive applications. Also we propose a novel data structure, named *Cube Mesh*, for the acceleration of the voxel-based terrain rendering in GPU ray casting. Applying the Cube Mesh to empty space leaping algorithms, we can reduce rendering time and computation errors as well as eliminate visual artifacts. In the pre-processing stage, it generates a set of cubes (Cube Mesh) fully enclosing the height field. It renders a terrain using GPU-based ray casting method with the Cube Mesh in rendering time. Since the Cube Mesh is a sort of bounding polyhedron containing terrain surface, we can achieve speedup as in empty-space leaping. Early ray termination is also applied for further acceleration.

In Sect.3, we explain our method in detail and we present acceleration technique using early ray termination. In Sect.4, we show experimental results. Lastly, we conclude our work.

R. Shumaker (Ed.): Virtual Reality, HCII 2007, LNCS 4563, pp. 71 – 79, 2007.

## 2 Related Work

In original Polygon Assisted Ray Casting algorithm, known as PARC [1],[2], a pair of bounding polygons is used to determine the distance between the nearest and the farthest voxels that possibly contribute to final image along each ray. The distance values can be obtained by projecting the bounding polygonal model. Once a distance has been computed for a ray, only the voxels between the nearest and the farthest samples are considered to determine the pixel color (Fig.1). Original PARC algorithm is a progressive-refinement approach using temporal coherence. In the initial frames, the rendering speed is relatively slow since it has to evaluate entire voxels in a volume data. Since the bounding polygon becomes tighter than that in the previous frame, we can progressively reduce rendering time by considering only the voxels that potentially contribute to final image.

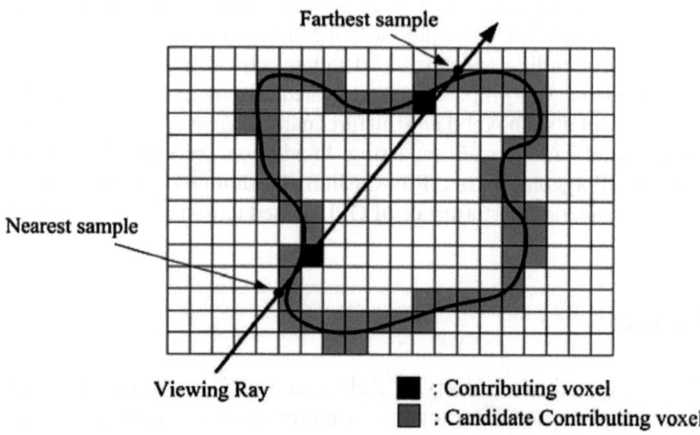


**Fig. 1.** An example of determining the meaningful voxels in PARC algorithm. A bounding polygon is used to determine the distance between the nearest and the farthest possibly contributing voxels along each ray.

Although original PARC is designed to accelerate volume ray casting method, it can be applied to height field rendering in Envelope method [3]. Envelope method uses graphics hardware and is expended voxel-based terrain method [4],[5]. It generates a bounding polygon mesh that encloses the terrain surface in rendering stage. However, since it produces a bounding polygon by considering only the maximum height values in each block, it has a problem of convexity.

As show in Fig. 2(a), Envelope method partitions height field data into $n \times n$ blocks (each block has $n \times n$ size). To make a polygon boundary, it selects vertices that have the maximum height value in each block. Then it connects the vertices to make a triangle mesh (Fig. 2(a)). However, this method has a critical drawback due to convexity of resulting mesh. Unless the block size is considerably small, a vertex might penetrate the generated polygon boundary (Fig. 2 (b)). This results in some visual artifacts on final image. Although small block solves the problem, it requires much preprocessing and rendering time to generate and manipulate denser triangle mesh.

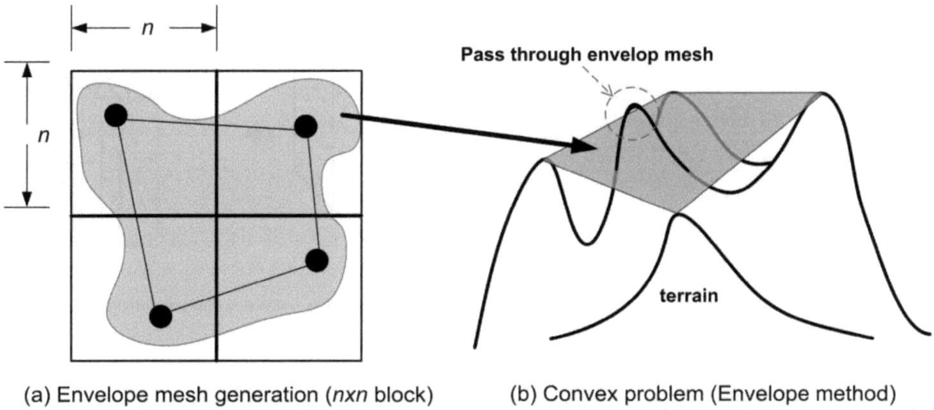


**Fig. 2.** (a) Previous method is applied *n*×*n* block to polygon boundary generation. (b) Result of convex problem when previous method applies the Envelop mesh to real-terrain data.

# 3 Efficient Height-Field Rendering

For the real-time rendering of height-field data, we exploited the voxel-based terrain rendering method, which is composed of preprocessing and rendering stage. In the preprocessing step, we generate a Cube Mesh that fully encloses the terrain surface. The size of the Cube Mesh is determined by pre-defined threshold values. In the rendering step, we display a terrain using three textures containing start position, direction and distance to exit point for each ray. While rasterizing the Cube Mesh, those textures are derived from depth values in graphic hardware. Additionally, we apply early ray termination as acceleration technique.

## 3.1 Cube Mesh

Our method divides an input height field into a quadtree (Fig.3) and generates a cube by considering errors $\varepsilon_h$ which enclose all terrain as shown in Eq. (1).

$$\varepsilon_h = \sqrt{\frac{\sum_{j=0}^{M-1}\sum_{i=0}^{N-1}(p_{i,j} - \varsigma)^2}{MN}} \tag{1}$$

In Eq. (2), the symbol Δ is difference value of maximum and minimum height and it is calculated in each block. In addition, the symbol ς is average value of all points. The error value $\varepsilon_h$ is the standard deviation for all terrain data. The symbol Δ is approximately proportion to error value $\varepsilon_h$. And the constant *c* control partition level of block. So, we can define partitioning condition from these parameters.

**where,** $\varsigma = \textit{average of all points}$ $\qquad \Delta = max - min$

$$\frac{\Delta}{\varepsilon_h} \geq c \ \textit{(partitioning condition)} \tag{2}$$

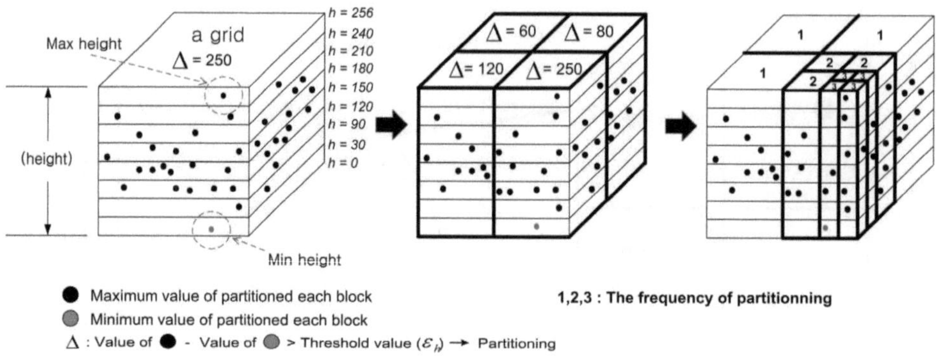


**Fig. 3.** An example of partitioning of height field data. When the difference of the maximum and the minimum value of a block is larger than the threshold $\varepsilon_h$, the block is recursively subdivided until the difference becomes less than $\varepsilon_h$.

As in most quadtree-based methods [6],[7],[8],[9], it trades off the size of quadrants for speedup. That is, if the block size becomes smaller, the efficiency of empty space skipping becomes higher since the distance between polygon boundary and the actual terrain surface is also decreased. However, we have to render a lot of polygons. Therefore we determine optimal block size by considering the maximum and the minimum values in preprocessing stage. In pre-rendering stage, firstly, we make once a unit cube that has a size of 1x1x1. And we exchange a unit cube for transformed cube through the calculated information (minimum value, maximum value and xy-coordinate) for each block. In other world, each block is translated and scaled as cube mesh in world coordinate. After transformation is finish about all unit cubes, we can show perfectly cube mesh that is applied adaptive quadtree. This result in a series of cubes inclosing each block called *Cube Mesh* (Fig.4).

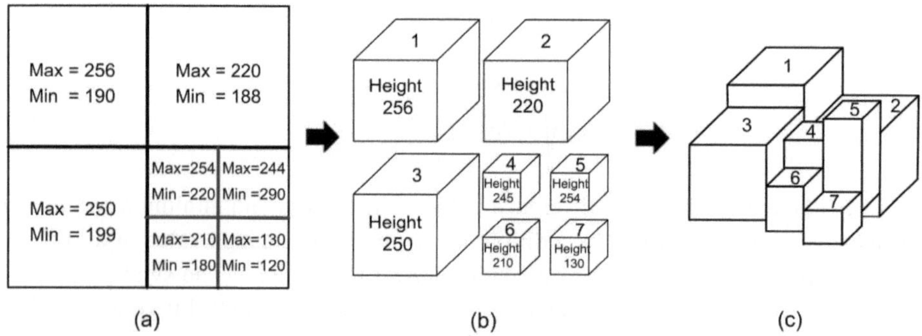


**Fig. 4.** In the preprocessing stage, (a) we get the minimum and the maximum height value for each block, (b) and make cube using the maximum value. The(c) show that a result image is put together all generated *Cube Mesh*.

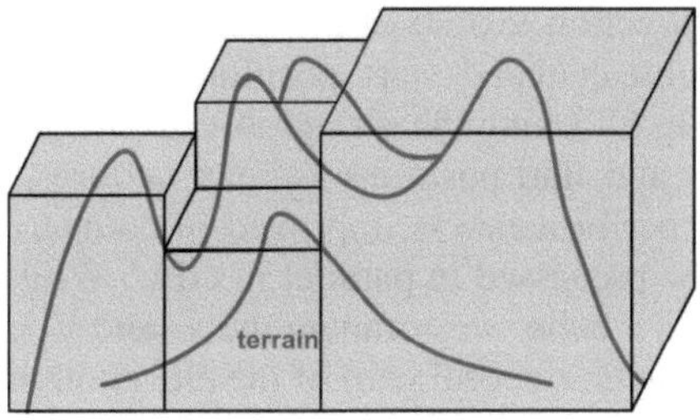


**Fig. 5.** Because each cubes in Cube Mesh perfectly enclose terrain surface in each region, it can solve convexity problem

As shown in Fig.5, Cube Mesh solves the convexity problem of Envelope method since each cube perfectly encloses terrain surface in that area and no vertex can be located outside of a cube. Because polygon mesh in Envelope method encloses terrain surface more tightly than Cube Mesh, its rendering time might be slightly faster than our method. However, when the size of cube is sufficiently small, the difference of rendering speed is negligible. Moreover, penetrated vertices causing severe artifacts are much more critical than rendering time.

### 3.2 GPU Ray Casting

Rendering stage of our method is further divide into two sub-steps. The first step renders the Cube Mesh to evaluate depth values of Cube Mesh. The second step actually renders a scene using GPU-based ray casting method [10],[11].

In the first step, the Cube Mesh is rendered once as triangle mesh to compute ray directions for current viewing condition required in the second rendering pass. We made pixel-shader program to perform volume ray casting [12],[13],[14],[15]. We stored coordinates of the front and the back faces of the bounding cubes into textures, then, we calculate the viewing directions for pixels by subtracting two textures [10].

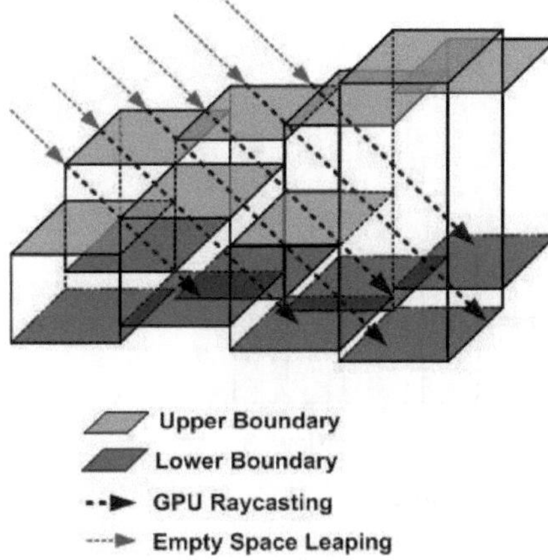


**Fig. 6.** The GPU ray casting using pre-calculated Cube Mesh in rendering stage

Since the calculated direction texture of the Cube Mesh is already reflected on the space leaping by the pre-calculated start position texture, we can easily perform empty space skipping (Fig.6). Using the elevation map (height field) and two textures storing the ray directions and start positions as color textures, we render the terrain in pixel shader. Rendering performance is improved in comparison to that of CPU because whole pixels can be processed in parallel in GPU. While traversing a ray as the amount of unit distance in a cube, we compute the x- and y- position of each sample, and compare the height value (z-coordinate) of the elevation map with y-coordinate of current sample position. If the ray still lies on the transparent region, it continues to advance. When it reaches the terrain surface (non-zero height value in elevation map), we compute real terrain surface point by linear interpolation. That is, if we assume the first inside sample for the ray is $P_i$ and previous sample point of $P_i$ is $P_{i-1}$, we compute exactly real terrain point through the interpolation of $P_i$ with $P_{i-1}$. In this case, although the preprocessing time is reduced compared with the Envelope method by rendering the triangle meshes using GPU, the total rendering time increases because ray casting method continuously requires sampling until ray traversal is terminated.

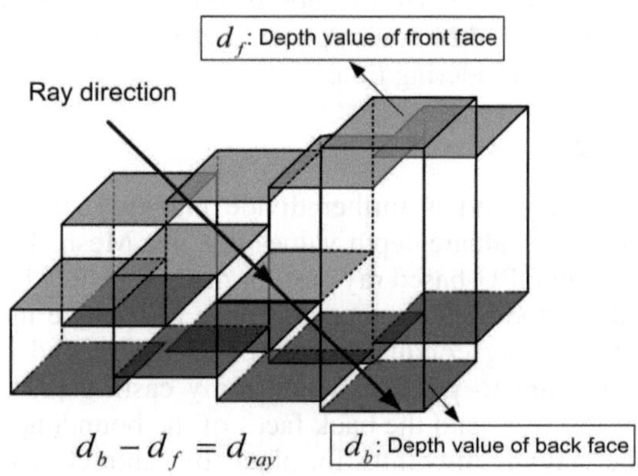


**Fig. 7.** The early ray termination, length of each ray is computed by subtracting depth of front face and depth of back face

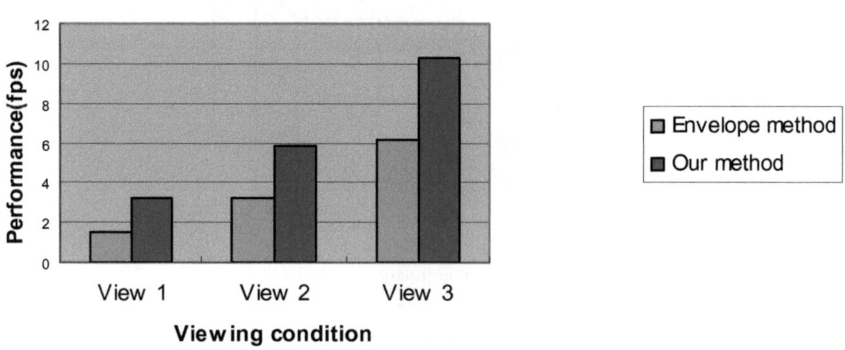


**Fig. 8.** A comparison of rendering speed of conventional method and outs for test dataset (Puget)

(a)

(b)

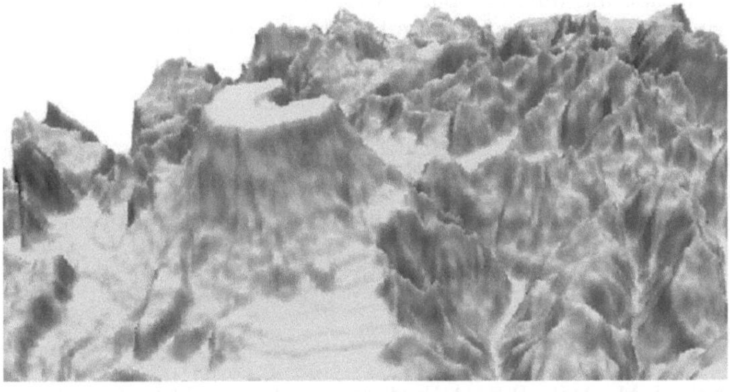

(c)

**Fig. 9.** A comparison of images produced by the conventional method and ours. (a) is an image produced by the Envelope method using the 16×16 blocks. (b) is generated by the Envelope method using the 8×8 blocks. (c) is resulting image of our method using adaptive quadtree.

Further acceleration is possible with early ray termination (Fig. 7). If we know exit position of ray traversal in advance, sampling and color computation do not require from that position. This improves the rendering performance. In preprocessing step, we store the minimum height values into each leaf node as well as the maximum values. By exploiting two boundaries (upper and lower boundaries), we can identify the interval of each ray that contributes to final image.

## 4 Experimental Results

Our method is implemented on a PC equipped with Pentium IV 3.0GHz CPU and 1GB main memory and NVIDIA Geforce 6600 graphic hardware. Puget height field data is well-known bench-marking data of which the resolution is 512×512. The view port size is 640×480.

Fig.8 shows the comparison of rendering time of the conventional method (Envelop) and our method. Our method is about twice faster than Envelope method since we use the Cube Mesh using adaptive quad tree. The Envelope method has not only a critical drawback of image distortion, but also is not use the early ray termination. But our method can reduces pre-processing time through the Cube Mesh using error metric. Also, since we can generate a tight boundary of top and bottom using Cube Mesh, we improve total rendering performance by early ray termination.

## 5 Conclusion

Recently, terrain visualization is important factor in the field of real-time computer games, flight simulations and GIS. The most important issue is to produce high quality images in real time. To render huge amount of height field data efficiently, we propose the Cube Mesh structure and GPU recasting using acceleration technique. Based on these methods, we can render the terrain scene fast with high image quality. Experimental results show that our method produces high quality images and requires less rendering time compared with the original GPU ray casting based terrain rendering method. Our algorithm has shown good speedups on a GPU/CPU by employing load-balancing. It can be used to render the virtual environment in several applications.

**Acknowledgments.** This research was supported by the MIC (Ministry of Information and Communication), Korea, under the ITRC(Information Technology Research Center) support program supervised by the IITA(Institute of Information Technology Assessment).

## References

1. Sobierajski, L.M., Avila, R.S.: A Hardware Acceleration Method for volumetric ray tracing. In: Visualization 1995 Proceedings, IEEE Conference, vol. 435, pp. 27–343 (1995)
2. Zuiderveld, K.J., Koning, A.H.J., Viergerver, M.A.: Acceleration of Ray-Casting Using 3D Distance Transforms. In: Visualization and Biomedical Computing Proceeding, pp. 324–333 (1992)

3. Jeong, T.S., Han, J.H.: A Shader-intensive Approach to Terrain Rendering. Samsung ElectronicGlobal Human-tech Thesis Winning Papers 11th (2006)
4. Lee, C.H., Shin, Y.G.: A Terrain Rendering Method Using Vertical Ray Coherence. The Journal of Visulaization and Computer Animation 8, 94–114 (1997)
5. Ming, W., Kaufman, A.: Virtual Flythrough over a Voxel-Based Terrain. In: Virtual Reality. Proceedings IEEE 13-17, pp. 53 – 60 (1999)
6. Lindstrom, P., Koller, D., Ribarsky, W., Hodges, L., Faust, M., Turner, G.: Real-Time Continuous Level of Detail Rendering of Height Fields. In: Proceedings of ACM SIGGRAPH 96, pp. 109–118 (1996)
7. Ulrich, T.: Continuous LOD Terrain Meshing Using Adaptive Quadtrees, Gamasutra (2000) http://www.gamasutra.com/features/200000228/ulrich_01.htm
8. Pajarola, R., Zurich, E.: Large Scale Terrain Visualization Using the Restricted Quadtree Triangulation, In: Proceedings of IEEE Visualization 98, p. 19 (1998)
9. Lim, S., Shin, B.: RPO: A Reserve-Phased hierachical min-max Octree for efficient space leaping. In: Proc. Pacific Graphics, pp. 145–147 (2005)
10. Krűeger, J., Wstermann, R.: Acceleration techniques for GPU-based volume rendering. In: Proceedings of IEEE Visualization, pp. 38–406 (2003)
11. Westermann, R., Ertl, T.: Efficiently using graphics hardware in volume rendering applications. In: Computer Graphics SIGGRAPH 98 proceedings, pp. 291–294 (1998)
12. Elvins, T.: A survey of algorithms for volume visualization. ACM SIGGRAPH Computer Graphics 26(3), 194–201 (1992)
13. Leovy, M.: Efficient ray tracing of volume data. ACM Transactions on Graphics 9(3), 245–261 (1990)
14. Danskin, J., Hanrahan, P.: Fast algorithms for volume ray tracing. In: Volume Proceeding of Volume visualization, pp. 91–82 (1992)
15. Lim, S., Shin, B.: Efficient space-leaping using optimal block sets. IEICE Transactions Information and System, E88-D(12), pp. 145–147 (2005)

# A Realistic Illumination Model for Stained Glass Rendering

Jung-A Kim, Shihua Ming, and Dongho Kim

Department of Media, Soongsil University
511 Sangdo-dong, Dongjak-gu, Seoul, Korea
{leo0621,mingshihua,dkim}@ssu.ac.kr

**Abstract.** In this paper we present an illumination model for rendering realistic stained glass which simulates the phenomenon of stained glass in real world. The optics for stained glass involves three basic physical mechanisms: diffuse light and specular highlight, Fresnel refraction, volume absorption; these dominate the appearance of stained glass. In this paper, we combine them to render realistic stained glass. Our approach avoids performing any expensive geometric tests, and involves no pre-computation; both of which are common features in previous work. The rendered stained glass images achieve excellent realism.

**Keywords:** stained glass, Fresnel refraction, light absorption, real-time rendering.

## 1 Introduction

Like all major art forms, stained glass has offered insights into the aesthetic sensibilities of cultures over time [4]. It usually sets into windows and the purpose of stained glass is not to allow those within a building to see out or even primarily to admit light but rather to control it. For this reason, stained glass windows have been described as 'illuminated wall decorations'. Effects of stained glass change along with illumination conditions. For example, appearances of stained glass are different in the morning or in the afternoon and also changes by the eye position. The photograph of stained glass in Fig. 1 illustrates different brightness of each piece of stained glass according to the view position. In computer graphics, despite the importance of illumination elements, stained glass rendering has not previously been treated realistically and a simple approximation with no luminous light component has been used.

In this paper, we propose an illumination model for rendering realistic stained glass. Generally speaking, the generation of stained glass involves three basic physical mechanisms: diffuse light and highlight, Fresnel refraction, and volume absorption. Diffuse light and highlight contribute to the brightness of stained glass which is typically white and changes along with the light source and the view position. Fresnel refraction dominates the amount of refracted (transmitted) light. Finally, volum absorption occurs in all stained glass and it is particularly important for the color of stained glass. So the rendered stained glass images achieve excellent realism.

We support fully dynamic lighting and viewing direction since there is no pre-computation involved. Our algorithm also runs entirely on the graphics hardware with no computation performed on the CPU. This is an important criterion in certain

R. Shumaker (Ed.): Virtual Reality, HCII 2007, LNCS 4563, pp. 80 – 87, 2007.

applications, such as games, in which the CPU is already extensively scheduled for various tasks other than graphics.

**Fig. 1.** Stained glass in Prazsky Hrad St. Vitus cathedral. The brightness of each piece of stained glass is difference in the eye position.

## 2 Related Works

Although stained glass has been subjected to a fair amount of research, a practical real-time stained glass rendering with an illumination model has not existed. In this section, we look at some of the earlier work in stained glass rendering and describe a few cases with particular relevance to our work.

A technique based on Voronoi regions [13] has been used in Photoshop [12]. The simplicity of this method makes it attractive, but in filter, the original image begins to reemerge as the tile size becomes small and in this case the filtered image resembles a mosaic much more than it does in a stained glass window. Recent pioneering works on image-based stained glass presented by Stephen Brooks [4] and a stained glass image filter proposed by Mould [3] achieved high degree in term of stained glass color but do not consider the illumination elements, so the results produced remain different from the appearance of real stained glass and do not support real-time rendering.

The work on rendering diamonds written by Sun et al. [1] resembles our work closely. In this work, they unify Fresnel reflection, volume absorption and light dispersion to render the diamonds. We adopted volume absorption technique [2] and conceived main idea in this work.

Although separate models have been developed for rendering a refraction model [11], volume absorption [2], there has not been a model which unify them for rendering stained glass. In this paper, we combine these phenomena with diffuse light and specular highlight to render the realistic stained glass.

# 3 Algorithm

The purpose of stained glass is primarily to see the fascinating colors and such effect is generated by the light which comes from outside. In this part we propose three step algorithm for rendering 'illuminated wall decoration' - stained glass. First, diffuse light and highlight contribute to the brightness of stained glass which are typically white and change along with the light source and the view position. Next, Fresnel refraction dominates the amount of transmitted light. Finally, volume absorption occurs in all stained glass which is particularly important for the color of stained glass.

We support fully dynamic lighting and viewing direction since there is no pre-computation involved

## 3.1 Diffuse Light and Specular Highlight

If illuminating light comes from behind stained glass, there are not only diffuse light, but also highlight on stained glass. As you see in Fig. 2, light comes with different

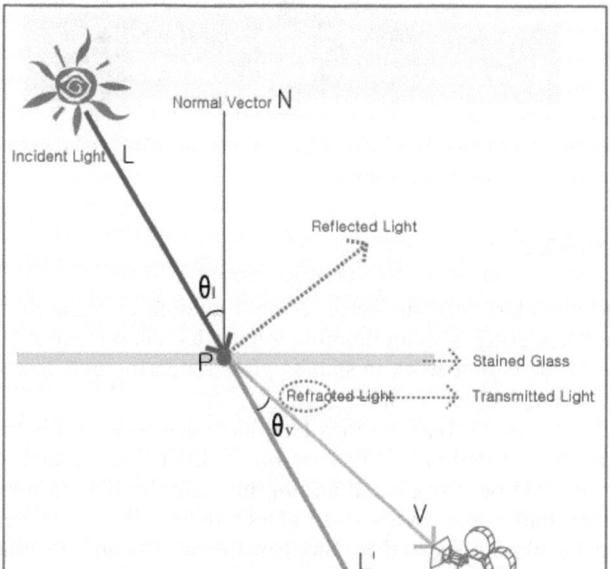


**Fig. 2.** Transmitted light is changing along with the angle between the light source and the eye position

angle according to the position of the light source. The amount of light entering into the stained glass surface is determined by incident angle $\theta_l$ between direction vectors of the normal and the light source. It corresponds to the diffuse component of light shading in conventional computer graphics. According to Eq.(1) we can calculate diffuse color $\boldsymbol{C}_d$.

$$C_d = C_g (L \bullet N) \tag{1}$$

Here, $\boldsymbol{C}_g$ indicates the color of the stained glass. $L$ and $N$ are the direction vector to the light source and the normal vector of the stained glass surface.

Highlight is another important factor for the amount of light. As you see in Fig. 2, when $\theta_v$ is equal to 0°, highlight is the brightest and gradually become less as $\theta_v$ increases. We can calculate highlight color $\boldsymbol{C}_h$ using Eq.(2)

$$C_h = C_g (V \bullet L')^n \tag{2}$$

where $\boldsymbol{C}_g$ is the color of the stained glass, $\boldsymbol{V}$ and L′ are the vector to the eye and the vector of transmitted light which is equal to the incident light vector $L$. n adjusts the intensity of highlight in the equation. As a result we can calculate the total light $\boldsymbol{C}_l$ by adding $\boldsymbol{C}_d$ and $\boldsymbol{C}_h$.

### 3.2 Fresnel Refraction

When light wave reaches the boundary of stained glass, some will be reflected and the other will refract (transmitted) at the boundary. The refraction ratio (the ratio of the refractive energy to the incident energy) depends on not only on the angle of incidence and the properties of the material, but also on the polarization of the incident light wave. According to Fresnel formulas [6] [7],

$$\begin{cases} R_{\parallel} = \left( \dfrac{n_2 \cos\theta_i - n_1 \cos\theta_t}{n2\cos\theta_i + n_1 \cos\theta_t} \right) = \dfrac{\tan^2(\theta_i - \theta_t)}{\tan^2(\theta_i + \theta_t)} \\ R_{\perp} = \left( \dfrac{n_1 \cos\theta_i - n2\cos\theta_t}{n_1 \cos\theta_i + n2\cos\theta_t} \right) = \dfrac{\sin^2(\theta_i - \theta_t)}{\sin^2(\theta_i + \theta_t)} \end{cases} \tag{3}$$

where $R_{\parallel}$ and $R_{\perp}$ (called Fresnel coefficients) correspond to polarizations that are parallel with and perpendicular to the incident plane. $n_1$ and $n_2$ are the refractive indices of the media on the incident and transmission sides, and $\theta_i$ and $\theta_t$ are angle of incidence and transmission. We approximate the Fresnel coefficient by the average of $R_{\parallel}$ and $R_{\perp}$ which determine the amount of reflection. This approximation is widely applicable because polarization is not important in most practical scenes [10]. We adopt this approximation in this paper. Since the transmitted light is obtained by subtracting the reflected light from total light, we can compute the resulting color as follows.

$$C_r = \left[ 1 - \frac{1}{2}(R_{\parallel} + R_{\perp}) \right] * C_l \tag{4}$$

### 3.3 Volume Absorption

Each piece of glass on stained glass has different light absorption capacity. In particular, black edges of stained glass can not transmit light because they are made of wax denture. In addition, volume absorption [2] influences the appearance of stained glass.

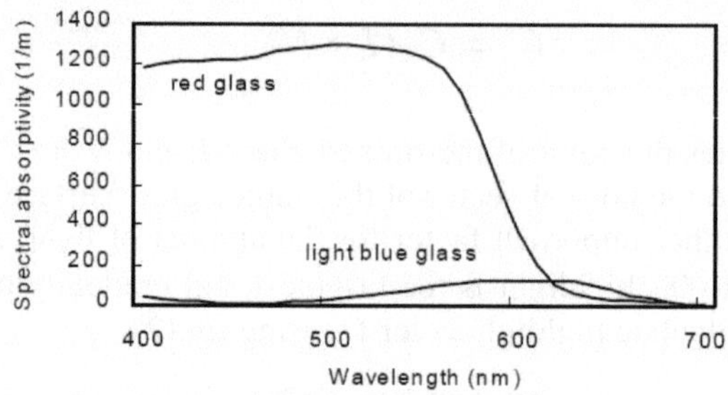


**Fig. 3.** Examples of spectral absorptivities

Figure 3 shows two typical spectral absorptivity curves: the curve for "light blue glass" is fairly smooth, while the one for "red glass" has an abrupt change. This can cause significant difference in the appearance of stained glass pieces made of "light blue glass" and "red glass."

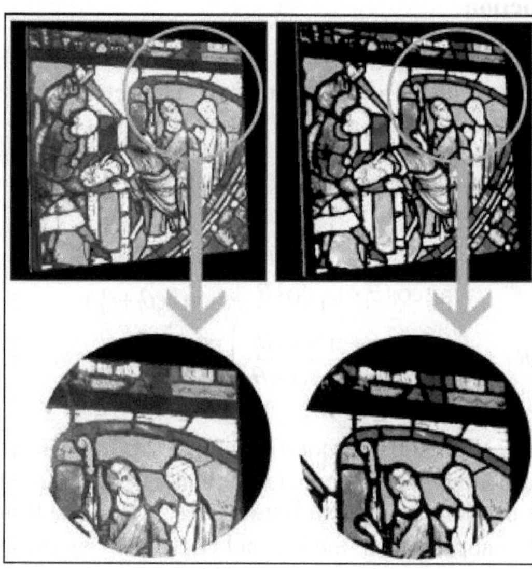

(a) (b)

**Fig. 4.** (a) The result without applying light absorption. (b) The result after applying light absorption.

According to the Bouguer-Lambertian law [5] [9] [14], the internal transmittance for light traveling from one point to another inside a transparent material is given by

$$T_{internal}\left(\lambda_i\right) = 10^{-a(\lambda_i)l}, \quad i = 1, \ldots\ldots, N \tag{5}$$

where $\alpha(\lambda_i)$ is the material's absorptivity, $\lambda_i$ is light wavelength, and $l$ is the length of the light path.

According to this law, increasing $l$ decreases the intensity and deepens color saturation of light. Thus, the resulting attenuated color can be obtained as follows.

$$C_{final} = C_r * T_{internal} \tag{6}$$

By combing Eq.(1), (2), (4), (6), the whole procedure can be represented by the following equation.

$$C_{final} = (C_d + C_h) * [1 - \frac{1}{2}(R_{\parallel} + R_{\perp})] * T_{internal} \tag{7}$$

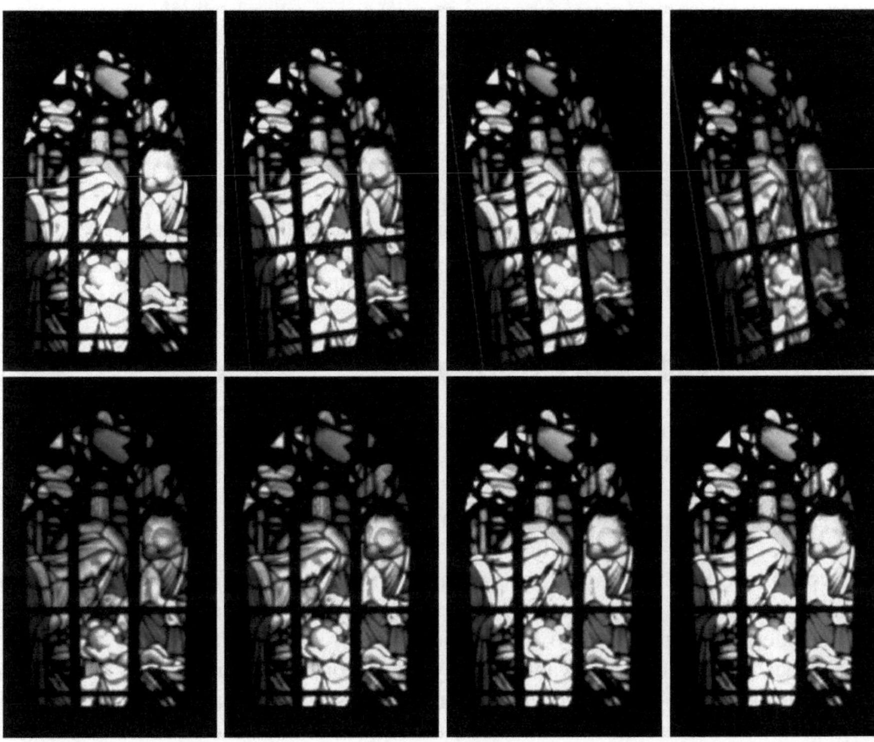

**Fig. 5.** Result image. Top row: the rendering results with various directions to the eye. Bottom row: the rendering results with various directions to the light source.

## 4 Results

The stained glass rendering algorithm was developed and implemented on a PC with a Pentium IV 3GHz CPU, 1GB memory and a nVIDIA GeForce 8800 graphics card. The algorithm was implemented using Microsoft DirectX 9.0 SDK and shader model 3.0. We calculate each pixel's direction of light and angle of gaze by using pixel shader. Thus, illumination can be calculated per pixel, including the amount of absorption depending on the wavelength.

The results of the proposed algorithm are shown in Fig.5. For this example, our algorithm can render at about 1400 frames per second with the resolution of 640x480.

**Fig. 6.** A selection of real stained glass and caustic phenomena

## 5 Conclusion and Future Work

We have combined the physical mechanisms for rendering realistic stained glass, including diffuse light, highlight, Fresnel refraction, and volume absorption. This work not only improves the capability of achieving excellent realism in rendering stained glass, but also provides fully dynamic lighting and viewing direction.

In real life, because of the participating media such as dusts and vapors in atmosphere, we can see the light rays directly which are transmitted from stained glass. We would like to add this phenomenon to our stained glass rendering algorithm, which might considerably improve the overall appearance of stained glass.

As another future work, we want to apply this algorithm to the field of nonphotorealistic rendering(NPR) of stained glass. Through this way we can produce more realistic images than before in the field of stained glass NPR. Next, in manufacturing stage of stained glass, bubbles and impurities might be contained in stained glass. They may generate spots and light dispersion on stained glass. This phenomenon could enhance the realism of stained glass rendering.

Finally, we plan to include caustic effect generated by light cast through stained glass such as Fig.6.

**Acknowledgments.** This work was supported by the Soongsil University Research Fund.

## Reference

1. Sun, Y., Fracchia, F.D., Drew, M.S.: Rendering diamonds. In: Proceeding of the 11th Western Computer Graphics Symposium, pp. 9–15 (2000)
2. Sun, Y., Fracchia, F.D., Drew, M.S.: Rendering the Phenomena of Volume Absorption in Homogeneous Transparent Materials. In: 2nd Annual LASTED International Conference on Computer Graphics and Imaging, pp. 283–288 (1999)
3. Mould, D. : A Stained Glass Image Filter. In: Proceeding of the 13th Eurographics Workshop on Rendering, ACM International Conference Proceeding Series, pp. 20–25 (2003)
4. Brooks, S.: Image-Based Stained Glass. IEEE Transactions on Visualization and Computer Graphics (TVCG) 12(6), 1547–1558 (2006)
5. MacAdam, D.L.: Color Measurement Theme and Variations, pp. 39–41. Springer, Heidelberg (1985)
6. DeLoura, M.: Game Programming Gems. Charles River Media (2000)
7. Born, M., Wolf, E.: Principles of Optics: Electromagnetic Theory of Propagation, Interference and Diffraction of Light. Pergamon Press, Oxford (1975)
8. Fernando, R., Kilgard, M.J.: The CG Tutorial: The Definitive Guide to Programmable Real-Time Graphics. Addison-Wesley Professional, Reading (2003)
9. Evans, R.M.: An Introduction to Color. John Wiley & Sons, New York (1961)
10. Cook, R. L., Torrance, K.E.: A Reflection Model for Computer Graphics. In: Proceeding of ACM TOG, vol. 1(1), pp. 7–24 (1982)
11. Emmering, R.T., London, R.A.: A refractive model for eclipsing binary radio pulsars In.: Astrophysical Journal, Part. 1, 363, 589–596 (1990) (ISSN 0004-637X)
12. O'Quinn, D.: Photoshop 6 Shop Manual. New Rides Publishing, Indianapolis (2001)
13. O'Rourke, J.: Computational Geometry. In: C. Cambridge University Press, Cambridge (1994)
14. Wyszecki, G., Stiles, W.: Color Science. Concepts and Methods, Quantitative Data and Formulas. Wiley, New York (1982)

# Visual Hull with Silhouette Maps

Chulhan Lee, Junho Cho, and Kyoungsu Oh

Department of Media, University of Soongsil, Korea
{dashans,junoeyo,oks}@ssu.ac.kr

**Abstract.** Visual hull is intersection of cones made by back-projections of reference images. We introduce a real-time rendering method of jaggy-free visual hull on programmable graphics hardware. Visual hull can be rendered quickly by using texture mapping approach. However, jagged artifacts are present near the edges of visual hull faces. In this paper, we solve the problem by using silhouette information. Our implementation demonstrates high-quality rendering results in real-time. Time complexity of our algorithm is *O(N)*, where *N* is the number of reference images. Thus, the examples in this paper are rendered over one hundred of frames per second without jaggies.

**Keywords:** Visual Hull, Image-based Rendering, Silhouette Map, GPU.

## 1 Introduction

Image-based modeling and rendering techniques take images of a scene as input, instead of 3D model containing geometry and material. The provided images are used to render new images from different camera locations. That has great benefits such as photorealistic results and short rendering time. Some image-based rendering algorithms, such as tour into the picture [2], concentric mosaics [13], and inverse displacement mapping [11], have constraints in the position or direction of view point. Visual hull algorithm, however, reconstructs 3D geometry of real objects from input images, so that we can freely look around [7]. That makes it possible to build immersive 3D environments, such as virtual tourism, video games and 3D interactive television.

Visual hull is an approximate shape representation of an object, which is actually the envelope of the true geometry. That is produced by intersecting silhouette cones of an object from all reference views. Each silhouette cone is formed by back-projecting the silhouette edges with camera calibration data. The intersection of these cones is the visual hull of an object. The region of the hull is an intersection set of maximal silhouettes [3].

Recently, by exploiting the capabilities of programmable graphics hardware, visual hull can be reconstructed and rendered in real time [4, 7, 9, 10]. Li, et al. [4] proposed a method for hardware-accelerated reconstruction and rendering of visual hull (HAVH). That uses projective texture mapping and alpha map trimming for reconstruction in image space without any numerical problems which exist for geometric intersection methods. It can be easily implemented on programmable graphics hardware and achieves high frame rates. However, the use of projective texture mapping

R. Shumaker (Ed.): Virtual Reality, HCII 2007, LNCS 4563, pp. 88–96, 2007.

for reconstruction causes artifacts near the boundaries of visual hull faces due to discrete representation of silhouette boundaries.

The visual hull can be constructed by 3D constructive solid geometry (CSG) intersections [5]. By combining HAVH with CSG, it can be rendered without jagged artifacts, since no sampling of discrete silhouette information is involved. Even this method can be accelerated by the GPU, the performance is still very low due to high fill-rate consumption. The time complexity of this algorithm is $O(N^2)$ in contrast to $O(N)$ for texture mapping based method, where $N$ is the number of silhouette cones.

Sen, et al. [12] introduced silhouette map algorithm to remove the jagged artifacts near shadow silhouette boundaries of standard shadow map. The silhouette map stores x and y coordinates of silhouettes. Silhouette boundaries are revised by using this silhouette information. This method is accelerated by graphics hardware and performed in real-time.

We combine the advantages of HAVH and silhouette map algorithm for visual hull rendering without serious jagged artifacts near the edges of visual hull faces. Our algorithm keeps high frame rates of HAVH without jaggies.

The remainder of this paper is structured as followed. In section 2, our jaggy-free visual hull algorithm with silhouette map is described. In section 3, implementation and rendering results of our method are presented. The conclusions and future works are summarized in section 4.

## 2 Algorithm

HAVH algorithm performs in high speed by using projective texture and alpha map trimming, but suffers from jagged artifacts that are present near the edges of visual hull faces. The artifacts are removed by solving the silhouette aliasing problem of projective textures. To remove these artifacts, we apply silhouette maps to HAVH without much modification of both methods.

Our algorithm consists of two main parts as shown in Fig. 1. When reference images captured from cameras are arrived, all the silhouette data related with reference images, such as silhouette mask, silhouette cone, and silhouette maps, are recomputed. With these silhouette data, the visual hull can be rendered from any novel viewpoint without jagged artifacts.

### 2.1 Silhouette Extraction

Silhouette extraction is only needed when reference images are newly changed. In this step, we first generate silhouette masks from reference images. The silhouette masks will be used to generate silhouette cones. To generate silhouette masks, foreground objects should be segmented from background images. Using image differencing technique [1], we can easily determine which pixels in each reference images correspond to foreground pixels and background pixels. Alpha values of background pixels are set to 0 and those of foreground are set to 1 (Fig. 2.a).

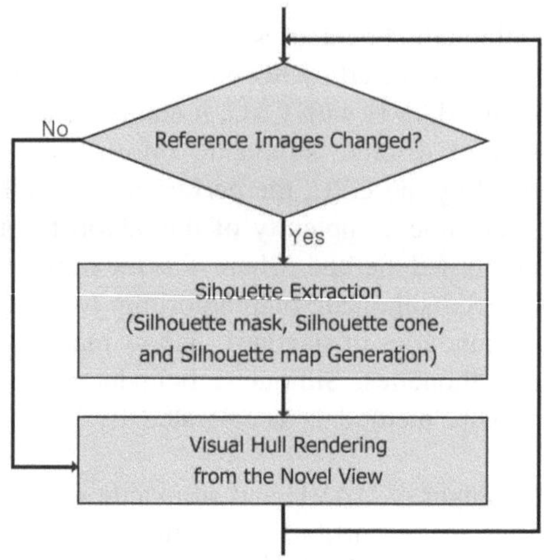


**Fig. 1.** Work flow of our algorithm

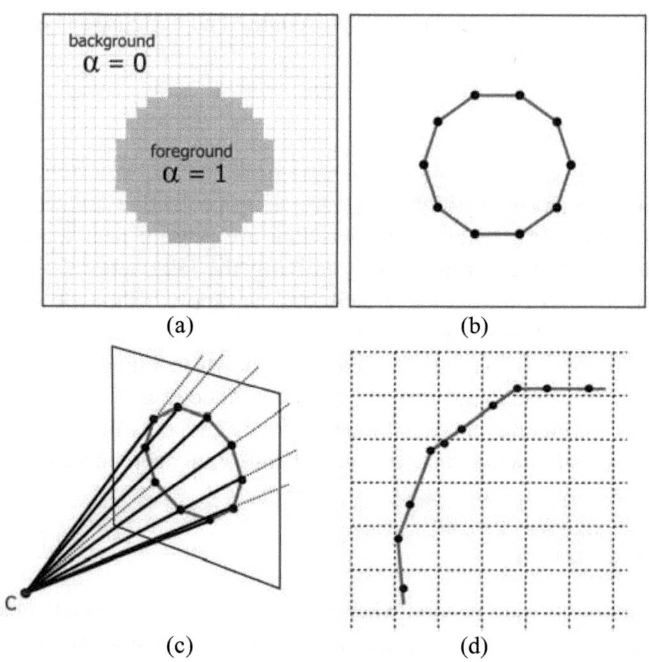


**Fig. 2.** Silhouette extraction can be divided into four major steps. (a) silhouette mask, (b) silhouette edges, (c) silhouette cone, and (d) silhouette map generation.

Secondly, silhouette edges are computed from silhouette masks. The silhouette edges on a silhouette mask is the collection of all edges separating the foreground

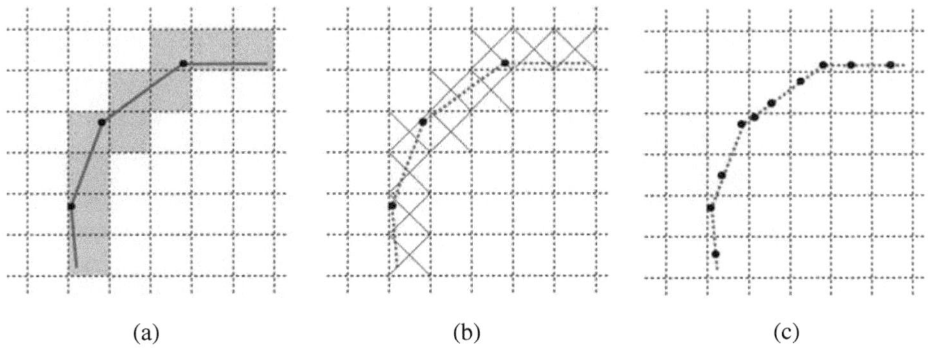


**Fig. 3.** Generation of silhouette maps. (a) rasterization of silhouette edges, (b) intersection test between silhouette edges and silhouette map texel, (c) the silhouette points stored in silhouette map.

object from the background (Fig. 2.b). We can obtain the silhouette edges using marching square algorithm [8].

After the silhouette edges from viewpoints are available, we can form silhouette cones and silhouette maps. To form a silhouette cone, the silhouette edges taken from each reference view are projected back into 3D scene space (Fig. 2.c). And using silhouette edges, silhouette maps are generated (Fig. 2.d). The Silhouette map stores silhouette points that provide information about the position of the silhouette edges. Every texel of the silhouette map stores (0.5, 0.5) as a default value, except when the silhouette edge pass through the texel. In this case, a point on the silhouette edge is stored in local coordinates. The fragment program picks a position of intersection between the silhouette edge and diagonals of current texel (Fig. 3).

## 2.2 Visual Hull Rendering

The visual hull is intersection of the silhouette cones from multiple viewpoints. The basic idea of HAVH to render visual hull is to trim silhouette cone surfaces with alpha maps. The alpha values of the reference image textures are set to 1 for foreground object and to 0 for background. Given a novel viewpoint, each silhouette cone is projectively textured by the reference images from all other views. In the alpha channel, alpha values from multiple textures are modulated. The result is that on a silhouette cone, only the region projected by all the other views gets the alpha value 1. This region is actually the reconstructed visual hull surface, which observes jagged artifacts along the intersection boundaries due to projective texture.

We are going to present advanced rendering algorithm to solve this aliasing issue. The visual hull is reconstructed by rendering silhouette cones. When silhouette cones are rendered, each silhouette cone is textured using reference images deformed by silhouette maps, except the view that produces the silhouette cone currently being rendered. That is, each pixel is projected onto all other reference views, and the reference image is sampled according to the projected position and following sampling rules with silhouette maps (Fig. 4).

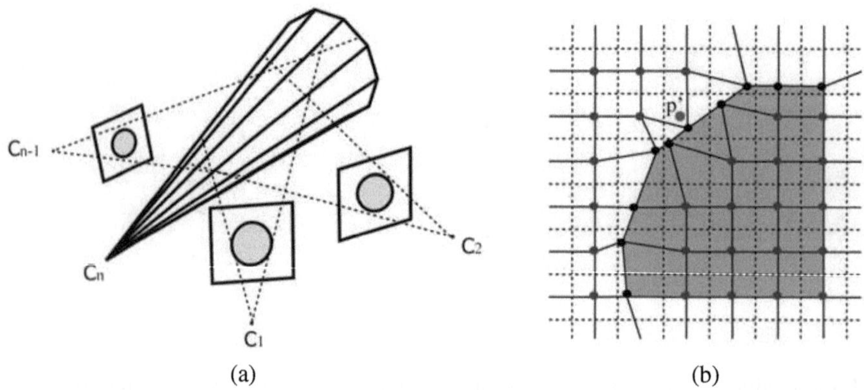


**Fig. 4.** Silhouette cone rendering with silhouette map. (a) when silhouette cone is rendered, (b) the point is projected to reference camera space. p' is the projected point and circles drawn in black indicate the silhouette points. Dotted lines are the silhouette map grid, and non-dotted lines are the reference image grid deformed by silhouette map.

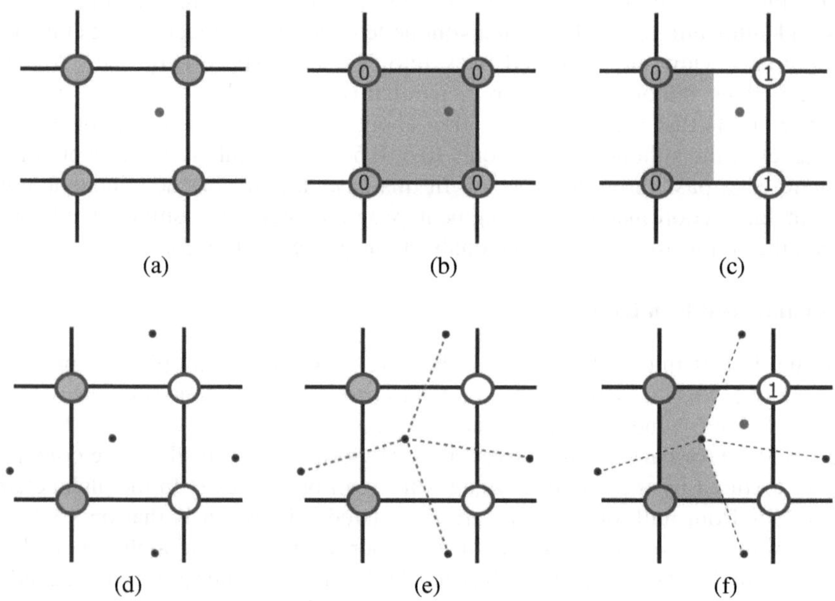


**Fig. 5.** Reference image sampling rules. (a) get 4 closest samples, (b) if these samples all agree, sample accordingly (c) if disagree, (d) get the silhouette point of its texel and 4 neighbors, (e) texel is divided into 4 skewed quadrants, (f) sample the corner of its skewed quadrant.

We decide if the projected point is in the region of silhouette boundary. We can get four closest reference image samples of the point, and compare the alpha values of the samples (Fig. 5.a). If they are same, this region is not intersected with the silhouette

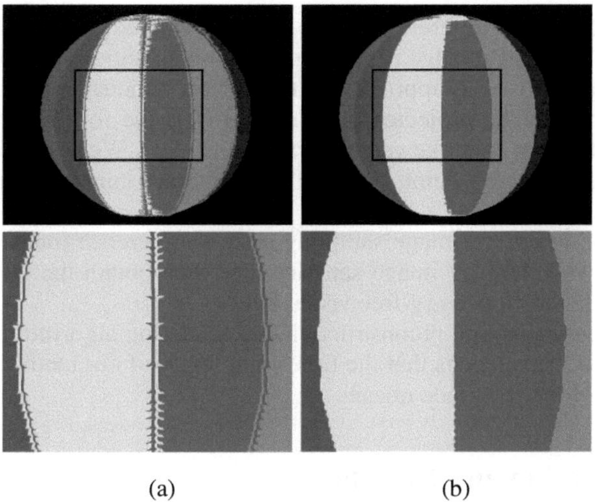


**Fig. 6.** Quality comparison of flat-shaded visual hull. (a) HAVH (b) jaggy-free visual hull with silhouette maps.

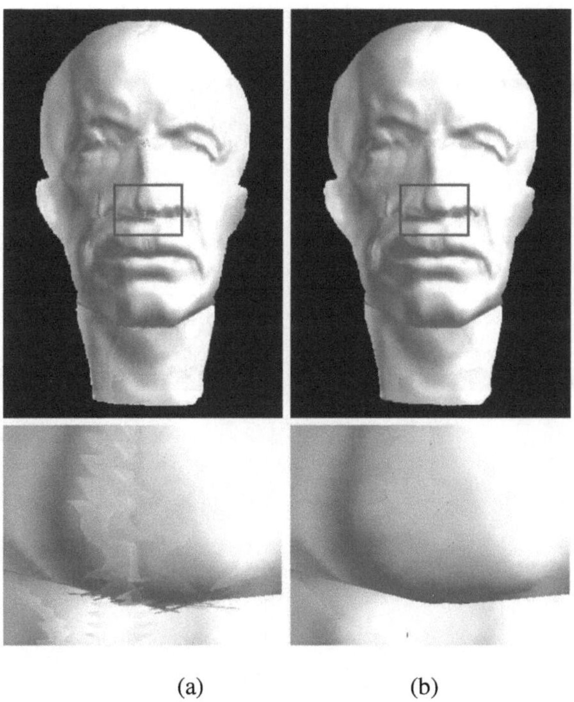


**Fig. 7.** Quality comparison of textured visual hull. (a) HAVH (b) jaggy-free visual hull with silhouette maps.

boundary (Fig. 5.b). The reference image is then sampled accordingly. If they disagree, however, a silhouette edge is passing through this region (Fig. 5.c). In this case, the silhouette map is used to approximate the correct silhouette edge. By connecting the silhouette point of the projected point's texel with the four neighbors (Fig. 5.d), the texel is divided into four skewed quadrants (Fig. 5.e). We determine the quadrant that contains the projected point, and use the reference image sample in the same quadrant (Fig. 5.f).

We iterate this reference image sampling over all reference images, and modulate the alpha values of reference image samples. We then obtain the intersection of silhouette cones, which is the jaggy-free visual hull.

This jaggy-free visual hull reconstruction and rendering algorithm is done in a single rendering pass. This means that the time complexity of our method is *O(N)*, where *N* is the number of the reference images.

## 3 Implementation and Results

We tested our algorithm on a Nvidia Geforce 7900 GTX graphics card with Direct3D and HLSL with shader model 3.0. We used synthetic 3D models and set 8 virtual cameras around the model (Fig. 6, 7). The resolution of acquired images was set to 640x480 pixels and rendered scene was also set to 640x480 pixels.

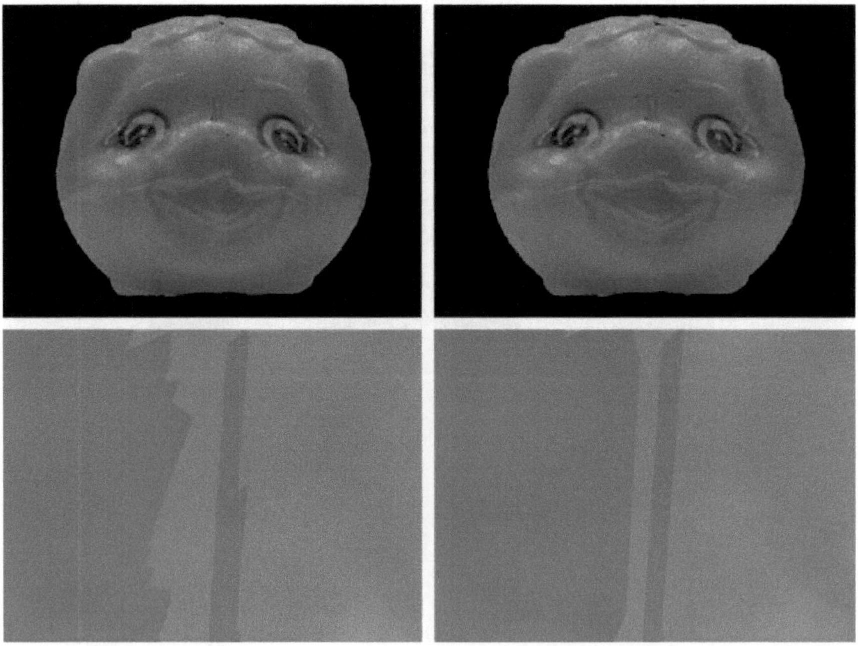

(a) (b)

**Fig. 8.** Quality comparison of visual hull from our real-time visualization system. (a) HAVH (b) jaggy-free visual hull with silhouette maps.

Under this setting, we have measured the rendering speed between HAVH and jaggy-free visual hull. The frame rates are 198 fps and 156 fps, respectively (Fig. 7). The average number of polygons of each silhouette cone was about 3500.

Our algorithm was also implemented in a real-time visualization system with cameras. We used 8 cameras to capture a real object (Fig. 8).

We could render up to 8 silhouette cones. The limitation of texture based visual hull reconstruction technique, like HAVH and our algorithm, is that the number of silhouette cones is restricted by the maximum number of available texture units. This problem can be solved with multi-pass rendering [6].

## 4 Conclusions and Future Works

In this paper we presented an algorithm which renders jaggy-free visual hull using silhouette maps. Our method solved aliasing problem of HAVH while keeping fast rendering speed.

All of the parts of our algorithm could be run on the GPU in real-time, except silhouette cone generation, which was computed on the CPU. If we can render to a vertex buffer from, the performance will be improved. That is because we can generate vertex buffers of the silhouette cone from silhouette edges internally on graphics hardware

## References


1. Bichsel, M.: Segmenting Simply Connected Moving Objects in a Static Scene. IEEE Trans. Pattern Anal. Mach. Intell. 16(11), 1138–1142 (1994)
2. Horry, Y., Anjyo, K., Arai, K.: Tour into the picture: using a spidery mesh interface to make animation from a single image. In: Proceedings of the 24th Annual Conference on Computer Graphics and interactive Techniques International Conference on Computer Graphics and Interactive Techniques, pp. 225–232. ACM Press/Addison-Wesley Publishing Co, New York (1997)
3. Laurentini, A.: The Visual Hull Concept for Silhouette-Based Image Understanding. IEEE Trans. Pattern Anal. Mach. Intell. 16(2), 150–162 (1994)
4. Li, M., Magnor, M., Seidel, H.: Hardware-accelerated visual hull reconstruction and rendering. In: Graphics Interface 2003, pp. 65–71 (2003)
5. Li, M., Magnor, M., and Seidel, H.: A hybrid hardware-accelerated algorithm for high quality rendering of visual hulls. In: Proceedings of the 2004 Conference on Graphics interface (London, Ontario, Canada, May 17 - 19, 2004). ACM International Conference Proceeding Series, Canadian Human-Computer Communications Society, School of Computer Science, University of Waterloo, Waterloo, Ontario, vol. 62, pp. 41–48 (2004)
6. Li, M., Magnor, M., Seidel, H.: Improved hardware-accelerated visual hull rendering. In: to appear in Vision, Modeling, and Visualization (November 2003)
7. Lok, B.: Online model reconstruction for interactive virtual environments. In: Proceedings of the 2001 Symposium on interactive 3D Graphics SI3D '01, pp. 69–72. ACM Press, New York, NY (2001)

8. Lorensen, W.E., Cline, H.E.: Marching cubes: A high resolution 3D surface construction algorithm. In: Stone, M.C. (ed.) SIGGRAPH '87. Proceedings of the 14th Annual Conference on Computer Graphics and interactive Techniques, pp. 163–169. ACM Press, New York (1987)
9. Matusik, W., Buehler, C., McMillan, L.: Polyhedral Visual Hulls for Real-Time Rendering. In: Gortler, S.J., Myszkowski, K. (eds.): Proceedings of the 12th Eurographics Workshop on Rendering Technique, June 25 - 27, 2001, pp. 115–126. Springer-Verlag, London (2001)
10. Matusik, W., Buehler, C., Raskar, R., Gortler, S.J., McMillan, L.: Image-based visual hulls. In: Proceedings of the 27th Annual Conference on Computer Graphics and interactive Techniques International Conference on Computer Graphics and Interactive Techniques, pp. 369–374. ACM Press/Addison-Wesley Publishing Co, New York, NY (2000)
11. Patterson, J.W., Hoggar, S.G., Logie, J.R.: Inverse Displacement Mapping. In: EUROGRAPHICS Conference Proceedings. Computer Graphics Forum 10(2), 129–139 (1991)
12. Sen, P., Cammarano, M., Hanrahan, P.: Shadow silhouette maps. ACM Trans. Graph. 22(3), 521–526 (2003)
13. Shum, H., He, L.: Rendering with concentric mosaics. In: Proceedings of the 26th Annual Conference on Computer Graphics and interactive Techniques International Conference on Computer Graphics and Interactive Techniques, pp. 299–306. ACM Press/Addison-Wesley Publishing Co, New York (1999)

# Region-Based Artificial Terrain Texture Generation

Qicheng Li[1], Chen Zhao[2], Qiang Zhang[2],Weining Yue[1], and Guoping Wang[1]

[1] Dep. of Computer Science & Technology, Peking University, Beijing, China
{lqc,yue,wgp }@graphics.pku.edu.cn
[2] Service Experience Research, IBM China Research Laboratory, Beijing, China
{zhaochen,zhqiang}@cn.ibm.com

**Abstract.** Terrain texture plays a great role on visualization in many 3D applications. Sometimes terrain texture is difficult to obtain in a desired area, thus a new approach to terrain texture generation based on satellite images is proposed to resolve this problem. We prepare a silhouette map and a satellite image for the desired terrain texture and colorize the two pictures with the same pattern according to the terrain features. Then a method of texture synthesis is adopted to generate the final terrain texture.

## 1 Introduction

For a long time research in terrain visualization has been concerned with developing techniques to cope with complex terrain geometries. While LOD terrain models as well as image based modeling and rendering techniques form the basis of any kind of large-scale, real-time terrain visualization, texturing techniques for terrain visualization have not been studied as much.

Terrain-texturing refers to the method used to fill the polygons that comprise the terrain database. The three primary texturing concepts tested were constant-color (CC), elevation-based generic (EBG), and photo-realistic (PR). The CC texturing concept represented an industry concept that has completed the process of Federal Aviation Administration (FAA) certification in the Capstone-program. The EBG texturing concept consisted of twelve equal-height coloring bands that correspond to different absolute terrain elevation levels, similar to the colors employed for Visual Flight Rules (VFR) sectional charts. The PR texturing concept was created by overlaying color ortho-rectified satellite imagery data onto a DEM database. And our terrain texturing method belongs to the third category.

Recently texture synthesis from samples has become a novel technology of texture generation. Compared with traditional texture mapping, texture synthesis from samples can avoid gaps and distortion. So we adopt texture synthesis from satellite imagery to generate the terrain texture.

## 2 Related Work

Texture synthesis has been an active area of research for many years. Numerous approaches have been proposed for texture analysis and synthesis. Here we briefly review some recent and representative works.

R. Shumaker (Ed.): Virtual Reality, HCII 2007, LNCS 4563, pp. 97 – 103, 2007.

### 2.1 Physical Simulation

One way to synthesize textures is to directly simulate their physical generation processes. Biological patterns such as fur, scales, and skin can be modeled using reaction diffusion [1] and cellular texturing [2]. These techniques can produce textures directly on 3D meshes so distortion problem in texture mapping is avoided. However, different textures are usually generated by different physical processes so these approaches are applicable to only a limited class of textures.

### 2.2 Markov Random Field

Many algorithms model textures by Markov Random Fields and generate textures by probability sampling [3]. Since Markov Random Fields have been proven to be a good approximation for a broad rang of textures, these algorithms are general and some of them produce good results. A drawback of Markov Random Field sampling, though, is that it is computationally expensive: even small texture patches can take hours or days to generate

### 2.3 Feature Matching

Some algorithms model textures as a set of features, and generate new images by matching the features in an example textures. Heeger and Bergen [4] introduced this problem to the computer graphics community in 1995. More recently, De Bonet and Efros and Leung [5] showed that a nearest-neighbor search can perform high-quality texture synthesis in a single pass, using multiscale and single-scale neighborhoods, respectively. Wei and Levoy [6] unify these approaches, using neighborhoods consisting of pixels both at the same scale and at coarser scales.

In this paper, we aim to introduce a texture synthesis based on feature matching approach to 3D terrain visualization. Our method can generate discretional terrain texture through simple interaction. This is a continued work of our terrain generation [7].

## 3 Terrain Texture Generation

The integrated terrain model requires both the geometrical data and upper information. The realistic upper information is the terrain color (texture) usually viewed from a vertical angle as those in aerial or satellite images. Such imagery, rare just ten years ago, is now widely available from commercial remote sensing agencies, such as Spot and Landsat. The aerial or satellite images are good sources to generate terrain texture. But the whole satellite image is not a Markov random field and we can not generate a terrain texture synthesis by sampling. However, various sub-regions of satellite images (such as forest, river, and plain) are Markov random fields, so we propose a region-based realistic terrain texture generation. Figure 1 is an example of satellite images.

### 3.1 Satellite Image Segment

This phase is to divide the satellite image into different regions and colorize the corresponding terrain type in the image. The colors selected to fill the image should be

**Fig. 1.** A satellite image. The region A, B, C, D, E, F are the texture feature areas.

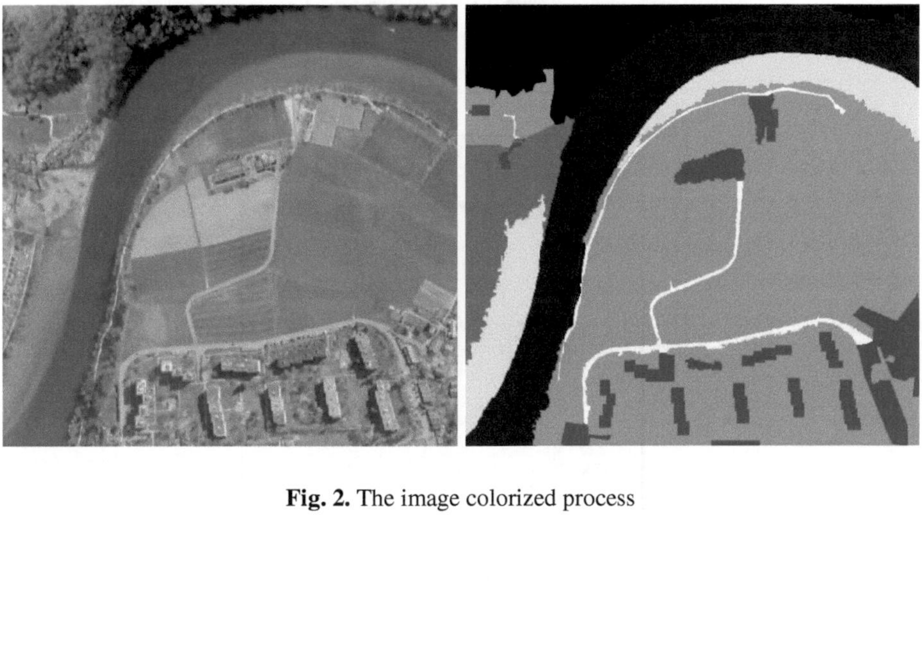

**Fig. 2.** The image colorized process

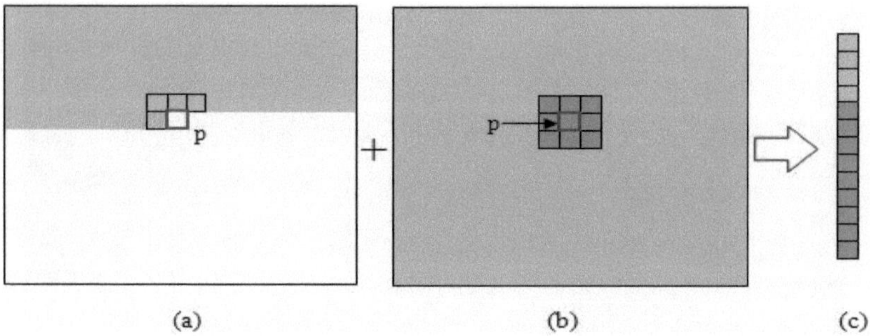


**Fig. 3.** The pixel feature vector set $\Psi$ , (a) the ***L***-neighbor pixels in the satellite image, (b) the 8-neighbor pixels in the colored image, (c) the pixel feature vector

recognized by computer easily, so we select the ultimate colors of RGB-space such as red (255, 0, 0), blue (0, 0, 255) and yellow (255, 255, 0). Because the content of the satellite image is very complex, none of image processing software can segment the image automatically. And we use Adobe-PhotoShop to colorize the image on hand (Figure 2).

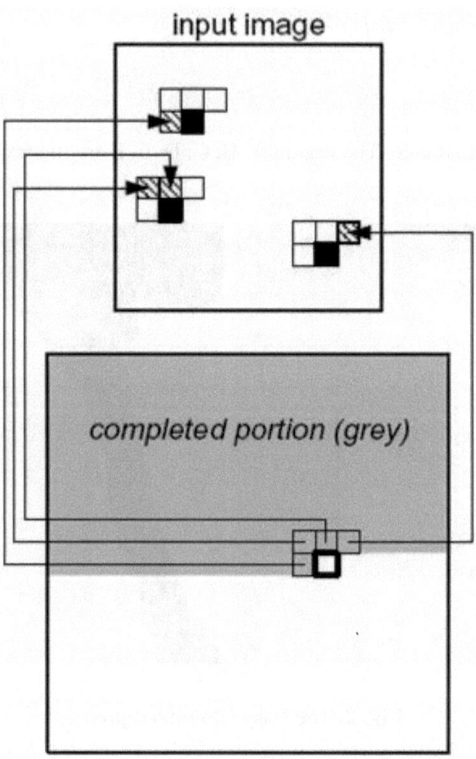


**Fig. 4.** Ashikhmin's approach

### 3.2 Texture Synthesis

For generating the desired terrain texture, we must prepare a terrain silhouette map. The terrain silhouette map is divided into several child-regions according to different terrain features. And we colorize the terrain silhouette map to get a colored terrain map. Now we have a satellite image $\boldsymbol{A}'$, the colored image $\boldsymbol{A}$ and the colored terrain map $\boldsymbol{B}$. Finally we synthesize the generated texture $\boldsymbol{B}'$ from the satellite image $\boldsymbol{A}'$, through which we choose the appropriate parts of the transform $\boldsymbol{A} \rightarrow \boldsymbol{A}'$ in synthesizing $\boldsymbol{B} \rightarrow \boldsymbol{B}'$. The texture synthesis is implemented as follows:

1. Build the pixel feature vector set $\Psi$ of the satellite image $\boldsymbol{A}'$, the elements of which are the RGB values of the $\boldsymbol{L}$-neighbor pixels in the satellite image and the 8-neighbor pixels in the colored image (Figure 3).

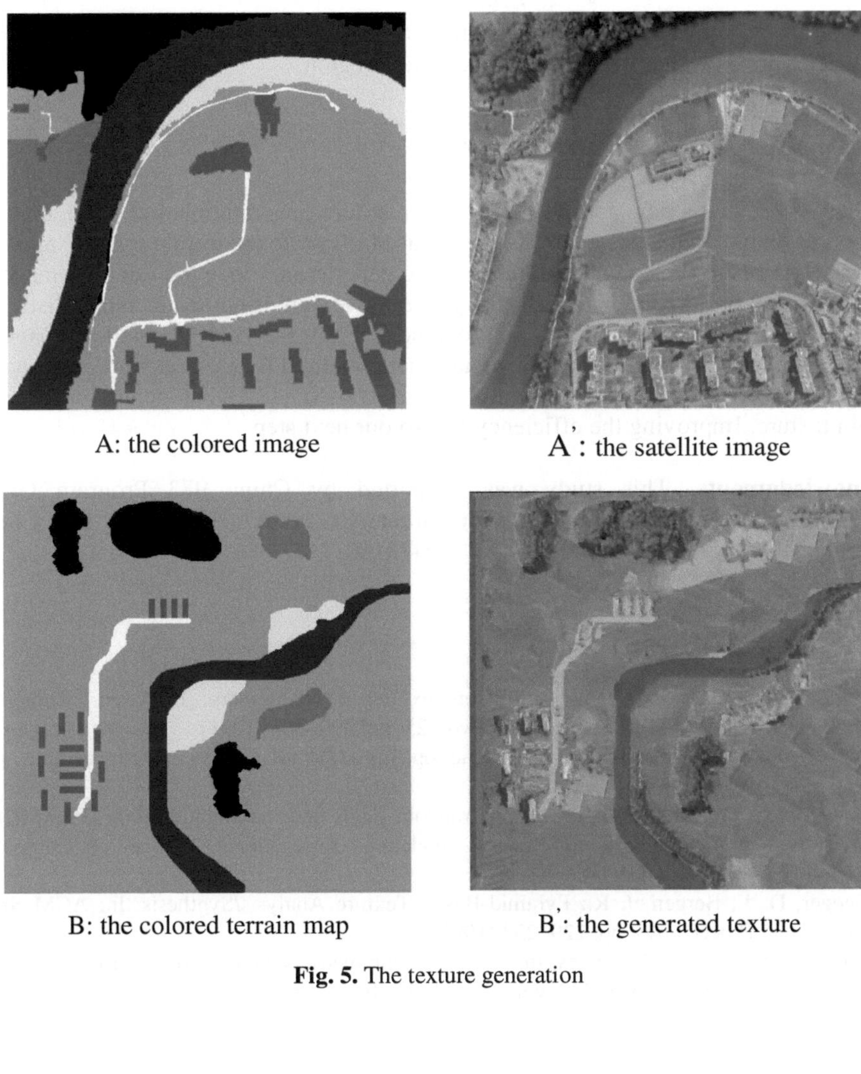

A: the colored image

A': the satellite image

B: the colored terrain map

B': the generated texture

**Fig. 5.** The texture generation

2. Synthesize the generated texture $\boldsymbol{B}'$ in scan-line order. For each pending pixel $\boldsymbol{p}$:
   a) Compute the feature vector $v_p$ of the pixel $\boldsymbol{p}$ according to colored terrain map $\boldsymbol{B}$ and the texture $\boldsymbol{B'}$ which has the established pixels in scan-line.
   b) Find the most ANN-suited pixel feature vector $v_{best-ann}$ from the set $\Psi$ by an approximate-nearest-neighbor search (ANN) [8] and get the most suited pixel $p_{best-ann}$.
   c) Find the most coherence-suited pixel $p_{best-coherence}$ according to a *coherence search*, based on Ashikhmin's approach [9].
3. Compare the $p_{best-ann}$ and the $p_{best-coherence}$, find out the best pixel $p_{best}$, and set the color of the best pixel $p_{best}$ to the pending pixel $\boldsymbol{p}$.

Through the aforementioned texture synthesis process, we can get an artificial terrain texture (Figure 5) which well matches the terrain region.

## 4 Conclusion and Future Work

We have presented a new approach for terrain texture generation based on regions. A method of texture synthesis from samples is used to create the terrain texture, and our approach adapts to the complex terrain texture generation. Since the satellite image is the resource of our texture synthesis, the generated texture is authentic and realistic.

There is still much room for improvement. First, the colored satellite image is created interactively, thus designing an automatic method is our next work. Secondly, the texture synthesis is a time-consuming process, especially when generating a huge terrain texture. Improving the efficiency is also our next step.

**Acknowledgments.** This study was supported by China 973 Program Grant No.2004CB719403, China 863 Program Grant No.2006AA01Z324075, and China National Natural Science Foundation No. 60473100.

## References

1. Witkin, A., Kass, M.: Reaction-diffusion textures. In: Sederberg, T. W.(ed.) Computer Graphics (SIGGRAPH'91 Proceedings), vol. 25, pp. 299–308 (1991)
2. Worley, S.P.: A cellular texture basis function. In: ACM SIGGRAPH 96 Proceedings, pp. 291–294 (1996)
3. Zhu, S., Wu, Y., Mumford, D.: Filters, random fields and maximun entropy (FRAME) – towards a unified theory for texture modeling. International Journal of Computer Vision 27(2), 107–126 (1998)
4. Heeger, D. J., Bergen, J. R.: Pyramid-Based Texture Analysis/Synthesis. In: ACM SIGGRAPH 95 Proceedings, pp. 229–238 (1995)
5. Efros, A., Leung, T.: Texture synthesis by non-parametric sampling. In: International Conference on Computer Vision '99, vol. 2, pp. 1033–1038 (1999)

6. Wei, L.-Y., Levoy, M.: Fast Texture Synthesis Using Tree-Structured Vector Quantization. In: ACM SIGGRAPH 00 Proceedings, pp. 479–488 (2000)
7. Li, Q., Wang, G., Zhou, F., Tang, X., Yang, K.: Example-Based Realistic Terrain Generation. In: Pan, Z., Cheok, A., Haller, M., Lau, R.W.H., Saito, H., Liang, R. (eds.) ICAT 2006. LNCS, vol. 4282, pp. 811–818. Springer, Heidelberg (2006)
8. Arya, S., Mount, D.M., Netanyahu, N.S., Silverman, R., Wu, A.Y.: An Optimal Algorithm for Approximate Nearest Neighbor Searching in Fixed Dimensions. Journal of the ACM 45(6), 891–923 (1998)
9. Ashikhmin, M.: Synthesizing natural textures. ACM Symposium on Interactive 3D Graphics, North Carolina, pp. 217–226 (2001)

# A Real-Time Color Quantization Scheme for Virtual Environments Navigation System*

Hun-gyu Lim and Doowon Paik**

School of Media, Soongsil University
Sangdo 5-dong, Dongjak-ku, Seoul, Korea
{hglim,dpaik}@ssu.ac.kr

**Abstract.** A navigation system for virtual environments using low-quality HMD(head mounted display) must quantize images when the system presents true-color image with restricted number of colors. Such navigation system quantizes an image by using fixed palette. If the system represents an image by using a variable palette which is made considering a region around the viewpoint then user can perceive a virtual environments more vividly because human visual system is sensitive to the colors variation in the region around the viewpoint. In this paper we propose a color quantization algorithm that quantize a region around the viewpoint more finely than other regions at each variation of viewpoint for virtual environments navigation system and compose virtual environments navigation system using proposed algorithm. The system quantizes an image at each variation of viewpoint and shows a quantized image to user through HMD. We tested user preferences for our proposed system and the results show that users preferred our system.

**Keywords:** Color quantization, navigation system, human color perception.

## 1 Introduction

A navigation system for virtual environments using low-quality HMD(head mounted display) must quantize images when the system presents true-color image with restricted number of colors. Color quantization is a process that reduces the number of colors used in an image, usually with the intention that the new image should be as visually similar as possible to the original image[1]. Several clustering algorithms are used in color quantization for improving correctness of quantization. Such algorithms are Octree[2][3], Median-cut[4], K-means[5] and Local K-means[6]. Moreover some algorithms tried to use CIE Lab, CIE Luv color space for improving correctness of quantization[7][8]. Recently quantization algorithm considering human color perception properties are proposed. One of these properties is that human visual system is sensitive to the color distortion in the homogeneous regions. Color quantization algorithm considering such property is proposed[9].

* This work was supported by Seoul R&BD Program(10581cooperateOrg93112).
** Corresponding author.

R. Shumaker (Ed.): Virtual Reality, HCII 2007, LNCS 4563, pp. 104 – 110, 2007.

Another property of human color perception is that human visual system is sensitive to a colors variation in the region around the viewpoint. Therefore if a region around the viewpoint is quantized more finely than other regions then the viewer can see the image more vividly. In virtual environments navigation system if user can vividly see a region around the viewpoint then user can perceive virtual environments more realistically.

In this paper we propose a color quantization algorithm that quantize a region around the viewpoint more finely than other regions at each variation of viewpoint and compose virtual environments navigation system using proposed algorithm. In the virtual environments navigation system user see a quantized image through HMD. The rest of the paper is organized as follows. In section 2, we describe color quantization method. In section 3, we describe experiments of proposed algorithm and system. In section 4, we discuss conclusions.

## 2 Color Quantization with Weight

In this paper we propose a color quantization algorithm in consideration of human visual sensitivity for color pattern variations of region around the viewpoint. The proposed algorithm make a palette at each variation of viewpoint. We use LKM clustering algorithm with weight value to quantize a region around the viewpoint more finely. If the region around viewpoint is quantized with a large number of colors then user can see the region around viewpoint more finely. Figure 1 shows the overall process of proposed algorithm. First, we translate RGB color space to CIE Luv color space for improving correctness of quantization[7][8]. Second, we assign weights to colors used in the image. Third, we execute LKM clustering algorithm. And then we reconstruct image using result. We will describe weight assignment and LKM clustering step because these steps play an important role in the process.

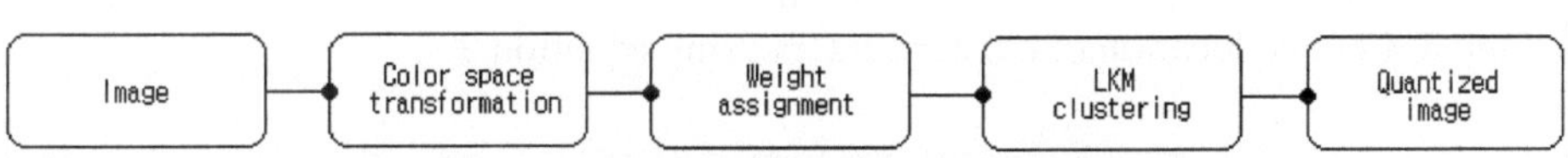


**Fig. 1.** Overall process diagram of proposed module

### 2.1 Weight Assignment

The proposed algorithm assigns different values to each color used in an image in order to quantize a region around the viewpoint with many colors. In LKM clustering algorithm a colors having high weight are quantized with a large number of colors. Therefore we assign high weight to the colors in a region around the viewpoint.

For weight assignment we use Gaussian kernel because weight of Gaussian kernel decrease according to distance from center[9]. In equation 1 $(i, j)$ represent coordinate of viewpoint and $G(x, y)$ represent weight of color of pixel coordinate $(x, y)$ in the image and $\sigma^2$ is variance of weight. The weighting value is normalized to lie within [0,1]. Figure 2 shows example of weight assignment using Gaussian kernel. The colors in a region around the viewpoint are assigned high weight value.

$$G(x,y) = \frac{1}{2\Pi\sigma^2} e^{\frac{(x-i)^2+(y-j)^2}{2\sigma^2}} \tag{1}$$

(a) viewpoint is center

(b) viewpoint is right bottom

**Fig. 2.** Example of weight assignment using Gaussian kernel

## 2.2 LKM Clustering

We use LKM clustering algorithm because LKM clustering algorithm is proven to be a fast algorithm[5]. The algorithm is described as in the following steps:

Step 1. Choose input data sets.
Choose input date sets among used color in image.
Step 2. Set initial cluster centers
Set initial cluster centers according to descending order of weight value
Step 3. Change location of cluster centers using equation 2

$$\overline{c_j}^{(t)} = \overline{c_j}^{(t-1)} + \alpha_t W_i \| c_i - \overline{c_j}^{(t-1)} \| \tag{2}$$

where $c_i$ is a color in input data sets and $\overline{c_j}$ is closest cluster center of $c_i$ and $t$ is execution counter. The adaptation parameter $a_t$ decrease exponentially. $W_i$ is weight value of the color $c_i$.
Step 4. Iterate Step3 for N times until some convergence criterion is met.

In step 1 input data sets are constructed by sampling the image in decreasing step sizes {1009, 757, 499. ...} because a result of algorithm using all used color in an image and a result of algorithm using sampled input data sets are similar and algorithm using sampled input data sets is fast[5]. In step 2 we set initial cluster centers according to descending order of weight value because LKM clustering algorithm quantize the colors of initial cluster centers with large number of colors. In step 3 $W_i$ is weight value of color $c_i$ which is calculated in weight assignment step.

# 3 Experiment

In experiment we quantize some images by using proposed algorithm and fixed palette to identify that a region around the viewpoint quantized by proposed algorithm is quantized with a larger number of colors than using fixed palette. The result of experiment shows that the region around the viewpoint quantized by proposed algorithm is quantized with a large number of colors than using fixed palette. Also we composed a navigation system using proposed algorithm and a fixed palette for experiment of user preferences.

## 3.1 Number of Quantized Colors in Region Around the Viewpoint

We quantize some images by using proposed algorithm and fixed palette to identify that a region around the viewpoint quantized by proposed algorithm is quantized with a larger number of colors than using fixed palette. Table 1 shows number of quantized color in a region around the viewpoint.

**Table 1.** Number of quantized colors in viewpoint

| Image | Proposed (number of colors) | Fixed palette (number of colors) |
|---|---|---|
| A | 75 | 51 |
| B | 82 | 61 |
| C | 44 | 37 |
| D | 97 | 68 |
| E | 53 | 28 |

In experiment we quantized true-color images to 256-color images and knew that number of quantized colors in a region around the viewpoint quantized by proposed algorithm is larger than number of quantized colors quantized by using fixed palette.

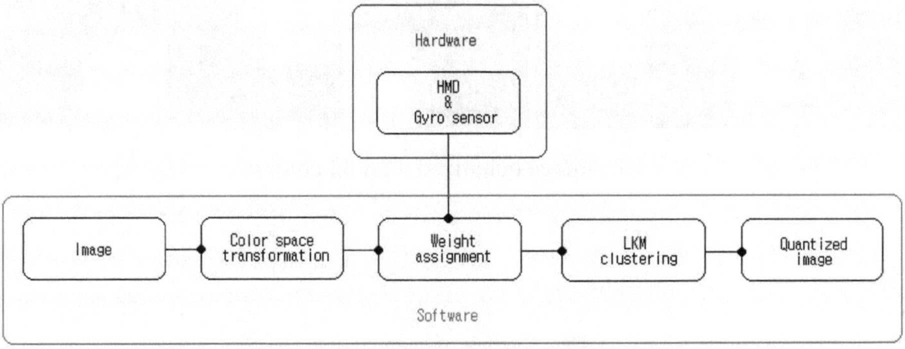


**Fig. 3.** Overall organization diagram of navigation system

**Table 2.** User preferences of each system

| Image | 32 color | | 128 color | | 256 color | |
|---|---|---|---|---|---|---|
| | Proposed (%) | Fixed colors(%) | Proposed (%) | Fixed colors(%) | Proposed (%) | Fixed colors(%) |
| A | 92 | 8 | 81 | 19 | 72 | 28 |
| B | 91 | 9 | 84 | 16 | 75 | 25 |
| C | 90 | 10 | 89 | 11 | 70 | 30 |
| D | 88 | 12 | 82 | 18 | 72 | 28 |
| E | 93 | 7 | 80 | 20 | 72 | 28 |

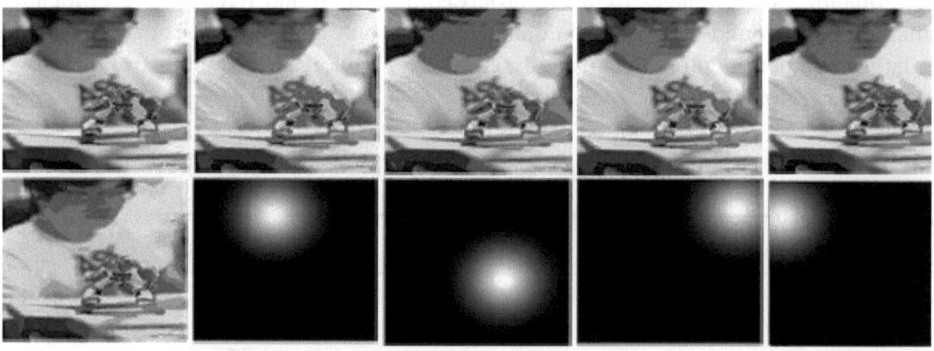

(a) image quantized with 128 color

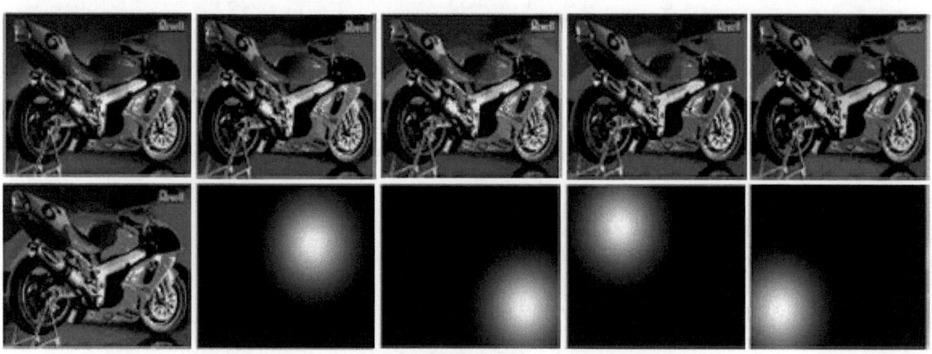

(b) image quantized with 32 color

| Original image | Quantized by proposed system | Quantized by proposed system | Quantized by proposed system | Quantized by proposed system |
|---|---|---|---|---|
| Quantized by system using fixed palette | user viewpoint | user viewpoint | user viewpoint | user viewpoint |

**Fig. 4.** result of quantization

### 3.2 Virtual Environment Navigation System

We composed virtual environments navigation system using proposed color quantization algorithm that quantize a region around the viewpoint more finely than other regions. In virtual environment navigation system user see a quantized image which is real-timely quantized through HMD. Composed virtual environments navigation system real-timely obtains information of user viewpoint and shows quantized image. Navigation system is composed of hardware and software. Hardware is composed HMD and Gyro sensor. Quantized image is seen through HMD and Gyro sensor translate information of user viewpoint by perceiving head movement. In software proposed algorithm is executed by using information of user viewpoint. Figure 3 shows the overall organization diagram of system.

### 3.3 User Preferences Test

We experiment with user preferences between proposed navigation system and the system using fixed palette. Table 2 shows the results of experiment with user preferences of systems. In each system user see an image which is quantized to 32, 128, 256 colors. Table 2 shows that user preferences of proposed system are higher than the system using fixed palette in most images and numbers of quantization colors. Also table 2 shows that user preferences are decrease according to the increase of numbers of quantization colors. Such results are caused by execution time of quantization. The execution time of quantization is increased according to the increase of numbers of quantization colors. Figure 4 shows quantized images which are quantized by each system.

## 4 Conclusions

In this paper we propose a color quantization algorithm that quantize a region around the viewpoint more finely than other regions at each variation of viewpoint and compose virtual environments navigation system using proposed algorithm. We experimented with user preferences between the system using proposed algorithm and the system using fixed palette. The results of research show that user preferences of proposed system are higher than the system using fixed palette in most images and numbers of quantization colors.

Also the experiment results show that user preferences decrease according to the increase of numbers of quantization colors. So we need to study for improving execution time of quantization and expand proposed system to 3D virtual environments.

## Reference


1. Clark, D.: Color quantization using octrees. Dr. Dobb's Journal, 54–57, 102–104 (Jan 1996)
2. Gervautz, M., Purgathofer, W.: A simple method for color quantization: octree quantization. In: Glassner, A. (ed.) Graphics Gems I, pp. 287–293. Academic press, San Diego (1990)

3. Kruger, A.: Median-cut color quantization. Dr. Dobb's Journal, pp. 46–54, 91–92, (September 1994)
4. Krishna, K., Ramakrishnan, K.R., Thathachar, M.A.L.: Vector Quantization using Genetic K-Means Algorithm for Image Compression. In Proceedings 1997 International Conference on Information, Communications and Signal Processing. ICICS, vol. 3, pp. 1585–1587 (1997)
5. Verevka, O., Buchanan, J.W.: Local K-means Algorithm for color image quantization,(1996)
6. Levkowitz, H.: Visualization, and multimedia applications, pp. 75–80. Kluwer Academic Publishers, Boston, MA (1997)
7. Kim, K.M., Lee, C.S., Lee, E.J., Ha, Y.H.: Color Image Quantization using Weighted Distortion Measure of HVS Color Activity. In: Proc. of International Conference on Image Processing, vol. 3, pp. 1035–1039 (1996)
8. Yoon, K.-J., Kweon, I.-S.: Color image segmentation Considering of human sensitivity, In: Proc.SPIE, vol.4572 (2001)
9. ftp://twikiedlab.cs.umass.edu/pub/Hanson570/WebHome/Gaussiankernel.pdf

# A Distributed Framework for Scalable Large-Scale Crowd Simulation

Miguel Lozano[1], Pedro Morillo[1], Daniel Lewis[2], Dirk Reiners[2], and Carolina Cruz-Neira[2]

[1] Departamento de Informática
Universidad de Valencia
Avenida Vicente Andrés Estelles, s/n
46100 Burjassot, (Valencia), Spain
{miguel.lozano,pedro.morillo}@uv.es
[2] Louisiana Immersive Techonologies Entreprise (LITE)
537 Cajundome Boulevard
Lafayette, LA 70506, USA
{daniel,dirk,carolina}@lite3d.com

**Abstract.** Emerging applications in the area of Emergency Response and Disaster Management are increasingly demanding interactive capabilities to allow for the quick understanding of a critical situation, in particular in urban environments. A key component of these interactive simulations is how to recreate the behavior of a crowd in real- time while supporting individual behaviors. Crowds can often be unpredictable and present mixed behaviors such as panic or aggression, that can very rapidly change based on unexpected new elements introduced into the environment. We present preliminary research specifically oriented towards the simulation of large crowds for emergency response and rescue planning situations. Our approach uses a highly scalable architecture integrated with an efficient rendering architecture and an immersive visualization environment for interaction. In this environment, users can specify complex scenarios, "plug-in" crowd behavior algorithms, and interactively steer the simulation to analyze and evaluate multiple "what if" situations.

## 1 Introduction

In less than a decade, the world has experienced a significant series of both man-made and natural disasters of unprecedented proportions, causing tremendous losses in terms of humans lives, as well as causing tremendous financial losses. The processes of responding, maintaining, and recovering from these disasters have made evident the strong needs to have better ways to train emergency responders, as well as to develop, analyze, and evaluate new effective approaches to incident management. Most of these incidents require well-coordinated and well-planned actions among all the different forces of emergency response within severe time constraints.

Furthermore, most of these incidents involve the population of the area in distress, requiring that the responders and government officials understand the impact of their actions on that population. Therefore, the ability of simulate the behavior of a crowd

R. Shumaker (Ed.): Virtual Reality, HCII 2007, LNCS 4563, pp. 111 – 121, 2007.

under different situations: stress, panic, danger, evacuation, as well as the ability to visualize it in the context it is being evaluated in is critical to develop a strong set of tools for emergency response. We propose a highly scalable distributed architecture integrated with an efficient rendering and immersive interactive space that can support large crowds with behaviors ranging from a single "mob mentality" to individualized behaviors for each member of the crowd. The key element of our architecture is the ability of handling the crowd control model and the realistic simulation all integrated in a real-time environment.

## 2 Background

Training emergency responders to effectively manage the kinds of large-scale disasters we face today needs to be approached through advanced computer simulations, visualizations and interactive environments. Traditional real-life training through mock-ups and actors [20] cannot provide a close reproduction of the complex interrelations among response forces, local, state, and federal officials, volunteers, and the affected population. The scale and extent of the situation lends itself to the application of virtual environments and simulation. A critical component of these environments is the ability of simulate large numbers of people within urban and transportation systems, with both crowd behavior as well as individual behaviors. However, there are several conflicting objectives involved in the real-time simulations of Emergency Reponses, especially when they are designed to study the behavior of citizens evacuating cities. On the one hand, this type of simulations must focus on rendering not only animated characters of humanoid appearance, but also the entire urban scenarios where they are located. On the other hand, these simulation systems should offer a wide rich variety of group and autonomous behaviors and actions associated with pedestrians in urban environments such as wandering, fleeing, panic, etc.

Crowd simulations have been used extensively in the entertainment industry to create realistic scenes containing large numbers of individuals. These techniques have been used to create crowd scenes in different movies, although the crowd models used in the entertainment industry are primarily concerned with creating visual realism, without regard to enabling robust behavior at the level of individuals. While these systems can create strikingly beautiful images, the level of behavioral realism is too low to be used for our purposes, and the simulations are far from interactive.

One traditional method of crowd simulation involves the use of a modified particle system, wherein each agent is represented by a single particle whose action is determined by a system of interaction rules [26]. This system is well suited to animating large crowds; however, the interaction rules are generally quite simple, limiting the complexity of behavior at the level of individuals.

There is typically a trade-off between maximum crowd size and behavioral richness, as increasing either rapidly increases the computational complexity of the simulation. Many crowd models, which are designed to accommodate large crowds, do away with individual behavior and instead focus on collective behavior of a crowd. Crowds have been divided at different levels in order to attempt to decrease the computational complexity of simulations. For example, the ViCrowd system [19] divides the simulation at the level of crowds, groups, and individuals. Modern variants of these crowd-oriented simulations use continuum dynamics to reach interactive simulation speeds for thousands of characters [32]. Although these approaches can display very populated and interactive scenes, their usability for emergency response plans is questionable as the higher-level behaviors are not based on individual behavior.

There have been efforts on developing smaller- scale systems that provide support for sufficiently advanced behavior. Consideration of crowd behavior can be incorporated into the design of buildings and public places [24], as well as be used to train emergency personnel in a variety of realistic environments, even the specific environment they will be working in. However, these models, although they provide a good crowd simulation for smaller areas, do not scale well when hundreds of thousands or even millions of characters are needed. For example, the United States military already uses a wide variety of simulation systems for training [8,24], however, these simulations lack a satisfactory crowd models [22] that reflect both mob behavior and individual behaviors.

In the area of virtual environments, we have not yet fully explored effective ways to produce crowd simulations. Several efforts are driven by extending the particle system approach with different level of details [3,30] in order to reduce the rendering and computational cost. Although these methods can handle crowd dynamics and display populated interactive scenes (10000 virtual humans), they are not able to produce complex autonomous behaviors for the individual virtual humans. Other approaches focus on providing efficient and autonomous behaviors to crowd simulations [4,9,21,23,27]. However, they are based on a centralized system architecture, and they can only control a few hundreds of autonomous agents with different skills (pedestrians with navigation and/or social behaviors for urban/evacuation contexts).

Although some scalable, complex multi-agent systems have been proposed [31], most efforts focus on the software architecture, forgetting the underlying computer architecture and graphics system. As a result, important features like inter-process communications, workload balancing, network latencies, or graphics optimizations are not taken into account. When we are considering Emergency Response simulations, we are looking at how to balance the cost of providing rich behaviors, rendering quality, and scalability in a fairly complex integrated system. This balance is strongly dependent on what we call system throughput, defined as the maximum number of characters that the integrated system can handle in real time without reaching the saturation point.

In order to provide a high system throughput, we propose a distributed framework based on a hybrid architecture model. This framework consists of a networked-server distributed environment to manage the inter-awareness among the crowd members, and among the crowd and the environment. In addition, in order to support consistency and autonomous behaviors for each character, we propose a centralized software architecture. The results presented in later sections of the paper that were obtained in the performance evaluation show that this architecture can efficiently manage thousands of autonomous agents.

## 3 Architectures for Distributed Environments and Crowds

From the area of distributed systems, we know three basic architectures are: centralized-server architectures [25,33], networked-server architectures [12,13] and peer-to-peer architectures [15]. Figure 1(top-left), shows an example of a centralized- server architecture. In the context of crowd simulation, we can consider the virtual world as a plane and the avatars as dots in the plane. In this architecture there is only a single server and all the client computers are connected to this server. The server has a complete image of the world and all the avatars, and the clients simply report the local changes to the server. In this way, everything is easily synchronized and controlled. However, the centralized server limits the scalability of the system.

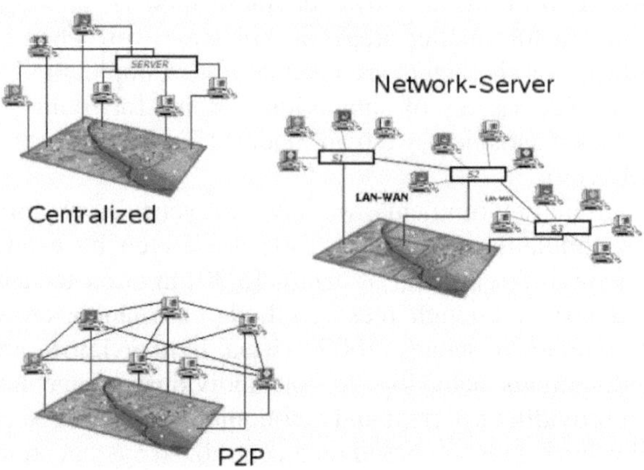


**Fig. 1.** Architectures for supporting distributed systems

Figure 1(right) shows an example of a networked-server architecture. In this scheme, there are several servers and each client is exclusively connected to one of these servers. Again, in the context of crowd simulation, this can be thought of as the large virtual space being partitioned across several servers and the clients are distributed according to the avatars that are populating each one of the areas. This scheme is more distributed than the client-server scheme, and since there are several servers, it considerably improves the scalability compared to the client-server scheme. Figure 1 (bottom-left) shows an example of a peer-to-peer architecture. In this scheme, each client computer is also a server. This scheme provides the highest level of load distribution. Although the earlier distributed architectures were based on centralized architectures, during the last few years architectures based on networked servers have been the main standard for distributed systems. However, in problems related to crowd simulation, each new avatar introduced in a distributed system represents an increase not only in the computational requirements of the application but also in the amount of network traffic [16,17]. Due to this increase, networked-server architectures struggle to scale with the number of clients, particularly for the case of MMOGs [1], due to the high degree of interactivity shown by these applications. As a result, Peer-to-Peer (P2P) architectures have been proposed for massively multi-player online games [7,15]. One of the challenges of P2P architectures for crowd simulation is making avatars aware of other avatars in their surroundings [28]. Providing awareness to all the avatars is a necessary condition to provide time-space consistency. Awareness is crucial for our framework to maintain a coherent and consistent crowd model in the virtual space.

In a networked-server architectures, the awareness problem is easily solved by the existing servers, since they periodically synchronize their state and therefore they know the location of all avatars at all times. Each avatar reports its changes (by sending a message) to the server that it is assigned to, and the server can easily decide which avatars should be the destinations of that message (by using a criterion of distance). There is no need for a method to determine the neighborhood of avatars, since servers know that neighborhood every instant.

## 4 Architecture for Crowd Simulation

From the discussion above it seems that the more physical servers the distributed environment (DE) relies on, the more scalable it is. On the contrary, features like the awareness and/or consistency are more difficult to be provided as the underlying architecture is more distributed (peer-to-peer architecture). Therefore, we propose a networked-server scheme as the computer system architecture for crowd simulation. On top of this networked-server architecture, a software architecture must be designed to manage a crowd of autonomous agents. In order to easily maintain the coherence of the virtual world, a centralized semantic information system is needed. In this sense, it seems very difficult to maintain the coherence of the semantic information system if it follows a peer-to-peer scheme, where hundreds or even thousands of computers support each one a small number of actors and a copy of the semantic database. Therefore, on top of the networked-server computer system architecture, we propose the software architecture as shown in Figure 2. This architecture has been designed to distribute the agents of the crowd in different server computers (the networked-servers). This centralized software architecture is composed of two elements: the *Action Server (AS)* and the *Client Processes (CP)*.

**The Action Server**. The Action Server corresponds to the *Action Engine* [10,11], and it can be viewed as the world manager, since it controls and properly modifies all the information the crowd can perceive. The Action Server is fully dedicated to verify and execute the actions required by the agents, since they are the main source of changes in the virtual environment. Additionally, another important parameter for interactive crowd simulations is the *server main frequency*. This parameter represents how fast the world can change. Ideally, in a fully reactive system all the agents send their action requests to the server, which processes them in a single cycle. In order to provide realistic effects, the server cycle must not be greater than the threshold used to provide quality of service to users in DEs [6,18]. Therefore, we have set the maximum server cycle to 250 ms. Basically, the AS consists of two modules: the Semantic Data Base and the Action Execution Module. The SDB represents the global knowledge about the interactive world that the agents should be able to manage, and it contains the necessary functionalities to handle interactions between agents and objects. The semantic information managed can be symbolic (eg: $object_i$ free true, $object_i$ on $object_k$, ...) and numeric (eg: $object_i$ position, $object_i$ bounding volume, ..), since it has been designed to be useful for different types of agents.

In order to manage the high number of changes produced, the AEM puts all the action effects in a vector (*vUpdates*) which reflects the local changes produced by each actuation (e.g.: an agent changes its position). Finally, when the server cycle has finished, this vector is sent to both, the clients and the SDB, which will update their correspondent environmental states (Figure 2).

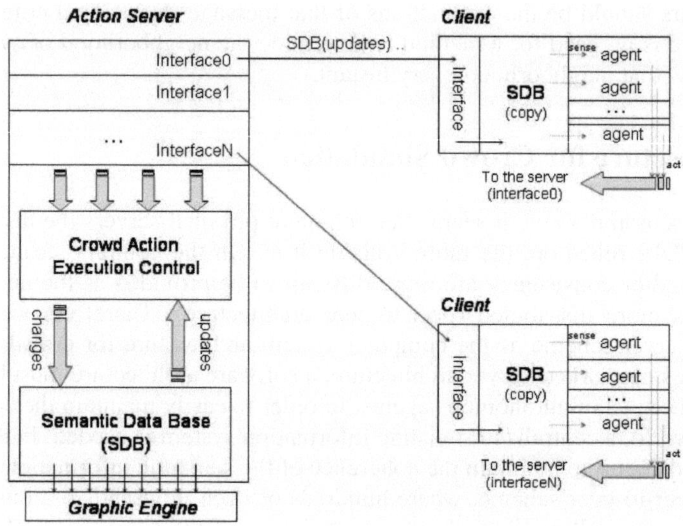


**Fig. 2.** The proposed software architecture

*The Clients.* Each process in a client computer manages an independent group of autonomous agents (a subset of the crowd), and it is executed in a single computer as a single process. This process has an *interface* for receiving and updating the information from the server, and a finite number of threads (each thread for an agent). Using this interface, a client initially connects to the Action Server and downloads a complete copy of the SDB. From that instant, agents can think locally and in parallel with the server, so they can asynchronously send their actions to the server, which will process them as efficiently as possible (since each agent is a process thread, it can separately access to the socket connected to the server). When a server cycle finishes (every 250 ms.), the accepted changes are submitted to all the clients interfaces, that will update their SDB copies. The proposed multi-threading approach is independent of the agent architecture (the AI formalism driving the agent behavior), that is out of the scope of this paper. However, the proposed action scheme guarantees the awareness for all agents [28], since all the environmental changes are checked in a central server and then broadcasted to the agents. Although time-space inconsistencies can appear due to agent asynchronies and network latencies, all these inconsistencies are kept below the limit of the server period.

A classical complex behavior required by many crowd systems is pathfinding (eg: evacuations). In our system, a Cellular Automata (CA) [2] is included as a part of the SDB, and each cell has precomputed the *k-best* paths of length *l* to achieve the exit cells. To calculate all the paths (k paths per cell; cell = 1m side square), we are using a variation of the A* algorithm. Our algorithm starts from each goal cell, and by inundation, we can select the k best paths that arrive to each cell. This let us to manage large environments and to reduce the correspondent memory problems. Furthermore, the calculation of complete paths is not interesting generally, as agents can only evaluate the k-first steps before deciding its next cell.

During the simulation time, each agent can access to its cell and decide the next one according to this information, and the set of heuristics defined (eg: waiting time, path congestion). As an example, Figure 3 shows 7 snapshots captured from 2 different simulations of the system running an evacuation with 8000 agents in a (200mx200m) area. Both simulations start from the same intial state (left), which corresponds to a normal random distribution of the crowd. In the first case (Figure 3a), we have placed 4 exits in each side of the simulated area, so the crowd try to escape through them. In the other case (figure 3b) there are 20 exit cells located on the top of the maze, and we can easily recognize them by following the different crowd flows. The figure 3 also shows both crowd situations at cycle 50,150 and 300, where several congestions has already produced due to the design of the environment (a maze with narrow doors).

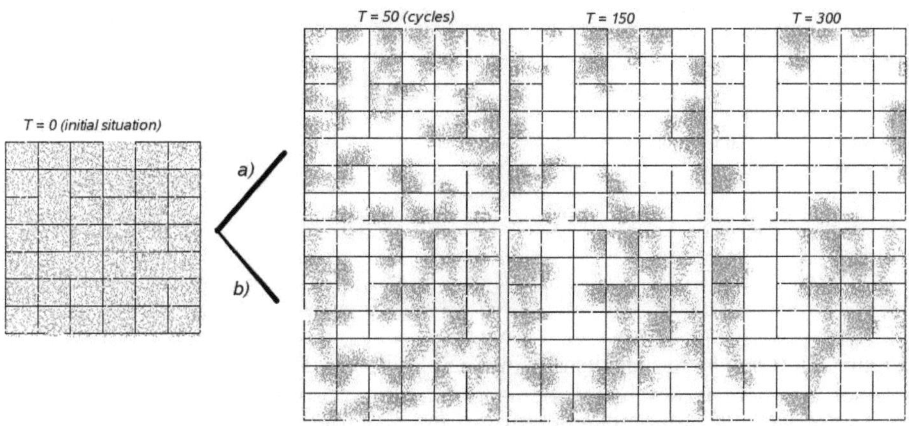


**Fig. 3.** Evacuation test with 8000 agents

On other hand, it is important to ensure that the system can render good images of the virtual world in real time. Our architecture allows for the rendering processes to become one of the clients. In this way, all the information about the position and changes in each individual avatar is available to the rendering system in the same timeframe as it is available to the computational clients. This allows us for the synchronized rendering of the crowd as well as to apply rendering optimization approaches based on the viewpoint.

## 5 Performance Test

In order to evaluated actual performance, we have performed measurements on a real system with this architecture. Performance evaluation is based on wandering agents, since this type of agents is the one that generate the highest workload to the AS (they simply move). As cited previously, the AS cycle has been set to 250ms. First, we have focused on system throughput (the maximum number of agents that the system can efficiently support), which in our architecture is limited by the AS throughput. Concretely, we have measured the AS throughput when it is fully dedicated to collision detection tasks. The rationale of this test is to evaluate the number of actions that the server is able to carry out in a single cycle, since this could be a plausible bottleneck. When an action is requested by an agent, the server basically must access its cell and then it must compute a set of simple distance checking against the agents which are sharing the same cell, as figure 4-right shows. If no collisions are produced, then this process continues until the 8 neighbor cells pass the same test.

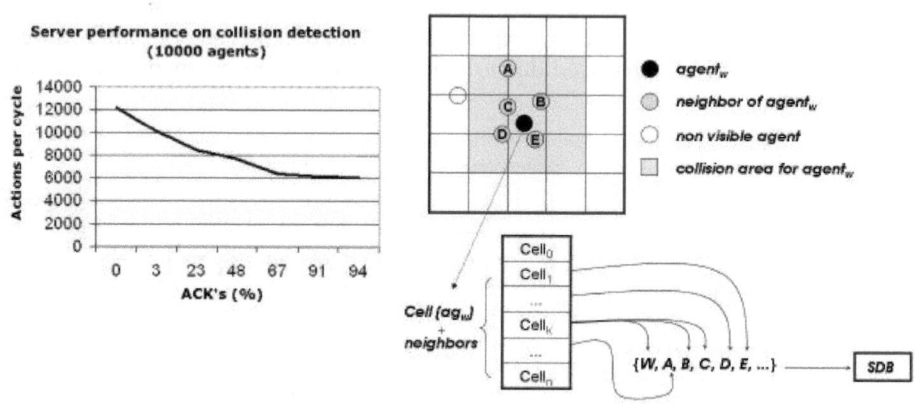


**Fig. 4.** Server Performance on Collision Test

Figure 4-left shows the results obtained in a collision detection test performed in a single server where 10.000 agents demand a random position as soon as they can, in order to saturate the server. The purpose of this experiment is to know how fast the server can run, in terms of the average of actions that it is able to process in a single cycle. As this value highly depends on the density of the crowd, we have represented this parameter as the percentage of finally executed actions (ACKs), since it is more informative for our purposes. Thus, an ACK percentage of 0% occurs when no motion is allowed because the crowd is completely full and no one can move. On the other hand, when all the agents pass a full collision test, all the actions are allowed (100% of ACKs) and all the agents finally move. In these experiments, this case (94% of ACKs) represents the worst case because the server needs to access to 8 + 1 cells and compute a variable number of distance checks for each action.

Figure 4-left shows that in the worst case (94% of ACKs) the server is able to process around 6000 actions in a single cycle (250 ms). However, when the density of the crowd increases the percentage of ACKs decreases because the probability of collision increases in very dense worlds. This will allow the server to finish the cell checking without visiting all the neighbors cells. As a consequence, the server can process a higher number of actions requests per cycle (12000 actions for a percentage of 0% ACKS). It is also worth mention that for a medium case (48% ACKs), the system can manage around 8000 agents.

## 6 Conclusions and Future Work

In this paper, we review the computer architectures used in the literature to support distributed environments and analyze how they can support the simulation of large crowds. Based on this analysis, we present a scalable hybrid distributed framework for large-scale crowd simulations. At the lowest level, the framework consists of a computer system based on a networked-server architecture, in order to achieve scalability while providing awareness and time-space consistency. At a higher level, our framework integrates a software architecture based on a centralized semantic information system that can easily maintain the coherence of the virtual world through a single copy of the semantic database. Performance evaluation results show that this architecture can efficiently manage thousands of individual, autonomous agents at interactive rates.

This preliminary work has assisted us to define the next steps. We plan to distribute the action server in multiple machines by using distributed databases techniques in order to improve the scalability. In addition, we plan to characterize the requirements of different kinds of autonomous agents. The idea is to use each client for supporting one (or more) kind of agents, according to the computational power of the client and the requirements of the agents. Thus, by properly balancing the existing load among the clients we expect to improve the system throughput. Furthermore, in the rendering side, we are looking into the extension of our scene-graph to make use of largely distributed graphics systems to avoid the rendering bottleneck. By using distributed rendering methods like sort-last composition we can keep the data transfer overhead minimal and use local graphics hardware in the servers to scale to interactively displayed scenes with hundreds of thousands or millions of avatars.

## References


1. Alexander, T.: Massively Multiplayer Game Development II. Charles River Media (2005)
2. Chenney, S.: Flow Tiles. In: Proceedings of the 2004 ACM SIGGRAPH-EuroGraphics Symposium on Computer animation. ACM Press, New York (2004)
3. Dobbyn, S., Hamill, J., O'Conor, K., O'Sullivan, C.: Geopostors: a real-time geometry/impostor crowd.
4. Donikian, S.: Informed virtual environments. In: Proceedings of the 2004 ACM SIGGRAPH/Eurographics (2004)
5. Fikes, R., Nilsson, N.: Strips: a new approach to the application of theorem proving to problem solving. Artificial Intelligence 5(2), 189–208 (1971)
6. Henderson, Bhatti, S.: Networked games: a qos-sensitive application for qos-insensitive users? In: Proceedings of the ACM SIGCOMM 2003, pp. 141–147. ACM Press / ACM SIGCOMM, New York (2003)
7. Gautier, L., Diot, C.: Design and evaluation of Mimaze, a multiplayer game on the internet. In: Proceedings of IEEE Multimedia Systems Conference (1998)
8. Karr, C.R., Reece, D., Franceschini, R.: Synthetic soldiers - military training simulators IEEE Spectrum 34(3), 39–45 (1997)
9. Iglesias, A., Luengo, F.: New goal selection scheme for behavioral animation of intelligent virtual agents. IEICE Transactions on Information and Systems

10. Iglesias, A., Luengo, F.: Behavioral Animation of Virtual Agents, In: Sixth International Conference on Computer Graphics and Artificial Intelligence, Limoges, France, May 2003, pp. 99–114 (2003)
11. Iglesias and F. Luengo.: Framework for simulating the human behavior for intelligent virtual agents. part I: Framework architecture. Lectures Notes in Computer Science, vol. 3039, pp. 239–236 (2004)
12. Greenhalgh, C., Bullock, A., Frion, E., Llyod, D., Steed, A.: Making networked virtual environments work. Presence: Teleoperators and Virtual Environments 10(2), 142–159 (2001)
13. Lui, J.C., Chan, M.: An efficient partitioning algorithm for distributed virtual environment systems. IEEE Trans. Parallel and Distributed Systems, 13 (2002)
14. Miller, D.C., Thorpe, J.A.: SIMNET.: the advent of simulator networking. In: Proceedings of the IEEE, vol. 8(83), pp. 1114–1123 (August 1995)
15. Mooney, S., Games, B.: Battlezone: Official Strategy Guide. BradyGame Publisher (1998)
16. Morillo, P., Orduña, J.M., Fernandez, M., Duato, J.: On the characterization of distributed virtual environment systems. In: Kosch, H., Böszörményi, L., Hellwagner, H. (eds.) Euro-Par 2003. LNCS, vol. 2790, pp. 1190–1198. Springer, Heidelberg (2003)
17. Morillo, P., Orduña, J.M., Fernandez, M., Duato, J.: Improving the performance of distributed virtual environment systems. IEEE Transactions on Parallel and Distributed Systems 16(7), 637–649 (2005)
18. Morillo, P., Orduna, J.M., Fernandez, M., Duato, J.: A method for providing qos in distributed virtual environments. In: (PDP'05). 13th EuroMicro Conference on Parallel, Distributed and Network-based Processing, IEEE Computer Society, Los Alamitos (2005)
19. Musse, S.R., Thalmann, D.: Hierarchical model for real time simulation of virtual human crowds. IEEE Transactions on Visualization and Computer Graphics 7(2), 152–164 (2001)
20. National Emergency Response and Rescue Training Center (NERRTC)
21. Nakanishi, H., Ishida, T.: Freewalk/ social interaction platform in virtual space. In: VRST '04. Proceedings of the ACM symposium on Virtual reality software and technology, pp. 97–104. ACM Press, New York, USA (2004)
22. Nguyen, Q.H., McKenzie, F.D., Petty, M.D.: Crowd Behavior Architecture Model Cognitive Design, In: Proceedings of the 2005 Conference on Behavior Representation in Modeling and Simulation (BRIMS), Universal City CA, May 16-19,2005, pp. 55–64 (2005)
23. Raupp, S., Thalmann, D.: Hierarchical model for real time simulation of virtual human crowds. IEEE Transactions on Visualization and Computer Graphics 7(2), 152–164 (2001)
24. Penn, A., Turner, A.: Space syntax based agent simulation. In: 1st International Conference on Pedestrian and Evacuation Dynamics, University of Duisburg, Germany (2001)
25. Quake: http://www.idsoftware.com/games/quake/quake/
26. Reynolds, C.W.: Flocks, Herds, and Schools: A Distributed Behavioral Model. Computer Graphics 21(4), 25–34 (1987)
27. Shao, W., Terzopoulos, D.: Autonomous pedestrians. In: SCA '05. Proceedings of the 2005 ACM SIGGRAPH/Eurographics symposium on Computer animation, New York, USA, pp. 19–28. ACM Press, New York, USA (2005)
28. Smith, R.B., Hixon, R., Horan, B.: Collaborative Virtual Environments, chapter Supporting Flexible Roles in a Shared Space. Springer-Verlag, Heidelberg (2001)
29. Singhal, S., Zyda, M.: Networked Virtual Environments. ACM Press, New York (1999)
30. Tecchia, F., Loscos, C., Chrysathou, Y.: Visualizing crowds in real time. Computer Graphics Forum, 21 (2002)

31. Tianfield, H., Tian, J., Yao, X.: On the architectures of complex multi-agent systems. In Proc. of the Workshop on "Knowledge Grid and Grid Intelligence", IEEE/WIC International Conference on Web Intelligence / Intelligent Agent Technology, pp. 195–206. IEEE Computer Society Press, Los Alamitos (2003)
32. Treuille, A., Cooper, S., Popovic, Z.: Continuum Crowds. In: ACM Transactions on Graphics, (SIGGRAPH), 25(3) (2006)
33. Unreal Tournament: http://www.unrealtournament.com/

# QEM-Based Mesh Simplification with Effective Feature-Preserving

Wei Lu, Dinghao Zeng, and Jingui Pan

State Key Lab for Novel Software Technology, Computer Science Editorial,
Department of Computer Science and Technology, Nanjing University
210093 Nanjing, China
hansh@mes.nju.edu.cn, dinghao_zeng@hotmail.com,
panjg@nanjing-fnst.com

**Abstract.** To preserve appearance attributes in a 3D model, a novel mesh simplification is proposed in this work based on the Quadric Error Metric (QEM). We make use of half-edge collapse method for mesh simplification and modify the QEM to solve the break between different texture coordinates. After analyzing several cases of the collapsing operation, a new formula on the cost of edge contraction is obtained to eliminate aberrances. Experimental results demonstrate that compared with other state-of-the-art techniques our algorithm can achieve satisfactory efficiency with desirable geometry and feature-preserving.

**Keywords:** mesh simplification, half-edge collapse, Progressive Meshes, the Quadric Error Metric, feature preserving.

## 1 Introduction

With booming of the Internet, 3D graphic visualization data composed by triangular meshes become one of the key media of network-based applications [1]. Due to the flexibility of geometric modeling operation and high rendering speed, triangular meshes are widely used for surface representation. Consequently, how to store, transmit and render large volumes of graphics data efficiently has become one of the most critical issues. Level-of-detail (LoD) techniques were introduced to solve this problem by decreasing object complexity and create a series of multi-resolution models for rendering [2]. Up to the present, lots of mesh simplification algorithms for LoD approximation have been developed. [3] shows an extensive review and comparison of these techniques.

Recently, edge collapse, the basis of many mesh compression algorithms [4-6], has become one of the most popular operations for simplifying models by iteratively contracting edges. However, as a simplified version of edge collapse, half-edge collapse operation can achieve similar results as other vertex placement schemes with no new points generated [7], contributing to saving storage, reducing bandwidth from RAM to GPU, and accelerating compression. So we choose it as the topological operator in this work and write a pair contraction as $v_s \rightarrow v_t$ ($v_s$ is the starting point and $v_t$ is the terminal point).

However, a common issue for edge collapse and half-edge collapse is how to choose the collapsing edge. When Hoppe first introduced the concept of Progressive Mesh

R. Shumaker (Ed.): Virtual Reality, HCII 2007, LNCS 4563, pp. 122 – 131, 2007.

(PM) [4] to represent triangular meshes based on edge collapsing and vertex splitting transformations, he minimized an energy function [8] for the selection. Progressive Meshes always generate accurate results, but as the expensive optimization procedure and the global error metric used in PM require much long time for contraction, it is unsuitable for practical applications.

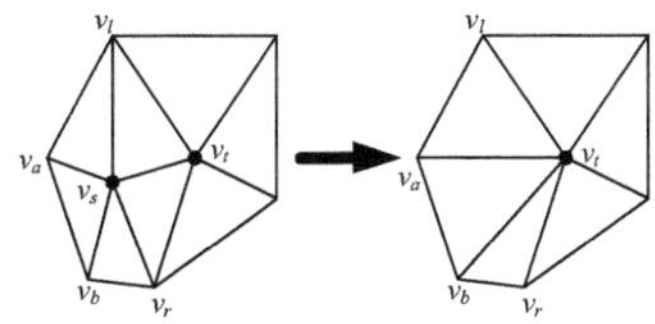


**Fig. 1.** Half-edge collapsing operation

**Fig. 2.** Six faces constituting the emerald model

The Quadric Error Metric (QEM) [5] proposed by Garland and Heckbert is a surface simplification algorithm which can produce high quality approximations of polygonal models at a high speed. The method makes use of matrix and achieves a trade-off between fidelity and efficiency. Kobbelt *et al.* [7] advanced a greedy algorithm based on QEM, which is one of the fastest mesh simplification methods for all algorithms developed so far. Even though QEM is a local error control method, the simplified meshes are usually as accurate as those produced by other global error control algorithms [1].

In practice, besides geometric features, meshes also hold material properties such as color values, normals and texture coordinates. In [9] Garland improved QEM to accommodate mesh decimation to preserve appearance attributes. Subsequently, Hoppe proposed a method based on QEM to deal with material properties which saves more storage [10]. However, both are based on the precondition that the values of material properties vary continuously over the surface. Yet it is not always the case. In this work, we develop a new mesh simplification algorithm based on QEM framework aiming at preserving textural discontinuities. A priority queue of the candidate edges keyed on the collapse cost is created to determine the quality of the approximations, and the essential issue is how to compute the costs. Beforehand we define a sharp edge [11] between discontinuity texture coordinates as a textural seam with the points on it as seam-points whilst the others as internal points. We formulate the cost of contraction and define the values of penalties for feature-preserving. Experimental results showed that for models with textural seams, our method can achieve a comparable efficiency with QEM and even a better result than PM.

## 2 Feature-Preserving Process

As the quality of the resulting model mainly depends on the collapse cost, different methods have been developed to find a good formula to compute it. But hardly can they achieve an ideal result in the case of meshes with textural seams as the Emerald model with six faces in Fig. 2. We have found a method based on iterative edge contraction and the Quadric Error Metric to decimate the Emerald model at different levels of detail and preserve its discrete properties.

## 2.1 Overview of QEM

A triangle can define a plane: $\mathbf{n}^T \mathbf{v} + d = 0$, where $\mathbf{n} = [a\ b\ c]^T$ is the unit normal vector of the plane with $a^2 + b^2 + c^2 = 1$. A given plane's error quadric defined in the QEM scheme 8 is $Q = (A, b, c) = (nn^T, dn, d^2)$.

Then the square distance from any point $v$ to the plane can be represented by the error quadric $Q(v) = D^2(v) = v^T A v + 2b^T v + c$.

After pair contraction, the quadric of the new point is the sum of two old vertices' quadrics 8. As half-edge collapse doesn't generate new point, it can be inferred that if $Q(v_s) > Q(v_t)$, the result point is $v_t$, otherwise it is $v_s$. The cost of contraction is $Cost(v_s, v_t) = (Q_s + Q_t)v_t$.

## 2.2 Analysis of Discrete Properties

As a vertex may have different attributes in different triangles, [12] proposed an intermediate abstraction called *wedge* to represent a set of vertex-adjacent corners whose attributes are the same. A vertex of the mesh is partitioned into a set of one or more wedges, and per wedge contains one or more face corners.

For meshes with textural seams, texture coordinates of internal points are continuous, and each of them corresponds to only one wedge. But a seam-point is probably partitioned into two or more wedges. After decimation, the potential changes in texture coordinate of a vertex will incur the appearance distortion. As a result, Garland 10 and Hoppe 4 took the appearance attributes into account when computing the contracting cost.

Most applications revealed that if two points of a collapsing pair $(v_s, v_t)$ are internal points, appearance distortion caused by contraction is less distinct than geometric errors. It is advised to follow the traditional QEM algorithm for this occasion, i.e. the appearance attributes won't be taken into account.

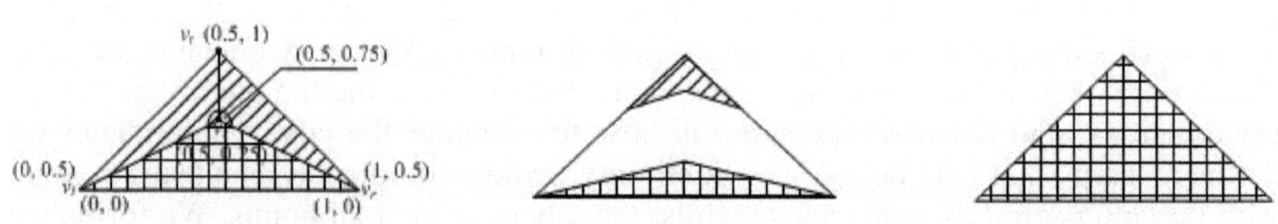


(a) (b) (c)

**Fig. 3.** Textural distribution of original Emerald model and modified Emerald model

Other than that occasion, we conclude three cases according to the type of $v_s$ and $v_t$.

*Case 1*: $v_s$ is a seam-point and $v_t$ is an internal point (see Fig. 3(a)) with two seams $(v_l, v_s)$ and $(v_s, v_r)$. After a half-edge collapse operation, $v_s$ is collapsed to $v_t$ and two incident triangles $(v_l, v_s, v_t)$ and $(v_s, v_r, v_t)$ vanish. However, the modified model in Fig. 3(b) leads to explicit textural distortion.

If we release the restriction of half-edge collapse and introduce new wedges (in this instance, the texture coordinate of $v_t$ is replaced by that of $v_s$), the texture is preserved yet with seams disappearing (see Fig. 3(c)). It shall cause errors if the seams are surface boundaries.

Hereby, this kind of vertex pair should be collapsed as late as possible. So the basic QEM formula is rewritten:

$$\mathrm{Cost}(v_s, v_t) = \mathrm{Dist}(v_s, v_t) + \alpha \bullet \mathrm{IsSeam}(v_s) \bullet (1 - \mathrm{IsSeam}(v_t))$$
$$\left( IsSeam(v) = \begin{cases} 1 & if\ v\ is\ the\ seam\text{-point} \\ 0 & otherwise \end{cases} \right) \quad (1)$$

where $\mathrm{Dist}(v_s, v_t) = (Q_s + Q_t)\, v_t$. The penalty $\alpha$ $\mathrm{Dist}(v_s, v_t)$ to postpone this kind of collapse operations.

*Case 2:* $v_s$ is an internal point and $v_t$ is a seam-point. After collapsing, the seam-point is fixed. In this case, we must find a proper wedge for replacement to eliminate distortion. According to the geometric structure, the wedges of $v_3$, $v_t$ and $v_s$ are continuous as they share one triangle (see Fig. 4(a)). So $w_0$ is continuous to $w_s$ and can be chosen to replace $w_s$.

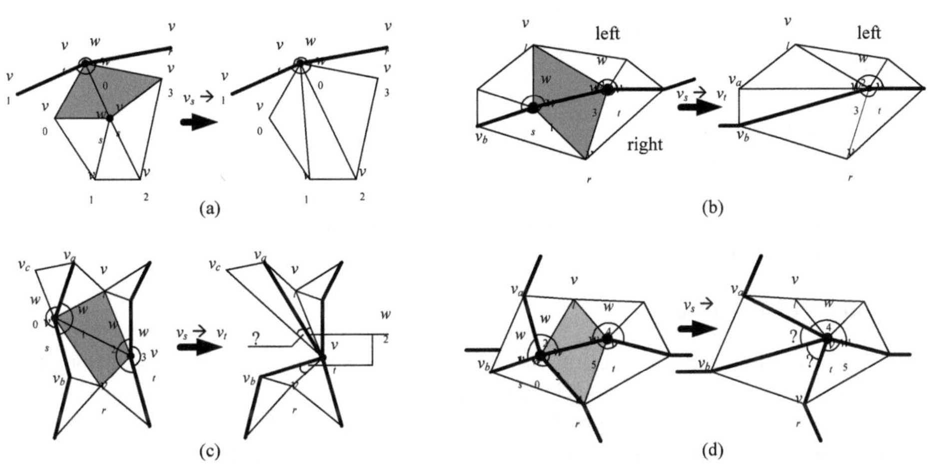


**Fig. 4. (a)** Half-edge collapsing from an internal point to a seam point; (b) Half-edge collapsing from a seam point to a seam point; (c) $v_s$ and $v_t$ on two different seams (d) Half-edge collapsing from a crossing point to a seam point

*Case 3:* Both $v_s$ and $v_t$ are seam-points. This occasion is much more complex so we classify it into four sub-cases.

In the first sub-case, the two vertices are exactly on the same seam as shown in Fig.4(b), and the primary issue, the same as Case 2, is how to choose a proper wedge for replacement. From Fig. 4(b), we know that $w_0$ and $w_2$ are continuous, while $w_1$ and $w_3$ are continuous. Then $w_2$ will replace $w_0$ and $w_3$ will replace $w_1$.

In the second sub-case, $v_s$ and $v_t$ are on two different seams yet edge $(v_s, v_t)$ isn't a seam (see Fig.4(c)). As no proper wedge could be found to replace $w_0$ in triangle $(v_s, v_a, v_c)$, textural feature of seam $v_a$ - $v_s$ - $v_b$ may be distorted. So we evaluate a higher cost for this kind of collapsing edges and amend Formula (1) as:

$$\begin{aligned} \mathrm{Cost}(v_s,v_t) &= \mathrm{Dist}(v_s,v_t) + \alpha \cdot \mathrm{IsSeam}(v_s) \cdot (1-\mathrm{IsSeam}(v_t)) \\ &\quad + \beta \cdot \mathrm{IsSeam}(v_s) \cdot \mathrm{IsSeam}(v_t) \cdot (1-\mathrm{IsSeam}(v_s,v_t)) \\ (IsSeam(v_s,v_t) &= \begin{cases} 1 & \text{if } (v_s,v_t) \text{ is a seam} \\ 0 & \text{otherwise} \end{cases}) \end{aligned} \tag{2}$$

and β Dist($v_s$, $v_t$).

As for the third sub-case, we firstly define a vertex on two or more different seams as a *crossing point*. In Fig. 4(d), $v_s$ is a crossing point on two seam: $v_b$ - $v_s$ - $v_t$ and $v_a$ - $v_s$ - $v_r$. $v_s$ are partitioned into four different wedges as $w_0$, $w_1$, $w_2$ and $w_3$, while $v_t$ holds two wedges as $w_4$ and $w_5$. Among these wedges, there are two continuous pair ($w_2$, $w_4$) and ($w_3$, $w_5$). After collapsing operation, $w_2$ is replaced by $w_4$. Since $w_3$ is unaffected, it won't be processed. However, suitable wedges cannot be found to replace $w_0$ and $w_1$ in the removed triangles ($v_a$, $v_b$, $v_s$) and ($v_b$, $v_r$, $v_s$) possibly leading to textural aberrance. So we alter the Formula (2) to back off these illegal operations:

$$\begin{aligned} \mathrm{Cost}(v_s,v_t) &= \mathrm{Dist}(v_s,v_t) + \alpha \cdot \mathrm{IsSeam}(v_s) \cdot (1-\mathrm{IsSeam}(v_t)) \\ &\quad + \beta \cdot \mathrm{IsSeam}(v_s) \cdot \mathrm{IsSeam}(v_t) \cdot (1-\mathrm{IsSeam}(v_s,v_t)) + \gamma \cdot \mathrm{IsCross}(v_s) \cdot \mathrm{IsSeam}(v_t) \\ (IsCross(v) &= \begin{cases} 1 & \text{if } v \text{ is a crossing point} \\ 0 & \text{otherwise} \end{cases}) \end{aligned} \tag{3}$$

Just as α and β, γ Dist($v_s$, $v_t$).

The forth sub-case is similar to the third one with the terminal point being a crossing point. Still referring to Fig. 4(d), $w_4$ and $w_5$ in the affected triangles can be properly replaced by $w_2$ and $w_3$ respectively. Then the corresponding cost is the same as that of collapsing an internal-point pair.

### 2.3 Values of Penalties

From the conclusion in last section, we know that α, β and γ must be large enough so that the costs of collapse edges yielding material distortion are larger than those of others. Consequently we will specify value for each penalty.

Firstly we discuss the value of α in Formula (1). It can be easily concluded that

$$\begin{aligned} \mathrm{Cost}(v_s,v_t) &> \max\{\mathrm{Dist}(v_i,v_j) \mid v_i \to v_j \in \mathrm{HEC}(M^n)\} \\ &= \max\{(\mathbf{Q}_i+\mathbf{Q}_j)v_j \mid v_i \to v_j \in \mathrm{HEC}(M^n)\} \end{aligned}$$

where HEC($M^n$) is a set of all the legal edges in $M^n$. Dist($v_i$, $v_j$) is the basic geometric error whose expression is

$$\mathrm{Dist}(v_i,v_j) = \sum_{t\in \mathrm{Tri}(v_i)} \mathrm{Area}(t) \cdot \mathrm{Dist}(v_j,t) + \sum_{t\in \mathrm{Tri}(v_j)} \mathrm{Area}(t) \cdot \mathrm{Dist}(v_j,t)$$

Tri($v$) is a set of all the incident triangles of $v$, Area($t$) is the area of triangle $t$ acting as a weigh for Dist($v$, $t$) - the distance from vertex $v$ to triangle $t$. Experiences indicate that by and large, Dist($v_i$, $v_j$) is smaller than double value of Dist($v_s$, $v_t$). Therefore we simplify the rule as Cost($v_s$ ,$v_t$) ≥2*Dist($v_s$ ,$v_t$).

As IsSeam($v_s$, $v_t$ ) = 1 brings on Cost($v_s$, $v_t$ ) = Dist($v_s$, $v_t$) + α., we can be obtained α≥Dist($v_s$ ,$v_t$).

Suppose *l*, *w* and *h* are length, width and height respectively of the bounding box of a grid, it is clearly that the distance of any two points on a grid won't be larger than the root of $l^2 + w^2 + h^2$. Defining $Max = \sqrt{l^2 + w^2 + h^2}$ , we modify the formula as:

$$\begin{aligned}
\mathrm{Dist}(v_s, v_t) &= \sum_{t \in \mathrm{Tri}(v_s)} \mathrm{Area}(t) \bullet \mathrm{Dist}(v_t, t) + \sum_{t \in \mathrm{Tri}(v_t)} \mathrm{Area}(t) \bullet \mathrm{Dist}(v_t, t) \\
&\le \sum_{t \in \mathrm{Tri}(v_s)} \mathrm{Area}(t) \bullet MaxDist + \sum_{t \in \mathrm{Tri}(v_t)} \mathrm{Area}(t) \bullet MaxDist \\
&= MaxDist \bullet \left( \sum_{t \in \mathrm{Tri}(v_s)} \mathrm{Area}(t) + \sum_{t \in \mathrm{Tri}(v_t)} \mathrm{Area}(t) \right) \\
&= MaxDist \bullet \left( \mathrm{TriArea}(v_s) + \mathrm{TriArea}(v_t) \right)
\end{aligned} \tag{4}$$

where $\mathrm{TriArea} = \sum_{t \in Tri(V_S)} \mathrm{Area}(t)$.

Since α (= $MaxDist \bullet (\mathrm{TriArea}(v_S) + \mathrm{TriArea}(v_t))$ ) is much larger than $\mathrm{Dist}(v_s, v_t)$, then $\mathrm{Cost}(v_s, v_t) \geqslant 2 * \mathrm{Dist}(v_s, v_t) \geqslant \mathrm{Dist}(v_i, v_j)$ (($v_i$, $v_j$) represents a majority of vertex pairs).

This restriction can only assure that the value of $\mathrm{Cost}(v_s, v_t)$ can be larger than most elements in HEC($M^n$) but not the whole set, as ($v_i$, $v_j$) isn't any two points on triangular meshes but merely represents a majority of edges. There may exist some collapse operations that won't cause appearance distortion though their decimation costs are larger than $\mathrm{Cost}(v_s, v_t)$. However we must evaluate a high cost for them since those operations can give rise to geometric errors to worsen visual quality. The experimental results proved it as well.

β is added to back off the collapse operations between two seam-points. The resulting geometric errors are similar to those caused by the operations from a seam-point to an internal point, so we can simply define β=α. The value of γ should be higher as 2α because appearance attributes of a crossing point are more distinct than those of others.

The final formula of the cost is:

$$\begin{aligned}
\mathrm{Cost}(v_s, v_t) = \mathrm{Dist}(v_s, v_t) &+ \alpha \bullet \mathrm{IsSeam}(v_s) \bullet (1 - \mathrm{IsSeam}(v_t)) \\
&+ \alpha \bullet \mathrm{IsSeam}(v_s) \bullet \mathrm{IsSeam}(v_t) \bullet (1 - \mathrm{IsSeam}(v_s, v_t)) \\
&+ 2\alpha \bullet \mathrm{IsCross}(v_s) \bullet \mathrm{IsSeam}(v_t)
\end{aligned} \tag{5}$$

where $\alpha = MaxDist \bullet (\mathrm{TriArea}(v_S) + \mathrm{TriArea}(v_t))$. The value of *MaxDist* is pre-calculated as it depends on the bounding box of a gird. For the arbitrary model, TriArea($v$) is the total area of all the incident triangles of $v$. After a collapse operation, all the triangles meeting at $v_S$ are integrated into the entire set of triangles of $v_t$: $\mathrm{TriArea}(v_t)\_new = \mathrm{TriArea}(v_S) + \mathrm{TriArea}(v_t)\_old$.

## 3 Implementation

The inputs of the algorithm are *VertexData* and *IndexData*: the former is a sequence of wedges denoting the attributes of per vertex in a grid model; the latter consists of wedges' indices for each triangle.

We introduce three temporary data structure: *PMVertex*, *PMWedge* and *PMTriangle* to simplify the implementation of the algorithm.

*PMVertex* contains attributes of a vertex (see in Fig. 5). *cost* and *to* are the key properties of the preferred collapsing edge with the lowest cost among all candidates.

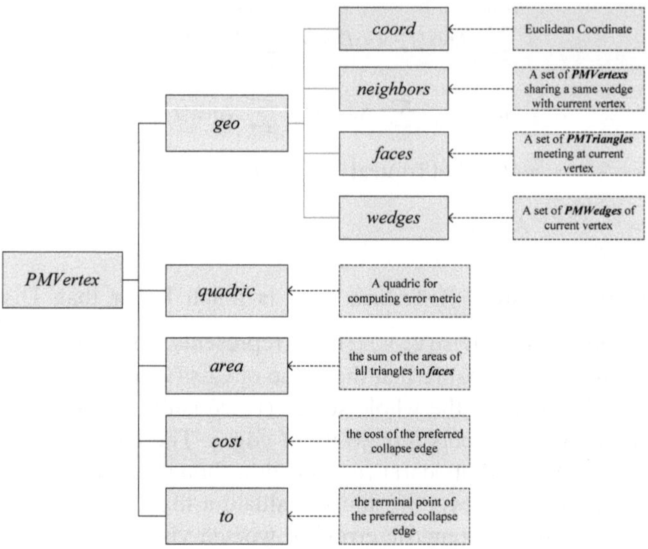


**Fig. 5.** Structure of *PMVertex*

*PMWedge* indicates a wedge represented as (*realIndex*, *vertex*), where *realIndex* is the index of current wedge and *vertex* is a *PMVertex* to memorize the corresponding vertex.

*PMTriangle* is a triangle with a triplet of wedges: ($w_0$, $w_1$, $w_2$). Its elements are three wedges of a triangle anti-clockwise.

Before the main algorithm is executed, *VertexData* and *IndexData* will be converted to temporary structures at first which means that the actual inputs are three sequences of *PMVertex*, *PMWedge* and *PMTriangle* as *vertices*, *wedges* and *triangles*.

In each iterative process, we first select the vertex *u* with lowest cost from the *vertices*, and collapse from *u* to *u.to*. The iterative procedure will be continued until the required resolution is reached. To simplify the selecting operation, we adopt the function in 11 to place all the vertex pairs in a heap keyed on cost with the minimum cost pair at the top. Time complexity will decrease from $O(n)$ from $O(\lg n)$.

The collapsing operation $\{u \rightarrow v\}$ is abstracted to seven steps:1. save neighbors of *u* as affected *PMVertex* for recomputing; 2. classify the relevant triangles of *u* into two sets: *removal*–the triangles to be removed; *replacement*–the triangles to be replaced; 3. find a proper substitute for the *replacement*'s wedge; 4. remove the *removal* set and delete the vertices of those triangles from their neighborhood; 5. substitute the *PMWedges* in *replacement*; 6. update quadrics and areas of incident triangles of *u* by adding them into those of *v* respectively; 7. recompute collapse cost for the affected *PMVertex* and update the heap. The modified *Triangles* can be regarded as the output.

## 4 Experimental Results

To verify the efficiency of the proposed simplification algorithm, we apply it to several ore models, and make a comparison with the PM operation and the original QEM algorithm. We performed the algorithm on an Intel Pentium IV with 2.94 GHz processor and 1 GB of memory.

The performances that we have obtained when building our multi-resolution structure from the full resolution mesh are presented in Table 1. Obviously our method is much more rapid than the PM operation. In [3] it reached a conclusion that QEM keeps ahead in speed compared with other algorithms, and as our method's speed is not far slower than it, it can be verified that the speed of the proposed algorithm is moderately outstanding.

**Table 1.** Multi-resolution construction time

| Mesh | Vertex | Triangles | Running Time (millisecond) | | |
|---|---|---|---|---|---|
| | | | Our method | PM | QEM |
| Emerald | 2502 | 5000 | 66 | 754 | 31 |
| Agate | 25002 | 50000 | 793 | 7484 | 496 |
| Cyrtospirifer rudkiensis | 30861 | 61718 | 952 | 9210 | 629 |

Compared the results obtained by our simplification algorithm with those generated by the other two techniques, we can assess the quality of the modified meshes. The comparison has been done using the publicly available *Metro* tool [13], which measures surface deviation and is thus biased towards simplification algorithms which use that criterion to guide compression. Fig. 6 summarizes the results derived from the Emerald model. Our method obtains results comparable to those of PM and

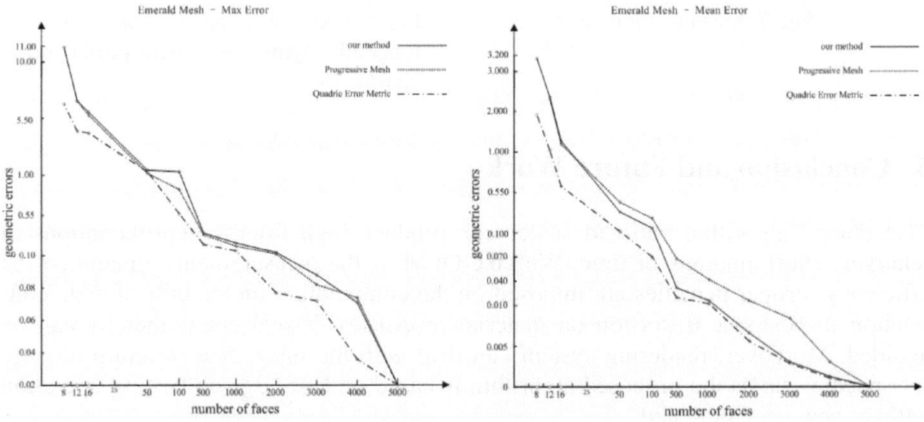


**Fig. 6.** Maximum and mean geometric error of Emerald

even better than PM for the mean error. As we processed the textural seams of the model, distinct errors are likely to be generated on these sharp edges. On the contrary, the PM algorithm left these edges unsettled. Then in the max errors of our method larger than those of PM. [3] has verified that the precision of QEM is impressive in the case with meshes without open boundaries. As the ore models are just without open boundaries, QEM surely achieves more accurate results.

Fig. 7 compares textural errors obtained on the Emerald model by our algorithm and the PM operation. Only from several certain angles with the resolution from 2000 to 500, our method produced more textural errors than that of PM. It is also because that only our method processed the textural seams. Thus from some angles the exposed seams lead to larger errors. For other cases especially ranging from 500 triangles to 12 triangles, our method achieved an apparently higher fidelity.

The visual quality of the approximations is illustrated in Fig. 8. The original models on the left have full resolution with 5000, 50000 and 61718 triangles respectively. The modified models to the right have 1000 and 150 triangles respectively.

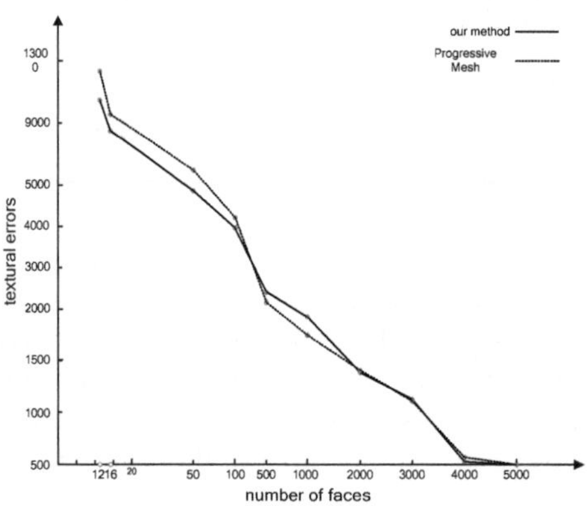


**Fig. 7.** Mean textural error

**Fig. 8.** Sequence of approximations of the Emerald, Agate and Cyrtospirifer rudkiensis

## 5 Conclusion and Future Work

The general algorithm outlined so far can produce high fidelity approximations in relatively short amounts of time. We take QEM as the measurement to maintain the efficiency. Proper penalties are imposed on the computation on the cost of edge contraction to postpone distortion on material properties. Visual errors thereby can be avoided. Moreover, rendering system can deal with the input data structure directly for speeding-up as the proposed algorithm is based on half-edge collapsing operation without new vertex created.

However, according to the experimental results it will take more than one second to simplify a meshes model with initially 60,000 faces, which cannot meet the requirement of many applications. As mesh simplification is a one-off process, we can record the relevant information throughout the algorithm, and make use of it to rebuild all the multi-resolution models during real-time rendering. In our future work, we will introduce a data structure to store multi-resolution models and develop an algorithm to rebuild those polygonal models from the data structure inversely.

**Acknowledgments.** The authors would like to thank the Department of Earth Science of Nanjing University for providing variety of ore models. This work is sponsored by the National Natural Science Foundation of China (No. 60473113) and the key Program of the National Science Foundation of China (No. 60533080)

## References

1. Dong, W.L., Li, J.K, Kuo, C.-C. J.: Fast Mesh Simplification for Progressive Transmission. In: Proceedings of IEEE International Conference on Multimedia & Expo, vol. 3, pp. 1731–1734 (2000)
2. Luebke, D., et al.: Level of Detail for 3D Graphics. Morgan Kaufmann, Seattle, Washington, USA (2002)
3. Cignoni, P., Montani, C., Scopigno, R.: A Comparison of Mesh Simplification Algorithms. Computers and Graphics 22, 37–54 (1998)
4. Hoppe, H.: New Quadric Metric for Simplifying Meshes with Appearance Attributes. In: Proceedings of IEEE Visualization'99, pp. 59–66
5. Kobbelt, L., Campagna, S., Seidel, H.P.: A General Framework for Mesh Decimation. In: Proceedings of Graphics Interface, pp. 43–50 (1998)
6. Hoppe, H.: Progressive meshes. In: Proccedings of SIGGRAPH'96, pp. 99–108 (1996)
7. Hoppe, H., DeRose, T., et al.: Mesh Optimization. In: Proceeding of SIGGRAPH92, vol. 27 pp. 19–26 (1992)
8. Garland, M., Heckbert, P.: Surface Simplification Using Quadric Error Metric. In: Proceedings of SIGGRAPH97, pp. 209–216 (1997)
9. Bouvier, E., Gobbetti, E.: TOM: Totally Ordered Mesh – A Multiresolution Structure for Time Cirtical Graphics Applications. International Journal of Image and Graphics 1, 115–134 (2001)
10. Garland, M., Heckbert, P. S.: Simplifying Surfaces with Color and Texture using Quadric Error Metrics. In: Proceedings of IEEE Visualization' 98, pp. 263–270 (1998)
11. Garland, M.: Quadric-Based Polygonal Surface Simplification. The PhD thesis in School of Computer Science, Carnegie Mellon University (May 1999)
12. Hoppe, H.: Effective Implementation of Progressive Meshes. Computer & Graphics 22, 27–36 (1998)
13. Cignoni, P., Scopigno, C.R., Metro, R.: Measuring Error on Simplified Surfaces. Tech. rep., Istituto I.E.I.-C.N.R., Pisa, Italy, January 1996. Technical Report B4-01-01-96(1996)

# Content Adaptive Embedding of Complementary Patterns for Nonintrusive Direct-Projected Augmented Reality

Hanhoon Park, Moon-Hyun Lee, Byung-Kuk Seo, Yoonjong Jin, and Jong-Il Park

Department of Electrical and Computer Engineering, Hanyang University, Seoul, Korea
{hanuni, fly4moon, nwseoweb, lakobe8}mr.hanyang.ac.kr,
jipark@hanyang.ac.kr

**Abstract.** In direct-projected augmented reality, the visual patterns for compensation may distract users despite users would not be interested in the compensation process. The distraction becomes more serious for dynamic projection surface in which compensation and display should be done simultaneously. Recently, a complementary pattern-based method of efficiently hiding the compensation process from users' view has been proposed. However, the method faced the tradeoff between the pattern imperceptibility and compensation accuracy. In this paper, we embed locally different strength of pattern images into different channels of the projector input images (AR images) after analyzing their spatial variation and color distribution. It is demonstrated that our content adaptive approach can significantly improve the imperceptibility of the patterns and produce better compensation results by comparing it with the previous approach through a variety of experiments and subjective evaluation.

**Keywords:** Nonintrusive direct-projected augmented reality, complementary pattern embedding, content adaptive.

## 1 Introduction

Direct-projected augmented reality (DirectAR) indicates a technique that displays (=projects) AR images on surfaces with arbitrary shape or color under arbitrary lighting environment without image distortion using a projector-camera pair. It needs the process of measuring the scene geometry and radiometry, and transforming the augmented reality images in advance, called usually compensation [1]. It is achieved by projecting code patterns using a projector, capturing the pattern images using a camera, and analyzing the camera images. In this process, the patterns are usually strongly perceptible and thus may visually intrusive to users. Moreover, in dynamic environments (e.g. camera, projector is moving, or geometry, photometry of surface is changing), the process of estimating the geometry and photometry of surface using visual patterns is not applicable any more [2]. To resolve these problems, there have been researches corresponding to projecting patterns invisibly or at high speed. We call them nonintrusive DirectAR.

Yasumuro et al. used an additional infrared projector to project near-infrared patterns which are invisible to human eyes [3]. Their system can augment medical

R. Shumaker (Ed.): Virtual Reality, HCII 2007, LNCS 4563, pp. 132 – 141, 2007.

images on dynamic human body without distortion and distraction. However, the frame rate is cut down by half because the system uses at least two projectors.

Raskar et al. have used special engineered digital light projector that is able to turn light on and off at a very high rate (over 1000Hz) [4]. This projector projects image bit-plane by bit-plane. Two of the 24 bit-planes are reserved to insert a light pattern and its complement. Because the switching is so fast, human eye is unable to distinguish between the bit-plane showing light pattern and the next one showing its complement.

Cotting et al. measured the mirror flip (on/off) sequences of a Digital Light Processing (DLP) projector for RGB values using a photo transistor and a digital oscilloscope, and imperceptibly embedded arbitrary binary patterns into projector input images (indicates augmented reality images in this paper) by adjusting the mirror flips to be aligned to the binary pattern for a very short period of time in such a way that the original projector input image values are approximated to the nearest values [5]. The adjustment can causes contrast reduction as explained in [6]. Moreover, sophisticated control of camera shuttering for detecting the short-term patterns is required.

There have been other types of nonintrusive DirectAR, which are not fully vision-based ones because they use physical sensors to measure the projected code patterns but use visual patterns and try to reduce pattern perceptibility. Summet and Sukthankar proposed a hand-held projected display whose location is tracked using optical sensors in conjunction with temporally-coded patterns of projected light and tried to minimize the extent of distracting temporal codes to small regions [7]. They projected a small pattern over located sensors instead of projecting a full-screen localization pattern, but left the rest of the projection area free for user display purpose. Lee et al. used the concept of frequency shift keyed (FSK) modulation to reduce pattern perceptibility [8]. That is, they selected either a bright red or a medium gray that, when rendered by their modified projector (removing the color wheel) appears to be a similar intensity of gray to a human observer, but are manifested as a 180Hz signal and a 360Hz signal respectively. The optical sensor can discriminate the signals. By using these two colors, they could hide code patterns in what appeared to be mostly gray squares.

Recently, Park et al. proposed a method that embeds complementary patterns into AR images based on a simple pixel operation without using sensors or special-purpose projectors [2]. In their method, code pattern images and their complementary (inverse) images are embedded into consecutive AR images by increasing and decreasing the pixel values of the AR image, or vice versa. If the frame rate of the sequence reaches the critical fusion frequency (75Hz according to Watson [9]), the odd and even frames are visually integrated over time, so that the embedded pattern image would be imperceptible to the users. The embedded pattern images are detectable using the camera synchronized with the projector. However, their method needs to deal with the tradeoff between the strength (visibility) of the embedded patterns and the accuracy of estimating the geometry and photometry of surface [2]. Bimber et al. attempted to fade patterns in and out within a short sequence of subsequent projector input images [6]. However, the frame rate is severely cut down. As a more effective method, we propose a content-adaptive pattern embedding method of minimizing the visibility of patterns while maintaining the compensation accuracy. We locally adjust the pattern strength and the embedding channel after analyzing the AR images based on the characteristics of human vision system. The advantage of using the characteristics of human vision system was also experimentally verified by other researchers [10].

With our approach, the patterns with the same strength can be more imperceptible by changing the embedding channel. And the strong pattern images minimize the compensation error in the region with high spatial variation and the compensation error due to weak pattern images in the region with low spatial variation is unnoticeable. It is demonstrated that our content adaptive method can significantly improve the imperceptibility of the embedded patterns and produce better compensation results by comparing it with the previous methods through a variety of experiments and subjective evaluation.

## 2 Embedding and Detecting Complementary Patterns

In this section, we briefly explain the method of embedding and detecting complementary patterns which indicate a pair of a pattern and its inverse. They are generated by adding and subtracting a color (or brightness) of successive AR images as shown in Fig. 1-(a) and Fig. 2-(a).

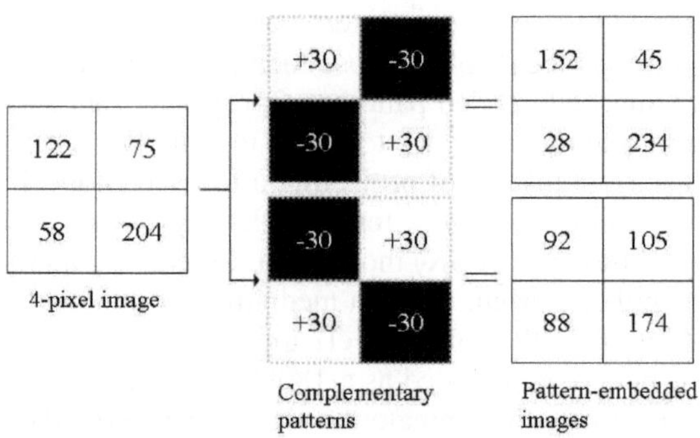


(a) pattern embedding

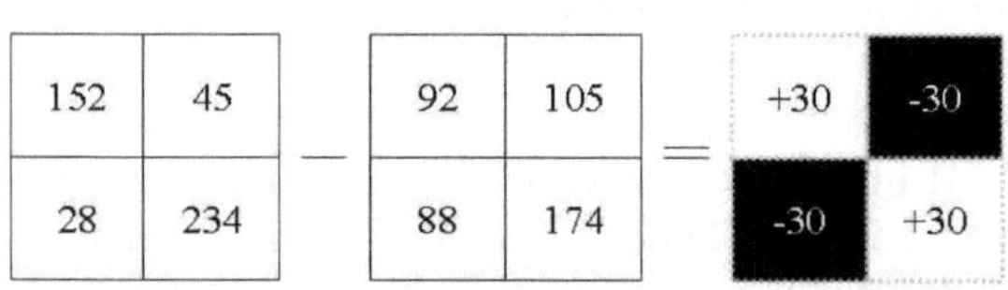


(b) pattern detection

**Fig. 1.** Example of embedding and detecting complementary patterns into a 4-pixel gray AR image

If complementary patterns are alternately projected at high speed, only the AR images will be perceived to the human eye because the human vision system integrates the amount of light seen over time in order to acquire an image as shown in Fig. 2-(c).

The detection of embedded pattern images is easily done by subtracting the odd and even frames of the camera image sequences and binarizing the result (see Fig. 1-(b)

and Fig. 2-(d)) once the camera is synchronized with the projector [2]. When the resulting images are noisy, the median filtering may be effectively applied to the images. In ill-conditioned environment, simple median filtering suffices. More sophisticated algorithms may be required under ill-conditioned experimental environments.

(a) pattern embedded AR images

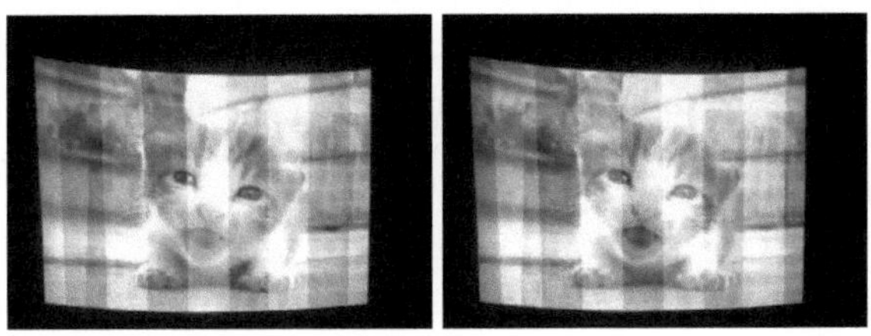

(b) camera images of projection of (a)

(c) image seen to the users

(d) extracted pattern from the images of (b)

**Fig. 2.** Example of embedding and detecting of code pattern for geometric compensation

## 3 Content-Adaptive Pattern Embedding and Detecting

In this section, we explain the content-adaptive method of embedding and detecting imperceptible pattern images. We locally embed patterns based on the analysis on the color distribution, spatial variation of AR images (= projector input images) as shown in Fig. 3. We divide the AR images into small $n \times n$ ($n < w, h$) blocks. $w$ and $h$ indicate the width and height of the AR images. For each block, we embed patterns with the strength proportional to the spatial variation into different channel depending on the color contribution.

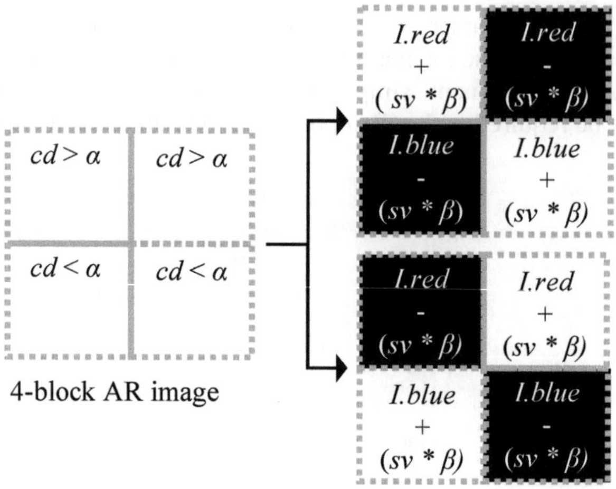


**Fig. 3.** Content-adaptive pattern embedding for a 4-block AR image. $\alpha$ and $\beta$ indicate user-defined constants. According to the color distribution (*cd* in Eq. (2)), the pattern images are embedded into different channels. According to the spatial variation (*sv* in Eq. (1)), the pattern images are embedded with different strengths.

The spatial variation is computed using a 2-D derivative filter as follows:

$$sv = \sqrt{\{F_h * I\}^2 + \{F_v * I\}^2} \qquad (1)$$

where * denotes spatial convolution, $F_h$ and $F_v$ denote horizontal and vertical derivative filters, respectively, and $I$ denotes projector input image. We use the filter kernel $\begin{bmatrix}-1 & 8 & -8 & 1\end{bmatrix}$ for derivative calculation.

The color distribution is analyzed in the YIQ color space. The transformation of RGB color space to YIQ color space is defined as

$$y = 0.299r + 0.587g + 0.114b,$$
$$i = 0.596r + 0.274g + 0.322b,$$
$$q = 0.211r + 0.523g + 0.312b.$$

Here, $i$ value is dominated by $r$ value while $q$ value is dominated by $g$ value. Therefore, we embed pattern images into the Q-channel in the region with a large value of $r$ while into the I-channel otherwise. Specifically, the color distribution value is computed as

$$cd = \operatorname{sgn}\left(\frac{\sum_N r/N}{\sum_N g/N} - 1\right) \quad \textit{where } N\text{: the number of pixels,} \qquad (2)$$

$$\operatorname{sgn}(x) = \begin{cases} 1 & x > 0 \\ 0 & x \le 0 \end{cases}.$$

The detection of embedded pattern images is not different from that of Section 2. Figure 5 shows the examples of detecting content-adaptively embedded patterns.

Although the patterns were embedded into locally different channels with locally different strengths, the pattern images were clearly extracted. It implies that the content-adaptive method does not influence the compensation accuracy.

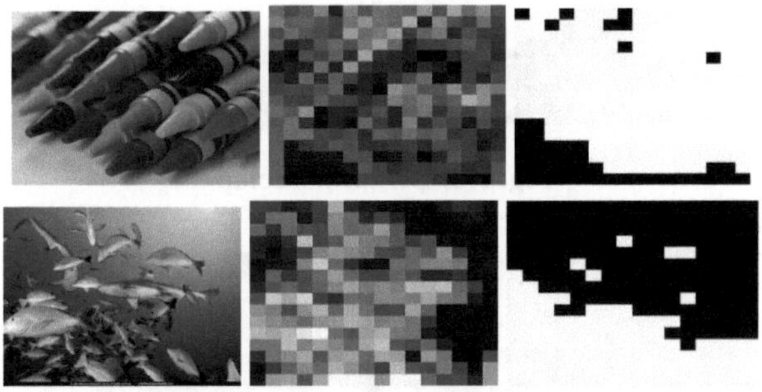

(a) original images and their derivative maps and color distribution maps

(b) non-adaptive (c) adaptive

**Fig. 4.** Content-adaptive pattern embedding for a real AR image. The derivative map has continuous values ranging from 0 to 1 while the color distribution map has two values, i.e. 0 and 1.

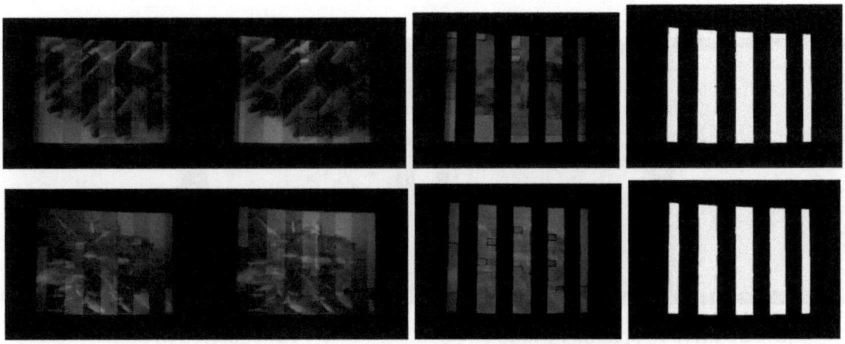

**Fig. 5.** Projection of adaptively pattern-embedded AR images, their difference images, and detected patterns. Even for the image having low spatial frequency and contrast all over, the weakly embedded pattern is also clearly detected.

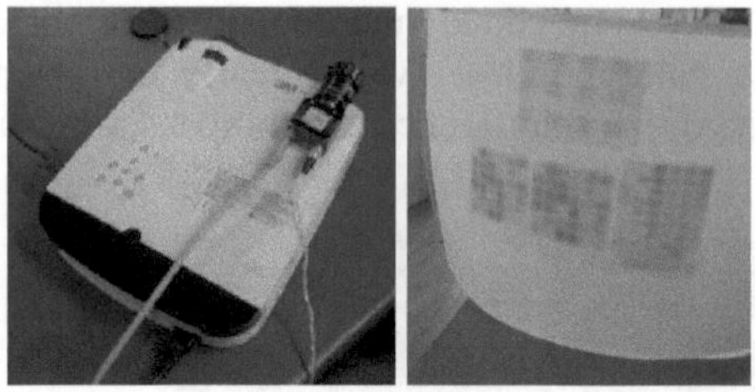

**Fig. 6.** Experimental setup

(a) original image and its projection (not compensated)

(b) non-adaptive

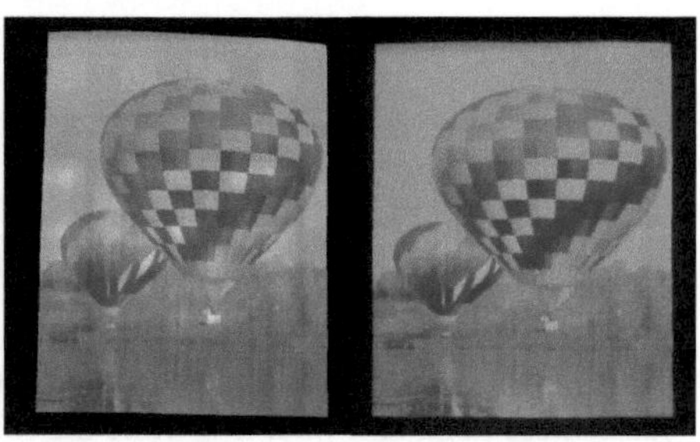

(c) adaptive to color distribution

(d) adatptive to spatial variation

(d) adaptive to both

**Fig. 7.** Comparison of compensation results using the non-adaptive embedding and adaptive embedding (for real image). Left images: modified projector input image, right images: compensated projection.

## 4 Experimental Results and Discussion

We created a projector-camera system which consists of a projector (3M DX60) and a camera (Prosilica EC 655C) as shown in Fig. 6. The camera was synchronized with the projector and it can capture the images projected by the projector without frame loss. A vertical synchronization (shortly, v-sync) signal of a VGA input signal connected to a projector was provided to an external trigger port of a camera as an external input signal. Input images with a resolution of 1024 by 768 pixels were used and the projection surface was non-planar and color-textured (see Fig. 6). The P matrices and nonlinear response functions of the projector and camera were computed in advance. Therefore, the system could work in real-time at a frame rate of 60Hz (= the refresh rate of the projector).

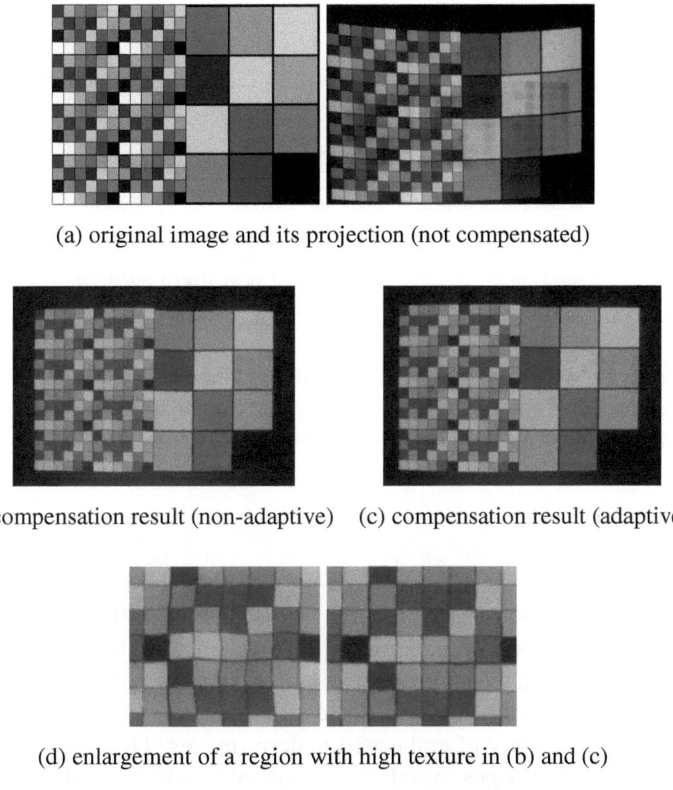

(a) original image and its projection (not compensated)

(b) compensation result (non-adaptive) (c) compensation result (adaptive)

(d) enlargement of a region with high texture in (b) and (c)

**Fig. 8.** Comparison of compensation results using the non-adaptive embedding and adaptive embedding (for synthetic image). The pattern strength was intentionally reduced to see the superiority of the adaptive embedding to the non-adaptive one.

Figure 7 and 8 show the compensation results for a real and synthetic image using content-adaptive embedding method and non-adaptive embedding method on the same experimental environment. The compensation results showed little difference.

Rather, the content-adaptive one outperformed the non-adaptive one in the region with high spatial variation as we see in Fig. 8[1]. Actually, the pattern strength was intentionally reduced for compensating the synthetic image. Thus, the overall compensation results were worse than those of the real image. However, the adaptive embedding method could reduce the compensation error in the region with high spatial variation by increasing the pattern strength.

To confirm the usability of the content-adaptive pattern embedding, we asked fourteen university students to complete a questionnaire based on their satisfaction of compensation results and the perceptibility of the embedded patterns. We divided the degree of user satisfaction and imperceptibility into ten levels. Figure 9 shows the results. It seems that users thought that the accuracies of both are similar but they suffered from the intrusiveness of patterns when using non-adaptive one. On the whole, they preferred adaptive one to non-adaptive one.

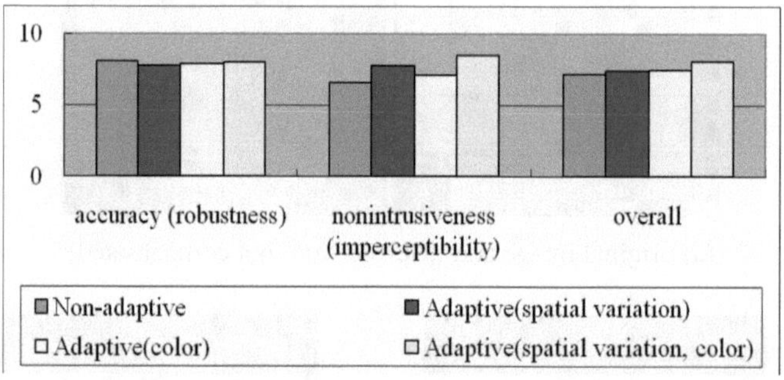


**Fig. 9.** Subjective evaluation on compensation results and pattern imperceptibility using the non-adaptive embedding and adaptive embedding. The overall rating was computed by averaging the two ratings for accuracy and nonintrusiveness.

## 5 Conclusion

In this paper, we proposed a content-adaptive method of embedding imperceptible pattern images and demonstrated that the method can significantly improve the imperceptibility of the embedded patterns on the one hand, produce better compensation results on the other hand, through a variety of experiments and subjective evaluation.

The block size for analyzing the color distribution and spatial variation would influence the imperceptibility of embedded pattern images. Therefore, it would also be valuable to divide AR images into different size of blocks depending on their spatial frequency and contrast, e.g. making a quad-tree.

**Acknowledgments.** This study was supported by a grant(02-PJ3-PG6-EV04-0003) of Ministry of Health and Welfare, Republic of Korea.

[1] Since the compensation error in the region with high spatial variation is usually well-perceptible, it is crucial to reduce the error.

## References


1. Park, H., Lee, M.-H., Kim, S.-J., Park, J.-I.: Surface-Independent Direct-Projected Augmented Reality. In: Narayanan, P.J., Nayar, S.K., Shum, H.-Y. (eds.) ACCV 2006. LNCS, vol. 3852, pp. 892–901. Springer, Heidelberg (2006)
2. Park, H., Lee, M.-H., Seo, B.-K., Park, J.-I.: Undistorted Projection onto Dynamic Surface. In: Chang, L.-W., Lie, W.-N. (eds.) PSIVT 2006. LNCS, vol. 4319, pp. 582–590. Springer, Heidelberg (2006)
3. Yasumuro, Y., Imura, M., Manabe, Y., Oshiro, O., Chihara, K.: Projection-based Augmented Reality with Automated Shape Scanning. In: Proc. of SPIE EI'05, vol. 5664 pp. 555–562 (2005)
4. Raskar, R., Welch, G. Cutts, M., Lake, A., Stesin, L., Fuchs, H.: The Office of the Future: A Unified Approach to Image Based Modeling and Spatially Immersive Displays. In: Proc. of SIGGRAPH'98 (1998)
5. Cotting, D., Naef, M., Gross, M., Fuchs, H.: Embedding Imperceptible Patterns into Projected Images for Simultaneous Acquisition and Display. In: Proc. of ISMAR'04 pp. 100–109 (2004)
6. Bimber, O., Grundhöfer, A., Zollmann, S., Kolster, D.: Digital Illumination for Augmented Studios. J. of Virtual Reality and Broadcasting (2006)
7. Available at: http://gonzo.uni-weimar.de/ bimber/Pub/DIAS.pdf
8. Summet, J., Sukthankar, R.: Tracking Locations of Moving Hand-Held Displays Using Projected Light. In: Proc. of Pervasive'05, pp. 37–46 (2005)
9. Lee, J.C., Hudson, S.E., Summet, J.W., Dietz, P.H.: Moveable Interactive Projected Displays Using Projectors Based Tracking. In: Proc. of UIST'05, pp. 63–72 (2005)
10. Watson, A.B.: Temporal Sensitivity. Handbook of Perception and Human Performance (1986)
11. Wang, D., Sato, I., Okabe, T., Sato, Y.: Radiometric Compensation in a Projector-Camera System Based on the Properties of Human Vision System. In: Proc. of PROCAMS'05 (2005)

# Lower Cost Modular Spatially Immersive Visualization

Frederic I. Parke

Visualization Sciences, College of Architecture, Texas A&M University
College Station, Texas, USA, 77843-3137
parke@viz.tamu.edu

**Abstract.** The development of lower cost modular spatially immersive visualization systems based on commodity components and faceted display surfaces is described. Commodity computers are networked to form graphics computing clusters. Commodity digital projectors are used to form surrounding rear projected faceted display surfaces based on polyhedral shapes. The use of these systems in the design and evaluation of human environments is discussed.

**Keywords:** spatially immersive visualization, modular visualization systems, lower cost visualization, graphics computing clusters.

## 1 Introduction

Access to computer simulation and computer based visualization has dramatically impacted our ability to understand data and design complex systems and environments. Immersive visualization, with its ability to present high quality interactive three-dimensional representations of complex systems, is the next step in this evolution. While standard visualization techniques provide 'windows' into virtual environments, immersive visualization provides the sense of being 'within' and experiencing the environments. However, immersive visualization has, until recently, been associated with complex, expensive, specialized systems used in applications such as scientific visualization, flight training and petroleum exploration where the benefits clearly justified the expense.

This paper explores the development, characteristics and potential of lower cost *modular* immersive visualization systems. We see the development and use of these systems as one way to extend and augment our ability to understand complex systems and complex data and to design and evaluate complex environments.

### 1.1 Impediments

While immersive visualization facilities are still relatively rare, they are becoming key facilitators for many research and industrial projects. Impediments to the broad use of immersive visualization have been:

1. high system cost – these systems, both hardware and software, have been expensive,
2. high cost of operation – specialist support staff and ongoing maintenance have been required,
3. accessibility – only a few systems are in place for a relative small number of users,

R. Shumaker (Ed.): Virtual Reality, HCII 2007, LNCS 4563, pp. 142 – 146, 2007.

4. software complexity – there are only a few 'off-the-shelf' applications; custom application software development is required for most new applications,
5. ease of use issues – special effort is needed to use these systems; they are not well integrated into workflows except for a few specialized problem domains, and
6. human factors issues – user fatigue, 'simulator sickness,' and the need to wear special viewing apparatus are a few of these issues.

Our goal, aimed at mitigating high system costs and limited accessibility, has been to develop very capable lower cost immersive visualization systems that are useful, cost effective and widely accessible. Such lower cost systems promise to enable much broader use in many disciplines.

## 2 Prototype Development

Technology now available enables spatially immersive visualization systems created using off the shelf components including high performance, relatively inexpensive, commodity computers and inexpensive commodity digital projectors. Flexible modular configurations utilizing polyhedral display surfaces with many identical modular components and networked visual computer clusters is one approach to such systems. This is the approach we have been pursuing.

Work is underway at the Texas A&M College of Architecture focused on developing and evaluating several prototypes of this class of systems to determine their practicality and effectiveness. Underlying concepts and issues related to the design and development of these systems are presented.

### 2.1 Spatially Immersive Systems

A spatially immersive visualization system consists of three major elements: computational infrastructure, surrounding display surfaces, and viewer tracking and interaction elements. We are exploring approaches to both the computational infrastructure and the display surface geometries used.

Current and near future technologies and computational economics allow the development of better and more cost effective spatially immersive visualization systems. In recent years, low cost commodity projectors have been replacing expensive projectors and commodity PC based graphics systems have been replacing expensive graphics systems.

A very compelling concept is collections or clusters of commodity computers networked to form powerful, inexpensive distributed parallel computing engines. This concept has been extended into visual computing with the development *tiled* display systems formed by dividing a two-dimensional display area into an array of adjacent regions or tiles [1]. Each of these regions is projected by one of an array of image projectors. This approach can support large, very high aggregate resolution displays.

## 2.2 Faceted Immersive Displays

Taking this approach one step further, spatially immersive systems are created by arranging the display tiles or *facets* into a surrounding three-dimensional display surface and creating a commodity based computational architecture optimized to support such immersive systems [2]. The computational infrastructure used is, as in the tiled display concept, a visual computing extension of the commodity computer cluster concept [3]. In such configurations, each facet need only display a relatively small portion of the total virtual environment. We have focused on faceted systems that are based on portions of the 24 face trapezoidal icositetrahedron shown in Figure 1. To date we have developed three, four, and five facet operational prototypes. A seven facet prototype is currently being developed. Figure 2 shows an early three facet prototype system and a current test-bed system using five display screens.

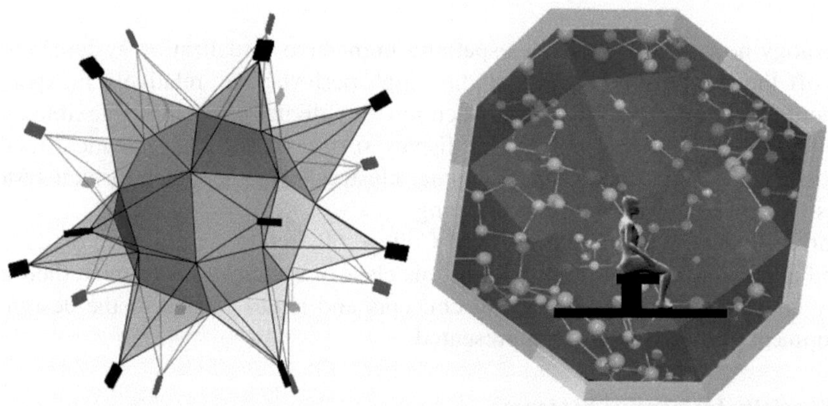

**Fig. 1.** On the left, a conceptual view of a 24 facet immersive system based on the trapezoidal icositetrahedron is shown. Also shown are the rear projector placements. On the right is a cross-section of a simulated 5 meter diameter 24 facet system.

## 2.3 Image Compensation

Since the display surfaces of immersive systems have often been curved and often required blending multiple projected images, expensive high light output CRT based projectors coupled with specialized optical image blending techniques have been the norm. These projectors allowed electronic warping of the projected images to compensate for various optical distortions.

The advent of commodity projectors based on solid-state light modulators such as DLP technology invite the development of immersive systems based on these lower cost devices. However, since the use of optical or electronic image correction with these projectors is very limited, the use of curved projection surfaces, especially rear projected surfaces, is difficult. This is one motivation for using faceted planar projection surfaces. The less than ideal optics used in commodity projectors coupled with the difficulty of precisely positioning the projectors has required the development of software based, primarily GPU based, approaches to compensating for geometric, intensity and color distortions in the projected images. This software image compensation has been informed by the work of Raskar [4] and Majumder [5].

### 2.4 Stereo Image Display

The use of commodity projectors also limits the available approaches to displaying stereo images. The active stereo imaging techniques usually employed in high-end systems require very high frame rates that only expensive projection systems can support. In addition, commodity graphics processors do not typically support tight frame synchronization across multiple systems. This tight synchronization is required for active frame sequential stereo techniques in multi-screen systems.

The frame rate limitations of commodity projectors and the lack of tight image synchronization in commodity graphics processors limit us to passive stereo display techniques. Anaglyphic stereo depends on separating the stereo images based on color. Polarization based stereo depends on separating the stereo images using polarizing filters. Anaglyphic stereo can be done with a single projector for each display facet. Polarization based stereo requires two projectors for each display facet. Both approaches require that the user wear glasses with color or polarizing filters to present each eye with the appropriate images.

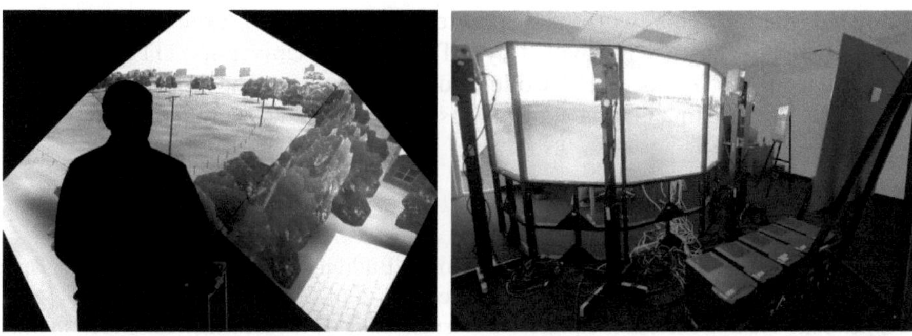

**Fig. 2.** On the left is a view of an early three facet prototype system in operation. On the right is a rear view of an operational five screen immersive system showing the backside of the display screens, projectors, computers and optical path folding mirrors.

## 3 Integration into Work Flows

As listed above, two of the impediments to using immersive systems are software complexity and lack of integration into workflows. While a number of software development libraries are available, only a few 'off-the-shelf' applications exist. The potential user is most often confronted with the daunting task of developing specialized software to support her tasks.

Our location in a college of architecture tends to focus our attention on the integration of these immersive systems into the design and evaluation of human environments. An approach we have been pursing is to develop 'bridging' software that allows users to make use of familiar design tools. The bridging software then facilitates easy translation of data and designs to the immersive systems.

Uses of our prototype systems have included the visualization of a nautical archeology site, the visualization of a currently inaccessible a historic cliff dwelling site and the interactive exploration of an underground leafcutter ant colony.

## 4 Future Modular Systems

Immersive systems based on rear projection technology have inherent difficulties including the need for large, usually high ceiling spaces, to accommodate the projection throw distances and the need for periodic calibration to maintain image alignment. Advances in large-scale flat panel image display technology promise effective alternatives to rear projection. Faceted display configurations could enable truly modular systems where the immersive environment is created by literally bolting together mass replicated modules. Each module would contain the required structural, computational, and display elements. The display surfaces of these modules might eventually utilize flat panel display technology such as organic LEDs. Our vision is that such truly modular systems would allow the widespread use of spatially immersive systems assembled where needed in modest sized spaces at relatively low costs.

**Acknowledgments.** This work is supported by NSF MRI grant CNS-0521110. Additional support has been provided by a Texas A&M University TITF grant and a seed grant from the Texas A&M College of Architecture. The images in Figure 1 were created by Christina Garcia at the Texas A&M Visualization Laboratory.

## References

1. Hereld, M., Judson, I., Stevens, R.: Introduction to Building Projection-Based Tiled Display Systems. IEEE Computer Graphics and Applications 20(4), 22–28 (2000)
2. Parke, F.I.: Next Generation Immersive Visualization Environments. In: Proc. SIGraDi 2002 Conf., Caracas, pp. 162–166 (2002)
3. Humphreys, et al.: WireGL: A Scalable Graphics System for Clusters. In: Proc. Siggraph 2001, pp. 129–140. ACM Press, New York (2001)
4. Raskar, R., et al.: Multi-Projector Displays Using Camera Based Registration. In: Proc. IEEE Visualization 99, San Francisco, pp. 161–168 (1999)
5. Majumder, A., Stevens, R.: Color Non-Uniformity in Projection-Based Displays: Analysis and Solutions. IEEE Trans.Visualization and Computer Graphics 10(2), 177–188 (2004)

# Designing Viewpoint Awareness for 3D Collaborative Virtual Environment Focused on Real-Time Manipulation of Multiple Shared Objects

Luciana Provenzano, Julie Delzons, Patricia Plénacoste, and Johann Vandromme

LIFL, Université de Lille 1, Cité Scientifique,
59655 Villeneuve D'Ascq Cedex - France
{luciana.provenzano,julie.delzons,patricia.plenacoste,
johann.vandromme}@lifl.fr

**Abstract.** In some collaborative manipulation activities – for example, medical experts making a diagnosis based on a 3D reconstruction of a human organ – remote participants may tailor their views on the shared object to their particular needs and task. This implies that each user has her viewpoint on the object. Awareness of viewpoint is then necessary both to coordinate each other and to understand remote users' activities. This work investigates how to provide the remote viewpoint awareness in a 3D collaborative desktop in which multiple shared objects can be independently positioned and manipulated to accomplish a common single activity. Preliminary results of ergonomic evaluations of the proposed metaphors are also provided.

**Keywords:** viewpoint, 3D virtual desktop, manipulation of 3D objects.

## 1 Introduction

In real life collaborative activities, some tasks are performed focusing on a specific aspect, and others require an overview of all participants' activity. Therefore, over a give period of time user attention is engaged in both individual and shared efforts [12], [13]. Consequently, Collaborative Virtual Environments (CVEs) have to manage subjective views on the shared data, independently navigation in common virtual space, shared and private mode of working, in order to actually support people's ability to collaborate [15]. In these workspaces, maintaining awareness of others – where partners are located, what they can see, what they are currently focused on, and what they are doing [1] – is an important factor for smooth and natural collaborations [2]. Particularly, in CVEs where distant users collaborate being concentrated on different parts of the shared data, the viewpoint awareness is necessary to coordinate each other and to understand remote users' activities.

Our research topic focuses on collaborative applications concerning the manipulation of multiple 3D shared objects. There are a lot of examples of possible collaborative activities that require distant users to manipulate shared objects. Let us consider for instance the following scenario. A group of mechanical engineers, geographically distant, is collaborating to design a new car. They could be discussing the engine

R. Shumaker (Ed.): Virtual Reality, HCII 2007, LNCS 4563, pp. 147 – 156, 2007.

structure and so they are concentrated on the same part (the engine), or be involved in individual tasks that may require to work on different parts of the car (for example, an engineer works on the front wheels and the other on the windscreen). So, the mechanical engineers might have different viewpoints on the same shared object (that is the car). Another example is given by three distant physicians (a radiologist, a surgeon and an oncologist) who make a diagnosis of a tumor by simultaneously analyzing a 3D reconstruction of a real patient's liver and the X-ray image. We can suppose that the radiologist examines the x-ray image, while the surgeon and the oncologist use the 3D model. The surgeon studies how to cut the liver (to extract the tumor) and the oncologist measures the tumor size. The three physicians cooperate to carry out the common activity (the diagnosis) but being concentrated on different objects and from distinct viewpoints, depending on their skills.

These and similar manipulation activities share three common features. The manipulated objects are the focus of the collaboration and so they are the only things that have to be shared among distant participants. There is no spatial relation among the manipulable objects. Finally, each user may have a different viewpoint on the shared objects, depending on the task she has to accomplish. Multiple perspectives can provide more insight into the task and might enable a group to accomplish it more efficiently. On the other hand, it is difficult to discuss and to coordinate each other since different viewpoints are employed [7], [16]. In a real context, a person working in a group can easily and naturally infer other partners' viewpoints because she can see them and their spatial position according to the common object.

This work deals with this specific problem: how to provide viewpoint awareness during a collaborative manipulation in a 3D virtual workspace in which distant users can not see one another and the manipulable objects can be independently positioned and oriented?

In this paper, we exploit two viewpoint metaphors: the "remote user's viewpoint" metaphor, which aims to provide any user with a global sense of where the other person's viewpoint is relative to a shared object, and the "local viewpoint" metaphor, which allows to share remote user's view on the common object. Our overall research hypothesis is that "local" viewpoint is more effective and useful than "global" viewpoint during a collaborative manipulation activity.

This paper first reviews the related research concerning the viewpoint awareness. It describes the experiment we conducted. Finally, it presents some of the observations, lessons learned and ideas for future explorations.

## 2 Related Work

The viewpoint is considered one of the main factors to maintain awareness in CVEs and it is widely exploited to reveal "what the remote users are looking at" both in navigation and visualization activities. A lot of techniques have been implemented to represent the viewpoint in CVEs.

In navigation activities, where users can independently move in the 3D shared workspace, the remote viewpoint is necessary to determine what a co-participant is referring to when she is out of view, distant or facing away. Dyck et al. [2] propose a number of embodiment enhancements, like the explicit representation of field of view, to support awareness of collaborators in their 3D collaborative workspace called Groupspace. In particular, the view cone approximates the viewable area of other users making it easier to see what is in their fields of view. A similar implementation is found in Hindmarsh et al. [6]. In their study of object-focused CVEs, also extend the embodiment's view by representing it as a semitransparent frustum, in order to provide action awareness. Park et al. [17] employ avatars with long pointing rays emanating from their hands to point at 3D model's features in a collaborative CAVE-based visualization tool for exploring multivariate oceanographic data sets. Schafer et al. [7] investigate egocentric/exocentric view combinations in a 3D collaborative virtual environment which represents the spatial problem the collaborators are working to resolve. The egocentric actor, who restricts the user to a first-person view of the space, is represented by a floating head avatar which shows her position and orientation. The exocentric view is restricted to an external view of the space.

On the other hand, the main issue for the collaborative visualisation of data is to provide collaborators with the remote user's focus of attention since each user can visualize data from different viewpoints. In CSpray [3], a collaborative 3D visualization application, the viewpoint concept is implemented by two techniques: eye cones and shared views. An eye cone is a simple embodiment in the form of a white eyeball placed at the camera position of a distant user and oriented towards the view direction of that camera. It represents the remote user's focus of attention. Shared views enable to share the viewpoint of any participant, by clicking over an eyeball, providing an "over the shoulder" viewpoint. Valin et al. [5] also exploit shared views to request another user's view or to send their view to the other users. Moreover, they use a 3D telepointer, positioned at the location of the user it represents, to point to remote user's focus of attention. Sonnenwald et al. [4] use multiple pointers – each showing the focus of attention and interaction state for one collaborator – to support mutual awareness when working in shared mode with their nanoManipulator Collaboratory System. The system also allows users to work independently in private mode. Finally, alternative views like radar views are common in 3D games, but do not show perspectives. 3D versions of the radar view have been developed, an example is the Grand Tour [2], to overcome problems in the 2D radar representation arising when users can move vertically and horizontally in the virtual space.

Our research differs from previous work for two main reasons: the collaborative activity we want to support is a synchronous and real-time manipulation of different parts of the same shared object and/or of multiple objects; the workspace is a non-immersive 3D virtual environment in which direct manipulation is applied in order to interact with the 3D objects in the environment. A detailed description is given in the following paragraph. In particular, the common objects can be independently positioned and oriented. Consequently, the viewpoint metaphors can not concern the 3D workspace as whole, since it is typical to each user, but they have to refer to every shared object.

## 3 Setting the Scene

There are bounds on the collaborative activities that we are trying to support in this research. Our boundaries involve the kinds of groups we are trying to support, the workspace environment where collaboration takes place, and the kinds of tasks that groups will undertake.

*Small groups and mixed-focus collaboration.* Small groups of between two and five people that work together but from different places. These groups often engage in mixed-focus collaboration, where people shift frequently between individual and shared activities during a work session.

*Workspace environment.* Many real-time groupware systems provide a bounded space where people can see and manipulate artifacts related to their activities. We concentrate on user-activity oriented desktop implemented as a closed space in which distant users cooperate to carry out a common single activity, by working on multiple shared objects. The shared objects are always kept visible and they can be privately placed and manipulated. Furthermore, each participant can arrange her own workspace to her liking, so that the workspace organization and the common objects arrangement are specific to each user. In these spaces, the focus of the activity is on the manipulable objects through which the task is carried out.

*Tasks.* Performance of physical manipulation on the existing shared objects.

## 4 The Remote User's Viewpoint Metaphor

This metaphor provides a global sense of where the other person's viewpoint is relative to a particular shared object, in order to have a roughly idea of what the others are looking at.

Specifically, we aim to reproduce the real situation in which a person working in a group knows other collaborators' perspective on the common object because she can see them. Let us consider this explanatory example. During a painting course, a group of students is asked to draw a statue placed in the centre of the room. Each student, owing to her physical position in the room, looks at it differently from the others and so she sees and draws different "aspects" of it. In particular, let us suppose that student A and student B are looking respectively at the front and back side of the statue. Even if the student B can not see the front side of the statue, because she is in the opposite position, she can have an idea of how student A perceives of it.

To this aim, our proposal is a wire sphere with a number of semicircles, one for each distant collaborator. The idea is that the sphere can be thought as the local user's virtual space surrounding the common object, and the semicircle as the representation of the remote user's viewpoint according to the local and remote object orientations. So this metaphor provides an egocentric representation of the remote perspectives since viewpoints are represented according to the local user's orientation of the common object.

The following figure (Fig. 1) shows the implementation of the remote user's viewpoint metaphor. The red semicircle placed on the left side of the wire sphere reveals the remote red user's viewpoint dependently on the local object orientation. So, the

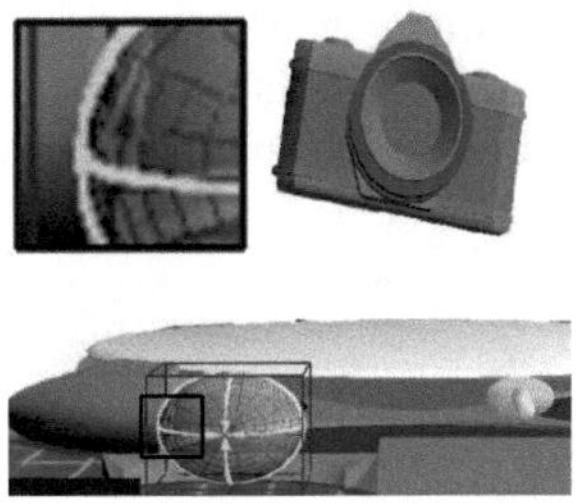

**Fig. 1.** The remote user's viewpoint metaphor

local green user can infer that the red user is looking at the left side of the camera (the camera on the table is the shared object).

We chose the semicircle shape to represent the remote user's viewpoint to correctly visualize the gaze orientation (the semicircle is a smiling mouth). The semicircle on the wire sphere does not reveal the physical distance between the object and the user, unlike the traditional radar map. Moreover, we use a wire sphere to enable to see the semicircle placed on its hidden surface. We implemented this metaphor like a 3D map, that is separately from the manipulated object, for two main reasons: to avoid surcharging the space around the object, and to keep the remote viewpoint always visible.

## 5 The Local Viewpoint Metaphor

The local viewpoint metaphor provides an "over the shoulder" [8] view on the shared object. The idea is to allow a user to instantaneously synchronize her viewpoint with that of a remote partner, seeing exactly what the other partner is looking at. In the painting course example, this metaphor corresponds to the teacher which takes one student's place in order to verify her painting. In fact, it is necessary for the teacher to share the student's viewpoint on the statue to understand if the drawing is correct.

The following figures show the implementation of this metaphor in our 3D collaborative workspace. Two users (the green and the blue) are collaborating in order to learn to use a camera (the object placed on the table), but every participant has a different viewpoint on the shared object (Fig. 2). At a certain point, the green user switches to the blue user's viewpoint (Fig. 3). So, the two users are now looking at the camera from the same viewpoint (the blue user's viewpoint).

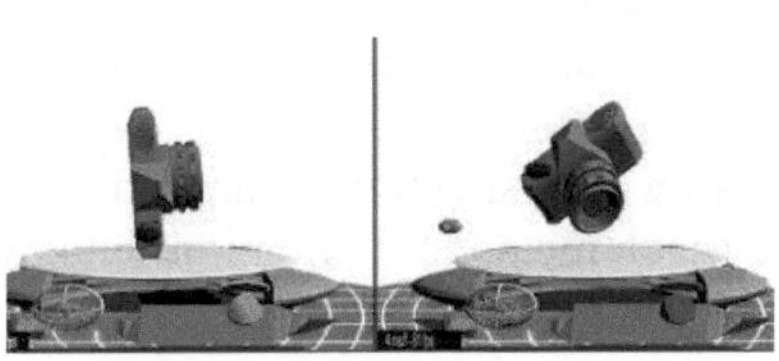

**Fig. 2.** The blue and green users' desktops, respectively on the left and the right

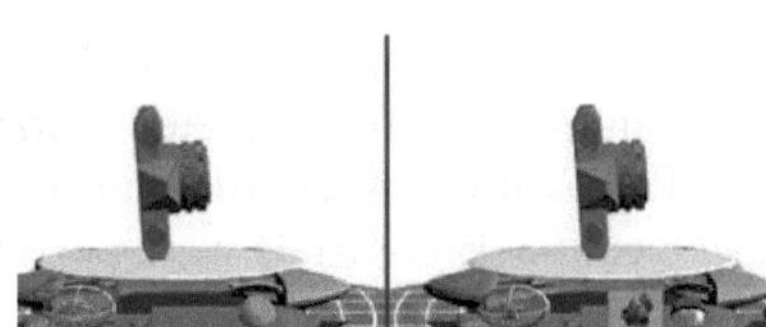

**Fig. 3.** The green user (on the right) switches to the blue user's viewpoint

If the green user wants to continue working privately, she selects the camera in miniature displayed beside the eye icon. This action causes the camera to be positioned according to her last orientation before sharing the other user's viewpoint (Fig. 4).

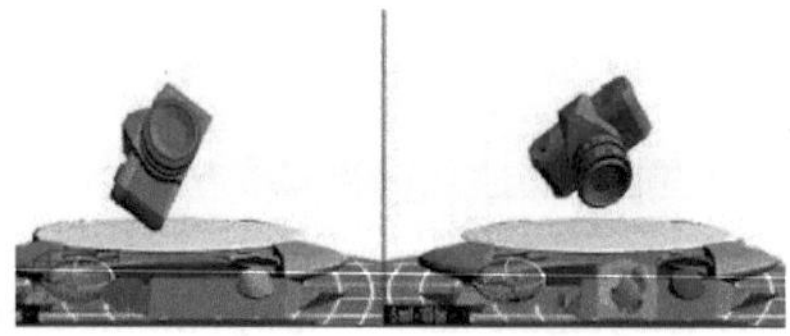

**Fig. 4.** Both users work privately, so the object orientation is local

# 6 Preliminary Usability Study

To test the understandability of our viewpoint metaphors we performed two experimentations, one for each metaphor. Our research hypothesis is that the "local viewpoint" is more intuitive and useful than the "global viewpoint" for a collaborative manipulation activity within our bounds.

*Procedure*
The experimental task, carried out in both the experiments, was a collaborative manipulation activity consisting in taking eight pictures, using a virtual Pentax camera, of a virtual person who was skiing. Participants were asked to set the virtual camera and to push on the shutter release button to take the photos. They manipulated the speed deal, the zoom ring and the aperture ring in order to choose the optimal settings to take good photos. The captured images could be viewed. Participants were asked questions such as: "in your opinion, how do I look at the camera?", "what is my camera orientation? (Could you rotate your camera according to my camera orientation?)", "my camera lens is in front of me, and the yours?". Each pair completed eight tasks corresponding to eight pictures taken according to different camera settings. They were seated back to back, so as not to be able to see each other's screen, and participants were asked to talk freely about the task.

Each trial took about an hour and consisted of a brief presentation to provide background information on the experiment, about 5 minutes for participants to get used to the system (individual practice), approximately half an hour to perform the given tasks, and about ten minutes for the participant to reply to a questionnaire about her experience of using the system. Finally, an informal debriefing discussion (approximately 15 minutes) was conducted before the participant left.

A VCR was used to record each participant's on-screen activities and audio from their perspective. Eight trials were performed for each metaphor validation.

*Subjects*
People participated in the experiments were divided into two homogeneous groups, each of them composed of 8 persons, 4 females and 4 males. Only one person was a computer scientist but the most had experienced a computer. Three persons knew 3D

virtual spaces, and five subjects played video games. None of them had a background in CVE technology. The average age of the participants was 32, with the youngest person being 24 years old and the oldest being 40 years old.

*Workspace settings*
The 3D workspace used for the experiments consisted of:

- a pointer, associated with the local user, to interact in the environment. So, the user selected an object in the scene and, once selected, she could manipulate it exploiting direct object manipulation [11];
- a telepointer (that is the local representation of the pointer associated with a distant user) to represent the remote user's focus of attention;
- colour changes of the public object subparts to show the remote user's action point ([9], [10], [11]);
- a clone representing the distant user in order to reinforce the co-presence during the collaborative activity;
- the virtual camera, that is the shared object, placed on the table;

The following figures (Fig. 5 and 6) show the 3D workspaces used to test out the remote user's viewpoint and the local viewpoint metaphors respectively.

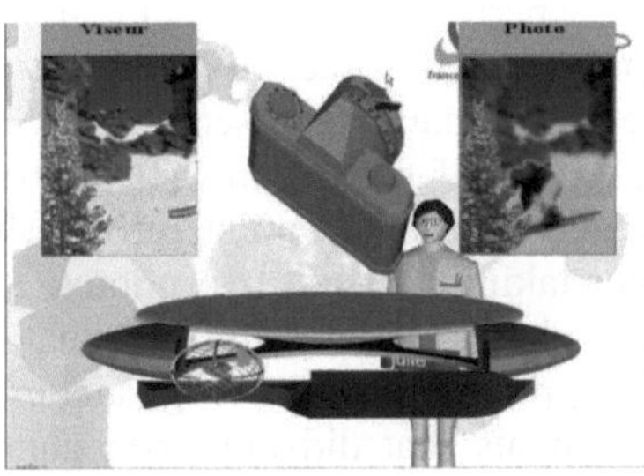

**Fig. 5.** 3D workspace used to study the "remote user's viewpoint" metaphor

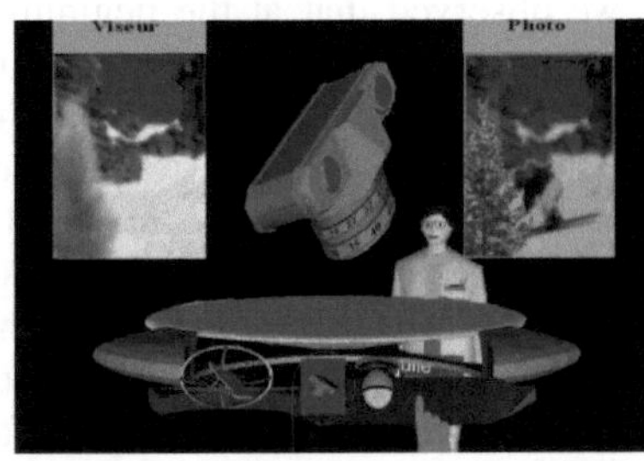

**Fig. 6.** 3D workspace used to study the "local viewpoint" metaphor

The experiments were conducted in the Virtual Reality Room of the GRAPHIX Laboratory, University of Lille 1, France. A Barco monitor displayed the 3D workspace used for the experiments. Each participant was provided with polarized glasses, a mouse and a space-mouse for the interactions.

*Discussion*
Our observations of the videos and debriefing discussions led us to the following interesting findings:

- during a manipulation activity, subjects are completely concentrated on the manipulated object so that they ignore the surrounding environment;
- the 3D virtual environment we proposed is perceived in two different ways: some users think that all participants share the same view on the common object, others think that the remote user looks at the object through the clone's eyes. Consequently, questions concerning the remote user's camera orientation, such as "how

do I look at the camera?", got the participants lost so that they thought they were wrongly accomplishing their task. This implies that participants did not understand that object orientation is local to each user.

These findings explain away the preliminary results we obtained:

- the local user's viewpoint metaphor is well-understood and efficiently used;
- subjects understand that the remote user's viewpoint metaphor represents the distant user's view on the shared object even if they find pretty difficult to infer how the distant partner is actually looking at it.

The eye metaphor has been correctly perceived by the most of the participants. The subjects immediately realised that the eye could be used to look at the object like the other user did. In fact, the answer to the question "what does it happen when clicking on the eye?" was often "I look at the camera from your viewpoint". Moreover, the subjects intuitively understood as well that, when sharing a distant user's viewpoint, their local orientation of the camera was piloted by the remote user. In other words, sharing the viewpoint causes the camera orientation to become public. Similarly, the miniature of the camera beside the eye was easily perceived as being "the local camera orientation before sharing the remote user's viewpoint".

Examining answers about the semicircle (for example, "what is the semicircle used for?"), we observed that at the beginning of the experimentation the semicircle had not been understood by the most of participants, even if somebody unconsciously replied "would the semicircle be your (the other participant) representation?". After accomplishing the whole task (eight photos), the most of participants (five persons) understood that the semicircle revealed the remote user's viewpoint on the shared camera. Specifically, two persons realised it after taking the first two photos, a participant at the fourth photo, and two at the seventh photo. One possibility is that these users were familiar with video games and so they applied their knowledge and experience to understand this metaphor. In fact, participants that did not understand the semicircle metaphor after completing the whole activity were not used to play video games and had never experienced 3D virtual spaces. Nevertheless, only one person among the last three replied that the semicircle is very hard to understand.

On the contrary, the percentage of correct camera orientations (31.25%) describes a different conclusion. Even if the semicircle revealed the remote viewpoint, it certainly required some real cognitive processing to understand what the other user was actually looking at. This may be because this metaphor is "statically" used by the subjects. In fact, we observed that the participants exploited this metaphor only when they were asked questions about the camera orientation. This is most likely due to the fact that the manipulated object (the virtual camera) was familiar and the activity to accomplish were relatively straightforward so that participants did not really need to know other viewpoint on the object to correctly attain their objective. These remarks are supported by the comments "the remote user's viewpoint awareness was not necessary for this specific manipulation task" and "the task was relatively straightforward to accomplish". Another possible explanation is that the remote user's viewpoint metaphor is separated from the manipulated object from the graphical point of view (in fact, the sphere is placed in the left bottom corner of the scene). Since the user is concentrated on the object during the collaborative manipulation she does not exploit this information because "it is not part of her focus".

In our opinion, people involved in a collaborative object manipulation need to know the collaborators' viewpoint only in the case of misunderstandings that hinder the activity. Also it could be most likely that the information required concerns "see exactly what the collaborator is looking at", rather than having a global idea. Sharing views, in this case, is more effective and efficient and allows users to quickly get the information needed to continue collaboration, without interrupting their main activity (the manipulation).

## 7 Conclusions and Future Work

This research investigated what kind of viewpoint awareness is more appropriate in a 3D collaborative desktop in which a group of persons, from different places, work together while they manipulate multiple shared objects in order to accomplish a common single activity. To this aim, each participant can position and orient the common objects to her liking to facilitate her manipulation task. So, different viewpoints on the shared objects can be employed.

We proposed two viewpoint metaphors: the remote user's viewpoint metaphor and the local viewpoint metaphor. The former aims to provide every user with the other person's viewpoint relative to the public object; the latter provides an "over the shoulder" viewpoint. We think that during a collaborative activity focused on the physical manipulation of existing objects, users need to share views rather than have a rough idea of what the distant partners are looking at. In fact, an "over the shoulder" viewpoint provides quickly the information necessary to solve a misunderstanding, without interrupting one person's private manipulation. Moreover, sharing views allow users to be involved in shared manipulation tasks, achieving therefore the mixed-focus collaboration [10], [12], [13], [7].

The preliminary results corroborate our hypothesis. The eye metaphor is more intuitive and pertinent to convey the awareness of viewpoint for collaborative manipulation activities within our bounds (paragraph "Setting the scene").

But having a global sense of where the other persons' viewpoints are relative to a shared object provides the implicit awareness of viewpoint that is typical of face-to-face collaborations. Is it therefore important to provide this kind of viewpoint awareness? To answer this question it should be necessary to experiment with a more difficult activity involving the manipulation of more complex objects.

Anyway, our preliminary study provides us with an important insight concerning how to design this kind of viewpoint awareness. So the global viewpoint awareness has to be strictly "linked" to the manipulable objects. This means that global viewpoint cues have to be graphically represented in the space which surrounds closely the focused object to be efficiently exploited. In fact, during a manipulation activity, persons are completely concentrated on the object to accomplish precisely their task. So everything outside this space is not considered.

A possible proposal is to exploit the telepointer to convey awareness of viewpoint. In fact, all subjects thought that the telepointer is very intuitive and helpful for helping collaboration. To this aim, it is necessary to add orientation to the telepointer to represent gaze direction. Moreover, a solution should be found to keep the "oriented" telepointer always visible.

Finally, we are investigating "rich telepointers" [14] to exploit telepointers in order to provide awareness of presence to avoid using clones.

## References


1. Gutwin, C., Greenberg, S.: The effects of workspace awareness support on the usability of real-time distributed groupware. ACM Transactions Computer-Human Interactions 6, 243–281 (1999)
2. Dyck, J., Gutwin, C.: Awareness. In: Collaborative 3D Workspaces. ACM Graphics Interface (2002)
3. Pang, A., Wittenbrink, C.: Collaborative 3D Visualisation with Cspray. IEEE Computer Graphics and Applications 17(2), 32–41 (1997)
4. Sonnenwald, D.H., Whitton, M.C., Maglaughlin, K.L.: Evaluating a Scientific Collaboratory: Results of a Controlled Experiment. ACM Transactions on Computer-Human Interaction 10(2), 150–176 (2003)
5. Valin, S., Francu, A., Trefftz, H., Marsic, I.: Sharing Viewpoints in Collaborative Virtual Environments. In: HICSS-34 Annual Hawaii International Conference on System Sciences (2001)
6. Hindmarsh, J., Fraser, M., Heath, C., Benford, S., Greenhalgh, C.: Object-Focused Interaction in Collaborative Virtual Environments. ACM Transaction on Computer-Human Interaction 7, 477–509 (2000)
7. Schafer, W.A., Bowman, D.A.: Evaluating the effects of frame reference on spatial collaboration using desktop collaborative virtual environments. Virtual Reality, vol. 7 (2004)
8. Stefik, M., Bobrow, D.G., Lanning, S., Tatar, D.: WYSIWIS revised: Early experiences with multi-user interfaces. ACM Transactions on Information Systems 5, 147–167 (1987)
9. Dumas, C., Degrande, S., Saugis, G., Chaillou, C., Plénacoste, P., Viaud, M.L.: Spin: a 3-D Interface for Cooperative Work. Virtual Reality Society Journal, Springer-Verlag, Heidelberg (May 1999)
10. Harrison, B.L. Ishii, H. Vincent, K.J.: Buxton: Transparent Layered User Interfaces: An Evaluation of a Display Design to Enhance Focused and Divided Attention. In: CHI'95 pp. 317–324 (1995)
11. Goebbels, G., Göbel, M.: On Collaboration in Distributed Virtual Environments. The Journal of Three Dimensional Images 14(4), 42–47 (2000)
12. Gutwin, C., Greenberg, S.: Design for individuals, design for groups: tradeoffs between power and workspace awareness. Computer Supported Cooperative Work, pp. 207–216 (1998)
13. Dourish, P., Bellotti, V.: Awareness and coordination in shared workspace. ACM Computer Supported Cooperative Work, 107–114 (1992)
14. Stach, T., Gutwin, C., Pinelle, D., Irani, P.: Rich Embodiments for Improving Awareness in Distributed Groupware. Technical Report HCI-TT-06-01 (2006)
15. Benford, S., Greenhalgh, C., Rodden, T., Pycock, J.: Collaborative Virtual Environments. Communication of ACM 44(7), 79–85 (2001)
16. Yang, H.: Multiple perspectives for collaborative navigation. In: CVE. Extended abstracts for the ACM Conference on Human Factors in Computer Systems, Springer, New York (2002)
17. Park, K. S., Kapoor, A., Leigh, J.: Lessons Learned from Employing Multiple Perspectives In: a Collaborative Virtual Environment for Visualizing Scientific Data. CVE CA USA (2000)

# Parallel Search Algorithm for Geometric Constraints Solving

Hua Yuan[1,2], Wenhui Li[1], Kong Zhao[3], and Rongqin Yi[1]

[1] Key Laboratory of Symbol Computation and Knowledge Engineering of the Ministry of Education, College of computer science and technology, Jilin University Changchun 130012, China
[2] School of Computer Science & Engineering, Changchun University of Technology Changchun 130012, China
[3] Suzhou Top Institute of Information Technology, Suzhuo 215311, China
yhyaya@126.com

**Abstract.** We propose a hybrid algorithm – (Parallel Search Algorithm) between PSO and simplex methods to approximate optimal solution for the Geometric Constraint problems. Locally, simplex is extended to reduce the number of infeasible solutions while solution quality is improved with an operation order search. Globally, PSO is employed to gain parallelization while solution diversity is maintained. Performance results on Geometric Constraint problems show that Parallel Search Algorithm outperforms existing techniques.

**Keywords:** geometric constraint solving, particle swarm optimization, simplex method, Parallel Search.

## 1 Introduction

Geometric Constraints Solving (GCS) are at the heart of computer aided engineering applications, and also arise in many geometric modeling contexts such as virtual reality, robotics, molecular modeling, teaching geometry, and so on. There are several approaches to solving the geometric constraint problem: the symbolic approach [1], the propagation approach [2], the graph analysis approach [3] and the numerical approach [4]. In solver based on the purely numerical approach, the geometric constraints between the geometric objects are expressed in the form of polynomial equations. The constraint problem is translated directly into a set of nonlinear equation and is solving using any of the available methods for solving nonlinear equation. The method most widely used is the well-know Newton-Raphson, [5] iteration. So the constraint problem can be transformed to an optimization problem.

The optimization methods are usually subdivided into local and global techniques. The former seek the local minimum of an objective function, without ensuring that the solution individuated is also a global minimum. The local techniques need an initial approximation; form which the algorithm, through an iterative procedure, finds the optimal solution evaluating a certain number of times the objective function. The global techniques do not require initial approximations, since they explore all the space of variables seeking the minimum of the objective function. But in these areas the algorithm

R. Shumaker (Ed.): Virtual Reality, HCII 2007, LNCS 4563, pp. 157 – 164, 2007.

may get into the local best solution because of its poor local searching capability. The Ref. [6] shows that using local optimization alone will produce inferior solutions in the target neighborhood. A common solution to this is the hybridization of a local search technique with a global search which is capable of spanning the search across different neighborhoods. As a try, a new hybrid optimization algorithm is introduced that integrates the global techniques- particle swarm optimization and the local techniques- simplex method in this paper.

Particle Swarm Optimization (PSO) is a population based optimization technique inspired by models of swarm and flock behavior [7]. It differs from other approaches by the inclusion of a solution velocity. Particles are connected both temporally and spatially to other particles in the population by two accelerations: each particle is attracted to its previous best position, and to the global best position attained by the swarm, where 'best' is quantified by the value of a state function at that position [8]. All particles follow the same behavior, quickly converging to a good local optimum of the problem. However, if the solution for the problem does not lie on a path between original particle positions and such a local optimum, then this convergence behavior prevents effective search for the global optimum. It may be argued that many of the particles are wasting computational effort in seeking to move in the same direction (towards the local optimum already discovered), whereas better results may be obtained if various particles explore other possible search directions.

As such, we apply the Particle Swarm Optimization Algorithm (by) as it has been shown [9] to produce good results due to its ability to explore the search space of candidate solutions in parallel. However using PSO alone typically gives slow convergence to the best possible solution as it lacks local information to determine the most promising search direction. Hence, in this paper, we propose a PSO-guided global search technique to speed up the rate of convergence while having the ability to escape from the local optimum through an extended Simplex search [10]. The Simplex search approximately finds a locally optimal solution to a problem with N variables when the objective function varies smoothly, and generates a new position by extrapolating behaviour of the objective function measured at each test point arranged as a simplex, then chooses to replace one of these test points with the new test point and so the algorithm progresses.

In the new algorithm, optimization is not solely done with PSOs due to their slow convergence in the final stages of the minimization. The purpose of the PSO is to perform an exploration for an approximative surface in the close vicinity of the real target. Thereafter a local search by the greedy algorithm will be more efficient (than the PSO) for the surface extraction. This new approach has been successfully applied to GCS and our experiments show the efficiency and robustness of our algorithm.

## 2 The Uses of Parallel Search in Solving Geometric Constraint

### 2.1 The PSO Algorithm

The Particle Swarm Optimization algorithm is optimization algorithm base on population, where the population is now called a swarm and each individual is called a particle [11], explores a multidimensional real number search space, each particle's position define a potential solution to problem. In PSO algorithms, a particle decides where to move next, considering its own experience, which is the memory of its best past position, and the experience of its most successful neighbour. So, there is a need to maintain and update the particle's previous best position ($p_{Best}$) and the best position in the neighbourhood ($g_{Best}$). There is also a velocity ($V_{id}$) associated with each dimension, which is an increment to be made, in each iteration, to the dimension associated (equation 1), thus making the particle change its position in the search space.

Assuming that the search space is D-dimensional, N is the size of the population, then with particle i represented $X_i = (x_{i1}, x_{i2}, \ldots, x_{id})$. Each particle $X_i$ also maintains a memory of its previous best position, $P_i = (p_{i1}, p_{i2}, \ldots, p_{id})$[12], the best previously visited position of the *i-th* particle is denoted as $p_{Best}$, at each iteration, the P vector of the particle with the best fitness in the local neighborhood, designated $g_{Best}$. The velocity of the *i-th* particle is represented as $V_i = (v_{i1}, v_{i2}, \ldots, v_{id})$, and its new position will be assigned according to the following two equations:

$$v_{id}^{k} = \omega_i \times v_{id}^{k-1} + c_1 \times rand() \times (pBest_i - x_{id}^{k-1}) + c_2 \times Rand() \times (gBest - x_{id}^{k-1}) \quad (1)$$

$$x_{id}^{k} = x_{id}^{k-1} + v_{id}^{k} \quad (2)$$

$x_{id}^{k}$ is the location vector, rand(), Rand() are two random numbers within the range [0, 1], $\omega$ is the inertia weight; $c_1$, $c_2$ is as the cognitive and social learning rate [13], trade- off the move direction of the global best particle had local best particle, while a small one, the particle may be far away from the goal area, while a big one, may be lead to sharp move to the solution space, even move over, suitable $c_1$, $c_2$ can avoid getting in local best solution. Usually, gives: $c_1 = c_2 = 2$ [14], algorithm can be written as follow:

step1. For each particle Initialise particle
step2. For each particle calculate the fitness value
    If the fitness value is better than the best fitness
    value ($p_{Best}$) in history
    Set current value as the new $p_{Best}$
step3. Choose the particle with the best fitness value of all the particles as the $g_{Best}$
    For each particle
    Calculate particle velocity according Eq. 1
    Update particle position according Eq. 2
while maximum iterations or minimum error criteria are not attained.

## 2.2 Simplex Optimization Algorithm

The Simplex Method is a zero-order deterministic method. It is suitable for the optimization of multi-dimensional object functions (OF). It is robust, but the convergence is quite slow in comparison with other methods of the same kind. A simplex is the simplest geometrical entity - with a finite volume - built by means of n+1 points, in the n-dimensional space. According to the method, reflections, contractions, expansions and reductions are performed, aiming to replace the vertex where the function has the higher value (in minimisation problems) with a more favourable one [15].

The simplest step is to replace the worst point with a point reflectedt through the remaining N points considered as a plane. If this point is better than the best current point, then we can try stretching exponentially out along this line. On the other hand, if this new point isn't much better than the previous value then we are stepping across a valley, so we shrink the simplex towards the best point.

Through a sequence of elementary geometric transformations, the initial simplex moves, expands, or contracts towards the minimum. At each step, the worst vertex with highest cost $x_{\max} = \arg\max_{x \in S} f(x)$ is replaced by one with smaller function value. At the beginning of each iteration, the worst vertex $x_{max}$ is selected and the centroid $x = \frac{1}{n}(\sum_{i=0}^{n} x_i - x_{\max})$ is computed. Then depending on $f(x_r)$, we perform the following operations to obtain the new vertex $x_{new}$ which replaces $x_{max}$ [16].

- *reflections* $x_r=(1+\alpha)x_{max}-\alpha x_n$
- *expansions* $x_e=(1-\gamma)\, x_{max} +\gamma x_n$
- *contractions* $x_c=(1-\beta)\, x_{max}+\beta\, x_n$

### 2.3 The Uses of Parallel Search in Solving Geometric Constraint

Generally, a geometric constraint problem can be first translated into a system of equations:

$$\begin{cases} f_1(x_0, x_1, x_2, \ldots, x_n) = 0 \\ \quad\cdots \\ f_m(x_0, x_1, x_2, \ldots, x_n) = 0 \end{cases} \tag{3}$$

Then the problem is how to solve this system of equations $F(X) = 0$; where $F= (f_1; f_2;\ldots; f_m)^T : R^n \rightarrow R^m$ is the equation vector and $X=(x_1; x_2;\ldots; x_n)^T$ is the vector of unknown variables. This system of equations can be solved iteratively by the Newton–Raphson method [17]. The iteration formula is $X_{k+1}= X_k - J(X_k)^{-1}F(X_k)$, where $J(X_k)$is the Jacobi matrix of $F(X)$at point $X_k$.

Unlike the other numerical methods, the optimization approach solves the system of equations $F(X)$ by converting it into finding $X$ at which the sum is minimal.

$$F(X) = \sum_{1} | f_i | \tag{4}$$

It is obvious that $F(X) = 0$ has a real solution $X^*$ if and only if *min* $F(X)$ is 0. The problem of solving a system of equations is thus converted into the problem of finding the minimum of a real multi-variate function. The problem now can be solved by various well-developed numerical optimization methods [18, 19, 20].

Since PSO methods are often trapped in local optima, we incorporated particle filtering framework with the simplex search. We choose the pipelining hybrid approach for our hybrid model [21], applies local and global search sequentially, where one creates data for the other, as the optimal result produced by Simplex will depend highly on the data, PSO will serve as a global search for the data, while the Simplex optimizes the given data efficiently. In this model, Simplex is applied to improve the local convergence of individuals in the population, followed by $p_{best}$ recombination to remove the local optima.

The process of PS in the geometric constraint solving is described as follow:

step1. Initialize the colony;
step2. Carry out iteration by the PSO, search the best individual $p_{best}$. If after some generations the best individual has not appeared, then turn to step 3.
step3. If after some steps search by simplex algorithm there is no better points than $g_{best}$, then stop; otherwise assuming to find a point p whose OF's is better than $p_{best}$, then produce a colony including p, return step 2.

step3 as follow:

Let $q_0$ be a starting point in simplex algorithm parameter space and let $\lambda_i$; i =1, . . . , n be a set of scales. Let $e_i$; i=1, . . . , n be n orthogonal unit vectors in n-dimensional parameter space, let $p_0$; . . . ; $p_n$ be (n+1) ordered points in n-dimensional parameter space such that their corresponding function values satisfy $f_0 \le f_1 \le, \ldots, \le f_n$, let $pbest = \sum_{i=0}^{n-1} p_i / n$ be the centroid of the n best (smallest) points, let $[p_i p_j]$ be the n-dimensional Euclidean distance from $p_i$ to $p_j$, let $\alpha$, $\beta$, $\gamma$ and $\sigma$, be the *reflection*, *contraction*, *expansion*, and *shrinkage* coefficient, respectively, and let T be the threshold for the stopping criterion. We use the standard choice for the coefficients: $\alpha$=1, $\beta$=0.5, $\gamma$=2, $\sigma$=0.5, T=$10^{-6}$.

3.1 given $q_0$ and $\lambda_i$, form the initial simplex as $q_i=q_0+\lambda_i e_i$, $i$=1,..., n,
3.2 relabel the n+1 vertices as $p_0,\ldots, p_n$ with $f(p_0) \le f(p_1) \le \ldots \le f(p_n)$,
3.3 get a *reflection* point $p_r$ of $p_n$ by $p_r=(1+\alpha)p_{best}-\alpha p_n$ where $\alpha=[p_r p_{best}]/[p_n p_{best}]$
3.4.1 if $f(p_r) \le f(p_0)$, replace $p_n$ by $p_r$ and $f(p_n)$ by $f(p_r)$, get an *expansion* point $p_e$ of $p_n$ by $p_e=(1-\gamma)p_{best}+\gamma p_n$ where $\gamma=[p_e p_{best}]/[p_n p_{best}]>1$
If $f(p_e)<f(p_n)$, replace $p_n$ by $p_e$ and $f(p_n)$ by $f(p_e)$. Go to step 3.5
3.4.2 else if $f(p_r) \ge f(p_{n-1})$, if $f(p_r) < f(p_n)$ replace $p_n$ by $p_r$ and $f(p_n)$ by $f(p_r)$, get a *contraction* point $p_c$ of $p_n$ by $p_c=(1-\beta)\, p_{best}+\beta\, p_n$, $\beta=[p_c p_{best}]/[p_n p_{best}]<1$
If $f(p_c) \ge f(p_n)$, *shrink* the simplex around the best vertex $p_0$ by $p_i=(p_i+p_0)\ \sigma$, $I \ne 0$, else replace $p_n$ by $p_c$ and $f(p_n)$ by $f(p_c)$, go to step 3.5
3.4.3 else replace $p_n$ by $p_r$ and $f(p_n)$ by $f(p_r)$
3.5 if $\sqrt{(\sum_{i=0}^{n} f(p_i) - f(p_{best})^2 / n)} < T$ , stop else go to step 3.2

Simplex search optimization algorithms are local optimization algorithms. Thus, for each (different) starting point, the optimization algorithm could converge to a different optimal solution. We constrain the parameter values to lie within a reasonable range and randomly choose six starting locations within this range.

## 3 Application Instance

The Fig. 1(b) is an auto-produce graph after some sizes of the Fig. 1(a) are modified by geometric constraints solver. From the above figures we can find out that once a user defines a series of relations, the system will satisfy the constraints by selecting proper state after the parameters are modified.

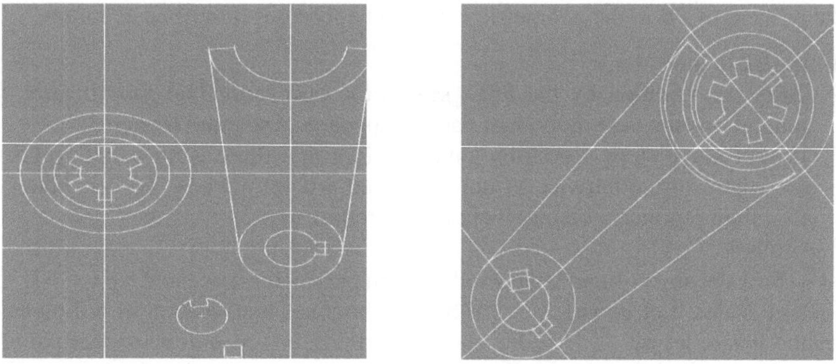

(a) (b)

**Fig. 1.** (a) Design Instance (b) Solving Result

### 3.1 CPU Time Comparison

For purpose of comparison a set of algorithm were tested including PS, PSO, Simplex method solves this case. The population-based algorithms used a population of 64 members. To allow direct comparison, in a given test case the same set of start points were used for each algorithm. Table 1 shows the same number of vars for each algorithm on test case, and the time required obtaining that result. The time results shown for PS, PSO and SM are the generation counts at which the minimum result was obtained, not the count for termination, which was fixed. For test case, the fastest time obtained by any algorithm, are highlighted.

**Table 1.** CPU time comparison of SP, PSO and SM

| Algorithm | 1 | | 2 | | 3 | |
|---|---|---|---|---|---|---|
| | Num of vars | Temporal/D | Num of vars | Temporal/D | Num of vars | Temporal/D |
| PS | 10 | 10 | 8 | 12 | 5 | 5 |
| PSO | 10 | 14 | 8 | 19 | 5 | 16 |
| SM | 10 | 37 | 8 | 39 | 5 | 26 |

It may be noted form Table 1 that time effectively found the global minimum in this case; new algorithm achieved this result faster than other algorithm. It achieved results as good as, or better, than all over algorithms, and its rate of convergence was highly competitive.

### 3.2 Success Rate Comparison

This experiment compares the efficiency of the PS algorithm to locate the known global optimum for GCS problem. We use PSO and SM as our basis for comparison, population initialization is done for 80 individuals. Our results are obtained using PS, PSO and SM. As seen in Table 2, PS has obtained the known global optima, a new global optima undiscovered by SM. Two other points are worth noting. Firstly, the low number of average generations required for PS can be explained by the fact that the PSO is to perform an exploration for an approximative surface. In comparison with PS, PSO produces inferior results. Hence, SM is more efficient (than the PSO) for the surface extraction. Secondly, a higher success rate is observed for PS. When PSO fails to produce an optimal solution, PS is able to complement this by location the optimum's basin through a global swarm search. Unlike PSO, it is less likely to be trapped in local optima, thus showing the efficiency of our simplex-based hybrid structure.

**Table 2.** Result of comparison efficiency in locating global optima

| Algorithm | $M_{best}$ | $M_{arg}$ | $R_s$ | $G_{avg}$ |
|---|---|---|---|---|
| PS | 14 | 14 | 100 | 0.10 |
| PSO | 11 | 11.3 | 70 | 6.71 |
| SM | 12 | 13.8 | 0 | 0.00 |

$M_{best}$ : best makespan obtained $M_{arg}$ : average makespan obtained
$R_s$ : success of obtaining optimum(%) $G_{avg}$ : average generation to reach optimum

The results show that the proposed algorithm is significantly higher than that obtained using the PSO on the convergence speed and ability of searching for approximate global optimal solution for solving geometric constraint problem.

## 4 Conclusions

The aim of the reaserch activity was the application of local and global optimisation techniques both of the deterministic and the stochastic type to solve geometric constraint problem. In this paper, we presented a simple new Evolutionary Programming algorithm called Parallel Search for globalized PSO-based evolution with localized Simplex search. It combines by improvement of the latter with simplex search and removal of local optima through the parallelism of PSO. While PSO is insufficient alone to locate the global optima, a hybrid of the above methods demonstrates synergism.

In this paper we have described a simple new Evolutionary Programming algorithm that utilizes concepts of PS. Tested on GCS problem, against PSO and SM, it has been demonstrated to exhibit superior performance. Examination of the results from the numerical experiments demonstrates population-based method PS and PSO, are competitive against simplex method. Within the population-based methods, PS outperformed the PSO in finding the global minimum on geometric constraint problems.

**Acknowledgements.** This research has been supported by National Nature Science Foundation of China. (Authorizing number: 60573182).

## References

1. Buchanan, S.A., de Pennington, A.: Constraint definition system: a computer algebra based approach to solving geometric problems. Computer Aided Design 25(12), 740–750 (1993)
2. Lee, J.Y., Kim, K.: Geometric reasoning for knowledge-based parametric design using graph representation. Computer Aided Design 28(10), 831–841 (1996)
3. Fudos, I., Hoffmann, C.M.: A graph-constructive approach to solving systems of geometric constraints. ACM Transactions on Graphics 16(2), 179–216 (1997)
4. Lamure, H., Michelucci, D.: Solving geometric constraints by homotopy. IEEE Transactions on Visualization and Computer Graphics 2(1), 28–34 (1996)
5. Johnson, L.W., Riess, R.D.: Numerical analysis, 2nd edn. Addison-Wesley, Reading (1982)
6. Liu, S., Tang, M., Dong, J.: Two Spatial Constraint Solving Algorithms. Journal of Computer-Aided Design & Computer Graphics 15(8), 1011–1029 (2003)
7. Kennedy J., Eberhart, R.C.: Particle Swarm Optimization. In: Proc of the IEEE International Conference on Neural Networks IV, pp. 1942–1948 (1995)
8. Eberhart, R.C., Shi, Y.: Particle swarm optimization: Developments, applications and resources. Proc Congress on Evolutionary Computation, 81–86 (2001)
9. Xie, X., Zhang, W., Yang, Z.: A dissipative particle swarm optimization. In: Proceedings of the 2002 Congress on Evolutionary Computation, vol. 2, pp. 1456–1461 (2002)
10. Nelder, J., Mead, R.: A Simplex Method for Function Minimization. Computer J. 7, 308–313 (1965)
11. Liu, S.G., Tang, M., Dong, J.: Two Spatial Constraint Solving Algorithms. Journal of Computer-Aided Design & Computer Graphics 15(8), 1011–1029 (2003)
12. Angeline, P.: Evolutionary Optimization versus Particle Swarm Optimization: Philosophy and Performance Difference, In: The 7th Annual Conference on Evolutionary Programming, San Diego, USA (1998)
13. Parsopoulos, K., Vrahatis, M.: Particle Swarm Optimizer in Noisy and Continuously Changing Environments. In: Hamza, M.H. (ed.) Artificial Intelligence and Soft Computing, pp. 289–294. IASTED/ACTA Press (2001)
14. Branke, J.: Memory Enhanced Evolutionary Algorithms for Changing Optimization Problems. In: Proc. of CEC 1999, pp. 1875–1882. IEEE Press, Los Alamitos (1999)
15. Gartner, B.: The Random-Facet Simplex Algorithm on Combinatorial Cubes. In: Random Structures & Algorithms 20(3), 353–381 (2002)
16. Walters, F., Parker, L.R., Morgan, S.L., Deming, S.N.: Sequential Simplex Optimization. CRC Press, Boca Raton, USA (1991)
17. Light, R., Gossard, D.: Modification of geometric models through variational geometry. Geometric Aided Design 14, 208–214 (1982)
18. Elster, K.J. (ed.): Modern mathematical methods of optimization. Akademie, Berlin (1993)
19. More, J.J., Wright, S.: Optimization software guide, SIAM (1993)
20. Nemhauser, G.L., Rinnooy Kan, A.H.G., Todd, M. (eds.): Optimization. Elsevier, Amsterdam (1989)
21. Xia, W., Wu, Z.: An effective hybrid optimization approach for multi-objective flexible job-shop scheduling problems. Computers & Industrial Engineering 48(2), 409–425 (2005)

# Scene Depth Reconstruction on the GPU: A Post Processing Technique for Layered Fog

Tianshu Zhou, Jim X. Chen, and Peter Smith

George Mason University George Mason University Member IEEE Computer Society
tzhou@gmu.edu, jchen@cs.gmu.edu, peter_smith@computer.org

**Abstract.** Realism is a key goal of most VR applications. As graphics computing power increases, new techniques are being developed to simulate important aspects of the human visual system, increasing the sense of 'immersion' of a participant in a virtual environment. One aspect of the human visual system, depth cueing, requires accurate scene depth information in order to simulate. Yet many of the techniques for producing these effects require a trade-off between accuracy and performance, often resulting in specialized implementations that do not consider the need to integrate with other techniques or existing visualization systems. Our objective is to develop a new technique for generating depth based effects in real time as a post processing step performed on the GPU, and to provide a generic solution for integrating multiple depth dependent effects to enhance realism of the synthesized scenes. Using layered fog as an example, our new technique performs per pixel scene depth reconstruction accurately for the evaluation of fog integrals along line-of-sight. Requiring only the depth buffer from the rendering processing as input, our technique makes it easy to integrate into existing applications and uses the full power of the GPU to achieve real time frame rates.

## 1 Introduction

For the past three decades, dramatic advances in computer graphics hardware and research have made it possible for computers and rendering systems to closely approximate the physical behavior of the real world. During this time, the graphics subsystem of the standard personal computer has risen in status from a simple peripheral device capable of nothing more than monochrome text displays, to a major computational component with a dedicated communication pathway to the CPU, capable of rendering hundreds of millions of lit, textured polygons per second. The current generation of graphics hardware, consisting of multiple processing units and containing more transistors than the motherboard CPU, is now capable of enormous computational power with a high level of parallelism. The addition of programmable logic to the graphics pipeline has endowed these devices with almost cinematic quality capabilities.

At the same time, it has been recognized that improved accuracy in physical simulations and light transport modeling has not yielded the same level of improvements in human perception of computer generated images [5]. Recently, increasing awareness of the human visual system has lead to an improved understanding of perception.

R. Shumaker (Ed.): Virtual Reality, HCII 2007, LNCS 4563, pp. 165 – 174, 2007.

This in turn started to influence the way to generate 3D graphics. We need to consider the human visual system in generating visually realistic images in order to improve immersion of the human participants in virtual environments (VE).

The effectiveness of sensory-immersion in virtual environments largely relies on the ability of synthesized scenes to match the user's sensory channel. In virtual environments, including augmented reality, simulators and games, perception enhancement through graphics generation process is a major area. Therefore, generating special effects to improve realism is an active research area.

Although we live in a 3 dimensional world, the scenes captured by human eye are 2 dimensional; similarly, everyday visual perception is based on interacting with a 3 dimensional world, but computer generated scenes are typically showed on a 2 dimensional display. Humans have learned to use additional information (depth cues) about the 3 dimensional world to process the 2 dimensional retinal images to perceive space and distance, through individual experiences. Accurate perception of distance from computer graphics is particularly important in immersive interfaces that aim to give a person the sensation of actually being in a virtual world that in fact only exists as a computer model. Adding depth cues into computer generated scenes helps depth perception in computer graphics match the capabilities of human visual system in understanding their real environment.

Effects such as depth of field and fog rely on accurate per pixel scene depth for quality results, yet existing scan-line techniques devote little effort towards generating accurate scene depth information, resulting in artifacts in the generated scenes. Alternatives, such as using special render targets, impose limitations and make system integration difficult.

In developing new techniques for generate depth based effects using rasterization, we developed a new post-processing based scene depth reconstruction technique that can be implemented entirely on the GPU. This technique decouples scene rendering from effects generation in the post-processing step, and allows easy integration of the technique into existing applications. In this paper, we present this new hardware oriented method and use layered fog as an example to demonstrate how this technique achieves high quality results in real time.

This paper is organized as follows: section 2 describes our new technique to reconstruct scene depth and 3D fragment position; section 3 presents how our new technique is used for generating layered fog, as well as the implementation details and integration of the technique to the existing rendering application; Section 4 shows the results; Section 5 concludes with future work.

## 2 Techniques

### 2.1 Scene Depth Reconstruction

There are currently two main approaches to generating scene depth information for depth based special effects, both of which lay down linear depth information to an alternate render target. The first is to use customized rendering shaders that can output linear scene depth values at the same time as rasterizing the scene in the frame buffer.

The second approach is a separate rendering pass to generate the depth information. The problem with the first approach is that the custom shaders can be difficult to integrate into existing rendering pipelines, while the second approach requires significantly more vertex and fragment processing power. In our new method, we reconstruct scene depth values directly from the depth buffer - a by-product of the normal rendering process that is usually discarded. While this solves many of the problems of other approaches, it presents some new ones. The contents of the depth buffer are non-linear, having been transformed by the modelview and projection matrices. In order to reconstruct the original scene depth information, we must transform these values back to linear values. A naive approach to this is to use an inverted modelview/projection matrix, along with normalized x and y values, to compute the full 3D fragment position relative to the camera. The inverse camera modelview matrix is then used to map this into a real world position. However, this is too computationally expensive, so we developed a more efficient method that allows us to reconstruct the fragment scene depth.

Given a point $p$ in world coordinates, the mapping to canonical viewing volume coordinates $p_0$, is done by the projection matrix $P$.

$$p_0 = P \cdot p \tag{1}$$

Perspective projection is characterized by the camera properties as follows:

$$P = \begin{bmatrix} \frac{2n}{r-l} & 0 & \frac{r+l}{r-l} & 0 \\ 0 & \frac{2n}{t-b} & \frac{t+b}{t-b} & 0 \\ 0 & 0 & \frac{f+n}{n-f} & \frac{-2f \cdot n}{f-n} \\ 0 & 0 & -1 & 0 \end{bmatrix} \tag{2}$$

Where $l$; $r$; $t$ and $b$ are the left, right, top and bottom edges of the view volume, and $n$ and $f$ are the near and far clipping planes respectively.

With Equation (1) and (2), we can deduce

$$z = \frac{-P_{34}}{\frac{z'}{w'} + P_{33}} \tag{3}$$

where $\frac{z'}{w'}$ is the depth value in the depth buffer, and

$$P_{33} = \frac{f+n}{n-f} \tag{4}$$

$$P_{34} = \frac{-2f \cdot n}{f - n} \quad (5)$$

In our new method, we use the normal rendering pipeline of the application to construct the scene in the frame buffer. We then capture the depth buffer before rendering a single, screen aligned polygon using vertex and fragment shaders, with the depth buffer as a texture. Our optimized algorithms in the shaders are used to reconstruct the scene depth values on a per-fragment basis from the nonlinear values in the depth texture. By taking full advantage of the GPU capabilities, we have reduced the computation to one addition and one division per pixel. As an additional benefit, by taking advantage of the vector capabilities of the GPU, this technique allows the scene depth values of up to four pixels to be computed in parallel if needed. Some special effects, such as depth-of-field can be implemented at this point since they require no further information [10]. However, for layered fog, we need the full 3D spatial position of the fragment.

**D Fragment Position Reconstruction.** With the scene depth of each fragment available, we can recover the fragment position easily by setting up a normalized eye-to-fragment vector. Given the four corner points of the screen aligned polygon and the camera position as input, the GPU hardware can be used to automatically interpolate the eye-to-fragment vector for use in the fragment shader. The fragment shader can then compute the fragment position relative to the camera given the eye-to-fragment vector and the depth value.

In the next section, we use layered fog as an example to demonstrate our new scene depth and fragment reconstruction technique in generating high quality depth based effects in real time with easy integration.

# 3 Layered Fog

Fog is formed by a suspension of water droplets in the atmosphere. It causes scattering of light amongst the water droplets, and therefore reduces the contrast of the scene. In computer graphics, the simplest fog model is homogeneous fog, which has a uniform density in all three dimensions. Layered fog, or height dependent fog, introduces a variation into the fog density dependent upon height.

## 3.1 Problems

In OpenGL, homogeneous fog functions are provided that allow the blending of the fragment color and a fog color based on the distance between the view point and the fragment. Unfortunately, these functions use the fragment depth as an approximation of distance, rather than the true Euclidean distance. This causes a problem when the viewpoint rotates, since the Z depth of an object can change while the Euclidean distance does not. The result of this is that objects can appear out of the fog, or disappear into the fog, simply as a result of rotating the viewpoint. Fig. 1. shows how these artifacts occur in OpenGL models. The grey gradient box represents the fog distribution. Although the Euclidean distance between viewpoint O and object point P does not change after the viewing plane rotates (viewing direction changes), the depth to P, however, is changed from $z$ to $z_{\alpha}$. As a result, the intensity of fogged fragment at point P will change.

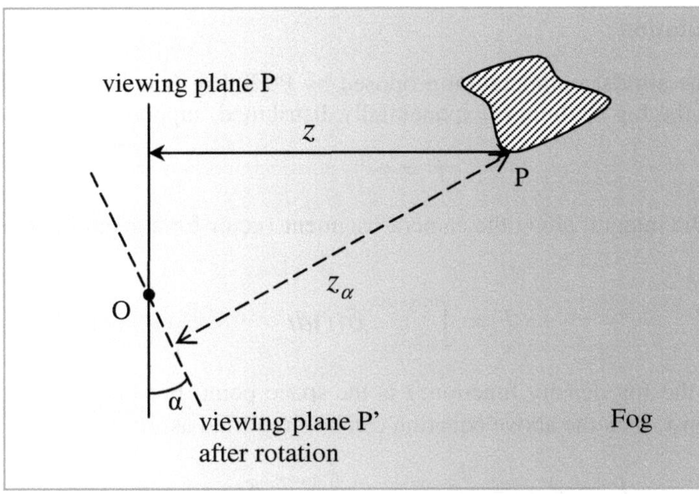


**Fig. 1.** Undesirable Artifacts of the Standard Fog Model

OpenGL provides a fog extension that allows per vertex specification of depth values for fog computation, enabling generation of effects such as height dependent fog. While it can be used to produce reasonable results, it also presents its own set of problems. Firstly, it can affect performance, since the additional per-vertex data required in this fog extension can potentially become a system bottleneck, in particular, demanding more CPU cycles and bus bandwidth. Secondly, since the depth value is provided once per vertex, it must be interpolated across the polygon. Large polygons can therefore make it very difficult to vary the fog density over small scales. The only way to improve this situation is to reduce the size of the polygons, which can cause further performance issues.

A great deal of effort has been devoted to generating atmospheric effects including fog using global illumination models[2]. While many can produce high quality results, they generally come with a price of high computational cost, and are not yet real time frame rates, particularly when integrated with generic visualization systems. An alternative is to generate visually pleasing fog effect without global illumination consideration. Perlin[6] documented a simple way of producing layered mist by integrating a vertical ray and then enlarging it along line-of-sight. A few techniques have been implemented using this idea, including texture table lookup [4], or pixel texture [3][1]. However, they are not fast enough.

In this paper, we accurately recover 3D fragment position based on scene depth reconstruction, and apply it when evaluating fog integral along line-of-sight to produce-realistic layered fog. Our new method performs fog computation entirely on the GPU at a post-processing step, achieving real time rendering and permitting easy integration into existing visualization applications.

### 3.2 Computation

We adopt the similar computation proposed by Perlin[6]. It is known[3] that the attenuation of the fog medium is exponentially distributed, suppose

$$f = e^{-F} \tag{6}$$

where $F$ is the integral along the camera-fragment vector for a given fog density function, then

$$F = \int_{camera}^{fragment} \delta(t)dt \tag{7}$$

where $\delta$ is the fog density function, $t$ is the space point. For layered fog, $\delta$ is only dependent on $y$, then the above equation can be simplified as

$$F = \frac{l}{\left| y_{fragment} - y_{camera} \right|} \int_{y_{camera}}^{y_{fragment}} \delta(y)dy \tag{8}$$

where $l$ is the Euclidean distance between the camera and the fragment. The blending result of the fog color and the fragment is computed by

$$C = f \cdot C_{frag} + (1 - f) \cdot C_{fog} \tag{9}$$

where $f$ is defined in Equation (6), $C_{frag}$ is the fragment color, $C_{fog}$ is the fog color.

Once the fragment position is computed based on scene depth reconstruction (details in section 2.1), the fog is computed by evaluating the fog density function along the line of sight, from the camera to the fragment (Equation (8)). This is done explicitly in the case of analytical functions (as in our example), or may use pre-computed integrals stored as a texture and provided to the fragment shader. Once the fog density has been evaluated for the fragment, the shader outputs the fog color and alpha value for blending with the scene fragment in the frame buffer.

### 3.3 Implementation

Our implementation is based upon a custom hierarchical scene management and OpenGL based rendering engine developed by the authors, although any OpenGL based rendering engine should be suitable. Written in C++, our application provides 'hooks' into various parts of the rendering pipeline, allowing us to easily insert our post processing algorithms. The rendering engine itself required no modification.

The first step is to render the scene into the frame buffer, which is done by the application as before. Once the scene rendering is complete, the scene post processing is triggered just prior to the frame buffer swap. At this point, the depth buffer is captured using the OpenGL copy-to-texture functionality. Next, the depth conversion parameters are computed based on the camera properties. The post processing is then initiated by drawing a screen-aligned polygon using the fog color, textured with the depth texture, and using custom vertex and fragment shaders written in the OpenGL Shading Language. The vertex shader is used to set up the eye-to-fragment unit vector, defined in real world coordinates. This is interpolated by the hardware pipeline, and delivered to the fragment shader for use in computing the fragment position. The depth conversion parameters needed for converting the depth buffer values are passed to the fragment shader as uniform variables. The fog computation is performed in the fragment shader based on Equation (8).

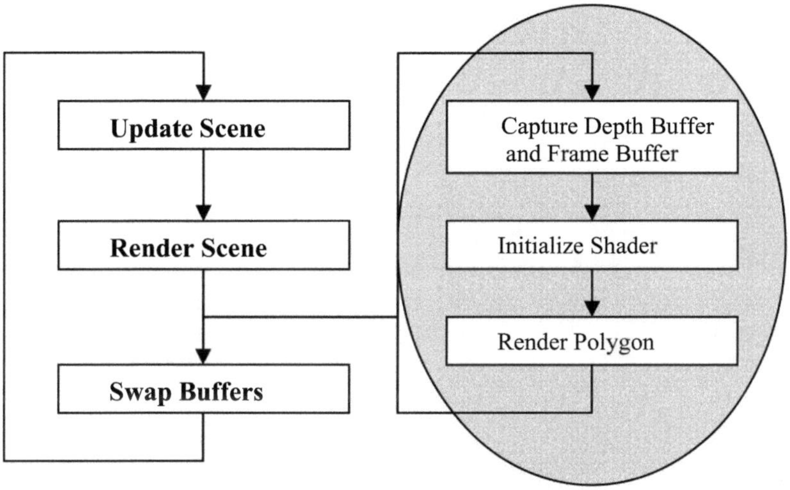


**Fig. 2.** Application Integration of The Post-processing

To blend the fog color with the fragment color, we take advantage of the standard OpenGL blending functionality and simply compute an alpha value in the fragment shader. The output from the fragment shader is a fragment color consisting of the RGB fog color, and the computed alpha (fog) value. The rendering pipeline takes care of the rest of the work by blending the fog color with the existing fragment in the framebuffer.

Fig. 1 shows the steps in our post processing implementation, and how it integrates into the rendering application.

# 4 Results

The algorithms in this paper have been implemented on a 2.8GHz Pentium IV platform, with 1GB RAM and an nVIDIA 6800 graphics card, running Linux.

**Fig. 3.** Layered fog in a city scene

A number of test scenes were chosen using different fog functions at differing screen resolutions, from 512 x 512 up to 1024 x 1024. Figures 3, 4, and 5 shows a selection of images generated using the technique. Figure 3 uses a simple exponential fog function, decreasing with increasing height, to simulate a typical city fog. Figure 4 uses a sinusoidal fog function to create a band of fog just above the surface of the water. Figure 5 uses a simple ramp function to simulate a dry-ice type fog in an indoor scene.

**Fig. 4.** Low level Sea Mist

**Fig. 5.** The Cloisters

Performance measurements showed that the technique takes from 0.4 up to a maximum of 2.1 milliseconds, depending upon the screen resolution and the type of fog implemented.

## 5 Conclusion and Future Work

The layered fog example demonstrates the effectiveness of our new GPU-based scene depth reconstruction technique. This technique has proved efficient and accurate when applied to generate other depth effects such as depth of field [10], and should prove effective for other depth cueing effects such as shadowing and motion blur.

Our GPU based integration framework presents easy integration of single effects into existing rendering applications, as well as combination of multiple effects through component level shader algorithms in the post-processing step. We are currently working on generating multiple depth effects using this integration framework in real time, with minimal impact of the existing rendering applications. The long term goal for this work is to improve realism and human immersion in the virtual environment, and in particular, to improve human subjects experience in perceiving distance and space in virtual environments.

## Reference:


1. Biri, V., Michelin, S., Arques, D.: Real-time animation of realistic fog. In: Rendering Techniques 2002 (Proceedings of the Thirteenth Eurographics Workshop on Rendering) (June 2002)
2. Cerezo, E., Perez, F., Pueyo, X., Seron, F., Sillionn, F.X.: A survey on participating media rendering technique. The Visual Computer 21(5), 303–328 (2005)
3. Heidich, W., Westermann, R., Seidel, H., Ertl, T.: Applications of pixel textures in visualization and realistic image synthesis. In: Proc. ACM Sym. On Interactive 3D Grahpics, pp. 127–134 (April 1999)
4. Legakis, J.: Fast muilti-layer fog. In Siggraph'98 Conference Abstracts and Applications, p. 266 (1998)
5. McNamara, A.: Visual Perception in Realistic Image Synthesis. Computer Graphics Forum 20(4), 211–224 (2001)
6. Perlin, K.: Using gabor functions to make atmosphere in computer graphics. http://mrl.nyu.edu/perlin/experiments/garbor/ (year unknown)
7. Rost, R.J.: OpenGL Shading Language, 2nd edn. AddisonWesley, London, UK (2006)
8. Woo, M., Neider, J., Davis, T.: OpenGL Programming Guide, 5th edn. Addison Wesley, Reading (2005)
9. Zdrojewska, D.: Real time rendering of heterogenous fog based on the graphics hardware acceleration (2004) www.cescg.org/CESCG-2004/web/Zdrojewska-Dorota/
10. Zhou, T., Chen, J.X., Pullen, M.: Accurate Depth of Field Simulation in Real Time. To appear in Computer Graphics Forum

# Part 2

# Interacting and Navigating in Virtual and Augmented Environments

# Independent Component Analysis of Finger Photoplethysmography for Evaluating Effects of Visually-Induced Motion Sickness

Makoto Abe[1], Makoto Yoshizawa[2], Norihiro Sugita[1], Akira Tanaka[3], Shigeru Chiba[4], Tomoyuki Yambe[5], and Shin-ichi Nitta[5]

[1] Graduate School of Engineering, Tohoku University,
[2] Information Synergy Center, Tohoku University,
[3] Faculty of Symbiotic Systems Science, Fukushima University,
[4] Sharp Corporation,
[5] Institute of Development, Aging and Cancer, Tohoku University
abe@yoshizawa.ecei.tohoku.ac.jp

**Abstract.** To evaluate the effects of visually-induced motion sickness that induces symptoms related to the autonomic nervous activity, we proposed a new method for obtaining the physiological index $\rho_{max}$, which represents the maximum cross-correlation coefficient between blood pressure and heart rate, with measurement of neither continuous blood pressure nor ECG but using finger photoplethysmography only. In this study, a blood pressure-related parameter was obtained using the independent component analysis of finger photoplethysmography. Two experimental trials in which subjects performed the Valsalva maneuver and then they watched a swaying video image were carried out to evaluate the adequacy of the proposed method. The experimental results have shown that the proposed method worked successfully as well as the conventional method.

**Keywords:** baroreflex, photoplethysmography, independent component analysis, visually-induced motion sickness.

## 1 Introduction

A human watching a moving image displayed on a wide-field display or screen often suffers from visually-induced motion sickness (VIMS) that induces symptoms related to the autonomic nervous activity such as nausea, vomiting, and dizziness. The previous study reported that the maximum cross-correlation coefficient ($\rho_{max}$) between blood pressure variability (*BP*) and heart rate variability (*HR*) whose frequency components were limited in the neighborhood of 0.1Hz was a useful index to evaluate the effects of VIMS on humans [1].

The present study has proposed a new method for obtaining $\rho_{max}$ with measurement of neither continuous blood pressure nor ECG but using finger photoplethysmography (PPG) only. In this study, *HR* was obtained from the foot-to-foot-interval (*FFI*) of the PPG signal, and *BP*-related information was obtained from parameters extracted by

R. Shumaker (Ed.): Virtual Reality, HCII 2007, LNCS 4563, pp. 177 – 184, 2007.

using the Independent Component Analysis (ICA). And an experiment with the Valsalva maneuver and the presentation of visual stimulation which induces VIMS was carried out to provide the validity of the proposed method.

## 2 Method with ICA

The proposed method using the ICA is as follows. 1) Let $x_1(t)$, $x_2(t)$, …, $x_m(t)$ be $m$ variables extracted from the PPG signal at time $t$. Define a feature vector $\boldsymbol{x}(t)$ as $\boldsymbol{x}(t)=[x_1(t), x_2(t), \ldots, x_m(t)]^T$ and define $\boldsymbol{X}$ *as* $\boldsymbol{X}=[\boldsymbol{x}(1), \boldsymbol{x}(2), \ldots, \boldsymbol{x}(t)]$. 2) Let $s_1(t)$, $s_2(t)$, …, $s_n(t)$ be $n$ unknown physiological parameters which are independent of one another at time $t$. Assume that the feature vector $\boldsymbol{x}(t)$ is given by a linear combination of $s_1(t)$, $s_2(t)$, …,$s_n(t)$. Define a parameter vector $\boldsymbol{s}(t)$ as $\boldsymbol{s}(t)=[s_1(t), s_2(t), \ldots, s_n(t)]^T$. Define $\boldsymbol{S}$ as $\boldsymbol{S}=[\boldsymbol{s}(1), \boldsymbol{s}(2), \ldots, \boldsymbol{s}(t)]$. 3) Thus, the matrix $\boldsymbol{X}$ is given by $\boldsymbol{S}$ as follows:

$$\boldsymbol{X}=\boldsymbol{A}\boldsymbol{S}$$

where, $\boldsymbol{A}$ represents an unknown constant mixing matrix consisting of coefficients of the liner combination. This equation shows that we need to estimate the independent component $\boldsymbol{S}$ and the mixing matrix $\boldsymbol{A}$ from the matrix of feature vectors $\boldsymbol{X}$. In this study, we used the ICA method in order to estimate $\boldsymbol{S}$ and $\boldsymbol{A}$. To separate linearly mixed independent source signals $\boldsymbol{X}$, we used a first fixed point algorithm (FastICA) presented by Hyvärinen and Oja [2] [3]. In addition, the number of feature variables $m$ was set to 7 and the number of independent variables $n$ did 4. Thus, $\boldsymbol{X}$ is 7×$k$ matrix, $\boldsymbol{S}$ is 4×$k$ matrix and $\boldsymbol{A}$ is 4×7 matrix, where $k$ is the number of heart beat.

Figure 1 shows the example of feature variables. One of the feature variables is the normalized pulse wave area (*NPWA*) [4]. This parameter shows the mean value of the pulsatile component of arterial blood volume.

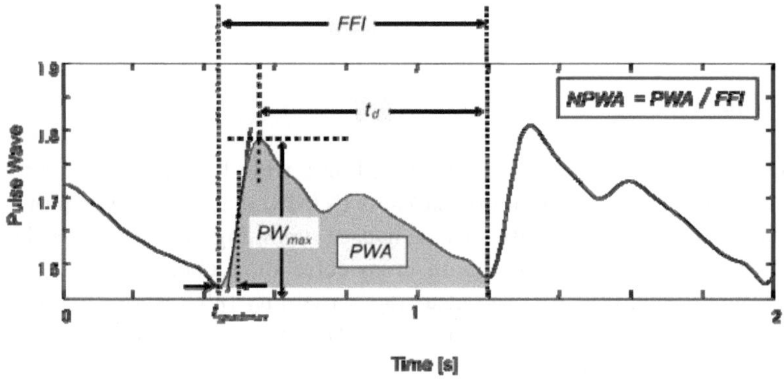


**Fig. 1.** Examples of feature variables and the definition of normalized pulse wave area (*NPWA*)

## 3 Experiment

In this study, healthy 15 subjects (12 males and 3 females, 23.6±2.6 yrs) participated in two consecutive trials. The first trial was the Valsalva maneuver to obtain the mixing matrix for each subject. The second one was the trial in which the subject watched the swaying video image.

### 3.1 Valsalva Maneuver

The Valsalva maneuver was performed by having the subject conduct a maximal, forced expiration against a closed glottis and keeping this condition for 1 minute. In general, baroreflex sensitivity of the subject on the Valsalva maneuver decreases and thus $\rho_{max}$ decreases.

ECG, continuous blood pressure and finger PPG of the subject was measured during the trial. Fig. 2 represents the protocol of the trial.

### 3.2 Trial with Swaying Video Image

After the Valsalva maneuver, all the subjects watched the swaying video image. Physiological parameters measured in this trial were the same as in the Valsalva maneuver.

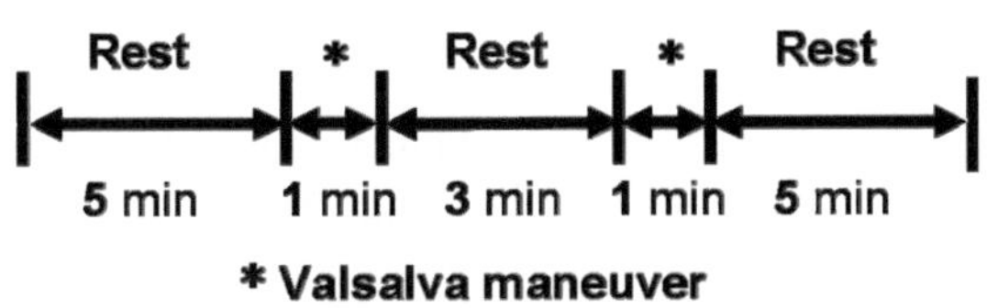


**Fig. 2.** The protocol of the Valsalva maneuver

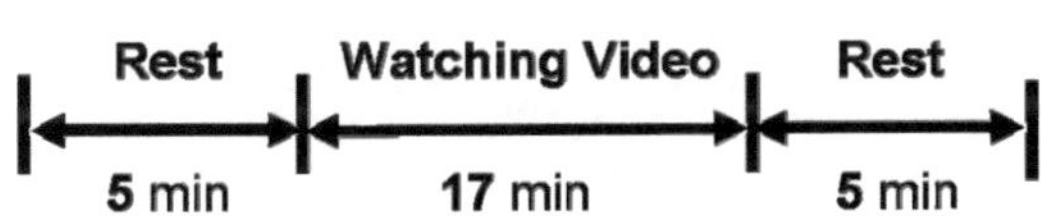


**Fig. 3.** The protocol of the trial with the swaying video image

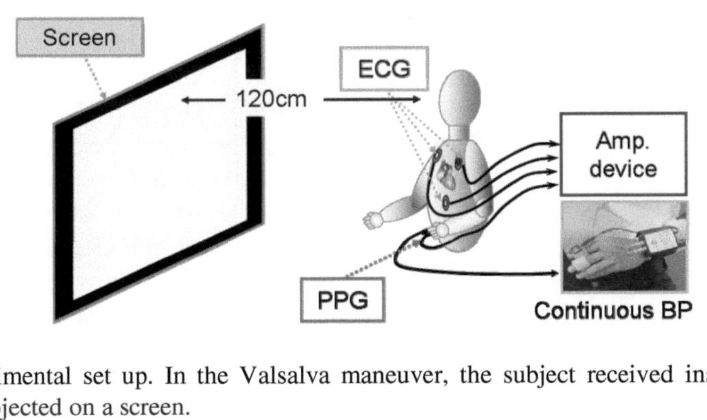


**Fig. 4.** Experimental set up. In the Valsalva maneuver, the subject received instructions by seeing text projected on a screen.

Figure 3 represents the protocol of the trial. After the second rest, the simulator sickness questionnaire (SSQ) [5] was charged on the subject. The total score (*TS*) of the SSQ is expected to show the intensity of VIMS. Fig. 4 shows the experimental set up.

## 4 Analysis

In the trial with the Valsalva maneuver, the beat-to-beat change was obtained from ECG. For each beat, the mean value of blood pressure and feature variables from PPG were calculated. The observed matrix $\boldsymbol{X}$ consists of feature variables from PPG. The mixing matrix $\boldsymbol{A}$ and independent component $\boldsymbol{S}$ were calculated with ICA for each subject. Let $\rho_{max}(BP)$, $\rho_{max}(NPWA)$ and $\rho_{max}(IC)$ denote $\rho_{max}$ between *HR* and *BP*, $\rho_{max}$ between *HR* and *NPWA*, and $\rho_{max}$ between *HR* and an independent component (*IC*), respectively. *IC* used in calculating $\rho_{max}$ was one that was most related to *BP* in all *IC*s.

In the trial with the swaying video image, the mixing matrix $\boldsymbol{A}$ obtained in the trial with the Valsalva maneuver was used to calculate *IC* for each subject. With the same way of analysis described above, $\rho_{max}(BP)$, $\rho_{max}(NPWA)$ and $\rho_{max}(IC)$ were calculated.

## 5 Results and Discussion

### 5.1 Valsalva maneuver

All subjects' data could successfully be obtained and analyzed in the Valsalva maneuver. Fig. 5 shows the change of $\rho_{max}(BP)$, $\rho_{max}(NPWA)$ and $\rho_{max}(IC)$. Each $\rho_{max}$ is

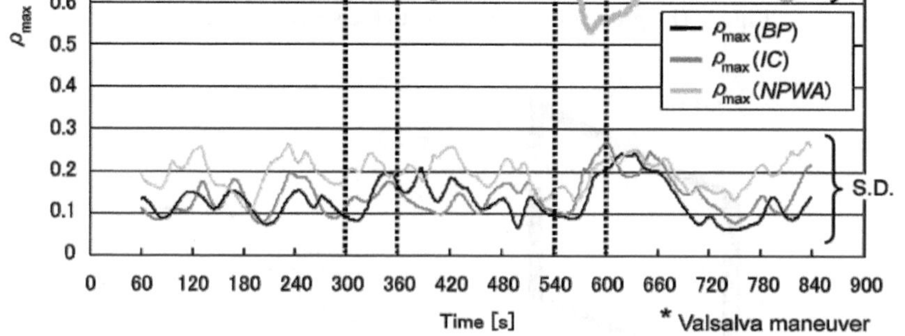


**Fig. 5.** Changes of $\rho_{max}$s averaged in all subjects in the Valsalva maneuver. $\rho_{max}(IC)$ represents $\rho_{max}$ calculated by using *IC* which was the most *BP*-related component.

the value averaged in all subjects and the standard deviation (S.D.) was shown in the lower part of the figure.

This result revealed that $\rho_{max}(IC)$ changed similarly to $\rho_{max}(BP)$. However the change of $\rho_{max}(NPWA)$ obtained from only the PPG signal was dissimilar to that of $\rho_{max}(BP)$.

### 5.2 Trial with Swaying Video Image

Fourteen subjects' data out of 15 could successfully be obtained in this trial. From the result of the subjective evaluation based on the SSQ, the median *TS* of 14 subjects was 17.7. All subjects were divided into two groups: "Sick" and "Well" groups. Sick group consists of 7 subjects with *TS* higher than 17.7 and Well group consists of 7 subjects with *TS* lower than 17.7.

Figure 6 shows changes of $\rho_{max}(BP)$, $\rho_{max}(NPWA)$ and $\rho_{max}(IC)$ averaged in 14 subjects. In this figure, $\rho_{max}(IC)$ changed more similarly to $\rho_{max}(BP)$ than $\rho_{max}(NPWA)$. $\rho_{max}(IC)$ was calculated by using the mixing matrix obtained from the result of the Valsalva maneuver. Therefore, this result suggests that the mixing matrix obtained in an experiment can be used for data set obtained in the other experiment. However, the change of $\rho_{max}(IC)$ did not completely correspond to that of $\rho_{max}(BP)$. This result suggested that the change of *BP* by autonomic nervous activity in the experiment with the Valsalva maneuver did not necessarily correspond to that in the experiment with the swaying video image.

Figure 7, 8 and 9 show changes of $\rho_{max}(BP)$, $\rho_{max}(NPWA)$ and $\rho_{max}(IC)$ averaged in 14 subjects, respectively. In these figures, each $\rho_{max}$ was compared between Sick and Well groups. The shadow shown in these figures represents the time interval in which the significant difference ($p<0.05$) between two groups was found by the Welch's t-test.

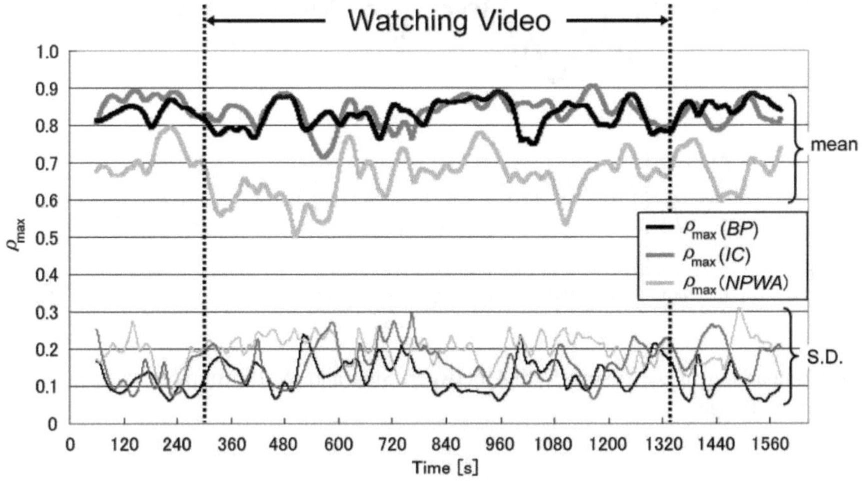


**Fig. 6.** Changes of $\rho_{max}$ averaged in 14 subjects in the trial with the swaying video image. $\rho_{max}(IC)$ represents $\rho_{max}$ calculated by using the mixing matrix obtained in the Valsalva maneuver.

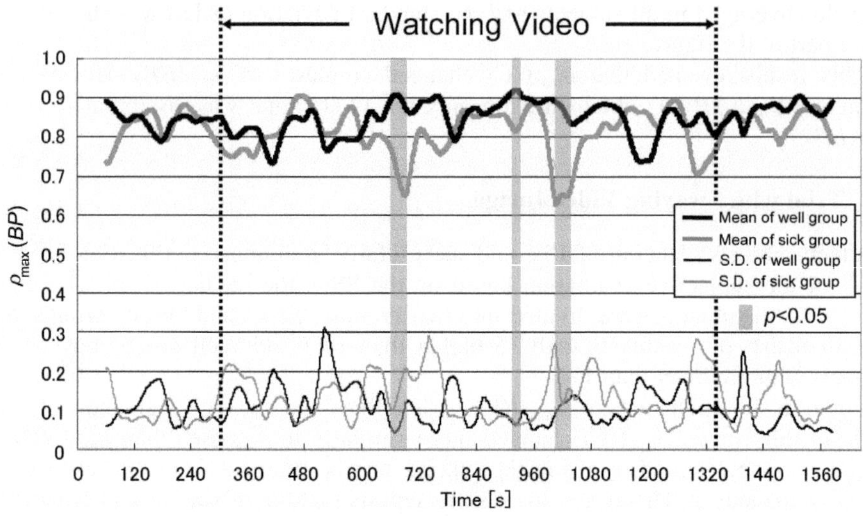


**Fig. 7.** Comparison in $\rho_{max}$ using *BP* between Sick and Well groups in the trial with the swaying video image

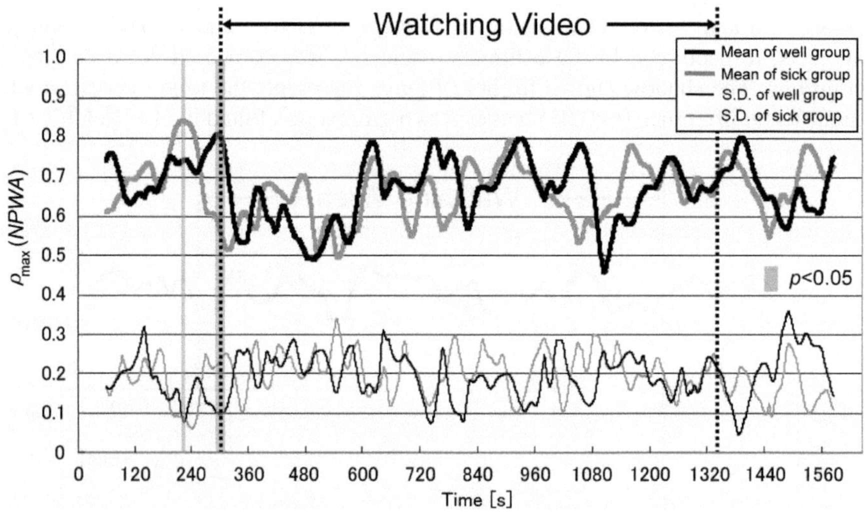


**Fig. 8.** Comparison in $\rho_{max}$ using *NPWA* between Sick and Well groups in the trial with the swaying video image

These results imply that $\rho_{max}(BP)$ and $\rho_{max}(IC)$ of Sick group was lower than those of Well group in the presentation of the video image. However, there was no significant difference in $\rho_{max}(NPWA)$ between two groups in the presentation. This fact suggests

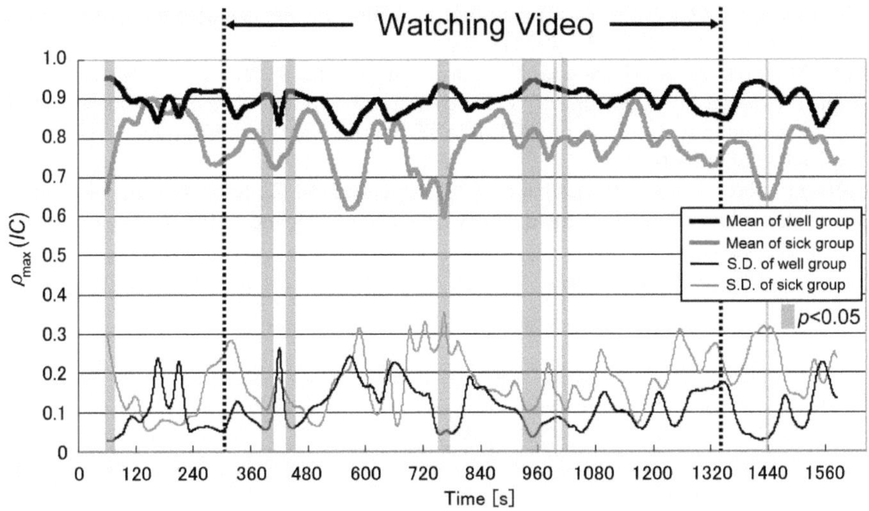


**Fig. 9.** Comparison in $\rho_{max}$ using *IC* between Sick and Well groups in the trial with the swaying video image

that symptoms of VIMS were caused by watching the swaying video image and it seems that the effects of it was strong especially at about 720 s and 960 s. However, $\rho_{max}(IC)$ did not necessarily correspond to traditional $\rho_{max}$ using *BP*.

## 6 Conclusion

This study has proposed a method for extracting the blood pressure-related parameter from photoplethysmography using the independent component analysis. From the experimental result, it was ascertained that the proposed method could extract the independent component related to *BP*. In addition, the effects of visually-induced motion sickness could be estimated with independent component which was obtained by using the mixing matrix calculated in the Valsalva maneuver. However, the physiological index $\rho_{max}$ using the independent component did not necessarily correspond to $\rho_{max}$ using blood pressure. Thus, we need to reveal the physiological reason of this result.

## References


1. Sugita, N., Yoshizawa, M., Abe, M., Tanaka, A., Yambe, T., Nitta, S., Chiba, S.: Biphasic Effect of Visually-Induced Motion Sickness Revealed by Time-Varying Correlation of Autonomic Nervous System. In: Proc. of the 11th International Conference on Human-Computer Interaction, Las Vegas, CD-ROM (2005)
2. Hyvärinen, A.: First and robust fixed-point algorithms for independent component analysis. IEEE Transactions on Neural Networks 10(3), 626–634 (1999)

3. Hyvärinen, A., Oja, E.: A fast fixed-point algorithm for independent component analysis. Neural Computation 9, 1483–1492 (1997)
4. Abe, M., Yoshizawa, M., Sugita, N., Tanaka, A., Chiba, S., Yambe, T., Nitta, S.: Physiological Evaluation of Effects of Visually-Induced Motion Sickness Using Finger Photoplethysmography. In: Proc. of SICE-ICASE International Joint Conference, Busan, 2006. pp. 2340–2343 (2006)
5. Kennedy, R.S., Lane, N.E., Berbaum, K.S., Lilienthal, M.G.: Simulator sickness questionnaire: An enhanced method for quantifying simulator sickness. Int. J. Aviation Psychology 3, 203–220 (1993)

# Virtual Gaze. A Pilot Study on the Effects of Computer Simulated Gaze in Avatar-Based Conversations

Gary Bente, Felix Eschenburg, and Nicole. C. Krämer

Department of Psychology, University of Cologne, Bernhard-Feilchenfeldstr.11, 50969 Cologne, Germany
{bente, felix.eschenburg, nicole.kraemer}@uni-koeln.de

**Abstract.** The paper introduces a novel methodology for the computer simulation of gaze behavior in net-based interactions. 38 female participants interacted using a special avatar platform, allowing for the real-time transmission of nonverbal behavior (head and body movement, gestures, gaze) as captured by motion trackers, eye tracking devices and data gloves. During interaction eye movement and gaze direction of one partner was substituted by computer simulated data. Simulated duration of directed gaze (looking into the face of the vis-a-vis) was varied lasting 2 seconds in one condition and 4 seconds in the other. Mutual person perception (impression ratings) and individual experience of social presence (short questionnaire) were measured as dependent variables. The results underline the validity of the computer animation approach. Consistent with the literature the longer gaze duration was found to cause significantly better evaluations of the interaction partners and higher levels of co-presence.

**Keywords:** Computer mediated communication, nonverbal behavior, social gaze, methodology, person perception, social presence.

## 1 Introduction

The lack of nonverbal signals has often been conceptualized as a deficit of computer mediated communication (CMC) with particular socio-emotional consequences, on one hand reducing social presence and leading to emotional impoverishment, on the other hand fostering the balance of power and influence and equalize participation through the absence of status signals [1]. Given this discrepancy it is meaningful to ask, under which circumstances the inclusion of nonverbal channels into CMC will enhance the experience of *social presence* [2, 3] and which particular cues lead to beneficial socio-emotional effects and which do not. Among the nonverbal communication phenomena so-called visual behavior [4, 5, 6], i.e. gaze and eye contact has received particular interest in communication research and social psychology. Social gaze serves as an indicator of covert cognitive processes and also constitutes a most powerful overt communicational social cue. Social Psychology has documented the prominent role of gaze behavior for the establishment of social relations, the fine tuning of interactions and the mutual attribution of mental states in social encounters [7, 8, 9, 10, 11] This holds not only for face-to-face interactions but also for virtual encounters with avatars and agents. While a series of studies explored the naturalness

R. Shumaker (Ed.): Virtual Reality, HCII 2007, LNCS 4563, pp. 185–194, 2007.

of simulated gaze in virtual environments [12] or the effects of pronounced social gaze, so-called supergaze [13], little is known yet about the effects of subtle variations in gaze duration, as they occur in real-life interactions [14]. In particular it is unclear in how far avatars can be used to effectively mimic gaze behavior, and whether the temporal thresholds for minimal and maximal exposure to directed gaze are comparable to those in real-life interactions. Against this background the current pilot study investigated the socio-emotional effects of different time patterns of simulated social gaze as embedded in ongoing avatar-mediated net-communications.

### 1.1 Gaze and Person Perception

There is ample evidence that gaze behavior has a strong impact on person perception and impression formation. It could be demonstrated that visual attention in particular increases liking [15]. Such effects however are nonlinear. Longer durations of directed gaze can be perceived as staring and evaluated as negative as gaze avoidance [16]. Also situational and personal variables seem to mediate the effects of social gaze [17, 18]. In addition to gaze duration also the gaze dynamics have a strong influence on likeability. Mason, Tatkow and Macrae [19] could show that averted gaze followed by directed gaze led to more favorable judgments of faces with respect to liking and attractiveness than did directed gaze followed by gaze aversion.

Besides liking and attractiveness gaze also influences other aspects of person perception and impression formation. For example people who maintain eye contact, especially when talking, are perceived as more dominant and powerful than those who tend to avert gaze [20, 21]. Moreover gaze aversion correlates with the perception of lower self-esteem [22] and increased state, trait and test anxiety, especially in women [23]. Common sense also associates gaze aversion with deception and untrustworthiness. Thus, it is not surprising that people who avert gaze are perceived as less credible and were more unlikely to be hired in an experimental job interview [24]. Although the reported effects of gaze behavior depend at least partly on the specific situations, averted gaze seems to be associated with less favorable traits and negative social evaluations [11].

### 1.2 Methodological Issues in Gaze Research

A closer look into the relevant literature reveals some basic methodological problems inherent in the experimental control of gaze and the establishment of causal relations between gaze and particular person perception effects. Existing knowledge on the effects of eye movement on person perception is mostly relying on either of two research strategies:

One strategy is based on the use of pre-produced or pre-recorded stimuli, i.e. photos [19, 25, 26] or video [11, 20, 21, 23, 27]. Such approaches have in common that they analyze impression effects from a passive observer's vantage point, i.e. they miss out on the interactive nature of gaze. Observers have no possibility to intervene or change the course of the conversation. Contingency aspects of behavior as e.g. mutual gaze or eye-contact thus are not covered by the experimental variations. Patterson [28, 29] criticizes the artificial separation of production and reception in most observer studies and doubts their generalisability.

The second strategy is based on the employment of confederates [8, 24, 30, 31] who are trained to exhibit a certain nonverbal behavior, e.g. gaze, while interacting with the subjects. Confederates can see the observer and contingently respond to him or her. To control the eye gaze and suppress spontaneous reactions however the confederates have to be trained very thoroughly and even after such training they might have problems to segregate the various nonverbal subsystems and to control particular aspects in a quantitatively predefined way (see [32]). More problems have been reported when using confederates in gaze studies. In a manipulation check of an experiment on the communication of facilitative conditions Kelly and True [33] found the interrater reliability on their confederates' gaze direction to be only .03. Burgoon, Manusov, Mineo and Hale [24] even speculate that their confederates' behaviour may have overridden their experimental manipulation.

Both research strategies suffer from the fact that the various nonverbal subsystems are interdependent not only within communicative acts of the interlocutors but also across interaction partners. To investigate the effects of isolated aspects of nonverbal behavior while preserving the natural contextualization of such cues it is therefore necessary to produce distinct variations of this particular aspect (gaze behavior) while leaving all other aspects of communicative behavior (head movement, gestures, body movement) unaffected. Also it is important that the participants are naïve about this manipulation, i.e. they are not consciously attentive to the cue under investigation. To solve these problems computer animation methodologies have been suggested recently [34, 35]. While early computer animation approaches only allowed for passive observation studies [14, 35, 36, 37] newer developments permit the experimental control of nonverbal cues during the course of an ongoing conversation. Such a methodology will be introduced in the following. Based on this we will report on a pilot study using the novel technology to determine the person perception effects of different levels of social gaze behavior.

## 2 Method

The pilot study is based on a recent development of an avatar platform, which is capable of transmitting head and body movements as well as hand gestures and gaze behaviors in real-time. Behavior is captured by standard capture devices (Polhemus®, Virtual Technologies Cybergloves®) and a special eye tracker (Mediascore®). Nonverbal communication data is transmitted via TCP-IP and can be buffered for algorithmic transformation or replacement by simulated data. Avatar animation is performed by means of a special AVI Codec transforming translation and rotation data into movements of a virtual character. Figure 1 shows the experimental setup during calibration, displaying a realistic avatar for feedback and adjustment.

To prevent influences of physical appearance the avatar used in our study was a very simplified cartoon-like androgynous character, with enlarged eyes, meant to facilitate the perception of gaze and eye movements (see figure 2).

**Fig. 1.** Experimental setup of the avatar platform

### 2.1 Participants

Seventy-six female undergraduates (between 19 and 55 years of age; m= 25.76; sd = 6.91) from University of Cologne participated in the experiment in return for course-credit or an incentive of 10 Euros.

### 2.2 Procedure

Two participants were invited for each time slot of the experiment. To avoid the participants meeting each other before the experiment they were invited to different floors at the laboratory building. Each participant was greeted by a female experimenter and led into the laboratory. While helping the participants into the sensor equipment the experimenter explained that the study involved avatar-mediated communication. After completing the calibration process the experimenter explained that the participants should get acquainted with each other by using avatar-mediated communication. As soon as the connection between the participants had been established, the experimenter started the recording of the interaction and left the room for ten minutes. After that, each participant was asked to fill out a questionnaire, was detached from the sensor equipment and paid for participating in the study.

### 2.3 Independent Variables

The experiment had a single-factor (short gaze vs. long gaze vs. real gaze) design. In each of the 38 dyads one participant saw the other's avatar with real eye data, whereas the other one saw an avatar with simulated eye data. Head, hand, torso and finger movement were directly mapped onto the avatar. There were two conditions of simulated gaze patterns. In the short-gaze condition the avatar offered eye contact (i.e. looked towards the participant) on an average of two seconds and looked away on an average of two seconds. In the long-gaze condition the avatar offered eye-contact on an average of four seconds and also looked away on an average of two seconds. Figure 2 shows three examples of different gaze directions.

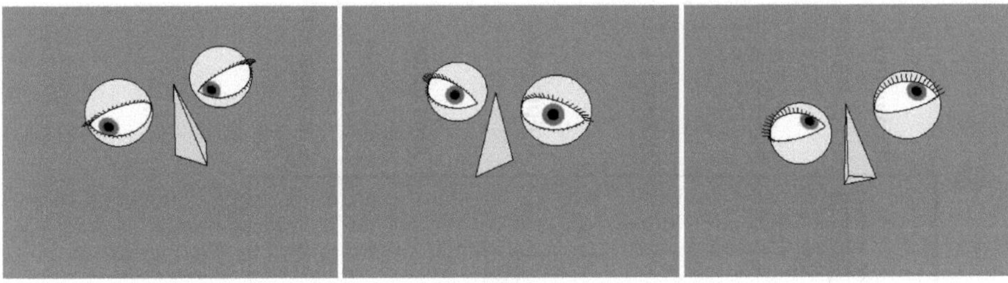

**Fig. 2.** Examples of averted gaze (left and right) and directed gaze (middle)

### 2.4 Dependent Variables

Person perception was assessed via a semantic differential on person perception developed by Krämer [38] and social presence was assessed with an instrument developed in a former study on social presence [39]. Specific items were added asking for technical problems or inconvenience in using the sensor technology. These items used a 5-point-Likert-scale of acceptance reaching from 1 (not at all) to 5 (extremely). Finally, the questionnaire included an item asking for the estimation of being looked at in percentage of time the conversation lasted.

## 3 Results

Factor analysis of the semantic differential for person perception revealed a three factor solution explaining 60.509% of the variance after Varimax rotation. The resulting factors could sensibly be named as evaluation (marker variable: "friendly-unfriendly"; factor loading: -.763), activity (marker variable: "active-passive"; factor loading: .920) and potency (marker variable: "dominant-compliant"; factor loading: .804). These were submitted to a single factor analysis of variance (ANOVA), which revealed a medium effect of gaze condition only on evaluation (df=2; F= 4.345; p =.017; $\eta 2 = 0.109$), but not on activity and potency. Bonferroni corrected post-hoc tests revealed significant differences between the long-gaze and the other two conditions (both $p < 0.05$).

Factor analyses on the social presence scale resulted into a three factor solution, explaining 51.27% of variance after Varimax rotation. The resulting factors were co-presence (marker variable: "I was often aware that we were at different places"; factor loading: -.841), ambiguity (marker variable: "My interlocutor was able to communicate his/her intentions"; factor loading: -.745) and contingency (marker variable: "My interlocutor's behavior did often influence my own behavior"; factor loading: .763). These factors were submitted to a single-factor ANOVA, which revealed a significant effect on co-presence (df= 2; F= 3.583; p = .033; $\eta 2 = .092$), but not on the other two factors. Bonferroni corrected post-hoc tests revealed a significant difference only between the long-gaze condition and the short-gaze condition (p= .027) on social presence.

Figure 3 summarizes the results for person perception and social presence factors across the three treatment conditions.

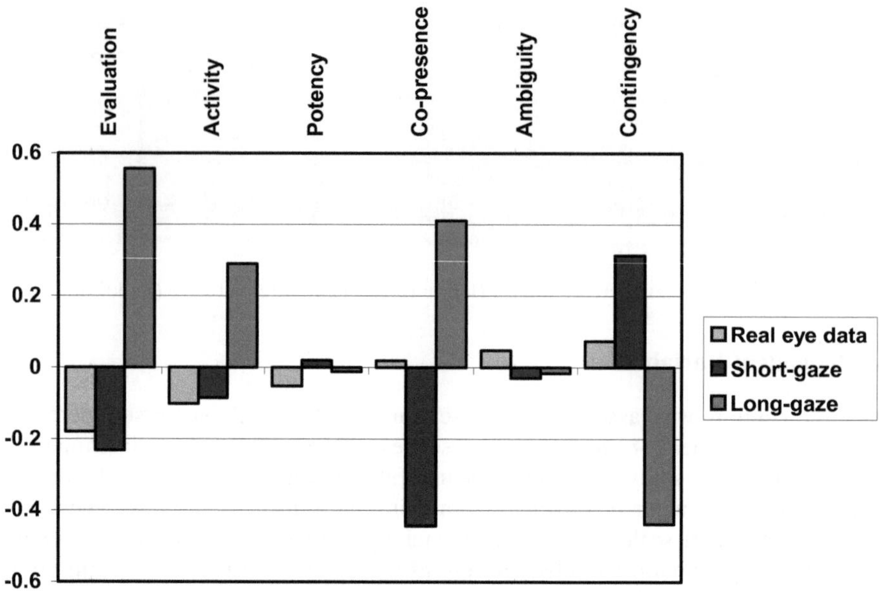


**Fig. 3.** Overview over the differences in the person perception and social presence factors

The questions on problems with the technology were analyzed on a single item basis. Each item's mean value was investigated and tested against the scale's mean value of 3 to decide whether there is a specific problem with the technology or not. Table 3 shows that all items scored significantly below the mean value of the scale. Thus, the technology was neither experienced as obtrusive nor as distracting during the interaction.

**Table 1.** Mean values and results of one-sample T-tests for the items on technological problems and obtrusiveness

| *Items* | *Mean* | *SD* | *t* | *df* | *p* |
|---|---|---|---|---|---|
| Did the headset limit your visual field? | 2.01 | 1.09 | -7.90 | 75 | .000 |
| Have you felt distracted due to the equipment? | 1.88 | .89 | -10.91 | 75 | .000 |
| Did you think a lot about the equipment during the interaction? | 1.82 | .83 | -12.47 | 75 | .000 |
| Did you feel alienated due to the equipment? | 1.92 | .86 | -10.93 | 75 | .000 |
| Did you worry about damaging the equipment during the interaction? | 1.21 | .52 | -29.74 | 75 | .000 |
| Did you feel limited in your freedom of movement? | 2.32 | 1.19 | -5.017 | 75 | .000 |

The last item under investigation was an estimation of the frequency of eye contact during the interaction given in percentage values. There were no significant differences between the real gaze condition (m = 51.38; sd = 19.78), the short-gaze condition (m = 49.02; sd = 27.32) and the long-gaze condition (m = 49.73 sd = 26.62). Surprisingly in all conditions the amount of perceived eye contact was estimated to cover around 50% of the interaction time. Thus the experimental variation did not pass the threshold of conscious registration but nevertheless induced significant person perception effects.

## 4 Discussion

Major advantages of using avatars in nonverbal communication studies could be demonstrated: (1) avatars allow to filter out the influence of physical appearance and thus help to establish direct causal relation between behavioral cues and impression formation (2) the relevant aspects of nonverbal behavior can be directly and reliably controlled, (3) uncontrolled aspects of nonverbal behavior keep their dynamic properties, leading to realistic overall impression and (4) the experimental variation can be overlaid to real-time interactions, thus placing the person perception and impression formation into an interactive process and not in a passive observer task. The results of our avatar study are consistent with the literature [11]. Longer phases of directed gaze, i.e. looking in direction of the partner for four seconds consecutively, produced more favorable results than shorter gaze periods (2 seconds). This significant result can also be interpreted as a successful treatment check, as the computer simulated gaze induced the expected impression effects. Interestingly the remarkable quantitative differences in gaze duration, though leading to different evaluations of the partners, did not pass the threshold of conscious registration. Eye contact in both conditions was estimated as covering about 50% of the interaction time. A number of questions however stay unanswered and have to be addressed in the next studies. As there is a confounding between the duration and the number of directed gazes as well as the overall percentage of directed gaze it is not possible to identify which parameter best reflects the psychological variance in person perception. This problem can be solved in future studies by applying systematic variation to all three aspects, which will also imply a control of total interaction time. Furthermore it remains unclear, how the duration of averted gaze is influencing the impression and how this aspect is interacting with duration of directed gaze. Another open problem concerns the type of relationship between gaze and evaluation. The identified differences can represent a segment of a linear relation as well as of a curvilinear one. It is most likely that a further prolongation of the directed gaze periods can lead to negative results as it is perceived as staring, or as non-contingent to ones own behavior. Future studies will have to clarify this relation more precisely and will aim at identifying possible thresholds for attention to and positive evaluation of directed gaze. The mentioned problems and open issues can well be addressed using the introduced platform within a programmatic research approach. Further improvements of the technology as under development will include ease of use in eye movement calibration and the provision of non-obtrusive remote eye-tracking and head tracking.

**Acknowledgements.** The presented research has benefited by funding from the German Science Foundation (DFG) within the project "Interaction, identity and subjective experience in virtual communication environments" (FK/SFB 427-B3) as well as from the European Commission as part of the Integrated Project "Psychologically Augmented Social Interaction Over Networks" (PASION, IST-FET Project no. 27654).

## References

[1] Kiesler, S., Siegel, J., McGuire, T.W.: Social psychological aspects of computer-mediated communication. American Psychologist 39(10), 1123–1134 (1984)
[2] Biocca, F., Harms, C., Gregg, J.: The Networked Minds Measure of Social Presence: Pilot Test Factor Structure and Concurrent Validity. In: Presence 2001. Philadelphia, PA (2001)
[3] Biocca, F.C., Harms, C., Burgoon, J.K.: Toward a more robust theory and measure of social presence: Review and suggested criteria. Presence-Teleoperators and Virtual Environments 12(5), 456–480 (2003)
[4] Exline, R.V., Gray, D., Schuette, D.: Visual behavior in a dyad as affected by interview content and sex of respondent. Journal of Personality and Social Psychology 1(3), 201–209 (1965)
[5] Exline, R.V.: Visual interaction: The glances of power and preference (1971)
[6] Fehr, B.J., Exline, R.V.: Social visual interaction: A conceptual and literature review, In: Siegman, A.W., Feldstein, S., (eds): Nonverbal behavior and communication 2nd ed. pp. 225–325 1987 Lawrence Erlbaum Associates, Inc 640 Hillsdale, NJ, England (1987)
[7] Argyle, M., Cook, M.: Gaze and mutual gaze, p. 210. Cambridge University Press, Oxford, England (1976)
[8] Abele, A.: Functions of gaze in social interaction: Communication and monitoring. Journal of Nonverbal Behavior 10(2), 83–101 (1986)
[9] Bavelas, J.B., Coates, L., Johnson, T.: Listener responses as a collaborative process: The role of gaze. Journal of Communication 52(3), 566–580 (2002)
[10] Kleinke, C.L.: Gaze and eye contact: A research review. Psychological Bulletin 100(1), 78–100 (1986)
[11] Larsen, R.J., Shackelford, T.K.: Gaze avoidance: Personality and social judgments of people who avoid direct face-to-face contact. Personality and Individual Differences 21(6), 907–917 (1996)
[12] Garau, M., Slater, M., Bee, S., Sasse, M.A.: The impact of eye gaze on communication using humanoid avatars. In: Proceedings of the SIGCHI conference on Human factors in computing systems, pp. 309–316. ACM Press, Seattle, Washington, United States (2001)
[13] Bailenson, J.N. Beall, A.C., Loomis, J., Blascovich, J., Turk, M.: Transformed Social Interaction, Augmented Gaze, and Social Influence in Immersive Virtual Environments. Human Communication Research 31(4), 511–537 (2005)
[14] Bente, G., Donaghy, W.C., Suwelack, D.: Sex differences in body movement and visual attention: An integrated analysis of movement and gaze in mixed-sex dyads. Journal of Nonverbal Behavior 22(1), 31–58 (1998)
[15] Mehrabian, A.: Relationship of attitude to seated posture, orientation, and distance. Journal of Personality and Social Psychology 10(1), 26–30 (1968)
[16] Argyle, M., Lefebvre, L., Cook, M.: The meaning of five patterns of gaze. European Journal of Social Psychology 4(2), 125–136 (1974)

[17] Ellsworth, P.C.: The Meaningful Look (Review of Argyle & Cook). Semiotica 24, 341–351 (1978)
[18] Williams, G.P., Kleinke, C.L.: Effects of mutual gaze and touch on attraction, mood, and cardiovascular reactivity. Journal of Research in Personality 27(2), 170–183 (1993)
[19] Mason, M.F., Tatkow, E.P., Macrae, C.N.: The Look of Love: Gaze Shifts and Person Perception. Psychological Science 16(3), 236–239 (2005)
[20] Brooks, C.I., Church, M.A., Fraser, L.: Effects of duration of eye contact on judgments of personality characteristics. Journal of Social Psychology 126(1), 71–78 (1986)
[21] Knackstedt, G., Kleinke, C.L.: Eye contact, gender, and personality judgments. Journal of Social Psychology 131(2), 303–304 (1991)
[22] Droney, J.M., Brooks, C.I.: Attributions of self-esteem as a function of duration of eye contact. Journal of Social Psychology 133(5), 715–722 (1993)
[23] Napieralski, L.P., Brooks, C.I., Droney, J.M.: The effect of duration of eye contact on American college students' attributions of state, trait, and test anxiety. Journal of Social Psychology 135(3), 273–280 (1995)
[24] Burgoon, J.K., Manusov, V., Mineo, P., Hale, J.L.: Effects of gaze on hiring, credibility, attraction and relational message interpretation. Journal of Nonverbal Behavior 9(3), 133–146 (1985)
[25] Baron Cohen, S., Wheelwright, S., Jolliffe, T.: Is there a language of the eyes? Evidence from normal adults, and adults with autism or Asperger syndrome. Visual Cognition 4(3), 311–331 (1997)
[26] Macrae, C.N., Hood, B.M., Milne, A.B., Rowe, A.C., Mason, M.F.: Are you looking at me? Eye gaze and person perception. Psychological Science 13(5), 460–464 (2002)
[27] Naiman, T.H., Breed, G.: Gaze duration as a cue for judging conversational tone. Representative Research in Social Psychology 5(2), 115–122 (1974)
[28] Patterson, M.L.: Functions of non-verbal behavior in social interaction. In: Giles, H., Robinson, W.P. (eds.) in Handbook of language and social psychology, pp. 101–120. John Wiley & Sons, Oxford, England (1990)
[29] Patterson, M.L.: Strategic functions of nonverbal exchange. In: Daly, J.A., Wiemann, J.M. (eds.) in Strategic interpersonal communication, pp. 273–293. Lawrence Erlbaum Associates, Inc, Hillsdale, NJ, England (1994)
[30] Iizuka, Y.: Gaze during speaking as related to shyness. Perceptual and Motor Skills, 78(3, Pt 2), pp. 1259–1264 (1994)
[31] Kleinke, C.L., Staneski, R.A., Berger, D.E.: Evaluation of an interviewer as a function of interviewer gaze, reinforcement of subject gaze, and interviewer attractiveness. Journal of Personality and Social Psychology 31(1), 115–122 (1975)
[32] Lewis, R.J. Derlega, V.J., Shankar, A., Cochard, E., Finkel, L.: Nonverbal correlates confederates' touch: Confounds in touch research. Journal of Social Behavior and Personality 12(3), 821–830 (1997)
[33] Kelly, E.W., True, J.H.: Eye contact and communication of faciliative conditions. Perceptual and Motor Skills 51(3), 815–820 (1980)
[34] Blascovich, J., et al.: Immersive virtual environment technology as a methodological tool for social psychology. Psychological Inquiry 13(2), 103–124 (2002)
[35] Bente, G., Krämer, N.C., Petersen, A., de Ruiter, J.P.: Computer animated movement and person perception: Methodological advances in nonverbal behavior research. Journal of Nonverbal Behavior 25(3), 151–166 (2001)
[36] Bente, G., Feist, A., Elder, S.: Person perception effects of computer-simulated male and female head movement. Journal of Nonverbal Behavior 20(4), 213–228 (1996)

[37] Bente, G., Petersen, A., Krämer, N.C., de Ruiter, J.P.: Transcript-based computer animation of movement: Evaluating a new tool for nonverbal behavior research. Behavior Research Methods, Instruments and Computers 33(3), 303–310 (2001)
[38] Krämer, N.C.: Bewegende Bewegung. Sozio-emotionale Wirkungen nonverbalen Verhaltens und deren experimentelle Untersuchung mittels Computeranimation. Pabst Science Publishers (2001)
[39] Rüggenberg, S., Bente, G., Krämer, N.: Virtual encounters. Creating social presence in net-based collaborations. In: Presence 2005, London, UK (2005)

# Evaluating the Need for Display-Specific and Device-Specific 3D Interaction Techniques

Doug A. Bowman, Brian Badillo, and Dhruv Manek

Center for Human-Computer Interaction and Department of Computer Science, Virginia Tech, 660 McBryde Hall, Blacksburg, Virginia 24061 USA
{bowman, bbadillo, dmanek}@vt.edu

**Abstract.** There are many visual display devices and input devices available to designers of immersive virtual environment (VE) applications. Most 3D interaction techniques, however, were designed using a particular combination of devices. The effects of migrating these techniques to different displays and input devices are not known. In this paper, we report on a series of studies designed to determine these effects. The studies show that while 3D interaction techniques are quite robust under some conditions, migration to different displays and input devices can cause serious usability problems in others. This implies that display-specific and/or device-specific versions of these techniques are necessary. In addition to the studies, we describe our display- and device-specific designs for two common 3D manipulation techniques.

**Keywords:** Virtual environments, display devices, input devices, 3D interaction techniques, migration, specificity.

## 1 Introduction

The number of different devices available for use in virtual environment (VE) systems is staggering [1]. Visual display devices include head-mounted displays (HMDs) and surround-screen, tabletop, and volumetric displays, just to name a few. Input devices include wands, pens, data gloves, pinch gloves, flying mice, gaming devices, PDAs, desktop 3D devices, and a whole host of home-brewed devices and research prototypes. Moreover, there is no standard set of devices for VEs.

This poses an interesting problem for designers and practitioners in the area of 3D user interfaces. Most well-known 3D interaction techniques (see [2]) were designed, implemented, and evaluated using only one set of devices. We call this the "native implementation" of the technique. For example, the native implementation of the Go-Go technique [3] uses an HMD and a tracked wand. While the characteristics of these devices may not have been explicitly considered in its design, the designer was no doubt influenced by the physical devices at his disposal. What is not known is how changes in displays or input devices will affect the usability of a technique.

Therefore, we are evaluating the effects of *migrating* 3D interaction techniques among display and input devices. If there are significant usability issues that arise due to migration, then the techniques might need to be redesigned for the new set of devices; we call these *display-specific* and *device-specific* techniques. Our research in

R. Shumaker (Ed.): Virtual Reality, HCII 2007, LNCS 4563, pp. 195–204, 2007.

this area is part of a larger research program into the use of *specificity* in 3D user interfaces in general [4]. We have also considered *domain-specific* 3D UIs [5].

In this paper, we describe our investigation of migration, which has addressed two research questions: 1) Can we demonstrate a *need* for display-specific and/or device-specific 3D interaction techniques, and 2) If the answer to the first question is yes, can we *design* display-specific and/or device-specific techniques with acceptable usability and performance? We describe three empirical studies addressing the first of these questions. The first two studies are described in detail in [6]; we only summarize them here. We also present two display- and device-specific techniques based on the results of the third study, and give preliminary results supporting their usability.

## 2 Related Work

Many authors have noted the importance of studying the differences between displays and the effects of displays on users, applications, and tasks [e.g., 7, 8]. Few, however, have provided empirical evidence of these effects.

A small number of studies have looked at the effects of particular display characteristics on interaction performance or usability. For example, Arthur [9] studied the effect of field of view in an HMD on performance in searching and walking tasks. Closer to our own work, Kjeldskov [10] reports an ambitious study on the usability of 40 common 3D interaction techniques in a semi-immersive curved display and a fully-immersive surround-screen display. He found qualitative differences in the usability of particular techniques between displays, but no quantitative data was collected. Our prior work [11] demonstrated a statistically significant difference in users' behavior between an HMD and a CAVE during a navigation task.

There have also been few studies that have explicitly addressed the impact of input devices on usability and performance in 3D interaction. The experiments of Zhai [12] and Hinckley [13] are notable exceptions. Still, we know little about the most appropriate mappings between input devices and 3D interaction techniques.

Finally, we note that there are certainly some examples of display-specific or device-specific 3D interaction techniques in the literature. LaViola's step-WIM [14], for example, is a CAVE-specific version of the World-in-Miniature technique [15]. Prior research has not, however, demonstrated the benefits of display- or device-specificity, and the topic of migration of 3D interaction techniques has not been studied systematically.

## 3 Displays, Devices, and 3D Interaction Techniques

In this section, we briefly introduce the VE displays, input devices, and 3D interaction techniques we have studied, and consider mappings among these components.

### 3.1 VE Displays

We have studied perhaps the two most common immersive visual displays: the CAVE [16] and HMD. Although these displays are well-known, it is useful to reflect on their characteristics that might have an effect on interaction. Table 1 summarizes a few of the differences that we have studied or encountered in our work (for more discussion of these issues, see [2]). Note that we are assuming a four-sided CAVE (three walls and a floor), currently the most common configuration.

**Table 1.** Selected differences between common CAVEs and HMDs

| *Characteristic* | *4-sided CAVE* | *HMD* |
|---|---|---|
| Field of view (FOV) | Wide | Narrow |
| Field of regard (FOR) | ~270° horizontal<br>~180° vertical | 360° horizontal and vertical |
| Occlusion issues | Incorrect occlusions possible | Correct occlusions |
| Visual quality | Variable (floor) | Variable (edges) |

A display's "field of view" (FOV) refers to the maximum number of degrees of visual angle that a user can see instantaneously, while "field of regard" (FOR) refers to the amount of the physical space surrounding the user (also measured in degrees of visual angle) in which visual images are displayed [2]. The CAVE has a wide FOV because a user can typically see between 90 and 180 degrees of the display at any time (depending on the stereo glasses that are used); HMDs typically have a narrow FOV between 30 and 60 degrees. On the other hand, tracked HMDs provide a 360-degree FOR because the user sees the VE no matter which direction he looks; a four-sided CAVE has a smaller FOR because of the missing back and top display surfaces.

Another difference between HMDs and CAVEs is the physical location of the display surfaces. In HMDs, the screens are fixed to the user's eyes, while in CAVEs, the screens are fixed in the environment. This leads to the issue of proper occlusion cues. In a CAVE, a virtual object that is "near" to the user can be occluded by a physical object (such as the user's hand) that is farther away, since all virtual objects are actually projected on the physical screens. This problem does not occur in HMDs.

Both CAVEs and HMDs may lack homogeneity in their visual quality. In 4-sided CAVEs, the floor is typically front-projected (i.e. from above). This means that users will cast shadows on the floor. In addition, the floor is often not made of high-quality screen material, and can get dirty. In HMDs, the visual quality is usually lower on the edges of the display, because of distortion caused by the device's optics.

### 3.2 3D Input Devices

We have evaluated two common VE input devices: tracked wands and Pinch Gloves. The tracked wand is perhaps the most common 3D input device used in VEs. It consists of a six-degree-of-freedom tracker embedded in a handheld device, which typically has several buttons, and in many cases a small joystick. Pinch Gloves are worn on the hands and have conductive cloth on the fingertips. "Pinching" two or more fingertips together generates a unique signal that identifies which fingers are touching. The gloves are often combined with six-degree-of-freedom trackers.

Both wands and tracked Pinch Gloves allow the user to provide continuous 3D input (e.g. for pointing, touching, or manipulating) as well as discrete input events (e.g. for selecting, grasping, or releasing). However, they also provide very different affordances to the user. Table 2 summarizes a few of these differences, focusing on those that may significantly affect 3D interaction.

**Table 2.** Selected advantages of wands and Pinch Gloves

| *Advantages of wands* | *Advantages of Pinch Gloves [17]* |
|---|---|
| Physical buttons minimize unintended triggering of events | The gloves are worn, leaving the hands free to do other tasks if needed |
| A single size fits most users' hands | Many more unique input events are possible |
| The device defines a unique orientation (e.g., pointing direction) | Gloves are light and flexible, reducing fatigue, and users can keep their hands in a comfortable posture |
| | Gloves afford two-handed input |

### 3.3 3D Interaction Techniques

Our studies have focused solely on 3D interaction techniques for the task of manipulation, since this is a fundamental yet highly interactive task in 3D user interfaces. Here we briefly describe the four techniques we have considered; we refer the reader to the cited references for more information.

The Go-Go technique [3] allows object manipulation at-a-distance by defining a non-linear mapping between the motion of the user's physical and virtual hands. In a small area surrounding the user, the virtual hand follows the physical hand, but outside this area, the virtual arm extends at a non-linear rate relative to the physical arm. This allows the user to select and manipulate objects both nearby and faraway.

HOMER [18] also addresses manipulation at-a-distance, and also provides scaled virtual hand movements to allow long-distance object manipulation. However, selection of objects in HOMER is done via ray-casting (pointing), which is typically faster and more accurate than selecting objects directly with the virtual hand.

The World-in-Miniature (WIM) technique [15] provides flexible object manipulation by allowing the user to work on small copies of the objects in the VE, rather than the objects themselves. The user holds a small copy of the entire VE in one hand, and selects and manipulates objects in the WIM with the other hand. These actions are reflected in the full-scale world.

Voodoo Dolls [19] is an extension of the WIM that provides more precision. Rather than always working at the scale of the entire VE, the user selects a "context" and is provided with a miniature of that context to hold in one hand, and then can manipulate other objects relative to the context with the other hand.

### 3.4 Mappings

The problem of mapping among displays, devices, and interaction techniques is not trivial. Clearly, not all combinations of these components will provide equivalent usability or task performance, and some combinations may not work at all. Ideally, designers would be able to choose one component and then use guidelines to make appropriate choices of the other components. For instance, many VE developers are constrained to a single visual display type. It would be quite useful to know which combinations of input devices and interaction techniques work well with that display. But as we have noted, the space of devices and techniques is very large.

Considering just the devices and techniques described above, there are 16 possible combinations, all of which would be candidates for a VE developer who needed to provide object manipulation in his/her application. However, each interaction technique has a native implementation. Go-Go, HOMER, and WIM were all originally designed for HMDs and wand-like input devices. Voodoo Dolls was also developed with an HMD, but used tracked Pinch Gloves as the input device.

## 4 Experiment I: Effect of Display Type on General 3D Manipulation Tasks

Our goal in this first experiment was to demonstrate that the properties of the visual display could have a tangible effect on 3D interaction tasks.

Our hypotheses were drawn from the comparison of the CAVE and HMD presented above. We imagined how these differences might affect the usability of 3D interaction tasks. The four hypotheses were:

1. Because of the limited vertical FOR in the CAVE (missing top screen), users will find the HMD more usable for selecting and manipulating objects at a height.
2. Because of the limited horizontal FOR in the CAVE (missing back screen), users will find the HMD more usable for placing objects behind them.
3. Because of the limited FOV in the HMD, users will find the CAVE more usable for tasks requiring interaction on both sides of their bodies.
4. Because of the issue of occlusion in the CAVE, users will find the HMD more usable for tasks requiring object placement very near to their bodies.

We designed a simple user study to test these four hypotheses using 3D selection/manipulation tasks in the CAVE and HMD. Using the Go-Go technique, subjects performed four "construction" tasks in both displays, and we recorded comments and subjective difficulty ratings for each task.

The results of the study strongly supported hypotheses 1 and 2. The missing sides in our four-screen CAVE indeed negatively impacted usability on tasks involving manipulation above and behind the user (requiring the user to change his/her view). Hypothesis 3 was also supported, although less strongly. The fourth hypothesis was not supported; occlusion was not an issue for the manipulation tasks we studied.

Overall, this study showed that display characteristics could significantly affect the perceived usability of 3D interaction tasks. However, these effects seemed to be general, rather than due to the specific interaction technique we used.

For details on the experimental design and results, we refer the reader to [6].

# 5 Experiment II: Effect of Display Type on Usability of a Specific 3D Manipulation Technique

Next, we wanted to show that the usability of a *particular* 3D interaction technique might depend on the display type. Specifically, this second experiment was intended to investigate what happens when a 3D interaction technique designed for one display type is used with a different display type. Our hypothesis was that we would find a significant decrease in usability when an interaction technique designed for one display is evaluated in another. To test this hypothesis, we chose to evaluate the WIM technique [15] in the HMD (its native display) and the CAVE, using the same WIM implementation in both displays.

Subjects performed 32 positioning trials in each display. Unlike experiment I, we gathered quantitative performance data in this experiment for the purpose of demonstrating a statistically significant difference between the two displays.

Results showed that selection time and errors were similar in both display types, but that manipulation time was significantly higher in the CAVE. While this supported our hypothesis that the non-native display would result in degraded performance, this result was less than satisfactory for two reasons. First, the absolute difference in performance was still relatively small. Second, the focus on quantitative performance produced results that were not helpful in terms of producing a CAVE-specific WIM technique. Further work was needed to demonstrate that overall usability suffers when migrating away from the native implementation, and that techniques could then be redesigned in a display-specific or device-specific manner.

For complete details on experiment II, we refer the reader to [6].

# 6 Experiment III: Effects of Display and Device Type on Usability of Specific 3D Manipulation Techniques

The goal of experiment III was to extend our previous results. We wanted to demonstrate that migration could cause significant usability problems for specific 3D interaction techniques. Furthermore, we wanted to study the effect of input device migration as well as display migration.

We chose to evaluate two displays (HMD and CAVE), two input devices (wand and Pinch Gloves), and three manipulation techniques (Go-Go, HOMER, and Voodoo Dolls), as described in section 3. The native implementations of the three interaction techniques use different input devices, although all of them were originally designed for the HMD. Unfortunately, there are very few well-known 3D interaction techniques that were developed for CAVEs originally.

## 6.1 Design

The three independent variables in the study were display device and input device (within-subjects), and interaction technique (between-subjects). Thus, each participant experienced four conditions.

A variety of measures were used to ensure that we were obtaining a good overall picture of usability. We asked participants to provide ratings of frustration, fatigue, difficulty, perceived speed, and perceived accuracy after each set of tasks. We also collected a think-aloud protocol for most of the tasks, in which participants verbalize their thought process and experience in performing a task; interviews were used following each condition to collect similar information. Observation by the experimenter provided another source of usability information. Finally, we measured actual performance on a few tasks, although this was not the focus of the experiment.

Six subjects, with an average age of 20, participated in the experiment. There was one female subject, and all subjects reported themselves to be novice users of VEs. Two participants were assigned to each of the three interaction techniques.

### 6.2 Equipment and Software

The HMD used in the experiment (and in the previous experiments) was a Virtual Research V8, with 640x480 resolution and a 60-degree horizontal field of view. The CAVE was a four-screen Fakespace CAVE of 10x10x9 feet. CRT projectors and active shutter glasses were used to provide stereoscopic graphics in the CAVE. Both displays and all input devices were tracked by an Intersense IS-900 VET tracker. The wand used in the experiment was the standard Intersense IS-900 wand, while the Pinch Glove conditions used a pair of Fakespace Pinch Gloves to which trackers could be attached. Finally, we used a tracked wireless mouse in the non-dominant hand for the Wand-Voodoo Dolls conditions, since the Voodoo Dolls technique requires two input devices (we did not have access to two wands).

The VE software was built on CHASM [20] and SVE [21], while tracker data was handled by DTK [22]. The same reference implementations of the three interaction techniques were used for all combinations of displays and devices.

### 6.3 Procedure

We designed a simple room environment for the study. The room contained a variety of realistic objects (tables, pictures, flowers, etc.) and was large enough to require manipulation at-a-distance. After a period of practice with the first assigned technique, display, and device, subjects were given a series of tasks to perform in this room. Tasks covered a range of difficulty levels, and included both near-space and far-space manipulations. Subjects repeated this set of tasks for each combination of displays and devices for their assigned interaction technique.

### 6.4 Results

The results of this study are quite rich due to the variety of measures that we used, and analysis is still ongoing. We have already identified several salient outcomes, however.

First, our overall conclusion is that naïve migration of these interaction techniques to different displays and input devices was largely successful. None of the techniques completely broke down or became unusable when used with non-native displays and devices. This was surprising, and might be used to argue that display- and device-specific techniques are not needed after all. We did find, however, several key usability problems for the migrated techniques, and we claim that these problems are significant enough to pursue further.

The native implementation of Voodoo Dolls uses the HMD and Pinch Gloves. Migrating this implementation to the CAVE did not result in serious usability problems. Using the wand with either display, however, we found that subjects reported much greater frustration and difficulty in completing certain tasks. We observed that users often bumped the two trackers into one another, lost tracking because one device was covering the other, or found their hands in odd positions when trying to rotate the context or place an object on the left side of the context. These problems were due to the bulkiness of the devices, the natural hand positions of users when holding the devices, and the fact that the reference implementation of Voodoo Dolls assumes that the user is holding the context object at its center.

For HOMER and Go-Go, recall that the native implementation uses the HMD and wand. We found that the HMD-Pinch Gloves and CAVE-wand combinations were still highly usable, but that the CAVE-Pinch Glove combination caused problems for the participants. Because of the missing back wall of the CAVE, most CAVE interfaces must provide a method to allow the user to rotate the environment around its vertical axis. This was required for our manipulation tasks, since users needed to be able to select and manipulate objects in the entire virtual room. In the CAVE-wand condition, this was not a problem, since the joystick on the wand could be used to rotate the environment, and users could even simultaneously manipulate an object (by holding a button) and rotate the environment by using two hands on the wand. In the CAVE-Pinch Glove condition, however, this was not the case. We provided object selection and release with one pinch gesture, and left and right rotations with two other pinches. It was difficult, if not impossible, for users to simultaneously hold a virtual object and rotate the environment. Interestingly, this problem did not occur until we had migrated the technique to both a new display and a new device.

## 7 Designing Display- and Device-Specific Techniques

With the need for display- and device-specific techniques established by our series of studies, the next step was to demonstrate successful technique redesigns for specific displays or devices. Based on the results of experiment II (section 5), we attempted to design a CAVE-specific WIM technique, but we lacked design guidance due to the performance-focused nature of the experiment. The redesigned technique did not improve the WIM's performance in the CAVE. We focus here on two redesigned techniques that were developed as a result of experiment III.

### 7.1 Wand-Specific Voodoo Dolls

To address the usability issues caused by migrating Voodoo Dolls to the wand input device, we designed a device-specific version of the technique. The redesigned technique has several key features:

- the side of the context doll, rather than its center, is attached to the non-dominant hand,
- the interaction positions are offset slightly away from the tracking devices, and
- the visual representations of the user's hands have the same shape and size as the tracking devices.

These changes were intended to reduce the occurrence of trackers colliding with one another, awkward hand positions, and tracker blockage. Although our follow-up usability study is still ongoing, preliminary results do indicate that these changes are having the desired effect and improving usability.

### 7.2 CAVE- and Pinch-Glove-Specific HOMER

The combination of a new display (the CAVE) and a new device (Pinch Gloves) caused usability problems for the HOMER and Go-Go techniques. Since the problems were the same for both techniques, we chose to implement a redesign for only one of them (HOMER). This display- and device-specific version of HOMER simply adds a second Pinch Glove on the user's non-dominant hand. This allows for many different combinations of pinches to indicate selections, releases, and world rotations. We have chosen to use the dominant hand to specify object selection and release, and two pinch gestures on the non-dominant hand to specify rotation of the VE. This allows users to manipulate objects and rotate the environment simultaneously with no fatigue and no conflicts. Early results indicate that this redesign is also quite successful.

## 8 Conclusions and Future Work

With the plethora of VE displays, input devices, and interaction techniques, finding appropriate combinations leading to usable 3D interaction is difficult. We have shown in this work that migration of 3D interaction techniques away from their native displays and devices can sometimes lead to significant usability issues. Although not always needed, in some cases display- and device-specific techniques can be designed to address these problems.

We are currently completing our study of the redesigned Voodoo Dolls and HOMER techniques, and expect to find that their usability greatly exceeds that of the unmodified versions. An open question, however, is whether the usability of the display- and device-specific techniques is equivalent to (or better than) the usability of the original, native implementations. In the future, we also plan to generalize our results into guidelines of two types: first, guidelines to help designers choose appropriate combinations of displays, devices, and techniques, and second, guidelines for managing the migration of techniques to new displays and devices.

## References

1. Sherman, W., Craig, A.: Understanding Virtual Reality: Interface, Application, and Design. Morgan Kaufmann, San Francisco (2003)
2. Bowman, D., et al.: 3D User Interfaces: Theory & Practice. Addison-Wesley, Boston (2005)
3. Poupyrev, I., et al.: The Go-Go Interaction Technique: Non-linear Mapping for Direct Manipulation in VR. ACM Symposium on User Interface Software and Technology (1996)
4. Bowman, D., et al.: New Directions in 3D User Interfaces. International Journal of Virtual Reality 5(2), 3–14 (2006)

5. Chen, J., Bowman, D.: Effectiveness of Cloning Techniques for Architectural Virtual Environments. IEEE Virtual Reality (2006)
6. Manek, D.: Effects of Visual Displays on 3D Interaction in Virtual Environments, M.S. Thesis, Dept. of Computer Science, Virginia Tech, Blacksburg, VA (2004)
7. Brooks, F.: What's Real About Virtual Reality? IEEE Computer Graphics & Applications 19(6), 16–27 (1999)
8. Lantz, E.: The Future of Virtual Reality: Head Mounted Displays versus Spatially Immersive Displays. ACM Press, New York (1996)
9. Arthur, K.: Effects of Field of View on Performance with Head-Mounted Displays, Dept. of Computer Science, University of North Carolina, Chapel Hill, NC (2000)
10. Kjeldskov, J.: Combining Interaction Techniques and Display Types for Virtual Reality. In: OzCHI. 2001. Perth, Australia (2001)
11. Bowman, D., et al.: Empirical Comparison of Human Behavior and Performance with Different Display Devices for Virtual Environments. Human Factors and Ergonomics Society Annual Meeting (2002)
12. Zhai, S., Milgram, P.: Human Performance Evaluation of Manipulation Schemes in Virtual Environments. Virtual Reality Annual International Symposium (1993)
13. Hinckley, K., et al.: Usability Analysis of 3D Rotation Techniques. ACM Symposium on User Interface Software and Technology (1997)
14. LaViola, J., et al.: Hands-Free Multi-Scale Navigation in Virtual Environments. ACM Symposium on Interactive 3D Graphics (2001)
15. Stoakley, R., Conway, M., Pausch, R.: Virtual Reality on a WIM: Interactive Worlds in Miniature. CHI: Human Factors in Computing Systems (1995)
16. Cruz-Neira, C., Sandin, D., DeFanti, T.: Surround-Screen Projection-Based Virtual Reality: The Design and Implementation of the CAVE. ACM SIGGRAPH (1993)
17. Bowman, D., et al.: Novel Uses of Pinch Gloves for Virtual Environment Interaction Techniques. Virtual Reality 6(3), 122–129 (2002)
18. Bowman, D., Hodges, L.: An Evaluation of Techniques for Grabbing and Manipulating Remote Objects in Immersive Virtual Environments. ACM Symposium on Interactive 3D Graphics (1997)
19. Pierce, J., Stearns, B., Pausch, R.: Voodoo Dolls: Seamless Interaction at Multiple Scales in Virtual Environments. ACM Symposium on Interactive 3D Graphics (1999)
20. Wingrave, C., Bowman, D.: CHASM: Bridging Description and Implementation of 3D Interfaces. Workshop on New Directions in 3D User Interfaces (2005)
21. Kessler, G., Bowman, D., Hodges, L.: The Simple Virtual Environment Library: An Extensible Framework for Building VE Applications. Presence: Teleoperators and Virtual Environments 9(2), 187–208 (2000)
22. Kelso, J., et al.: DIVERSE: A Framework for Building Extensible and Reconfigurable Device Independent Virtual Environments. IEEE Virtual Reality (2002)

# Human Computer Intelligent Interaction Using Augmented Cognition and Emotional Intelligence

Jim X. Chen and Harry Wechsler

Computer Science Department, George Mason University, Fairfax, VA 22030, USA
{jchen, wechsler}@cs.gmu.edu

**Abstract.** Human-Computer Interaction (HCI) has mostly developed along two competing methodologies: direct manipulation and intelligent agents. Other possible but complementary methodologies are those of augmented cognition and affective computing and their adaptive combination. Augmented cognition harnesses computation to exploit explicit or implicit knowledge about context, mental state, and motivation for the user, while affective computing provides the means to recognize emotional intelligence and affects human-computer interfaces and interactions people are engaged with. Most HCI studies elicit emotions in relatively simple settings, whereas augmented cognition and affective computing include bodily (physical) embedded within mental (cognitive) and emotional events. Recognition of affective states currently focuses on their physical form (e.g., blinking or face distortions underlying human emotions) rather than implicit behavior and function (their impact on how the user employs the interface or communicates with others). Augmented cognition and affective computing are examined throughout this paper regarding design, implementation, and benefits. Towards that end we have designed an HCII interface that diagnoses and predicts whether the user was fatigued, confused, frustrated, momentarily distracted, or even alive through non-verbal information, namely paralanguage, in a virtual reality (VR) learning environment.

## 1 Introduction

Augmented cognition extends users' abilities to improve their performance and provide for graceful degradation. "the field of Augmented Cognition has the explicit goal of utilizing methods and designs that harness computation and explicit knowledge about human limitations to open bottlenecks and address the biases and deficits in human cognition" (http://www.augmented.cognition.org). Here, it is the computer or avatar rather than the human user that has its cognition augmented to overcome biases and enhance its performance. Towards that end, one seeks to design and implement a closed loop that becomes aware of subjects' intentions and emotions. Face analysis and processing is integral to this endeavor. There is feedback based among others upon facial displays, the interface is adaptive, and anticipation is driven by predictions. Both context and the subjects' (mental states) models are attended to or inferred to leverage the connections between personal appearance, cognitive state, and behavior, for an enhanced authentication of user identity and/or purposeful activity and their

R. Shumaker (Ed.): Virtual Reality, HCII 2007, LNCS 4563, pp. 205–214, 2007.

interpretation. Augmented cognition parses both covert and overt communication and supports switching among contexts.

The questions augmented cognition addresses are not limited to human identity. They are also about what the (face) messages convey and the reasons behind them, the place and time (sequence), and the channels of communication used. W5+ (see Sect. 4) is a succinct framework that encompasses such queries. It bears a close relationship to several new disciplines related to human-computer intelligence interaction, including aware computing, cognitive prostheses, human-centered computing, and pervasive and ubiquitous computing. Yet another emerging discipline, socially aware computing [35], takes into account the social context in support of group activities. Belief networks [33] are the method of choice to model and implement augmented cognition.

Paralanguage, part and parcel of augmented cognition, refers to any (nonverbal) communication that goes beyond spoken words and includes inflection, emotions, and gestures. Sadness, according to Knapp and Hall [26], is communicated when "the inner corners of the eyebrows are drawn up. The skin below the eyebrows is triangulated, with the inner corner up. The upper-eyelid inner corner is raised." The medium of paralanguage or non-verbal face (and body) display plays a major role in Human authentication / face recognition and avatars' design. Face communication includes gestures to modify and/or help with understanding, e.g., nodding or shaking the head, frowning for puzzlement, and raising the eyebrows for questioning. Gaze direction reveals mental state and social contact, e.g., intimacy, directness, and honesty [3].

Immersive virtual environments can increase access for learners in regular physics and math education curriculum, by providing 3D abstraction for those concepts that cannot be represented in alternative delivery formats [5]. The integration of augmented cognition with avatars allows the learning system to adapt to learners' affective and mental states. When the Human-Computer Intelligent Interaction (HCII) perceives the learning user's frustration, it replaces challenging problems with comfortable review materials and explanations. The new HCII paradigm will have profound and broad impact in learning, training, and gaming applications that are yet to be conceived and developed.

## 2 Learning Systems

ScienceSpace, an NSF funded project, is a set of immersive virtual worlds designed to aid students in mastering challenging concepts in science [37]. It consists of three worlds — NewtonWorld, MaxwellWorld, and PaulingWorld. NewtonWorld provides an environment for investigating the kinematics and dynamics of one-dimensional motion. MaxwellWorld supports the exploration of electrostatics, leading up to the concept of Gauss's Law. PaulingWorld enables the study of molecular structures via a variety of representations, including quantum-level phenomena. Through multisensory immersion in three-dimensional synthetic environments, learners themselves become part of the physical phenomenona, gaining direct experiential intuitions about how the natural world operates. MUVE: Multi-User Virtual Environment, is another NSF funded project for creating multi-user virtual environments that use digitized museum resources to enhance middle school students' motivation and learning about science and its impacts on society [6]. MUVEs enable multiple simultaneous participants to access virtual architectures configured for learning, to interact with digital artifacts, to represent themselves through graphical "avatars," to communicate both with other participants and with computer activities of various types. We also build a computational steering system for learners to understand the concepts of velocities and pressures, but without any previous knowledge of the differential continuity equation and Navier-Stokes equations for incompressible flow [5]. By looking at a fluid flow area, students can see the propagations of the pressures and velocities, and understand Navier-Stokes equations which govern the fluid flow field as a whole. The animated process gives much insight to the meanings of the parameters, variables, and the dynamic processes of the equations. We have been integrating the learning systems with HCII that is discussed below. The smart user interface responds to learner's activity and progress, while at the same time learns about users' inner emotion and motivation. The implication of this development is broad and profound.

## 2 Paralanguage

Emotions have an affective valence, i.e., a positive or negative feeling. Surprise is considered to be valence neutral, before giving way to happiness or sadness. Interest, however, is an inner or cognitive state rather than just an emotion [9]. The genetic narrative for facial displays, modulated by specific survival needs, led Panksepp [32] and Gray [23] to suggest specific biological drives that explain the "basic" emotions witnessed. Rather than merely serving as the means for communication, the drives are special routines or programs that provide an indication for intention and predict human behavior. Ortony and Taylor [31] model anger as a mix of several drives "The furrowed brow might accompany frustration or puzzlement; the open set mouth, pre adapted attack; the compressed lips, resolve; the raised upper eyelids, increased vigilance and attention" [9]. The drives themselves can be further decomposed or assembled from sub-drives and so on. Facial display and emotional state are not necessarily equivalent [20]. There are, however, many possible associations, e.g., the intention to fight and the display of anger. Staring, usually rude, is used for control and power. Medusa's look petrifies humans. People "face off" and "face down," when competing. "Saving face" and "losing face" are related to dignity. Expressions affect or reinforce emotions.

Fernandez-Dols et al. [16] discuss inconsistencies in the way emotions and facial expressions are linked. The same ambiguities, which affect natural language processing, hamper paralanguage too. The consequences are observed by all but the intentions are hidden. The observables are expressed using communication via either regular language or paralanguage. The search or inference, for the physiological processes behind the observed or expressed behavior, is similar to that expressed by Hidden Markov Models (HMM). The problem raised by Fernandez-Dols et al. [16] is that "emotions are particularly opaque to and challenge language."

The empirical but standard approach for studying emotions goes back to Darwin's *The Expression of the Emotions in Man and Animals*. The approach, more recently associated with Izard [24] and summarized by Ekman [13], has been idealistic in its belief in universal emotions. According to the idealistic view, there are basic emotions, whose production (modulated by culture) and (innate) recognition has been regulated by evolutionary needs. Today, however, one is constantly aware about and seeks individual (rather than universal) profiles and preferences. Emotions are further driven by context and motivation. Human behavior is situated, and above all, sequenced or time dependent rather than static.

According to Ginsburg and Harrington [22], "emotion is action in context." The alternative view ultimately espoused by Fernandez-Dols et al. [16] is that "facial expressions are not 'persistent' objects or concepts but 'rather experienced only once and not unique' events." According to this view, the facial expression is an icon, which suggests similarity rather than a pointer to some static and unique emotions.

## 3 Face Expressions

The expressions the idealistic approach finds to be universal include anger, disgust, fear, joy, sadness and surprise. "These signals emerge in infancy and on a reliable timetable. They are almost certainly unlearned. The smile and surprise appear 'first' at birth. Thalidomide babies born blind, deaf, and armless show them" [29]. The computer study of face expressions traces its origins to the Facial Action Coding System (FACS), which is based on measurements of facial actions [12]. FACS defines a repertoire of Action Units (AU) that is driven by the complex interplay between the skull/cranium and bones, the soft tissue / flesh, and the muscles.

The analysis of face expressions serves several purposes. Among them, indexing of inner states and emotion displayed, either spontaneous or deliberate, for augmented cognition. Similar to pose detection, which leads to subsequent face recognition indexed for that particular pose, one trains on face recognition constrained by the specific face expressions displayed. Face expression analysis requires image acquisition, image representation, and classification. The methods used to represent face expressions involve the aggregation of deformations starting from some neutral state. The methods are similar to those employed to define and encode the face space or those used to transform and warp faces for animation and virtual reality. The latter capture the dynamic aspect and bear resemblance to motion analysis, e.g., (dense) optical flow and tracking [38]. Another alternative, MPEG-4-SNHC [27], includes analysis, coding, and animation (of talking heads).

Facial expressions are deformations that result from the contractions of facial muscles. "Typical changes of muscular activities are brief, lasting for a few seconds, but rarely more than 5s or less than 250 ms. 'Timing of' facial expressions can be described with the aid of three temporal parameters: onset (attack), apex (sustain), and offset (relaxation)" [15]. Demographics, factors related to denial ("occlusion") and deception ("masking"), and the geometry and ambient lighting experienced during the image acquisition process, affect the analysis of face expressions. The representations used are local, e.g., Gabor filters, or global, e.g., PCA. Classification aggregates and relates among temporal information, e.g., HMM or (recursive) neural networks. A note of interest is that aphasics, people who show deficit in understanding spoken language, are "unusually sensitive to deceitful behavior and significantly more accurate than controls at detecting lies" possibly from "the growth of compensatory skills" [14].

Donato et al. [10] report on an extensive study concerning the automatic classification of facial expressions from image sequences. The methods used include analysis of facial motion through estimation of optical flow; holistic spatial analysis, such as PCA, independent component analysis (ICA), local feature analysis (LFA), and LDA; and methods based on the outputs of local filters, such as Gabor wavelet representations and local PCA. Best performance on classifying twelve facial actions of the upper and lower face were obtained using Gabor wavelets and ICA. Local filters, high spatial frequencies, and statistical independence were found most important for classifying the facial actions. Cohn et al. [8] have measured facial expressions over intervals from four to twelve months, and found that individual differences were stable over time and "sufficiently strong that individuals were recognized on the basis of their facial behavior alone at rates comparable to that for a commercial face recognition system." They conclude that "facial action units convey unique information about person identity that can inform interpretation of psychological states, person recognition, and design of individual avatars."

Fidaleo and Neumann [17] partition the face into local regions of change, which are labeled as co-articulation (CoArt) regions. Each of the local CoArt regions displays its own texture while actuated by a limited number of facial muscles or degrees of freedom, and the coupling between such regions is limited. Significant reduction in the dimensionality of the facial gesture data can be further achieved using PCA. One of the important innovations made comes from using Gesture (second d-order) Polynomial Reduction (GPR) to model and learn the G-manifolds or trajectories that correspond to different facial gesture movements and/or speech (viseme) sequences. GPR overcomes the limitations of the discrete face space defined by CoArt. Both the input and output space for GPR are continuous. GPR drives 2D Muscle Morphing animation where a mass – spring muscle system drives the control points. Synthesis for direct animation, driven by GPR modeling, is achieved by using a single camera and varying the settings in terms of user models, context, and lighting. An added advantage of GPR comes from the use of intensity for the gestures analyzed. Fidaleo [18] describes a new approach that integrates analysis and data-driven synthesis for emotive gesture and speech analysis, on one side, and 3D avatar animation, on the other. This is essential for the development of intelligent human-machine interfaces.

## 4 W5+

Non-verbal information or paralanguage facilitates now a special type of communication, where the ultimate goal is to probe the inner (cognitive and affective) states of the mind before any verbal communication has been even contemplated and/or expressed. The existing work on facial processing can be extended to task relevant expressions rather than the typical arbitrary set of expressions identified in face processing research. This is characteristic of the *Nominalistic* approach and leads incrementally to W5+ [11] and HCII via traditional HCI and dynamic Bayesian (belief) networks (DBN) approaches as described next.

HCI has mostly developed along direct manipulation and intelligent agents (also known as delegation) [28]. These methodologies can be contrasted as the computer sitting passively waiting for input from the human vs. the computer taking over from the human. Another dimension for HCI is that of affective computing [36], which is concerned with the means to recognize "emotional intelligence." Most HCI studies elicit emotions in relatively simple settings, whereas emotional intelligence includes both bodily (physical) and mental (cognitive) events. There are many interacting but hidden factors behind the display of expressions, and a probabilistic approach that includes uncertainty in their interpretation is required. The usual approach involves Bayesian networks, in general, and Hidden Markov Models, in particular.

The ultimate goal for smart interfaces is to expand and complement the human perceptual, intellectual, and motor activities. The old debate between direct manipulation and delegation using software agents has led to the realization that what is really needed is "to look at people, to understand them, and to adapt to them" [7]. This leads to HCII (see Fig. 1) in general, and W5+, in particular, which are adaptive and smart.

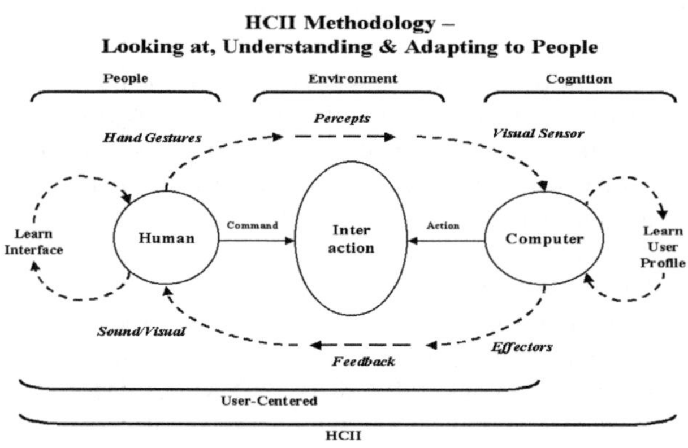


**Fig. 1.** Human-Computer Intelligent Interaction

The range of questions W5+ can answers includes queries about location (*where*), identity (*what* and *who*), time (*when*), motivation *(why*), and modality (*how*). W5+ integrates parsing and interpretation of non-verbal information with a computational model of the user, which in turn feeds into processes that adapt the interface to enhance user performance and provide for rational decision-making. The availability of users' embodied cognitive models is used in an adaptive fashion to enhance human-computer interactions and to make them appear intelligent, i.e., causal, to an outside observer. HCII promotes human activity and creativity. It combines the (computational) ability to perceive multimodal affordance (input) patterns, reasoning and abstraction, learning and adaptation, and meaningful communication. These concepts, akin to perceptual intelligence [34], echo those of Kant, for whom "perception without abstraction is blind, while abstraction without perception is empty."

To reach the sophisticate characteristic of HCII, one needs to (a) perceive users' behaviors; (b) infer users' cognitive and affective states on the basis of those behaviors; (c) adapt to help the users achieve their goals; and (d) improve the quality of interactions for users [11]. Adaptive interfaces are especially needed in situations where the user may become confused and frustrated in carrying out tasks with a computer application. Time stamped records for both explicit and implicit user behaviors are maintained for dynamic modeling purposes. These behaviors are natural forms of non-verbal communication that signal particular affective states such as confusion, frustration, fatigue, stress, and boredom. The record of explicit and implicit behaviors serves as input to a computational model of embodied cognition, e.g., ACT-R/PM cognitive architecture [4]. ACT-R/PM is a framework to create models of cognitive processing out of fundamental building blocks of cognition, perception and motor control. The outputs from ACT-R/PM drive HCII to align itself with the user's task and cognitive states, subject to the affective states mentioned above. The range of adaptations includes (i) presentation of pertinent tutorial information; (ii) reduction or enhancement of visual and auditory stimulation; (iii) emphasis of the most relevant information and de-emphasis of secondary information (for the subtask at hand); (iv) acceleration or deceleration of the pace of interaction; and (v) dynamic adjustment of the reactivity of the input devices in response to transient physical motor problems. ACT-R/PM enables HCII to react to a problem or specific need after it occurs, i.e., reactive adaptation, as well as to anticipate an upcoming problem or need and act before it occurs, i.e., proactive adaptation.

A cognitive model solves the same tasks as humans do using similar cognitive steps. An embodied cognitive model is endowed with affective states to match the user's states, and with the ability to perceive and interact with an external world in a similar way as the user does. Embodied cognition uses affective sub – symbols and their degree of belief, derived earlier by the perceptual and behavioral processing modules. Building models of embodied cognition calls for a specific cognitive architecture, e.g., ACT-R, Soar, EPIC, 3CAPS, which includes a relatively complete and well validated framework for describing basic cognitive activities, possibly at a fine granularity. Currently the framework that works best for building models of embodied cognition appears to be ACT-R/PM, a system that combines the ACT-R cognitive architecture [2] with a modal theory of visual attention [1] and motor movements [25].

ACT-R/PM is a hybrid production system architecture, which represents knowledge at both a symbolic level (declarative memory elements and productions) and subsymbolic level (the activation of memory elements, the degree of association among elements, the probability of firing productions, etc). ACT-R/PM contains precise (and successful) methods for predicting reactions times and probabilities of responses that take into account the details of and regularities in motor movements, shifts of visual attention, and capabilities of human vision. The task for the embodied cognition module is to build a detailed mapping of interpretations, i.e., motion/affective states, for parsed sensory-motor data within the ACT-R/PM model. One can extend ACT-R/PM to make it a true model of embodied cognition by incorporating the effects of affect on performance.

The scope for W5+ and HCII extends beyond cognitive and affective states and includes understanding and/or ascribing intentions. The tentative narrative for such an expansion comes from the discovery of mirror neurons in Broca's and pre-motor cortical areas of the brain, which fire when performing an action or when observing the same action performed by another subject [19] [30]. Such neurons, a kind of mind readers making predictions on others' expected behavior, appear to be important for imitation learning and for encoding the intentions behind particular actions. Lack of the mirror neurons is conjectured to be responsible for autism.

## 5 Integration of Learning and HCII

We are developing an online math education system with combination of networking, computer graphics, data mining, data access and data base management technologies to facilitate student online education [21]. The features of interaction, intelligent evaluation, distributed access, and data management are characteristics of such physical environments. An added student profiling system aims for achieving high grades for elementary school students. The system provides an interactive mathematical learning environment that is personalized to each student with intelligent state feedback to tailor the appropriate mathematics exam data set for the student in order to evolve his/her mathematical skills. If the student responds correctly, he/she will be challenged with a more difficult test question set. If he/she responds incorrectly, an easier question set will be administered at the next round. On the completion of the academic assessment, the student receives feedback that shows the correct answers of each question, the difficulty level of the questions, the student□s final score to each set, and a predicted score along with probability bands that show satisfactory performance ranges.

A simple application of the HCII is to identify the learner's current states: positive (happy, successful, advantage, etc.) and negative (unhappy, frustration, retreat, etc.). In the learning system, the current state of the learner along with his/her current physical and verbal commands, in addition to performance, are used to compose the system feedback. The response includes decisions on levels of performance, problem sets, and contents of learning. The interactions, in addition to text and graphics, include a virtual human instructor that provides communications in facial animation and verbal feedback. The virtual instructor complements the learning environment with rich, face-to-face learning interactions. It can demonstrate complex tasks, employ locomotion and gesture to focus students' attention on the most salient aspect of the task, and convey emotional responses in the learning process. The animated instructor is an expression of the system in response to the student's activity and emotion.

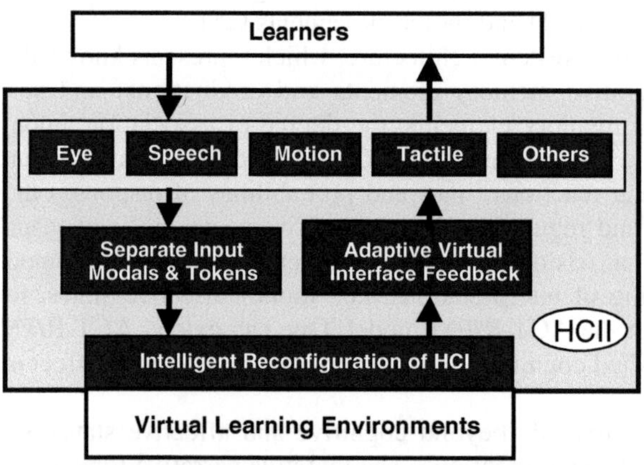


**Fig. 2.** Integration of learning and HCII

The boundaries between the 'real world', augmented reality, and virtual environments are blurred to create a mixed reality: an adaptive and virtual reality human computer interface for VR learning environments. On one hand, we employ VR technologies to build HCI and simulate complex phenomena to help learning. On the other, we seek to enhance the real environment instead of replacing it. The result is an emerging ecosystem that interfaces people and computing devices, promotes mutual understanding, decreases the cognitive load experienced by the user, and leads to optimal sharing of the computational load.

Our system architecture includes sensory input and output, adaptive virtual interface, and the intelligent reconfiguration of the HCI depending on the learner's profile/preference (Fig. 2). At the design stage, our sensory input includes eye tracking, voice recognition, VR 3D position/orientation tracking, and tactile sensory devices. Each sensory input is used to control all possible HCI input components, while multiple sensory input forms can dynamically reconfigure according to the learner's ability and/or preference. The implementation stage of this project emphasizes on eye tracking and voice recognition.

## References


1. Anderson, J.R., Matessa, M., Lebiere, C.: ACT-R: A Theory of Higher Level Cognition and Its Relation to Visual Attention. Human-Computer Interaction 12, 439–462 (1997)
2. Anderson, J.R., Lebiere, C. (eds.): Atomic Components of Thought. Erlbaum, Hillsdale, NJ (1998)
3. Baron-Cohen, S., Cross, P.: Reading the Eyes: Evidence for the Role of Perception in the Development of a Theory of Mind. 'Mind and Language 7, 182–186 (1992)
4. Byrne, M.D., Anderson, J.R.: Perception and Action. In: Anderson, J.R., Lebiere, C. (eds.) Atomic Components of Thought, pp. 167–200. Erlbaum (1998)
5. Chen, J.X.: Learning Abstract Concepts. Computers & Graphics 30(1), 10–19 (2006)
6. Chen, J.X., Yang, Y., Loftin, R.B.: MUVEES: a PC-based Multi-User Virtual Environment for Learning. In: IEEE Virtual Reality (VR'03), pp. 163–170. IEEE Computer Society Press, New York (April 2003)
7. Cipolla, R., Pentland, A. (eds.): Computer Vision for Human-Machine Interaction. Camb. Univ. Press, Cambridge (1998)
8. Cohn, J., Schmidt, K., Gross, R., Ekman, P.: Individual Differences in Facial Expression, In: Int. Conf. on Multimodal User Interfaces, Pittsburgh, PA, pp. 491–496 (2002)
9. Cole, J.: About Face. MIT Press, Cambridge, MA (1998)
10. Donato, G., Bartlett, M.S., Hager, J.C., Ekman, P., Sejnowski, T.J.: Classifying Facial Actions. IEEE Trans. on Pattern Analysis and Machine Intelligence 21(10), 974–989 (1999)
11. Duric, Z., et al.: Integrating Perceptual and Cognitive Modeling for Adaptive and Intelligent Human-Computer Interaction. In: Proc. IEEE 90(7), 1272–1289 (2002)
12. Ekman, P., Friesen, W.V.: Facial Action Coding System (FACS): A Technique for the Measurement of Facial Actions. Consulting Psychologists Press, Palo Alto, CA (1978)
13. Ekman, P.: An Argument About Basic Emotions. Cognition and Emotion 6, 162–200 (1992)
14. Etkoff, N.L., et al.: Lie Detection and Language Comprehension. Nature 405, 139 (2000)
15. Fasel, B., Luettin, J.: Automatic Facial Expression Analysis. Pattern Recognition 36, 259–275 (2003)
16. Fernandez-Dols, J., et al.: The Meaning of Expressions: Views from Art and Other Sources. In: Anolli, L., et al. (eds.) Say not to Say: New Perspectives on Miscommunication, IOS Press, Amsterdam, Trento, Italy (2001)
17. Fidaleo, D., Neumann, U.: Coart: Coarticulation Region Analysis for Control of 2D Faces. Computer Animation, 17–22 (2002)
18. Fidaleo, D.: G-Folds: An Appearance Based Model of Facial Gestures for Performance Driven Facial Animation, PhD Thesis, University of Southern California (2003)
19. Fogassi, L., Ferrari, P.F., Gesierich, B., Rozzi, S., Chersi, F., Rizzolatti, G.: Parietal Lobe: From Action Organization to Intention Understanding. Science 308, 662–667 (2005)
20. Friedlund, A.J.: Evolution and Facial Action in Reflex, Social Motive and Paralanguage. Biological Psychology 32, 3–100 (1991)

21. Fu, G.: A New Strategy for K-12 Students to Learn Math, Dissertation Proposal. George Mason Univ. (2004)
22. Ginsburg, G.P., Harrington, M.E.: Bodily States and Context in Situated Line of Actions. In: Harre, R., Parrot, W.G. (eds.): The Emotions. Social, Cultural and Biological Dimensions, Sage, London (1996)
23. Gray, J.A.: The Neuropsychology of Anxiety. Oxford University Press, Oxford (1982)
24. Izard, C.E.: The Face of Emotion, Appleton-Century-Crofts (1971)
25. Kieras, D.E., Meyer, D.E.: An Overview of the EPIC Architecture for Cognition and Performance with Application to Human Computer Interaction. Human-Computer Interaction 12, 391–438 (1997)
26. Knapp, M.I., Hall, J.A.: Nonverbal Communication in Human Interaction, 6edn., Wadsworth
27. Koenen, R.: MPEG-4 Project Overview, ISO/IEC JTC1/SC29/WG11 (2000)
28. Maes, P., Shneiderman, B.: Direct Manipulation vs. Interface Agents: a Debate. Interactions, vol. 4(6), ACM Press, New York (1997)
29. McNeill, D.: The Face - A Natural History, Little, Brown and Company (1998)
30. Nakahara, K., Miyashita, Y.: Understanding Intentions. Science 308, 644–645 (2005)
31. Ortony, A., Taylor, T.J.: What's Basic About Emotions. Psychological Review 97, 315–331
32. Panksepp, J.: Toward a General Psychobiological Theory of Emotions. Behavioral and Brain Sciences 5, 405–467
33. Pearl, J.: Probabilistic Reasoning in Intelligent Systems: Networks of Plausible Inference. Morgan Kaufmann, Seattle, Washington, USA (1988)
34. Pentland, A.: Perceptual Intelligence. Comm. of ACM 43(3), 35–44 (2000)
35. Pentland, A.: Socially Aware Computing and Communication. Computer 38(3), 33–40 (2005)
36. Picard, R.: Affective Computing. MIT Press, Cambridge, MA (1998)
37. Salzman, M.C., Dede, C.J., Loftin, R.B., Chen, J.X.: Understanding How Immersive VR Learning Environments Support Learning through Modeling. Presence 8(3), 293–316 (1999)
38. Wechsler, H., Duric, Z., Li, F., Cherkassky, V.: Motion Estimation Using Statistical Learning Theory. IEEE Trans. on Pattern Analysis and Machine Intelligence 26(4), 466–478 (2004)
39. Wechsler, H.: Reliable Face Recognition Systems: System Design, Implementation, and Evaluation. Springer, Heidelberg (2006)

# Interactive Haptic Rendering of High-Resolution Deformable Objects

Nico Galoppo[1], Serhat Tekin[1], Miguel A. Otaduy[2], Markus Gross[2], and Ming C. Lin[1]

[1] Department of Computer Science, University of North Carolina, Chapel Hill, North Carolina, 27599-3175, U.S.A
[2] Computer Graphics Laboratory, ETH Zentrum, Haldeneggsteig 4, CH - 8092 Zurich, Switzerland
{nico, tekin, lin}@cs.unc.edu
{otaduy, grossm}@inf.ethz.ch

**Abstract.** We present an efficient algorithm for haptic rendering of deformable bodies with highly detailed surface geometry using a fast contact handling algorithm. We exploit a layered deformable representation to augment the physically based deformation simulation with efficient collision detection, contact handling and interactive haptic force feedback.

**Keywords:** Haptic Display, Collision Detection, Deformable Models.

## 1 Introduction

Haptic rendering of forces and torques between interacting objects, also known as 6 degree-of-freedom (DoF) haptics [11], has been demonstrated to improve task performance in applications such as molecular docking, nano-manipulation, medical training, and mechanical assembly in virtual prototyping. Haptic display of complex interaction between two deformable models is considered especially challenging, due to the computational complexity involved in computing contact response and performing proximity queries. Such queries include collision detection, separation distance, and penetration depth, between two deformable models at force update rates [11] and [14].

Dynamic contact scenarios arise when objects with rich surface geometry are rubbed against each other while they bounce, roll or slide through the scene. They are computationally costly to simulate in real time and particularly difficult to perform with 6-DoF haptic manipulation. We present an efficient algorithm for 6-DoF haptic rendering of deformable bodies with high-resolution surface geometry using approximate but stable contact forces to achieve interactive haptic force feedback rendering. We propose a two-level layered model representation for deformable objects in the scene to augment a fast physically based deformable model simulator with efficient collision detection, contact handling and stable force feedback rendering.

A fast collision detection module is essential to compute contact force at sufficiently high rates that enable haptic rendering. Our method exploits the layered model representation in a fast image-based collision detection algorithm using parallelized

R. Shumaker (Ed.): Virtual Reality, HCII 2007, LNCS 4563, pp. 215–223, 2007.

operations on graphics hardware, such that the actual cost depends on the size of the contact area, not directly on the resolution of the deformable mesh.

We have developed novel and efficient solutions for contact force computation that interacts with haptic force feedback at haptic update rates in a stable manner using virtual coupling. We demonstrate our haptic rendering algorithm on various scenarios, such as those shown in Fig. 1.

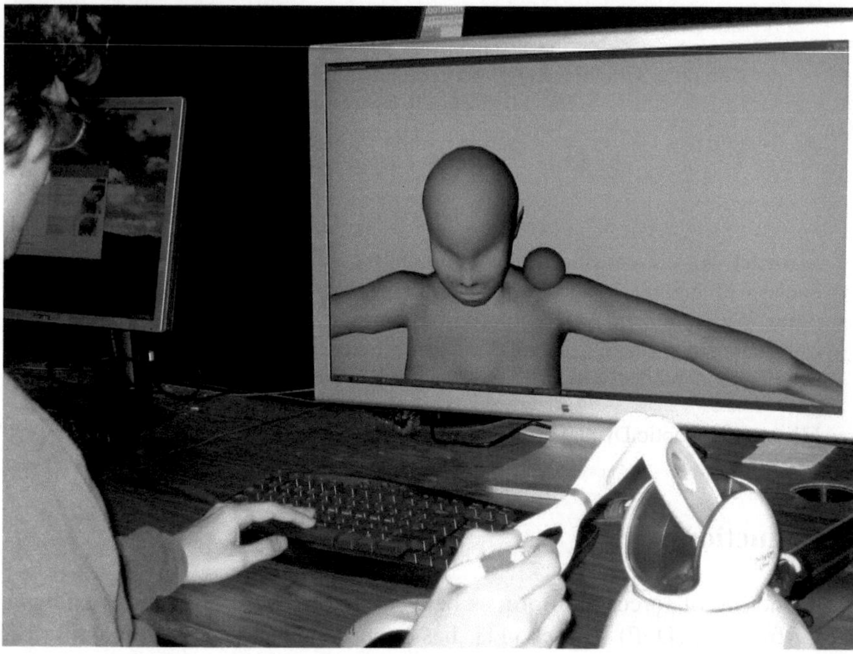

**Fig. 1.** A user interacting with a soft body using a haptic device

The rest of the paper is structured as follows. Section 2 discusses the related work on dynamic simulation and haptic rendering of deformable models. We introduce our novel representation and give an overview of our approach in Section 3. Section 4 presents our proximity query algorithm and Section 5 describes our penalty-based method for rendering collision response. Finally, we show results in Section 6 and conclude with possible future research directions in Section 7.

## 2 Related Work

Physically-based simulation of deformable bodies has been widely studied in computer graphics and haptic rendering during the last two decades [17]. We focus our discussion here on work directly related to our approach.

Continuum mechanics methods are commonly used to simulate deformable objects and some of these methods have been used for haptic rendering or other interactive applications. Some of the examples include linear FEM with matrix condensation [1],

[5], and [6], corotational linear FEM for stable large deformations [12], the boundary element method [9], or quasi nonlinear elasticity with precomputation of response functions [4]. For contact handling, penalty methods are easy to implement but rely on existence of interpenetration and suffer from loss of passivity, although recent local models alleviate the latter problem [10]. Constraint-based methods, which have a higher computational cost but handle nonpenetration accurately, have been applied in a variety of formulations. Cotin et al. [4] applied equality position constraints at contacts, and solved for contact forces using Lagrange multipliers. Duriez et al. [5] and [6] eliminated sticking problems by adopting Signorini's contact model, and formulating a linear complementarity problem (LCP). This approach proves to model contact effectively for deformable bodies, but it is not directly applicable to rigid bodies, because the system may be over-constrained.

## 3 Overview

In this section, we first introduce the representation we use in this work, and then give an overview of our haptic rendering pipeline.

### 3.1 Representations and Key Concepts

Our haptic rendering algorithm exploits the following key concepts:

- A two-level layered model representation for deformable objects, illustrated in Figure 2. The low-resolution proxies are used to accelerate collision detection and haptic force rendering, whereas a high-resolution tetrahedral mesh is used to achieve highly detailed deformations. See Fig. 2 for an example.

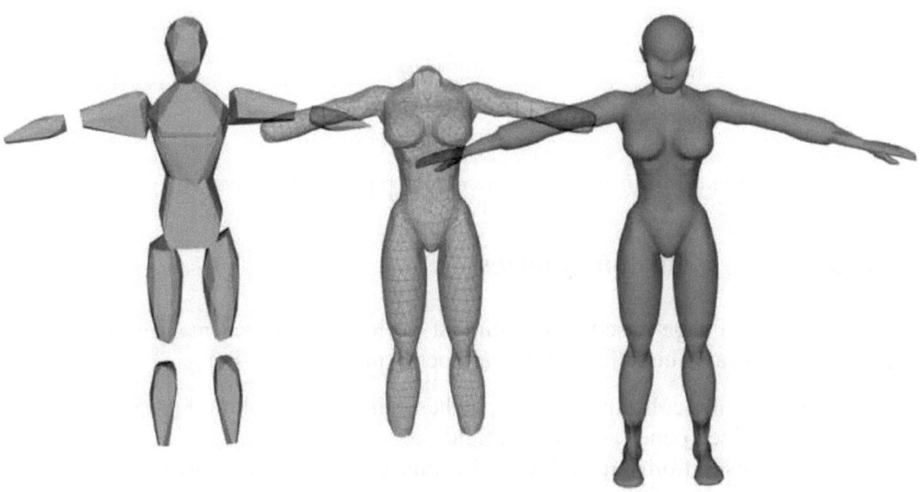

**Fig. 2.** Our layered representation of a human model. In green on the left are low-resolution proxies used for collision detection and haptic interaction; in the middle the deformable tetrahedral mesh; on the right, the highly detailed surface mesh with deformable skin.

- Using a two-stage collision detection algorithm for layered deformable models, our proximity queries are scalable and output-sensitive, i.e. the performance of the queries does not directly depend on the complexity of the surface meshes but rather on the area of the contact patch.
- Using penalty-based collision response, implicit integration of motion equations and virtual coupling of contact forces to the haptic tool, we provide fast and responsive contact handling, alleviating the time-step restrictions of previous impulsive methods.

We simulate the deformable material with a fast rotationally invariant FEM simulator with implicit integration to guarantee stability [12]. Our mathematical formulation of dynamic simulation and contact processing, along with the use of dynamic deformation textures, is especially well suited for realization on commodity SIMD or parallel architectures, such as graphics processing units (GPU), Cell processors, and physics processing units (PPU).

### 3.2 Haptic Rendering Pipeline

We use the haptic rendering pipeline and the multi-rate architecture similar to the one presented by Otaduy and Lin [15], along with virtual coupling introduced by Colgate et al. [2] and [3]. Fig. 3 shows the overall haptic rendering pipeline of our system.

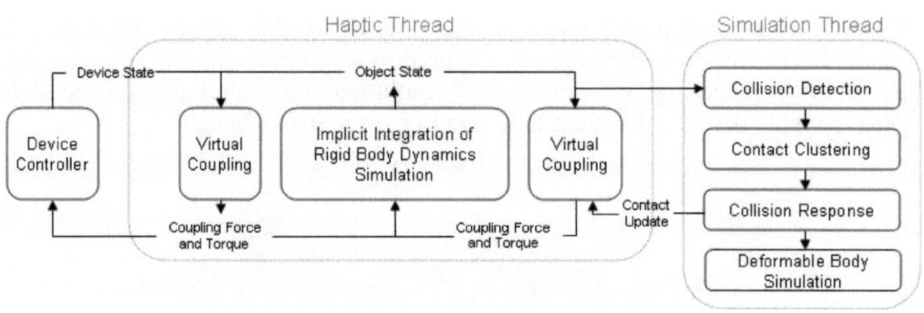


**Fig. 3.** The overall haptic rendering pipeline of our system

## 4 Accelerated Collision Queries

We propose a fast image-based algorithm that exploits our representation of soft characters. Our accelerated collision queries are performed in three steps:

1. Identify potentially colliding contact patches using low-resolution proxies.
2. Compute localized penetration depth fields.
3. Collect high-resolution skin surface collisions and directional penetration depths.

The last two steps are performed using image-space techniques with the aid of graphics hardware, achieving fast collision detection results at haptic update rates. Our method shares the two-step approach of others used for rigid bodies [13] or rigid bodies with a deformable surface layer [8]. But unlike these methods, our collision query algorithm also performs hierarchical pruning to eliminate large portions of the objects from collision queries, by exploiting the skeletal nature of the models. The worst-case cost of our collision detection is $O(n)$ for a pair of tested objects with $n$ surface nodes; the actual cost depends on the size of the contact area.

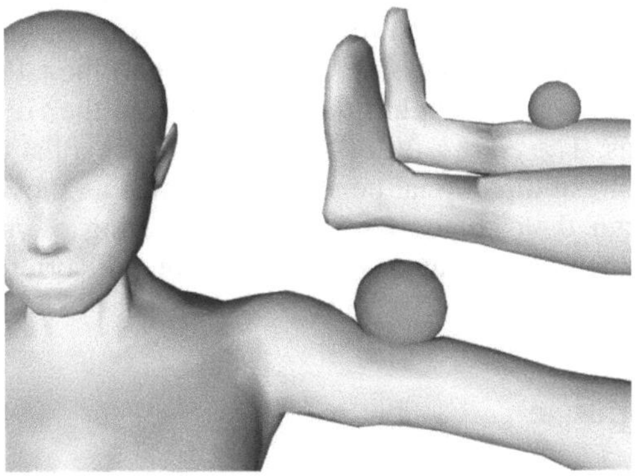

**Fig. 4.** Different collision scenarios with contact response on the human skin model. The contact areas are associated with the low-resolution detected areas in Figure 5.

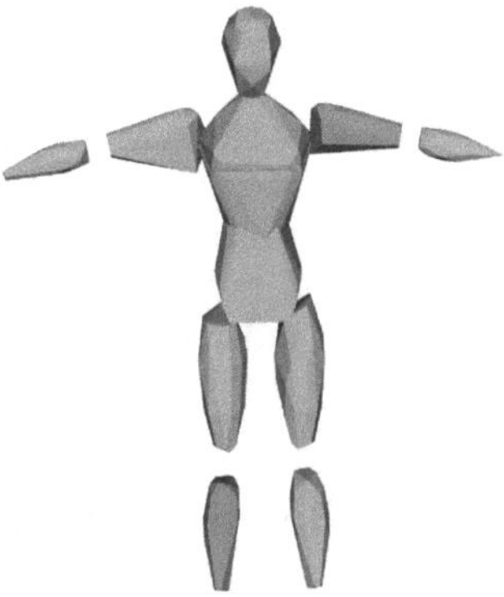

**Fig. 5.** Collision pruning. Only the area around the bone proxies colored in red are considered for high-resolution collision detection.

Our accelerated proximity query algorithm starts by performing object-space collision detection between low-resolution polygonal proxies. In a pre-process, we first perform an approximate convex decomposition of the input models, creating a set of coarse, convex proxies with a few tens of vertices each, as shown in Figure 3. The union of all proxies represents an approximate bounding volume of the model, where each deformable skin vertex is associated with at least one proxy. At runtime we use the maximum skin displacement of all vertices to compute a conservative bound of the proxy. We identify potentially intersecting surface patches and a penetration direction for each contact region, using a fast collision detection algorithm for convex objects [7].

We then refine the query result by considering a localized height-field representation of the deformable geometry parameterized on a 2D domain. We have developed an image-space algorithm for computing directional penetration depth between deformable models that is well suited for parallel implementation on GPUs that achieves fast computation at haptic update rates. We assume that, within regions of contact, the surfaces can be described as height fields. The directional penetration depth can then be defined as the height field difference between the intersecting patches, in the local direction of penetration [13]. Given a contact region between two skin surface patches, we identify a contact plane $D$ as the plane passing between the contact points and oriented according to the contact normal $\mathbf{n}$. In a first pass we rasterize the high-resolution surface geometry using an orthogonal projection $P$ aligned with the normal $\mathbf{n}$ of contact plane $D$ and use a simple fragment program to write out depth to the frame buffer. In the next pass, we subtract the depth, which yields positive values where the patches intersect in the image plane. The resulting localized penetration depth field is stored in the graphics hardware texture memory.

Finally, we check for high-resolution skin surface collisions and collect colliding skin vertices, again with the aid of graphics hardware. For each vertex of the skin mesh, we use the projection matrix associated with $P$ to determine its position in the image plane and read back its penetration depth value from GPU texture memory to the CPU. Note that in practice this last step is performed in a forward algorithm using a fragment program on the GPU, because reading back individual values to the CPU is potentially very slow. Moreover, in this way we exploit the parallelism in the GPU hardware to do the projection transforms. The end result of this final stage is a list of colliding skin vertices, along with their local directional penetration depths, as shown in Figure 4. The penetration depths can then be used for haptic rendering of net reaction forces and torques using a penalty-based approach, which we will briefly describe next.

## 5 Penalty-Based Collision Response

The collision query returns the contact normal and penetration depth for each colliding point while preserving the original high-frequency geometry. As a result, penalty-based collision response forces can be computed on a per point basis. We compute the reaction forces based on a force-displacement relationship between the surface points $s_1$, $s_2$ and the penetration depth $\boldsymbol{\delta}$. A spring of zero rest length is attached between $s_1$, $s_2$ which results in the force $\mathbf{F_p} = -k\,\boldsymbol{\delta}$, where $k$ is the stiffness of the spring. The stability problems introduced by stiff springs can be countered by adding a damping term, which gives $\mathbf{F_p} = -(k\,\boldsymbol{\delta} + d\,\boldsymbol{\delta}')$. Here $d$ is the damping constant and $\boldsymbol{\delta}'$ is the relative velocity in the direction of contact normal. Once given the penetration depth, to compute the force feedback is very fast and takes little time to display the resulting forces and torques to the user.

## 6 Results

We have tested our novel haptic rendering algorithm on deformable models of high complexity (consisting of many tens of thousands of surface elements) with rich surface deformation. The low-resolution proxies are simplified down to a few hundred of triangles, which is roughly the size that can be handled by existing collision detection techniques [14]. In the case of the head model in Fig. 6, which has 44,000 deformable vertices, we were able to obtain per-vertex penetration depth information within 2 msec for touching one and within 6 msec for two of them in contact. The gear model in Fig. 7 has 29,000 vertices each and takes about 3 msec for two gears in contact to compute the penetration depth between them. The pumpkin model (Fig. 8) consists of 30,000 vertices each and also takes roughly 3 msec to perform the proximity queries between two such models in contact. These timings include the transfer of the contact information to the deformation domain, where it is directly available for dynamics computation.

**Fig. 6.** Models used for benchmarking collision detection performance. Shown are a head model, a pumpkin model and a deformable gear with respectively 44K, 30K and 29K vertices.

Using our scalable and output-sensitive collision detection algorithm, we compute object penetration depth that captures the original high-frequency geometry, and we then display dynamic effects due to surface deformation that would otherwise be missed, such as the deformation on the bottom of the pumpkins and the dynamic rolling behavior of the gears due to the deformation of its teeth.

In Fig. 1, we show a scene where the user uses a haptic device, PHANTOM 1.5, to push a human body model with high-resolution features on its surfaces. This model consists of 3563 vertices and 10,340 tetrahedral elements (see Fig. 2, 4, and 5). Figure 7 shows two more screenshots of the user touching the model's upper leg and its arm/shoulder respectively. The proximity queries for haptic rendering take less than 2 msec on this model. All contacts on the surface have global effect on the entire deformable layer, they are processed simultaneously and robustly. Without any precomputation

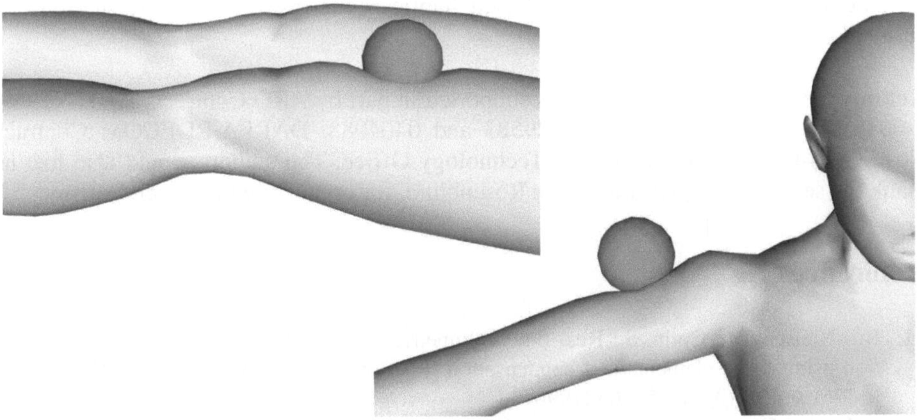

**Fig. 7.** The haptic tool (the green sphere) is in continuous contact with the human skin. Our algorithm computes skin deformation and force feedback to the user at interactive rates.

of dynamics or significant storage requirement, we were able to haptically render the human model and other benchmarks shown in this paper at interactive rates, on a 3.2 GHz Pentium 4 PC with NVidia GeForce 7800.

Our approach is considerably faster than other methods that enable large time steps, such as those that focus on the surface deformation [1] and corotational methods that compute deformations within the entire volume [12], with more stable collision response. Our approach can also handle many more contact points than novel quasi-rigid dynamics algorithms using LCP [16], while producing richer deformations for haptic rendering.

## 7 Conclusion and Future Work

We have presented an interactive 6-DoF haptic rendering algorithm for deformable bodies with high-resolution surface geometry and large contact regions. We have overcome the computational challenges of this problem by adapting a novel layered representation of deformable models where physically based deformation and haptic force feedback are computed in a multi-level algorithm. Based on this representation, we have also presented efficient collision detection which enables fast contact response for haptic manipulation of deformable models.

The use of a layered representation obviously poses some limitations on the type of deformations that can be modeled, but they are well suited for many real-world models, such as human bodies and soft objects that deform up to 30-40% of its radius. Our representation can be extended to articulated, flexible bodies that undergo skeletal deformations, by augmenting the generalized coordinate set of the core representation to include multi-body systems.

We plan to apply our algorithm and representation to the simulation of virtual human with skeletal control and plausible collision avoidance. Further optimizations of the algorithm and the steady growth of parallel processors offer possibilities for interactive, detailed physically-based haptic rendering of skin deformations in surgical simulator.

**Acknowledgements.** This work was supported in part by ARO Contracts W911NF-04-1-0088, NSF awards 0400134, 0429583 and 0404088, DARPA/RDECOM Contract N61339-04-C-0043 and Disruptive Technology Office. The authors would also like to thank the session chair, Dr. Lawrence Rosenblum, for organizing this special session.

## References

1. Bro-Nielsen, M., Cotin, S.: Real-time volumetric deformable models for surgery simulation using finite elements and condensation. In: Computer Graphics Forum, (Eurographics'96), vol. 15(3), pp. 57–66 (1996)
2. Colgate, J.E., Brown, J.M.: Factors affecting the z-width of a haptic display. In: IEEE International Conference on Robotics and Automation, pp. 3205–3210 (1994)
3. Colgate, J.E., Stanley, M.C., Brown, J.M.: Issues in the haptic display of tool use. In: Proc. of IEEE/RSJ International Conference on Intelligent Robots and Systems, pp. 140–145 (1995)

4. Cotin, S., Delingette, H., Ayache, N.: Realtime elastic deformation of soft tissues for surgery simulation. IEEE Trans. on Visualization and Computer Graphics, vol. 5(1) (1999)
5. Duriez, C., Andriot, C., Kheddar, A.: A multithreaded approach for deformable/rigid contacts with haptic feedback. In: Proc. of Haptics Symposium (2004)
6. Duriez, C., Dubois, F., Kheddar, A., Andriot, C.: Realistic haptic rendering of interacting deformable objects in virtual environments. Proc. of IEEE TVCG, 12(1) (2006)
7. Ehmann, S.A., Lin, M.C.: Accelerated proximity queries between convex polyhedra by multi-level Voronoi marching. In: Proc. of International Conference on Intelligent Robots and Systems (2000)
8. Galoppo, N., Otaduy, M.A., Mecklenburg, P., Gross, M., Lin, M.C.: Fast simulation of deformable models in contact using dynamic deformation textures. In: Proc. of ACM SIGGRAPH/Eurographics Symposium on Computer Animation, pp. 73–82 (2006)
9. James, D.L., Pai, D.K.: Artdefo: Accurate real time deformable objects. Proc. of ACM SIGGRAPH (1999)
10. Mahvash, M., Hayward, V.: High-fidelity passive force-reflecting virtual environments. IEEE Transactions on Robotics 21(1), 38–46 (2005)
11. McNeely, W., Puterbaugh, K., Troy, J.: Six degree-of freedom haptic rendering using voxel sampling. Proc. of ACM SIGGRAPH, pp. 401–408 (1999)
12. Muller, M., Dorsey, J., McMillan, L., Jagnow, R., Cutler, B.: Stable real-time deformations. In: Proc. of ACM SIGGRAPH Symposium on Computer Animation (2002)
13. Otaduy, M.A., Jain, N., Sud, A., Lin, M.C.: Haptic display of interaction between textured models. In: Proc. of IEEE Visualization (2004)
14. Otaduy, M.A., Lin, M.C.: Sensation preserving simplification for haptic rendering. In: Proc. of ACM SIGGRAPH, pp. 543–553 (2003)
15. Otaduy, M.A., Lin, M.C.: Stable and responsive six degree-of-freedom haptic manipulation using implicit integration. In: Proc. of World Haptics Conference (2005)
16. Pauly, M., Pai, D.K., Guibas, L.J.: Quasirigid objects in contact. In: Proc. of ACM SIGGRAPH/Eurographics Symposium on Computer Animation (2004)
17. Terzopoulos, D., Witkin, A.: Physically based models with rigid and deformable components. IEEE Computer Graphics and Applications 8(6) (1988)

# Collaborative Virtual Environments: You Can't Do It Alone, Can You?

Arturo S. García, Diego Martínez, José P. Molina, and Pascual González

LoUISE Research Group
Instituto de Investigación en Informática de Albacete, Universidad de Castilla-La Mancha
Campus Universitario, Avda. España s/n, 02071 Albacete (Spain)
{arturo, diegomp1982, jpmolina, pgonzalez}@dsi.uclm.es

**Abstract.** Many Collaborative Virtual Environments (CVEs) have been developed to date. However, when focusing our attention on the way users perform their task in these systems, there is still little research on understanding the impact of different platforms on the collaboration experience. This paper describes not only a CVE, in this case, one that reproduces a block building game; but also an experiment that was carried out to evaluate both the interaction using different input and output technologies and the impact of collaboration on task performance and overall experience.

**Keywords:** Virtual Reality, Collaboration, Performance.

## 1 Introduction

Virtual Reality (VR) is usually related to technologies such as three-dimensional graphics, touch and force feedback, and spatialized sound. VR developers use all those technologies trying to achieve one common aim, which is to make users experience the Virtual Environment (VE) as a real one. If that environment is meant for multiple users joining the virtual space from different physical locations, for the purpose of a particular task or just to serve as a social meeting place, there is one more technology that gets involved: computer networks.

Nowadays, there is a common agreement that using computers to connect people together and allow them to collaborate is a must, having the potential in communication that computer networks and specially Internet provide. The technology has been successfully applied to the field of individual work, as most of the current applications are focussed on a single user that, in general, produce a result or reach a goal. At present, the research community is trying to change this limited focus, so that several users can use one application at the same time, in other words, participate simultaneously in the production of a result or collaborate to reach a goal. An example of this is the design of a 3D model of a single piece or a whole environment, which is usually tackled by a single engineer or artist using their CAD/CAM or 3D authoring tool, but now it is possible to work together with other people, collaborating in its realization, as in [1].

R. Shumaker (Ed.): Virtual Reality, HCII 2007, LNCS 4563, pp. 224–233, 2007.

On the other hand, VR seems to be suitable to simulate a virtual space where tasks take place and where people, even geographically distributed, collaborate to reach a common goal. This leads to a definition of Collaborative Virtual Environments (CVEs) that is concise, clear and widely accepted [2]: *CVEs are a form of telecommunication technology that bring together co-located or remote, participants within a spatial social and information context.*

In this context, this paper describes an educational and collaborative building game and its evaluation. Even though other similar systems can be found in the bibliography [3][4][5], none of these ones tackles the problem as the reproduction of a real game, but as a puzzle similar to the Rubik's cube, Heldal et al. 2005 [3]; as the building of a gazebo, Roberts et al. 2003[4]; or as a two-handed 3D modeller, Kiyokawa et al. 1996 [5].

Besides, focusing our attention on the way users perform their task in these systems, there is still little research on understanding the impact of different platforms on the collaboration experience –see, for instance, Heldal et al. 2005 [3]-. However, it is even more difficult to find studies which compare individual versus collaborative performance on the same task. Ruddle et al. 2002 [6], focused on cooperative manipulation, and Hendal et al. 2006 [7], continuing the work done in [3], may be the only published works on this regard. However, as these last studies are focused on only one task, there is a question how general the findings are. For that reason, we aim to study collaboration when performing different tasks in different situations and to compare the results with the ones obtained from performing the same tasks in the same situations by an individual user, and even to compare those results with the real physical game.

This paper is organized as follows: firstly, section 1.1 shows an introduction to the topic of the CVE developed, and section 2 gives a brief description of its architecture; after that, section 3 describes the evaluation carried out; finally, section 4 shows the results of that evaluation.

### 1.1 VRPrismaker

Education usually relies on games, and many games are considered to be not merely entertainment but pedagogical tools. Games usually imply several participants, sometimes as opponents, in other cases as members of the same team that collaborate to achieve a common goal. Education and entertainment, often referred as edutainment, are then fields where collaboration can be studied and, considering the application of VR to them, they also allow to study collaboration in CVEs. One of those games is Prismaker, a game designed for children over three years old, consisting of several types of blocks with which different models can be built.

As part of two previous projects, our research group carried out the implementation of two different computer versions of this game. The first of them was a desktop application that was written in Java3D. The second one [8] was similar to the previous one, but this time the environment was completely immersive. However, none of these two previous versions allowed to study Prismaker as a game where several people can collaborate, simultaneously, to build a model, as both applications were single-user. Thus, a third project was proposed to obtain, based on the code written for the immersive version, a CVE in which several participants can join the game and play together, some of them wearing helmets and gloves, and others using a standard desktop. This CVE is described in the following section.

## 2 CVRPrismaker

*Collaborative Virtual Reality Prismaker* (CVRPrismaker) is a CVE developed as an experimental platform where collaboration in cyberspace can be studied and compared to collaboration in real places. Focus is then on communication and interaction between subjects, but also on interaction with the models and the computer itself, and how all these factors have an impact on collaboration.

The immersive version of Prismaker tried to replicate precisely the interaction of the real game, in other words, by means of a tracking system and a pair of data-gloves the user can use his or her own hands to build models by grabbing, assembling and dropping blocks using several gestures.

In this case, the user can basically perform two actions: pick up an object and drop an object. Performing an action in different places of the scene may result in a different outcome (for example, dropping a block on another one will join them and dropping it on another point of the space will make the block stay in that position). Therefore, the system takes into account not only the action that the user carries out, but also the context in which it is carried out.

Since one of the objectives of this project was to get insight into the interaction within these systems, it was also developed another version that made use of a conventional desktop system, but with adapted interaction to overcome the limitations of this platform (for example, restricting the rotations to 90 degrees).

### 2.1 Description of the Collaborative System

The most important aspects that define a collaborative system are the following:

*Collaboration*: Users of CVRPrismaker are able to work following different strategies, from splitting the models to building in separate parts and joining them later, working by turns or even simultaneously on the same model. Therefore, the strategy of collaboration is freely decided by users while using the system.

*Communication*: There are two types of communication in the system. As regards to the communication between users, it was thought that voice communication was the more important mean of communication in this system. Although in this first development the users shared the same space, and so they can speak freely, in the future it is planned to make use of voice transmission through the network.

To solve the problem of the communication between collaborative systems, it was chosen a moderator that controlled the actions carried out by the clients. With this moderator and its set of clients, the system turns to be a client-server architecture.

*Information Sharing*: Another important issue of every collaborative system is the information sharing between users. In CVRPismaker, users share the blocks they are using to build models, and the model they are building. Thus, the user's awareness of the state of the world becomes one of the main concerns. More precisely, it is important to be aware of the position of the other users' hands, as well as what model is building. In order to do so, the users must be placed in the right position so that they are able to see their partner, as well as to locate them in the 3D space.

## 2.2 Network

There are several options to consider when choosing the appropriate architecture for a CVE, from client-server, to peer-to-peer, or even more complex hybrid models [9]. Among them, a client-server architecture was chosen for implementing CVRPrismaker. In this system, the server is responsible for managing the incoming connections and ensuring the consistency of the data over the network. The server, however, does not store a copy of the scene model. Instead, each client keeps its own copy, which is modified according to the update messages sent by the server.

The server acts then as a moderator in the working group and resolves, in real time, the conflictive situations that arise between users, such as ownership of objects, making their collaboration possible.

## 2.3 Consistency and Synchronization

Each object of the virtual world has a unique identifier. This identifier is generated by the server and allows clients to reference objects in a non-ambiguous way. Furthermore, each client also keeps its own client identifier.

To keep consistency, each client sends an interaction request each time a virtual action on an object happens. If the objects are not already locked, the server will lock them. This exclusion over the objects is held until the interaction ends, which avoids conflicts as it is impossible to produce two different actions over the same object at the same time.

To keep all the clients synchronized, for each interaction request received that can be satisfied, the server sends an interaction acknowledgement to each client indicating the objects taking part and the necessary data. This way, each change in the state of the world happens in the same order and with the same data in all the clients.

## 2.4 Hardware and Software Platforms

For the development of this system, an immersive VR setup was used. It was composed of a HP Compaq XW6000/PL station (dual 2.4GHz Intel Xeon, 512 MB, 3Dlabs Wildcat III 6110), an Ascension Flock of Birds tracking system with three trackers, a pair of Fakespace Pinch Gloves and a ProView XL35 stereoscopic head mounted device (Fig. 1a and 1b).

For the desktop system, a HP Compaq XW4000 (P4 2.4 GHz Intel, 512 MB, NVIDIA Quadro4 900 XGL) station was used with a conventional mouse, desktop and keyboard (Fig. 1c). Some keys of the keyboard were labelled with symbols representing its associated function, to make it easier for the user to use (Fig. 1d).

As regards the software platform chosen, the development of the system mostly relied on VRJuggler [10], mainly because its easy management of hardware devices. Regarding the graphics API, OpenGL was selected as it is a standard supported by many different platforms. The VRML/X3D file format is used to store the scene model, the user-built models and the users' avatars. Finally, a free and widely used library for network games, Raknet (by Rakkarsoft [11]), was selected for the transmission of data over the network.

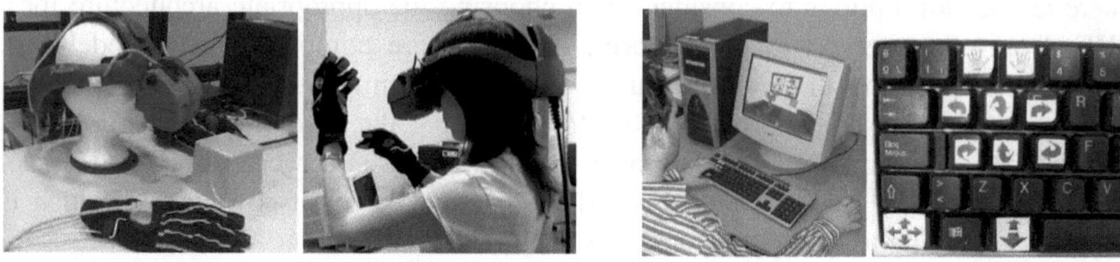

(a) (b) (c) (d)

**Fig. 1.** Hardware used in the immersive (a-b) and desktop configuration (c-d)

# 3 Evaluation

This section describes the experiment that has been carried out as a first approach to the evaluation of some parameters in this kind of systems. With this experiment, we want to evaluate not only the usability of different input technologies but also the performance of the different platform configurations. This way, it is not only our interest to test an immersive platform, but also to check if a desktop-based system is also useful as a platform for a CVE. The satisfaction of the users taking part in the evaluation was also taken into account.

Obviously, it was also our purpose to evaluate the performance of the system in each different platform in terms of collaboration support. To get insight into all these issues, it was decided to carry out an experiment that allowed us to test the following hypothesis: Collaborative work is more efficient than individual work.

## 3.1 Description of the Experiment

In order to verify the initial hypothesis, an evaluation with real users was designed. In this experiment, a set of independent participants passed through several tasks, and the time taken to fulfil each task was annotated.

The participants built two different models. These models where designed with collaboration in mind, so that one of them was difficult to divide and the other one had easily distinguishable subparts. Fig. 2 shows the instructions given to the participants to help them in their tasks.

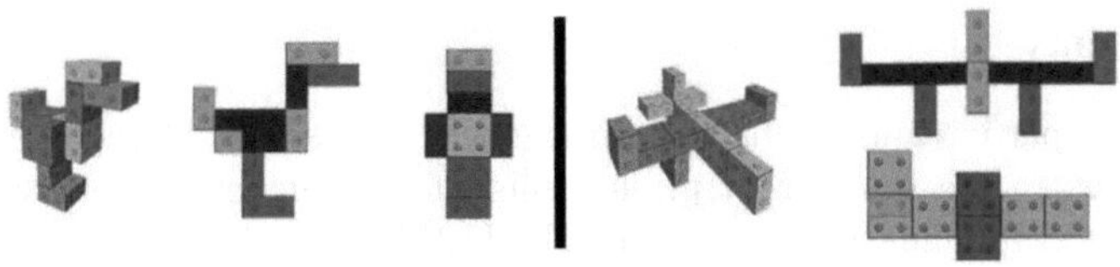

**Fig. 2.** Instructions given to users

As measuring the performance at different platforms was one of the objectives of the experiment, the participants had to fulfil their tasks using the real game, the desktop based system and the immersive one. There was only one immersive system available for this experiment, and so the combination of the platforms used by each couple is the one shown in table 1.

**Table 1.** Tests done by each participant

| *Individual Tasks* | *Collaborative Tasks* |
|---|---|
| Real (R) | Real – Real (R-R) |
| Desktop system (D) | Desktop – Desktop (D-D) |
| Immersive System (I) | Immersive – Desktop (I-D) |
| | Desktop – Immersive (D-I) |

As a result, each participant completed 3 x 2 = 6 individual tasks (3 platforms x 2 models) and 4 x 2 = 8 collaborative tasks (4 platforms x 2 models). When designing the tests, the order in which each task was taken was modified so that some users started with the individual tasks and others with the collaborative ones. This was done so to avoid any influence of learning on the measures related to performance.

### 3.2 Virtual Environment

The VE (Fig. 3) consists of a 3x2m room where the following objects can be found: Blocks (basic units used to build models), Boxes (place where the user can get new blocks), Table (place to build the models on), Shelves (place to store user-created models), and Picture (instructions of how to build two test models).

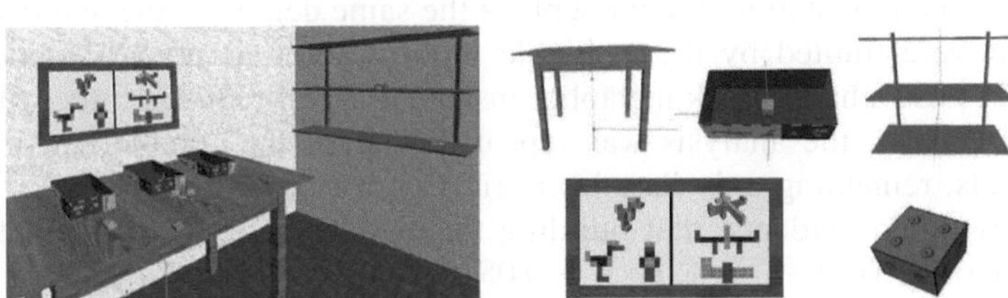

**Fig. 3.** The virtual room and the elements it comprises

### 3.3 Participants

The number of participants in the experiment was 18 people, 11 men and 7 women. The differences in the number of participants of each gender, as shown in former experiments, was thought to not affect results [12].Finally the age of the participants was varied from 19 to 31 years old.

## 4 Results and Analysis

In order to analyze the data gathered during the experiment, different ANOVA (*ANalysis Of VAriance*) were carried out to confirm if the differences observed in data were significant or not, in particular when any of the tests previously described was performed in less time than the rest, and more specially when that test was carried out in pairs.

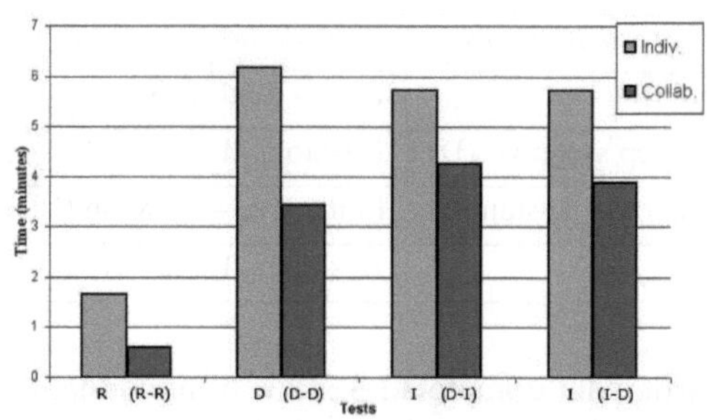


**Fig. 4.** This bar chart shows mean completion times for the first object (Duck)

After performing ANOVA with the selected data, the result of the analysis showed that completion times were not independent from the platform used, whether real or virtual, individual or collaborative, as $F(6,42) = 21.94$; $p < 0.05$ for the first object –the duck-, and $F(6,42)=7.54$ ; $p < 0.05$ for the second object –the airplane-. Having a look at the bar charts shown in Fig. 4 and Fig. 5, it can be clearly stated that there is one platform that outstands from the others, as the average time took by users using the real game (R, as single user, and R-R, working in pairs) is less than using any VE. This means that, even though we tried to reproduce in the VE the naturalness of the real game, the implementation did not achieve the same degree as the real one, mostly because they were limited by the available input devices as regards manipulation, which forced to use a hand-block metaphor instead of a full-realistic finger-block one.

After this finding, the analysis was repeated without the completion times from real game trials, remaining only data from trials performed with the VEs. This time, ANOVA showed no evidence that building the first object was different from one platform to another ($F(4,30) = 1.08$; $p > 0.05$), even though the completion times in collaborative tests were slightly lower. However, this was not the case for the second object, for which ANOVA showed that there was a significant difference in time ($F(4,30) = 3.15$; $p < 0.05$). This outcome confirmed our expectations when designing the experiment and choosing the two objects to build, as the first one –the duck- was supposed to be difficult to split in parts that could be completed by pairs of participants in parallel, so it was not expected any significant improvement in time when performing the task in pairs. On the other hand, the second object –the airplane- was thought to be easier to divide in smaller objects which could be build by a different participant of each pair, and then put all them together, so some improvement in time was expected in comparison with single user trials.

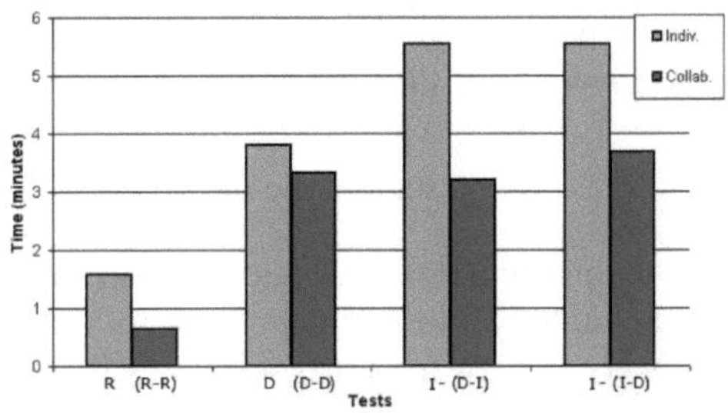


**Fig. 5.** This bar chart shows mean completion times for the second object (Airplane)

Finally, the analysis was repeated once again without the completion times from individual tests, so that only collaborative tests in VEs were taken into account this time, using ANOVA to check if any particular pair of platforms performed better than the others. This time, the results for the duck model ($F(2,18) = 0.91$; $p > 0.05$) and for the airplane model ($F(2,18) = 0.27$; $p > 0.05$) showed no evidence of significant difference in data gathered for each pair of platforms. This means that performance in collaboration does not depend on platforms but on the models to build, as stated before. However, these results may be a consequence of the presence of the desktop platform in every pair, lacking this study of completion times when performing the tasks in a pair of immersive environments. Better completion times may be expected if tested with this combination, as a better perception of the space seems to make manipulation easier in comparison to the desktop setup, mostly as the third dimension is concerned, which causes problems to desktop users.

**Table 2.** Ease of use of each setup, as perceived by participants

| *Single user* | *Score* | | | | | *Avg.* | *Collaborative* | *Score* | | | | | *Avg.* |
|---|---|---|---|---|---|---|---|---|---|---|---|---|---|
| | 1 | 2 | 3 | 4 | 5 | | | 1 | 2 | 3 | 4 | 5 | |
| Real (R) | 6 | 4 | | | | 1.4 | Real– Real (R-R) | 10 | | | | | 1.0 |
| Desktop (D) | 1 | 3 | 5 | 1 | | 2.6 | Desktop – Desktop (D-D) | 3 | 5 | 2 | | | 1.9 |
| Immersive (I) | 1 | 1 | 3 | 3 | 2 | 3.4 | Desktop – Immersive (D-I) | 5 | 1 | 3 | 1 | | 2.0 |
| | | | | | | | Immersive – Desktop (I-D) | 2 | 3 | 2 | 3 | | 2.6 |

In addition to completion times gathered from the trials, each participant filled in a questionnaire, answering some questions about their own experience when using each platform, a questionnaire that was designed to get insight into the problems each user may have faced when using each platform, and whether they preferred to work alone or collaborate in pairs.

Table 2 shows the scores given by users as regards the operation of each platform in particular. In the questionnaire, they were asked to mark, with a number from 1 to 5, the perceived ease of use of the platform, bearing in mind that a value of 1 meant it was easy to use, and a value of 5 meant that it was difficult to use. At the end of each row in the table, it is shown the average score for the corresponding setup, computed by summing all scores given and then dividing them by the total number of participants. For instance, the average score for the (D-I) setup is $\frac{1\times5+2\times1+3\times3+4\times1}{10}=2.0$, as can be seen in the table.

As it can be expected, the participants gave better marks to the real game, as it was not hampered by input technology. Surprisingly enough, the desktop is the second most valued system by users, which in turns makes it also the preferred VE when collaborating with other users. This may be caused by the way rotations were performed in the desktop environment, not as smooth as in the immersive environment but in successive amounts of 90 degrees, which was introduced to facilitate the task to users. Following that finding, it can be observed that the combination desktop-immersive systems is the third most valued. As the desktop was found easier to use by single users, this result is not surprising, as it gives us the perception of the user from the desktop side of the coupled systems, no matter which platform used the other participant.

In the questionnaire given to participants, there was also a blank space for them to express their thoughts regarding the collaboration with their mate in trials. Only one of them complained about being hindered by the other user, the rest of them used that blank space to suggest improvements to the system, and to comment about the operation of the input and output devices. Regarding the immersive system, some of the participants complained about the amount of wires around them, as well as the weight of the helmet and the fatigue it caused to them. As for the desktop system, the comments were related to problems when perceiving the third dimension (moving blocks further or closer), which may have been solved by using stereo graphics, not used in this experiment.

## 5 Conclusions and Future Work

In this paper, it has been described a CVE that reproduces a block building game, a system that has been named CVRPrismaker. Besides, it has also been described an experimental evaluation of the VE in different setups, real and virtual, individual and collaborative, and the results of that experiment have been presented and analyzed.

As the most important conclusion, this evaluation has showed significant differences in performance depending on the task, which should be taken into account by designers when assessing the suitability of collaborative systems. This result has been confirmed using different ANOVA studies, which have also shown that users collaborating in the VE employed less time than performing the tasks in an individual way. Another conclusion of the evaluation is that the VE can be experienced using immersive devices as gloves and goggles as well as conventional devices such as mouse and keyboard, resulting in similar outcomes.

As a future work, it is planned to carry out a new evaluation using immersive systems at both ends of the collaborative system, and also study collaboration in Internet as opposed to a local network. Both issues are currently under development.

**Acknowledgments.** This work has been partially supported by the Ministerio of Educación y Ciencia of Spain (CICYT TIN2004-08000-C03-01), and by the Junta de Comunidades de Castilla-La Mancha (PAI06-0093).

## References

1. Caligary TrueSpace 7 (Last visit 09-02-07) http://www.caligari.com/
2. Roberts, D., Wolff, R.: Controlling Consistency within Collaborative Virtual Environments. In: 8th IEEE International Symposium on Distributed Simulation and Real Time Applications DS-RT, Budapest (2004)
3. Heldal, I., Steed, A., Schroeder, R.: Evaluating Collaboration in Distributed Virtual Environments for a Puzzle-solving Task. In: HCI International 2005, the 11th International Conference on Human Computer Interaction. Las Vegas (2005)
4. Roberts, D., Wolff, R., Otto, O., Steed, A.: Constructing a Gazebo: Supporting Teamwork in a Tightly Coupled, Distributed Task in Virtual Reality. Presence: Teleoperators and Virtual Environments 16(6), 644–657 (2003)
5. Kiyokawa, K., et al.: VLEGO: A Simple Two-Handed Modeling Environment Based on Toy Blocks. In: Proc. ACM Virtual Reality Software and Technology, pp. 27–34 (1996)
6. Ruddle, R.A., Savage, J.C.D., Jones, D.M.: Symmetric and Asymmetric Action Integration During Cooperative Object Manipulation in Virtual Environments. ACM Transactions on Computer-Human Interaction 9(4), 285–308 (2002)
7. Heldal, I., Spante, M., Connel, M.: Are Two Heads Better than One? Object-focused Work in Physical and in Virtual Environments. In: 13th ACM Symposium on Virtual Reality Software and Technology (VRST 2006), Cyprus (2006)
8. Molina, J.P., García, A.S., Martínez, D., Manjavacas, F.J., Blasco, V., López, V., González P.: The development of glove-based interfaces with the TRES-D methodology. In: 13th ACM Symposium on Virtual Reality Software and Technology (VRST). Cyprus, pp. 216–219 (2006)
9. Singhal, S., Zyda, M.: Networked Virtual Environments: Design and Implementation. Addison Wesley, London, UK (1999)
10. Juggler,VR.: (Last visit 09-02-07) http://www.vrjuggler.org/
11. Rakkarsoft.: Raknet. (Last visit 09-02-07) http://www.rakkarsoft.com/
12. García, A.S., Molina, J.P., González, P.: Exemplar VE design guidance tool for selection and manipulation interaction techniques. In: HCI International 2005, the 11th International Conference on Human Computer Interaction, Las Vegas (2005)

# Development of Wide-Area Tracking System for Augmented Reality

Hirotake Ishii, Hidenori Fujino, Bian Zhiqiang, Tomoki Sekiyama, Toshinori Nakai, and Hiroshi Shimoda

Graduate School of Energy Science, Kyoto University,
611-0011 Kyoto, Japan
{hirotake, fujino, bianzq, sekiyama, nakai, shimoda}@uji.energy.kyoto-u.ac.jp

**Abstract.** In this study, two types of marker-based tracking systems for Augmented Reality were developed: a tracking system using line markers and a tracking system using circular markers. Both markers were designed for use inside buildings such as nuclear power plants, which are very complicated and in which it is difficult to paste many large markers. To enlarge the area in which tracking is available using only a limited number of markers, a hybrid tracking method and a two-layer tracking method were also developed. The experimental evaluation shows that both methods can increase the available area compared to legacy methods such as single-camera tracking and simple square markers.

**Keywords:** Augmented reality, Marker-based tracking, Wide area tracking.

## 1 Introduction

A promising application of Augmented Reality (AR) is the maintenance support of large plants such as nuclear power plants and chemical plants. The safety and efficiency of the maintenance work can be improved by applying AR, for example, by navigating workers toward their work place and indicating dangerous locations [1]. To apply AR to such maintenance support tasks, some improvements of tracking technology that measures the user's viewing position and orientation in real time are necessary because existing tracking technologies are affected easily by metal, magnetic fields, and sounds, and therefore cannot be used in the plants. The authors, therefore, designed two types of fiducial markers and developed algorithms to recognize them on camera images using image-processing techniques and those results are used for tracking [2]. Using the newly designed markers and algorithms, it became possible to execute tracking inside the plant buildings both stably and accurately. Nevertheless, a persistent problem is that many markers must be pasted and their positions must be measured in advance to execute tracking in a wide area. Preparation of the markers is too burdensome for practical use. In this study, therefore, a hybrid tracking method and a two-layer tracking method were developed to enlarge the area in which tracking can be done using only small number of markers.

R. Shumaker (Ed.): Virtual Reality, HCII 2007, LNCS 4563, pp. 234–243, 2007.

# 2 Tracking Method Using Line Markers

## 2.1 Design of Line Marker and Tracking Algorithm

A typical marker tracking method is ARToolKit [3]. However, ARToolKit can recognize a marker only when the distance between the marker and the camera is very short. We must use very large markers when we want to use ARToolKit on the condition that the distance between the markers and the camera is very long. Unfortunately, it is difficult to paste large square markers inside buildings such as nuclear power plants because many instruments are installed inside such buildings: few large spaces can be used for the markers. However, many pipes with thin rectangular surfaces exist in nuclear power plants and chemical plants. The authors considered that these surfaces are useful for pasting the markers and designed line-shaped markers as shown in Fig. 1. The line marker is a combination of black elements: each element corresponds to one bit. The square element signifies "0". The double-sized rectangle element denotes "1". The total number of elements is 11. Therefore, one line marker can express an 11-bit code. Of its 11 bits, 7 express the ID, whereas the remaining 4 bits are the Hamming code. Using this coding method, 128 kinds of line markers can be made with arbitrary one-bit error correction. The shape of the line marker is almost a single *line*. Consequently, it is easy to paste them on the pipes that are ubiquitous in the plants. Details of how to recognize the markers on images captured by a camera are described in the literature [2].

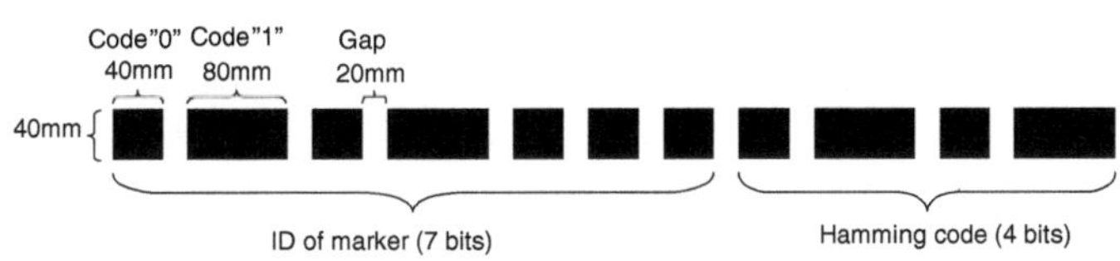


**Fig. 1.** Line marker design

To obtain a unique solution of the relative position and orientation between the camera and the markers, at least four feature points must be recognized on the camera image. These feature points must not be on the same line and the accuracy depends on the distances between the feature points. Therefore, the authors decided to obtain two feature points from each line marker (two terminals of the line marker), so that at least two line markers must be recognized on the camera image simultaneously.

The P3P solution algorithm and nonlinear algorithm are adopted to calculate the relative position and orientation from *n* feature points and minimize the error between the estimated position of the four feature points calculated using the tracking result and the actual position on the camera image.

## 2.2 Performance Evaluation of Line Marker

A laboratory experiment was conducted to evaluate the maximum detection distance and the accuracy of the developed methods. Six line-code markers of about 50 cm were pasted in a room (10 m × 20 m), as shown in Fig. 2. Then the camera was moved in the room with 1 m steps. The estimated and actual positions and orientations of the camera were compared.

Figure 3 shows the estimated camera position error. The maximum detection distance at which the markers were recognized without any failure was about 11 m and the maximum distance with some recognition failure was about 17 m under the condition that an XGA black-and-white camera with 6.37 mm focal length lens was used. About 96% of the tracking was executed with less than 30 cm position errors when the markers were recognized without any failure.

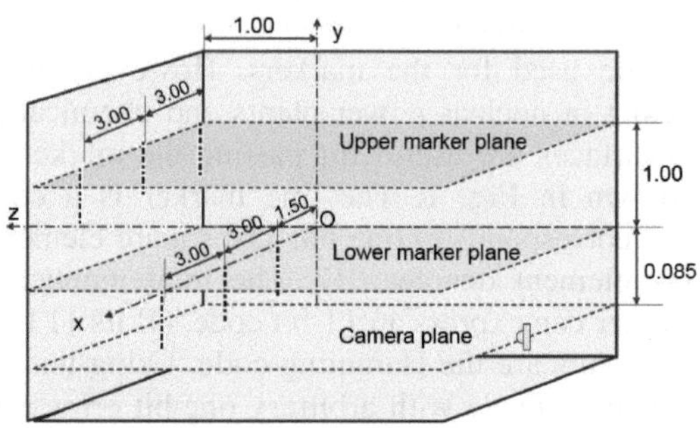


**Fig. 2.** Experimental Setup (Unit: m)

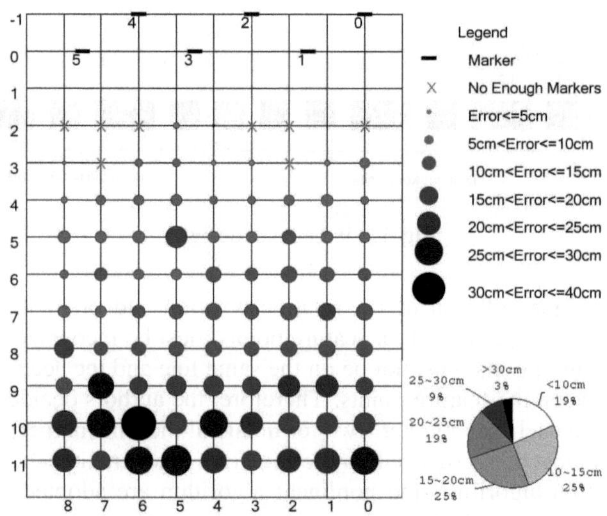


**Fig. 3.** Estimated camera position error

## 2.3 Development of Hybrid Tracking Method

The tracking method described in 2.1 and 2.2 is useful at a longer distance than a legacy tracking method like ARToolKit; moreover, it uses very slim markers that can be pasted easily inside a complicated structure. However, to execute tracking, at least two line markers must be captured by a camera (in the case of ARToolKit, one marker is sufficient for tracking). Therefore, the number of line markers that must be pasted in the working environment is much larger than the case of ARToolKit. One candidate to solve this problem might be the use of a wide-angle camera that can capture wide angle images that include more markers. But the resolution of the images captured with a wide angle camera becomes very low and the distortion of the images also becomes very large. This might decrease the maximum detection distance and the tracking accuracy.

In this study, therefore, a hybrid tracking method using a multi-camera unit and gyro-sensor was developed to enlarge the area in which tracking is available with a limited number of markers.

**Tracking with a Multi-camera Unit.** In this study, a multi-camera unit with three cameras which view angle is about 40 degrees was developed as shown in Fig. 4. These three cameras are located with about 40 degrees relative angle and can capture three-times-wider angle images than a single camera. Of course, using the multi-camera unit, the users can obtain a three-times-wider angle of view than in the case of a single camera without increasing the number of markers pasted in the environment. However, tracking can not be executed by a tracking algorithm developed only for a single camera when two line markers are captured separately by two cameras. In this study, therefore, a new tracking algorithm for multi-camera units was developed.

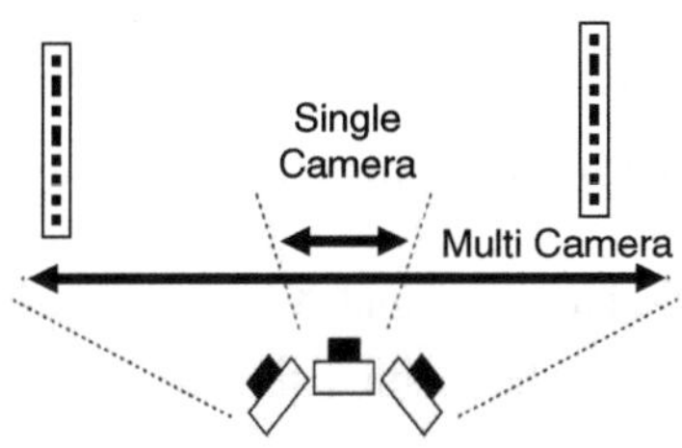


**Fig. 4.** Extension of Viewing Angle using a Multi-Camera Unit

In this study, a condition by which all line markers must be mutually parallel was introduced to simplify the tracking algorithm considerably. Many pipes in the plants are parallel. Therefore, the condition will not spoil the applicability of the line marker.

Details of the tracking algorithm for the multi-camera unit are as follows:

Assume that three-dimensional positions of the pasted markers, the relative position and orientation among three cameras and the inertial parameters of the cameras are measured in advance. The transformation equation for mapping a point $\mathbf{x} = (x, y, z, 1)^T$ in the camera 1 coordinate system to a point in the screen coordinate system of camera j is the following.

$$\begin{pmatrix} u \\ v \\ 0 \\ 1 \end{pmatrix} = \mathbf{PT_j x} = \begin{pmatrix} t_{j11} & t_{j12} & t_{j13} & t_{j14} \\ t_{j21} & t_{j22} & t_{j23} & t_{j24} \\ t_{j31} & t_{j32} & t_{j33} & t_{j34} \\ 0 & 0 & 0 & 1 \end{pmatrix} \begin{pmatrix} x \\ y \\ z \\ 1 \end{pmatrix} \tag{1}$$

Therein, $\mathbf{T}_j$ (j=1,2,3) is a transformation matrix from the camera 1 coordinate system to the camera j coordinate system, and $\mathbf{P}$ is a projection matrix of the cameras.

1. Capture the line markers by three cameras and recognize them. Select two line markers which the distance is longest. Adopt the tracking algorithm for a single camera if the selected markers are in the same image. Assume that one of the line markers is captured by camera j and that the other line marker is captured by camera k if the selected markers are captured by different cameras.
2. Set the terminals of the line marker captured by camera j as $f_1$ and $f_2$; set the terminals of the line marker captured by camera k as $f_3$ and $f_4$. where $f_1$ and $f_3$ are the same side of the line markers.
3. Find two lines, respectively, through $f_1$ and $f_2$, $f_3$ and $f_4$. Equations of the lines in each camera coordinate are

$$a_1 u + b_1 v + c_1 = 0, a_2 u + b_2 v + c_2 = 0. \tag{2}$$

4. Substituting $u$ and $v$ obtained from eq. (1) into eq. (2) produces

$$\begin{array}{ll} (a_1 t_{j11} + b_1 t_{j21})x + & (a_1 t_{k11} + b_1 t_{k21})x + \\ (a_1 t_{j12} + b_1 t_{j22})y + & (a_1 t_{k12} + b_1 t_{k22})y + \\ (a_1 t_{j13} + b_1 t_{j23})z = A & (a_1 t_{k13} + b_1 t_{k23})z = B \end{array} \tag{3}$$

5. Equation (3) is two planes in the camera 1 coordinate; each plane includes a line marker.
6. Set normal vectors of the planes $\mathbf{v_1}$ and $\mathbf{v_2}$; then the direction of the line markers in the camera 1 coordinate is obtainable using eq. (4) because the two line markers are parallel.

$$\mathbf{d} = \frac{\mathbf{v}_1 \times \mathbf{v}_2}{\left|\mathbf{v}_1 \times \mathbf{v}_2\right|} \tag{4}$$

7. The vector from one terminal to the other of the line marker captured by camera j can be expressed as

$$\mathbf{m_j} = \mathbf{R_j} \mathbf{d} l = \left(m_{j1}, m_{j2}, m_{j3}\right)^T, \tag{5}$$

where the length of the line marker captured by camera j is $l$ and the rotation matrix of transformation matrix $\mathbf{T_j}$ is $\mathbf{R_j}$.
8. Set the positions of the terminals of the line marker captured by camera j in the screen coordinate system $(u_{f1}, v_{f1})$ and $(u_{f2}, v_{f2})$. Terminals of the line marker can be expressed as $(\alpha u_{f1}, \alpha v_{f1}, \alpha)^T$ and $(\beta u_{f2}, \beta v_{f2}, \beta)^T$. Then the following equation is obtainable.

$$\begin{pmatrix} \alpha u_{f1} \\ \alpha v_{f1} \\ \alpha \end{pmatrix} + \begin{pmatrix} m_{j1} \\ m_{j2} \\ m_{j3} \end{pmatrix} = \begin{pmatrix} \beta u_{f2} \\ \beta v_{f2} \\ \beta \end{pmatrix} \tag{6}$$

9. Obtain $\alpha$ and $\beta$ from eq. (6). Substituting them into eq. (7) produces the positions of terminals of the line marker in the screen coordinate of camera 1.

$$\mathbf{f}_1 = \left(\mathbf{PT}_\mathrm{j}\right)^{-1} \begin{pmatrix} \alpha u_{f1} \\ \alpha v_{f1} \\ \alpha \end{pmatrix} \quad \mathbf{f}_2 = \left(\mathbf{PT}_\mathrm{j}\right)^{-1} \begin{pmatrix} \beta u_{f2} \\ \beta v_{f2} \\ \beta \end{pmatrix} \tag{7}$$

10. Repeating 6, 7 and 8 for camera k produces positions of the terminals of the line marker captured by camera k in the screen coordinate of camera 1.

The four terminals of the two line markers captured by the three cameras in the screen coordinate of camera 1 are obtainable using the algorithm given above. Then the same algorithm can be adopted for the case of a single camera.

**Tracking with a gyro-sensor.** Using the multi-camera unit described above, the number of the line markers that must be pasted in the environment can be decreased at a certain level. But when a part of the line marker is hidden by a user's body or tools used for maintenance, the tracking will not be able to continue. In this study, therefore, a hybrid tracking method that combines a gyro-sensor and the line marker has been developed. From the gyro-sensor, only the orientation is obtainable at all times, but the output is not so accurate and the cumulative error will increase as time passes. Therefore, the gyro-sensor is useful only for a very short period of time.

The process using the gyro-sensor and the line marker is divisible into three parts.

*A case in which more than two markers can be captured by a camera.* In this case, the position and the orientation of the camera are calculated based on the two line markers and an output from the gyro-sensor is recorded. Then the amount of the error of the tracking result based on the two line markers is estimated. A weighted average of the tracking result based on the two line markers and the output from the gyro-sensor is calculated if the amount of the error is larger than a threshold value. The result is used as the final tracking result. Otherwise, the tracking result based on the two line markers is used directly as the final tracking result. The accumulated error of the gyro-sensor is corrected if the amount of the error is smaller than a threshold value.

*A case in which only one marker can be captured by a camera.* In this case, the position of the final result of the previous frame is set as the position of a temporary tracking result. The output from the gyro-sensor is also set as the orientation of the temporal tracking result. Then the position of the line marker on the camera image is estimated using the temporary tracking result. The temporary tracking result is adjusted nonlinearly to minimize the difference between the estimated position and the actual position of the marker on the image. The adjusted result is used as the final tracking result.

*A case in which no marker can be captured by a camera.* In this case, the output from the gyro-sensor is used as the orientation of the final tracking result; the position of the final result of the previous frame is used as the position of the final tracking result. Therefore, if the camera moves in parallel, the error of the final tracking result will be the amount of the parallel movement.

### 2.4 Performance Evaluation of Hybrid Tracking

To evaluate the effectiveness of introducing the hybrid tracking method, an evaluation experiment was conducted in a room of Fugen, which is a real but retired nuclear power plant in Japan. Figure 5 shows that 15 line markers were pasted in a room (8 m × 9.5 m) and the multi-camera unit with a gyro-sensor was moved along the two routes, as shown in Fig. 5. Figure 6 shows a comparison between the case of the hybrid tracking and the case of a single camera. In this case, an assumption is made that the output of the gyro-sensor is reliable for 500 ms after no markers can be captured by the multi-camera unit.

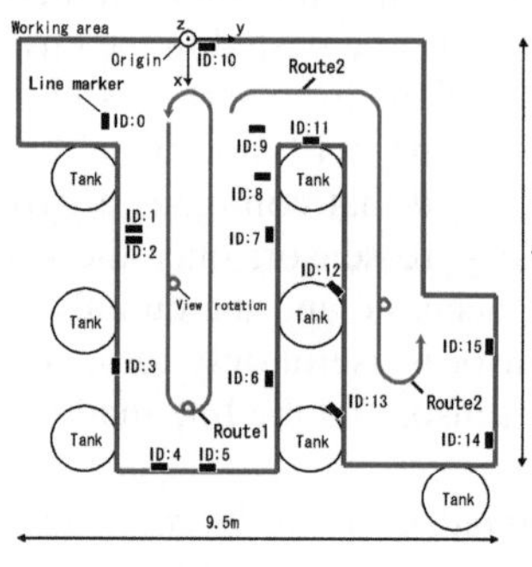


**Fig. 5.** Marker layout for the evaluation experiment

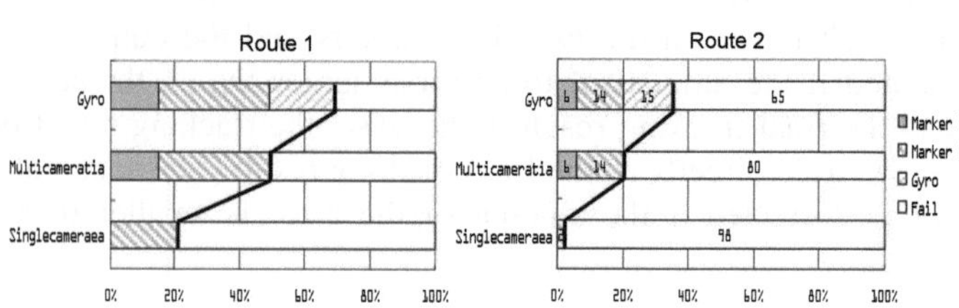


**Fig. 6.** Comparison between hybrid tracking and single camera

Figure 6 shows that the areas for which the tracking are available with the hybrid tracking method are 3 times (Route 1) and 17 times (Route 2) larger than when using the single camera. This result confirmed that the hybrid tracking method can enlarge the available area without increasing the number of markers.

# 3 Tracking Method Using Circular Markers

## 3.1 Basic Idea of Circular Marker Design

The edges of the square on the image become jagged, as shown in Fig. 7, if a square is captured by a low resolution camera from a long distance. This jagged edge affects the accuracy of the tracking strongly because the tracking calculation for square markers like ARToolKit is based on the intersections of the four lines that the jagged edges form. In contrast, even if a circle is captured from a long distance, a center of the circle can be recognized accurately, as shown in Fig. 8. Therefore if a marker consists only of circles and the tracking calculation is based on the center of the circles, the accuracy of the tracking will not decrease even if the marker is captured from a long distance.

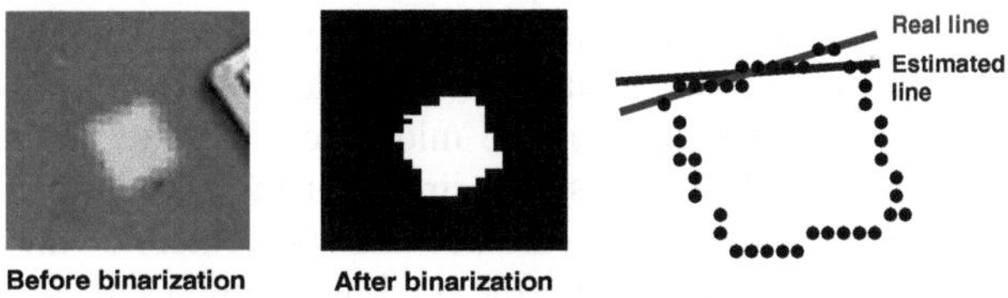


**Fig. 7.** A square captured from a long distance and estimated lines

**Fig. 8.** Recognition of circle centers in severe conditions

Another idea to design a new marker is the relationship between a number of markers captured by a camera and the distance between the camera and the markers. Figure 9 shows that the captured markers become very numerous and the size of the marker on the image becomes very small when the distance between the camera and the markers is long. It therefore becomes difficult to obtain plural feature points from one marker because the marker size on the image is too small, but plural feature points are obtainable from plural markers. Moreover, the distances among the feature points can be long because markers can be pasted so as not to be so near with each other. On the other hand, when the distance between the camera and the markers is short, the number of the captured markers becomes small and the size of the markers on the image becomes very large. In this case, it becomes possible to obtain plural feature points from one marker because the marker size on the image is sufficiently large.

Based on the idea described above, the authors have designed circular markers as shown in Fig. 10. This marker consists of one black outer circle (with thickness of 30% of the marker radius), one white center circle (the radius is 30% of the marker

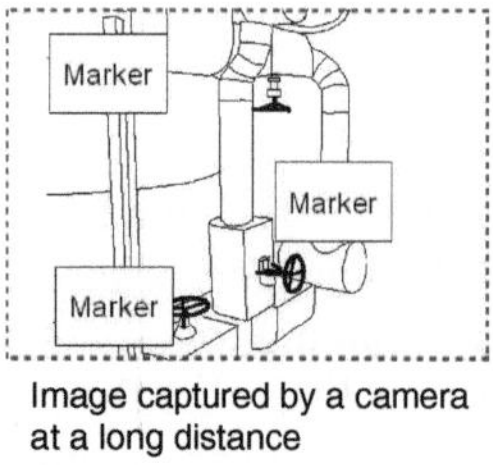


**Fig. 9.** Relationship between a number of captured markers and the camera distance

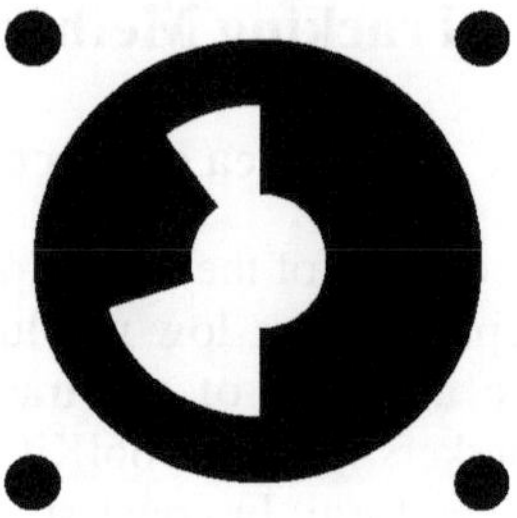

**Fig. 10.** Design of a circular marker

radius), and a middle circle (with thickness of 40% of the marker radius), which consists of 10 black or white fans that represent a binary code and four small circles (the radius is 24% of the marker radius) at the corner of the marker.

The black outer circle and the white center circle are used for determining the threshold to analyze the binary code of the middle circle. The markers that can be used simultaneously are 99. The four small circles at the corners can be recognized when the marker is captured at a short distance and the centers of these small circles are used as four feature points to execute the tracking using a P4P solution. Thereby, even if only one or two markers are captured by a camera because the distance between the camera and the markers is too short, the tracking can be continued if the marker size on the image is sufficiently large. Therefore the marker shown in Fig. 10 is useful in two-layer modes: long distance mode with plural markers, and short distance mode with single marker.

### 3.2 Performance Evaluation of Circular Marker

To estimate the maximum detection distance of the circle marker, one circular marker was pasted on a wall and the maximum distance was measured under the condition that the tracking system can correctly recognize the code of the circular marker. The circular marker diameter was changed from 3 cm to 10 cm by 1-cm steps. For comparison, one square marker (ARToolKit) was pasted on a wall and its size was changed from 3 cm to 10 by 1-cm steps. 128 markers with binarized patterns were registered to the ARToolKit system in advance. The result shown in Fig. 11 verifies that the maximum detection distance of the circular marker is about twice that of the square marker.

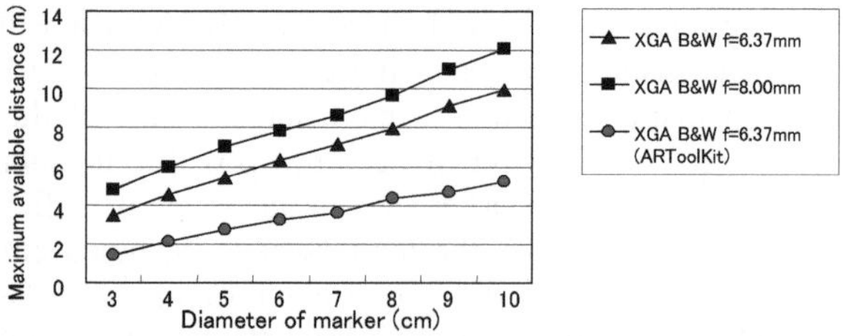


**Fig. 11.** Comparison of maximum detection distance (a circular and a square marker)

To confirm that the circular marker is useful for two-layer tracking, a simple experiment was conducted. In the experiment, five circular markers of 8 cm diameter are pasted on a wall and the camera (Dragonfly II XGA black-and-white) was moved from a short distance (about 30 cm) to a long distance (about 8 m). This experiment verified that the tracking can be executed properly at all distances. In addition, the mode change between the tracking using single marker and the tracking using plural markers were unnoticeable to the extent that the calibration of the camera lens distortion was done properly.

Evaluation of the tracking accuracy using circular markers has not been done yet, but the tracking accuracy depends on the layout of the feature points obtained from the markers. Therefore, when the circular markers are pasted in a condition that the centers of the circular markers are on the terminals of the line markers, the tracking accuracy will be nearly equivalent to that of the case of the line markers. Concrete evaluation of the accuracy using the circular markers will be conducted as future work.

## 4 Summary and Future Works

In this study, a hybrid tracking method and a two-layer tracking method were developed to enlarge the area in which tracking is available using only a limited number of markers. These tracking methods were developed separately and can not be used simultaneously. Future work will integrate these methods into a single tracking method to cover short distances and long distances seamlessly.

## References

1. Navab, N.: Developing Killer Apps for Industrial Augmented Reality: Computer Graphics and Applications. IEEE 24(3), 16–22 (2004)
2. Ishii, H., Fujino, H., Bian, Z., Sekiyama, T., Shimoda, H., Yoshikawa, H.: Development of Marker-based Tracking Methods for Augmented Reality Applied to NPP Maintenance Work Support and its Experimental Evaluation, In: 5th Intl. Topical Meeting on Nuclear Plant Instrumentation, Control and Human-Machine Interface Technologies, pp. 973–980 (2006)
3. Kato, H., Billinghurst, M., Poupyrev, I., Imamoto, K., Tachibana, K.: Virtual Object Manipulation on a Table-Top AR Environment, In: International Symposium on Augmented Reality, pp. 111–119 (2000)

# An Efficient Navigation Algorithm of Large Scale Distributed VRML/X3D Environments

Jinyuan Jia[1,2], Guanghua Lu[2], and Yuan Pan[2]

[1] School of Software Engineering, Tongji University,
Jiading District, Shanghai, P. R. China
csjyjia@yahoo.com.cn
[2] Zhuhai College of Jilin University,
Jinwan District, Zhuhai, P. R. China, 519041
{Lunikko, panyuanpy}@163.com

**Abstract.** Typical shortest-path search algorithm, e.g. Dijkstra algorithm, is difficult to implement in VRML/X3D world directly due to the simplicity of VRML/X3D programming. By using JavaScript with good cross-platform and compatibility with VRML, this paper proposed an efficient back-traceable climbing (BTC) based navigation algorithm, by improving Hill Climbing search algorithm with the destination oriented guidance and loop removal, and amplifying it with simple data structure and flexible interfaces. The BTC based navigation algorithm performs greatly better than Dijkstra algorithm in terms of efficiency, consumed memory and the number of accessed nodes. It also possesses the merits of simplicity, easy implementation and reliability. Experimental results also show that it can provide real-time virtual navigation services with enough precision for large scale VRML/X3D environment.

## 1 Introduction

Distributed virtual environment (DVE) becomes worldwide popularly with its immersion, interaction and imagination. VRML/X3D, as the second generation Web language after HTML, thoroughly changes the tedious interfaces and weak interactions of traditional Web applications. People can easily construct their own virtual world with VRML/X3D on Internet. However, with the size of virtual environments increasing, users usually feel lost during walkthrough in VRML/X3D environments and could not reach the destination they intended in advance. Too long time meaningless wandering with disorientation also makes users frustrated and loss the patience and interests to roam in virtual environments. Therefore, it is quite meaningful to provide efficient navigation algorithms for guiding users to walkthrough in large scale VRML /X3D environments. The research about this topic also attracts more and more attentions [1-6]. In this paper, we introduced an efficient navigation algorithm for guiding users to explore VRML/X3D environment effectively.

In Section 2, we summarize some related works concerning navigation algorithms of VEs. The proposed back-traceable climbing method is outlined roughly in Section 3 and illustrated in detail in Section 4 respectively. Experimental results and performance

R. Shumaker (Ed.): Virtual Reality, HCII 2007, LNCS 4563, pp. 244–252, 2007.

analysis are given in Section 5. The paper concludes in Section 6 by summarizing our contribution and discussing some thoughts concerning future work.

## 2 Related Works

Basically, navigation denotes the process of "wayfinding" to define an optimal path from one location to another in a VR environment which may be assisted by the underlying system. This is such a wide research area that it is difficult to summarize all of published works in this paper. Only typical or newest navigation techniques are addressed here.

A good survey on navigation algorithms of VEs was given by Ropinski *et al* [7]. Salomo *et al* [8] plans path for virtual avatars automatically and interactively with Probabilistic Road Map (PRM). Christie *et al* [8] specifies camera path according to some height information embedded into building models in VEs. Currently, there are three typical methods to search for the shortest path in VEs. The first one is classical Dijkstra algorithm [6][9-11]; the second one [12] is $A^*$ based search method and the last [4] is grid based search method.

However, these three shortest path search algorithms are addressed to general virtual environments, not VRML/X3D environments, and they become impractical to implement due to the weak and simple programming capability of VRML/X3D provided. The navigation algorithm for VRML/X3D environments requires high efficiency, cross-platform, simplicity and easy implementation. Li *et al* [11] implemented their improved Dijkstra algorithm with Java Applet, its drawback is that the users with Window platforms have to download and install JVM inconveniently before running this algorithm. That might make those novice users lose their patience to go on walkthrough your VRML environments.

In this paper, we solved this problem by (*a*) improving traditional $A^*$ algorithm with Back-Traceable Climbing maneuver; (*b*) making it simple enough for JavaScript programming; (c) implementing our proposed BTC based algorithm with JavaScript, Java Script possesses cross-platform and compatibility.

## 3 Major Idea of BTC Based Navigation Algorithm

### 3.1 Modeling Road Network Topologically

In realty, roadway not only has physical connectivity (without isolated points), but also logical connectivity, for two arbitrary points of roadway, you can always reach from one point to the other. Considering the fact that changing direction is required only at the crossing points of roadway, physical roadway is represented topologically with the road network model as shown in Fig. 1.

In the model above, the color circle denotes node, the number within the circle denotes the ID to identify this node, the connected line segment between two nodes is the edge and the number along the edge is the weight of path. In each node, two kinds of data are required to store, one is its absolute coordinate in VRML/X3D world, the other the lengths of all its incident edges. Generally, the nodes and their adjacency relationships in road network are represented with the data structure, *adjacent list*, which could be provided only in Java, C++ and other advanced programming languages.

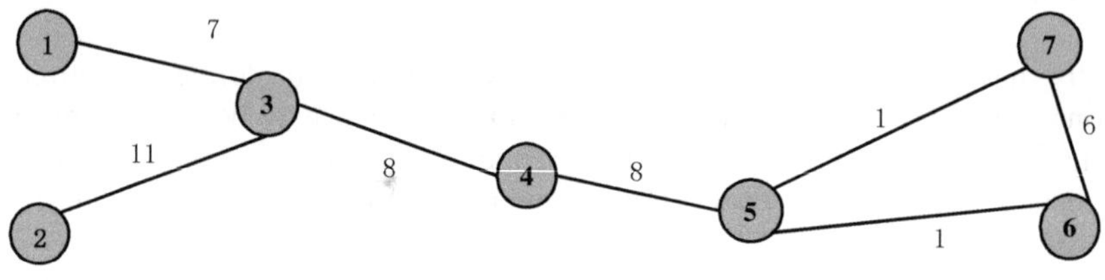


**Fig. 1.** Road network Model for Roadway

### 3.2 Heuristic Searching with Hill Climbing

Heuristic search is a search strategy to consider the applicable knowledge of problem space, dynamically determine the priorities of rules and choose the best rule of problem solving. Usually, it need to establish the *Open* list to record those nodes which have been produced but not traversed, and the *Closed* list to record those un-traversed nodes for maintaining the node data used in searching procedure.

Hill Climbing is a classical heuristic search strategy, at next step of search, the best node always is chosen to expand. It does not preserve the subsequent nodes and father of current node, during the path-searching, it only searches partially the solution state space and reduces the cost of dynamical maintenances by canceling the *Open* list. Thus, it possesses the merits of low time complexity, high efficiency and low memory cost. However, due to no historical records preserved, it has no back-tracing and restoring mechanism in case of “apexes”, “basins”, “ridges” and so on. So it easily falls into an optimal solution locally and even is unable to reach the final solution globally. Only back-traceable climbing can help overcome the drawback of traditional heuristic search with blind climbing.

### 3.3 Evaluation Function

In our proposed algorithm, the heuristic searching in AI is applied to navigation problem of road network. To an heuristic searching scheme [5], the best nodes for the optimal navigation path, it is important to design a good evaluation function, $f(m) = g(m) + h(m)$, for choosing the best node to expand at each step. Here, we improved two components $g(m)$ and $h(m)$ respectively. Firstly, $g(m)$ is set as the weight of $N_m N_{m-1}$, the edge from the node $N_m$ to its father $N_{m-1}$, instead of the total path from the starting node to the current node $N_m$. Secondly, the distance $Sqrt((x_1 - x_2)^2 + (x_1 - x_2)^2)$ from the current node to destination is chosen as $h(n)$, and is further simplified as, $h(n) = |x_1 - x_2| + |y_1 - y_2|$ for removing computation of square roots. The function h(m) is to guide the searching to the nodes more hopeful to reach destination and avoid its blind searching along locally optimal directions. The function g(m) is to prevent the searching repetitively along wrong paths or loops.

### 3.4 Back-Traceable Climbing Maneuver

The back-traceable climbing maneuver is employed in our algorithm to avoid tramping into a locally optimal solution. our algorithm design a new data structure, valid node list VNL, instead of the open list and close list of traditional heuristic searching methods, to save those traversed nodes and current nodes which are chosen to expand at next step. Comparing to open list and closed list in traditional heuristic searching, VNL does not need recording all the nodes of road network and sorting priority of the list of expandable nodes, and thereby, dynamical maintenance operations are reduced a lot. Furthermore, two definitions are given at first to illustrate our BTC based navigation algorithm.

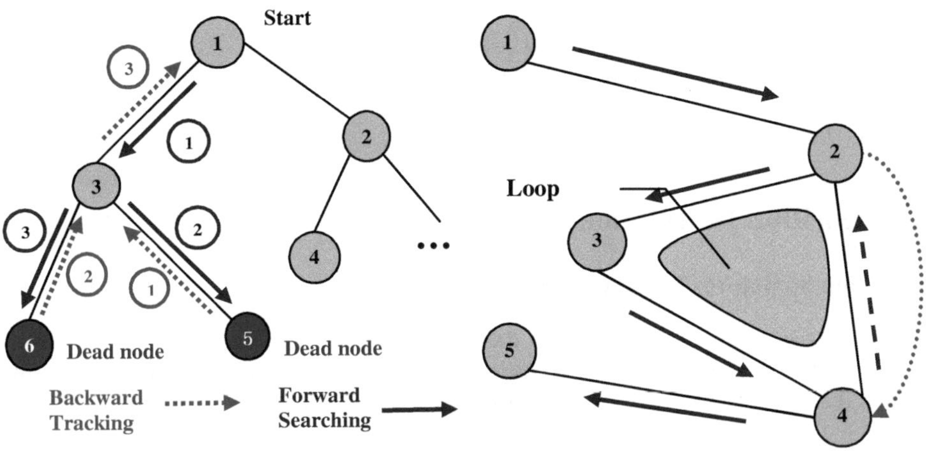


**Fig. 2.** Back-traceable Climbing Algorithm and Loop Removal

**Definition 1.** Dead Node is the node which has either no subsequent nodes or whose subsequent nodes all have been included in VNL already. If such dead nodes be found during path searching, then back-track processing has to do.

**Definition 2.** Active Node is the node which is not dead nodes and does not appear in VNL as well. During path searching, all active nodes can be chosen as candidates to expand at next step.

Two key points of BTC based navigation algorithm are how to give the back-tracking and ending condition of heuristic searching for the navigation path.
Here, the back-traceable condition of heuristic search is given as follows:

If the subsequent ones of current node all are dead nodes, then, go back (back-tracking) to its father node and expand. The detailed back-tracking process is depicted as in Fig. 2. The ending condition is given as follows:

- If the current node just is the destination, then searching succeed and return;
- If VNL becomes empty, then the searching fails and exits.

### 3.5 Loop Removal

Since the BTC based method only can give a locally optimal solution (not globally optimal solution) at each step, it cannot avoid the loop during searching for path. Therefore, it is necessary to judge where loops form and remove them from VNL in time during BTC based path searching, here, a simple loop removal method is proposed as follow. For the current node $N_c$ and a subsequent node of it $N_s$, let us check if a loop can be formed after $N_s$ is added and how the loop can be removed from current path in advance. A simple loop determination and loop removal method is suggested as the following steps:

(1) *search* $N_s$ in VNL = $\{N_i\}$, $i = 1..m$, by comparing it with each element $N_i$;
(2) *if* it is not found in VNL, *then return* with 'no loop found', *else* do following loop removal processing:
   a) *locate* its position in VNL, say $N_s == N_k$ ($k \leq$ m);
   b) *delete* all the nodes ($N_{k+1}, N_{k+2}, \ldots, N_m$) behind $N_k$ from VNL;
   c) *append* $N_c$ into VNL;
(3) *fetch* next active subsequent node $N_{ss}$ of $N_c$, *goto* (1).

## 4 Algorithm Description

### 4.1 Data Structures Based on VRML

Based on the script of VRML, two data structures are designed specially for road network as shown in Fig. 5, one is *node list* to store geometric information of all the nodes, the other is *adjacent edge list* to represent the adjacency relationships of two connected nodes (edges).

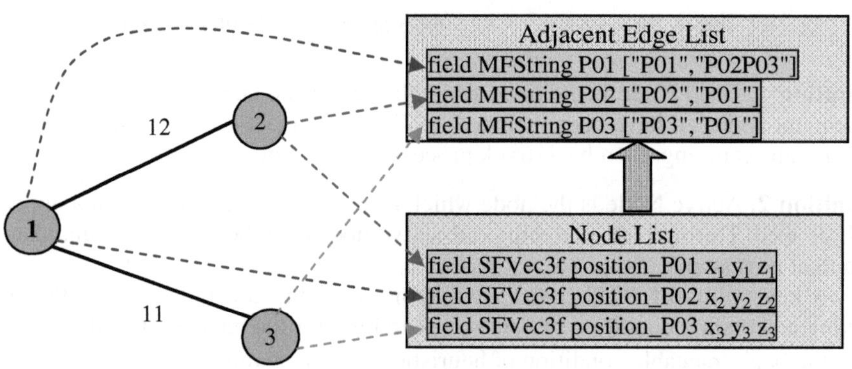


**Fig. 3.** Two data structures: (1) Adjacent Edge List (AEL) and (2) Node List (NL)

1) MFString, a field variable to store multiple string variables, can be used to store the adjacency relationship of any two connected nodes. Here, the array MFString[0..*n*] is used to represent the adjacent edge list, MFString[0] notes the VRML node P01 itself. MFString[1], field MFString P01

["P01","P02P03"], notes the two adjacent nodes P02 and P03 (two edges) of P01. MFString[2], field MFString P02 ["P02","P01"], notes the only one adjacent node P01 of P02. MFString[3], field MFString P03 ["P03","P01"], notes the only adjacent node P01 of P03.

2) SFVec3f, a VRML variable to store the coordinates of a 3D point (*x, y, z*), can be used to represent the location coordinates of a node for road network, for example, field SFVec3f position_P01 x1 y1 z1 notes the 3D coordinates (x1, y1, z1) of P01.

### 4.2 Computing Self-intersections of a Single Canal Surface

Based on BTC maneuver and VRML data structures, the algorithm of near shortest path search is sketched roughly as follows.

Notes: the beginning node: *start*, the ending node: *destination*, the current node: *c*, the subsequent node of *c* is *i*.

Step1【Initialization】VNL = {*start*} ; *c* = *start*;

Step2【Judge if VNL is empty】**if** VNL == Ø **exit**;【Searching fails】

Step3【Judge if searching succeed】**if** *c* has any active subsequent node *i*, **get** one of them;

**if** *i* == *destination*, **return**;【searching succeed】

Step4【Judge if active nodes exist】**if** *c* has no active subsequent node,

**then**【backtracing】

**mark** *c* as the dead node;

**delete** *c* from VNL;

**goto** Step 2;

Step5【Judge if loop met】**if** *i* can be found in VNL,

**then**【loop removal】

**delete** all the nodes behind *i* in VNL;

**append** *c* into VNL;

**get** the next active subsequent node *i* of *c*;

Step6【go forward】**if** *destination* can be found from the field of adjacent node of *i*,

**then append** *i* into VNL; *c* = *i*; **goto** Step 3;

Step7【expand the best subsequent node of *c*】

**append** the active subsequent node *i* of *c* with the smallest f(*i*) into VNL;

*c* = *i*; **goto** Step 3■

## 5 Experimental Results and Performance Analysis

An example, a transportation map of Zhuhai City, Guangdong, P. R. China as shown in Fig. 4, was chosen to implement with Java Script. and a road network with 153 nodes totally was created artificially, in which, the red circles correspond to the nodes of Zhuhai road network. To evaluate the performance of our proposed virtual

(1) (2)

**Fig. 4.** (1) Road network of Zhuhai City, (2) Virtual Zhuhai Campus of Jilin University

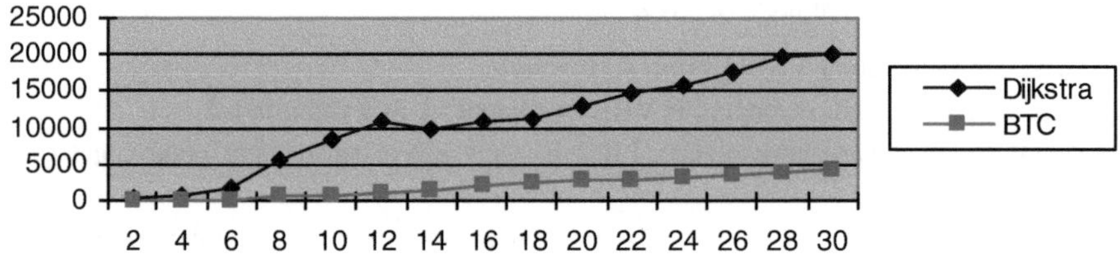


**Fig. 5.** Comparison on the Number of Accessed Nodes

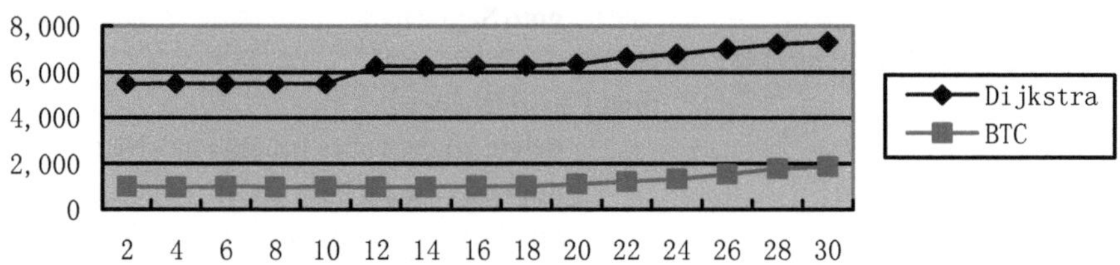


**Fig. 6.** Comparison on Memory Costs of Two Algorithms

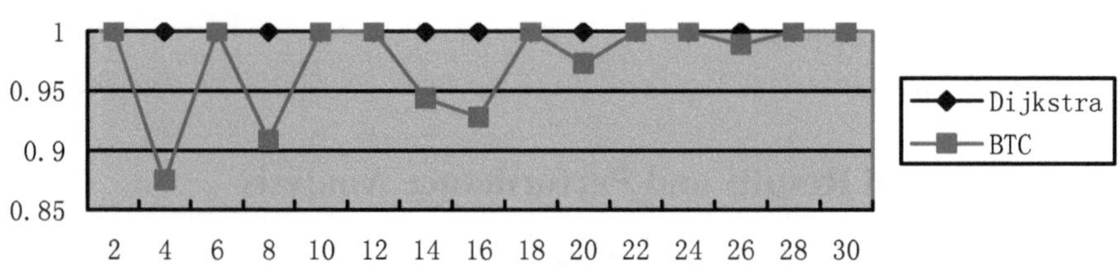


**Fig. 7.** Comparison on the Exactness of Resulting Paths

navigation algorithm, both classical Dijkstra algorithm and our own algorithm have been implemented with Java script programming at Pentium 4, 2.8 GHz CPU and 1GB RAM. The comparing experimental results and performance analysis are illustrated from Fig. 5 to Fig. 7 in terms of the number of accessed nodes, consumed memory and exactness respectively.

The following notations are given for performance analysis:

**BL** = Total length of the path generated by BTC algorithm;
**DL** = Total length of the path generated by Dijkstra algorithm;
**Exactness** = BL / DL * 100%.

Above experimental data as shown in Fig. 5 imply that BTC has strong directionality and only deal with the nodes and their sub-nodes along the route oriented to the destination during searching. Thereby, the total number of nodes accessed by BTC should be proportional to the length (the number of nodes) of the final path. However, the number of nodes traversed by Dijkstra algorithm should increase exponentially with the size of road network, and the number of nodes traversed by BTC algorithm is extremely less than by Dijkstra algorithm as shown in Fig. 6. Similarly, the memory cost of BTC is far from the memory cost of Dijkstra algorithm as well, as shown in Fig. 7, it always maintains a low level stably without leaping acutely with the size of road network increasing, for example, the memory cost of Dijkstra algorithm for processing the path with more than 10 nodes is 1000KB (about 1MB) more than for processing the path with less than 10 nodes. But, BTC removes dynamical maintenance of Open list by improving traditional climbing manner, and thereby achieves much lower memory cost than Dijkstra algorithm, however, the next node at each step expanded by BTC algorithm only is a locally optimal solution currently, that might not become a globally optimal solution finally. Usually, the exactness of BTC could not reach 100%, as shown in Fig. 8, its exactness fluctuates seriously at the topology of road network for a small scale virtual environment, however, the fluctuation becomes slightly and the exactness goes increasing stably with VRML environment being larger and larger.

Classical Dijkstra algorithm is a brute force searching algorithm, it expands the next node blindly according to equal probability criterion for all subsequent nodes, without considering the orientation and position of destination its time complexity is

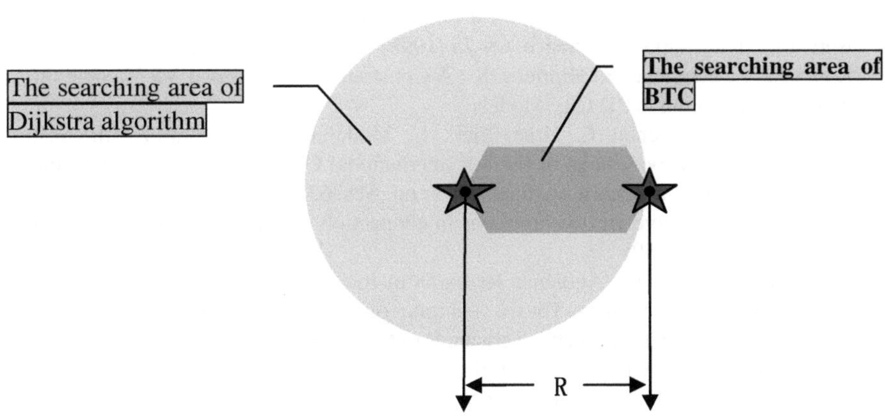


**Fig. 8.** Searching areas of Dijkstra algorithm and BTC

*O* ($n^2$), where *n* is total number of nodes of road network, so the search area of Dijkstra algorithm is the yellow circle with the beginning node as its center and the distance to destination as its radius in Fig. 8.

## 6 Conclusion

We proposed a high efficient BTC based navigation algorithm and implemented it in our big VRML world (Virtual Zhuhai Campus of Jilin University, http://soft.jluzh.com/yanshi/school/index.htm) by using JavaScript purely. Thereby, it owns the merits of JavaScript programming, cross-platform and free-plugin, and facilitates users to login VRML world and walkthrough with navigation services on Internet conveniently. Due to the limit of JavaScript itself, this algorithm may not achieve the most ideal effects. However, it can get the optimal or near-optimal paths in most cases. Huge practical tests also have shown that this algorithm can completely satisfy both requirements of real-time walkthrough and navigation exactness on Internet.

One important advantages of this algorithm is the low cost and fewer traversing nodes, but it just reduces the exactness of the resulted navigation path in the case of loops and backtracking. Theoretically, this drawback could be overcome by devising a better evaluation determinant. It will be regarded as our future work.

## References


1. Knight, C., Nunro, M.: Virtual but Visible Software. In: Proceedings of IV00, International Conference on Information Visualization. IEEE CS Press, Washington, DC, USA (2000)
2. Chittaro, L., Coppola, P.: Animated Products as a Navigation Aid for E-commerce. In: CHI00. Proceedings of Computer Human Interaction, pp. 107–108. ACM Press, Netherlands (2000)
3. Bowman, D.A., Koller, D., Hodges, L.F.: 3D User Interface Design. In: Course Notes of SIGGRAPH '00, ACM Press, New York (2000)
4. Chittaro, L., Ranon, R., Ieronutti, L.: Guiding Visitors of Web3D Worlds through Automatically Generated Tours. In: Proceedings of Web3D, pp. 27–38. ACM Press, New York (2003)
5. Bowman, D.A., Koller, D., Hodgesm, L.F.: 3D User Interface Design. In: Course Notes of SIGGRAPH '00, ACM Press, New York (2000)
6. Benjamin, Z.F., Charles, N.E.: Shortest Path Algorithms: An Evaluation Using Real Road Networks, Transportation Science, 65–73 (1998)
7. Ropinski, T., Steinicke, F., Hinrichs, K.: A Constrained Road-Based VR Navigation Technique for Travelling in 3D City Models
8. Christie, M., Languenou, E., Granvilliers, L.: Modeling camera control with constrained Hyper tubes. In: Proceedings of the 8th International Conference on Principles and Practice of Constraint Programming, Ithaca, NY, pp. 618–632 (2002)
9. Dijkstra, E.W.: A note on two problems in connection with graphs. Numerical Mathematics, pp. 269–271 (1959)
10. Jang, S.D.: The Use and Audience Research of Interactive Multimedia Tours Guide Systems in Museums. Masters Thesis, Institute of Communication Technology, National Chiao Tung University, Hsinchu, Taiwan, R.O.C. (1994)
11. Li, T.Y., Gan, L.K., Su, C.F.: Generating Customizable Guided Tours for Networked Virtual Environments. In: Proceedings of NCS'97 (1997)
12. Luger, G.F.: Artificial Intelligence Structures and Strategies for Complex Problem Solving, Fourth edn. China Machine Press (2004)

# Development of a Handheld User Interface Framework for Virtual Environments

Seokhwan Kim[1], Yongjoo Cho[2], Kyoung Shin Park[3], and Joasang Lim[2]

[1] Department of Computer Science, Sangmyung University, Seoul, Korea
[2] Division of Digital Media Technology, Sangmyung University, Seoul, Korea
[3] Multimedia Engineering, Dankuk University, Cheonan, ChungCheongnam-do, Korea
ycho@smu.ac.kr

**Abstract.** This paper describes a design and implementation of a new handheld user interface framework called HIVE. HIVE provides the familiar 2D user interface on a mobile handheld computer to support user interactions in a virtual environment. It provides a scripting language based on XML and Lua to ease the development of handheld user interfaces and to increase the reusability of the interface components. This paper also discusses the use of the HIVE framework to develop a couple of handheld user interface applications for virtual environments to show usability.

## 1 Introduction

Interaction is a critical component in virtual reality [2]. The virtual interface is the virtual representation of physical user interfaces, such as menu, buttons, sliders, and dials, floating in a 3D virtual environment. It is the most commonly used interaction method in the virtual environment since it uses the familiar desktop PC user interface widgets. However, it is difficult for novice users to manipulate such interfaces in the virtual environment using 3D input devices, such as a wand or a virtual glove. In addition, every visual manifestation of interaction device for the virtual interfaces must be created in the virtual environment, which takes lots of efforts.

In the past, there have been a few attempts of using other computing devices, such as Personal Digital Assistants (PDAs) or notebook computers, to support user interactions in the virtual environment [1,8,10,11,12]. For instance, a 2D map interface is used to help users navigate and collect data easily in a Virtual Field [8]. A PDA interface was built for users to select virtual fish and to view detailed information about the selected fish in Virtual Aquaria [11]. In Virtual Harlem, AMIS (Annotator Management Interface System) allows users to view a list of virtual annotations or see the locations on a 2D map. Then, users can select one of the annotations from the list or from the map to play the annotation back within the virtual environment [10].

However, it is difficult to create handheld user interfaces for virtual environments since it requires lots of domain knowledge, such as user interface design, mobile systems, networking programming, and virtual reality. Also, these interfaces are specifically developed for certain virtual environments, and hence they cannot be easily reused in other VR systems. Thus, some researchers have developed several toolkits

R. Shumaker (Ed.): Virtual Reality, HCII 2007, LNCS 4563, pp. 253–261, 2007.

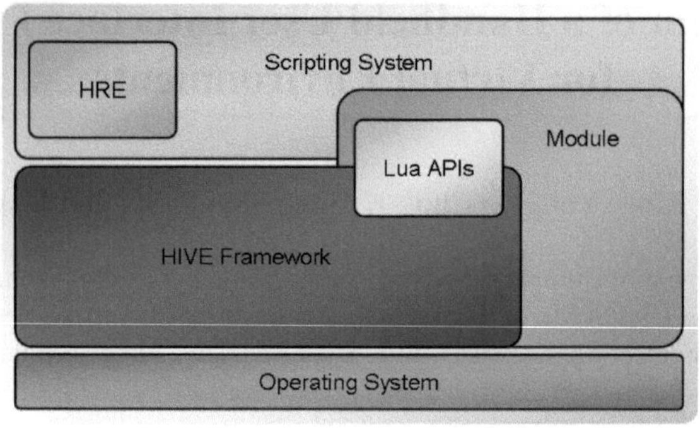


**Fig. 1.** The Architecture of the HIVE Framework

that allow the easy creation of such handheld virtual interfaces, such as Tweek [6], VIST [9], and Glass library [5].

In this paper, we present an overview of a new handheld user interface framework called HIVE (Handheld-based Interface development framework for Virtual Environments). HIVE is designed to ease the development of virtual interfaces by providing reusable interface components and a powerful scripting language. This paper first presents related works on handheld user interface toolkits. It then describes the detail design and implementation of the HIVE framework. It also discusses two handheld user interface applications designed with HIVE, and then it concludes with the future research directions.

## 2 Related Works

A handheld device, such as PDA is small, lightweight, and portable, while it has enough power to handle multimedia data, such as a large chunk of texts, sounds, and movie clips. Also, it supports most of graphical user interface (GUI) available in the desktop computer which is very familiar to many users. Due to this fact, recently there are many works done on utilizing such devices (i.e., PDA) as the user interaction aids for virtual environments, which usually implement WIMP (Windows, Icons, Menus, Pointer) user interfaces on handheld devices. However, most of them are designed for specific VR applications, and hence, they are not easily applicable to other virtual environments. Also, building such handheld user interfaces requires a lot of different knowledge domains, such as user-interface programming, network programming, 3D graphics, and virtual reality. Hence, researchers have developed a few toolkits for easy construction of such handheld virtual interfaces.

Tweek is a handheld user interface design toolkit with the abstract communication architecture and the dynamic loading mechanism for extensibility of GUI components. Tweek incorporates a 2D GUI system to help user interaction in a virtual environment. It is built on top of C++, Java, Java Beans™, XML, and CORBA. It consists of three major components: the GUI client system, the server interacting with the virtual environment, and the middleware. The middleware is based on CORBA to manage the inter-language communication between a VR application written in C++ and the Java-based GUI interface. While it is a powerful toolkit for the handheld user interface development, it requires a steep learning curve from the developer due to the knowledge requirements on various domains. Also, the developers need to re-write and compile their Java codes even for a very little modification, thereby increasing the development time.

VIST is a toolkit for constructing handheld user interfaces designed to increase reusability by using dynamic loading mechanism and a glue scripting language. It employs a dynamic loading mechanism to rapidly prototype handheld applications by assembling various user interface components. Unlike Tweek, VIST employs a light-weight simple component model that simplifies the development of interface components. However, the VIST's scripting language is not rich enough to describe all the logics of the virtual interactions. Hence, most functionality has to be implemented in low-level modules and its scripting language only supports the interoperability among such modules. This weak scripting capability would increase the development time unless a lots of low-level interaction modules are already available.

The Glass library provides similar features to Tweek and VIST. It is designed for distributed computing systems based on cluster computers. It also offers a GUI design tool that enables developers to easily create GUI-based handheld interfaces without programming. However, it is not extensible compared to other toolkits since it only provides three types of event templates: simple, exit, and skin. The "simple" event sends the associated event number to the interested nodes of the clustered system to process the event. The "exit" event is used to terminate the application. The "skin" event is used to change the background image of the handheld device. An important feature of the Glass interface is that it treats a handheld device as one of the cluster nodes, which makes the interface quite coherently tied to the VR applications.

## 3 HIVE Framework

Fig. 1 shows the architecture of HIVE (Handheld-based Interface development framework for Virtual Environments). HIVE is divided into a core system, which is the main executable program, and a collection of modules. The modules include standard user interface components provided along with the core program, such as button or list; new modules can be added by UI module developers. The core system includes Lua C API wrapper classes and HIVE Runtime Environment (HRE). HRE interprets the HIVE script and then divides it into HIVE Runtime Script Language (HRSL)—a Lua script—and HIVE Module Description Language (HMDL) code. HRE then initializes all modules specified in the HMDL script and displays the GUI modules on the main HIVE Window. HIVE Window is a parent window of all HIVE visual modules, which have visual representations that would be shown on the screen. HIVE Window also serves as the entry point of the framework. That is, when HIVE Window is executed, it loads all the binary images of components of the HIVE framework and executes them.

The left image of Fig. 2 shows the function prototypes of a module defined for Microsoft Windows platform. When the HIVE framework loads a module, it also initializes and checks the available messages from the module. When making a GUI module, developers should implement at least five export functions and a Lua

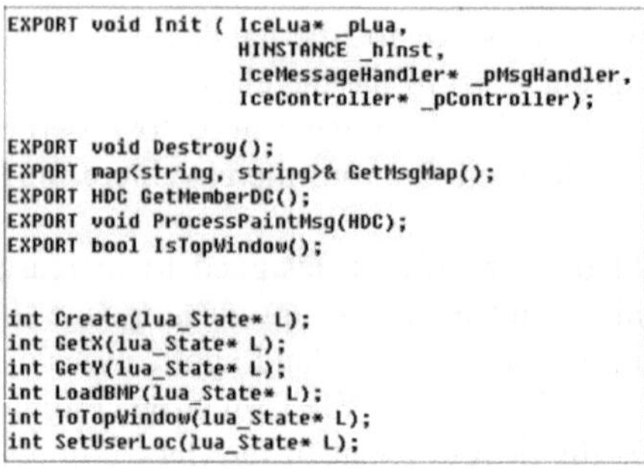

```
EXPORT void Init ( IceLua* _pLua,
                   HINSTANCE _hInst,
                   IceMessageHandler* _pMsgHandler,
                   IceController* _pController);

EXPORT void Destroy();
EXPORT map<string, string>& GetMsgMap();
EXPORT HDC GetMemberDC();
EXPORT void ProcessPaintMsg(HDC);
EXPORT bool IsTopWindow();

int Create(lua_State* L);
int GetX(lua_State* L);
int GetY(lua_State* L);
int LoadBMP(lua_State* L);
int ToTopWindow(lua_State* L);
int SetUserLoc(lua_State* L);
```

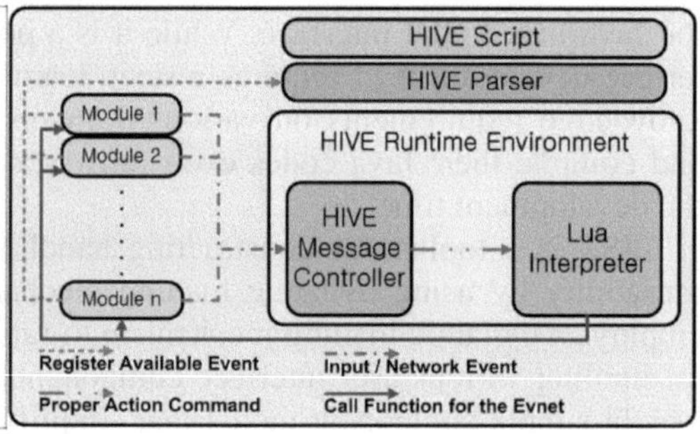


**Fig. 2.** Function prototypes of the HIVE Module (left) and Detailed System Design of the HIVE Framework (right)

function called by the HIVE framework. The HIVE framework calls "Init()" function defined in the dynamic library module to process any startup code of the module, while "Destroy()" is used for cleaning up. "GetMsgMap()" function is also called to find out the events that the module can handle. "ProcessPaintMsg()" is called whenever the visual component needs to be redrawn. Finally, "IsTopWindow()" function checks whether the module is on top of other component modules or not.

The right image of Fig 2 shows the overall layout of the HIVE framework's event and message flows. The HIVE modules generate events based on the user's input or other stimulus, such as a network packet reception, an input from a web camera, and so on. The events are, then, sent to the HIVE message controller in the HRE. Then, the message controller checks whether the event handler for the event exists in the runtime environment. If the handler is found, the mapped event processing routine written in Lua is called, which will be shown in the HIVE Window.

### 3.1 HIVE Scripting

HIVE provides a higher-level scripting system that is executed by HIVE Runtime Environment (HRE). The scripting system consists of HIVE Module Description Language (HMDL) and HIVE Runtime Script Language (HRSL) code. HMDL is designed based on the XML script code, for easy configuration and extensibility. HMDL is intended to specify the description of module by describing the module's name, executable component file, and event associated with the module. It also defines the position, orientation, and size of the GUI component modules to be laid out on the HIVE Window. Finally HMDL defines the event handler code and the initialization script codes written in HRSL, inside <SCRIPT> and <EVENT> tags of HMDL. HRSL incorporates the Lua script language [7].

The script code starts with the element "HIVE." After this element, user can write Lua script for global initialization or HMDL code. With given HMDL code, the framework loads the dynamic library files listed by the attribute "file" of the XML element, "GUI_MODULE" or "MODULE." GUI_MODULE defines a graphical module that has a visual representation shown on the screen, whereas the MODULE can work without any visual representation, such as the network communication

```
<GUI_MODULE file = "Block.dll">
    <NAME>block</NAME>
    <SCRIPT>
    </SCRIPT>
    <POSITION x = "20" y = "10" z = "0"/>
    <ORIENTATION x = "0" y = "0" z = "0"/>
    <SIZE x = "198" y = "705" z = "0"/>
    <EVENT type = "MOUSE_LEFT_BUTTON_UP">

    </EVENT>
    <EVENT type = "MOUSE_LEFT_BUTTON_DOWN">
        ProcessBtnDown (block.GetX(), block.GetY())
    </EVENT>

    <EVENT type = "MOUSE_LEFT_BUTTON_UP">
        ProcessBtnUp()
    </EVENT>

    <EVENT type = "MOUSE_LEFT_BUTTON_DOWN_AND_MOVE">
        ProcessBtnDownAndMove()
    </EVENT>
</GUI_MODULE>
```

**Fig. 3.** An Example of the HIVE Script Code

module. For the GUI_MODULE, the framework reads "POSTION", "SIZE", "ORIENTATION", which defines the layout of each GUI component on the HIVE Window.

Fig. 3 shows an example of HIVE script illustrating a GUI module. The name of the module is block. The script loads the "Block.dll", a Windows dynamic linking library file. After loading the DLL, the framework registers the functions provided by the module. In the script, accessing the module functions can be done by the following the dot (.) notation: <module_name>.<module_function>. For example, "block.GetX()" allows the scripting tool to access the function named "GetX()" of the module, whose name is "block". The element "EVENT" has an attribute "type," which specifies the name of the event.

As shown in Fig. 3, the block module contains MOUSE_LEFT_BUTTON_UP MOUSE_LEFT_BUTTON_DOWN_AND_MOVE, and so on. When a user clicks on the left mouse button, the block module sends the message named MOUSE_LEFT_BUTTON_DOWN and, then, triggers a HRSL code fragment, ProcessBtnDown(…). The XML element "SCRIPT" is used to define initialization of HRSL codes, such as function definitions and global variables. These code fragments between the elements "SCRIPT" are executed when the program starts.

### 3.2 HIVE Runtime Environment (HRE)

HIVE Runtime Environment (HRE) is the virtual platform that executes HRSL using the Lua interpreter and stores the functions and global variable data. HRE is designed around the Lua runtime environment. The Lua runtime environment exists in the form of dynamic or static library as well as binary executables specific to the platforms. HRE contains the Lua environment as a form of static library to increase the reliability of the HIVE framework and to minimize the number of components of the framework for easier deployment.

HRSL can have functions and data written in Lua, which are maintained in HRE during run-time. HRE is designed to raise the reusability of modules. For example, a map view interface application (which will be described in section 4.2) marks the location of items with blue rectangles to be shown on the display device. Adding or removing these items can be easily modified on the HRSL script without rewriting and rebuilding the low-level components.

In addition, the map view interface marks the current location of the user in the virtual environment as a red rectangle. To show the current location, the interface application should get the location data from the virtual environment through a network or other medium. However, the 3D virtual world coordinate also needs to be converted to the 2D display device coordinate since the 3D world and 2D application have different coordinate system. This converting routine is typically declared in the low-level module, especially in VIST. Using HIVE, this routine can be easily implemented in the HRSL script.

## 4 HIVE Applications

We developed two handheld user interface applications using HIVE for virtual environments to show the usability of this framework.

### 4.1 The Block Simulator Interface for Tangible Moyangsung

Tangible Moyangsung is a virtual heritage edutainment system that employs the tangible interfaces to help a group of users to learn collaboration while they work together for repairing a destroyed virtual Moyangsung castle [3]. In this system, a war story is presented to players to increase the engagement. The mission of the game is for players to walk around the castle to find a destroyed part of the wall and then repair the wall by putting the tangible blocks (i.e., Tetris-pattern blocks made of transparent acryl) on the board before the enemies invade. When the players get close to a broken wall in the virtual environment, they would see the pattern of the destroyed wall on the tangible (10 x 10 grid) board interface, and then the players should put blocks in the correct position on the pattern appeared on the board to repair the destroyed wall of the virtual castle. the block simulation handheld user interface.

Tangible Moyangsung is currently installed in the X-edu studio at Jeonju University. The tangible interface used in this project helps users to easily layer the blocks in the virtual environment compared to the traditional virtual interface, such as 3D block placement interaction using a 3D input device. However, this interface is not easily deployed in other places without the hardware because it is fixed on a table. Thus, we used the HIVE framework to develop a handheld user interface that simulates the board interface for the Tangible Moyangsung system. This block simulator interface is designed for a user to manipulate the blocks with more familiar drag-and-drop mechanism. The user simply select a block from the block palette with a mouse or stylus, and drag-and-drop it to the appropriate place on the board. This mobile-version block interface is still a lot easier than the virtual interface. The left image of Fig. 4 shows the destroyed part of virtual Moyangsung and the right image of Fig. 4 shows the block simulator interface built using the HIVE framework.

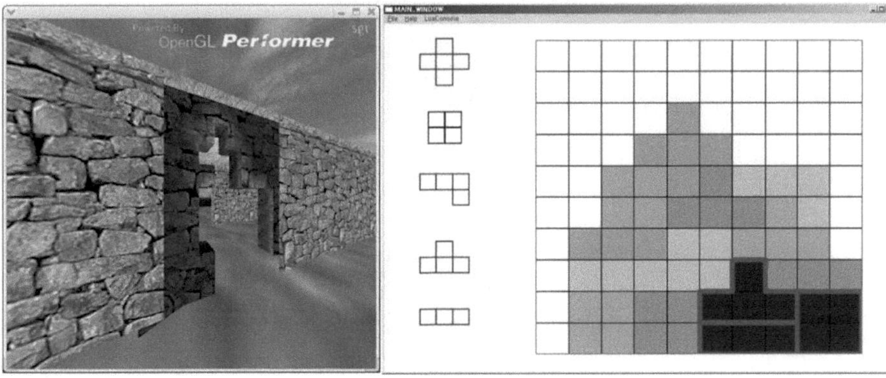


**Fig. 4.** The Moyangsung VR system (left), and the block simulation handheld user interface (right)

For the block simulator interface, we created three low-level modules: network, block, and grid modules. The network module, which is a non-GUI module, processes communication between the interface and the game context server of the Moyangsung system to control the virtual environment. The block GUI module is designed for block manipulation (such as, moving a block over a window area or presenting the mouse cursor on the screen). User's manipulation of a block generates an event and passes it to the HIVE script system. Then, the script system processes the event handler, and then sends a command to the grid module. The grid GUI module checks where the block is placed on the board and generates an event to the script environment that eventually calls the network module to communicate with the game context server.

### 4.2 The Interactive Map View Interface for Digital Goguryeo

Digital Goguryeo is a virtual heritage application that reconstructs the Goguryeo mural painting tomb, Anak No.3 [4]. It is designed to create an interactive learning environment that enriches the users' understanding of the past and to present Goguryeo history and culture comprehensively. In this environment, users explore the painted chambers and corridors as they exist at the present time. When they are close to the painting, the two dimensional painted figures become life-sized three dimensional characters, giving narrations about cultural artifacts and interactively ask and answer questions on the context of the paintings.

The right image of Fig. 5 shows the interactive map view interface for the Digital Goguryeo application. It shows the user's current location in the virtual environment as a red rectangle and also highlights the location of ten important cultural relic items in the tomb presented as blue rectangles. Using this interface, the user can mark his/her current VE location or take a memo with a stylus on the touch screen window. In this interface, the locations of items are received from the virtual environment when the program starts and they are specified in a HIVE script so that the interface designer can easily modify them.

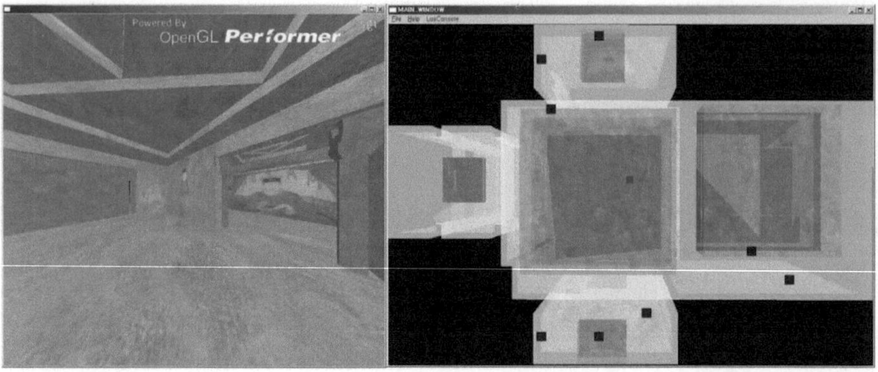


**Fig. 5.** Digital Goguryeo inside the tomb view (on the left) and the top-down map view interface (on the right)

# 5 Conclusion and Future Work

In this paper, we presented a new handheld user interface framework called HIVE (Handheld-based Interface framework for Virtual Environments). HIVE is designed for the rapid prototyping of user interfaces on a handheld computer to support user interactions in a virtual environment. HIVE incorporates a simple module-based architecture and a higher-level scripting system, to make this toolkit easy to learn and to increase reusability and extensibility. In HIVE, Lua is used to support a powerful scripting tool that enables developers to easily add interface logics in the script without modifying the low-level modules. A couple of handheld user interface applications were also developed to illustrate some features of the HIVE framework.

In the future, we will develop more general 2D GUI modules (such as, sliders and menus) and specific VR interaction modules (such as, selection, navigation, and manipulation) to simplify the development process of virtual interfaces. We will also conduct a user study of developing handheld user interfaces using HIVE in comparison with a low-level visual embedded C++ language and other toolkits such as VIST to investigate if HIVE increases productivity and reusability.

# Reference

1. Benini, L., Bonfigli, M.E., Calori, L., Farella, E., Ricco, B.: Palmtop Computers for Managing Interaction with Immersive Virtual Heritage, In: Proceedings of EuroMedia, pp. 183–189 (2002)
2. Burdea, G., Coiffet, P.: Virtual Reality Technology. John Wiley & Sons, Inc, New York, N. Y (1994)
3. Cho, H., Lee, B., Lee, S., Kim, Y., Cho, Y., Kang, S., Park, S., Park, K., Hahn, M.: The Development of a Collaborative Virtual Heritage Edutainment System with Tangible Interfaces. In: Harper, R., Rauterberg, M., Combetto, M. (eds.) ICEC 2006. LNCS, vol. 4161, pp. 362–365. Springer, Heidelberg (2006)

4. Cho, Y., Park, K., Park, S., Moon, H.: Designing Virtual Reality Reconstruction of the Koguryo Mural. In: Luo, Y. (ed.) CDVE 2005. LNCS, vol. 3675, pp. 194–201. Springer, Heidelberg (2005)
5. Guimaraes, M.P., Gnecco, B.B., Zuffo, M.K.: Graphical interaction devices for distributed virtual reality systems, In: Proceedings of ACM SIGGRAPH international conference on Virtual Reality continuum and its applications in industry, pp. 363–367 (2004)
6. Hartling, P., Bierbaum, A., Cruz-Neira, C.: Tweek: Merging 2D and 3D Interaction in Immersive Environments. In: Proceedings of the sixth World Multiconference on Systemics Cybernetics and Informatics (2002)
7. Ierusalimschy, R.: Programming in Lua, 2nd edn. Open Source Press (2006)
8. Johnson, A., Moher, T., Cho, Y., Edelson, D., Russell, E.: Learning Science Inquiry Skills in a Virtual Field. Computers & Graphics 28(3), 409–416 (2004)
9. Park, K., Cho, Y.: A Toolkit for Constructing Virtual Instruments for Augmenting User Interactions and Activities in a Virtual Environment. In: Negoita, M.G., Howlett, R.J., Jain, L.C. (eds.) KES 2004. LNCS (LNAI), vol. 3215, pp. 103–109. Springer, Heidelberg (2004)
10. Park, K., Leigh, J., Johnson, A., Carter, B., Brody, J., Sosnosok, J.: Distance Learning Classroom Using Virtual Harlem. In: Proceedings of the Seventh International Conference on Virtual Systems and Multimedia, pp. 489–498 (2001)
11. Wetzstein, G., Stephenson, P.: Towards a Workflow and Interaction Framework for Virtual Aquaria. VR for Public Consumption, IEEE VR Workshop (2004)
12. Wloka, M., Greenfield, E.: The virtual tricorder: a uniform interface for virtual reality, In: ACM Symposium on User Interface Software Technology, pp. 39–40 (1995)

# Time-Varying Factors Model with Different Time-Scales for Studying Cybersickness

Tohru Kiryu[1], Eri Uchiyama[1], Masahiro Jimbo[1], and Atsuhiko Iijima[2]

[1] Graduate School of Science and Technology, Niigata University,
[2] Graduate School of Medical and Dental Sciences, Niigata University,
8050-Ikarashi-2, Niigata 950-2181, Japan
kiryu@bc.niigata-u.ac.jp

**Abstract.** We have investigated cybersickness in terms of image motion vectors, visual characteristics, and the autonomic nervous regulation. We obtained the RR interval, respiration, and blood pressure time-series and estimated the low-frequency (LF) and high-frequency (HF) power components to determine the some sensation intervals. Then, we traced the time-series of the LF component backwards to find out the local minimum as the onset. An experiment consisted of five consecutive exposure sessions of the same first-person-view video image. In the unpleasant group from fifteen healthy young subjects, the LF/HF increased with respect to the number of trials and a significant difference was confined between two groups. The trigger points concentrated around the specific segments. Within the unpleasant group, eyes did not follow the camera motion around the trigger points. Accordingly, it recommends to monitor image motion vectors as a trigger factor and autonomic nervous regulation as an accumulation factor for studying cybersickness.

**Keywords:** cybersickness, image motion vectors, autonomic nervous regulation, trigger factor, accumulation factor.

## 1 Introduction

In applications of virtual reality and virtual environments, sickness discomfort and aftereffects due to visual stimuli have been reported. This type of visually induced motion sickness, sometimes referred to as "cybersickness" since early 1990s [1], could be caused by the mismatch between the visual and vestibular cues [2], [3]. Cybersickness symptoms produce more disorientation and nausea than oculomotor-related symptoms [4]. Studies on cybersickness have appeared in three major fields regarding display devises and images, sensory and cognitive systems, and the autonomic nervous regulation. For evaluating the effects by display devises and images, geometric pattern or optic flow images by an optokinetic rotating drum, and virtual images by computer graphics have been used [5]-[7]. So *et al.* [8] proposed a metric for quantifying virtual scene movement by the spatial velocity, but the images were virtual scenes. Thus, there have been a few studies in quantifying real video image features as visual stimuli [9]. Study on sensory systems by eye movement [7] showed that subjects with poor visual acuity experienced greater visually induced motion

R. Shumaker (Ed.): Virtual Reality, HCII 2007, LNCS 4563, pp. 262–269, 2007.

sickness and visual fixation reduced sickness but had no affect on vection. Neuroscientific models [3], [10] further dealt with vestibular and proprioceptive inputs in relation to sensory conflict or sensory rearrangement. In addition to the visual stimuli, unpleasant sensation for individual subjects has been assessed by autonomic-nervous-activity-related indices with a relatively long time-scale: they have been estimated from biosignals including heart rate, blood pressure, finger pulse volume, respiration rate, skin condition, and gastric myoelectrical activity [11]. On the other hand, there is a popular subjective index: the Simulator Sickness Questionnaire (SSQ) [12].

We have investigated cybersickness in terms of the autonomic nervous regulation and showed the time-frequency structure of image motion vectors under cybersickness [13]. The results demonstrated that specific camera motion could evoke some sensation including cybersickness. In this paper, we propose a time-varying factors model with different time-scales for describing cybersickness with the trigger factors and the accumulation factor. The trigger factors have a short time scale and could be related to display devises and images, and sensory and cognitive systems. On the other hand, the accumulation factor has a long time scale and could be evaluated by the autonomic nervous regulation after specific visual stimuli.

# 2 Methods

## 2.1 Time-Varying Factors Model

Unpleasant sensation has been assessed by the change in autonomic-nervous- activity (ANA)-related indices estimated from biosignals induced by sensory stimuli. We assumed that cybersickness is caused by an accumulation factor and trigger factors (Fig. 1). An accumulation factor has a long time scale because it relates to background activity, while trigger factors have a short time scale because of direct effects on vision or brain. Major trigger factors from outside in cybersickness could be luminance and camera motion.

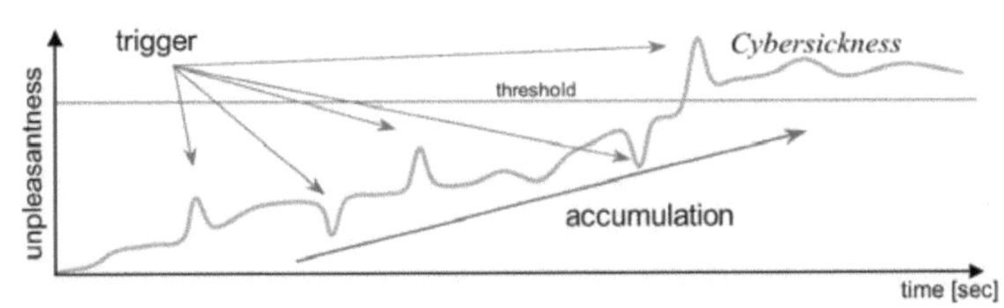


**Fig. 1.** Time-varying factors model with trigger factors and accumulation factor

## 2.2 Experimental Protocol and Analysis

Subjects continuously viewed a 2-min-long mountain biking video image five times for 10-min (Fig. 2): the video image was taken from a first-person viewpoint. The video camera attached at the bike produced shaken or off-centered vection-inducing camera motion. The video image was back-projected onto a 70-inch screen by XGA video projectors with over 2500 ANSI lumens, and the illumination in the room was 10 lux. The distance between a subject and the screen was adjusted to near 1.7 meters for setting the horizontal and vertical view angle at 22° and 17°, respectively.

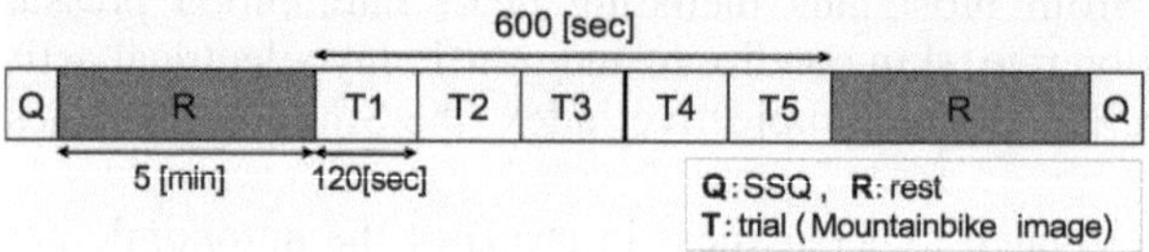


**Fig. 2.** Experimental protocol

Measured ANA-related biosignals were ECG, blood pressure, and respiration at a sampling frequency of 1000 Hz with 12-bit resolution. The time-varying behaviors of ANA-related indices were the candidates for presenting an accumulation factor. A subjective index, SSQ, was also obtained before and after five consecutive exposure sessions (Fig. 2). Besides, we asked subjects to press the button at any time they felt unpleasant sensation. As trigger factors, both the property of video image and the vision characteristics should be treated. We represented the camera motion by image motion vectors and acquired eye movement by the limbus tracker.

Determining the input visual stimulus for unpleasant sensations is difficult because the process from visual stimulus to ANA-related indices is relatively complicated. For quantifying the input visual stimulus, we estimated the zoom, pan, and tilt components of the image global motion vector (GMV) that is used in image data compression [14]. We calculated the correlation coefficient between the GMV and eye movement, $\gamma_{GMV\text{-}eye}$, every 10-sec, as the visual characteristics.

### 2.3 Some Sensation Intervals and Trigger Points

For evaluating the output unpleasant sensation, we determined the some sensation interval (SSI) by ANA-related indices and then searched the triggered onset of the input trigger factors. Actually, the focused frequency bands for ANA-related indices were 0.04–0.15 Hz (Mayer wave related frequency band) and 0.16–0.45 Hz (Respiratory Sinus Arrhythmia related frequency band). We obtained the time-series of the ANA-related indices every frame (30 frame/sec) with a 10-s interval from the RR interval, respiration, and blood pressure time-series by the continuous Wavelet transform. After estimating the averaged low-frequency and high-frequency (HF) power components during a preceding rest period, we determined the SSI based on the following ANA-related conditions (Fig. 3) [9], [13]: the LF component is greater than the 120% of the averaged LF component,

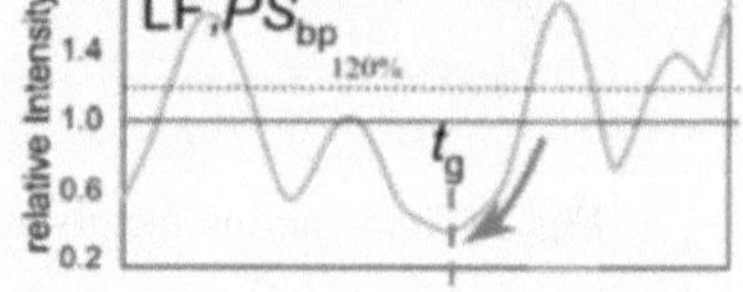


**Fig. 3.** ANA-related conditions

the HF component is less than the 80% of the averaged HF component. Then, we determined the onset of SSI that could be triggered, tracing the time-series of the LF component backwards to find out the local minimum. Actually, we used the LF and HF components from the RR interval, HF component from respiration (PSresp), and LF component from blood pressure (PSbp).

Consequently, we monitored the accumulation factor by LF/HF every 10-sec in relation to the autonomic nervous regulation and the trigger factors in the GMV around the SSI. The SSI was practically determined by the two combinations: HF and LF; PSresp and PSbp.

## 3 Results

Fifteen healthy young male subjects (21.9 ± 0.9 yrs. old) participated in the experiments. In our experiments, nine subjects reported unpleasant sensations and six subjects did not, as determined by the subjective button press and the total severity of SSQ between before and after exposure. We averaged the LF/HF time-series within each group and evaluated the time-varying behavior.

### 3.1 Trigger Factors and Accumulation Factor

Fig. 4 shows the time-series of averaged LF/HF for two groups and the subjective button press events in the unpleasant group. In the unpleasant group, the averaged LF/HF gradually increased with respect to the number of tasks and a significant difference ($p < 0.01$) with a long time interval appeared between two groups, especially in the 4th and 5th tasks after 320-sec. Significant difference ($p < 0.05$) between groups was confirmed in 1st, 4th, and 5th tasks. Significant difference ($p < 0.01$) between 1st task and other tasks was confirmed in the unpleasant group, and after 3rd task in the non-unpleasant group. Almost all the subjective button press events located over the zones in which averaged LF/HF in the unpleasant group significantly larger than that in the non-unpleasant group.

Fig. 5 shows the time-series of averaged LF/HF, the subjective button press events, and the time-distribution of trigger points in the unpleasant group. Trigger points

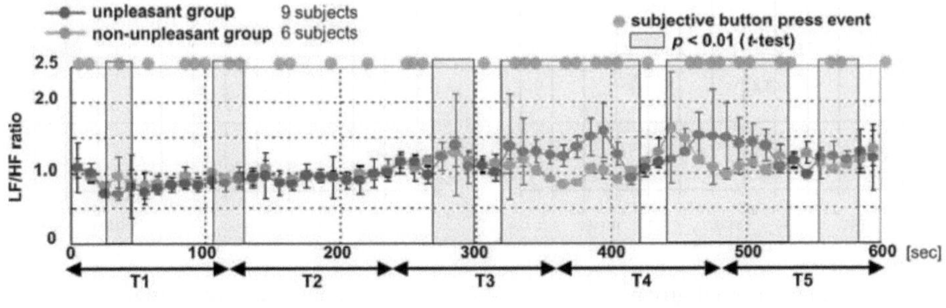


**Fig. 4.** Time-series of averaged LF/HF and the subjective button press event. Gray zones indicate the significant differences between two groups ($p < 0.01$).

concentrated around subjective button press events. There were many trigger points in the 3rd and 4th tasks. Regarding the time-distribution of the 73 trigger points at each 10-sec segment for the 120-sec task, the trigger points located around the 31–40-s and 71–90-s segments in a task.

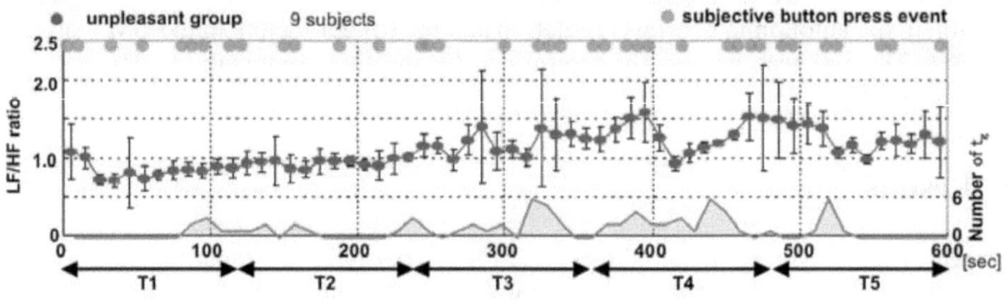


**Fig. 5.** Time-series of averaged LF/HF, the subjective button press events, and the time-distribution of trigger points for the image session with the highest unpleasant score

### 3.2 GMV and Eye Movement

We studied the relationship between the pan component and the horizontal eye movement because our preliminary study demonstrated greater cybersickness for the pan components than for others. Within the unpleasant group, $\gamma_{GMV\text{-}eye}$ showed resemble behavior in time for five consecutive tasks and decreased around the 81–90-s segment (Fig. 6) where the trigger points showed a peak for a task [13]. That is, eyes did not follow the camera motion around the peaks of ANA-related trigger points. For the non-unpleasant group, $\gamma_{GMV\text{-}eye}$ also decreased around the 81–90-s segment, but the time-varying behavior was different among tasks.

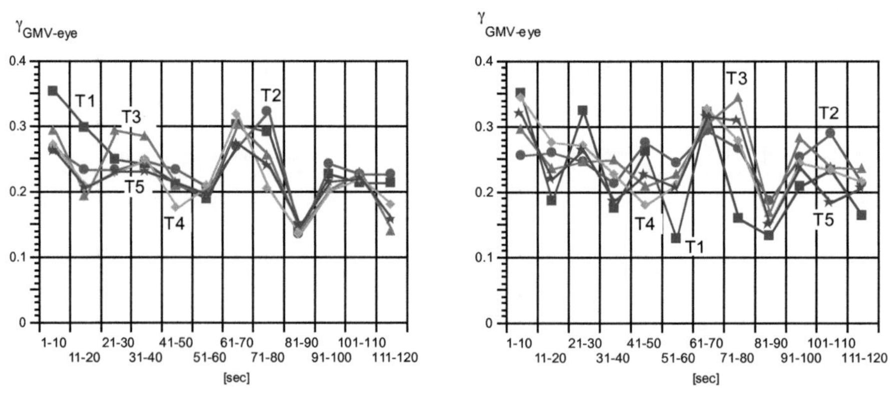


(a) unpleasant group (b) non-unpleasant group

**Fig. 6.** Correlation coefficients $\gamma_{GMV\text{-}eye}$ every 10-sec segment for each task

# 4 Discussion

We obtained a noticeable time-distribution of trigger points for expecting the trigger factors and a significantly increasing behavior of LF/HF for unpleasant group (Fig. 4). For the 3rd and 4th tasks, unpleasant sensation was greatly expected due to the subjective button press and time-distribution of trigger points. For these tasks, the averaged LF/HF significantly increased. Thus the LF/HF would be useful for evaluating the accumulation factor. Besides, concentrated trigger factors most likely cause the increase in the LF/HF: the less the localization of trigger points, the less the increase in the LF/HF with respect to time. Hence, the specific behavior of image motion vectors could disturb the autonomic nervous regulation and produce the accumulation factor. The time-frequency structures of motion vectors in relation to cybersickness were presented in the previous literature [13]: regarding the specific time-frequency structures of GMVs over 0.5 in the normalized power around trigger points, it included low frequencies ranging 0.3–2.5 Hz in three GMV components.

However, the disturbance of autonomic nervous regulation was not always related to the unpleasant sensations. According to the relationship between the unpleasant score and the number of trigger points per minute for ten different image sections in the 18-min-long first-person-view video images, there were trigger points that cause some other sensations, but not cybersickness [13]. In this experiments, subjects answered a simple questionnaire (unpleasant, not specified, non-unpleasant) for specific impressed image sessions after the 18-min-long task. For the image session with the lowest unpleasant score (car race), we observed the different time-varying behavior of averaged LF/HF and the subjective button press events (Fig. 7), although this was a supplemental study because the subjects were not fully the same as those in Figs. 4 and 5. Note that the number of trigger points per minute was the same as that in the image session with the highest unpleasant score. Comparing to Fig. 4, the averaged LF/HF did not demonstrate steady increase. Besides, there were not a tight relationship between localization of trigger points and subjective button press events.

We extracted some sensation intervals and determined the triggered onsets, tracing the time-series of the LF component backwards in time. It was reported that there was a time delay in the autonomic nervous regulation after visual stimuli, according to the results of the transient visual-autonomic responses [15]. Although visual stimuli in our

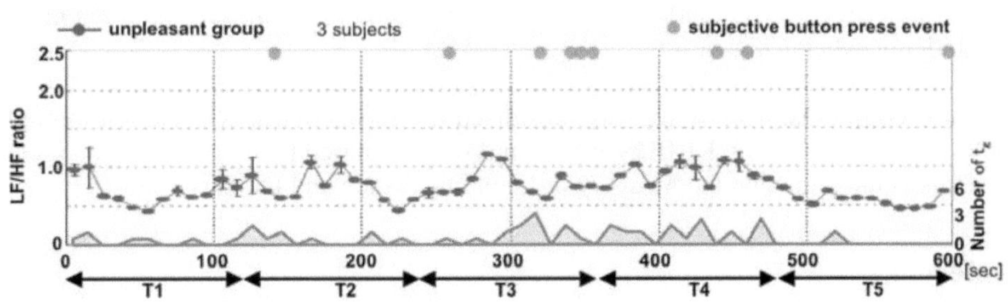


**Fig. 7.** Time-series of averaged LF/HF, the subjective button press events, and the time-distribution of trigger points for the image session with the lowest unpleasant score

experiments might be weak, the similar development of symptom could occur. Conventional studies with rotating drum and prolonged virtual environment exposure reported that sickness symptom increased as a function of time for more than several tens of minutes [16], [17]. However, we confirmed that steady accumulation did not occur in the ten different image sections of the 18-min-long first-person-view video images including mountain bike and car race. Thus, the accumulation did not simply increase with respect to time. Accumulation factor most likely links to specific trigger factors according to Figs. 5 and 7. The features and timings of specific trigger factors should be further studied.

In our experiments, the correlation coefficient between GMV and eye movement, $\gamma_{GMV\text{-}eye}$, and the power spectrum pattern of eye movement demonstrated a distinguishable feature for the unpleasant group. As an additional study, we estimated the coherence function between the pupil diameter (output) and the illuminance (input) every 10-sec for different seven young subjects (23.9 ± 1.8 yrs. old). The coherency between the pupil diameter and the illuminance in the focused frequency range, 0.35-0.45 Hz, was practically used to be compared with the ANA-related indices. According to the preliminary experiment, the unpleasant group demonstrated higher coherence even over 0.4 Hz. The vision characteristics could be related to the potential feature inducing unpleasant sensation. As a result, the unpleasant group was sensitive for visual stimuli.

A dynamic threshold could exit between positive and negative sensations even for the same stimuli, depending on the capacity of autonomic nervous regulation affected by the cardiovascular system. Preventing unpleasant sensations is a key point for sustaining sufficient effectiveness and motivation in the progression of recovery. Since the heart rate is different between virtual and real exercises, activation of muscle contraction even in virtual environment could suppress cybersickness. Further study on the difference between real and virtual exercises in terms of the time-varying factors model will reveal hints to design continuous repetitive virtual tasks.

## 5 Conclusion

We confirmed accumulation and trigger factors of a simple time-varying factors model, studying cybersickness in terms of image motion vectors, visual characteristics, and autonomic nervous regulation. Hence, it should recommend to monitor image motion vectors as a trigger factor and autonomic nervous regulation as an accumulation factor for studying cybersickness.

**Acknowledgments.** This study was subsidized the Japan Keirin Association through its Promotion funds from KEIRIN RACE and was supported by the Mechanical Social Systems Foundation and the Ministry of Economy, Trade and Industry.

## References

1. McCauley, M.E., Sharkey, T.J.: Cybersickness: perception of self-motion in virtual environments. Presence 1, 311–318 (1992)
2. Reason, J.T., Brand, J.J.: Motion Sickness. Academic Press, London (1975)

3. Bles, W., Bos, J.E., de Graaf, B., Groen, E., Wertheim, A.H.: Motion sickness: only one provocative conflict? Brain Research Bulletin 47, 481–487 (1998)
4. Stanney, K.M., Kennedy, R.S., Drexler, J.M., Harm, D.L.: Motion sickness and proprioceptive aftereffects following virtual environment exposure. Applied Ergonomics 30, 27–38 (1999)
5. Cobb, S.V.G., Wilson, J.R., Nichols, S., Ramsey, A.: Virtual reality-induced symptoms and effects (VRISE). Presence 8, 169–186 (1999)
6. Hu, S., Davis, M.S., Klose, A.H., Zabinsky, E.M., Meux, S.P., Jacobsen, H.A., Westfall, J.M., Gruber, M.B.: Effects of spatial frequency of a vertically striped rotating drum on vection-induced motion sickness. Aviation Space Environment Medicine 68, 306–311 (1997)
7. Webb, N.A., Griffin, M.J.: Optokinetic stimuli: motion sickness, visual acuity, and eye movements. Aviation Space Environment Medicine 73, 351–358 (2002)
8. So, R.H., Ho, A., Lo, W.T.: A metric to quantify virtual scene movement for the study of cybersickness: Definition, implementation, and verification. Presence 10, 192–215 (2001)
9. Kiryu, T., Yamada, H., Jimbo, M., Bando, T.: Time-varying behavior of motion vectors in vection-induced images in relation to autonomic regulation. In: Proc. 26th Annu. Int. Conf. IEEE/EMBS, pp. 2403–2406 (San Francisco, 2004)
10. Yates, B.J., Miller, A.D., Lucot, J.B., Physiological, J.B: Physiological basis and pharmacology of motion sickness: an update. Brain Research Bulletin 47, 395–406 (1998)
11. Cowings, P.S., Naifeh, K.H., Toscano, W.B.: The stability of individual patterns of autonomic responses to motion sickness stimulation. Aviation Space Environment Medicine 61, 399–405 (1990)
12. Kennedy, R.S., Lane, N.E., Berbaum, K.S., Lilienthal, M.G.: Simulator sickness questionnaire: An enhanced method for quantifying simulator sickness. Int. J. Aviation Psychology 3, 203–220 (1993)
13. Kiryu, T., Nomura, E., Iijima, A., Bando, T.: Time-frequency structure of image motion vectors under vection-induced cybersickness. In: Proc. 11th Int. Conf. Human-Computer Interaction, 2358.pdf (Las Vegas, 2005)
14. Jinzenji, K., Watanabe, H., Kobayashi, N.: Global motion estimation for static sprite production and its application to video coding. In: IEEE ISPAC'98, pp. 328–332 (1998)
15. Wood, S.J., Ramsdell, C.D., Mullen, T.J., Oman, C.M., Harm, D.L., Paloski, W.H.: Transient cardio-respiratory responses to visually induced tilt illusions. Brain Research Bulletin 53, 25–31 (2000)
16. Stanney, K.M., Hale, K.S., Nahmens, I., Kennedy, R.S.: What to expect from immersive virtual environment exposure: influences of gender, body mass index, and past experience. Hum. Factors 45, 504–520 (2003)
17. Howarth, P.A., Finch, M.: The nauseogenicity of two methods of navigating within a virtual environment. Applied Ergonomics 30, 39–45 (1999)

# A True Spatial Sound System for CAVE-Like Displays Using Four Loudspeakers

Torsten Kuhlen[1], Ingo Assenmacher[1], and Tobias Lentz[2]

[1] Virtual Reality Group, RWTH Aachen University,
Seffenter Weg 23, 52074 Aachen, Germany
[2] Institute of Technical Acoustics, RWTH Aachen University,
Neustraße 50, 52066 Aachen, Germany
{kuhlen,assenmacher}@rz.rwth-aachen.de,
tobias.lentz@akustik.rwth-aachen.de

**Abstract.** The paper introduces an audio rendering system based on the binaural approach, which allows a real-time simulation of spatially distributed sound sources and, in addition to that, near-to-head sources in room-mounted virtual environments. We have been developing a dynamic crosstalk cancellation, allowing the listener to freely move around without wearing any headphones. The paper gives a comprehensive description of the system, concentrating on the dual dynamic crosstalk cancellation and aspects of the integration of a real-time room acoustical simulation. Finally, two applications are described to show the wide applicability of the system.

**Keywords:** Virtual Reality, 3D Audio, Spatial Acoustics, Binaural Synthesis.

## 1 Introduction

In contrast to the human visual system, the human auditory system can perceive input from all directions and has no limited field of view. As such, it provides valuable cues for navigation and orientation in virtual environments. With respect to immersion, the acoustic sense is a very important additional source of information for the user, as acoustical perception works precisely especially for close auditory stimuli. This enhances the liveliness and credibility of the virtual environment. The ultimate goal thus would be the ability to place virtual sounds in any three dimensions and distance around the user in real-time. However, although multimodality is a crucial feature in Virtual Reality, the acoustical component is often neglected. While with head-mounted displays it might be quite acceptable to wear headphones, in CAVE-like environments loudspeakers are favored. Therefore, we have been developing a high-quality sound system based on the binaural approach. This approach is a powerful method for generating spatially distributed sounds, as a binaural signal represents the sound pressure at the eardrum of the listener. In contrast to other loudspeaker-based systems, the main benefit is the ability to reproduce near-to-head sources realistically. The binaural approach relies on crosstalk compensation when loudspeakers are used instead of headphones, which in existing systems only works when the user's head is

R. Shumaker (Ed.): Virtual Reality, HCII 2007, LNCS 4563, pp. 270–279, 2007.

positioned in a "sweet spot". Since in a virtual environment a user is typically walking around however, we have developed a dynamic crosstalk suppression which even works properly for a moving user. In particular, we are using a setup of four loudspeakers, where only two of them are active at a time in a way that a full 360 degrees rotation for the listener is provided. In addition to that, we coupled the acoustical rendering system with a visual VR system in order to realize a multi-modal dynamic virtual environment where the user and all sound sources can freely move without constraints, including near-to-head sources. With our approach, a versatile and stable real-time binaural sound system based on loudspeakers with dynamic crosstalk cancellation is available, generating congruent visual and acoustical scenes. One of the major contributions of this comprehensive system is the realization as a software-only solution that makes it possible to use this technology on a standard PC basis.

The remainder of this paper is structured as follows. First, we will give a brief overview of different reproduction approaches. We will, however, concentrate on the dynamic binaural synthesis approach with crosstalk cancellation and present this in more detail. After that, we briefly discuss aspects of the integration of a real-time room-acoustical simulation in our system. Room acoustics is an important aspect of a virtual environment, as sound is never correct without reference to the room it is present in. Two showcase applications will be presented in section 4 to show the width of applications that are possible to realize with a system like this. After that, a short discussion will end the paper.

## 2 A Brief Taxonomy of Audio Rendering in VR Systems

### 2.1 Panning

A popular technique for spatial acoustic imaging can be found in the intensity panning approach. Here, sound source distance and position is modeled by modifying the amplitude on the output channels of a predefined static loudspeaker setup. Such a multi channel audio is often used in home cinema systems to surround the listener with sound and also work quite well for VR applications which do not require a very exact placing of virtual sound sources. However, intensity panning is not able to provide authentic virtual sound scenes. In particular, it is impossible to crate virtual near-to-head sound sources, although these sources are of high importance in direct interaction metaphors for virtual environments, such as by-hand-placements or manipulations. Therefore, we will not discuss it in more detail.

There are mainly two different techniques reproducing a sound event with true spatial relation, i.e. wave field synthesis and the binaural approach. The following sections will briefly introduce principles and problems of these technologies.

### 2.2 Wave Field Synthesis

The basic theory of the wave field synthesis (WFS) is the *Huygens' principle.* An array of loudspeakers (ranging from just a few to some hundreds in number) used to reproduce a complete wave field. The simulation reproduces the sound field by virtually placing an array of microphones in the field that would be used to record a sound event at these points [3]. Placing loudspeakers at these points can reproduce an entire wave field for this area. Hence, this approach is especially adequate for multi-user virtual environments, where even non-tracked moving users get the real spatial sound impression.

The main drawback, beyond the high effort of processing power, is the size of the loudspeaker array. Furthermore, mostly solutions have been presented so far, where the sound field is only reproduced in one horizontal plane by a line of loudspeakers instead of a two-dimensional array. The placement of the loudspeakers in immersive projection-based VR displays with four to six surfaces as in CAVE-like environments is nearly impossible without any severe compromises. However, for semi-immersive displays like an L-shaped bench or a PowerWall, wave field synthesis is an excellent option when the focus is on multi-user virtual environments [12].

### 2.3 Binaural Synthesis

In contrast to wave field synthesis, a binaural approach does not deal with the complete reproduction of the sound field. It is convenient and sufficient to reproduce the sound field only at two points, the ears of the listener. In this case only two signals have to be calculated for a complete three-dimensional sound scene. The procedure of convolving a mono sound source with an appropriate pair of Head-Related Transfer Functions (HRTFs) in order to obtain a synthetic binaural signal is called *binaural synthesis*. The synthesized signals contain the directional information of the source, which is provided by the information in the HRTFs.

A *static binaural synthesis* transforms a sound source without any position information to a virtual source being related to the listener's head. This already works for a non-moving head, as the applied transfer function is related to the head and not to the room. For a moving head, this implies that the virtual source moves with the listener. For the realization of a room-related virtual source, a *dynamic binaural synthesis* has to be applied, where the HRTF must be changed when the listener turns or moves his head. In a VR system, the listener's position is always known and can also be used to realize a synthetic sound source with a fixed position corresponding to the room coordinate system. The system calculates the relative position and orientation of the listener's head to the imaginary point where the source should be localized. By knowing the relative position and orientation, the appropriate HRTF can be chosen from a database. It is also possible to synthesize many different sources and to create a complex three-dimensional acoustic scenario.

**Headphones versus Loudspeakers.** From a technical point of view, the presentation of binaural signals by headphones is the easiest way since the acoustical separation between both channels is perfectly solved. However, unsatisfying results are often obtained in the subjective sense of listeners. Furthermore, when the ears are covered by headphones, the impression of a source located at a certain point and distance to the listener often does not match the impression of a real sound field.

Another point is that while wearing a head-mounted display (HMD) in combination with headphones may fit quite well, in projection-based VR displays the focus is on non-intrusive components, i.e., the user should be as free as possible of any wearable hardware. This leads to the need for loudspeaker based reproduction techniques not only for the WFS approach, but also for the binaural synthesis.

The problem with loudspeaker reproduction of binaural signals is the crosstalk between the channels that destroys the three-dimensional cues. The requirement for a correct binaural presentation is that the right channel of the signal is audible only in the right ear and the left one is audible only in the left ear. This problem can be solved by a crosstalk cancellation (CTC) filter which is based on the transfer functions from each loudspeaker to each ear. For a static CTC system the four transfer functions from the speakers to the ears are used to calculate the filters for the elimination of crosstalk at one specific point. A detailed description of static CTC systems can be found in [2]. A static CTC system may only be quite acceptable for desktop VR systems with a user sitting in front of a monitor. In all other cases, it is necessary to adapt the CTC filters in real-time dependent on the current position and orientation of the listener [5]. While static CTC systems are state of the art, a newly developed, purely software-based approach of such a dynamic CTC – allowing a user to freely move within immersive virtual environments without wearing headphones – will be described in the next section.

Table 1 summarizes the benefits and drawbacks of the particular audio rendering approaches for different VR displays. For a high-quality integration of spatial audio into a virtual environment, only WFS and dynamic binaural synthesis with loudspeakers come into question. While WFS is rather costly and can only be installed in

**Table 1.** Assessment of available audio rendering approaches for different VR display technologies (LS: Loudspeaker, HP: Headphones, BS: Binaural Synthesis, WFS: Wave Field Synthesis). The benefits and drawbacks of the particular approaches are described in section 2. The last row depicts our approach introduced in this paper.

| | Desktop VR | HMD | Non-immersive Projection | Immersive Projection | Remarks |
|---|---|---|---|---|---|
| **Panning (LS)** | 😐 | 😐 | 😐 | 😐 | No near-to-head sources |
| **WFS (LS)** | ☺ | ☺ | ☺ | ☹ | High quality, high costs, multi-user |
| **Static BS, HP** | 😐 | ☹ | ☹ | ☹ | Sound moves with user |
| **Dyn. BS, HP** | 😐 | ☺ | 😐 | 😐 | Bad naturalness of presented sounds |
| **Static BS, LS** | 😐 | ☹ | ☹ | ☹ | Sweet Spot: user may not move |
| **Dyn. BS, LS** | ☺ | ☺ | ☺ | ☺ | **Flexible, low costs, user-centered** |

non- or semi-immersive environments without compromises, binaural synthesis promises to cope with few loudspeakers and flexible setup. Additionally, in particular near-to-head sound sources can be very precisely reproduced by the binaural approach. Especially for direct interaction such as by-hand placements or manipulations), which are preferred interaction metaphors in virtual environments, most objects reside within the grasping range and thus rather near to the user's head. Although no systematic studies have been carried out so far, there are strong hints that for such near-to-head sources, the binaural approach produces better results than WFS. A major drawback of the binaural synthesis is that it cannot be used in multi-user environments, however.

**Dynamic 360 degrees Crosstalk Cancellation.** To reproduce the binaural signal at the ears with a sufficient channel separation without using headphones, a CTC system is needed [9, 6]. Getting the CTC work in an environment where the user should be able to walk around and turn his head, a dynamic CTC system which is able to adapt during the listener's movements [5, 7] is required. The dynamic solution overrides the sweet spot limitation of a normal static crosstalk cancellation.

Figure 1 (left) shows the four transfer paths from the loudspeakers to the ears of the listener ($H_{1L}$) illustrates the transfer function from loudspeaker 1 to the left ear). A correct binaural reproduction means that the complete transfer function from the left input to the left ear, including the transfer function $H_{1L}$, is meant to become a flat spectrum. The same is intended for the right transfer path, accordingly. The crosstalk indicated by $H_{1R}$ and $H_{2L}$ has to be canceled by the system.

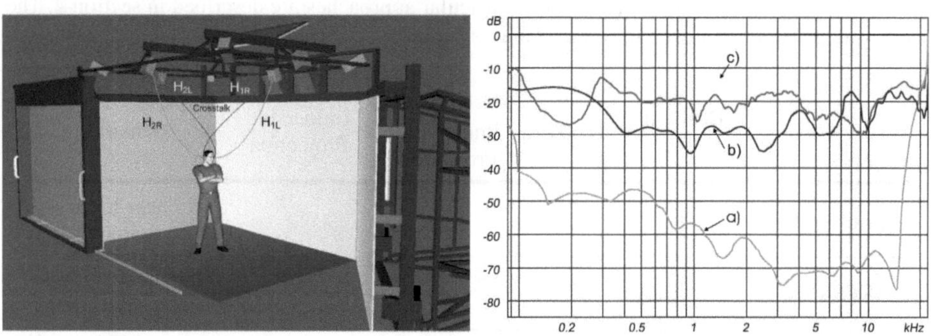


**Fig. 1.** *Left*: The CAVE-like environment at RWTH Aachen University. Four loudspeakers are mounted on the top rack of the system. The door, shown on the left, and a moveable wall, shown on the right, can be closed to allow a 360 degree view with no roof projection. *Right*: Measurement of the accessible channel separation using a filter length of 1,024 taps. a) calculated, b) static solution, c) dynamic system.

Since the user of a virtual environment is already tracked to generate the correct stereoscopic video images, it is possible to calculate the CTC filter on-line for the current position and orientation of the user. The calculation at runtime enhances the flexibility of the acoustic system regarding the validity area and the flexibility of the loudspeaker setup which can hardly be achieved with preprocessed filters. As a consequence, a database containing 'all' possible HRTFs is required. For our system, we use a database with a spatial resolution of one degree for both azimuth and elevation. The HRTFs were measured at a frequency range of 100Hz – 20kHz, allowing a cancellation in the same frequency range.

To provide a full head rotation of the user, a two loudspeaker setup will not be sufficient as the dynamic cancellation will only work in between the angle spanned by the loudspeakers. Thus, a dual CTC algorithm with a four speaker setup has been developed, which is further described in [8]. With four loudspeakers eight combinations of a normal two-channel CTC system are possible and a proper cancellation can be achieved for every orientation of the listener. An angle dependent fading is used to change the active speakers in between the overlapping validity areas of two configurations. Each time the head-tracker information is updated in the system, the deviation of the head to the position and orientation compared to the information given that caused the preceding filter change is calculated.

To classify the performance that could be reached theoretically by the dynamic system, measurements of a static system were made to have a realistic reference for the achieved channel separation. Under absolute ideal circumstances, the HRTFs used to calculate the crosstalk cancellation filters are the same as during reproduction (individual HRTFs of the listener). In a first test, the crosstalk cancellation filters were processed with HRTFs of an artificial head in a fixed position. The calculated channel separation using this filter set is plotted in Figure 1 (right) a). Thereafter, the achieved channel separation was measured at the ears of the artificial head, which had not been moved since the HRTF measurement (Figure 1 (right) curve b)). In comparison to the ideal reference cases, Figure 1 (right) curve c) shows the achieved channel separation of the dynamic CTC system. The main difference between the static and the dynamic system is the set of HRTFs used for filter calculation. The dynamic system has to choose the appropriate HRTF from a database and has to adjust the delay and the level depending on the position data. All these adjustments cause minor deviations from the ideal HRTF measured directly at this point. For this reason, the channel separation of the dynamic system is not as high as one that can be achieved by a system with direct HRTF measurement.

## 3 Dynamic Real-Time Room-Acoustics

For VR applications, it is not only important to have a flexible and precise reproduction system, but also the synchronization between the presented aural cues and the visual scene (or other modalities) is very important. The synchronization aspect does not only cover the correct timing of the presentation, but also the validity of all the cues with respect to the presented scenery. In that sense, for a correct auditory rendering, the virtual room has to be taken into account.

For that purpose, we coupled our reproduction system, which is controlled by a VR application, with the room-acoustics simulation software RAVEN [10], which enables us to simulate the dynamic room impulse responses for moving sources in real-time. RAVEN is basically an upgrade and enhancement of the hybrid room acoustical simulation method by [14]. Image sources are used for determining early reflections in order to provide a most accurate localization of primary sound sources (precedence effect [4]) during the simulation. Scattering and reverberation are estimated on-line by means of an improved stochastic ray tracing method. This aspect is an innovation in real-time virtual acoustics, which is to be considered as an important extension of the perceptive dimension. Since this contribution focuses on the implementation and applications of the complete system, no further details are presented here. A detailed description of the implementation and test results can be found in [11]. However, our complete system of binaural reproduction with dynamic crosstalk cancellation and room-acoustical simulation is currently able to simulate up to 10 moving sources with 2 seconds reverberation in real-time on today's standard PCs.

## 4 Applications

### 4.1 Interactive Concert Hall

As a case study application which features all aspects of complex acoustical sceneries, we developed a simulation of an existing convention center, the Eurogress located in Aachen, which is occasionally used as a concert hall. The concert hall has a volume of approximately 15.000m³. In this application, users can freely move within the scenery and study, for example, different listening positions and source configurations. In addition to that, they are able to move really close to the sound sources that are located in the scenery, grab them and move them around, while at all the time, the simulation produces a correct binaural representation at the ears of the listener. As sound sources, we modeled five instruments, two violins, a viola, a cello and a double bass.

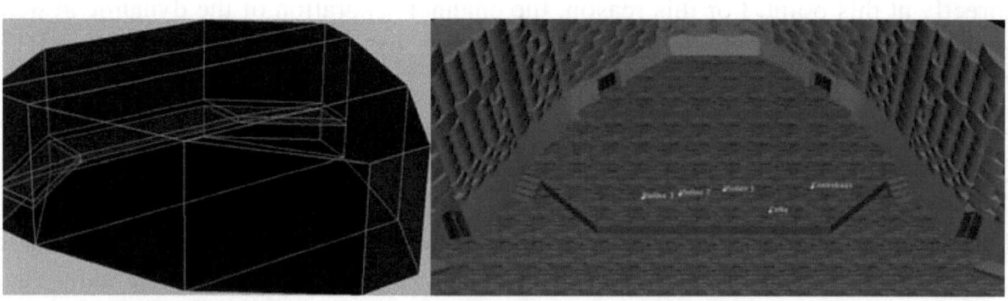

**Fig. 2.** *Left*: The room model used for the room acoustical simulation. *Right*: View from above the balcony on to the stage on the visual model of the concert hall. The labels indicate the positions of the sound sources in the scene at the beginning of the application. During the simulation, sound sources as well as listener positions may vary without constraints.

A source material we used midi tracks for each instrument, as it is difficult to get musical tracks in the field of classic music as anechoic and truly channel separated material. The five instruments are placed on stage of the concert hall, see Figure 2 (right).

The basis for the room-acoustical simulation is a reduced model of the visual model, see Figure 2 (left), and consists of 105 polygons and 74 planes respectively. This model has to be created before the simulation, as currently it is not possible for us to dynamically change the room-geometry during the simulation run. Although it is kept quite simple, the model contains all indoor elements of the room which are acoustically of interest, e.g., the stage, the skew wall elements, and the balustrade. Details of small elements are neglected and represented by equivalent scattering. Surface properties and coefficients are defined through standardized material data (ISO17497-1, ISO354:2003). For demonstration purposes, we implemented that users can switch between free-field simulation and room-acoustical simulation during the application run, allowing to pair-compare the difference in the sound-field with and without room-acoustics.

Although no formal studies in this environment were carried out, the responses to this dense and interactive scenario by users are very positive. The localization with enabled room-acoustics seems to be less precise, as there are more cues in the signal due to the simulated reflection of the walls, but the overall immersion is much higher, as the sound becomes more vivid and realistic. In addition to that, the presentation of a room inside a 360 degree CAVE-like environment in addition to a 360 degrees dynamic sound field with near-to-head sources seems to compensate the imperfection of the installation, e.g., as we do not compensate reflections from the real projection walls of the projection device in the binaural signal.

### 4.2 A Visuo-Acoustic VR Study in Neuro-Psychology

The audio rendering system has recently been integrated into *NeuroMan*, a toolkit developed at RWTH Aachen University which allows for VR-based behavioural studies in the neuro-psychological field [13]. Currently, a study is being carried out which aims at developing a three-dimensional cube-shaped paradigm to assess visual, auditory as well as cross-modal cueing effects on spatial orientation of attention. Up to now, cueing effects have only been assessed in two-dimensional space. In the three-dimensional space it remains unclear if cues need to have exactly the same spatial position as the target stimulus in order to provoke an optimal validity effect.

The cube is constructed with cues and targets being presented at exactly the same spatial positions in both the visual and the auditory modalities at an L-shaped workbench. The auditory condition is realised by the audio rendering system presented in the previous sections. The spatial positions in the cube are marked by virtual loudspeakers placed at all eight corners of the cube (see Figure 3 (left)). Spatial cueing is provided by changing the colour of one of these loudspeakers, whereas the loudspeaker itself topples down to serve as a target. There are valid as well as invalid cues (in an 80:20 ratio). The response times depending on the spatial position of these cues in relation to the target position are measured in milliseconds. A preliminary test with

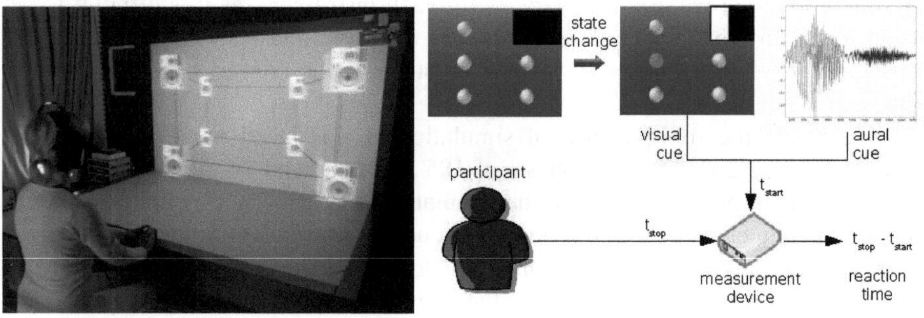


**Fig. 3.** *Left*: A VR-based neuro-psychological study about cross-modal cueing, performed on an L-bench and making use of the audio rendering system. *Right*: The experiment's setup and schematic view of the reaction time measurement.

9 volunteers has shown that the dynamic binaural approach based on loudspeakers is particularly suitable to perform such experiments and by far preferable to a headphones solution.

## 5 Discussion

We developed and integrated techniques to realize a fully dynamic acoustic-visual VR environment. We put emphasis on the interactivity aspect of the system, realizing a physically plausible real-time simulation of sound sources located in a room, where both are possible: the listener as well as the sources can be moved independently without constraints. The 360 degrees CTC system enables the use of a flexible, yet low cost, sound installation in CAVE-like environments without the need for headphones. This realizes a non-intrusive technology that can be used directly without further calibration. The complete system is the basis for extensive research on the interplay between acoustic and visual modalities on different levels. While one aspect covers the very basic interactions on a perceptive level, another focus will be research on a subjective level, where immersion or presence aspects will be focused on. Another great challenge will be the work on dynamic room simulation, where users will be able to change parameters of the room-acoustical simulation on-line, e.g., changing the room geometry or wall materials and inspect the differences in the sound-field. This, of course has the precondition of a simulation that has, as an on-line simulation comparable results (in terms of correctness and quality) to off-line simulations usually employed in room acoustical simulation.

**Acknowledgements.** The work in this paper is part of the DFG project KU 1132/3 and VO600/13. The authors kindly thank the German Research Foundation (DFG) for their support and funding. In addition, we would like to thank Solveyg Anders and Walter Sturm, University Hospital Aachen, for their collaboration in the study about cross-modal cueing, funded by the Interdisciplinary Center for Clinical Research (IZKF BIOMAT).

## References


1. Steinberg Media Technologies GmbH: ASIO2.0 Audio Streaming Input Output Development Kit, (2007) last visited: 12.02.2007 URL: http//www.steinberg.net
2. Bauck, J., Cooper, D.H.: Generalization Transaural Stereo and Applications. In: Journal of the AES 44, 683–705 (1996)
3. Berkhout, A.J., Vogel, P., de Vries, D.: Use of Wave Field Synthesis for Natural Reinforced Sound. In: Proceedings of the Audio Engineering Society Convention 92 (1992)
4. Cremer L., Müller, H. A.: Die wissenschaftlichen Grundlagen der Raumakustik. S. Hirzel Verlag (1978)
5. Gardner, W.G.: 3-D audio using loudspeakers; PhD Thesis, Massachusetts Institute of Technology (1997)
6. Kirkeby, O., Nelson, P.A., Hamada, H.: Local sound field reproduction using two loudspeakers. Journal of the Acoustical Society of Amerika 104, 1973–1981 (1998)
7. Lentz, T., Schmitz, O.: Realisation of an adaptive cross-talk cancellation system for a moving listener. In: Proceedings of the 21st Audio Engineering Society Conference, St. Petersburg (2002)
8. Lentz, T., Behler, G.: Dynamic Cross-Talk Cancellation for Binaural Synthesis in Virtual Reality Environments. In: Proceedings of the 117th Audio Engineering Society Convention, San Francisco, USA (2004)
9. Møller, H.: Reproduction of artificial head recordings through loudspeakers, vol. 37 (1989)
10. Schröder, D., Lentz, T.: Real-Time Processing of Image Sources Using Binary Space Partitioning. Journal of the Audio Engineering Society 54,Nr.: 7/8, 604–619 (2006)
11. Schröder, D., Dross, P., Vorländer, M.: A Fast Reverberation Estimator for Virtual Environments. In: Audio Engineering Society, 30th international Conference, Saariselka, Finnland (2007)
12. Springer, J.P., Sladeczek, C., Scheffler, M., Jochstrate, J., Melchior, F., Fröhlich, B.: Combining Wave Field Synthesis and Multi-Viewer Stereo Displays. In: Proc.of the IEEE Virtual Reality 2006 Conference, pp. 237–240 (2006)
13. Valvoda, J.T., Kuhlen, T., Wolter, M., Armbrüster, C., Spijkers, W., Vohn, R., Sturm, W., Fimm, B.: NeuroMan: A Comprehensive Software System for Neuropsychological Experiments. CyberPsychology & Behaviour 8(4), 366–367 (2005)
14. Vorländer, M.: Ein Strahlverfolgungsverfahren zur Berechnung von Schallfeldern in Räumen. ACUSTICA 65, 138–148 (1988)

# Design and Evaluation of a Hybrid Display System for Motion-Following Tasks

Sangyoon Lee[1], Sunghoon Yim[2], Gerard Jounghyun Kim[1,*], Ungyeon Yang[3], and Chang-Hun Kim[1]

[1] Dept. of CSE, Korea Univ.
Seoul 136-701 Korea
gjkim@korea.ac.kr
[2] VR Lab, Dept. of CSE, POSTECH
Pohang Kyoungbuk 790-784 Korea
[3] VR Team, Digital Content Research Division, ETRI
Daejeon 305-700 Korea

**Abstract.** Hybrid display systems are those that combine different types of displays to exploit the complementary characteristics of the constituent display systems. In this paper, we introduce a hybrid system that combines a stereoscopic optical see-through head-mounted display (HMD) and a large projection display for an application in a multi-user ship painting training scenario. The proposed hybrid system's projection display provides a large FOV and a physical metaphor to the ship surface with natural depth perception, while the HMD provides personal and unoccluded display of the motion training guides. To quantify its effectiveness, we conducted a human subject experiment, comparing the subject's motion following task performance among three different display systems: large projection display, head-mounted display, and hybrid. The preliminary results obtained from the experiment has shown that given the same FOV, the hybrid system performed, despite problems with registration between the real and virtual worlds, up to par with the head-mounted display, and better than the projection display. Thus, it is expected that the hybrid display will result in higher task performance with the larger FOV factor available.

## 1 Introduction

In virtual or mixed reality systems, usually visual display systems of a single type are combined to achieve certain functionality, for example, a large FOV or stereoscopy [1, 3]. On the other hand, hybrid display systems are those that combine different types of displays, equally to meet certain visual needs, but by exploiting the complementary characteristics of the constituent display systems. For example, Ilie et al. introduced a hybrid display system that consisted of a high-resolution stereoscopic head-mounted display (HMD) and a low resolution wide FOV projector display to provide an effective imagery to surgical trainees who needed to be spatially aware of one's surroundings, yet be able to concentrate on a central object [4].

* Correspondence author.

R. Shumaker (Ed.): Virtual Reality, HCII 2007, LNCS 4563, pp. 280–289, 2007.

Another avenue to leverage on the merits of the head-mounted display and wide FOV projection display is in a multi-user motion training scenario (note that in [4], although the application domain was also a training system, the training occurred through passive first-person viewpoint visualization). One particular application is the training for spray painting of ships. Spray painting of ships requires careful timing and following regular motion profiles to ensure uniform paint thickness on the surface. We can envision a VR-based training system in which only a large projection display is used with its zero parallax plane corresponding to the ship surface. In addition, with stereoscopic support (e.g. shutter glass or light polarization), one can simulate the required close-range 3D motion profiles to train a user. The problem is that it is difficult to display the motion training guide because of the occlusion by the hands on which the virtual spray gun must be rendered (and overlaid). The same system can be realized using an HMD, however, it is expected that the use of a large projection would be better because of the large FOV, and the natural physical metaphor to the ship surface (and depth perception). A hybrid display, e.g. HMD + projection display, offers a solution; the projection still provides the large FOV and physical metaphor, and the HMD provides unoccluded motion guides for the hands. In addition, the hybrid system allows multiple users to train at the same time.

In this paper, we present a hybrid system that combines a large projection display and an optical see-through HMD to be used as a display system for training ship spray-painting. To quantify its effectiveness, we conducted a human subject experiment, comparing the subject's motion-following task performance among three different display systems: (large) projection only, head-mounted display only, and hybrid. This paper is organized as follows. In the next section, we review the work related to the hybrid visual display systems. Section 3 describes the details of our hybrid display system, and Section 4 steps through the human subject experiment and the derived results. Finally, we conclude the paper with an executive summary and directions for future research.

## 2 Related Work

The concept of the hybrid display was first introduced in 1991 by Feiner and Shamash who combined an HMD and a flat panel display to provide personal context information [2]. Others have attempted to mix different types of displays as well. Researchers from the Fraunhofer Institute developed a visualization system that combined a central autostereoscopic 3D display with surrounding 2D displays [7]. However, in general, not much work has been published regarding system designs nor usability of hybrid display systems.

Our idea of using the projection surface metaphorically mapped to a virtual object (in this case, the painted ship surface) is similar to the work on life-sized projector-based dioramas by Low et al. [6]. Their work aimed at creating life-sized immersive virtual environments by projecting on physical objects that roughly approximated the geometry of the objects it was to represent.

An HMD with a wide field of view is hard to come by because of the technical (e.g. wide angle folding optics), economical (e.g. high resolution) and ergonomic (e.g. light weight) difficulties. Slater and Usoh simulated a wider FOV by rendering the foveal region normally and by compressing more of the scene into the outer regions of the display area [8]. Yang and Kim also have shown that the effective FOV could potentially be increased up to twice the physical FOV by scaling down the imagery without significant distortion in depth perception when multimodal interaction is used [11].

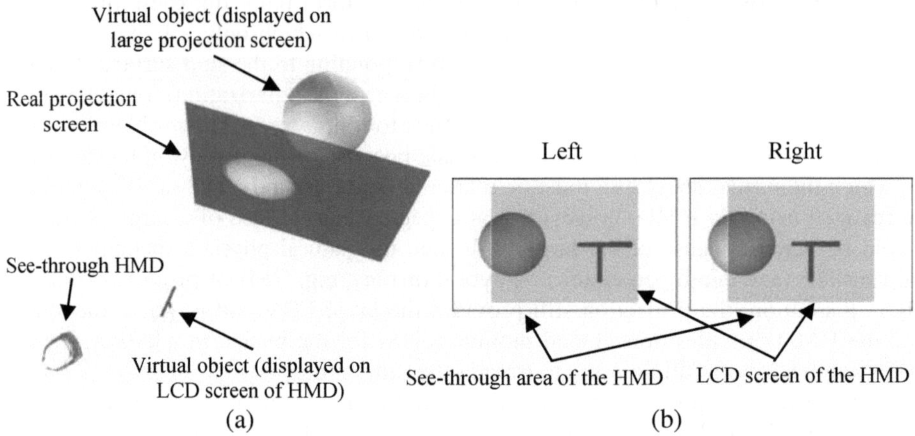


**Fig. 1.** An illustration of combining the images displayed on the projector screen and displayed on the LCD screen of the see-through HMD. (a) An example of the configuration using both the large screen and the see-through HMD. (b) Combined stereoscopic image pair shown through the see-through HMD.

## 3 Implementation of a Hybrid Display System

In this section, we describe implementation details of our hybrid display system that consists of a rear-projected large display and a see-through HMD. The large display had the screen size of 140cm × 105cm, and used two projectors for passive stereoscopy with circular polarized light filters. Each projector supported a resolution of 1280 pixels × 1024 pixels. The optical see-through HMD (called Deocom SX-500) had a resolution of 1280 pixels × 1024 pixels, an aspect ratio of 5:4, and a vertical FOV of 27.4°. The circular polarized light filters were also attached to the HMD, so users could see both the stereoscopic image displayed on the large projection screen and that displayed on the LCD screen of the HMD at the same time (see Figure 1).

The projection models for the large display and for the HMD were different from each other in order to correctly register images on the projection screen and on the LCD screen of the HMD. While the standard perspective (on-axis) projection model was used for the HMD, an off-axis (head-coupled) perspective projection model was used for the large display. The viewing frustums for the large display and for the HMD were made to be seamlessly combined, by adjusting the near and far clipping planes for each display For head tracking, the Intersense IS-900 VE head tracker was attached to the HMD, and the offset to the center position between the left and right eyes from the tracker sensor was estimated with the 3D CAD model of the HMD provided by the HMD manufacturer. Images for the large display and for the HMD were generated from two separate PCs, which were connected to same tracker sever through the VR Peripheral Network [9].

Although each parameter for the projection models was carefully and precisely measured, it was not enough to correctly register images on the projection screen and on the LCD screen of the HMD. It was because the IPD of the HMD (which was fixed at 6.5cm) could be different from those of users. In order to match the distance between the centers of two images for left and right eyes with user's IPD (which was measured with a pupilometer), we performed a simple calibration procedure. In the procedure, the user was required to adjust the viewport positions (the first two parameters of OpenGL glViewport() function) of stereo pair images rendered with her/his IPD. The detailed procedure followed the steps below:

- *Step 1*: Display two identical reference left eye images (e.g. blue painting gun) each on the projection screen and on the see-through HMD screen.
- *Step 2*: For a given user, while wearing the see-through HMD, adjust the viewport parameters for the HMD using the joy stick on the wand until the two images are reasonably fused and registered.
- *Step 3*: Repeat Steps 1 and 2 for the right eye.

The hybrid display system was applied to a simple painting-training application using the Ghost metaphor [10]. In the application, users could paint on a virtual object (displayed on the large projection screen at a distance of 2m) in a given pattern with a virtual blue painting gun controlled by (and drawn at the position of) a wand, while following the guided motion of a virtual yellow painting gun. An example is shown in Figure 3.

# 4 Experiment

## 4.1 Independent and Dependent Variables

The independent and dependent variables considered in the experiment are shown in Tables 1 and 2, respectively. We compared three display types: using a large display only (PROJECTOR), using a see-through HMD only (HMD), and using both a large display and a see-through HMD (HYBRID). Each display type could be simply set up by adjusting the near and far clipping planes for each display system, because the positions of target objects were fixed and the virtual painting gun (or user's hands) and the viewpoints could be located only in the given range (note that the guide painting gun moved through the predefined paths). Since the paths of the guide motion might have an effect on the dependent variables, the different types of the guide motion (or painting pattern) were also considered as an independent variable. The FOV of the see-through area was set approximately equal to that of the HMD to make the experiment conditions the same. In other words, FOV was not a factor in this experiment.

## 4.2 User Tasks

In the experiment, each participant carried out six types of the painting task: three types for training and three types for actual trials. The task types are described below:

**Table 1.** The independent variables considered in the experiment

| Level | Description |
|---|---|
| | *Display Type* |
| PROJECTOR | All objects are displayed only on the large screen. |
| HMD | All objects are displayed only on the LCD screen of the see-through HMD. |
| HYBRID | Target objects are displayed on the large screen, and the painting guns (including the guide gun) are displayed on the LCD screen of the see-through HMD. |
| | *Guide Motion (or Painting Pattern) Type* |
| Level | Description |
| HORIZONTAL | The guide painting gun moves mainly in a horizontal direction (The painting pattern is horizontal). |
| VERTICAL | The guide painting gun moves mainly in a vertical direction (The painting pattern is vertical). |
| CIRCULAR | The guide painting gun moves through a circular path (The painting pattern is circular). |

**Table 2.** The dependent variables considered in the experiment

| Name | Description |
|---|---|
| PD | The average position difference between the user and the guide motions. |
| OD | The average orientation (represented by unit quaternions) difference between the user and the guide motions. |
| PPD | The average distance between the given painting pattern and the user painting result. |

- *Training Task 1*: Spraying red paint freely on a gray square plane (side length = 90cm) located about 2m ahead (see Figure 2).
- *Training Task 2*: Spraying red paint on the gray plane in a "horizontal" pattern while following the motion of a yellow guide painting gun. The guide gun moved in horizontal direction only for 10 seconds, and its orientation was not changed (see Figure 3).
- *Training Task 3*: Spraying red paint on the gray plane in a "vertical" pattern while following the guide motion. The guide gun moved in vertical direction only for 10 seconds, and its orientation was not changed.
- *Actual Task 1 (HORIZONTAL)*: Spraying red paint on a gray sphere (radius = 30cm) located about 2m ahead, while following the motion of the yellow guide painting gun for 10 seconds. The painting pattern was "horizontal," but the orientation of the guide gun, as well as its position, was changed (see Figure 4a).
- *Actual Task 2 (VERTICAL)*: Spraying red paint on the gray sphere, while following the guide motion for 10 seconds. The painting pattern was "vertical," but the orientation of the guide gun, as well as its position, was changed (see Figure 4b).
- *Actual Task 3 (CIRCULAR)*: Spraying red paint on the gray sphere, while following the guide motion for 30 seconds. The painting pattern was "circular," but the orientation of the guide gun, as well as its position, was changed (see Figure 4c).

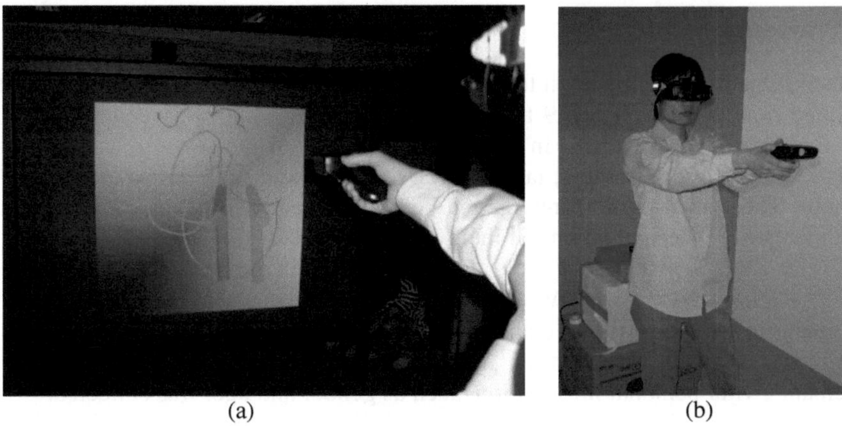

Fig. 2. Training Task 1: Free spray without the guide object. (a) A snapshot of a participant's carrying out the training task 1 with PROJECTOR. (b) A front view of him.

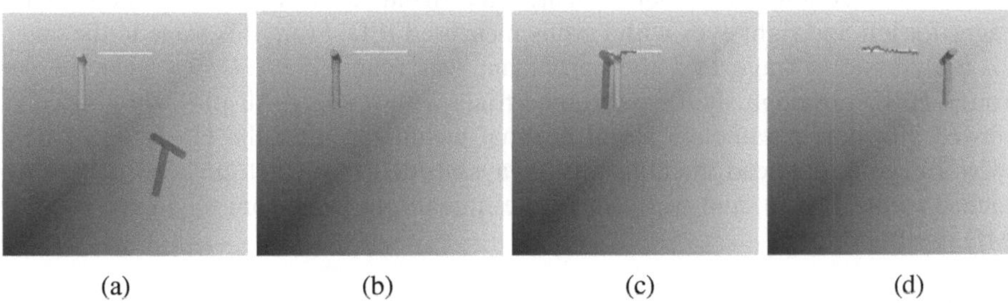

Fig. 3. Training Task 2: Spraying the paint in the given horizontal pattern while following the guide motion. (a) Initial state. (b) Matching the position and orientation of the painting gun with those of the guide painting gun. (c) Spraying the paint while following the guide motion. (d) Task completion.

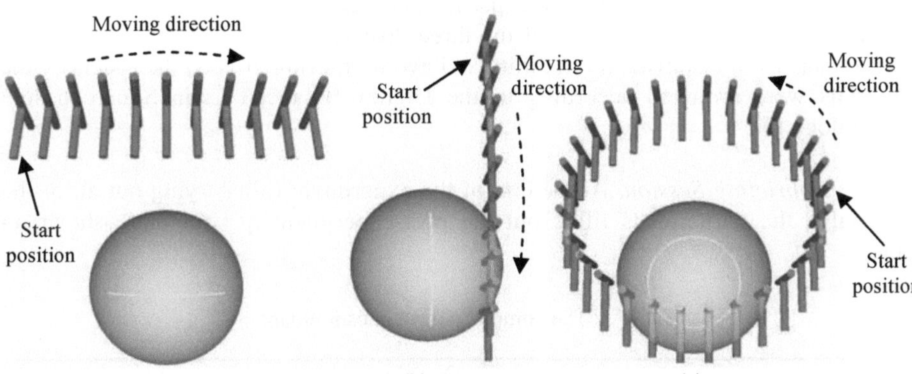


Fig. 4. The position and orientation of the guide painting gun profile at every second for each Actual Task. (a) For Actual Task 1: The total path length of the guide motion was about 35cm. (b) For Actual Task 2: The total path length of the guide motion was about 21cm. (c) For Actual Task 3: The total path length of the guide motion was about 63cm.

### 4.3 Procedure

Eighteen subjects participated in the experiment. Each participant visited our lab at an appointed time and performed 9 trials (1 trial for each task-display combination or 3 trials for each display system) in different orders. All of the sessions including preliminaries, calibration, training, task, as well as discussion time, lasted approximately one hour. The age of participants ranged between 19 and 35 (mean = 23.5 and standard deviation = 3.6), and among of them were 2 females.

*Stage I: Preliminary Session.* We introduced the experiment to the subject with the participant instruction which elaborated on the system and devices used in the experiment, as well as the task to be performed. After the introduction, the participant's vital personal information,′such as gender and age, was collected.

*Stage II: Calibration Session.* First, the participant's inter-pupil distance (IPD) was measured with a pupilometer. And then, we performed the calibration procedure described in Section 3 in order to match the distance between the centers of two images for left and right eyes with her/his measured IPD. From this stage to the end of task trial session (Stage IV), the participant was required to always wear the see-through HMD although she/he performed trials with the large display only, since the adjusted viewport parameters might become unsuitable after the HMD was put off and worn again, the head tracking was always needed (note that the head tracker was attached to the HMD), and we wanted to eliminate the bias from having to wear the HMD itself.

*Stage III: Training Session.* To understand how to operate and carry out the required task, the participants were given a period of training prior to the actual task session. The training involved carrying out the three tasks designed for training (described in Section 4.2) with all of the three display systems.

*Stage IV: Task Trial Session.* Each participant performed the three actual tasks (described in Section 4.2) with all of the three display systems ($3 \times 3 = 9$ trials). In order to enhance the statistical reliability and avoid ordering effects, the orders of the nine trials were arranged according to the Digram-Balanced Latin Square design methodology [5].

*Stage V: Debriefing Session.* At the end of the experiment (after trying out all of the nine trials), the participants filled out the post-experiment questionnaire shown in Table 3.

**Table 3.** The comprehensive questionnaire.

| No. | Question |
|---|---|
| 1 | Was there any abnormal incidence while performing the given tasks? |
| 2 | During the task trials, what virtual objects did you mainly gaze on? |
| 3 | Did you experience any inconvenience in using the system? If you did, please describe. |

## 5 Results

The means and the standard deviations of the dependent variables collected in the task trial session are summarized in Figures 5–6. A two-way within-subject ANOVA was applied on the dependent variables. The ANOVA results for the display type are also shown in Figures 5–6. According to the ANOVA, there were statistically significant differences among the display types for all of the dependent variables. However, the SNK (Student-Newman-Keuls) post hoc multiple comparison test revealed that only PROJECTOR was in a different group, that is, there was no significant difference between HMD and HYBRID. This means that HMD (the display type using HMD only) and HYBRID (the display type using both the large display and the HMD) exhibited higher task performance than PROJECTOR (the display type using the large display only). When PROJECTOR was used, the guide painting gun was often occluded by the wand or the participant's hands. However, when HMD and HYBRID were used, the painting gun was not occluded, since the LCD image of the HMD was always drawn on the real objects. In the debriefing session, seven participants reported this occlusion problem. We think that the occlusion problem of PROJECTOR had a negative effect on carrying out the given tasks.

On the other hand, as for the guide motion (or painting pattern) factor, the ANOVA revealed that there were significant differences for PD (position difference between the user and guide motions) and OD (orientation difference between the user and guide motions) but not for PPD (distance between the given painting pattern and the user painting result) (see Figure 6). However, there was no significant interaction between the display type and the guide motion type for all of the dependent variables (for PD, $F_{4,68} = 1.11$, $p = 0.36$, for OD, $F_{4,68} = 1.16$, $p = 0.34$, and for PPD, $F_{4,68} = 2.27$, $p = 0.07$). This means that the guide motion type alone had an effect on the task performance, but it did not have any mutual influence on the effects of the display type.

According to the replies to the questionnaire of the debriefing session, two participants reported that they had felt a little dizzy because the head belt of the HMD was too strongly tightened. Eleven participants replied to the second question that they had mainly gazed on the guide painting gun during the task trials, and the others replied that they had mainly gazed both on the target object and on the guide painting gun in an alternating fashion. As for the inconvenience in using the system, four participants pointed out the problem that the images projected on the large screen were dark. This problem was due to using the polarized light filters for stereoscopic imaging, and the brightness reduction caused by the half mirror installed in the HMD for providing the optical see-through function. We believe that the brightness reduction problem can be resolved simply by using brighter projectors. Two participants reported that the images displayed on the large projection screen and those on the LCD screen of the HMD were not fully registered, that is, the paint was sprayed on slightly different spots from the intended ones (at which they pointed the painting gun) for HYBRID. However, the experimental results show that the hybrid display system performed, despite the registration problem, up to par with the HMD.

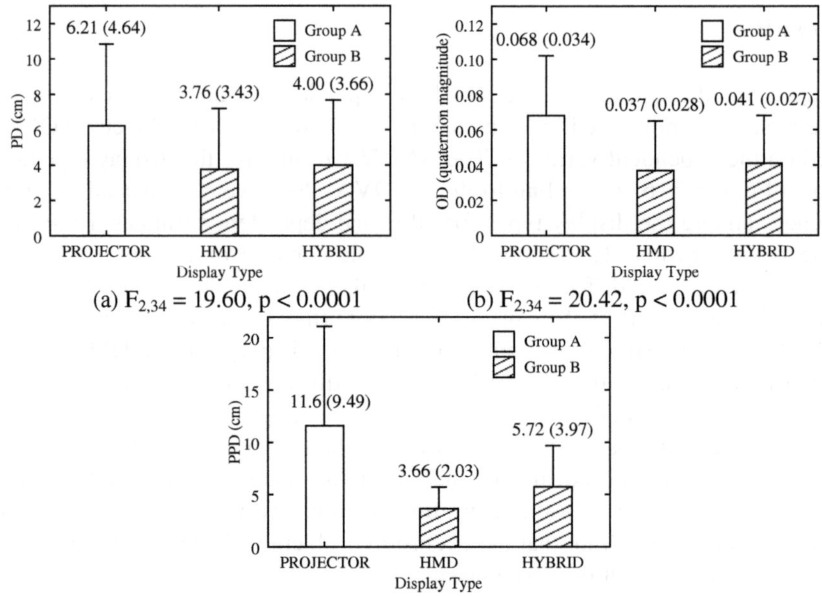


(a) $F_{2,34} = 19.60$, $p < 0.0001$ (b) $F_{2,34} = 20.42$, $p < 0.0001$

(c) $F_{2,34} = 27.52$, $p < 0.0001$

**Fig. 5.** Three task performance results for the display types: the means and (parenthesized) standard deviations, the ANOVA results, and the SNK-grouping results ($\alpha = 0.05$)

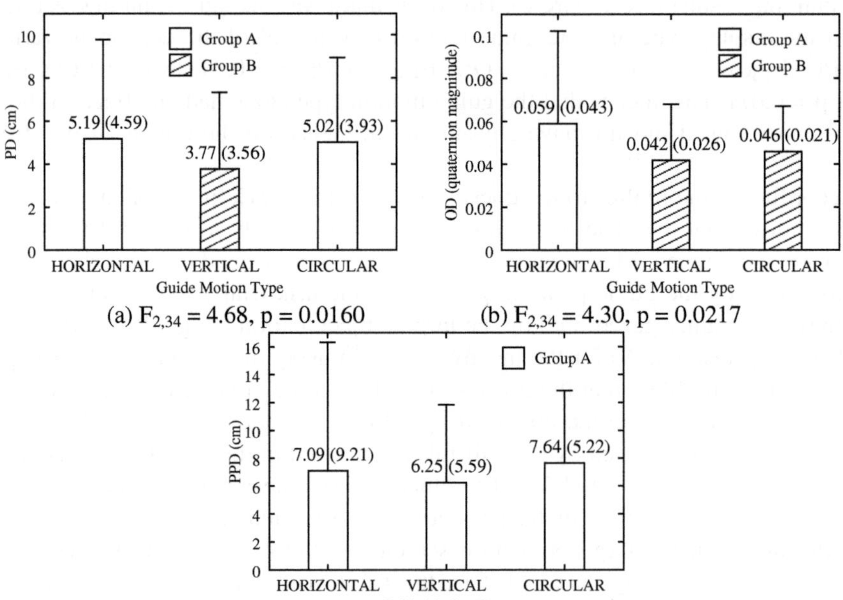


(a) $F_{2,34} = 4.68$, $p = 0.0160$ (b) $F_{2,34} = 4.30$, $p = 0.0217$

(c) $F_{2,34} = 0.81$, $p = 0.4537$

**Fig. 6.** Three task performance results for the guide motion types: the means and (parenthesized) standard deviations, the ANOVA results, and the SNK-grouping results ($\alpha = 0.05$)

## 6 Conclusions and Future Work

In this paper, we demonstrated that using a hybrid display that consisted of a large projection display and a see-through HMD was better for the guided-motion-following tasks than just using the large display only, thanks to the advantage of the HMD that eliminated occlusion of the guide motions. Although there was no significant difference between using the hybrid display and using the HMD only, we believe that using the hybrid display would have an advantage over the HMD only, because the hybrid display can provide much wider FOV (which was not a factor in the experiment in this work) than the HMD. Our future work is to experimentally validate this claim and to upgrade and deploy our system for a real industrial usage.

**Acknowledgement.** The authors would like to thank ETRI for its financial support. This work was also supported in part by MIC & IITA through IT Leading R&D Support Project.

## References

1. Cruz-Neira, C., Sandin, D.J., DeFanti, T.A.: Surround-Screen Projection-Based Virtual Reality: The Design and Implementation of the CAVE. In: Proc. of the ACM SIGGRAPH (1993)
2. Feiner, S., Shamash, A.: Hybrid User Interfaces: Breeding Virtually Bigger Interfaces for Physically Smaller Computers. In: Proc. of the ACM UIST (1991)
3. Hereld, M., Judson, I.R., Stevens, R.L.: Introduction to Building Projection-Based Tiled Display Systems. IEEE Computer Graphics and Applications 20(4), 22–28 (2000)
4. Ilie, A., Low, K.-L., Welch, G., Lastra, A., Fuchs, H.: Combining Head-Mounted and Projector-Based Displays for Surgical Training. Presence: Teleoperators and Virtual Environments 13(2), 128–145 (2004)
5. Keppel, G.: Design and Analysis: A Researcher's Handbook. Prentice-Hall, Upper Saddle River, NJ (1991)
6. Low, K.-L., Welch, G., Lastra, A., Fuchs, H.: Life-Sized Projector-Based Dioramas. In: Proc. of the ACM VRST (2001)
7. Pastoor, S., Lie, J.: 3-D Display and Interaction Technologies for Desktop Computing. In: Javidi, B., Okano, F. (eds.): Three-Dimensional Television, Video, and Display Technologies, pp. 315–356. Springer-Verlag, Berlin (2002)
8. Slater, M., Usoh, M.: Simulating Peripheral Vision in Immersive Virtual Environments. Computers & Graphics 17(6), 643–653 (1993)
9. Talyor II, R.M., Hudson, T.C., Seeger, A., Weber, H., Juliano, J., Helser, A.T.: VRPN: A Device-Independent, Network-Transparent VR Peripheral System. In: Proc. of the ACM VRST (2001)
10. Yang, U., Kim, G.J.: Implementation and Evaluation of "Just Follow Me": An Immersive, VR-Based, Motion-Training System. Presence: Teleoperators and Virtual Environments 11(3), 304–323 (2002)
11. Yang, U., Kim, G.J.: Increasing the Effective Egocentric Field of View with Proprioceptive and Tactile Feedback. In: Proc. of the IEEE VR (2004)

# Orientation Specific and Geometric Determinant of Mental Representation of the Virtual Room

Zhiqiang Luo and Henry Been-Lirn Duh

Centre for Human Factors & Ergonomics, School of Mechanical & Aerospace Engineering, Nanyang Technological University, Singapore
peterluo@pmail.ntu.edu.sg, mblduh@ntu.edu.sg

**Abstract.** Subjects in the experiment reported observed the same spatial layout in the rectangular room and the cylindrical room from the exocentric ( $45^0$ ) perspective first and then the egocentric ( $0^0$ ) perspective. The mental representations of space were testified by the judgment of relative direction between objects. The results showed that subjects represented the spatial horizontal relation more accurately along the imagined direction that paralleled to the wall in the rectangular room but along the imagined direction that was ever faced in the cylindrical room. The rectangular room better facilitated the coding of spatial vertical information than the cylindrical room. Subjects could respond faster when retrieving the spatial relations in the direction faced during the observation. The data indicated that the orientation-specific representation was constructed and the environmental geometry could influence the accuracy of spatial direction in mind.

**Keywords:** Virtual Reality, Mental Representation, Perspective, Geometry.

## 1 Introduction

Understanding the structure of space is one natural activity when people explore the three-dimensional (3D) space. Although large numbers of studies have brought insights into the mechanisms of spatial memory during navigation, most of them concerned two-dimensional (2D) navigation. The main reason might be that the height of perspective is not changed during the navigation. For instance the navigator on the plane observes the space constantly through the eye-level perspective while the orientation may update dynamically. Thus most research pays no much attention to the effect of verticality on the representation of space. The present study approaches the verticality of space by changing the viewpoint from the exocentric perspective to the egocentric perspective.

The egocentric perspective means the perspective of a ground-level observer within the space, whereas the viewpoint of exocentric perspective is external to the space, for example the viewpoint of map reader. Subjects in the study of Shelton and McNamara [8] learned the spatial layout of a large-scale virtual environment from either the egocentric perspective or the exocentric perspective. They found that

R. Shumaker (Ed.): Virtual Reality, HCII 2007, LNCS 4563, pp. 290–299, 2007.

subjects seemed to represent the space according the direction faced in the first leg of route. Luo and Duh [5] classified the exocentric perspective in more details. In their study subjects observed the spatial layout in the room through one of five perspectives distributed on the vertical plane, and then took the direction judgment task. They found that the accuracy of representation of the vertical link among the spatial layout decreased as the perspective elevated in the room. Subjects with the mid-exocentric ($45^0$) perspective better encode the horizontal link among the spatial layout in the rectangular room. The perspective changed along the vertical dimension affects the spatial process of verticality on space. The process of verticality in memory was observed to be independent of the process of horizontal dimension [3]. The change of verticality could be a source of disorientation in space. Subjects in the Passini study [6] needed knowledge about vertical relationships to make decisions about the use of stairways and elevators.

Perspective elevation can also influence the performance of the task in the 3D space. In the research about designing the format of the aviation display, Wickens and colleagues found that the display showing the view from the egocentric perspective better supports the local guidance in which the egocentric frame of reference plays the critical role [10]. The display showing the view from the exocentric perspective, especially when the degree of elevated viewpoint is $45^0$, enhances the understanding of spatial structure and support the awareness in space, in which the exocentric frame of reference takes main functions [4]. Further, they proposed that the split-screen display that depicted the space from both the egocentric and exocentric perspectives at the same time may resolve the perceptual ambiguities. The experimental result suggested that this split-screen display provide the better support for the continuous task of local awareness and guidance and poor support for some of global situation awareness (SA) tasks [9].

From a spatial reference point of view, the environmental geometry can take function as the exocentric frame of reference to influence the representation of space. Hartley, Trinkler and Burgess [1] changed the geometry of the arena that was enclosed by walls, and found that subjects marked the cue object based on the distance to the walls. They suggested that geometry of the arena acted as a cue to the orientation. One salient feature of room space is the external constraint, the room wall. The geometry of room is assumed to influence the representation of the spatial layout in the room. But Shelton & McNamara [7] found that after the wall was changed from rectangular shape to the cylindrical shape, the orientation-specific representation of space was still observed.

To summarize the previous findings, perspective elevation could influence the representation of space, but providing the exocentric view during the navigation could improve the spatial awareness. In the present study, the effect of combining the exocentric and immersive (egocentric) views on the representation was studied further. Subjects observed the spatial layout in the room first from the exocentric perspective and then the egocentric perspective. The mental representation was tested by the same spatial task. It was assumed that the orientation-specific mental representation could be constructed after the observation. Another objective of the present study was to investigate the role of environmental geometry in representing the spatial layout. Two rooms, the rectangular room and the cylindrical room, were simulated by computer software. The room axes defined by the wall were more salient in the rectangular room than in the cylindrical room. The salient room axes might interfere the coding of space. It was hypothesized that subjects could better represent the spatial layout in the cylindrical room than in the rectangular room.

## 2 Method

### 2.1 Participant

There were 24 students, 12 males and 12 females, from Beijing Jiaotong University joining the experiment. They received 10RMB per one hour for participation.

### 2.2 Materials

The virtual scene was constructed in EON (Eon Reality Company, 2004), and showed on the i-glass HMD (i-O Display Systems, LLC) with the $26.5^0$ diagonal field of view. Four virtual environments were created: the experimental and practice rectangular virtual rooms, the experimental and practice cylindrical rooms. The difference between the experimental and practice rooms was that the experimental room comprised 7 virtual objects inside whereas the practice room was empty. The rectangular room was measured 8 m × 6 m × 6 m in virtual space. The radius of cylindrical room was 4m and the height was 6m in virtual space.

The exocentric view presented the layout of floor from the viewpoint at 4 meters above each floor. Specifically, the viewpoint was a view forward and downward from one short the wall in the rectangular room or was lying on the corresponding position in the cylindrical room, and its projection on the floor was 4 meters from the centre of floor. The elevation angle of viewpoint was $45^0$ that was computed with respect to the floor. The egocentric view presented the layout of the floor from the eye-level height (1.7m) above the floor. The elevation angle of viewpoint was set to $0^0$, meaning that participant's eyesight looked forward. The geometric field of view (GFOV) of both the exocentric and egocentric view was set at $75^0$.

There were 7 objects located on the floor, including the lamp, teapot, chair, missile, stoneware, hammer and pillar. Three of objects were higher than the height of the egocentric perspective. The visual views used in the experiment are shown in Figure 1. When taking the test, subjects would point out the target direction in front of a board via a laser pointer.

### 2.3 Procedure

In order to assess participant's memory, subjects first took a memory test. Subjects were required to scan 9 objects printed on a paper for 30 seconds and then generated these objects at the corresponding positions on a blank paper with the same size.

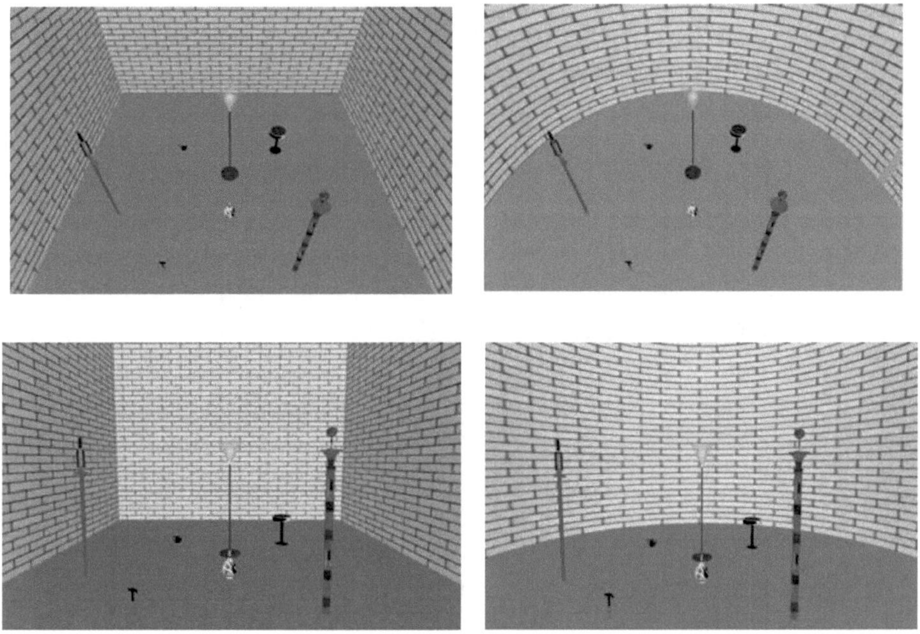

(a) (b)

**Fig. 1.** (a) the exocentric view (above) and the egocentric view (down) in the rectangular room; (b) the exocentric view (above) and the egocentric view (down) in the cylindrical room

These 9 objects were not used in the virtual room. Subjects who correctly recalled more than 5 objects were allowed to proceed to the next phase. All subjects could recall more than 6 objects in this test.

Subjects were then randomly allocated into 2 groups with gender balance. One group subjects observed the spatial layout in the rectangular room and another observed the same layout in the cylindrical room. Subjects observed the 7 experimental objects printed as 3D objects on a paper. After they could associate each object with the unique name, they wore HMD and were instructed to first watch an empty virtual room. Subjects observed from the exocentric ( $45^0$ ) perspective. After subjects were familiar with this perspective and felt comfortable with wearing HMD, the experimenter displayed the experimental virtual room containing 7 objects viewed from the same perspective. Subjects spent 2 minutes learning the location of each object. During observation the experimenter helped them to recognize the virtual objects if necessary. Then, experimenters would display the empty virtual room again and subjects would watch the empty room from the egocentric ( $0^0$ ) perspective. After subjects were familiar with this perspective, the experimenter displayed the experimental virtual room viewed from the egocentric perspective. They also spent 2 minutes observing the experimental spatial layout from the egocentric perspective.

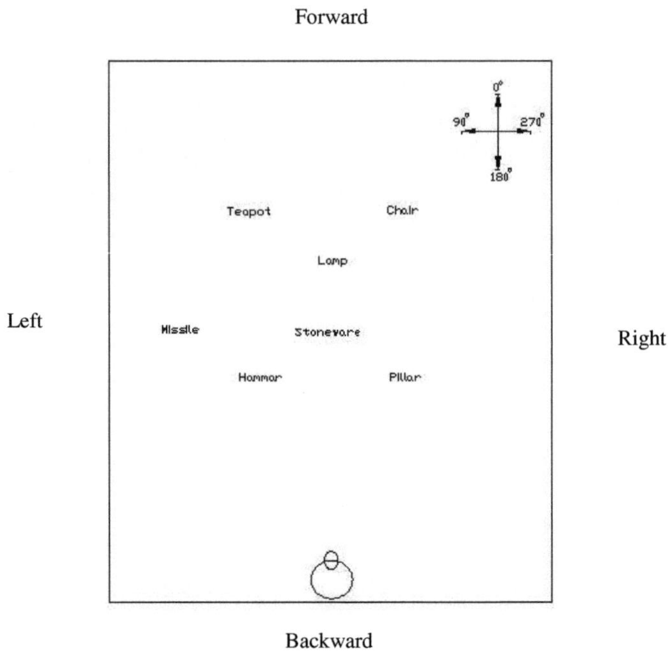


**Fig. 2.** The spatial layout in the rectangular room and four imagined facing directions

After observing visual scenes, all subjects' mental models of the space were assessed by the judgment of relative direction task (JRD, e.g. "Imagine you are standing at A object and facing B object, point to C object", [2]). Subjects were required to point to the specific position of the target object, for example, the top of the stoneware. When performing the task, subjects stood at the mark in front of a board and used a laser pointer to point out the direction. The coordinate of the centre of two eyes was recorded. Each test trial was constructed from the names of three objects. The experimenter recorded the response time and the coordinates of the laser point on the board. The judged direction of each trial could be computed by the coordinates of the laser point and the centre of two eyes. The total time for the experiment was approximately 60 minutes.

The experimental design manipulated the room style ( two different rooms, the between-subjects variable) and the imagined facing direction (the within-subjects variable). The imagined facing direction included there categories, the forward, left/right, and backward directions. The direction defined by the standing position (the A object above) and the facing object (the B object above) required in the JRD task was labeled. The $0^0$ direction was defined from Stoneware to Lamp (paralleling to the long walls of the rectangular room) and the degree of direction increased counterclockwise (see Figure 2). The $90^0$ direction was defined from Stoneware to Missile model, paralleling to the short wall of room. The $180^0$ direction was opposite to $0^0$ direction while the $270^0$ direction was opposite to the $90^0$ direction. The backward direction includes all directions at the range from 90 degree to 270 degree.

The left/right direction includes the two directions: $90^0$ and $270^0$ . The forward direction includes the other directions at the range from $270^0$ to $360^0$ and from $0^0$ to $90^0$.

The dependent variables were the horizontal and vertical angular errors and the response latency. The angular error was measured as the angular difference between the actual direction of target and pointing direction. The response latency was measured as the time from the presentation of question to the end of response.

## 3 Result

All dependent measures were analyzed using a split-plot factorial ANOVA with terms for the room style and imagined direction. Room style was between-participant and imagined direction was within-participant. An $\alpha$ level of .05 was used.

As shown in figure 3, the effect of imagined direction on the judgment of horizontal direction was significant, $F(2,44) = 3.64$, $p = .034$. The main effect of room was not significant. Interaction between the imagined direction and room style was significant, $F(2, 44) = 9.23$, $p < .01$. Further ANOVA was computed in each room. In the rectangular room, subjects performed worse when imagining forward than when imagining left or right or backward direction; in the cylindrical room, subjects performed worse when imagining left or right direction than when imagining forward or backward direction.

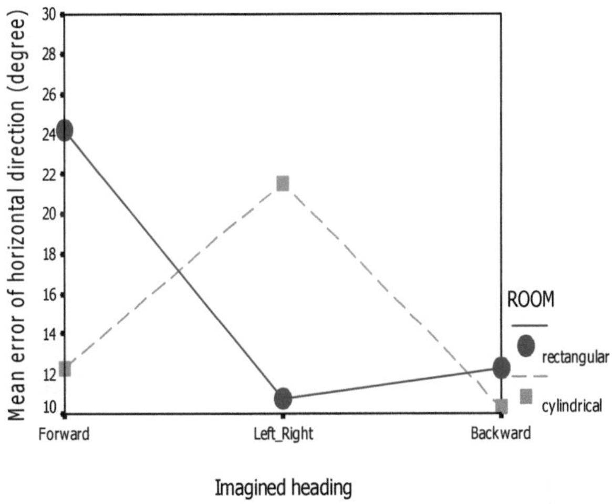


**Fig. 3.** Angular error in judgments of relative horizontal direction as a function of imagined direction and room style

The effect of room style on the judgment of vertical direction was significant, $F(1,22) = 35.91$, $p < .01$, depicted in Figure 4. The mean of vertical angular error (M = 18.25) in the cylindrical room was larger than that (M = 10.58) in the rectangular room. The effect of imagined direction on the judgment of vertical direction was also significant, $F(2,44) = 10.54$, $p < .01$. Interaction between the imagined direction and room style was significant, $F(2,44) = 10.32$, $p < .01$. Further ANOVA was computed in each room. The significant effect of the imagined direction was only observed in the cylindrical room. The performance was worse when subjects imagined left and right direction, whereas better in the backward direction.

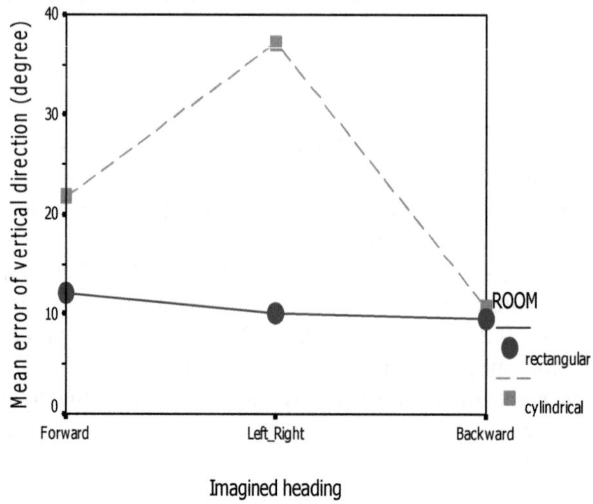


**Fig. 4.** Angular error in judgments of relative vertical direction as a function of imagined direction and room style

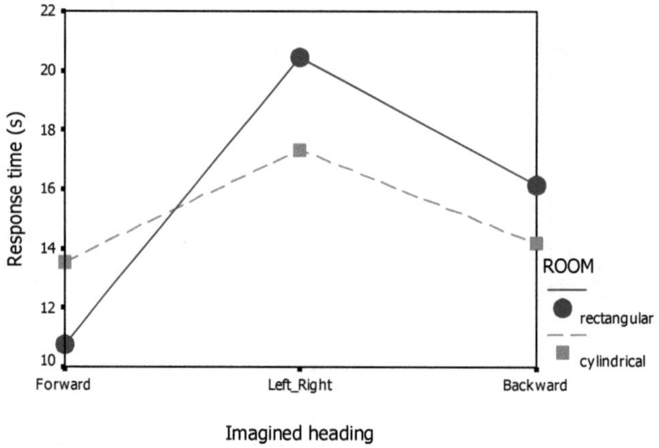


**Fig. 5.** Response latency to perform the task as a function of imagined direction and room style

The effect of imagined direction on the response time was significant $F(2,44) = 6.74$, $p < .01$; depicted in figure 5. Subjects were faster to response when imagining forward direction than when imagining left or right or backward direction. The effect of room style was not significant. There was no interaction between the room style and imagined direction.

## 4 Discussion

The goal of study was to determine the role of perspective change and the room geometry on the mental representation. Subjects in the experiment observed the spatial layout first from the exocentric perspective and then from the egocentric perspective. The result showed that the spatial relations among objects could be represented more accurately in memory along specifically preferred orientations. Moreover, subjects could respond faster when imagining forward direction than left or right or backward direction. The room geometry interacted with the participant's orientation in the room to influence the representation of spatial layout.

The representation of spatial horizontal links among the layout was influenced by both the orientation to observe the layout and the room geometry. In the rectangular room, performances were better for the two directions paralleled to the room walls than for the directions misaligned with room walls. This finding was consistent with the previous study, revealing the effect of salient room axes defined by room walls on the representation of space [7]. But in the cylindrical room where the room axes defined by the room walls were not as salient as those in the rectangular room, the main effect of the egocentric orientation was observed. The data related with the horizontal links among objects supported the first hypothesis that the orientation-specific representation of spatial layout was constructed after the observation.

Performance of judging the vertical direction was different in two rooms. The performance to judge the vertical direction was better in the rectangular room than in the cylindrical room. The result did not support the second hypothesis. The data suggested that the salient room axes could facilitate the coding of vertical information among the layout. Easton and Sholl [2] pointed out that people need to construct the exocentric coordinate over the reference object to retrieve the direction information when they judged the relative direction between objects. Luo and Duh [5] suggested that the spatial vertical information was mainly interpreted with respect to the exocentric reference provided by the environment. The efficiency of constructed exocentric coordinate was determined by the ecological properties of structure, such as the height information. Therefore, if the room wall provided better cues for the height information, the room wall could take main function to affect the coding of spatial vertical information. Compared with the cylindrical wall, the linear wall of the rectangular room better provided cues to explain the height information. It was demonstrated by the result: there was no the main effect of the egocentric direction on the judgment of vertical direction in the rectangular room whereas the effect of the egocentric direction was observed in the cylindrical room.

It was noteworthy that the patterns between the judgments of the spatial horizontal and vertical directions were different in the present experiment. The results revealed that coding of the spatial vertical information was independent with the spatial horizontal information among the same layout, as suggested in the study [3]. Few studies investigated the spatial process on the vertical dimension, but Wilson et al [11] took a preliminary study about the vertical information represented asymmetrically in memory. The additional evidence for this difference was also drawn from the later description of strategies subjects used to perform the spatial task. Most subjects (90%) reported that they first retrieved the horizontal direction of target and then judged the vertical direction.

Subjects responded fastest to retrieve the spatial relations when imagining the forward direction. It further supported the orientation-specific property of the mental representation of spatial layout. Subjects faced the forward direction when they observed the spatial layout. The familiar view should be more salient in memory than the novel views that were imagined from the new viewpoints. The process to imagine the view from the new viewpoint might involve either the viewer rotation or the object rotation [12]. The additional mental process delayed the response to figure out the direction of target.

## 5 Conclusion

The important conclusion of present study includes two aspects. First, the orientation-specific representation was constructed when people observed the virtual room-sized space first from the exocentric perspective and then from the egocentric perspective. Second, the room geometry tended to interact with the orientation facing the spatial layout to influence the mental representation of the space. In terms of the spatial vertical knowledge, the study suggested that the coding of spatial vertical information was affected by both the orientation to the space and the environmental geometry.

Subjects observed the same spatial layout from two static viewpoints on the vertical dimension in the present experiment. Our future study will investigate whether the continual change of perspective from the exocentric viewpoint to the egocentric viewpoint influences the representation of space. The successful views during the vertical movement might improve the spatial knowledge about the verticality.

## References


1. Hartley, T., Trinkler, I., Burgess, N.: Geometric determinants of human spatial memory. Cognition 34, 39–75 (2004)
2. Easton, R.D., Sholl, M.J.: Object-array structure, frames of reference, and retrieval of spatial knowledge. Journal of Experimental Psychology: Learning, Memory, and Cognition 21(3), 483–500 (1995)
3. Gärling, T., Böök, A., Lindberg, E., Arce, C.: Is elevation encoded in cognitive maps? Journal of Environmental Psychology 10, 341–351 (1990)
4. Hickox, J.C., Wickens, C.D.: Effects of elevation angle display, complexity, and feature type on relating out-of-cockpit field of view to an electronic cartographic map. Journal of Experimental Psychology: Applied 5, 284–301 (1999)
5. Luo, Z., Duh, H.B.L.: Perspective dependence on direction judgment in a virtual room space. In: Proceedings of Human Factors and Ergonomics 50th annual meeting, San Francisco, USA 2006 (2006)
6. Passini, R.: Wayfinding in Architecture. Van Nostrand Reinhold, New York (1984)

7. Shelton, A.L., McNamara, T.P.: Systems of spatial reference in human memory. Cognitive Psychology 43, 274–430 (2001)
8. Shelton, A.L., McNamara, T.P.: Orientation and perspective depdence in route and survey learning. Journal of Experimental Psychology: Learning, Memory, and Cognition 30, 158–170 (2004)
9. Wickens, C.D., Olmos, O., Chudy, A., Davenport, C.: Aviation display support for situation awareness (No. ARL-97-10/LOGICON-97-2). University of Illinois, Aviation research Lab, Savoy, IL (1997)
10. Wickens, C.D., Prevett, T.T.: Exploring the dimensions of egocentricity in aircraft navigation play. Journal of Experimental Psychology: Applied. 1, 110–135 (1995)
11. Wilson, P.N., Foreman, N., Stanton, D., Duffy, H.: Memory for targets in a multilevel simulated environment: Evidence for vertical asymmetry in spatial memory. Memory & Cognitio 32, 283–297 (2004)
12. Wraga, M., Creem, S.H., Proffitt, D.R.: Updating displays after imagined object and viewer rotations. Journal of Experimental Psychology: Learning, Memory, and Cognition 26, 151–168 (2000)

# Towards Transparent Telepresence

Gordon M. Mair

Transparent Telepresence Research Group, Department of Design, Manufacture, and Engineering Management, University of Strathclyde, 75 Montrose Street, Glasgow G1 1XJ, Scotland, UK
g.m.mair@strath.ac.uk

**Abstract.** It is proposed that the concept of transparent telepresence can be closely approached through high fidelity technological mediation. It is argued that the matching of the system capabilities to those of the human user will yield a strong sense of immersion and presence at a remote site. Some applications of such a system are noted. The concept is explained and critical system elements are described together with an overview of some of the necessary system specifications.

**Keywords:** Telepresence, teleoperation, displays, immersion, mixed-reality.

## 1 Introduction

This paper is concerned with immersion in a remote real world environment, literally *tele-presence*, as opposed to immersion in a computer-generated environment as found in virtual reality. The author will therefore argue that it is justifiable to assert that a state of *transparent telepresence*, in which the technological mediation is transparent to the user of a telepresence system, can be closely approached through the use of technology alone. It is recognised that "immersion" is not necessarily "presence" and that other factors also contribute to a sense of presence. However it is suggested that in this telepresence context they are of secondary importance to the fidelity of the human–computer/machine/product interface and associated communication and remote site equipment.

### 1.1 Defining Transparent Telepresence

Over half a century ago the science-fiction author James Blish [1] explained the concept of telepresence in a short story about a worker, located on a moon of Jupiter, who carried out work through remote control of a vehicle in the planet's atmosphere. He even used the equivalent of a head-mounted-display. The term itself was first mooted in print by Marvin Minsky [2]. Today the term has come to be used in a manner that has wider connotations. This is despite a number of writers providing useful and practical definitions throughout the last one and a half decades, e.g. [3], [4], [5]. What is apparent is that today "presence" is often, but not always, used as an abbreviation for "telepresence" and it is also inclusive of virtual reality and the experience of being immersed in a virtual world. The explication of "presence" is still

R. Shumaker (Ed.): Virtual Reality, HCII 2007, LNCS 4563, pp. 300–309, 2007.

a matter for discussion with many scholars offering interesting perspectives, for example the International Society for Presence Research web site [6] has a comprehensive statement on the topic. Also Sadowski and Stanney discuss the characterisation of presence in [7], in this they provide a comprehensive literature review and suggest that "one must be afforded both technological and experiential immersion to maximize the likelihood of high levels of presence".

This paper acknowledges the widely accepted view that in the general case technological fidelity is insufficient for full presence, e.g. Heeter [8] states "perfectly mediated sensory stimuli do not automatically induce continuous presence". She discusses how the sense of presence can be different for different individuals and vary from moment to moment. Sanchez-Vives and Slater [9] and Welch [10] point out that the amount of control we have over the remote environment is also important. However it is this author's contention that *transparent telepresence* [11] is a special case and may be defined as *the experience of being fully present interactively at a live real world location remote from one's own physical location.* In this situation the technological mediation should provide both the multi-sensory input necessary to represent the remote environment, and the ability to interact with that environment in a natural and instinctive manner, thus providing most of the criteria for a sense of presence. Transparent telepresence is therefore a goal rather than an existing state, it is a goal that is unlikely to be achieved for decades but it does provide an objective and quantifiable target.

Another justification for adopting this technological approach is that the experience of presence in itself is difficult to measure, particularly if it is "second order" [6], [12], i.e. technologically mediated experience as opposed to "first order" mediated only by human senses. In attempting to measure presence numerous questionnaires have been created, e.g. [13] and their validity discussed e.g. [14] which includes a comment that other approaches such as ethnographic studies could be more appropriate. Witmer et.al [15] provide a review of the chronological development of questionnaires since the early nineteen nineties, also Ma and Kaber [16] include comments on the difficulty of using questionnaires and measuring presence in general. Finally in [17] Slater argues that post experience questionnaires alone cannot be used to assess presence in virtual environments. However in adopting the ultimate goal of transparent telepresence the question of how to measure presence becomes redundant since transparent telepresence will, by definition, allow the system user to feel present at the remote site. This technological approach can ultimately only provide perceptual, rather than physical, equivalence of the remote site. To provide even apparent physical equivalence a means of bypassing our normal sensory system and sending information on the remote site directly to the appropriate locations in the brain would be necessary as happens with VR in fictional stories such as Neuromancer [18].

As a final comment in this section it should be noted that, particularly in Europe, the term "Mixed Reality" is currently popular. This follows from the observation that technologically mediated experiences occur along a Reality-Virtuality continuum [19]. At one end of this is unmediated reality and at the other is a fully computer generated virtual environment. As we move along the continuum from the real environment we experience Augmented Reality, this occurs when computer generated information can be superimposed on the real world. We can then move further along and find Augmented Virtuality where the computer generated environment may have real world entities superimposed. Moving further we find at the extreme end we have a fully computer generated environment. An interesting example of a mixed reality system is described in [20] where a tripod mounted display is used to provide real world images of a site of historical interest combined with computer generated images of the scene as it would have existed in historical times. Currently a number of large-scale European funded projects focusing on mixed-reality are underway, information on these and further links can be found at [21]. Transparent telepresence will sit very close to Reality on this continuum since although it constitutes a technologically mediated experience it is the real world in real time that is being considered albeit at a site physically removed from the system user.

Ultimately a full Product Design Specification should be achievable for a Transparent Telepresence System based on technological transparency. This goal perhaps appears contrary to the zeitgeist in presence research however since transparent telepresence is a special case of presence the author suggests that this approach of attaining a high fidelity representation of the mediated environment will provide an "absolute" specification or datum, from which to compare other systems at an objective and unambiguous level.

## 1.2 Application and Justification of Transparent Telepresence

The ability to apparently exist interactively in a remote real world location has many applications, a more detailed account can be found in [22]. Applications include the ability to carry out work in remote hazardous or unpleasant environments, e.g. bomb disposal and decommissioning of radioactive nuclear facilities; remote surgery, particularly where a specialist would find it impossible to be physically present such as in a battlefield; space and planetary working although transparency will never be fully achieved due to the distances and subsequent communication time delays involved. Entertainment and education could be exciting applications where the system user could experience coral reefs, rain-forests, foreign cities and people, as though physically there. A trend that is emerging in the developed countries is that their demographics are changing such that average age the population is increasing as the percentage of older people increases. With advancing age also often comes a decrease in mobility, thus transparent telepresence could provide a means for this part of the population to continue contributing to society, earning income, and end generally enjoying a better quality of life. This would also apply to those with disabilities that may prevent them participating in many activities they would otherwise pursue. Finally business applications where eye-to-eye contact and one to one conversations or round table meetings are involved could produce economic and environmental rewards. For example $CO_2$ emissions would be reduced by reducing the need for air travel, also the actual cost of the travel would be removed. Additionally unusual situations can arise that restrict travel, e.g. where there is a terrorist alert, disruptive weather, or even concern over a possible pandemic.

## 1.3 Structure of a Transparent Telepresence System

The basic elements of a transparent telepresence system are shown in Figure 1. In a basic system there is the home site, the remote site, and a communications link between them. In order to address the problem of technological transparency the elements have to be able to provide a high fidelity interface between the hardware and the human at the home site, and between the hardware and the environment at the remote site. The human machine interface requires careful consideration of the displays and controls, a wide variety of both are currently available. Similarly the sensors at the remote site have to acquire information to a degree of precision that will be suitable for technological transparency of the display and the actuators have to respond in such a manner to very closely emulate the control signals. The computer interface at both home and remote sites needs to be able to process the data being transferred at a speed sufficient for transparency, and the communication link needs to have a bandwidth capable of transmitting all of the data at a fast speed although of course over very long distances the speed of light is obviously a limiting and noticeable factor. These aspects are now considered more fully.

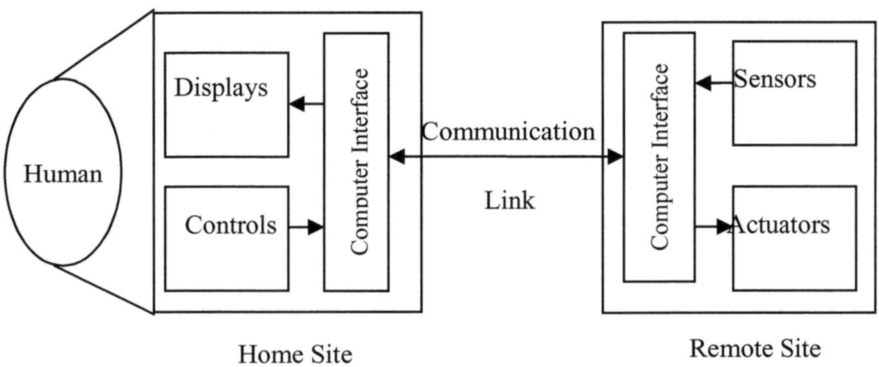


**Fig. 1.** Basic Elements of a Transparent Telepresence System

# 2 Transparent Telepresence System Elements Overview

## 2.1 Home Site Human - System Interface Ergonomics

Technologically mediated experiences involve real world ergonomic problems for the system users. For example for extended operation, the working environment should usually be comfortable with respect to ambient temperature, airflow, and noise levels. However if fully transparent telepresence is to be experienced then it may be reasonably argued that these factors should be the same as the remote environment. Thus we have a dichotomy, full immersion in the remote site may cause uncomfortable working conditions for the system user, but making them comfortable will destroy the fidelity of the representation of the remote site. The solution will be dependent on the application, i.e. if it is important for application then the remote conditions can be emulated, if not then the comfort of the user will be paramount. Other aspects of the system user must be fully considered such as anthropometrics, physiology, anatomy, and psychology. For example if a head mounted display is being used then consideration must be given as to how its weight and balance on the head affects the joints and muscles of the wearer, otherwise strain and fatigue may result. Unnatural forces on joints, tendons, and muscles must also be avoided. MacCauley Bell provides a discussion on Ergonomics in Virtual Environments in [23], and more general information on ergonomics can be found in [24] which includes established design guidelines. The basis of this technological approach is that by considering the human senses as having discrete just noticeable differences (JNDs) based on the Weber fraction [25] we can compare these directly for each sense with a technological capability that can provide a perceptual equivalent

### 2.2 Home Site Displays and Remote Site Sensors

A wide range of displays are available for technologically mediated experience however only a few types are appropriate for transparent telepresence. For our purposes we require displays that are capable of providing immersion and also of displaying a live representation of the remote site. This should apply for as many of the senses as possible and for transparent telepresence should include visual, aural, haptic, olfactory, and vestibular, (gustatory sensing will normally be unnecessary).

Similarly at the remote site a wide variety of sensors may be used. These should be compatible with the home site displays and provide enough information for the fully immersive experience. In this paper we will assume that the resolution of the remote site sensor and the home site display are approximately the same. The exception to this will be the aural system where the Nyquist sampling theorem states that the sampling rate must be at least twice the frequency of the original signal. This theorem can be applied to all the senses but audio is the most critical in this respect.

**Visual Displays.** Considering firstly the visual sense the likely displays will either be of the head mounted display (HMD) or wide angle screen type. Humans have a field of view of just over 180 degrees horizontally and 120 degrees vertically [26], [27]. To the best of the author's knowledge at the time of writing there is no head mounted display capable of providing this. It is possible to achieve wide-angle immersion through the use of projection systems as can be found in large format cinemas and theme parks, however none of these provide the live video required for transparent telepresence. Additionally we have the ability to perceive depth through the use of stereoscopy. This means that the display will also require the ability to present images as they would be seen by both the left and right eye of the user. With respect to resolution, humans can detect the separation of two points that are separated by 60 seconds of arc [28], this can provide an indication as to the resolution required for the display. The dynamic range of the display is also important, at any level of light adaptation the eye can see detail at a contrast ratio of 10,000:1 and therefore the ability to produce a display capable of this [29] is important for transparent telepresence. Additional aspects that need to be considered include colour fidelity, frame rate, and he need to provide a natural operation of both accommodation and vergence of the eye.

**Visual Sensors.** In order to create a stereo image two perspectives will be required. Had we simply required a relatively narrow field of view then this would not present a significant problem since two matched cameras could be used separated by the average pupilliary pitch of approximately 63mm. If the system is to be for a single user wearing a head mounted display then the problem is ameliorated since the cameras can be mounted on a motorized sensor platform whose movements are slaved to the movements of the user located at the home site, an early visual telepresence system designed by a member of the author's Transparent Telepresence Research Group (TTRG) is described in [30]. However for a real time fully immersive large screen display for a number of viewers there are considerable difficulties. For example the cameras have to acquire an image with a wide enough field of view to provide an immersive experience to all of the viewers simultaneously. To achieve this at a high enough resolution, without image distortion, for technological transparency it is likely that a cluster of cameras would be required. However two of these clusters would be necessary for stereoscopic viewing and if a spherical field of view was necessary then one camera cluster would be seen by the other and stereoscopy would be lost at certain angles. Another alternative is to use a single cluster with a very large number of small cameras pointing in directions that will allow two spherical stereoscopically separated images to be acquired. These cameras will also need to be able to acquire the images at the appropriate resolution and dynamic range suitable for display at the home site.

**Aural Displays.** Hearing is particularly important for a sense of presence [31]. In the transparent telepresence context the displays would be either binaural headphones or surround sound speakers. The headphones would be most likely to be used in conjunction with a head mounted display for single user applications. Binaural headphones provide the listener with a sense of direction for the sound source that, unlike stereo headphones, is external to the head and can be located on a 360 degree sphere. The surround sound speakers with the immersive screen would be suitable for multiple users.

**Aural Sensors.** To acquire binaural sound for the single user headphones a dummy head fitted with microphones located where the tympanic membrane of the user's head would be. Ideally the head could be fitted with artificial pinnae corresponding the shape of the user's external ear and the head would have the same head related transfer function (HRTF) as the user's head. This allows accurate recording of interaural time differences (ITDs) and interaural intensity differences (IIDs). Head movements are also important for identifying the direction of sound [32], see [33] for a practical experiment using artificial pinnae on a mechatronic sensor platform.

**Haptic Displays.** The haptic sense is comprised of touch and kinaesthesia. Touch or tactile information results from cutaneous stimulation that provides the brain with knowledge of external stimuli acting on the skin. Whereas kinaesthetic information provides the brain with knowledge from internal sensors indicating the position of, and forces acting on, the body's limbs and joints. Thus haptic displays need to provide both tactile information such as the shape, roughness or smoothness, temperature, wetness or dryness, etc. of an object; and kinaesthetic information such as the forces being applied to grasp the object, it's weight, and the position or velocity of the grasped object etc. There is significant ongoing research work in this field, e.g. [34] provides one example. An early example of a TTRG system can be found in [35].

**Haptic Sensors.** In order to detect information at the remote site that can inform the haptic displays of the home site complementary sensors are required. For tactile sensing the field of robotics has yielded a variety of touch sensors that provide information on the shape of an object through arrays of pressure sensors on gripper fingertips. Again they do not approach the resolution required for transparency. Similarly a remote slave arm could be instrumented at appropriate locations with strain gauges to act as force and torque sensors. These would provide information to be communicated to the home site which would alter the forces being experienced by the user who would be wearing a master arm with motorized joints which could emulate the forces being experienced by the slave arm at the remote site.

**Olfactory Displays.** Estimates of the number of identifiable sensations of odour vary between $10^4$ [36] and $10^6$ [37]. A number of factors are important in producing an effective olfactory display, some of these are; the odorant concentration, the duration of exposure, the flow rate, the directionality, and the adaptation time. Very little odorant will be necessary to create an olfactory image [38]. Adaptation occurs with all senses but it is particularly noticeable with olfaction and gustation, it is the decrease in sensitivity that occurs when a sense is exposed to constant stimulus. Some very specific "displays" exist at present, for example the generation of the smell of freshly baked bread in a supermarket, however there are no existing full olfactory telepresence displays and work is still at the research stage on this.

**Olfactory Sensing.** In order to detect "smells" chemical sensors would need to be used. Arrays of sensors have been used to produce input for neural networks and other systems in an attempt to identify smells [39]. This leads on to an interesting problem for telepresence olfaction. Should the specific odour be identified at the remote site, the identity of the odourant signaled to the home site, and then requisite odour selected for display from an existing library. This would be the simpler solution but would only be applicable for a finite number of odours. Alternatively the exact chemical composition and structure could be identified at the remote site, this information communicated to the home site, where it would then be synthesized to replicate the smell. This would be extremely difficult since the precise nature of how the chemical composition affects the odour is not fully known. At the moment there is no known method of creating an olfactory telepresence system that can operate in real time across a wide range of odours.

**Vestibular Displays and Sensors.** The vestibular sense is part of the body's proprioceptive system and various studies have been carried out to determine JNDs and sensitivity, e.g. [40]. These are most familiar to visitors of theme parks where they experience virtual rides on flying vehicles or submarines, and to pilots using flight simulators. These motion platforms, usually of the six axis Stewart Platform type, are essentially vestibular displays since they convey a sense of motion and orientation to our bodies through manipulation of our vestibular system. When combined with visual cues the brain can be tricked into believing it is moving over long distances and accelerating, decelerating, or simply traveling at a constant velocity. These displays are not yet normally used with telepresence systems. Sensors would be located on the vehicle or other sensor platform containing the cameras etc. at the remote site. They would be likely to be gyroscopes and accelerometers to provide absolute information on velocity, acceleration, deceleration, and orientation of the remote system

### 2.3 Home Site Controls and Remote Site Actuators

The controls should adhere to all ergonomic principles for ease of use. An interesting possibility is the use of a direct EEG based brain-computer interface (BCI) for control. As well as being investigated to aid physically disabled individuals [41] it has also been used for navigation in virtual environments [42], [43]. The possibility of hybrid systems incorporating BCI for control with more conventional technology for displays is an interesting one. At the remote site the actuators may be motors controlling the movements of an anthropomorphic arm and gripper. As such they will require resolution comparable with home site controls and good repeatability. The technology for these elements is similar to that of industrial robotics, with the exception that for transparency anthropometric manipulators should be used.

### 2.4 Home and Remote Site Computer Interfaces and Communications Link

At the home site these will handle the signals from the controls and change them into a format for transmission to the remote actuators, and also handle the incoming signals from the remote sensors and translate them into suitable values for use by the displays. At the remote site the data from the sensors will be processed before transmission to the home site, for example image compression algorithms [44] will probably be used to reduce the data required for the video and audio information. The control signals will be received from the home site and translated into appropriate signals for the actuators. For transparent telepresence a broadband connection will be necessary, mostly to cope with the video information. Audio, haptic, olfactory, and vestibular senses will require much lower bandwidth. The processing time for all of this information introduces delays into the system. For transparency these need to be minimised a various writers have presented values for the maximum delay allowable. One of the lower values indicated is 17ms [45] for HMD operation although delays up to 300 ms could be tolerated as a maximum for teleoperation [46].

## 3 Discussion

The paper has postulated that if appropriate technology can be created, then the mediation between the human and the telepresence system can approach transparency. This would allow full immersion in the remote environment, and the author strongly suggests, although this is open to argument, that this would also allow full "presence" in the remote environment to be experienced.

## References

1. Blish, J.: Bridge. Astounding Science Fiction. pp. 57–82 ( February 1952)
2. Minsky, M.: Telepresence. Omni. 2, 45–52 (1980)
3. Schloerb, D.W.: A quantitative measure of telepresence. Presence 4(1), 64–80(1995)

4. Sheridan, T.B.: Defining our terms. Presence 1(2), 272–274 (1992)
5. Draper, J.V., Kaber, D.B., Usher, J.M.: Telepresence. Human Factors 40(3) (1998)
6. International Society for Presence Research. The Concept of Presence: Explication Statement. (2000) Retrieved 8th February 2007 from http://ispr.info/
7. Sadowski, W., Stanney, K.: Presence in Virtual Environments. In: Stanney, K.M. (ed.) Handbook of Virtual Environments, Lawrence Erlbaum Associates, Mahwah, NJ (2002)
8. Heeter, C.: Reflections on real presence by a virtual person. Presence, 12(4), 335–345 (August 2003)
9. Sanchez-Vives, M.V., Slater, M.: From presence to consciousness through virtual reality. Nature Reviews: Neuroscience 6 (April 2005)
10. Welch, R.B., Blackmon, T.T., Liu, A., Mellers, B.A., Stark, L.W.: The effects of pictorial realism, delay of visual feedback, and observer interactivity on the subjective sense of presence. Presence 5, 263–273 (1996)
11. Mair, G.: Transparent telepresence research. Industrial Robot, vol. 26(3), pp. 209–215, MCB University Press (1999)
12. Lombard, M., Ditton, T.B., Crane, D., Davis, B., Gil-Egui, G., Horvath, K., Rossman, J., Park, S.: Measuring Presence: A literature-based approach to the development of a standardized paper-and-pencil instrument. In: Third International Workshop on Presence, Delft 2000 (2000)
13. Witmer, B.G., Singer, M.J.: Measuring Presence in Virtual Environments: A Presence Questionnaire. Presence: Teleoperators and Virtual Environments, 7(3) (1998)
14. Slater, M.: Measuring Presence: A Response to the Witmer and Singer Presence Questionnaire. Presence: Teleoperators and Virtual Environments 8(5), 560–565 (1999)
15. Witmer, B.G., Jerome, C.J., Singer, M.J.: The Factor Structure of the Presence Questionnaire. Presence 14(3), 298–312 (2005)
16. Ma, R., Kaber, D.B.: Presence, workload and performance effects of synthetic environment design factors. Int. J. Human-Computer Studies 64, 541–552 (2006)
17. Slater, M.: How Colorful Was Your Day? Why Questionnaires Cannot Assess Presence in Virtual Environments. Presence: Teleoperators and Virtual Environments 13(4), 484–493 (2004)
18. Gibson, W.: Neuromancer. Victor Gollancz Ltd (1984)
19. Milgram, P., Takemura, H., Utsumi, A., Kishino, F.: Augmented Reality: A class of displays on the reality-virtuality continuum. SPIE, vol. 2351, Telemanipulator and Telepresence Technologies (1994)
20. Schnadelbach, H., Koleva, B., Flintham, M., Fraser, M., Izadi, S., Chandler, P., Foster, M., Benford, S., Greenhalgh, C., Rodden, T.: The Augurscope: A Mixed Reality Interface for Outdoors. In: Proceedings of SIGCHI Conference on Human Factors in Computing Systems 2002, vol. 4, pp 9–16. Minneapolis, USA (2002)
21. Keho the place for the Presence community. Retrieved 8th February 2007 from http://www.peachbit.org
22. Mair, G.: Telepresence - The Technology and its Economic and Social Implications. In: Proc. Technology and Society at a Time of Sweeping Change. International Symposium on Technology and Society, June 1997, Glasgow, pp. 118–124 (1997)
23. Bell, M, Pamela, R.: Ergonomics in Virtual Environments. In: Stanney, K.M. (ed.) Handbook of Virtual Environments, pp. 807–826. Lawrence Erlbaum Associates, Mahwah, NJ (2002)
24. Pheasant, S.: Ergonomics Standards and Guidelines for Designers. British Standards Institution, Milton Keynes, 1987 (1987)

25. Geldard, F.A.: The Human Senses, 2nd edn. John Wiley and Sons Inc, New York, NY (1972)
26. Kalawsky, R.S.: The Science of Virtual Reality. Addison-Wesley, London, UK (1993)
27. May, J.G., Badcock, D.R.: Vision and virtual environments. In: Stanney, K.M (ed.) Handbook of Virtual Environments, Lawrence Erlbaum Associates, Mahwah, NJ (2002)
28. Hochberg, J.E.: Perception, 2nd edn. Prentice Hall, New Jersey (1978)
29. Ledda, P.: High Dynamic Range Displays. Presence, 16(1) (February 2007)
30. Heng, J.: The design and application of a unique anthropomorphic sensor platform. PhD. thesis Dpt. of DMEM, University of Strathclyde, Glasgow, UK (Unpublished 1995)
31. Gilkey, R.H., Weisenberger, J.M.: The Sense of Presence for the Suddenly Deafened Adult - Implications for Virtual Environments. Presence, 4(4), 357–363 (1995)
32. Wenzel, E.M.: Localization in virtual acoustic displays. Presence 1(1), 80–107 (1992)
33. Harrison, C., Mair, G.: Mechatronics applied to auditory localisation for telepresence. Mechatronics Journal 9, 803–816 (1999)
34. Pongrac, H., Farber, B.: A model of Haptic Perception for Determining the Feedback Requirements in Telemanipulation Systems. In: Joint International COE/HAM-SFB453 Workshop on Human Adaptive Mechatronics and High Fidelity Telepresence, October 6, 2005, Tokyo, Japan (2005)
35. Khalil, T.: A Novel Anthropometric Master-Slave Arm System for Telepresence. (Unpublished) PhD. thesis Dpt. of DMEM, University of Strathclyde, Glasgow, UK (2000)
36. Axel, R.: The Molecular Logic of Smell. Scientific American Special Edition, Secrets of the Senses 16(3) (2006)
37. Drawert, F.: Biochemical formation of aroma components, In: Proceedings of the International Symposiun on Aroma Research, Zeist, The Netherlands, May 26-29, 1975, pp. 13–39 Pub by Wageningen Centre for Agricultural Publishing and Documentation (1975)
38. Schiffman, H.R.: Sensation and Perception: an Integrated Approach, fifth edn. John Wiley and Sons, Inc, New York, NY (2001)
39. Gutierrez-Osuna, R.: Pattern Analysis for Machine Olfaction: A Review. IEEE Sensors Journal 2(3), 189–202 (2002)
40. Richerson, S.J., Morstatt, S.M., O'Neal, K.K., Patrick, G., Robinson, C.J.: Effect of lateral perturbations on psychophysical acceleration detection thresholds. Journal of NeuroEngineering and Rehabilitation, 3(2) (2006)
41. Kauhanen, L., Nykopp, T., Lehtonen, J., Jylanki, P., Heikkonen, J., Rantanen, P., Alaranta, H., Sams, M.: EEG and MEG Brain-Computer Interface for Tetraplegic Patients. IEEE Transactions on Neural Systems and Rehabilitation Engineering, 14(2) (2006)
42. Leeb, R., Scherer, R., Lee, F., Bischof, H., Pfurtscheller, G.: Navigation in Virtual Environments through Motor Imagery. In: 9th Computer Vision Winter Workshop, CVWW'04 2004, pp. 99–108 (2004)
43. Friedman, D., Leeb, G.C., Steed, A., Pfurtscheller, G., Slater, M.: Navigating Virtual Reality by Thought: What Is It Like? Presence 16(1), 100–110 (2007)
44. Ahlvers, U., Zoelzer, U., Heinrich, G.: Adaptive coding, reconstruction and 3D visualisation of stereoscopic image data. In: Proceedings Visualisation, Imaging, and Image Processing. VIIP 2004; Marbella, Spain, September 2004 (2004)
45. Adelstein, B.D., Lee, T.G., Ellis, S.R.: Head Tracking Latency in Virtual Environments: Psychophysics and a Model. In: Proc. Human Factors and Ergonomics Society 47th Annual Meeting. Denver, Colorado 2003, pp. 2083 –2087 (2003)
46. Sheridan, T.: Space teleoperation through time delay: Review and Prognosis. IEEE Transactions on Robotics and Automation, vol. 9(5) (1993)

# Towards an Interaction Model in Collaborative Virtual Environments

Diego Martínez, José P. Molina, Arturo S. García, and Pascual González

Lab. of User Interfaces and Software Engineering (LoUISE),
Instituto de Investigación en Informática de Albacete,
University of Castilla-La Mancha, Albacete, Spain
{diegomp1982,jpmolina,arturo,pgonzalez}@dsi.uclm.es

**Abstract.** This paper highlights some of the current problems in CVE development. These problems are mainly due to a lack of a good interaction model guiding the behaviour of the environments. This paper introduces the definition of a model based on the idea of the *interaction views*. The key concepts for understanding *interaction views* are also given during the explanation of the model. The paper also describes a reference architecture based on this model which can be found useful for the design of modelling tools, and a prototype application that helps understanding both the architecture and the model.

**Keywords:** Virtual Reality, Interaction, Collaboration.

## 1 Introduction

Collaborative Virtual Environments (CVEs) have been a topic under intensive study in the last few years. The current status of the technology, which allows computers with a good graphical performance and VR devices at lower prices, has boosted this research. Many techniques and ideas have arisen, and researches have shown many of the best properties of CVEs, such as presence and object manipulation. Furthermore, many technologies and tools have emerged around these kinds of systems: techniques for managing groups, frameworks for building distributed environments and interconnecting them. All these tools together with the tools typical for VEs (OpenGL, VRML/X3D, etc.) should provide enough support to implement useful environments as this is the current interest of developers. In the last years, developers are no longer looking for environments which look and feel like real, but environments that offer the user an efficient way to achieve a goal.

However, when looking at the systems described in the literature [1,2,3,4,5,10], most of them can be categorized in two main families: commercial and experimental environments. The first family of these systems allows a high scalability but its members doesn't benefit from the best properties of CVEs. The second family of systems refers to the experimental systems used by researchers. They benefit quite well from the features found in CVEs, but focusing on just one feature that is,

R. Shumaker (Ed.): Virtual Reality, HCII 2007, LNCS 4563, pp. 310–319, 2007.

somehow, evaluated. In both cases, collaboration is faced exclusively from the point of view of information sharing. The more common techniques used are:

- **Collaboration Buses:** Many systems, like MOVE [7] or like MPEG´s back channels [1,6], use an event dispatcher connecting all the clients in the CVE and that, in addition, can be used to build a higher level of abstraction through the definition of communication protocols between objects.
- **Shared Scene Graph:** This solution is more appropriate for VR applications, and it is used in other platforms such as DIVE[3,4] or MASSIVE[1]. All the users share the same definition of the position and status of each object in the environment. The shared information is all contained in the scene and clients do not communicate with each other directly, but trough modifications in the Scene Graph. This technique encapsulates all the details which allow users to share a common world.

These techniques allow different users to communicate, but they do not deliver messages according to other factors like the identity of the user or their interests. Even in those projects that actually try to build generic environments –as the ones cited before- little effort has been done in defining ways to process and map interactions. This fact makes the development of CVEs a difficult task [7,11]. In this paper, we explain an interaction model for CVEs, which is based on one of the implicit properties of VEs: the physical representation and the definition of interactive areas.

In order to illustrate this model, a reference architecture is also given, and a prototype application is described. The prototype is called CVRPrismaker, which defines a virtual room where several users can collaborate playing with a block-based construction game named Prismaker, similar to the more popular LEGO but this time any face of the box-shaped blocks can be connected to any other block. The design of CVRPrismaker includes the key aspects of the approach presented here. Besides, to carry out its development in a systematic way, the TRES-D methodology has been used [9]. The relevant aspects of CVRPrismaker will be detailed during the explanation of the model: both highlighting the points that established the basis for this model, and also showing the deficiencies in its design. Possible improvements are also shown during that explanation. However, event though CVRPrismaker perfectly serves as a testbed for many of the key elements in CVEs, it is just a prototype implementation, and a new system based on a mature implementation of this model is currently under development. Flexibility is the main objective for this implementation. The system will allow the easy definition of a high set of object's behaviours and will be easy to integrate with many other business models.

## 2 The Proposed Model

As pointed out in the previous section, the collaborative interaction model for CVEs described in this paper is based on the physical representation. Given the nature of interactions in VEs, a physical representation must be given for every object that allows interaction (even data and other "logical" elements). The user will have to deal with these physical representations to produce its interactions to the system.

Usually, these features are translated in CVEs with the usage of a scene-graph, which holds the information about each object's position and status, enriched which some other "semantic" features (material, weight…). To guide interaction, the system applies some "general" rules to every object.

Instead of using this approach, this model is based on the definition of several geometric views of the same object: one or more *appearance views*, and one or more *interaction views*. The *appearance views* can be exchanged based on the object state or the LOD required. The *interaction views* establish the conditions to determine whether a user action may change the state of objects of the world.

To help understand the behaviour of the model, some key concepts are explained:

- **Action:** Any user input, a contact in a data glove, a key press… is considered as an *Action*. *Actions* are no more than messages, and thus, they need something to process that message. The *interaction views* in the objects will be those filters, and they will tell if this *Action* ends up changing the state of the world or not.
- **Interaction:** If the appropriate *Action* is performed over the appropriate object, the target object will produce an *Interaction*. *Interactions* are responses of the system to a user action through a given object that may change the state of the world. Given that every change in the world will be due to an *Interaction*, it is important that all the clients who have the target object in their scene graphs perform the *Interactions*. Also, given the distributed nature of the virtual environment, the execution of the *Interactions* must be synchronized with the other clients granting exclusive access to the necessary objects. A tight control over *Interactions* becomes necessary to achieve consistency.

### 2.1 The Geometrical Actions

The interaction management done in the system is based on the concepts above and on one main idea: given that everything in a Virtual Reality application will have a physical representation, it is considered easier to give user *Actions* a representation too, and so it is done in this model. As it has been said when *Actions* were defined, they represent users inputs in the form of a message. That message is of a symbolic type, that is, a tagged value. But, in addition to that, the model associates a geometrical representation to each message. This representation is the part of the space where this message is propagated.

This geometrical representation is usually not as complex as the rendered geometry and, in fact, it is currently implemented by using simpler geometries, more precisely sets of spheres. The system will process each of the user *Actions* propagating the resulting messages to the different objects accessible in his scene graph.

### 2.2 The Interaction Tree: A Layered Scene Graph

The proposed model, as most VE applications, uses a kind of Scene Graph, but of a completely different kind. As every Scene Graph, it contains the definition of the position and status of every object in the VE. But the information available for each object is different. Each object is defined as a set of different views. Some of the views define the appearance of the object, while others define the kind of action that will trigger an interaction over the object.

**The Appearance view.** Every object in the scene will have one or more appearance views. This view or set of views defines the "visual" aspect of the object and contains information usually complex and useless for its use in interaction decisions. The union of all the appearance views of the objects of one environment would correspond to the classical definition of Scene Graph given in the literature. To manage this information, standardized Scene Graphs such as OpenSceneGraph or OGRE could be used.

The model defines a restrictive interface to the actual "appearance Scene Graph" used, which only allows it to define the positions of the objects, its appearance and the definition of one objects position relative to another object. This restricted interface is one of the key concepts that allow the model to keep its independency from the actual Scene Graph used in the implementation. Only the appearance views will be Scene Graph-dependant.

**The Interaction views.** Apart from the "visual" view available for every object, if the object allows any interaction to the user, it will contain (al least) one interaction view.

An *interaction view* determines the geometrical place where a user can perform his or her *Actions* to trigger an *Interaction* over the target object. Also, every *interaction view* contains the conditions the user *Action* has to fulfil to trigger the *Interaction.* These conditions may vary from one object to another and they are based on the geometries of both the *interaction view* and the user *Action* itself, and in the status of the objects involved in the *Interaction*.

For this purpose, the *interaction views* are defined basically as set of very simple geometries, for instance spheres as in the implementation of CVRPrismaker. This technique was inspired in our prototype implementation. The approach followed for this implementation distinguished two views, a graphical view and a 'logical' view. The logical definition described the volumes in every object where interactions could be performed (see figure 1).

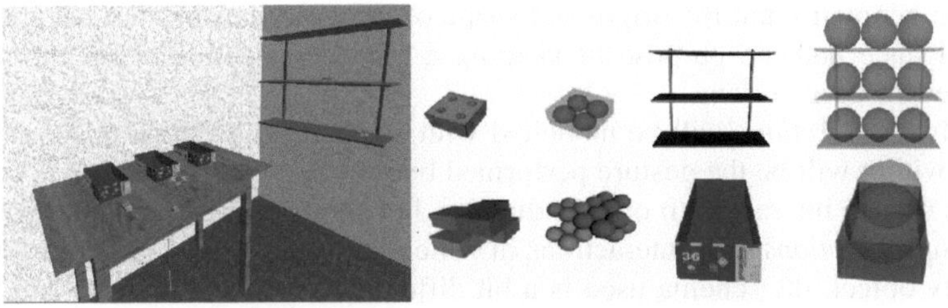

**Fig. 1.** Logical Views used for CVRPrismaker

The idea underneath is that users are not interested on the whole object, but only on those regions where he or she can perform any interactions; i.e. the selves only could contain nine objects, so nine interactive areas were defined. Boxes did the same, they defined the spaces were users would interact to pick/release objects.

Even though these areas are used in these two objects to model receivers to the user actions, the definition given for pieces and figures gave them a different meaning. These reduced geometries could also be used to define the constraints that determined whether two figures could be joined or not. This use is explained more in depth in point 2.3.

After some study on these ideas, some other concepts raised. When studying the interactive regions of an object, it is often easy to identify relations between these regions. These relations would allow their division into different views according to some predefined features:

- **Object's functionality:** Each *interaction view* would contain the regions with an associated functionality.
- **User identity:** The *interaction view* will contain the interactive regions accessible for each kind of user in the system.
- **User message:** The object will contain a view for each kind of message the object can process, i.e. if we implement a system where a user can produce 'pick' and 'drop' messages using his gloves, each object would define two *interaction views*, the first for the 'pick' and the second one for the 'drop' messages.

The *interaction views* available for a user define his capabilities over each object. These objects are complete objects, that is, full functionality can be accessed. Furthermore, they process all the *Interactions* produced in the system, even if they come from other users with different *interaction views*. The limitation is for the local user: he can only trigger the *Interactions* available though his *Interaction views*.

Overall, *interaction views* might be considered like *filters*. Those filters are placed in the Scene Graph associated to an object and they process the messages propagated to the object. A*ctions* will be detected by those filters according to the message propagated into the *Action* and to the geometries of both the *Action* (message) and the *interaction view* (receiver).

### 2.3 The Handheld Objects as *Action* Modifiers

All along this paper it has been said that each of the user's *Actions* would have an associated geometry, but the origin and shape of those *Actions* has not been specified. This avoidance had the purpose of keeping a broad conception about the available geometries for user *Actions*.

Initially, user *Actions* will be modelled with a sphere in a virtual position, and the message within will be the gesture performed by the user. This definition is enough to allow the user to interact with objects directly, but some other behaviours would need more complex *Actions*. For interactions in which the user must use a tool to operate a third party object, the schema used is a bit different. It is not the user's hand but the handheld object position the one which is interacting. In CVRPrismaker, the logical geometry of the object was used to test whether the interaction could be performed. Under this focus, CVRPrismaker's handheld figures transformed the received single-sphere *Actions* into *Actions* with a different message and the geometry of the handheld figure. This way, every object held by the user would transform the *Actions* received, modifying both its geometry and its content according to its own rules.

This behaviour can be used in general modelling tools to manage de assemble/disassemble operations. The object to assemble, i.e. a girder, would transform the spherical 'drop' user message as follows: Its content would be transformed into a 'join' message, and the geometry used would be the interactive areas placed in the points where the girder can be assembled to a structure.

Also, a bigger concept of transitivity can be used, allowing the successive concatenation of filters/modification of the user *Actions*.

### 2.4 Interaction Views as *Action* Receivers

This usage of the *interaction views* is one of its simpler uses, but defines an efficient and flexible way to manage interaction. As seen in most VR systems, it is possible to identify a reduced set of messages: due to user inputs (drop, pick, point, etc), or to the used tools (cut, lift, etc). If an interaction view for each of these possible *Actions* is defined, the definition of the world is faced from a very flexible way: if all the *interaction views* available for a given message (i.e. pick) are put together the result will be the Scene Graph of the virtual regions where that action may have an effect (the regions where the user can perform the 'pick' operation).

For each message, a different geometry with the relevant elements to process that message will be used. This geometry may not be a part of the own object, as a result of the own meaning of the message studied. Also, this separation allows us to differentiate which data/geometry will be used to represent the object when processing a given message.

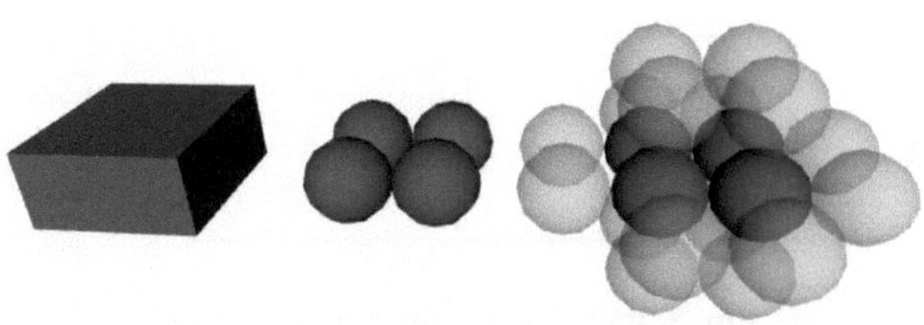

**Fig. 2.** Views needed for a correct design of CVRPrismaker

In CVRPrismaker, only one *interaction view* was defined for every object. When facing the definition of the pieces, the *interaction view* was well suited to manage 'pick' messages, but not so well suited to the 'join' user's messages. CVRPrismaker should have used the *interaction views* shown in the figure 2: one to process 'pick' messages and a different one for 'drop' messages.

For modelling tools, the interaction data needed to 'join' pieces is about the regions where new pieces can be added (16 for each of the Prismaker pieces). These areas will be spaces around the places where elements may be connected. This can be faced as defining the correct places where pieces or connectors may fit, building the *interaction view* joining these places.

## 3 A Reference Architecture

At this point, an example implementation of this model is given. The design is simple but faces the challenges of CVEs. Like the model, this architecture uses a distributed

Scene Graph that keeps the same status in every client. The key to achieve consistence is that ***Committed Interaction***s are shared by all the clients. All the clients execute the same ***Interaction***s in the same order and with the same operands (objects and discrete data). This feature will be transparently managed by the system. Even though this feature would be enough to assure system's consistency, the periodical retransmission of the object's status would avoid completely any possible loss of consistency.

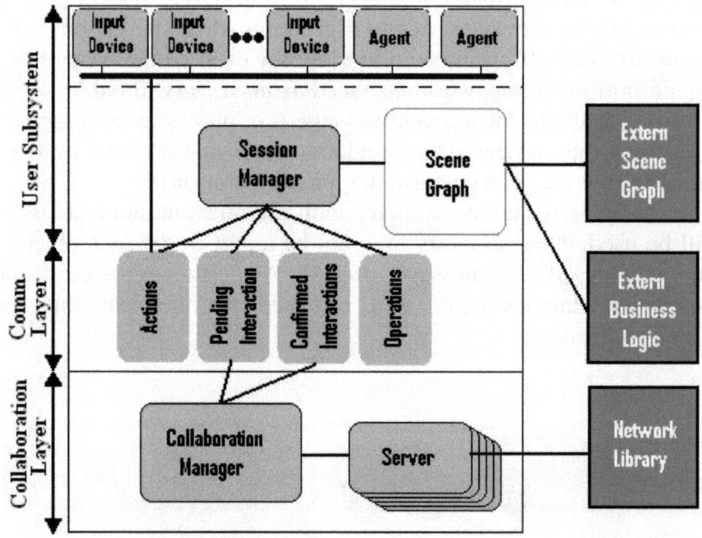


**Fig. 3.** Purposed architecture overview

This design of the system uses a generic Scene Graph and a Network library. These elements could be taken from the commercial products available. The current implementation of the model is considering OGRE and Raknet as a suitable solution for this purpose, but other tools could be used.

### 3.1 User Subsystem

It controls one user's view of the world. It contains a copy of the Scene Graph where the appropriate *interaction views* will be loaded. The *Session Manager* is responsible for feeding the Scene Graph with the *Action*s produced. To achieve this purpose, it is responsible of two main tasks:

- **Controlling user actions:** This system will send the *Action* messages produced by the user to the appropriate objects, and will ask for the necessary permission to perform an *Interaction* when this situation occurred.
- **Receiving confirmed interactions:** It will receive all the change messages from the connected clients. These messages will be delivered to the appropriate *interaction view* in the Scene Graph, that executes the *Interaction* appropriately.

### 3.2 Communication Layer

This layer represents the communication between the user subsystem and the rest of the virtual environment. Through this layer user actions will be declared, checked and, in the appropriate cases, shared to all the other clients. It is implemented as a set of four mailboxes:

- **Actions Mailbox:** All the *Actions* messages produced in the subsystem are sent to this mailbox. The actions are produced by any of the elements in the first sublayer of the User subsystem. These are the *Active Objects* in the Scene Graph and may represent anything able to produce an *Action*. This would include both users and other intelligent behaviours like Agents.
- **Pending Interactions Mailbox:** When an *Action* has fulfilled the conditions of an *interaction view*, it is inserted in this mailbox. The *Collaboration Layer* will determine if the *Interaction* will be executed or not. This decision is made according to the mutual exclusion conditions available over the involved objects.
- **Confirmed Interactions Mailbox:** When the *Collaboration Layer* finds a *Pending Interaction* that can be executed, a message is sent through the *Network library* to all the clients in the system (including the producer's client). Once the messages are received, they are inserted in each on the Confirmed Interactions Mailbox. This is a 'synchronized' mailbox.
- **Operations Mailbox:** Once a client is notified to perform a given *Interaction* over one object, the appropriate actions are taken. Many of these actions will depend on the logic under our interface layer but many others will have to modify this interface itself, modifying the interaction Scene Graph also. This is not a problem itself but, as many systems do, it is common that the drawing of the world is done together with the calculation of the state for the next frame (interaction processing). As this model does not use Scene Graph replication for drawing, those actions that may change the position, appearance and status of the objects in the scene graph are stored here until the drawing is completed.

### 3.3 Collaboration Layer

This layer is responsible for making all the clients in the system share the same status of the Scene Graph. To control this, the *Collaboration Layer* will have to send to all the connected users every operation changing the state of the Scene Graph. As the only element which can change the state of the Scene Graph are interactions, this layer will be responsible for making sure that all the *Interactions* on the system are sent to the rest of the clients. Also, the *Collaboration Layer* is responsible for telling whether a user *Interaction* can be performed over a given object, or whether the object is being modified by other client and the *Interaction* must be ignored.

## 4 More Complex Behaviours

The usage of the *interaction views* shown in this paper is very simple. It just uses the *interaction views* to distinguish between the available messages propagated over the system. This view is very restricted, and more complex definitions might be given if the differentiation of the *interaction views* of the objects in a Scene Graph is done according to other concepts.

If we identify the different views according to the identity of the user, we would be working on a hierarchical environment, where every user would only access the allowed *interaction views*. The *interaction views* could be aware of the internal structures of the organization and provide *interaction views* only for members of a given group or even only for a given user (personal objects).

Also, patterns could be identified so that the users in the system are classified under a given set of roles. This way, it would be the user's role, and not its own identity the one which would determine the *interaction views* to load in the local copies of the Scene Graph.

If the differentiation of the views is done according to the user's knowledge of the object, we come up with a different philosophy. If the interactive regions of the object are differentiated according to the experience needed to understand and use the objects correctly, then an adaptive environment could be defined, with simplified views for novel users and other more complicated for experts.

Also, this model differentiates object's appearance from their functionality. This way it would be possible for two users to have different *appearance views* of the same object. This could be permitted to allow a higher adaptation of the environment. These users would be able to collaborate using their common *interaction views*.

Also, the *appearance views* available could be dependant of the *interaction views* available, allowing one user to see one representation of one object (i.e. a mailbox) while another user, i.e. the owner, can have a completely different perception of that same object (i.e. a 'new staff' folder in his desk).

All in all, *interaction views* are a very new concept and more study over its applicability is still necessary.

## 5 Conclusions and Future Work

This paper has given an introduction to the *interaction views*. These views allow a new way of defining the objects in the environments; these objects will have a 'layered' definition where they will define both its external appearance, and the relevant geometry for each kind of the available interactions over the object.

Using this concept, an interaction model has been proposed, and a simple execution workflow, assuring the more important properties of the environment, explained. Following this model, and with the purpose of benefiting from our experience in modelling tools, a reference architecture for a CVE has been proposed.

This definition, however, makes a very limited usage of the potentialities of the *interaction views* concept. As a future work, we will keep studying this concept, and a more elaborated proposal will rise.

The final goal is the definition of an application that could work as a skeleton for CVEs. This skeleton would define a clear set of rules that would dictate the way objects are managed in the VE and the logical way through which user actions are filtered and how those actions would be mapped into interactions. Thus, users of this system would only need to define the objects in its VE and, if any kind of new object is needed, define the behaviour of these objects.

**Acknowledgements.** This work has been supported by the Ministerio de Educación y Ciencia of Spain (CICYT TIN2004-08000-C03-01), and the Junta de Comunidades de Castilla-La Mancha (PAI06-0093).

## References

1. Joslin, C., Di Giacomo, T., Magnenat-Thalmann, N.: Collaborative Virtual Environments –From Birth to Standardization. In: IEEE Communications Magazine 42, 28–33 (2004)
2. Oliveira, J.C., Shirmohammadi, S., Georganas, N.D.: Collaborative Virtual Environments Standards: A Performance Evaluation. In: IEEE DiS-RT99 Workshop Proceedings, pp. 14–21
3. Frecon, E.: DIVE: A generic tool for the deployment of shared, virtual environments. In: Proc. of ConTEL 2003, vol. 1, pp. 345–352 (2003)
4. Frécon, E., Stenius, M.: DIVE: a scaleable network architecture for distributed virtual environments. Distrib. Syst. Engng. 5, 91–100 (1998)
5. Steed, A., Tromp, J.G.: Experiences with the Evaluation of CVE Applications. In: Proc. of CVE'98, University of Manchester, U.K., pp. 123–130 (1998)
6. Walsh, A., Bourges-Sevenier.: The MPEG-4 Jump-start Prentice Hall PTR
7. García, P., Montalá, O., Rallo, R., Gómez, A.: MOVE: Component Groupware Foundations for Collaborative Virtual Environments. In: Proc. of 4th International Conference on Collaborative Virtual Environments, 2002 Bonn, Germany, pp. 55–62 (2002)
8. Rousseau, M., Slater, M.: A Virtual Playground for the Study of the Role of Interactivity in Virtual Learning Environments. In: Proc. of PRESENCE 2005: The 8th Annual International Workshop on Presence, London, UK, International Society for Presence Research, pp. 245–253 (2005)
9. Molina, J.P., García, A.S., Martinez, D., Manjavacas, F.J., Blasco, V., López, V., González, P.: The development of glove-based interfaces with the TRES-D methodology. In: Proc. of ACM VRST 06, Limassol, Cyprus, pp. 216–219 (2006)
10. Steed, A., Frecon, E.: Construction of Collaborative Virtual Environments. In: Sánchez, M.I. (ed.): Developing Future Interactive Systems, Idea Group 2005, pp. 235–267 (2005)
11. Goebbels, G., Laliot, V., Göbel, M.: Design and evaluation of team work in distributed collaborative virtual environments. In: Proc. of ACM VRST'03, Osaka, Japan, pp. 231–238 (2003)

# C-Band: A Flexible Ring Tag System for Camera-Based User Interface

Kento Miyaoku[1], Anthony Tang[2], and Sidney Fels[2]

[1] NTT Cyber Solutions Laboratories, NIPPON TELEPHON AND TELEGRAPH
1-1 hikarinooka Yokosuka-shi Kanagawa, Japan
miyaoku.kento@lab.ntt.co.jp
[2] University of British Columbia,
Vancouver, British Columbia, Canada
{tonyt,ssfels}@ece.ubc.ca

**Abstract.** This paper proposed a new visual tag system for enhancing real-world media interaction using handheld camera devices. This paper also described performance evaluations of the prototype, and its applications. C-Band is based on a ring with a color pattern code. A C-Band tag can provide a self-contained URL, and is flexible enough to allow various aesthetic designs for the tag's surface. Furthermore, the tag's structure is useful for building interactive techniques. Taken together, these features suggest that C-Band is an effective method to build various attractive camera-based media interactions.

**Keywords:** Visual Tag, Color-Difference Signal, Camera, Mobile Terminal.

## 1 Introduction

One of the most promising goals in mobile computing is linking real-world objects such as paper, panels, labels and screens to digital data. This will allow real world objects to be used as input keys to trigger various applications [1,2] Among the many approaches to realizing this vision, we are most interested in camera-based techniques because of the ubiquity of mobile phones and other devices with high-resolution cameras (Figure 1).

Visual tags such as QR code [3] are very attractive since they can contain a practical amount of application data such as a URL, and the computational cost for decoding is quite low so they can be mounted on even low power mobile devices such as cell phones. However, current existing visual tags are aesthetically inflexible. They often can not fit into surrounding graphical design. This limitation reduces the popularity of using visual tags in camera-based interaction systems.

To overcome this limitation, we proposed a new color ring based visual tag system called "C-Band". Using a color difference-based encoding provided by the ring gives C-Band tags sufficient design flexibility to allow integration with various graphic designs (Figure 2). We built a prototype using a preliminary algorithm and evaluated its basic performance. The evaluations show that a C-Band tag containing 28 bytes

R. Shumaker (Ed.): Virtual Reality, HCII 2007, LNCS 4563, pp. 320–328, 2007.

can be effectively extracted from a 640×480 pixel resolution image. These features suggest that C-Band is an effective method to build various camera-based interactions. We describe some possible applications in this paper.

**Fig. 1.** Linking real world objects with digital data

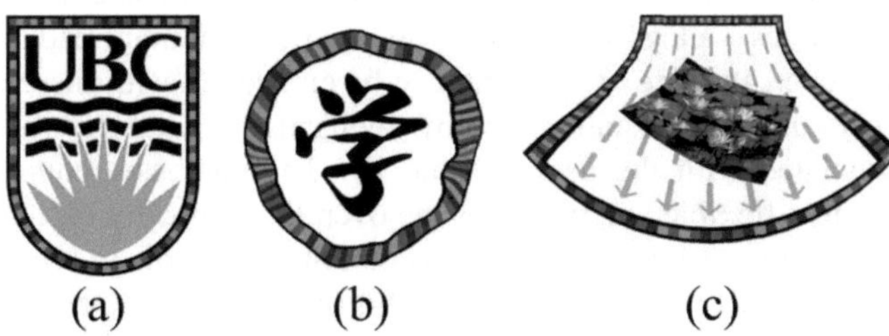


**Fig. 2.** Feasible C-Band tag designs

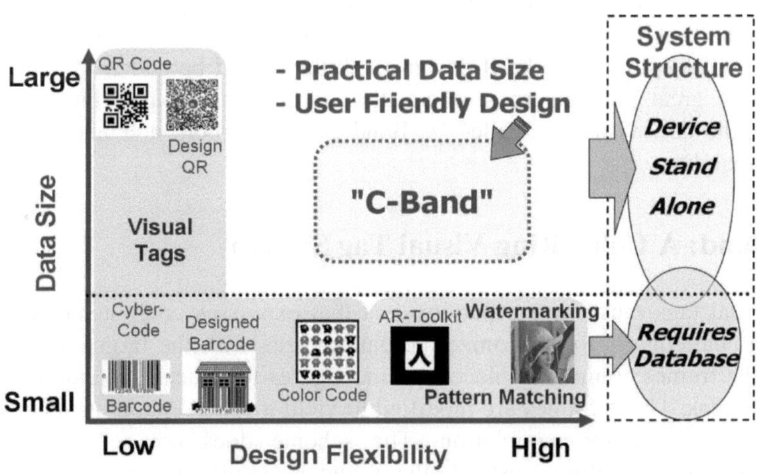


**Fig. 3.** Design space of camera based tagging systems

## 2 Related Work

There are three main approaches to embedding camera readable data into an object/image: (1) visual tags: placed on the object and scanned [3-7]; (2) digital image watermarking: dormant and imperceptible information is embed via digital encoding [8,9], and (3) image feature pattern matching: the image itself is used as data [10] .

Some explicit visual tag systems support a very large data size so that the tag can contain various kinds of data such as URLs, e-mail addresses, and so on. This flexibility enables the tag system to stand alone (i.e. no database lookup), and facilitates building many applications in a simple and cost-effective way. Also, systems to decode visual tags are usually very simple and processed rapidly so that they can be executed on common cell phone devices. However, their designs are aesthetically inflexible and cannot provide any human-readable semantic information. Moreover, they often disrupt the attractiveness of the overall graphical design.

Watermarking techniques [8,9] and image feature pattern matching techniques [10] can place data into any image without compromising the aesthetic quality. This means that these techniques integrate tagged areas with human-readable semantic information. However, the size of data that can be embedded with these techniques is usually relatively small and static, thereby requiring a database to look up the information associated with the data, i.e. the ID. The database requirement makes these approaches less flexible and increases the overall complexity of the system.

In summary, existing techniques that allow common cameras to scan data create a tradeoff between data size and aesthetic flexibility (Figure 3). DataGlyph [11] can well integrate relatively large amounts of data into images. Unfortunately, it is expensive to extract DataGlyph from images captured by common image sensors. Its response speed is a problem when it runs on common cell phone devices.

These observations indicate that the visual tag system still the most reasonable approach to build phone camera based interaction systems, as some interactions requires high response speeds. If design flexibility could be added to visual tags, it would have great potential to promote the use of camera based interactions. Our proposal, the new visual tag called "C-Band", achieves both practical data size and design flexibility.

## 3 C-Band: A Color Ring Visual Tag System

Since visual tags must have a pattern area that expresses computer-readable data, the main challenge is to harmonize the pattern area with the target. Our approach utilizes the frames commonly placed around figures to indicate, to emphasize, or to mark off areas. These frames are modified to yield a visual encoding scheme that is based on frame color modulation. The scheme does not rely on geometric information for decoding; instead, the scanner simply detects sequential color differences. Consequently, the tags can have various shapes and surface designs (Figure 2).

### 3.1 Structure of C-Band Tag

Figure 2 shows examples of C-Band tags. A C-Band tag consists of a content area and a frame surrounding the content area. The ring surface is divided into color sectors, and the number of color sectors depends on the size of the embedded data. Each ring has black edges to enhance the accuracy of ring component extraction. A thin white margin between the ring and the content area is usual to ensure reliable detection.

### 3.2 Color Difference-Based Encoding Method

To achieve tag shape flexibility, C-Band uses a simple hue-difference based encoding method using 3 colors to encode information [12]. With this method, a hue-increase between colors of a pair of successive color-sectors on the ring expresses a single bit; the hue-increase of $2/3\pi$ indicates "0", and $4/3\pi$ indicates "1". For example, using a color wheel representation with (R)ed (hue=0 or $2\pi$ ), (G)reen (hue=$2/3\pi$) and (B)lue (hue=$4/3\pi$), color changes from R→G, G→B and B→R indicate '0', and color changes from R→B, B→G, and G→R indicate '1'. A binary sequence that includes $n$-bit data and $c$-bit checksum can be transformed into a color pattern using this encoding method. The pattern expressing $n+c$ color differences is placed on the ring in a counter-clockwise direction. As a sector is required to delineate the start and end of the pattern, the ring is divided into $n+c+2$ sectors to express $n$-bit data.

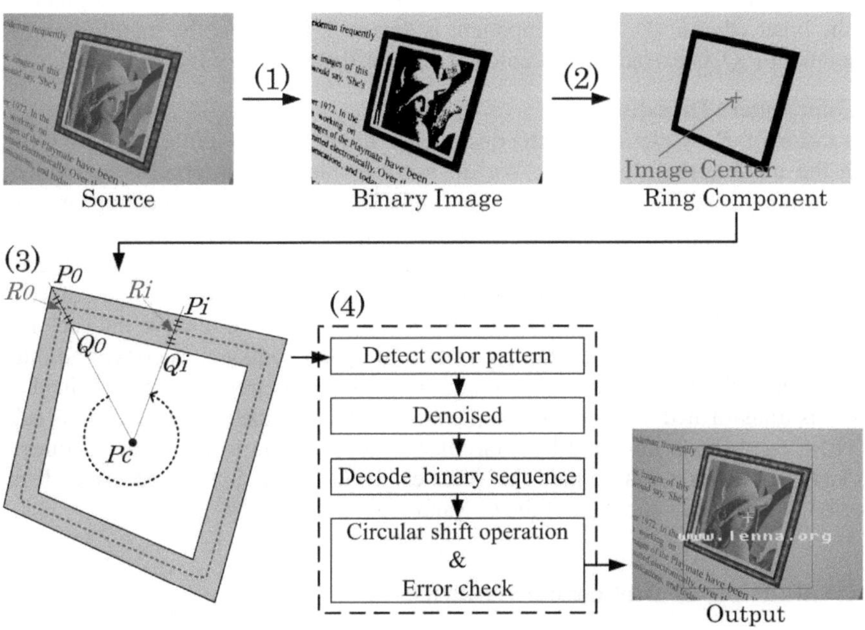


**Fig. 4.** C-Band Tag Detection Process

### 3.3 Detection Processes

We designed a preliminary algorithm to detect and decode a C-Band tag. When the user captures a tag, the tag is detected and interpreted by the algorithm. The algorithm, outlined in Figure 4, consists of the following four stages:

(1) Binarization
The original RGB color image is transformed into a binary image by applying a preset threshold to the luminosity of each pixel. The luminosity, Y, is calculated by the equation: $Y = 0.299*R+0.587*G+0.114*B$.

(2) Ring component extraction
After labeling all connected components in the image, a ring component candidate is selected by considering the shape and the positional relationship with the image center and other components.

(3) Ring skeleton extraction
Pixels at the boundary between different colors including the edge are often mixed making it difficult to accurately detect the color changes at these points. To decrease the effect of color mixing, we use a thinning algorithm to extract the most reliable pixels. We use the following algorithm:
The pixel sequence $R_i$ on the ring skeleton is extracted. First, $P_c$ inside the ring component is selected. The pixel sequence $P_i$ $(i = 0,..,N-1)$ is the sequence of ordered pixels appearing on the outer edge of the ring component in a counter-clockwise direction. For each $i$ $(i = 0,..,N-1)$, the intersection point $Q_i$ between the segment $P_iP_c$ and the inner edge of the ring component is detected, and then, the middle point $R_i$ of the segment $P_iQ_i$ is extracted as a color pixel near the middle of the sector.

(4) Color Pattern Decoding
Each color of $R_i$ is classified into one of the three primary colors (R,G,B) simply using the maximum color value. We do not use hue for this process to reduce the computational cost. From this, we obtain the RGB color sequence that appears around the ring (such as {R, R, R, G, G, G, B, B, B, *R*, G, G, G}) as the pixel sequence $R_i$.

This sequence is denoised and reduced to form the RGB color pattern for decoding: first, repeated colors mark a sector and are reduced to a single color in the sequence; second, if a color sector only has a single pixel, we remove the sector from the sequence as noise. In the example above, the color sequence is converted into the color pattern of {R, G, B, G} (note that *R* is removed as noise). The obtained color pattern is transformed into a binary sequence by applying the above transitions rules.

Then, every code obtained by a circular shift operation to the binary sequence is checked. If no error is found, the scanner decides that a tag and its code were detected which yields the data of the C-Band tag.

## 4 Evaluation of Basic Performance

We prototyped the C-Band system (Figure 5) using a Windows PC and a webcam (Sony PCGA-UVC11A, Lens: F3.4 focal length f=5mm (35mm film conversion f=40mm); Focus range: 3cm to infinity). We used standard PC equipment for ease of implementation; in practice, the algorithm is simple enough to run on a standard mobile phone. Our prototype uses Microsoft's DirectShow technology, and can process white-balanced images (provided by the webcam) at 15-30fps depending upon camera resolution. In our tests, the tags expressed 16-bit CRC check bits. When the data size is $n$-bit, the ring of the tag is divided into $n+18$ sectors. The tags were printed by a small common inkjet printer (HP Deskjet 5740).

### 4.1 Performance Under Indoor Lighting

The basic detection performance of the system was tested under indoor fluorescent lighting. The system processed 1000 image frames in which a tag was captured continuously. We measured how many times the system could detect and decode the tag's data correctly. Note that, because of the CRC check bits, the system never incorrectly decoded a tag (a false positive). Thus, detection reliability is dependent only on the percentage of correct detections (the hit rate) in the 1000 trials.

There is a tradeoff between camera resolution and detectable data size, because data size depends on how many color sectors are used: each color sector must be captured with enough pixels to detect its color accurately. This experiment was intended to determine the smallest detectable data size for each resolution under ideal conditions.

We tested square tags containing data ranging from 4 bytes to 32 bytes. The height of each printed tag was 5cm. The width of the ring of these tags was 1/14 of the height of the tag, or 3.6mm. The tags were detected by a camera set 7cm in front of the tag. In this case, the captured tag was in the center of the image and the height of the tag is about 80% of the height of the image. We tested camera resolutions of 640x480, 320x240 and 160x120 pixels. Figure 5 shows the results of these tests.

With images of 640x480 pixel resolution, the system achieved over 90% detection reliability for tags of up to 28 bytes. 320x240 pixels images attained 90% reliable detection for the square tag of up to 16 bytes, and the oval tag of up to 20 bytes. Finally, 8 byte tags were reliably detected almost 100% of the time even with 160x120 pixel resolution.

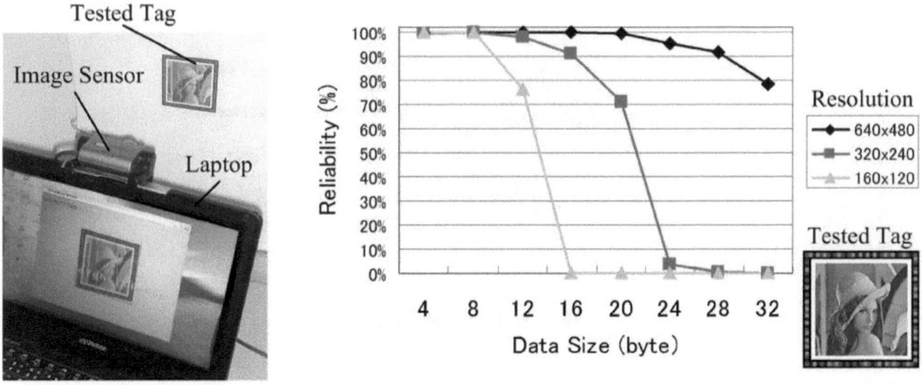


**Fig. 5.** Relationship between detection reliability and data size

### 4.2 Processing Speed

The processing speed of the detection system was checked by using a small laptop (Victor MP-XP7310) which has a Pentium M 1Gz CPU. Under the same condition as the experiment in Section 4.1, 1000 captured images were processed and the average processing time for each image was calculated. The processing times were 68.0msec, 14.8msec and 3.5msec for 640×480 pixels, 320×240 pixels and 160×120 pixels, respectively. The labeling process in the ring component extraction occupies the longest processing time, and ring skeleton extraction is also takes long. Extrapolating this performance to current cell phone technology (100MHz to 425MHz processors), we would expect a 2 to 10 times increase in processing time; however, implementing the image processing functions on a GPU (Graphics Processing Unit) - commonly found in newer mobile phones - would significantly decrease the processing time.

## 5 Potential Applications

With a prototype C-Band system in place, we explored a variety of application contexts for camera-based interaction. Due to space limitations, we describe the most salient and interesting explorations here.

(1) Paper Keypad
A paper keypad is a paper slip which shows several tags that contain a character code, a symbol code or a command code (Figure 6). The paper keypad can be used as a portable input method for small camera devices. Since existing visual tags can not contain a figure on their surface, an embedded character must be shown next to a visual tag. C-Bands around each letter allow the desired characters to be pointed at and selected directly, improving text entry speed and accuracy.

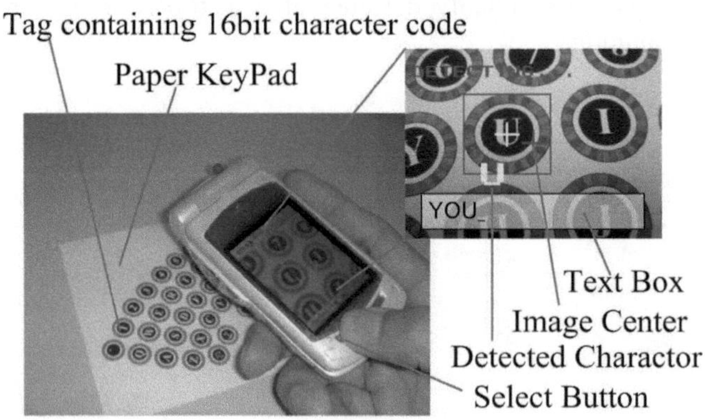


**Fig. 6.** Paper Keypad

(2) Large screen interaction
C-Band tags can also contain animation as semantic information which is not possible with the other tagging systems. We built a whack-a-mole game (Figure 7) to exploit

this feature. In the game display, nine C-Band tags indicate the holes of the moles. Each C-Band tag (hole) has a small ID. A user points and shoots by using a camera device. Since C-Band tags can occupy a large space in the game UI as holes, they can be detected much better and from wider ranges than is possible by placing small matrix codes beside the holes. Test users enjoyed this game and generally seemed to like the feel of the UI graphics design.

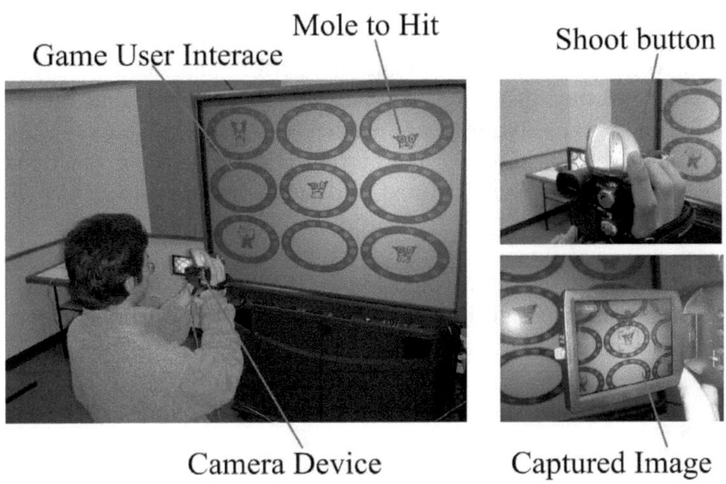


**Fig. 7.** C-Band based Whack-a-Mole game screen

(3) Hot Frame - Physical URL
The evaluations showed that the tag can directly provide a short URL which can be expressed by 28 bytes or fewer. A C-Band frame works both as a URL source and as a cue to indicate a hotspot area. As shown in Figure 2 (a), C-Band can also be used as a part of the graphical design of a frame. QR-code tags require more than 1cm space if the camera has 0.3mm resolution. If the figure is restricted to a 3cm×3cm space it is not efficient to use a QR-code as shown in Figure 8. However, C-Band can use this space effectively by forming its shape to fit around the figure. This feature makes C-Band a reasonable way to attach a physical URL to small figures like trademarks.

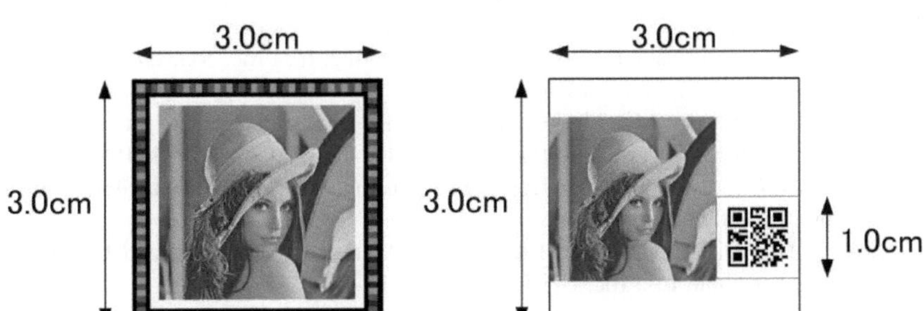


**Fig. 8.** Adding a URL tag to small, fixed space

## 6 Conclusion

We created a new flexible visual tag system, "C-Band", to promote the use of camera-based interaction. Experiments under indoor lighting with a proof-of-concept system showed that a tag with up to a 28 byte data can be detected well by a 640×480 pixel camera. We also showed that C-Band allows designers to be flexible and creative in embedding C-Band tags into graphical objects (Figure 2). We believe that these features of C-Band will encourage the adoption of camera-based interaction via visual tags. We continue to work on resolving the remaining issues with this technology. The most important task is to evaluate its performance under various lighting conditions. We confirmed that the prototype could work under some outdoor lighting conditions, but more extensive tests are needed. Also, we will improve the detection algorithm to increase robustness, as the current algorithm, while functional, is quite rudimentary. We plan to install C-Band into smart phones and PDAs to make the system truly practical.

**Acknowledgments.** The authors would like to thank members of the HCT Lab and NTT Cyber-Solutions Laboratories for their support. This work was done while the first author was visiting the University of British Columbia.

## References

1. Brush, A.J.B., Turner, T.C., Smith, M.A., Gupta, N.: Scanning Objects in the Wild: Assessing an Object Triggered Information System. In: Proc.Ubicomp2005, pp. 305–322 (2005)
2. Rekimoto, J., Nagao, K.: The World through the Computer: Computer Augmented Interaction with Real World Environments. In: Proc. UIST'95, pp. 29–36 (1995)
3. QR-code.com, http://www.qrcode.com/
4. Semacode, http://semacode.org/
5. Rekimoto, J., Ayatsuka, Y.: CyberCode: Designing Augmented Reality Environments with Visual Tags. In: Proc. DARE2000, pp. 1–10 (2000)
6. Toye, E., Sharp, R., Madhavapeddy, A., Scott, D.: Using Smart Phones to Access Site-Specific Services. IEEE Pervasive Computing 4(2), 60–66 (2005)
7. ColorZip, http://www.colorzip.com/
8. Alattar, A.M.: Smart images using digimarc's watermarking technology. in Security and Watermarking of Multimedia Contents II, Proc. SPIE, vol. 3971, pp. 264–273 (2000)
9. Nakamura, T., Katayama, A., Masashi Yamamuro, M., Sonehara, N.: Fast Watermark Detection Scheme for Camera equipped Cellular Phone, In: Proc. NUM2004, pp. 101–108 (2004)
10. Kato, H., Billinghurst, M.: Marker tracking and HMD calibration for a video-based augmented reality conferencing system. In: Proc. IWAR1999, pp. 85–94 (1999)
11. Moravec, K.L.C.: A grayscale reader for camera images of Xerox DataGlyphs. In: Proc. BMVC, pp. 698–707 (2002)
12. C-blink: A Hue-Difference-Based Light Signal Marker for Large Screen Interaction via Any Mobile Terminal. In: Proc. UIST 2004, pp. 147–156 (2004)

# A Framework for VR Application Based on Spatial, Temporal and Semantic Relationship

Changhoon Park[1], TaeSeok Jin[2], Michitaka Hiroseo[3], and Heedong Ko[4]

[1] Dept. Of Game Engineering, Hoseo University,
29-1 Sechul-ri, Baebang-myun, Asan, Chungnam 336-795, Korea
chpark@office.hoseo.ac.kr
[2] Dept. of Mechatronics Engineering, DongSeo University,
San 69-1 Churye-dong, Sasang-ku, Busan 617-716, Korea
[3] The University of Tokyo,
4-6-1 Komaba, Meguro-ku, Tokyo 153-8904, Japan
[4] Korea Institute of Science and Technology,
39-1 Hawolgok-dong, Sungbuk-gu, Seoul 136-791, Korea

**Abstract.** This paper proposes a framework for VR application based on 3 different kinds of hierarchical structures for spatial, temporal, and semantic relationship. To achieve this, we incorporate scene graph, time graph, and ontology into the framework. This approach will enable to integrate synthetic space, real space, and knowledge seamlessly as a new way of developing immersive tangible space.

**Keywords:** Framework, Immersive Tangible Space, Spatial relation, Temporal relation, Semantic relation, Scene Graph, Time Graph, Ontology, Seamless Integration.

## 1 Introduction

Recently the Systems Technology Division in Korea Institute of Science and Technology (KIST) is continuously researching and developing the core technology for the intelligent HCI. It has launched a project named "Tangible Space Initiative (TSI)." The art of TSI is based on the concept of tangible space where several physical objects of real space are integrated into virtual objects of synthetic space. Thus, the space creates a new kind of living environment for human which exceeds all the spatial and physical limits.

In TSI, more effective VR interface metaphor is sought: a user may experience an interaction environment that is realized by both physical and virtual means. TSI effort is led by three parallel and cooperative components: Tangible Interface (TI), Responsive Cyber Space (RCS), and Tangible Agent (TA). TI covers how the user sees and manipulates the 3D cyber space naturally. RCS creates and controls the virtual environment with its objects and behaviors. TA may sense and act upon the physical interface environment on behalf of any components of TSI. (Ko, 2002).

R. Shumaker (Ed.): Virtual Reality, HCII 2007, LNCS 4563, pp. 329–337, 2007.

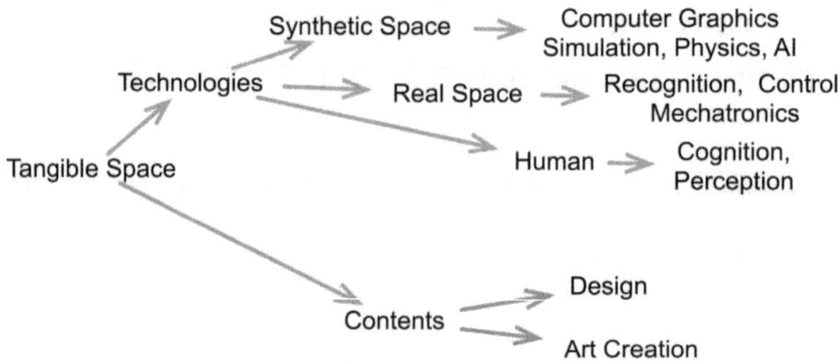


**Fig. 1.** The initiative involves experts from diverse related fields such as virtual reality (VR), intelligent control, human robotics, image processing, multimedia database, and artificial intelligence

This paper will propose a framework in order to facilitate the research of TSI. For the seamless integration between synthetic and real spaces, we believe that it is important to integrate diverse technologies into the framework. So, the framework will be designed to support adding new functions independently. Then, various experts can focus on their business without understanding others. And, different TSI applications need different functions. So, it will be needed to organize our framework based on XML description. Then, we can optimize and build various applications for fast test.

In this section, we have introduced the motivation of this research relating to TSI. Section 2 will review a framework named NAVER(Networked and Augment Virtual Environment aRchitecture) based on distributed micro-kernel. In section 3, spatial, temporal, and semantic hierarchical structures are explained. Then, we explain about the implementation and present some results that have been achieved. Finally, we concluded in section 5 with possibilities for future work.

## 2 Related Work

We have been developing a framework named NAVER, which was developed for the Gyeongju VR Theater of the World Culture EXPO 2000 in Korea from September 1 to November 26, 2000. This VR Theater is characterized by a huge shared VR space with tightly coupled user inputs from 651 audience members in real time. Large computer-generated passive stereo images on a huge cylindrical screen provide the sensation of visual immersion. The theater also provides 3D audio, vibration, and olfactory display as well as the keypads for each of the audience members to interactively control the virtual environment. At that time, the goal of NAVER was to coordinate both virtual world and various devices [1].

In recent, NAVER introduced the concept of module to facilitate adding new functions such as handling new input device, visual special effect and so on. And, it is important to support the integration of diverse techniques for synthetic or real space. Therefore, module will enable to extend function of NAVER without detailed understanding or modifying the kernel [2].

Module is defined as a set of callback functions and XML-based specification. These functions will be invoked by the simulation loop of the kernel. As a building block, some of modules can be chosen and plugged into the kernel without modifying the kernel. And, XML description allows specifying a configuration of modules without programming. So, we can configure and optimize NAVER for a specific application or content with evaluating and finding functions causing bad performance. NAVER consists of several modules listed in Table 1. And, we have been developing modules for augmented reality, physics, character animation and so on.

**Table 1.** NAVER modules

| Modules | Description |
|---|---|
| nvmVRPNClient | This module manages a communication with a VRPN server in which various peripheral devices are connected. |
| nvmDisplay | This module is used to display the virtual world into multiple PCs. |
| nvmLoader | This module is used to load the models to construct the scene graph |
| nvmScenario | This module controls the development of stories in virtual environment |
| nvmNavigation | This module is used to change the camera position and orientation. |

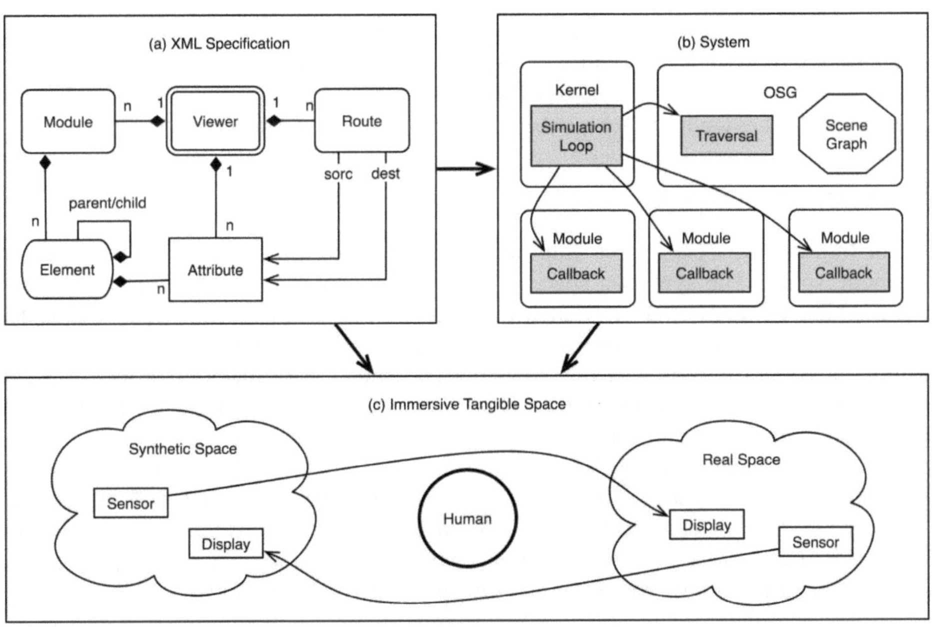


**Fig. 2.** NAVER enables to define and manage both synthetic and real spaces by means of XML specification consisting of one viewer, and a set of modules and routes. Route is provided to make modules work together by sending and receiving events among them.

# 3 Three Hierarchical Representations

In this section, we explain how to use spatial, temporal, and semantic relationship for the seamless integration between synthetic space, real space, and knowledge as a new way of developing immersive tangible space. These relationships will be organized into a tree-like hierarchical structure. The structure allows repeating information using parent and child relationship. This provides an efficient way of managing and accessing complex data.

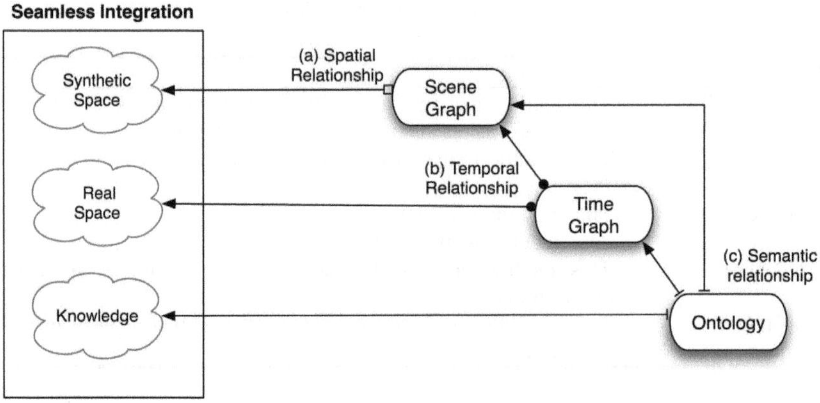


**Fig. 3.** (a) Scene graph is used to construct a synthetic space by describing its spatial relationship. (b) Time graph enables to synthetic and real space over time by describing the temporal relationship of scene graph and modules for real space. (c) Ontology is used for a domain-specific knowledge which will be applied to manage time graph and scene graph.

## 3.1 Spatial Relationship

In our framework, scene graph is introduced as a way of representing and managing a synthetic space. The synthetic space is then broken down into a hierarchy of nodes representing either spatial groupings of objects, settings of the position of objects, animations of objects, or definitions of logical relationships between objects. The leaves of the graph represent the drawable geometry, their material properties, and multimedia such as video and audio. This enables to organize synthetic so that it can be rendered quickly and efficiently.

Scene graph enables to organize how some object is located in synthetic space in relation to some reference object so that it can be rendered quickly and efficiently. This means that we can modify and reference spatial relationship of everything in synthetic space. Three are two different spatial relationships when we apply scene graph: Bounding volume hierarchy and transform hierarchy as below.

**Bounding Volume Hierarchy.** In order to be able to exploit the spatial locality of a scene graph, we need to introduce the concept of bounding volumes for each node. At the bottom of the hierarchy the size of the volume is just large enough to encompass a single object tightly. As you walk up the hierarchy each node has its own volume which tightly encompasses all the volumes beneath it. Bounding Volume Hiearchies are useful for speeding up efficient culling and speeding up collision detection between objects. Bounding volumes change as the transformations and geometry of scene graph nodes change over time.

**Transform Hierarchy.** All nodes should contain their linear transformation relative to their parent. The transformation hierarchy includes all of the root nodes and root node descendants that are considered to have one or more particular locations in the synthetic space. In this way, the node defines its own local coordinate system relative to its parent. We can transform points in the local coordinate system of the node to the world coordinate system by concatenating all the transformation matrices of nodes in the path from the root node of the scene graph to the current node.

And, we will access scene graph to make not only dynamic and complex synthetic space but also real-time rendering. In general, scene graph is closely related to the performance of culling and state sorting. Culling is the process of removing the objects from a scene that won't be seen on screen. The hierarchical structure of the scene graph makes this culling process very efficient. And, state sorting is the process that all of the objects being rendered are sorted by states such as textures, materials, lighting values, transparency, and so on. Then, all similar objects are drawn together. In our framework, scene graph and its traversing will be updated during run-time to make better performance.

### 3.2 Temporal Relationship

We introduce a timing model to make more complex and dynamic tangible space which can change its presentation of synthetic space and configuration of real space dependent on not only event but also time. Our framework will use a timing model to control the change of scene graph and modules.

It should be noted that scene graph can include time dependent objects such as keyframe animation, video and audio as well as static. And, module can be added to handle new device as described before. Therefore, timing model enables to describe temporal composition of everything of synthetic and real space. This means we can integrate synthetic and real space by means of a timing model.

We propose a timing model by extending SMIL [1] (Synchronized Multimedia Integration Language), XML-based language to integrate a set of independent multimedia objects into a synchronized presentation. In our framework, this time graph will be used to control not only 3D objects of synthetic space but also interaction devices of real space over time. And, it also enables to schedule event routing between different spaces. Thus, we can build more complex and dynamic VR applications with integrating synthetic and real things at the same context.

---

[1] The World Wide Web Consortium (W3C) for encoding multimedia presentations for delivery over the Web developed SMIL. SMIL integrates a set of independent multimedia objects into a synchronized presentation. This means SMIL is not a content media type because it doesn't define any particular type of media. Instead, the author can describe a composition of existing multiple media with referring other files in other format.

In SMIL, there are 3 timing container elements for a structured composition. Each element specifies different temporal relationships between their children. The seq element specifies its children handled in sequence, one after the other. The par element specifies that its children be handled in parallel. The excl element activates only one of its children at a time. Thus, it is allowed to construct a hierarchical or structured timeline by nesting 3 timing containers. It means that any child of a timing container element can be an element for media object or other timing containers [3,4].

And, SMIL has a set of attributes to control timing of media object elements and composite elements. Elements have a begin, and a simple duration. The begin can be specified in various ways – for example, an element can begin at a given time, or based upon when another element begins, or when some event happens. It should be noted that this model is dynamic because we can't expect when event happens such as mouse click.

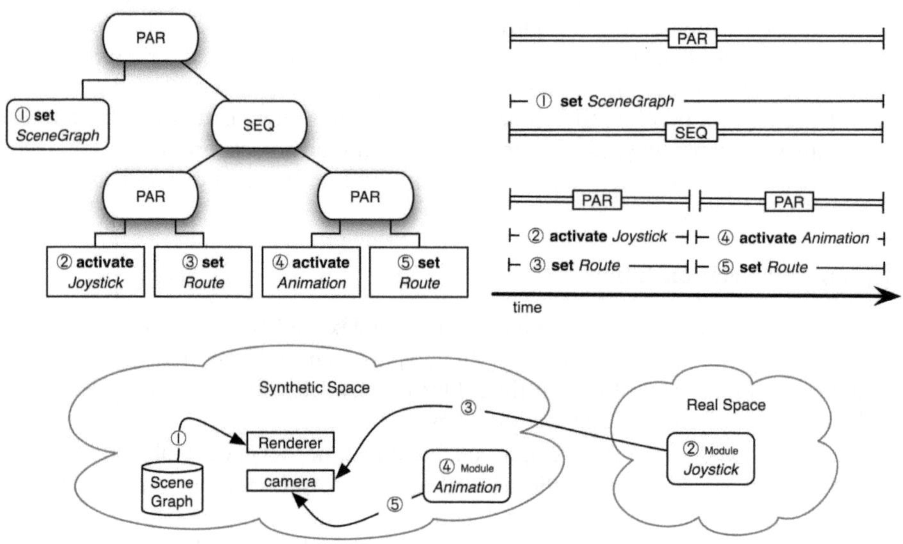


**Fig. 4.** The root of time graph is a *par* node so its children will be processed in parallel. Then, we can invoke an action ① to assign a scene graph for a visual rendering of synthetic space. At the same time, there is a *seq* node including two *par* nodes. And, the first *par* node has 2 commands ② and ③ as its children. ② will activate a module for joystick in real space. At the same time, ③ makes a path from the joystick to the camera of synthetic space. Then, it will be allowed to navigate synthetic space by controlling joystick. After this, ④ and ⑤ make a camera path animation with activating a module to generate animation and routing its result to the camera. Actually, timing attributes like begin and duration are not explained here.

### 3.3 Semantic Relationship

This framework use ontology to make knowledge driven tangible space based on semantic relationship. Ontologies provide the theoretic and axiomatic basis to underlying knowledge bases. Based on this formalization, we will express semantic relationships between synthetic and real space. Thus, the supporting framework enables to perform reasoning by inference on the content and the semantics of both synthetic and real spaces.

And, semantic information can be used to perform knowledge driven rendering, interaction, integration and so on. Ontology allows describing domain concepts by means of their properties as well as their relationship. This means that we will use ontology to define domain specific knowledge besides scene graph for spatial relation and time graph for temporal relation. After all, these information will facilitate the development of VR applications with supporting semantics based description and control.

**Semantic-based Culling.** Culling removes objects that are outside the viewing frustum from the rendering process. In a networked virtual environment, state updates will not be exchanged between players if they can't see each other any reason in a shared virtual space. We'd like to use domain-specific knowledge to improve culling for rendering and network.

**Semantic-based LOD.** Accounting for level of detail involves decreasing object complexity as it moves away from the viewer or according other metrics such as object eye-space speed or position. We'd like to change not only the complexity of geometry but also various behaviors depending on semantics. This approach will help analysis and manipulate scientific data in virtual space. Ontology will be used to define complexity mapping and semantic distance.

**Semantic-based Highlighting.** When a modeler makes a scene graph, he gives some name to a node of scene graph or texture to represent what it is. Then, we will use this name to define a domain specific ontology. By using this ontology, we can have a kind of context. This context helps system intelligent with understanding a scene graph. For example, there is node named door. Then we can add transform to its parent in order to open the door when an avatar is close to the door. And, if a name of texture includes "stone", system can set its mass or features to the objects which has the texture especially for physics simulation.

**Semantic-based Interaction.** In our approach we use ontologies to process the user's input and context semantic integration in order to manipulate virtual devices in a virtual environment. We use a domain independent device conceptualization as part of the ontology describing general virtual entities of virtual devices in combination with a domain dependent world application conceptualization that describes the application environment. This ontology in collaboration with the context information will compute the semantic integration [5.6].

## 4 Implementation

NAVER can be download from http://naver.imrc.kist.re.kr. This site provides information about new feature, getting started and installation. In recent, the part of visual rendering has changed from OpenGL Performer to OpenSceneGraph. And, many modules for such as physical simulation, character animation, bump mapping, particle system, and augmented reality have been developing based on Cal3D[2], osgART[3] and so on.

**Fig. 5.** A complex rigid body System was the recent demo based on NAVER. Providing an interactive rigid body simulation that allows the user to interactively build a different configuration of rigid bodies and simulate them to see how the domino effect is generated with a help of multi-modal interaction including SPIDER(right), and speech command.

## 5 Conclusion

We have presented a framework for the development of immersive tangible space by integrating synthetic and real spaces seamlessly. To achieve this, scene graph, time graph and ontology are integrated into the framework for spatial, temporal and semantics relationship respectively. The scene graph is used for the composition of synthetic space. By using scene graph, we can coordinate and interconnect synthetic space and various devices over time managed by scene graph and modules. Ontology allows organizing a domain specific knowledge in order to build intelligent tangible space.

**Acknowledgments.** This research was supported by the Academic Research fund of Hoseo University in 2006. ( 20060091)

## References

1. Park, C., Ko, H., Kim, T.: NAVER: Design and Implementation of VR Framework for Gyeongju VR Theater. Computer and Graphics 27(2), 223–236 (2003)
2. Park, C., Hirose, H., Ko, H.: A Platform for Interactive VR Storytelling. In: Pan, Z., Aylett, R., Diener, H., Jin, X., Göbel, S., Li, L. (eds.) Technologies for E-Learning and Digital Entertainment. LNCS, vol. 3942, pp. 193–202. Springer, Heidelberg (2006)

---

[2] Cal3D is a skeletal based 3D character animation library written in C++ in a platform-/graphic API-independent way. It supports combining animations and actions through a "mixer" interface.

[3] OSGART is a cross-platform library that simplifies the development of Augmented Reality applications by merging computer vision based tracking with OSG rendering.

3. Ayers, J., et al.: Synchronized Multimedia Integration Language (SMIL) 2.0. World Wide Web Consortium Recommendation (2001) http://www.w3.org/TR/2001/ RECsmil20-20010807/
4. Schmitz, P.: Multimedia Meets computer Graphics in SMIL2.0: A Time Model for the Web. WWW 2003, pp. 45–53 (2002)
5. Kalogerakis, E., Christodoulakis, S., Moumoutzis, N.: Coupling ontologies with graphics content for knowledge driven visualization. In: Virtual Reality, 2006, pp. 25–29 (2006)
6. Irawati, S., Calderón, D., Ko, H.: Spatial Ontology for Semantic Integration in 3D Multimodal Interaction Framework. In: Proceedings of ACM International Conference on Virtual Reality Continuum and its Applications, June 2006, pp. 129–135 (2006)

# How Much Information Do You Remember? -The Effects of Short-Term Memory on Scientific Visualization Tasks

Wen Qi

Department of Industrial Design,
Eindhoven University of Technology,
P.O.Box 513, 5600MB, Eindhoven,
The Netherlands
w.qi@tue.nl

**Abstract.** In this paper we describe our experiences and lessons learned from two user studies about the effects of short-term memory on data analysis tasks with graphical user interface and virtual environment. Visualization is a powerful tool for representing scientific data for analysis purpose. Current research progress enables us to create a high fidelity visual representation of scientific data. However, the value of traditional graphical user interface and Virtual Reality (VR) as human computer interface in data analysis via visualization tool is questioned by the domain scientists. We carried out two user studies that asked users to perform data analysis tasks. The first user study compared the user performance on selecting and manipulating transfer function (TF) with different graphical user interfaces in volume visualization to search certain structures within a 3D data set. The second user study investigated the performance difference of immersive VR, fish tank VR and haptic-based fish tank VR systems on four generic visualization tasks. The two user studies indicates that short-term memory plays an important role in 3D user interaction during data analysis task. The pitfall of 3D user interface design for scientific visualization is that too many efforts have been put into the interface itself or technology, rather than designing user interface to match or amplify human capabilities, for instance the limit amount of short term memory and its importance in data analysis process.

## 1 Introduction

Three-dimensional (3D) interaction with scientific data involves studying visualization methods to faithfully represent data, on the one hand, and designing interfaces that truly assist users in the data analysis process, on the other hand. However, manipulating and viewing data in order to reveal valuable information effectively and efficiently is still not an easy task. Some of the bottlenecks are the huge amount of data and the ability to visualize and understanding these data. Scientific visualization investigates possible methods to translate data into a visible form that highlights important features, including commonalities and

R. Shumaker (Ed.): Virtual Reality, HCII 2007, LNCS 4563, pp. 338–347, 2007.

anomalies. The progress in visualization by itself does not guarantee that users will be able to work more efficiently and effectively. In his review paper,"Top Ten Questions in Scientific Visualization", Chris John pointed out that one of the ten problems in scientific visualization research is still human computer interaction (HCI) [1]. HCI research has become more and more important in the area of scientific data visualization. Since 3D interface is so immature, developing technology is still the main research activity. 3D interface developers argue that interfaces or interaction techniques are extremely complex to design and make, and that the demand for the function that interfaces can provide has always outdriven the demand for better usability. Until recently, the focus of 3D user interfaces and interaction research has shifted from emphasizing design hardware (e.g. development of 6 DOF input devices and 3D output devices) or software toolkits to paying more attention to studying the user with currently available knowledge from cognition, psychology.

In this paper, we specifically study how the human computer interface influences user performance in scientific visualization through two kinds of user interface: graphical user interface for TF specification and VR as interface for generic visualization tasks.

## 2 User Study I

The TF is a critical component of the direct volume rendering process. It specifies the relation between scalar data (e.g. densities measured by CT or MRI imaging), and possibly also their first- or second-order derivative values, and optical characteristics, such as color and opacity [2]. The most common method is the trial-and-error method. It involves manually editing the TF by modifying a graphical curve and/or by adjusting numerical parameters, and visually inspecting the resulting image.

The trial-and-error method provides only minimal visual feedback in TF specification, and we therefore have devised an experiment by which we explore the usefulness of additional information in this trial-and-error method. More specifically, we aim to assess the effects of the following additional feedbacks: 1) data-dependent information, such as the histogram; 2) data-independent information, such as suggested or standard TFs. We also wanted to investigate the effect of a graphical user interface with a limited number of DOFs.

Our experimental hardware setup consists of a DELL graphics workstation (Pentium IV, 2.4 GHz, 512 MB RAM, ATI *FireGL 4* graphic card). The TF specification is implemented by means of a texture look-up table with the help of hardware-accelerated 3D texture mapping.

The experiment involves five interface conditions. The baseline interface with free-style control, referred to as condition 1, consists of parts 1a and 1b in Figure 1. With this free-style interface, a user has full control over the TF. The part 1a allows the user to manipulate the TF by creating and moving control points of a piecewise linear function along the horizontal and vertical direction within a 2D interaction area. The panel 1b controls the course of the experiment.

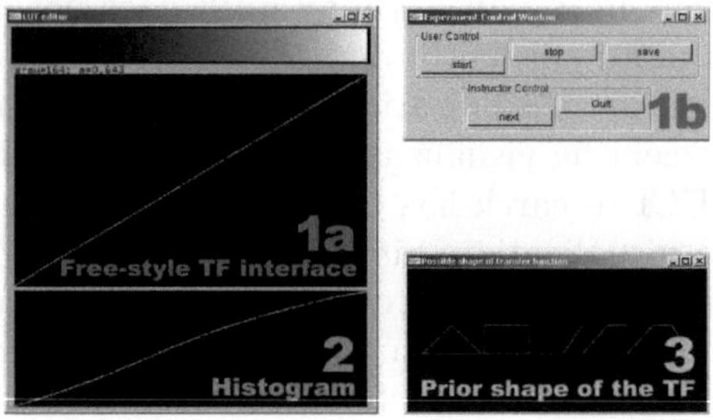


**Fig. 1.** The user interfaces for experimental conditions 1 (part 1), 2 (part 1+2), 3 (part 1+3) and 4 (part 1+2+3)

Experimental condition 2 includes data-dependent information, and consists of parts 1 and 2 in Figure 1. A cumulative histogram and free-style TF interface are presented at the same time. Experimental condition 3 includes data-independent information, and consists of parts 1 and 3 in Figure 1. In condition 4, both data-dependent and data-independent information are offered, so that all parts in Figure 1 are presented. The interface for our final condition 5 is shown in Figure 2. It is a user interface that allows for a number of piecewise-linear TFs, and that does not provide (data-dependent) histogram information. Each kind of TF is represented by a graphical icon. The available TF graphical representations have only few control points and limited DOFs. This implies that the shape of a graphical representation cannot be altered.

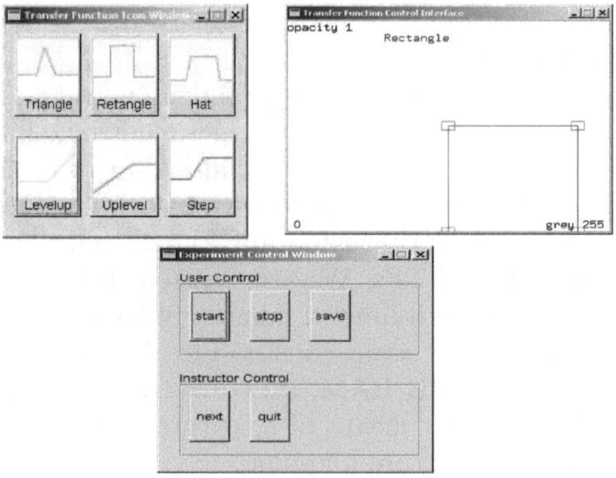


**Fig. 2.** The user interface for experimental condition 5

There were 13 subjects in the experiment. Each subject participated in all conditions (within-subject design). Each participant performed four tasks in each

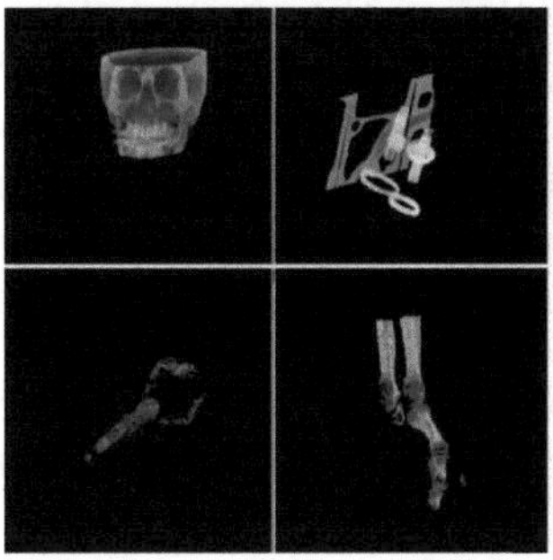

**Fig. 3.** The required structures being rendered with four data sets

of the five interface conditions. Each task involved a different data set ("head", "engine", "lobster", and "foot"), and required the subjects to visualize a predescribed structure within the data as good as possible (Figure 3). For example, one task is to ask the subjects to find out one TF that can create a 3D image that contains only the bone structure of the skull. The dependent variables recorded during the experiment were the following:

- the total number of the mouse clicks during a task;
- the number of the mouse clicks for each icon in condition 5;
- the time needed to finish an task;
- the rendered image produced at the end of a task.

The subjects were given several questions to answer after the experiment. More specifically, the questionaires contained the following parts:

- Their agreement or disagreement with general usability statements about the system, such as: "It was easy to use the system";
- Questions addressing the usability of the individual interfaces.
- In order to assess the task performance, they were asked both to rate the output images individually and to express their preferences for all pairwise combinations of output images;

### 2.1 Results

There are no significant differences of the time spent among the five conditions for the "lobster", "head", and "foot" data set, respectively. For the "engine" data set, the order of the conditions with respect to performance time is one to five from faster to slower. For the "engine" data set, "Analysis of Variance" (*ANOVA*) with repeated measures indicates that there are significant differences among the five interface conditions, $F(4, 52)=9.141$, $p < 0.05$ . The post hoc test shows that between condition 1 and 5, condition 2 and 5, and condition 3 and 5, there are significant differences in the response time. Condition 4 and 5 do not demonstrate a significant difference. *ANOVA* on the number of mouse clicks for all four tasks shows that there are no significant effects in either of the four data sets among the five conditions.

This subjective evaluation is based on the answers from the questionnaire. The results are mainly summarized along several important characteristics, such as, effectiveness, efficiency, satisfaction and overall image quality.

**The difficulty of the tasks.** The tasks with these four data sets presented different levels of difficulty for the subjects. The task with the "engine" data set has been recognized as the easiest one. The most difficult task is the one with the "head" data set.

**The task performance by the image quality.** The image quality is scaled by how close the produced image is compared with the original goal. With the "engine" and "head" data set, the task performance in condition 5 is the worst. However, the best performance has been achieved in condition 5 with "lobster" data.

**Effectiveness.** In terms of effectiveness, Condition 4 gets the highest rank, with condition 2 as the close second. Condition 5 is considered as the least effective.

**Efficiency.** Efficiency was defined as "how fast the user feels that he can finish the task" with each of those interfaces. Condition 4 again scores best, while condition 5 is the worst.

**Satisfaction.** The subjects are requested to give an evaluation on "the arrangement of the five interfaces". The results illustrate that condition 4 still gets the highest appreciation. Condition 5 scores higher in this attribute than in the previous attributes.

## 3 User Study II

The second user study compares three kinds of VR systems: HMD based VR, fish tank VR and fish tank VR with haptic feedback. Relative performance of these systems is compared over four generic tasks involving the visualization of volumetric data. The rendering paradigms are only tested in their most common configurations: inside-out for HMD and outside-in for fish tank.

### 3.1 Apparatus

All three systems display the volumetric data using the Visualization Toolkit (VTK). To enable real-time interaction, we chose Marching Cubes as the primary algorithm and render isosurfaces of the volumetric data.

**Immersive HMD VR system.** The immersive VR system uses a V8 HMD from Virtual Research System. Head tracking is performed via a 3rdTech HiBall tracking system. The outward-looking HiBall sensor is mounted on the back of the HMD (Figure 4b). We used a DELL Precision 530 (dual 2.8-GHz Xeon with

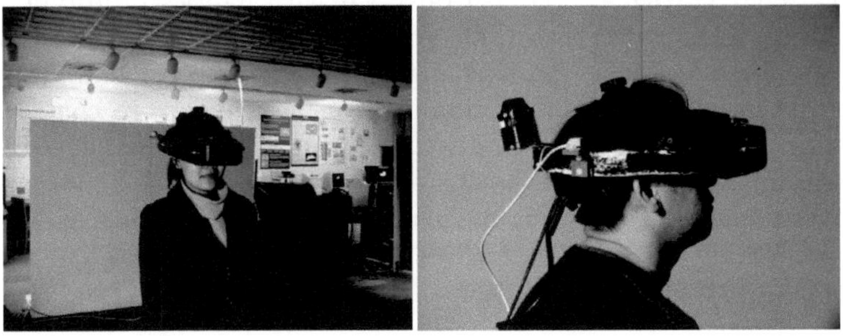

**Fig. 4.** Head-mounted display system: head-mounted display with head sensor

2GB RDRAM) and an NVidia *Quadro FX 1000* graphics card. The working space for a user in this VR system is about 4.5 meters wide by 7 meters long by 4 meters tall (15 feet × 23 feet × 13 feet) as shown in Figure 4.

**Fish-tank VR.** The second VR system is based on the concept of fish tank VR introduced by Colin Ware [4]. The central computing platform of this VR system is identical to the HMD system with the following additional components:

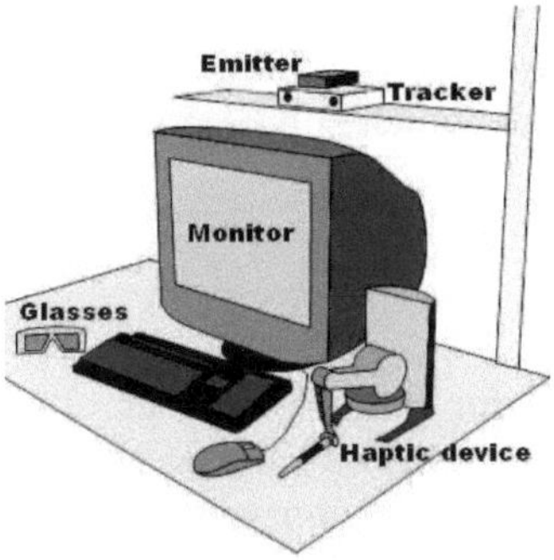


**Fig. 5.** A diagram of the fish tank VR system

- A 17-inch CRT monitor with a refresh rate of 100 Hz to support stereo display, an infrared emitter and shutter stereo glasses from StereoGraphics.
- A PHANTOM Desktop$^{TM}$ haptic device. In fish tank VR mode, the PHANTOM was used to rotate the volume around its center only.
- A DynaSight 3D optical tracker for measuring the 3D position of a target (reflective disc) attached to the front of the stereo glasses.

The hardware components are organized to enable accurate and easy calibration (Figure 5).

**Fish-tank with Haptics.** The fish tank VR with haptics prototype uses the same hardware setup as the fish tank VR system, except that the PHANTOM also provides force feedback. An axis-aligned on-screen icon follows the stylus's motion in 3D, producing an effect similar to using a mouse to control the on-screen cursor. The haptic representation of volumetric data employed different force models for different objects within the volume: viewers felt the outside surface of spheres and ellipsoids, but the inside of long curved tubes and cylinders.

### 3.2 Data and Tasks

Simulated volumetric data are generated to act as trials during our studies. A random number of two to four types of differently-shaped objects (sphere, ellipsoid, cylinder, and curved tube) are inserted at random positions (details are found in [5]). The objects' properties (such as size, shape) and the density of each volume form experimental conditions that vary between trials. The bounding box of the volume is subdivided into eight equally-sized subregions within which object density may differ. Subregions are labeled with unique numbers (1 through 8).

Subjects are asked to complete fours tasks within each trial. Each task involves judging the properties of a specific object or of the overall volume, specifically:

- *Shape task:* Subjects identify the number of differently-shaped objects within the volume and name the objects.
- *Size task:* Subjects report how many differently-sized spheres exist.
- *Density task:* Subjects identify the densest subregion in the volume.
- *Connectivity task:* Subjects report how many curved tubes exist in the volume, and then determine which subregion(s) the longest curved tube passes through.

### 3.3 Results

Forty subjects volunteered for our experiment, 33 males and 7 females. The subjects were randomly assigned into one of the three display system groups. Two measures of performance were derived for each trial a subject completed: response time $rt$ and error rate $\widehat{P_e}$ . A single $rt$ value representing the total time in seconds needed to complete all four tasks was captured for each trial. Four separate $\widehat{P_e}$ values for the four tasks subjects completed were also generated.

For $rt$ statistics, trials were divided by display system (HMD, fish tank, or fish tank with haptics). For $\widehat{P_e}$ statistics, trials were divided by display system (HMD, fish tank, or fish tank with haptics) and task (shape, size, density, or connectivity). The logarithm of $rt$ in average and $\widehat{P_e}$ for different conditions were then compared (using $ANOVA$ with a 95% confidence level for $\lg(rt)$, Chi-Square test for $\widehat{P_e}$).

In summary, the following significant differences in performance were identified:

1. The HMD group had significantly longer $rt$, compared to both the fish tank and the haptic groups. Using haptics in the fish tank also resulted in longer $rt$.

2. For most tasks (counting number of different shapes and number of curved tubes and finding the densest subregion), the HMD group had higher $\widehat{P_e}$, compared to both the fish tank and haptic groups.
3. In counting number of different sizes about sphere objects, none of these three groups is accurate. The HMD group made significantly more errors than the fish tank and the haptics group in case only one size of sphere was present. In case more than one size was present, subjects from all three groups mainly underestimated the number of sizes on average.
4. For identifying the subregions that the longest tube passes through during the connectivity task, the HMD group had higher chances in both missing the right subregions and misjudging the wrong subregions, compared to both the fish tank and the haptic groups.

Subjective measurements were obtained through analysis of the post-experiment questionnaires. The answers indicated that overall, subjects preferred the haptic and HMD VR systems due to perceived ease of use, presence, and immersion. We summarize our findings over the following categories of questions we asked.

**Overall perception of the VR systems.** This category asked about the perception properties and characteristics of a VR system, including the immersion, presence, depth, and spatial relationships. For the question: "the extent that you felt you were within a virtual environment", the HMD system ranked significantly higher than the fish tank and haptics systems, $F(2, 37) = 5.481, p = 0.008$, with a post-hoc comparison between HMD and haptic of $p = 0.006$. There was also a significant difference on the question: "the extent you had a sense of acting in the virtual space, rather than operating something from outside". The HMD system ranked significantly higher than the other two systems, $F(2, 37) = 15.666, p = 0.001$.

**Usability of a VR system.** The ease of learning and using a VR system is the main focus of this category. Although subjects from all three groups felt their system was easy to use, the HMD group ranked highest for the perceived difficulty in carrying out their tasks. Moreover, HMD subjects reported a significantly higher demand for memorizing than the other two groups, $F(2, 37) = 5.534, p = 0.008$. Finally, HMD subjects were less confident about the accuracy of their answers, $F(2, 37) = 5.521, p = 0.008$.

## 4 Discussion

A further analysis through the knowledge of engineering psychology and perception explains the reasons of such performances for those tasks. Human beings have two different storage systems with different durations: working memory and long term memory [6]. Working memory is the temporary, attention-demanding store that a human user uses to retain new information until he or she uses it [7].

A human user uses working memory as a kind of "workbench" of consciousness where he or she examines, evaluates, transforms, and compares different mental representations. A human user might use working memory, for example, to carry his or her mental arithmetic or predict what will happen if he or she set a TF one way instead of another. Working memory is used to hold new information (for instance the resulting image with one TF setting) until a human user gives it a more permanent status in memory, that is, encodes it into long term memory.

Several experiments have demonstrated the transient character of working memory [8]. Estimates generally suggest that without continuous rehearsal, little information is retained beyond 10 to 15 seconds. This transient character of working memory presents a serious problem for those work domains/tasks when information can not be rehearsed because of time constraint [9].

Working memory is also limited in its capacity (the amount of information it can hold) [10]. And this limit interacts with time. Experiments show that faster decay is observed when more items are held in working memory, mainly because rehearsal itself is not instantaneous [11]. The limiting case occurs when a number of items can not successfully be recalled even immediately after their presentation and with full attention allocated to their rehearsal. The limiting number is sometimes referred to as the memory span.

Task analysis can suggest that TF specification is a task that puts high demands on working memory from a user. When a user uses a TF interface to search for required results or structures, he or she continuously inputs different parameters for the TF through the interface and judges whether or not the corresponding rendering results are the ones he or she needs. Often he or she needs to retrieve previous settings that are better after comparison. A user needs to perform so many interactions (modifying the TF parameters and observing the corresponding visual feedbacks) and has to hold mapping information between TF setting and visual feedback with respect to each data set in working memory, which introduces more possibilities for error. The graphical user interface of trial-and-error method proposed by many researchers did not present any mechanism to relief the workload of memory. Clearly, the limited capability of working memory has a major impact on the effectiveness and efficiency of an TF interface. On the other hand, it also indicates that a user interface will be more efficient and effective if it can relieve the workload of a user's working memory during the specification process.

The second user study showed that immersive virtual environment highly increased the immersion and presence experiences of the subjects, but asked subjects to memorize the data structure heavily so that they could perform the tasks. In the absence of an overview capability, subjects were forced to make an internal representation of the total volume; the dense nature of the data removed visible landmarks that can normally provide such a frame of reference. The time needed to complete tasks in the HMD system was significantly longer, compared to both the fish tank and the fish tank with haptics systems. It is due to the reported inability of HMD subjects to remember where they had previously seen target items within the volume because of the high density of data sets. They would often have to re-search the volume for objects they had previous located, but had "lost"as they walked into a different region.

## 5 Conclusion and Future Work

In this paper, based on the results of two user studies, we emphasize the importance of short-term memory on the data analysis tasks and propose the factor of short-term memory should be taken into account while designing 3D user interface for data visualization applications. The perception and cognition skills of a human user play an important role in determining the success or failure of a 3D interface or interaction technique.

**Acknowledgments.** This project is funded by SenterNovem as part of the Innovation Oriented Research Program (IOP-MMI) supported by the Dutch Ministry of Economic Affairs. We would like to thank the NIH National Research Resource in Molecular Graphics and Microscopy at the University of North Carolina at Chapel Hill, which is supported by the NIH National Center for Research Resources and NIH National Institute of Biomedical Imaging and Bioengineering grant 5-P41-RR02170-21.

## References

1. Johnson, C.R.: Top scientific visualization research problems. IEEE Computer Graphics and Applications 20(6), 2–6 (2004)
2. Lichtenbelt, B., Crane, R., Naqvi, S.: Introduction to Volume Rendering. Prentice-Hall, New Jersey (1998)
3. Qi, W., Martens, J.-B.: Transfer Function Specification with Trial-and-error Interface for Volume Visualization: A User Study. In: The IASTED International Conference on Human Computer Interaction 2005, November 14-16, Phoenix, USA pp. 50–57 (2005)
4. Ware, C., Arthur, K., Booth, K.S.: Fish tank virtual reality. In: Proceedings of CHI 93, pp. 37–42. ACM and IFIP (1993)
5. Qi, W., Taylor, R., Healey, C., Martens, J.B.O.S.: A comparison of immersive HMD, fish tank VR and fish tank with haptics displays for volume visualization, In: Proceedings of the 3rd symposium on Applied perception in graphics and visualization 2006, pp. 51–58, ACM (2006)
6. Wickens, D.C., Hollands, G.J.: Enginerring Psychology and Human Performance. Prentice-Hall, New Jersey (1999)
7. Baddeley, A.D.: Working memory. Clarendon, Oxford (1986)
8. Brown, J.: Some tests of the decay theory of immediate memory. Quarterly Journal of Experimental Psychology 10, 12–21 (1959)
9. Moray, N.: Handbook of perception and human performance. Wiley, New York (1986)
10. Baddeley, A.D.: Human memory. Allyn and Bacon, Boston (1990)
11. Melton, A.W.: Implications of short-term memory for a general theory of memory. Journal of Verbal Learning and verbal Behavior 2, 1–21 (1963)
12. Bowman, D.A., Kruijff, E., LaViola, J.J., Poupyrev, I.: 3D User Interfaces: Theory and Practice. Addison-Wesley, New Jersey (2004)

# Super-Feet: A Wireless Hand-Free Navigation System for Virtual Environments


Beatriz Rey[1], Jose A. Lozano[1], Mariano Alcañiz[1], Luciano Gamberini[2], Merche Calvet[1], Daniel Kerrigan[2], and Francesco Martino[2]

[1] LabHuman, Institute of Research and Innovation in Bioengineering
Universidad Politécnica de Valencia, Camino Vera s/n
46022 Valencia, Spain
{beareyso,jlozano,malcaniz}@mediclab.upv.es
mercalga@teleco.upv.es

[2] Human Technology Lab, Department of General Psychology
University of Padova
{luciano.gamberini,francesco.martino}@unipd.it
daniel.kerrigan@tiscali.it



**Abstract.** Navigation is a fundamental task in virtual environments. Some of the metaphors that are used to determine where users want to be placed at each moment are based on physical locomotion. Usually, these techniques require the use of several sensors and complex algorithms. In this paper, we present Super-Feet, a wireless navigation system controlled by natural movements without requiring invasive methods or devices. It uses a low-cost infra-red system to detect the instantaneous position of both feet and this information is translated into a walking and rotation velocity in the environment. Preliminary results show that Super-Feet navigation is more accurate but slower than joypad based navigation systems.



**Keywords:** User Interface Events, Navigation in Virtual Environments, Virtual Reality Ergonomics.


## 1 Introduction

Navigation is a fundamental task in real and virtual environments. Users of virtual environments need methods to change their instantaneous position. In order to define a navigation system, there are two components of locomotion that have to be controlled: the direction and the velocity of motion. Different travel techniques have been developed to control these parameters based on several assumptions, and different classifications have been proposed to describe these travel techniques.

One of these classifications is based on the interaction metaphors that are used to control the navigation. Bowman [1] organizes travel techniques by six common metaphors: physical locomotion, steering, route-planning, target-based, manual manipulation and scaling. All of these techniques have different advantages and disadvantages that can make them more or less suitable depending on the application. However, the most natural techniques for the user are based on physical locomotion.


R. Shumaker (Ed.): Virtual Reality, HCII 2007, LNCS 4563, pp. 348–357, 2007.

In this paper, we present Super-Feet, a system based on the physical locomotion metaphor. In the following points, we will describe more in detail other developments that have been made in navigation systems based on this kind of metaphor, so we can analyze the advantages and disadvantages of our proposal compared with these systems.

### 1.1 Physical Locomotion Navigation Systems

The first approximation that can be thought as a way to move inside virtual environments is to use exactly the same movements as in the real world, that is, to physically walk. This technique is natural, provides vestibular cues and promotes spatial understanding [1]. Real walking navigation systems have to be based in a wide-area tracking system that detects the instantaneous position of users while they walk. An example of this kind of tracking systems is the HiBall Tracker [2, 3, 4]. A HiBall (infrared sensing system) is fixed to each object that has to be tracked, pointing towards the ceiling, where a system of fixed infrared beacons is placed. This optical tracking system provides six degrees of freedom. Real walking is also used in other kind of applications, such as augmented reality outdoor systems, allowing users to move in a wide area in the real world. An example is the mobile augmented reality system (MARS) [5] which uses GPS and inertial/magnetometer orientation sensors to detect the position and rotation of the user.

An approach that can take the benefits of the naturalness of the movements without requiring the use of a wide-area tracking system is walking in place. This technique allows movements along big distances in the virtual environment while remaining in a small area in the real world.

One of these systems is the Virtual Treadmill [6], a system which tracked head motion of users and detected steps using a neural network. It requires that participants reproduce the physical head motions generated during actual walking but without physically locomoting. The pattern analyzer determines if users are walking in place, and if this is the case, makes them move forward in the direction of gaze.

As Templeman describes [7], the U.S. Army Research Institute in conjunction with the University of Central Florida's Institute for Simulation and Training also proposed a system for walking in place based in vertical motion of the feet. The movement starts when the foot is moved above a vertical threshold. The rotation is controlled by an electromagnetical tracker placed between the shoulders.

A system based on a similar approach is the one developed by Grant and Magee [8]. In this case, the movement of the user was controlled by moving the foot forward or backward over the floor. The rotation is calculated as the average direction between both feet. An electromagnetic tracker is also used in this case.

*Gaiter* system [7] is also based on stepping movements. Different movements of the legs are used to control the velocity and direction of motion. In order to track these movements, electromagnetic trackers are attached to the knees to control translation and rotation of the lower leg. Besides, the system also uses force sensors on shoe insoles to follow the different forces that are apply to the ground. A step occurs when a foot looses the contact with the floor.

In other cases, physical locomotion techniques are used with complex mechanical devices, such as treadmills, bicycles and wheelchairs. Templeman [7] classifies mechanical locomotion systems in unidirectional and multidirectional ones. Unidirectional systems limit movement to one direction, and a special action is necessary for rotating in the virtual environment. One of the first systems to be used was the treadmill proposed by Brooks [9]. This system has a handle to control the rotation. On the other hand, multidirectional systems allow users to move in any direction. One example of this kind of systems is the omni-directional treadmill [10]. This system is composed of two perpendicular treadmills, one inside of the other, which allow users to walk in any direction. Iwata [11] proposed a torus-shaped surface as a locomotion interface. This system uses twelve sets of treadmills which are connected side by side and driven to perpendicular direction. The effect of infinite surface is generated by the movement of these treadmills. The Sarcos Treadport is a locomotion interface consisting of a large tilting treadmill, an active mechanical tether, and a CAVE like visual display. The treadmill employs orthogonal overlapping bands to create a totally walkable two-dimensional surface. The tether's linear axis is motorized to push or pull on the user, thereby simulating unilateral constraints, slope, and inertial forces that intensify the walker's physical effort [12]. The main problem of these kinds of systems is that their complexity generates limitations and constraints on the natural movements of users.

Some studies have compared different physical locomotion navigation techniques. Slater [13] compared their virtual treadmill with walking in place and concluded that users without previous navigation experience reported a higher subjective presence when they walk in place using the virtual treadmill than when they fly along the environment (hand-pointing navigation method). Usoh [14] added real walking as a third condition, and found that the simplicity, straightforwardness and naturalness of real walking was significantly better in the real walking system. Besides, both kinds of walkers had higher subjective presence than flyers.

Some approximations combine different navigation metaphors. An example is the Step WIM [15]. In order to move in large areas, this system presents a world in miniature (WIM) that appears below the users' feet so their real position in the virtual environment coincide with their position in the WIM. A special interface has been designed for the feet, so that users can tap their toes or heels to decide when they want to be translated to other places in the virtual environment. This interface (Interaction Slippers) [16] is made embedding a wireless trackball device into a pair of slippers.

## 2 Technical Aspects

The main objective of this work has been to develop a hand-free navigation system that leaves a greater freedom for other interactions with the system using the hands. The system has to be applied in settings of reduced dimensions and without requiring complex devices that can be invasive for the user.

A physical locomotion approach was selected. The use of real walking systems [4, 5] was discarded, as the use of this kind of systems in a small area is not suitable to control movement in big virtual environments. On the other hand, as one of our goals is simplicity, we also decided to avoid systems based on mechanical devices, such as treadmills [9, 10, 11].

Super-Feet can be included in the category of walking-in-place devices. Similarly to other approaches [6, 7, 8], our system has to be based on some kind of tracking device in order to know the position and movement of the parts of the body that control the advance velocity and rotation inside the virtual environment. All these systems are based on electromagnetic tracking devices, used with force sensors in the case of *Gaiter*. In our case, we have decided to use optical tracking, because this technology is less sensitive to noise, and our hardware configuration does not require an excessive workload for the computer. Besides, it is not a problem to have a direct line-of-sight between the camera and the tracked objects.

Super-Feet has to detect instantaneous movements of the feet and associate them to velocities in the virtual world. According to previous studies [13, 14], the naturalness of movements seems to be related with higher presence in the virtual environment, so we have decided to use an approach based on natural feet movements as similar as possible to real walking.

### 2.1 Hardware Configuration

Super-Feet detects the movements of the users' feet in a non-invasive way using a low cost infra-red commercial tracking system: Optitrack [17]. This commercial system includes an infra-red camera which is connected to the computer via USB interface. Optitrack includes an application programming interface that is used to communicate and obtain information from the camera. The object tracking that can be made using this technology is very precise and reliable. Reflective markers have to be placed on objects to be tracked and inside the field of view of the camera. Once the camera has been connected, LEDs emit infra-red light which is reflected when it comes in contact with the markers. The camera can then receive the reflected light and determine the position of the markers.

This commercial system has been used to prepare the physical configuration associated to Super-Feet, as can be observed in Figure 1.

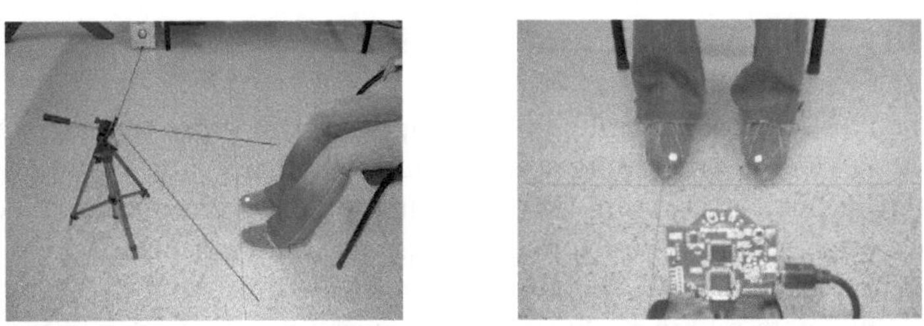

**Fig. 1.** In the left image, the relative position of the user and the infra-red camera can be observed. The right image shows a view of the reflective markers from the camera perspective.

Users will be seated on a chair during the exposition to the virtual environment and move their toe tips up and down, and laterally, to control the different movements in the virtual world. The Optitrack camera will be placed on a tripod in front of the user.

The user has to wear two flexible plastic covers (similar to sockets) that can be adapted for different feet sizes. Each of these covers has a circular reflective marker on it.

### 2.2 Software Tools

The functionality of the system has been implemented in a software library that can be used from external applications. The library has been developed using the Visual C++ programming environment and makes use of the functions provided by the Optitrack API. The library has been adapted for its use from Brainstorm eStudio software [18], which has been used to program the environments used during the ergonomic evaluation.

### 2.3 System Description

While both feet are still and placed at equal distances to the symmetry axis, walking and rotation velocity are zero.

In order to start moving, the user has to move alternatively up and down toe tips from each foot. The markers are placed in the toe tips, so the rest of the leg and the heel can remain fixed. The system calculates the individual vertical velocity of each foot. A filtering is applied to the calculated velocities in order to achieve smoother variations and movements. The walking velocity that is obtained is proportional to the minimum of these two vertical velocities. If users move feet quickly, they will achieve greater velocities in the virtual environment.

If the user moves a foot away from the symmetry axis of the image, the camera acquires a rotation velocity in the direction of the displacement. The modulus of this rotation velocity is proportional to the distance to the symmetry axis of the image which is calculated at the beginning of the session as the mean point between the two markers. In order to calculate this position, an initial calibration process is required which takes only a few seconds during which the user has to remain still in the repose position.

## 3 Usability Test: Method and Results

We performed an ergonomic evaluation of Super-Feet in order to understand the usability of the device in performing some basic movements in a digital environment. We decided to adopt as a criterion for this evaluation the performance of a device that is commonly used in similar tasks, namely a joypad, and performed what is called a 'comparative evaluation' [19]. The movements selected for the tests were the following: a pre-defined path within a labyrinth-like environment; a double curve corridor; a rectilinear path along a corridor; a free walk in a two-floors indoor space in search of three specific items.

The labyrinth tested the usability of the devices in terms of accuracy and speed. Participants did not have to choose directions and were instructed to complete the route as fast as possible and without colliding with the walls. We measured the overall time spent, the overall length of the route covered, the number of impacts on the wall and the number of changes in directions.

In the double curve route corridors, participants were instructed to complete the route in the shortest possible path in order to check the accuracy of the device. We measured the overall length of the route covered, the number of impacts on the wall, the time to complete the task and the number of changes in direction.

In the rectilinear path, participants were asked to walk as fast and as straight as possible. The two devices were calibrated in order to have the same peak velocity, so that we could compare the time spent to accomplish the task. We also measured the number of changes in directions in order to assess the ease of maintaining a straight direction.

The final task was designed to examine longer and more variegated courses of action with a video-analysis, which will not be discussed here. For the purposes of this evaluation we only considered performance in terms of number of items found and time taken to find each one of them.

All data were collected by a special software within a User-Interface Events (UIE) paradigm, based on the automatic gathering of the user's operations on the interface together with their time of occurrence [20].

### 3.1 Design and Procedure

Three different devices were compared:

1. Super-Feet: Participants used Super-Feet to move around the environment and, simultaneously, to explore it visually.
2. Super-Feet and HeadTracker: Participants used Super-Feet to move around the environment. To explore it visually they could either move with Super-Feet as in he previous condition, or rotate their head without changing their position in the environment, thanks to a Head-Tracking System (HTS) (Intersense Intertrax2). In this way they could choose to decouple movement and visual exploration.
3. Joypad: Participants used a two-stick joypad. The stick on the left was used to move on the horizontal plane as in Super-Feet, while the right stick allowed visual exploration.

The participants were divided in three groups of 12 people (6 men and 6 women), and assigned to one condition each. All participants executed the four tasks in the

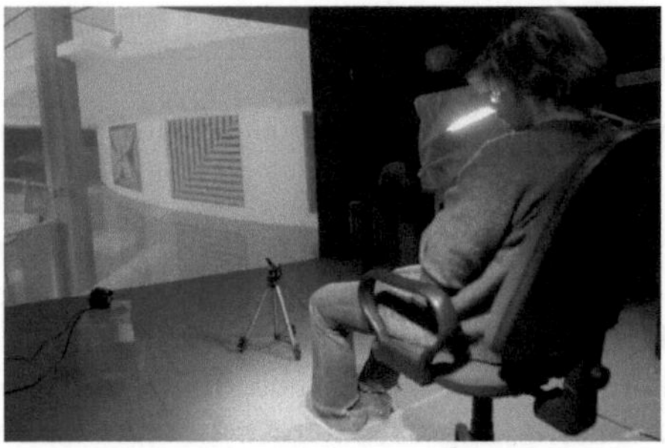

**Fig. 2.** The experimental setting

same order. Before the task series, participants signed an informed consent and had a training session of at least 5 minutes in a special digital environment to practice with their own experimental device until they declared to have understood its functioning.

The experimental setting was the same for all of them: they were positioned at a 2.83 meters distance from the screen, sitting, and the OptiTrack camera was at 65cm distance from the heels. The dimensions of the screen were 3.20×2,40 meters (see figure 2). Participants were not familiar with any of the device employed in the experiment.

## 4 Results

A one-way, between-subjects ANOVA was used to compare different measures in the three conditions. In the *first task*, the end of the labyrinth is reached more fastly with the joypad [$F_{(2,35)}$ =8,774, $p$ < 0,002], even though with a longer route than with the Super-Feet ($F_{(2,35)}$=3,338, p<.05; Tukey HSD Test, p<.05) (figure 3). This could mean that Super-Feet allows to draw more precise trajectories, but with a higher expenditure of time. There was no significant difference in the amount of collisions, but they were rare events, since the environment was large enough to avoid them. Similarly, there was no significant difference in the amount of direction changes.

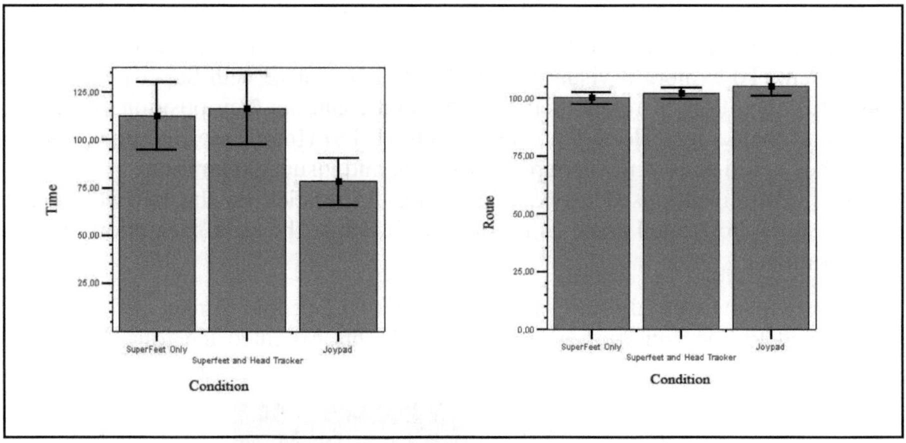


**Fig. 3.** Time to accomplish the first task (left), route length (right) in the three conditions

In the *double curve task*, where speed did not count, no significant difference was found among the three conditions in any measure. This could be related to the fact the devices differ only in the trade-off between accuracy and time.

Therefore, the result of the *third task*, where participants had to cover a straight corridor in the shortest time, is of great interest. In fact, we found a better performance in the condition with the Joypad [$F_{(2,35)}$=4,002, P<.03] (figure 4).

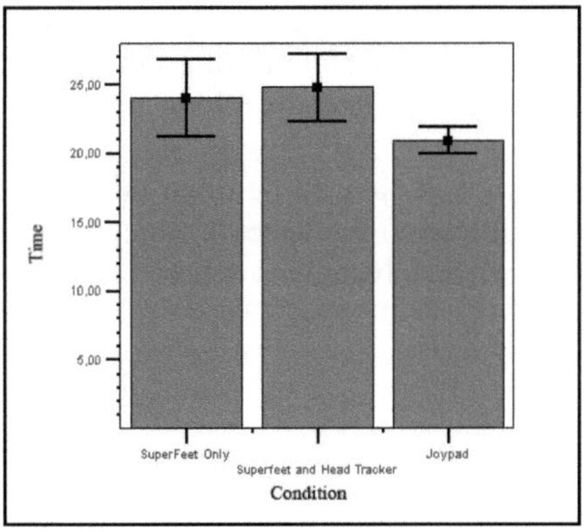


**Fig. 4.** Differences in time necessary to complete the task in the three conditions

Since the peak speed of Super-Feet and Joypad is almost the same, the difference between the two devices may suggest that it is more difficult do keep a peak speed for a long while by moving the feet fast instead of just by keeping a stick pressed. Super-Feet engages the body more directly with physical effort, and in fact in these two conditions the variance is greater, probably due to different physical endurance. No comparison was made on the directional changes since they only occur once.

We did not find any significant difference in the performance indexes in the *fourth task* (number of items found, time taken to find each item) even though the task required visual exploration, which could have favoured the conditions with Headtracker and Joypad. Super-Feet was able to produce the same performance as the other conditions even though it did not allow an independent visual exploration.

## 5 Conclusions

The results of the usability test show that there were no significant differences in performance indexes between Super-Feet and the Joypad. This allows us to conclude that Super-Feet can be used as a navigation system with similar results to the ones achieved with a commonly accepted navigation device as the joypad.

As we have told in the introduction, the use of one navigation device or another for a particular virtual environment will depend on the specific purpose of this environment. Super-Feet was designed to achieve two basic goals, which are simplicity and the possibility of leaving user's hands free. The main advantages that have been obtained with this system when compared with other physical locomotion systems are:

1. It does not require the complexity of mechanical devices such as treadmills. That makes it more portable and less invasive for the user.
2. It is based on feet movements, so hands are left free for other interactions inside the virtual environment.
3. It is not based on electromagnetical tracking devices, so it is less sensitive to noise and interferences.

In synthesis, Super-Feet seems more physically engaging and a more accurate device than the Joypad, which may be useful or not according to the task. When speed is required at the expenses of accuracy and for a long time, then a joypad may perform better.

In any case, more research will have to be done in specific applications of Super-Feet to analyze how it contributes to the specific objectives of these applications and which are its advantages and disadvantages when compared with other navigation systems.

## References

1. Bowman, D.A., Kruijff, E., LaViola Jr., J.J., Poupyrev, I.: 3D User Interfaces. In: Theory and Practice, Addison-Wesley, Boston (2004)
2. Ward, M., Azuma, R., Bennett, R., Gottschalk, S., Fuchs, H.: A demonstrated optical tracker with scalable work area for head-mounted display systems. In: Proceedings of the 1992 Symposium on Interactive 3D Graphics, Computer Graphics, vol. 25 (2), pp. 43–52 (1992)
3. Welch, G., Bishop, G.: SCAAT: Incremental tracking with incomplete information. In: Proceedings of SIGGRAPH 97, Computer Graphics Proceedings, Annual Conference Series 1997, pp. 333–344 (1997)
4. Welch, G., Bishop, G., Vicci, L., Brumback, S., Keller, K., Colucci, D.: The HiBall Tracker: High-Performance Wide-Area Tracking for Virtual and Augmented Environments. In: Proceedings of the ACM symposium on Virtual reality software and technology 1999, pp. 1–10 (1999)
5. Höllerer, T., Feiner, S., Terauchi, T., Rashid, G., Hallaway, D.: Exploring MARS: developing indoor and outdoor user interfaces to a mobile augmented reality system. Computer & Graphics 23, 779–785 (1999)
6. Slater, M., Steed, A., Usoh, M.: The virtual treadmill: A naturalistic metaphor for navigation in immersive virtual environments. In: Goebel, M. (ed.): First Eurographics Workshop on Virtual Reality Eurographics Assoc.1993, pp. 71–86 (1993)
7. Templeman, J.N., Denbrook, P.S., Sibert, L.E.: Virtual Locomotion: Walking in Place through Virtual Environments. Presence 8(6), 598–617 (1999)
8. Grant, S.C., Magee, L.E.: Navigation in a virtual environment using a walking interface. In: Goldberg, S.L., Ehrlich, J.A. (eds.): The Capability of Virtual Reality to Meet Military Requirements. pp. 81–92, NATO, New York (1998)
9. Brooks, F.P., Airey, J., Alspaugh, J., Bell, A., Brown, R., Hill, C., Nimscheck, U., Rheingans, P., Rohlf, J., Smith, D., Turner, D., Varshney, A., Wang, Y., Weber, H., Yuan, X.: Six generations of building walkthrough: final technical report to the national science foundation (Tech. Rep. No. TR92-026). Department of Computer Science, The University of North Carolina, Chapel Hill, NC, 1992 (1992)
10. Darken, R., Cockayne, W., Carmein, D.: The Omni-Directional Treadmill: A Locomotion Device for Virtual Worlds. In: Interaction. Proceedings of UIST'97, pp. 213–222. ACM Press, New York (1997)
11. Iwata, H.: Walking about virtual environments on an infinite floor. In: IEEE Virtual Reality Conference 1999, p. 286 (1999)
12. Hollerbach, J., Xu, Y., Christensen, R., Jacobsen, S.: Design Specifications For The Second Generation Sarcos Treadport Locomotion Interface. In: Proc. ASME Dynamic Systems and Control Division, DSC (2000)

13. Slater, M., Usoh, M., Steed, A.: Taking Steps: The Influence of a Walking Technique on Presence in Virtual Reality. ACM Transactions on Computer-Human Interaction 2(3), 201–219 (1995)
14. Usoh, M., Arthur, K., Whitton, M.C., Bastos, R., Steed, A., Slater, M., Brooks Jr., F.P.: Walking > Walking-in-Place > Flying, in Virtual Environments. In: Proceedings of the 26th Annual Conference on Computer Graphics and Interactive Techniques 1999 pp. 359–364 (1999)
15. LaViola Jr, J.J., Acevedo Feliz, D., Keefe, D.F., Zeleznik, R.C.: Hands-Free Multi-Scale Navigation in Virtual Environments. In: Proceedings of ACM Symposium on Interactive 3D Graphics 2001, pp. 9–15 (2001)
16. La Viola Jr., J.J., Keefe, D.F., Zeleznik, R.C., Acevedo Feliz, D.: Case Studies in Building Custom Input Devices for Virtual Environment Interaction. In: IEEE VR Workshop 2004 (2004)
17. NaturalPoint Homepage: http://www.naturalpoint.com
18. Brainstorm Multimedia Homepage: http://www.brainstorm.es
19. Bowman, D.A., Gabbard, J.L.: A survey of usability evaluation in Virtual Environments: Classification and Comparison of Methods. Presence 11(4), 404–424 (2002)
20. Hilbert, D.M., Redmiles, D.F.: Extracting Usability Information from user Interface Events. ACM Computing Surveys 32(4), 384–421 (2000)

# Psychophysical Approach to the Measurement of Depth Perception in Stereo Vision

Humberto Rosas, Watson Vargas, Alexander Cerón, Dario Domínguez, and Adriana Cárdenas

Unversidad Militar Nueva Granada,
Cra 11 No. 101-80 Bogota, Colombia
chrosasg@yahoo.com, wlvargas@yahoo.com, aceronc@umng.edu.co,
fracumng@umng.edu.co, elsac@umng.edu.co

**Abstract.** In stereo vision, the measurement of depth perception remains an enigmatic question. On the basis of geometric optics, numerous hypothesis and mathematical formulations have been proposed for explaining the mechanism of depth perception responsible of vertical exaggeration, although none of them have shown to be entirely satisfactory. We believe that stereo vision is not merely determined by geometry elements but also by mental factors that interact through a psychophysical process. Our initial observations refer to stereo-drawings that suggest a logarithmic correlation between real depth (stimulus) and perceptual depth (sensation), according to the psychophysical Fechner's law. On this new approach, experimental data is being obtained in order to determine the Fechner's constant for the sensorial modality of stereo vision, and to establish the logarithmic equation that rules the stereoscopic relationships between real and sensorial space. This equation might involve possibilities for technological developments, and it is the next step of our current research.

**Keywords:** Depth perception, psychophysics, stereo vision.

## 1 Introduction

The theme of stereoscopic depth perception has called the attention of many investigators, particularly concerning the geometry of the stereo-model perceived in the observer's mind. Normally, the vertical magnitudes of the perceptual image do not keep proportionality with those of the real object. For example, in the stereoscopic observation of aerial photographs, it is well known that the stereo model is viewed vertically exaggerated compared to the actual terrain. The problem of measuring this vertical exaggeration lays on the fact that no method for scaling depth impression has been developed. It is generally accepted that stereoscopic depth impression increases with parallax, but no mathematical equation connecting these two variables is still known. Upon the basis of geometric relationships apparently existing between real object and perceptual stereo-model, different mathematical equations for vertical exaggeration have been proposed [5][7][8][9][10][11][12][17][18][19][20], though none of them has received general acceptance. It looks as if geometric optics had not been an appropriate approach in the search for a solution.

R. Shumaker (Ed.): Virtual Reality, HCII 2007, LNCS 4563, pp. 358–366, 2007.

Such a controversial situation concerning depth perception and vertical exaggeration has provided reasons for the perceptual stereo-model to be considered as a "mystery" [2], and the search for determining its vertical exaggeration to be regarded as a "Quixotic effort" [20]). It has been observed that an atmosphere of skepticism seems to have caused a stagnation of the investigations in this field [16]. Indeed, since long ago the purely geometric approach to stereo vision has fall in an evident sterility. This is the reason for no recent literature to have been produced on this field.

From a different point of view, we have been working on the hypothesis that the real 3D model becomes a visual stimulus able to produce a sensation in the form of a perceptual image. In other words, the stereoscopic vision is not a simple matter of geometric optics but a problem connected with a mental process. Therefore, the solution to this problem should to be searched in the field of psychophysics.

## 2 Stereovision from the Geometric Point of View

### 2.1 Monocular Vision

According to geometric optics, the human eye behaves as a camera. Its crystalline plays the roll of lens, and its retina acts like a film where images are recorded and transmitted to the brain. From experience it is assumed that the retinal image provides an exact mental reproduction of the object shape at a given scale (Fig.1). This correspondence between retinal image and object shape, which is valid in monocular vision, it is not so in stereovision. In this last case, 3D objects are perceived deformed in their third dimension.

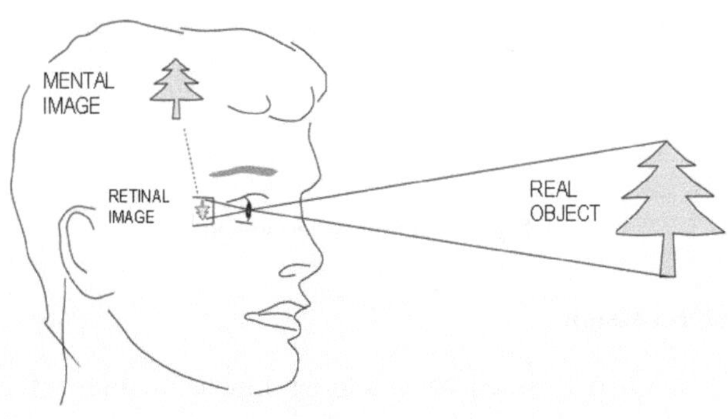


**Fig. 1.** Monocular vision

### 2.2 Binocular Vision

In this case, 3D objects are perceived through a pair of retinal images which are transmitted to the brain, where they are fused and converted into a mental 3D model. Because of the eye separation, the two retinal images are not identical but show small disparities (parallaxes) which vary directly with object heights. Certainly, parallax becomes the key to depth perception. It is well known that two plane views of a 3D object contain geometric information enough for the object to be reconstructed in its three dimensions. This is just the golden rule of photogrammetry. Therefore, it sounds reasonable to imagine that human brain acts like a photogrammetrist who builds a 3D model out of two plane retinal images. In Fig 2, natural stereovision is illustrated by showing how a three-dimensional object represented by a pyramid, is viewed and perceived in the brain.

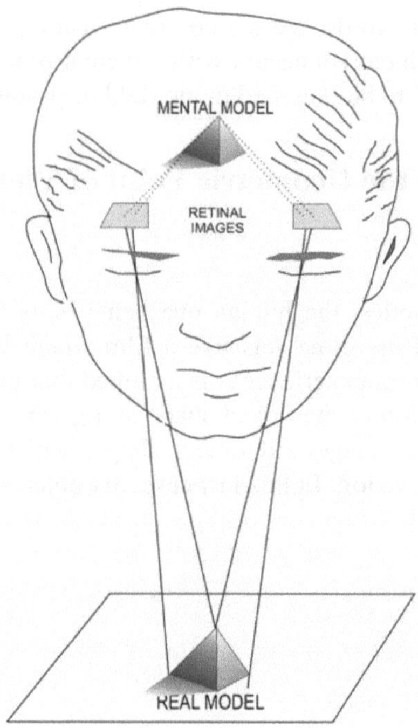


**Fig. 2.** Natural stereo vision

## 2.3 Artificial Stereovision

Artificial stereovision is performed when a three-dimensional object, instead of being viewed directly, is perceived through a pair of plane images. A typical example is the stereoscopic observation of aerial photographs. Fig. 3 illustrates the three-dimensional perception of an area of land by stereoscopic observation of a pair of aerial photographs taken form two positions of the plane. In this instance, what the observer views is a terrain model formed geometrically by intersection of optical rays. The characteristics of such geometric model depend on the geometry under which photographs were accomplished, and also on the geometry of rays under which photographs are observed.

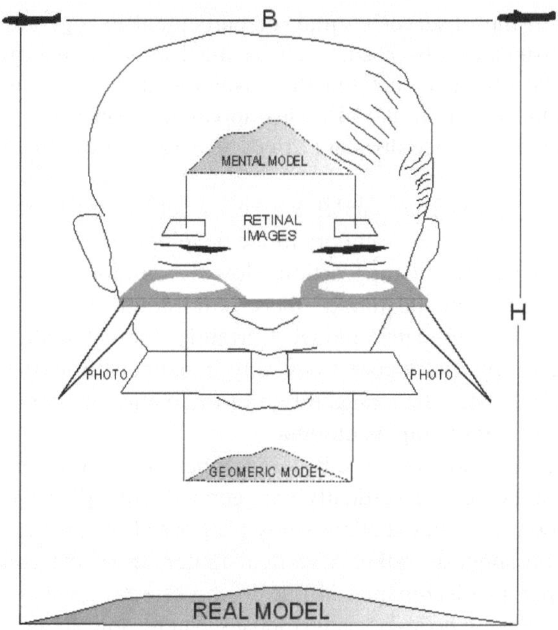


**Fig. 3.** Artificial stereo vision

## 2.4 Vertical Exaggeration

The concept of vertical exaggeration is crucial for solving the problem of depth perception, for it represents the ratio of perceptual depth to real depth. In a geometric sense, vertical exaggeration is defined as the ratio of vertical scale to horizontal scale. Due to the fact that investigations on artificial stereovision have normally been limited to the standards of pocket and mirror stereoscopes, it is normal that the geometric model shows an exaggeration in its vertical scale, a reason for which the expression "vertical exaggeration" has been coined. However, the term "exaggeration" may result confusing for it does not necessary means an increase of vertical scale. There may be cases in which the geometric model shows no exaggeration at all, that is, its vertical exaggeration is equal to 1, or even it may be vertically flattened rather than exaggerated, which means that its vertical exaggeration is less than 1.

## 2.5 Ambiguity Related to Vertical Exaggeration

In the geometric approach to stereovision, there has prevailed the tendency to believe that the geometric model is equivalent in shape to the mental one, and that consequently both models would share the same vertical exaggeration. This erroneous belief has caused an ambiguity in the use of the term "vertical exaggeration", and creates the convenience of differentiating the vertical exaggeration of the model generated geometrically, or geometric exaggeration, from the vertical exaggeration of the model perceived in the observer's mind, or perceptual exaggeration. In 1956, some geometric inconsistencies observed, such as the lack of convergence under which stereovision can be obtained, created the suspicion that we do not see the outside world but or mental impressions [14]. This apparent inconsistence was explained by the fact that such a divergence does not affect the stereoscopic fusion of images in the brain [15].

The belief that the external model we see would correspond in shape to what we perceive in mind, led several authors to the development of mathematical formulations for determining vertical exaggeration. However, although none of them has been valid for measuring the mental model, there is no doubt that most of them are perfectly applicable to the geometric model. Certainly, the calculation of the geometric exaggeration is a simple procedure frequently explained in textbooks. The question changes when it deals with the exaggeration of the mental model, or perceptual exaggeration, which continues being an enigma.

Normally, authors who have used stereoscopes in their observations report the mental image to be perceived vertically exaggerated [5][7][8][9][10][11][14][17][18][19][20]. On the contrary, an excellent study [13] based on a neural approach through natural stereovision suggests rather a vertical flattening of the mental image. In our opinion, such apparent discrepancy is due to the effect of viewing distance, taking into account that those who used stereo lenses where able to view at a shorter distance, in comparison with those who applied natural stereo vision. It is also important to note that the use of a stereo-pair allows a constant parallax to be used at different distances, while in natural stereovision parallax decreases with viewing distance. It is interesting to note that, although vertical stereoscopic perception is determined by binocular disparities, no explicit neural response connected with the perception of depth has been observed [1].

## 3 Stereovision from the Psychophysical Point of View

In the authors' opinion, stereoscopic perception is influenced both by geometric and mental factors. The mental model represents a visual sensation determined by the stimulus of the object being observed. Such an object may be either a real model in the case of natural stereovision, or a geometric model in the case of artificial stereovision. This feature establishes a psychophysical connection between image (sensation) and object (stimulus), according to the logarithmic Fechner's law [3], which establishes that the intensity of the sensation is proportional to the logarithm of the corresponding intensity of the stimulus that is

$$R = K \mathrm{Log} S \tag{1}$$

Being R the intensity of sensation (perceptual depth), K a constant characteristic for each sensorial modality, and S the intensity of the stimulus (real depth).

The validity of the Fechner's law has been recognized not only in humans but also in animals, like insects [12]. Electrophysiological evidences have shown some retinal cells to be logarithmically related to stimulus intensity [4][6].

# 4 Graphic Indication of Psychophysical Relationships in Stereovision

Figs. 4 and 6 show two stereo-pairs to be viewed with the aid of a pocket stereoscope. For the case of no stereoscope availability, these two stereoscopic images are represented in perspective (figures 5 and 7 respectively). In both, stereoscopic and perspective figures, a 4cm squared base pyramid showing 8 levels of depth sensation can be seen. Level 1 corresponds to the pyramid base, and level 8 to its vertex. Each of these levels is located at a parallax interval of 1mm. At first glance, in can be observed that, although parallax is constant (1mm) for the eight levels, the level intervals are not perceived to be equal but they seem to decrease upwards. At this point it is important to note that, according to geometry, real depth intervals are directly proportional to parallax. However, this proportionality which is valid for the real space, does not look to be so for the perceptual space, where equal parallaxes do not yield equal depth sensations or perceptual depths.

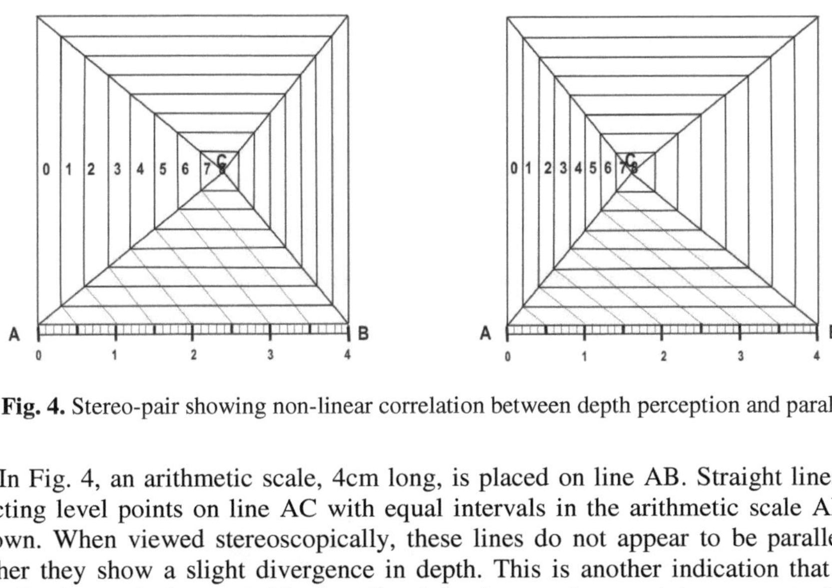


**Fig. 4.** Stereo-pair showing non-linear correlation between depth perception and parallax

In Fig. 4, an arithmetic scale, 4cm long, is placed on line AB. Straight lines connecting level points on line AC with equal intervals in the arithmetic scale AB, are drown. When viewed stereoscopically, these lines do not appear to be parallel, but rather they show a slight divergence in depth. This is another indication that equal parallax intervals do not yield proportional depth sensations, and that perceptual depth is not connected linearly either with parallax or with real depth.

In Fig. 6, the arithmetic scale showed in Fig. 4 was replaced for a logarithmic one, representing parallax logarithms. The process followed in the calculations is shown in table 1. The parameter of proportionality C required for fitting a logarithmic scale into line AC, 4cm long, was calculated by dividing the higher logarithm value of 1+Δp (0.255) by 4. In order to handle logarithmic numbers grater than one, parallax intervals were taken from a point of origin equal to 1. If the logarithmic scale AB is correlated with the perceptual scale AC by means of straight lines, these lines show up as parallel in the perceived stereo model. Such a parallelism would indicate that

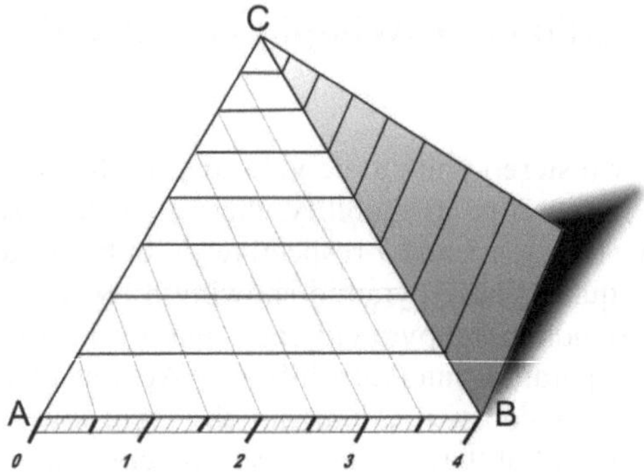


**Fig. 5.** Perspective representation of Fig 4

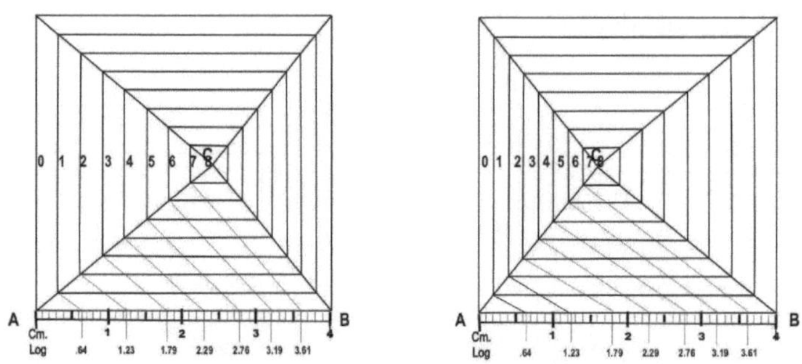


**Fig. 6.** Stereo-pair showing logarithmic correlation between depth perception in parallax

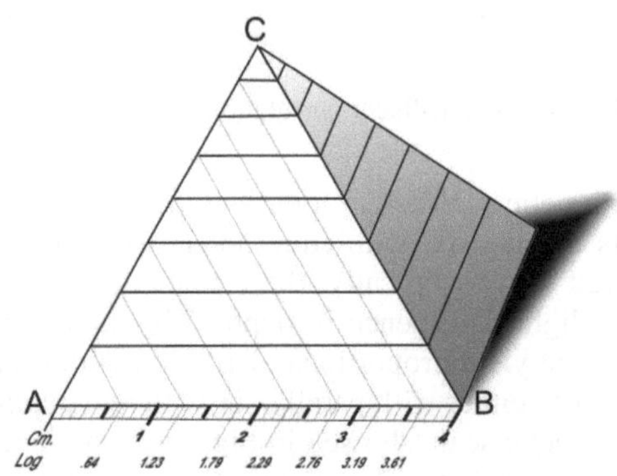


**Fig. 7.** Perspective representation of Fig 6

depth sensation varies proportionally to the parallax logarithm. Since parallax is a linear function of real depth, it follows that perceptual depth (sensation) varies proportionally to the logarithm of real depth (stimulus), according to the psychophysical Fechner's law (Equation 1).

On the assumption that the Fechner's low is valid for the stereoscopic vision, as it is for many other sensorial modalities, we are working on collecting experimental data which will allow us to correlate real depth versus perceptual depth in order to obtain the Fechner' constant K. We believe that this psychophysical approach will yield a mathematical expression for the perception of depth in stereoscopic vision.

**Table 1.** Construction of Figure 6

| Level | $\Delta p$ (mm) | $1+\Delta p$ (mm) | $\log(1+\Delta p)$ | C=4 / 0.255 | $C\log(1+\Delta p)$ |
|---|---|---|---|---|---|
| 0 | 0 | 1.0 | 0.000 | 15.58 | 0.00 |
| 1 | 1 | 1.1 | 0.041 | 15.68 | 0.64 |
| 2 | 2 | 1.2 | 0.079 | 15.58 | 1.23 |
| 3 | 3 | 1.3 | 0.114 | 15.68 | 1.79 |
| 4 | 4 | 1.4 | 0.146 | 15.58 | 2.29 |
| 5 | 5 | 1.5 | 0.176 | 15.68 | 2.76 |
| 6 | 6 | 1.6 | 0.204 | 15.58 | 3.19 |
| 7 | 7 | 1.7 | 0.230 | 15.58 | 3.61 |
| 8 | 8 | 1.8 | 0.255 | 15.68 | 4.00 |

## 5 Conclusions and Perspective

The availability of a psychophysical formulation for depth perception would permit that the problem of vertical exaggeration and other enigmas concerning the stereoscopic vision can be solved.

As mentioned before, vertical exaggeration is a crucial factor of depth perception, for it is given by the ratio of perceptual depth to real depth. In fact, the possibility for determining the vertical exaggeration, both in natural and artificial conditions, would make it possible, for example, the artificial reproduction of natural stereoscopic effects. Consequently, a reliable psychophysical formulation of the stereoscopic phenomenon -which is our primary goal-, might have possibilities for technological developments.

**Acknowledgments.** The authors express their appreciation to Dr. Gotfried Konecny from the Institute for Photogrammetry and Geoinformation, Hannover, for his valuable comments and analyses concerning the scope of this investigation.

## References

1. Backus, B.T., Fleet, D.J., Parker, A.J., Heeger, D.J.: Human Cortical Activity Correlates With Stereoscopic Depth Perception. J. Neurophysiology, 86 (2001)
2. Collins, S.H.: Stereoscopic Depth Perception. Photogrammetric Engineering 47(1), 45–52 (1981)
3. Fechner, G. T.: Elemente der psychophysik, vol. 1, [Elements of psychophysics (vol. 1)]. Breitkopf and Härte,Leipzig, Germany (1889)
4. Fuortes, M.K.: Inhibition of impulses in the visual cells of limulus. J. Physiol. 148, 270–278 (1959)

5. Goodale, E.R.: An Equation for Approximating the Vertical Exaggeration of a stereoscopic view. Photogrammetric Engineering 19(4), 607–616 (1953)
6. Hartline, H.K., Ratliff, F.: Visual receptors and retinal interaction. Science 164, 270–278 (1957)
7. La Prade, G.L.: Stereoscopy – a More General Theory. Photogrammetric Engineering, vol. 38 (1972)
8. La Prade, G.L: Stereoscopy – Will Data or Dogma Prevail? Photogrammetric Engineering 39(12), 1271–1275 (1973)
9. La Prade, G.L.: Stereoscopy: Manual of Photogrammetry, American Society of Photogrammetry, FourthEdn., Ch. X, pp. 519–534 (1978)
10. Miller, C.L.: The Stereoscopic Space- Image. Photogrammetric Engineering 26(54), 810–815 (1958)
11. Miller, C.L.: Vertical Exaggeration in the Stereo Space-Image and its use. Photogrammetric Engineering 26(5), 815–818 (1960)
12. Moore, A. R., Cole, W.H.: The Response of Popillia Japonica to Light and the Weber-Fechner Law, The journal of General Physiology (1920)
13. Farley, N.J., Todd, J.T., Perotti, V.J., Tittle, J.S.: The Visual Perception of Three-Dimensional Length. Journal of Experimental Psychology 22(l), 173–186 (1996)
14. Raasveldt, H.C.: The Stereomodel, How It is Formed and Deformed. Photogrammetric Engineering 22(9), 708–726 (1956)
15. Rosas, H.: Vertical Exaggeration in Stereo-Vision. Theories and Facts: Photogrammetric Engineering and Remote Sensing 52(11), 1747–1751 (1986)
16. Rosas, H.: A new approach to photogrammetric plotting: International Archives of Photogrammetry and Remote Sensing, vol. 29, Part. B2, ISPRS, Washington, D.C. U.S.A. In: Salzman, M. H. (1950) Note on Stereoscopy: Photogrammetric Engineering, 16(3), pp. 475–477 (1992)
17. Thurrell Jr., R.F.: Vertical Exaggeration in Stereoscopic Models. Photogrammetric Engineering 19(4), 579–588 (1953)
18. Treece, W.A.: Estimation of Vertical Exaggeration in Stereoscopic Viewing of Aerial Photographs. Photogrammetric Engineering 21(9), 518–527 (1955)
19. Yacoumelos, N.G.: The Geometry of the Stereomodel: Photogrammetric Engineering, 38(8) (1972)
20. Yacoumelos, N.G.: Comments on Stereoscopy: Photogrammetric Engineering 39(3), 274 (1973)

# Measurement of Suitability of a Haptic Device in a Virtual Reality System

Jose San Martin[1] and Gracian Trivino[2]

[1] Universidad Rey Juan Carlos, 28933 Móstoles, Spain
jose.sanmartin@urjc.es
[2] European Centre for Soft Computing, 33600 Mieres, Spain
gracian.trivino@softcomputing.es

**Abstract.** In the context of the optimization of the mechanical platform of a virtual reality system involving a haptic device, this paper introduces two tools in order to help the designer for obtaining the best positioning of the device respect to the application workspace. With this purpose we have defined a measure called Average Volumetric Manipulability, of how the application workspace fits in with the volume where haptic device provides its best performance. Also, we have defined other measure called Useful Manipulability which takes in account the frequency with which each zone of the application workspace is visited during the simulation process. The practical use of these measures is demonstrated using them during the design and development of a real application.

**Keywords:** Virtual reality, Haptic interface, Manipulability, Mechanical Performance.

## 1 Introduction

The design of a virtual environment in occasions involves the integration of different mechanical devices. The mechanical system can include manipulators that, depending on the configuration can reach more or less easily the different points of the workspace.

In case of not redundant manipulators, every point of the space can be only reached by a certain configuration of joints of the kinematics chain. The value of the angle of every joint, the geometry of arms of the manipulator, besides the relation that exists between the length of links of a manipulative arm, as main characteristics, determine the efficiency in the transmission of force and speed to the end of the manipulator (End Effector). A criterion of design of a system that contains haptic devices is maximizing this efficiency. A tool to obtain this goal will be to quantify the quality of the relative geometric positioning of each manipulator respect to the virtual environment workspace.

This work is part of a multidisciplinary project for the development of a Minimally Invasive Surgery Trainer (MIST) [1] where we have needed to optimize the mechanical relative positioning of the haptic devices in the system platform.

R. Shumaker (Ed.): Virtual Reality, HCII 2007, LNCS 4563, pp. 367–375, 2007.

## 2 Manipulability

Manipulability of a device is its ability to move freely in all directions into the workspace [2]. The first formulation that allowed a mathematical simple quantification was brought up by Yoshikawa [3]. We use the formulation of Manipulability proposed by Cavusoglu et al. [4]:

$$\mu = \sigma_{min} (J_u) / \sigma_{max} (J_u). \tag{1}$$

Where:

$\sigma_{min}$ and $\sigma_{max}$ are the minimum and maximum singular values of $J_u$, upper half of the manipulator Jacobian matrix.

So the first step in the study of Manipulability is the analysis of the kinematics of a manipulator, in this case we have used the PHANToM OMNi of SensAble Technologies (Fig. 1).

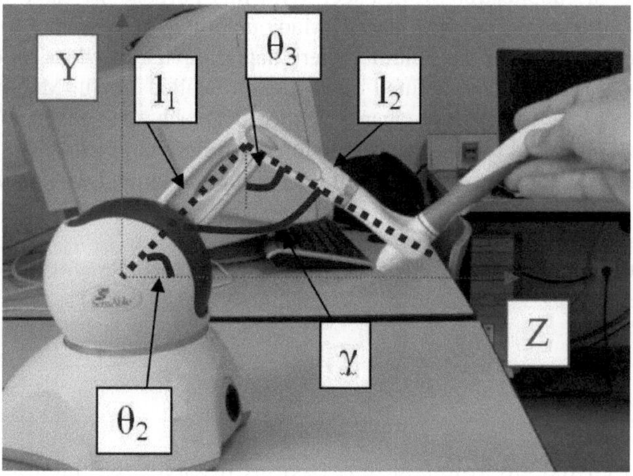


**Fig. 1.** OMNi arms $l_1$=129mm y $l_2$=133 mm. Angle inter-arms $\gamma$. Angles $\theta_1$ y $\theta_2$.

From the geometrical relations we obtain:

$$x = (l_1 \cos\theta_2 + l_2 \sin\theta_3)\sin\theta_1$$

$$y = l_1 \sin\theta_2 - l_2 \cos\theta_3$$

$$z = (l_1 \cos\theta_2 + l_2 \sin\theta_3)\cos\theta_1$$

The analysis of the kinematics of the device allows us to calculate the Jacobian matrix associated to this device [5].

$$J = \begin{pmatrix} l_1\cos(\theta_2) + l_2\sin(\theta_3) & 0 & 0 \\ 0 & l_1\cos(\theta_2 - \theta_3) & 0 \\ 0 & -l_1\sin(\theta_2 - \theta_3) & l_2 \\ 0 & 0 & -1 \\ \cos(\theta_3) & 0 & 0 \\ \sin(\theta_3) & 0 & 0 \end{pmatrix}$$

From Jacobian we calculate using (1) the Manipulability measure. Figure 2 shows the YZ-map of Manipulability obtained for the OMNi.

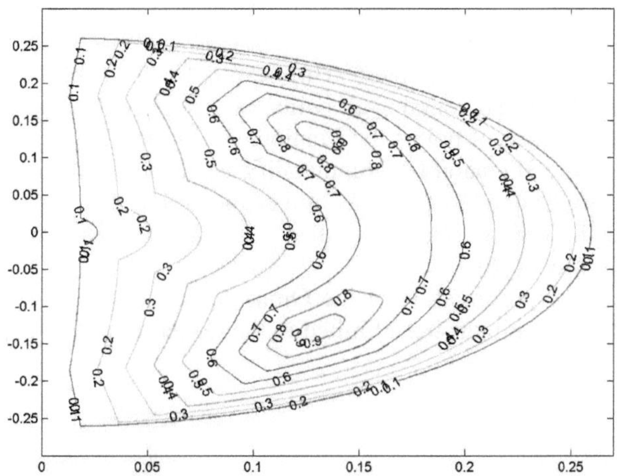


**Fig. 2.** Map of Manipulability values for plane YZ. Axes in millimetres.

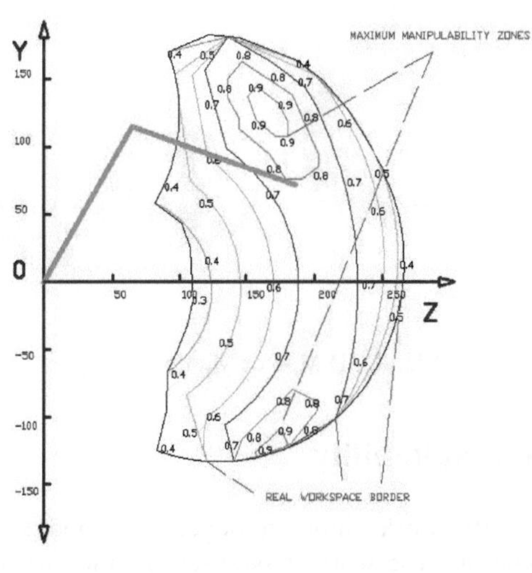


**Fig. 3.** Manipulability map of PHANToM OMNi for the plane YZ considering movement restrictions. Arms of the manipulator in bold lines. Axes in millimetres.

Now we must take into account that, due to the mechanical restrictions during its implementation, the device has a limited area of work that includes all those points that it is capable of reaching. We have called Real Workspace (RW) to the extension of useful workspace of the OMNi, obtaining the map of Manipulability showed in Fig. 3. Note that this map extends in the plane YZ and includes the drawing of a RW borderline obtained by measuring manually the OMNi device range of angles $\theta_2$ and $\theta_3$.

Note that, as it was expected, the OMNi mechanical design includes in the RW the best values of Manipulability.

## 3 3D Map of Manipulability

We can extend the map 2D developed previously by analyzing the behaviour of the device in its whole surrounding space. This RW defined in 3D is a volume of the space near of the OMNi that contains all points of the space that the End Effector can reach. If we assign to each of points the Manipulability measure calculated by (1), the resultant volume is the 3D map of Manipulability associated to the device.

This map constitutes one important feature of the OMNi that we can consider to be physically joined the device. We can realize this map as a zone of influence of the device in its environment [6].

Figure 4 shows a representation of the Omni device together with its 3D map of Manipulability. Note that it has been limited to the OMNi Real Workspace.

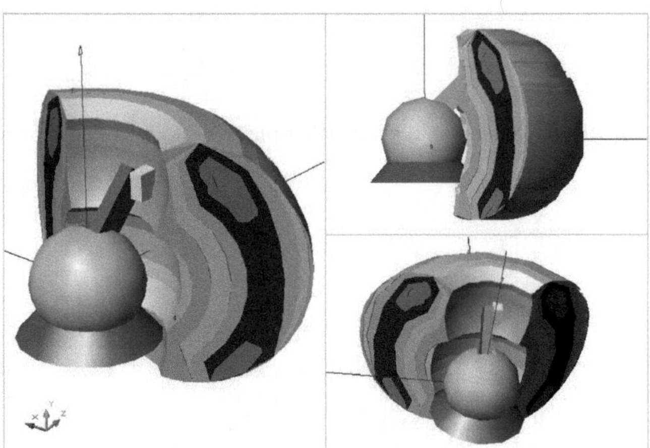

**Fig. 4.** 3D Map of Manipulability

## 4 Measurement of Suitability

There are several scientific works aimed to develop methods of optimizing the use of manipulators [7]. Some of these works have used the measure of Manipulability as a criterion of optimization [8], [9]. The design of a virtual reality system requires positioning the Application Workspace (AW) inside the 3D map of Manipulability. This intersection affect zones with different values of μ (different colored volumes $v_i$ in figure 4). The measure we need must provide the quality of the mechanical positioning of an OMNi respect of the AW.

For a given a positioning of the device in a simulation platform, and therefore an AW divided in different sub-volumes of Manipulability, we define the "Average Volumetric Manipulability" $\mu_v$ [5] as:

$$\mu_v = \frac{(\mu_1 \cdot v_1 + \mu_2 \cdot v_2 + \mu_3 \cdot v_3 + \ldots\ldots\ldots \mu_n \cdot v_n)}{V_T} \tag{2}$$

Where:

$V_T$ is the total volume of the intersection:

$$V_T = \sum_{i}^{n} v_i = v_1 + v_2 + \ldots + v_n$$

This measure assigns each sub-volume the weight of its correspondent Manipulability calculating then the average value over the total volume. We can use $\mu_v$ for qualifying the configuration of a device (with its RW) respect to a determinate application (with its AW). From our experience using this measure, we can affirm that, if we design a mechanical platform that produces an Average Volumetric Manipulability of a value rounding 0.8 or even 0.9, we can consider the fitting of the AW inside of RW as excellent.

The practical use of this concept has the difficulty of finding the best mechanical device positioning in a very large space of search.

Our first approach is to use a set of empirical rules in order to help in the searching of a good configuration. Unfortunately using this procedure does not assure we have obtained the best solution.

To solve partially this problem, we have developed an automatic searching process based on Simulated Annealing [10]. Every step of the simulated annealing algorithm the system searches randomly a solution near the current one, according to a probability that depends on the current temperature (similar to the metallurgy concept of Annealing). The algorithm allows calculating an optimal positioning of AW that produces a maximum value of the cost function $\mu_v$.

Studying the possibilities of improving the previous results we have seen that our application has zones of AW which are more used than others. These are, for instance in a surgical operation simulation, the specific areas where the surgical intervention is effectuated. It is desirable that the haptic device provides its best performance in these zones. We propose, for the cases in which the use of the workspace is not homogeneous, to perform an additional analysis taking in account this heterogeneity. It involves the study of the End Effector movement across the AW during the simulation process.

Considering a discretized AW using a tri-dimensional grid of cells (i, j, k), we define a new measure called "Useful Manipulability" for each AW configuration respect to RW using the formula:

$$\hat{\mu}_v = \sum_{ijk} \mu_{vijk} \cdot f_{ijk} \tag{3}$$

Where:

$\mu_{v\,ijk}$ is the Volumetric Average Manipulability of a cell.

$f_{ijk}$ is the frequency of visits sampled during a simulation session in each cell.

Note that if the size of cells (i,j,k) is small enough we can consider that Manipulability is constant and we can use the more simple formula:

$$\hat{\mu}_v = \sum_{ijk} \mu_{ijk} \cdot f_{ijk} \quad (4)$$

Where:

$\mu_{ijk}$ is the Manipulability of a cell.

With this criterion the best positioning of the OMNi in terms of frequency of use will produce maximum value of $\hat{\mu}_V$.

## 5 Results

We have used the above defined measures to calculate the grade of suitability of a manipulator in a real application. The application consists of the positioning of an OMNi device used as a component of the mechanical platform of a Minimal Invasive Surgery Trainer [1]. We have used a set of simple geometrical shapes to model the internal cavity of a human shoulder (Figure 5). In a previous work we have shown the use of this kind of geometrical shapes to make easier the task of fitting the manipulator RW with the AW [9].

Figure 5 shows the AW corresponding with a virtual model of this AW. The upper part represents the subacromial cavity and the cylindrical sized one situated below represents the glenohumeral cavity. The figure shows two different volumes of intersection between the AW and the 3D map of Manipulability.

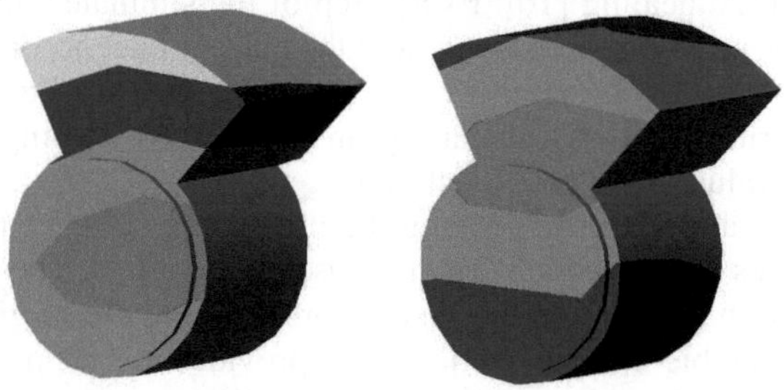

**Fig. 5.** Two possible configurations of AW respect to OMNi location

Option 1 (Table 1). In this option we have situated the AW in such position that optimizes the operation into the glenohumeral zone. This positioning provides an Average Volumetric Manipulability $\mu_v$=0.8073 (fig. 5-left).

After the mentioned process of discretization, considering the frequency of use of the different volumes we have obtained a Useful Manipulability of $\hat{\mu}_V$ =0.8026.

**Table 1.** Option 1. Optimizing glenohumeral zone.

| $V_i$ (mm$^3$) | Volume Figure | μ | $\mu_i \cdot v_i$ |
|---|---|---|---|
| V1=11177 |  | μ=0.9-1 | 10786 |
| V2=16269 | 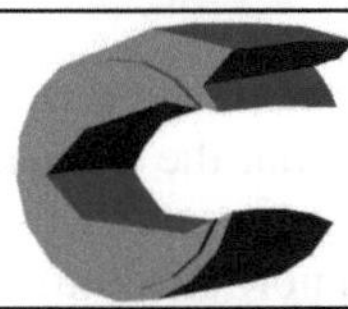 | μ=0.8-0.9 | 14073 |
| V3=22612 | 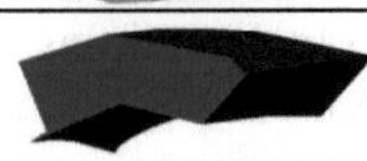 | μ=0.7-0.8 | 17298 |
| V4= 12101 |  | μ=0.6-0.7 | 8047 |
| $V_T$=62159 | | $\mu_v = \frac{\sum_i \mu_i \cdot v_i}{V_T}$ | 0.8073 |

**Table 2.** Option 2. CG at maximum Manipulability zone.

| $V_i$ (mm$^3$) | Volume Figure | μ | $\mu_i \cdot v_i$ |
|---|---|---|---|
| V1=16238 | 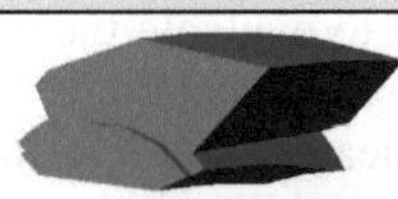 | μ=0.9-1 | 15426 |
| V2= 29282 | 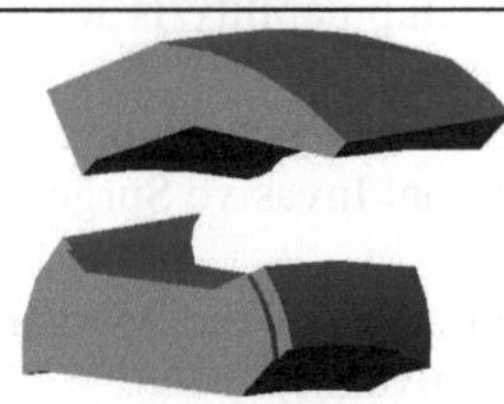 | μ=0.8-0.9 | 24890 |
| V3=16639 | 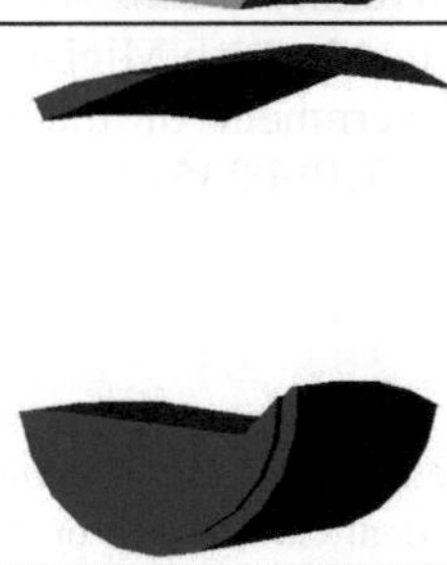 | μ=0.7-0.8 | 12562 |
| $V_T$=62159 | | $\mu_v = \frac{\sum_i \mu_i \cdot v_i}{V_T}$ | 0,8507 |

Option 2 (Table 2). This configuration consists of positioning the maximum Manipulability zone in the centre of gravity of the whole AW. This option tries to distribute the available Manipulability between the two operation workspaces. This option provides an Average Volumetric Manipulability: $\mu_v$=0.8506 (fig. 5-right).

Considering the frequency of use of the different volumes we have obtained a Useful Manipulability of $\hat{\mu}_V$ =0.8022.

Note that the option 2 is the best election in terms of Average Volumetric Manipulability, while the result is similar taking in account the frequency of use. We can say that the improvement of $\mu_v$ in the positioning represented by option 2 has been obtained for zones rarely visited in the course of a normal simulation.

An improvement of this positioning was obtained using an automatic searching process based on Simulated Annealing [11]. With this procedure we have obtained the maximum value of $\hat{\mu}_V$ =0.8685. This value corresponds with positioning the centre of gravity of AW at the position XYZ (-9, 130, 100) mm from the origin at the centre of the OMNi.

## 6 Conclusions

In this work we analyze the problem of optimize the positioning of a manipulator inside of the application workspace of a virtual reality system.

We have introduced two measures of the quality of this positioning: The concept of Average Volumetric Manipulability is useful to evaluate the performance that we can expect from a specific mechanical positioning of a haptic device in the virtual reality system platform. As a complement of this measure, the Useful Manipulability measures the grade in which the available Manipulability is located in the spatial zones were the manipulator is used more frequently.

The advantage of using these two measures has been demonstrated practically during the design and development of a Minimal Invasive Surgery Trainer.

**Acknowledgements.** The authors are grateful to the Modeling and Virtual Reality Group (GMRV) of the Rey Juan Carlos University.

This work has been partially funded by the Spanish Ministry of Education and Science (grant TIC2003-08933-C02-01), Government of the Community of Madrid (grant GR/SAL/0940/2004 and grant S-0505/DPI/0235).

## References

1. Bayona, S., Garcia, M., Mendoza, C., Fernandez, J.M.: Shoulder Arthroscopy Training System with Force Feedback, In: International Conference on Medical Information Visualisation-BioMedical Visualisation (MedVis'06)2006, pp. 71–76 (2006)
2. Murray, R.M., Li, Z., Sastry, S.S.: A mathematical introduction to robotic manipulation. CRC Press, Inc, Boca Raton, FL (1994)
3. Yoshikawa, T.: Manipulability and redundancy control of robotic mechanisms, Robotics and Automation. In: Proceedings of IEEE International Conference on (Mar 1985), vol. 2, pp. 1004–1009 (1985)

4. Cavusoglu, M. C., Feygin, D., Tendick, F.: A Critical Study of the Mechanical and Electrical Properties of the PHANToM Haptic Interface and Improvements for High Performance Control. Teleoperators and Virtual Environments, 11(6), 555–568 (2002)
5. Yoshikawa, T.: Foundations of Robotics: Analysis and Control. MIT Press, Cambridge, MA (1990)
6. Sobh, T.M., Toundykov, D.Y.: Optimizing the tasks at hand [robotic manipulators]. Robotics & Automation Magazine, IEEE 11(2), 78–85 (2004)
7. Alqasemi, R.M., McCaffrey, E.J., Edwards, K.D., Dubey, R.V.: Analysis, evaluation and development of wheelchair-mounted robotic arms. Rehabilitation Robotics 2005, ICORR 2005. In: 9th International Conference on 28 June-1 July 2005. pp:469–472 (2005)
8. Guilamo, L., Kuffner, J., Nishiwaki, K., Kagami, S.: Manipulability optimization for trajectory generation. Robotics and Automation 2006, ICRA 2006. In: Proceedings 2006 IEEE International Conference on May 15-19, 2006. pp: 2017–2022 (2006)
9. San Martin, J., Trivino, G.: Mechanical performance of a manipulator in virtual reality systems. In: 2nd International Conference on Computer Graphics Theory and Applications. GRAPP 07 March 2007 (Accepted, in press)
10. Kirkpatrick, S., Gelatt, Jr., C.D., Vecchi, M.P.: Optimization by Simulated Annealing, Science (220), 671–680 (13 May 1983)
11. Aragon, C.R., Johnson, D.S., McGeoch, L.A., Shevon, C.: Optimization by Simulated Annealing: An Experimental Evaluation; Part II, Graph Coloring and Number Partitioning. Operations Research 39(3), 378–406 (1991)

# IMPROVE: Advanced Displays and Interaction Techniques for Collaborative Design Review

Pedro Santos[1], André Stork[1], Thomas Gierlinger[2], Alain Pagani[2], Bruno Araújo[3], Ricardo Jota[3], Luis Bruno[3], Joaquim Jorge[3], Joao Madeiras Pereira[3], Martin Witzel[4], Giuseppe Conti[4], Raffaele de Amicis[4], Iñigo Barandarian[5], Céline Paloc[5], Maylu Hafner[6], and Don McIntyre[7]

[1] Fraunhofer-IGD, A2,
{Pedro.Santos,Andre.Stork}@igd.fhg.de
[2] TU-Darmstadt, FB21,GRIS,
{Thomas.Gierlinger,Alain.Pagani}@igd.fhg.de
[3] INESC-ID,
{brar,jota.costa,bruno,jaj,jap}@inesc-id.pt
[4] GraphiTech,
{martin.witzel,giuseppe.conti,raffaele.de.amicis}@graphitech.it
[5] VICOMTech,
{Inigo.Barandarian,Celine.Paloc}@vicomtech.es
[6] UNIMEP,
MayluHafner@yahoo.com.br
[7] Lighthouse,
don.mcintyre@urbanlearningspace.com

**Abstract.** In this paper we present evaluation results of an innovative application designed to make collaborative design review in the architectural and automotive domain more effective. Within IMPROVE, a European research project in the area of advanced displays, we are combining high resolution multi-tile displays, TabletPCs and head-mounted displays with innovative 2D and 3D Interaction Paradigms to better support collaborative mobile mixed reality design reviews. Our research and development is motivated by application scenarios in the automotive domain involving FIAT Elasis from Naples, Italy and in the architectural domain involving Page/Park architects from Glasgow, Scotland. User evaluation took place at Glasgow (UK), Naples (ITA) and Darmstadt (GER), where we tested the integrated IMPROVE prototype application. The tests were conducted based on several heuristics such as ergonomics and psychomotorial factors and they were conducted based on guidelines recommended by ISO 9241 to verify whether the developed interfaces were suitable for the applications scenarios. Evaluation results show that there is a strong demand for more interactive design review systems, allowing users greater flexibility and greater choice of input and visualization modalities as well as their combination.

## 1 Introduction

Design Review is one of the most prominent areas benefiting from Virtual Reality and Immersive Projection Technologies. Today Virtual Reality is used to present design alternatives, but fully interactive commercial VR or AR design review applications

R. Shumaker (Ed.): Virtual Reality, HCII 2007, LNCS 4563, pp. 376–385, 2007.

are still being developed or not available. Use cases generally comprise many observers in front of a back projection wall discussing a design decision on a virtual model. This is why in IMPROVE we include support for large single- or multi-tile displays as well as support for TabletPCs. In the above mentioned scenarios we can have users controlling what is visualized on the power-wall from their TabletPCs and vice versa. In addition we also aim at supporting mobile mixed reality using optical see-through HMDs which allow architects to go on site or meet around a table to look at the virtual model of a new building inserted into the real environment featuring the same lighting and reflections as the surroundings.

Components of the IMPROVE system tested by users and performance aims:

- 2D Interaction techniques as well as 3D Interaction techniques for 3D environments were assessed, as is the case when users use a TabletPC to alter the design of a model or proceed to attach annotations or choose material properties or when they use a stereo optical see-through HMD or stand in front of a Power-wall. In any case both performance and learnability were assessed.
- For the combination of display technology and rendering techniques the image quality was assessed, e.g. a comparison between standard OpenGL Lighting and GPU-based pre-computed radiance transfer.
- For the HMD ergonomic issues have been addressed such as brightness, weight, display resolution and power consumption.
- Marker-less tracking for mobile mixed reality environments has been paid special attention during the tests with respect to tracking accuracy, tracking speed, tracking area and final cost of the system.
- The mobile video transmission component has been tested to analyse whether image quality and latency times are enough for the target scenarios. Stereo video stream transmission is used to transmit high quality rendered images to a mobile user receiving the compressed 3D stereo video stream and decompressing it onto the optical stereo-see-through HMD.

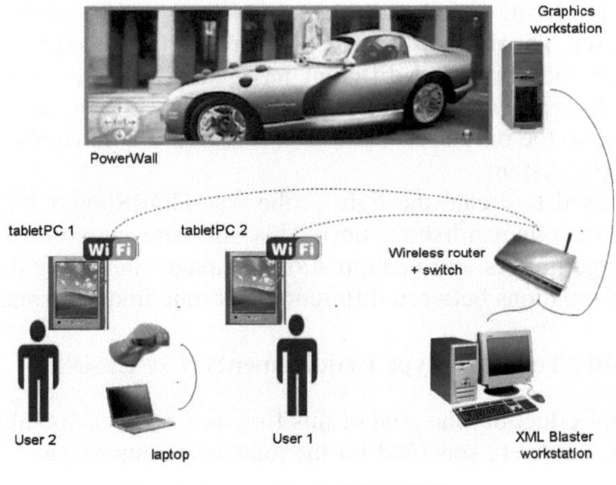


**Fig. 1.** A possible IMPROVE Setup

The tests of the interaction scenarios are presented in another paper in this conference. Here we present the tests of the supporting components to IMPROVE in Darmstadt on July 19th., 2006.

## 2 Rendering Component Usability Tests

The usability test for the rendering component was conducted to answer three questions:

- Is the rendering quality convincing?
- Is the rendering speed adequate for an interactive walk-through.

The problem with the first two questions is to find a measure for the subjective statements of being "convincing" and being "fast enough". To answer the first question we decided to take a comparative approach. We provided the user with a rendering we judged as being convincing and asked him to compare the quality of the IMPROVE renderer to this reference image. The second question was handled by giving the user a navigation task he had to accomplish in the 3D environment. We provided 3D environments of different complexity and asked the user whether the response time of the system was good enough to accomplish the task.

### 2.1 Systems Setup and Features

The location of the test was the laboratory of the department A2 of IGD in Darmstadt. We were using a standard pc, namely

- CPU: Intel Pentium4 3 GHz
- Memory: 2 GB Ram
- Graphics Board: Nvidia GeForce 6600
- Operating System: Windows XP Professional Service Pack 2

To assess the rendering speed and quality we were using a desktop version of the IMPROVE renderer. The desktop version of the renderer was equipped with a simple QT user interface and supported different navigation modes, switching of lighting environments and preprocessing models. For this test we concentrated on rendering quality and speed, so the only user interaction required was navigation to evaluate the response time of the system.

The software used to create the light probe was HDRShop 1 from University of Southern California (www.hdrshop.com). This software supports the generation of high dynamic range images and manipulation of images including different selection modes and transformations between different panoramic image formats.

### 2.2 First Usability Test Prototype Requirements (Use Cases)

As stated in the introduction, the goal of this first user test was to validate three of the performance aims that were specified for the rendering component.

- The first one is the rendering speed
- The second goal was to validate the rendering quality.

- The third performance aim we wanted to validate is the time that is needed to capture a lighting environment by generating an HDR light probe.

### 2.3 Usability Test Description

The usability test of the rendering component was divided into two parts. The first one was concerned with the evaluation of the rendering engine itself, namely the rendering speed and quality. The second part was about generating new lighting input for the renderer (i.e. light probe acquisition).

### 2.4 Rendering Speed and Quality

The first three questions of the user test were designed to evaluate the rendering quality. The user was presented three still images (screenshots) of the same scene rendered using different renderers. The images are shown in Fig. 2..

**Fig. 2.** Screenshots of the same scene rendered with different quality

Image a) was generated using the second version of the IMPROVE renderer. This version supports high dynamic range reflections and direct visualization of the light probe image. Image b) was rendered using the first version of the IMPROVE renderer which supported only low dynamic range reflections and low dynamic range background images. Image c) was generated using the mental ray offline renderer. This rendering uses final gathering for environment lighting and ray tracing for calculating reflections. It should be noted, that the images a) and c) were rendered without any tone mapping while image b) has a simple tone mapping applied which is the reason for the shift in the car color. This only affects the saturation of the lacquer, not the quality of the reflections. The more washed out look of the reflections is due to the low dynamic range reflection map.

Given these three images the users were asked to rate the quality of the rendering on a scale from 1 to 5 with 5 representing the best rendering quality. The expected ordering of the images was

- Image b) worst quality of the three images
- Image a) medium quality
- Image c) highest quality

The next two questions in the user test were about the rendering speed. The users were asked to navigate the camera from a default starting point in front of a car into the position of a driver sitting in the car and looking out of the front window. The navigation was done using a mouse to drive an "examine viewer" (i.e. moving the mouse with left button pressed rotated the object about it's center, moving the mouse with middle button pressed pans the scene, moving the mouse with right button pressed zooms in/out). The user was asked to repeat the navigation in two scenes. The first one is the low resolution Lotus scene (see 1). This scene has 230.000 triangles (110.000 lit using PRT, 120.000 for background and glass). This scene was rendered at about 60 frames per second on the test system. The car model was downloaded from the internet (see http://dmi.chez-alice.fr) and was generated using some digital content creation tool (i.e. a 3D modeler, not a CAD system). The second scene showed a BMW model that was generated from CAD data (see figure 2). This model was composed of 1.35 million triangles (1.2 million lit using PRT, 150.000 for background and glass). This scene was rendered on the test system at approximately 10 frames per second.

| | |
|---|---|
|  |  |
| Initial position of the camera | Traget position of the camera |

**Fig. 3.** BMW scene

For each of the scenes we measured the time the user required to finish the navigation and afterwards asked him whether he felt the response time of the system was fast enough to accomplish this task. The answer was given on a scale from 1 to 5 with 5 meaning the rendering was fast enough and 1 meaning the rendering was too slow.

## 2.5 Questionnaire Analysis

We had six test users, all with experience in navigating in 3D programs. None of the users had generated a light probe before.

Figure 4 shows the results for the first three questions about the rendering quality. The average scores show the expected result. The image generated with the first version of the IMPROVE renderer (Picture b) was rated to have the lowest quality of the series with 2.33 out of 5 points. The image generated with the second version of the IMPROVE renderer (Picutre a) was rated to be of medium quality (score 3.83 out of 5) and the image generated with the offline renderer (Picture c) was rated to be the most convincing one of the series (score 4.0 out of 5). This result shows that the quality of the current IMPROVE renderer is relatively close to the quality of the offline renderer (3.83 compared to 4.0). This basically means that the real-time rendering algorithm we chose for the IMPROVE renderer (Precomputed Radiance Transfer) is adequate for rendering scenes like the one used in this test (static geometry under low frequency lighting). However, even the score of the offline renderer did not reach the maximum of 5.0 in this test. The reason for this is most likely the fact that the materials that were used on the model are relatively simple. The lacquer of the car is a Phong material, the interior has only diffuse materials assigned. By using more advance materials / shaders it should be possible to increase rendering quality.

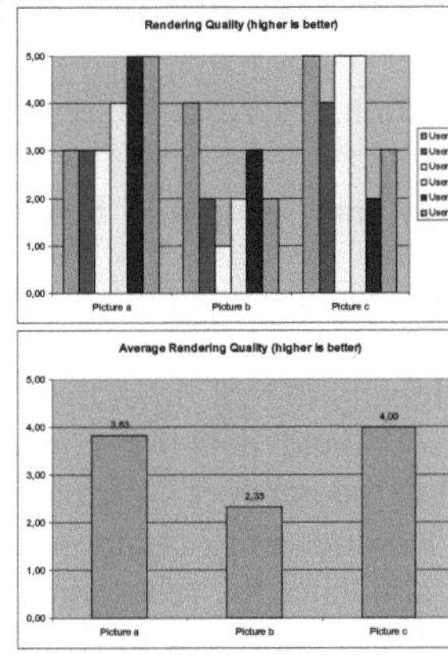


**Fig.4.** Rendering Quality

The results of question number four about the rendering speed are shown in figure 5. The graph on the right-hand side displays the average rating of the rendering speed in the two test scenes. It can be seen, that the rendering speed in the low polygon scene (Lotus scene) is judged to be fast enough (5.0 out of 5.0) for easy navigation. Although the scores for the complex scene (BMW scene) are considerably lower (3.17 out of 5.0) the rendering speed of this scene was still acceptable for the majority of the users. On the other hand a look at figure 6 reveals that the navigation in the complex BMW scene was harder due to the lower response time of the system. Compared to the simple Lotus scene the users needed more than twice the time to complete the navigation. This result suggests that increasing the rendering speed should not be of high priority in the next development phase. Although higher rendering speed of complex models will increase the usability of the system, the rendering quality (more specifically the quality of materials / shaders) seems to be a more pressing problem since no configuration in the rendering quality test reached the top score of 5.0 points.

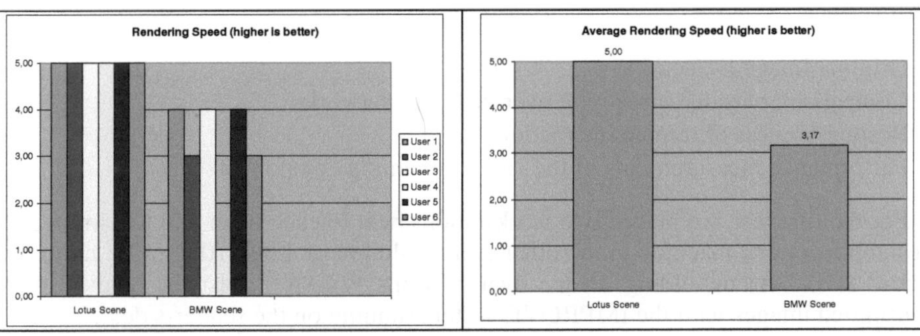


**Fig. 5.** Rendering Speed

## 2.6 Conclusion

This first evaluation of the rendering component suggests that the priority of the development should be on the improvement of the supported materials / shaders. The rendering speed is adequate for small to moderate size scenes (100.000 to 500.000 triangles). For complex scenes (around 1 million triangles) the rendering speed is acceptable, but improving the speed would increase usability. The light probe acquisition is possible in the estimated time (below one hour), but requires some training to achieve good results.

# 3 Video-Streaming Component Usability Tests

This section describes the results of the video-streaming component tests.

## 3.1 Systems Setup and Features

Since the video-streaming component is to be used to support mobile HMD users who do not have the local processing power for high-quality rendered images to be computed locally in real-time, the stereo video-streams need to be transmitted over wireless or narrow-band network connections. In addition, also the sender side can be connected to the network over narrow-band connections in worst case. Therefore we tested the video-streaming component under such circumstances. The different bandwidths where simulated by restricting the throughput at the switches the two computers were patched to. In addition to that the video-streaming sender component allows to explicitly predefine the data throughput of the stream, which was defined as follows:

- UMTS (300 Kbps video stream throughput)
- DSL (650 Kbps video stream throughput)
- WLAN (3000 Kbps video stream throughput)

The reason why we did not set the amount of video data produced to rates higher than 3000 Kbps is because the image quality would not get any better at higher values, when we compared the original stream and the encoded/decoded stream on the same computer for the resolutions we tested.

We did four tests, three with test candidates and one to measure transmission performance:

- Original Image Detection
- Comparison of video-streaming over different networks
- Responsiveness of remote interaction
- Performance measurements of the video-streaming component

For the first test, we placed two workstations next to each other and transmitted the Desktop from one machine to the other at a resolution of 1280x1024 (40% more data than 2 x SVGA) upholding 25 fps over 54Mbps WLAN to test the quality of the transmitted images with the IMPROVE system running on the sender-side.

For the second and third test the sender was set to a resolution of 1600 x 600 with a color depth of 32bit and the compressor was set to keep up a target frame-rate of 25fps on sender-side. The stream throughput to be generated was set to one of the three throughputs we wanted to test over the three different network bandwidths.

For dual channel video-streaming we use two identical threads on the sender-side which compress the images for the left eye and the images for the right eye respectively, which means left and right viewport on a horizontal span Desktop. Alternative implementations which embed both streams in one are described in D20. However since the streams are to be decompressed by two separate low-power, small form factor and low-consumption mobile computers, we split them into a dual channel stream with one channel sent to each machine. The streams are synchronized from the sender to the two receiving sub-notebooks on the receiver-side which decompress and display the streams on the user's HMD.

In the last test we measured the performance between two workstations simulating different stream throughputs, networks and screen resolutions.

For the user tests we conducted we tested 13 individuals, 9 male and 4 female, with ages ranging between 20 - 30 years and a background in computer graphics, architecture and design.

### 3.2 Usability Test 1 - Original Image Detection

In the first test, the video-streaming is already taking place in 54Mbps WLAN conditions at 3000 Kbps, when the user is invited to enter the room where the test takes place. The application transmitted over the network by the video-streaming component is the current IMPROVE prototype system featuring a PRT (Pre-computed Radiance Transfer) rendered car model which remains static in its position (figure 8).

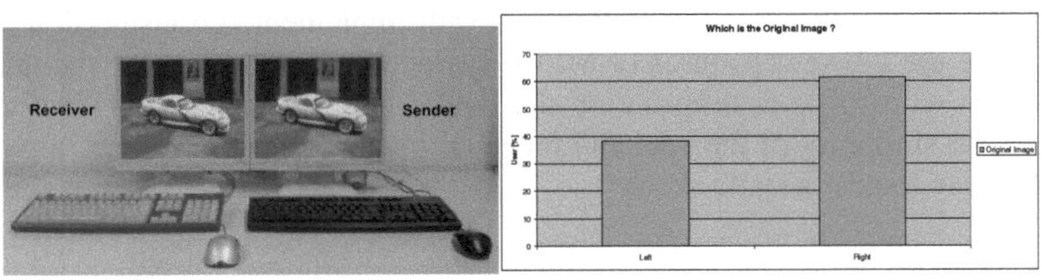


**Fig. 6.** Video-streaming Test Setup / Which is the original image ?

The user is then asked to find out which is the original image and which the received to see whether he can tell the difference at highest quality and almost loss-less compression. In fact the original image is the right one in Fig. 6. and differences can only be detected at very close range. The 60% of the test candidates that identified the original image correctly pointed out, that they found out it was the right image due to smooth transitions on edges which would have a sharp contrast in the original image.

As can be observed in figure 9 the outcome is pretty balanced. Although the majority of the test candidates identified the original image correctly in an average time of 14,7 seconds, the image quality appears not to have deteriorated much, because almost half of the candidates could not identify the sender correctly.

### 3.3 Usability Test 2 - Comparison of Video-Streaming over Different Networks

For the second test we setup the sending workstation to a resolution of 1600 x 600 horizontal span, the compressor was set up in two channel synchronized mode to uphold a framerate of 25 fps on the sender side at three different throughput rates sent over three different network simulations:

- UMTS (384 Kbps video stream)
- DSL (768 Kbps video stream)
- WLAN (3000 Kbps video stream)

The first question was on how the candidates rated the similarity between received and sent images. A car model was used as content and remained static in the scene.

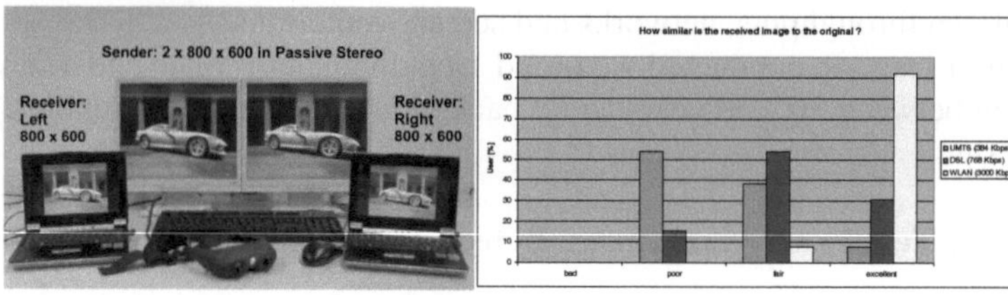


**Fig. 7.** User Test 2 - How similar is the received image to the original ?

As would be expected the results (Figure 9) confirm that more candidates perceive the images to be similar to each other the better the connection is. However interestingly for the static scene and for all types of connections the similarity is not rated bad by anybody. We assume that in addition to a well implemented transmission pipeline this is due to the inherent features of MPEG4 which gradually increase the quality of an image by sending delta information the longer it is not changed. Therefore most users find the similarity of the sent and received images fair to excellent in particular the longer they look at a static scene.

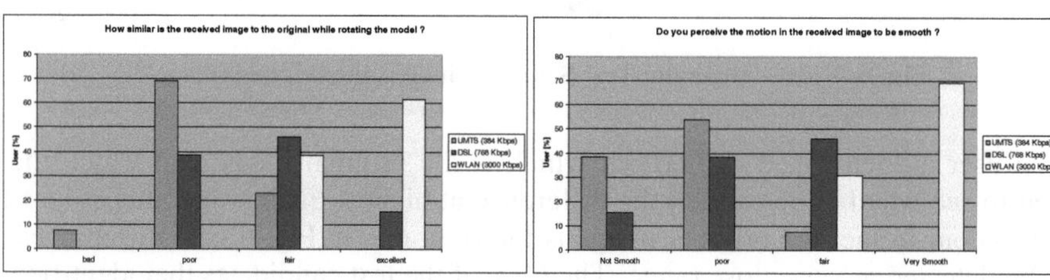


**Fig. 8.** User Test 2 - How similar is the received image to the original while rotating the model ? / Is the motion smooth ?

The second situation (figure 10) was to confront the candidates with moving images which cause much more traffic due to ever-changing image information. For this purpose the model of the car is rotated on the sender-side by using the keyboard tracking emulation inbuilt in the IMPROVE system. Compared to the static images we notice a slight shift in perception towards worse quality which was to be expected. However, only very few users consider the similarities to be bad even in worst bandwidth conditions. Mostly candidates complain about sharp edges turning soft and fuzzy. One candidate complained about seeing a few artifacts during transmission when we simulated UMTS bandwidth conditions.

The third question regarded motion smoothness. We asked the test candidates whether they were satisfied with the smoothness of motion in dynamic scenes over three different network types.

From the results we can conclude, that if Video-streaming is to be used at high resolutions for mobile collaborative applications such as the IMPROVE system, we need to ensure at least DSL transmission rates.

### 3.4 Usability Test 3 - Testing Remote Interaction Performance

In the third part of the test, the users were asked to remotely interact with a simple game, a maze. The outcome of those tests will be presented in the conference.

## 4 User Tests of the Supporting Hardware

We conclude that the rendering component and the video streaming component have both successfully been tested and yielded good results.

The speed of the rendering component is acceptable. The rendering quality is close to the quality of offline rendering if only scenes with static geometry and low frequency environment lighting are considered. The focus of the further development of the rendering component should be on supporting more advanced materials to increase the rendering quality. The acquisition of light probes that can be used with the rendering component is possible in less than an hour, but some experience and training is required to achieve acceptable results.

Concerning the video streaming, we have come to the conclusion that for mobile application within IMPROVE we need at least a network connection of 1 Mbps and above which is feasible since network operators start providing for higher bandwidth UMTS connections. The quality of the images transmitted is adequate for architects and automotive designers resulting in only minimal quality differences at such appropriate bandwidths. Due to the fact that we use dual channel transmission to two separate receivers we can use small form factor devices for decompression in mobile environments.

**Acknowledgements.** This work has partially been funded by European Commission Grant IMPROVE IST-2003-004785.

## References

1. Debevec, P.E., Malik, J.: Recovering High Dynamic Range Radiance Maps from Photographs. Computer Graphics, In: SIGGRAPH 1997, vol. 31, pp. 369–378 (1997)
2. Debevec, P.: Rendering synthetic objects into real scenes: Bridging traditional and image-based graphics with global illumination and high dynamic range photography. In: SIGGRAPH 98 (July 1998)
3. Drummond, T., Cipolla, R.: Real-Time visual tracking of complex structures. IEEE Transaction on Pattern Analysis and Machine Intelligence 27, 932–946 (2002)
4. Fiorentino, M., de Amicis, R., Monno, G., Stork, A.: SpaceDesign: A Mixed Reality Workspace for Aesthetic Industrial Design, In: Intl. Symposium on Augmented and Mixed Reality, Darmstadt, ISMAR 2002 (2002)

# Comparing Symptoms of Visually Induced Motion Sickness Among Viewers of Four Similar Virtual Environments with Different Color

Richard H.Y. So* and S.L. Yuen

Department of Industrial Engineering and Logistics Management
Hong Kong University of Science and Technology,
Clear Water Bay, Kowloon, Hong Kong SAR
rhyso@ust.hk

**Abstract.** This paper reports an experiment conducted to study the effects of changing scene color inside a virtual environment on the rated levels of nausea among sixty-four viewers. Current theory on visually induced motion sickness suggests that changing the color of dynamically moving visual stimuli, while keeping everything equals, will not affect the rated sickness symptoms of the viewers. Interestingly, a recent study by another authors reported that color do affect levels of visually induced motion sickness. Preliminary results of this experiment suggest that while exposure duration to the visual stimuli significantly increased the rated levels of nausea and simulator sickness questionnaire scores (*$p<0.001$, ANOVAs*), changes of color did not affect the levels of sickness. Reasons for the conflicting results are discussed in the paper.

## 1 Introduction

Occurrence of visually induced motion sickness (VIMS) has been associated with the presence of visually induced self-motion illusion (vection) in the absence of appropriate vestibular stimuli and / or responses. One example is to visually navigate through a virtual environment (VE) while sitting stationary. It is well known that the perception of visual motion in human follows the magnocellular visual pathways that involve m-type (or parasol) ganglion cells that are color-blind (the two visual systems theory: Schneider, 1967). This suggests that, giving all things equal, changing the color of objects inside a VE but keeping the same contrast ratios and luminance (or gray scale) levels will not affect the reported symptoms of the viewers. With much interest, the authors read Bonato *et al.* (2004) which reported that color of the visual stimuli can affect symptoms of VIMS. Does this imply that the traditional association between the magnocellular visual pathways and VIMS has been mistaken? An experiment has been conducted to investigate the effects of changing color of objects inside a VE on symptoms of VIMS among sixty-four viewers.

* Corresponding author.

R. Shumaker (Ed.): Virtual Reality, HCII 2007, LNCS 4563, pp. 386–391, 2007.

## 2 Objectives and Hypothesis

The objective of this experiment was to study whether rated levels of visually induced motion sickness (VIMS) associated with a virtual reality (VR) simulation would change when the color of that corresponding VE was changed. We hypothesize that color would have no significant influence on the rated levels of VIMS (H1). This hypothesis is consistent with the two visual systems theory by Schneider (1967) that states that the ambient vision, which is responsible for detecting motion, is insensitive to color.

## 3 Methods and Design

### 3.1 Manipulation of Color While Keeping Other Things Equal

A full-factorial between-subject design was used. The color of the virtual environments (VEs) was the only independent variable and had four levels: (i) blue-colored sea with brown-colored floor; (ii) green-colored sea with brown-colored floor; (iii) blue-colored sea with gray-colored floor; and (iv) green-colored sea with gray-colored floor (snap-shots of these four VEs will be shown during the presentation at the conference). The Paint Shop Pro® version 6 was used to manipulate the color. The color of the sea and the ground were manipulated because they occupied about half of the field-of-views during the VR simulation. The sky also occupied a large portion of the field-of-view but it was difficult to change the blue sky to another natural color (e.g., cloudy white) without affecting the spatial frequencies. In this study, we avoided unnatural combinations of color (e.g., red sea and a green sky). The four VEs have been carefully manipulated to produce similar spatial frequencies (their spatial frequencies were not significantly different using t-tests: $p>0.9$). To calculate the spatial frequencies, 4800 snapshots (2 snapshots per second) were taken from each of the four VR simulations. These snapshots were captured at a resolution of 495 pixels (horizontal) x 115 pixels (vertical) to match the resolution of the VR4 head-mounted display (HMD) used in the study. An image analysis of these 4800 snapshots shows that the views of the sea and the ground occupy an average of about 28% of the total field-of-view. To facilitate spatial frequency estimation, these snapshots were converted to portable gray map (pgm) files according to Hoffmann (2005).

The average radial spatial frequency of each group of 4800 snapshots taken from the same VR simulation was then calculated using the 'combined' method adopted from So, Ho and Lo (2001). This published method is also illustrated and explained at www.cybersickness.org. The experiment had thirty-two male and thirty-two female Chinese participants between 19 and 27 years old. They were randomly assigned to one of the four VEs so that each VE was viewed by eight male and eight female participants. All participants were healthy. A color blindness test was conducted before the experiment to ensure they did not have color blindness. They were paid US$6 per hour to compensate for their time and travel expenses. The experiment was approved by the human subject committee of the Hong Kong University of Science and Technology.

### 3.2 Measurements

A 7-point nausea rating scale was used to measure the level of nausea (Golding and Kerguelen, 1992; Webb and Griffin, 2002) and a four-point vection rating scale was used to measure the level of self-motion (Hettinger et al., 1990). Both scales have been used in previous studies of VIMS (So, Ho and Lo, 2001; So, Lo and Ho, 2001). In addition, the 27-symptom simulator sickness questionnaire (SSQ) was also used (Kennedy et al., 1993). Data from the pre-exposure and post-exposure SSQs were used to calculate the nausea sub-score (N), oculo-motor sub-score (O), disorientation sub-score (D) and the total SSQ score (TS). Besides subjective measures, objective postural tests were used to quantify the ability of participants to balance themselves before and after VR exposures. In this study, the sharpened Romberg (also known as the tandem Romberg) (e.g., Hamilton *et al.,* 1989; Cobb and Nichols, 1998), the stand-on-preferred-leg (SOPL), and the stand-on-non-preferred-leg (SONL) (e.g., Kennedy *et al.*, 1997) tests were used. In all three tests, the durations that participants could balance themselves without changing the required posture were measured (referred to as the balancing time) as well as the amount of head sway (Kennedy and Stanney, 1996).

### 3.3 Procedures

A Virtual Research VR4 LCD Head-Mounted Display (HMD) with a field-of-view of 48° × 36° was used to present the virtual environments. This HMD has a resolution of 495 pixels (horizontal) × 115 pixels (vertical). VR simulations were rendered by the dVISE software running on a Silicon Graphic ONXY II Infinite Reality workstation at a frame rate of 30 frames per second. A Polhemus 3-Space magnetic tracker was used to measure the head position and orientation during the VR simulation as well as during the postural tests.

Before the experiment, all participants were educated on the meaning of vection and the meanings of the symptoms used in the SSQ. After that, they were given three minutes to try out the VR apparatus and to personalize the adjustment of the apparatus before they were asked to fill in a pre-exposure SSQ. If the participants had a total score of 10 or more (corresponding to more than one slight sickness symptom), they were asked to rest in an air-conditioned room for 10 minutes and to complete the pre-exposure SSQ again. If their scores were still 10 or more, they were asked to come back on a later date. This practice is consistent with that of Stanney *et al.* (2003). After the pre-exposure SSQ, participants had to carry out four trials of sharpened Romberg tests followed by three trials of SOPL and SONL tests. They would then be assigned randomly to one of the four VR simulation conditions. The exposure time was 40 minutes. During the exposure, participants viewed the VE through the HMD and they were navigated along a pre-determined path inside the VE. The same path was used for all participants and they could change their viewpoints by turning their heads although participants were asked to keep their heads facing forward unless they were instructed otherwise. To encourage the participants to be more attentive, they were asked to turn their heads to one side every 30 seconds and to report verbally what they saw. The direction of turning was randomized. This method to encourage involvement was adopted from So, Lo and Ho (2001). During the 40-minute exposure and at every 5-minute interval, participants were asked to rate their nausea feelings verbally according to a 7-point nausea rating (0 to 6) and their feeling of self-motion according to a 4-point vection rating (0 to 3). After the exposure, participants completed a post-exposure SSQ and performed another four trials of sharpened Romberg tests followed by three trials of SOPL and SONL tests. Participants who gave a rating of 6 on the nausea scale (i.e., moderate nausea and want to stop) were allowed to terminate their exposure and complete the post-exposure SSQ and the postural tests. We assumed that the nausea and vection ratings of these subjects remained the same for the time beyond their termination time. In other words, if a participant scored a rating of 6 on the nausea scale and a rating of 2 on the vection scale after 30-minute exposure, the estimated nausea and vection ratings at 35 minutes and beyond would be 6 and 2, respectively.

## 4 Results and Discussion

The data followed a normal distribution. Preliminary results of ANOVAs indicate that exposure duration had significant effects on both nausea and vection ratings ($p<0.001$). However, both color and gender did not significantly affect the nausea and vection ratings ($p>0.1$). Student-Newman-Keuls (SNK) tests showed that nausea ratings increased significantly from 0 minutes to 25 minutes and did not change significantly from 25 minutes to 40 minutes.

The simulator sickness questionnaire (SSQ) total scores taken after the exposure (i.e., post-SSQ scores) were significantly greater than those scores taken before the exposure (i.e., pre-SSQ scores) ($p<0.01$). For each participant, the differences between the post-SSQ scores and the pre-SSQ scores were the differences between the corresponding post-exposure scores and the pre-exposure scores. Results of ANOVAs show that color had no significant effect on the differences between the post- and the pre-SSQ total score ($p>0.3$). Both the balance times and the root-mean-square (r.m.s.) head deviations during the balancing periods of the postural tests along the six directions (fore-and-aft, lateral, vertical, roll, pitch and yaw) were analyzed. Results of ANOVAs indicate that the r.m.s. head deviations along yaw and roll axes collected from the sharpened Romberg tests and r.m.s head deviations along pitch axis collected from the SOPL tests collected after the exposure were significantly greater than those collected before the exposure ($p<0.05$). However, these significant increases due to exposure to the VR simulation were not significantly affected when VEs with different color combinations were used ($p>0.05$).

The preliminary results of this experiment clearly support hypothesis H1 that the rated levels of VIMS of participants navigating through a VE will not be affected when its color is changed while keeping a similar level of average spatial frequencies. In this study, the change of color was limited to the choices of natural color (e.g., blue or green for the sea).

The current findings contradict with the results of Bonato *et al.* (2004). Further analyses reveal that in Bonato's study, effects of color were significant on rated levels of headache but not on rated nausea. Also, the methods to manipulate the color of the visual stimuli in the two studies are very different. For example, in Bonato's study, the comparison was conducted between conditions with and without color while in the current study, the comparison was conducted among conditions with different colors. Another reason for the differences in the results of the two studies may be due to the differences in the portion of the field-of-views in which the changes of color had occurred.

## 5 Conclusions

Viewing a 40-minute dynamically moving virtual reality (VR) simulation significantly increased the rated levels of nausea ($p<0.001$), vection ($p<0.001$), and SSQ scores ($p<0.05$) among sixty-four viewers.

Measures of head deviations during sharpened Romberg tests and Stand-on-Preferred-Leg tests conducted after the 40-minute VR exposure were significantly greater than those measured before the exposure ($p<0.05$).

While the 40-minute VR exposure could significantly increase both the rated levels of sickness and postural stability as measured by head deviations, changing the color of the virtual environment by about 28% did not affect the rated levels of sickness nor postural stability measurements.

**Acknowledgement.** The authors would like to thank the Hong Kong University Grants Council and Hong Kong Research Grants Council (HKUST6154/04E) for partially supporting this study.

## References

1. Bonato, F., Bubka, A., Alfieri, L.: Display color affects motion sickness symptoms in an optokinetic drum. Aviation, space, and environmental medicine 75, 306–311 (2004)
2. Cobb, S.V.G., Nichols, S.C.: Static posture tests for the assessment of postural instability after virtual environment use. Brain Research Bulletin 47(5), 459–464 (1998)
3. Golding, J.F., Kerguelen, M.: A comparison of the nauseogenic potential of low-frequency vertical versus horizontal linear oscillation. Aerospace Medical Association 63, 491–497 (1992)
4. Hamilton, K.M., Kantor, L., Magee, L.E.: Limitations of postural equilibrium tests for examining simulator sickness. Aviation, Space, and Environmental Medicine 60, 246–251 (1989)
5. Hettinger, L.J., Berbaum, K.S., Kennedy, R.S., Dunlap, W.P., Nolan, M.D.: Vection and simulator sickness. Military Psychology 2(3), 171–181 (1990)
6. Hoffmann, G.: Luminance models for the grayscale conversion. (2005) http://www.fho-emden.de/ hoffmann/index.html
7. Kennedy, R.S., Lane, N.E., Berbaum, K.S., Lilienthal, M.G.: Simulator sickness questionnaire: An enhanced method for quantifying simulator sickness. The International Journal of Aviation Psychology 3(3), 203–220 (1993)
8. Kennedy, R.S., Berbaum, K.S., Lilienthal, M.G.: Disorientation and postural ataxia following flight simulation. Aviation, Space, and Environmental Medicine 68(1), 14–17 (1997)
9. Kennedy, R.S., Stanney, K.M.: Postural instability induced by virtual reality exposure: Development of a certification protocol. International Journal of Human-Computer Interaction 8(1), 25–47 (1996)

10. So, R.H.Y., Ho., A., Lo, W.T.: A metric to quantify virtual scene movement for the study of cybersickness: Definition, implementation, and verification. Presence 10(2), 193–215 (2001)
11. So, R.H.Y., Lo, W.T., Ho, A.T.K.: Effects of navigation speed on motion sickness caused by an immersive virtual environment. Human Factors 43(3), 452–461 (2001)
12. Schneider, G.E.: Contrasting visuomotor functions of tectum and cortex in the golden hamster. Psychologische Forschung 31, 52–62 (1967)
13. Stanney, K.M., Hale, K.S., Nahmens, L.: What to expect from immersive virtual environment exposure: influence of gender, body mass index, and past experience. Human Factors 45, 504–520 (2003)
14. Webb, N.A., Griffin, M.J.: Optopkinetic stimuli: motion sickness, visual acuity, and eye movements. Aviat Space Environ Med 73, 351–358 (2002)

# Effects of Global Motion Included in Video Movie Provoking an Incident on Visually Induced Motion Sickness

Hiroyasu Ujike

Institute for Human Science and Biomedical Engineering
National Institute of Advanced Industrial Science and Technology
Central 6, 1-1-1 Higashi, Tsukuba 305-8566 Japan
h.ujike@aist.go.jp

**Abstract.** The present study examined the effect of global motion combinations on visually induced motion sickness, presenting global motion analyzed from the video movies that induced the VIMS incident in Japan in 2003. The stimulus movie was presented on LC displays, whose size was either 20 or 37 inch with viewing distance of one meter. The results showed that when the extent of pitch and yaw motion was reduced to one third of from the original motion of the movie had larger effect than when other types of motion was reduced the same ratio of extent. This may be related to the fact that the original movie included larger amount of yaw motion. Moreover, we found that the lager display pro-duced larger total scores, and also larger "Disorientation" sub-socres, of SSQ than the smaller display. This may suggest the discomfort for the larger and smaller displays are produced by mainly different mechanisms.

## 1 Introduction

Recent evolution of moving image technique makes movies more enjoyable and video games more attractive. With computerized system, the creators can easily produce visual images, which simulate motion and actions in virtually three-dimensional space. Moreover, people can take video movies more easily and enjoy them with larger TV screen than ever before. The broad diffusion of these techniques, however, increases the possibility for us to be suffered from visually induced motion sickness. The visually induced motion sickness is often recognized as just a minor annoyance and not signifying any serious medical illness. The sickness may, however, cause a risk in any particular tasks, even in daily life.

Actual incidents of visually induced motion sickness (VIMS) were socially reported in Japan in 2003 and 2006, although the latter is uncertain as to whether it was VIMS. About the incident in 2003, local junior high school students, total of 294, had watched a 20-minitute movie presented on a large screen in an auditorium during class. The movie was shot by a handheld video camera, and includes unexpected whole image motion and vibration, which were caused by both intended and unintended camera motion. During and after the class, some of the students complained of feeling nausea and head ache; finally 36 students were treated at a hospital for a symptom of motion sickness (Ujike, Nihei and Ukai).

R. Shumaker (Ed.): Virtual Reality, HCII 2007, LNCS 4563, pp. 392–396, 2007.

In order to reduce the risks for us to suffer VIMS while keeping attractiveness and enjoyment of watching visual images created by the latest technique, we need to clarify the factors affecting the sickness, and to develop an evaluation method of visual images in terms of the sickness. The literature (Lo and So, 2001) categorized the causative factors of cybersickness as the following three: (i) how moving image is presented, (ii) who watches moving image, and (iii) what is presented as moving image. This categorization is important and can be applied also to VIMS. In the categories, the third item, 'what is presented', is my concern in the present study, because visual mo-tion might be a primary cause of VIMS while the other factors will enhance or attenuate the VIMS.

In my earlier studies, my colleagues and I had investigated the effects of global motion, both one directional rotation and also reciprocating rotation along different three axes, those as roll, pitch and yaw (Ujike, Yokoi and Saida, 2004; Ujike, Ukai and Saida, 2004; Ujike, Kozawa, Yokoi and Saida, 2005). In those studies, we found that (i) visual roll motion can be the most effective and visual yaw motion can be the least effective, and (ii) a certain range of rotational velocity is effective for VIMS. In the present study, the experiment examined the effect of global motion combinations on visually induced motion sickness, presenting global motion that was analyzed from the video movies that induced the incident in the local junior high school in Japan in 2003.

## 2 Methods

### 2.1 Observers

One hundred and thirty-four adults, aged 19-72 years (mean: 36.2, SD: 9.74; 92 females and 33 males), participated in the study as observers, after giving their informed written consent in accordance with the Helsinki Declaration, and were free to withdraw at any time during the experiment. The study was approved by the Ethics Committee of the National Institute of Advanced Industrial Science and Technology. The ob-servers were naïve as to the purpose of the experiments, and had normal or collected-to-normal visual acuity.

**Fig. 1.** City scene image presented to observer. The image was textured to inside wall of a sphere, at which center a virtual camera was set to make a movie image. The camera motion was applied from the global motion analyzed from the movie of the incident in Japan in 2003.

## 2.2 Visual Stimuli and Apparatus

The stimulus was video image that was comprised of five-minutes gray image, 20-minutes video footage, and another two-minutes gray image, which were presented in this order. We used four different 20-minutes video footages, each of which was made as CG movie of virtually produced city scene (Fig. 1). The camera motion in the CG movie was basically reproduced based on the camera motion estimated in the video movie that induced the incident in Japan in 2003. The difference among the four movies was the extent of motion of the different types of camera motion. The first one was produced with the original motion. The second was with reduced roll motion whose extent was one third of the original. The third was with reduced zoom motion whose extent was one third of the original. Finally, the fourth was with reduced pitch and yaw motion whose extent was one third of the original.

Four different small experimental booths were set up side by side; each of the booths was mostly enclosed by blackout curtain, was set up with a LC display, the chin-, head- and arm-rests, with a viewing distance of 1.0 m. There were two different size of the LC display, 20 inch (or 22.7 x 17.0 deg) and 37 inch (or 34.1 x 25.9 deg).

The height of the LC display was adjusted so that the center of the display was the same as vantage point of observers. The experimental room was light-proofed, and the light other than the display was turn off during the experiment.

On one of the armrest, a response box was fixed. The response box has a button and a four-way joystick. The button was pressed when a small red dot was appeared for a short period on a movie image, in order to keep the observers eyes on the display screen. The joystick was used for observers to evaluate discomfort in a four point scale.

## 2.3 Procedures

Before the experiment, each of the four different movie was allocated to different ob-servers, so that total number, gender, age and susceptibility to motion sickness of ob-servers are almost equally appeared in each movie. Susceptibility to motion sickness was self-reported by each observer before the experiment.

The experiment was mostly done using all four different stimulus displays (the two for 20 inch, the other two for 37 inch) simultaneously, depending on observers' participation. Each experimental session started with asking observers to do Simulator Sickness Questionnaire, and then, observers fix their heads at chin- and head-rests, and their arms on armrests. They watched the video movie for 27 minutes; during this time, observers were asked, every one minute, to report about one of SSQ score, "General discomfort" in four alternatives: "None," "Slight," "Moderate," and "Severe"; they report the score using the four-way joystick. The observers also need to respond by pressing the button on the response box when a small red dot was appeared for a short period on a movie image; the position and time (three times every minute) of the appearance of the was randomized. Just after finishing watching the video movie, they started, again, SSQ, and then they did it another three times every 15 minutes.

## 3 Results and Discussions

Averaged SSQ total score across all the observers shows three things: The first one was that the score dramatically increased just after finishing watching the video, and then, gradually decreased with trials after finishing the video movies. The second one was that the scores obtained with the movie including the original motion was always the largest among the different movies. The third one was that the scores obtained with the movie including the reduced pitch and yaw amplitude was the smallest after the immediately-after-the-watching trial. This indicates that the effect of pitch and yaw was relatively larger than that of other global motion.

To see detail of the effects of different stimulus movies, the results were separately analyzed for different display size. Then, we found that for the larger stimulus display, the SSQ total scores obtained with the movie including the reduced pitch and yaw amplitude was the smallest after watching the movie, while for the smaller stimulus display, the SSQ total scores for different stimulus movie was almost the same. This indicates that the effect of pitch and yaw was relatively larger for the larger display than for the smaller display.

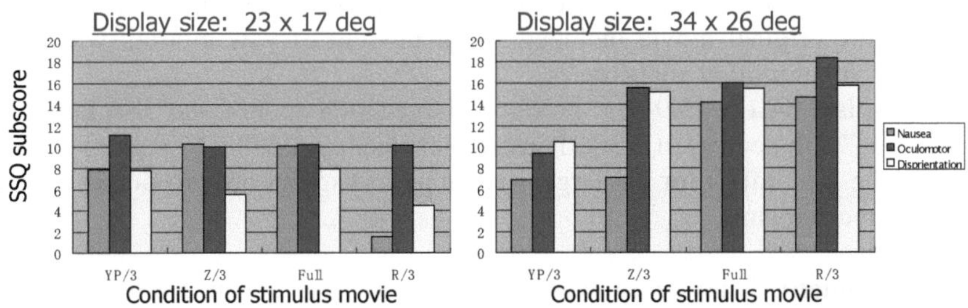


**Fig. 2.** SSQ sub-scores for different conditions of stimulus movie and for different display size. The different colors of the bar show the different sub-scores: Blue for "Nausea," beige for "Oculomotor," and yellow for "Disorientation." Abbreviations on the horizontal line indicate condition o stimulus movie: "YP/3" for the reduced pitch and yaw motion, "Z/3" for the reduced zoom motion, "R/3" for the reduced roll motion, and "Full" for the original motion of the stimulus movies.

To see more details of the effects of different stimulus movies, the results were separately analyzed for different sub-scores of SSQ, which are "Nausea," "Oculomotor," and "Disorientation," for different display size. The results were shown in Fig.2. From the figure, we found the following three. Firstly, the scores are generally larger for the larger display than the smaller display. This is the effect of display size. While previous reports had been focused on the effects of more larger display, our results showed the effects still exists for the smaller size that we used. Secondly, the "disorientation" sub-scores relatively increased for the larger display than for the smaller display. This may suggest that the discomfort for the larger and smaller displays are produced by mainly different mechanisms. That is, the movie in the larger display induced discomfort mainly through equilibrium mechanism, while the movie in the smaller display induced discomfort mainly through other mechanism.

Thirdly, sub-scores of the reduced pitch and yaw motion was relatively smaller than the other conditions of the movie. This may be because the original motion included relatively larger amount of Yaw motion, which was found by our quantitative analysis through global motion analysis of the original movie.

Averaged discomfort scores of every one minute during watching seemed relatively correlated to relative increment and decrement of each type of global motion. Moreover, the scores overall gradually increased during watching. Therefore, we speculated that there are two types of effects: the transient and sustained effects of VIMS.

## 4 Summary

In the study, we found the following:

1. The effect of reducing pitch and yaw motion from the original motion of the movie shown on site of the VIMS incident happened in Japan in 2003 was larger than the effects reducing same ratio of the other types of motion. This may be related to the fact that the original movie included larger amount of yaw motion, which found based on global motion analysis.
2. Lager display, 34.1 x 25.9 deg, produced larger total scores, and also larger "Disorientation" sub-socres, of SSQ than smaller display, 22.7 x 17.0 deg. This may suggest the discomfort for the larger and smaller displays are pro-duced by mainly different mechanisms.

**Acknowledgement.** This study was subsidized by the Japan Keirin Association through its Promotion funds from KEIRIN RACE and was supported by the Mechanical Social Systems Foundation and the Ministry of Economy, Trade and Industry.

## References

1. Lo, W.T., So, R.H.Y.: Cybersickness in the presence of scene rotational movements along different axes. Applied Ergonomics 32(1), 1–14 (2001)
2. Ujike, H., Ukai, K., Nihei, K.: Survey on Motion Sickness-like Symptoms Provoked by Viewing a Video Movie during Junior High School Class. Displays (submitted).
3. Ujike, H., Yokoi, T., Saida, S.: Effects of virtual body motion on visually-induced motion sickness. In: Proceedings of the 26th Annual International Conference of the IEEE EMBS, pp. 2399–2402 (2004)
4. Ujike, H., Ukai, K., Saida, S.: Effects of motion types and image contents on visu-ally-induced motion sickness. Transactions of the Virtual Reality Society of Japan 9(4), 377–385 (2004)
5. Ujike, H., Kozawa, R., Yokoi, T., Saida, S.: Effects of rotational components of yaw, roll and pitch on visually-induced motion sickness. In: Proceedings of the 11th International Con-ference on Human-Computer Interaction (2004)

# Individualization of Head-Related Transfer Function for Three-Dimensional Virtual Auditory Display: A Review

Song Xu[1], Zhizhong Li[1,*], and Gaviriel Salvendy[1,2]

[1] Department of Industrial Engineering, Tsinghua University, Beijing, 100084, P.R. China
[2] School of Industrial Engineering, Purdue University, West Lafayette, IN 47907-1287, USA
zzli@tsinghua.edu.cn

**Abstract.** This paper sums up the previous research on Head-Related Transfer Function (HRTF) individualization for three-dimensional (3D) virtual auditory display. Papers which involve experiment research, theoretical computation research, and applications of 3D virtual auditory display based on HRTFs have been reviewed. The necessity of HRTF individualization is discussed based on the review of previous experimental comparison between non-individual and individual HRTFs. At last the seven potential methods of individualization of HRTFs are summarized.

**Keywords:** Three-Dimensional Virtual Auditory Display; Head-Related Transfer Function (HRTF); Individualization.

## 1 Introduction

From the viewpoint of human perception, the reality of virtual environment depends on the visual channel, auditory channel, tactual channel, and so on. Compared with visual cues, auditory cues are often given "minimal attention" during the design of virtual environment or simulation [1]. However, auditory cues play an important role in the construction of virtual environment. As one of the important presentation modality of information, auditory display has been widely applied into not only the fields which need both visual and auditory channels such as military training, computer game, geographic information system, control room of nuclear power or chemical plant but also the fields where visual channel is not often used such as the assistance system or navigation system for visually impaired people [2-5]. Except common auditory display, three-dimensional (3D) auditory display is also widely applied in many fields [6]. All kinds of evidences show that the research of 3D auditory display has a promising future.

The construction of 3D auditory display depends on one core technology named Head-Related Transfer Function (HRTF). Currently, non-individual HRTFs are widely used in 3D virtual auditory display. However, some reports suggest that individual HRTF may be necessary in some applications since non-individual HRTFs may cause high error rate and low performance in sound localization. It is therefore of importance to investigate whether HRTFs should be individualized or not and how to

[*] Corresponding author.

R. Shumaker (Ed.): Virtual Reality, HCII 2007, LNCS 4563, pp. 397–407, 2007.

individualize them. This paper aims: 1) to review previous research on the individualization of HRTFs; 2) to discuss the necessity of individualization of HRTFs; 3) to sum up the methods used to individualize HRTF for the design of auditory display. Papers ranging from 1977 to 2006 selected from international journals and conferences have been reviewed which involves experiment research, theoretical computation research, and applications of 3D auditory display.

The rest part of this paper will be arranged as follows: section two introduces the concept and the background of virtual auditory display and HRTFs; section three reviews previous research on HRTFs individualization and discuss the necessity of HRTFs individualization; the methods of individualizing HRTFs are reviewed in section four; the last section is the conclusion of this paper.

## 2 Three-Dimensional Auditory Display and HRTFs

### 2.1 Three-Dimensional Auditory Display

**Virtual Auditory Display.** In real life, the importance of hearing as a spatial sense cannot be "overstated since the auditory field of regard is considerably more extensive than the visual field" [7]. Spatial information has more usually been presented using visual displays because the spatial acuity of the visual channel is much better than that of the auditory channel [8]. The term "auditory display" is associated with the use of both speech and non-speak sound in computational settings to present information to end users [9]. A virtual auditory display (VAD) is a system for generating spatialized sound to a listener [10]. Akio Honda defined a virtual auditory display as a system for generating sounds with spatial positional characteristics and conveying them to a listener [11].

Many researches in difference fields have reflected that the system with auditory display can improve the operator performance [2-3] [12-17]. Even the military standard of the U.S.A., MIL-STD-1472F, points out that auditory display should be preferred to provide under some conditions [18].

**Three-Dimensional Auditory Display.** In complex auditory displays with potentially sonic events occurring simultaneously, it becomes difficult to isolate currently important information. If these events are rendered as if originating from different directions, the separation is made substantially easier [19]. It is so-called three-dimensional (3D) auditory display. Several researches in the fields such as aviation indicate that the performance can be significantly improved in the system with 3D auditory display compared with common auditory display [4-5] [20].

The spatial or 3D aspect of the human perception of sound is one key feature of our sense of hearing that has been underexploited for blind people. 3D Auditory display has many promising applications for navigation in non-visual environment. Some researches have paid attention to this important issue [2] [19] [21-23]. They indicate that auditory navigation is possible without any visual feedback. Another interesting application of 3D sound is for purposes of alerting and attention management in multi-task decision environments [23-24]. With virtual reality being more popularly used in industries such as communication, entertainment, and military training, more and more attention will be paid on the technology of 3D sound.

## 2.2 Head-Related Transfer Function (HRTFs)

Blauert pointed out that "the sound signals in the canals (ear input signals) are the most important input signals to the subject for spatial hearing" [25]. He also pointed out that the quality of spatial hearing could be easily influenced by the change of signals at ears. People can localize a sound position/direction as one of the auditory ability with head-related transfer functions (HRTFs) which is defined as the Fourier transforms of the ratio of the sound pressure at the entrance to that at the center of the head in a free sound field in the frequency domain [26]. The physical structures of the head, external ears and the torso transform the spectrum of a sound as it travels from sound source to the ear canal [27].The physical transform of sound waves is characterized by the concept of HRTF. When a listener hears through headphones sounds that have been filtered with HRTFs measured from his or her own ears, a "virtual acoustic environment" results. The listener feels the sounds appear to originate from well-designed directions in the space surrounding the subject [28].

## 2.3 The Acquisition of Head-Related Transfer Function

The acquisition of accuracy HRTF is crucial to the generation of 3D sound. Basically there are two ways to obtain HRTF data: theoretical computation and experimental measurement.

**Theoretical Computation.** HRTF can be computed according to acoustic diffraction theory based on the simplification of human models such as headless model, spherical head model [29-30], ellipsoidal head model [31], and snowman model [32-33]. The irregular shape of human, especially the complex shape of head and external pinna is not sufficiently considered in these simple models. To consider the irregular shape of human head, external ear and torso, numerical mathematical tools such as BEM (Boundary Element Method) [33-34], NNA (Neural Networks Analysis) [35], Genetic Algorithms [36], and Wavelet Analysis [37] may be used. The accuracy of these computational methods still needs to be improved according to compare with data from experiment measurement [38].

**Experiment Measurement.** Since the first human experiment of HRTF measurement in which 10 subjects participated were measured in 1989 by Wightman [39], the measurement procedures and accuracy have been greatly improved [27] [40-43]. There are a great many databases of HRTFs which are widely used by other researchers: 1) KEMAR HRTF database by MIT Media Laboratory (http://www.media.mit.edu) [44-45]; 2) CIPIC HRTF database by the CIPIC Interface Laboratory of University of California at Davis (http://interface.cipic.ucdavis.edu) [43]; 3)database of HRTFs by the Advanced Acoustic Information Systems Laboratory of Tohoku University of Japan in 2001 (http://www.ais.riec.tohoku.ac.jp); 4) database by Nagoya University in Japan (http://www.itakura.nuee.nagoya-u.ac.jp/hrtf); 5) IRCAM HRTF Database from France (http://www.ircam.fr/equipes/salles/listen/ index.html); 6) database by Kresge Hearing Research Institute of University of Michigan [28]. Other HRTFs databases include the database collected by Shouichi Takane in Japan [46], mannequin database measured by Bovbjerg [42], database measured by Knowles Electronic Manikin for Acoustic Research (KEMAR) [41] and so on. Experimental methods to measure HRTF data have some disadvantages. First, experimental methods need some high-quality environments (e.g. anechoic chamber) and elaborate physical apparatuses (e.g. probe mice phone); second, it is very difficult to get HRTF data at some special directions (e.g. at the point where the elevation is less -50 degree); third, there is too much work to do in order to get individualized HRTF data.

## 3 Why Individualization of HRTFs

### 3.1 Errors Using Non-individual HRTFs

Early studies show that a given subject's judgments of apparent position are determined to some extent by "idiosyncratic features" of that subject's own HRTFs [47-49]. Kistler [49] analyzed the HRTF of 10 subjects at 265 different positions using principal components analysis (PCA). The validation experiment suggests that subjects normally resolve front-back and up-down ambiguities by analyzing the fine spectral detail provided by their own HRTFs. The unmatched HRTFs may influence the performance of listeners. The influence of sound location resulted from unmatched head size was investigated by Xie [50]. The result implies that an unmatched listener's head size is one of the main causes of side image direction distortion in virtual sound reproduction. One location experiment using non-individualized head-related transfer function measured from 16 subjects was conducted by Wenzel [51]. The result reveals that most listeners showed high rates of front-back and up-down confusions that increased significantly for virtual sources with non-individualized HRTF compared to the free-field stimuli.

### 3.2 Comparison Experiments

Whether the individual HRTFs can significantly improve sound localization performance or not should be further investigated by comparison experiments.

M¢ller presented a localization experiment, in which 20 subjects listened to binaural recordings whose HRTFs were from the ears of 30 humans [52]. The result indicates that the recordings with a random subject can produce high error rate in sound location. Although the "typical" HRTF can reduce error rate, it is still high compared with that in real life. In another experiment M¢ller compared the real-life listening, individual binaural, non-individual binaural, and mixed binaural listening by four types error (cone of confusion error, out-of-cone error, within-cone error, median-plane error, and distance error). The experiment result shows that: 1) individual binaural recordings are capable of giving an authentic reproduction for which localization performance is preserved when compared to that of real life; 2) nonindividual recordings also result in an increased number of distance errors, although this effect is less pronounced than increase of median-plane errors; 3) use of nonindividual recordings results in an increased number of median-plane error occurring not only in terms of movements to nearby directions but also to directions further away [53].

Middlebrooks compared virtual localization performance under conditions in which virtual audio was synthesized by targets' own ears and from the ears of other subjects. The experiment result shows that in other-ear conditions, all error measures tended to increase in proportion to the inter-subject differences in DTFs (Directional

Transfer Functions which examines inter-subject differences in the directional components of subjects' HRTFs) [28].

Experiments including 12 subjects were conducted by Väljamäe. The results show a significant increase in presence ratings of individualized binaural stimuli compared to responses to stimuli processed with generic HRTFs [54].

The evaluation of performance by artificial head was conducted. The results showed that the best artificial head had an error rate of 37% in the median plane. Also the best human heads performed with an error rate of 32% compared with the real life error rate of 10%. There was a large difference between the performance of different artificial-head and human head recordings with the real life condition [52] [55-56].

In conclusion all evidences listed above indicate that HRTFs vary significantly from listener to listener. Dramatic perceptual distortions can occur when one listens to sounds spatialized with non-individualized HRTF. From theoretical analysis and experiment validation, individualized HRTF can increase the location cues which are necessary for the reduction of spatial location error, especially at the elevation location. Therefore, it is necessary to individualize the HRTFs.

# 4 The Methods of Individualize HRTFs

The methods getting individual HRTFs draw some attention from researchers. According to literatures dozens of studies have explored the solutions to individualize HRTFs. In summing up it may be stated in the following methods:

*(1) The direct HRTF measuremen:* The method can get the most accurate HRTF, but it is the most time-consuming. It is not feasible to measure every consumer's HRTF before the costumer use virtual auditory products based on HRTF technology [57]. Hence this method is not practical for commercial use.

*(2) Partial individualization by averaging HRTFs or using typical HRTFs:* Averaged HRTF is partially individualized HRTF compared with randomly using HRTFs of other's. It can be obtained by averaging the HRTFs measured from real persons. The second partial individualized HRTFs can be obtained using typical mannequin [45]. The third way is by theoretical computation based on geometric models such as spherical model, snow man model and so on [58-59].

*(3) Individualization by subjective selection*: In this method individual HRTF can be obtained by listener's subjective selection. Two methods were found in literature. Two selection-steps method proposed by Seeber is one subjective selection method which gives random access to sounds filtered with HTTFs [60]. In a first selection step a group of HRTFs is chosen out of which a final HRTF is singled out in a second step according to multiple criteria. The results show that the selection minimizes the variance of the localization responses and the number of inside-the-head localizations. Localization error as well as the number of front-back confusions is small [60]. DOMISO (Determination method of Optimum Impulse-response by Sound Orientation is proposed by Saito in which listeners are asked to choose their most suitable HRTFs from among many HRTF data based on tournament-style listening tests [61]. Validity experiments show that the virtual sound localization performance listening using HRTFs fitted with this method was similar to the performance of subjects using their own HRTFs [10] [61]. The differences in sound localization performance for

real sound sources between the fitted HRTFs and their own HRTFs is also investigated [11]. The result of experiment in which 40 subjects participated shows that sound localization performance using fitted HRTFs was similar to performance using own HRTFs. DOMISO has some advantages as follows: 1) the task for a listener is simple and little physical restriction exists; 2) the time cost for individualization is very short compared with the measurement of listener' HRTFs; 3) an additional signal compensation is not required because of the use of the VAD system to be individualized in DOMISO [10].

*(4) Individualization by scaling/grouping non-individual HRTFs*: Compared with direct measurement of HRTF, grouping non-individual HRTFs, is one tradeoff method to provide relative individualized HRTFs. Experiments conducted by Wightman shows that the several alternative sets of HRTFs are necessary to produce a usable auditory system [62].

*(5) Individualization by theoretical computation:* The individual HRTF can be also obtained by theoretical computation based on the individualized anthropometry [31] [43] [63]. This method sounds very easy and feasible; however, compared with experimental method it is not very accurate because the method of theoretical computation bases on simplified geometric models (irregular model needs efficiency algorithm) [38]. It is not easy to consider complex anthropometry parameters in computation method.

*(6) Indirect individualization by physical features:* Wenzel studied the individual differences in sound localization [48]. The result shows that although listeners are uniformly accurate when judging source azimuth, individual differences are the greatest in judgment of source elevation. Further research founds that a listener's accuracy in judging source elevation can be predicted from an analysis of the acoustic characteristics of the listener's outer ears. The researcher believes that many of the individual differences in localization behavior are traceable to individual differences in outer-ear acoustics. Hence, individual HRTF can be indirectly obtained using a certain level of correlation between similarity of physical shapes and similarity of HRTFs between individuals [35] [57] [64-66]. For example, the method can individualize HRTF by the relationship between human's anthropometric data and HRTF features. However, how to choose the anthropometric parameters and validate the method is worth further study.

*(7) Individualization by tuning:* Active Sensory Tuning (AST) is a general technique for searching through large multidimensional parameters spaces to optimize subjective criteria. Runkle proposed the model and presented the use of AST in fitting generic HRTFs to individual listeners in spatialized audio [67]. Another similar method proposed by Andreas Silzle pointed that the tuning and selection of HRTF by tuning experts can be done individually for every wanted direction [68]. The resulting HRTFs have clearly reduced coloration and improved global localization although.

## 5 Conclusions

The paper reviews the previous research on HRTF individualization and discusses the necessity of HRTF individualization and the potential methods according to literatures. Almost seventy papers ranging from 1977 to 2006 selected from international journals and conferences have been reviewed. They involve experiment research, theoretical computation research, and applications of 3D virtual auditory display based on HRTFs. Experiment researches show that the use of non-individual HRTF can cause high error rate and low performance. The comparison experiments by a few studies show that it is necessary to individualize HRTF in order to obtain accuracy localization and high quality auditory display. Seven potential methods are summarized. Generally speaking, 3D virtual auditory display has promising further; however, there is large room to improve the current methods if they are applied in commercial fields due to the problems such as high complexity, low accuracy, and convenience.

## References


1. Stanney, K.M.: Handbook of Virtual Environment. Lawrence Erlbaum Associates, Inc., (1999) (update on 13th October, 2006) http://vehand.engr.ucf.edu/handbook
2. Loomis, J.M., Golledge, R.G., Klatzky, R.L.: Navigation System for the Blind: Auditory Display Modes and Guidance. Presence: Teleoperators and Virtual Environments 7(2), 193–203 (1998)
3. Holland, S., Morse, D., Gedenryd, H.: AudioGPS: Spatial Audio Navigation with a Minimal Attention Interface. Personal and Ubiquitous Computing 6(4), 253–259 (2002)
4. Simpson, B.D., Brungart, D.S., Gilkey, R.H., Cowgill, J.L., Dallman, R.C., Green, R.F.: 3D Auditory Cueing for Target Identification in a Simulated Flight Task. In: Human Factors and Ergonomics Society (HFES), 2004 Annul Meeting (2004)
5. Veltman, J.A., Oving, A.B., Bronkhorst, A.W.: 3-D Audio in Fighter Cockpit Improves Task Performance. The International Journal of Aviation Psychology 14(3), 239–256 (2004)
6. Oving, A.B., Veltman, J.A., Bronkhorst, A.W.: Effectiveness of 3-D Audio for Warnings in the Cockpit. The International Journal of Aviation Psychology 14(3), 257–276 (2004)
7. Bolia, R.S.: Special Issues: Spatial Audio Displays for Military Aviation. The. International Journal of Aviation Psychology 14(3), 233–238 (2004)
8. Shinn-Cunningham, B.: Applications of Virtual Auditory Displays. In: Proceedings of the 20th international Conference of the IEEE Engineering in Biology and Medicine Society,1998, vol. 20 (3), pp. 1105–1108 (1998)
9. Dereck, B., Ballas, J.A., McClimens, B.: Perceptual Issues for the Use of 3D Auditory Displays in Operational Environments. In: ACM International Conference Proceeding Series; Proceedings of the 1st International Symposium on Information and Communication Technologies (Session: HCI), Dublin, Ireland, 2003 vol.49, pp. 445–448 (2003)
10. Iwaya, Y.: Individualization of Head-related Transfer Functions with Tournament-style Listening Test: Listening with Other's Ears. Acoustical Science and Technology 27(6), 340–343 (2006)
11. Honda, A., Shibata, H., Gyoba, J., Saitou, K., Iwaya, Y., Suzuki, Y.: Transfer Effects on Sound Localization Performances from Playing a Virtual Three-Dimensional Auditory Game. Applied Acoustics, pp.1–12 Doi: 10.1016 (in press, 2006)
12. Veitenruber, J.E.: Design Criteria for Aircraft Warning, Caution, and Advisory Alerting Systems. Journal of Aircraft 15, 574–581 (1978)
13. Blatner, M.M., Sumikawa, D.A., Greenberg, R.M.: Earcons and icons: Their Structures and Common Design Principles. Human Computer Interaction 4, 11–44 (1989)

14. Begault, D.R., Wenzel, E.M.: Techniques and Applications for Binaural Sound Manipulation in Human-Machine Interfaces. International Journal of Aviation Psychology 2(1), 1–22 (1992)
15. Gaver, W.W.: Using and Creating Auditory Icons. In: Kramer, G. (ed.) Auditory Display: Sonification, Auditfication, and Auditory Interfaces, Addison-Wesley, London, UK (1994)
16. Brock, D., McClimens, B.: Cognitive Models of the Effect of Audio Cueing on Attentional Shifts in a Complex Multimodal Dual-Display Dual-Task. In: Proceedings of the 28th Annual Meeting of the Cognitive Science Society, Vancouver, BC, 2006 (2006)
17. Walker, B.N., Lindsay, J.: Navigation Performance with a Virtual Auditory Display: Effects of Beacon Sound, Capture Radius, and Practice. Human Factors 48(2), 265–278 (2006)
18. MIL-STD-1472F, Human Engineering Design Criteria for Military Systems Equipment and Facilities. pp. 42–53 (1999)
19. Cooper, M., Petrie, H.: Three-Dimensional Auditory Display: Issue in Applications for Visually Impaired Students. In: Proceedings of ICAD 04-Tenth Meeting of the International Conference on Auditory Display, Sydney, Australia, 2004 (2004)
20. Brock, D., Stroup, J.L., Ballas, J.A.: Effects of 3D Auditory Display on Dual Task Performance in a Simulated Multiscreen Watchstation Environment. In: Proceedings of the Human Factors and Ergonomics Society 46th Annul Meeting, pp. 1570–1573 (2002)
21. Cooper, M., Pearson, M.D., Petrie, H.: The Computer Synthesis and Reproduction of 3D Sound Environments research towards an implementation for blind students. In: Proceeding of Audio Engineering Society 16th International Conference on Spatial Sound Reproduction, Rovaniemi, Finland, 1999 (1999)
22. Keating, D.A.: The Generation of Virtual Acoustic Environments for Blind People. In: Proceeding of 1st European Conference on Disability, Virtual Reality and Associated Technologies, Maidenhead, UK, 1996, pp. 201–207 (1996)
23. Lokki, T., Gröhn, M.: Navigation with Auditory Cues in a Virtual Environment. IEEE Multimedia 12(2), 80–86 (2005)
24. Ballas, J.A., Kieras, D.E., Meyer, D.E., Brock, D., Stroup, J.: Cueing of Display Objects by 3D Audio to Reduce Automation Deficit. In: Proceedings of the Fourth Annual Symposium on Situational Awareness in the Tactical Environment, Patuxent River, MD, 1999 (1999)
25. Blauert, J.: Spatial Hearing, pp. 78–89. MIT Press, Cambridge, MA, England (1997)
26. Blauert, J.: Spatial Hearing: The Psychophysics of Human Sound Localization (Revised edition). The MIT Press, Cambridge, Mass (1996)
27. Middlebrooks, J.C.: Individual Differences in External-ear Transfer Functions Reduced by Scaling in Frequency. Journal of the Acoustical Society of America 106(3), 1480–1492 (1999)
28. Middlebrooks, J.C.: Virtual Localization Improved by Scaling Non-individualized External-Ear Transfer Functions in Frequency. Journal of the Acoustic Society of America 106(3), 1493–1510 (1999)
29. Cooper, D.H.: Calculator Program for Head-Related Transfer Function. Journal of the Audio Engineering Society 30(1/2), 34–38 (1982)
30. Duda, R.O., Martens, W.L.: Range Dependence of the Response of a Spherical Head Model. Journal of the Acoustic Society of America 104(5), 3048–3058 (1998)
31. Algazi, V.R., Duda, R.O., Thompson, D.M.: Use of Head-and Torso Methods for Improved Spatial sound Synthesis. In: Proceeding of AES 113th Convention, Los Angeles, CA, 2002 (2002)

32. Gumerov, N.A., Duraiswami, R.: Modeling the Effect of a Nearby Boundary on the HRTF. In: Proceedings of the 2001 IEEE International Conference on Acoustic, Speech, and Signal, 2001 vol.5, pp. 3337–3340 (2001)
33. Gumerov, N.A., Duraiswami, R., Tang, Z.H.: Numerical Study of the Influence of the Torso on the HRTF. In: Proceedings of IEEE International Conference on Acoustics, Speech, and Signal Processing (ICASSP '02), Orlando, Florida, 2002 pp. 1965–1968 (2002)
34. Katz, B.F.G.: Boundary Element Method Calculation of Individual Head-related Transfer Function (I): Rigid Model Calculation. Journal of the Acoustic Society of America 110(5), 2440–2448 (2001)
35. Lemaire, V., Clérot, F., Busson, S., Choqueuse, V.: Individualized HRTFs from Few Measurements: a Statistical Learning Approach. In: Proceedings of International Joint Conference on Neural Networks, Montreal, Canada, July 31-August 4, 2005 pp. 2041–2046 (2005)
36. Cheung, N.M., Trautmann, S., Horner, A.: Head-related Transfer Function Modeling in 3-D Sound System with Genetic Algorithms. Journal of the Audio Engineering of Society 46(6), 531–539 (1998)
37. Lo, T.F., Wu, Z.Y., Chan, F.H.Y., Lam, F.K., Chan, J.C.K.: Wavelet Analysis of Head-Related Transfer Functions. In: Proceedings of the 20th Annual International Conference of the IEEE Engineering in Medicine and Biology Society, Hong Kong, P. R. China, 1998, vol.20 (3), pp. 1549–1552 (1998)
38. Cheng, C.I., Wakefield, G.H.: Introduction to Head-Related Transfer Functions (HRTFs): Representations of HRTFs in Time, Frequency, and Space. Journal of the Audio Engineering Society 49(4), 231–249 (2001)
39. Wightman, F.L., Kistler, D.J.: Headphone Simulation of Free-Field Listening. I: Stimulus Synthesis. Journal of the Acoustic Society of America 85(2), 858–867 (1989)
40. Wightman, F.L., Kistler, D.J.: Headphone Simulation of Free-Field Listening. II: Psychophysical Validation. Journal of the Acoustic Society of America 85(2), 868–878 (1989b)
41. Brungart, D.S., Rabinowitz, W.M.: Auditory Localization of Nearby Sources Head-Related Transfer Functions. Journal of Acoustic Society of America 106(3), 1465–1479 (1999)
42. Bovbjerg, B.P., Christensen, F., Minnaar, P., Chen, X.: Measuring the Head Related Transfer Functions for an Artificial Head with a High Directional Resolution. 109 AES Convention (2000)
43. Algazi, V.R., Duda, R.O., Thompson, D.M., Avendano, C.: The CIPIC HRTF Database, In: IEEE Workshop on Applications of Signal Processing to Audio and Acoustics, New Paltz, New York, USA, October 21-24, 2001, pp. 99–102 (2001)
44. Gardner, B., Martin, K.: HRTF Measurements of a KEMAR Dummy-Head Microphone, MIT Media Lab Perceptual Computing Technical Report #280, (1994) (update on October13th, 2006) http://www.media.mit.edu
45. Gardner, W.G., Martin, K.D.: HRTF Measurement of A KEMAR. Journal of the Acoustic Society of America 97(6), 3907–3908 (1995)
46. Takane, S., Suzuki, Y., Miyajima, T., Sone, T.: A New Method for High Definition Virtual Acoustic Display. In: Proceedings of the 8th International Conference on Auditory Display 2002, pp. 213–218 (2002)
47. Bulter, R.A., Belendiuk, K.: Spectral Cues Utilized in the Localization of Sound in the Median Sagittal Plane, vol. 61, pp. 1264–1269 (1977)

48. Wenzel, E., Wightman, F., Kistler, D., Foster, S.: Acoustic Origins of Individual Differences in Sound Localization Behavior. Journal of the Acoustic Society of America 84 (Suppl.1S79) (1988)
49. Kistler, D.J., Wightman, F.L.: A Model of Head-Related Transfer Function Based on Principal Components Analysis and Minimum-Phase Reconstruction. Journal of the Acoustic Society of America 91(3), 1637–1647 (1992)
50. Xie, B.S.: Effect of Head Size on Virtual Sound Image Localization. Applied Acoustics 21(5), 1–7 (2002)
51. Wenzel, E.M., Arruda, M., Kistler, D.J., Wightman, F.L.: Localization Using Nonindividualized Head-Related Transfer Functions. Journal of the Acoustic Society of America 94(1), 111–123 (1993)
52. Møller, H., Jensen, C.B., Hammershøi, D., Sørensen, M.F.: Using a Typical Human Subject for Binaural Recording, In: 100th Auditory Engineering Society Convention, Copenhagen, May 11-14 1996 (1996)
53. Møller, H., Sørensen, M.F., Jensen, C.B.: Binaural Technique: Do We Need Individual Recordings. Journal of Audio Engineering Society 44(6), 451–469 (1996)
54. Väljamäe, A., Larsson, P., Västfjäll, D., Kleiner, M.: Auditory Presence, Individualized Head-Related Transfers Functions, and Illusory Ego-Motion in Virtual Environments, In: Proceedings of Seventh Annual Workshop Presence 2004, Valencia, Spain, 2004, pp. 141–147 (2004)
55. Møller, H., Sørensen, M.F., Hammershgi, D.H, Jensen, C.B.: Head Related Transfer Function of Human Subjects. Journal of the Audio Engineering Society 43(5) (1995)
56. Minnaar, P.J., Olesen, S.K., Christensen, F., Møller, H.: Localization with Binaural Recordings from Artificial and Human Heads. Journal of the Audio Engineering Society 49(5), 323–336 (2001)
57. Zotkin, D.N., Duraiswami, R., Davis, L.S.: HRTF Personalization Using Anthropometric Measurements, In: IEEE Workshop on Applications of Signal Processing to Audio and Acoustics, New Paltz N.Y, 2003 pp. 157–160 (2003)
58. Duda, R.O.: Modeling Head Related Transfer Functions. In: Proceeding of Twenty-Seventh Annual Asilomar Conference on Signals, Systems and Computers, Asilomar CA, USA 1993, vol. 2, pp. 996–1000 (1993)
59. Algazi, V.R., Duda, R.O.: Estimation of A Spherical-Head Model from Anthropometry. Journal of Audio Engineering Society 49(6), 472–478 (2001)
60. Seeber, B., Fastl, H.: Subjective Selection of Non-individual Head-Related Transfer Functions, In: Proceeding of ICAD 2003, pp. 259–262 (2003)
61. Saito, K.Y., Iwaya, Y., Suzuki.: The Technique of Choosing the Individualized Head-Related Transfer Function Based on Localization. Technical Report of IEICE 2004, vol. (104), pp. 1–6 (2004)
62. Wightman, F.L., Kistler, D.J.: Multidimensional Scaling Analysis of Head-Related Transfer Functions, In: IEEE Workshop on Applications of Signal Processing to Audio and Acoustics, 17-20 October 1993, pp. 98–101 (1993)
63. Terai, K., Kakuhari, I.: HRTF Calculation with Less Influence from 3-D Modeling Error: Making a Physical Human Head Model from Geometric 3-D Data. Acoustical Science and Technology 24(5), 333–334 (2003)
64. Zotkin, D.N., Duraiswami, R., Davis, L.S., Mohan, A., Raykar, V.: Virtual Audio System Customization Using Visual Matching of Ear Parameters. In: Proceedings of IEEE 16th International Conference on Pattern Recognition 2002 vol. 3, pp. 1003–1006 (2002)

65. Jin, C., Leong, P., Leung, J., Corderoy, A., Carlile, S.: Enabling Individualized Virtual Auditory Space Using Morphological Measurements. In: Proceeding of the First IEEE Pacific-Rim Conference on Multimedia (International Symposium on Multimedia Information), pp. 235–238 (2000)
66. Inoue, N., Kimura, T., Nishino, T., Itou, K., Takeda, K.: Evaluation of HRTFs Estimated Using Physical Features. Acoustical Science and Technology 26(5), 453–455 (2005)
67. Runkle, P., Yendiki, A.: Gregory H. Wakefield, Active Sensory Tuning for Immersive Spatialized Audio. In: Proceeding of International Conference on Auditory Display (ICAD 2000), Atlanta, GA (2000)
68. Silzle, A.: Selection and Tuning of HRTFs, AES 112th Convention, Munich, Germany, May 10-13, pp. 1–14 (2002)

# Facial Expression Recognition Based on Hybrid Features and Fusing Discrete HMMs

Yongzhao Zhan and Gengtao Zhou

School of Computer Science and Telecommunication Engineering, Jiangsu University, Zhenjiang 212013, Jiangsu, China
yzzhan@ujs.edu.cn, zhougengtao@163.com

**Abstract.** Most of facial expression recognition methods generally use single feature extraction method currently. These methods can not extract effective features for each feature area. A method of facial expression recognition based on hybrid features and fusing discrete HMMs is presented in this paper. In this method, texture feature for the eye area is extracted by using Gabor wavelet transformation, and shape variety feature for the mouth area is extracted by using AAM. In the process of recognition, discrete HMM is adopted for expression recognition in each expression area respectively. The recognition results are fused by means of integrating the probability of each expression in each area with its weight obtained by contribution analysis algorithm, and the final expression is determined as which with the maximal probability. Experiments show that our method can get high recognition rate.

**Keywords:** pattern recognition, facial expression recognition, hybrid feature extraction, Gabor wavelet transformation, active appearance model.

## 1 Introduction

Expression recognition is the basis of emotion understanding, and it is one of the effective approaches for computer to understand human emotion. Automatic facial expression recognition has many potential applications in areas such as human-computer interaction, emotion analysis, interactive video, indexing and retrieval of image and video database, image understanding and synthetic face animation.

Facial expression recognition is to classify expression according to the movement feature and deformation feature of face based on vision characteristic. Expression results in facial deformation consequentially, and Facial deformation includes the information of expression classification. If we want to get the expression information, we must get the facial deformation information firstly. Facial deformation includes two aspects: facial texture variety and facial shape variety. In 1990s, with the development of techniques of facial detection and recognition, the techniques of facial expression recognition developed quickly. The existing methods for facial expression recognition usually only use one kind of the feature described above, that is texture variety feature or shape variety feature [1-2], and these methods can not give attention to two kinds features. At the same time, the texture variety feature is obvious than shape variety feature in some

R. Shumaker (Ed.): Virtual Reality, HCII 2007, LNCS 4563, pp. 408–417, 2007.

feature areas such as areas of eye and eyebrow, but in other feature areas such as area of mouth shape variety feature is obvious than the texture variety feature. So if we only use one kind of the features, we can not recognize facial expression effectively. In this paper, we present a method of facial expression recognition based on hybrid features and fusing discrete HMMs. We use different methods to extract expression features for different expression areas and use HMM to recognize expression in each expression area respectively first. Then we fuse each probability of expression in each expression area by the weight obtained by contribution analysis algorithm. Finally, we use the expression with maximal probability as the recognition result.

## 2 Expression Image Preprocessing

Expression image preprocessing includes face sub-image segmentation, circumrotation revision and image normalization. There are many methods for face detection by far [3], because the emphasis of this paper is facial expression feature extraction and facial expression recognition, not face detection. We use Adaboost algorithm [4] to detect face sub-image. Because some times eyes may close, in this paper we use the position of the two eyebrows to fix on the angle should to rotate in the process of circumrotation revision.

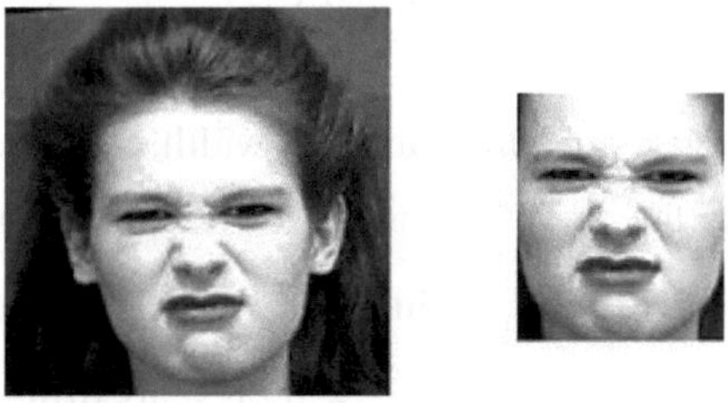

**Fig. 1.** Result of expression image preprocessing

Grayscale equalization is to eliminate the influence due to illumination variety and ethnicity. Although the extracted features based on Gabor transformation is not insensitive to illumination variety, grayscale equalization can improve the results. This task can he achieved by amending grayscale histogram to change the mean of the gray values of images and square error. The histogram amending equation is as below:

$$\overline{I}(x,y) = \frac{\sigma_0}{\sigma}\left(I(x,y) - \mu\right) + \mu_0, \tag{1}$$

where $I(x, y)$ and $\overline{I}(x, y)$ are the intensities of pixel (x,y) before and after grayscale equalization respectively, $\mu_0, \sigma_0$ are the mean and the covariance value of the equalized image, and $\mu$ , $\sigma$ are those values of the original image. By grayscale equalization, all the values of the mean and covariance of the different gray-value image can be adjusted to the same. The goal of scale normalization, which can be implemented by the strategy based on bilinear interpolation, is to transform the expression sub-images into ones with normal size so as to extract expression features conveniently and easily. The expression image preprocessing result is shown in Fig.1.

## 3 Hybrid Feature Extraction

In this paper, for the areas that have obvious texture variety feature such as areas of eye and eyebrow, we use Gabor wavelet transformation to extract their texture feature, and for the areas that have obvious shape variety feature such as area of mouth, we use active appearance model to extract their shape variety feature.

### 3.1 Feature Extraction for Areas of Eyes and Eyebrows Based on Gabor Wavelet Transformation

A Gabor filter is a complex sinusoid modulated by a 2D Gaussian function and is an important tool for signal processing in space and frequency fields. 2D Gabor wavelet transformation has wide applications in such research areas as image processing and pattern recognition etc.

A 2D Gabor wavelet kernel function is defined as equation (2):

$$\Psi_j\left(\vec{k},\vec{x}\right)=\frac{\left|\vec{k}_j\right|}{\sigma^2}\exp\left(-\frac{\left|\vec{k}_j\right|^2\left|\vec{x}\right|^2}{2\sigma^2}\right)\left(\exp\left(i\vec{k}_j\times\vec{x}\right)-\exp\left(-\frac{\sigma^2}{2}\right)\right), \tag{2}$$

where $i$ stands for complex operation and the width of kernels is controlled by the parameter $\sigma = 2\pi$ . $\vec{k}_j$ is the wave vector and different Gabor wavelet functions can be defined by selecting different values of $\vec{k}_j$ . The vector $\vec{k}_j$ is defined as: $\vec{k}_j = k_v\left(cosj, sinj\right)^T$ , where $k_v = 2^{-(v+2)/2}\pi$ represents different frequency of a kernel wavelet and $\varphi$ represents the orientation of Gabor wavelet. Because expression features are mainly described by high frequency components, we employ a discrete set of 3 different higher frequencies, indexing $v = 0,1,2$ , and six orientations, indexing $j = \frac{\pi}{6},\frac{2\pi}{6},\frac{3\pi}{6},\frac{4\pi}{6},\frac{5\pi}{6},\pi$ . Thus, we have defined a family of $3\times6$ Gabor wavelet kernel functions to extract expression features.

Gabor wavelet transformation at one lattice is defined as a convolution as below;

$$G_j=\Psi_j\left(\vec{k},\vec{x}\right)*I\left(\vec{x}\right)=\iint\Psi_j\left(\vec{k},\vec{x}\right)I\left(\vec{x}\right)dxdy\ , \tag{3}$$

where $I\left(\vec{x}\right)$ represents gray-level lattice image and $\Psi_j$ is No.j kernel function and $\vec{x} = \left(x, y\right)$ represents the coordinates of a given pixel. The results of transformation are described by complex values, so we can calculate their amplitudes as the final transformation results.

We must fix on the region that will be executed by Gabor wavelet transformation before feature extraction. In this paper, we use the method based on gray information and Harris corner detection [5] to detect the position of the two eyes, and select a region that includes the eye and eyebrow according to the position of eyes, here the region is $100 \times 35$, and execute Gabor wavelet transformation in the selected region. We select $5 \times 5$ grid as transformation unit, shown in Fig. 2, and use the module of transformation result as feature parameter. For the texture feature extracted by Gabor wavelet, every frame includes $20 \times 7$ feature parameters. Assume there are 10 frames in every expression sequences, so there are 1400 feature parameters in a total. We adopt these feature parameters to train the model of the eye and eyebrow, and to get six probabilities of belonging to the 6 expressions.

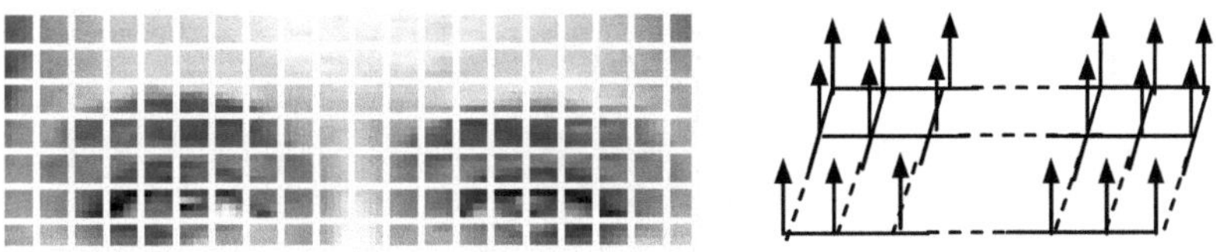

**Fig. 2.** The latticing of eyes region and the feature vector graph based on Gabor wavelet transformation

### 3.2 Feature Extraction for the Area of Mouth Based on Active Appearance Model

Active Appearance Model (AAM) is to build objects' shape and appearance model through statistical study for objects' shape and texture. It derives from ASM, but it needs training of object's texture. ASM is presented by Cootes [6] first. ASM build shape model through studying the shape information of the training samples, and it does not consider enough for the object's texture information (color or gray information). But AAM consider this problem, and it can obtain better detection result through training the shape and texture information of the model.

AAM is an optimizing problem. It synthesizes the appearance model from the image and model parameters, and minimizes the difference between the model's appearance and actual image through adjusting the model's parameters. The difference vector is defined as: $\delta I = I_i - I_m$, here $I_i$ is the texture vector of current image, $I_m$ is the texture vector for synthetic model. In order to get the optimizing model matching the image, we minimize the gray difference vector $\Delta = |\delta I|^2$ through adjusting the model's parameters. Because the model may have many parameters, and this causes the optimizing problem to a multi-dimension optimizing problem. Usually select iteration algorithm to minimize model's parameter $\Delta$.

In order to reduce the searching region of AAM and reduce computing, we use the position of eye fixed by using the method mentioned above as the initial search position. Fig. 3 shows the result of AAM. After detecting the position of mouth, we select the height and width of the mouth stretched, the horizontal and vertical displacement of the left and right corner of the mouth, and the vertical displacement of the middle point of upper and lower lips as the feature parameters of the mouth region. Definition of feature vector for the mouth area is shown in Table 1. For the shape variety features extracted through AAM, every frame includes 8 feature parameters. Assume there are 10 frames in every expression sequences, so there are 80 feature parameters in an expression sequence. We adopt these feature parameters to train the model of the mouth region, and to get six probabilities of belonging to the 6 expressions.

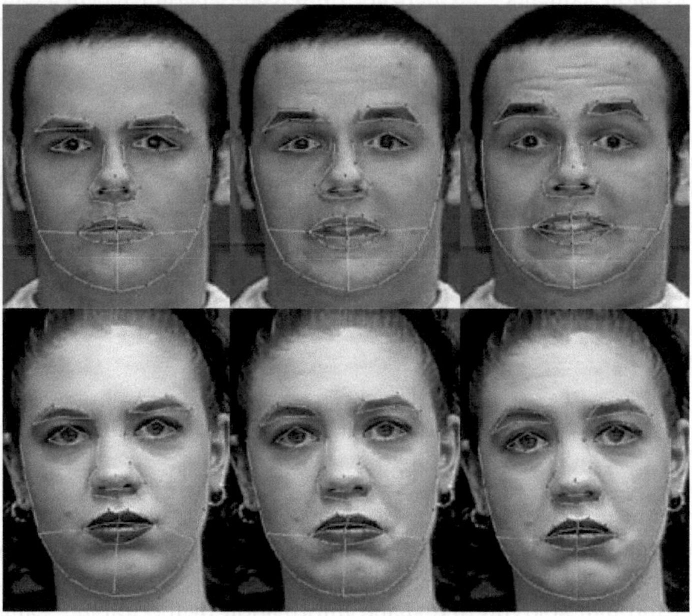

**Fig. 3.** Detection result of AAM

**Table 1.** Definition of feature vector for the mouth area

| dimension | physical meaning | dimension | physical meaning |
|---|---|---|---|
| 1 | width of mouth | 5 | vertical displacement of middle point of upper lip |
| 2 | height of mouth | 6 | vertical displacement of middle point of lower lip |
| 3 | vertical displacement of left mouth corner | 7 | horizontal displacement of left mouth corner |
| 4 | vertical displacement of right mouth corner | 8 | horizontal displacement of right mouth corner |

# 4 Facial Expression Recognition Based on Hybrid Features and Fusing Discrete HMMs

Hidden Markov Model is composed of two stochastic processes, one is inherent limited Morkov chain, and the other is stochastic process of observation vector correlating with the each state of Morkov chain. The two stochastic processes associate to each other, and describe the statistical characteristic of signal synchronously. The characteristic of Morkov chain is opened out by signal observed. Because the image sequences have some time interval, the extracted features from the image sequences are also discrete. In order to correctly classify the discrete features, we use discrete HMM as a feature classification model.

A standard Hidden Markov Model can be denoted by five parameters [7]:

$$\lambda = (N, M, \pi, A, B). \tag{4}$$

Here, $N$ is the state number of model, $q$ denotes the state in time $t$, $1 \le q_t \le N, 1 \le t \le T$, $T$ is the length of observation sample sequence.

$M$ is the observation number of each state, assume $o_t$ is the possible observation in time $t$, so $0 \le o_t \le M-1$.

$\pi_N$ is initial state distributing probability, it is a $N$ dimension vector, $\pi = \{\pi_i\}$, here $\pi_i = P(q_1 = i), 1 \le i \le N$.

$A_{N\times N}$ is state transition matrix, denotes the probability form state $i$ to state $j$, $A = \{a_{ij}\}$, here $a_{ij} = P(q_{t=j} / q_{t-1} = i), 1 \le i, j \le N$, and they must meet $a_{ij} \ge 0, \sum_{j-1}^{N} a_{ij} = 1, \quad 1 \le i \le N$.

$B_{M\times N}$ is observation probability matrix, denotes the probability of $o_t$ in time $t$ and state $j$, $B = \{b_j(o_t)\}$, here, $b_j(o_t) = P(Ot = ot / qt = j)$, $1 \le j \le M, 0 \le ot \le M-1$ and $b_j(o_t) \ge 0, \quad 1 \le j \le N$, in the same time $\sum_{o_t=0}^{M-1} b_j(o_t) = 1, 1 \le j \le N$.

Usually let $\lambda$ denote the parameters of HMM, it includes an initial state distributing vector and two probability matrixes, $\lambda = (\pi, A, B)$. In order to describe the actual temporal process, we must build HMM accurately, that is to determine the parameter $\lambda$. Parameter $\lambda$ of HMM can be calculated by the probability value $P(O / \lambda)$, this probability is needed when calculating the back probability, here $O = (o_1, o_2, \ldots o_T)$ is observation sample sequence. We select $T$ frame expression images from neutral frame to maximal expression frame as an expression image sequence. In order to calculate the probability $P(O / \lambda)$, we must select the state number $N$ and the observation number $M$, and then calculate the initial probability distributing vector, state transition matrix and observation probability matrix.

In this paper, we select $N = 4$. Considering the generality of our model, that is the expression is not always change from neutral frame to maximal expression frame, the expression state can skip among each other, the topological structure of our HMM is shown in Fig. 4, which makes the state can transit from each other. At the same time, because we assume the expression always from neutral frame, so we confine the initial probability vector, that is $\pi_i = 1 (i = 0), \pi_i = 0 (i \neq 0, i < N)$. Because the key points of mouth can move along the negative direction X-axes or Y-axes of the image, the observations we obtain are negative. These observations can not directly input to HMM. We must normalize them to the range of $[0, M-1]$.

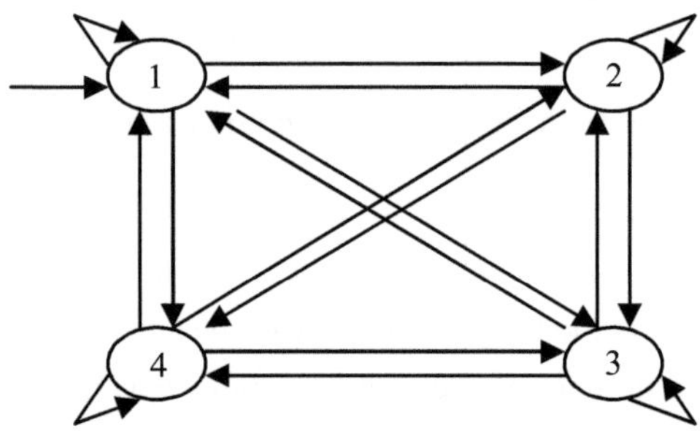


**Fig. 4.** Topological structure of our HMM

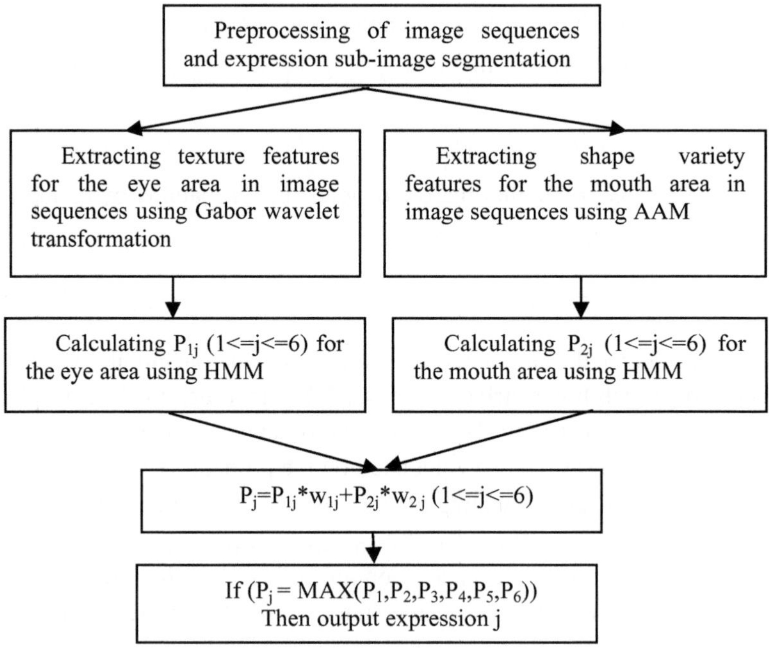


**Fig. 5.** Scheme chart of expression recognition

**Table 2.** Weights for each expression areas

| weight | angry | sad | disgust | happy | fear | surprise |
|---|---|---|---|---|---|---|
| Mouth area $\omega_1$ | 0.57 | 0.55 | 0.41 | 0.29 | 0.34 | 0.50 |
| Eye area $\omega_2$ | 0.43 | 0.45 | 0.59 | 0.71 | 0.66 | 0.50 |

The process of facial expression recognition is shown in Fig. 5. We preprocess the testing image sequences and segment expression sub-images such as eye area, mouth area fist. Then we extract texture features for the eye area in image sequences using Gabor wavelet transformation and extract shape variety features for the mouth area in image sequences using AAM parallel. After that, we use HMM to recognize expression in each expression area respectively, and then fuse each probability of expression in each expression area by the weight obtained by contribution analysis algorithm. Finally, we use the expression with maximal probability as the recognition result. Assume the probability of the expression in each expression area is $p_{ij}(1 \le i \le 2, 1 \le j \le 6)$, we can calculate the fusing probability for the six expressions by $p_j = \sum_{i=1}^{2} \omega_{ji} p_{ij} (1 \le j \le 6)$. If $p_j = MAX(p_1, p_2, p_3, p_4, p_5, p_6)$ then we output expression $j$.

The weight of contribution to each expression area for each expression is fixed by using contribution analysis algorithm when training template [8]. Here the weight of contribution to each expression area for each expression is defined as follows:

$$\omega_j = \frac{1}{n}\sum_{t=1}^{n} \frac{\operatorname{cov}(\hat{\theta}(y_t), \hat{\phi}_j(x_{tj}))}{\operatorname{var}\theta(y_t)} \qquad (j = 1, 2) \quad . \tag{5}$$

Here, $\theta(y_t) = \sum_{j=1}^{2} \phi_j(x_{tj}) + \varepsilon_t$ , $\theta(y_t) = \sum_{j=1}^{2} \phi_j(x_{tj}) + \varepsilon_t$ , $\theta(y_t)$ is function of Euclid distance $y$ which is the distance between the probability of expression image sequence $t$ and the probability of template. $\phi_j(x_{tj})$ is quadratic function of probability $x_{tj}$ which is probability of the expression image sequence $t$ in expression area $j$ . $\varepsilon_t$ is stochastic error, $\hat{\phi}_{tj}(x_{tj})$ and $\hat{\theta}(y_t)$ are optimal functions which are iterated by using ACE (Amended Conditional Expectation) algorithm. In this paper, $n = 10$ . The weight of contribution to each expression area for each expression is shown in Table 2.

## 5 Experiment Results and Comparisons with Other Works

Our algorithm is experimented on Cohn-Kanade facial expression database. Firstly, we select 10 image sequences for each expression to train model. Then, we select 40 image sequences from different persons to test. There are 240 image sequences in total. The recognition data and recognition rate of the six expressions are show in Table 3, the average recognition rate is about 90.42%. Experiments show that facial expression recognition based on hybrid features and fusing discrete HMMs can effectively recognize the six basic expressions of image sequence.

In order to validate the advantage of facial expression recognition based on hybrid features and fusing discrete HMMs, we respectively experiment three facial expression recognition methods, which are the method of single feature and single HMM, the method of hybrid features and single HMM, and the method of hybrid features and fusing discrete HMMs. The training templates and testing samples are same with previous method.

**Table 3.** Experiment results

| | happy | surprise | sad | fear | angry | disgust | Recognition rate |
|---|---|---|---|---|---|---|---|
| happy | 38 | 1 | 0 | 1 | 0 | 0 | 95% |
| surprise | 1 | 39 | 0 | 0 | 0 | 0 | 97.5% |
| sad | 0 | 0 | 34 | 0 | 3 | 3 | 85% |
| fear | 2 | 1 | 0 | 37 | 0 | 0 | 92.5% |
| angry | 0 | 0 | 0 | 4 | 35 | 1 | 87.5% |
| disgust | 0 | 0 | 3 | 0 | 3 | 34 | 85% |

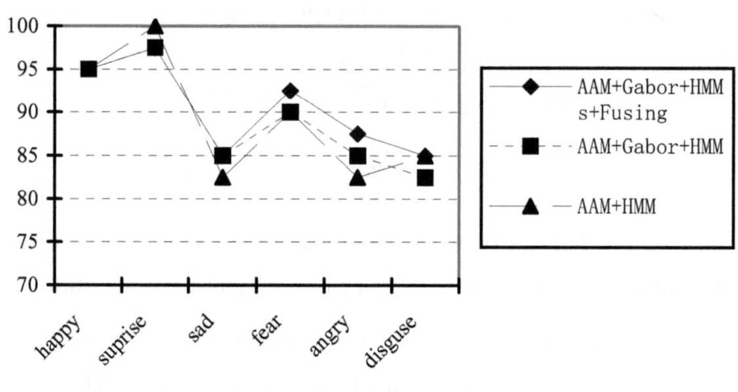


**Fig. 6.** Experiment results of the three methods

Fig. 6 shows the experiment results about the three methods. From Fig. 6, we can find that the average recognition rate in the method of this paper is higher than the other two methods, especially for some easily confused expressions, for example sad, angry and fear, our method has obvious higher recognition rate. But for the surprise expression, the recognition rate in our method is lower than the method AAM plus HMM. The main reason is that surprise expression has obvious shape deformation features in the areas of eyes and mouth. So the method of AAM+HMM has better performance for recognizing the surprise expression.

## 6 Conclusion

The methods about how to effectively extract expression features and recognize expression is studied in this paper. Firstly, we segment the face image from each image in the image sequence, and execute the operations of gray and scale normalization, circumrotation revision for the sub-face image. Then a hybrid feature extraction method based on AAM and Gabor wavelet transformation is presented in this paper. After that, we use HMM to recognize expression in each expression area respectively, and then fuse each probability of expression in each expression area by the weight obtained by contribution analysis algorithm. Finally, we use the expression with maximal probability as the recognition result. Experiments show that our method can recognize the six basic expressions effectively. Especially for the easily confused expressions such as angry, sad, fear, our method also can recognize much better.

**Acknowledgements.** We would like to express our thanks to Carnegie Mellon University Robotics Institute, they offer us the database of Cohn-Kanade facial expression for testing our method. This paper is supported partly by National Natural Science Foundation of China under Grant No. 60673190, and the advanced Professional Talent Research Foundation of Jiangsu University of China under Grant No.05JDG020.

## References

1. Fasel, B., Luettin, J.: Automatic Facial Expression Analysis: A Survey. Pattern Recognition 36, 259–275 (2003)
2. Aleksic, P.S., Katsaggelos, A.K.: Automatic Facial Expression Recognition Using Facial Animation Parameters and Multistream HMMs. IEEE Transactions on Information Forensics and Security 1, 3–11 (2006)
3. Liang, L., Ai, H., Xu, G., Zhang, B.: A Survey of Human Face Detection. Chinese Journal of Computers 25, 449–458 (2002)
4. Yang, G., Huang, T.S.: Human Face Detection in Complex Background. Pattern Recognition 27, 53–63 (1994)
5. Yang, C., Zhou, G., Zhan, Y.: Eye Feature Extraction Based on Gray Information and Harris Corner Detection, In: IeCCS'06 (2006)
6. Cootes, T.F., Taylor, C.J., Cooper, D.H., Graham, J.: Active Shape Models-Their Training and Application. Journal of Computer Vision and Image Understanding 61, 38–59 (1995)
7. Rabiner, L.R.: A Tutorial on Hidden Markov Models and Selected Applications in Speech Recognition. In: Proceedings of the IEEE, vol. 77, pp. 257–285 (1989)
8. Zhan, Y., Cao, P.: Research and Implementation of Emotional Feature Extraction and Recognition in Speech Signal. Journal of Jiangsu University 26, 72–75 (2005)

# Part 3

# Industrial Applications of Virtual Reality

# Sketch Based Modeling System

Hideki Aoyama and Hiroki Yamaguchi

Keio University, Department of System Design Engineering
3-14-1 Hiyoshi, Kohoku-ku, Yokohama, Japan
haoyama@sd.keio.ac.jp, yamaguchi@ina.sd.keio.ac.jp

**Abstract.** In the design process of the external form of a product, sketching is applied for creating and embodying idea. Sketches are able to reflect the aesthetic sense of designers the most easily, making them the most efficient design tool. Sketches can be classified into thumbnail sketches, rough sketches, and rendering sketches according to the embodied idea. Rough sketches are used for developing the idea. In this paper, a system to support the rough sketching process and evaluate the designed product shape using 3D models constructed from the rough sketch is described. This system has a function for extracting and generating sketch lines drawn by a designer, a function for interactively modifying sketch lines, and a function for constructing 3D models from rough sketches. In order to support rough sketching, algorithms which automatically extract/generate the desired sketch-lines are proposed and implemented as a system. A method to construct 3D models form sketch lines is also proposed and implemented as a system.

**Keywords:** Style design, idea embodiment, 3D model construction, Sketch, Sketch supporting system.

## 1 Introduction

Circumstances surrounding product development are significantly changing, and it is becoming increasingly difficult to differentiate the functionality and economic efficiency desired with the progress of manufacturing technology. As a result, design is increasingly playing a larger role in the selection of products as awareness of its importance grows.

Various computer aided systems are effectively working for design and manufacturing processes. In design processes, computer aided design systems (CAD systems) are utilized for detail design of functional parts. However, currently used CAD systems have the following problems;

- form definition processes are complex,
- the designed form depends on the primitive shapes of the using CAD system, and
- creativity of idea is obstructed by the complex operations.

Therefore, support performance for appearance design and basic design of 3D-CAD systems is extremely poor. Since the design of the appearance configuration is a creative endeavor which strongly depends on aesthetic sense of designers, it is difficult for designers to make use of this aesthetic sensitivity due to the complicated

R. Shumaker (Ed.): Virtual Reality, HCII 2007, LNCS 4563, pp. 421–430, 2007.

operations of 3D-CAD systems which interfere with the ideas of designers. Design shapes created are thus limited by the capability of 3D-CAD systems, which lead to the need for systems with high operability which do not interfere with the ideas of designers.

In the process of embodying the external form of a product, design is firstly created by sketching. Designers embody the form from the image while they sketch over and over again. Sketches are able to reflect the aesthetic sense of designers the most easily, so they can be said to be the most efficient design tool. Sketches can be classified into thumbnail sketches, idea sketches, rough sketches, and rendering sketches according to the embodied idea level [1]. Among these, rough sketches are sketches which are located midway between thumbnail sketches and rendering sketches and used to develop the idea. After the image which forms the basis of a product is represented in the thumbnail sketches, rough sketches are drawn to advance the idea based on the thumbnail sketches. In the rough sketch process, designers draw many lines for a line expressing a product, and a clear line is finally determined. Drawing rough sketches expands the idea developed in the thumbnail sketches.

In this study, the authors proposes a sketch support system which uses a tablet PC as the input device of sketch lines to automatically extract or generate the desired sketch-lines from information on drawn lines as the rough sketches, and which can also interactively modify extracted or generated lines. In order to evaluate the designed product shape, a system which automatically constructs 3D models from rough sketches is also proposed. The proposed systems: the sketch support system and the 3D model construction system, are implemented and there effectiveness are confirmed by basic experiments.

## 2 Proposed System

### 2.1 Background of Proposed System

Figure 1 shows an example of rough sketches drawn by a car designer in the process of embodying the external form from images. As shown in this figure, first, the designer thinks of and develops ideas, and creates the whole shape desired gradually while drawing a one silhouette line which expresses the outline of the car many times over each other. Based on these lines, the designer redraws the thick and wide line for a silhouette line of the whole shape, and decides the designed shape of the car.

Recently, digital sketch systems for drawing sketches on computer directly using a pen tablet and tablet PC are introducing for practical use. Being used digital sketch systems are more convenient than traditional sketching using a paper and a pencil in painting compared to coloring and shading. However, with regard to drawing lines which is the most important process in sketching to advance an idea, the advantages of digitization cannot be applied. When using digital sketch systems, designers advance their ideas while drawing one silhouette line many times and embodying the desired lines while deleting the unwanted lines.

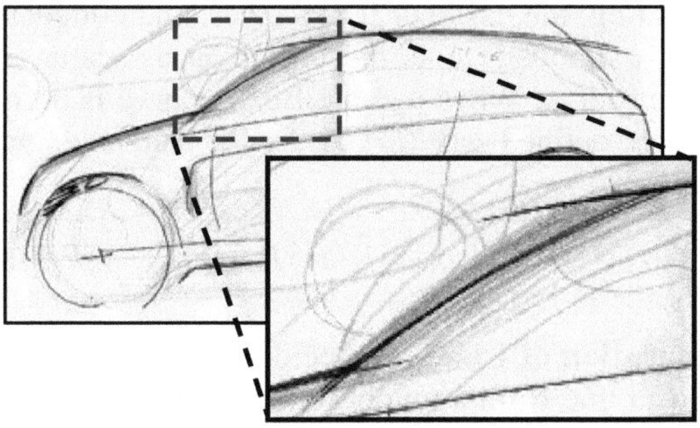

**Fig. 1.** Example of rough sketch

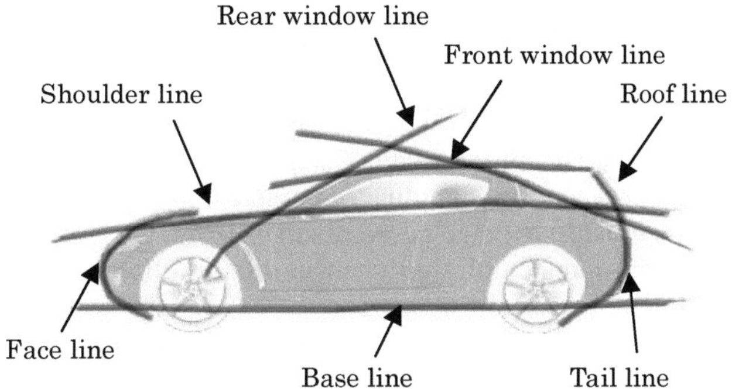


**Fig. 2.** Silhouette lines expressing car body form

## 2.2 System Configuration

In view of the above mentioned circumstances, the authors have developed a sketch support system applying the advantages of sketch digitization. This system has a function for extracting and generating sketch lines, function for interactively modifying sketch lines, and function for constructing 3D models from rough sketches. From the information on sketch lines input to the tablet PC, a line is extracted or generated automatically. By overwriting new lines to an extracted or generated line, this line can be modified interactively. In addition, 3D models can be constructed from 2D sketches generated in this way and the design can be evaluated in the 3D form.

## 2.3 Function for Automatically Extracting and Generating Sketch Lines

**Input of Lines.** In the initial process of aesthetic design, designers embody their image by drawing the external form of a product using silhouette lines. Silhouette lines express boundaries of brightness on the object when parallel rays are applied. Figure 2 shows the silhouette lines expressing the side shape of a car. In the case, the side car shape is represented by seven silhouette lines.

This system extracts or generates the line for a silhouette line which is drawn as many lines in his/her thinking process by a designer. Upon deciding a silhouette line by extracting or generating, the designer lays a layer, and completes the side shape of a car. When deciding a silhouette line, the line input as scattered points is approximated to a cubic Bezier curve. When a cubic Bezier curve is defined as $Q(t)$, and the control points of $Q(t)$ are defined as $Pi(i = 0 - 3)$, $Q(t)$ can be expressed by the following equation (1).

$$Q(t) = (1-t)^3 P_0 + 3t(1-t)^2 P_1 + 3t^2(1-t)P_2 + t^3 P_3 \quad (1)$$

**Extraction and Generation of Lines.** To decide the evaluation criteria in the extraction and generation of a line from a number of lines, the authors interviewed car designers and obtained information on how designers feel when sketching; designers feel that they draw a good line when their arm is moving smoothly and that dynamic lines are drawn with momentum.

From the knowledge, pen pressure and drawing speed in drawing lines were incorporated as evaluation standards for the automatic extraction of lines. A line was then extracted based on the following evaluation standards (a) - (c), and a new line was generated from a number of lines in the following way (d).

(a) The line with the least number of sign changes of acceleration between adjacent points at discrete points on an input line is extracted.
(b) The line with the greatest average-pen-pressure is extracted.
(c) The line with least number of sign changes of the difference in pen pressures extracted is extracted.
(d) The line is newly generated by connecting the mean positions of a number of lines smoothly.

The above (a) and (c) are the processing of evaluation standards capturing the designer's feelings that good design lines appear when the designer's arm is moving smoothly. The processes (a) and (b) mean line extraction in which change in velocity and pen pressure in sketching is the least. The above (b) is the processing based on the judgment that a designer will apply more pressure himself/herself when lines are drawn with momentum. The above (d) is based on the judgment that designers will draw the desired sketch lines themselves many times unconsciously while drawing sketch lines over and over again, and this is the process of finding the average of sketch lines drawn.

Figures 3 and 4 are examples of distribution of pen pressure and acceleration when drawing a sketch line. According to the evaluation standards, the result of extraction based on the process (a) is shown as Figure 5.

## 2.4 Modifying and Fairing Sketch Line

**Modification of Sketch Lines.** After the line is extracted/generated from many lines by the above processes (a) - (d), the extracted/generated line needs to be modified interactively based on the designer's evaluation. This system can therefore modify the line interactively by adding new lines to a line extracted/generated after a line is extracted/generated from many lines by the above processes (a) - (d). As shown in figure 6(a), when sketch lines are added to an extracted/generated line, a new line is determined as the position average of the extracted/generated line and added lines as shown in figure 6(b). This process is effective for the case that a designer would want to modify an extracted/generated line partly while confirming the shape little and little. In other case, a designer wants to modify a line by validating added lines and connecting them to a line already drawn smoothly as shown in Figure 6(c). This process is also effective for the case that added lines changes from an extracted/generated line to a large degree.

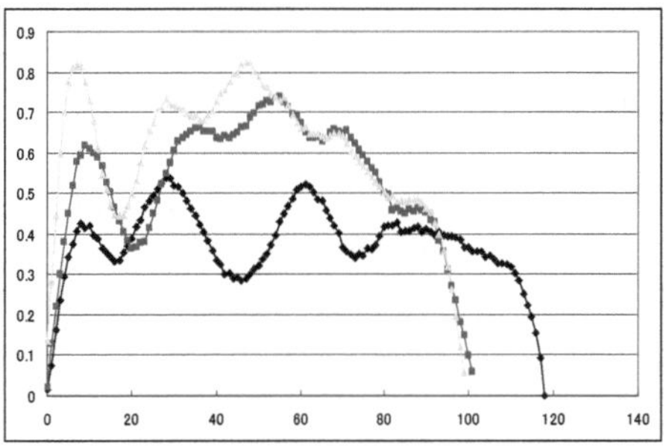


**Fig. 3.** Distribution of pen pressure

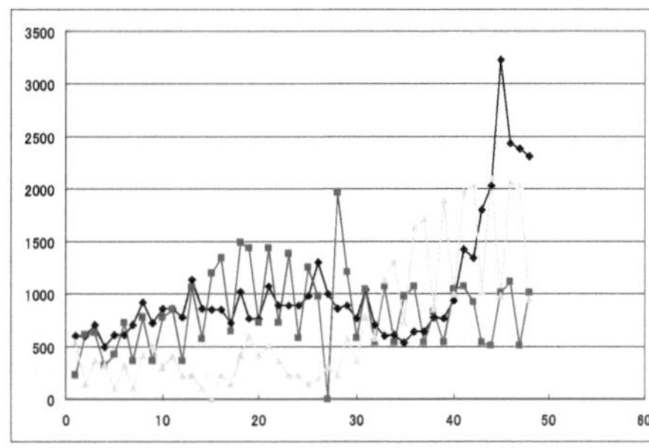


**Fig. 4.** Distribution of acceleration

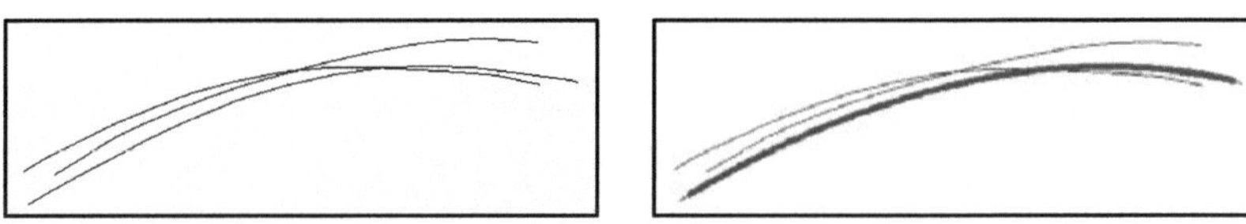

(a) Input sketch lines (b) Result of extraction

**Fig. 5.** Example of sketch line extraction

**Fairing Sketch Line.** It is known that designers draw sketches by controlling the curvature of lines unconsciously [2]. Therefore, the aesthetic degree of an extracted and generated sketch line or modified sketch line can be evaluated by curvature distribution which is represented as the curvature logarithm chart. In the chart, the horizontal axis is defined as $\overline{\rho}$ represented in equation (2), and vertical axis is defined as the frequency of appearance $\overline{S}$ represented in equation (3).

$$\overline{\rho} = \log_{10} \frac{\rho}{S_{all}} \tag{2}$$

$$\overline{s} = \log_{10} \frac{s}{S_{all}} \tag{3}$$

where, $\rho$ : curvature, $S_{all}$ : entire length of curve, $s$ : curve length of with $\rho$ .

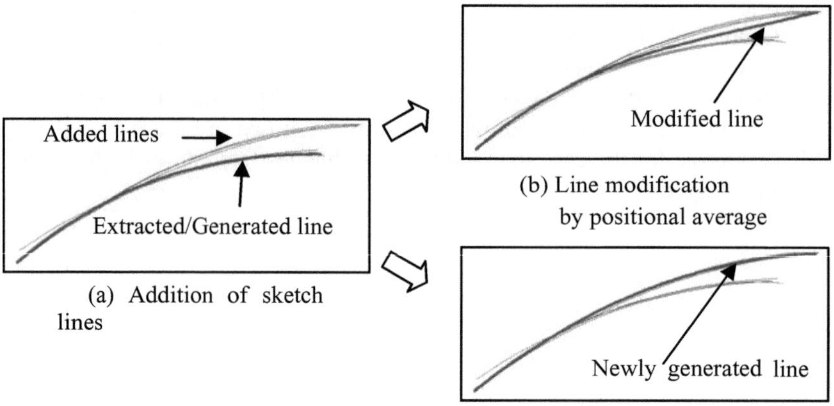


(a) Addition of sketch lines

(b) Line modification by positional average

(c) Validation of new input lines

**Fig. 6.** Modification of sketch lines

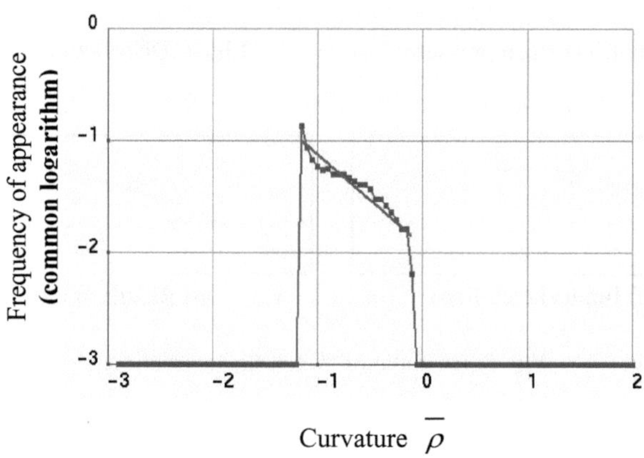


**Fig. 7.** Curvature logarithm chart

Figure 7 shows an example of the curvature logarithm chart. The chart shows the relationship between curvature and the length rate for curvature and represents the rhythm of curvature. A curve with a uniform curvature rhythm is called a rhythm curve which shows the linear property in the chart. A rhythm curve is seen on industrial products admired for design and beautiful natural objects. A sketch line drawn by a designer is evaluated from the view points of curvature distribution and the faired line can be generated by making the line the linear property in the chart.

### 2.5 Implementation Results of System

Figure 8(a) shows the rough sketch of the side view of a car drawn on a tablet PC. This figure 8(b) shows the results of extracting and generating each silhouette line

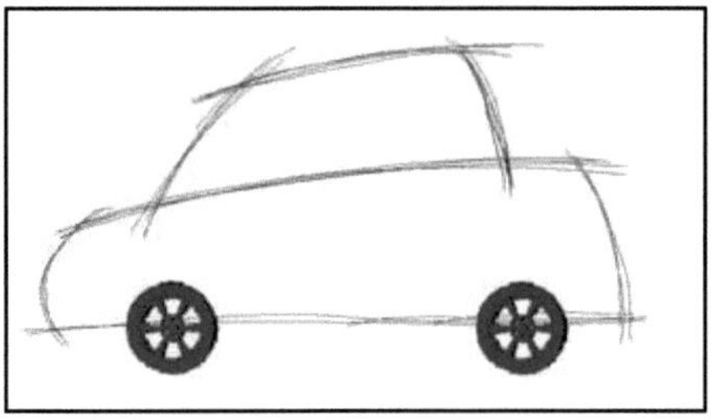

(a)Input sketch lines

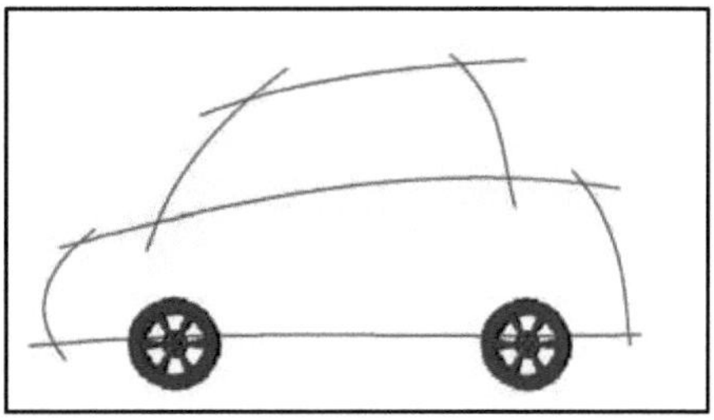

(b)Extracted or generated lines

**Fig. 8.** Extraction and generation of sketch line

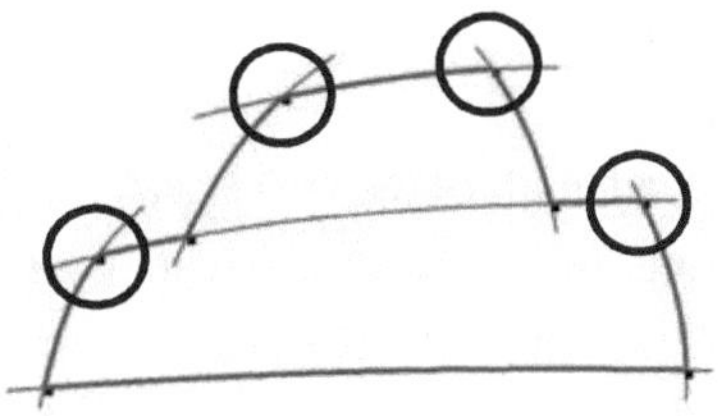

**Fig. 9.** Positions of connecting curves

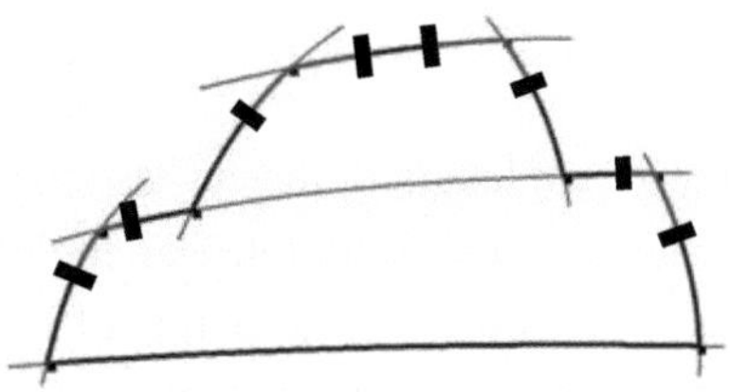

**Fig. 10.** Division of basic lines

according to the evaluation criteria for sketch lines described above. These extracted/generated lines can be modified respectively.

## 2.6 Definition of Connecting Lines

As shown in figure 2, the side view sketch of a car drawn with the basic lines seems to be angulated wholly due to positional continuity only at the connected points of the basic lines. In order to connect the basic lines with higher-dimensional continuity, connecting lines should be constructed between the basic lines at the four points as shown in Figure 9.

In order to make connecting lines, the basic lines are divided at constructed spaces as shown in Figure 10. Then, the connecting lines are constructed in the spaces. To construct the connecting lines with higher-dimensional continuity between the basic lines defined by cubic Bezier curves, the lines defined by the control elements [3] and the control points are used.

When two Bezier curves $A(t)$ and $B(t)$ are connected smoothly, formulas (4) and (5) must be established.

$$\frac{dA(1)}{ds_1} = \frac{dB(0)}{ds_2} \tag{4}$$

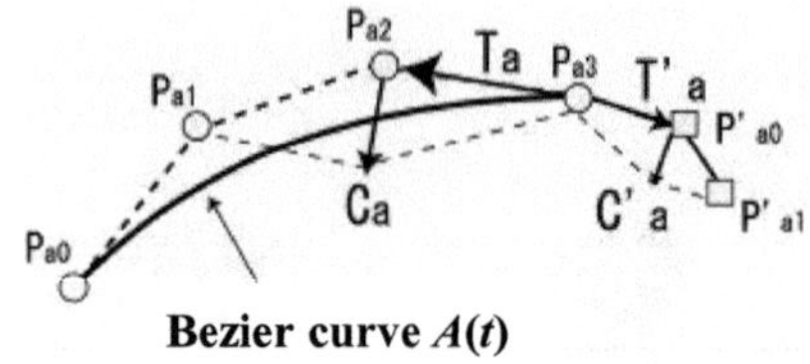


Fig. 11. Tangent vectors and curvature vectors in curve *A(t)*

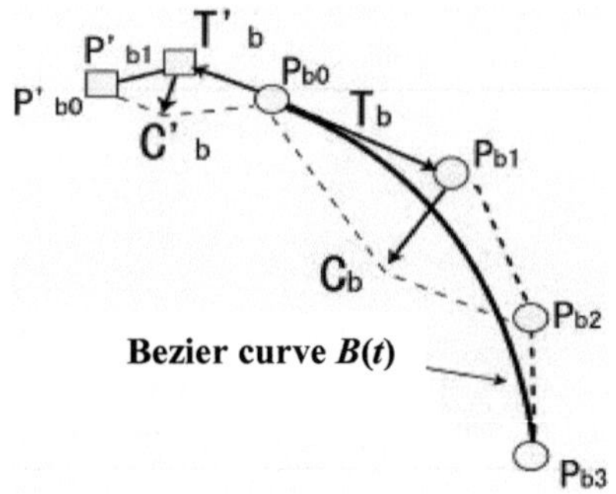


Fig. 12. Tangent vectors and curvature vectors in curve *B(t)*

$$\frac{d^2A(1)}{ds_1^{\ 2}} = \frac{d^2B(0)}{ds_2^{\ 2}} \tag{5}$$

where, $s_1$ : arc length of the curve $A(t)$, and $s_2$ : arc length of the curve $B(t)$.

When $p_{a0} \sim p_{a3}$ are defined as the control points of the curve $A(t)$, and $p_{b0} \sim p_{b3}$ are defined as the control points of the curve $B(t)$, equations (6) and (7) are established according to precondition equations (4) and (5).

$$T_a = s \cdot T'_a \tag{6}$$

$$C_a = s^2 \cdot C'_a \tag{7}$$

where, $s$ is the proportion of arc lengths of the curves $A(t)$ and $B(t)$, $T_a$ and $T'_a$ are the tangent vectors, and $C_a$ and $C'_a$ are the curvature vectors at connecting point as shown in figure 11. The control elements $P'_{a0}$ and $P'_{a1}$ of the curve $B(t)$ can be then derived.

In the same way, the following equation is also established in the case of the curve $B(t)$. $s$ is the proportion of the arc lengths of the curves $A(t)$ and $B(t)$, and $T_b$ and $T'_b$ are the tangent vectors, and $C_b$ and $C'_b$ are the curvature vectors at connecting point as shown in Figure 12. Thus, the elements of control points $P'_{b0}$ and $P'_{b1}$ can be calculated.

Thus, control points $p_{t0}$ and $p_{t1}$ are derived according to the four elements of the control points.

$$p_{t0} = (1-t) \cdot P'_{a0} + t \cdot P'_{b0} \tag{8}$$

$$p_{t1} = (1-t) \cdot P'_{a1} + t \cdot P'_{b1} \tag{9}$$

Therefore, a smooth connecting curve $C(t)$ between the curve $A(t)$ and the curve $B(t)$ can be expressed by equation (10).

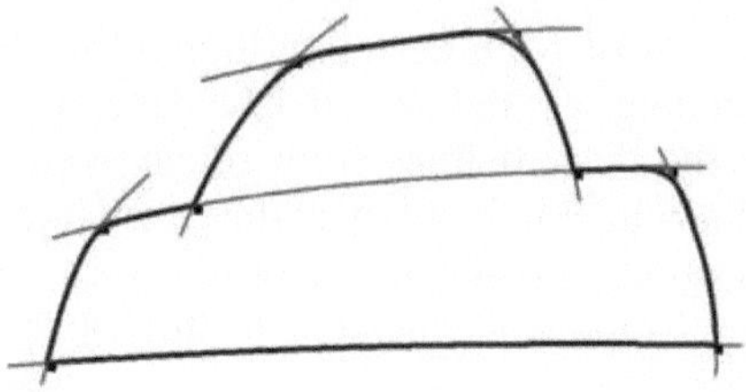

**Fig. 13.** Basic lines with smooth connecting lines

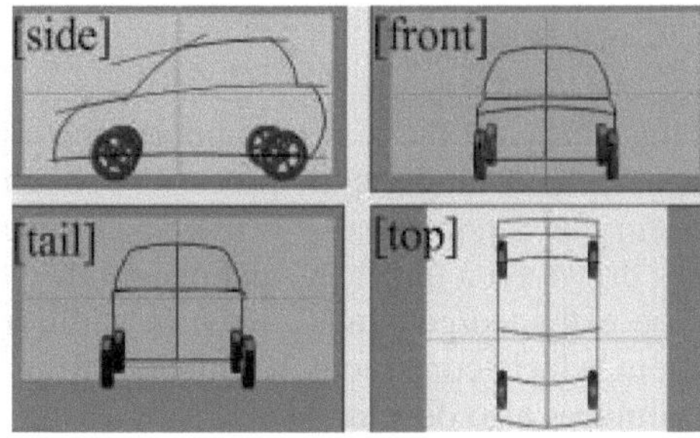


**Fig. 14.** Example of sketches to construct 3D model

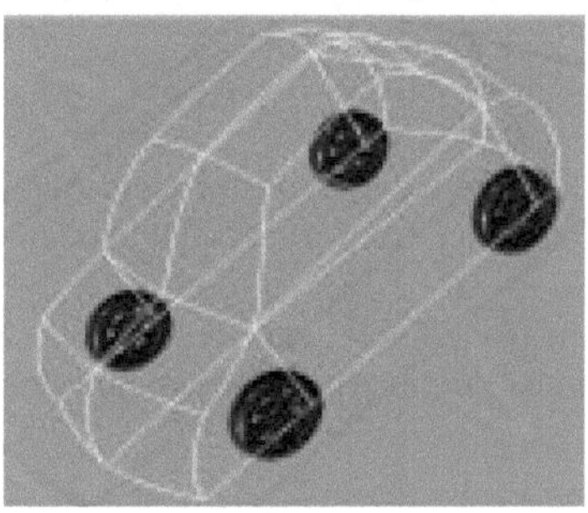

**Fig. 15.** Constructed 3D model represented as wire frame

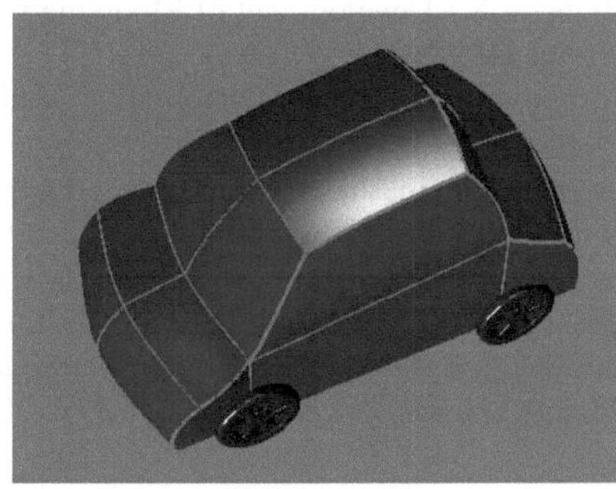

**Fig. 16.** Constructed 3D model represented as surface model

$$C(t) = (1-t)^3 \cdot P_{a3} + 3(1-t)^2 \cdot t \cdot p_{t0} + 3(1-t) \cdot t^2 \cdot p_{t1} + t^3 \cdot P_{b0} \quad (10)$$

Figure 13 shows the basic curves with smooth connecting curves. The roundness at the connecting points can be changed by the parameters of the connecting curves.

## 2.7 3D Modeling System

In order to construct the 3D models from 2D sketches, it is essential to decide the target object of design and determine the constraint conditions on modeling. In this paper, the target object of design is assumed to be a car body and the side view sketch consists of seven silhouette lines. The front view, top view, and back view are also drawn with silhouette lines which correspond to seven basic lines of the side view as shown in figure 14.

A system to automatically construct the 3D model from the sketches drawn with silhouette lines of the side view, front view, top view, and back view as shown in figure 14 was developed. Figures 15 shows the 3D wire frame model constructed from the sketches shown in figure 14. And figure 16 shows the 3D surface model of this with cubic Bezier surfaces.

## 3 Conclusions

In this study, in the aim to support creating process of form design, a digital sketch system which supports the process of rough sketching was developed. The developed system can automatically extract and generate the desired lines from rough sketch lines drawn on a tablet PC and can modify the lines interactively by adding new lines to the extracted/generated lines. In addition, in order to evaluate the design form, a system which constructs 3D models from 2D information generated in this sketch system was also developed.

## References

1. Shimizu, Y.: Development of Modeling by Sketch (in Japanese), pp. 2–9, Japan Publishing Service (1998)
2. Toshinobu, H.: Study of Quantitative Analysis of the Characteristics of a Curve? Forma 12, 55–63 (1997)
3. Aoyama, H., Inasaki, I., Kishinami, T., Yamazaki, K.: A New Method for Constructing a Software Model of Sculptured Surfaces with C2 Continuity from a Physical Model. Advancement of Intelligent Production, 7–12 (1994)
4. Yoshida, S., Miyazaki, S., Hoshino, T., Ozeki, T., Hasegawa, J., Yasuda, T., Yokoi, S.: Spatial Sketch System for Car Styling Design. International Archives of Photogrammetry and Remote Sensing, XXXIII, Part B5, 919 (2000)

# Ergonomic Interactive Testing in a Mixed-Reality Environment

Monica Bordegoni, Umberto Giraudo, Giandomenico Caruso, and Francesco Ferrise

Politecnico di Milano, Dipartimento di Meccanica, Via G. La Masa 34,
20158 Milano, Italy
{monica.bordegoni,umberto.giraudo,giandomenico.caruso,
Francesco.ferrise}@polimi.it

**Abstract.** The field of computer graphics is greatly increasing its overall performance enabling consequently the implementation of most of the product design process phases into virtual environments. The deriving benefits of using virtual practices in product development have been proved intrinsically highly valuable, since they foster the reduction of time to market, process uncertainty, and the translation of most prototyping activities into the virtual environment. In this paper we present the developed platform in mixed environment for ergonomic validation. Specifically we defined a methodology for testing both aspects related to design and ergonomic validation by allowing the tester to interact visually and physically with the car dashboard control devices and related interface by the mean of a rotatory haptic device. By experimental session it has been highlighted that it is possible gathering qualitative data about the design, and finding typical occlusion problems, but also quantitative data can be collected by testing the infotainment interface and the consequent users' distraction during the device use.

**Keywords:** Mixed environments, ergonomic analysis, tactons.

## 1 Introduction

Nowadays, it is possible to find on the market more and more software tools able to describe and validate different aspects of the to-be product such as finite element analysis, photo realistic rendering, up to ergonomic validation tools.

More specifically, the research in the field of ergonomic validation in a digital context intends to provide designers with tools supporting the validation of the postural and interaction issues between the human and the final product without the requirement to build a physical prototype.

In this direction much effort has been spent, for example, in the automotive domain, and in particular in the interior layout of the vehicles; ergonomic interior design of a vehicle based on virtual prototypes and virtual manikins has been described in [1]. The approaches described in [1] and [2] are not oriented to analyze the final configuration of the product but instead to improve design activities already in the concept phase.

Two different ergonomic methodologies are currently in use: static and dynamic analysis. The first one intends to validate the postural aspects of a human under

R. Shumaker (Ed.): Virtual Reality, HCII 2007, LNCS 4563, pp. 431–440, 2007.

certain working conditions [3] (e.g., Driving a car, sitting on a desk...); the second one [4] relates to the possibility of verifying postural parameters under dynamic conditions and verify certain types of interaction with the product (e.g., Grasping, touching a button, reaching an object). The classic approach used in industry consisting in programming the movements of a virtual mannequin by means of direct manipulation. This approach is time consuming to apply especially where the environment is encumbered because the collisions are not automatically avoided [5]. A mixed mock-up refers to the combination of both real and virtual models in one unique simulation environment Virtual Reality can add realism and improve analysis method in ergonomic design; [6; 7; 8]. The main feature of a mixed mock-up is that it enables the integration of a real operator within the real-time ergonomic analyses system. Mixed mock-ups have proved to be time and cost effective when used for evaluating and comparing design variants. [7; 8]

In this sense an enrichment may be provided by haptic interfaces in ergonomic analysis by adding to the simulations the sense of touch [9] [10].; One of the main disadvantages of current infotainment systems on vehicles is related to the level of interaction required for accessing to the increased number of controls. The current trend [11] tends to reduce the number of control devices by grouping them in fewer multi-functional knobs; still an open question remains whether a single command is effectively better performing in controlling complex and different functions of the vehicle in regards to the related safety issues [12]. In this paper we propose an approach and a methodology based on advanced VP, VR and haptic devices to carry out ergonomic tests; we have developed and applied the methodology in immersive and mixed environments related to interior design evaluation of a concept car in. Specifically we wanted to test three different conditions with different methods for controlling a haptic knob in order to understand whether a smart haptic feedback (tacton) [13; 14] is really effective in conveying information to the user and by consequence reducing his distraction from the driving conditions.

## 2 The Experimental Set Up

Virtual reality systems require different media to reproduce real conditions in a virtual environment; to develop our experiment a specific hardware and software set up has been created by combining different commercial solutions as it will be presented in the following.

### 2.1 Motion Tracking System

In order to obtain the head tracking we use the VICON 460 motion capture system (www.vicon.com). The VICON system is composed by a hardware component (high frequency cameras, IR flashes and data station) and software applications for the complete control and analysis of motion capture Optical motion capture is the recording of movement of an entity in a given physical space for supporting the reproduction of the action in a digital environment by the mean of high-resolution cameras (six in our case).The user, whose motion is to be captured, has a number of reflective markers attached to his body, in well-defined positions. The markers are spheres that reflect infrared light from the strobes back into the camera. For this full body capture, spheres of 14 millimeters diameter are used. Markers set-up consists fundamentally of the markers' correct positioning on the subject who is going to do the movements. It is necessary to stick them onto the user's body considering that they must be seen as clearly as possible by the cameras, and that they must fit at best with the digital human model previously created.

VICONiQ 2.0 is the central application of the VICON software suite used to collect and process the raw video data. It takes the two-dimensional data from each camera, combining it with calibration data to reconstruct the equivalent digital motion in three dimensions. After this reconstruction the data may be passed, live or recording, to other VICON applications for analysis and manipulation or to third party applications (in our case UGS Jack) such as those used for digital animation or virtual environments.

### 2.2 The Head Mounted Display

For the visualization of the interior of the vehicle we have used a stereoscopic see-through head mounted display. The nVisor ST is a high-resolution see-through head-mounted display designed for augmented reality applications requiring a wide field-of-view format with superior SXGA image quality (www.nvisinc.com). High efficiency optics incorporating reflective-transmissive polarizer's increase light-throughput, presenting a high-contrast virtual image while allowing 50% light transmission from the environment. The use of this HMD allows the simultaneous visualization of the virtual environment created with the ergonomic testing software UGS Jack and the physical environment. The physical environment is composed by a block of foam for providing kinesthetic feedback of the arm rest and thc display controlled by the haptic device.

### 2.3 Ergonomic Validation Software

UGS Jack (http://www.ugs.com/products/tecnomatix/human_performance/jack) is an ergonomic and human factors tool to support designers to improve the ergonomics of product designs and workplace tasks in various industrial fields. This tool enables the users to position, with an accurate biomechanical methodology, digital humans in virtual environments permitting furthermore the assignment of different tasks and analyzing their performances. For our purposes, we decided to make use of Jack because it allows realizing and testing the virtual environment in a simple and effective way. In our case, we have used a virtual cockpit realized from our Department, and Jack suit software package has given us the possibility to import three-dimensional objects deriving from different CAD platforms. More important, we have the possibility to obtain the stereoscopic image of the eyes perception of the digital human. This feature allows us to obtain two video signals to reconstruct the depth of the scene and therefore providing a stereo image in the HMD. Still it was not so immediate to define a correct parameter of the stereo settings since the default stereo vision does not provide a correct size of the represented object. To obtain a proper tuning of the visualization parameters (parallax, interpupillar distance, etc) we have developed a methodology [15], which consists on considering a physical object whose we, have a digital version and superimposing the digital image.

## 2.4 The Haptic Knob

In order to define the command interface of the on-board infotainment system, we made use of a haptic knob similar to the BMW iDrive's design. As haptic device we have used one of the haptic knob realized in our Department [16] connected to the visual interface realized with Adobe Flash. The main idea consists of creating an integrated haptic control system that allows the final user to receive both visual and kinesthetic information. Concerning the specific design implemented in our experimental session, we defined seven different haptic behaviors occurring in different situations controlled by the Flash interface. The very first design is defined by an homogeneous behavior with a step every 18 degrees with high torque values, substantially this design represents a typical not actuated knob with no specific characteristics.

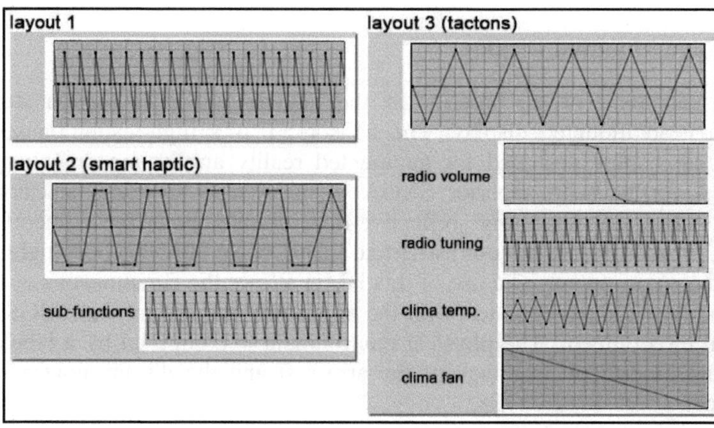


**Fig. 1.** Haptic rendering design

The second behavior, specifically implemented to be coherent with the Flash interface, is based on a step every 36 degrees with static load between the steps and with strong torque values. In the third situation, where we intend to provide the feeling of the action to be accomplished, we introduced an haptic metaphor (tacton) [13] [17] trying to assimilate the concept of increasing or diminishing a function X to the increment/decrease of perceived forces. For the radio controls, we implemented the viscosity function. In this situation the knob stands in the zero position and the tester by turning the knob clockwise can feel higher opposing forces and in the other direction diminishing forces. In this layout no stepping solution is implemented. A second design refers to the implemented fan-control testing conditions. In this layout the knob has a relative positioning and by turning the knob clockwise, the tester can feel a step every 30 degree and there is an increment of released torque forces (or decrease in case of turning in the opposite direction). This defines a very first study for our research group for investigating haptic metaphor issues in a very simple way, certainly more complex situations may be implemented as well.

### 2.5 Interactive Interface

We considered using Adobe Flash since it is an extremely flexible and advanced platform for creating the interactive interface of the infotainment system. Using Flash we have designed and displayed the interface relates to the radio and fan control functions in an extremely credible way. Secondly, due to the property of Action Script programming language it has been possible to define a knob on the interface whose movements and actions were coherent with the haptic knob. Concerning the interface to simulate the infotainment system, we have designed an interface representing all the typical functions available in a car as radio, navigation system, ventilation control, etc. Still in order to simplify the simulation and the accomplishment of the tasks by the user we limited our study to the radio and fan control functions.

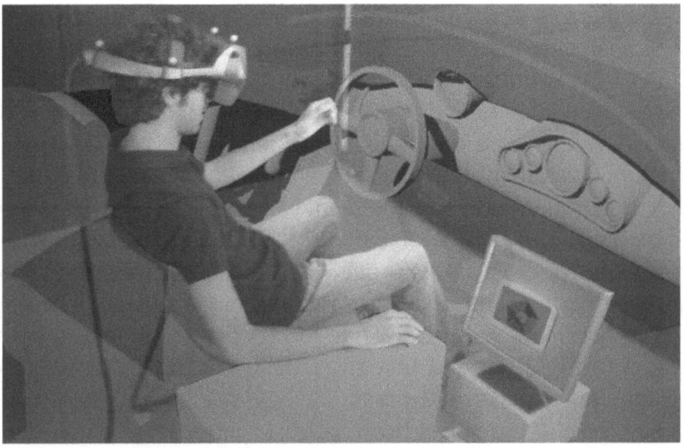

**Fig. 2.** Experimental setup

To enter in the sub menu we provide a button placed beneath the knob, to confirm his selection the tester has just to press down the knob prompting the enter command. Once entered in the sub level (either relative to the radio or to the fan controls) the tester is presented a main screen (formally level 1) where all the current settings are displayed. Concerning the specific contextual sub-menus, we intentionally adopted three different graphical layouts in order to highlight differences between them in terms of performance. For what concerns the radio tuning sub menu, we defined a slide bar displaying all different radio station and different FM values; concerning the volume we decided to implement just a numeric volume with no other spatial reference. Concerning the temperature and fan settings in the ventilation sub menus we defined rotatory virtual knob in order to provide a direct spatial correspondence between the actual physical knob and the virtual, as it happens with the main menus.

## 3 The Experimental Protocol

Usually the design process involves different activities strictly correlated to different media as paper sketching, tablet drawing and by using CAD software. Each of these media is able to provide different support to the designer, but actually the representation of the space is subjective (for what concerns the sketching) or is not directly comparable to the physical world (in the case of CAD representation). This lack of direct interaction may easily lead to design errors or to the definition of misleading parameters.

The question we want to address is how much is a virtual validation quantitatively able to improve the solution of a design in terms of quality and number of solved errors before the starting of the production? Is it possible to measure it?

In order to provide an answer to this question we have defined an experiment relative to error recognition in a comparative methodology between 2D displays and immersive environment. We have considered a 3D file of the interior of a sport car partially modified in order to insert typical design errors. The implemented errors were belonging to two different categories: postural and functional. To the first category belong typical errors deriving from a not correct positioning of the mannequin in the early design phase, that are pedals positioning, gear lever positioning, positioning and dimensions of the armrests. To the second category belong slightly harder mistakes to be recognized in a typical CAx environment like A-pillar occlusion of the street. Problems deriving from the incorrect dimensioning of the steering wheel that causes a partial occlusion of the gauges behind, body parts like the tester's arm occluding other functional parts like the display in the car, and the positioning of the commands knob. To run the test we have invited 10 external testers with no previous experience in immersive environment, but with a design background (product design or mechanical engineering) and a specific interest in car design. The experiment has been organized in two main sessions of five testers per group and in both of them the tester were asked to highlight and recognize design mistakes, furthermore we set a time limit of 2 minutes to perform the task.

In the first session the tester has been asked to navigate through the virtual environment of the car's interior (in the same way as it happens in any CAD interface) with the support of a 3D mouse (www.3dconnexion.com). In the second session the second group of testers had to navigate through the virtual environment in an immersive situation with a stereoscopic occlusive HMD (head mounted display) and with the head movement tracked by the VICON tracking device; specifically the tester had to sit on a chair simulating the seat on a car interior.

The second hypothesis proposes a novel methodology for defining a global validation of the infotainment system on board by the use of an haptic knob. As previously illustrated the extreme complexity of the menus and the necessity of having a visual feedback from the on-board display, the time required for accomplishing certain functions may lead to distractions for the driver with inherent consequences for his own safety. Specifically in the praxis it is relative hard to define a testing in the actual environment of use before the release of the vehicle. Usually tests are conducted singularly on the interface [18] or relatively to the position of the knob within the car interior. In this context we are proposing a methodology based on mixed reality tools to validate a car interior and contextually different infotainment system layouts by the use of an haptic knob.

To run the test we have developed a single graphical interface with three different interaction layouts by the use of the haptic knob. Relatively to the knob we wanted to test the effectiveness of conveying significant information in order to reduce the time spent in watching the display [19]. To achieve a comparable result we have proposed the three different behaviors previously described.

To run the test, 10 external testers with no previous experience in virtual environments or design field have been invited. They have been provided with a seat and HMD see-through stereoscopic display tracked by the VICON tracking device, a display and the haptic knob, both of them coherent in terms of position with the visualized car model. The main condition was that the tester had to keep a driving position watching straightforward simulating real driving conditions while seating in this position the testers had to perform some interaction tasks with the infotainment system. Specifically the tester was asked to switch on the radio, change the radio station, set the volume, change the temperature of the air conditioning and set the fan. The tester had to perform these tasks in random order using all the three different layouts and providing a qualitative evaluation for each task afterwards. In order to avoid learning curve issues and make the results comparable, the three different layout of interaction have been selected randomly, for instance the first tester had to test the acoustic feedback first, then the normal layout and then the smart haptic layout. To accomplish the following task the tester has been tracked with the VICON optical system and by retrieving head measurement it has become possible to quantitatively define the distraction of the infotainment system as amount of time spent in watching the display.

# 4 The Experimental Result

## 4.1 The First Experiment

The first experiment has clearly highlighted the benefits deriving from an immersive environment for validating project features, still with some qualitative differences. On the basis of ten testers, the five performing the test with a typical CAD interface have, on average, been able to find fewer mistakes within the assigned time frame (75% recognized on 45% for the CAD group) and with a drastic difference in terms of typology. In fact the testers who performed the test in a virtual environment have been able to find at first mostly functional errors (86% compared to just 10% of the CAD group) compared to the other group that has at first found postural errors. Certainly it must be considered the great differences in terms of navigation in the virtual space, with a CAD interface since it becomes much more difficult to interpret the actual sitting in the car, and by consequence it is possible to find out more localized errors.

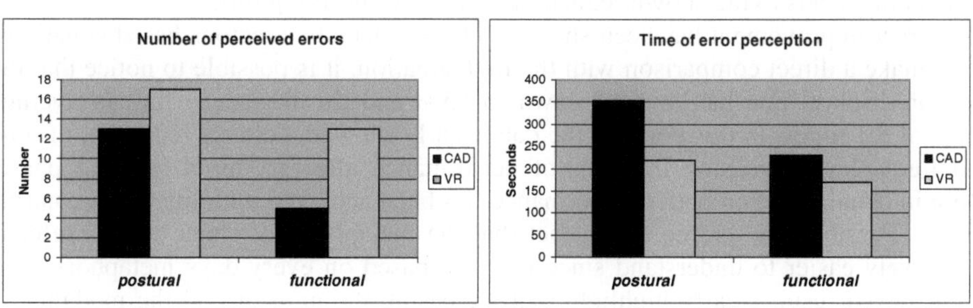


**Fig. 3.** First experiment results

On the other side, if we define the term error accuracy as the number of reported errors in absolute values, it can also be highlighted that the immersive environment is highly better performing with an average of 5 found errors compared to the average of 3.6 of the other group with an average time of 1'17" compared to 1'52".

An interesting issue regards the number of wrongly identified mistakes that has been bizarrely high for the immersive environment tester (3.4 in average), this can be possibly be explained with the fact that people were relatively eager in identifying mistakes and this lead them to be hyper critical to some design details.

As result of this experiment it has been shown that immersive environment are intrinsically able to provide a better validation of the project both in terms of accuracy and time required to accomplish the analysis. On counterparts, and specifically in our experiment set-up, with an immersive environment, it is not possible to perceive details which are not directly within the field of view, and, as it has been shown, some features may be not recognized (as the pedals asymmetry position) and may cause problems in the later phases of the design process.

### 4.2 The Second Experiment

The second experiment was intended to provide an interface-ergonomical validation within the context of a mixed reality environment. By the analysis it has resulted that summing up different levels of feedbacks, is drastically able to improve the infotainment controls functionality and by consequence reducing the distraction of the driver. In the first layout, using the haptic knob with no specific behavior, the testers had to check the effectiveness of his actions on the display with great frequency and for longer time (12.9 times in average). Specifically, because of the homogeneous scale of the angular movement, the amount of time spent in observing the single menus and sub-menus has been approximately constant throughout the testing session (25" in average). It could be expected to have a lower value for what concerns the audio controls because of the intrinsic acoustic feedback, but in our test the radio connections were not integrated and they were merely control functions.

In the second situation, with an adaptative sound feedback, all the testers have been able to reduce the frequency of observation of the display (9.4 times), but still not so drastically to reduce the time required for receiving a visual feedback (17" in average). Like in the previous situation, between the two control situations no great discrepancy has appeared. Possibly the reduction of the frequency of observation is a direct result deriving from the duplication of information via haptic and acoustic channel that leads to the shown reduction of display observing time.

A great improvement has been shown with the adaptative tactons based situations, if we make a direct comparison with the first situation, it is possible to notice that the eyes-on-display time has levered down to 55% and the frequency has an average value of 8.1 times. In this context, the data clearly showed a drastic reduction of time and frequency, increasing in terms of performance after an initial learning phase. More in detail, an even better performance has been achieved with the clima controls testing. Possibly this is due to the fact that the metaphors to which tactons refer is cognitively easier to understand since they are based on every days metaphors. Still the achieved result clearly highlight that increasing the number and the modality of

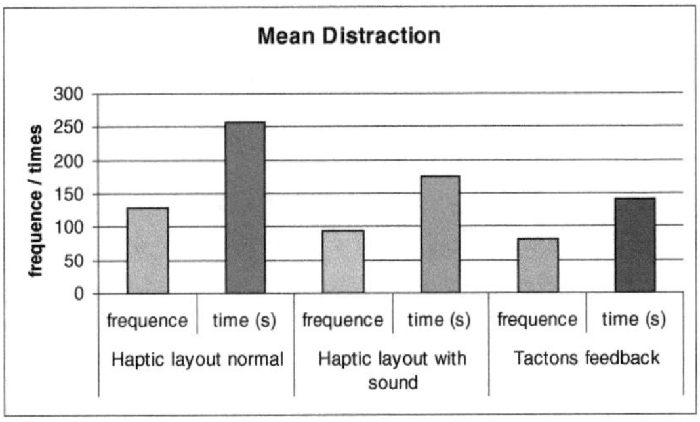


**Fig. 4.** Second experiment results

provided feedbacks for certain operations it becomes possible to define novel metaphors so that the visual display of information decreases its importance in the time.

Furthermore it is possible to affirm that the obtained results are interesting since the provided simulation is not effectively defining a real situation with force feedbacks or representing real driving conditions, still permitting a comparative result in absolute terms between different interaction layouts.

## 5 Conclusion and Future Developments

In this paper we have presented the results of our experimental sessions inherent to immersive and mixed reality environments. In the first experiment we have highlighted the great benefits deriving from using VR instead of typical CAD environments. In the second experiment we have a proposed a methodology based on mixed environment for supporting different aspects of the ergonomics of a car interior and, furthermore defined a set up for validating an infotainment interface in simulated driving conditions. Concerning the haptic interface we have tested different behaviors and we have validated the initial hypothesis suggesting that an increment of information leads to lower the requirement of attention by the user by conveying them into the tactile channel.

## References

1. Vogt, C., Mergl, C., Bubb, H.: Interior Layout Design of Passengers Vehicles with RAMSIS. Human Factors and Ergonomics in Manufacturing. vol. 15(2), pp. 197–212 Wiley Spring (2005)
2. Colombo, G., Cugini, U.: Virtual Humans and Prototypes to Evaluate Ergonomics and Safety. Journal of Engineering Design. (Taylor & Francis) 16(2), 195–207 (2005)
3. Mergl, C., Bubb, H., Vogt, C., Kress, H.: Ergonomic layout process for a driver working place in cars, SAE international (2006)
4. Wang, X., Chevalot, N., Monnier, G., Trasbot, J.: From motion capture to motion simulation: an in-vehicle reach motion database for car design. In: SAE International conference, Detroit, USA (2006)

5. Chan, A., MacLean, K.E., Mc Grenere, J.: Identififying haptic icons under workload. In: Proceedings of Word Haptics Conference, IEEE-VR2005, Pisa, Italy (2005)
6. Di Gironimo, G., Monacelli, G., Martorelli, M., Vaudo, G.: Use of Virtual Mock-Ups for ergonomic Design, In: Proceedings of 7th International Conference ATA, Florence (May 23rd – 25th 2001)
7. Desinger, J., Breining, R., Robler, A., Ruckert, D. Hofle, J.J.: Immersive Ergonomic Analyses of Console Elements in a Tractor Cabin. In: The 4th Immersive Projection Technologies Workshop, Ames, IA.
8. Desinger, J., Breining, R., Robler, A.: ERGONAUT: A Tool for Ergonomic Analyses in Virtual Environments. In: 6th Eurographics Workshop on Virtual Environments, June 1 – June 2, 2000, Amsterdam, Netherlands (2000)
9. Burdea, G., Coiffet, P.: Virtual Reality Technology, 2nd edn. John Wiley & Sons, Hoboken. New Jersey (2003)
10. Sherman, W.R., Craig, A.B.: Understanding Virtual Reality: Interface, Application, and Design, 1st edn. Morgan Kaufmann, Seattle, Washington, USA (September 2002)
11. Hassel, L., Hagen, E.: Evaluation of a dialogue System in Automotive Environment. In: Proceedings of 6th SIGdial conference, Sep. 2-3 2005, Lisbon, Portugal (2005)
12. Rydstroem, A., Bengtsson, P., Grane, C., Brostroem, R., Agarh, J., Nilson, J.: Multifunctional system in vehicles: a usability evaluation. In: Proceedings of CybErg 2005, the fourth international Cyberspace conference on Ergonomics, Johannesburg, International Ergonomics Association Press (2005)
13. Brown, L.M., Brewster, S.A., Purchase, H.C.: A first investigation into the effectiveness of Tactons. In: Proceedings of the 1st Joint Eurohaptics Conf. and Symp. On hpatic interfaces for Virtual Environment and Teleoperator Systems. WHC 2005 Pisa, Italy (2005)
14. Mac Lean, K., Enriquez, M.: Perceptual Design of Haptic Icons. In: Proceedings of Eurohaptics, Dublin, Ireland, pp. 351–363 (2003)
15. Bordegoni, M., Caruso, G., Ferrise, F., Giraudo, U.: A mixed environment for ergonomics tests: tuning of the stereo viewing parameters. In: Proceedings of Eurographics, Italian Chapter, Trento (February 14-16, 2007)
16. Colombo, G., De Angelis, F., Formentini, L.: A mixed virtual reality – haptic approach to carry out ergonomics test on virtual prototypes. In: Proceedings of TMCE 2006, April 18-22, Ljubljana, Slovenia (2006)
17. Chedmail, P., Maille, B., Ramstein, E.: Accessibility and ergonomics study with virtual reality, a state of the art. Mécanique & Industries 3, 147–152 (2002)
18. Nielsen, J., Mack, R.L., Wiley Summerskill, S.J., Porter, J.M., Burnett, G.E.: Usability inspection methods. New York (2004)
19. Burnett, G.E, Porter, J.M.: Ubiquitous computing within cars: designing controls for non visual use. International Journal of Human-Computer Studies 55, 521–531 (2001)

# Designer-Centered Haptic Interfaces for Shape Modeling

Monica Bordegoni and Umberto Cugini

Politecnico di Milano, Dipartimento di Meccanica,
Via G. La Masa 34, 20158 Milano, Italy
{monica.bordegoni,umberto.cugini}@polimi.it

**Abstract.** This paper presents some results of a research project aiming at developing haptic tools for virtual shape modeling resembling the real tools like rakes and sandpaper used by modelers and designers in the real workshop. The developed system consists of a CAS (Computer Aided Styling) system enhanced with intuitive designer-oriented interaction tools and modalities. The system requirements have been defined on the basis of the observation of designers during their daily work and translating the way they model shapes using hands and craft tools into specifications for the modeling system based on haptic tools. The haptic tool and the interaction modality developed for exploring and sanding a surface is presented in the paper.

**Keywords:** Haptic interfaces, designer-centered user interface, 3D interaction techniques, shape modeling.

## 1 Introduction

The conceptual design phase of new products having aesthetic value presents several critical issues that contribute in making the overall design process costly and time consuming. Two main practices are used for representing concepts of new products: hand-made prototypes and 3D digital models. Hand-made prototypes are created by skilled modelers by modeling malleable materials with their hands, and/or using very basic tools [1]. This practice is expensive and requires long time of execution. Besides, some reverse engineering techniques are required for building the digital model of the physical prototype for subsequent manufacturing activities. The other practice consists of designers making digital models using CAS (Computer Aided Styling) or CAD (Computer Aided Design) tools. In general, designers consider these tools too technical, and lacking intuitive user interfaces. Furthermore, there is the subsequent necessity to physically build the prototype for evaluating the most important qualities of the model: aspects such as proportions and quality of surface are evaluated by observing and touching the object. In order to create physical prototypes, some expensive and time consuming rapid prototyping or milling techniques are used, which needs 3D digital models as starting point.

The idea of bridging physical and virtual modeling by maintaining the effective and performing aspects of digital modeling and enriching tools with some new modalities of interaction more oriented to exploiting designers' skills is at the basis of the

R. Shumaker (Ed.): Virtual Reality, HCII 2007, LNCS 4563, pp. 441–450, 2007.

research work described in this paper. The research activities have been carried out in the context of the research project T'nD - Touch and Design (www.kaemart.it/touch-and-design) funded by the FP6-IST Programme of the European Union. The project intends to define free-form shape modeling tools based on novel haptic interaction techniques that can be easily used by designers in their activity for incrementing their performances, and by modelers who are able to preserve their manual skillfulness and at the same time be integrated into the digital process for the development of new industrial design products [2].

The paper presents the novel shape modeling system developed within the context of the T'nD project. The system is based on a designer-cantered approach, is friendly and intuitive to use for designers, and couples the effective functionalities of current CAS tools with user friendly modalities which allow designers to make use of ways of working and tools similar to the ones used in the real workshop.

Section 2 presents the users' requirements defined on the basis of observing designers' ways of working. Section 3 describes the overall architecture and components of the developed shape modeling system based on 3D haptic tools, and section 4 describes the sanding tool used for shape refinement and exploration. Finally, Section 5 includes conclusions and a discussion about future development activities.

## 2 Users' Requirements

In order to achieve the goal of proposing an intuitive and easy-to-use shape modeling system, the research activity supported by the cognitive psychologists involved in the project has focused on the observation and analysis of modelers' activities performed in the real workshop [3]. The intention was to gather information about the different modeling techniques used by modelers and designers at work, their gestures, the used tools, and the modalities used for checking the quality and characteristics of the in-progress models. Therefore, practices and hand modeling activities performed by modelers of the project industrial partners (working in the car design and domestic appliances design sectors) have been observed and analyzed. During some study case sessions modelers have been asked to create the physical model of an object using different techniques, in order to gather information about the various approaches used in relation to different materials and tasks: some modelers were asked to create a hand-hold vacuum cleaner using hard resin, other modelers were asked to make the same object using foam material and clay.

Video recordings of the modeling sessions have been tabulated in a process chart, including: timing, duration of events, activities and tools, and target of the actions. Subsequently, a quantitative analysis of gestures for each session (characterized by the kind of material used, the modelers' or designers' skills, the expected level of accuracy and the overall complexity of the mock-up) has been performed. Finally, main gestures have been selected and described on the basis of qualitative and quantitative information, such as: aim and modus operandi of the tool, tool movements, hands movements, shape evaluation tasks, similarity with other tools, etc.

Concerning the gestures performed by the modeler, they are influenced by several factors. We can identify two main types of gestures: ergotic gesture which is performed by the modeler when working on the shape, and exploratory gesture which is performed for evaluating the quality of the shape. The analysis of ergotic gestures also provides hints about how the tools are used. Conversely, exploratory gestures occurred without the use of any tools.

## 2.1 Ergotic Gestures and Tools

The analysis of the recorded modeling sessions have highlighted that approximately 75% of the object modeling actions are done using five tools. In order to define which tools are more effective and useful than others, we have decided to classify the tools on the basis of the comparison of the total time of usage, and the number of times they were used. In fact, we noticed that if a tool was used for a longer time, it did not necessarily demonstrate its importance.

Concerning the tools, we can state that the movement performed for scraping material is representative enough of most of the gestures families occurring during the process. This type of action is rather qualitative, and we can affirm that the same gesture is used both for shaping and finishing a surface, and is also used either for large surfaces or for details. Concerning the type of tools, rakes are used for removing thick layers of material, while sandpaper is used for finishing the surface and eliminating small defects. Both hands are often used in order to work with strength and accuracy. A single stroke allows obtaining a wide curved surface, instead of a number of small flat surfaces, which have to be refined further.

## 2.2 Exploratory Gestures

After working the piece of material with the tools, the modeler had the necessity to check whether the physical mock-up had the expected proportions and quality of shape. Different approaches were used for assessing the correctness of the work regarding the various aspects. For example, modelers checked the object dimensions and the profile and the curvature continuity through the use of both vision and touch. These evaluations depended on the expected level of accuracy, on the scale and size of the mock-ups, and on the strategy used by the modeler. For instance, in the case of car design, the expected level of accuracy was very high: several measurements were done, many marks were placed on the mock-up, and the outcome dimensional precision of the mock-up was in the order of tenth of millimeters. According to our observations, the most commonly used validation modalities were based on the use of touch and surface contact. These validations occurred during the sculpting activities as well as during the finishing activities and affected an average of 5% of the whole object modeling time. They were used to test the final shape (sculpting steps), and to ensure the obtaining of high quality surface (finishing steps).

Concerning tactile verifications, they were carried out in different ways, and each of them had different goals. Rapid sweeps on surface appeared often while sculpting or finishing the mock-up and more particularly when the modeler had to remove dust. This action carries information not exactly about the precise curvature of the shape, but rather about the detection of irregularities or variations on the curvature. For example, a bump or a hole can be detected very quickly. Thus, a curvature variation is detected and not the curvature itself; this method allows to detect features otherwise unrecognizable just by visual observation.

Another method is based on long sweep performed along the surface, that are iterative movements, back and forth or from side to side, through which the modeler gets information about curvature variations more than curvatures themselves. In addition, a long sweep movement was performed with both hands encompassing the mock-up; it was used for exploring the symmetry of the mock-up. The information was slowly and hardly treated, and it was necessary to repeat this movement several times in order to integrate the information acquired in the various steps more precisely.

It has to be pointed out that the work was made all the time under visual control and that the very first and intuitive way to check shape was through its visual observation. For doing this, the modeler stopped working and started observing the mock-up. In this way two aspects were mainly observed: the object curvatures and its symmetry. The mock-up cannot be evaluated in a global way that is all its aspects at the same time. Therefore, the modeler generally performs local checks. The user holds the mock-up at the eyes level, orients it in order to observe the contour only, and turns it to observe different aspects sequentially. Another common technique is based on the use of the reflection lines of light and shading, which has been extensively simulated in computer aided design systems.

In conclusion, tactile and kinesthetic inputs seem to complete visual information, still ambiguous about the three dimensions, and help to construct a more precise 3D mental representation of the concept [4].

### 2.3 Analysis and Conclusions

The gestures and tools analysis has shown that the most common actions are scraping, surface quality check and finishing actions, and the related tool, which are respectively: rakes, hands and sandpaper. Figure 1 shows some typical actions performed by modelers and tools used during the manual modeling sessions.

The results of this study have been used for designing and developing the interaction modalities and tools of the system.

**Fig. 1.** Typical actions performed by modelers while modeling objects manually, and related tools

## 3 Shape Modeling System Based on 3d Haptic Tools

The design and development of the innovative modeling system developed within the context of the research has started with the definition of its requirements. From a human-computer interaction and usability perspective, the system intended to provide haptic tools and modeling operators for scraping and finishing surfaces which support a way of working for users which is very much similar to the one used in their daily physical work. Therefore, the system should allow users to generate digital shapes using a CAS tool integrated with interaction devices and modalities which are similar to the ones supported by rakes and sandpaper tools used for modeling and finishing the object surfaces in real life.

Therefore, in order to satisfy the requirements, the system consists of the integration of haptic interfaces into a digital design tool. Haptic technology supports the possibility of touching virtual objects and perceiving their physical properties [5]. In this way besides the usual visual perception of the object, a kinesthetic knowledge of the object can also be achieved defining a more comprehensive perception of it.

The analysis of the state of the art of technology available showed that an extended version of the FCS-HapticMaster (www.moog-fcs.com/robotics) haptic technology would have been the most appropriate hardware solution for the implementation of the system [6]. In fact, the device provides an adequate workspace and rendered force (250 N), appropriate stiffness and supports from 3 to 4 degrees of freedom (DOF). The FCS-HapticMaster technology has been used as basic platform for the system development, equipped with a strong and stiff 6 DOF device carrying simulated modeling tools.

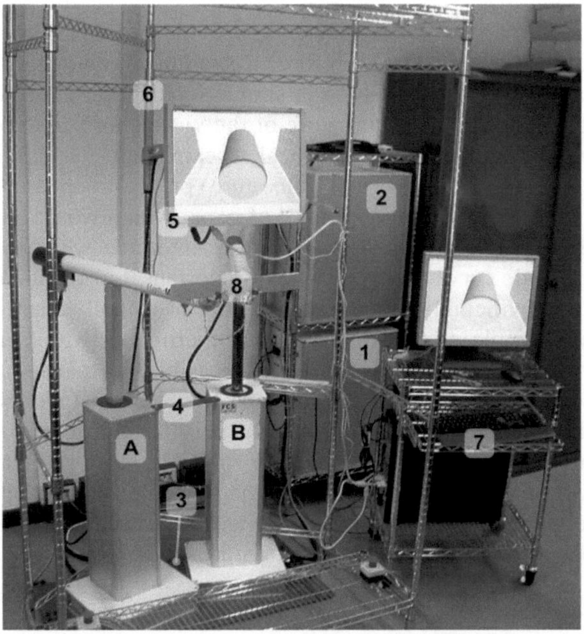


**Fig. 2.** Haptic modeling workstation set-up

The haptic modeling workstation consists of several hardware and software modules [7]. They include commercially available components and custom components that have been developed as part of the research project. Figure 2 depicts the hardware configuration of the system. The visible components are two FCS-HapticMasters (A, B) complete with their controller boxes (1, 2) and mounting hardware (3, 4), a suspended display (5) with its mounting rack (6) and a computer workstation (7). The configuration of the system is based on the use of two FCS-HapticMasters (A, B) as each device does not provide a sufficient number of DOFs useful for supporting the simulation of the movement and of the exertion of reaction forces as required by the scraping and sanding tools.

Ad-hoc end-effectors meeting the application specifications have been developed. Users' activities that the project aims to simulate include scraping a piece of clay, check the surface quality and sand the surface. Therefore, two tools have been developed: scraping tool for material removal, and the sanding tool for surface quality check and surface finishing operations. The configuration of the haptic system is such that the two tools can be easily replaced so that the user can switch between the various actions he intends to perform. The application must also change its behavior accordingly by switching between different operational modes. The end-effector shown in the picture is the scraping tool (8). The second end-effector for surface finishing has been developed and is described in details in the following section.

## 4 Haptic Tool for Exploring and Sanding a Shape

As previously said, the system was expected to provide a tool for checking the surface quality and sanding the surface. Therefore, a sanding system has been developed consisting of a sanding tool that allows the simulation of a piece of sandpaper, where the curvature actually follows the curvature of the virtual surface to be sanded. Since the device is new, it required psychophysical research into the difference perceived between a single curvature ("cylindrical" curvature) piece of paper, or a double curvature ("spherical" or "saddle" curvature) piece of paper which would in practice have to wrinkle in real life. It is considered that even an interface which would only have plane motion and single curvature would yield important information on the degree of fidelity needed to convincingly emulate the feeling of actually sanding a virtual surface. Even such a simple setup would allow experiments with completely virtual experiences with tools not available or indeed possible, in real life, such as adding instead of removing material by virtual sanding. The rotational workspace of the tool is the same as that of the human hand. It is usually limited to ± 30° in fore-aft tilt relative to the human arm, but the freedom in roll is at least 120°, and in fact more than that if the extra roll at the elbow joint of the human arm is taken into account. In order to accurately and realistically representing the surface shape, the implementation of the sandpaper tool supports double curvature.

### 4.1 Hand Interface for Rendering the Surface Curvature

Surface curvature can be rendered to the human hand by presenting the proper alignment of the surface at all places of contact between the hand and the surface. Conceptually, the surface can be subdivided into patches for some or all fingers or groups of fingers, and the palm of the hand (Figure 3 a). This gives great flexibility in the type of surface curvature to render, and the maximum deflections possible. However, it would imply that every patch needs actuation in depth, and possibly also in two degrees of rotational freedom. Since it was our aim to present surfaces of G2 (geometric curvature continuity) complexity only, it has been decided to create an interface which is itself a contiguous surface of exactly this complexity. This will typically take the form shown in Figure 3 b, with the number of degrees of freedom discussed in the following.

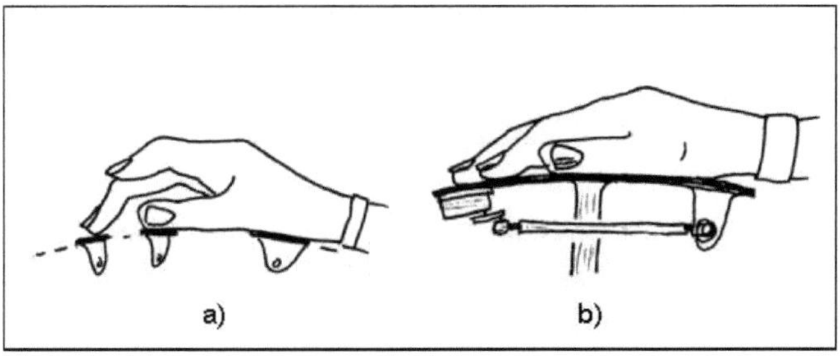


**Fig. 3.** a) Surface curvature rendering. b) DOF representation of surface curvature interface.

A piece of sandpaper, or rather the underlying surface of the work piece contacted, has curvature in addition to orientation. Our system is limited to the G2 curvature, which is the degree of "roundness" of the surface, similar to the second derivative of a curved line on a flat surface. From mathematical theory, we know that the curvature has three degrees of freedom:

- Orientation of the first principal direction.
- Curvature in the first principal direction.
- Curvature in the second principal direction, which is at right angles to the first.

The user will move the surface patch over the virtual surface, when exploring or virtually sanding a surface. It has been noticed that in most of the cases it is sufficient to continuously adapt the G2 curvature of the patch symmetrically, to the local curvature of the surface under exploration, instead of providing higher derivatives. If the hand is relatively large in relation to the radii of curvature of the surface under exploration, and if the curvature of the surface is changing rapidly, then human users may well extract a cue about the nature of the surface, from the longitudinal changing of the curvature under the moving hand, i.e. by feeling the traveling bumps passing under the hand. Emulating this moving curvature would require higher orders of derivatives of the surface than G2, starting with the third derivative. Third derivatives indicate a linearly changing G2 curvature, if nonzero in a certain direction. Actuating certain third derivatives would allow users to feel how they are approaching and passing corners first feeling the increase of the curvature under the hand when approaching the corner, then feeling the symmetry of the curvature when at the most curved point of the corner, and then feeling the decreasing curvature under the patch when moving away from the high point of the corner.

The hardware device consists of a structure that is covered by a tactile patch. The patch is supported and controlled from the centre, where the G0 location, G1 attitude orientation and G2 curvature of the patch are defined. The tool is based on a ting structure consisting of a plane structure based on semi-stiff radial ribs placed at 120° intervals, forced by the actuators to the desired cross-sections of the surface to the desired curves, and with the webs between the radial ribs filled in by some form of semi-stiff concentric webbing. The resulting structure looks like an umbrella. The important difference to a foil umbrella is that the area between the radial ribs will be stiffened by circular elements. These need to be fairly stiff in out of plane bending, but at the same time variable in length to accommodate the compression and stretching of these concentric perimeter curves. Figure 4 shows a closer look of the device, complete with the custom elastic surface that was made from thin plastic sheet. The numbers in the figure identify the components of the device. In particular, the picture shows the following main components:

- flexible spokes made of harmonic steel. There are three spokes spaced at 120 degrees from each other (number 1);
- guy wires used to transform the traction force exerted by the servo motors via the nylon cables, into a torque (number 2);
- the elastic surface, driven by the flexible spokes (number 5);
- hexagonal stud that serves as the base component supporting all the other components (number 6).

**Fig. 4.** Detailed view of the sanding tool device structure

This combination of stiffness can be achieved by making the rings out of sheet material such as stiff paper or plastic, placed on end to give out of plane bending stiffness, and folded into a zig-zag or concertina pattern to accommodate length changes. The resulting rings look like a cookie cutter, or like certain table placemats (Figure 5 a). Depending on the coarseness of the webbing of the supporting structure, the final surface is smoothed to the touch. The tool has a smooth, stretching surface. This consists of a number of layers of lycra pre-stretched to avoid wrinkling when "compressed". The number of layers and the thickness of the material can be adapted to the smoothness required. The system computes information about the surface curvature according to the haptic tool position. This information is used for shaping the tool according to the surface curvature (Figure 6 b).

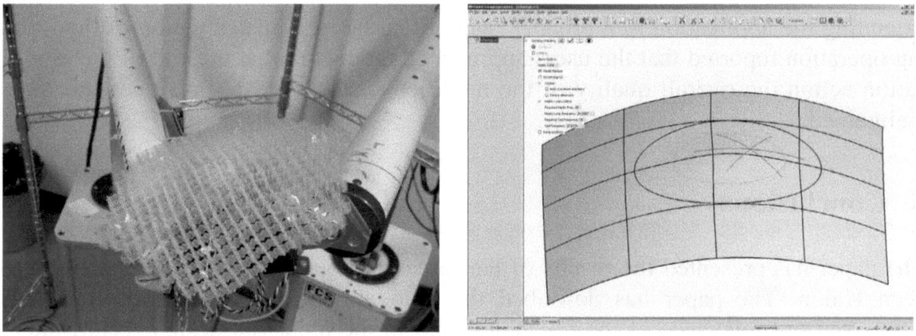

a) b)

**Fig. 5.** a) Views of the sanding tool device without the cover; b) area explored using the sanding tool

The sanding tool is easily manipulated by the user as it was a real piece of sandpaper. The user is free to move and rotate the tool around the three axes in order to feel the surface curvature of the object. When the user moves the hand the device deforms according to the surface curvature (Figure 6 b). The same device is used for adding material to a shape by means of an inflating operator. When the system is operating in this modality, the user exerts some forces over the surface, and a proportional layer of material is added.

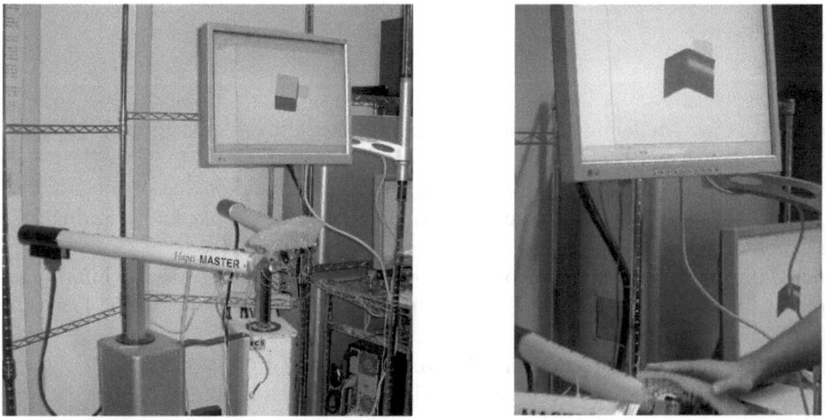


a) b)

**Fig. 6.** a) T'nD system equipped with the sanding tool; b) The sanding tool device deforms according to the surface curvature

For what concerns the evaluation of the sanding tool, the users who tried the system reported that the force feedback provided by the device was good. The current device allows the perception of convex shapes with a minimum radius. The perception of these types of shapes is good. Additional research activities are required for extending the application to a broader range of surfaces. The evaluation of the inflating operation reported that the users appreciated the fact that at the end of the modification action the overall quality of the modified surface was always guaranteed and maintained.

## 5 Conclusions

The paper has presented the results of the research project T'nD funded by the European Union. The paper has described the motivations that justify the project, the objectives and relevance of the research topics in the industrial design sector, the requirements collected by interviewing and observing designers at work, and the analysis performed for designing the system. Furthermore, the paper has presented the achieved results that consist in the identification of the system functionalities resembling ways of operating of designers and modelers, in the study and implementation of the haptic tools. In particular, the paper has presented the haptic tool developed for exploring and sanding a surface. The tools have been tested by end users who have reported easiness of use, fidelity of the force feedback provided. The perception about the effectiveness of the system was quite positive, despite the fact that the kinds of surfaces that can be rendered are currently limited. One of the major problems concerning the system usability reported in the users' tests is related to the lack of co-location of the haptic and visual perceptive spaces. In this sense, a better visualization system, based on stereo viewing, would certainly improve the overall users' perception, and consequently the system usability aspects.

## References

1. Yamada, Y.: Clay Modeling: techniques forgiving three-dimensional form to idea, San'ei Shobo Publishing Co (1997)
2. Bordegoni, M., Cugini, U.: Haptic modeling in the conceptual phases of product design, Virtual Reality Journal, Special Issue on Haptic Interfaces and Applications. Springer Computer Graphics Format 9(1), (2006)
3. Giraudo, U., Bordegoni, M.: Using observations of real designers at work to inform the development of a novel haptic modeling system, In: Proceedings of ICMI'05, Trento, Italy (2005)
4. Poitou, J.P.: La dissonance cognitive, A.Colin, Paris (1974)
5. Burdea, G.: Force and Touch Feedback for Virtual Reality, John Wiley & Sons, New York (1996)
6. Bordegoni, M., et. al.: Deliverable D1 Hardware and software technology and cognitive ergonomics update. T'nD project public report (2004) www.kaemart.it/touch-and-design
7. Bordegoni, M., Cugini, U.: A conceptual design tool based on innovative haptic devices, In: Proceedings of DETC'06, ASME, Philadelphia (2006)

# An Egocentric Augmented Reality Interface for Spatial Information Management in Crisis Response Situations

Anthony Costello and Arthur Tang

Media Interface and Network Design (M.I.N.D.) Laboratories
Department of Industrial Engineering and Management Systems
University of Central Florida, Orlando, Florida
khtang@mail.ucf.edu

**Abstract.** In emergency operations centers, operators are challenged with managing and analyzing massive amounts of information in a timely manner. With the advent of motion tracking systems and low-cost, high-performance graphics workstations, novel spatial augmented reality (AR) interfaces are becoming technologically feasible. AR interfaces have very unique characteristics as compared to other media and computer interfaces: users interact with the computer system through body motion in a volumetric space, instead of via a two-dimensional surface. We have created three prototype immersive AR computing interfaces for emergency operation center. User interacts with the information using a pair of motion tracked pinch gloves, and information is displayed through a head-tracked optical see-though head mounted display. The emergency operator uses intuitive grab and release gesture to move and manipulate the digital information in the environment analogous to interaction of everyday life objects.

**Keywords:** Augmented Reality, Human Computer Interaction, Spatial Interface.

## 1 Introduction

In Emergency Operations Centers, operators are challenged with managing and analyzing massive amounts of information in a timely manner. Teams of people may be assigned to collect, collate and transpose this information into an accurate depiction of the crisis situation in order to make timely decisions. As we move into the digital era where most information is managed and stored digitally, legacy computer interfaces are being stretched far beyond their practical limits to meet interaction requirements such as ever increasing information loads and activity levels. These issues are far more critical in the high-stress and information intensive environments of Emergency Operation Centers.

### 1.1 Prototype Concept

With the advent of motion tracking systems and low-cost, high-performance graphics workstations, novel spatial augmented reality (AR) interfaces are becoming technologically feasible. AR interfaces have very unique characteristics as compared to

R. Shumaker (Ed.): Virtual Reality, HCII 2007, LNCS 4563, pp. 451–457, 2007.

other media and computer interfaces. For instance, AR facilitates interaction paradigms that allow users to interact with a computer system through body motion in a volumetric space, instead of via two-dimensional surfaces. These spatial characteristics can potentially be powerful "cognitive artifacts" [1] or "intelligence amplifying systems" [2] that enhance human cognitive activities, such as attention, planning, decision making, and procedural and semantic memory. Volumetric AR interfaces make use of a greater range of human sensorimotor capabilities, and can potentially increase the communication bandwidth between the user and the computer by cutting the ties to that technological ancestor – the typewriter.

We created several prototype immersive AR computing interfaces in an emergency operation center setting. Users view the information via a see-through head mounted display (HMD) and interact with information objects using a pair of motion tracked pinch gloves. The emergency operator uses intuitive grab and release gestures to move and manipulate the digital information in an egocentric workspace. This interaction paradigm is designed to be analogous to the way humans interact with objects in everyday life. Critical information such as incident reports in text form, audio records (e.g. radio communications from emergency responders) or video records (e.g. visuals of hurricane damage) are streaming into the workspace through an "inbox" analogous to the "inbox" in conventional email client software. The emergency operator can then organize the incoming information spatially, and register the information spatially to the physical workspace.

## 2 Theoretical Background

Before exploring how to optimize the interface for digital information organization, it is worth exploring how humans organize information in everyday life.

### 2.1 Spatial Cognition and Information Organization

If an Emergency Operation Center operator were in charge of analyzing physical versions of documents (e.g., faxes, reports, forms), how would the operator organize the documents to facilitate the cognitive process? Typically, the paperwork would be placed on a desk for the operator. As the number of paperwork increased, along with the diversity of information they contained, the operator's first instinct would probably be to cluster the paperwork according to some criteria, and to spread the cluster of paperwork out across the desk. This action, referred to by Kirsh as "spatially decomposing a task" [3], is an initial effort to organize the information without the benefit of context. As Aaltonen and Leikoinen observed, "many of our structuring actions serve to reduce the descriptive complexity of our environments" [4]. The operator's instinctive step, therefore, can be viewed as an initial effort to use objects in the environment to simplify the task of organization until a more efficient method can be devised. As the operator learns more about the relationships between different documents, piles will inevitably form. Malone poses four reasons for the creation of such paper piles: "(1) the mechanical difficulty of creating labeled file folders, binders and so forth, especially if multiple levels of classification are desired, (2) the cognitive difficulty of creating appropriate categories and deciding how to classify information in a way that will be easily retrievable, (3) the desire to be reminded of tasks to be done, (4) the desire to have frequently used information easily accessible" [5].

In other words, when confronted with disordered information, humans utilize skills and techniques to decrease cognitive load by first organizing it at a high level—in this case, spatially. This higher-level organization usually results in a loose, generalized set of clusters (e.g., individual piles of papers), which form a starting point for further analysis [3]. The next step is to analyze the characteristics of each object, noting both unique and common attributes. An iterative process follows where clusters are reorganized, eliminated or parsed down to smaller clusters. During the organization process and any associated tasks upon which the organization effort depends, humans must constantly recall where they left objects or where objects belong. Put simply, humans will make an effort to use spatial decomposition to decrease cognitive load while organizing information in their world.

Whether using a physical desktop in the real world or a virtual desktop on a 2-dimensional computer screen, humans use tools in the external world to help them organize information. Therefore, an appropriate organization paradigm for human operators would most likely involve a compromise between highly organized documents in file folders and a more loose organization of document piles spread out spatially in front of the user [6].

### 2.2 Information Organization and Human Information Processing

If reduction of cognitive load is a natural goal for humans when engaging in the organization of information, then it is necessary to explore how information organization fits into overall human information processing.

During the *perception stage*, stimuli are perceived through detection, recognition, identification or categorization [7]. It is important to note that attentional resources are finite and will limit the number of stimuli that can be processed in this manner. The *cognition stage* processes the stimuli through both working and long-term memories. Working memory is characterized, in part, by it's vulnerability to interference and limited capacity, whereas long-term memory serves as the brain's permanent storage system. During the *cognition stage*, attention resources are required to make comparisons between perceived stimuli and information stored in long-term memory. If a physical reaction is chosen during the cognitive stage, it is carried out in the *motor response stage*. This physical response also draws from attention resources [7].

As information is processed through each stage, it is evident that attentional resources are critical throughout the process. Working memory, in particular, has been a focus of research since it is an attention-demanding store where humans "examine, evaluate, transform and compare different mental representations" [7]. Some of this research has yielded results that may help shed light on why humans organize information the way they do.

Baddeley [8] broke working memory down into three sub-processes: the visuospatial sketchpad, the phonological loop and the episodic buffer. These sub-processes are governed by a central executive component that modulates attention to each. The visuospatial sketchpad is particularly important to this discussion since it forms "an interface between visual and spatial information, accessed either through the senses or from LTM [long term memory]" [8]. Wickens and Holland [7] tell us that mental rotations (i.e., figuring out how landmarks on a map correspond to the world in front of us) involve mental rotations of the information. This information is stored in the visuospatial sketchpad, but also involves central executive. Therefore, systems that help reduce the difficulty of mental rotations will further offload cognition.

George Miller [9] maintains that working memory can handle 7 chunks +/-2, providing full attention is utilized [7]. If information is properly chunked, it can be processed more effectively, easing the demand on attention resources. This suggests that the format of the material before it is perceived may dictate whether or not the human will have to devote greater cognitive and attentional resources to process it. This format change may be in how each unit of information is represented, or how the information is represented as a whole. If it is represented in such a way as to promote recognition rather than recall, the information will be processed to a certain degree prior to entering working memory—further reducing load on attention resources. Hence, a worthy goal would be to design a tool that may allow the user to manipulate and/or visualize data in such a way to promote chunking and recognition.

Returning to the discussion regarding methods through which humans organize information, varying the presentation of the information may affect how well humans can remember a given item or group of items by providing a mnemonic structure to the data. Fiore, Johnston and van Duyne [10] maintain that mnemonics of this type "(1) help the trainee organize the information conveyed; (2) facilitate the assimilation of new information with related prior knowledge; and, (3) deepen processing and make the information easier to remember".

Furthermore, information presentation may affect how humans perceive and associate in coming stimuli (e.g., visual) with information that already resides in memory. In the case of interface design, visual data can be presented with context to further aid the linking of semantic information with relevant spatial information. Visual context, or "the global configuration of all items", may aid both the ability to recall information and the ease by which subjects locate embedded target information during visual search [11]. Furthermore, Chun [12] maintains that contextual encoding may be intrinsic to how humans selectively process and encode information because memory capacity is limited. According to Tulving's [13] encoding specificity principle, the effect of relevant context (e.g., geographical map presentation) may help a human remember other information associated with that location (e.g., the status of emergency responders) simply because contextual information is closely related (or is identical to) the semantic information regarding that location. Therefore, designing displays that provide relevant visual context may further assist the human operator in recalling relevant information when performing tasks of a spatial nature (e.g., IOC operators attempting to remember information regarding specific events at specific locations).

### 2.3 Information Visualization and Spatial Cognition

Many traditional information systems and visualization such as graphs, diagrams, and signage make extensive use of spatial cues to facilitate human cognitive process. Modern information visualization techniques have a great potential to further augment the limitation of human cognitive process. Card, Mackinlay and Schneiderman [14] maintain that externalizations and visualizations of information may actually augment the processing capability of a user by reducing load on their working memory. Combining techniques in visualization with the capabilities inherent to augmented reality may serve to improve spatial cognition and further offload working memory.

According to Biocca, Tang, Owen and Xiao [15], "Augmented reality (AR) techniques enhance the perception of reality through the use of computer-generated virtual annotations". Not to be confused with Virtual Reality (VR), AR does not completely immerse the user in a virtual world. Rather, AR "enhances the user's senses by overlaying a perceptible virtual layer on the physical world" [4]. Tang, Owen, Biocca and Xiao indicate that "[AR's] ability to overlay and register information on the workspace in a spatially meaningful way allows AR to be a more effective instructional medium" [16]. Experimental results of Tang et al. indicate that using AR as an instructional medium increase spatial task performance and reduce mental workload [16].

It is possible that designing an interface that closely parallels the spatial organization techniques used in our everyday lives may decrease cognitive load and demands on operators' limited attentional resources. To this end, using techniques in information visualization and the capabilities of AR interfaces could possibly help support the process of spatial organization without increasing demands on cognitive processes.

## 3 Prototype Interface

Three prototype AR interfaces was developed to illustrate the idea of egocentric spatial interface for digital information in the emergency operation setting. The prototypes were developed using ImageTclAR [17]. The prototypes were running on a commodity class PC with Microsoft Windows XP.

### 3.1 Projection-Based Augmented Reality

In the projection-based AR prototype, the digital information was projected on a table top projection. The operator manipulates the digital information using a traditional mouse. This prototype is different from the traditional computer desktop interfaces in the sense that the display surface is horizontal rather than vertical. The horizontal display surface epitomizes the everyday processing and organization of paperwork, in contrast to the typical vertical display in most computer interface. Furthermore, the prototype has a larger display size than typical compute display, which facilitates the organization of digital information in a spatial context.

### 3.2 Video See-Through Augmented Reality

In the video see-through AR prototype, a video see-through HMD were constructed with a camera attached to an opaque HMD. Digital information was overlaid on the video stream captured by the camera. The camera also kept track of the fiduciary marks attached on the table such that the digital information rendered can be registered spatially on the table. User's hands motion were tracked by the fiduciary mark on the gloves. A pair of virtual cursors were attached to the position of each of the user's hands. A pair of pressure sensors were attached to the thumb of each glove to detect the gesture of the pinch of the thumb and index finger. When the cursor is in contact with a virtual object, the user can pick and lift the virtual object by pinching the thumb and the index finger. The user can release the object to the environment by letting go the pinch gesture.

### 3.3 Optical See-Through Augmented Reality

In the optical see-through AR prototype, the digital information was displayed through an optical see-through HMD. User's head motion was tracked using an Intersense IS-900 room-based motion tracker. Computer graphics were rendered in real time based on the head motion data from the tracker. User manipulated the digital information using a pair of motion tracked pinch gloves. A virtual cursor was attached to the position of each of the user's hands. The video see-through AR prototype incorporated a similar virtual object manipulation method as optical the optical see-through AR prototype, by pinching and release the thumb and the index finger.

## 4 Future Work

We are designing a user study to evaluate the effectiveness of the spatial AR interface as compared to traditional interfaces currently deployed in emergency operations centers. Subjects will be asked to organize incoming critical incident information in a digital format using our prototype interface. The rate at which information arrives will vary to generate different levels of stress and mental workload throughout the task. An array of measurements will be used to assess user's task performance and traits. Quantitative measurements will assess subjects' response time and error rate. Subjects' situation awareness will be measured using the Situation Awareness Global Assessment Technique [18]. Pre-test and Post-test questionnaires will be used to measure subjects' perceived memory, mental workload, meta-cognition, subjective situation awareness, spatial ability, and sense of presence. The study seeks potential empirical evidence indicating that successful spatial information techniques using advanced spatial AR interfaces can improve user's performance and enhance interface usability, usability, enabling users to find, manipulate, and remember digital information better than current interface paradigms.

## References

1. Norman, D.: Things that make us smart: defending human attributes in the age of the machine. Addison-Wesley Publishing Co, Menlo Park, CA (1993)
2. Brook, F.: The computer scientist as toolsmith II. Communication of the ACM 39(3), 61–68 (1996)
3. Kirsh, D.: The intelligent use of space. Artificial Intelligence 73, 31–68 (1995)
4. Aaltonen, A., Lehikoinen, J.: Exploring augmented reality visualizations. In: Proceedings of Working Conference on Advanced Visual Interfaces, Venezia, Italy (2006)
5. Malone, T.: How do people organize their desks? Implications for the design of office information space. ACM Transactions on Office Information Systems 1(1), 99–112 (1983)
6. Jones, W.: The spatial metaphor for user interfaces: experimental tests of reference by location versus name. ACM Transactions on Office Information Systems 4(1), 42–63 (1986)

7. Wickens, C., Hollands, J.: Engineering psychology and human performance. Prentice-Hall, Inc, Upper Saddle River, NJ (2000)
8. Baddeley, A.: Is working memory still working? European Psychologist 7(2), 85–97 (2002)
9. Miller, G.: The magic number seven, plus or minus two: some limits on our capacity for information processing. Psychological Review 63, 81–97 (1956)
10. Fiore, S.M., Johnston, J., van Duyne, L.: Conceptualizing the training space: constructing hierarchies to integrate time and space for distributed debriefings. In: In: Proceedings of Human Factors and Ergonomics Society 48th Annual Meeting, New Orleans, LA (2004)
11. Chun, M., Jiang, Y.: Implicit, long-term spatial contectual memory. Journal of Experimental Psychology: Learning, Memory and Cognition 29(2), 224–234 (2003)
12. Chun, M.: Contextual cueing of visual attention. Trends in Cognitive Sciences 4, 170–178 (2000)
13. Tulving, E.: Elements of episodic memory. Oxford University Press, New York, NY (1983)
14. Card, S., Mackinlay, J., Schneiderman, B.: Readings in information visualization: using vision to think. Morgan Kaufmann Publishers, San Francisco, CA (1999)
15. Biocca, F., Tang, A., Owen, C., Xiao, F.: Attention funnel: omnidirectional 3D cursor for mobile augmented reality platforms. In: Proceedings of CHI '2006, Conference on Human Factors in Computing Systems. Montréal, Cananda (2006)
16. Tang, A., Owen, C., Biocca, F., Xiao, F.: Comparative effectiveness of augmented reality in object assembly. In: Proceedings of ACM CHI '2003, Conference on Human Factors in Computing Systems, Fort Lauderdale, FL (2003)
17. Owen, C., Tang, A., Xiao, F.: ImageTclAR: a blended script and compiled code development system for augmented reality. In: Proceedings of STARS2003, The International Workshop on Software Technology for Augmented Reality Systems, Tokyo, Japan (2003)
18. Endsley, M.: Theoretical underpinnings of situation awareness: a critical review, In: Endsley, M. (ed.): Situation Awareness Analysis and Measurement, pp. 1–24. Lawrence Erlbaum Associates, Mahwah, NJ (2000)

# A Reconfigurable Immersive Workbench and Wall-System for Designing and Training in 3D Environments*

Jesús Gimeno[1], Marcos Fernández[1], Pedro Morillo[2], Inmaculada Coma[1], and Manuel Pérez[1]

[1] Instituto de Robótica
Universidad de Valencia
Polígono de la Coma, s/n
46980 Paterna, (Valencia), Spain
jgimeno@robotica.uv.es

[2] Louisiana Immersive Techonologies Entreprise (LITE)
University of Louisiana at Lafayette
537 Cajundome Boulevard
70506 Lafayette, (LA), USA
pedro@lousiana.edu

**Abstract.** Virtual and Augmented Reality have been widely used in many scientific fields for the last two decades in order to visualize complex data and information. Although both techniques are oriented to show users complex 3D environments by means of an intuitive and easy mechanism, they use to become useless to manipulate the information in an intuitive and realistic way. In this paper, we present SOROLLA, a new concept of workbench designed for virtual and augmented reality purposes and specially oriented to the fields of tele-education and engineering. Unlike other proposals, SOROLLA not only allows an easy utilization and configuration, but also shows a cost-effective immersive visualization system based on off-the-shelf elements. The initial results using our workbench and wall-system show that both efficiency and user satisfaction are higher than the ones obtained using conventional devices.

**Keywords:** Virtual Workbench, VWB, Virtual Reality, Augmented Reality, Virtual Prototyping, Immersive Visualization Systems.

## 1 Introduction

Nowadays, new visualization technologies and multimodal user interaction offer users a new way to easily fulfill their tasks. In this sense, both Virtual Reality (VR) and Augmented Reality (AR) techniques have been extensively employed in the last two decades in order to visualize complex data and information in many scientific fields [15]. The use of these techniques has become especially relevant when inherently complex information (usually composed of a huge amount of data) is represented

* This paper is supported by both the Spanish MEC under grant DPI2006-14928-C02-02 and the European Commission Network of Excellence INTUITION IST-NMP-1-507248-2.

R. Shumaker (Ed.): Virtual Reality, HCII 2007, LNCS 4563, pp. 458–467, 2007.

using classic visualization devices: the entire plan of a skyscraper, the design of a route for a road traversing hundreds of miles, a high quality representation of the human body for anatomy and surgery instruction, etc.

One of the most affordable VR devices oriented to this type of applications is the Virtual Workbench. The term Virtual Workbench (VWB) refers to a small semi-immersive visualization device consisting of a projection screen under which virtual environments are backprojected stereoscopically [17,23]. A VWB uses to join cutting-edge input devices, advance visual mechanisms and even audio capabilities and creates a new "front-end" interface for the VR applications. The manipulation of the new and complex information elements using a Virtual Workbench has led to evolve the classic metaphors in the human-computer interaction process towards new interaction styles. Even though these new styles are oriented to show users complex 3D environments by means of an intuitive and easy mechanism, they have three main important problems. Firstly, they do not offer optimal capabilities to manipulate information in an intuitive and realistic way. For instance, it is not very realistic to manipulate the 3D visualization of a virtual terrain using a classic device (2D mouse or a spaceball) that limits the motion control in a plane. Second, they impose a qualitative variation in the way of working when a WBS is used as work tool in professional activities as CAD/CAM design, graphic design, etc. By their nature, these professional activities have require workers to perform well-established actions using the computer for their working life, and therefore the transition to the new environment becomes a hard adaptation or even the rejection of the new working environment. Finally, the investment in new adapted devices (to be presented as general purposes devices for virtual reality applications) is not only resulting in high costs, but also is releasing products that lack easy usability.

In this paper, we present SOROLLA, a new concept of workbench designed for virtual and augmented reality purposes and specially oriented to the fields of tele-education and engineering. SOROLLA is a new system consisting of a 3D visualization and manipulation software and a special hardware. This hardware is composed of a virtual reality workbench and a wall projection system, both of them including stereo viewing and tracking capabilities. The main premises in the design of SOROLLA are an easy utilization and configuration and also a framework based on inexpensive off-the-shelf elements. Taking into account the increase in importance achieved by the new paradigms of visualization and interaction, our system offers the next features: a suitable visualization more according to the handled information, an interaction mechanisms for properly modifying the real data in the virtual environment and a software that takes advantages of these visualization and interaction features. This paper also presents a set of preliminary experiments oriented to evaluate the initial performance of SOROLLA. Our results suggest that SOROLLA performs slightly better that some classical immersive visualization devices in terms of easiness of adaptation to the new device, and also to the new interaction styles.

The rest of the paper is organized as follows: Section 2 describes the related previous work in the area of semi-immersive visualization systems and virtual workbenches. Section 3 describes the software and hardware architecture of SOROLLA. Next, Section 4 establishes a realistic environment for the preliminary performance evaluation of SOROLLA and discuses the first obtained results. Finally, Section 5 presents some concluding remarks.

## 2 Related Work

Traditionally, the Virtual Workbenches have been used for Virtual Reality purposes because users not only can visualize three-dimensional objects and spaces, but also they can interact and travel through the scenes [17,23].

The development and commercialization of products based on Virtual Workbenches have been led by both public organizations [9,11,13,14,16,18,27] and privates companies [2,3,4,22]. Although most of the proposed designs follow the same pattern using a single mode of visualization, the main important structural differences among the different proposals are related to the position and location of the screen. In this sense, [9, 14, 16] take advantage of the initial design [17,23] where a fixed screen is set as a regular element of the framework. Some products offer more versatility allowing the user to modify the initial orientation screen [4], or even the height of the single projection surface [5]. Another system includes an additional screen in order to create an L-shaped projection table [3]. Concerning to the stereo-projection techniques, most of Virtual Workbenches incorporate passive stereo and only few products incorporate active stereo projection to allow a group of users to share the same workbench (using infrared glasses) [1,11,18].

Since this type of devices was initially presented for medical purposes [17] where 3D virtual widgets interact with real surgical tools, some areas of the advance medicine such as neurosurgery [23,9] or bronchial surgery [14] incorporated prematurely the use of virtual workbenches as a part of their surgery procedures. Nowadays, Virtual Workbenches are used in many different fields such as collaborative design [1,18], industrial maintenance training [27], hydraulics [13], physics [16] and applied social psychology [11].

The cost of immersive VR devices is the major barrier to its wider use and application. Therefore, some universities and commercial initiatives have oriented the research towards to launch low-cost immersive visualization devices. However, from our knowledge, only a initial prototype has been proposed to reduce the costs of manufacturing Virtual Workbenches [1]. In this proposal, the reduction of the final cost is based on using some low-cost interaction devices involved in the architecture of the system, and without redesigning any other additional aspect.

## 3 System Description

The system architecture of SOROLLA consists of two major elements. On the one hand, a projection and visualization subsystem allows projecting stereoscopic images to the user for any of the two feasible configurations. On the other hand, an interaction subsystem makes an abstraction of all the different input data (using a shared data structure) that the system can offer to the VR application running on SOROLLA. In this sense, this data structure includes information about the user's point of view obtained from the capture of the head position and also about the current position and type of gesture obtained from the virtual reality glove.

**Framework and Projection System.** The hardware architecture of SOROLLA consists of a visualization subsystem together with a projection subsystem and has been designed to join the comfort of a regular virtual workbench and the group work capacity of a projection-wall system. In this sense, our system includes two visualization modes associated with the two different included screens called *work mode* and *presentation mode*. The first 50-inch screen is linked to the surface of the workbench forming an angle which value can be configured manually to reduce the reflection of external lights. However, the second 100-inch screen is placed perpendicular to the surface of the workbench acting as a presentation screen. Both visualization modes include stereo visualization based on active projection. This feature, achieved by means of passive stereo glasses offers a more realistic and comprehensive visualization of the virtual scene. The projection subsystems is composed of two standard projectors including circular filters. These filters polarize the left and right eye images from the projectors while the user wear low cost, lightweight polarized glasses to direct the left/right images into the correct eye. Figure 1 shows a detailed schematic of SOROLLA when it is configured using the work or presentation mode. As shown in this figure, in order to make the system more compact, the optical path was folded 90-degrees using a mirror and, therefore, the images are obtained by back-projecting from both projectors (left/right images) onto any of the screens.

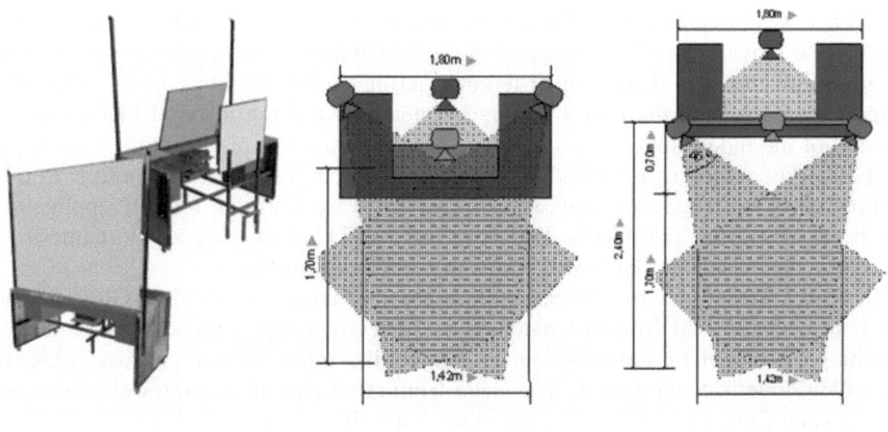

**Fig. 1.** A schematic views of the projection and visualization subsystems included in the design of SOROLLA: (left) A perspective view of the workbench showing both configuration modes, (center) A schematic plan view of the field-of-view (FOV) of the capture system when the work mode or the presentation mode (right) have been selected

One of the key aspects in the design of SOROLLA was to develop a compact (and therefore a portable) immersive visualization system. Since the compactness has an effect on the storage and transport costs, our device can be packed and shipped in a hard-shell flight case with dimensions of about 185x80x95 cm.

**The Multimodal Interaction System.** SOROLLA extends the classic style of interaction based on the desktop metaphor with new styles of interaction from three-dimensional virtual environments such as direct manipulation of 3D objects and multi-user interaction. These features have been implemented into the interaction subsystem. This subsystem is composed of a optical capture system based on webcams and two tracked pinch gloves. The capture system employs four standard webcams (C1,C2,C3 and C4 )and a custom software to obtain the final 2D/3D coordinates associated to optical tracking devices. The trackers have been designed as a multiple color light-emitting diodes (LED) covered with an spreading spherical screen in order to avoid the extreme directionality of the regular LEDs. By using the stereoscopic principle and performing an initial camera calibration, two of the cameras (C1 and C2 are installed on the upper corner of the workbench) obtain the 3D position of the trackers differentiated by their colors. This low cost capture system can detect the position of several trackers simultaneously inside a visual field of three meters with an approximate error radius of 1cm. Although high-cost solutions based on infrared capture systems (such as ART[2], ViCom [20] or IR-PRO) could offer a lower positioning error, our approach not only provides a sufficient precision for our purposes, but also is more robust and reliable to the common and unintentional movements in the framework of the workbench. Unlike infrared capture systems, our approach avoids recalibrations when variations of the camera position greater than one degree occurs, since it includes color information about the existing trackers.

The classic interaction style based on the desktop metaphor is implemented using the camera C3 (located behind the screen to remove occlusions), which objective is to capture the movements of the users on the screen and move the cursor to the specified positions. In order to deal with different lighting conditions, an adaptive algorithm detects the contact of the user's fingers by means of placing infrared LEDs fixed on the end of the index finger of each glove. The camera C4 is placed in the central part of the workbench focusing ahead on the users. The purpose of this camera is to offer compatibility with existing and well-known software libraries for AR applications (such as ARToolkit [6], osgART [19] or ARTag [12]) where a single camera can recognize square marker patterns located in real environments.

SOROLLA includes two tracked pinch gloves (named as Thimble-Glove) which offer an accurate and low-cost mechanism of recognizing natural gestures such as grabbing an object or initiating an action. Unlike other similar products [25], the Thimble-Glove is a wireless device made from cloth and incorporates electrical sensors in each fingertip. This device provides not only information about pinching gestures of the user's hand, but also tracking information since (like a virtual stick) it incorporates infrared LEDs fixed on the fingertip of the index finger. Since Thimble-Glove does not includes external measurement devices such as a goniometers or flexometers it does not require any type of recalibration. The wireless communication of data included in Thimble-Glove is based on a commercially-available device known as "mote" which is a generic sensor node platform that integrates sensing, computation, and communication.

Figure 2 shows an example of different views of the Thimble-Glove in use. This figure emphasizes the compactness and lightweightness of the device which consists of wired connections from the covered fingertips to the wrist where the "mote" is adjusted by Velcro strips.

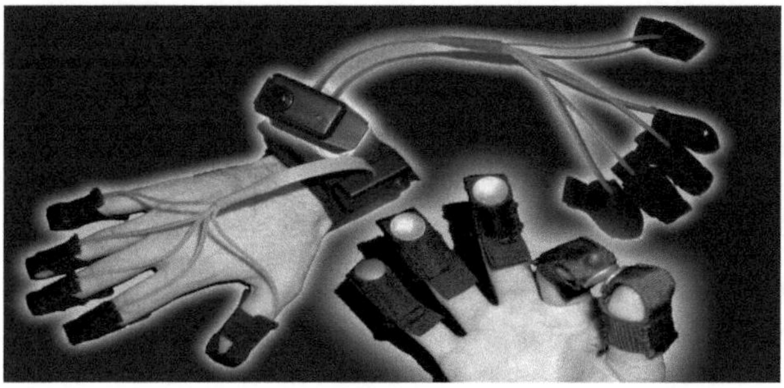

**Fig. 2.** Different views of the same Thimble-Glove. The wireless device consists of a mote motherboard, five contact switches and infrared LEDs fixed on the fingertip of the index finger.

Since in the design of this device we have avoided the idea of assembling a totally covered virtual glove, Thimble-Glove fits easily into any hand, regardless of size or hand preference. Moreover, it overrides the hygienic problems related to sweating problems (hyperhidrosis) when the device is used for exhibition or demonstration purposes.

In order to facilitate compatibility to any type of applications, SOROLLA provides two different types of connectivity based on sockets and VRPN [26]. When a third party (VR or AR) application selects a connection type based on sockets, a server is listening for a network connection on a predefined port, and once a connection is established it starts sending a XML message describing all the devices included in the interaction subsystem (Thimble-Gloves and capture system). Moreover, a VRPN server defines three determined devices (called tracker2d, tracker3d and th-glove). When third party applications are launched on SORLLA, they only have to register and include (using the proper function defined in the VRPN protocol) these three devices as regular elements in their software architecture.

## 4 Applications and Experiments

We have designed a set of preliminary experiments oriented to evaluate the initial performance of our virtual workbench [8,21]. These experiments consist in testing and evaluating the behavior of a benchmark applications on SOROLLA compared to a regular desktop monitor fitted with a hand-tracked interaction device (usually called Desktop VR [24]) and a four-sided CAVE [10]. In our case, the human performance and behavior have been tested in terms of navigation (or exploration) and interaction (or manipulation) in the 3D virtual world. The reason of this type of evaluation lies in the fact of SOROLLA has been defined as a generalist device designed to VR and AR purposes. Our benchmark includes two different multiplatform Virtual Reality applications called VALLE [7] and VISUALG. VALLE is a roadway design system based on Virtual Reality technologies where users design roads and skid trails to follow the natural topography and contour, minimizing alteration of natural features. The navigation mechanisms permit users to navigate through 3D landscapes and city models to evaluate the impact of the designed roads. On the other side, VISUALG is a training software program based on Augmented Reality to provide a method for disseminating expertise on ocular surgery procedures and other complex processes related to ocular physiology. VISUALG merges a full 3D model of the ocular anatomy and images from real users in real time and provides an excellent training interface where all the element belonging to the ocular anatomy can be manipulated. This application was chosen as an example of AR software where the interaction and manipulation of the elements in the 3D virtual environment are extensively exploited.

In order to obtain these results we organized a evaluation session at our laboratories in early June 2006. In this experiment, a selected set of 40 students and staff of our university were invited to test SOROLLA in a session of two hours of duration. All the participants performed the same sequence of six exercises (three executed on VALLE and the rest executed on VISUALG) using the three different immersive visualization devices. The evaluation test (see Figure 3) lasted roughly one hour and a half including a brief training, the exercises, and the time to fill out the final evaluation forms. The participants ranged in the age from 19 to 55 years and 22 (55%) were men. The educational levels among the participants ranged from grade school through doctoral level.

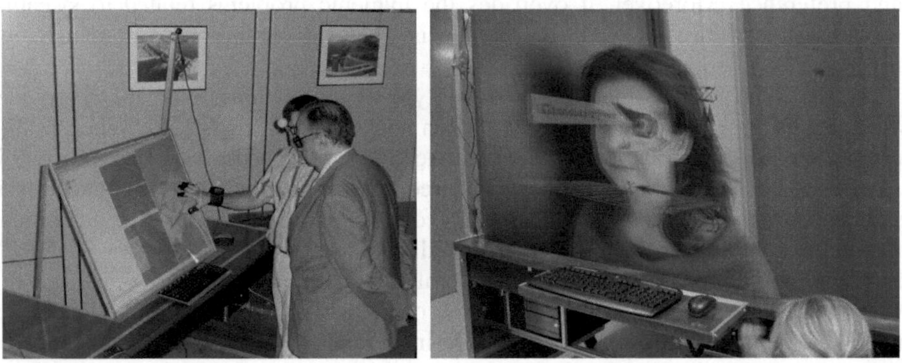

**Fig. 3.** Some snapshots of VALLE and VISUALG running on SOROLLA during the evaluation session

The evaluation session was divided in different phases. First, a brief training video showed the participants the objective of the experiment, the relevant points and what they should do in each one of the six exercises in the three immersive visualization devices. The basic personal information such as sex, age and academic level was also gathered in this phase. Next, an instructor showed the participants the basic operations and commands of both hardware (SOROLLA, Desktop VR and CAVE) and software (VALLE and VISUALG) for short periods of time before the real experiments. Once all the experiments were completed, the participants answered verbally several questions targeting some relevant aspects (interactivity, presence, etc) concerning the exercise. Finally, they scored the three devices in a scale from 0 (worst) to 10 (best) following the next aspects: visual realism of the simulated 3D environment (VR3D), easiness of adaptation to the new device (EAND), easiness of adaptation to the new interaction style (EAIS), degree of immersion (DI) and degree of usability (DU). Table 1 shows the results of this evaluation session. This table shows the average and the standard deviation of the obtained results for the different immersive visualization devices.

**Table 1.** Comparative results of Desktop-VR, CAVE and SOROLLA obtained in the evaluation session

| | *Desktop-VR* | | *4-sided CAVE* | | *SOROLLA* | |
|---|---|---|---|---|---|---|
| | *Average* | *Std. Dev.* | *Average* | *Std. Dev.* | *Average* | *Std. Dev.* |
| *VR3D* | 5.70 | 1.45 | 8.50 | 1.17 | 8.10 | 1.05 |
| *EAND* | 8.90 | 0.76 | 6.60 | 1.30 | 8.30 | 0.95 |
| *EAIS* | 9.10 | 0.80 | 6.40 | 1.10 | 8.50 | 1.07 |
| *DI* | 5.50 | 1.28 | 9.00 | 0.90 | 8.40 | 0.89 |
| *DU* | 6.50 | 1.62 | 5.70 | 1.60 | 7.70 | 1.65 |

The results presented in Table 1 seem to indicate that the perception of visual realism (VR3D) is significantly related to the projection mechanism included in the system. In this sense, although the CAVE system obtained the best results due to the screen size, it is possible to appreciate that SOROLLA has a similar performance. The reason of this similitude could be caused because both SOROLLA and the 4-sided CAVE used in our experiments offer a similar final quality of the projected images.

Concerning to the easiness of adaptation to the new device (EAND), it is noticeable how the Desktop-VR has obtained the best scores. This apparently surprisingly result is not strange because this type of environments is currently used by the subjects with only a few extra additions mainly related to the 3D render quality. In the case of the two actually new immersive environments, it is possible to emphasize that our virtual workbench performs better than the tested 4-sided CAVE. In absolute terms, the reason of this behaviour may be because SOROLLA has been provided with some interaction devices oriented to offer to the users similar elements of interaction to the ones they are used to for the most usual tasks (menus, buttons, etc.). However, elements like FlySticks, 3D mouses, wands or data gloves are completely new to the CAD/CAM users when they are participating in a CAVE experience. The aspect of the easiness of adaptation to the new style of interaction (EAIS) has very similar results than the EAND, the reason is that SOROLLA has been designed taking into account the use of 2D interaction techniques for common tasks meanwhile in the CAVE system the interaction style is more revolutionary and involves new ways of working to perform the most common tasks. Concerning to the aspect of the feeling of immersion (DI), and as we expected, the CAVE environment has obtained the best scores. However, SOROLLA obtained proper results (in terms of feeling of immersion when specially the projection mode is selected) because the use of a large-screen graphics display surface, a high quality stereo projection and the head tracking.

Finally, SOROLLA received the top score when the users evaluated the general usability of the system (DU). The reason of this high-unexpected acceptance could be our virtual workbench not only offers a new interaction mechanism (oriented to improve the classical 3D object manipulation and navigation in virtual environments), but also it still keeps some of the familiar desktop mechanisms which allow the users feel more comfortable performing regular task like file system administration, etc.

## 5 Conclusions

In this paper, we have proposed SOROLLA a new virtual workbench designed for virtual and augmented reality purposes. We have compared the performance and user satisfaction of our system with some devices specifically designed for the same purposes and the obtained results have been very encouraging.

The reason for these results could be caused by the *"evolutionary"* approach suggested by SORROLLA. The system proposes to introduce new 3D interaction styles to traditional 2D/3D desktop-like applications, but centering the interaction on actual 3D aspects of the object manipulation and scene navigation. Moreover, it maintains the classic management of the 2D elements included in most of applications (menus, buttons, scroll-bars, etc) by using a touch screen interface. The fact of maintaining this interaction style makes people more comfortable and self-confident within the new environment because they perform their regular tasks in the same manner in which they did in their usual workspaces. This transition probably will not be needed in the future when desktop metaphors are not so assumed by people that have worked for long periods of time using this paradigm. Meanwhile, the use of smooth transitions between interaction styles, maybe a good way to gain acceptance for the new generation of multimodal interfaces.

## References

1. Andujar, C., Fairen, M., Brunet, P.: Affordable Inmersive Projection System for 3D Interaction. In: 1st Ibero-American Symposium on Computer Graphics, Proceedings of Ibero-American Symposium on Computer Graphics (SIACG'02), Guimeraes, Portugal, pp. 1–9 (2002)
2. Advanced Realtime Tracking GmbH, A.R.T. Infrared Tracking System. Information brochure ( April 2001).
3. Barco CONSUL, http://www.barco.com/VirtualReality/products/product.asp?element=313
4. Barco TAN, http://www.barco.com/VirtualReality/products/product.asp?GenNr=968
5. Barco BARON, http://www.barco.com/corporate/products/product.asp?GenNr=324
6. Billinghurst, M., Kato, H., Poupyrev, I.: Artoolkit: A computer vision based augmented reality toolkit. In: Proceeding of IEEE Virtual Reality 2000, New Jersey, USA. IEEE Press, New York (2000)
7. Bosch, C., Ballester, F., Otero, C., Fernández, M., Coma, I., Togores, R., Pérez, M.A.: VALLE®R: A highway design system in a virtual reality environment. In: Proceedings of the 11th International Conference on Computing and Decisión Making in Civil and Building Engineering (ICCBE-06), Montreal, Canada (2006)
8. Bowman, D.A., Johnson, D.B., Hodges, L.F.: Testbed Evaluation of Virtual Environment Interaction Techniques. In: Proceedings of the ACM symposium on Virtual Reality Software and Technology (VRST-99), London, United Kingdom, pp. 26–33 (1999)
9. Chua, G.G., Serra, L., Kockro, R.A., Ng, H., Nowinski, W.L., Chan, C., Pillay, P.K.: Volume-based tumor neurosurgery planning in the Virtual Workbench. In: Proceedings of IEEE VRAIS'98, pp. 167–173. IEEE CS Press, Atlanta, USA (1998)
10. Cruz-Neira, C., Sandin, D., DeFanti, T.: Surround-Screen Projection-Based Virtual Reality: The Design and Implementation of the CAVE. In: Proceedings of the ACM SIGGRAPH Computer Graphics Conference, pp. 135–142. ACM Press, New York (September 1993)

11. Di Fiore, F., Vandoren, P., Van Reeth, F.: Multimodal Interaction in a Collaborative Virtual Brainstorming Environment. In: Luo, Y. (ed.) CDVE 2004. LNCS, vol. 3190, pp. 47–60. Springer, Heidelberg (2004)
12. Fiala, M.: Artag revision 1, a fiducial marker system using digital techniques. In: National Research Council Publication 47419/ERB-1117 (November 2004)
13. Fok, S.C., Xiang, W., Yap F.F.: Internet-enabled Virtual Prototyping Workbench for Fluid Power Systems. In: Proceedings of International Conference on Fluid Power Transmission and Control (ICFP 2001), Quan Long, China (2001)
14. Heng, P.A., Fung, P.F., Wong, T.T, Leung, K.S., Sun, H.: Virtual Bronchoscopy. International Journal of Virtual Reality, vol. 4(4), pp. 10–20, IPI Press (2000)
15. Kim, G.: Designing Virtual Reality Systems: The Structured Approach. Springer, Heidelberg (2005)
16. Koutek, M., van Hees, J., Post, F.H., Bakker, A.F.: Virtual Spring Manipulators for the Particle Steering in Molecular Dynamics on the Responsive Workbench. In: Proceedings of Eurographics on Virtual Environments '02, pp. 55–62 (2002)
17. Kruger, W., Bohn, C.A., Frohlich, B., Schuth, H., Strauss, W., Wesche, G.: The Responsive Workbench. IEEE Computer Graphics and Applications 14(3), 12–15 (1994)
18. Kuester, F., Duchaineau, M.A., Hamann, B., Joy, K.I., Ma, K.L.: The Designers Workbench: towards real-time immersive modeling. In: Stereoscopic Displays and Virtual Reality Systems VII, Washington, USA, vol. 3957, pp. 464–472, The International Society for Optical Engineering (2000)
19. Looser, J., Grasset, R., Seichter, H., Billinghurst, M.: OSGART - A pragmatic approach to MR, In: Proceedings of the IEEE/ACM International Symposium on Mixed and Augmented Reality (ISMAR), Santa Barbara, USA (2006)
20. MacIntyre, B., Coelho, E.M., Julier, S.J.: Estimating and adapting to registration errors in augmented reality systems. In: Proceeding of IEEE Virtual Reality 2002, Orlando, USA, pp. 73–80. IEEE Press, Orlando, Florida, USA (2002)
21. Marsh, T.: Evaluation of Virtual Reality Systems for Usability. In: Proceedings of ACM SIGCHI 99, Pittsburgh, USA, pp. 61–62 (1999)
22. Murray, N., Roberts, D.: Comparison of head gaze and head and eye gaze within an immersive environment. In: Proceedings of the International Symposium on Distributed Simulation and Real-Time Applications (DS-RT'06), Torremolinos, Spain, pp. 70–76 (2006)
23. Poston, T., Serra, L.: The Virtual Workbench: Dextrous VR. In: Proceedings of Virtual Reality Software and Technology (VRST 94), pp. 111–121. IEEE CS Press, Los Alamitos, USA (1994)
24. Robertson, G., Czerwinski, M., Dantzich, M.: Immersion in Desktop Virtual Reality. In: Proceedings of Symposium on User Interface Software and Technology (UIST), Alberta, Canada, pp. 11–19 (1997)
25. Seay, A.F., Ribarsky, W., Hodges, L., Krum, D.: Multimodal Interaction Techniques for the Virtual Workbench. In: Proceedings of ACM SIGCHI 99, Pittsburgh, USA, pp. 282–283 (1999)
26. Taylor, R.M., Hudson, T.C., Seeger, A., Weber, H., Juliano, J., Helser, A.T.: VRPN: a device-independent, network-transparent VR peripheral system. In: Proceedings of the ACM symposium on Virtual Reality Software and Technology 2001(VRST-2001), Bannf, Canada, pp. 55–61 (2001)
27. Wang, Q.H., Li, J.R.: A Desktop VR Prototype for Industrial Training Applications. In: Journal of Virtual Reality, vol. 7(3), pp. 187–197. Springer Verlag, Heidelberg (2004)

# VR-Based Virtual Test Technology and Its Application in Instrument Development

Tiantai Guo[1] and Xiaojun Zhou[2]

[1] China Jiliang University, Hangzhou 310018, P.R. China
guotiantai@163.com
[2] Zhejiang University, Hangzhou 310009, P.R. China
sky@zju.edu.cn

**Abstract.** Test plays a very important role in manufacturing, but the general practice so far cannot fully meet the demands of flexibility and efficiency required by a fast-changing market. To supply a new and flexible approach to the solution of various complex engineering testing problems, the concept of "VR-based virtual test technology" was put forward in the authors' previous works, which can be regarded as the combination of these three technologies: virtual reality (VR), test technology and computer simulation. This paper is the deepening of the authors' previous works. After elucidating the theoretical model of VR-based virtual test technology, its application in instrument development is discussed, and finally a prototype VR-based instrument development system is given to show the initial effects of the approach. The conclusion is that VR-based virtual test technology can play a very important and active role in testing and instrument development.

**Keywords:** Virtual reality (VR), test technology, computer simulation, instrument development, virtual test technology.

## 1 Introduction

Test plays a very important role in manufacturing, but the general practice so far can not fully meet the demands of flexibility and efficiency required by a fast-changing market. For example, in many cases tests can only be made with equipments with limited functions, detection of machine parts' faults and failures is often not timely, and test of nanometer-scale or large-scaled machineries and robots working in environments inconvenient for human beings has caused much concern.

Virtual reality (VR) offers a new solution to these problems. VR is a technology which has found successful application in many fields like medical training, education, computer games, molecule simulation, robot control, machine tool simulation, flight, ship and vehicle simulators, etc. [1]-[4] VR is a computer system used to create an artificial world in which the user has the impression of being in that world and with the ability to navigate through the world and manipulate objects in the world.

After exploring the requirements and features of VR, test technology and computer simulation, the authors put forward the concept of "VR-based virtual test technology" in previous research works, which can be regarded as the combination of these three

R. Shumaker (Ed.): Virtual Reality, HCII 2007, LNCS 4563, pp. 468–477, 2007.

technologies: VR, test technology and computer simulation, where VR supplies the interface and environment for test activities to take place, test technology shows the immediate aim and use of the approach, while computer simulation supplies the necessary algorithms for the solution of engineering test tasks.

To make VR-based virtual test technology practical in engineering, both theoretical research and prototype development are necessary. On the basis of the authors' previous researches, this paper put forward a modified theoretical model of VR-based virtual test technology. Furthermore, this paper gives a prototype application of VR-based virtual test technology in instrument development to show the initial effect of VR-based virtual test technology. The conclusion is that VR-based virtual test technology can play a very important and active role in testing and instrument development, with the rapid progress of computer technology and the coming up of more affordable and practical VR peripherals.

# 2 VR-Based Virtual Test Technology

## 2.1 VR-Based Virtual Test Technology (VRVTT)

"VR-based virtual test technology" is a concept put forward by the authors in previous works as an attempt to supply a new approach to the solving of difficult engineering test problems such as the testing of mechanisms of nanometer scale, or equipments working in areas difficult to access by traditional ways, and the basic idea is first to generate a virtual test environment with computer software supported by appropriate computer hardware and VR peripherals in accordance with specific applications, in which virtual reality (VR) serves not only as an interface but also as an interaction tool between the user and the virtual test environment, and then the test processes are interactively planned, optimized and simulated in a virtual test environment, while intermediate and final test results are visualized, analyzed and replayed in dynamic 3D forms. [5] [6].

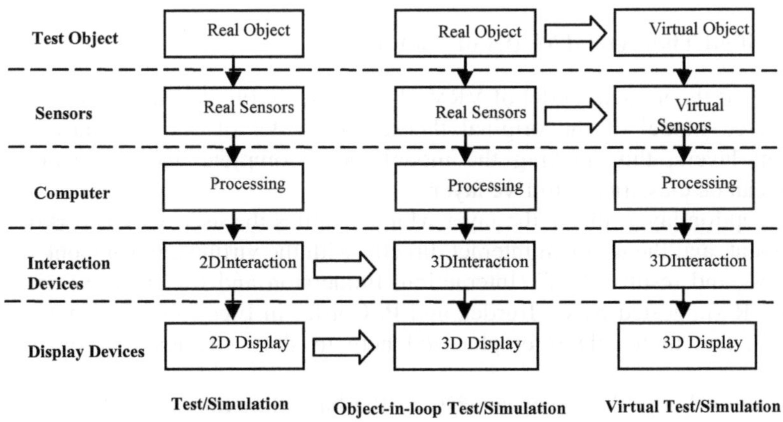


**Fig. 1.** Progress of test and simulation

Fig.1 shows the progress of test and simulation, which shows a definite trend of substituting existing 2D interaction modes with 3D interaction devices such as space-balls and trackers, and 2D display is giving way to 3D displays. This is what VR is expected to be doing so far. Furthermore, by substituting real objects with virtual (imaginary) objects, and real sensors with virtual sensors, we get VR-based virtual test technology (abbreviated as VRVTT henceforth), which can be used to simulate available test system for tutorial and training purposes, or to design new test equipments to show the principles and configurations of the equipments under design, or eventually to perform virtual tests completely in virtual test environment on the basis of theoretical modeling and simulation. Accordingly, the virtual test environment can either be a replica of actual world scenes, or any imagined or designed environment generated by computer.

VRVTT is a combination of these technologies: virtual reality (VR), computer simulation, test technology. VR supplies a platform for all the design, simulation and test activities, and computer simulation supplies the system with algorithms to make full use of the obtained data (real or virtual), while test is the direct purposes of the technology.

Depending on the function and whether real (physical) test object exists, the implementation of VRVTT drops under four categories (as shown in Table 1): physical test, object-in-loop test simulation, VR-based test and simulation, and complete VR-based test. The first two categories are the traditional way of conducting test and simulation, while the latter two are the trend of test and simulation technologies.

**Table 1.** Categories of VR-based virtual test technology

| | **With real test object** | **Without real test object** |
|---|---|---|
| Test | **Physical test** | **Complete VR-based test** |
| Simulation | **Object-in-loop simulation** | **VR-based test and simulation** |

## 2.2 Modified Theoretical Model of VRVTT

The modified theoretical model of VRVTT is shown in Fig.2. This model expands the three-layered model of the original theoretical model of VRVTT into five inter-dependent layers, thus making the model more complete and practical. So now VRVTT can be classified into five layers:

1) Perception layer: this is the layer which supplies the user with a working virtual environment, and the user can interact directly with the virtual environment and check the process and results. "3Is" (Interaction, Immersion and Imagination) are the features of VR suggested by G. Burdea and P. Coiffet in Electro'93 International Conference[7], and their role is emphasized here to show the leading role of VR in VRVTT.

2) Function layer: this layer consists of the basic functions of VRVTT, including measurement, detection, test, simulation and training.

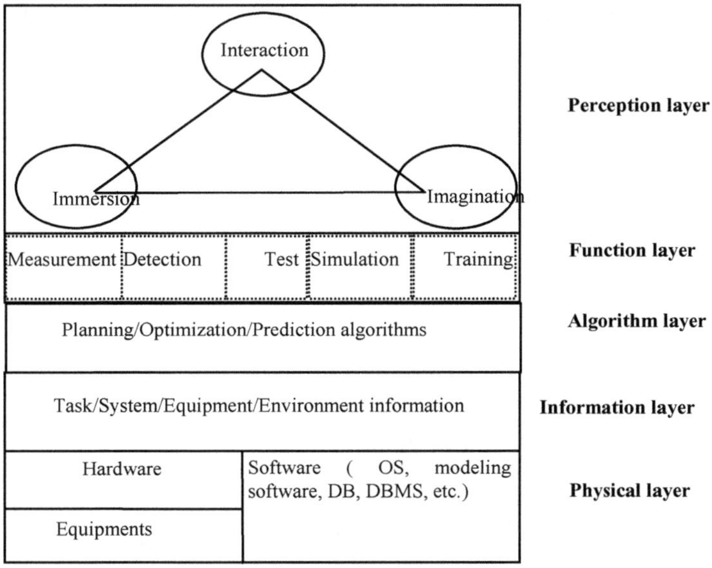


**Fig. 2.** Modified theoretical model of VRVTT

3) Algorithm layer: this layer integrates the algorithms necessary for the operation of VRVTT, such as planning algorithm, optimization algorithm, prediction algorithm, signal processing algorithms, etc.

4) Information layer: this layer includes the information of task description, measurement, detection and test system, equipment, environment, sensors, etc.

5) Physical layer: this layer is the physical basis of VRVTT, and it's made up of three parts:

a. *Hardware,* such as computer, peripherals, head-mounted display (HMD), etc.;

b. *Equipments,* which are a part of VRVTT when hardware-in-loop measurement, detection and test is performed;

c. *Software,* such as operating system (OS), modeling software, database (DB), database management system (DBMS), etc.

## 2.3 Mathematical Model of VRVTT

Theoretically speaking, VRVTT can be regarded as a reproduction of a real (physical) measurement, detection and test system, or merely an imaginary (virtual) visualization of a test system under design or simply in planning. To be of practical value, VRVTT must be similar to its physical or anticipated counterpart in features (geometrical, kinetic, dynamic, etc.), functions and working principles. Mathematically, the test process can be described as:

$$T = \{q0, c, \delta, qf\} \tag{1}$$

Where T is the test process, while q0 is the initial (starting) conditions, c is the constraints, δ is the operations taken, and qf is the final conditions. Formula (1) shows that the test process is a process in which the system transits from the initial state to the final state under certain constraints, with the interference from users. The test task can be understood as finding a path (practical and/or optimal) between the initial state and the final state, and this concerns the application of such algorithms as planning, decision, optimization, prediction, signal processing, system recognition, pattern recognition, etc.

### 2.4 The Working Principles of VRVTT

As has been discussed above, VRVTT is supposed to perform these basic functions: measurement, detection, test, simulation and training. Among these, simulation is the most important, since VRVTT has to go through a period of completely-virtual test, i.e., VR-based simulation of test processes and results, before it can be combined with real (physical) equipments to perform real tasks.

In the simulation function of VRVTT, prediction is very important, which includes applying the available test principles and experiences to the solution of real task. After the test scheme is decided and parameters properly selected, the aim of the simulation is to get a useful prediction of the performance of the real system, and display it in a virtual test environment.

The predictive test in VRVTT is based on the fact that many machine parts are made from the same type or similar type of materials, dimensions and shapes, the properties of the materials used are familiar to the manufacturers, and the effect of dimensions and shapes on the performance can be deduced from past test data.

The predictive test in VRVTT is to find and simulate the causal relation between the results and the type of materials, dimensions and shapes of the parts. Suppose the causal relation under consideration be expressed as:

$$Y(t)=F(u(t),\ a(t)) \qquad (2)$$

Where t is time, Y(t) represents test results or output, u(t) represents the variables which form the input or reason of the system, a(t) represents other unclear factors or noises which also affect the system, and F() is the mathematical expression of the causal relation between the input and output of the system.

Since the input of the system can be simulated by the system by imitating physical systems or following relevant regulations, and noises can be added into the system without much difficulty, Eq. (2) will be useful in predicting the test process and results if the causal relation between the input and output of the system can be obtained. This relation can be obtained in many ways, and one effective method is through the technique of system recognition, which is based on the obtained data in the past, i.d., Y(t), u(t)(t=1, 2, 3, ……, n).

VRVTT receives instructions from user through man-machine interface, and collects information of the test system, object and environment. Based on the a priori knowledge and algorithms in databases, VRVTT performs functions like control, prediction, collision detection, process optimization, simulation, decision-making, etc. As its output, VRVTT shows the simulation process and results in a virtual environment by means of measurement, detection and test process visualization, results visualization, results analysis, and process replay, etc.

# 3 Application of VR-Based Virtual Test Technology in Instrument Development

## 3.1 Application of VR-Based Virtual Test Technology in Instrument Development

Nowadays developers of instruments are facing more and more pressures from the market, since the development cycle has to be shortened, and the flexibility of the whole development process needs to be increased. To meet such demands, virtual instruments (VI) have been adopted in many industries where instruments are needed [8][9]. The basic idea of VI is to replace the old-fashioned application-specific instruments with computer hardware and software, most typically by replacing the signal acquisition and processing units with computer algorithms, and replacing the old display panels and screens with computer display. In this way, a computer can be turned into a versatile data-processing instrument, which can serve more functions than the old application-specific instruments, thus reducing development cost drastically.

But VI has its disadvantages too. Besides the configuration of screens, buttons, knobs, switches and keypads on the front panel of the instrument, the users also want to know the complete appearance of the instrument in real applications, its working principles, signal flowcharts, wiring system, hardware configuration, display results, etc., preferably in visual and interactive forms, and this is exactly what VR-based virtual test technology is good at. So VR-based virtual test technology supplies a novel approach for instrument development, since the user can implore the instrument to be designed before it is made in a 3D virtual environment, and networked development can be easily implemented.

VRVTT can be very different for different applications, so here the case of non-destructive test (NDT) is taken as an example. Among various NDT methods, ultrasonic NDT has become the most important method adopted in many fields such as airplane, ship, automobile industries, medical science etc. for the detection of internal defects in metal and nonmetal parts[10]-[12]. This is due to the ultrasonic wave's special advantages of high sensitivity, good direction, strong penetration ability, and being harmless to human body. But in China, many manufacturers still use the traditional method of manual test, which requires the participation of professional personnel, and the efficiency and accuracy are rather limited.

VRVTT can do quite a lot in partly solving this problem. By setting up a model of the test system under design in advance in computer, the cost is greatly reduced, and flexibility is increased, since the model can be modified without causing much trouble. What's more, by performing virtual test and simulation in a computer-generated virtual environment, the professional personnel and skillful operators can both be trained in an effective way. Finally, since NDT industry has accumulated large quantities of test principles and experiences, which can be used to form knowledge bases and guidelines for the test tasks, intelligent prediction of test process and results are made not only possible but also practical. In fact, the state-of-the-art of ultrasonic NDT is to develop auto-detection systems and prediction models, and show test results in 3D rather than 2D.[13][14]

### 3.2 A Prototype VR-Based Instrument Development System

A prototype virtual ultrasonic NDT system (VNDTS) is developed to show the application of VR-based virtual test technology in instrument development, and shows how a simple but helpful virtual test system can be implemented on a personal computer without much cost. Research work under study includes modeling of the NDT system, analysis of the NDT system, simulation of the NDT process, prediction and display of NDT results, and finally, the practical virtual test of real objects.

VNDTS adopts a client/server (C/S) configuration, and TCP/IP is used for communication protocol. VNDTS combines techniques such as Hypertext Markup Language (HTML), VRML, Servlet and Java to supply the system with various functions. On the server side, application programs include user management server, VRML world generating server and virtual testing server; client runs on webpages, which are downloaded with HTTP protocol, with Java Applet and VRML browser supplied. VRML supplies 3D viewing of the scenes, while Java Applet supplies user interface, deals with application protocol communication between client and server, communicates with VRML space through External Authoring Interface (EAI), downloads local models to client, and submits test results to server, etc. WWW server manages information on webpages, Java Applet, VRML files and virtual tests. Application server supplies services for clients through the webpages.

The handling of user's task can be on the server side or on the client side. If it is done on the server side, when the server accepts the requirement, a server application program will be run, and then the results will be transferred back to the client. The server is the core of the system, and supplies most of the functions, while the configuration of the client can be highly flexible. The C/S structure facilitates the software system, simplifies the client software, and makes the use of VNDTS very convenient and easy.

Client can be a simple PC which has access to the Internet, while the server is the essential part of the system. For the sake of economy and convenience, VRML, HTML and JAVA are chosen for 3D modeling tool, webpage display and implementation of complex algorithms respectively.

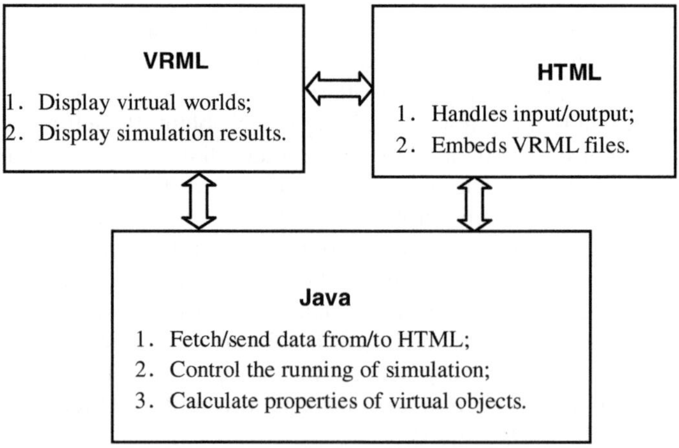


**Fig. 3.** Working principle of VNDTS

The working principle of VNDTS is shown in Fig. 3. VRML and Java Applet are put into the same web page, and Java Applet serves as the core of simulation control. VRML does not have calculation function itself, and such functions are all implemented with Java. The 3D world browser used is CosmoPlayer.

When the system is started, it first enters a HTML mainpage to allow the user to select from several options. After the selection of system function and parameters, VNDTS allows the user to view 2D teaching materials or enters 3D display and interaction mode. VNDTS receives instructions and requirements from user through man-machine interface, and collects relevant information for the special task. After requirements are handled and calculations made, the results are sent back to the client.

Fig. 4 shows some pictures of VNDTS, which shows how a simple but helpful VR-based test system can be implemented on a personal computer without much cost. In Fig. 5, (a) shows a test table in a virtual test environment, and the user can interact with it by using the buttons supplied by CosmoPlayer. (b) shows a pseudo 3D display of NDT result, thus supplying more information than a 2D image. (c) is an image in 2D, but color information is emphasized to help user locate the defects. (d) is the window where user can input the test data and parameters. Work under research is trying to combine the technique of scientific visualization with VR, so as to create 3D and vivid images of the tested part and internal defects.

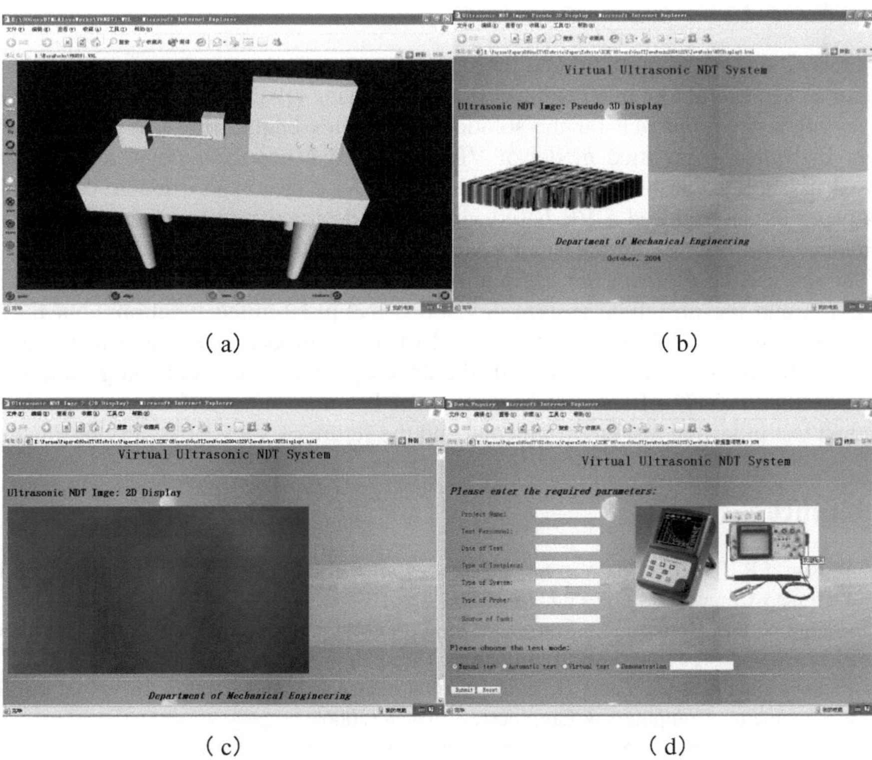


**Fig. 4.** Pictures of a virtual ultrasonic NDT system

Main difficulties in developing VNDTS lie in modeling, including the geometrical, physical and movement modeling of both the virtual environment and test equipment and object. Users often ask for scenes as real as possible, and refreshing of scenes as fast as possible, while these contradictory requirements both mean huge demand of storage and calculation time. To ease this bottleneck, many ideas have been put forward, like LOD (level of detail) [15][16], in which scenes are represented in different levels of detail according to the direction and distance of the viewer, and image-based rendering[17][18], in which images are used directly to form a part of the virtual environment, especially when large area of background is concerned.

There are many kinds of data with different data format and time sequence flowing in VNDTS: data from VR peripheral equipments, data from computer vision module, data from database system, data created within VNDTS during the test and simulation process, data from actual test equipment and test object in the case of partially virtual VNDTS, etc., and some of them are contradicting to each other. All these must be coordinated and integrated into VNDTS. Technologies like data fusion, multi-sensor fusion, fuzzy pattern recognition and neural network can be used to solve this problem.

Though the system is just a prototype system with limited functions, the pictures show the potential of this approach in the field of test and simulation.

## 4 Conclusions

Test technology is facing more and more challenges, and simulation is proved to be an economic and useful tool in reducing cost and increasing reliability and products' quality. To supply a new approach for the solution of complex engineering test problems, this paper first gave a modified model of VR-based virtual test technology, and then discussed its application in instrument development. As a prototype example of VRVTT, this paper also introduced a VR-based virtual non-destructive-test system which is implemented with HTML, Virtual Reality Modeling Language (VRML) and Java.

Though for the moment the application of VRVTT is still immature and not very common, and the prototype system developed has just limited functions, but the effects are quite good, showing the potential of this approach in test and instrumentation, and it can be expected that with the development of test technology and computer hardware and software techniques, it'll become more and more practical to conduct test in virtual test environments, and the future of VRVTT is very promising.

## References

1. Wilson, J.R., D'Cruz, M.: Virtual and interactive environments for work of the future. Int. J. Human-Computer Studies 64, 158–169 (2006)
2. Pouliquen, M., Bernard, A., Marsot, J., et al.: Virtual hands and virtual reality multimodal platform to design safer industrial systems. Computers in Industry 58, 46–56 (2007)
3. Pan, Z., Cheok, A.D., Yang, H., et al.: Virtual reality and mixed reality for virtual learning environments. Computers & Graphics 30, 20–28 (2006)
4. Egerstedt, M., Hu, X., Stotsky, A.: Control of mobile platforms using a virtual vehicle approach. IEEE Transactions On. Automatic Control 46(11), 1777–1782 (2001)

5. Tiantai GUO. Research on the Theory and Applications of VR-based Testing [PhD thesis]. Zhejiang University, Hangzhou, P. R. China. (August 2005) (In Chinese)
6. Guo, T., Zhou, X., Zhu, G.: Application Of CBR In VR-Based Test And SimilationSystem. In: Proc. of 2003 International Conference on Machine Learning and Cybernetics. Xi-an, China, 2-5 November 2003, pp. 2337–2340 (2003)
7. Burdea, G., Coiffet, P.: Virtual Reality Technology New York: A Wiley-Interscience Publication, John Wiley & Sons, Inc., pp. 1–14 (1994)
8. Taner, A.H., Brignell, J.E.: Virtual instrumentation and intelligent sensors. Sensors and actuators 61, 427–430 (1997)
9. Hubert, C.G., McJames, S.W., Mecham, I., et al.: Digital imaging system and virtual instrument platform for measuring hydraulic conductivity of vascular endothelial monolayers. Microvascular Research 71, 135–140 (2006)
10. Ullah, F., Kaneko, S.: Using orientation codes for rotation-invariant template matching. Pattern Recognition 37(2), 201–209 (2004)
11. Yin, X., Morris, S.A., O'Brien Jr., W.D.: Experimental Spatial Sampling Study of the Real-Time Ultrasonic Pulse-Echo BAI-Mode Imaging Technique. IEEE Transaction on Ultrasonics and Frequency Control 50(4), 428–440 (2003)
12. Ma, H.W., Zhang, X.H., Wei, J.: Research on an ultrasonic NDT system for complex surface parts. Journal of Materials Processing Technology 12(9), 667–670 (2002)
13. Sadoun, B.: An efficient simulation scheme for testing materials in a nondestructive manner. Information Sciences 137, 43–51 (2001)
14. Fenster, A., Surry, K., Smith, W., et al.: 3D ultrasound imaging: applications in image-guided therapy and biopsy. Computers & Graphics 26, 557–568 (2002)
15. Jeong-Hwan, A., Dong-Keun, L., Ho, Y.-S.: Compact representation of 3D models using mesh merging[C]. TENCON '97. IEEE Region 10 Annual Conference. Speech and Image Technologies for Computing and Telecommunications Proceedings of IEEE, 1, 323–326 (1997)
16. Gobbetti, E., Bouvier, E.: Time-critical multiresolution rendering of large complex models[J]. Computer-Aided Design 32(13), 785–803 (2000)
17. Mukaigawa, Y., Mihashi, S., Shakunaga, T.: Photometric image-based rendering for virtual lighting image synthesis[C]. In: Augmented Reality 1997 (IWAR '99) In: Proceedings. 2nd IEEE and ACM International Workshop on, 1999, pp. 115–124 (1999)
18. Hansard, M.E., Buxton, B.E.: Image-based rendering via the standard graphics pipeline[C]. Multimedia and Expo 2000, ICME 2000. In: 2000 IEEE International Conference on. 2000, vol. 3, pp. 1437–1440 (2000)

# An Integrated Environment for Testing and Assessing the Usability of Information Appliances Using Digital and Physical Mock-Ups

Satoshi Kanai[1], Soh Horiuchi[1], Yukiaki Kikuta[2], Akihiko Yokoyama[2], and Yoshiyuki Shiroma[3]

[1] Hokkaido University, Japan
kanai@ssi.ist.hokudai.ac.jp
[2] Cs Lab. Co. Ltd., Sapporo, Japan
[3] Sapporo City University, Sapporo, Japan

**Abstract.** Executing user-test of information appliances costs much due to fabrication of physical functional mockups, the securing of human subjects for the test, and preparation of testing facilities. Results of the user test have to be manually analyzed by usability engineers, and the analysis takes a couple of weeks. In this paper, we propose an integrated software and hardware environment for prototyping and assessing usability of information appliances where the users can operate a user-interface either of a 2D digital mockup or 3D digital mockup or a physical-mockup of the appliance under the test. This function enables engineers to test and evaluate the usability of the appliances both from the cognitive aspect and from the physical aspects.

**Keywords:** User Interface, Usability Test, Digital Mockup, Physical Mockup.

## 1 Introduction

Recently, information appliances such as digital consumer electronics have spread to general users. Product design conscious of "usability" of user interfaces (UIs) is needed in the manufacturers. As a method of usability assessments, "user-test" is recognized as the most objective one where the end users are directly involved in the test process. However, executing user-test of information appliances usually costs much due to fabrication of physical functional mockups, securing of human subjects for the test and preparation of testing facilities. Results of the user test have to be manually analyzed by usability engineers, and the analysis usually takes a couple of weeks. Therefore, an advanced environment for the user-test is strongly needed to remove the cost and the time barriers of executing the test.

In this paper, we propose an integrated software and hardware environment for prototyping and assessing usability of information appliances where the users can operate a user-interface either using a 2D digital mockup, 3D digital mockup or a physical mockup of the appliance under the test. This function enables engineers to test and evaluate the usability of the appliances both from the cognitive aspect and from the

R. Shumaker (Ed.): Virtual Reality, HCII 2007, LNCS 4563, pp. 478–487, 2007.

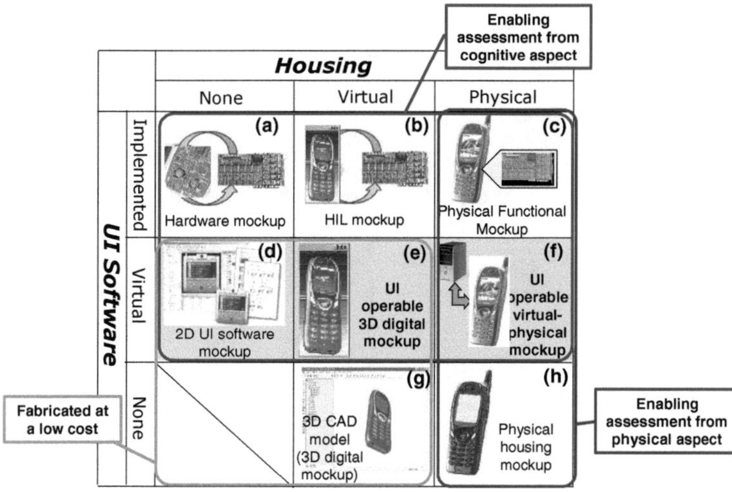


**Fig. 1.** Different kinds of mockups in developing information appliances

physical aspects, and to choose an optimal combination of the housing models and UI models according to the product type, constraints of cost and time, and required reliability of test results.

In the following sections, related works and features of the proposed environment are described, and detail functions of the environment are explained. Finally, an application of the environment

## 2 Related Works

As for the user test of information appliances, different kinds of mockups could be made corresponding to different embodiment combinations of the housing and UI software as shown in Figure 1. In user-test, developers have to evaluate these mockups from physical aspect and from cognitive aspect. Among those mockups, our environment deals with 2D UI software mockup (Figure-1 (d)), UI operable 3D digital mockup (e), and UI operable virtual-physical mockup (f).

As for 2D UI software mockup, there are some commercial prototyping tools [1,2] which have a UI simulation function. Moreover, there are a few tools which have usability assessments functions [3,4]. However, these tools were designed to develop UI for standard PC or mobile phone, and it is difficult for subjects to operate their UI with sufficient reality when executing the user test for appliances.

UI operable 3D digital mockups have been studied which consist of a virtual housing model (CAD model) and virtual UI software [5,6,7]. The virtual UI software can enhance the reality of interaction. However, these mockups do not necessarily provide functions of defining and executing the state-transition UI behaviors. The mockup

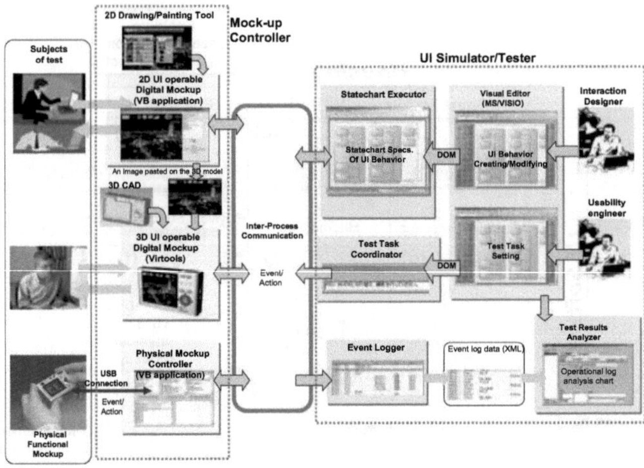


**Fig. 2.** An Overview of Testing and Assessing Environment

also does not have a physical housing, so that the usability assessment from physical aspect is ignored in this type of mockup.

On the contrary, UI operable virtual-physical mockup has a physical housing mockup and a virtual UI software simulation function [8,9,10,11]. The subjects can directly grasp a physical housing and can manipulate the UI elements on it. However, these mockup need the fabrication of the housing models and hardware connection between the physical mockup and UI software simulator.

The tools described above only have a function of UI simulation and of executing user test only by using one of the 2D digital mockup, 3D digital mockup or physical mockup. There is no tool so far where usability engineers can seamlessly shift the type of mockup for the test from the virtual one to the physical one.

## 3 Overview of the Testing and Assessing Environment

Figure 2 shows the proposed testing and assessing environment. The environment mainly consists of the mockup viewer/controller part and the UI simulator/tester part. These two parts can be communicated by socket-communication via network. The mockup controller part includes the 2D UI operable digital mockups, 3D UI operable digital mockup, and the physical mockup controller. A physical functional mockup can be connected to this environment via the controller. On the other hand, the UI simulator/tester part includes statechart executer, test task coordinator, event logger and test result analyzer.

In the working situation, a tester operates the digital or physical mockup, then an event published from the mockup is sent to the statechart executer. And an action published from the statechart executer is then returned to the mockup to make the indicated status of UI changed. The statechart executer carries out a transition of UI state and generates an action based on the predefined statechart specification.

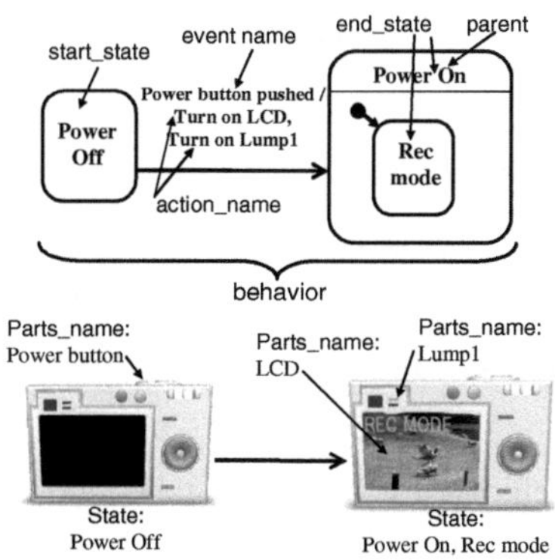


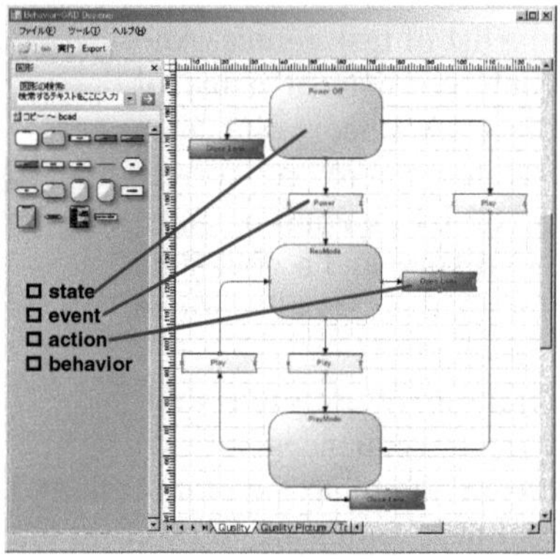


**Fig. 3.** UI behavior model based on Statechart **Fig. 4.** MS/Visio-based Statechart editor

# 4 User Interface Simulator / Tester

## 4.1 Statechart Executer

In the statechart executer, UI behavior is processed in response to incoming events such as mouse click issued from a test subject either on the 2D digital, the 3D digital or the physical mock-up. UI behavior data model uniformly represents event-driven behaviors on the appliance's side which describe how status on the output devices (CRT, LCD, lumps etc.) of the appliance changes as a result of the event from the input devices (buttons, dials, etc.). This event-driven behavior is modeled by the Statechart [12].

The UI behavior model mainly consist of "state", "event", "behavior" and "action" as shown in Figure 3. A state represents an identical physical status of the UI. An event represents a user's action inputted into the UI such as "a power button is pushed", and brings on a transition from one state to the other state. An action is expresses dynamic change occurred on the appliance. A change of the LCD property such as "turn on a LCD from dark to blue" is an example of the action. A behavior expresses a transition between two states, and is defined as a combination of two states before and after the transition, an event causing the transition and a sequence of actions of the appliance caused by the transition.

As shown in Figure 4, the statechart specification of the UI behavior can be schematically created and edited by a commercial visual editor (MS/Visio), and the statechart executer can directly read the document-object-model of Visio. Interaction designers can easily input and edit the UI behavior specification in graphical way.

## 4.2 Test Task Coordinator

In a user test, subjects are asked to complete a set of "task" by operating the UI, and his/her actual UI operations for each task are logged to evaluate the usability. In the standard [13], a task is defined as "the activities undertaken to achieve a goal". As shown in Figure 5, in our test task coordinator, a task is modeled by a start state, goal

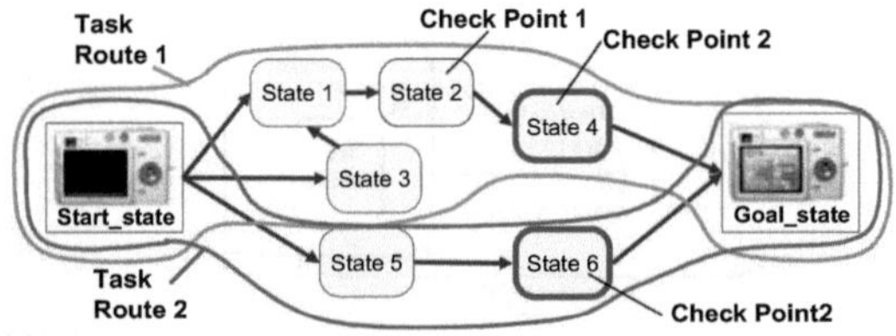

Fig. 5. Task, Checkpoint and Route

state and a list of task routes. And a task route consists of a list of checkpoints. A checkpoint is a certain state where a correct sequence of UI operations must pass. A start state and a goal state both refer to the "state" defined in the Statechart.

Generally there are often multiple correct sequences of UI operations to complete a certain task and to achieve a goal. In our task model, multiple correct task routes are allowed in one task by defining the different set of checkpoints shown in Figure 5. If actual number of input events from the continuous checkpoints stays within a predetermined number of time, or if actual elapsed time of the operation between these checkpoints stays within a specified time limit, the operations are judged to be correct. In this way, examiners of user-test can define alternatives of task routes, and can flexibly adjust a range of correct UI operations for the task when evaluating the number of error operations and task completion in the test results analysis.

After defining tasks, the test task coordinator indicates a predefined goal of each task in the form of an imperative sentence when a new test starts. "Switch shooting mode" is a typical example of the goal. The goal is indicated on another window of the screen just above the 3D digital mock-up as shown in Figure 8.

### 4.3 Test Results Analyzer

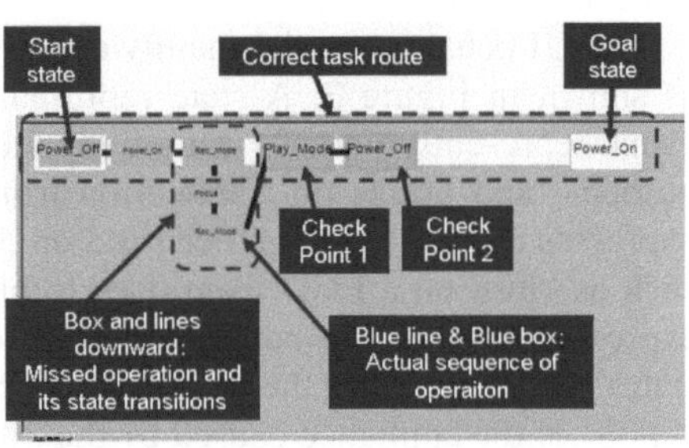

Fig. 6. Operational log analysis chart

The test results analyzer compares the event log data from the subject's operation with the test task data and UI behavior specification, and outputs measures of the usability assessments. We adopted the following four measures of usability assessment based on three basic notions of usability (effectiveness, efficiency and satisfaction) defined in ISO 9241-11 [13]; 1) number of events inputted in each task and in each subject, 2) elapsed time in each task and in each subject, 3) personal task achievement ratio, and 4) scores for SUS questionnaire.

An actual sequence of state-transitions operated by a subject is automatically compared with the one of correct task routes defined in the test task data, and the result of the comparison is graphically displayed in the form of "operational log analysis chart" on the lower part of the screen. Figure 12 shows the notation of this operational log analysis chart. Each rectangle shows a state, and a line between two rectangles does a transition between states. A left-most rectangle in the chart indicates a start state, and a right-most rectangle does a goal state. The upper most horizontal white straight line indicates transitions (behaviors) on a correct task route, and every rectangle with orange edges on this line except both ends corresponds to each checkpoint. While the blue rectangles and blue lines indicate actual operation sequence of the subject. If a subject does UI operations whose elapsed time or number of events between two neighboring check points exceeds the predefined bounds, the tool judges that a subject did a wrong operation on the UI, and draws additional blue rectangles and blue lines in downward direction corresponding to these wrong operations. Therefore, as a depth of the chart becomes larger, the examiner of the user test can easily recognize that the subject did more missed operation in this task.

# 5 Mockup Viewer/Controller

## 5.1 2D UI Operable Digital Mockup

In case of simulating UI behavior of appliances where all of the UI elements such as LCD, buttons and lamps are placed in one surface of the appliances, 2D UI operable digital mockups is sufficient. Therefore, we build a Visual Basic application for 2D UI operable digital mockup as shown in Figure 7. In this mockup, images of menus and icons displayed on LCD and ones of buttons are painted using 2D drawing or painting tool by interaction designers in advance. Then a 2D spatial arrangement of these images and change of the display status of these images are defined in an XML document according to the format of our extended vision of UsiXML[14] which is one of the Model Driven Architecture methodologies of developing the UI application.

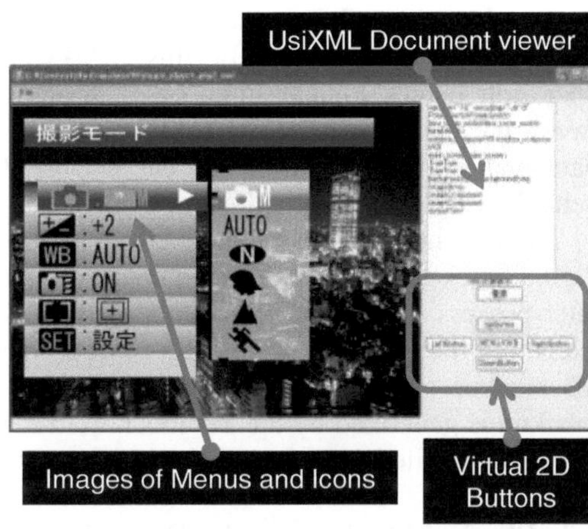


**Fig. 7.** 2D UI operable digital mockup

When executing UI simulation and user test, the incoming events such as mouse click issued from a test subject on the mockup are sent to the statechart executer via inter-process communication, and an action published from the statechart executer is then returned to the mockup to make the indicated UI status of the mockup.

## 5.2 3D UI Operable Digital Mockup

In case of simulating UI behavior where UI elements are placed in multiple surfaces of the appliances, 2D UI operable digital mockups is insufficient and a digital mockup with 3D housing shape data is needed. To build this 3D UI operable digital mock-up, we used a commercial Web3D programming tool (Virtools) and added two functions of UI simulations to the tool.

The 3D CAD data is imported to the tool in the format of 3D-XML [15]. The 3D-XML format includes the assembly configuration information which describes relationships among an assembly and parts. 3D-XML format includes the assembly configuration information which describes relationships among an assembly and parts. In the 3D CAD data of the housing, a 3D object which becomes a target of an event or an action has to be modeled as a single part in the assembly. A button, a switch, a LCD screen and a LED are typical examples of such objects. A usability engineer interactively ties each of events or actions in the behavior data to the name of a part selected from the list. Consequently this operation makes logical links between the part names of 3D CAD data and events or actions in UI behavior data.

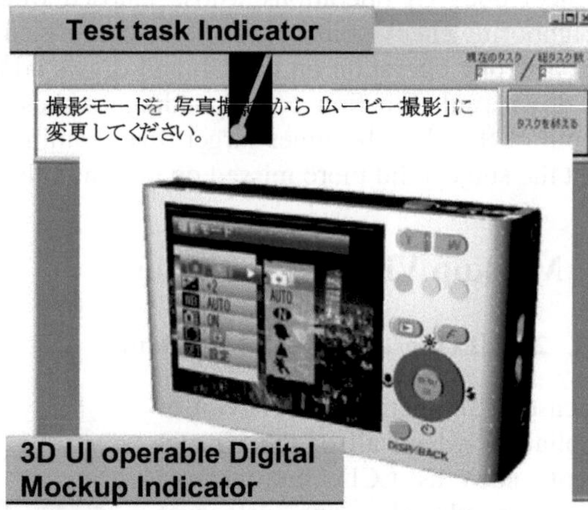


**Fig. 8.** 3D UI operable digital mockup

The mechanism of executing UI simulation and user test on this 3D UI operable digital mock-up is as same as the one of 2D digital mockup as shown in Figure 8. The inter-process communication function was developed and built in the tool. When executing the 3D mockup, the 2D mockup described in 5.1 is also executed with this 3D mockup simultaneously. An image data displayed on the LCD part on this 3D mockup is generated by the 2D mockup in real time, and is pasted on the 3D mockup via a scratch file by the image sharing function which we developed.

### 5.3 Physical Mockup and Its Controller

In the 2D or 3D digital mockups described above, the user has to complete his/her operations on the UI completely on a computer screen, and this sometimes makes the test results inaccurate. To solve the problem, we also developed the physical mockup controller which enables us communication between a variety of physical input and output devices and the statechart executer. Physical dials, buttons, lumps, LCDs and LEDs placed on the physical housing model are connected to this controller, and can be directly operated by the test subjects.

Moreover, to reduce the time and cost of fabricating the physical mockup, we can connect the RFID embedded physical mockup [16] to the controller. Figure 9 shows an example of this RFID embedded physical mockup of a digital camera. In this RF-ID embedded physical mockup, 2mm x 2mm small RFID tags are stuck at the position of buttons on the mock-up, and a subject puts a glove-type wearable RFID R/W on his/her arm where small antennas of the R/W are attached to each fingertip. When the subject is operating the mock-up, physical contact between the RFID tag in the button and his/her fingertip is detected by the wearable RFID R/W. The tag's ID code is sent to the physical mockup controller.

A button with a RFID tag is very small and is easily attached to and detached from the mock-up surface, because of its wireless and powerless communication functions. The position of buttons or switches on the mock-up can easily be repositioned. Therefore redesign-and-test activities can be repeated in a short cycle.

By integrating these physical mockups with the 2D and 3D digital mockups, the usability engineer can seamlessly shift the type of mockup for the test from the virtual one to the physical one, so that more accurate results of operation can be obtained.

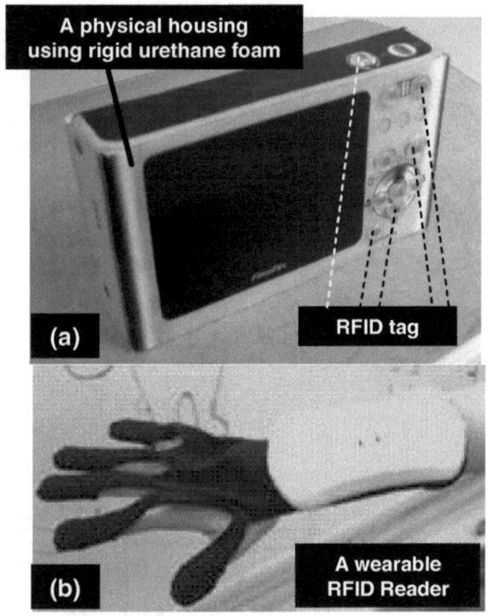


**Fig. 9.** RFID embedded Physical Mockup

# 6 Examples of Usability Testing and Assessment

User tests using the UI operable 3D digital mock-up ("3D-DMU") and RFID embedded physical mockup ("PMU") were done to verify an effectiveness of the environment. A 3D-DMU and PMU of a digital camera (Fuji-Fine Pix Z1) on the market shown in Figure 8 and 9 were built for the test. These two types of mock-ups (3D-DMU and PMU) are operated by two subject groups each of which consists of 7 subjects who did not have experiences of operating this camera. The test results of 3D-DMU and PMU were compared and analyzed.

We set two test tasks; turning on the camera (task-1), and setting self-timer's duration to 2 second (task-2). To complete the task-1, the subject has to open the lens cover on the front side of the housing. While in the task-2, the subject has to pus several buttons on the back side.

Figure 10 shows two operational log analysis charts for the task-2 when using the 3D-DMU (Figure 10-(a)) and the PMU (Figure 10-(b)). A wider line on the chart indicates more subjects passed over the route of operations. It was found that the sequences of operations including wrong operations were very similar to each other in the 3D-DMU and in the PMU, and that many subjects stepped to a wrong way at a state of "Rec_Mode". By observing this state on the 3D-DMU, it was found that many subjects did not notice that the self-time setting was allocated to the downward cursor button, and found that many of them pushed the center button instead of the downward one. This result suggested that many subjects could not recall the

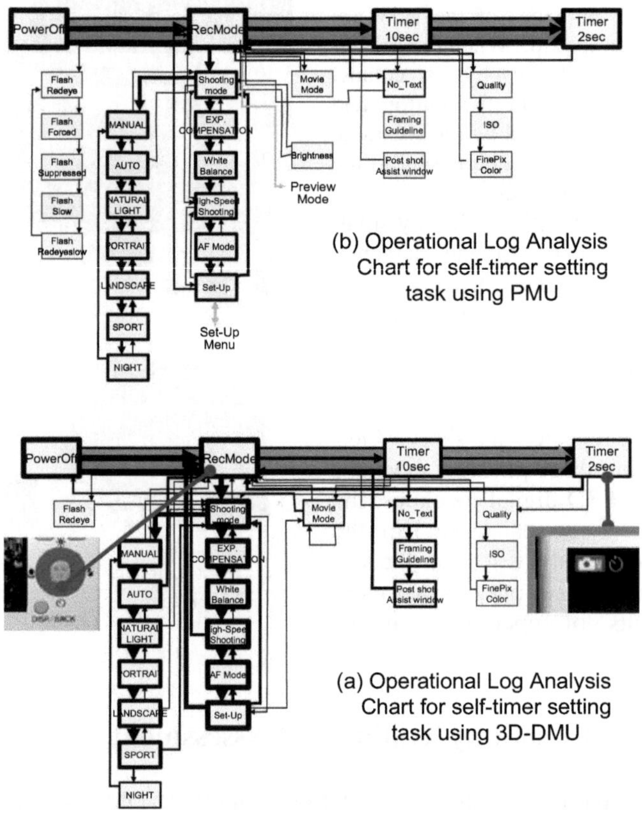


**Fig. 10.** A difference of operational log analysis chart using 3D-DMU and PMU

"self-timer" from the small icon indicated on the housing surface just under the downward cursor button as shown in Figure 10-(a). The shape and size of this self-timer icon should be redesigned.

# 7 Conclusions

An integrated software and hardware environment was proposed for prototyping and assessing usability of information appliances. The users could operate a user-interface either using a 2D digital mockup, 3D digital mockup or a physical-mockup of the appliance under the test. This function enabled engineers to test and evaluate the usability of the appliances both from the cognitive aspect and from the physical aspects. The results of the user test using a 3D digital mock-up in comparison with those of a physical mockup of the digital camera confirmed an effectiveness of our proposed environment.

**Acknowledgements.** This work was financially supported by a grant-in-aid of Intelligent Cluster Project (Sapporo IT Carrozzeria) funded by MEXT.

## References


1. Protobuilder, http://www.gaio.co.jp/product/dev_tools/pdt_protobuilder.html
2. Rapid Plus, http://www.e-sim.com/products/rapid_doc/index-h.htm
3. Avrahami, D., et al.: Forming Interactivity: A Tool for Rapid Prototyping of Physical Interactive Products. In: Proceedings of the ACM Symposium on Designing Interactive Systems, pp. 141–146 (2002)
4. Lee, K.P.: User-Participatory Testing Using Web, In: Proceedings of HCII 2003 (2003)
5. Kuutti, K., et al.: Virtual prototypes in usability testing, In: Proceedings of the 34th Hawaii International Conference on System Sciences 2001, vol. 5 (2001)
6. Bruno, F., et al.: A new approach to participatory design: usability tests in virtual environment, In: Proceedings of Virtual Concept 2005 (2005)
7. Kanai, S., et al.: Digital Usability Assessment for Information Appliances using User-Interface operable 3D Digital Mock-up. In: Proceedings of Virtual Concept 2006, HUCEID-P235, vol. 2, Springer, Heidelberg (2006)
8. Verlindern, J., et al.: Qualitative comparison of Virtual and Augmented Prototyping of Handheld Products, In: Proceedings of International Design Conferences, pp. 533–538 (2004)
9. Nam, T.-J.: Sketch-Based Rapid Prototyping Platform for Hardware-Software Integrated Interactive Products, In: Proceedings of CHI'05 2005, pp. 1689–1692 (2005)
10. Aoyama, H.: Development of system using mixed reality technology for evaluating designability and operability of product. In: Proceedings of Virtual Concept 2006, WoIM-P188, vol. 2, Springer, Heidelberg (2006)
11. Hartmann, B., et al.: d.tools: Visually Prototyping Physical UIs through Statecharts, In: Proceedings of UIST 2005 (2005)
12. Horrocks, I.: Constructing the User interface with Statecharts. Addison-Wesley, London, UK (1998)
13. ISO9241-11: Ergonomic requirements for office work with visual display terminals (VDTs) – Part 11: Guidance on usability (1998)
14. Vanderdonckt, J., et al.: UsiXML: a User Interface Description Language for Specifying Multimodal User Interfaces, In: Proceedings of W3C WMI'2004 (2004)
15. 3D-XML: http://www.3ds.com/3dxml
16. Horiuchi, S., et al.: Low-cost and rapid prototyping of UI-embedded mock-ups using RFID and its application to usability testing, In: Proceedings of HCII 2005 (2005)

# A Virtual Environment for 3D Facial Makeup*

Jeong-Sik Kim and Soo-Mi Choi**

Department of Computer Engineering, Sejong University, Seoul, 143-747, Korea
jskim@sju.ac.kr, smchoi@sejong.ac.kr

**Abstract.** We simulate the application of facial makeup in 3D by means of multi-sensory interaction which integrates a haptic interface with stereo visual perception. We aim to allow a user to simulate the facial makeup within an immersive virtual environment. To allow interactive 3D makeup process, we start by acquiring surface elements of a face which is enhanced by adjusting its texture and skin tone. Then the user can begin a virtual makeup session using 2D pixel-based paint model by grasping a haptic handle and looking at an autostereoscopic display. The use of this model avoids the texture distortion seen in existing 3D painting systems.

**Keywords:** Virtual makeup simulation, Haptic interface, Facial beautification.

## 1 Introduction

Visual perception of the face is a function of four qualities: color, texture, size, and shape. Many researchers have shown that people from most cultures prefer faces with a brownish color and a smooth texture. For centuries, cosmetics have been used to improve the color and texture of people's faces and make them more 'beautiful'. More recently, researchers in computer graphics and multimedia have developed several applications related to makeup, as well as cosmetic surgery and dentistry [1-3]. These applications have generally focused on changing the 2D texture of the face using a 2D graphical user interface. In contrast, we propose a framework to simulate the application of real makeup in 3D using haptic and stereo visual display techniques, and we also provide facial enhancement tools.

Existing makeup systems can be classified into 2D picture-based and 3D model-based approaches. Most simulators such as *FaceFilter Studio*, *VirtualMakeOver*, *MAGGI*, and *Makeup Pilot*, adapt a 2D picture-based environment as a lightweight solution with a simple interface. These systems have a simple 2D interface which supports various makeup tools, such as foundation, lip-liner, lip-stick, eye-shadow and eye-liner. However, they have low quality graphics and limited interactivity. *FaceFilter Studio* [4] is the most clearly related existing system to our work. It provides a 2D picture-based skin enhancement tool and a brush-based makeup tool, which we extend to 3D. *VF Pro* [5] is a 3D system that uses a template face model to provide more convincing visualization of a face, but it has no other advantages over

* This work was supported by the Seoul R&BD (Research and Business Development) program.
** Corresponding author.

R. Shumaker (Ed.): Virtual Reality, HCII 2007, LNCS 4563, pp. 488–496, 2007.

2D picture-based applications. Table 1 itemizes the differences between the 2D and 3D approaches. Neither type of system supports user-centric interaction because a user can only simulate a makeup under limited resource of the system.

**Table 1.** Comparison between 2D picture-based and 3D model-based applications

| | 2D picture-based makeup | 3D model-based makeup |
|---|---|---|
| Representation | Only 2D image | 3D model and 2D texture image |
| Interface | 2D mouse and 2D display | 2D mouse and 2D display |
| Painting model | 2D pixel-based painting | 3D mesh-based painting |
| Platform | Local and Web | Local |

There are several 2D painting systems based on haptic interaction. Baxter et al. [6] provided physical sensations to a user who is 'painting' on a canvas using physics-based 3D brush models. In order to simulate real painting, they used a bi-directional painting transfer model and deformable brushes. The work of Adams et al. [7] proposed interactive 3D painting system that uses a haptic interface. In order to overcome parameterization problems that hamper existing 3D painting applications, they proposed a unified sample-based approach to represent the geometry and texture of the 3D object as well as that of the brush. The generalization of 2D pixel-based paint models to sampled points allows this application to simulate the painting of 3D objects. We use 2D pixel-based paint models to allow a user to simulate the application of real makeup to their own face.

We aim to overcome the limitations of the existing makeup applications, while adding a skin enhancement technique and the ability to modify skin tone. To do this, we have developed a method of 3D facial filtering and a model of makeup application. We first create a 3D face model using a 3D scanner. Then the user can adjust skin tone and enhance the skin texture. Finally, the user can use a haptic handle to simulate a makeup session while seeing its own face displayed in 3D.

The remainder of this paper is laid out as follows: We give an overview of our technique in Section 2. Next, in Section 3, we present the surface elements that we use to represent faces, and surface-elements based graphic renderer, and an auto-stereoscopic visualization method. In the same section, we also describe our method of facial skin enhancement and our haptic-based makeup application. Experimental results are provided in Section 4. Finally, we draw some conclusions and make some suggestions for future work in Section 5.

## 2 3D Facial Makeup Simulation

This section describes the behavior of our 3D facial makeup simulation from the user's point of view. We also clarify the benefits of our approach.

In essence, our 3D facial makeup framework provides the user with a real 3D face model and a multi-sensory interface. It consists of three components: a pre-processing facial skin filter, a graphic renderer, and a model of haptic-based makeup application. Figure 1 is an overview of this framework.

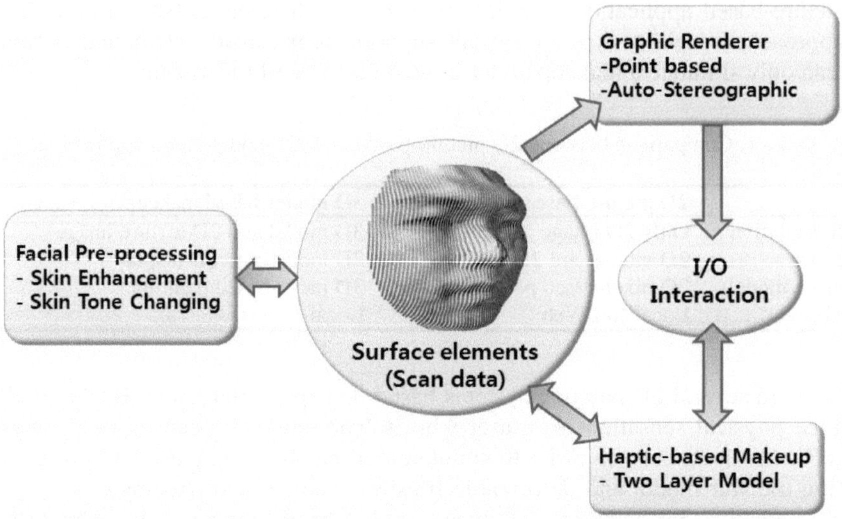


**Fig. 1.** An overview of the 3D facial makeup simulation system

We acquire a 3D facial model using Cyberware 3030 scanner. This device extracts the geometry and texture of a head from two viewpoints, using a low-intensity laser and a high quality video sensor. After the facial model has been input into the makeup application, the user grasps a haptic handle while looking at a 3D auto-stereoscopic display in order to simulate the makeup process. The integration of haptic feedback with stereo visual cues provides a real sensation of putting makeup on.

The user can also change the model's skin tone and adjust the texture of the skin using methods such as automatic brightness and contrast adjustment, smoothing, and noise removal, during a pre-processing step. The user can then set eight lights to optimize visual effect of the makeup. The user can go on to use a sponge-like tool that locally changes the skin tone. Attributes such as the size of the 'sponge' that the makeup contains, the amount of moisture, and the magnitude of the haptic feedback, can all be adjusted. The user can also remove makeup.

# 3 Methods

We will now provide more detail about the implementation of our makeup simulation technique. In particular, we will explain how the surface elements are combined with our skin enhancement methods and the haptic makeup application. We implemented our system using the OpenGL graphics library and the OpenHaptics library.

## 3.1 Surface Element Representation

Polygon-based rendering is ubiquitous, but it has limited performance in an environment in which a complex scene is linked to a physical simulation, so that the resolution of the model may vary. Surface elements [8] can be created by sampling a textured model using ray-casting, or acquired by a 3D scanner. At each surface point sampled, a surfel (surface element) is created, with a position, color, and a normal vector, and any local shading attributes. Surfels can model a whole unbroken surface, and form the basis of a multi-resolution representation which is suitable for the dynamic graphics and complex simulations. A surfel representation requires no connectivity information, unlike a mesh-based representation. This allows us to support discrete processes such as skin enhancement and makeup application.

### 3.2 Rendering of Surface Elements

Our graphic renderer is based on two techniques. One is the EWA (Elliptical Weighted Average) splatting technique [9] that we have developed for rendering surfels. The other is the auto-stereoscopic rendering.

We render a facial model by using a disk renderer, a disk blending renderer, or an EWA splatting renderer. The disk renderer colors disks at the position and orientation of each surfel. This method is fast, but there may be artifacts at the intersections between disks. EWA splatting solves this problem. In this method the surfels are projected into a depth buffer, and then a low-pass filter and a warped reconstruction filter are applied.

3D stereo rendering can give the user the experience of real depth perception that can only be obtained through binocular depth cues. To get binocular depth cues, one picture per eye is necessary. It can be implemented by column prisms on the surface of an LCD display. In terms of software, we first create an image for each eye. Then we send the left image to the odd columns and the right image to the even columns of the OpenGL stencil buffer. Then we can render the scene on a single display. This is sometimes called vertically interlaced D4D stereo [10]. When a user is in a position where two images can be seen with the respective eye, user will experience depth from the binocular depth cues without any special glasses. For the freedom of movement, we can track the position and orientation of the user's head using infrared sensors and a reflecting head frame.

### 3.3 A Haptic-Based Model of Makeup Application

To simulate the application of makeup, a user grasps the stylus of the haptic device, and controls a sponge-like graphic model on the screen which contacts the surface of the facial model. At this time, the results of an action depend on several factors: the current color, the magnitude of the force applied by the user, the simulated moisture content of the makeup, and the size of the sponge. The sponge is modeled by surface voxels. The surface voxels representation reduces the numbers of operations required for the detection of, and response to, the resulting forces. In order to paint on to a 3D facial surface, we use a two-layer painting model based on 2D pixel buffer. A basic layer stores the color of the underlying facial surface, while the color of the second layer is determined by the sponge tool. During a makeup operation, we first determine the surfels involved in the collision between the sponge and the facial surface. Next we project these samples into the painting buffer. We then blend the surface and the sponge color, using the formula of Equation 1, and finally we re-project mixture on to the facial surface. Figure 2 shows the main steps in a makeup operation.

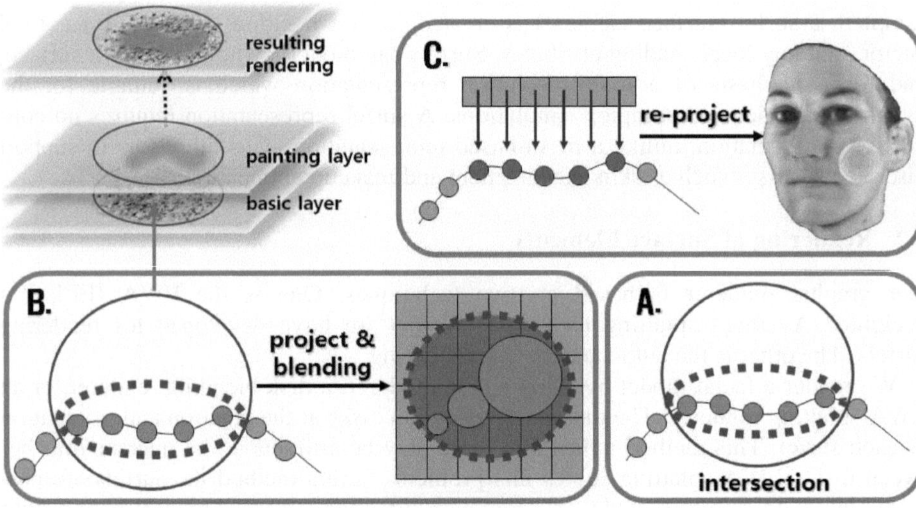


**Fig. 2.** A makeup operation based on two color layers

We use a rendering method to process collisions and to compute the force between the objects. The position of the haptic end-effector corresponding to the HIP (haptic interface point) is discretized by a haptic encoder, and that information is then used to compute the force resulting from the collision. Once collision detection is complete, we can calculate the IHIP (ideal haptic interface point) which is the contact orientation. After this, we compute the penetration depth vector connecting the IHIP to the HIP. Finally we apply the resulting force to the haptic stylus.

We used the OpenHaptics library to implement the necessary procedures [11]. This library uses a multi-threading and a synchronization technique to render forces and to keep the graphics and haptics in step. We also mix the high-level representation of the surface, consisting of the surfels, with a low-level triangle meshes to improve performance. We represent the facial model using a form of BSP (binary space partitioning) tree and an axially aligned bounding culling technique. This accelerates the local processing needed for collision detection and force determination.

### 3.4 3D Facial Skin Texture Enhancement and Tone Alteration

We use filtering to change the texture of the surface elements, using three kinds of filters without affecting any geometric information. We first generate a 2D image of the 3D facial surface, which can be obtained from the projection part of the EWA splatting algorithm. Then we apply smoothing, automatic contrast and brightness adjustment, and remove the noise from the image. Finally we re-project the resulting image back into 3D space. A low-pass Gaussian filter, based on a 7x7 or 15x15 convolution mask is used to smooth the skin texture. A median filter removes noise. And histogram equalization, based on statistical information about the skin colors, is used to adjust brightness and contrast.

Unlike the texture filters, changes of skin color are performed in 3D. A user first selects one of eight template colors. The color of each surfel can then be changed as follows;

$$C = C_b*I + C_p*(1-I). \tag{1}$$

Where $C$ is the resulting color, $C_b$ is the color of the base layer, $C_p$ is the previous color, and $I$ is the intensity derived from the haptic interaction. The intensity is determined as follows;

$$I = I_G*I_M*I_F. \tag{2}$$

Where $I_G$ is the Gaussian weight, $I_M$ is the moisture content of the makeup and $I_F$ is a weight derived from the haptic force. This means that the colors generated during the makeup process dependent on the simulated moisture, the magnitude of the haptic force, and the Gaussian coefficient relating the distance of the surface elements from the center of the sponge. Equation 1 defines the resulting color by haptic interaction.

# 4 Experimental Results

Our hardware environment consists of a Cyberware™ 3030 3D scanner, SensAble™ PHANToM haptic device, and a SeeReal™ auto-stereoscopic display (or simply 3D display). Figure 3 shows a skin adjustment and a makeup simulation using the haptic device and the auto-stereoscopic display.

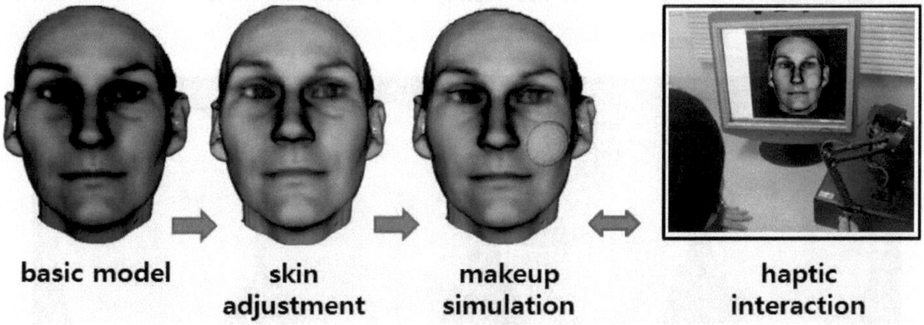


**Fig. 3.** The results of a makeup session using a haptic device and an auto-stereoscopic display: (from left to right) basic model, skin adjusted model, makeup result of using a rouge-like color, haptic interaction

## 4.1 A Calibration of an Auto-Stereoscopic Display

Without binocular depth cues, a user cannot get a good simulation of the makeup application process. An auto-stereoscopic display allows the user much better depth perception than most 2D monitors using monocular depth cues. To see left and right images with corresponding eyes in the 'sweet spot', it is necessary to determine the optimal distance from the user to the display screen. It is also needed to adjust the stereo rendering parameters: depth and the gap between the user's eyes. The auto-stereoscopic display has a viewing angle of ±20º and, for the best 3D sensation, the user must stay 70-75 cm from the screen.

### 4.2 Experimental Data and Graphic/Haptic Rendering Performance

Our face models came from the Max Planck Institute for Biological Cybernetics [12], and this geometric data is used throughout the makeup simulation. Figure 4 shows the difference between the surfels obtained from a model and from the scanner. The scanner achieves a better density, and this affects the image quality. The average number of surfels in our face models is between 200,000 and 300,000. We use 2D pixel-based paint models to allow a user to simulate the application of real makeup to their own face.

The performance of the graphic and the haptic rendering during simulation of the makeup process is compared in Table 2. This performance was measured using a conventional display. On the stereoscopic display the performance is roughly half as good.

**Table 2.** Approximate graphic and haptic performance during 3D facial makeup simulation

| | Graphic frame rate | Haptic frame rate |
|---|---|---|
| Point renderer | 90 FPS | 1000 Hz |
| Disk renderer | 60 FPS | 1000 Hz |
| Blending disk renderer | 40 FPS | 1000 Hz |
| EWA Splatting renderer | 3 FPS | depends on graphic performance |

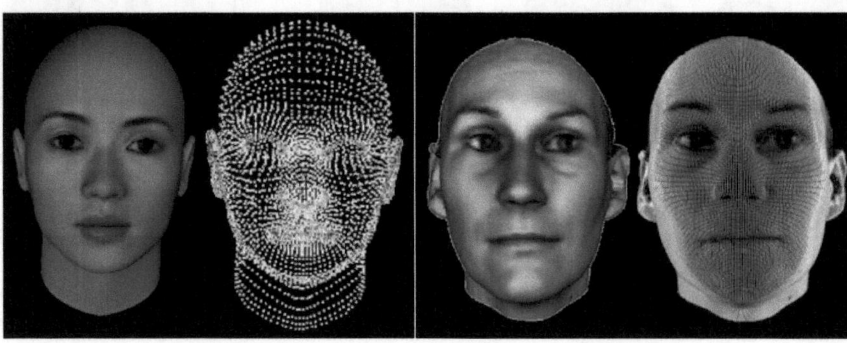

**Fig. 4.** 3D face models: (left) template model from the FaceGen modeling tool; (right) Cyberware™ 3D scan data from the Max Planck Institute

### 4.3 Facial Skin Enhancement

Figure 5 shows the result of skin enhancement using filters, while Figure 6 shows skin tones corresponding to five representatives of the eight template colors. The time

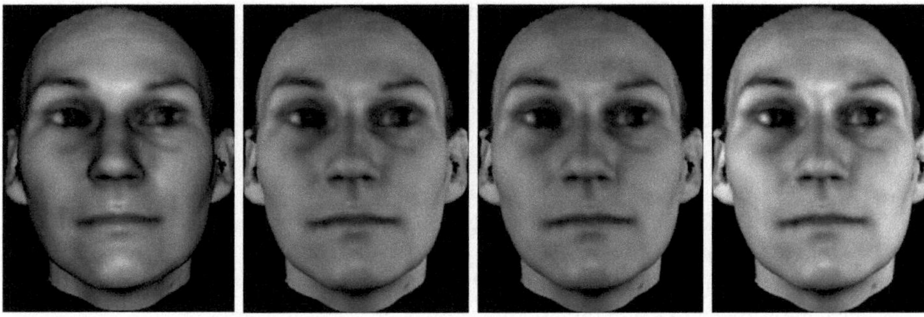

**Fig. 5.** Texture enhancement: (from left to right) basic model, smoothed model, noise-free model, model after contrast adjustment

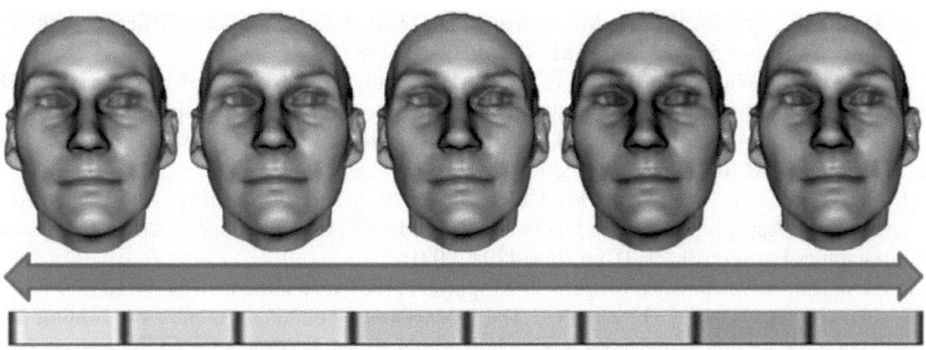

**Fig. 6.** Changes in facial skin tone using template colors

required for smoothing, noise removal, and contrast and brightness adjustment are of the order of 0.5 to 1.0 seconds.

## 5 Conclusions and Future Work

We have designed a framework for simulating facial makeup using a multi-sensory interface that integrates a haptic device with an auto-stereoscopic display. The user is provided with a three-dimensional illusion during interaction with our surfel-based face model. This is achieved with a surfel-based graphic renderer and a two-layer paint model. By pre-processing the appearance of the facial skin, we were able to reconstruct an acceptable 3D face model from 3D scanner data.

In the near future, we will improve the speed of the EWA splatting algorithm using a GPU. Also, while facial models obtained from the scanner have a good density of surface elements, we need a higher density in creased region. This can be achieved with a multi-resolution representation. Additionally, we will enhance our method of haptic interaction by using virtual coupling which interacts between objects instead of the point-object based haptic interaction.

As 3D digital content becomes more ubiquitous, and techniques for 3D display and haptic interaction continue to improve, we envisage that our approach will be utilized in areas such as fashion, games and medicine.

## References


1. Schmidhuber, J.: Facial Beauty and Fractal Geometry. Technical report, IDSIA-28-98, IDSIA 1998 (1998)
2. Eisenthal, Y., Dror, G., Ruppin, E.: Facial attractiveness: Beauty and the machine. Neural Computation 18(1), 119–142 (2006)
3. Leyvand, T., Cohehn-Or, D., Dror, G., Lischinkski, D.: Digital Face Beautification. In: ACM SIGGRAPH 2006, Technical sketches (2006)
4. FaceFilter Studio 2, Software available at http://www.reallusion.com/facefilter
5. VirtualFashion Professional, Software available at http://virtual-fashion.com
6. Baxter, B., Scheib, V., Lin, M., Manocha, D.: DAB: Interactive Haptic Painting with 3D Virtual Brushes. Proc. of ACM SIGGRAPH, 461–468 (2001)
7. Adams, B., Wicke, M., Dutre, P., Gross, M., Pauly, M., Teschner, M.: Interactive 3D Painting on Point-Sampled Objects. In: Symposium on Point-Based Graphics 2004 (2004)
8. Pfister, H., Zwicker, M., Baar, J.V., Gross, M.: Surfels: Surface Elements as Rendering Primitives. ACM SIGGRAPH, 335–342 (2000)
9. Ren, L., Pfister, H., Zwicker, M.: Object Space EWA Surface Splatting: A Hardware Accelerated Approach to High Quality Point Rendering. In: Eurographics 2002, Computer Graphics Forum, vol. 21(3), pp. 461–470 (2002)
10. Dodgson, N.A.: Autostereoscopic 3D Displays. IEEE Computer 38(8), 31–36 (2005)
11. Itkowitz, B., Handley, J., Zhu, W.: The OpenHaptics Toolkit: A Library for Adding 3D Touch Navigation and Haptics to Graphics Applications. In: Proc. of 1st Joint Eurohaptics Conference and Symposium on Haptic Interfaces for Virtual Environment and Teleoperator Systems 2005 (2005)
12. Max Planck Institute for Biological Cybernetics, Facial database available at http://faces.kyb.tuebingen.mpg.de

# A Virtual Space Environment Simulation System

Chaozhen Lan, Qing Xu, Jiansheng Li, and Yang Zhou

Institute of Surveying & Mapping, 450052, Zhengzhou, China
Lan_cz@163.com

**Abstract.** Visiting the outer space freely was the human imagination until recently. Virtual environments of the space will be the way for people to "visit" the space to study their motion and interrelationships. This paper assembles a scalable, immersive virtual environment system called the Virtual Space Environment Simulation System (VSESS) that allows users to visualize objects and physical phenomena in near-earth space and provides a brief sketch of the design thinking of such system. The software architecture of the VSESS is designed incorporate the various simulation, analysis and visualization elements of the system into a single, integrated environment. The system employs a VR system with double projector to build immense 3-D environment and applied to some actual space projects and they demonstrate the efficacy of the concept and the processing.

**Keywords:** space system, virtual simulation, virtual space environment, VR.

## 1 Introduction

Until very recently, visiting the outer space freely was the human imagination - a notoriously poor form of transport. The variety, complexity, size, and in outer space conspire against using just the mind to comprehend the motion of satellites, other physical phenomena in outer space, and their interplay. For example, because of the complexities of orbital motion, examining the orbital elements for even a few spacecrafts does not provide an understanding of the positional relationships of the spacecrafts or of the motion of the bodies involved.

Unfortunately, people cannot look to space flight to provide insight, much less the ability to partake of the outer space's wonders - the time when a common person can visit the outer space freely lies in the distant future. Even when outer space travel becomes possible, the cost required will preclude visiting more than a few planets. We believe that, for the foreseeable future, virtual environments of the space that are based on orbital motion information and accurately portray each body's appearance will be the only - and most illuminating - way for people to "visit" the space to study their motion and interrelationships.

On the other hand, because of the cost and in many cases the unfeasibility of simulating spacecraft missions in a terrestrial environment, computer based simulation systems are a possible alternative. As graphics techniques for photo-realistic visual simulation have evolved over the last ten years it is now possible to simulate scenes of high complexity. Simulation systems using advanced visualization techniques can be

R. Shumaker (Ed.): Virtual Reality, HCII 2007, LNCS 4563, pp. 497–503, 2007.

used for applications such as mission planning and rehearsal. Such systems allow alternative mission scenarios to be explored for modest cost and no risk. Another important use of the visual simulation software is to provide a tool for generating mission concepts to a wider audience. A visual simulation which can be understood at a glance will often generate the enthusiasm and advocacy which words alone cannot achieve [1].

Several systems have been developed to promote insight into selected aspects of orbital spacecrafts' relationships and appearance [2~6], but they provide a limited solution. We therefore assembled a more complete scalable, immersive virtual environment system called the Virtual Space Environment Simulation System (VSESS) that allows its user to visualize objects and physical phenomena in near-earth space.

We undertook the VSESS project to improve comprehension and appreciation of the complexity, motion, and splendor of near-earth space. To do so, the VSESS must (1) accurately portray the orbital behavior of satellites, planets, and other bodies, and (2) function in a virtual environment. Additionally, the system needs to

- provide a flexible, 3D graphical user interface for immersive operation, graphically model all bodies in near-space in 3D and to the same scale;
- accurately portray the objects and their locations;
- provide analytical capability and visualization of results, and
- maintain an interactive frame rate.

In this article we describe how we met these requirements.

## 2 Architecture Overview

The software architecture of the VSESS is designed incorporate the various simulation, analysis and visualization elements of the system into a single, integrated environment. Fig.1 shows the major software modules of VSESS and their interrelationships.

There are six primary software modules and a database which comprise the VSESS. The six software modules are (1) Simulation Controller, (2) Scenario Manager, (3) Space Objects Simulator, (4) Space Environment Simulator, (5) Analysis Module, and (6) 3D Display Engine. The database is The Satellites Orbit Database.

The Simulation Controller is responsible for controlling the whole simulation process while running. The Scenario Manager Module has two main functions: (1) Objects Manager. This module deals with all kinds of objects in the simulation scenario including space-base objects and ground-base objects. We can easily add, delete, modify and operate any object through this module; and (2) Time Manager. By using the Time Manager, user can set start, end time and time step for simulation and can also make time speed up or speed down freely. Time can be animated forward, reverse and in real-time to simulation.

Space Objects Simulator is one of the core sub-systems in VSESS. It provides multiple analytical and numerical propagators (Two-body, J2, J4, SGP4) to compute satellite position data in a wide variety of coordinate types and systems. For the novice, Space Objects Simulator provides the Orbit Wizard to guide the user through quick creation of commonly-used orbit types such as geostationary, circular, critically-inclined, sun synchronous, molniya, and retrograde. For ground-base objects, this module also has the ability to calculate their position and velocity for analysis, visualization.

The Space Environment Simulator provides the cabebility of numcal caculation for the basic space environment elements such as atmosphere, Magnetosphere, Ionosphere, and etc.

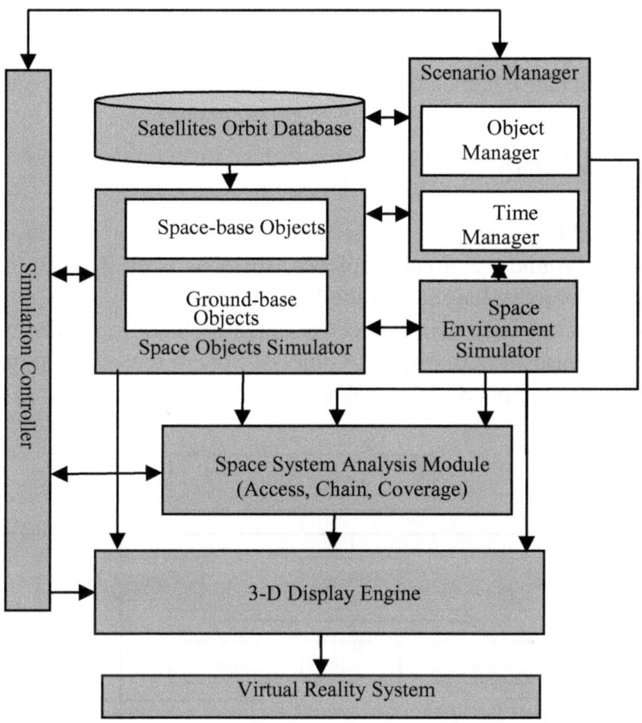


**Fig. 1.** Major Software Modules & Their Interrelationships

The Space System Analysis Module is another core sub-system in VSESS. It has the ability of access, chain and coverage analysis. VSESS allows user to determine the times one object can see, another object. In addition, user can impose constraints on accesses between objects to define what constitutes a valid access. The Chain module allows users to extend the pair-wise analysis capabilities to include accesses to and from satellite constellations, ground station networks, groups of targets and multiple sensors. The Coverage module allows user to analyze the global or regional coverage provided by a single satellite or a constellation of satellites while considering all access constraints. Specific results are generated based on detailed access computations performed to grid points within an area of coverage.

The last important module is the 3D Display Engine. This Display Engine brings 3-D viewing capability to the VSESS environment. This engine takes advantage of today's readily available workstations graphics engines to provide state-of-the-art interactive graphics performance. It displays all near-earth space information from VSESS using realistic and dynamic 3-D views of space, airborne and terrestrial assets, space environment, and orbit trajectories.

The only database in VSESS is the Satellite Orbit Database. This database uses the STK satellite database as its data source. STK satellite database is available on its web site (www.STK.com) and updated every week. The most extensive database, from which all of our other databases are derived, is an up-to-date catalogue of over 8,000 objects. This database is maintained by U.S. Space Command. It contains data on Two-Line Element sets (TLEs), Space Surveillance Catalog (SSC) numbers, common names for satellites, launch dates, launch times, apogee, perigee, activity state and more.

## 3 Objects of VSESS

Objects are the building blocks of a VSESS simulation scenario. Platforms in VSESS include satellites, grounds stations, airplanes, ships as well as earth, moon and sun. Fig. 2 contains the objects diagram for the VSESS.

We build the space system using object-oriented methodology. The basic space object types – Space base and Ground base objects, Sphere (celestial bodies) and Stars – are all derived from the Space-object, which is the root object for the system.

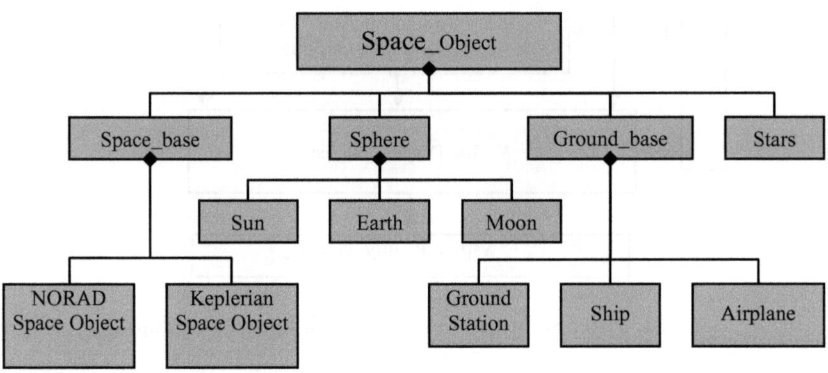


**Fig. 2.** Object Definition

The sun, moon and earth objects are derived from the Sphere object. The Earth object is considered to be at the origin of the VSESS and the magnitude of its position is always zero. The physical constants describing the Earth include mass, mean equatorial radius, flattening coefficient and rotational rate. The Sun and Moon objects are internally predefined and the user has limited control over their initial conditions. They are propagated using algorithms based on general perturbation theory as described in [7]. The propagation modules are accurate enough to allow modeling of solar and lunar eclipses.

The NORAD Space Object defines circular or elliptical orbits about the earth by using the NORAD SGP4 or SDP4 orbit propagators, while the keplerian space object also defines orbits by using analytical and numerical propagators (Two-body, J2, J4,etc.)

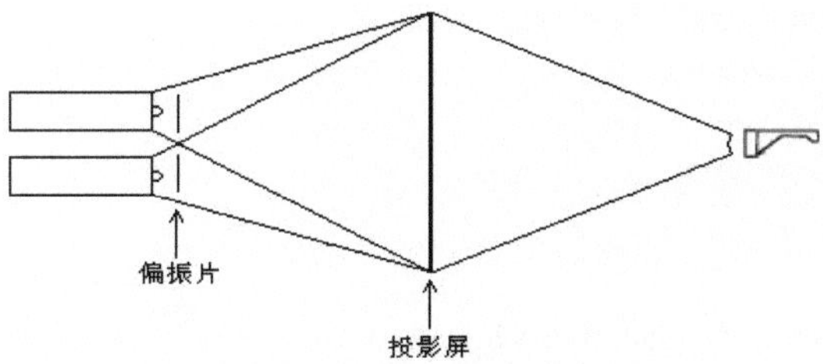


**Fig. 3.** VR system of VSESS

**Fig. 4.** Projectors of the VR system

## 4 System Implementation

We built the A Virtual Space Environment Simulation System using object-oriented methodology on the system of Windows XP based on the design way given in this paper. All modules were written in C++ with Microsoft Visual C++ 6.0. We employ a simple VR system (shown in Fig. 3) with double projector to build immense 3-D environment, Fig. 4 shows the projectors of the VR system. The software uses 3-D view to make all the information of the result of simulation and analysis visible. The 3-D view were developed by using OpenGL API functions and achieve a frame rate of between 40 and 60 frames per second depending on the number of satellites being propagated

**Fig. 5.** Visible Magnetosphere in VR system

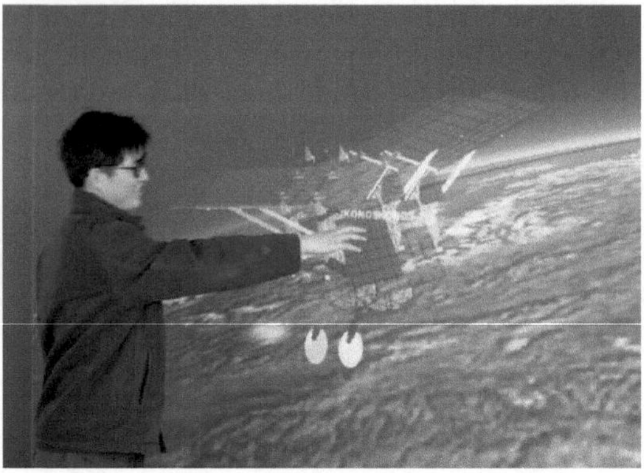

**Fig. 6.** Spacecraft simulation in VR system

and their orbits in our VR system. Fig. 5 shows the visible magnetosphere in our VR system. Fig. 6 presents spacecraft simulation on orbit, and a 3-D view of a close-up satellite's model, Earth surface and the result of sensors simulation. Earth texture and colors are based on NASA data and images from Planetary Arts and Sciences.

## 5 Conclusion and Future Work

VR tools and computer simulation can play an important role in the field of space designs and applications. The simulation techniques with advanced scene generation technology and analysis capability can produce new tools with applications in mission planning, rehearsal and presentation. The purpose of the design of VSESS is to provide near-earth space environment simulation and analysis system and decision makers with intuitive insight involving the near-Earth astro-dynamics problem domain. This paper provides a brief sketch of the design thinking of such software. The system we developed is applied to some actual space projects and they demonstrate the efficacy of the concept and the processing.

We plan to expand the software in several ways. First, we intent to improve the analysis capability of space system. We also intend to model and simulate the near earth space environment and then develop a capability to compute the effect of satellite in space environment in VR environment.

## References


1. Stephenson, T., Gelberg, L.: MARC-A System for Simulation and Visualization of Space Mission Scenarios. IEEE AES Magazine, 14–19 (1989)
2. Mara, S.: Visim. J. British Interplanetary Society, 46, 203–208 (1993)
3. McGreevey, M.: Virtual Reality and Planetary Exploration. In: Wexelblat, A. (ed.) Virtual Reality and Planetary Exploration, pp. 163–198. Academic Press, New York (1993)

4. Ocampo, C.: Computer Graphics Applied to the Visualization of Two-Body Orbital Mechanics Problems. In: Proceedings Of the 28th Aerospace Sciences Meeting, pp. 1–15. AIAA Press, Easton, PA, AIAA-90-0075 (1990)
5. Pickover, C.A.: A Vacation on Mars-An Artist's Journey in a Computer Graphics World. Computers & Graphics 16, 9–13 (1992)
6. Analytical Graphics, Inc. Getting Started with Satellite Tool Kit (STK) Version 4.2.
7. Bayliss, S.S.: Interplanetary Targeting Program, Aerospace TOR-0059 (6773) (1971)

# Collaborative Design Prototyping Tool for Hardware Software Integrated Information Appliances

Tek-Jin Nam

Department of Industrial Design, Korea Advanced Institute of Science and Technology, 373-1, Kusung-Dong, Yusung-Gu, Daejeon, 305-701, Korea
tjnam@kaist.ac.kr

**Abstract.** Simple and rapid prototyping is important for collaborative design where end users are involved in the design process from the early phase. This paper presents a collaborative design prototyping tool for hardware software integrated information appliances, such as mobile phones and digital cameras. It supports the collaboration between designers and users for identification of user needs and evaluation of design. The tool consists of STCtools (State Transition Chart tools) software, hardware modeling materials, physical user interface toolkits for software hardware integration, and Augmented Reality desk (ARdesk) for interactive simulation. STCtools allow users to prototype the behavioral aspect of information appliances using states and events. Using the hardware modeling materials and the physical user interface toolkit, designers and end-users explore hardware aspects together. ARdesk is a workbench where the interactive sketch display is projected onto an invisible paper marker of the hardware model using the projection based augmented reality technique. Three collaborative design workshops of designing a portable device for theme park users were accomplished with the prototyping tool for qualitative evaluation. The results suggested that the tool supported collaborative design by iterative concept development and active interactions between designers and end users.

**Keywords:** Collaborative Design, Information Appliance Design, State Transition, Augmented Reality, Prototyping, Hardware Software Integration.

## 1 Introduction

Collaborative design is a user-centered design method where end users are involved in the design process from the early phase. It becomes a key method for human-centered design as satisfying users' emotional and mental value becomes important for successful products. By working together with end users, designers can get sufficient understanding of the user's functional and emotional needs. One of the important collaborative design techniques is to run a collaborative design workshop where designers and end users work together to search for new concepts, find design problems and evaluate early concepts. Simple and rapid prototyping is important in collaborative design because the concepts have to be readily explored, visualized and evaluated.

Collaborative Design has a significant historical meaning in the development of design methodology [1]. Early cases of user participation related to the introduction

R. Shumaker (Ed.): Virtual Reality, HCII 2007, LNCS 4563, pp. 504–513, 2007.

and development of new technology can be found in the Scandinavian countries [2]. Recently, with growing interests in reflecting the end users' needs in information system designs, application of collaborative design is increasing in the human computer interaction field. Its application is also expanding in design fields such as product, interior and visual design.

On the other hand, many new information appliances are produced with the rapid development of digital technology. As human experience or interaction with the artifacts is emphasized in these projects, the new fields, such as information design and interaction design, the software aspects of a product, such as the contents and user interface, have to be considered together with the hardware aspects. To accomplish collaborative design in the new design projects, the software aspects and the integration need to be considered. Most preceding researches on collaborative design [3] have been focused on hardware centered methods. Also, areas related to hardware and software integration at the early process of design did not gain much attention. Currently, the integration of hardware and software can not be easily achieved without close interdisciplinary collaboration. There are little research works on collaborative design prototyping tools.

This paper presents a prototyping tool that can be used in information appliance design projects for collaboration between designers and end users at the early stage of the projects. It also presents a user trial of the collaborative prototyping tool in a design project.

## 2 Proposed Collaborative Design Prototyping Tool for Hardware-Software Integrated Information Appliances

A collaborative design prototyping tool for digital product developments needs to address various issues. First of all, general users who are not skilled at concept actualization should be able to visualize ideas rapidly, easily and effectively as professional designers do. Especially, methods to naturally express abstract ideas of needs and wants should be considered. Also, the final idea actualized by the prototyping tool should be directly related to or give inspiration to the design solution that the design team is developing. Flexible applications need to be supplied in order to apply it to various themes and circumstances in a collaborative design workshop. Moreover, the interaction and structural aspects of the software need to be considered as well as the functional and emotional aspects of the product's hardware.

A set of collaborative design prototyping tool for information appliances is proposed to satisfy these needs. The set is composed of i) STCtools(State Transition Charts tools) software for prototyping the software aspects of collaborative design prototyping, 2) a modeling material for collaborative hardware prototyping iii) a physical interface toolkit for hardware and software connection, and iv) Augmented Reality desk for the hardware and software integrated simulation.

### 2.1 STCtools for Collaborative Software Prototyping

STCtools is based on STC(State Transition Chart) that was suggested in the previous research by Nam [4]. STC is a means to model a digital product's information structure or a user interface flow. During a product's interface or content development, this allows a designer to articulate essential states and events that trigger changes between the states. STC can be compared with STD(State Transition Diagram) that is often used in the software engineering field. Tools based on STD, such as Statechart [5], visual STATE[6] and SDL[7], were developed but they were mainly for software engineers. In collaboration design, visualization that allows the users to understand information structure and abstract concepts at ease is an important issue. Existing software engineering tools show little considerations for visual factors such as screen layout, text, or icons. It also does not support sketching.

STC uses a familiar method to both designers and users, sketching, which has been commonly used in software concept development as well as in hardware concept development of digital products. Users can more readily suggest and verify diverse interface concepts through post-its and whiteboard that are familiar to both designers and users [4]. STCtools was developed to support a more dynamic and iterative design process of the post-it and whiteboard method by applying digital technology.

**Modules of STCtools Software.** With STCtools users can create the states of STC and assign events that cause transitions between the states. Users can interactively execute mid or final results of STC as an interactive simulation. STCtools consists of three software modules to support these functions. The first module, STCmake, has the function to rapidly sketch states and edit already drawn graphic elements, as if sketching the main states of a digital product on post-it notes. Fig. 1 (left) shows a screen layout of STCmake. Icons on draw, select and delete are provided to support basic sketching function. STCtools run on a pen input computing environment. Short pen clicks were applied to divide continuously drawn elements in the sketching process. According to the properties, the divided sketch elements can be assigned as sketch of hardware appearance, content elements and interface elements such as buttons. A dialog box window, where the properties of a screen element can be assigned, opens when a property icon is clicked [Fig. 1 right].

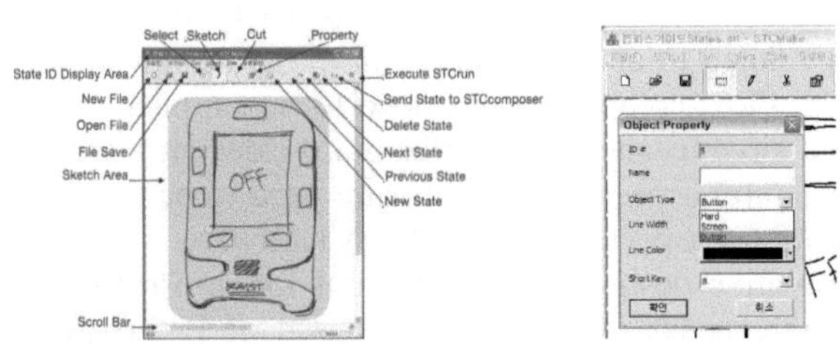


**Fig. 1.** Screen layout and user interface elements of STCmake (left), Dialogue window to define the properties of the sketch element (right)

The states made from STCmake are wirelessly transmitted to the next software module, STCcompose. STCcompose structures the relationships of the states made from STCmake and defines the events that cause transitions between the states. Navigational structure of user interface or contents can be explored through these event definitions. STCcompose provides a wide workspace for the defining procedure of the states' structure [Fig. 2 left]. Basic functions such as zoom, pan, slider bars are provided to shift the view of the workspace. Transitions within states can be defined by adding an arrow on to the interface element.

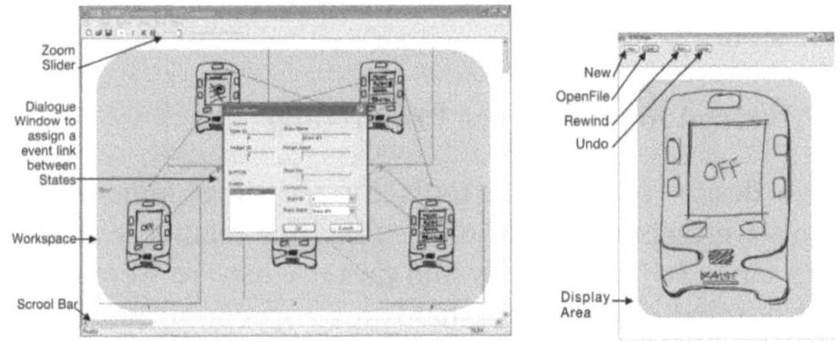


**Fig. 2.** Screen layout and user interface elements of STCcompose (left) and STCrun (right)

The last software module, STCrun, enables the STC results composed in STCcompose to be tested promptly. Additional interface was minimized to test the actual functioning process of the final STC made by STCmake and STCcompose. Basic functions such as file open, in case a previously saved STC exists, file run and return to the initial state are provided with icons [Fig. 2 right]. Any changes are instantly updated whenever a state or an event has been added since the three software modules are linked in real time. STCrun can be executed from the menu category in STCcompose or STCmake.

**Hardware Configurations of STCtools.** Fig. 3 (left and right) shows the two main hardware configurations that are used with the STC software modules. The first composition uses a combination of a Tablet PC and a small-sized PDA. STCmake and STCrun run on a PDA while STCcompose and STCrun are used on a Tablet PC. This can be used effectively to develop the software interface to inspect the small sized information appliances, contents, or screen element. Also, its portability makes it easy to use in a collaborative design workshop that is performed at the actual usage environment. The second composition, composed of a Tablet PC and an electronic whiteboard with a sketch input device such as Mimio, can be used when a larger sketching area is required.

**Fig. 3.** Portable system composition using a PDA and a Tablet PC(left), System composition using a Tablet PC and an electronic whiteboard (right)

STCtools software modules were developed under Visual C++.net environment. STCmake and STCrun were converted to Embedded C++ 3.0 and developed in to two different versions because they needed to support both the PDA and desktop PC environment. The hardware used were iPAQ PDA and Compaq TC100 Tablet PC. A general internet environment using TCP/IP transmission protocol was used for wireless data transmission.

### 2.2 Modeling Material for Hardware Prototyping

The collaborative design prototyping tools for the development and evaluation of hardware concepts were composed of tools suited for relatively small digital product modeling. Velcro tape, Styrofoam, clay and poster adhesive were used as prototyping materials [Fig. 4 left and middle]. The hardware aspects of digital products, such as portability, scale, proportion and balance, could be examined by using these prototyping materials. The hardware prototypes would be used to demonstrate the usage situation of a digital product or discuss the situation in detail. Along with these modeling materials, existing digital products, such as mobile phone, digital camera, PDA and remote control, could be supplied additionally to the users to readily comment on similar or referential hardware elements [Fig. 4 right].

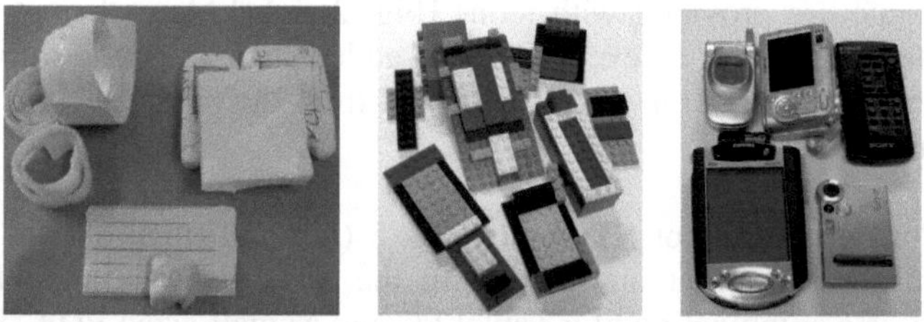

**Fig. 4.** Hardware modeling materials such as velcro, styrofoam, clay (left) and Lego (middle), Digital devices for reference (right)

### 2.3 Physical Interface Toolkit for Hardware and Software Linkage

A distinctive feature of the collaborative design prototyping tool suggested in this paper is that the software prototype result can be easily linked to the external hardware. STCtools would be used to develop the software concept and various materials would be used to examine the alternatives of hardware aspects. A physical interface toolkit, a set of physical user interface components and a key encoder, connects the hardware and the software [Fig. 5 left]. The key encoder is a device that can convert the signals of external input devices, such as buttons, into simple keyboard input signals in order to link it to the software. Buttons of various sizes were supplied as physical interface elements. An adhesive material, UHUtac® [8], was used on these buttons to allow it to stick on STCtools hardware sketches or mockups made of modeling materials [Fig. 5 right]. The buttons were connected to the computer through the encoder by two strands of wire. The button value was set to be automatically assigned by simply pressing a button when states were to be created or an interface element

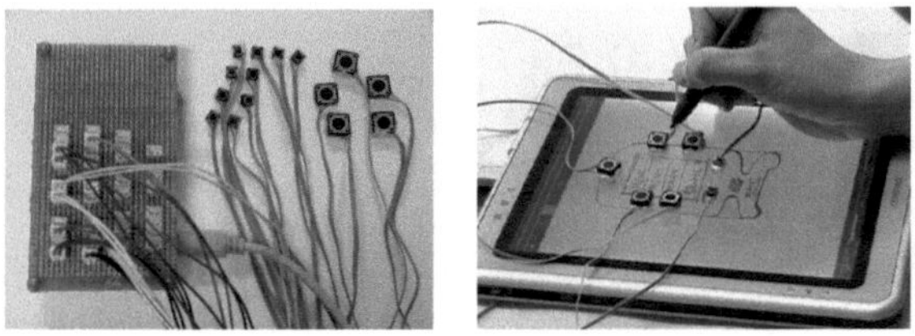

**Fig. 5.** Encoder and buttons of various sizes (left) Integration of physical interface elements and STCtools (right)

was to be specified in STCtools. Wired buttons were replaced by wireless input device using infrared signal for convenient use. However, button size and reception distance appear as limitations when using wireless input devices.

### 2.4 Augmented Reality Desk (ARdesk)

The final component of the collaborative design prototyping tool is Augmented Reality desk for integrated simulation. It is useful to have a large electronic workspace when using the STCComposer module of STCtools. This workspace can be provided on ARdesk when being used for hardware software integrated simulation. ARdesk is an electronic whiteboard equipped with video projection based Augmented Reality features. It has a screen with two video projectors. The rear video projection is used for the electronic whiteboard. On the surface of the desk, a pen input device, Mimio®[11], is installed. The front video projection is used to overlay virtual display onto a real paper marker on a hardware model. Different sized paper markers can represent the various sized display parts of an interactive product. The interactive simulation created in STCtools with sketches are captured and projected onto the paper markers. The front projection overlays the software display onto the marker attached to foam mockups. When a foam mockup with a maker is located on the ARdesk, users can touch and operate the physical user interface elements. This interactively updates the projected display of state sketches. ARdesk supports seamless transition between state compositions and the tangible usage experience of the intermediate or final results.

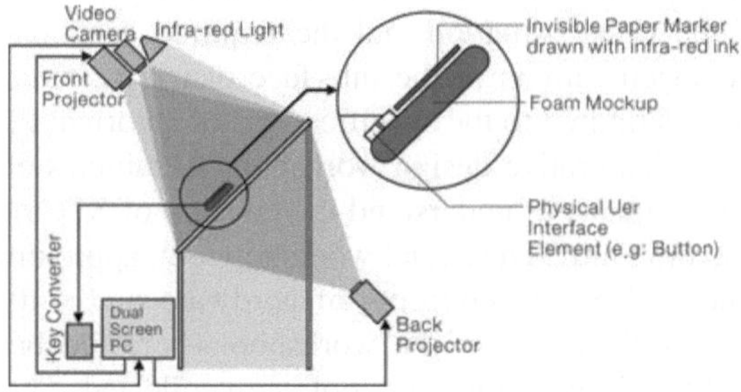


**Fig. 6.** The configuration of ARdesk

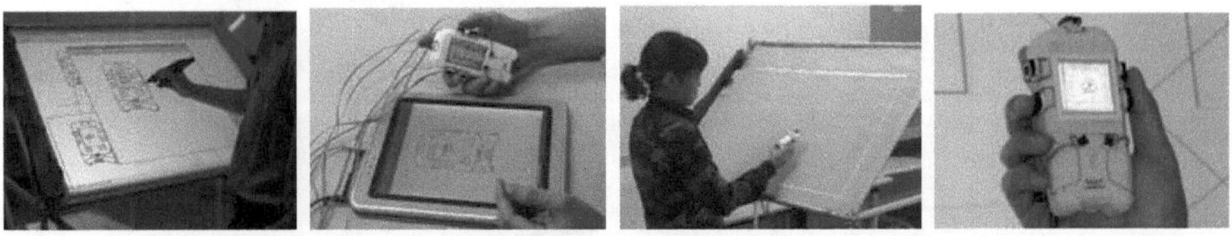

**Fig. 7.** Usage Scene of ARdesk (from left, composing scene, PUI widgets attached on a foam mockup, conducting integrated simulation on ARdesk, Virtual STCrun image projected onto the foam mockup)

To build a more compact configuration of the ARdesk, tracking and video projection was installed on the front side [Fig. 6]. The projector and the camera for marker detection was integrated and attached to a single tripod. The captured screen image of STCrun is projected onto the paper marker while the camera detects the identity and location of the marker. The invisible paper marker was made with infrared ink. The camera with an infrared filter could detect the marker pattern without interfering the projected video image on the surface of the paper marker [Fig. 7]. ARtoolkit[10] was used for marker tracking.

## 3 Case Study of Collaborative Design Workshop Using the Prototyping Tool

Collaborative design workshops were held for qualitative evaluation of the prototyping tool. Three teams of two designers and two users participated in the workshops. The one designer helped users in the workshop while the other designer controlled process of the workshop. STCtools with a PDA and a Tablet was used for the first team. The other teams used STCtools with a Tablet PC and an electronic whiteboard. The hardware modeling material, the physical interface toolkit and ARdesk were also provided for all three teams.

The theme of the design project for the collaborative design workshops was to design a portable digital information device for theme park visitors. Portable information device is a representative information appliance where the hardware and software are combined. Moreover, this theme was selected because general users would be able to think readily of the usage situation and the required functions. To simplify the design problem, the specifications of the interface elements, button type and screen size of target device was limited to the specifications of a normal PDA.

Prior to the actual collaborative design workshop, 10 minutes of practice time was given to allow the participants to understand the concept of STCtools and other components of the prototyping tool. The actual workshop took approximately 1 hour when the participants generated design concepts of hardware and software. An informal interview session was followed after the workshop where feedbacks on the overall design project, usability of the prototyping tool were collected. The workshop session was vide recorded for further analysis.

### 3.1 Result and Interpretation

The focus of the observation was on whether users can use STC to suggest and examine the software aspects of digital products without difficulty and whether the prototyping tool is effective in the collaborative design process. Within about 10 minutes, the users adapted quickly to the STC technique. Active participation was made on making and organizing the states by using STCtools. It can be interpreted that STC technique can be effectively used by general users without professional skills. Both the designers and users who participated in the workshop operated the STCtools software but the designer who was well acquainted with the use of the software performed the main operation.

The greatest effect that was achieved by using STCtools is thought to be the process of connecting the structured states by using STCcompose to examine the structure and add events. The enlargement, reduction, movement function of the workspace provided in STCcompose was effectively used and the creation of events and rearrangement of states were performed freely. Also, the mid-results were frequently checked by using STCrun.

Through this process, it was found that the problems presented in the design process could be reexamined and the discussion process concerning detailed problems and solutions are repeated through the use of STCrun. For example, during the third workshop, the number of states increased from 14, at the first STCrun, to 20, at the final step. This shows that a more detailed concept is discussed and added after making the first result. Also, more ideas could be linked to the next step because suggestions on the new states can be instantly recorded by using STCmake.

The biggest difficulty experienced by the participants who used the PDA and Tablet PC composition was making states by using STCmake. The screen size of the PDA used by the users for STCmake was limited to 5x6cm. All the physical user interface elements and contents had to be presented in this space. Because of this limitation in space, the users had to express their concept sketches in reduced sizes. Difficulties of using PDA pen input were also found. Unlike sketching on paper, additional usability problems such as the lack of tactile feedback and unnatural sketch posture emerged as problems. These problems were not significant in the Tablet PC and electronic whiteboard hardware configuration.

Although STCtools was used to materialize various ideas on software aspects, there were difficulties in expressing all the concepts proposed by the users. During the workshop, the users proposed ideas on various input-output interfaces. For example, ideas on windows and scrolling text that frequently supply information on events in theme parks were proposed. Also, new input methods such as pen and touch screen were proposed. These input methods however, were not easily implemented using STCtools.

The users used pen and paper along with STCtools during the initial concept discussion process. Often, basic concepts were developed by pen and paper before performing the procedures by STCmake. This suggests that even though STCtools is provided, this method of concept development process does not need to be blocked because users feel natural with the traditional sketching method. This shows that a more natural combination between traditional media and STCtools need to be considered.

Suggestions on the use of physical toolkits for the integration with hardware modeling material was limited mainly to the inspection of size and the use of buttons to check the final results using STCrun. The hardware linkage method used in the workshop was to perform the steps to register the specified key values on to the buttons when the sketch element properties produced in STCmake are defined. The integration did not occur as actively as expected because the connection process of these hardware buttons and sketch elements did not go well. Also, the problem of having to relocate the initial hardware buttons occurred because the screen view on STCmake did not exactly match the screen view on STCrun.

Participates often attached PUI widgets (buttons) on the surface of the device running STCmake, while states were created and refined. They also used ARdesk to examine the simulations and to combine the display of sketch simulation and the foam mockup. The intermediate results were refined by iteratively repeating these steps.

The concepts proposed by users using the prototyping tool were more concrete and realistic. Along with the analysis of basic functional needs that can be acquired from general user participatory design workshops, specific cases of the kind of interface the users feel comfortable with and the contents a product should contain were proposed. Moreover, STCtools was found to facilitate the interaction between users and designers from the initial stage and enable recurring idea development. The workshop participants made several comments of criticism on the usability of STCtools but they highly approved of the contributions the new tool makes on concept proposal and development.

## 4 Discussion

In STCtools, the concept of State Transition used in software engineering was developed into a tool familiar to both user and designer. However, as the workshop revealed, more function and interface is required to develop it into a more complete prototyping tool. Another issue that needs to be considered is the tradeoff between the completeness of the tool and acceptability of the user. Various supplement devices (e.g. Hierarchy, Concurrency, Communication factors used in Statechart [7]) are required to achieve a complete software prototyping system. These supplement features can make the interface more difficult for general users. Therefore, a sufficient examination is needed for an adequate level of tradeoff.

The difference between general software development tools and STCtools is in the concern on the integration with physical interface elements. The hardware toolkit supplied at the present is limited to physical interface elements with buttons of various sizes. Research on methods to link various other input devices, such as slider, pen and joystick, is required. Also, research for a more convenient method to integrate these elements, such as wireless connection, is needed as well. With an increased variety of hardware modeling material, improvement of toolkit elements linkage method (wireless connection) and use of new technology (e.g. Flexible Display, flexible Touch screen, etc.), the toolkit will become more freely usable.

Integration with traditional media is another factor to consider. Traditional media such as pen and paper is used at the initial design stage when users make sketches.

Rather than excluding the use of traditional media, a way to naturally integrate it with new digital tools is required.

# 5 Conclusion

This paper presents a collaborative design prototyping tool that can be used for hardware and software combined digital product design as a method for user centered design. This tool composed of STCtools, hardware materials, physical interface toolkit and ARdesk can be used effectively by users and designers together in exploring all aspects of information appliances. It is a good example of augmented reality application in prototyping for design.

The collaborative design method proposed in this study is expected to be effectively applicable in existing product or system designs as well as digital product designs. It is especially expected to act as an objective backup on design proposals in professional design companies or design departments inside companies. Also, it can be used effectively as a collaborative design tool among designers and professionals of other fields or designers themselves, and can support an iterative design process. Moreover, problems of the existing research method concerning the weak link between user studies and the actual design concept development can be partially overcome. In conclusion, this research is expected to rationalize the digital product development process by including collaborative design at the initial concept design stage of digital products.

# References

1. Cross, N.: Developments in Design Methodology, Umi Research Pr. (1984).
2. Clement, A., Besselaar, P.: A Retrospective Look at PD Projects. Communications of the ACM 36(6), 29–37 (1993)
3. Scrivener, S., Ball, L., Woodcock, A. (eds.): Collaborative Design. Springer, Heidelberg (2000)
4. Nam, T-J.: Designing Information Appliances: the evaluation of a design process framework based on a designer-friendly prototyping environment, In: Durling, D., Shakelton, J. (eds.): Common Ground, The proceedings of Design Research Socety International conference 2002 (2002).
5. Harel, D.: Statecharts: a visual Formalism for complex systems, The Science of Computer Programming, pp.231–274 (1987)
6. IAR: IAR visualSTATE for Embedded Systems, (2006) http://www.iar.com
7. SDL: What is SDL (2006) http://www.sdl-forum.org/SDL
8. UHUtac: (2006) http://www.uhu.de
9. Mimio: (2006) http://www.mimio.com
10. Billinghurst, M., Kato, H.: Collaborative Mixed Reality, In: Proc ISMR'99, Yokohama, Japan (1999)

# Improving the Mobility Performance of Autonomous Unmanned Ground Vehicles by Adding the Ability to 'Sense/Feel' Their Local Environment

Siddharth Odedra*, Stephen D. Prior, and Mehmet Karamanoglu

Department of Product Design and Engineering, Middlesex University, London
N14 4YZ, United Kingdom
s.odedra@mdx.ac.uk

**Abstract.** This paper explores how a 'learning' algorithm can be added to UGV's by giving it the ability to test the terrain through 'feeling' using incorporated sensors, which would in turn increase its situational awareness. Once the conditions are measured the system will log the results and a database can be built up of terrain types and their properties (terrain classification), therefore when it comes to operating autonomously in an unknown, unpredictable environment, the vehicle will be able to cope by identifying the terrain and situation and then decide on the best and most efficient way to travel over it by making adjustments, which would greatly improve the vehicles ability to operate autonomously.

**Keywords:** Unmanned, Autonomous, Mobility, Situational Awareness, Way Finding, Terrain, Reconfigurable, Intelligent Wheels.

## 1 Introduction

Robots are fast becoming perceptive, and autonomous systems are already a reality. One class of robot, which has the hardest task in terms of autonomous navigation, is the Unmanned Ground Vehicle (UGV). The main reason for this is the fact that they need to travel over different types of unknown terrain and avoid a number of variable obstacles. An example of how tough it is to negotiate autonomously in an unknown environment was demonstrated at the first DARPA Grand Challenge in 2004, where all the systems failed the course due to not being able to sense and adapt to situational changes [1].

To be able to operate fully autonomously on land, a UGV must be able to know as much as possible about its environment in order to be able to decide the best route from A to B in the quickest and safest way possible. It gathers this information using input sensors, which can include light, ultrasonic, infrared and even 3D scanners such as Laser Radars (LADAR), and the system builds up a picture of the obstacles and terrain ahead using the information received from these inputs.

Sensors are therefore very important, particularly for autonomous UGV's who use them to help build up this picture of the environment in order to make decisions.

* Corresponding Author.

R. Shumaker (Ed.): Virtual Reality, HCII 2007, LNCS 4563, pp. 514–522, 2007.

Remote controlled or tele-operated robots have the added decision making of human operators who make decisions on what they see from real-time video feedback, whereas UGV's need more information about their local environment to make the same decisions even if this information is as trivial as knowing the difference between hard and soft ground, which a human operator usually determines by sight alone.

This leads onto how we (humans) take it for granted that we can recognise any object or environment and its properties by its appearance, but this isn't true, we only know this information by previously encountering it and remembering its properties, as with any learning experience. Therefore, if this can be added to UGV's it will ultimately create a system which grows more knowledgeable with experience and therefore more capable of being autonomous.

The need to know the difference between terrain types to be able to successfully travel over it is displayed in the latest Land Rover Discovery where a system known as 'terrain response' is available to the driver. This system reconfigures engine, transmission, suspension, brakes and traction settings to improve handling and performance in order to be able to negotiate in the safest and most efficient way over certain terrain types [2]. This also demonstrates that a human driver needs to select the terrain type by sight alone and the vehicle settings adjust to suit, therefore if the vehicle had the ability to detect the terrain type then it would create an autonomous or in this case an automatic system.

### 1.1 Motivation

Unmanned vehicles technology has advanced a great deal over the last decade and is at the forefront of military capabilities, with current research and development on unmanned systems focused on making them more perceptive and autonomous for use on the battlefield as seen in the U.S Army's Future Combat Systems program [3]. The use of robotics in the military is fundamentally to save the lives of soldiers and the more a system can become autonomous then it lowers the need for human presence on the battlefield.

This paper has been completed as an early part of the research being carried out in this area and will act as a review over the work done in the field of terrain detection for unmanned ground vehicles and breaks up the components to do with terrain sensing in terms of terrain types and available sensors, which will ultimately help ongoing research in the field.

## 2 Review of Prior Research

Previous work has been done in this area and is known as terrain classification, terrain trafficability or terrain traversability. Most work has been done in the area of terrain classification by using vision systems or 3D radars to build up a map of the terrain by its appearance alone, but how can this represent if the terrain is safe to travel over or how best to tackle it. This paper outlines work carried out in the area of unmanned systems and terrain and is by no means all the work completed in the field, but a selection of a range of methods used to identify terrain.

Lacroix et al [4] use a vision-based system to segment the terrain into four categories, flat, uneven, obstacle and unknown. The system would look at certain areas and segment them into cells, which it then labels as one of the four categories.

Dupont, Moore et al [5] from the Florida State University (also known as FAMU-FSU) offer a system that does not replace the vision detection method but instead compliments it in order to offer a system that can 'see' and 'feel' the terrain just as humans do in order to determine the terrains properties. Sadhukhan's [6] thesis on autonomous ground vehicle terrain classification using internal sensors firstly justifies terrain detection by say that a system can manoeuvre better over a surface that it has more knowledge about and then goes onto say how different terrains require different driving techniques and uses the tendency to get stuck in mud by driving too fast over it, as an example. The main work done by FAMU-FSU is using internal sensors to classify terrain by measuring the robots internal vibration as it travels over different terrain, and also the use of neural networks in terrain identification.

Iagnemma et al [7, 8] from the Massachusetts Institute of Technology (MIT) have done a lot of work on terrain classification especially in the area of space rovers and planetary exploration. Their work includes classifying terrain by measuring internal states such as torque and wheel angular and linear speed to name a few. Their main work is determining soil shear from two key parameters, cohesion of the soil and internal friction angle.

Seraji [9] and Howard [10]of the Jet Propulsion Laboratory (JPL) have developed a system that does not identify the terrain but instead detects its traversability. They used a vision system to create a traversability index using fuzzy rules to detect terrain using four key elements: roughness, slope, discontinuity and hardness. Roughness indicates coarseness and surface irregularity; slope looks at the surfaces incline/decline; discontinuity looks at the end of the surface such as cliffs; and the surface hardness is measured to see how it affects traction. The rules for each are set such as roughness is smooth, rough or rocky and slope is classified as flat, sloped or steep. The system uses this information to detect the terrains traversability and identifies it simply as a low, medium or high risk.

Manduchi, et al [11] are working on the dynamic response of a vehicle on different terrain. They also discuss how the compressibility of obstacles can help to determine whether they should be avoided or traversed and this will greatly reduce the number of unnecessary avoidances. Their work focuses more on obstacle detection/avoidance than terrain detection but the system offers a combined approach. The system uses a contact type sensor on the front of the vehicle in the form of a spring and damper configuration, which tests the compressibility of the object. Their recent work uses a LADAR system to detect obstacles and classify terrain using vision based information.

Thrun [12] and the Stanford Racing team were the first team to complete the second DARPA Grand Challenge in 2005 with their vehicle known as 'Stanley', which won them the $2 million prize. Their system used a combination of camera vision and LADAR systems to learn about what is, and how to select the safest terrain to traverse. Stanley was successfully able to cope with the desert terrain after learning from previous encounters by using machine learning algorithms, which meant Stanley grew smarter with experience and eventually became a master of finding safe paths and avoiding obstacles [13].

# 3 Terrain

Terrain can be defined as any land surface and is known in geographical terms as the 'lay of the land'. There are many different types of terrain whether it is indoors or outside, but as yet there is no explicit list of terrain types available. Many researchers have their own classification of terrain types with some as simple as the system demonstrated by Lacroix et al [4], which identifies terrain as: flat, uneven, obstacle, and unknown; as previously mentioned. Table 1 below is an early list of the terrain types we have compiled, with their standard traversable properties which is by no means a complete list of every possible type.

**Table 1.** Terrain types and their properties

| | | | Effect of weather | | |
|---|---|---|---|---|---|
| | Terrain type | General surface properties | Sun | Rain | Snow/ice |
| | Sand | sinkage, slippage | hot | hydrocolloid | n/a |
| | Mud | sinkage, slippage | soft | liquefaction | hard |
| Harder >> | Clay | slippage, sinkage | hard | liquefaction | slippage |
| | Rocks | uneven, hard | dry, hot | slippage | slippage |
| | Forest | long grass, foliage, | dazzle | marsh | hard |
| | Short grass | can get tangled | $\mu = 0.35$ | $\mu = 0.2$ | $\mu = 0.15$ |
| | Gravel | loose, uneven, slippage | dry, hot | slippage | slippage |
| | Dirt track | dusty, level | dry | liquefaction | slippage |
| << Easier | Paved road | gaps, flat, high friction | $\mu = 0.7$ | $\mu = 0.5$ | $\mu = 0.08$ |
| | Ashphalt | flat, high friction | $\mu = 0.8$ | $\mu = 0.4$ | $\mu = 0.06$ |
| | Concrete | flat, high friction | $\mu = 0.7$ | $\mu = 0.5$ | $\mu = 0.08$ |

## 3.1 Weather Conditions

All the different terrain types change with different weather conditions as seen in Table 1 above. These conditions will change the terrain's properties therefore certain measurements cannot be taken accurately to be used to identify the terrain. This means that for every different outdoor terrain type there is more than one condition for each weather condition, so the 16 terrain types listed in the table each have 3 different conditions making 48 different types of terrain parameters to identify.

## 3.2 Other Factors

Other factors that affect terrain detection are the gradient or slope of the land, and positive and negative obstacles. Positive obstacles include vegetation, rocks, fences and hills; negative obstacles include potholes, cliffs and valleys; and in the case of road driving then drain covers and curbs would pose problems.

# 4 Sensors

A short review of sensor types and their properties has been conducted to see what is currently used to detect terrain and what types are available (see Table 2).

**Table 2.** Sensor types and their detection properties in reference to terrain

| Sensor | Type | Properties |
|---|---|---|
| Optical - Visible Spectrum | Passive | Range data with stereo pairs.<br>Colour differences.<br>Texture difference. |
| Optical - Infrared | Passive | Detects water absorption.<br>Detects mineral reflection. |
| Optical - Infrared (thermal) | Passive | Can differentiate between object types. |
| Touch - Contact switch | Passive | Feels for solid objects. |
| Touch - Antennae | Passive | Measures antennae deflection. |
| Chemical | Passive | Detects certain chemical presence. |
| LADAR | Active | Range finder, single and 2 axis scanning.<br>Can detect water.<br>Can differentiate objects from one another. |
| RADAR | Active | Range finder using reflection.<br>Frequency dependant material classification.<br>Can see through weather conditions. |
| SONAR (Ultrasound) | Active | Range finder using reflection. |
| X-Ray | Active | Can see through materials. |

## 4.1 What Parameters to Measure?

The problem with detecting terrain is to firstly select which parameters are best to measure in order to find a distinct difference. The question then arises as to what properties will show a distinct difference in all conditions? Questions have to be asked about what does the system need to know about the terrain it is about to encounter, for example, it will need to know if the wheels will slip or sink; and then the right type of sensor can be sourced

## 4.2 Current Work on Touch/Feel Sensors

There is ongoing worldwide research being carried out on giving robots the ability to feel and mimic human touch.

The first type of feel sensor is being developed for use in minimally invasive surgery. Maheshwari [14] and Saraf [15] have developed these sensors by using metal and semiconducting nanoparticles in a small area which are so precise that they can feel the shape of the head on the back of a coin. Future work with these touch sensors is in detecting cancer cells by feeling their hardness.

Another type of feel sensor is the artificial robotic whisker developed by Schultz et al [16] that can accurately sense different shapes and textures. It has been developed to mimic the way animals, such as rats use their whiskers to build up a picture of their environment and to test the hardness of objects. They work by measuring the 'bending moment' or torque deflection at the base of the whisker using piezoelectric strain gauges. These are then put in an array and can extract an entire shape.

**Table 3.** DARPA Grand Challenge 2005 top 5 sensor review

| Team | Vehicle | Vision | LIDAR | | RADAR*** |
|---|---|---|---|---|---|
| | | | Short Range* | Long Range** | |
| Stanford | Volkswagen Touareg | 1 | 5 | 0 | 1 |
| Red Team | M998 HMMWV | 1 | 6 | 1 | 1 |
| Red Team Too | H1 Hummer | 1 | 6 | 1 | 1 |
| Team Gray | Ford Escape Hybrid | 2 | 3 | 1 | 0 |
| Team Terramax | Oshkosh MTVR Truck | 2 | 3 | 1 | 0 |

* Short Range LIDAR type used is typically the SICK LMS (Range <25m).
** Long Range LIDAR type used is typically the SICK LMS (Range <80m).
*** Long Range RADAR is typically <200m.

## 4.3 Why Sense Terrain?

Terrain is an important element in autonomous driving because if a vehicle cannot travel over a certain terrain type but does not know this, then it will become stuck and ultimately fail its mission. There are a number of ways of looking at this issue as seen in Fig 1. There can be non intelligent systems that are built to cope with a lot of different terrain types, such as 4x4 vehicles that can drive over almost any rough terrain but if it was to become stuck due to sinkage or slippage then it would fail; therefore, for autonomous solutions it is best to give the vehicle the ability to sense the terrain. There are two ways to navigate autonomously over terrain, the first is to have a system which detects that it cannot cope with a certain terrain type and therefore avoid it to prevent getting stuck, but this creates a system which is limited to where it can go. The second solution is a system that can sense the terrain and have the ability to 'morph' in order to adapt to changes, which would ultimately create a system without limitations on where it can go.

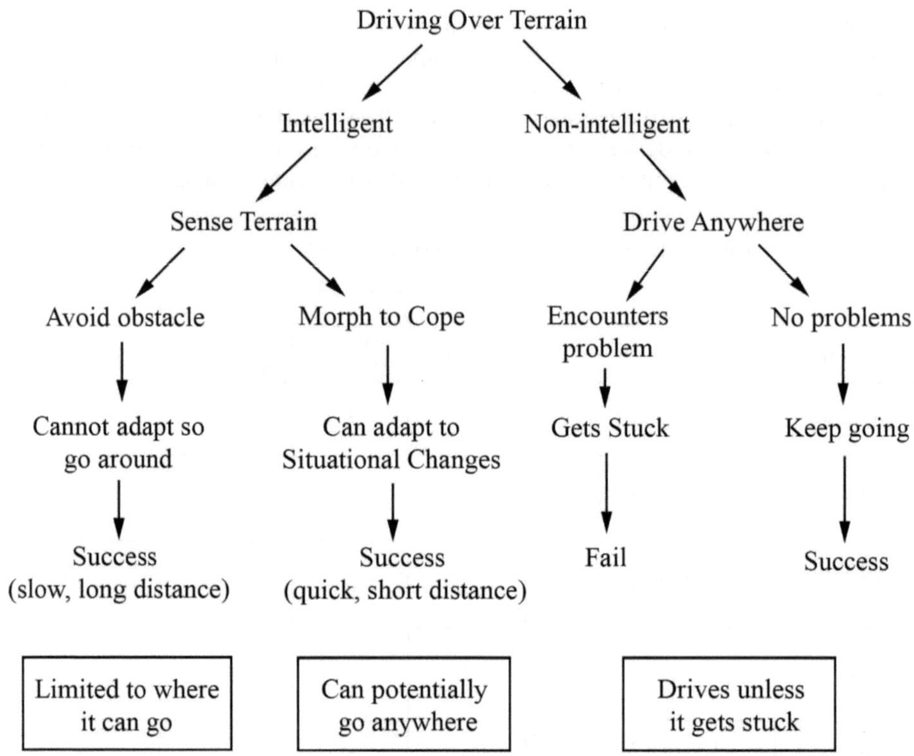


**Fig. 1.** A flow diagram of driving over terrain, using intelligent and non-intelligent systems

## 5 Conclusion

Looking at the terrain types in Table 1, it will be harder to independently class terrain and label each one because of the number of variations and changes in them, therefore only the right parameters must be measured in order to give a distinct difference between types. Another way to tackle the terrain detection issue is to only search for, or sense the relevant attributes to do with traversability such as hardness, sinkage and slippage as well as its gradient and flatness, but this will create a system that is looking for 'safe' rather than a system that can cope with any terrain type, and this is what most current terrain detection systems do by using vision systems and 3D radars to build up maps of areas or analyse terrain by its appearance and surface properties to search for the safe flat ground as done by the winners of the DARPA Grand Challenge 2005 (see Table 3).

The two terrain detection methods discussed earlier not using vision systems are the soil cohesion and internal friction angle work done by Iagnemma et al [7, 8], and internal vibration sensing done by Dupont et al [5]. The problem with internal vibration detection system is that it informs the systems its reaction to the terrain after, or as it travels over it which can be too late. It doesn't tell you if it is traversable, for example if it was stuck in mud, as described by Sadhukhan [6], and the wheels were slipping, then the system would think it is still moving over a smooth surface because there is no vibration. The benefit of this system is that it can assist a system to feel the terrain by measuring its own reaction to it, and if it had the ability it could make changes to adapt to the situation.

Manduchi [11] and JPL's work on contact sensing is more relevant to feel/touch sensing but it then leads onto the issue of the time consuming feeling around at low speeds and has the same issues as SLAM (Simultaneous Localisation and Mapping) in what comes first, testing the environmental properties or actually operating in those environments.

## 6 Future Work

The concepts discussed in this paper will help ongoing research on reconfigurable mobility systems for UGV's, where the vehicle can use the information about its local environment to be able to 'morph' into the right configuration in order to suit the terrain and environment, therefore adding the ability to take more risks in unstructured, unknown environments.

Earlier work done at Middlesex University [17] on reconfigurable mobility systems include a concept known as intelligent wheels (Fig 2), which can change in size and form to adjust diameter, ground clearance, surface area and traction. The system will ultimately use the embedded sensors to carry out analysis on the local environment and using information learnt from previous experiences, the system could make adjustments to best suit the situation.

**Fig. 2.** Intelligent wheels conceptual model and prototype

## References

1. Vance, A.: DARPA's Grand Challenge proves to be too grand. (2004) cited; Available from: http://www.theregister.co.uk/2004/03/13/darpas_grand_challenge_proves/
2. Vanderwerp, D.: What Does Terrain Response Do? (2005) cited; Available from: http://www.caranddriver.com/features/9026/what-does-terrain-response-do.html
3. Shachtman, N.: Undead Warrior. 2006 [cited; Available from: http://www.defensetech.org/archives/cat_fcs_watch.html

4. Lacroix, S., Chatila, R., Fleury, S., Herrb, M., Simeon, T.: Autonomous Navigation in Outdoor Environments: Adaptive Approach and Experiment. In: IEEE International Conference on Robotics and Automation 1994 (1994)
5. DuPont, E.M., Moore, C.A., Roberts, R.G., Collins, E.G., Selekwa, M.F.: Online Terrain Classification for Mobile Robots. In: ASME International Mechanical Engineering Congress and Exposition Conference (2005)
6. Sadhukhan, D.: Autonomous ground vehicle terrain classification using internal sensors, in Department of Mechanical Engineering. The Florida State University (2004)
7. Iagnemma, K., Dubowsky, S.: Terrain Estimation for High-Speed Rough-Terrain Autonomous Vehicle Navigation. In: SPIE Conference on Unmanned Ground Vehicle Technology IV 2002 (2002)
8. Iagnemma, K., Shibly, H., Dubowsky, S.: On-Line Terrain Parameter Estimation for Planetary Rovers. In: IEEE International Conference on Robotics and Automation (2002)
9. Seraji, H.: Safety measures for terrain classification and safest site selection. Autonomous Robots, (21), 211–225 (2006)
10. Howard, A., Seraji, H.: Vision-based terrain characterization and traversability assessment. Journal of Robotic Systems 18(10), 577–587 (2001)
11. Manduchi, R., Castano, A., Talukder, A., Matthies, L.: Obstacle Detection and Terrain Classification for Autonomous Off-Road Navigation. Autonomous Robots 18(1), 81–102 (2005)
12. Thrun, S., Montemerlo, M.: DARPA Grand Challenge 2005 Technical Paper 2005 Stanford Racing Team (2005)
13. Orenstein, D.: Stanford team's win in robot car race nets $2 million prize. (2005) cited; Available from: http://news-service.stanford.edu/news/2005/october12/stanleyfinish-100905.html
14. Maheshwari, V., Saraf, R.F.: High-Resolution Thin-Film Device to Sense Texture by Touch in Science 2006, pp. 1501–1504 (2006)
15. Saraf, R.F., Maheshwari, V.: Nanodevice for Imaging Normal Stress Distribution With Application in Sensing Texture and Feel' by Touching, Nebraska Univ Lincoln (2004)
16. Schultz, A.E., Solomon, J.H., Peshkin, M.A., Hartmann, M.J.: Multifunctional Whisker Arrays for Distance Detection, Terrain Mapping, and Object Feature Extraction. In: 2005 IEEE International Conference on Robotics and Automation (2005)
17. Gaspar, T., Rodrigues, H., Odedra, S., Costa, M., Metrolho, J.C., Prior, S.: Handheld devices as actors in domotic monitoring system. In: IEEE International Conference on Industrial Informatics, INDIN '04 2004, pp. 547–551 (2004)

# A Novel Interface for Simulator Training: Describing and Presenting Manipulation Skill Through VR Annotations

Mikko Rissanen[1,*], Yoshihiro Kuroda[2,**], Tomohiro Kuroda[3,*], and Hiroyuki Yoshihara[3,*]

[1] Graduate School of Informatics, Kyoto University
[2] Graduate School of Engineering Science, Osaka University
[3] Division of Medical Informatics, Kyoto University Hospital
[*] Division of Medical Informatics, Kyoto University Hospital Shogoin Kawahara-cho 54, Sakyo-ku, 606-8507 Kyoto, Japan
{Mikko, TKuroda, Lob}@kuhp.kyoto-u.ac.jp
[**] Dept. of Medical Science and Bioengineering, Osaka University, Machikaneyama 1-3, Toyonaka-Shi, 560-8531 Osaka, Japan
YKuroda@bpe.es.osaka-u.ac.jp

**Abstract.** Virtual reality (VR) based skill training simulators are highly interactive computer systems that allow for training of e.g. manipulation skills. In the most complex domains, such as in surgery, teaching correct manipulation requires expert's judgement and instructions. Video annotation has enabled presentation of explicit principles of manipulation that are highlighted on a recorded demonstration of an expert. In VR, similar annotation methods have been applied even though interactivity of VR allows for novel kinds of representations of annotated data. This paper presents an annotation model and an interface that uses interactivity of VR as an advantage on reading the annotations, which has potential to convey the principles of manipulation through multiple modalities to novices. The design of the model is based on behavioural parameters of the simulation – features which cannot be accessed in the real world. This approach has potential to enhance efficiency of VR simulator based skill training.

**Keywords:** Virtual Reality, Open Skill, Annotation, Multimodal Feedback.

## 1 Introduction

To learn manipulation skills, such as sculpting or closing incisions by suturing using surgical instruments, requires much practice. Even though significant learning theories have been proposed, it has been acknowledged that the current theories are incapable of explaining certain aspects of skill. It has always been difficult to distinguish mere motor skill and the cognitive part of human actions [1]. For example attention and proper focusing are difficult to be measured during a performance.

R. Shumaker (Ed.): Virtual Reality, HCII 2007, LNCS 4563, pp. 523–532, 2007.

The most complex manipulation skills are open, i.e. the environment varies during each case in which the skill has to be applied. Domains in which open skills are required are for example team sports, martial arts and surgery.

The traditional approach to learn movements and motor skills is based on observation and mimicry of expert's examples with the aid of the expert's verbal instruction. According to learning theories, in order to gain a skill, one must first learn rules about what to do in which situation and then manage to absorb the rules into almost automatic behaviour through repetition. The use of verbal instruction is mainly dictated by the nature of the real world. In practise, the rules are learned case by case and they become greater in amount and more accurate in details during experience. Further in this text, these rules are called *relationships within manipulation*. True expertise is described as problem-solving without any deliberate attention to the rules learned in the beginning. The relationships are observed almost automatically.

Simulator training offers the possibility to gain experience without consequences in case of failures that are an essential part of learning. Simulators have been extended from aviation to fields that require a safe environment for practise of manipulation skills. Surgical simulators have become a popular subject of research and even industrial development. The focus of research has been strongest on technology. Development of skill assessment methods has begun only recently. Relatively little research exists on teaching methods of manipulation skills. Except for a few attempts on haptic guidance [2,3] and application of Virtual Fixtures [4], the teaching methods in VR usually replicate the ones in the real world even though in a fully digital world there are very few physical limitations. Record and Replay approach (e.g. [2,3,5]), in which expert's actions are recorded and perceptualized to the trainee by using some experimental method, has been found possible. However, as development of Record and Replay training systems usually aim to fully automatic human-machine-human transfer of skill, it may not be the most suitable approach for complex open skills that are taught in the real world under experts' instruction. Research so far has not managed to address the need of expert's insight in the Record and Replay approach.

Using the traditional teaching media, for example text-books and videos, *annotation* has been found useful as the means to highlight the essential from the other content. Through video annotation, general principles of manipulation can be represented: arrows and other illustrations overlaid on a video clip demonstrating an example performance are so called external annotations that intend to convey a message to the viewer. For the learner, presentation of the principles supports the cognitive part of learning. Similar annotations have been implemented into VR training simulators, but the main point of VR – interactivity – has been forgotten in the design. Since interaction modelling in training simulation allows realistic interaction, interactivity should be included into annotations as a basic characteristic.

This paper presents an annotation model that allows expert's insight to be encapsulated into Record and Replay VR and to be represented in intuitive manner to the novices. Two main advantages are introduced: 1) Relationships within manipulation can be explicitly perceptualized to the user in terms of the essential information determined by an expert. 2) The relationships can be presented to several sensory channels making the feedback to the user multimodal. The design of the model is based on behavioural parameters of the simulation that are recorded as time-series – features which cannot be accessed in the real world. This approach can enhance efficiency of VR simulator based skill training by reducing the expert's one-on-one instruction and by providing only the relevant feedback to the user.

## 2 Related Work

Two aspects of previous work on VR have to be examined: training simulators using advanced teaching methods and VR annotation systems.

### 2.1 Training Simulators

Conventional training simulators only replicate reality so that realistic interaction modelled in the system allows for practise in a safe environment. Record and Replay approach [2,3,5] has been demonstrated to be possible and even beneficial for some parts in learning of simple skills [2,3]. However, teaching of the most complex open skills would require insight of the experts that is not modelled in the system. In other words, even if Record and Replay was implemented in simulators allowing for training of open skills, the expert would still be needed.

One of the restrictions of the real world is that the intentions, priorities of sub-goals and the significant features of the manipulation can only be described verbally. VR allows access to the whole digital environment, which gives the system's developers freedom to use teaching methods different to the real world. So far, only haptic guidance gives alternative means for representation of the example manipulation than in the real world. Approaches based on visualization, for example Just Follow Me [6], mainly replicate the real world methods with the only difference being that the replayed expert's performance is overlaid onto the user.

This review shows that VR is too often viewed as a mere training environment. Teaching features of VR have not been studied rigorously to the date at the level of complex, open manipulation skills. Yokokohji *et al.* [5] presented their research questions "What is the essential data to be recorded for transferring the skill?" and "What is the best way to provide the data to the trainee?" in 1996. These are questions that have not been answered during this decade. Most skill-transfer systems attempt to transfer skills through a single holistic method. Yet, that approach has not been found to have clear training advantage. Since automatic skill-transfer seems a goal of the far future, current VR training simulation should be designed as a teaching tool. The model presented in this paper is oriented more on the expertise itself than on engineering solutions by harnessing the power of annotation of manipulation level behaviour into the training simulation using multiple modalities.

### 2.2 VR Annotation Systems

As envisioned by Shaffer *et al.* [7], annotations could be a significant part of a future's training environment that is built around a simulation engine. In the following, the most recent attempts of VR annotation are compared.

Welch *et al.* [8] introduced a VR recording system for surgical training as knowledge mediator and included annotation as description of the surgical procedure's stages and key events. Aubry *et al.* [9] presented VR annotation as an improvement for product design in collaborative virtual environments. Their model is capable of coupling the knowledge level ontologies with the annotations. As the model is intended to support design processes, the manipulation level that would be needed in training simulators has not been addressed.

These text-based systems mainly implement the traditional video annotation methods into 3D VR. As the aim has been on transfer of knowledge, transfer of manipulation skills has not been addressed in the previous VR annotation systems. Annotation systems developed so far have not attempted to include interactivity of VR as a basic feature of annotations, which provides a new research opportunity.

## 3 VR Annotation for Training Open Manipulation Skills

Annotation required to represent expert's insight on very complex principles and case-dependant relationships of manipulation has to include interactivity of virtual training environments into the fundamental design. Fig. 1 shows the general idea of how interactive training simulation is annotated. The basic features of annotation are discussed in detail below: target and media of annotation, representation of annotated data and anchoring.

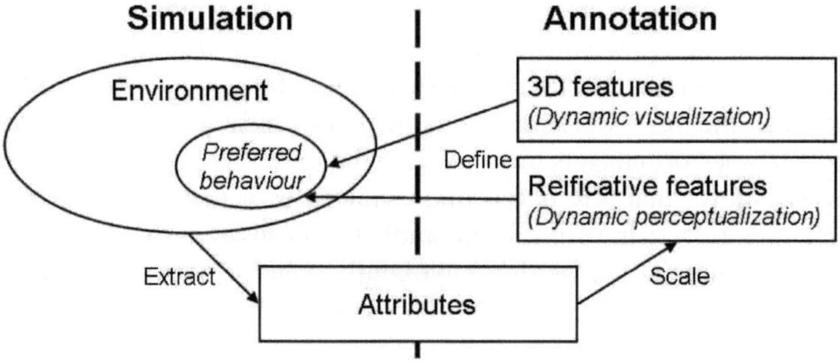


**Fig. 1.** Annotation of interactive simulation. Preferred behaviour of the simulated environment is annotated as *3D* and *reificative features*. Reificative features facilitate understanding of complex concepts by highlighting the essential from the whole data. They can be perceptualized dynamically using any modality, whereas 3D features can only be visualized. Simulation's attributes act as scaling factors on the reificative features, for example that length of an incision made by a surgeon depends on the size of the limb. 3D features are naturally in right scale without any modifications.

Using the Record and Replay approach, highlighting is done on the expert's recorded performance. *3D features*, such as lines indicating correct directions or highlighted surfaces of a target, are visualized dynamically on the expert's pre-recorded performance. *Reificative features* are used to explain information that is otherwise hard to understand. The concept of reification is explained below by describing the target, representation and anchoring of annotations as well as the process of making them.

### 3.1 Target of Annotation

Fig. 2 illustrates the data that can be annotated. A recording API allows a simulator's developer to include any behavioural parameter (BP) to be recorded as time-series. Thus, dynamics of the interactive simulation can be accessed.

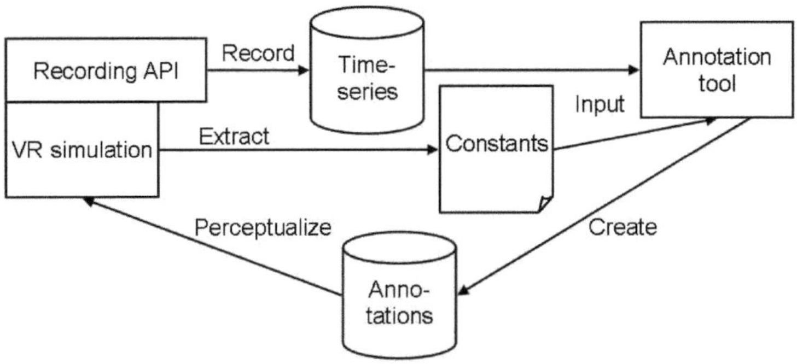


**Fig. 2.** Annotation of interactive VR simulation. Time-series can be recorded from any variable in the simulation. Constants are extracted attributes of the simulation that can be included into the annotations. Annotations are represented to the user through multi-modal perceptualization.

*Time-series* are the most significant data form that can be annotated. In practice, time-series are recorded behavioural parameters (RBPs). Time-series data can consist of any number of dimensions. Typically, the data covers a timestamped 3D coordinates (x, y and z). 2-dimensional time-series would consist of a timestamp and a single value changing over time. Thus, dynamics of the simulation are accessible.

*Constants* are pieces of data that do not change. An example of a constant is for example length of a virtual tool or general stiffness of an elastic model. The annotator binds the constants to BPs. Constants act as scaling factors to time-series data so that, for example, force that the user should exert depends on size or stiffness of the target. The constants are derived from the attributes of the simulation which are included into 3D and interaction models in most of the advanced simulation software.

Using these two simple data formats, their combination allows complex relationships to be made between several variables of the virtual environment: time-series scaled by constants or relationships between several time-series.

### 3.2 Annotation Process

Visualization of the recorded behavioural parameters is the basis for support of the annotation process. Conventional video annotation software allows sound waves to be represented graphically so that the annotator can select segments on the timeline accurately. For the proposed model, similar approach was chosen with the distinction that there can be multiple layers of data that can be annotated separately. Multiple

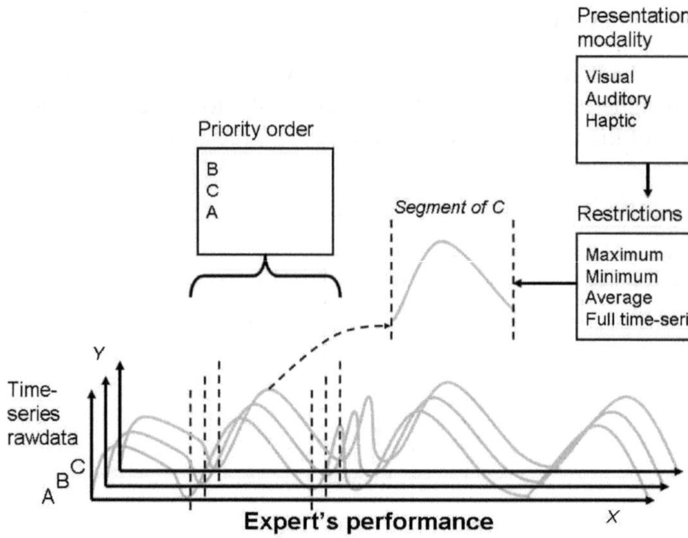


**Fig. 3.** Annotation process. Expert's performance is first visualized, then segmented, and finally content of annotations determined: priorities between time-series; segment-specific definitions of restrictions and presentation modality.

layers allow different segmentation of the time-series of RBP. Characteristics that can be determined for each segment of time-series are presented in Fig. 3.

*Priorities* between the factors in manipulation are described as a percentage of what the skill is composed of. For example, the annotator could determine that the most important factor for success is correct amount of power, whereas accuracy of contact location is only secondary factor.

*Restrictions* are set to every BP: maximum, minimum, average or full time-series can be selected. Restrictions are applied to single segments of example performances which are then aggregated to a so called general description of skill when statistical variance of data in a number of segments is calculated. This allows implementation of rules that, for example, would describe a skilful manipulation as amount of power that is not to be exceeded or acceleration profile during a motion. Restrictions are illustrated later in Fig. 3.

*Modality* can be chosen between visual, auditory and haptic sensory channels.

### 3.3 Representation of Annotations

The purpose of this annotation model is to perceptualize principles of manipulation to the user in an intuitive manner. Annotations can be represented on any modality by following the Virtual Fixtures concept [4]. Two time-series of RBPs, the pre-recorded examples and the user's live recording, provide an ideal feedback on performance for simple as well as for complex manipulations. Fig. 4 illustrates how different representations can be generated from the rawdata.

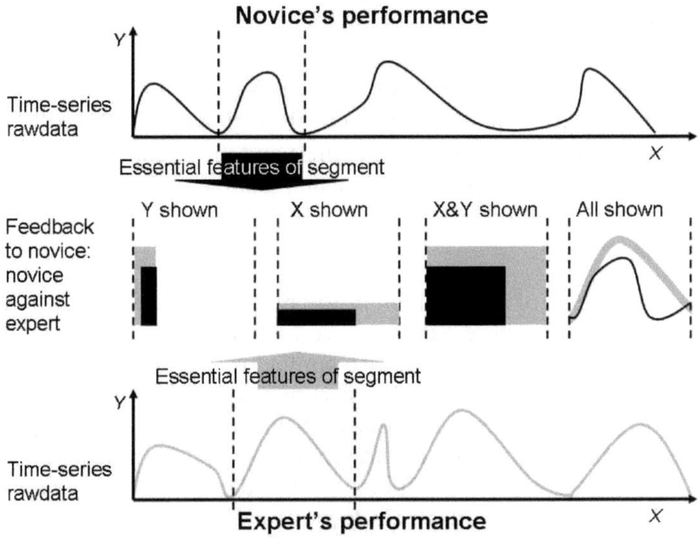


**Fig. 4.** Simulation's preferred behaviour, caused by expert's performance, is represented on the essential features only as Virtual Fixtures. The novice's performance is shown against the one or many expert's performances according to restrictions annotated. Using several modalities, many layers of time-series can be perceptualized at once. Thus, the annotator is given a choice of priorities of relationships that should be learned from the simulation.

Knowledge of Result (KR) and Knowledge of Performance (or Process, KP) are terms used in motor learning research to categorize feedback to the trainee (see e.g. [1]). *Guidance hypothesis* suggests that simple tasks require KR only after several trials, whereas the most complex skills demand constant KP [10]. KR can be implemented using a simple triggering system coupled with the recording API, so that at the end of recording a segment, KR is displayed.

Mapping of modalities is based on guidelines on multimodal representation of information [11]. Visualization is the most suitable method for representing complex information. In addition to complexity, visualization allows the user to plan the actions when the preferred future behaviour is shown. Auditory feedback is mapped to temporal data and haptic feedback (mostly vibro-tactile) is the best modality to represent simple one-dimensional restrictions as warnings.

### 3.4 Anchoring

Time-series of RBPs regulate also the anchoring. An example of dynamic anchoring is a contact point (vertex of a mesh) that the user touches virtually through a haptic device. ID of the vertex changes over time during manipulation, and thus the time-series of the vertex' position provides a dynamic anchor for the annotation that appears at the contact point when there is any contact. Appearance of any annotation can be controlled in a similar way by setting the anchor to some time-series.

## 4 Discussion

In brief, the proposed annotation extends previous VR annotation to truly interactive simulation, displays "the essential information" through a kind of Virtual Fixtures and has the potential to bridge the motor performance and the cognitive part of training by presenting the essential relationships within manipulation explicitly.

### 4.1 Novelty

Basically, representation of annotations in the proposed annotation model is based on Virtual Fixtures [4]. These sensory overlays were originally intended as a support for telemanipulation tasks, but also applied in training. The most significant advantage of the proposed model is that it conveys only the essential information from the expert's point of view to novices using recorded manipulations as the annotated media. In comparison to previous research, Virtual Fixtures in the proposed model only restrict manipulation on the parts that the expert sees important. For simple closed skills, holistic view of Virtual Fixtures may be enough as a training aid. Complex open skills require more advanced feedback, which is achieved by applying the proposed model to a working interface implemented onto a training simulator.

VR annotation models presented so far has mostly covered somewhat static data. The proposed model is capable of representing highly dynamic data extracted from an interactive simulation. Interactivity, which is the most essential feature of skill training simulators, is now a fundamental part of the design: the simulator shows how the environment should behave and overlays the user's performance against the desired one.

Hutchins *et al.* [12] studied representations of objects in virtual training environments. In their framework, multiplicity and augmentation of representations were some of the main aspects: an object does not need to have only one representation, such as mimetic behaviour of the real world often preferred in training simulation, since virtuality allows several representations. Our work falls into this category: unlike in the real world, the environment's behaviour is perceptualized on multiple modalities and the recorded expert's performance is displayed to the user only for the essential parts. The essential part is annotated into the system by the expert.

### 4.2 Advantages

The proposed model intends to support especially complex, open skills. Explicit representation of relationships, that in the real world are learned case by case, have the potential of enhancing the link between mere motor performance and the cognitive part of training.

As a note to possible technical issues concerning implementation of the model on a real training simulator, the authors wish to highlight that specifications of the simulator itself do not restrict the annotation model at all. Only the data that can be recorded and the attributes of the simulation act as the annotation media. In practice, there will be only minor technical problems in the implementation since data processing and storage technologies are already very advanced.

### 4.3 Future Directions

As the model supports teaching (expert's involvement) and learning (novice's involvement), a working interface based on the model is the main topic of the future research. The extent of complexity is to be addressed in future studies on transferring a skill through annotated VR in comparison to non-annotated VR.

Automation for selection of optimal feedback modalities is another topic of the future. The priorities between BP's and their restrictions as well as user's preferences could play a significant role in the design, since there are individual differences on the optimal feedback channels.

## 5 Conclusion

Previous studies have not managed to address the need of expert's insight in the Record and Replay approach. The proposed annotation model is capable of representing the essential information from recorded experts' examples when replaying the annotations to the user. Replay of annotations is interactive so that the essential parts of both the example and the user's performance are displayed at once. As an enhancement to previous VR annotation designs, the proposed model includes interactivity as the key feature of reading annotations.

The proposed model shows potential to bridge mere motor performance and the cognitive part of skill training, which is expected to promote learning of complex, open manipulation skills. Attention is explicitly drawn to relationships within the manipulation that are difficult to learn. In the real world, the relationships are learned case by case. Using the proposed model, the relationships are represented though several modalities whereas in the real world verbal description is often the only feasible feedback option. Thus, a novel interface for simulator based training of manipulation skills was achieved on a theoretical level. The interface would not depend on specifications of the simulator itself, but only on the data that can be recorded. This approach has potential to enhance efficiency of VR simulator based skill training by reducing the expert's one-on-one instruction and by providing optimal feedback to the simulator's user.

Future work will cover automated representation of annotations on the most suitable modalities. Then, the learning effect can be compared between the annotated and non-annotated training approaches.

**Acknowledgements.** The authors would like to thank Dr. Naoto Kume, Dr. Megumi Nakao, Mr. Masayuki Kawasaki, Dr. Keisuke Nagase and Mr. Stéphane Aubry for their support. This study was funded by Grant-in-Aid for Scientific Research (S) (16100001), Young Scientists (A) (18680043) and Exploratory Research (18659148) from The Ministry of Education, Culture, Sports, Science and Technology, Japan, and by Nakajima Fund.

## References

1. Sherwood, D.E., Lee, T.D.: Schema Theory: Critical Review and Implications for the Role of Cognition in a New Theory of Motor Learning. Research Quarterly for Exercise and Sport, American Alliance for Health, Physical Education, Recreation, and Dance, vol. 74(4), pp. 376–382 (2003)
2. Teo, C.L., Burdet, E., Lim, H.P.: A Robotic Teacher of Chinese Handwriting. In: Proc. of the Symposium on Haptic Interfaces for Virtual Environment and Teleoperator Systems 2002, pp. 335–341 (2002)
3. Saga, S., Vlack, K., Kajimoto, H., Tachi, S.: Haptic Video. In: Proc. of SIGGRAPH 2005, DVD-ROM (2005)
4. Rosenberg, L.B.: Virtual fixtures: Perceptual Tools for Telerobotic Manipulation. In: Proc. of the IEEE Annual Int. Symposium on Virtual Reality 1993, pp. 76–82 (1993)
5. Yokokohji, Y., Hollis, R.L., Kanade, T., Henmi, K., Yoshikawa, T.: Toward Machine Mediated Training of Motor Skills -Skill Transfer from Human to Human via Virtual Environment-. In: Proc. of the 5th IEEE International Workshop on Robot and Human Communication 1996, pp. 32–37 (1996)
6. Yang, U., Kim, G.J.: Implementation and Evaluation of "Just Follow Me" : An immersive, VR-based, Motion-Training System. In: Presence: Teleoperators and Virtual Environments, vol. 11(3), pp. 304–323. MIT Press, Cambridge (2002)
7. Shaffer, D., Meglan, D., Ferrell, M., Dawson, S.: Virtual Rounds: Simulation-based Education in Procedural Medicine. In: SPIE vol. 3712: Battlefield Biomedical Technologies (1999)
8. Welch, G., State, A., Ilie, A., Low, K.-L., Lastra, A., Cairns, B., Towles, H., Fuchs, H., Yang, R., Becker, S., Russo, D., Funaro, J., van Dam, A.: Immersive Electronic Books for Surgical Training. In: IEEE Multimedia, vol. 12(3), pp. 22–35. IEEE Computer Society Press, Los Alamitos (2005)
9. Aubry, S., Lenne, D., Thouvenin, I., Guénand, A.: VR Annotations for Collaborative Design. In: Proc. of Human-Computer Interaction International, CD-ROM (2005)
10. Schmidt, R.A., Young, D.E., Swinnen, S., Shapiro, D.C.: Summary Knowledge of Results for Skill Acquisition: Support for the Guidance Hypothesis. Journal of Experimental Psychology: Learning, Memory, and Cognition 15(2), 352–359 (1989)
11. Nesbitt, K.: Designing Multi-sensory Displays for Abstract Data. PhD Thesis, School of Information Technologies, University of Sydney (2003)
12. Hutchins, M., Adcock, M., Stevenson, D., Gunn, C., Krumpholz, A.: The Design of Perceptual Representations for Practical Networked Multimodal Virtual Training Environments. In: Proc. of Human-Computer Interaction International, CD-ROM (2005)

# Evaluation of Interaction Devices for Projector Based Virtual Reality Aircraft Inspection Training Environments

Sajay Sadasivan[1], Deepak Vembar[2], Carl Washburn[3], and Anand K. Gramopadhye[1]

[1] Department of Industrial Engineering, Clemson University
[2] Department of Computer Science, Clemson University
[3] Aircraft Maintenance Technology, Greenville Technical College
{sajay@clemson.edu}

**Abstract.** The Aircraft maintenance and inspection is a complex system wherein humans play a key role in ensuring the worthiness of the aircraft. Traditional visual inspection training consisted mainly of on-the-job training (OJT). While OJT provides novice inspectors with the hands-on experience critical to effective transfer, it lacks the ability to provide real-time feedback and exposure to various scenarios in which to inspect.

With advances in technology, computer simulators have been developed to train the novice inspector and reduce the learning curve inherent with transitioning from the classroom to the workforce. Advances in graphics and virtual reality (VR) technology have allowed for an increase the sense of involvement in using these simulators. Though these simulators are effective, their deployment in aircraft maintenance training schools is limited by the high cost of VR equipment. This research investigates the effectiveness of different interaction devices for providing projector based simulated aircraft maintenance inspection training.

**Keywords:** computer input devices, industrial inspection, virtual reality, human computer interaction.

## 1 Introduction

Human inspection reliability plays an important role in guaranteeing the airworthiness of the aircraft fleet. Training has been found to be a useful tool in improving the reliability of the human inspector. Previously, this training consisted mainly of on-the-job training (OJT). However, with advances in technology, computer simulators have been developed to train the novice inspector in the inspection procedures and reduce the learning curve inherent while transitioning from the classroom to the workforce. Using advances in graphics and virtual reality technology, there is an increase the sense of involvement in using these simulators. Research conducted at Clemson University has investigated the use of virtual reality (VR) for aircraft maintenance inspection training and has been successful in demonstrating that there is significant performance improvement following training. The above mentioned

R. Shumaker (Ed.): Virtual Reality, HCII 2007, LNCS 4563, pp. 533–542, 2007.

inspection training simulator is immersive and was implemented using a head mounted display (HMD) and a 6-DOF mouse. Development of virtual reality (VR) simulators has kept up with the advances in technology and there is a tendency to fall into the trap of 'gold plating'. This results in the technology being expensive and its benefits are lost as the colleges and small aviation maintenance firms can't afford to implement such solutions. There is a need to have a selective fidelity approach to find the trade-offs in using VR simulators for training. As a first step to address this problem, current research evaluates the level of presence experienced by participants performing a visual inspection task using a VR cargo-bay simulator at different levels of immersion ranging from complete immersion using a HMD (Head Mounted Display) to a very low level of immersion using a basic desktop. As a part of this study, different interfaces need to be developed for the simulator for the different levels of immersion fidelity conditions to find the best interface for each display condition. Projector based VR is becoming popular and has an advantage as most classrooms already have the equipment. The challenge in implementing projector based VR lies in the trainee's interaction with the VR environment. This research investigates the effectiveness of different interfaces using a modified off-the-shelf gamepad for providing projector based simulated aircraft maintenance inspection training.

## 2 Background

Aviation industries need qualified and proficient aircraft maintenance technicians to keep aircraft in peak and safe operating condition, by performing scheduled maintenance, making repairs, and completing inspections required by the Federal Aviation Administration (FAA). Growth in air traffic, due to anticipated economic and population growth, coupled with the need to replace retiring experienced aircraft maintenance technicians, are two factors contributing to the strong employment outlook [1, 2]. Unfortunately, aircraft technical programs and curricula have not kept pace with technology changes to the aircraft and the maintenance environment. Most importantly, students do not receive hands-on inspecting experience and, as a result, are not adequately prepared for the transition to the workplace. A major limitation has been the inability of the programs to create realistically the experience of the complex aircraft maintenance environment, especially wide-bodied aircraft. Most schools do not have hangars to house such planes and the cost of having a wide-bodied aircraft is prohibitive. Further emphasizing the problem, the training provided to students on smaller aircraft does not necessarily transfer to wide-bodied aircraft. Thus, students trained via traditional methodology are confronted with on-the-job situations that require them to provide quick and correct responses to stimuli in environments where they have no previous experience and a situation where inspection and maintenance errors can be costly and at times, catastrophic [3]. A system is needed that realistically mimics the complex aircraft maintenance environment for use in the education and training of aircraft maintenance technicians. In response to this need, recent research efforts have looked at closing this gap by using technology to bring the complex wide-bodied aircraft maintenance environment into the classroom.

Visual inspection by humans is a widely used method for the detection and classification of nonconformities in industry. In the aviation industry, sound aircraft inspection and maintenance are an essential part of safe and reliable air transportation. Aircraft inspection is a complex system with many interrelated human and machine components [4]. 90% of all aircraft inspection is visual in nature conducted by human inspectors [5]. Thus it is critical that a high level of inspection performance is achieved but human inspection is not 100% reliable [6, 7]. It is critical to deploy strategies that will reduce human error and improve human performance. Human inspectors have the flexibility to adapt to various tasks and scenarios and improving their inspection process could increase their effectiveness.

Training has been shown to be effective in improving visual inspection performance [8].

With computer technology becoming cheaper, the future will bring an increased application of advanced technology in training. Many of these training delivery systems, such as computer-aided instruction, computer-based multimedia training, and intelligent tutoring systems, are already being used today.

In the domain of visual inspection, the earliest efforts to use computers for off-line inspection training were reported by Czaja and Drury [9], who used keyboard characters to develop a computer simulation of a visual inspection task. Since these early efforts, low fidelity inspection simulators with computer- generated images have been used to develop off-line inspection training programs for inspection tasks [10]. Similarly, human performance using a high fidelity computer simulation of a printed circuit board inspection has been studied [11] while another domain which has seen the application of advanced technology is radiology.

However, advanced technology has found limited application for inspection training in the aircraft maintenance environment. Currently, most of the applications are restricted to complex diagnostic tasks in the defense and aviation industries. The message is clear: we need more examples of advanced technology applied to training for inspection tasks, examples that draw on proven principles of training.

The use of offline virtual reality (VR) technology has been studied to overcome the problems with inspection errors and the limitations of 2D simulators [12]. Virtual reality (VR) technology offers a promising approach. It has been shown that in aircraft inspection tasks there are positive transfer effects between virtual and real world environments [13]. In addition, the participants who experienced high involvement in the simulator felt that these experiences were as natural as the real world ones. Using VR, the research team can more accurately represent the complex aircraft inspection and maintenance situation, enabling students to experience the real hangar-floor environment. The instructor can create various inspection and maintenance scenarios by manipulating various parameters reflective of those experienced by a mechanic in the aircraft maintenance hangar environment. As a result, students can inspect airframe structure as they would in the real world and initiate appropriate maintenance action based on their knowledge of airframe structures and information resources such as on-line manuals, airworthiness directives, etc. The trainee can be exposed to the various defect types and locations before they move on to the inspection of an actual aircraft. In a VR simulator, the trainee can receive performance feedback in an inspection task, during and after the task. Process feedback can also be provided to the trainee after task completion.

For virtual environments, presence, the subjective experience of being in one place or environment even when physically situated in another, becomes the most important criterion. The success of using VR as a tool for training and job aiding therefore should be highly dependent on the degree of presence experienced by the users of the virtual reality environment. The problem with the design of training systems using VR is that designers attempt to replicate as many physical and functional stimuli as possible in the training device. This leads to the devices getting too expensive and there is also the risk of them having higher fidelity on some aspects than others based on the available technology that could lead to ineffective simulators. The higher fidelity in control interfaces can add additional workload that may be detrimental to task performance and learning. It is thus necessary to evaluate the design and carefully determine the extent to which fidelity should be built in. Here the concept of selective fidelity [14, 15] can be used which would be more focused on trainee learning requirements than on analytical and technological shortcomings.

# 3 Methodology

This research looks at the effect of control fidelity on task performance and presence in a virtual reality aircraft inspection training simulator based on a projector based display. A modified Witmer and Singer [16] Presence Questionnaire is used to assess presence and inspection accuracy is used to assess task performance.

## 3.1 Participants

This study used 18 volunteers from Clemson University as participants. The age of the participants ranged from 22 to 36 years. They were screened for visual acuity (20/20 natural or corrected) and color vision. It has been demonstrated [17] that student subjects can be used in lieu of industrial inspectors.

## 3.2 Stimulus Material and Equipment

There are two key control aspects which must be considered for interaction with the simulator: the first is the user's ability to change view and the second is his ability to select targets. In the HMD-based VR simulator, trainee manipulated his view of the environment by naturally walking and looking around in the environment, as the view was mapped to the position and orientation of a 6DOF tracker attached to the HMD (Figure 1). Additionally, the trainee selected defects using a cursor controlled by a hand held 6-DOF mouse. In the projector-based VR simulator, the trainee's position and orientation is fixed (facing the screen) and the view is limited to the display on the screen. To manipulate the environment in the projector-based VR, the trainee must consciously change the view. Three interaction techniques were prototyped and evaluated for interacting with the projector based simulator.

The principal hardware components are described as follows. Ascension Technology Corporation's Flock of Birds (FOB) tracking system is used for rendering the virtual scenario with respect to the participant's movements where applicable. A 1024x768 resolution projector, displaying the VR environment on a screen approximately 12 feet in front of the participant was used while the control interface was a Gravis Eliminator Pro gamepad (Figure 2) which has a directional D-pad joystick and 10 buttons. In all the conditions, the simulator is launched on a 1.5GHz dual Xeon processor Dell personal computer with an NVidia GeForce 6800 Ultra graphics card, running the Linux (Fedora Core 4) operating system.

In all three interface conditions, the buttons 1-4 on the gamepad were used to control the motion of the user – step left, right, front and back - which can be compared to walking in the VR environment. This control was available at all times. The participant selected defects by guiding the targeting cursor onto the defect and pressing button 5 on the gamepad.

The first interface (A) is the lowest fidelity control condition. Here the manipulation of the D-pad joystick was used to change the view of the environment – rotate left, right, up or down - relative to the original view. This can be compared to the head orientation in the HMD. The targeting cursor was fixed at the center of the display. The user had to manipulate the environment to align the defect with the targeting cursor and press button 5 on the gamepad for defect selection.

The second interface (B) the user could manipulate both the environment and the targeting cursor. The joystick was overloaded to provide both orientation and targeting information. The trainee would have to switch between using the joystick to change the view of the environment and controlling the cursor to target defects on the screen. This was accomplished by having the participant depress button 6 to toggle between the orientation and targeting control. In the orientation control mode the manipulation of the joystick was used to change the view of the environment – rotate left, right, up or down - relative to the original view. In the targeting mode, the trainee selected defects by guiding the targeting cursor onto the defect and pressing button 5 on the gamepad. The orientation was fixed in this mode but the position controls (buttons 1-4) were active.

**Fig. 1.** HMD

**Fig. 2.** Gravis gamepad

**Fig. 3.** FOB tracker

The third interface (C) was the highest fidelity control condition. In this control condition, the orientation information was streamed from the Flock of Birds (FOB) tracker (Figure 3) and the manipulation of the gamepad was used to change the view of the environment. Rotating the gamepad left, right, up or down caused the orientation to rotate left, right, up or down relative to the original view. In this interface, the targeting cursor could be controlled by the D-pad joystick and defects were selected by pressing button 5. The cursor could be controlled concurrently with the orientation control. In addition to this, by depressing button 6 the participant can toggle to a mode in which the orientation is fixed and the targeting cursor can be controlled using the joystick for target selection within the view. Depressing button 6 toggles the stat of the interface and the orientation control is activated mapping the current position of the gamepad to the orientation of the scenario.

**Fig. 4.** Aft cargo bay

**Fig. 5.** Familiarization scenario

The scenarios used in this study are variations of a virtual reality model of an aircraft aft cargo bay similar to the one in a Lockheed L1011 aircraft (Figure 4).

Five variants of the cargo bay scenario were used for this study: A familiarization scenario (Figure 5) with the different types of defects highlighted was the first scenario. The purpose of this scenario is to familiarize participants with virtual reality and to allow them to become accustomed to the cargo bay environment. This scenario also presents highlighted examples of the five different types of defects used in the study. Defect types are crack, corrosion, broken electrical conduit, abrasion and hole.

The second scenario was the selection training scenario (Figure 7) where the trainee could get acclimated to the control interface and practice manipulating their view in the environment. This scenario also displayed various targets in the cargobay environment which the participants could practice selecting using the defect selection mechanism.

**Fig. 6.** Selection training scenario

**Fig. 7.** Inspection task scenario

Participants perform the inspection task using three additional multiple defect inspection scenarios. These scenarios (Figure 7) were constructed to be equivalent in task difficulty (identical distribution of defect types and similar locations) and contain twenty-two defects of the five above-mentioned types.

### 3.3 Procedure

The participants were first asked to complete a consent form, a demographic questionnaire, and given instructions to ensure their understanding of the experiment. All the participants were then immersed in the familiarization scenario to familiarize them with VR, the cargo bay environment, and the different types of defects. This was followed by introducing the participant to the control mechanism followed by a two minute manipulation and defect selection practice scenario with the first interface. They were then asked to perform an inspection task in a multiple defect environment using the same interface. The task involved the participants searching for defects in the virtual inspection scenario. Once they found a defect, they marked it in the scenario by using the target selection mechanism. If the selection was correct, the defect was then highlighted in red. The task was a paced task limited to 5 minutes. A subjective questionnaire was administered after this. This process of defect selection training followed by the inspection task followed by the questionnaire was then performed by the participants with the second interface and so on for all three interfaces. The order in which the participant encountered each of the interfaces was counterbalanced. One of the multiple defect inspection scenarios were presented for each inspection task. The three multiple defect inspection scenarios were counterbalanced to assure that the inspection task was performed an equal number of times in each of the task scenarios for each interface condition.

The questionnaires used for evaluating the participant's perceptions of the interfaces and the training environment were recorded on a 5 point Likert Scale, with 1 being strongly disagree, 5 being strongly agree, and 3 being neutral. A majority of the questions dealt with the perceived ease of use of the interface for navigation within the virtual environment as well as the interaction capabilities or short-comings of either of the input devices for defect selection. The results of the data collected are presented in the next section.

## 4 Results

### 4.1 Performance Measures

The mean number of hits for each condition is as shown in Figure 8. The results were analyzed initially using an ANOVA using the PROC MIXED procedure in SAS V9. There was no significant difference found between the three interface conditions for the number of correct defect selections (Hits).

### 4.2 Subjective Measures

The subjective questionnaire (Table 1) was administered after each interface condition. The scores were analyzed for each question using a Friedman Test on the interfaces blocking on the participants. Then (if significant) a Fisher's protected LSD procedure was used to compare the pairs of means. There was no significant difference between the three control conditions except for questions 6 and 12. The LSD procedure applied to the two questions showed that all the conditions were significantly different. For question 6, interface B scored higher than A and interface

C scored higher than both A and B. For question 12, interface C scored higher than A and interface B scored higher than both A and C.

**Table 1.** Subjective Questionnaire

| |
|---|
| 1. The environment was responsive to the actions that I initiated. |
| 2. The interactions with the environment seemed natural. |
| 3. I was involved by the visual aspects of the environment. |
| 4. The mechanism which controlled movement through the environment seemed natural. |
| 5. I was able to anticipate what would happen next in response to the actions that I performed. |
| 6. I could examine objects from multiple viewpoints. |
| 7. I was involved in the simulated inspection experience. |
| 8. The control mechanism was distracting. |
| 9. There was no delay between my actions and expected outcomes. |
| 10. I adjusted quickly to the interface used for the virtual environment experience. |
| 11. I felt proficient in moving and interacting with the virtual environment using this interface. |
| 12. I could effortlessly manipulate the mechanism for defect selection in the virtual environment. |
| 13. It was easy for me to select defects using this interface. |
| 14. The control devices interfered with performing the task. |
| 15. I could concentrate on the task rather than on the mechanisms used to perform the task. |
| 16. I would personally prefer this interface for inspection training using virtual reality. |

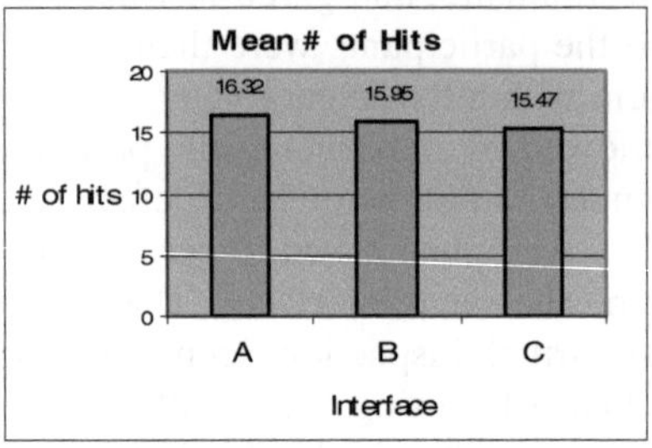


**Fig. 8.** Performance Measures

## 5 Discussion

Based on these results we see that there was no difference in the participants' performance for the different control fidelity conditions. This could be explained by the additional workload experienced by the participants in using the higher fidelity interfaces that may have negated the benefits of greater control in the paced task.

The participant's perception of presence in the environment seems to be equivalent with the three control conditions. Increasing the control fidelity allowed for greater interaction with the environment and this was perceived by the participants in their response to question 6. In interface B, independent control of the targeting cursor allowed the participants to select a defect from multiple orientations while the FOB based interface in addition allowed for quick movements allowing greater control of the orientation.

The results of Question 12 are slightly surprising as the FOB based interface had concurrent control of the cursor using the D-pad joystick with the orientation control using the FOB. This could be explained by the experimenter's observation that some participants tended to not use the concurrent control of the cursor. The combination of the two control levels of the targeting cursor using the joystick (concurrent or in fixed orientation mode), and the orientation control using the gamepad may have induced a high level of workload in the search task and the participants may have chosen to discard the higher level of interaction control to optimize the workload level [19].

During the debriefing session at the end of the experiment, the participants noted that they had difficulties in targeting the cursor while using the first interface in which it was fixed at the center. Although many participants found this interface the easiest to get used to, they complained of lack of fine cursor control and hence frustration with selecting defects in the environment. In the second interface, when they had control over the environment versus the cursor movement, they observed that the selection process was much simpler than the first interface. However, some participants noted that it would have been helpful to have a visible toggle notification to inform them of the mode they were presently in. Some participants also noted that although they had to repeatedly look down at the gamepad to ensure that they were pressing the correct buttons due to their inexperience with the gamepad, they got used to the interface after a while. In case of the third interface, since many of the participants had not used an immersive VR environment before, found that they needed some time to get acclimatized to the controls in the environment. While they found that the FOB was responsive to their actions, they suggested that they had difficulties in manipulating the cursor and the gamepad simultaneously, especially while looking up at the ceiling. They observed that they had to overcome this effect by using the toggle button to freeze the frame and then selecting defects.

## 6 Conclusion

Based on these results revisions are made for the design of the prototype interaction devices for the projector based virtual reality aircraft inspection simulators. Considering the complexity and cost of the FOB based gamepad interface, it is recommended to explore other off-the-shelf solutions to interact with the projector based environment. New video game control devices can be explored to enhance the fidelity of the regular gamepad interface. The Wiimote from Nintendo and Sony's PS3 controller can be explored for providing enhanced orientation and position information. In addition to evaluating performance and presence, it is recommended to evaluate workload while evaluating these interfaces.

## References


1. Federal Aviation Administration - Pilot and Aviation Maintenance Technician Blue Ribbon Panel, Pilots and Aviation Maintenance Technicians for the Twenty First Century – An Assesment of Availability and Quality (August 1993)
2. Federal Aviation Administration, Training and Certification in the Aircraft Maintenance Industry – Specialist Resources for the 21st Century (1996)
3. National Transportation Safety Board, National Transportation Safety Board Report #N75B/AAR-98/01 (1998)

4. Drury, C.G., Prabhu, P.V., Gramopadhye, A.K.: Task analysis of aircraft inspection activities: methods and findings. In: Proceedings of the Human Factors Society 34th Annual Meeting, Santa Monica, CA 1990, pp. 1181–1185 (1990)
5. Drury, C.G.: The Maintenance Technician in Inspection, Human Factors in Aviation Maintenance Phase 1: Progress Report, FAA, Washington, DC, pp. 45–91 (1991)
6. Chin, R.: Automated visual inspection:1981 to 1987. Computer Vision Graphics Image Process 41, 346–381 (1988)
7. Drury, C.G.: Inspection performance. In: Salvendy, G. (ed.) Handbook of Industrial Engineering, pp. 2282–2314. Wiley, New York (1992)
8. Gramopadhye, A.K., Drury, C.G., Prabhu, P.V.: Training strategies for visual inspection. Human Factors and Ergonomics in Manufacturing 7(3), 171–196 (1997)
9. Czaja, S.J., Drury, C.G.: Training programs for inspection. Human Factors 23(4), 473–484 (1981)
10. Gramopadhye, A.K., Drury, C.G., Sharit, J.: Training for decision making in aircraft inspection. In: Proceedings of the Human Factors and Ergonomics Society 37th Annual Meeting 1993, pp. 1267–1271 (1993)
11. Drury, C.G., Chi, C.-F.: A test of economic models of stopping policy in visual search. IIE Transactions, 382–393 (1995)
12. Duchowski, A.T., Medlin, E., Gramopadhye, A.K., Melloy, B.J., Nair, S.: Binocular eye tracking in VR for visual inspection training. In: Proceedings of Virtual Reality Software & Technology (VRST). Banff, AB, Canada, ACM, pp. 1–8 (2001)
13. Vora, J., Nair, S., Gramopadhye, A.K., Melloy, B.J., Meldin, E., Duchowski, A.T., Kanki, B.G.: Using Virtual Reality Technology to Improve Aircraft Inspection Performance: Presence and Performance Measurement Studies. In: Proceedings of the Human Factors and Ergonomic Society 45th Annual Meeting 2001, pp. 1867–1871 (2001)
14. Schricker, B.C., Lippe, S.R.: Using the High Level Architecture to Implement Selective-Fidelity. In: Proceedings of the 37th Annual Symposium on Simulation April 18 - 22, 2004. Annual Simulation Symposium, p. 246. IEEE Computer Society, Washington, DC (2004)
15. Andrews, D.H., Carroll, L.A., Bell, H.H.: The Future of Selective Fidelity in Training Devices Armstrong Lab Wright-Patterson AFB OH Human Resources Directorate Final Rrport # ADA316902 (1996)
16. Witmer, B., Singer, M.: Measuring presence in virtual environments: A Presence Questionnaire. Presence: Teleoperators and Virtual Environments 7(3), 225–240 (1998)
17. Gallwey, T.J., Drury, C.G.: Task complexity in visual inspection. Human Factors 28, 595–606 (1986)
18. Wickens, C.D., Hollands, J.: Engineering psychology and human performance. Prentice Hall, Upper Saddle River (2000)

# IMPROVE: Collaborative Design Review in Mobile Mixed Reality


Pedro Santos[1], André Stork[1], Thomas Gierlinger[2], Alain Pagani[2], Bruno Araújo[3], Ricardo Jota[3], Luis Bruno[3], Joaquim Jorge[3], Joao Madeiras Pereira[3], Martin Witzel[4], Giuseppe Conti[4], Raffaele de Amicis[4], Iñigo Barandarian[5], Céline Paloc[5], Oliver Machui[6], Jose M. Jiménez[7], Georg Bodammer[8], and Don McIntyre[9]

[1] Fraunhofer-IGD, A2
[2] TU-Darmstadt, FB21,GRIS
[3] INESC-ID
[4] GraphiTech
[5] VICOMTech.,
[6] Trivisio GmbH
[7] MED
[8] STT,
[9] Lighthouse

{Pedro.Santos, Andre.Stork}@igd.fhg.de, {Thomas.Gierlinger, Alain.Pagani}@igd.fhg.de, {brar, jota.costa, bruno, jaj, jap}@inesc-id.pt, {martin.witzel, giuseppe.conti, raffaele.de.amicis}@graphitech.it, {Inigo.Barandarian, Celine.Paloc}@vicomtech.es, machui@trivisio.de, georg.bodammer@microemissive.com, jmjimenez@stt.es, don.mcintyre@urbanlearningspace.com



**Abstract.** In this paper we introduce an innovative application designed to make collaborative design review in the architectural and automotive domain more effective. For this purpose we present a system architecture which combines variety of visualization displays such as high resolution multi-tile displays, TabletPCs and head-mounted displays with innovative 2D and 3D Interaction Paradigms to better support collaborative mobile mixed reality design reviews. Our research and development is motivated by two use scenarios: automotive and architectural design review involving real users from Page\Park architects and FIAT Elasis. Our activities are supported by the EU IST project IMPROVE aimed at developing advanced display techniques, fostering activities in the areas of: optical see-through HMD development using unique OLED technology, marker-less optical tracking, mixed reality rendering, image calibration for large tiled displays, collaborative tablet-based and projection wall oriented interaction and stereoscopic video streaming for mobile users. The paper gives an overview of the hardware and software developments within IMPROVE and concludes with results from first user tests.


## 1 Introduction

Design Review is one of the most prominent areas benefiting from Virtual Reality and Immersive Projection Technologies. Use cases generally comprise many observers in


R. Shumaker (Ed.): Virtual Reality, HCII 2007, LNCS 4563, pp. 543–553, 2007.

front of a back projection wall discussing a design decision on a virtual model. The user's visual experience is further enhanced by the possibility of individually rendering the 3D stereoscopic images of a model for each user's point of view. Recent developments allow up to 4 tracked users [Fröhlich04].

In the last couple of years Augmented Reality ceased to be used only for maintenance and training but also in design and design review (e.g. see ARVIKA project homepage: www.arvika.de). Typically video-based AR is applied to augment physical models with design alternatives e.g. new virtual dash boards (VW), alternative wheel designs (Audi). However Interaction and collaboration seldom take place in such applications.

SpaceDesign [Fiorentino02] was one of the first creative and generative tools allowing a user equipped with stereoscopic optical see-through glasses to sketch free-form surfaces directly in 3D augmenting a physical model underneath.

Schmalstieg [Schmalstieg 06] explored the possibilities of mobile collaborative AR within their Studierstube system supporting various applications from scientific visualisation to interactively experiencing math and esp. geometry.

With AR technology maturing, companies such as BMW [Klinker02] became curios and interested whether AR can be used in large(r) environments enabling mobile users to compare virtual with real models by walking around them in presentation facilities.

## 2 Application Scenarios

For us this was the starting point for brainstorming the possibilities of Mixed Reality in the design process with representatives from automotive industry and architecture. One thing important to note is that the two branches are completely different in structure. Car makers are big companies that to a great extent have pushed VR technology in the last 15 years whereas the architecture branch is characterized by many small enterprises that cannot afford expensive VR installations.

Discussions with architects revealed the following needs:

1. Starting a new Building: Early shape studies integrating new building in its surroundings and the landscape – Support by sketching capabilities on the construction site using Tablet-PCs for early sketches and optical see-through glasses for visualising the sketch in its physical environment.
2. Refinement of early sketches in the office: Collaborative Review and interactive presentation to customers using HMDs supporting multiple viewports. Pen-based direct 3D interaction is envisaged for creating annotations and change orders.
3. Final Design: Presentation of final design on construction site for multiple users. Again, HMDs and large area tracking is needed. The correct lighting of the virtual model with respect to the lighting conditions at the construction site is important.

**Fig. 1.** Onsite sketching and collaborative indoor reviewing scenarios (conceptual sketches)

In contrast to the architects, whose scenarios are centred around the use of HMDs indoor or on location, the representatives from automotive industry are familiar with large area displays and want to improve and extend the use of large single- or multi-tile projection technology.

The automotive scenarios look as follows:

1. The reviewers in front of the large projection wall shall be equipped with Tablet PCs. The Tablet PC shows the scene on the wall in reduced resolution from the same viewpoint unless a user decouples from the wall. Decoupled users can create annotations and suggestions for changes using handwritten input on their Tablet PC and "re-connect to the wall" at will.
2. Multiple users can work side-by-side to the wall in an AR setup performing direct 3D interaction with 3D pen.
3. Single users in front of the wall can directly interact with the wall using hand gestures.

To improve geometric and colour consistency of high resolution walls more efficient calibration techniques are required.

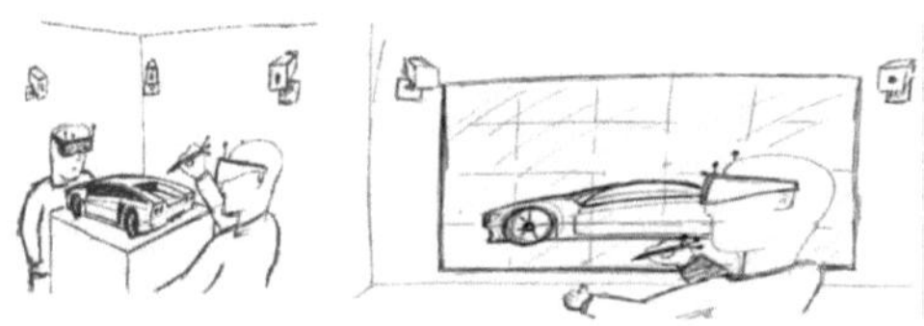

**Fig. 2.** Collaborative cAR design review scenario combining large and head mounted displays (conceptual sketches)

## 3 Requirements

Analysing the mobile collaborative scenarios (indoors and outdoors) from both branches entails that a combination of state-of-the art and progress in the following areas is needed to answer the requirements:

- lightweight, power efficient stereoscopic optical see-through HMDs
- large area multi user tracking
- augmented reality rendering
- collaborative interaction techniques spanning display walls, Tablet PCs and direct 3D interaction
- image calibration techniques
- image (video) transmission techniques to ensure highest possible rendering quality for mobile users using limited computational and graphics power

The authors are aware of no comparable approach that offers that unique combination of technologies and techniques. The most comparable work is probably done by Regenbrecht et al [Regenbrecht02] while IMPROVE is wider in scope and spans more diverse environments and scenarios. IMPROVE not only contributes to the mixed and augmented reality field with that combination of techniques listed above but also with new achievements such as taylor-made organic light emitting display (OLEDs) by the consortium partner Micro Emissive Displays (MED), efficient image calibration techniques, innovative interaction techniques, pre-computed radiance based rendering and optimized video transmission for mobile users.

# 4 IMPROVE System Architecture

This chapter presents the general IMPROVE architecture (Fig. 3). We will analyze the different components subsequently.

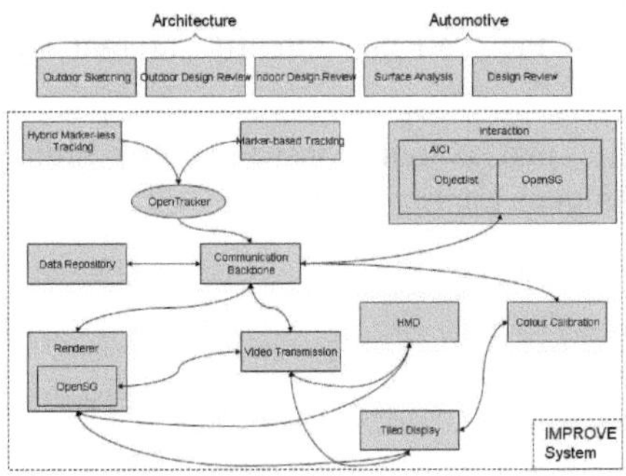


**Fig. 3.** IMPROVE System Architecture

*Communication Backbone:* The communication backbone is one of the internal modules which is part of the IMPROVE system i.e. the AICI framework and is responsible for providing to the other internal modules a simple interface to support the communication. This communication interface allows other modules or the main interface view of the application access to the following functionalities:

- Connection to the distributed server i.e. an instance of the XMLBlaster server available in the network
- Login and Logout to the distributed server using a username for identification
- Subscription of an interest to receive a network message of a given type
- Sending mechanism to publish messages of a given type to the network

**Fig. 4.** Creation of annotations and material property changes

Messages can be object updates, navigation messages or session messages, i.e.: one instance could broadcast an update to an already existing annotation on the OSGA communication backbone.

In the AICI system the communication is accessible trough the Communicator which is the internal module of the system that interacts with the OSGA communication layer which provides a simple interface to create an XMLBlaster Client with the ability to communicate with the distributed server which is an XMLBlaster server instance running in the network.

Interaction: The architectural indoor interaction subsystem supports interaction between users during collaborative reviews. The system operates as two or more IMPROVE instances connected, through OSGA, to the communication backbone. The IMPROVE instances interact by sending and receiving IMPROVE entity messages.

The scenario presents two or more architects in a collaborative design session or an architect and a client on a collaborative review session. In both situations (collaborative sessions), all actors use Tablet PCs. The Space Mouse is also supported in addition to the Tablet PC pen. Furthermore the scenario supports users with HMDs who visualize models on top of a table or outdoors and can be shown design alternatives by architects using TabletPCs. In the automotive scenario the setup may involve a collaborative design session in front of a powerwall. In all cases there are a variety of interaction modalities to provide input to the TabletPCs or powerwall.

**Fig. 5.** Creation shapes and annotation in front of a Power-wall with a TabletPC

Collaborative entity messages can be divided into two groups: Shape editing and Annotation editing. Shape messages are only used during collaborative design sessions between architects. Clients are not allowed to create new shapes. Annotation entity messages are available on both design sessions and review sessions.

In the moment possible shapes are restricted to primitive shapes like cones, cylinders and cubes (Fig. 5). We plan to also be able to create free-form surfaces.

Annotations use the Post-It metaphor. Users can take notes of their comments and then stick them to objects. This is done by choosing an appropriate anchor on the object to stick the note to. Post-It notes will always face the user. All commands are broadcast to the OSGA communication backbone.

The IMPROVE system includes the following interaction modalities:

- Laser Interaction – For Powerwall interaction (Fig.6). TabletPC uses the pen for the same effect;
- Voice Activation commands – Available on both indoor and outdoor scenarios;
- Smart Widget – The Powerwall scenario relies on a mobile device input to create annotations. The mobile device is chosen over other solutions because of its lightweight, user familiarity and ubiquity.

- Multi-modal interaction developed focus on using Laser interaction as main interaction modality and Voice or Smart Widgets as backup modalities. The interaction techniques described in the following sections describe the solutions we implemented using the presented methods.

*Annotation Interaction.* Annotation interaction uses Laser Interaction as a pointing device and Smart Widgets as annotation input device.

*Menu Interaction.* Some actions will only be available though a menu. Unfortunately the standard way to access a menu - mouse right-click - is not available on the Powerwall scenario. To overcome this problem we devised a menu activation gesture to be executed with the laser - This interaction was also adapted to the Tablet PC pen interaction. To activate menu options a gate mechanism adopted. This allowed the users to navigate the menu and activate menu options on a single stroke, as depicted on Figure 6.

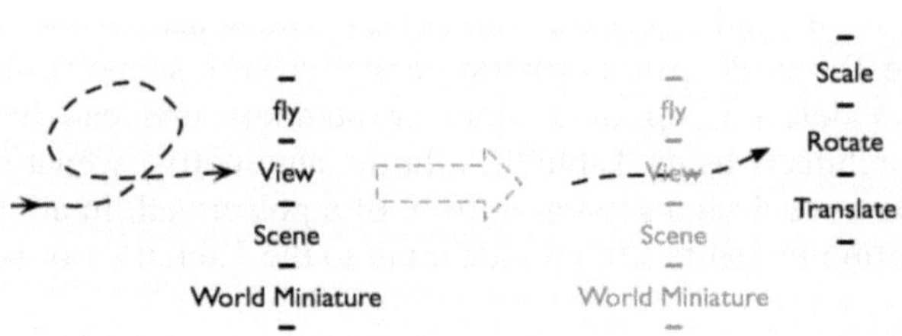


**Fig. 6.** Menu interaction example. User executes a gesture and a gate menu appears. New menu options appear in front on the laser postion for a fluid interaction.

*Object Selection.* To solve the laser limitation, we developed a novel selection interaction: To select an object you circle the object. In order to select several objects, just selected one or more at the same time. Moreover, the selections are cumulative, thus each selection adds the objects to the selection group. An empty selection resets the objects selected (Fig. 7).

*Navigation Interaction*

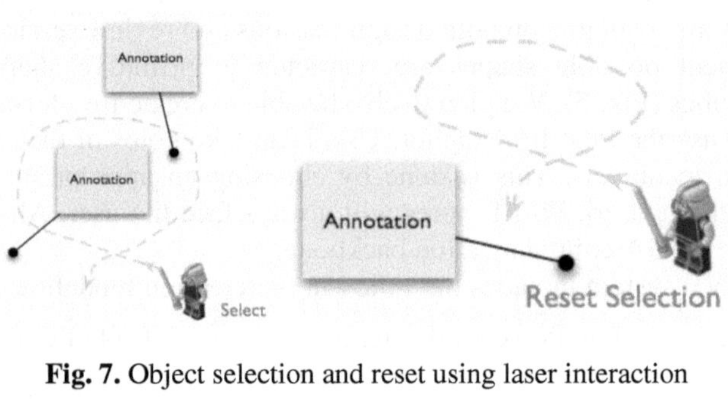


**Fig. 7.** Object selection and reset using laser interaction

*Context Menu.* Some options are only applied under a certain context. To satisfy this need, context menus automatically popup when a one or more objects become selected (Fig.8).

*Rendering:* The aim of the first prototype of the rendering component was to extend the OpenSG scenegraph library to support Precomputed Radiance Transfer. This first implementation was rather designed to get a correctly working implementation of the algorithm up and running than being tuned for high performance. This approach resulted in a CPU implementation of the run-time calculations of the PRT algorithm which was relatively easy to debug. However, doing the convolution of lighting and transfer function on the CPU prevents one from using display lists or vertex buffers to accelerate the rendering. The results of the lighting calculation have to be transferred to the graphics board every frame which eliminates the possibility of caching. For the second version of the renderer we have moved the convolution to the graphics board which significantly increases the performance of the renderer. Further more we have worked on moving the PRT preprocess from a per-vertex basis into texture space (which is not finished yet) and we have implemented a full HDR rendering pipeline which includes HDR reflection maps. The following sections give some detail about these improvements.

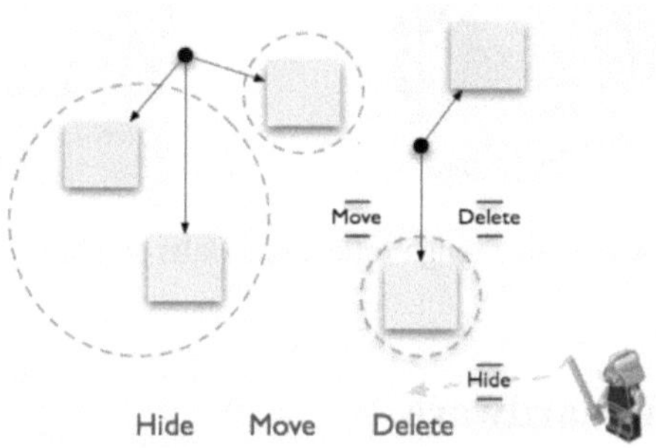


**Fig. 8.** Context Menu appears whenever a new object is selected. The available options depend on the selected objects type.

*PRT Runtime calculation on GPU.* The run-time calculation of the PRT algorithm boils down to a simple dot product between the coefficient vectors of SH-projected lighting and transfer functions. To perform this calculation using the GPU it is necessary to supply the per-vertex coefficient data to the graphics board. This is usually done using OpenGL vertex attributes, a general notion of data associated with a vertex. However OpenSG does not currently support the abstract vertex attributes, but only standard per vertex data like texture coordinates. Therefore we store the SH coefficients as texture coordinates. OpenSG supports up to 8 texture coordinate sets. We use up to 6 of these sets for the SH coefficients and also the secondary color property of a vertex, which allows us to support PRT rendering with up to five bands (i.e. 25 coefficients per vertex, stored in 6*4 texture coordinates + 1 secondary color coordinate). The first two texture coordinate sets are not used since they are used for standard texture mapping. The last information that is necessary to compute the PRT lighting on the GPU is the coefficient vector of the environment light. Since this vector is constant for the whole object we don't provide it as vertex attributes but as uniform variables. The coefficient vectors of the light and the transfer function at a vertex can now be scalar multiplied in a vertex shader. However, this implies that we cannot use the simple OpenSG materials anymore but have to apply custom vertex and fragment shaders to the model. Fortunately the VRED editor does also support SHL materials (i.e. shaders written in the OpenGL shading language), so we can still use this tool for material application.

*High Dynamic Range reflections.* The OpenSG version we used during the development of the first prototype (version 1.6) did not support floating point texture formats and offscreen render targets. This prevented the use of high dynamic range reflection maps as well as the direct visualization of the light probe as the background of the scene. However in the current version of OpenSG (1.8) support for floating point textures and high dynamic range image formats (namely RGBE (.hdr) images) has been implemented. This allows us to use the light probe of a scene directly in shaders. A comparison between low dynamic range reflections and backgrounds and high dynamic range reflections and background is shown in Fig. 9. It should be noted that the only difference between the two renderings is the texture image format.

**Fig. 9.** Comparison of Low dynamic range reflections (left) and high dynamic range reflections (right)

## 5 Improve System Hardware

*HMD:* For the mobile outdoor and indoor design review sessions Trivisio has developed a first prototype HMD using OLED Technology. The first prototype is using an evaluation board from MED to drive the OLED QVGA microdisplays. To connect to VGA signals from a PC an external converter is used.

To allow for marker-less tracking we have integrated a VRmagic model "VRmC-3". This camera has a resolution of VGA (640x480) and offers progressive scan which is useful for tracking purposes. The refresh rate is up to 48fps. In the standard configuration the camera offers a field of view of 52° diagonal which seems to be suitable for a tracking camera and can be changed by replacing the lens. The interface is USB 2.0 which is standard for such cameras. Trivisio and IGD have experience with this type of camera from former projects. The mechanical design is only a first concept and the aesthetic aspects should be improved in the next steps. The focus is

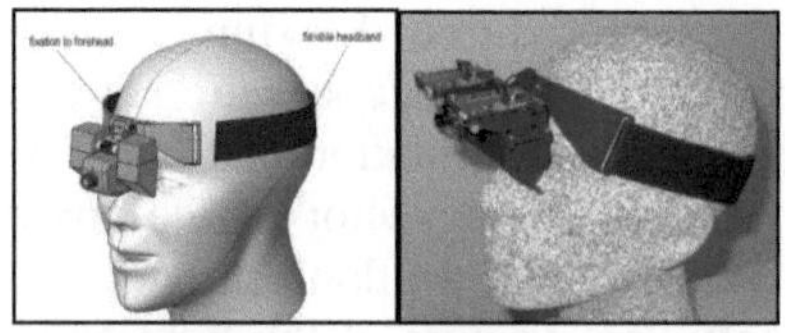

**Fig. 10.** HMD, fixation points to user's head

on functionality. The fixation to user's head is realized by a flexible headband as discussed and accepted with the projects's users and as this is the experience of Trivisio for the best and most ergonomic solution (see Fig. 10). In the case of calibration problems some additional sensors must be integrated or additional head fixation points such as nose-bridge must be added to the second prototype.

The two optical units are containing the optical components as described above including the microdisplays. The top covers can be removed and give an easy access to replace the microdisplays. Both units can be adjusted by a central screw to adapt the individual user's interpupil distance (IPD) by a linear sliding movement. The hinge connects the optical units to a forehead support and its angle can be adjusted to the individual user's forehead. The hinge can also be used to flip up the HMD to unblock user's sight quickly. Currently the FOV (field-of-view) is: virtual image: 17,6° diagonal, 10,66° vertical, 14,16° horizontal.

*Powerwall:* The Powerwall is a Tiled Display System (see Fig. 11). In this setup, the projection screen is divided in a number of tiles. Each tile receives the projection from on or two projectors (two in the case of stereoscopic walls). Each projector is individually connected to the video output of a single PC. All the PCs are arranged in a cluster configuration. The system additionally has a server, which role is to subdivide the image into individual image parts, and to send the image parts to the PCs over a network (usually using TCP/IP).

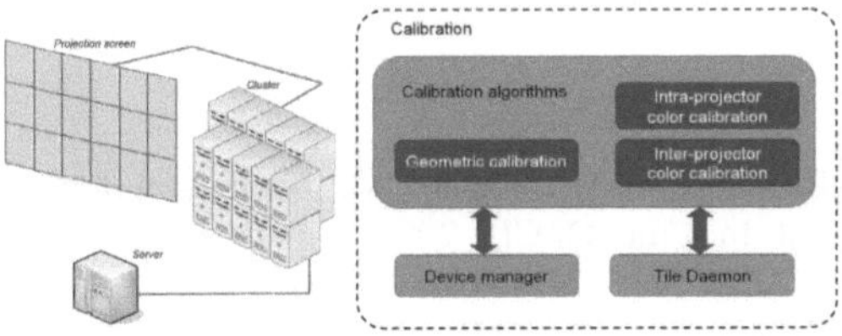


**Fig. 11.** The Powerwall

For the first prototype we used the HEyeWall from the Fraunhofer IGD in Darmstadt, Germany for the Powerwall component. The HEyeWall is a stereoscopic Powerwall, made out of 24 tiles (arranged in a 6x4 grid). Each tile is a part of the screen which receives the projection of two projectors (one for each eye). The total number of projectors is thus 48. Each projector connects to a PC, and the 48 PCs are used as a cluster of PCs. One supplementary PC serves as general server. Inside one tile, the right-eye and left-eye images are overlapping. When used in a monoscopic configuration, both projectors show the same image, resulting in an improved brightness. In the stereoscopic configuration, the images produces by each projector correspond to slightly different camera poses. The right-eye and left-eye signals are separated by specific goggles using Infitec Filters. The overall resolution of the HEyeWall is 6144 x 3072 pixels, for an image size of about 6m by 3m.

The calibration module is the software application used to calibrate the Powerwall. This application has three main components: The Calibration algorithms, the Device manager and the Tile Daemon (see Fig.11). The Calibration algorithms component is software that runs on the server of the Powerwall. It is used to conduct one of the three possible calibration processes: the geometric calibration calculating the distortion compensation, the intra-projector color calibration using software shading table adaptation and the inter-projector color calibration doing the characterization of the projectors and then the color transformation so all tiles look the same.

## 6 Conclusion

We have presented the IMPROVE application scenarios and details of almost each individual component of IMPROVE. Additional components are marker-less and marker-based tracking as well as stereo video-streaming to allow for remote rendering of high quality images and wireless transfer to the HMD. The Communication Backbone linking all parts of the system has been presented as well as our interaction approaches with TabletPCs, Powerwalls and HMDs. High Dynamic Range Images are used for calculation of lighting, soft shadows and reflections. We have presented a new HMD and Color Calibration for the HEyeWall. We plan to continue our development of the IMPROVE system based on the OpenSG framework. In a separate paper also within this conference we discuss results of the first user tests.

**Acknowledgements.** This work has been partially funded by European Commission Research Grant IMPROVE IST-2003-004785.

## References

1. [Regenbrecht02] Regenbrecht, H., Wagner, M.: Interaction in a Collaborative Augmented Reality Environment. In: Proc. Of CHI 2002, Minneapolis, Minnesota, USA, April 20-25, 2002, pp. 504–505. ACM Press, New York (2002)
2. [Schmalstieg06] Schmalstieg, D.: Designing Immersive Virtual Reality for Geometry Education, IEEE Virtual Reality, Alexandria, VA, USA, March 27, IEEE 2006. Virtual Concept 2006 Short Article Title Paper Number -11- Copyright Virtual Concept (2006)
3. [Klinker02] Klinker, G., Dutoit, A.H., Bauer, M., Bayer, J., Novak, V., Matzke, D.: Fata Morgana – A Presentation System for Product Design, In: Intl. Symposium on Augmented and Mixed Reality, Darmstadt, ISMAR 2002 (2002)
4. [BernEppstein03] Bern, M., Eppstein, D.: Optimized color gamuts for tiled displays. In: SCG '03. Proceedings of the nineteenth annual symposium on Computational geometry, San Diego, California, USA, pp. 274–281. ACM Press, New York (2003)
5. [Brown05] Brown, M., Majumder, A., Yang, R.: Camera-Based Calibration Techniques for Seamless Multi-Projector Displays. IEEE Transactions on Visualization and Computer Graphics, vol. 11(2) (2005)
6. [Debevec97] Debevec, P.E., Malik, J.: Recovering High Dynamic Range Radiance Maps from Photographs, Computer Graphics, vol. 31, pp. 369–378, In: SIGGRAPH 1997 (1997)
7. [Debevec98] Debevec, P.: Rendering synthetic objects into real scenes: Bridging traditional and image-based graphics with global illumination and high dynamic range photography. In: SIGGRAPH 98 (July 1998)
8. [Drummond02] Drummond, T., Cipolla, R.: Real-Time visual tracking of complex structures. IEEE Transaction on Pattern Analysis and Machine Intelligence 27, 932–946 (2002)

9. [Fiorentino02] Fiorentino, M., de Amicis, R., Monno, G., Stork, A.: SpaceDesign: A Mixed Reality Workspace for Aesthetic Industrial Design, In: Intl. Symposium on Augmented and Mixed Reality, Darmstadt, ISMAR 2002 (2002)
10. [Fröhlich04] Fröhlich, B., Hoffmann, J., Klüger, K., Hochstrate, J.: Implementing Multi-Viewer Time-Sequential Stereo Displays Based on Shuttered LCD Projectors, 4th Immersive Projection Technology Workshop, Ames, Iowa, May 2004 (2004)
11. [Kato00] Kato, H., Billinghurst, M., Poupyrev, I., Ikamoto, K., Tachibana, K.: Virtual object manipulation on tabletop AR environment. In: International Symposium on Augmented Reality, 2000, pp. 111–119 (2000)
12. [Kresse03] Kresse, W., Reiners, D., Knoepfle, C.: Color consistency for digital multi-projector stereo display systems: the HEyeWall and the Digital CAVE. In: EGVE '03. Proceedings of the workshop on Virtual environments 2003, Zurich, Switzerland, pp. 271–279. ACM Press, New York (2003)
13. [Lepetit05] Lepetit, V., Fua, P.: Monocular Model-Based 3D Tracking of Rigid Objects: A survey. (October 2005)
14. [Lowe01] Lowe, D.: Distinctive image features from scaleinvariants keypoints. International Journal of Computer Vision 20(2), 681–682 (2001)
15. [Majumder00] Majumder, A., He, Z., Towles, H., Welch, G.: Achieving color uniformity across multi-projector displays. In: VIS '00. Proceedings of the conference on Visualization '00, Salt Lake City, Utah, United States, pp. 117–124. IEEE Computer Society Press, Washington, DC, USA (2000)
16. [Majumder03] Majumder, A., Jones, D., McCrory, M., Papka, M.E., Stevens, R.: Using a Camera to Capture and Correct Spatial Photometric Variation in Multi-Projector Displays, In: IEEE Workshop on Projector-Camera Systems (PROCAMS 2003) (2003)

# Developing a Mobile, Service-Based Augmented Reality Tool for Modern Maintenance Work

Paula Savioja, Paula Järvinen, Tommi Karhela, Pekka Siltanen, and Charles Woodward

VTT Technical Research Centre of Finland, P.O. Box 1000, FI-02044 VTT, Finland
Paula.Savioja@vtt.fi, Paula.Jarvinen@vtt.fi, Tommi.Karhela@vtt.fi, Pekka.Siltanen@vtt.fi, Charles.Woodward@vtt.fi

**Abstract.** In the VTT PLAMOS (Plant Model Services for Mobile Process Maintenance Engineer) project new tools were developed for modern maintenance work carried out in industrial plants by either the plant personnel or personnel of an industrial service provider. To formulate the requirements for new tools the work of a maintenance man was studied with a particular method, the Core-Task Analysis which has its roots in study and development of work in complex settings. The aim was to develop and create concepts for novel tools that would support the development of good work practices in a situation where the work is concurrently undergoing several transformations. Hence, the new tools should have potential to enable and affect new ways of working.

## 1 Introduction

Maintenance of an industrial plant is work that strives for keeping the process equipment within the plant in a condition that is required to reach the production goals. The process equipment consists of all the physical equipment within the plant, such as pumps, pipes, and tanks. The professional maintenance both installs and repairs the equipment so that it functions in the intended way.

Increasing complexity of industrial plants lays growing demands on the operating personnel who take care of the plants. Advanced technology is used to access information related to the equipment maintained. Even though current maintenance and automation systems enable storage and browsing of equipment and process related data, the systems do not solve many of the common problems the maintenance personnel are facing, e.g.: How to locate the equipment needing maintenance? How to get intuitive and easily understood information about the plant floor equipment and their state? How to combine data from several sources without accessing many different applications with different user interfaces?

The problems are expected to become even more difficult in the future as changes also take place in the business environment. Traditionally the lifecycle management of an industrial facility, such as a process plant, has been divided between three main groups of players: owners/operators of the plant, system/component providers, and

R. Shumaker (Ed.): Virtual Reality, HCII 2007, LNCS 4563, pp. 554–563, 2007.

engineering consultants. However, since owners/operators are increasingly outsourcing parts of their operations, new business opportunities occur for industrial service providers. While the change creates new business opportunities, it also creates new demands for software applications. The challenges are related to the application interoperability, as well as human system interfaces.

Traditionally the maintenance workers have worked for years in the same plant, knowing the process and equipments almost by heart. While the machinery becomes increasingly complicated and maintenance is outsourced or carried out with a smaller amount of on-site maintenance personnel, the need for intuitive user interfaces for locating the equipments and viewing the product and process information is increasing.

Huge amounts of data created and maintained during the plant lifecycle is currently stored in diverse databases, which has non-standard interfaces for user interaction and information exchange. There is an increasing need to be able to use the information through unified, standardized interfaces, regardless of what application the information is stored in. The companies providing outsourced services can serve several plants that are owned and operated by different owner/operators. However, the outsourcing leads to true benefit only if the service company is capable of utilizing information from all the repositories via standard interfaces. Currently, there are ongoing industrial efforts (Mimosa 2006, OPC 2006) that aim at standardization of how the plant lifecycle information will be expressed in different contexts. This information model (also known as plant model) will form a basis for application interoperability in the industry, provided that services based on the model are specified simultaneously with the plant model standardization.

The aim of the Plamos project was to create new tools for maintenance work which would promote the development of good work practices in the partly transforming context of the work. In order to understand the requirements for the new tools it is essential to understand the practice in which the tool will be used.

## 2 The Research Approach and Process

In the Plamos project the technology development was approached from two different perspectives: Agile prototyping and human-centred design. The two approaches were used simultaneously and the processes kept each other informed by conducting project meetings in which findings were discussed.

In order to select the suitable technologies to be used in the tool development a few feasibility assessments were conducted. The technical feasibility studies were:

- *Augmented reality* where the user views real-time video of the machinery in the plant, and the information of the target object is augmented to the live video stream.
- *On-line simulation*, where the user sees calculated variables from the process based on measurements from the control system. The simulation results are shown to the user in the augmented reality view.

- *Plant model -based information management* where information from various sources is presented to the user in a uniform view. Information gathering is based on *a plant model* which is a conceptual, semantic model that describes the plant structures as well as the functions of the process and automation. It contains the plant information commonly represented in various different documents.
- *WLAN positioning* where the user gets position information in real time. The information was presented to the user with a floor plan of a building.

A handheld small size tablet PC, equipped with a video camera was selected to be used in the development process. All the above mentioned technology studies were conducted using the tablet PC. The small screen size of the tablet PC introduced some extra challenges for the user interface design. But the size of the device was considered to be small enough for the mobile maintenance engineer to carry along during routine job.

Another branch of research started a human-centred design process (ISO 13407:1999) the aim of which was to ensure the usability of the solutions being developed. The objective in the preliminary phases of the research was to understand the changes taking place in the context of maintenance work and with that knowledge generate functional requirements for the novel work tools.

The method used the user study was Core-Task Analysis (CTA). CTA is a work analysis method developed to study different kinds of work taking place in complex, dynamic, and uncertain environments (Norros 2004). It aims to identify *the core task* of a particular work; the essence of the activity which stays the same from situation to situation independently e.g. of the organisation of the work and the specific tools being used. CTA also studies the work practices that produce good results i.e. practices that promote reaching the objectives of work in varying conditions.

In the Plamos project CTA was carried out by conducting interviews and workshops. Altogether 15 maintenance engineers from three different companies were interviewed with semi-structured interviews concerning their work, its organization, current tools, changes having taken place etc.

Management and strategic level management personnel participated in a workshop concerning the objectives of different stakeholders in maintenance work. Models of maintenance activity and the changes taking place in the business environment w were produced in the workshops.

After the technical feasibility studies and the analysis of the core task the work continued as a software development process. Figure 1 outlines the phases of the development process.

The outputs of the CTA were transformed to requirements for an information system including use case scenarios, system functions and a data model. The user interface prototype was designed based on the requirements and priorities of the user needs. In the design phase the interfaces to the different components of the system were planned including the process and simulation systems, data storages and the augmented videos. Finally, the system was implemented with Java in the Eclipse platform (a vendor-neutral open development platform by the Eclipse Foundation (Eclipse 2006)).

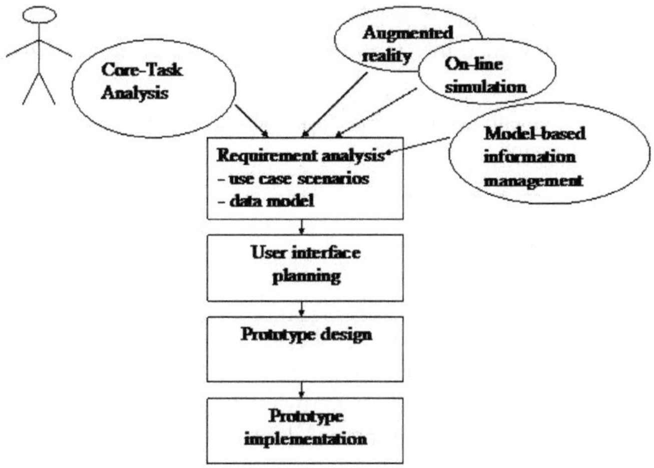


**Fig. 1.** The Plamos development process

# 3 Results

In the project a concept for a new tool and an interactive prototype were developed based on the understanding of maintenance work that was acquired through analysis of the core task.

## 3.1 The Requirements from Analysing the Core Task

The core-task analysis aims at identifying what are the objectives of a given work that do not depend on the particular organisation of the work. In addition, in core-task analysis the means to achieve the objectives are identified. In this project we tried to use this knowledge to derive requirements for a new work instrument for maintenance work.

The objectives (core task) of maintenance work were discussed in both the interviews of the employers and in the management workshops. There were varying conceptions of what should be considered the objective in maintenance. In the following we have adopted broadest possible conception including all the aspects of the objectives that came up in data collection. The objectives in industrial maintenance are:

1. Availability of the maintained process
2. Quality of the end product
3. Safety of the plant and of the plant personnel
4. Life-cycle management of the plant
5. Development of the production process
6. Cost efficiency of maintenance

These objectives were broken down into means to reach them. Most of the means relate to *repair of failed equipment*, *anticipation of equipment failure*, and *reaction to equipment failure* (see also Reiman & Oedewald 2004). Next, the different means were analysed and transformed into requirements for the new tools (Table 1).

**Table 1.** Deriving requirements with the core task approach. Only the requirements related to employers' tools are presented.

| **Objective** | **Means to achieve** | **Requirements for an employer's tool – what should the tool do?** |
|---|---|---|
| Availability of the maintained process | • Efficient repair – shortening the down time<br>• Acquiring process knowledge<br>• Acquiring equipment knowledge<br>• Calibration of the equipment<br>• Optimizing the whole<br>• Maintaining appropriate culture | – Locate the equipment<br>– Increase understanding of the process<br>– Help in the use of manuals in the field |
| Cost efficiency in maintenance | • Anticipation of equipment failures (analysis of process data)<br>• Maintaining in advance<br>• Optimising repair | – Analyse of process data<br>– Organise the work in tasks<br>– Create task order |
| Quality of the end product | • Acquiring/maintaining process knowledge<br>• Calibration of the equipment | – Increase understanding of the process<br>– Help in the use of manuals in the field |
| Safety of the plant and of the plant personnel | • Planning the maintenance<br>• Appropriate work culture | – Report problems and equipment failures<br>– Provide safety information and manuals |
| Life-cycle management of the plant | • Planning the maintenance | – Organising the work in tasks and task order |
| Development of the production process | • Acquiring/maintaining process knowledge | – Increase understanding of the process |

### 3.2 The Concept for a New Tool

The interaction concept of the new tool was inspired by the analysis of current practice of maintenance work. Modern maintenance work is conducted by either plant personnel or a separate service provider. Independent of the organisation, the work area typically consists of the whole plant. The maintenance men move around and carry the equipment with them. They need as much information as possible on hand all the time since the situations in which the information is needed are often unexpected and emergent. Thus the concept of a mobile device providing access to different kinds of data was developed. The device uses augmented reality techniques that help personnel e.g. in locating and identifying equipment and providing additional information. The features presented below help carrying out work at unfamiliar plant sites and also help in working more efficiently.

### 3.3 The Prototype

For the prototype we first identified the users of the mobile tool and sketched three use case scenarios. The users and scenarios were formed based on the results of the core-task analysis and workshops with the company representatives. The identified user groups were maintenance engineers, operating personnel, design and assembly engineers, and new employees. Three different usage scenarios were developed as follows:

1. *Assembly of new equipment.* The assembly engineer is not familiar with the site and the main problems are how to find the right position for the equipment and how the final equipment will show up at the site. In this scenario the use of augmented reality is most feasible.
2. *Maintenance of the process.* An operation engineer notices an exception in the process and goes on-site to see what's going on. He/she gets process and simulation data to the mobile device and can monitor and trend the process variables on-site with the mobile terminal.
3. *Repair.* A maintenance engineer gets each day a list of 1- 10 tasks including failures, repairs and maintenance tasks. To be able to carry out the tasks the engineer needs information from several sources: fault and correction history, maintenance manuals, safety instructions, the availability of spare parts, manuals from the component manufacturers etc. The data is typically located in different heterogeneous systems. The mobile Plamos-tool will deliver the information with one uniform interface to the user on-site. The user can also update the status of the repair task.

The analysis of the use case scenarios produced the prototype (Figure 2). We ended up in a solution where the same user interface serves all user groups. It turned out that each user group had overlapping data needs and building own separate interfaces for each use case was not reasonable. We organised the user interface according to the data contents instead of user functions. The user interface is divided into different views that the user can browse. The views are Tasks, Equipment, Augmented reality and Failure notice. In the Tasks view (Figure 3) the user gets a list of the tasks for each day and sees the necessary details to do the job: the equipment involved, the task description, the contact persons etc. The user makes the report of the completed task using the same view.

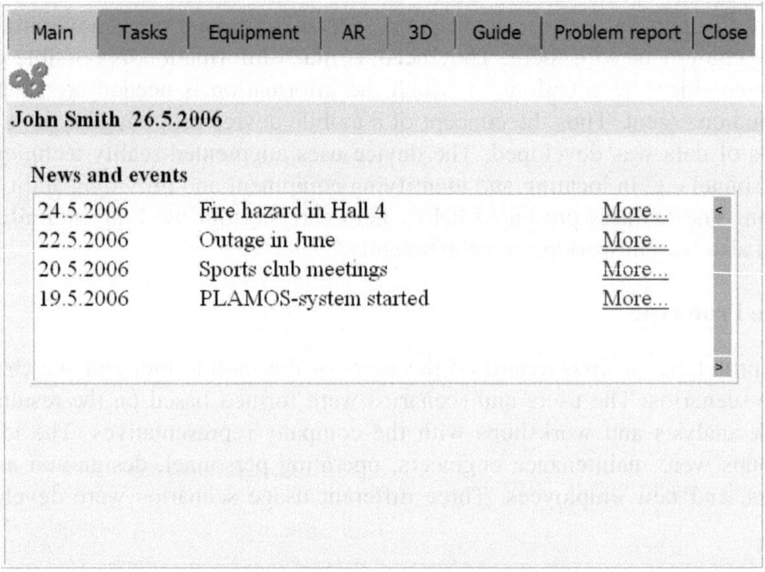


**Fig. 2.** Plamos prototype (the main page). The different views can be accessed through the tabs on top of the screen.

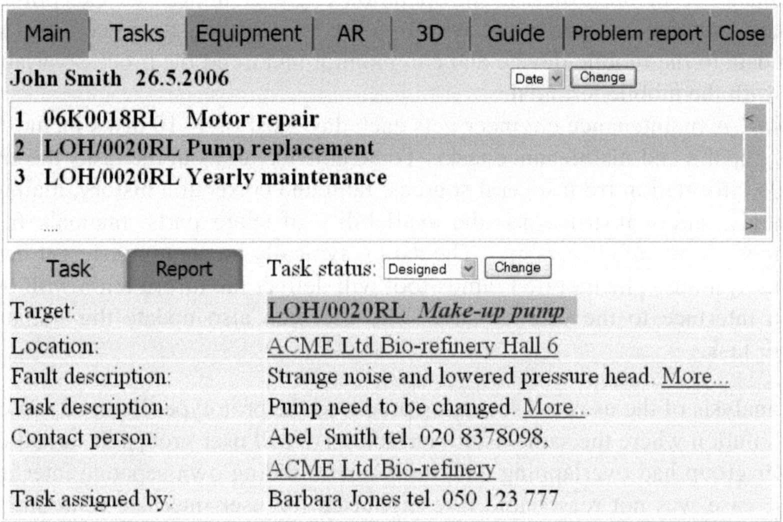


**Fig. 3.** The task view. The tasks are presented as a scroll list in the upper window. In the lower part of the screen there is additional task related information, for example the specific equipment that the task is related to. The Equipment can be located by selecting the task and then the AR view.

**Fig. 4.** The augmented reality (AR) view of the prototype. The identification of the object is carried out with black and white 2-dimensional matrix. Other possibilities for identification were also tested.

The Augmented reality view shows the augmented scene of the identified object (Figure 4). In the view information from the plant databases and the automation system is combined and presented to the user by augmenting it in the real-time video stream. The information is always presented on top of the equivalent equipment so that it is intuitively combined with the right part of the process.

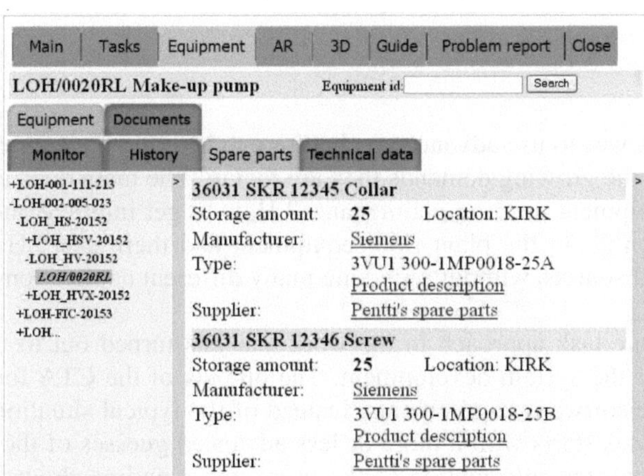


**Fig. 5.** The equipment view of the Plamos prototype. In this view data from many sources is combined.

In the Equipment view (Figure 5) the user can browse the function and equipment hierarchy and get information about the system or sub system: The fault history, the spare parts, technical data, assembly manual, instructions for use, maintenance manuals, safety instructions, failure identification manuals, and diagrams of the system.

The Failure report view (Figure 6) is meant for reporting the failures the maintenance and operation personnel detects during their daily work. The notices will be collected into data storage and they will be used as source data for planning the maintenance work. The user can navigate to the failure report view from the AR-view, in which he has identified the object to report on. In this case the report form will be prefilled with the equipment information.

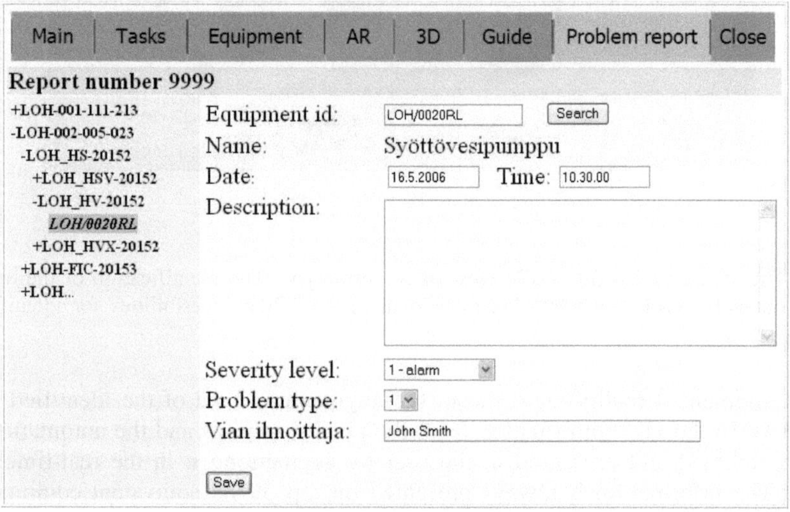


**Fig. 6.** The failure report view

# 4 Discussion

Our original task was to use advanced technology to help the maintenance and operating personnel in the growing demands they are facing. The main questions were: How to locate the equipment needing maintenance? How to get intuitive and easily understood information about the plant floor equipment and their state? How to combine data from several sources without accessing many different applications with different user interfaces?

The use of core-task approach in the work analysis turned out to be a very good starting point for the system development. The outputs of the CTA formed an excellent basis for the software requirements. Instead of the typical situation where the requirements analysis starts with a more or less advanced guesses of the user needs we had fresh and analyzed information of the users' tasks and needs in our hands. The data modelling, use case planning, and the design of the user interface were straightforward. We believe that we succeeded in creating a prototype that meets the user needs very well. Also the augmented reality turned out to be a natural interface for delivering equipment information to users.

The locating of the equipment and the augmented reality were tested in an experimental industrial environment. Experiments were made both with tracking objects using matrix codes and markerless tracking using WLAN positioning. The matrix code tracking worked well and the user got process and simulation data of the identified object on an augmented reality view. Our goal to locate the equipment and get intuitive and easily understood information was well achieved. The markerless tracking was not equally successful due to the immaturity of WLAN technology of in-door positioning. For the same reason we had to leave out the guidance of the employee to the object device from our concept. We could not get accurate enough information of the user's location in the building. We believe that this feature is possible to implement in the near future when the accuracy of the WLAN positioning is improved or alternative positioning mechanisms emerge.

Our third goal, to combine data from several sources was achieved by using standard interfaces such as MIMOSA OpenO&M and OPC Unified Architecture.

The final usability tests with real users will be done in the applied research phase of the project. A group of industrial partners will test the tool in real industry environments. The tool development continues in co-operation with the partners aiming at the commercialisation of the tool.

Some new ideas for the use of the technology also emerged from the experiments. Similar device that uses AR and simulation technology and plant modelling could be used in professional training of plant personnel. The users could walk around the plant and get information about different equipment and sub processes directly when at the site. We believe that this would make the theoretical learning, e.g. about the process, more concrete and would thus enhance learning.

**Acknowledgements.** The authors would like to thank the personnel of M-Real, UPM Kymmene, and YIT Services who participated in the study. The authors would also like to thank the whole Plamos project team.

## References

1. Eclipse (2006) http://www.eclipse.org/org/
2. ISO 13407:1999. Human-centred design processes for interactive systems. International standard. International Standardization Organization. Geneve
3. Mimosa (2006). OpenO&M, http://www.mimosa.org/
4. Norros, L.: Acting Under Uncertainty. VTT Publications, Espoo (2004)
5. Reiman, T., Pia, O.: Kunnossapidon organisaatiokulttuuri.Tapaustutkimus Olkiluodon ydinvoimalaitoksessa. Espoo, VTT Tuotteet ja tuotanto. 62 s. + liitt. 8 s. VTT Publications; 527 (2004)
6. OPC 2006. OPC Foundation, http://opcfoundation.org

# Augmented Reality System for Development of Handy Information Device with Tangible Interface

Hidetomo Takahashi, Shun Shimazaki, and Toshikazu Kawashima

Graduate School of Tokyo Institute of technology,
2-12-1 Oookayama, Meguro-ku
152-8552 Tokyo , Japan
{takahashi.h.am,shimazaki.s.aa,kawashima.t.ad}@m.titech.ac.jp

**Abstract.** In development of a handy information device, for example, a smart phone, the repetition of prototyping, evaluating and correcting are indispensable for ensuring stability of grasp, operationality and non-fragility. Because those properties are not able to be evaluated by common digital product development systems. In addition, operationality of these products greatly changes by shape of product, arrangement of buttons, output of implemented programmes etc. However, there is no system that makes the user evaluate efficiently and totally such a product. Therefore, the goal of this research is to develop the augmented reality system with the tangible interface that can tactually present the outline shape of the product model for efficiently product development.

**Keywords:** handy information device, stability of grasp, operationality.

## 1 Introduction

A handy information device equips various functions such as communication, data viewer and music player etc with a compact body. Those functions should be easily made available. In development of such a device, the repetition of prototyping, evaluating and correcting is indispensable for ensuring stability of grasp, operationality and non-fragility. Since those properties cannot be evaluated by common digital product development systems. In addition, operationality of these products greatly changes by shape of product, arrangement of buttons, output of implemented programmes etc. However, there is no system that enables the user to evaluate efficiently and totally such a product.

Attempt to evaluate the product based on the function model of man's hand are researched for such a problem[1]. Moreover, attempt to evaluate the usability are performed by using a digital prototype on the computer[2]. Both using virtual mock-up and Real mock-up with mixed reality technology is developed[3].

To present the grasping feel of a virtual object, some researches are performed. The system that applied a parallel manipulator was developed[4]. The system that some rings installed in the finger are driven with the wire was developed[5]. The system attached on the user's hand, so called exoskeleton type device was developed[6]. However, these systems has the limitation of the numbers of contact point and the

R. Shumaker (Ed.): Virtual Reality, HCII 2007, LNCS 4563, pp. 564–573, 2007.

location. So these system are not able to generate real grasping feel. On the other hand, the attempt where it tries to present arbitrary shape by using the balloon is proposed[7]. This system cannot present a shape accurately.

Then, the goal of this research is to develop an augmented reality system that enables a user to evaluate the stability of grasping and the operationality etc. of the product under the design. In this paper, an outline of the proposed system is described and the characteristic of the prototyped system are described.

## 2 Augmented Reality System for Development Handy Information Device

Fig. 1 shows the overview of our proposed system. In this system, watching detailed image of the product under design, the user is able to grasp the outline shape represented by the tangible interface to evaluate the stability of grasp and the operationality. At the same time, the operation of the user is recorded by video camera and the video signal is send to PCs by both NTSC and IEEE1394, simultaneously.

The video signal of IEEE 1394 is captured as video streaming by PC1. Then the hand image is extracted by using the brightness of the image in each flame. On the other hand, the signal of NTSC is captured as video streaming by PC2. The markers image are extracted, then the position and posture is calculated from the position of the markers in the screen. The position and posture is sending to PC1 by TCP/IP.

The detailed product image is generated from the 3D-CAD model and the position and posture received from PC2. The output image of the emulator which executes the target program, is captured from a part of the window and glued to the part corresponded the output screen of the detailed image. Finally, the hand image and the detailed image of the product are composted and displayed.

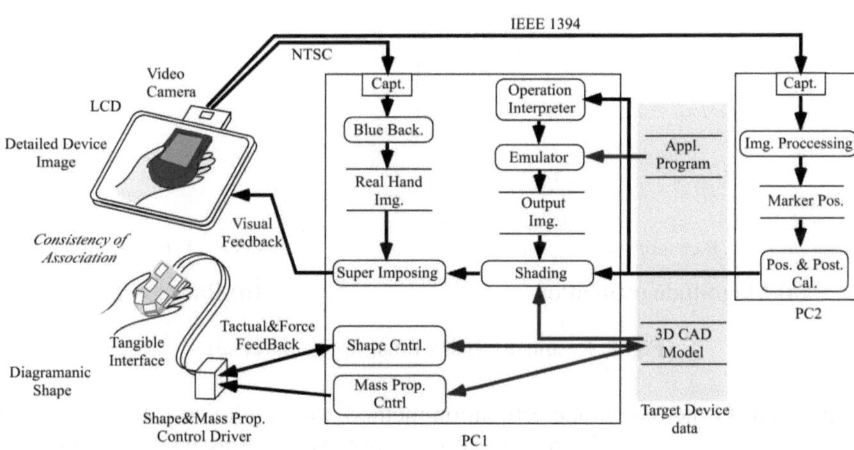


**Fig. 1.** Overview of Augmented Reality System for development of handy information Device

## 3 Tangible Interface

In this chapter, some characteristic of haptic perceptions relevant to the interface and the configuration of a tangible device is described.

### 3.1 Haptic Sensation of Hand

Width discrimination was investigated by A G Dietze et al[8]. The result was given as Weber's ratio:0.02 for clamping between thumb and index finger. Then it corresponds 1mm for 50mm width. S. Mcknight et al[9] reported that discrimination of radius of 5cm sphere by clamping between two fingers was 1.29mm. Two point discrimination threshold is thought as an indication for simplification of shape. It changes by the part of hand. Valbo A. B. et al[10] reported 1–3mm for fingertip, about 10mm for palm. It is considered that the roundness of the edge strongly affects perception of local shape for a product. So the sensation of the edge is measured by the experiment described as below:

Subjects: 4, male, twenties, right hand(right-handed)

Specimens: cylinders of Ø0.5,1.5,3,5,8,10,14,20 mm.

Load: 200g (including weight of the moving part)

Each specimen is fixed on the block, and vertically pushed on test region with the equipment composed of a linear slider.

Region(Dir): index fingertip(**L**,**T**), index finger cushion(**T**), palm/base of the thumb(**L**,**T**), Dir: **L**ongitudinal/ **T**ransversal.

Method: magnitude estimation(Ø0.5=1, Ø20=100, answered value: *E* ) rating scale method(None(N),Very Small(VS), Small(S), Slightly Small(SS), Slightly Large(SL), Large(L),Very Large(VL)).

Trial: random, 3 times, no visual information.

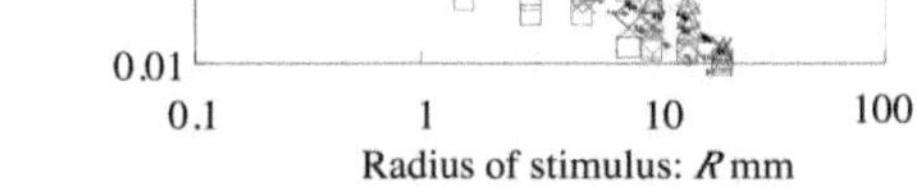


(a) Magnitude estimation

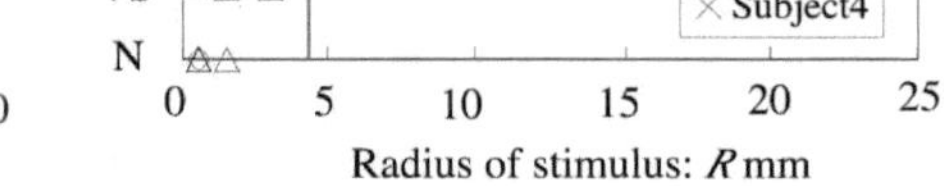


(b) Rating scale

**Fig. 2.** Results for Index fingertip(Transversal)

In the result of the magnitude estimation method, the involution rule is approved to the stimulation radius and the reciprocal of answer strength as well as other senses. The values are from -0.34 to -1.39. The most sensitive result index fingertip (transversal) is displayed in Fig. 2. From the result of the rating scale method, the stimulation not felt large was less than 5mm for the finger, and less than 3mm for the palm. When the display of detailed shape by the sight is compared with a sense of touch presentation of the outline shape, this value becomes important.

### 3.2 Interface Design

Checking specification of typical smart phones such as HP/iPaq hw6515, HTC/P4350, Palm/Treo 700w and RIM/Blackberry 8700g etc., the size of height is from about 110mm to 130mm, width is about from 55mm to 70mm, and depth is about from 15mm to 25mm. The weight is about from 135g to 220g. The outline shape of those is platy and the change in the main shape is contour.

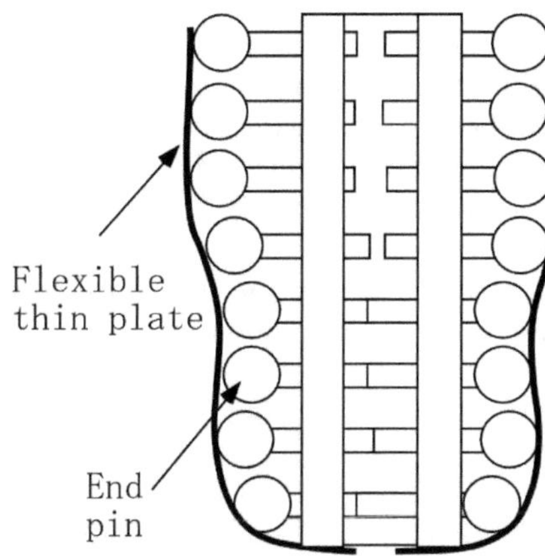


**Fig. 3.** Shape presentation method of tangible interface

The tangible interface displays the outline shape of a product by controlling the position of right and left eight end pins as shown in Fig. 3, and connecting between them with an flexible thin plate. The shape cannot be automatically changed, because the setting of the plate on the pin must be manually executed.

The position of end pin is controlled by a R/C servo motor and each pin is locked with the brake at an arbitrary position. The mechanism is shown in Fig. 4 and 5. The shaft connected with the end pin is passed through a release spring and the hole of the frame, and connected with the stroke control wire. The rotation of the shaft is locked by the plane on the cylindrical surface and the lock plate. The shaft is put between two brake plates, which is looped by a brake wire. The one end of the wire is fixed on the frame and the other end is connected to the R/C servo motor through a tension spring. The stroke of the end pin and the brake force are controlled by rotation angle of the R/C servo motor. The thickness between the bottom board and the top board is changed by the rack-and-pinion. There are 16 R/C servo motors for position control, 16 motors for brakes, and 2 motors for thickness control. So the shape of the device can change as follows: the end pin width is 50-70mm and the thickness are 14-24mm. And the weight of the interface is about 130g.

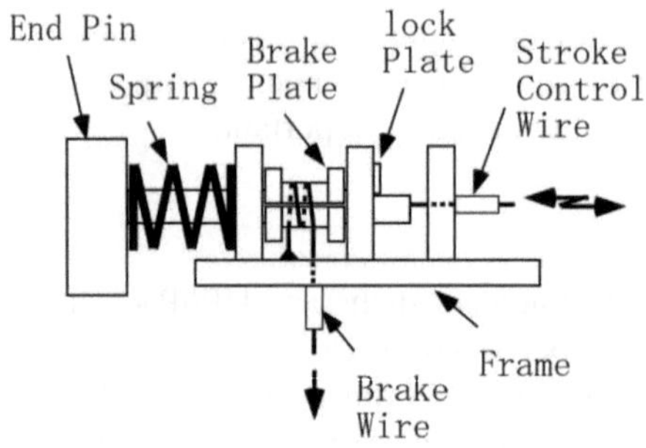


**Fig. 4.** Shape Control Mechanism

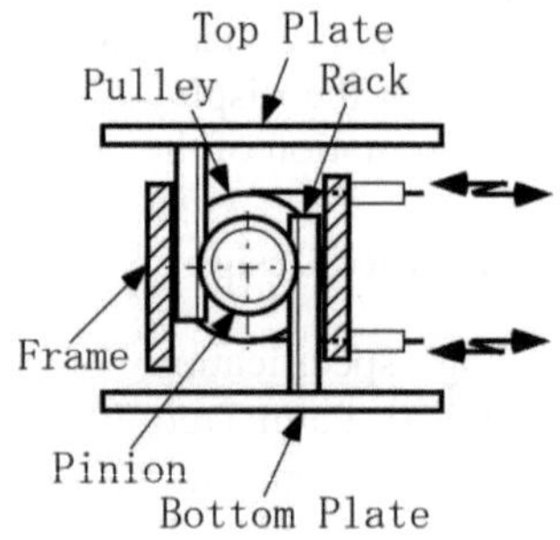


**Fig. 5.** Thickness Control Mechanism

The schematic of shape control system is shown in Fig.6. A R/C servo motor controller is able to control 12 R/C servo motors, then three motor drivers are used. The R/C servo motor controllers connect with a PC by daisy chain connection through RS232C signal line. Slack sensors are connected to I/O lines of a PIC. The PIC send the status of slack sensors to the control PC with a level converter IC through RS232C.

The maximum error of end pin positioning is 0.5mm, and it is thought that it is enough accuracy for man's perception resolution.

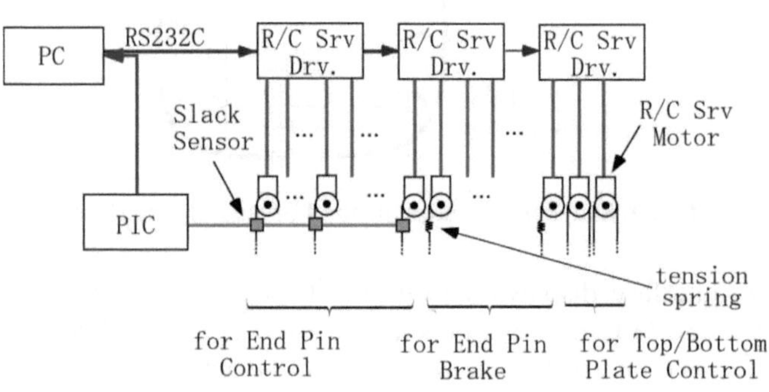


**Fig. 6.** Schematic of shape control system

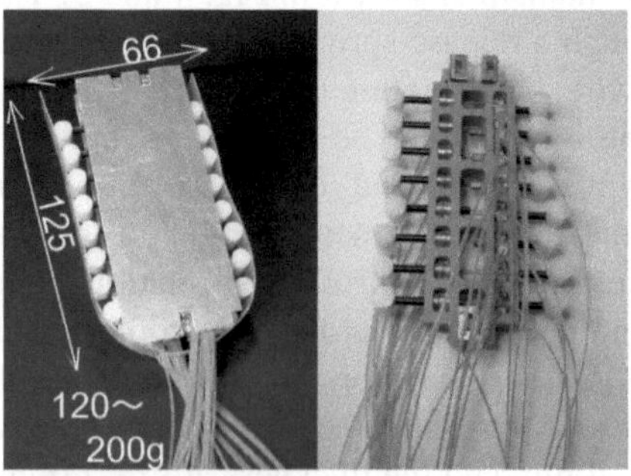


**Fig. 7.** Tangible interface

**Fig. 8.** R/C servo motor unit

# 4 Position and Posture Measurement System

The position and posture measurement of markers is executed in order of the extraction of marker's image from a screen of video streaming and the calculation of the marker coordinate in the world coordinate system. In this chapter, the principle of measurement and the digital image processing is described. Then the evaluation of the measurement system is described.

## 4.1 Principle of Position and Posture Measurement

There is few systems that can accurately and stably measure the position and posture in comparatively near field within arm's reach without receiving the influence of LCD and the motor. So a positional posture measurement system with two dimensional marker and a single camera was developed in this research.

The coordinate system is defined as shown in Fig. 9. There are three coordinate systems, world, screen and marker, each system is stand by right down subscript *w*,*s* and *m*, respectively. It assumes that the origin of the screen coordinate system is fitted to the origin of the world coordinate system. *L* means the distance between the screen and the reference point of the video camera.

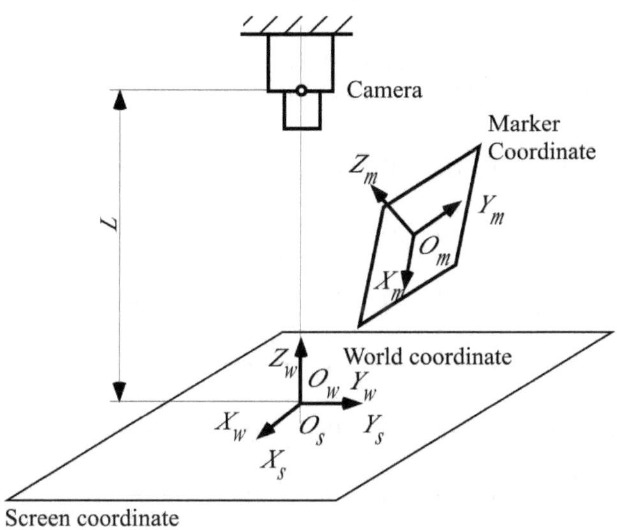


**Fig. 9.** Coordinate System

When the starting point position of the marker coordinate system is assumed to be $c_x$, $c_y$, and $c_z$ here, posture is shown with Roll-pitch-yaw angle $\theta_r$, $\theta_p$, and $\theta_y$, and the marker coordinates of n piece in the marker coordinate system are assumed to be $\mathbf{M}$ = [$A_0$, $A_1$, ... , $A_{n-1}$], the marker coordinates in the world coordinate system are expressed by the next equation. Each position is expressed in homogeneous coordinate, so the dimension is four.

$$ {}^{w}\mathbf{M} = \mathbf{Trans}\left(c_x, c_y, c_z\right)\mathbf{RPY}\left(\theta_r, \theta_p, \theta_y\right)\mathbf{M} \tag{1} $$

Here, **Trans**() and **RPY**() mean a homogeneous transformation matrix of translation and Roll-pitch-yaw, respectively. Therefore, the position of the markers on the screen coordinate is represented by

$$ {}^{s}\mathbf{M} = \mathbf{Proj}(L)\ {}^{w}\mathbf{M}\,, \tag{2} $$

where **Proj**() means perspective transformation matrix with one vanishing point.

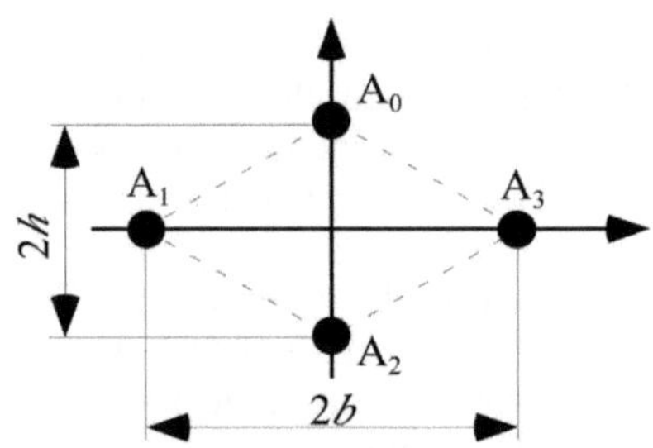


**Fig. 10.** Marker

The markers are set as shown in Fig.10. Is assumes that the position of the markers on the screen are represented by $x_{pi}, y_{pi}$, $i = 0,1,2,3$. From the Eq.(2),

$$ \begin{bmatrix} 1 & 0 & \frac{x_{p0}}{L} & 0 & h & 0 & 0 & 0 & \frac{h\,x_{p0}}{L} \\ 0 & 1 & \frac{y_{p0}}{L} & 0 & 0 & 0 & h & 0 & \frac{h\,y_{p0}}{L} \\ 1 & 0 & \frac{x_{p1}}{L} & -b & 0 & 0 & 0 & \frac{-b\,x_{p1}}{L} & 0 \\ 0 & 1 & \frac{y_{p1}}{L} & 0 & 0 & -b & 0 & \frac{-b\,y_{p1}}{L} & 0 \\ 1 & 0 & \frac{x_{p2}}{L} & 0 & -h & 0 & 0 & 0 & \frac{-h\,x_{p2}}{L} \\ 0 & 1 & \frac{y_{p2}}{L} & 0 & 0 & 0 & -h & 0 & \frac{-h\,y_{p2}}{L} \\ 1 & 0 & \frac{x_{p3}}{L} & b & 0 & 0 & 0 & \frac{b\,x_{p3}}{L} & 0 \\ 0 & 1 & \frac{y_{p3}}{L} & 0 & 0 & b & 0 & \frac{b\,y_{p3}}{L} & 0 \end{bmatrix} \begin{bmatrix} c_x \\ c_y \\ c_z \\ R_{00} \\ R_{01} \\ R_{10} \\ R_{11} \\ R_{20} \\ R_{21} \end{bmatrix} = \begin{bmatrix} x_{p0} \\ y_{p0} \\ x_{p1} \\ y_{p1} \\ x_{p2} \\ y_{p2} \\ x_{p3} \\ y_{p3} \end{bmatrix} \tag{3} $$

is obtained. Where $R_{ij}$ means an element of Roll-pitch-yaw matrix indexed by $i$ and $j$. Then rewrite this equation,

$$ \mathbf{C}\,\mathbf{X} = \mathbf{Y}\,. \tag{4} $$

By using psudo-inverse matrix $\mathbf{C}^{+} = \mathbf{C}^{T}(\mathbf{C}\,\mathbf{C}^{T})^{-1}$, Eq.(4) is solved by

$$\mathbf{X} = \mathbf{C}^{+}\mathbf{Y}. \tag{5}$$

This solution gives the ratio of each variable

$$\mathbf{X} = \lambda \begin{bmatrix} c_x & c_y & c_z & R_{00} & R_{01} & R_{10} & R_{11} & R_{20} & R_{21} \end{bmatrix}^T \tag{6}$$

However, from Eq.(6) the following equations are obtained,

$$tan\theta_r = \frac{R'_{10}}{R'_{00}} = \frac{\lambda\, R_{10}}{\lambda\, R_{00}}, \quad tan\theta_p = -\frac{R'_{20}}{R'_{00}} cos\,\theta_r = -\frac{\lambda\, R_{20}}{\lambda\, R_{00}} cos\,\theta_r. \tag{7}$$

Therefore,

$$\lambda = \frac{R'_{00}}{cos\theta_r\, cos\,\theta_p}, \quad \theta_y = sin^{-1}\left(\frac{R'_{21}}{\lambda\, cos\,\theta_p}\right). \tag{8}$$

At last, all unknowns are solved

$$C_x = \frac{C'_x}{\lambda}, \quad C_y = \frac{C'_y}{\lambda}, \quad C_z = \frac{C'_z}{\lambda}. \tag{9}$$

### 4.2 Implementation

In order to get marker's position and orientation, the image of a markers are extracted from a scene of the video, then calculation is done, as follows:

1. Binarizing: A scene is captured from the video, then the image is converted to binary image based on brightness information.
2. Labeling: The binarized image has some domains, each domains are labeling by modified border following method.
3. Selecting: The marker images are identified from the labeled domains by area and circle-ness of domains. The circle-ness is defined by a ratio between area and border length.
4. Calculation: The position and posture is calculated from the marker positions by above principle.

These procedures are implemented by using Directshow API which is one of multimedia expansions of Direct-X.

### 4.3 Evaluation of Measurement System

In order to evaluate this algorithm, the measurement was done in the 135 kinds of conditions, position: $C_z$=225,250,275mm, $C_x$, $C_y$=-25, 0, and 25mm, posture: $\theta_r$, $\theta_p$, $\theta_y$ = -20, 10, 0, and 20° , by using the machining center: Toyoda Machine Works PV-5 with a swiveling angular table and an inverted fluorescent light. In this measurement, the marker of B:55mm H:40 and radius:10mm was used. And the camera distortions had been calibrated by the method based on the work[11].

The average position error of $C_x$, $C_y$ and $C_z$ was 0.2mm, and maximum error was 0.43mm. The average posture error of $\theta_r$, $\theta_p$, and $\theta_y$ was 0.09°, 0.27°, and 0.4°, respectively. These measurement were done within video frame rate.

# 5 System Construction

The systems mentioned above were integrated, and system construction was done. The Clie (Palm OS) emulator was adopted as a target device. The input of the target device is executed as follows; The position on a virtual device of the thumb is calculated from the location information of the marker put on the thumb, and tap operation timing confirmed as an input from the keyboard on the system. Then the cursor on the emulator is moved according to the calculated position and mouse event is executed. Other specifications are follows:

PC1:CPU:Athlon XP3000+/2GB/GPU:NVIDIA GeForce6600/Windows XP
PC2:CPU:Pentium IV3.8GHzX2/2GB/GPU:NVIDIA Quadro FX1400/Windows XP
Video Camera: Sony Handy cam DCR-PC110.

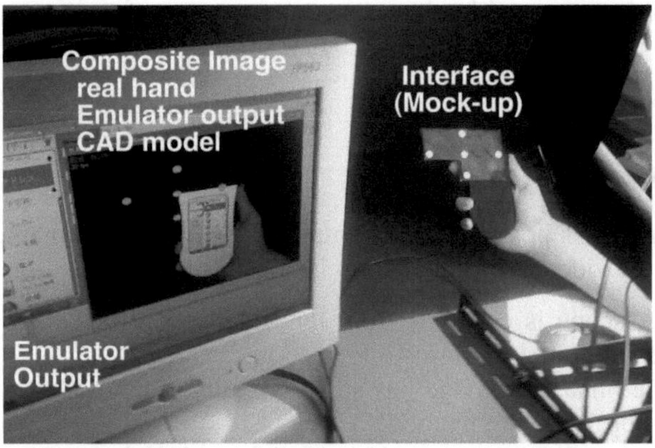


**Fig. 11.** Operating situation of system

A basic operation experiment was conducted by using this system, and it confirmed the following;

1. It synchronizes with the movement of the interface and a virtual model with the hand image moves by the video frame rate.
2. The action of the target device can be imitated by the operation similar to a real machine on this system.

# 6 Conclusions and Future Work

In order to realize efficiently product development for handy information device, an augmented reality system with a tangible interface is proposed and proto-typed. The basic characteristics are described.

In the future, the influence on the shape perception of the difference between sight information and sense of touch information will be quantitatively evaluated by using this system. And the effectiveness of this system in the product development will be evaluated.

## References

1. Endo, Y., Kanai, S., et al.: A development of a system for Ergonomic design by integrating a digital hand with product models(4th Report) (in Japanese) pp. 23–24(2006)
2. Horiuchi, S., Kanai, S., et al.: A research on usability assessment system using digital prototype for information appliances, 2006 The Japan Society for Precision Engineering (in Japanese) pp.26–27 (2006)
3. Iwata, H.: Artificial Reality with Force-Feedback: Development of Desktop Virtual Space with Compact Master Manipulator. ACM SIGGRAPH 2(4), 165–170 (1990)
4. Kimishima, Y., Aoyama, H.: Evaluation method of style design by using mixed reality technology, 2006 The Japan Society for Precision Engineering,(in Japanese) pp. 26–27 (2006)
5. Walairacht, S., Koike, Y., Sato, M.: A New Haptic Display for Both-Hands-Operation: SPIDAR-8; ISPACS'99 In: 1999 IEEE International Symposium on Intelligent Signal Processing and Communication Systems, Phuket, Thailand, pp. 569–572 (1999)
6. http://www.immersion.com/3d/products/cyber_grasp.php
7. Ono, N., Yano, H., Iwata, H.: Image projection to the Volumetric Display, TVRS,10,2, (in Japanese), pp. 209–216 (2005)
8. Dietze, A.G.: Kinesthetic discrimination: The difference limen for finger span (1961)
9. McKnight, S., Melder, N., Barrow, A.L., Harwin, W.S., Wann, J.P.: Psychophysical Size Discrimination using Multi-fingered Haptic Interfaces (2004)
10. Valbo, A.B., Johanson, R.S.: The tactile sensory innervation of glabrous skin of the human hand. In: Gordon, G. (ed.) Active Touch. 2954, Pergamon Press, New York (1978)
11. Tsai, R.Y.: A Versatile Camera Calibration Technique for High-Accuracy 3D- Machine Vision Metrology Using Off-the-Shelf TV Cameras and Lenses, IEEE Journal of Robotics and Automation,vol. RA-3(4) (1987)

# Which Prototype to Augment? A Retrospective Case Study on Industrial and User Interface Design

Jouke Verlinden[1], Christian Suurmeijer[2], and Imre Horvath[1]

[1] Delft University of Technology, Faculty of Industrial Design Engineering, Landbergstraat 15, 2628 CE, Delft, The Netherlands
{j.c.verlinden,i.horvath}@tudelft.nl
[2] Benchmark Electronics, Lelyweg 10, 7602 EA Almelo, The Netherlands
christian.suurmeijer@bench.com

**Abstract.** Emerging augmented reality and tangible user interface techniques offer great opportunities towards delivering rich, interactive prototypes in product development. However, as most of these are evaluated outside the complexity of. Design practice, little is known about the impact of these prototypes on the resulting product or the process. As a part of a larger multiple-case study approach, this study attempts to explore cues to characterize and improve the design practice of information appliances by performing a retrospective case study. The development of a handheld digital oscilloscope was chosen as an exemplar, embodying complexity in both form giving, interaction and engineering aspects. Although some of the employed techniques have grown obsolete, reflection on this development project still forecasts interesting and useful issues that should be considered while developing new design support methods and techniques.

**Keywords:** Information Appliances, Industrial Design, Case Study, Design Support.

## 1 Introduction

Tangible Prototypes and scale models play an important role in the design of physical artifacts. In the field of Industrial Design, ergonomic, aesthetic, mechanic, and manufacturing aspects all need consideration and physical models are often used for exploration, verification, communication, and specification. As summarized in the following section, the combination of physical and virtual artifact models offers new opportunities. It could improve the outcome of the design process, creativity of the designer, and innovativeness of the product. Our focus is on so-called Augmented Prototyping technologies that include principles of projection or video mixing to establish a dynamic prototype at a relatively low cost. We have implemented a number of such systems. This collection has a use of Augmented Prototyping, although a robust evaluation and comparison of other prototyping means is lacking. The resulting systems also showcase the power of tangible computing as natural, embodied interaction. Of course, the use of physical mockups are not a necessary

R. Shumaker (Ed.): Virtual Reality, HCII 2007, LNCS 4563, pp. 574–583, 2007.

condition for success; for example Schrage [11] argues that the insistence of using full size clay models impeded American car manufacturers in maintaining their domestic market share in favor of foreign companies that switched to rapid/virtual prototyping techniques. This leads to our primary interest in question what these advanced prototyping technologies offer for current and future design practice.

| Category | Geometric Modeling | Interactive Painting | Layout Design | Information Applicances | Automotive Design | Augmented Engineering |
|---|---|---|---|---|---|---|
| Impression |  |  | 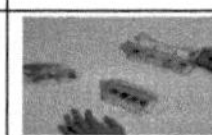 |  |  |  |
| Functionality | General-purpose 3D modeling of surfaces. | 2D painting on 3D surfaces. | Real-time simulations projected on floor plans. | Projection of screens on physical mockup, supporting interaction. | Projections on clay or foam models. | Visualization of engineering aspects in physical context. |
| Application fields | Sculpting/ detailing of shapes. | Exploration of styling curves, material/texture study. | Urban planning, interior architecture. | Usability testing. | Principle styling curves, component selection, material/color exploration. | Simulation of behavior, manufacturing aspects. |

**Fig. 1.** Existing Augmented Prototyping Applications (adapted from [13])

### 1.1 Emerging Prototyping Technologies

The concept of Augmented Prototyping employs mixed reality technologies to combine virtual and physical prototypes. One of the objectives is to create product models with an embodied/tangible high level of engagement and with a shorter manufacturing time than high-fidelity physical prototypes. At present, a collection of Augmented Prototyping systems have been devised, which can be summarized in the following categories: Geometric Modelling, Interactive Painting, Layout design, Information Appliances, Automotive design, and Augmented Engineering. These are summarized in Figure 1, more details and references are specified in [13]. Of particular interest are the Information Appliances, which are difficult to evaluate with solely physical or virtual prototypes – augmentation to project the screen helps in assessing both physical and cognitive ergonomics. Furthermore, it enables easy rearrangement of keys or exploring interaction techniques (joysticks, touch screens).

From the field of tangible user interfaces, the disposal of physical sensors and actuators or "phidgets" [5] extend the capabilities to simulate and evaluate product interaction. Systems as Switcheroo [1], Calder [8] and [7] offer less cumbersome systems by using passive or active RF wireless communications. STCtools [10] and d.tools [6] offer platforms to model and evaluate interaction on physical mock-ups in the conceptual design stage. Both Kanai and Ayoama [12] present usability measurement methods to fine-tune operability by statistical analysis, which makes sense in detailing stages of design.

Other categories from Figure 1 that are relevant in this discussion are Interactive painting and layout design; both illustrate the naturalness of the interaction, while complicated simulations can be included. For example the Urp system projected calculated shadows, reflections, and wind turbulence on a urban design plan; when buildings were moved, the virtual simulations were updated in real-time. For industrial design engineering, one could extend such simulations to for example mould flow simulations or finite element analysis.

### 1.2 Multiple Case Study Approach

Although the technologies described in the previous section offer appealing solutions, there is a lack of knowledge on how such advanced prototyping technologies are assessed in practice. Most studies evaluate systems with small groups of people, solely relying on students, and cannot reflect on the overall impact such means has on the design process. The usefulness of such techniques in a design or engineering setting is of a different order than testing internal validity of a tool. Amongst others, Gill et al [4] involves professional design teams, but only for specific activities, which is difficult to judge in complex product realization.

We chose the method of multiple case studies to produce a deep and accurate account of all prototyping and modeling activities [14]. Our approach harbors two types of case studies ("pre"and "post"). In the "pre" phase, three different product realization processes are empirically followed (see following section). These represent a range of industrial design engineering domains, which were considered to be susceptible to support by interactive augmented prototyping [13]. The chosen design domains are: 1) Information Appliances, 2) Automotive, and 3) Furniture. At present, the three "pre"case studies are being finalized. This specific article reports on the case study on Information Appliances, focused on the development of a handheld oscilloscope sold by a large measurement maker in the United States. However, due to the fact that not all conclusions could be finalized, the main contribution of this article is to indicate the complexity of such product development processes and the variety of prototypes. After a short description on the case study approach, we will report on the project characteristics and its implicit complexity. The type of product also yields specific bottlenecks, which are described in section 4. Section 5 contains preliminary conclusion and a specification of future work.

## 2 Retrospective Case Approach

The research questions formulated in the introduction section are stated as "how" and "why", suggesting investigations of exploratory, descriptive or explanatory nature. In particular, the instrument of case studies seems to be applicable. As described by Yin [15], a crucial aspect of case study is the combination of the multiple sources of evidence (triangulation). Observations, artifact models, documentation, interviews are all be consulted to establish causal relationships. This provides a means for internal validation. Furthermore, the case study requires a case study protocol: a public document that acts as an agreement on what will be studied between investigator and the subject/company of interest. This section will discuss the details of this specific study.

### 2.1 Case Selection

Our criteria for case selection were: i) The domain should be identifiable with industrial design engineering products and processes, ii) the domains can be accessed by the researcher in terms of time, resources and openness, iii) the selection of cases should cover a diverse range of products. In meeting the second criterium, finding a representative case in the field of information appliances proved to be difficult, as most developing products are shielded from competitors and external observers are not allowed. As a matter of fact, the only remaining option was to select a product development process that had finalized. In the context of the product design portfolio of the particular manufacturer, we specifically selected the first comprehensive handheld digital oscilloscope – offering both color and black and white LCD displays -as a representative and well-documented example. The resulting product (which is still on the market today) has increased the reputation of the company's brand while the development included a number of design and engineering challenges. As this product development process happened between 1996 and 1999, the developed case study protocol had to be adapted to cater for an historic analysis. The second author acted as the main guide to this process, he was involved in various aspects of the product development as industrial designer. He re-established contact with other former team members/stakeholders and provided access to archived material.

### 2.2 Sources of Evidence

Information sources for this study comprised of the following: 1) The existing product, 2) interviews with several people of the original design team, including the lead user interface designer and industrial designer, 3) Archived documentation: product specifications (both UI and electrical engineering), several versions of the product development schedule and related resource planning, and 4)Several product and services commercial material with references to this particular product development process. In a period of three months, these data were studied and meetings were planned with former stakeholders. The findings of the study will be presented for verification to all key stakeholders (in principle, the lead industrial and interaction designers). Furthermore, the bottlenecks will be validated by an external expert committee, which will consider the multiple cases in order to harmonize and differentiate bottlenecks and further cues for Interactive Augmented Prototyping. The strategy and procedure of this component has been specified in [14].

### 2.3 Case Study Components

As Yin specifies, common components of case studies are: 1.) a study's questions (typically 'how' and 'why' questions), 2) its propositions, if any, 3) its units of analysis (measures), 4) the logic thinking the data to the propositions, and 5) criteria for interpreting the findings [15]. The case specific questions, closely associated with anticipated results and data collection methods are presented in the Table 1.

## 3 Handheld Oscilloscope Design and Realization Processes

The client in this case was a large electronic measurement and diagnostics devices manufacturer. Its brand has a reputation for portability, ruggedness, safety, ease of use and rigid standards of quality. The company in question already had a handheld digital multi-meter with some oscilloscope functions. By demand of the customer base, a dedicated oscilloscope seemed a logical extension of the existing product range. The handheld oscilloscope is intended to be used by service personnel to perform all types of diagnostics in the field. The whole project can be characterized as a typical human-centered design project; it featured usability engineering techniques like concept testing (in focus groups), paper prototyping, and virtual prototyping evaluation on PCs with physical mockups attached. [9]. Most of these evaluations were facilitated by external UI evaluation experts and took place in the United States, as the prospective users were considered to be more outspoken and less trained (i.e. more faultfinding) than Europeans.

**Table 1.** Pre Case study analysis structure

| *Case study question (and related propositions)* | *Result* | *Data collection methods* |
|---|---|---|
| When in the design process are concept utterances generated and used? (P1) | Timeline with design representations | Interviews, planning inspection, pictures of prototypes, design services presentations.. |
| What are the characteristics of these concept utterances? (P2, P5) | List of characteristics | Structured interviews of stakeholders, confrontations with visual materials, product inspection |
| Which product modeling aspects play a role in these utterances? (P1, P4) | List of aspects per prototype | Structured interviews, |
| What topics are dealt with as group activities? Who are involved? (P3) | Addition to the timeline of topics: product modeling aspects and who is involved. | Planning documents, interviews |
| Which bottlenecks occurred during concept uttering? | Collection of bottlenecks, tied to list of concept utterances and timeline/activities. Classification of bottlenecks (impact on overall process) | Product inspection, interviews with stakeholders, process reflections. |

**Table 2.** Product development timeline

| *Design phase* | *Start date* | *Activities* | *Prevalent Design representations* |
|---|---|---|---|
| Market study | March 1996 | Exploration market opportunity | -design sketches<br>-rough foam models<br>-interface on paper |
| Definition | July 1997 | Validation of initial concept: technology, market and user research | -3d renderings<br>- foam models<br>- paper test model |
| Conceptualization | March 1998 | Creation of design concepts and design specifications. | - machined sight model<br>- 3d cad surface model<br>- interaction simulation on laptop with ' foilkeys' on front (connected to laptop)<br>- state transition charts for specifying interaction. |
| Detailing | April 1999 | Implementing all relevant aspects of software/hardware. | -Stereolithography model<br>-Casted models<br>-Software alpha release tested with users |

The development project timeline is depicted in Table 2. It was based on the structured development method that defined milestones, to deliverables and responsibilities.

The design of the handheld digital oscilloscope included accessories, packaging, and documentation. In particular, new measurement probes were developed in a modular fashion (fitting a multitude of interchangeable tips). Furthermore, the official black and white display was extended by a color version. This mainly affected graphical design, although the size of the screen was increased a few millimeters, which required changes in the key layout. After this project, other alterations of the oscilloscope were developed to suit specific tasks, e.g. power quality measurement and servicing MRI/CT scanners.

### 3.1 Stakeholders

The development team of this product represented a large number of disciplines. The stakeholders and their most significant information exchange paths are shown in Figure 2. This includes Industrial Design (ID), User Interface Design (UID), Product Planning (product marketing), core technology research and development (technology Innovation), Sales, Mechanical Engineering (ME), Software Engineering (SE), Electrical Engineering (EE), Factory Engineering (FE), and packaging. Not depicted in the figure are project planning and prospective clients. Most stakeholders were employees and had experience with project-based organizations.

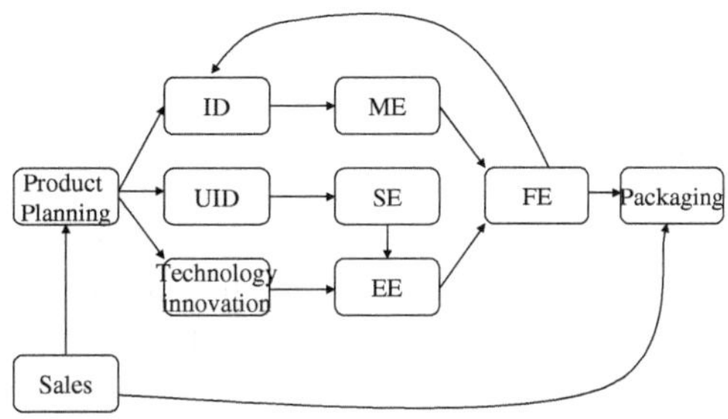


**Fig. 2.** Flow among internal stakeholders during the development process

The followed development method defined clear boundaries and interfaces between these groups. The product-planning representative steered both the design and technical development. For the technical innovation, this included the development of new sampling and processing chips (ASICs, DSPs), graphical processing units and related custom-made components. For the Interface Design the focus was on the product housing and the button layout. Past products had rather conservative form factors, which were considered to be outdated by the product planning. For User Interface Designers, the main responsibility was to develop a function requirements and a function hierarchy that would best fit the tasks of electronics diagnostics in the field. The development progressed in three parallel tracks with little interaction, delivering the physical design to the Mechanical Engineers, the User Interface Design to the Software Engineers, and the specialized components to the electronics engineers. The end result was then forwarded to the factory engineers who were responsible for the shop floor planning, manufacturing preparation and so on. Some additional information flows can be identified, namely the dimensional data to the packaging department, the involvement of the sales department in both marketing and packaging aspects, and the consultation of the Factory Engineers by the Industrial Designers to test the manufacturability of particular designs. Unfortunately, our case study has not yet evaluated this development process. In its complexity and diversity of disciplines, one could assume to find a number of conflicts of interest among the groups, or particular cultural aspects that influence the decision making process. Such aspects are worthwhile to investigate, as advanced prototyping systems could visualize or bridge those gaps and to find consensus or to acknowledge a certain degree of pluralism.

## 3.2 Design Challenges

In our initial interviews with the industrial and user interface design representatives, the following topics were considered to be large challenges in the development of this particular product.

- Fitness to task; The task analysis and related navigation structure and mental maps have been given a lot of attention by the user interface designers.
- Making a complex tool accessible to lower educated users. Simple and flat navigation structure was essential for the success of this product
- Screen layout; the limited resolution was a primary concern from start. Font design and graphical layout of presenting measurement data took a considerable amount of time, as extreme conditions (large numbers or information) had to be considered. The introduction of the color version ignited a (unavoidable) repetition of this effort.
- Grasping, ergonomics; as the handheld microscope has a considerable weight (2 kilograms) and size (26x17x6 cm) while the usage context can be quite harsh, the ease of grasping and holding the device for longer periods of time is important. Extra straps and holders were devised to cater for such requirements.
- Button layout; careful placement and size of the keys was crucial. As the digital oscilloscope has more advanced functions than analogue ones (e.g. storing and recalling measurement data, filters and triggering), the keys cannot be directly copied from analogue counterparts. Furthermore, there were technical constraints in locating soft keys as close to the display as possible.
- Probes; the use of the oscilloscope is not limited to operating the console (keys). Picking and touching the intended signals is of crucial, being able to shift between tips and clamps when necessary. Safety regulations also introduced extra complexities, as outdoor measurement of high voltages/frequencies requires physical barriers.

Although this study is unfinished, the design challenges show resemblance to other handheld appliances.

## 3.3 Characteristics of the Employed Prototypes

Based on planning documents and interviews, we could recreate the following overview of physical models shown in Table 3. We have disregarded all specific prototypes geared towards electronics engineering. In the use, we differentiated between exploration (diverging), verification (evaluation), communication, and specification objectives, as proposed by Geuer [3]. Based on project planning and memory recollection, the amount of prototypes and the duration that it took to develop and use them was estimated. In further discussions, we tried to differentiate the impact that these prototypes had on the development of the handheld oscilloscope. It is interesting to relate the impact to its use, explorative and verifying types of prototypes seem to have a larger significance on the project than specification models. However, this strongly depends on the definition of "impact", something that we will revisit extensively in the cross case analysis (not in this paper). Based on the judgment of the second author, coverage of aspects and fidelity level for each of these prototypes has been estimated; this is depicted in the Appendix.

**Table 3.** Prototype characteristics

| *Type* | *Use* | # | *Duration (lead+lifetime)* | *Impact on project* |
|---|---|---|---|---|
| Sketch prototype (foam) | Exploration of dimensions and overall shape. | 10 | 2 weeks | Large |
| User interaction prototype (PC-based simulation with physical keys on mockup) | Verification and specification of User Interface. | 1 | 2 months | Little |
| User experience prototype ( milled) | Specification and communication of shape details and surface tuning | 1 | 2 months | Little |
| Mechanical prototype (SLA) | Exploration of inside construction | 3 | 3 months | Medium |
| Test prototype (PU vacuum casting) | Specification of shell parts. | 1x20 | 2 months | Little |
| FOOT/SOOT (first/second out of tool) | Exploration in tolerancing and material finish ("feel"). | 2 | 4 months | Little |
| Null series (moulded) | Verification of software and manufacturing | 50 | 4 months | Large |

The interviewed design stakeholders expressed some additional remarks on strengths and weaknesses of these prototypes. A main weakness of the sketch prototypes (foam mockups) is that it does not support exploration of the graphical user interface and interactive behavior; the user interaction prototype had an extremely large lead-time and was not easily adapted. Conversely, this PC-based simulation did offer a good platform for usability analysis (related to the user's tasks) and acted as a concise specification of the UI for the software engineers. The User Experience prototype functions as a "design freeze", at approximately 80% of completion of the design aspects. The resulting milled mockups acted as a good internal promotion material and yielded managerial commitment.

Some of these statements can be translated in requirements for prototyping tools, many of these are already supported partially by techniques discussed in section 1.1.

## 4 Bottlenecks in the Development Process

The retrospective case study has not yet been completed. Definite challenges and bottlenecks have yet to be verified and validated with similar design processes. Furthermore, the technology employed in this project has been subsided by more capable ones, in particular in the field of graphic design and industrial design.

Bottlenecks that could be alleviated by augmented reality systems include:

- The separation between prototypes for interaction and industrial design.
- Specific flexibility in key layout/control selection in consideration with technical feasibility of placement (collisions with internal components etc).
- Complexity of the process, although no related bottlenecks have been not found up to this date.
- Development of embedded graphical user interfaces, with limitations in resolution and size.

Furthermore, prototyping activities in the early part of the project seem to have had a larger impact (combined with their explorative nature). It is interesting to acknowledge that similar opportunities arise later on, at the FOOT/SOOT stage (First out of Tool/Second out of tool). As a final note, we should acknowledge that studying design scenarios of the present might not generate the best solutions for the future. Our only hope is that the inspection of a number of diverse product designs might identify blind spots.

## 5 Conclusions and Future Work

This article presented intermediate results of a retrospective case study, covering issues in both industrial and user interface design. Although the product itself is meant for a specialized target group (diagnostics of electronic equipment), the characteristics show similarities to other information appliances. In our quest to develop advanced prototyping techniques that have a positive impact on the overall development process, a number of bottlenecks have been identified from revisiting the material and interviews. However, this work has not been completed yet, more effort will be put in investigating issues on project complexity and organizational bottlenecks. Furthermore, the findings will be combined with the currently running case studies.

**Acknowledgments.** The authors would like to thank all people could contribute to this historical study, in particular Maarten van Alphen at Benchmark.

## References

1. Avrahami, D., Hudson, S.E.: Forming interactivity: a tool for rapid prototyping of physical interactive products, In: proceedings of DIS '02, 2002, pp. 141–146 (2002)
2. Dourish, P.: Where The Action Is: The Foundations of Embodied Interaction. MIT Press, Cambridge (2001)
3. Geuer, A.: Einsatzpotential des Rapid Prototyping in der Produktentwickelung. Springer Verlag, Berlin (1996)
4. Gill, S., Johnson, P., Dale, J., Loudon, G., Hewett, B., Barham, G.: The Traditional Design Process Versus a New Design Methodology: a Comparative Case Study of a Rapidly Designed Information Appliance. In: The Proceedings of the Human Oriented Informatics & Telematics Conference (2005)

5. Greenberg, S., Fitchett, C.: Phidgets: easy development of physical interfaces through physical widgets. In: proceedings of UIST '01, 2001, pp. 209–218 (2001)
6. Hartmann, B., Klemmer, S.R., Bernstein, M., Abdulla, L., Burr, B., Robinson-Mosher, A., Gee, J.: Reflective physical prototyping through integrated design, test, and analysis. In: Proceedings of UIST 2006, pp. 299–308 (2006)
7. Horiuchi, S., Kanai, S., Kishinami, T., Hosoda, S., Ohshima, Y., Shiroma, Y.A.: A new virtual design mockup for digital devices with operable GUI using RFID chip and Mixed Reality. In: Proceedings of Virtual Concept 2005, p. 154 (2005)
8. Lee, J.C., Avrahami, D., Hudson, S.E., Forlizzi, J., Dietz, P.H., Leigh, D.: The calder toolkit: wired and wireless components for rapidly prototyping interactive devices. In: Proceedings of DIS '04, pp. 167–175 (2004)
9. Mayhew, D.: The Usability Engineering Lifecycle. Morgan Kaufman, Seattle, Washington, USA (1999)
10. Nam, T.-J.: Sketch-Based Rapid Prototyping Platform for Hardware-Software Integrated Interactive Products. In: Proceedings of CHI'05, 2005, pp. 1689–1692 (2005)
11. Schrage, M.: Cultures of Prototyping. In: Winograd, T. (ed.) Bringing Design to Software, ACM Press, New York (1996)
12. Verlinden, J., Nam, T.-J., Aoyama, H., Kanai, S.: Possibility of applying Virtual Reality and Mixed Reality to the Human Centered Design and Prototyping for Information Appliances. In: Research in Interactive Design, vol. 2, Springer, Heidelberg (2006)
13. Verlinden, J., Horvath, I., Edelenbos, E.: Treatise of Technologies for Interactive Augmented Prototyping, In: Proceedings of Tools and Methods of Competitive Engineering (TMCE) 2006, pp. 523–536 (2006)
14. Verlinden, J., Horvath, I.: Framework for testing and validating Interactive Augmented Prototyping as a Design Means in Industrial Practice. In: Proceedings of Virtual Concept 2006 (2006)
15. Yin, R.: Case Study Research: Design And Methods. Sage Publications, United Kingdom (1988)


## Appendix: Specification of Prototyping Aspects

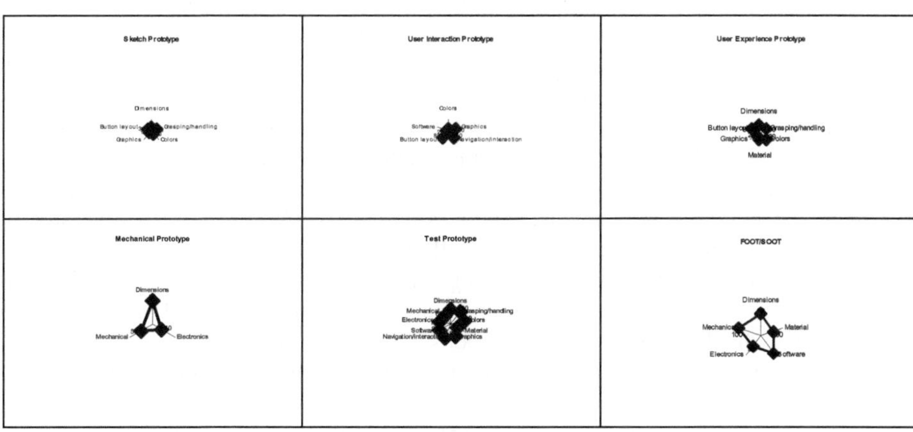

# Simulators for Driving Safety Study – A Literature Review

Ying Wang[1], Wei Zhang[1], Su Wu[1], and Yang Guo[2]

[1] Department of Industrial Engineering, Tsinghua University, Beijing 100084, China
[2] Intelligent Systems Center, University of Missouri - Rolla, Rolla, MO65401, USA
wang-ying03@mails.tsinghua.edu.cn

**Abstract.** Driving simulator is an important facility for driving safety study. This paper introduced three well-know large-scale moving-base driving simulators and two fixed-base simulators. Driving simulator has a broad range of applications of driving safety study, from driver's behavior study to vehicle device and technology study, the paper reviewed seven main research aspects including behavior study, driver education and training, transportation infrastructure, medicine and therapy, ergonomics, Intelligent Transportation System, and administrative method.

**Keywords:** Driving simulator; Driving safety; Moving-base; Fixed-base.

## 1 Introduction

Automobile driving simulator is a rather new application of computer technology compared to the flight simulator used in aerospace industry for almost fifty years. As the performance of computers has greatly improved, coupled with a drastic decrease in cost, it has made it possible for automotive industry to develop useful simulators of ground vehicles at a reasonable cost, relying instead on the use of actual vehicles for testing and development. In the early 1980s, the full-scale driving simulators developed by Daimler-Benz and the Swedish National Road and Transportation Research Institute (VTI) were of the most well-known in the world [1]. During the next 10 years, leading automobile manufacturers and research institutes like General Motors (GM), Ford, Mazda began to develop their own simulators one after another. At the end of 1993, National Highway Traffic Safety Administration (NHTSA, USA) developed the National Advanced Driving Simulator (NADS) in the University of Iowa, which cost more than 10 million dollars and was well-known as the largest simulator in the world. Today's driving simulators vary greatly for different applications, ranging from low-level inexpensive desktop-mounted systems with single-monitor display, to high-level expensive installations capable of replicating large amplitude driving motions with a moving base and detailed virtual driving environments[2].

The driving simulator has a broad range of applications from driver's behavior study to vehicle device technology study. Because it provides an environment that is both safe and replicable, driving simulator is ideal for driving safety study and driver

R. Shumaker (Ed.): Virtual Reality, HCII 2007, LNCS 4563, pp. 584–593, 2007.

training. The simulator can safely measure driver reaction to unsafe and even life-threatening situations [3]. Dutta et al. used a mid-level driving simulator to evaluate and optimize factors affecting understandability of various message signs [4]. Liu and Wen investigated the effects of two different display modes (head-up display (HUD) vs. head-down display (HDD)) on the driving performance and psychological workload ratings of drivers operating commercial vehicles in Taiwan [5]. Desktop driving simulators have also been used to investigate the situation awareness and workload in driving while using adaptive cruise control and cellular phones. By using driving simulators instead of driving on real roads, these studies eliminated the danger of accidents due to wrong operations or cellular phone distraction [2]. In addition, training of new drivers on a simulator eliminates the danger of wrong operations and allows the drivers to experience some designed dangerous situations. Simulators can be also used in carefully controlled experimental studies, in which the experimental variables are isolated from other factors that might influence driver performance [3]. For example, driving simulation is a useful way to evaluate road sign design. By measuring subjects' performance, one can quantitatively tell which design of road signs has the highest satisfaction and the best recognition and reaction of the testing drivers [6] [7].

The use of driving simulation for driving safety study is increasing with the reduction of simulator cost and the improvement of hardware/software technology. Software advances make it possible for researchers to design specific testing situations in a virtual environment. Nowadays, worldwide universities, research institutes and authorized organizations are using simulators in driving safety studies, just as NHTSA, VTI, University of Michigan Transportation Research Institute (UMTRI), University of Iowa, Monash University Accident Research Center (MUARC, Australia), and Institute for Transportation Studies in University of Leeds (UK). This paper will introduce several well-known large-scale simulators and other mid-level simulators, then review the use of simulators in driving safety studies.

# 2 Well-Known Simulators

Driving simulators are diversified from simple desktop fix-based one that costs only thousands dollars to large-scale moving-based one that costs up to millions of dollars. However, all of them can be well used for different purposes if technical parameters are well controlled.

## 2.1 NADS at the University of Iowa (USA) [8]

The National Advanced Driving Simulator (NADS) is the most sophisticated research driving simulator in the world. Developed by the NHTSA, and located at the University of Iowa's Oakdale Research Park, the NADS offers high-fidelity, real-time driving simulation. It consists of a large dome in which entire cars and the cabs of trucks and buses can be mounted. The vehicle cabs are equipped electronically and mechanically using instrumentation specific to their make and model. At the same time, the motion system, on which the dome is mounted, will provide 400 square meters of horizontal and longitudinal travel and nearly 360 degrees of rotation in either direction. The effect will be that the driver will feel acceleration, braking and steering cues as if he or she were actually driving a real car, truck or bus. Fig. 1 shows the configuration of the NADS.

**Fig. 1.** The NADS at University of Iowa

As a national leading simulator, the NADS was charged with many kinds of research projects and contributed a lot of valuable publications. They are focused on five research areas: a) driver distraction relating to wireless voice communication devices; b) driver behavior including young driver risk, driver validation and driver reaction to thread separation scenarios; c) drugs and driver impairment including vision validation test and pharmaceutical project; d) advanced vehicle system including electronic stability control, evaluating lane change collisions, safety vehicles using adaptive interface technology, agricultural virtual proving ground, and Crash Avoidance Metrics Partnership (CAMP); f) advanced simulation including visual database development, advanced simulator research consulting, and software support.

## 2.2 Simulator III at VTI (Sweden) [9]

Simulator III at the VTI was introduced in April 2004, after several years of intensive development work. Simulator III is built around a real vehicle chassis and a sophisticated motion system, which enables fast acceleration. The surroundings are simulated and displayed to the driver via three main screens and three rear view mirrors. Under the chassis is a vibration table to simulate contact with the road surface, providing a more realistic driving experience. The driving dynamics are also very advanced and on the forefront of what can be done with current technology. Together this creates a unique simulator that provides an extremely realistic experience. Because of the modular construction, the various subsystems can be adapted to suit the needs of each individual research project. The driving simulator can be fully adapted for private cars and trucks by means of a chassis interchange system. In the future, it will also be possible to use it to simulate rail traffic.

**Fig. 2.** Simulator III at the VTI, left-side is the appearance of simulator outside the dome, mid-side is the system control center, right-side is the view inside dome

The application of Simulator III was broad from studies concerning driver behavior, the human-machine interface and the effects of tiredness and drugs to projects concerning environmental issues, road and landscape design, tunnel design, the reactions of the body, drivers with reduced functionality and new subsystems in vehicles. The effects of noise and vibrations on driver performance are examples of other areas that may be studied using the simulator. One exciting area is how the new technology influences driving, for example the use of mobile telephones. VTI has performed this type of test in the simulator, which would have been impossible in a real traffic environment for safety reasons. Recently, the simulator has also been used for the planning of the Northern and Southern Link Roads in Stockholm, for example, in order to determine the positioning of road signs and for reasons of aesthetic design.

### 2.3 Other Moving-Base Simulators

Except the large-scale simulators with extendable motion area as NADS and VTI, most of other moving-base simulators were not so expensive and area consuming, although they are still much more costly and complex compared with fixed-base simulators. Many research institutes developed such kind of simulators, for example, Institute of Industrial Science in the University of Tokyo, driving simulator in VIVW at Würzburg University in Germany, National Institute of Advanced Industrial Science and Technology (Japan), and DaimlerChrysler Research Center. Fig. 3 is the simulator developed at the University of Tokyo. It was developed for human, vehicle and traffic research. It is equipped with a 360-degree omni-directional image generation system, 6 DOF motion platform with turn table and flexible layout cabin. A macroscopic and microscopic traffic simulation system is embedded into the driving simulator. That is called KAKUMO. KAKUMO can generate virtual traffic in the simulator scenario in real time, with up to 100 surrounding vehicles created and controlled independently [10].

### 2.4 Fixed-Base Simulators

Though fixed-base simulator is not as fabulous as the advanced moving-base one, its low cost and convenience makes it more popular in driving related research and training. In recent years, traffic safety issues got more and more attention both in academic area and administrative organizations, consequently, a great deal of universities and institutes purchased or developed driving simulators. However, due to limited resources, most of researchers could not afford such sophisticated moving-base one, then, fixed-base simulators become the better choice. On the other hand, despite continuous improvement in driving simulation techniques and equipment capabilities over the years, subjects in a driving simulator still interact with a simplified environment and perceive less as compared to real-world driving [8]. That is to say, although the fidelity of moving-base is attractive, whether human's behavior can be established better is not sure. Therefore, fixed-base simulators are also reliable and adoptable for human factors research.

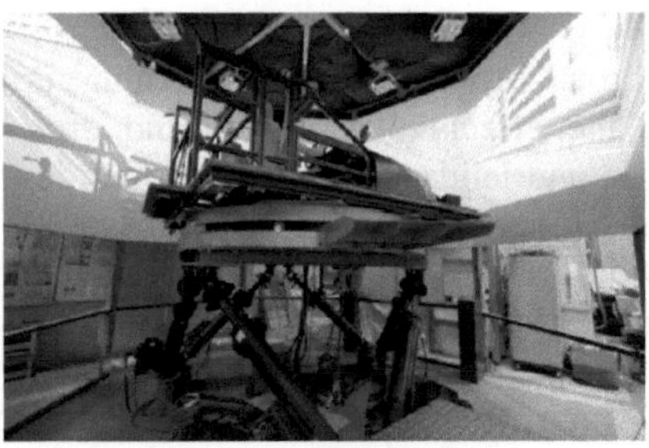

**Fig. 3.** The Universal Driving Simulator in the University of Tokyo

**Fig. 4.** Globalsim Simulator at UMTRI

**GlobalSim Simulator at UMTRI (USA) [11].** University of Michigan Transportation Research Institute (UMTRI) is a world-leading research institute in traffic safety area. GlobalSim DriveSafety Research Simulator is their primary simulator used for studies of in-vehicle devices (navigation systems, cell phones), driver workload, the effects of health on driving (e.g., Alzheimer's disease, driver age), and other topics.

The driving simulator has a full size vehicle cab with a touch screen center console, a computer-controlled, projected LCD speedometer/tachometer cluster, operating foot controls, and torque motor to provide realistic force feedback. The in-cab sounds are generated by software and presented by a 10-speaker system from a Nissan Altima, supplemented by a 4-speaker system for road sounds. To provide realism, the cab has limited vertical vibration, and for use in warning systems, a haptic feedback seat. Road scenes are projected on 3 forward screens almost 16 feet from the driver (120 degree field of view) and a rear channel 12 feet away (40 degree field of view). Each channel has a resolution of 1024x768 and updates at 60 Hz. Scenes are currently daytime only, though bad weather (fog, rain, snow) can be simulated. Traffic is programmable, either following the general rules of the road or as scripted. The vehicle dynamics can be changed. Driver and vehicle performance (steering wheel angle, speed, lane position, etc.) are recorded at up to 30 Hz by the main simulator computer. In addition, driver actions (their face, hands, the instrument panel feet and foot controls) and parts of the road scene can be recorded by an 8-camera video system onto a quad split image. Control is achieved using 8x4 and 16x16 video switchers, and a 12x4 audio mixer.

## 3 Driving Safety Study

As an important approach for driving safety study, driving simulators have been used by many researchers for a variety of studies. Table 1 shows the research issues of driving safety study using simulators. Some typical research literatures are reviewed in the following sub-sections.

**Table 1.** Driving safety study using driving simulators

| Number | Aspects of study | Study issues |
|---|---|---|
| 1 | Driver behavior study | |
| | | - Influence of distraction or impairment (cellular phone use, fatigue, etc.) |
| | | - Driving performance or behavior measurement (gap acceptance, lane change, speeding, passing vehicles, etc.) |
| | | - Characteristic of young drivers (risk taking, drinking) |
| | | - Collision |
| 2 | Education and training | |
| | | - Novice driver training |
| | | - Accident avoidance training |
| | | - Education of holding safe views in driving |
| 3 | Design and evaluation of transportation infrastructures | |
| | | - Traffic sign system |
| | | - Road markings, road-block, speed Hump and other infra on road |
| | | - Road surfaces, tunnel, bridge |
| 4 | Medicine and therapy application | |
| | | - Drugs and alcohol |
| | | - Clinical Trials Support |
| | | - Crash Biomechanics |
| 5 | Ergonomics and cognitive study | |
| | | - Visual and auditory obstacle in driving |
| | | - Haptic feedback on simulator |
| | | - Motion sickness |
| | | - Old drivers |
| 6 | Intelligent Transportation System (ITS) study | |
| | | - Adaptive Cruise Control system |
| | | - Head-Up Display and Head-Down Display |
| | | - Collision and accident warning system |
| | | - Other new in-vehicle technologies |
| 7 | Administrative method evaluation | |
| | | - Design and evaluation of the new policies |
| | | - Urban and rural traffic environment |

### 3.1 Driving Behavior Studies

**Influence of Distraction or Impairment.** Since conducting impaired driving test is risky on real road, many researchers have turned to use virtual driving simulation as the main approach. Wittmann et al. (2006) used driving simulation approach for evaluating the effects of visual display position on driving performance. To determine the relative safety of onboard display positions while driving, participants performed a lane-keeping task in a driving simulator. Concurrently, they reacted to a light by pushing the brake pedal. A secondary task was projected onto a display at one of the seven different locations in the cockpit. Behavioral data, eye movements, and subjective rating scales showed that the manipulation of display information during driving disturbed drivers' performance exponentially as a function of distance between the line of sight to the outside primary task and the onboard display position. Vertical eccentricity had a greater detrimental effect than horizontal distance. Under a certain condition with a high secondary task load, reaction time of pushing the brake to the outside stimulus nearly doubled with a diagonal eccentricity of 351 as compared to lower eccentricities. Subjective workload measures complement the behavioral data of clear detrimental effects with eccentricities of at least 351 [12]. Sung et al. (2005) used driving simulation for studying effects of oxygen concentrations on driver fatigue [13].

There are still lots of studies that investigate the influence of cellular phone use while driving in a simulator [14] [15]. These studies aim to understand how serious the distraction is due to cellular phone use. Simulator system can collect detailed driving performance data (e.g. gas control, brake control, steering, speed selection, etc.) and conduct quantitative study afterwards. The similarity of these studies is that both tests involve higher driving risks due to increased mental workload or impairment. It is needed to note that this kind of experiments can not be easily conducted in real driving condition due to risk concerns. So in this condition, driving simulation becomes a useful approach for this kind of performance measurement when there is risk effect.

**Driving Performance or Behavior Measurement.** Another kind of study using driving simulation is driving performance measurement. Real condition driving is difficult to track driver's operations while a simulator allows convenient collection of every operation data. For example, Salvucci, & Liu (2002) explored the time course of lane changing, including driver's control and eye movement behavior, using a fixed-base, medium-fidelity driving simulator and 11 participants. In the experiment, drivers were required to navigate a simulated multi-lane highway environment. Then the driver data were segmented into standardized units of time to facilitate an analysis of behavior before, during, and after a lane change. Results of this analysis showed that (1) drivers produced the expected sine-wave steering pattern except for a longer and flatter second peak as they straightened the vehicle; (2) drivers decelerated slightly before a pass lane change, accelerated soon after the lane change, and maintained the higher speed up until the onset of the return lane change; (3) drivers had their turn signals on only 50% of the time at lane-change onset, reaching a 90% rate only 1.5-2 s after onset; (4) drivers shifted their primary visual focus from the start lane to the destination lane immediately after the onset of the lane change. These results show that using simulators is an effective way of operation data collection. However, on the other hand, the result (1) also indicates that the steering behavior for driving in a simulated environment may have difference from driving a real vehicle. This implies that driving simulator fidelity or validity could be a research problem in order to make use of the measured data. If the validity is low, then the measured data is meaningless [16].

**Young Driver's Risk Taking.** Driving simulator is an ideal instrument to do experiments that was risky on real road. Leung (2005) conducted a single-blind randomized study with young and mature drivers to assess how age, combined with a modest dose of alcohol, influenced performance on a driving simulator. The driving tasks included detecting the presence of a vehicle on the horizon as quickly as possible, estimating the point on the road that an approaching vehicle would have passed by the participants' vehicle (time-to-collision) and overtaking another vehicle against a steady stream of oncoming traffic [17].

### 3.2 Design and Evaluation of Transportation Infrastructures

**Traffic Sign System.** Driving simulation is a useful method for traffic sign design and evaluation. By conducting evaluation in a virtual environment and allowing drivers drive in that simulator, it helps evaluate and optimize the sign in very early stage, accordingly reduces cost and improves design quality and usability. In a study conducted by Upchurch et al. (2002), the design and placement of exit sign of Boston Central Artery-Tunnel (Interstate 93) through downtown Boston was simulated and evaluated. Before the study, reconstruction of the Central Artery is needed to improve traffic operations by reducing the number of exits and entrances on Interstate 93 from the current 27 exits and entrances (two-directional total) over 3 mi to 14. Yet, the reduction of the exit signs may cause drivers-especially unfamiliar drivers to have difficulty obtaining guidance information for their exit. This can lead to driver frustration and a reduction in safety caused by abrupt lane changing and other maneuvers. To address these problems with improved sign design and placement, a study using a driving simulator was undertaken. A computer-generated roadway through the tunnel was developed to replicate the tunnel geometry (including horizontal and vertical curvature and ceiling height) and sign placement. Test subjects drove through the simulated tunnel to evaluate the developed signing alternatives [6].

### 3.3 Intelligent Transportation System Study

**Adaptive Cruise Control Systems (ACCs).** In contrast with the rapid developed new technology in automobile industry, driver's adaptation seems always far more behind. Hence, use of driving simulators to measure and evaluate the new in-vehicle devices is a wise choice for manufactures avoiding inconvenience in factual application. Hoedemaeker (1998) has conducted a study aimed at assessment of driver behavior in new technology at that time, particularly Adaptive Cruise Control Systems (ACCs). In this study, benefits and drawbacks of Adaptive Cruise Control Systems (ACCs) were assessed by having participants drive in a simulator. The four groups of participants taking part differed on reported driving styles concerning Speed (driving fast) and Focus (the ability to ignore distractions), and drove in ways which were consistent with these opinions. The results show behavioral adaptation with an ACC in terms of higher speed, smaller minimum time headway and larger brake force. Driving style group made little difference to these behavioral adaptations. Most drivers evaluated the ACC system very positively, but the undesirable behavioral adaptations observed should encourage caution about the potential safety of such systems [18].

### 3.4 Administrative Method Evaluation

Driving simulation has also been used for traffic administration measurement. In the study conducted by Uzzell and Muckle (2005), the change of driving behavior was observed in driving simulation. By testing different engineering solutions for "quiet lanes"program, different driving behaviors and effectiveness were observed and evaluated. The background of the study: The growth in motorized traffic on rural lanes in the UK has increased the dangers of, and dissuades people from, walking, cycling or horse riding on roads in the countryside. A UK Government initiative, "Quiet Lanes", aims to address this contra-sustainability development and make rural lanes safe and attractive for non-motorized users. Although traffic calming measures have been employed in urban areas, their translation into more environmentally sensitive rural areas has been problematic, largely on aesthetic grounds as they often have an urban appearance. Innovative solutions are necessary to reduce traffic speed but it would be prudent to assess experimentally the likely effectiveness and acceptability of any new measures before they are built. This paper discusses the use of simulated environments by means of manipulated color photographs to predict changes in driving behavior associated with changing road environments. It was found that respondents were able to differentiate between the different simulated engineering solutions and their suggested driving behavior accurately reflected that associated with road use under similar conditions elsewhere [19].

## 4 Conclusions

Using driving simulator is becoming a more and more important approach for driving safety study due to its advantages, such as safety, low cost, repeatability and controllability for experiment. Due to the rapid progress of computer technology, a lot of advanced driving simulators were developed for improving transportation research, such as the NADS and VTI. Meanwhile, many research institutes who are professional on transportation and accidents study support the development of simulators and road safety powerfully, such as the NHTSA, UMTRI and MUARC. It can be predicted that more and more people will share the benefits from driving simulators with the technological upgrading of high-level simulators, and wide spread of mid-level or low-level simulators.

## References


1. Yoshimoto, K., Suetomi, T.: The History of Research and Development of Driving Simulator in Japan. In: Proceedings of Driving Simulation Conference Asia/Pacific, 2006 ,Tsukuba, Japan (2006)
2. Wang, Y., Zhang W., Zhang, E.D., Zeng, H., Leu, M.C.: Development of A Low-cost Driving Simulation System for Safety Study and Training. In: Proceedings of Driving Simulation Conference Asia/Pacific 2006, Tsukuba, Japan (2006)
3. Technical Specifications for the Simulator from the Driver Simulator Laboratory Center for Intelligent Systems Research, (2006) http://www.cisr.gwu.edu/lab_simulator.html

4. Dutta, A., Fisher, D.L., Noyce, D.A.: Use of a Driving Simulator to Evaluate and Optimize Factors Affecting Understandability of Variable Message Signs. Transportation Research Part F 7, 209–227 (2004)
5. Liu, Y.C., Wen, M.H.: Comparison of Head-up Display (HUD) vs. Head-down Display (HDD): Driving Performance of Commercial Vehicle Operators in Taiwan. Int. J. Human-Computer Studies 61, 679–697 (2004)
6. Upchurch, J., Fisher, D.L., Carpenter R.A., Dutta, A.: Freeway Guide Sign Design with Driving Simulator for Central Artery-Tunnel:Boston Massachusetts. Transportation Research Record, n 1801, 02-2981, 9–17 (2002)
7. Dutta, A., Carpenter, R.A., Noyce, D.A., Susan, S.A., Fisher, D.L.: Drivers' Understanding of Overhead Freeway Exit Guide Signs: Evaluation of Alternatives with Advanced Fixed-base Driving Simulator. Transportation Research Record, n 1803, 02-2618, 102–109 (2002)
8. The National Advanced Driving Simulator at University of Iowa.: http://www.nads-sc.uiowa.edu/
9. VTI, Swedish National Road and Transportation Research Institute.: http://www.vti.se/templates/Page_3257.aspx
10. Suda, Y., Shladover, S.E., Takahashi, Y., Onuki, M., Matsushita, K., Kanoh, M., Honda, K., Shiraishi, T.: Validation of the Universal Driving Simulator with Interactive Traffic Simulation. In: Proceedings of Driving Simulation Conference Asia/Pacific 2006, Tsukuba, Japan (2006)
11. University of Michigan Transportation Research Institute.: http://www.umtri.umich.edu
12. Wittmanna, M., Kiss, M., Gugg, P., Steffen, A., Fink, M., Pöppel, E., Kamiya, H.: Effects of Display Position of a Visual In-Vehicle Task on Simulated Driving. Applied Ergonomics 37, 87–199 (2006)
13. Sung, E.J., Min, B.C., Kim, S.C., Kim, C.J.: Effects of Oxygen Concentrations on Driver Fatigue during Simulated Driving. Applied Ergonomics 36, 25–31 (2005)
14. Liu, Y.C.: Effects of Taiwan In-Vehicle Cellular Audio Phone System on Driving Performance. Safety Science 41, 531–542 (2003)
15. Haigney, D.E., Taylor, R.G., Westerman, S.J.: Concurrent Mobile (cellular) Phone Use and Driving Performance: Task Demand Characteristics and Compensatory Processes. Transportation Research Part F 3, 113–121 (2000)
16. Salvucci, D.D., Liu, A.: The Time Course of a Lane Change: Driver Control and Eye-Movement Behavior. Transportation Research Part F 5, 123–132 (2002)
17. Leung, S., Starmer, G.: Gap Acceptance and Risk-Taking by Young and Mature Drivers, both Sober and Alcohol-Intoxicated, in a Simulated Driving Task. Accident Analysis & Prevention 37, 1056–1065 (2005)
18. Hoedemaekera, M., Brookhuis, K.A.: Behavioural Adaptation to Driving with an Adaptive Cruise Control (ACC). Transportation Research Part F 1, 95–106 (1998)
19. Uzzell, D., Muckle, R.: Simulating Traffic Engineering Solutions to Predict Changes in Driving Behaviour. Transportation Research Part F 8, 311–329 (2005)

# A Virtual Reality-Based Experiment Environment for Engine Assembly Line Workplace Planning and Ergonomics Evaluation

RunDang Yang[1,2], XiuMin Fan[1,2], DianLiang Wu[1,2], and JuanQi Yan[1,2]

[1] CIM Institute of Shanghai Jiaotong University, Shanghai 200030, China
[2] Shanghai Key Laboratory of Advanced Manufacturing, Shanghai 200030, China
yrd@sjtu.edu.cn

**Abstract.** In this paper, an integrated virtual assembly simulation experiment environment of interactive workplace planning, assembly process simulation and ergonomics evaluation is built and it provides a new ways and means for interactive and visualized workplace design and process planning. A simple and effective method of measuring the movement manipulating data of operator is presented and can provide data source for ergonomics evaluation of the operator. In order to obtain these data in VE, movement data of the operator in real environment is transformed into VE and is related with virtual objects by the corresponding relation between VH and real hand (RH). Based on these data, the operator's fatigue index and energy consumption can be calculated. The conformability and fatigue of users for repetitive assembly operations are quantitatively evaluated to reduce the health problems of operators because of unreasonable layout and repetitive work.

**Keywords:** Virtual reality; Workplace planning; Virtual assembly; Data acquisition and processing; Ergonomics evaluation.

## 1 Introduction

To obtain optimizational assembly process and workplace layout, traditional workplace planning relies on the judgment and experience of industrial engineers and the repeated testing and improvement using physical model. At present, the method of automobile engine plant is to stop the production line specifically for the trial assembly. If a problem discovered in the course of the trial assembly. The problem is returned and improved the products assembly design in CAD or revised the assembly process and workplace planning information. This repeatedly suspended for trial assembly is not only a waste of resources but also affects the production progress.

To reduce/replace the trial assembly times of certification process design and workplace planning rationality, this paper proposes a solution: Workplace panning and assembly simulation virtual experiment environment (WPASVEE) is built using virtual reality (VR) technology. In WPASVEE, operators interactively implement workplace planning and assembly simulation by virtual hand (VH) using data gloves, position tracking device (Flock of Birds, FOB) and stereo glasses. Movement data of

R. Shumaker (Ed.): Virtual Reality, HCII 2007, LNCS 4563, pp. 594–603, 2007.

the operator can be real-time collected in the process of assembly. The quantitative indexes and evaluation methods of suitable for WPASVEE are built and a unified map relation of human motion data from WPASVEE to real environment is established. The conformability and fatigue of users for repetitive assembly operations are quantitatively evaluated to reduce the health problems of operators because of unreasonable layout and repetitive work.

## 2 Related Works

Applying computer-aided ergonomics to new product design improves the efficiency of product design and used [1]. The method has a potential to improve assembly productivity and ergonomics and offer a better understanding among product designers and production engineers in product development processes [2].

Chryssolouris [3] develops a virtual assembly work cell. Taking high-speed boat propeller as an example qualitatively evaluates human-process-related factors in the virtual assembly work cell. In the process of assembly, the qualitative evaluation of human-process-related factors such as the perception of the working environment, the interface with the work cell layout, the reachability of mounting locations, and the handlability of production component and tools, and the qualitative evaluation of human-process characteristics related to critical performance issues, such as the lifting capacity, the energy expenditure and the manual task cycle time, are implemented. However, the virtual assembly work cell doesn't support yet an exact representation of reality or specialized process characteristics.

Jayaram [4] introduces quantitative ergonomic analysis tools in real time for occupational ergonomic studies. The "Virtual Assembly Design Environment" (VADE) is used as VE. Human model is modeled using commercial ergonomics tool and is integrated into the VADE. Operators control the human model using interactive devices and implement assembly operation simulation. Finally, ergonomic issues are quantitatively analyzed in JACK according to operation-process data.

Rajan [5] develops an integrated VR-based environment JIGPRO for the analysis of assembly product and jig designs. CAD models of assembly product, jig and virtual hand are imported into the JIGPRO for assembly process simulation and accessibility analysis to ensure well capability of assembly and ergonomic for tools and fixtures designs.

A.Sundin [6] describes a case study of bus development and manufacturing process and presents a work process for analysis of time and ergonomic aspects in early design phases. The study focuses on a work process to visualize manual assembly and work postures for workers.

## 3 The Frame Structure of WPASVEE

The frame construction of WPASVEE is shown in Fig.1. The inputs of the WPASVEE are CAD assembly models and assembly process and workplace table that are obtained according to production standard and assembly sequence. They are transformed into the WPASVEE by secondary development interface.

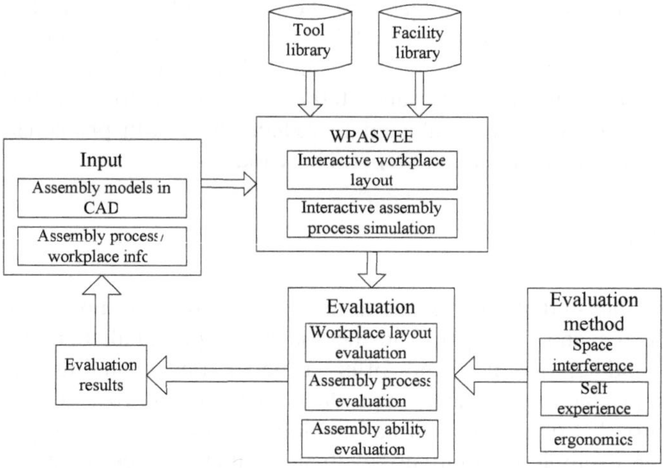


**Fig. 1.** The frame structure of virtual experimental environment

User can interactively layout workplace facilities and simulate assembly tasks according to the whole space of the workplace, facilities chosen and experiential knowledge using VR devices in the WPASVEE. In order to judge the reasonableness of the workplace design, on one hand, the workplace design is evaluated according to operator's the subjective experience; the other, it is quantitative evaluated by calculating LI and energy consumption according to the establishment of evaluating index, calculation equation and the operator movement data collected in the process of assembly. Finally, to improve design, the evaluation results will be returned to the CAD product design and assembly process/ workplace design. Ergonomic problems can be evaluated and found in early design phases. Assembly process and workplace layout are verified and evaluated before real production using VR technologies, thereby shortening the development cycle of new products, reducing costs and enhancing the competitiveness of their products.

# 4 The Key Technologies in the Virtual Experiment Environment

## 4.1 The Evaluation Methods Ergonomics-Based

The evaluation and analysis methods ergonomics-based are built in virtual experiment environment. The movement of data operator is recorded in the process of interactive operation. Fatigue index and energy expenditure of the operator are calculated and analyze based on these data.

NIOSH lifting equation [7-9] is to analyze fatigue grade for manual operation. The purpose of the method is to avoid or reduce the occurrence of lifting related low back pain(LBP), reduce other musculoskeletal disorders associated with lifting. The equation meets three criteria: biomechanical, physiological and psychophysical limitation. It provides with evaluating the lifting capacity of workers and meets acceptable lifting capacity of 75% of females (99% males). The outputs of the equation are Recommended Weight Limit (RWL) and Lifting Index (LI), where, LI is the ratio of the load lifted to the RWL.

For ergonomic risk assessment certain calculations determining workload are necessary. Energy consumption can be calculated applying mathematical methods. Energy consumption usually is transformed into metabolic energy expressed in vats (W), kcal/h or kcal/min. Further, energy consumption is equated to corresponding work severity categories [10].

Variables involved in the process of calculation are described in Table.1.

**Table 1.** The ergonomic models used in the WPASVEE

| NIOSH equation | Energy consumption equation |
|---|---|
| $RWL = LC \cdot HM \cdot VM \cdot DM \cdot AM \cdot FM \cdot CM$<br>Where<br>RWL: recommended weight limit(kg)<br>LC: load constant=23kg<br>HM: horizontal multiplier<br>VM: vertical multiplier<br>DM: distance multiplier<br>AM: asymmetric multiplier<br>FM: frequency multiplier<br>CM: coupling multiplier<br><br>LI=L/RWL<br>Where<br>LI: lifting index<br>L: load weight(kg) | $A=\left(F\cdot H_n+\frac{F\cdot L}{9}+\frac{F\cdot H_O}{2}\right)\cdot K\cdot n$<br>Where<br>A: amount of work(J)<br>F: force applied(N)<br>Hn: distance, in which the object is lifted(m)<br>Ho: distance, in which the object is lowered(m)<br>L: distance the object is moved horizontally(m)<br>K: coefficient(biomechanical criterion)characterizing moving individual sections of the body and equal to 6<br>n: number of equal technological cycles in the given or shift |

For NIOSH equation, LI<1.0 will protect most workers, LI>1.0 exists potential hazard to most workers and LI>3.0 nearly all workers are at increased risk.

For energy consumption, Institute of Health of Chinese Academy of Medical Sciences [11] studies the relation between working time and energy consumption for representative 262 kinds occupation in china. The conclusion is the limitation value of energy consumption should be from 1400 to 1600kcal in a working day (8 hour) and can't exceed 2000kcal.

## 4.2 Operator Movement Data Acquisition

The VH isn't completely corresponding with RH from the overall perspective because it is controlled by increment of tracker in WPASVEE. Moreover, the operator can't fully immersed in VE because he is replaced by VH and no virtual human in VE. It is very difficulty to obtain parameters needed of the above quantitative evaluation criteria and methods from the process of VA. Therefore, movement data obtained must be transformed into WPASVEE and associated with the operation objects together by the corresponding relation between the VH and the RH.

Two FOBs, which the corresponding coordinates are the CB and CH respectively, is fixed on the operator's left hand (right hand in the same way) and vertebra surface as shown in Fig. 2. Co coordinates of the human operator.

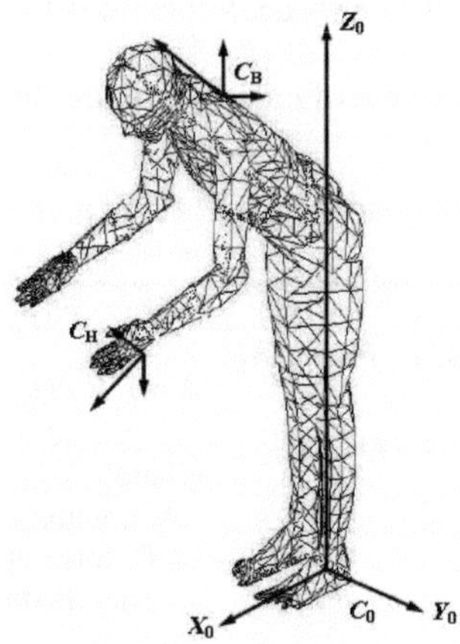


**Fig. 2.** Fixture location of FOB

The measurement steps include:

(1) Data samples. In a workplace, for each operation object (directly manipulated by hand) corresponds to a set of data; the each group data collected include starting and ending points in two parts, respectively.

(2) Data calibration. Before the operation began, the pose of the operator is calibrated firstly: the waist of the operator should be straight; position and orientation matrix $M_{B0}$ of the FOB on the waist is recorded when FOB is activated.

(3) Data collection. In the process of VA, position and orientation matrix $M_B$ of the FOB on the waist and $M_{VH}$ of the FOB on the hand are recorded when operation object is first grasped. The coordinate origin of the object grasped is $P_0(x, y, z)$ under the world coordinate system and the quality of the object is $L_{avg}$. The position and orientation matrix $M_B{}'$ of the FOB on the waist and $M_{VH}{}'$ of the FOB on the hand are recorded when the object is released, the coordinate origin of the object released is $P_1(x, y, z)$. Existing data are replaced by current data at each releasing the object until assembly tasks are over.

(4) Determining fixed transformation. The position and orientation matrix $M_{H-FOB}$ is a fixed transformation of FOB on data gloves relative to VH.

### 4.3 Operator Movement Data Processing

The known quantities include arbitrary point $p_0$ and normal vector $n_0$ of the workshop ground in WPASVEE, the operator's height $h$ and the ratio coefficient $\mu$ between waist joint and $h$ in the process of solving.

Data processing process is divided into the following six steps :

(1) Solve the position and orientation matrix $M_{B-V}$ of the FOB on the operator's back in WPASVEE when the VH is corresponding with the RH and when VH counterparts. The method includes:

Step1 : Solve the position and orientation matrix $M_{VH-FOB}$ of FOB on the RH relative the VH in WPASVEE:

$$M_{VH-FOB} = M_{H-FOB} \times M_{VH} \tag{1}$$

Step2 : Solve the position and orientation matrix $M_{H-V}$ of the RH in WPASVEE:

$$M_{H-V} = (M_{H-FOB})^{-1} \times M_H \tag{2}$$

Step3 : Solve the fixed transformation matrix $M_{VH-H}$ between the RH in WPASVEE and the VH:

$$M_{VH-H} = M_{V-H} \times M_{VH}^{-1} \tag{3}$$

Step4 : Solve the position and orientation matrix $M_{B-V}$ of FOB on the operator's back in WPASVEE:

$$M_{B-V} = (M_{VH-H})^{-1} \times M_B \tag{4}$$

(2) Build the coordinate system $C_0$ of the operator in WPASVEE:

The Z axis is upward vector and perpendicular to the ground through the center O1 point of the lumbar; X axis is an intersection line between sagittal plane of the operator and the ground; and Y axis is defined according the right rules, as C0 illustrated in Fig. 3. The calculation method shown in Fig. 3: A is origin point of $M_{B0}$, B is origin point of $M_B$, $A'$ and $B'$ are projective points form the point A and B to the ground, $O_1$ is central point of waist joint of the operator, and CD parallels to $A'B'$ through the point $O_1$.

Known quantity: The coordinate value of the point A and B are $(x_A, y_A, z_A)$ and $(x_B, y_B, z_B)$, respectively.

The solving steps are:

Step1 : Calculate the coordinate value of $A'$ and $B'$ by the point and normal vector of the ground and coordinate of the point A and B, then the direction of X axis of $C_0$ should be $\overrightarrow{A'B'}$.

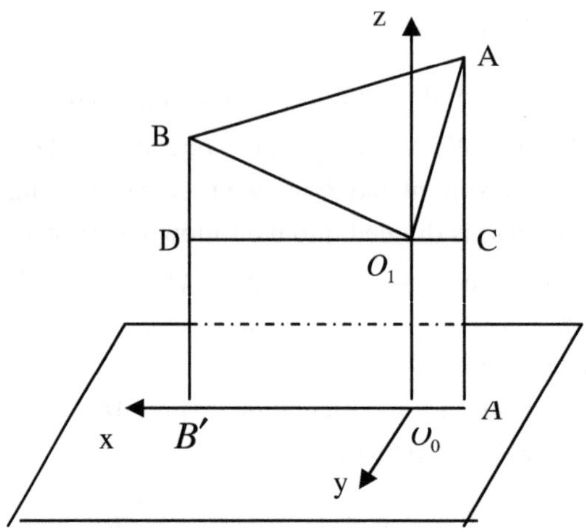


**Fig. 3.** Coordinate system in virtual environment

Step2 : The length of $O_0A'$ is calculated by the equation:

$$\left(|BB'|-h\cdot\mu\right)^2+\left(|A'B'|-|O_0A'|\right)^2=\left(|AB'|-h\cdot\mu\right)^2+|O_0A'|^2 \quad (5)$$

Step3 : The coordinate of $O_0$ is calculated according to the length of $O_0A'$ and the coordinate of $A'$ and $B'$;

Step4 : Build the CS $C_0$ whose z axis is normal vector of the ground, x axis is $\overrightarrow{A'B'}$, y axis meets the right rules and origin point is $O_0$.

(3) Solve the horizontal position H (distance of hands from midpoint between ankles) and vertical position V (the starting height of the hands from the ground).

Step1 : Build the coordinate system $C_0$ of the operator in WPASVEE according to the methods and principles above.

Step2 : Solve the matrix $M_{B-V}'$ and $M_{VH}'$ by transformation $M_{B-V}$ and $M_{VH}$ to CS $C_0$ ;

Step3 : Obtain the origin point $P(x,y,z)$ of the position and orientation $M_{VH}'$ ;

Step4 : Then, obtain the horizontal position $H=x$ and vertical position $V=z$ of the RH.

(4) Solve the rotation angle A of the operator in the process of operating a object.

Step1 : Solve the matrix $M_{B0}'$ by transformation $M_{B0}$ to CS $C_0$;

Step2 : Calculate the increment matrix $\Delta M_{B-C}$ from $M_{B0}'$ to $M_{B-V}'$ ;

Step3 : Calculate the angle A of $\Delta M_{B-C}$ around z axis of CS $C_0$.

(5) Calculate the vertical distance D

Step1 : For each set data obtained, its start point $P_0(x_0, y_0, z_0)$ and end point $P_1(x_1, y_1, z_1)$ of $M_{VH}{}'$ are calculated using the above method, respectively.

Step2: Calculate the vertical distance D of RH from start point to end point, $D' = z_1 - z_0$, $D = |D'|$

(6) Calculated the horizontal distance L and the lifting height $H_m$ or the lowering distance $H_n$

Step 1 : $h = P_{1z} - P_{0z}$ ,if $h \geq 0$, then, $H_n = 0$ and if $h < 0$, then $H_m = 0$ and $H_n = |h|$ ;

Step2 : Calculate the projective points $P_0'(x, y, z)$ and $P_1'(x, y, z)$ by projecting $P_0(x, y, z)$ and $P_1(x, y, z)$ to the ground of the plant floor ;

Step3 : Calculate L : $L = \left|P_0'P_1'\right|$。

These relevant data are obtained by the above measurement and processing methods. The fatigue index and energy consumption will be calculated by incorporated these data into the NIOSH equation and energy equation in Table 1.

## 5 Example

In order to verify above theories and methods, an example of the workplace planning of engine crankshaft in assembly line is given. The virtual scene of workplace layout and assembly operation is described in Fig. 4. In the workplace, first, crankshaft is assembled to cylinder body by crane; second, five bear caps are assembled to cylinder body to fix the crankshaft; then ten bolts is inserted into ten tap holes on five bear caps; finally, the ten tap holes are tightened by tool to fix the crankshaft on the cylinder body.

**Fig. 4.** Data measurement of operator in VA

In the process of assembly operation, three FOBs are fixed on both hands and back of the operator. Before the operation began, the operator should calibrate his pose firstly. The position and orientation matrix of each FOB are recorded when the object is grasped and released by VH. When these data are collected, the data needed for planning and evaluation workplace is obtained according to above methods. The results are shown in Fig. 5 for the operator in the crankshaft assembly workplace.

Based on the above data and the calculation methods in Table 1, the fatigue index of operator is $CLI = 0.474$ , and energy expenditure is 2128J through calculating in the workplace of crankshaft assembly,. In order to the correctness of and evaluation models and data measurement and treatment methods are verified by commercial software JACK.

In JACK (Fig.6), set parameters include operating frequency of Labor experienced cycles and rest interval. These parameters should be set up in line with the WPASVEE. The results is calculated, LI equivalent to the value of 0.465; 525kcal task is in a cycle energy consumption. WPASVEE with the experimental data is very close to that from an engineering point of view, the outcome is feasible.

```
Task# Description Avg. Load Max. Load O.H. O.V. D.H. D.V. Dist O.A. D.A.
100 安装轴瓦1 0.037 0.4 25.912 71.507 29.746 96.621 25.114 1 1
200 安装轴瓦2 0.037 0.5 29.746 73.621 37.963 99.163 25.542 1 1
300 安装轴瓦3 0.037 0.5 30.963 94.163 34.638 68.625 25.538 1 1
400 安装轴瓦4 0.037 0.5 30.010 91.490 26.210 65.621 25.869 1 1
500 安装轴瓦5 0.037 0.5 25.058 90.623 26.313 63.677 26.946 1 1
600 轴承盖1 0.507 1 26.056 71.624 51.249 101.391 29.767 1 1
700 轴承盖2 0.507 1 26.062 71.623 49.289 105.142 33.519 1 1
800 轴承盖3 0.507 1 26.054 71.624 59.097 104.775 33.151 8.973 8.9
900 轴承盖4 0.507 1 26.059 71.623 54.990 105.361 33.738 1 1
1000 轴承盖5 0.507 1 26.064 71.623 55.692 106.317 34.694 8.976 8.6
1100 螺栓1 0.047 1 26.064 71.623 54.476 108.492 36.869 8.962 9
1200 螺栓2 0.047 1 43.433 79.617 51.523 104.924 25.307 1 1
1300 螺栓3 0.047 1 47.924 82.199 55.798 107.220 25.021 1 1
1400 螺栓4 0.047 1 47.923 82.200 53.639 107.966 25.766 1 1
1500 螺栓5 0.047 1 47.922 82.200 52.532 109.716 27.516 1 1
1600 螺栓6 0.047 1 57.083 82.711 50.370 110.499 27.788 1.840 2
1700 螺栓7 0.047 1 57.084 82.711 55.224 109.422 26.711 1.840 1
1800 螺栓8 0.047 1 59.518 81.653 51.199 112.732 31.079 1 1
1900 螺栓9 0.047 1 57.055 83.724 52.487 114.337 30.613 42 42.694
2000 螺栓10 0.047 1 57.055 83.724 51.664 111.701 27.977 0.921 9.724
```

**Fig. 5.** The data result file of operator in crankshaft assembly workplace

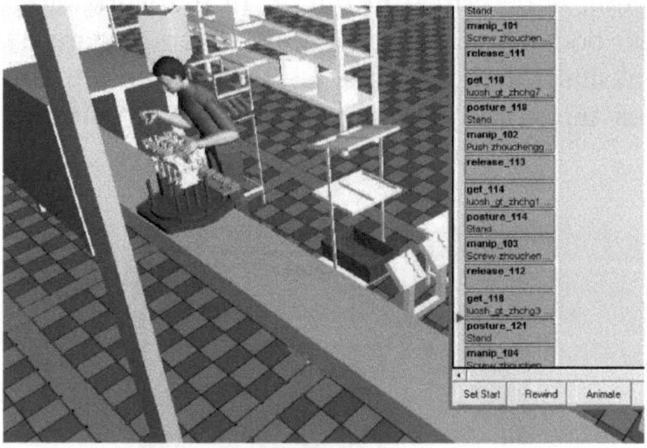


**Fig. 6.** The assembly tasks simulation in JACK

## 6 Summary

Traditional assembly line planning and ergonomics evaluation is implemented through the collection plentiful movement data of operator. The method is time-consuming and expensive. A large amount of data is needed for solving new similar problems such as evaluation the conformability and efficiency of the operator; and then the results are verified and further improved in the physical environment.

An integrated virtual experiment environment is built for interactive workplace planning, assembly simulation and evaluation. The environment provided a new way and mean for interactive and visual workplace design and process planning.

**Acknowledgments.** The work is supported by the National High Technology Research & Development Program of China (Grant No. 2006AA04Z141) and the Key Project from Science & Technology Commission of Shanghai Municipality (Grant No. 065115008). The authors are also grateful to the editors and the anonymous reviewers for helpful comments.

## References

1. Badler, N.: Virtual Humans for Animation, Ergonomics, and Simulation. In: Proceedings of the IEEE Non Rigid and Articulated Motion Workshop 1997, pp. 28–36 (1997)
2. Wilson, J.R.: Virtual Environments Applications and Applied Ergonomics. Applied Ergonomics 30, 3–9 (1999)
3. Chryssolouris, G., Mavrikios, D., Fragos, D.: A Virtual Reality-based Experimentation Environment for the Verification of Human-related Factor in Assembly Processes. Robotics and Computer-Integrated Manufacturing 16, 267–276 (2000)
4. Jayaram, U., Jayaram, S., Shaikh, I., Kim, Y.J., Palmer, C.: Introducing Quantitative Analysis Methods into Virtual Environments for Real-time and Continuous Ergonomic Evaluations. Computer in Industry 57, 283–296 (2006)
5. Rajan, V.N.: Accessibility and Ergonomic Analysis of Assembly Product and Jig Designs. International Journal of Industrial Ergonomics 23, 479–487 (1999)
6. Sundin, A., Christmansson, M., Larsson, M.: A Different Perspective in Participatory Ergonomics in Product Development Improves Assembly Work in the Automotive Industry. International Journal of Industrial Ergonomics 33, 1–14 (2004)
7. Waters, T.R., Baron, S.L., Kemmlert, K.: Accuracy of Measurements for the Revised NIOSH Lifting Equation. Applied Ergonomics 29, 433–438 (1998)
8. Temple, R., Adams, T.: Ergonomics Analysis of a Multi-task Industrial Lifting Station Using the NIOSH Method. Journal of Industrial Technology 16, 1–6 (2000)
9. Workplace Safety and Health, National Institute for Occupational Safety and Health (NIOSH), DHHS (NIOSH) Publication No. 2003-116.
10. Garg, A., Chaffin, D.B., Herrin, G.D.: Prediction of Metabolic Rates for Manual Materials Handling Jobs. American Industrial Hygiene Association Journal 6, 661–674 (1978)
11. Metabolism Calorimetric Measurement of Human Engineering, the National Standards of the People's Republic of China GB/T 18048-2000, General Bureau of Technical Supervision of the People's Republic of China (2000)

# Part 4

# Health, Cultural, Educational and Entertainment Applications

# Video Game Technologies and Virtual Design: A Study of Virtual Design Teams in a Metaverse

Shaowen Bardzell[1] and Kalpana Shankar[2]

[1] School of HPER, Indiana University, 1025 E 7th Street, Rm 394, Bloomington, IN 47405, USA
[2] School of Informatics, Indiana University, 1900 E 10th Street, Rm 1032, Bloomington, IN 47406, USA
{selu,shankark}@indiana.edu

**Abstract.** Massively Multiplayer Online Games (MMOGs) are no longer just games. "Metaverses," a variant of these games, which include Second Life and Active Worlds, represent some of the most immersive, interactive possibilities for learning, simulation, and digital design in use today. They also increasingly blur distinctions between work and play, as well as user and designer, prompting questions about the nature and practice of virtual design, that is, design that is practiced inside virtual reality by and on 3D avatars. This paper describes results from a qualitative study of collaborative design practices within Second Life, a popular metaverse and design environment. We analyze design processes, including the artifacts that avatar-designer create and use in the design activities.

**Keywords:** metaverse, virtual design teams, collaboration, artifacts, designers, boundary objects.

## 1 Introduction

The advent of collaborative virtual environments (CVEs) places geographically dispersed collaborators inside of 3D virtual reality as embodied agents (Snowdon et al., 2001). Coinciding with the emergence of such environments is the growing popularity of massively multiplayer online games [MMOGs]. One variant of these games is the "metaverse," which is a participant-created virtual space. Examples include Second Life, Active Worlds, and There. Metaverses bring these parallel streams together; using game technologies, they offer complex character animation and interactive possibilities. Like CVEs, they offer sophisticated social and communication interfaces. They have progressed far beyond gaming: they are the site of collaborative design and building projects, mixed reality events, and MTV marketing efforts. Thus, metaverses lead naturally to the use of CVEs for both serious and pleasurable purposes (Benford et al., 2001).

Most events and locations in Second Life are made possible in part through their design and "builds." *Design* in Second Life typically involves creating custom 3D environments, called "builds," which include buildings, furnishing, and animated and interactive artifacts. As a multi-user platform, Second Life offers many features to

R. Shumaker (Ed.): Virtual Reality, HCII 2007, LNCS 4563, pp. 607–616, 2007.

encourage and support collaboration. The question that this paper addresses is how the convergence of virtual collaboration and video game technologies affects design practices in Second Life.

This study follows two design teams designing spaces and artifacts in Second Life through a combination of observations and interviews, noting the design environment, activities, interactions, and conversations among team members. One group (70 active members) uses Second Life for risk management and disaster relief training. This group owns two virtual islands; their design is influenced by dioramas often used by emergency services. The other team consists of 25 entrepreneurial designers dedicated to recreating the clothing and animations of a specialized sexual fetish. In this paper, we report preliminary findings (November 2006 to January 2007) of the study and explore several key collaborative design issues, including tracing how a design idea is initiated, negotiated (among various collaborators), and implemented; and how it becomes integrated in other design activities.

## 2 Related Work

The study of design in metaverses such as Second Life presents intriguing relations between work and play as well as business and pleasure. The notion of collaborative design has been one of the central research foci in the field of computer-supported cooperative work (CSCW). Since the design process is both creative and personal, it highlights the tensions between the individual and the team when design activities take place in a group setting. Twidale and his colleagues believe the interplay between private and communal design is an important aspect of design and emphases the need to support the individual's freedom of expression as well as the formalization of design ideas so as to be shared and used effectively among team members (Twidale et al, 1993). In an ethnographic study of graphic designers' work, Murray finds briefing and job scheduling two of the most essential tasks in providing the necessary context, structure, and division of labor to ensure success (Murray, 1993). The meanings are negotiated and co-constructed by members of the team, and they are context-dependent and non-stable. In a metaverse such as Second Life, these design-related sense-making, support, and coordinating activities are also embodied, using the virtual body as a representational medium for communication and interaction. The 3D immersive environment allows direct manipulation of artifacts in-world, enabling participants to interact with each other and the artifacts naturally (as if in real life). However, since team members are scattered across different time zones and continents, it problematizes design processes.

Understanding the sociality of work in all of its manifestations has been the going concern of CSCW, which has been motivated by the role of language, the coordination of work processes, and the development of collaborative tools. However, more recently, the process by which objects, physical or digital, become accepted by all of the communities and individuals who have some jurisdiction over them requires numerous negotiations about their form, function, ownership, and purposes. There has been some discussion of how these processes transpire in various aspects of engineering design. Star and Griesemer (1989) call such objects, which mediate between communities of practice and help achieve standardization and consensus among them "boundary objects." This theoretical construct has taken hold in much of CSCW literature to describe and theorize many kinds of digital objects that serve as what Henderson (1991) calls "social glue" between individuals and groups responsible for working together. Databases, sketches, and any other artifacts mediate and facilitate distributed cognition and organizational memory (Ackerman and Halverson, 1999), shared meanings of critical working terms (Lutters and Ackerman, 2002), and establish jurisdictional expertise in projects. How "boundary objects" function and become stabilized has not been explored in virtual reality environments, though Prasolova-Forland and Divitini (2003) has explored how virtual reality spaces themselves can function as boundary objects and the implications for the design of artifacts. Guimarães (2005) explores the role of objects and knowledge about them in terms of trade, which is also an important mechanism for establishing and maintaining standards. In the teams we observed, the products of design work are not the only the boundary objects that engender trust in teams. Contracts, shared language, and Second Life itself are essential to bringing together multiple stakeholders.

## 3 Data Collection and Analysis Methodology

The subjects for the study are recruited from various Second Life electronic distribution lists and discussion forums. During the study, the researchers conducted both ethnographic observations and interviews to understand collaborative design practices.

As an exploratory first step, the researchers developed a sensibility toward design in Second Life. This included developing familiarity with Second Life as a content authoring tool, by creating some original content. It also included spending time informally in "sandboxes," which are free content development areas open to the public, whose contents are deleted on a daily basis; the purpose of these informal observations were not to study any one in particular, but rather to get a feel for the vocabulary, practices, and space-time of Second Life content creation.

For the formal study, we first conducted exploratory interviews with the team leaders to understand the big picture and explore the domain believed to be important to the study. Ethnographic observations ensued, followed by structured interviews after each observation session. We then performed content analysis on chat logs collected during observations and interviews. This technique is used to identify keywords of interest, themes repeated by designers, and sequences of actions (e.g., history, consequence, repetition, etc.) performed during design activities. The results of the analysis provided a foundation for correlating the observations with open-ended interviews that we also administered to give the researchers the flexibility to explore questions and topics of interest.

## 4 Results

Our preliminary findings show patterns that reflect what we know about the use of information technologies in other kinds of computer-supported communication and

CSCW. In what follows, we summarize the results in the following five areas: work environment, virtual teams, design process, artifacts, and organizational knowledge.

## 4.1 Work Environment

Content creation in Second Life takes place on virtual land, which is not only a diegetic visualization of the world, but also a metaphor for server space. In other words, land costs money, and paying for it is equivalent to paying hosting costs. Because one cannot build without land, Second Life makes available a limited number of public sandbox spaces, mentioned above, in which users can develop content and save it to their inventories before it is automatically removed. For those doing serious work in Second Life, acquiring land of one's own, and paying for it, is essential.

Both of the teams we studied had acquired their own land for private development. When first acquired, land is typically presented as a more or less featureless, flat field. Since Second Life land initially lacks context, it is common for design teams to construct contexts appropriate to their situations, to make their design activities meaningful. For example, the disaster relief team constructed a virtual town and a virtual hospital on the land they own to create a situated context for the design activities. For the clothing and animation design team, rather than creating these specialized clothing and intimate animations out in the middle of a featureless field, the team first created a virtual house, complete with tall trees, a shaded garden and an enclosed shed, which provide a sense of context, scale, and visual coherence for their work. They designed and built this home setting not with the intention of selling the house (or copies of it), but rather to create for themselves a design environment that meets the specific needs and situation of the team. This practice demonstrates that members of the team regard their land, their development space not merely as physical coordinates in 3D virtual environment but as a socio-cultural construct (Harrison & Dourish, 1996; Wright et al., 2005).

"Land" converted into a meaningful place or context is the diegetic space in which design occurs, but designers also work in the non-diegetic Second Life content authoring environment. The authoring environment in Second Life includes a simple primitive-based 3D modeling environment, in which users create models out of simple shapes, such as cubes, cones, and spheres, which they can then position, scale, and distort; a scripting language (Linden Scripting Language, or LSL); and the capacity to import external media assets, including 2D bitmap graphics, or textures, to map onto 3D models, and 3D character poses and animations.

Significantly, the authoring environment is not separate from the rest of the virtual world. That is, Second Life content is not authored in an external application and then imported into the world; instead, one's avatar develops content in-world. This makes Second Life a social authoring environment, where a group of people can literally develop and modify builds simultaneously and in the same space, and in fact such collaboration is quite common. Further, as seen from our observations and interviews of both teams, collaborators often define their roles during building, with one person specializing (for example) in Photoshop and textures, while another specializes in building design/architecture, and in scripting. In addition, there will be people who are in charge of design research and content generation (as in the case of disaster relief training team). Both teams have a leader who coordinates and manage all activities, and personnel. He is generally the one who sends out group notices and leads design and evaluation meetings.

### 4.2 Virtual Teams

While the setting is important in contextualizing the design activities of the virtual teams we studied, the composition of the team also demonstrates direct connections to how team members conduct design activities. According to Cohen and Bailey (1997), a team is "a collection of individuals who are independent in their tasks, who share responsibility for outcomes, who see themselves and who are seen by others as an intact social entity embedded in one or more larger social systems and who manage their relationships across organizational boundaries." This is evident in Second Life as well. Like other social groupings in MMOG, persistent groups in metaverses are formed to enhance human-human and human-artifact interactions in-world. Unlike most of the group construction in MMOG in which collaboration is essential in accomplishing a difficult game task (Duchenault et al., 2004), the rationale behind group formation in metaverses often has more to do with commerce, education, business/professional networking, shared hobbies, and so on. In Second Life, an individual can belong to up to 25 groups. Of special note are the group titles, which appear in-world beside people's names, signifying group membership.

The two design teams in Second Life we followed take advantage of the grouping mechanism to create team identity, solidify shared responsibility for outcomes, and facilitate group communications. Since group names appear over avatar heads along with their names, they provide instant contextual information to everyone within view of the avatar. Wearing a group title not only indicates affiliation with the group, but because an avatar can only have one group title active at a time, it also suggests that one is "working" when that tag is active, since commonly avatars activate different groups when they engage in different activities.

Grouping enhances the way team members communicate and conduct their work. The two teams we observed send meeting notices, event information, and new product/build releases to group members via the "Group Notices" mechanism, which is only available to group members. The access restriction settings established by groups also determine and structure team interactions: only team members are allowed to access lands owned by the team, and by the same token, only team members can build or edit artifacts on shared lands.

For a team to succeed, there needs to be a clearly defined purpose that is accepted and followed by all team members. These group-only and group-specific mechanisms that the two teams use to coordinate and restrict teamwork greatly enhances and promotes team identity. CSCW research shows that when people first enter group setting, they often have different kinds of knowledge and conflicting goals (Ackerman, 2001). Both teams we observed demonstrated that grouping over time incorporates people into a shared sense of purpose, where participants' orientations and objectives are rearticulated and reconfigured. Since common grounds and understanding are established, it is easier to foster knowledge-sharing across the teams.

Though space and grouping provide a coherence and identity to members, we also observed a fair amount of off-topic behavior. Some members of the disaster relief team, for example, have face-to-face relations in real life; as a result, during collaboration in-world, their discussions sometimes drifted to the personal. One member of the clothing/animation team revealed during an open-ended interview that she had several email and IM exchanges with the spouse of the team leader, which helped her obtain deeper understanding of the work patterns and habits of her team leader. Off-topic behavior demonstrates that personal and emotional relationship building is essential in the emergence of trust, effective communication, and effective leadership and teamwork (Powell et al, 2004).

### 4.3 Design Process and Coordination

The overall design process used by the two teams we observed fell into two categories: what Rosson and her colleagues (1988) call a phased development approach versus an incremental approach. The disaster relief team adapts the phased development approach to compartmentalize design activities into design, implementation, and evaluation; while the clothing/animation team uses incremental method where the design and implementation are highly intertwined and iterative; they spend little time on explicit evaluation during the design process. The difference in approaches, of course, is presumably related to the nature of the design project as well as team size. The disaster relief training team has about 70 people and the resources needed to devote to different tasks, especially the evaluation of their training materials, given that they are accountable to the government agencies that fund their projects. The smaller intimate clothing/animation team, on the other hand, needs to produce products in a short time frame to meet market needs and beat the competition; as a result, design and implementation are done simultaneously in a timely fashion. The user testing is literally done after products are launched, when they are in the hands of the users.

It is evident from our observations and interviews that regardless of the approach, both teams follow a member co-created vision as opposed to sheer intuition during design. In general, the two teams start with information gathering, which involves needs assessment (in the case of the disaster relief training team) and comparative analysis of competing lines (in the case of the clothing/animation team). Information and ideas are then passed through multiple meetings where group discussions take place for refinement of ideas and resolving problems. Only when a common frame of reference is achieved can the team begin working together successfully. Collaboration intensifies during the actual design phase where work planning, coordination among different designers, maintaining shared understanding (of the tasks and objectives) across the team, learning (of how to work with team members and team lead), negotiation (of tasks, time, workload, etc.) all have to happen in harmony. Both teams rely not only the in-world communication channels (e.g., IM, chat) to collaborate, but make use of other mechanisms, such as VoIP (Skype), email, and Google chat. These alternates are popular among team members because of the intrinsic limitations of in-world chat/IM systems for long-period collaboration. Research has shown that since people generally speak more and faster than when typing, the adoption of multi-modal communication greatly enhances team performance (Sallnäs, 2001), and both teams accordingly have adopted communications technologies external to Second Life.

### 4.4 Artifacts

Trust within a team often coalesces around shared documents and artifacts (Star and Griesmer, 1989). The disaster relief team we observed is a particularly strong example of a community that relies upon artifacts and policies to maintain effective collaboration with stakeholders, which include officials from the federal government (whom they term "content experts" who possess and transmit knowledge about the disaster scenarios to be modeled), educators working with students who are to use the scenarios, and other design businesses in Second Life from whom off-the-shelf artifacts are occasionally purchased. But when time concerns are pressing, there is little luxury for allowing trust to unfold organically. In one interview, the team leader noted that he outsources some of his design work, but "outsourcing takes experience…you really need to breathe [Second Life] air to work effectively…know the SL community and identify good designers." He felt that trust is built through the design portfolios and good customer relations when working with content experts, who may not understand the capabilities of SL. –As the team leader noted, "Our target audience and content experts know little about virtual environments let alone web conferencing…so we really had to take the bull by the horns and show them what could be done." For example, the team built a virtual auscultation tool (to hear heart sounds and murmurs) just to show a team of nurses (content specialists) what could be done with Second Life – "a carrot", the team leader called it.

### 4.5 Organizational Knowledge

Our findings suggest that for virtual design teams in Second Life, the process of creating new information and synthesizing that information to create shareable knowledge is dependent upon negotiating several themes that are central to understanding how organizations learn and grow: the harvesting of tacit knowledge and its contributions to innovation strategies. Although the concept of tacit knowledge has its roots in the philosophy of Michael Polanyi (1966), more recently organizational theorists have used his central paradigm of "we do not know what we know" to understand and harness the knowledge of individuals who constitute organizational settings (Nonaka, 1994).

Not surprisingly, establishing and harnessing tacit knowledge – often acquired through activities outside of Second Life- is essential to the pursuit of design activities in Second Life. Tacit knowledge, a personal and implicit knowing that which is difficult if not impossible to articulate and capture for re-use, is often conceptualized as "embodied" knowledge. This kind of knowledge is often perceived to be the most crucial to organizational functioning, but the most maddening to harness. Although tacit knowledge is often acknowledged to be most readily exchanged in face-to-face interactions, Lave and Wenger (1991) and Wenger (1997) have argued that deliberately creating and engaging in larger "communities of practice" that share informal conversation as well as formal tasks is one way to get around the "body problem".

The design teams we observed in Second Life share a sense of joint enterprise that is enriched by the constant sharing of information to develop and strengthen group identity. Although it would seem that sharing tacit knowledge in a community of practice is complicated by a computer-mediated environment, many previous studies have shown empirically that computer-mediated communication and virtual design contribute to the sharing of design knowledge benefit from and are not harmed by the mediated form of communication (Woo, Clayton, et al, 2003).

The world of Second Life and its affordances appeared to contribute to a sense of shared enterprise and knowledge sharing. A member of the clothing/animation team commented on this when she told the researchers that she and her business partner were able to meet in Second Life in a way that would not have been possible in the real world, and they could bring their knowledge and experiences from outside of Second Life to their business in it by allowing them to design artifacts that would not have been as easily made or sold.

## 5 Discussion

Observation and interviews of the two Second Life design teams reveal interesting and challenging aspects of Second Life as a collaborative design platform, especially in relation to the issue of embodiment.

A number of CSCW studies show technical problems have a negative impact on team members' perception of and experience with team performance (Kayworth & Leidner, 2000; van Ryssen & Godar, 2000, cited in Powell et al, 2004). The common Second Life performance problems (e.g., lag, low frame rates) make communication difficult, highlighting the issue of awareness of the presence of team members in collaborative design settings. According to Sallnäs (2001), the notion of "presence" is related to the feeling "as if being more or less physically inside a computer-generated environment that feels like reality" (Sallnäs, 2001). The subjective perception of team members (represented by their avatars), coupled with one's psychological state of being in-world is what makes the feeling of "being there" possible. In demonstrating a newly built tool, the disaster relief training team spent a significant portion of its time and effort ensuring that everybody was present and looking at the same artifact under discussion. The perceptual disconnect and the psychological uncertainty with the team as a whole, brought on largely due to the partial rezzing of the avatars of the team members (i.e., lack of embodiment), greatly undermined team performance.

Interestingly enough, embodiment also factors in design research. One member of the clothing/animation team, who specializes in design research, often seeks out avatars in clubs to test out competitors' intimate animations. After the intimate encounter, she reports back to her team her (and her partners') reactions to the intimate animations. This type of research would not be possible were it not for the sexual desire of the partners she meets in clubs (who are often there to meet partners for cybersex), and she indicates that finding partners is even easier, because a real-life picture of herself is available in her profile, and men find her attractive.

## 6 Conclusion and Future Work

The Second Life environment, which unifies authoring, social interaction, and avatar action, create an unusually strong bond among avatars, environments, artifacts, and authoring tools. In unifying these, which have traditionally been spread across multiple windows, applications, and temporalities, Second Life constructs a unity around the avatar that is much stronger than traditional CVEs and CSCW applications, and the new unity also affects the practice of design.

Timeliness of delivery, good working relations, and designs that work are essential to creating an environment of trust, whether in work or play. Uncertainties are managed through use and re-use of artifacts and traces, but in virtual reality, we have found that the unfolding of the design process itself is a boundary object (and not just the end product of that process). In this phase of our research, we have identified collaborative design process and practices as well as some boundary objects and in subsequent stages, we expect to map them more systematically.

**Acknowledgments.** The authors wish to acknowledge the two teams who participated in this study and our colleague Jeffrey Bardzell for his insightful comments on the paper.

## References

1. Ackerman, M.S.: The Intellectual Challenge of CSCW: The Gap Between Social Requirements and Technical Feasibility. In: Carroll, J. (ed.) Human-Computer Interaction in the New Millennium, pp. 303–324. ACM Press, New York (2001)
2. Ackerman, M.S., Halverson, C.: Organizational Memory: Processes, Boundary Objects, and Trajectories. In: Proceedings of the IEEE Hawaii Int. Conf. of Syst. Sciences 1 (1999)
3. Benford, S., Greenhalgh, C., Roden, T., Pycock, J.: Collaborative virtual environments. Communications of the ACM 44(2), 79–85 (2001)
4. Cohen, S.G., Bailey, D.E.: What Makes Teams Work: Group Effectiveness Research from the Shop Floor to the Executive Suite. Journal of Management 23(3), 239–290 (1997)
5. Ducheneaut, N., Moore, R.: The Social Side of Gaming: A Study of Interaction Patterns in A Massively Multiplayer Online Game. In: Proceedings of CSCW'04, Chicago, IL, November 6-10, 2004, pp. 6–10. ACM Press, New York (2004)
6. Guimarães, M.J.L.: Doing Anthropology in Cyberspace: Fieldwork Boundaries and Social Environments. In: Hine, C. (ed.) Virtual Methods: Issues in Social Research on the Internet, pp. 141–157. Berg Press, Oxford (2005)
7. Harrison, S., Dourish, P.: Re-place-ing space: The roles of place and space in collaborative Systems. In: Proc. of CSCW'96. ACM Press, New York (1996)
8. Henderson, K.: Flexible Sketches and Inflexible Data Bases: Visual Communication, Conscription Devices, and Boundary Objects in Design Engineering. Science, Technology, and Human Values, vol. 16, pp. 448–473 (2005)
9. Lave, J., Wenger, E.: Situated Learning: Legitimate Peripheral Participation. Cambridge University Press, Cambridge, UK (1991)
10. Lutters, W.G., Ackerman, M.S.: Achieving Safety: a Field Study of Boundary Objects in Aircraft Technical Support. In: Proceedings of the 2002 ACM Conference on Computer Supported Cooperative Work, New Orleans, LA. pp. 266–275 (2002)

11. Murray, D.: An Ethnographic Study of Graphic Designers. In: Proc. of ECSC'94 (1994).
12. Nonaka, I.: A Dynamic Theory of Organizational Knowledge Creation. Org. Sci. 5, 14–37 (1994)
13. Powell, A., Piccoli, G., Ives, B.: Virtual Teams: A review of Current Literature and Directions for Future Research. The Data Base for Advances in Information Systems 35(1), 6–36 (2004)
14. Prasolova–Forland, E., Divitini, M.: Collaborative Virtual Environments for Supporting Learning Communities: An Experience of Use, Proceedings of the 2003 International ACM SIGGROUP Conference on Supporting Group Work, pp. 58–67 (2003)
15. Rosson, M., Maass, S., Kellogg, W.: The Designer As User: Building Requirements for Design Tools from Design Practice. Communications of the ACM 31(11) (1988)
16. Rutter, J., Smith, G.W.H.: Ethnographic Presence in a Nebulous Setting. In: Hine, C. (ed.) Virtual Methods: Issues in Social Research on the Internet, Berg Press, Oxford (2005)
17. Sallnäs, E.: Collaboration in Multi-Modal Virtual Worlds: Comparing Touch, Text, Voice, and Video. In: Schoreder, R. (ed.) The Social Life of Avatars: Presence and Interaction in Shared Virtual Environments, Springer-Verlang London Ltd (2001)
18. Snowdon, D., Churchill, E.F., Munro, A.: Collaborative virtual environments: Digital spaces and places for CSCW. An Introduction. In Churchill, E., Snowdon, D., Munro, A. (eds): Collaborative Virtual Environments: Digital Places and Spaces for Interaction Springer-Verlang London Ltd (2001) http://www.cvebook.com/pages/chapter1.php
19. Star, S.L., Griesmer, J.: Institutional Ecology, 'Translations,' and Boundary Objects: Amateurs and Professionals in Berkeley's Museum of Vertebrate Zoology, 1907-39 Social Studies of Science 19, 387–420 (1989)
20. Twidale, M., Rodden, T., Sommerville, I.: The Designers' Notepad: Supporting and Understanding Cooperative Design. In: Proc. of ECSC'93 (1993)
21. Wenger, E.: Communities of Practice. Cambridge University Press, Cambridge, UK (1998)
22. Woo, J.-H., Clayton, M., Johnson, R., Flores, B., Ellis, C.: Sharing Tacit Design Knowledge in a Distributed Design Environment (2003) Report available: http://www.aia.org/SiteObjects/files/Woo_color.pdf
23. Wright, P., McCarthy, J., Blythe, M., Coyne, R., Boeher, K.: Space, place, and experience in Human-Computer Interaction. In: Proc. of Interact'05. ACM Press, New York (2005)

# Visuo-Haptic Blending Applied to a Tele-Touch-Diagnosis Application

Benjamin Bayart[1], Abdelhamid Drif[1], Abderrahmane Kheddar[1,2], and Jean-Yves Didier[1]

[1] UEVE/CNRS Informatique, Biologie Intégrative et Systèmes Complexes (IBISC) France
[2] AIST/CNRS Joint Japanese-French Robotics Laboratory (JRL), Tsukuba, Japan
{bayart,adrif,didier}@iup.univ-evry.fr, kheddar@ieee.org

**Abstract.** This paper introduces a concept of augmented reality haptics close to its vision equivalent, namely the blending of information between direct input, measured in the real world, with virtual ones, computed from a VR simulation, related to the explored real world. Hence, we propose blending functions enabling the transition of haptic features, applied for forces and for position switch. Finally, to demonstrate our concept, a tele-operative system dedicated to the tele-touch-diagnosis, is presented and used for scenarios of comparison between real and virtual objects as well as experimental results.

**Keywords:** Augmented Haptics, tele-operation, Haptic blending.

## 1 Introduction

One of the main purposes of classical vision-based Augmented Reality (AR) is to merge real and virtual worlds, related to each other, in a same display environment. A common use of this functionality is to enhance lacking information or missing parts in images of real objects using a virtual model. Nonetheless, as pointed in [1], the AR concept extends to all the other human senses: sight, touch, smell, taste and hearing. Our work, first introduced in [2] focuses on extending AR to haptic, which is the branch of Virtual Reality (VR) focusing on simulating and stimulating the human sense of touch. Indeed, the haptic component may either enhance or be enhanced to provide, similarly to vision-based AR, extra information. We define the term of Augmented Haptic when the haptic feedback is overloaded, partially or completely, with extra haptic cue(s). We can instance this idea with the following examples:

- Increase the value of the forces fed back to reveal a default: feeling small bumps or holes on a surface;
- Add buzzing to the haptic feedback, to warn the user: prevent the operator to touch a sensitive part;

In this paper, we discuss the possibility to conceive augmented reality haptic using the same schemes as its vision equivalent. Both of them consist in blending information between direct input, measured in the real world, with virtual ones,

R. Shumaker (Ed.): Virtual Reality, HCII 2007, LNCS 4563, pp. 617–626, 2007.

computed from a related VR simulation, running in parallel, as shown in figure [1]. Hence, in the first part of the paper, related works are compiled, followed by the study of the augmented haptic feedback and the presentation of our haptic rendering switches. Finally, our tele-touch-diagnosis setup is presented as well as experiments based on these functions in the last part.

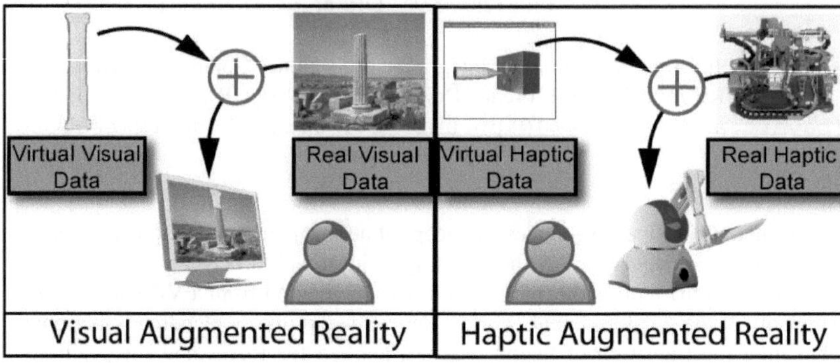


**Fig. 1.** Similarly to typical visual AR, we propose extensions to haptic, when users are either fed back with real haptic data, virtual ones or a mix of both

## 2 Related Works

The originality of our work is based on the modification of the haptic features fed back to the operator. We believe that our concept illustrates the terminology of Augmented Haptic, even if the notion of haptic augmented reality has already been expressed in different applications.

In [3], the augmented reality system merges in real-time synthetic haptic input into the user's perception of the real environment in addition to visual augmentation. This allows user interaction between virtual and real objects. In [4] the calibration method has been improved and allowed a better integration of haptics into visual AR. In [5], the authors designed and implemented an AR system called VisHap that uses visual tracking to seamlessly integrate force with tactile feedback. This system is capable of generating a ``complete" haptic experience, which avoids drawbacks inherent in attaching the haptic device to the user. Nonetheless, despite the use of the term Augmented Haptic in these researches, none so far have tried to define clearly the concept of augmented haptic or tried to blend real and virtual forces. A first proposal has been attempted in [6]. Actually, their approach aimed at combining passive haptic, resulting from the real interaction with a simple flat board, and virtual forces computed to simulate buttons. In [7], [8], the haptic feedback is also used to provide additional non-passive information in case of insufficient control conditions. These works illustrate properly the second category of the taxonomy presented in [2], namely Enhanced Haptic, where the haptic component is used to bring extra-information, different from the lonely manipulation of the distant part.

The next section provides a general presentation on the Augmented Haptic rendering applied to the comparison and blend between real and virtual haptic features.

# 3 Revisiting the AR Concept

## 3.1 Real and Virtual Calibration

The AR concept lies upon the merge of two worlds, a real and a virtual one. We define $\mathrm{O}_R$ and $\mathrm{O}_V$, respectively, as the set of real and virtual objects of each world, and $O_R \in \mathrm{O}_R$ and $O_V \in \mathrm{O}_V$ as particular related objects of these sets. When there is a perfect geometrical calibration between the pair $O_V \times O_R$, through a unique homogeneous $4 \times 4$ transformation matrix T, we can write:

$$\forall x_R \in O_R, \exists x_V \in O_V / x_V = T \times x_R . \tag{1}$$

When adding any other virtual object $O_V{}'$, the transformation $T_o$ between $O_V$ and $O_V{}'$ is computed and consequently the transformation between $O_R$ and $O_V{}'$.

## 3.2 Information Blending

From the generalization of the AR concept, a typical haptic augmented reality consists in rendering blended data, the one coming from a interaction with $O_R$ through $S_R$, sensory sampling the real world, the other generated from a virtual object parallel interaction of $O_V$ through $S_V$, simulated equivalent sensors in the virtual world, once a initial calibration has been done. Let $B$ be the blending function between data vector $d_V$ obtained from a mapping of $S_V$, and $d_R$ obtained from a mapping measurement $S_R$, that is

$$d = B(d_V, d_R) . \tag{2}$$

where $d$ is the vector of rendered data parameter to the operator. We may also define the two following properties:

$$B(d_V, 0) = d_V \text{ and } B(0, d_R) = d_R . \tag{3}$$

Which represents respectively an exclusive real and virtual feedback.

In vision-based AR, this interaction is made through the visual channel, and where the color $C_R$, the contrast $L_R$ ...are part of $d_R$. The result is the merging of a virtual image onto the representation of the real one. Nonetheless, we extend the concept to haptics considering that possible haptic data consist in the interaction force $F$ (including frictions), temperature $\theta_R$, etc. Then we consider the virtual haptic vector

$h_V$ obtained from a mapping of $S_V$, and the real haptic vector $h_R$ obtained from a mapping measurement $S_R$.

Augmenting haptics during the exploration is nearly impossible to make without an intermediary interface capable of rendering artificial haptic information on the top of, or instead of missing, real haptic data. Hence, instead of having a direct contact, an haptic sampling device is required in order to collect directly haptic data, in the same way a camera does in vision based AR. These devices fall into haptic feedback teleoperators' technology, and various robotic designs can be considered. Haptic sampling devices can therefore be remotely placed. Assuming the use of a non-direct haptic device for the exploration, we introduce $P_m$ the master haptic probe.

### 3.3 Haptic Blending

We then offer to the operator to explore by touch a given object as fully virtual or fully real or a parameterized blending of both. Let $P_R$ be a real haptic probe, its purpose being to sample haptic information from a real object's surface $O_R$ ; $P_V$ is a virtual probe, purpose of which is to compute forces from an interaction with a virtual object $O_V$. $P_R$ is a chosen point on the sampling haptic device, that is controlled directly from the operator instructions through the master haptic interface $P_m$. $P_V$ is a numerical representation of $P_R$ that is controlled also from operator instructions through the same haptic interface. There are several robust and efficient methods to couple the virtual and real probes and the haptic display device, readers may refer to [9], [10]. Haptics AR is then reduced to express the blending function $B$ in eq. (2). Furthermore we assume that a full or a partial 3D (i.e. at areas of interest) model of $O_R$ exists in the form of numerical data represented by $O_V$.

A linear α-blending could be for instance

$$h = \alpha \times h_V + (1-\alpha) \times h_R \ . \tag{4}$$

where α is a tunable parameter which reflects the blending balance. $\alpha = 1 \rightarrow h = h_V$ and when $\alpha = 0 \rightarrow h = h_R$. α could be a scalar common to each component of $h_{i\in\{V,R\}}$ or a transpose of a vector $a$ in which each component may have a different value of $\alpha \in [0,1]$ interval.

$$a = (\alpha_1, \alpha_2, \ldots \alpha_n)^T \text{ and } h = a^T \times h_V + (1-a)^T \times h_R \ . \tag{5}$$

Here, there is not distinction between all the components of $h_{i\in\{V,R\}}$, but we will need to differentiate between positions and forces according to discrepancies that may appear between what is expected and what is really sensed. The developed theory, although simple, has been formalized in order to ease its implementation. Hence depending on the knowledge about the discrepancies' location, two strategies are proposed:

**Known discrepancies' location.** When exploring an impaired object, if the location of the discrepancies are known (or accurately determined in real-time by using several kind of sensors), recovering virtual patches are placed at appropriate spots. We however add a thick virtual border between the virtual patches and real object in order to avoid discontinuity in haptic rendering and smooth the transition. If $\alpha$ is the thickness of the virtual border, the blending will smooth the transition and avoid the instability occurring when switching from one feedback to the other. Actually $\alpha$ varies as follows:

– outside the deteriorated zone : $\alpha = 0$ and real forces are sent back to the user
– in the transition part:
  - from 0 to 1, i.e. from real to virtual
  - from 1 to 0, i.e. from virtual to real
– -within the deteriorated zone : $\alpha = 1$ and virtuall forces are sent back to the user

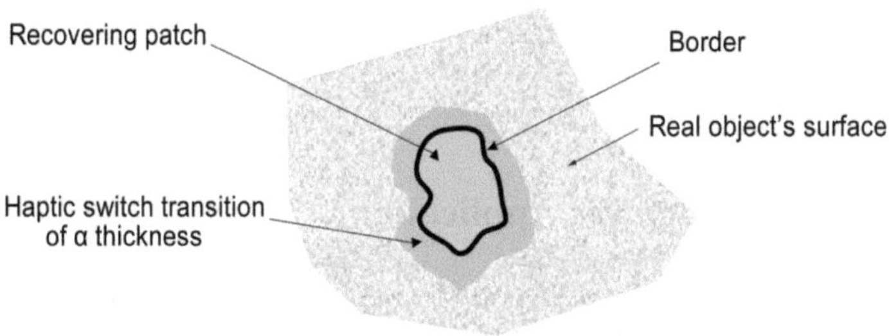


**Fig. 2.** Concept of the patch recovering the impaired zone of the object. The size of the patch is wider than the hole in order to ensure continuity in haptic rendering.

**Unknown discrepancies' location.** A situation may occur when the positions of $P_R$ and $P_V$ do not match along either normal or orthogonal direction, due to an unknown discrepancy (e.g. presence of crack, whole, bump on $O_R$ without being on $O_V$ ). In such a case, $\alpha$ cannot be tuned automatically, from the position knowledge. Thus, a continuous control and comparison method is proposed to warn the operator about this discrepancy, and allow him to take the decision to investigate what the difference is about. In order to make the operator perceive the difference state, we need to provide switching at will (tuning $\alpha$ to either 0 or 1) allowing him to touch locally exclusively either the real object $O_R$ or the virtual one $O_V$ .

The switching, presented in the following algorithm, processes as follows: when a discrepancy is noticed by the position comparison function $C$ , a warning and a trajectory logging process are triggered. The non-operating probe is stopped at the first discrepancy point and the operating one continues exploration. When the operator decides to switch the mode (real or virtual) of exploration, a force field is generated along the saved trajectory for backtracking to the first point. When the operator reaches this point, the probes are switched and bilaterally coupled, and the exploration resumes in the other mode.

```
For each haptic step t do
  Send Pm to distant setup and receive Pr and Fr
  Insert Pm to the simulation and calculate Pv and Fv
    if (Exploration==Real) then
      if (C(Pr,Pv)==FALSE) then
        Record Pr in RPr, Pv=STAYS, WARNING, endif
      Apply Fr (real force)
    else if (Exploration==Virtual) then
      if (C(Pr,Pv)==FALSE) then
        Record Pv in RPv, Pr=STAYS, WARNING, endif
      Apply Fv (virtual force)
    else SWITCH
      if From Real to Virtual then
        Pr=Replay RPr
        Apply F=B(Pm,Pr)
      else
        Pv=Replay RPv
        Apply F=B(Pm,Pv)
      endif
    endif
endfor
```

## 4 A Tele-Touch-Diagnosis Application

As pointed out, a tele-operated haptic device is required to modify the haptic feedback. Hence we designed a system dedicated to the exploration of a remote object, comparing its surface and geometry with their theoretical values.

### 4.1 Setup Description

The whole teleoperative system comprises three major components.

A standard PHANToM Omni interface, ref figure 3.A, taken as a master haptic device, that measures the user's position in space and that applies feedback forces on the user's hand.

A remote *xyz* cartesian robot taken as a slave robot, equipped with a sensing exploratory probe, ensuring position remote control, as shown in figures 3.B This device has been designed for virtual and augmented reality applications involving multimodal interactions [11].

A software implementation designed as a multi-threaded application including:

- a slave controller implemented to initialize the slave robot configuration and to supervise the position servo-control.
- a thread dedicated to the VR simulation where a virtual scene of the distant environment is reproduced using OpenGL for the visual display
- a haptic thread, using the HDAPI library from Sensable Technologies, dealing with the control force feedback mapping.

Working within a local network, the delay is less than 1msec.

**Fig. 3.** The different components of the setup. A: The master device. B: the distant haptic robot C: The VR simulation.

## 4.2 Virtual and Real Slave Registration

Since we would like to interact with both real and virtual environments, a calibration procedure is requested. Actually, the geometrical transform between the tip of the probe and the explored object is to be known at anytime. We call $T_{xy}$ the geometrical transform between the local coordinate system of an object Y (called $\{y\}$) and an object X (called $\{x\}$).

The first step of our calibration procedure aims at determining the pose of the probe ($p$) at the initial start. This is performed using a camera ($c$) and several ARToolkit-like markers. Once the camera calibrated using Zhang's method [12], one marker is stuck on the object ($o$) while a second one is placed at the basis ($b$) of the probe. We note that the transformation between the tip and the basis of the probe is known since it consists in a rigid transformation ($T_{p0b}$). Then we can determine $T_{co}$ and $T_{cb}$ .The transformation between the tip of the probe and the object is then expressed as follows:

$$T_{p0b} = T_{pb} \times T_{co}^{-1} \times T_{cb} \ . \tag{6}$$

The second step consists in expressing the pose of the tip of the probe anytime. The probe being mounted on the distant robot equipped with position sensors, the transformation $T_{pp0}$ of the slave device when we move the probe at any time $t$ is known and then the current relation between the probe and the object is:

$$T_{po} = T_{pp0}(t) \times T_{p0b} \ . \tag{7}$$

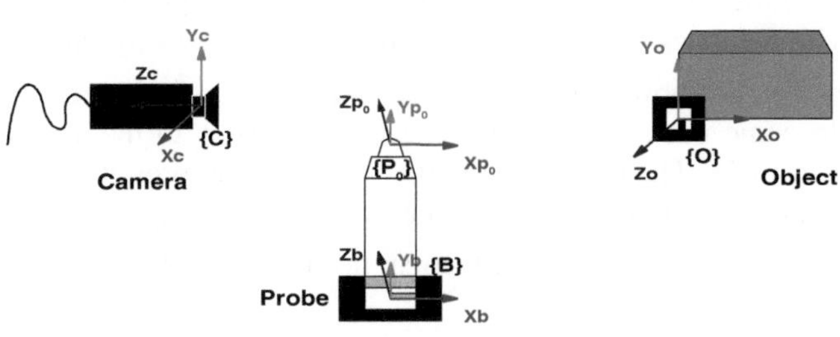


**Fig. 4.** Coordinates systems relationships between the camera, the probe and the object

## 5 Experimentation and Results

In order to assess the benefits of our method, we designed two experiments where users have to explore a impaired objects in both situation where the location of the deteriorated part is known or unknown.

### 5.1 Known Discrepancies Location

As discussed in 3, if the location of the damages is known, we propose to recover the determined spots with virtual patches, as shown in figure 2. Thus we tried our blending method on a specific case where the location of the hole is known. Figure 5 presents the result of the transition.

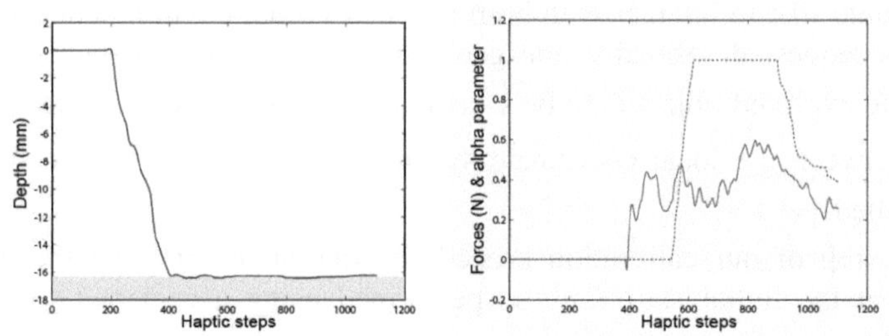


**Fig. 5.** Recordings of the probe position from the start point (at depth=0) to the surface of the object (at depth=-16.5) (left image) and the forces applied on the user's device and the α parameter (right image)

### 5.2 Unknown Discrepancies Location

Figure 6 shows the second used scenario, where the location is not known and where two kinds of discrepancies subsist between the real object and the virtual. The real object $O_R$ consists in a flat surface with a hole on its right, while the virtual one *Ov*, representing the original object, is a flat surface with a hole on its left. On the different pictures, the light gray probe represents the real one $P_R$ while the light orange the virtual one $P_V$. In step A, when starting the exploration, with real haptic feedback, both probe's position match. In B, a difference of position appears between them. In this case, our strategy consists in allowing the real probe to continue to move and explore with feedback from $O_R$, while the virtual probe stays at the first location of discrepancy *Dp*, as shown in C; Moreover, the path of *Pr* is recorded and allows the operator to come back to *Dp* when the user switches to the virtual exploration mode, as shown in D. Then, the exploration resumes, as presented in E, with now feedback from the VR simulation, i.e. forces when interacting with $O_V$ .Similarly in F, there is a difference of position and the real probe stays still while the virtual probe continues.

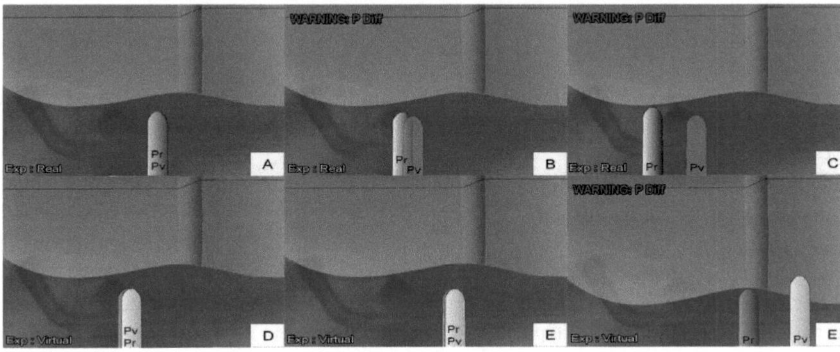


**Fig. 6.** The 6 steps of the scenario used to explore the real and the virtual object. The mode of exploration as well as the warning are visually displayed similarly to our VR application.

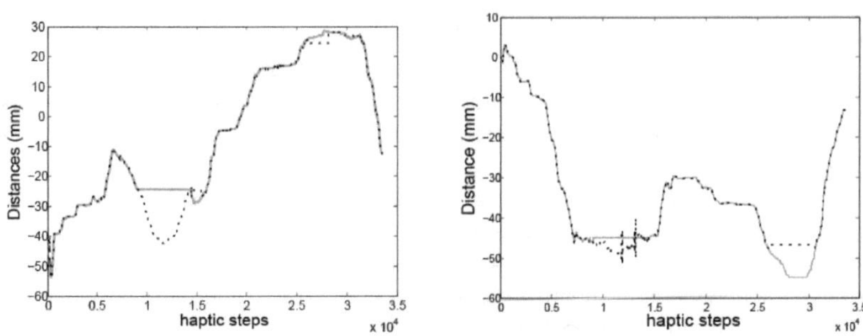


**Fig. 7.** The figures present the recording of the real probe $P_R$ (dark dotted line), and the virtual probe's movement $P_V$ (light continuous line), along the tangential direction (left) and the normal direction (right)

## 6 Conclusion and Future Work

In this paper, we introduce a generalization of the AR concept dedicated to the merge of visual and haptic information coming from real and virtual worlds, especially using an α-blending method. In order to ascertain the benefits of such theory, we present the setup we developed in order to allow a tele-touch-diagnosis, merging real and virtual information data, in the cases when the location of impairment is known or unknown. Several issues remain and need to be investigated further, such as the possible use of these concepts, the design of specific setups, etc.

In the future, a longer test will be proposed to users to determine the defective part(s) on several objects without prior knowledge about the damage location and investigation with other haptic features.

## References


1. Azuma, R., Baillot, Y., Behringer, R., Feiner, S., Julier, S., MacIntyre, B.: Recent advances in augmented reality. In: IEEE Computer Graphics and Application 21(6), pp. 34–47 (2001)
2. Bayart, B., Kheddar, A.: Haptic augmented reality taxonomy: haptic enhancing and enhanced haptics. In: EuroHaptics 2006, pp. 641–644 (2006)
3. Vallino, J., Brown, C.M.: Haptics in augmented reality. In: Proceedings of the IEEE International Conference on Multimedia Computing and Systems (1999)
4. Bianchi, G., Knoerlein, B., Szekely, G., Harders, M.: High precision augmented reality haptics. In: EuroHaptics 2006, pp. 169–177 (2006)
5. Ye, G., Corso, J.J., Hager, G.D., Okamura, A.M.: Vishap: Augmented reality combining haptics and vision. In: Proceedings of IEEE International Conference on Systems, Man and Cybernetics 2003, pp. 3425–3431 (2003)
6. Borst, C.W., Volz, R.A.: Evaluation of a haptic mixed reality system for interactions with a virtual control panel. Presence: Teleoperators & Virtual Environments 14(6), pp. 677–696 (2005)
7. Hwang, G., Aarno, D., Hashimoto, H.: Haptic guidant bilateral teleoperation for single-master multi-slave system. In: EuroHaptics 2006, pp. 401–406 (2006)
8. Turro, N., Khatib, O., Coste-Maniere, E.: Haptically augmented teleoperation. In: Proceedings of IEEE International Conference on Robotics and Automation, Seoul, Korea, 2001, pp. 366–392 (2001)
9. Hannaford, B.: A design framework for teleoperators with kinesthetic feedback. IEEE Transaction on Robotics and Automation (1989)
10. Hashtrudi-Zaad, K., Salcudean, S.E.: Analysis and evaluation of stability and performance robustness for teleoperation control architectures. In: IEEE International Conference on Robotics and Automation 2000 (2000).
11. Kheddar, A., Drif, A., Citerin, J., Le Mercier, B.: A multilevel haptic rendering concept. In: Eurohaptic 2004 (2004)
12. Zhang, Z.: Flexible camera calibration by viewing a plane from unknown orientations. In: International Conference on Computer Vision 1, p. 666 (1999)

# Design of Water Transportation Story for Grand Canal Museum Based on Multi-projection Screens

Linqiang Chen[1], Gengdai Liu[2], Zhigeng Pan[2], and Zhi Li[3]

[1] Department of Computer Science, Hangzhou Dianzi University, Hangzhou 310000,China
[2] State Key Lab of CAD&CG, Zhejiang University, Hangzhou, 310058, China
[3] Ningbo Institute of Technology, Zhejiang University, Ningbo, 315100, China
chenlinqiang@163.com, {liugengdai,zgpan}@cad.zju.edu.cn,
iback1121@yahoo.com.cn

**Abstract.** This paper presents a method for cultural heritage exhibition. A design scheme of multi-projection screens based digital storytelling system for the Grand Canal Museum in China is introduced. The task of this system is to exhibit a famous Chinese painting on a large display wall dynamically. In order to display this painting in a large display wall, the painting have to be repainted with very high resolution and segmented into many smaller tiles for being projected onto the large wall. Additionally, in order to make this static painting attractive and charming, the technology of digital storytelling is used. So a script called *water transportation story* is composed elaborately by us to show the magnificent scene along the Grand Canal.

**Keywords:** digital heritage, multi-projection screens, virtual reality, digital storytelling.

## 1 Introduction

China is an ancient country with long history and glorious culture. A large quantity of artworks has been handed down from generation to generation. However, some forms of art have disappeared with time elapsing. We should study how to combine traditional culture and modern technology, use novel technology to preserve and exhibit traditional art and even create new forms of art more than only study how to preserve the cultural relics.

In this paper, a multi-projection screens based digital storytelling system for the Grand Canal Museum is presented. The task of this system is to exhibit a famous Chinese painting on a large display wall dynamically [1]. The famous ancient painting, *Qingming Festival by The Riverside* that is done in Song dynasty is a rare realistic painting and thought to be a world-class cultural relic. It is about 500 centimeters long and 25 centimeters wide. This painting gives us a bird's eye view of the flourishing scene of Bianliang, the capital of Song dynasty. It was painted from a panoramic view and detailed scenes along the river that stretched for dozens of miles were covered. A part of this painting is showed in Figure 1.

To display this large Chinese painting dynamically and keep artistic appeal, we did a multi-projection system for the Grand Canal Museum. The museum arranged specially

R. Shumaker (Ed.): Virtual Reality, HCII 2007, LNCS 4563, pp. 627–632, 2007.

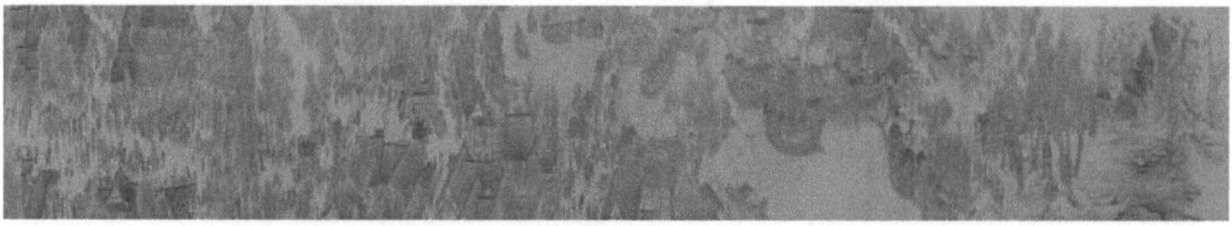

**Fig. 1.** The painting of *Qingming Festival by The Riverside*

a huge hall for this system. In the hall, there is a very large wall with 6 meters high and 12 meters long, which is used as large screen. The surface of this wall is specially treated so that it can give good diffuse reflection. The painting, *Qingming Festival by The Riverside* is repainted by artists and then is projected on the large screen. The music and commentary is played synchronously as the video goes on so that he flourishing scene of the capital of Song dynasty shows before us vividly, as if we stand in the real street of the ancient city.

It is necessary to make the objects on this still painting locomotive, so as to enhance the expression force of this famous painting. Therefore, the method of applying IBR (Image Based Rendering) technology and computer animation to create a 2D picture with locomotive 3D objects on it and display the video on a large screen is used. To reconstruct the realistic scene in the past, we use the technology of digital storytelling. We compose a script, which consists of 11 scenarios.

In the next section, the related works about digital cultural heritage and digital museum are introduced. And in the third section, we described the multi-projection systems in detail. Then the script we composed is introduced. Finally, we give the conclusion and future work.

## 2 Related Works

The technology of digital museum is an effective method to preserve those natural and cultural heritage. More and more specialists in heritage preservation and computer science are engaged in this field. Hu[2] made a summary of the application of virtual reality and digital media in the field of digital museum.

As for the current research situation of digital museum, there are four main aspects focused by researchers in the world. The first one is the digitization, storage and display of cultural relics. Liu[3] introduced how to digitize, process and exhibit the Dunhuang frescoes using computers. Wang[4] introduced how to capture and process the model of Terracotta Warriors in Emperor Qinshihuang's mausoleum, and presented a method of texture mapping. The second aspect involves virtual museums on the Internet. Kwon[5] presented the key techniques of digital museum on the internet, and a general scheme of the modeling, management, storage and transmission of large quantity of data of digital museum. The third aspect is concerning how to create the avatar-based multi-user immersive virtual museum. Usaka[6] presented the prototype system of an immersive virtual museum. The terminal users can enter the virtual museum as avatars via Internet to visit all the exhibits in it and can communicate with other users.

The forth aspect is the application of virtual reality in the real museums. Lin[7] implemented the PC Cluster-based CAVE system, named PCCAVE, which has been applied to display virtual cultural sites. Pletinckx[8] introduced the application of virtual reality in a real museum at Ename, Belgium. Ding[9] presented a large screen projection system using 3 projectors to display an ancient street in Hangzhou, China. In our work, the most important distinction is that the display wall is much larger and much more projectors are employed.

## 3 Projection System

The display wall in the museum is 6 meters high and 12 meters wide. We have to design a multi-projection screens based projection system in terms of the size of the wall. Therefore a PC-based multi-channel VR projection system is employed in order to project a high-resolution storytelling video on so large a display wall. Considering the area of the wall, the distance between the wall and the projectors and brightness those projectors can give off, we decided to use 30 projectors, 31 high-performance PCs and a clustering multi-channel switch.

Those 30 projectors compose a 3*10 projectors matrix, and accordingly the whole screen is split into 30 rectangular tiles, each of which is covered by the image from one projectors. C/S architecture can be used in this projection system. The video is played and every frame is segmented into 30 tiles in the PC server. Then each segment is transmitted to the corresponding client PC through switch synchronously. Each client connected with a projector is responsible for rendering one tile and projecting this tile to the proper position on the large wall. The architecture of projection system used in our system is shown in Figure 2.

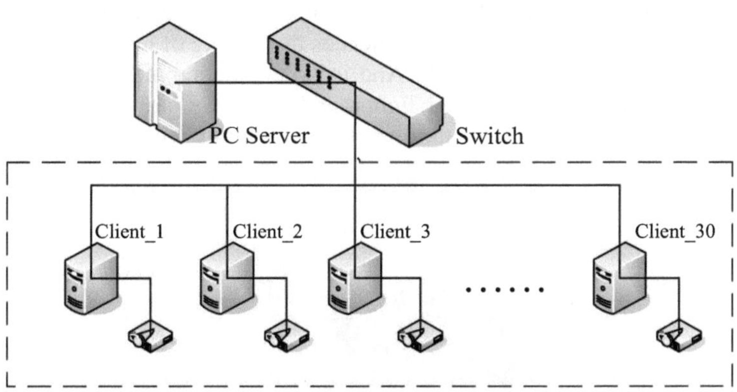


**Fig. 2.** The framework of projection system

In order to guarantee that the video on the large wall is consistent and these 30 tiles are seamlessly stitched, geometric calibration must be used. But the manual calibration is boring, especially for so many projectors, because the position and orientation of every projector should be adjusted. So we decided to use software geometric calibration to stitch all the tiles seamlessly and automatically. Multiple mapping matrices are used for tiled display during software geometric calibration as Zhou describes[10]. Multiple matrices are computed for each projector to map each pixel on the projected screen to the frame buffer. The method goes as follow: firstly, feature points for each projector are displayed alternatively. Secondly, feature points for each projector are taken photos. Then, the calibration algorithm starts to recognize the feature points and calculate the mapping matrices and the effective projection regions. Multiple mapping matrices method means that one matrix on each calibration point must be calculated and then the corresponding point in the frame buffer can be found. Then all other pixels will be mapped to the frame buffer like texture mapping. This method guarantees that there's no overlap region and gaps between two adjacent projectors. The configuration of this system has to be high, especially the memories and network cards of PC server and throughput and bandwidth of the multi-channel switch due to the large quantity of data.

In our system, every frame of the video must be segmented into 30 tiles and all the data of these tiles have to be transmitted through the switch, which put heavy burden on the PC server and the multi-channel switch. So we have to reduce the resolution of the video. However, because the distance between the wall and the audiences is far enough, the question caused by lower resolution can be ignored and the final result is quite acceptable.

# 4 Implementation of the System

## 4.1 Creation of the Video

The video is created with Maya[11], Photoshop and After Effects[12]. Maya is used for 3D modeling, Photoshop is used for images and textures edit, and After Effects is used for video edit and mix. In order to give audiences the feeling of historical grandeur, the hue of the video is dim and yellowish. And in order to combine 3D objects with 2D background harmoniously, textures, lights and shadows are created and edited elaborately. Figure 3 shows a 3D walking horse in harmony with the background.

**Fig. 3.** The horse in harmony with the background

## 4.2 Design of Storytelling

In order to make this static painting attractive and charming, the technology of digital storytelling is used. So a script called *water transportation story* is composed elaborately by us to show the magnificent scene along the Grand Canal. This story is composed of many scenarios. For example, in the first scenario called *Transportation Start*, many porters carried goods onto the boats by the riverside, and then boatmen ferried the goods along the river. There are some other locomotive objects in the river or by the riverside, such as carriages, mill wheels, pedestrians and other workers as shown in Figure 4.

**Fig. 4.** The turning mill wheel and working people

**Fig. 5.** Scenario 1 of the story

Many other scenarios then follows, such as *Listening To Music in Yangzhou* and *The Shadow of Tongzhou* Pagoda, etc. Each scenario tells a historic story happened at a famous place along the Grand Canal. The final result of first scenario is shown in Figure 5.

## 5 Conclusion and Future Work

A multi-projection screens based projection system has been introduced to cultural heritage exhibition. In this system 30 projectors, 31 high-performance PCs and a multi-channel switch are used in order to project the painting on a very large display wall. We use software calibration method for all the projectors in stead of manual calibration because the manual calibration method is too boring and software calibration can lead better result. We repaint the original painting and put some locomotive 3D objects on it to make the scene more lively and magnificent. To discover the story hidden behind the famous painting, a script composed of 11 scenarios is plotted.

In this paper, we present our design plan and the system will be implemented in the future. At present, our system can only play pretreated video and there is no interactive capability. In the real implementation, we intend to make this system interactive. So the audiences can enjoy the novel experience brought about by the interactive storytelling. Another point could be improved lies in the architecture of the projection system. We can change it to meet the problems caused by simple C/S architecture.

**Acknowledgements.** This research work is co-supported by NSFC project on "Virtual Olympic Museum"(grant no:60533080) and 863 project on "Digital Media Authoring Platform"(grant no:2006AA01Z335).

## References

1. Li, Z., Liu, G.D., Pan, Z.G.: Story of Ancient Water Transportation: Design of A Virtual Presentation System. The 4th Workshop on Digital Museum and Digital Heritage (2006)
2. Hu, W.X., Pan, Z.G., et al.: Digitized World Heritage Protection Methods. Journal of System Simulation 15(3), 315–318 (2003)
3. Liu, Y., Lu, D.M., et al.: Dunhuang 285 Cave Multimedia Integrated Virtual Exhibit. Journal of Computer-Aided Design & Computer Graphics 16(11), 1528–1533 (2004)
4. Wang, J., He, M.Y., et al.: Research on Digitizing Processing of The Terracotta Warriors And Horses of The Qin Dynasty. In: Proc. of GMAG'03, pp. 201–207. IEEE Press, New York (2003)
5. Kwon, Y.M., Kim, I.J., et al.: Virtual Heritage System: Modeling, Database & Presentation. In: Proc. of VSMM'01, IEEE Press, New York (2001)
6. Usaka, T., Sakamura, K.: A Design and Evaluation of the Multi-User Virtual Environment Server System for the Digital Museum. In: Proceedings of the 13th TRON Project International Symposium, pp. 60–69. IEEE Press, New York (1996)
7. Lin, B.W., Pan, Z.G., Yang, J., Shi, J.Y.: PC-Based High Performance CAVE System. Journal of Computer-Aided Design & Computer Graphics 15(6), 724–729 (2003)
8. Pletinckx, D., Callebaut, D., et al.: Virtual-Reality Heritage Presentation at Ename. In: IEEE Multimedia, vol. 7, pp. 45–48. IEEE Press, New York (2000)
9. Ding, J.H., Wang, Y.G., Pan, Z.G.: Hefang Street Walkthrough Based on Large - Scale Projector System. Journal of Hangzhou Dianzi University 25(1), 56–59 (2005)
10. Zhou, R., Lin, H., Shi, J.Y.: Geometric Calibration on Tiled Display Using Multiple Matrices. In: Proceeding of Pacific Graphics 2005, pp. 97–99 (2005)
11. Autodesk Maya Documentation, http://www.autodesk.com/maya
12. Rankin, J., Ulrich, A.: Adobe After Effects 6.5 Magic. New Rider Press (2005)

# VIDEODOPE: Applying Persuasive Technology to Improve Awareness of Drugs Abuse Effects

Luciano Gamberini, Luca Breda, and Alessandro Grassi

Human Technology Lab
Department of General Psychology
University of Padua, Italy

**Abstract.** *Videodope* is an interactive digital environment that is meant to show the short-, medium- and long-run effects of psychoactive substances on the human organism. Its purpose is to increase the users' knowledge of these effects, which is often based on misconceptions and legends, and to provide a feedback on their level of information, with preventive purposes. These kind of educational games have the advantage of being more persistent, ubiquitous, informative, anonymous and multi-medial than a normal lecture. However, they have to be perceived as credible and plausible to the user in order to be persuasive, especially since the target is constituted of young people familiar both with the technology and with the subject. In this paper, we will describe the process of designing and evaluating the videogame in the field, as well as the insights provided by the participants who took part to the evaluation.

## 1 Theoretical Background

This paper describes a digital environment devoted to an application in the area of persuasive technologies. This area studies the use of technical artifacts designed to modify the users' believes, attitudes and behaviors without any explicit persuasive message, and without any coercion or defeat [1]. These technologies are applied to education, to provide interactive lessons on selected subjects or to promote specific types of safety behaviors in the users [2]. Tools such as educational videogames can be able to capture the user by adopting a language they like [3] and offer the advantages of scalability, persistency, ubiquity, anonymity, multimodality and can store, access, and manipulate huge volumes of data [1]. It can approach users in situations where a physician or an educator would be perceived as inadequate or even hostile, and can be used in a variety of settings, individual or shared, local or networked.

One area of intervention that seems particularly challenging is the prevention of psychoactive substance abuse. In Italy, where this software was developed and tested, the highest consumers of psychoactive substances are people aged 15 to 24, as emerged from an anonymous survey conducted on a random sample of respondents from a representative amount of municipalities [4]. The contexts in which the assumption is more likely to occur are connected to night aggregation (concerts,

R. Shumaker (Ed.): Virtual Reality, HCII 2007, LNCS 4563, pp. 633–641, 2007.

private parties, clubs and discos), and specific music genres [5]. The increased use of cannabis and cocaine, the great diffusion of so-called 'designer drugs' where psychotropic molecules are combined and manipulated to obtain new effects, and the multiple abuse of different substances depict a complex phenomenon that needs adequate tools to be coped with [5, 6]. Becker's underlies that the use of substances has sub-cultural roots [7]; any 'deviance' is conceived as the consequence of the acquisition of norms and values from the group of belonging. The reason for trying and assume a substance is mediated by the sub-cultural context to which the person belongs, whose believes and information are also responsible for shaping the way in which the risk associated to the consumption of substances is perceived [7]. It has been shown for instance that the dangerousness of risky behaviors such as driving upon assumption of psychoactive substances [8] or the addictiveness of certain substances [9] are generally underestimated. The interactive environment that we present here is called 'Videodope', and is meant to provide information on the consequences of the abuse of psychoactive substances in order to improve awareness in the target users and t counter the commonsensical knowledge that often informs risky behaviors. It may represent an effective way to approach adolescents and young adults with an informative proposal that is consonant with their own language, with the kind of music and graphics they are accustomed with and that can be offered directly in the places they use to go. Classic preventive strategies may look boring, ridiculous or even hostile. Even though an educational videogame seems more adequate to reach young people where they aggregate and have fun, in order to be convincing it must take into account the habits and environment in which consumers leave. In fact, a determinant role in a persuasive process is played by the relevance and appropriateness of the way in which the information is proposed, as well as by the credibility of such information [10, 11, 12]. Dutta-Bergman, for instance, conducted a study on health information available on the Internet and found that it the more complete it was perceived, the more credible is was judged [13]. This concern about credibility has informed the development and testing of Videodope, which will be described in the following paragraphs.

## 2 The Digital Environment

Videodope is a non -immersive virtual environment developed with Virtools Dev 3.0 and 3D Studio Max. It contains an informative module and a comprehension check. The former is based on the idea of showing a model of a human being. The organs affected by a selected drug appear in transparency, along with the information on the damages derived from abuse. The other module is a quiz-like test, with questions related to the information displayed in the previous module. Finally, to make the environment plausible with respect to the users' tastes, the appearance and the clothes of the human body were accurately designed so as to look similar to those of club-goers.

The navigation in Videodope starts by clicking on the related icon; the user selects the human model's gender and a type of drug among several possible ones: alcohol, hallucinogens, amphetamine, cannabis, cocaine, ecstasy, heroin and ketamine. By clicking on the icons surrounding the 3D avatar, the user can see on the right side of the screen a description of the physiological consequences of the selected drug on that organ, as well as the legal and social ones (Figure 1). This exhibition of a cause and effect relation is a well-known persuasive strategy in this kind of educational tools [1].

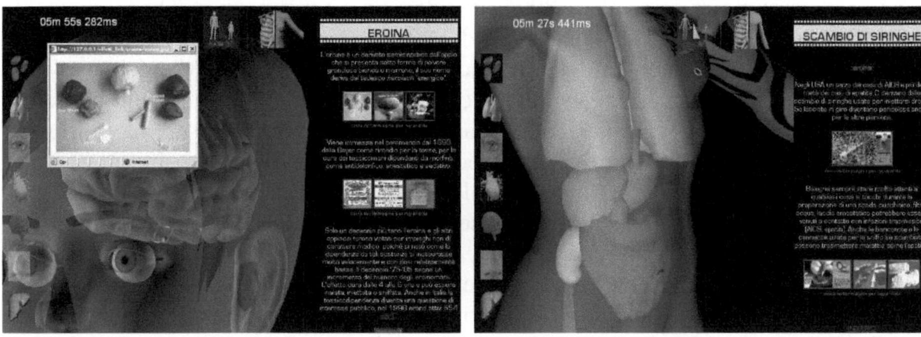


**Fig. 1.** The transparent man and woman bodies with the organs icons and the text frame with images and links on the right of the screen

A different background music for each substance was also implemented on the interface. Since this version of the game was meant to be evaluated on the field, we wanted to have comparable sessions across the different users. Therefore, the session had a pre-defined length of at maximum 6 minutes, after which the user was presented with the starting screen, and once selected a certain type of drug it was not possible to go back and change, until the end of the whole session. By pressing the bar on the keyboard, the user could enter the 10 items quiz session. Feedback on the correctness of the answer was provided. (Figure 2). After a usability test on the prototype, conducted within our laboratory with a cognitive walk-through with experts [14] and students, and leading to some adjustments in the questionnaire format, in the layout of the images, and in the variety of the background music, Videodope was ready to be evaluated in the field.

**Fig. 2.** Two screenshots of a wrong and right answer message in the final session of the game

## 3 In-Field Evaluation

The purpose of the evaluation was to collect the users' acceptance of the videogame as an informative tool. It was important to involve target users of Videodope, namely people aged 15 to 24, and to locate the test in a context similar to those in which drug consumption is likely to occur. Therefore, we conducted the evaluation during an Italian music summer festival in 2006 attended by young people. The participants were 49 people (38 males, 11 females) aged 24.7 on average (s.d. 6.32).

Our station was located in a tent adjacent to the main stage where it was also possible to get some refreshments, and access the Internet. The equipment consisted of a projector and a big screen, a tablet pc and two amplifiers. The users sat in front of the screen and interacted with the projected digital environment by using mouse and keyboard (Figure 3). The experimenters only intervened in case of need.

The participants took one individual sessions with the Videodope environment, with the informative module regarding one drug of their choice and the quiz module. They were explained the goal of the game, its component and its functioning. They were advised that they could stop the informative module and take the quiz earlier. Finally, they were announced that after the game they would have been administered a questionnaire. At the end of the navigation and the quiz session, they were lead to a different table to filled in a 12-items paper and pencil questionnaire. The questionnaire contained items on the credibility of the Videogame, on the perceived completeness of the information provided, on its appeal and usability. The questionnaire also collected socio-demographic information on the respondents and measured their familiarity with Internet, videogames, rave parties and drugs.

**Fig. 3.** Two scenes from the evaluation with users in the field

## 4 Results

### 4.1 Relevance of the Sample

Participants were mostly workers or students, with a slight prevalence of the latter, 12 of them hold a university degree, 10 a high school diploma, 26 a college degree. 73%

of them came from the North of Italy. Their familiarity with drugs is reported in Table 1.

The table highlights a prevailing consume of cannabis and alcohol in the sample, since 4.2% of the respondents declared to have never drunk some alcohol and nobody declared to have never tried cannabis. This means that we were able to reach the target. By replacing the 7 points in the Likert scale with numerical values (1= once a week, 7= never), we could compare the familiarity with the different substances in several subgroups. A comparison by age (16/23 versus 24/45) revealed no significant difference, whereas groups divided by occupation had a significant different in familiarity with substances, with students scoring higher ($T(40) = 2.37$; $p = .023$). A significant difference was also found in groups divided by familiarity with rave parties: rave-goers, which represented a 58.3% of the sample, declared a consume of drugs higher than the other ($T(38) = 2.38$; $p = .023$). Their expertise with Internet was low, and 36% declared that they never used a videogame.

The mean score they achieved in the quiz was of 6.7 right answers out of 10.

**Table 1.** Percentages of drug's consume within participants

| | *Several times a week* | *Once a week* | *Once a month* | *Rarely* | *Once in a life tim e* | *I used* | *Never* | *Tot.* |
|---|---|---|---|---|---|---|---|---|
| *Alcohol* | 72.9 | 16. 7 | 2.1 | 0 | 0 | 2.1 | 4.2 | 1 00 |
| *Hashish/ Marijuana* | 62.5 | 6.3 | 18.8 | 4.2 | 0 | 8.3 | 0 | 1 00 |
| *Cocaine* | 4.2 | 2.1 | 2.1 | 10.4 | 16. 7 | 14. 6 | 50 | 1 00 |
| *Mushrooms* | 0 | 0 | 4.2 | 10.4 | 8.3 | 6.3 | 70. 8 | 1 00 |
| *Ecstasy* | 4.2 | 0 | 2.1 | 6.3 | 4.2 | 6.3 | 77. 1 | 1 00 |
| *Amphetamine* | 0 | 2.1 | 0 | 12.5 | 0 | 4.2 | 81. 3 | 1 00 |
| *LSD* | 0 | 0 | 2.1 | 6.3 | 0 | 6.3 | 85. 4 | 1 00 |
| *Heroine* | 0 | 0 | 2.1 | 0 | 2.1 | 2.1 | 93. 8 | 1 00 |
| *Other* | 0.4 | 0 | 0.4 | 5.4 | 4.6 | 8 | 81. 2 | 1 00 |

### 4.2 Videodope Relevance and Usability

It seemed that Videodope was not taken as a game, since users tried to be informed about situations that resembled their real-life ones: the gender of the videogame was mostly the same of the user and the most selected drugs were cannabis, which as also the most commonly used in the sample (14 people), or hallucinogens. The interest was high, as can be inferred from the fact that 90% of the respondents declared that they would have tried again the environment spontaneously if there were a chance, and almost 70% would have liked to navigate for more sessions in order to find out information about other substances.

Regarding credibility, completeness, appeal and usability of the interface, they were investigated by measuring the agreement with some statements on a 5-point Likert scale (1: I agree - 2: I almost agree - 3: I do not agree nor disagree- 4: I disagree a bit- 5: I totally disagree). It seems that the dimensions to which designers paid a special attention were evaluated positively (fig. 4).

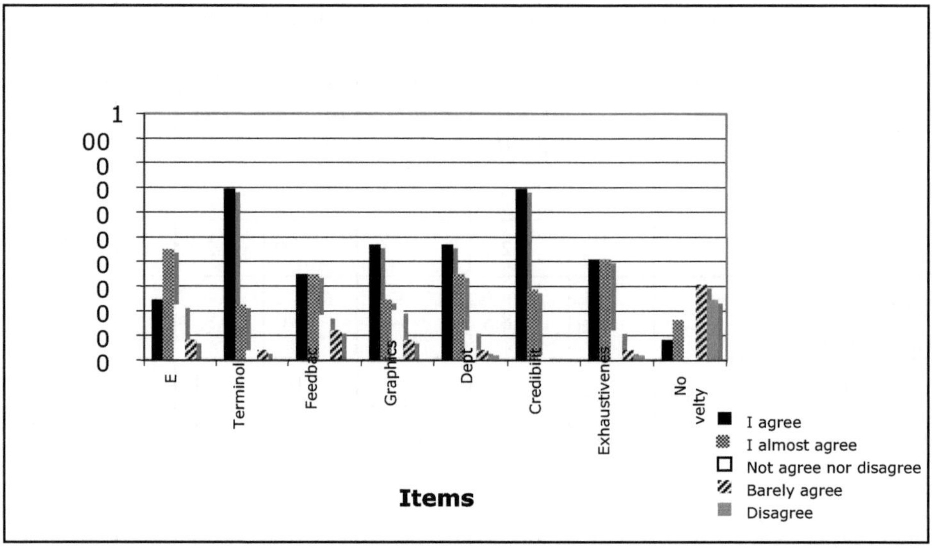


**Fig. 4.** Percentages of evaluation of some Videodope's dimensions provided by participants

Most respondent agreed that the 'information seemed credible' (item 6), which was an essential requisite for Videodope. Regarding the perceived quality of the information provided, a great percentage of agreement was collected for the items investigating the comprehensibility ('the terminology sued in the game was easy to comprehend', item 2), exhaustiveness ('the game provides an exhaustive amount of information', item 7) and depth of the information ('Videodope was useful to deepen my knowledge of substances', item 6). About novelty, a fair part of respondents declared that Videodope matched with what they already knew on the subject ('the information provided are different from the ones that I already knew', item 8). This may suggest both that the information was plausible to them and that it could have been presented in such a way as to privilege what is not known.

A group of items was meant to investigate the usability of the game in terms of effectiveness and satisfaction. Regarding the graphic appearance ('I was satisfied with the graphic appearance of the game, item 4'), responsiveness ('to all my action corresponded a good response from the game', item 3) and ease of finding the information of need (item 1), the agreement was slight lower than with the other aspects but still in the positive half of the scale. The questionnaire concluded by asking for suggestions on the way in which the game could be improved. Respondents mentioned the possibility of introducing a higher amount of images showing the consequences of the substances on the organs, for instance before-and-after the consumption. They also suggested to insert autobiographic narratives from witnesses that can testify of their own experience with heavy abuse of the substances. They also suggested to add more curious information and statistics, to increase its multi-mediality by inserting videos, and to provide a final score in the quiz, as in the other videogames. Some of them suggested to increase the rhythm and the speed of the game. Ideal locations for Videodope were the Internet (73.5%), secondary schools (69.4%), primary schools (49%) and discos or pubs (24.5%), with people who already use substances as the most recommended target, followed by 'who is willing to try some'.

## 5 Conclusions

The location for the evaluation proved adequate to the purpose of approaching target users. The interest for the game was high and the overall evaluations received by Videodope as a credible, complete and appealing tool were positive. The results of the questionnaire suggest to push even more on the game metaphor to meet the users' expectations, while at the same time making the information more surprising, visual and multimedial. Making Videodope available over the Internet could be a next step in order to take full advantage of the ubiquity and anonymity of a digital environment.

## References

1. Fogg, B.J.: Persuasive technology. Morgan Kaufmann, San Francisco, CA (2003)
2. Squire, K.: Video games in education. International Journal of Intelligent Games & Simulation, 2(1) (2003)
3. De Aguilera, M., Méndiz, A.: Video Games and Education (Education in the Face of a "Parallel School"). ACM Computers in Entertainment, 1(1) (2003)
4. Ministero della Solidarietà Sociale: Relazione annuale al Parlamento sullo stato delle tossicodipendenze in Italia (2005) From http://www.governo.it
5. De Matteis, C.: Discoteca e nuove professioni. Dinamica Universitaria, Bologna (1997)
6. Bagozzi, F.: Generazione in ecstasy: droghe, miti e musica della generazione techno. Edizioni Gruppo Abele,Torino (1996)
7. Gourley, M.: A subcultural study of recreational ecstasy use. Journal of sociology 40(1), 59–73 (2004)

8. Neale, J.: Driving on Recreational Drugs: a qualitative investigation of experiences from behind the wheel. Drugs: education, prevention and policy, 8(4) (2001)
9. Milanese, R., Zanellato, L., Pastore, M., Melosi, S.: La rappresentazione del consumatore di ecstasy: i risultati di una ricerca empirica. Bollettino per le Farmacodipendenze e l'Alcolismo, XXIII(1), 1–12 (2002)
10. Fogg, B.J., Marshall, J., Kameda, T., Solomon, J., Rangnekar, A., Boyd, J., Brown, B.: Web credibility research: A method for online experiments and early study results. In: Proceedings of CHI'01, Extended Abstracts on Human Factors in Computing 2001, pp. 295–296 (2001)
11. Ilgen, D.R., Fisher, C.D., Taylor, M.S.: Consequences of Individual Feedback on Behavior in Organizations. Journal of Applied Psychology 64(4), 349–371 (1979)
12. DiMicco, J.M., Pandolfo, A., Bender, W.: Influencing group participation with a shared display. In: Proceedings of the ACM Conference on CSCW, Chicago, Illinois, pp. 614–623 (2004)
13. Dutta-Bergman, M.J.: The Impact of Completeness and Web Use Motivation on the Credibility of e-Health Information. The. Journal of Communication 54(2), 253–269 (2004)
14. Gamberini, L., Valentini, E.: Web usability Today. In: Riva, G., Galimberti, C. (eds.) Toward cyberpsychology, vol. 2, p. 312. IOSPress, Amsterdam (2001)
15. Berdichevsky, D., Neuenschwander, E.: Toward an ethics of persuasive technology. Communications of the ACM 42(5), 51–58 (1999)
16. Brookhuis, K.A., de Waard, D., Samyn, N.: Effects of MDMA (ecstasy), and multiple drugs use on (simulated) driving performance and traffic safety. Psychopharmacology 173, 440–445 (2004)
17. Century Council: Alcohol 101 software can help colleges tackle high-risk drinking problems. Education Technology News (2003)
18. Inaba, D.S., Cohen, W.E.: Eccitanti, sedativi, psichedelici: effetti fisici e mentali delle sostanze psicoattive. Piccin Nuova Libraria, Padova (1993)
19. Karat, J., Karat, C.M., Ukelson, J.: Affordances, motivation, and the design of user interfaces. Communications of the ACM archive 43(8), 49–51 (2000)
20. Khaslavsky, J., Shedroff, N.: Understanding the seductive experience. Communications of the ACM 42(5), 45–49 (1999)
21. King, P., Tester, J.: The landscape of persuasive technologies. Communications of the ACM 42(5), 31–38 (1999)
22. Mantovani, G., Spagnoli, A.: (a cura di): Metodi qualitativi in psicologia. Bologna: Il Mulino (2003)
23. Marlatt, G.A.: Harm reduction: come as you are. Addictive behaviors 21(6), 779–788 (1996)
24. Martin, B.R.: Marijuana: psychopharmacology. In: The fourth generation of progress, Raven Press, New York (1995)
25. Mathias, R.: Like methamphetamine, "ecstasy" may cause long-term brain damage. NIDA Notes, 11(5) (1996)
26. Nechama Tec, Ph.D.: Reflections on the Positive Consequences of Illicit Drug Usage by the Younger Generation. Br. J. Addict, vol. 71, pp. 343–351 (1976)
27. Picard, R.W., Wexelblat, A.: Future Interfaces: Social and Emotional. CHI, April 20-25, 2002, Minneapolis, MN, pp. 698–699 (2002)
28. Purgato, A., Gamberini, L.: Play Safety: Virtual Environments as a persuasive tool to contrast risky behaviours in youth. Annual Review of CyberTherapy and Telemedicine 3, 243–245 (2005)

29. Ricautre, G.A., McCann, U.: Recognition and management of compications of new recreational drug use. The Lancet 365, 2137–2144 (2005)
30. Salvini, A., Testoni, I., Zamperini, A.: Droghe. Tossicofilie e tossicodipendenza. UTET Università, Torino (2002)
31. Squires, D., Jenny Preece1, J.: Predicting quality in educational software: Evaluating for learning, usability and the synergy between them. Interacting with Computers 11(5), 467–483 (1999)
32. Ungerleider, J.T., Fisher, D.D., Fuller, M., Caldwd, A.: The "Bad Trip" – the etiology of the adverse LSD reaction. American Journal of Psychiatry 124, 1483–1490 (1968)
33. Yacoubian, G.S., Miller, S., Pianim, S., et al.: Toward an ecstasy and other club drug (EOCD) prevention intervention for rave attendees. Journal of Drug. Education 34(1), 41–59 (2004)

# AR Pottery: Experiencing Pottery Making in the Augmented Space

Gabjong Han[1], Jane Hwang[1], Seungmoon Choi[1], and Gerard Jounghyun Kim[2]

[1] Virtual Reality and Perceptive Media Laboratory
Department of Computer Science and Engineering
POSTECH, Republic of Korea
{hkj84, jane, choism}@postech.ac.kr
[2] Computer Science and Engineering Department
Korea University, Republic of Korea
gjkim@korea.ac.kr

**Abstract.** In this paper, we apply augmented reality to provide pottery design experiences to the user. Augmented reality offers natural 3D interaction, a tangible interface, and integration into the real environment. In addition, certain modeling techniques impossible in the real world can be realized as well. Using our AR system, the user can create a pottery model by deforming a virtual pottery displayed on a marker with another marked held by the user's hand. This interaction style allows the user to experience the traditional way of pottery making. Also provided are six interaction modes to facilitate the design process and an intuitive switching technique using occlusion-based interface. The AR pottery system can be used for virtual pottery prototyping and education.

**Keywords:** Augmented reality, pottery making, 3D modeling, deformation.

## 1 Introduction

Pottery has been an important part of cultural heritage in Korea, East Asia and perhaps all over the world. While there are many convenient desktop modeling tools and techniques that allow us to easily design various types of 3D models, they are not readily applicable to providing the "feel" of the traditional pottery making process, that is, most geometric modeling tools are targeted toward just providing certain modeling functionality. Traditional potteries are modeled almost simultaneously as the user applies deformation directly to the clay on a rotating platform, after which colored patterns are added using special materials and procedures.

To elevate the modeling process to an experience, we propose to use augmented reality (AR) technology. Augmented reality is particularly attractive for this application domain, because the pottery making process can be situated in the real environment very easily. A completely virtual environment is an alternative, but would be much harder to construct and would be less convincing and immersive. In

R. Shumaker (Ed.): Virtual Reality, HCII 2007, LNCS 4563, pp. 642–650, 2007.

addition, the markers that serve as placeholders for the virtual pottery (in the augmented space), although limited, offer tangibility, a property that is deemed very important in an artistic process such as pottery making. Although not implemented in this work, simple actuating devices such as a vibrator can be easily attached to the tangible marker/prop for a more realistic physical experience. 3D Manipulation of the markers/props is very easy and natural. Unlike in the completely virtual space, the finished virtual pottery design can be placed (e.g. just to see how the pottery design would go with ambience of one's office) anywhere within the augmented real space by moving the marker/prop.

The pottery model in our system is represented as a Bezier volume with control points for determining its overall shape. We use two markers that are detected and recognized by the camera for their relative positions and orientations in the augmented space. One marker represents the rotating platform (on which the evolving pottery design is visualized), and the other one held by the user represents the tool tip or user's hand. The virtual pottery can be deformed, by direct interaction and manipulation, with the tool tip marker in various ways, in a manner similar to the real pottery making process. We believe that the augmented reality is an appropriate media technology (only next to experiencing it for real) to teach, demonstrate and experience (second hand) pottery making, a process in which direct interaction and tangibility are the most important experiential qualities.

This paper is organized as follows. The next section reviews work related to 3D modeling interfaces, in particular, to digital pottery modeling. Section 3 describes our AR based pottery modeling system, followed by results in Section 4. Finally, we conclude this paper in Section 5.

## 2 Related Work

There are various previous research projects that have explored 3D based modeling in AR/VR environment. In this section, we will present a brief overview on 3D geometric model representations, 3D modeling interfaces, and digital pottery modeling systems.

### 2.1 Representing 3D Models

There are several ways of representing 3D models in the VR/AR environments. The polygon (or triangle) based model is the most popular representation format in 3D applications because it is the basis of the current rendering hardware. However, it is difficult to model objects with smooth curves or surfaces with individual polygons. Many mathematical curve and surface primitives, such as B-splines, NURBS, and Blobby objects, can be used for this purpose [1-3]. However, to form complex objects, they have to be patched together and deforming them either locally or globally may involve a complicated representation and process [4]. As such, more intuitive "object-level" deformation techniques have been proposed over the years. Free form deformation techniques (and their variants) [5-7] is one such approach that uses control points (or wires) to determine the overall shape of a target object. A more direct approach would be also possible, for example, allowing the user to modify the locations of individual vertices, and having the system to compute or remesh the resulting shape. However, this would be much more computing intensive. In our case, we took an approach to apply free form deformation but at a high degree of granularity to achieve more directness (See Section 3.2).

### 2.2 3D Modeling Interfaces for Pottery Making

Although not entirely intuitive, most 3D object modeling functionalities are possible with the 2D desktop interfaces (e.g. keyboard, mouse, and tablet). Few researchers have attempted to use 3D VR/AR interfaces instead as it is a very natural application domain for 3D interfaces (e.g. 6DOF trackers and immersive display) [8-11], mapping the 3D (hand or hand-held pointer) actions directly (or indirectly) to the shape of the object. Other variants involve two hand interaction, 3D gesture driven systems, or even ones with haptic/tactile feedback [12, 13]. Also note that modeling systems not only require specifications of 3D shapes for which 3D interfaces might be appropriate for, but also many other miscellaneous commands and alphanumeric input for which traditional 2D interfaces would suffice.

A few modeling systems specific for pottery have been developed. The system developed by Korida et al. uses a stereoscopic display and a glove based gesture for pottery modeling [14]. The Virtual Clay system by McDonnel et al. employed haptic feedback to simulate the shape manipulation with clay [15]. A similar system by Kameyama used a 3D mouse and a tactile feedback device [16]. In terms of interaction and the overall process, these systems lack reality in terms of providing the actual experience of pottery making.

## 3 AR Pottery Modeling System

### 3.1 System Overview

The AR pottery system consists of a computer, a USB camera and three markers (See Figure 1). The first marker represents the rotating platform on which the evolving virtual pottery design is overlaid, the second, a tool tip which is the physical mean through which the shape of the virtual pottery changes, and the third, a tangible menu/button system for making miscellaneous commands. The system is implemented using the ARToolkit [17] that is capable of recognizing the three specially made markers, and computing the positions and orientations of the markers relative to the camera coordinate system. What is shown to the user, through a monitor or a head mounted display (HMD), is the imagery taken by the camera overlaid with 3D virtual objects (namely the pottery, tool tip, and 2D buttons) as seen from the camera where the markers are supposed to be seen. Thus, the user can hold the tool tip marker, and touch the virtual pottery to change its shape or interact with the 2D button for other functions.

**Fig. 1.** AR pottery system: the set-up (left), close up view of the display (right)

### 3.2 Pottery Model Representation

The pottery model in our system is a mesh of quadrilaterals (i.e. each with 4 vertices). A control grid is overlaid upon the model and by manipulating points (e.g. red points in the left part of Figure 2) on the control grid through interaction, the target mesh is deformed according to the usual free form deformation technique [5]. Strictly speaking, this is an indirect way of changing the shape (as opposed to what we are claiming). However, by offering a high resolution control grid, the process can be regarded practically direct. Once the vertices change their locations by free form deformation, each polygon is rendered as a smooth Bezier surface patch with 4 x 4 control points by the OpenGL. The needed control points, 16 of them (white little circles in the middle part of Figure 2), are created on the fly by interpolating among the four original vertices (See Figure 2). Currently, the C-1 continuity is not guaranteed among the polygons.

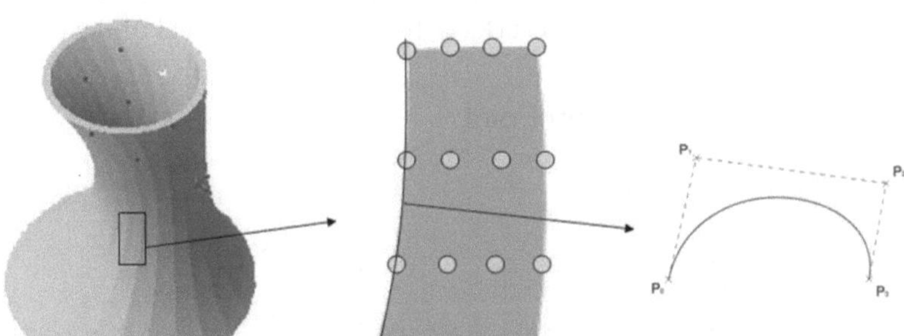

**Fig. 2.** Curved surface rendered as a Bezier surface by OpenGL

### 3.3 Interaction Design in AR Pottery

The main and the most important task in AR pottery is shape modeling. The interaction was modeled after the real pottery shaping process as much as possible.

That is, just as in the real situation, the scene is augmented with a rotating piece of clay, and by touching its (rotating surface), a shape change symmetric to the rotating axis occurs. Because it is difficult to detect human hands/fingers (which is used in the real pottery making), we use the hand-held marker instead, on which a virtual finger is drawn.

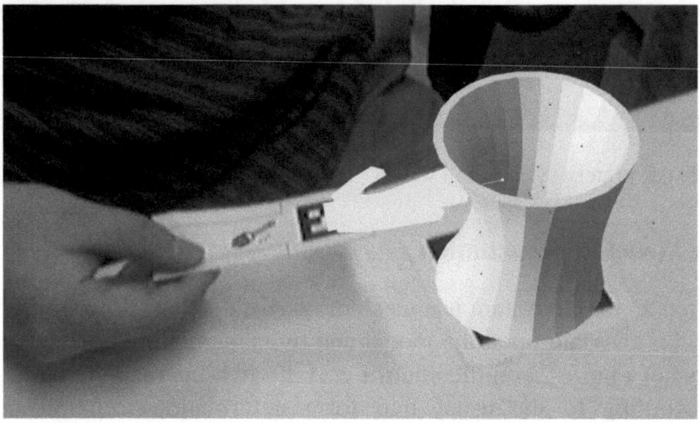

**Fig. 3.** Changing the shape of the pottery with the tool tip marker

A fast and simple ray-vs.-polygon collision detection method is used to make the interaction between the hand and the pottery possible. The virtual hand/finger is internally modeled as a line segment and its collision with any of the polygons of the pottery is checked. If a collision is detected, the collision point and the penetration depth are calculated and used as input to the deformation handler. Figure 4 illustrates this process. The penetration depth is the perpendicular distance from the end point of the tool tip to the penetrated polygon surface (this along the normal of the polygon).

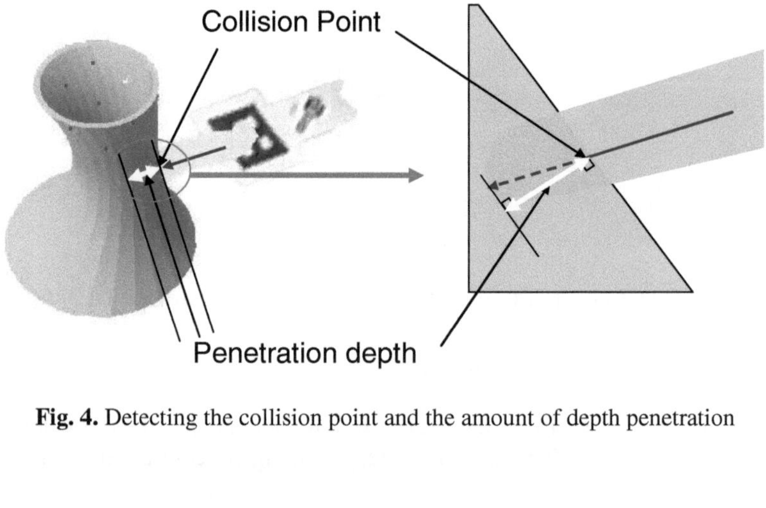


**Fig. 4.** Detecting the collision point and the amount of depth penetration

In the free-form deformation technique (such as ours), the control points determine the shape of the deformable body. The penetration depth and direction between tool tip and virtual pottery determines the amount of translations of the control points. The control points are manipulated according to the following six methods (also see Figure 5).

- Poke: The pottery stands still (not rotating) and when the user pushes a part of the pottery (with the tool tip), the corresponding part moves in accordingly.
- Push: The pottery stands still (not rotating) and when the user pushes a part of the pottery (with the tool tip), the corresponding and the opposite parts moves in together accordingly.
- Symmetric Push: The pottery is rotating in effect, and when the user pushes a part of the pottery, the shape is deformed in symmetric manner just as in real pottery making.

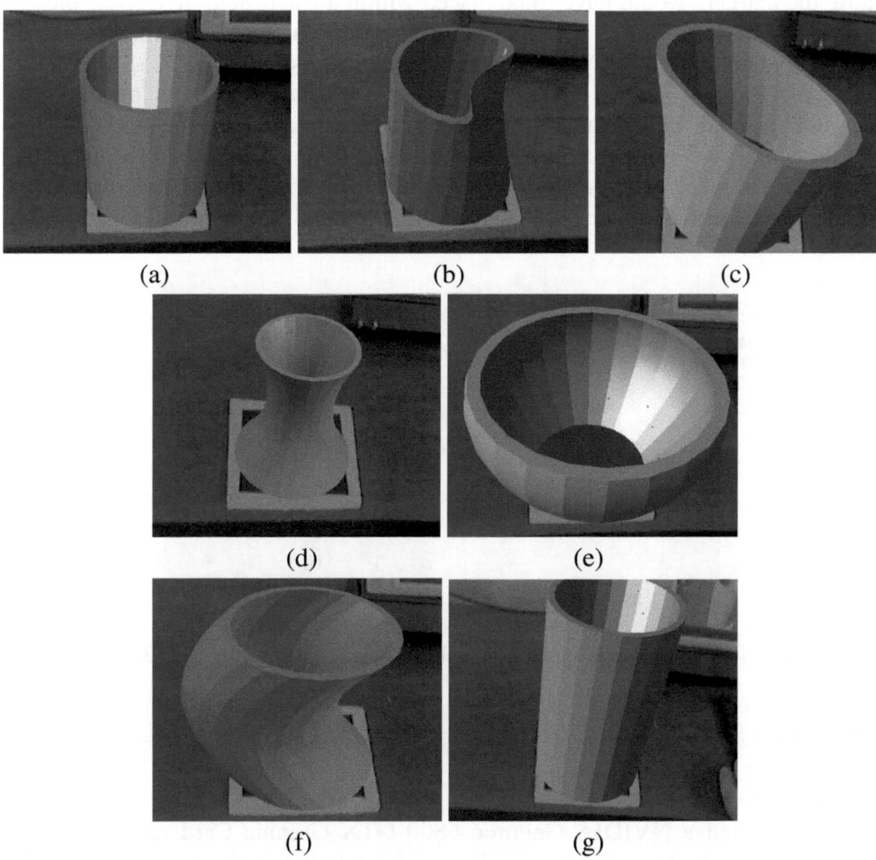

**Fig. 5.** Different interaction methods: (a) Original default model, (b) Poking, (c) Pushing, (d) Symmetric push, (e) Symmetric pull, (f) Bending, and (g) Stretching

- Symmetric Pull: The pottery is rotating in effect, and when the user selects a part of the pottery and pulls it out, the shape is deformed in symmetric manner. Note that although inspired by the real pottery making process, this is not possible in reality.
- Bend: The pottery stands still (not rotating) and when the user pushes a part of the pottery (with the tool tip), the corresponding "waist" of the pottery is pushed causing a bending effect.
- Stretch: The pottery is either scaled up or down in the y direction (height adjustment).

### 3.4 Switching Between Interaction Modes

In order to allow various ways to change the shape of the pottery, six different modes are used as explained in the previous section. To realize this, one approach is to use a number of different marker props. However, this can be very confusing, especially because the markers would have to be placed within a small field of view of the paper in a crowded manner, or/and the shape of the marker has to be designed in a way to reflect its content (e.g. "Push" tool marked with the letters "P,", "U,", "S," and "H"). In general, recognizing such a specific form reduces the robustness of the marker recognition. Instead, we use the third marker as a switch to change the mode of the tool tip. In particular, we use the occlusion based interaction proposed by [18] in which an interaction is invoked when a marker is occluded by the finger. Thus, as shown in Figure 6, arrow buttons can be invoked to cycle through different tool tip modes easily.

(a) (b)

**Fig. 6.** Switching between interaction modes of the tool tip using the OBI interface

## 4 Results

We have implemented our system on an Intel Pentium 4 3.60GHz computer with 1.00GB RAM and a NVIDIA GeForce 6800 GTX Graphic Card (256 RAM). Our system runs in runs in real time at about 20~30 frames per second. We used the ARToolkit [17] and OpenGL [19] to detect the markers and draw and overlay the virtual objects, respectively. Figure 7 shows examples of potteries created using our system in the matter of minutes.

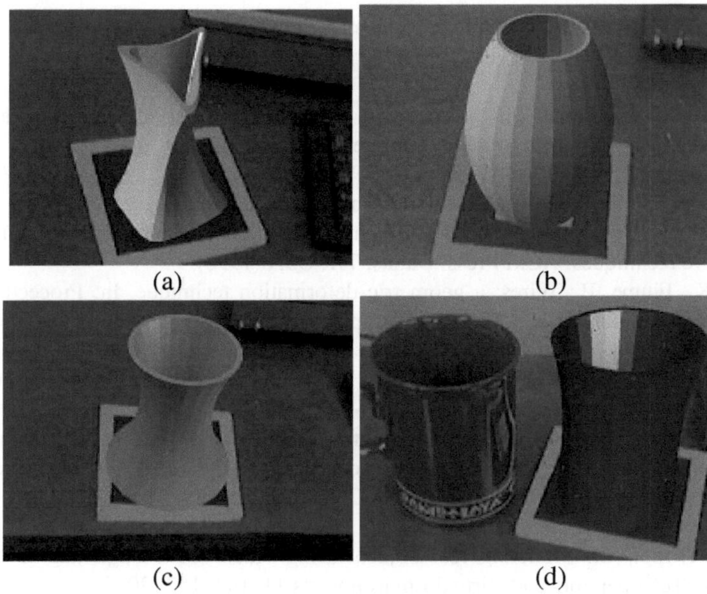


**Fig. 7.** Various potteries created by the AR pottery system

# 5 Conclusion and Future Work

In this paper, we described an AR based pottery modeling system. With the proposed system, the use can make the pottery intuitively (direct manipulation and real life inspired interface) and very easily (only a USB camera and a few sheets of markers) but, above all, gain a close to life experience. This system can be extended in various ways, e.g. adding more hands for collaboration, bare hand interaction, adding more functions (like surface painting) and processes (e.g. pottery baking), and making the experience even more physical through vibratory feedback simulating a form of haptics. We are also investigating the usability of the system in terms of task performance and user experience.

**Acknowledgments.** This project was supported by the grant from the Korea MIC's ITRC (CGVR) program.

# References

1. Liu, D., Hoschek, J.: GC1 continuity conditions between adjacent rectangular and triangular Bezier surface patches. Computer-Aided Design 21, 194–200 (1989)
2. Lamousin, H.J., Waggenspack, Jr, N.N.: NURBS-based free-form deformations. Computer Graphics and Applications, IEEE 14, 59–65 (1994)
3. Watt, A., Watt, M.: Advanced animation and rendering techniques. ACM Press, New York (1991)

4. Barr, A.H.: Global and local deformations of solid primitives. In: Proceedings of the 11th annual conference on Computer graphics and interactive techniques, pp. 21–30. ACM Press, New York (1984)
5. Sederberg, T.W., Parry, S.R.: Free-form deformation of solid geometric models. In: Proceedings of the 13th annual conference on Computer graphics and interactive techniques, pp. 151–160. ACM Press, New York (1986)
6. Coquillart, S.: Extended free-form deformation: a sculpturing tool for 3D geometric modeling. In: Proceedings of the 17th annual conference on Computer graphics and interactive techniques. ACM Press, Dallas, TX, USA (1990)
7. Singh, K., Fiume, E.: Wires: a geometric deformation technique. In: Proceedings of the 25th annual conference on Computer graphics and interactive techniques. ACM Press, New York (1998)
8. Liang, J., Green, M.: A highly interactive 3 D modeling system. Computers & graphics 18, 499–506 (1994)
9. Piekarski, W., Thomas, B.H.: The Tinmith system: demonstrating new techniques for mobile augmented reality modelling. In: Proceedings of the Third Australasian conference on User interfaces - vol. 7, Australian Computer Society, Inc., Melbourne, Victoria, Australia, 2002 (2002)
10. Lee, J., Hirota, G.: Modeling real objects using video see-through augmented reality. Presence: Teleoperators and Virtual Environments 11, 144–157 (2002)
11. Wong, J.P.Y., Lau, R.W.H., Ma, L.: Virtual 3D Sculpting. Journal of Visualization and Computer Animation 11, 155–166 (2000)
12. Buchmann, V., Violich, S., Billinghurst, M., Cockburn, A.: FingARtips: gesture based direct manipulation in Augmented Reality. Proceedings of the 2nd international conference on Computer graphics and interactive techniques in Australasia and South East Asia, pp. 212–221. ACM Press, Singapore (2004)
13. Phantom Haptic Devices. Sensable Technologies, Inc., Woburn, MA (2006)
14. Korida, K., Nishino, H., Utsumiya, K.: An Interactive 3D Interface for a Virtual Ceramic Art Work Environment. In: Proceedings of the 1997 International Conference on Virtual Systems and MultiMedia, p. 227 (1997)
15. McDonnell, K.T., Qin, H., Wlodarczyk, R.A.: Virtual clay: a real-time sculpting system with haptic toolkits. In: Proceedings of the 2001 symposium on Interactive 3D graphics, pp. 179–190. ACM Press, New York, NY, USA (2001)
16. Kameyama, K.: Virtual clay modeling system. In: Proceedings of the ACM symposium on Virtual reality software and technology, pp. 197–200. ACM Press, Lausanne, Switzerland (1997)
17. Kato, I.P.H., Billinghurst, M.: ARToolkit User Manual, Version 2.33. Human Interface Technology Lab, University of Washington (2000)
18. Lee, G.A., Kim, G.J., Billinghurst, M.: Immersive authoring: What You eXperience Is What You Get (WYXIWYG). Communications of the ACM 48, 76–81 (2005)
19. The OpenGL® API 2.1. SGI, Sunnyvale, CA (2006)

# An Optical See-Through Augmented Reality System for the Treatment of Phobia to Small Animals

M. Carmen Juan[1], Mariano Alcañiz[1], Jérôme Calatrava, Irene Zaragozá[1], Rosa Baños[2], and Cristina Botella[3]

[1] MedICLab (Universidad Politécnica de Valencia), Valencia, Spain
[2] Dep. de Personalidad, Evaluación y Tratamientos Psicológicos, U. de Valencia, Spain
[3] Dep. de Psicología Básica y Psicobiología. Universitat Jaume I, Castellón Spain
mcarmen@dsic.upv.es, malcaniz@degi.upv.es, irzaal@aaa.upv.es, rosa.banos@uv.es, botella@psb.uji.es

**Abstract.** This paper presents an optical see-through (OST) Augmented Reality (AR) system for the treatment of phobia to small animals. Our group has already presented two AR systems for this treatment. The first system was a video see-through (VST) AR system. The second one was a markerless AR system. And now, we present a third version using an OST approach. To check whether the OST AR system is more or less effective than the OST AR system, we have carried out an experiment comparing both systems. In this paper we focus on the anxiety level of participants during the experiment. Results show that both systems provoke anxiety in participants even if they do not have fear to cockroaches/spiders. OST AR system provokes slightly more anxiety than the VST AR system.

**Keywords:** Augmented Reality, Optical see-through, virtual therapy, phobia to small animals.

## 1 Introduction

The term Augmented Reality (AR) is used to describe systems that blend computer generated virtual objects with real environments.

AR has been used in many fields such as military, entertainment, etc. AR has been recently used for the treatment of different psychological problems. Our group developed an AR system for the treatment of acrophobia using immersive photography [1]. Other problem that we also have treated is the phobia to small animals where two different versions of the same system have been presented. The first system was a video see-through (VST) AR system [2][3]. It was a marker-based tracker, used a colour camera and a VST Head-Mounted Display (HMD). In these works, it was demonstrated that, with a single one-hour session, patients significantly reduced their fear and avoidance. Initially, the system was tested in a case study, and then was tested on nine patients suffering phobia of small animals. The second system was a markerless AR system [4], where the markers were not visible to the user. This second system incorporated two cameras: one colour camera for capturing the real

R. Shumaker (Ed.): Virtual Reality, HCII 2007, LNCS 4563, pp. 651–659, 2007.

world without visible markers and one infrared camera for capturing the real world whereby it was possible to distinguish markers drawn with a special ink.

In this paper we present a new version of these systems for the treatment of phobia to small animals that uses an optical see-through (OST) HMD and an infra-red (IR) bullet camera.

This is not the first time an OST HMD has been used in AR, but it is the first time it has been used for the treatment of phobia to small animals.

In this paper, we are going to cite several AR systems that use OST HMD for different purposes. Grasset et al. [5] proposed an OST AR system for collaborative applications where users are around a table. They can interact with AR applications such as architectural design, gaming and planning simulation. Ivanovic and Plate [6] implemented an OST AR system which shows elements of structures that are hidden behind the already built buildings. Ozbek et al. [7] presented a gaming environment. Leebmann [8] presented an OST AR system as a tool for disaster management such as earthquakes. Schwald and Laval [9] presented an AR system for training and assisting in maintaining equipment in industrial context.

# 2 OST AR System for the Treatment of Phobia to Small Animals

## 2.1 Hardware

The system requires a camera to capture the real world in order to determine where the virtual elements will exactly have to be drawn.

We have used an infrared (IR) camera, but it could also be possible to use a color camera. After processing the captured image, the system obtains the real camera position and orientation relative to physical markers, and determines where the virtual elements have to be drawn. In this case, only these elements are drawn because the user is seeing the real world. For achieving this, we have used the LitEye-500 OST HMD. A more detailed description of these elements is included next.

- An image of the monocular OST HMD used, LitEye-500, can be seen in Fig. 1.a. The resolution of the HMD enables 800x600 with a FoV of 28 degrees.
- Fig. 1.b shows the IR bullet camera used. It has a 715 nm IR filter and comes in a lipstick sized tube 2.5 inches long, with a diameter of 0.8125 inches. The diagonal FOV of the camera is 92 degrees. The image sensor is 1/3" CCD with 290,000 CCIR pixels, capable of delivering a video stream at a frame rate of 30 fps in several image formats, among them 640x480. The output of the camera is a composite video signal. A regulated 12 VDC power supply is needed for proper operation. USB2.0 Video Grabber converts a video composite signal into a USB 2.0 signal. It delivers a frame rate of up to 30 fps at a resolution of 640x480. The device is compliant with DirectShow.

## 2.2 Software

We programmed the system using C++ and ARToolKit with Virtual Reality Modeling Language (VRML) support to incorporate AR options. The system uses visible markers.

ARToolKit is an open source vision tracking library that enables the easy development of a wide range of Augmented Reality applications. It was developed at Washington University by Kato and Billinghurst [10]. The required elements for the application are: a USB or FireWire camera, and a marker. Markers are white squares with a black border inside of which are symbols or letter/s. ARToolKit uses computer vision techniques to obtain the position and orientation of the camera with respect to a marker. Virtual elements are drawn on these markers. ARToolKit includes code for image acquisition, the detection of markers in the video stream, the calculation of the three-dimensional position and orientation of the markers, the identification of markers, the computation of the position and orientation of the virtual objects relative to the real world, and the rendering of these virtual objects in the corresponding video frame.

a) b)

**Fig. 1.** a) The LiteEye-500 monocular OST HMD. b) The IR bullet camera used.

The virtual elements that appear in the system are spiders and cockroaches. The three-dimensional models of these virtual elements were constructed using Autodesk 3D Studio Max.

The graphical user interface was created with the OpenGL Utility ToolKit (GLUT)-based user interface library (GLUI).

Sound support is provided by the OpenAL sound library.

As the system is OST, the calibration process is much more complicated than in a VST system because the human subject is an inseparable part of the eye-display system. Several procedures of calibration for OST system have already been proposed, for example: [5] [11] [12]. Kato and Billinghurst proposed a calibration method for OST HMD based on marker tracking [10]. We have adapted it for the calibration of the OST HMD used.

The third version of the system uses the same four VRML models as the first system used. We have three different spiders and one cockroach. For each type of animal, three models have been created; a non-moving, a moving and a dead animal. To obtain as real a result as possible the moving cockroach is animated with moving legs and moving tentacles, and the spiders move their legs.

When the animals are killed the system produces a sound similar to that of a real animal being killed. The system includes two sounds: a squirting sound similar to the sound of a real can of insecticide; and a squishing sound similar to that of a real cockroach or spider being crushed.

### 2.3 Description of the System

The system uses an OST HMD with an infrared camera to capture the scene. The video of the infrared camera is treated by the system and using ARToolKit is possible to establish the position and orientation of the IR camera respect to the marker. After this step, the system draws animals in the right place.

The system loads a calibration file. The calibration process has to be realized before running the system. This process was realized and a default calibration file was created. The system loads this file and normally works properly, but for better results this process should be realized for each user (differences in visual perception among users).

The functionality of the system is the same as the VST AR system [2]. Therefore, in this paper we only comment on its functionalities briefly.

- The user can select the number of animals to appear:
  - one animal
  - increase/reduce in three animals
  - increase/reduce in 20 animals
- The animal/s can increase/reduce its/their size
- The animals can move or stop
- It is possible to kill animals using two different elements. When this occurs the system plays a sound related to the tool used and one or more dead animals appear.
- If the spider system is used, it is possible to choose among three types of spiders.

## 3 Study

To check whether the OST AR system is more or less effective than the optical see-through AR system, we have carried out an experiment comparing both systems. In this paper we focus on the anxiety level of participants during the experiment.

### 3.1 Participants

In total, 23 subjects took part in the experiments: 11 men and 12 women.

The interval of age lies between 20 and 44. Mean age of the subjects is 31.2 years.

Participants were divided into two groups: low fear subjects, with fear score equal or less than 50 (13 people) and more fear subjects, with fear score more than 50 (10 people).

Participants were counterbalanced and assigned to one of two conditions: a) Participant first used the VST AR system and later the OST AR system, b) Participant first used the OST AR system and later VST AR system. Therefore, four different groups have been defined:

G1 - Participants with low fear (LF) use first the OST AR system.
G2 - Participants with low fear use first the VST AR system
G3 - Participants with more fear (MF) use first the OST AR system.
G4 - Participants with more fear use first the VST AR system

4 participants were not asked for the anxiety level during the experiment. As a result, the participants that answered for the anxiety level in the four groups were:

1. 5 people
2. 7 people
3. 3 people
4. 4 people

We have to highlight that the anxiety level was only asked the first time the participant used one of the systems. That is, if a participant used first the OST AR system, he/she was asked for the anxiety during this experiment and he/she would not be asked for the anxiety when he/she would use later the VST AR system.

### 3.2 Measures

We have used several common testing tools, which we adapted to our AR system. In this paper we only cite measures related with the results presented here.

- *Fear and avoidance scales.* These scales were adapted from Szymanski and O'Donohue questionnaire [13]. Participants rate the level of fear/avoidance on a 0-10 scale.
- *Subjective units of discomfort scale (SUDS).* Following [14], we asked the participant to rate her maximum level of anxiety on a 0 to 10 scale (0=no anxiety, 10=high anxiety).
- *Consent form:* The participant read and signed a consent form accepting the treatment that he/she was going to receive, allowing us to videotape the sessions, and allowing us to use his/her data in our research.

### 3.3 Study

First, participants filled out the fear and avoidance questionnaire for cockroaches and spiders. If the score was higher for cockroaches, this was the animal that would be shown during the experiment, otherwise, spiders would be shown.

The higher score is also used for assigning participants to the group with less fear (<=50) or to the group with more fear (>50). After that, participant was assigned to one of the two groups of systems (use first the OST or the VST). This assignation was done in order to counterbalance the experiment.

Before using one of the two systems, a narrative was introduced so that the experience had more sense and interest to them. Then, the first exposure session began. During this first exposure session, participants were asked about their current level of fear. They were asked three times: at the beginning of the session, when animals crossed his/her hand and at the end of the session. In order to measure the anxiety, we used SUDs; as it has been commented, the scale used ranges from 0 to 10, whereby 0 is the minimum fear level and 10 the maximum fear level.

## 4 Results

Examples of a participant using the OST AR system are shown in Fig. 2-4.

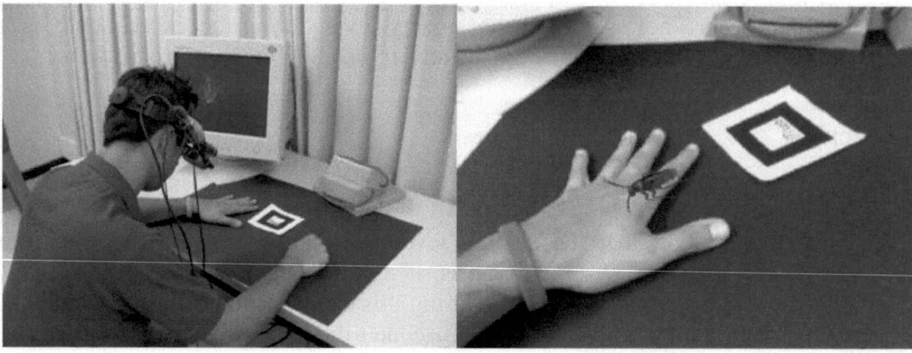

a) b)

**Fig. 2.** Participant lets a cockroach approach and cross over his hand. a) Participant b) Participant's view.

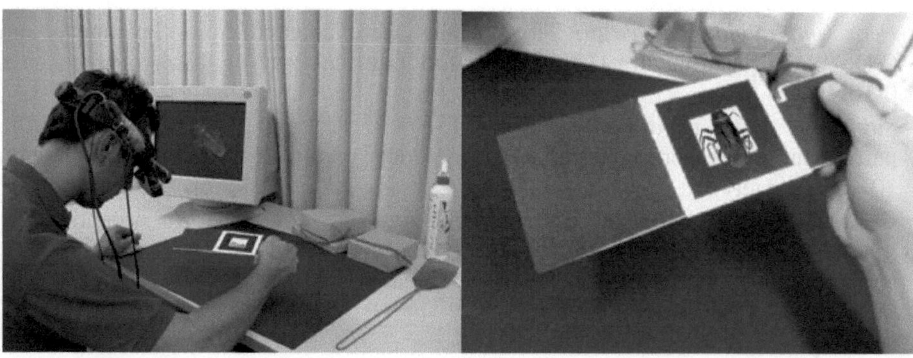

a) b)

**Fig. 3.** Participant looking closely at the animal. a) Participant b) Participant's view.

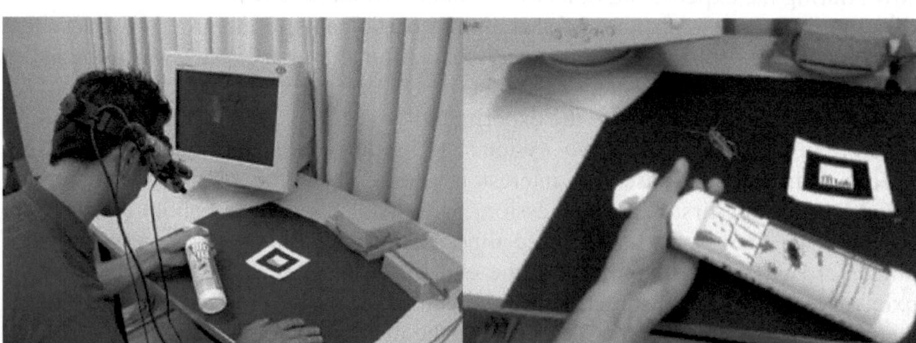

a) b)

**Fig. 4.** Participant killing a cockroach. a) Participant b) Participant's view.

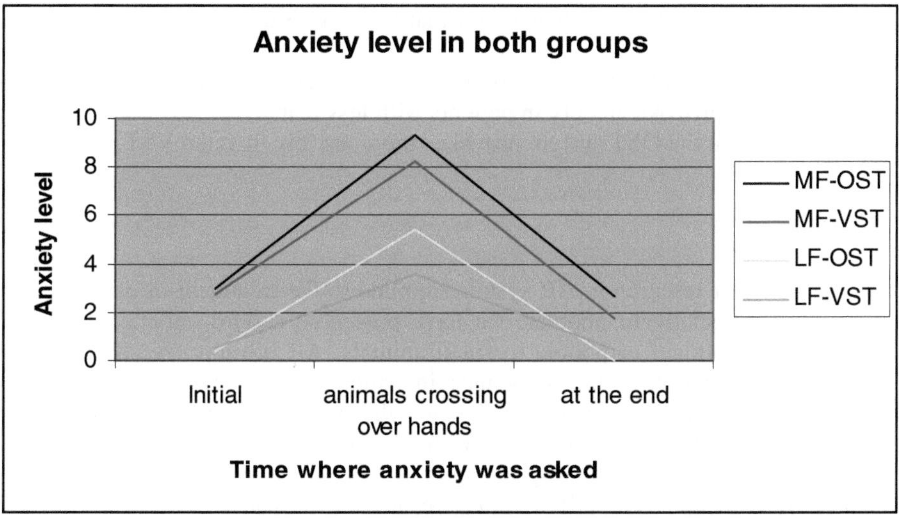


**Fig. 5.** Mean Anxiety Level in both groups

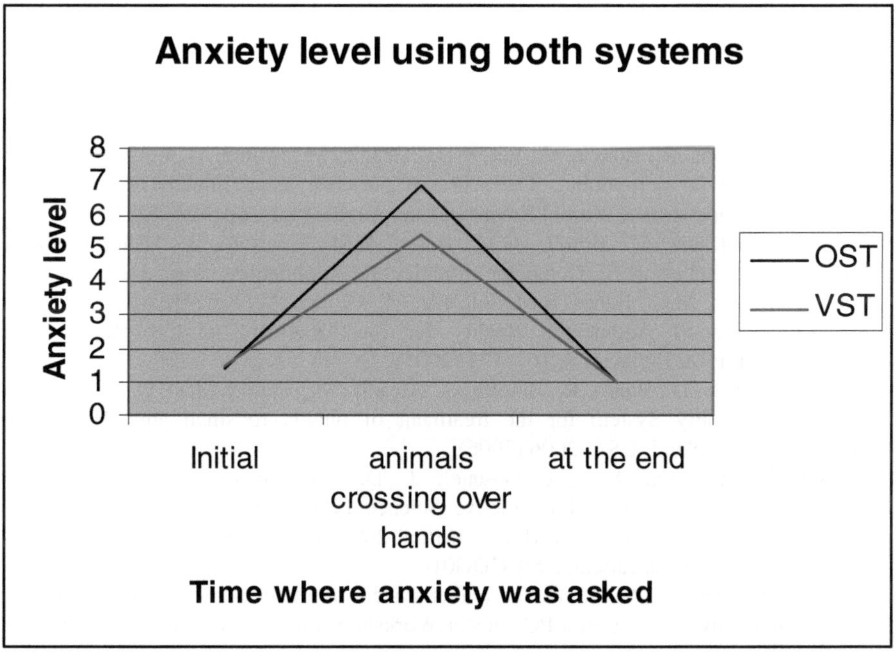


**Fig. 6.** Mean Anxiety Level using both systems

The means of the anxiety level of the four groups described in section 3.1 during the exposure sessions are presented in Fig. 5. We also have grouped participants by the system used and not by the fear score, that is, G1+G3 and G2+G4. These means are presented in Fig. 6.

Fig. 5 shows that both systems provoke more anxiety in participants with more fear, but they also provoke anxiety in patients with less fear.

Fig. 6 shows that the OST system provokes more anxiety than the VST.

## 5 Conclusions

Following with our research in AR systems applied to the treatment of psychological problems and especially to phobias, we have presented a third version of our AR system for the treatment of phobia to small animals. AR has already proved that is effective for reducing fear and avoidance in patients' suffering from this type of phobia [2] [3]. But we would like to develop the best AR system for this type of phobia and this is why we are working on the development of different AR systems. In this paper, apart from presenting our OST AR system, we have presented results comparing it with the VST AR system. Results show that both systems provoke anxiety in participants even if they do not have fear to cockroaches/spiders. OST AR system provokes slightly more anxiety than the VST AR system.

The study's main shortcoming is the small sample size. We need to study both systems with larger samples.

## References

1. Juan, M.C., Baños, R., Botella, C., Pérez, D., Alcañiz, M., Monserrat, C.: An Augmented Reality System for acrophobia: The sense of presence using immersive photography, Presence: Teleoperators & Virtual Environments, August Issue, pp. 393–402 (2006)
2. Juan, M.C., Alcañiz, M., Botella, C.M., Baños, R.M., Guerrero, B.: Using augmented reality to treat phobias. IEEE Computer Graphics and Applications 25(6), 31–37 (2005)
3. Botella, C., Juan, M.C., Baños, R.M., Alcañiz, M., Guillen, V., Rey, B.: Mixing realities? An Application of Augmented Reality for the Treatment of Cockroach phobia: Cyberpsychology & Behavior 8, 162–171 (2005)
4. Juan, M.C., Joele, D., Baños, R., Botella, C., Alcañiz, M., van der Mast, C.: A Markerless Augmented Reality System for the treatment of phobia to small animals, Presence Conference, Cleveland, USA, 2006 (2006)
5. Grasset, R., Decoret, X., and Gascuel, J. D. Augmented Reality Collaborative Environment: Calibration and Interactive Science Editing, Proceedings of 3th Virtual Reality International Conference (Laval Virtual 2001) last visited February 2007 (2001) http://artis.imag.fr/Publications/2001/GDG01/
6. Ivanovic, A., Plate, J.: An augmented reality system on the construction site for different users Virtual Environment on a PC Cluster Workshop, Protvino, Russia, 2002, pp. 77–84 (2002)
7. Özbek, C., Giesler, B., Dillmann, R.: Jedi Training: Playful Evaluation of Head-Mounted Augmented Reality Display Systems, In: SPIE Conference Medical Imaging, San Diego, USA, SPIE CMI, 2004, vol. 5291, pp. 454–463 (2004)

8. Leebmann, J.: Application of an augmented reality system for disaster relief International Archives of the Photogrammetry, Remote Sensing and Spatial Information Sciences, vol. XXXIV-5/W10, (2006) last visited February 2007 http://www.photogrammetry.ethz.ch/tarasp_workshop/ papers/leebmann.pdf,
9. Schwald, B., Laval, B.: An augmented reality system for training and assistance to maintenance in the industrial context. In: International Conference in Central Europe on Computer Graphics, Visualization and Computer Vision, pp.425–432 (2003)
10. Kato, H., Billinghurst, M.: Marker tracking and HMD calibration for a video-based augmented reality, Conferencing system. In: 2nd IEEE and ACM International Workshop on Augmented Reality (IWAR'99), San Francisco (California), pp. 85–94 (1999) (last visited February. 2007) http://www.hitl.washington.edu/artoolkit,
11. Owen, B.C., Zhou, Ji, Tang, A., Xiao, F.: Display-Relative Calibration for Optical See-Through Head-Mounted Displays. In: Third IEEE and ACM International Symposium on Mixed and Augmented Reality (ISMAR'04) 2004, pp. 70–78 (2004)
12. Genc, Y., Tuceryan, M., Navab, N.: Practical solutions for calibration of optical see-through devices, pp. 169– 175 (2002)
13. Szymanski, J., O'Donohue, W.: Fear of spiders questionnaire. Journal of Behavior Therapy and Experimental, Psychiatry 26(1), 31–34 (1995)
14. Wolpe, J.: The practice of behavior therapy. Pergamon Press, New York (1969)

# Summary of Usability Evaluations of an Educational Augmented Reality Application

Hannes Kaufmann[1] and Andreas Dünser[2]

[1] Interactive Media Systems Group, Vienna University of Technology
Favoritenstrasse 9-11/188/2, A-1040 Vienna, Austria
kaufmann@ims.tuwien.ac.at
[2] HIT Lab NZ, University of Canterbury, Private Bag 4800
8140 Christchurch NZ
andreas.duenser@hitlabnz.org

**Abstract.** We summarize three evaluations of an educational augmented reality application for geometry education, which have been conducted in 2000, 2003 and 2005 respectively. Repeated formative evaluations with more than 100 students guided the redesign of the application and its user interface throughout the years. We present and discuss the results regarding usability and simulator sickness providing guidelines on how to design augmented reality applications utilizing head-mounted displays.

**Keywords:** augmented reality, usability engineering, formative evaluation, geometry education.

## 1 Introduction

Our work is based on the educational Augmented Reality (AR) application Construct3D [1-3]. This system deploys AR to provide a natural setting for face-to-face collaboration of teachers and students. The main advantage of using AR is that students actually see virtual three dimensional objects. With traditional methods students have to rely on 2D sketching or calculating and constructing objects using pen and paper or CAD software. Direct manipulation and dynamic interaction with virtual 3D objects using tangible interaction devices are key features of Construct3D. In our standard setup users are wearing a see-through head-mounted-display; a pen and a panel are used for direct interaction in 3D space. Head, pen and panel are fully tracked in 3D which allows users to walk around objects and to view them from different perspectives (Fig. 1).

By working directly in 3D space, complex spatial problems and spatial relationships may be comprehended better and faster than with traditional methods. Our system utilizes collaborative AR as a medium for teaching, and uses 3D dynamic geometry to facilitate mathematics and geometry education.

Over the course of 6 years Construct3D has been developed, improved, tested and evaluated with more than 100 students in over 500 teaching lessons. Pedagogical theories such as constructivism and activity theory influenced the design of the

R. Shumaker (Ed.): Virtual Reality, HCII 2007, LNCS 4563, pp. 660–669, 2007.

collaborative educational AR hardware setup and content design. Technical details and pedagogical uses of Construct3D (including teaching content) have been published by the first author before [2-4].

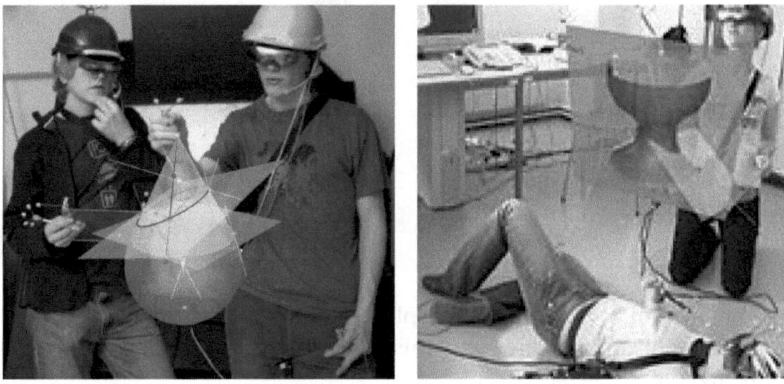

**Fig. 1.** Students working with Construct3D

The development process of Construct3D resembles the usability engineering methods of virtual environments suggested by [5]. The first informal evaluation in 2000 helped to compile a detailed user task analysis whereas expert guideline-based evaluations occurred numerous times during the development process. Visiting teachers and researchers evaluated the system and provided useful feedback. Two formative evaluations in 2003 and 2005 had a big impact on the design and development of Construct3D. In this paper we summarize three usability evaluations conducted in 2000, 2003 and 2005 and will present the lessons learned.

## 2 Construct3D

Construct3D is based on the Studierstube AR system [6]. It promotes and supports exploratory behavior through dynamic 3D geometry. A fundamental property of dynamic geometry software is that dynamic behavior of a construction can be explored in real time by interactively moving individual defining elements such as corner points of a rigid body. Users can see which parts of a construction change and which remain the same. The histories of constructions as well as dependencies between geometric objects are maintained. Experiencing what happens under movement facilitates better comprehension of a particular construction and geometry in general.

The menu system is mapped to a hand-held tracked panel called the personal interaction panel (PIP) [7]. The PIP (Fig. 2) allows the straightforward integration of conventional 2D interface elements like buttons, sliders, dials etc. as well as novel 3D interaction widgets. Passive haptic feedback from the physical props guides the user when interacting with the PIP, while the overlaid graphics allows the props to be used as multi-functional tools. Students can for instance position

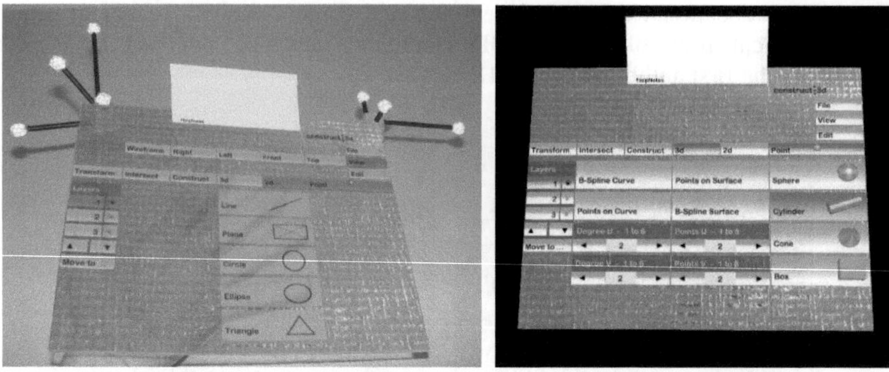


**Fig. 2.** Left: Menu system of Construct3D displayed on the PIP. In a help-box (on top) further details and help on application features are provided. Right: 3D submenu displayed for the user working with the red color scheme.

written notes onto the tablet which might help them during their work in the virtual environment.

All construction steps are carried out via direct manipulation in 3D using a stylus tracked with six degrees of freedom. In order to generate a new point the user clicks with his pen exactly at the location in 3D space where the point should appear. Users can easily switch between point mode (for setting new points) and selection mode (for selecting 3D objects).

Desktop CAD systems typically have a very steep learning curve and offer an abundance of features in deeply nested menus. For Construct3D we focused on a simpler menu system, which is easy to learn and intuitive to use. In addition we accommodated to the fact that menu widgets seen through a HMD need a certain size in order to be usable. Organizing the functions proved difficult under these conditions as the number of program functions increased over time. We finally organized the menu – according to a user task analysis, experts' guidelines and experience by logic grouping of functionality – into five submenus accessible via tabs (Fig. 2), with frequently used functions being visible all the time. This provides relatively quick access to all program functions. The menu concept is similar to that used in traditional desktop CAD menu systems known by many students, while avoiding excessive interface modes.

**Hardware Setups.** The standard immersive setup used for Construct3D supports two collaborating users wearing stereoscopic see-through head mounted displays (HMDs) (see Fig. 1) providing a shared virtual space. The users interact with the system using pen and pad props (Fig. 2). Both users see the same virtual objects as well as each others' pens and menu systems which provides a global shared space. In addition it allows users to help each other (i.e. with the menu system) if necessary. Position and orientation of head and hands are tracked using a 4-camera infrared-optical tracking system. In a co-located setup - such as the one used for our evaluations - one dedicated host with two graphic ports renders stereoscopic views for both users.

# 3 Usability Studies

We report and compare a first informal user study and formative usability studies completed in 2003 and 2005. Based on feedback from many trials with high school students and a first informal evaluation in 2000 [8] we continuously improved Construct3D over a course of 5 years.

All usability enhancements were conducted with the intention of improving collaborative learning and teaching. As usability can only be improved in accordance with users' needs and application specific strengths and weaknesses, the guidelines mentioned here cannot be applied directly to other applications without careful adaptation.

## 3.1 1st Informal Evaluation – 2000

In our first evaluation [8] with 14 students we observed the students' interaction with the system. We obtained very positive and encouraging feedback and a number of problems were pointed out. During the evaluation it was gratifying for us to see users work with Construct3D in a very constructive manner. They did not need a long introduction to the system but applied their experience with 2D user interfaces to the 3D interface. After completing the task, some walked around the objects, viewing them from different sides or got down on their knees and looked at the scene from below. Half of the students felt that working with Construct3D for the first time was easier than their first experience with a desktop CAD package.

Hand-eye coordination showed to be very difficult when spotting a point accurately in 3D space without haptic feedback or constraints. All students reported problems with setting points at given coordinates. As a consequence we implemented raster and grid functions. About constructing in VR, students especially liked walking around and inside objects, the "playful" way of constructing, and that spatial relationships and complex three dimensional designs are directly visible. The clear structure of Construct3D's menu system and the audio help system were mentioned positively.

At that time Construct3D was still a static modeling tool and did not provide dynamic features. Insights gained from the first evaluation (i.e. the difficulty for highly accurate 3D interaction) and the understanding that students would educationally benefit from 3D dynamic geometry encouraged us to change Construct3D into a dynamic 3D geometry application.

## 3.2 2$^{nd}$ Evaluation Study - 2003

In 2003 we conducted a study based on interviews and the standardized ISONORM 9241/10 usability questionnaire [9]. We designed a number of training exercises that fit the Austrian descriptive geometry curriculum of 11$^{th}$ and 12$^{th}$ grade [4]. Using Construct3D, 15 high school students (9 male, 6 female) worked on these exercises with the aid of their teachers. All students attended geometry classes (descriptive geometry) since the beginning of grade 11. Each of them participated in 5 training sessions lasting 6 hours. Our main objective was to assess the usability of our system and its potential as an educational tool for real high school work. At the end of all training sessions students had to answer an ISONORM usability questionnaire. Two questions regarding self-descriptiveness of the application had to be removed since they were related to desktop applications only. Afterwards students answered general questions regarding user acceptance, user behavior, technical requirements and organizational aspects.

**Results.** A closer look at the data (Figure 2) reveals that the categories "suitability for learning" and "suitability for task" received the highest rating which is very important in this context. In our opinion the highest priorities for an educational application that complies with pedagogic theories such as constructivism are that it (1) is easy to use and requires little time to learn, (2) encourages learners to try new functions and (3) can be used consistently and is designed in a way that things you learned once are memorized well. These are exactly the items that students rated very high. Almost all students reported that they could imagine using the current version of Construct3D in high school or university education.

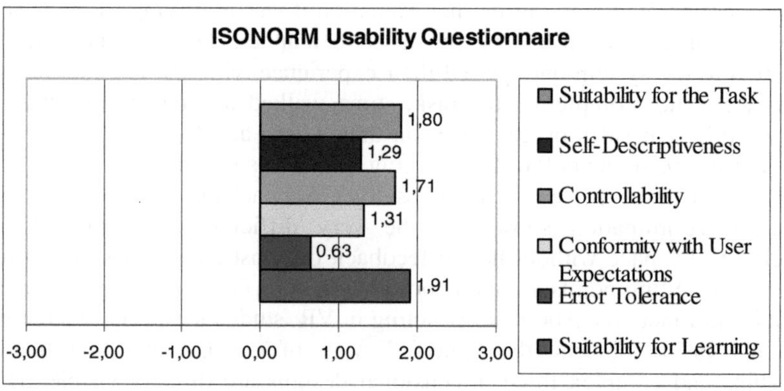


**Fig. 3.** Results of the ISONORM [9] usability questionnaire in 6 categories

The categories "self-descriptiveness" and "conformity with user expectations" got lower ratings than the rest. Self-descriptiveness of Construct3D was improved by adding better labeling and a help-box on the panel in order to explain all menu items.

As a result of this usability study the user interface was completely redesigned. The menu system was restructured (Fig. 2) to make features that are used most frequently easily accessible. In addition the visual design of geometric objects was enhanced considerably. The purpose of visual design of objects constructed by the user is to support the user's understanding of a construction. Unlike desktop visualization of the same content, using stereoscopic see-through HMDs requires to deal with limited contrast, resolution and viewing angle. Moreover, the system should present scenes of high depth complexity in a clear way, providing an improved insight into the construction. Among the techniques employed in Construct3D to support these goals are the use of transparencies for geometric objects to allow students to see inside objects (Fig. 1), consistent color coding to allow distinguishing between multiple users' contributions (which is especially important in distributed remote teaching scenarios), separation into layers to support semantic structuring of a construction, and automatic previewing of new objects. Details of the improvements are given in [3].

### 3.3 3rd Evaluation Study - 2005

In the 2005 evaluation 47 students were solving tasks with Construct3D in AR while another group of 44 students solved the same geometric problems with an educational desktop application called CAD3D [10] (which is used in Austrian high schools). Participants were Austrian high school students aged between 16 to 19 years (M = 17.49, SD = .79; 44 (48.4%) male and 47 (51.6%) female). Students attended 6 training sessions which lasted 45 minutes with one week pause in between. In both groups a tutor supervised two students working on the geometry tasks. The tutors explained the tasks to the students and supported them if they needed help.

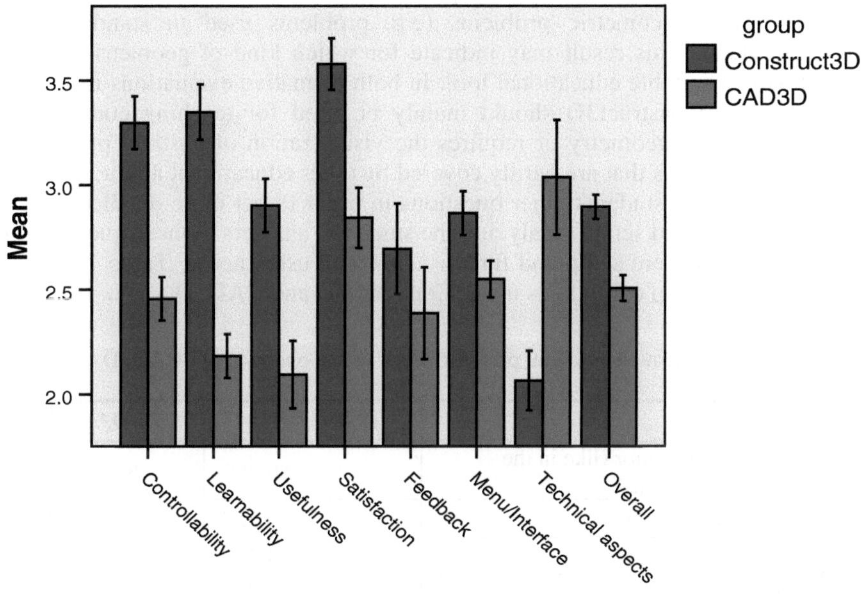


**Fig. 4.** Usability ratings of students working with Construct3D and CAD3D (4-point Likert scale; 1-min, 4-max = best; error bars ± 1.96 * standard error)

To assess usability we adapted questions of 8 established usability questionnaires to develop a questionnaire (7 scales (see Fig. 4); 28 questions in total) better suited for the range of applications tested. The questions were taken from the Questionnaire for User Interface Satisfaction, Perceived Usefulness and Ease of Use, Purdue Usability Testing Questionnaire, Computer System Usability Questionnaire, Practical Heuristics for Usability Evaluation (all at [11]), Software Usability Measurement Inventory [12], SUS [13] and the ISONORM [9] usability questionnaire.

**Results.** The analysis of the usability questionnaire showed that students using Construct3D gave higher ratings ($p < .01$) for all categories (Controllability, Learnability, Usefulness, Satisfaction, Feedback, and Menu/Interface) except technical aspects (e.g. robustness) than students using CAD3D. This indicates that the AR based geometry education application Construct3D is a highly usable system which - from a usability perspective - has several advantages over the traditional desktop based application. Especially user satisfaction, learnability and controllability got high ratings. However the low ratings for technical aspects suggest that there are still some issues regarding technical robustness that have to be addressed. Infrequent system crashes and minor technical problems can reduce motivation of participants and usability of the system.

Comparing the results of the 2003 and 2005 evaluations illustrates that conformity with user expectations (2003) / satisfaction (2005) was improved throughout the years. Suitability for the task got quite high ratings in the 2003 evaluation. In 2005 students rated usefulness, the equivalent scale, somewhat lower. In the 2005 evaluation a more extensive training setup was realized and thus students worked on a broader variety of geometric problems (e.g. problems used in standard school curriculum). Hence, this result may indicate for which kind of geometric problems Construct3D is a suitable educational tool. In both formative evaluations its strengths became obvious. Construct3D should mainly be used for teaching content which utilizes 3D dynamic geometry or requires the visualization of abstract problems. In addition these are areas that are hardly covered by other educational applications.

We also asked the students other questions in order to get more detailed feedback on the training task and setup. Analyzing the students' answers to these questions may help to refine our system setup and further adapt it to users needs. Table 1 shows the preferred training setup of students using Construct3D and CAD3D.

**Table 1.** How would you prefer to work with Construct3D / CAD3D

| | *Construct3D* | *CAD3D* |
|---|---|---|
| 2 students, one tutor (like in the training sessions) | 80.95% | 86.00% |
| 1 student, one tutor | 9.52% | 4.65% |
| 2 students, without tutor | 4.76% | 2.33% |
| alone | 4.76% | 4.65% |

There were no significant differences regarding the preferred training setup between students working with Construct3D and CAD3D. Most of the students liked the setup we used for the trainings in our study: 2 students working with one tutor.

Regarding the potential use of Construct3D in educational institutions we asked the students if they would like to use Construct3D in school in a setting similar they worked with (1 to 2 students) given the technical equipment would be affordable for schools. The majority of students would like to use Construct3D in school (yes = 64.44%, rather yes = 26.67%); 8.89% would rather not like to use the system in schools. Students' comments on the potential problems of using Construct3D in schools were mainly concerned with lack of finances and the robustness of hardware and software.

## 4 Simulator Sickness

As described earlier, Construct3D requires users to wear a HMD. In the second evaluation study (2003) some of the students reported negative side effects after working in the virtual environment, a condition known as simulator sickness, which is similar to motion sickness [14]. One female student reported headache and eye strain after 20 minutes of work in the virtual environment but did not stop working and wanted to use Construct3D again. In retrospect we know that our evaluation sessions lasting one hour were simply too long for continuous work with a HMD. Since negative side effects are a general potential problem when working with HMDs and influence the user's subjective experience of a VR/AR environment considerably they are relevant to all VR/AR applications that use these displays. We identified some possible reasons of such negative side effects that may be relevant to our virtual environment such as accommodation problems, low frame rate, lag or bad fitting helmets. If not taken into account, symptoms experienced by users affected by simulator sickness can drastically diminish usability of a system [15].

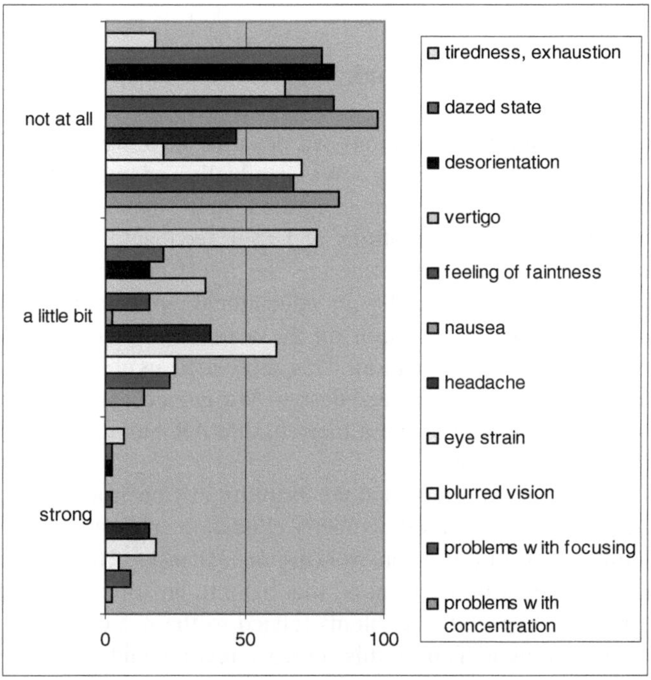


**Fig. 5.** Percentage of users reporting a specific symptom is shown (0% = reported by no user; 100% = reported by all users)

In order to minimize the chance of users suffering from symptoms of simulator sickness we limited training sessions to a maximum of 45 minutes in our third evaluation study (2005). Furthermore we replaced the hard plastic helmet (Fig. 1, left) which caused pressure on some students' forehead or even headache with a relatively lightweight bicycle crash helmet (Fig. 1, right). Students also were asked to take a rest when they felt the need to. After they finished the training sessions with Construct3D we asked them to which extent they actually did experience specific symptoms related to simulator sickness (questionnaire; 11 questions). Fig. 5 shows the percentage of participants having experienced a specific symptom 'not at all', 'a little bit' or 'strong' during or while having worked with Construct3D.

75.56% of the 47 participants felt a moderate amount of tiredness or exhaustion and 61.36% reported a little bit of eye strain. There were also some participants who reported having experienced some headache (37.78%) and vertigo (35.56%). Most of these symptoms may be related to the use of a HMD. Thus although we limited training time there still seem to persist issues with respect to some simulator sickness symptoms, especially exhaustion and eye strain. However in general most of the participants did not report having experienced severe problems.

In accordance with our observations and other studies we recommend limiting HMD usage to 20-30 minutes per session. Based on our experience image quality of HMDs but especially lag and quality of tracking data contribute most to the reported effects.

## 5 Conclusion and Future Work

In this summary of usability evaluations we describe how we managed to improve usability of Construct3D iteratively. We gradually adapted, reconfigured and redesigned hard- and software and integrated new interaction techniques and interfaces according to our observations and user feedback. A number of studies report that cognitive overhead in mastering the interface can hinder training and learning of the task [16]. Especially in educational applications it is of utmost importance to focus students' attention on the actual task and to reduce cognitive overhead needed to use the application. This motivated us to put a lot of time and effort into interaction and user interface design. We gained valuable results from the evaluations which helped us to create a more usable AR-based learning environment with improved user satisfaction.

In our latest evaluation we found that the usability of Construct3D was rated higher than the usability of a desktop based geometry education application. This may be due to the more intuitive workflow when working on 3D tasks. However there are still technical issues (e.g. software robustness) that have to be solved in order to improve usability even further. Especially problems related to the use of HMDs and tracking latency need careful thought. Thus at this stage we recommend to limit usage times of head mounted displays in immersive training setups. For an educational application such as Construct3D we envision its integration into courses; therefore temporally limited usage is very reasonable in this context.

Developers of AR-based applications face specific hard- and software related issues that are different from those of desktop based GUI or WIMP design. No set of common design guidelines exist yet that would facilitate or streamline the development of easy to use AR systems [15].

Regarding future work we plan to use Construct3D as a tool for evaluating various aspects of virtual learning environments in our future research including a comprehensive pedagogic evaluation, studying e.g. teaching styles/methodology or transfer of learning to tasks in the real world.

## References


1. Kaufmann, H., Schmalstieg, D.: Mathematics and geometry education with collaborative augmented reality. Computers & Graphics 27, 339–345 (2003)
2. Kaufmann, H.: Geometry Education with Augmented Reality. Ph.D. Thesis. Vienna University of Technology (2004) http://www.ims.tuwien.ac.at/research/construct3d/videos.php
3. Kaufmann, H., Schmalstieg, D.: Designing Immersive Virtual Reality for Geometry Education. In: Proceedings of IEEE Virtual Reality Conference 2006, Alexandria, Virginia, USA 2006, pp. 51–58 (2006)
4. Kaufmann, H., Papp, M.: Learning Objects for Education with Augmented Reality. In: Proceedings of EDEN 2006 (European Distance and E-Learning Network) Conference, Vienna 2006, pp. 160–165 (2006)
5. Hix, D., Gabbard, J.L.: Usability Engineering of Virtual Environments. In: Stanney, K.M. (ed.) Handbook of Virtual Environments - Design, Implementation, and Applications, pp. 681–699. Lawrence Erlbaum Associates, Mahwah, New Jersey (2002)
6. Schmalstieg, D., Fuhrmann, A., Hesina, G., Szalavári, Z.S., Encarnacao, L.M., Gervautz, M., Purgathofer, W.: The Studierstube augmented reality project. Presence - Teleoperators and Virtual Environments 11, 33–54 (2002)
7. Szalavári, Z.S., Gervautz, M.: The Personal Interaction Panel - A Two-Handed Interface for Augmented Reality. Computer Graphics Forum 16, 335–346 (1997)
8. Kaufmann, H., Schmalstieg, D., Wagner, M.: Construct3D: a virtual reality application for mathematics and geometry education. Education and Information Technologies 5, 263–276 (2000)
9. Prümper, J.: Der Benutzungsfragebogen ISONORM 9241/10: Ergebnisse Zur Reliabilität und Validität. In: Liskowsky, R. (ed.): Software-Ergonomie '97, Stuttgart (1997)
10. Stachel, H., Wallner, J., Pfeifer, M.: CAD-3D für Windows. (2003) http://www.geometrie.tuwien.ac.at/software/cad3d/
11. Perlman, G.: Web-Based User Interface Evaluation with Questionnaires. (accessed Feb. 15th 2006) http://www.acm.org/~perlman/question.html
12. Kirakowski, J., Corbett, M.: SUMI: the Software Usability Measurement Inventory. British Journal of Educational Technology 24, 210–212 (1993)
13. Brooke, J.: SUS: a quick and dirty usability scale. In: Jordan, P.W., Thomas, B., Weerdmeester, B.A., McClelland, I. (eds.): Usability Evaluation in Industry. Taylor and Francis, London, pp. 189–194 (1996)
14. LaViola Jr., J.J.: A discussion of cybersickness in virtual environments. ACM SIGCHI Bulletin 32, 47–56 (2000)
15. Dünser, A., Grasset, R., Seichter, H., Billinghurst, M.: Applying HCI principles to AR systems design. In: MRUI'07: 2nd International Workshop at the IEEE Virtual Reality 2007 Conference, Charlotte, North Carolina, USA (2007)
16. Dede, C., Salzman, M.C., Loftin, R.B.: ScienceSpace: Virtual Realities for Learning Complex and Abstract Scientific Concepts. In: Proceedings of IEEE VRAIS '96, pp. 246–252 (1996)

# VR-Based Self Brain Surgery Game System by Deformable Volumetric Image Visualization


Naoto Kume, Kazuya Okamoto, Takashi Tsukasa, and Hiroyuki Yoshihara

JSPS Research Fellow, Kyoto University Hospital, Japan
Graduate school of Informatics, Kyoto University, Japan
Graduate school of Informatics, Kyoto University, Japan
Department of Medical Informatics, Kyoto University Hospital, Japan
kume@kuhp.kyoto-u.ac.jp
kazuya@kuhp.kyoto-u.ac.jp
ttsukasa@kuhp.kyoto-u.ac.jp
lob@kuhp.kyoto-u.ac.jp


## 1 Background

Virtual reality (VR) based system has an advantage to provide an experience which never be realized in the real world. In these years, medical training simulators are developed by VR-based system. The aim of medical VR training system is to teach the actual manipulation in surgery. At the same time, the most important feature is that the system can teach anatomical and physiological behaviors. Interactive learning by VR system is expected to motivate active learning effectively. Hence, this study aims to provide a game system which does not require completely accurate simulation for a teaching material. However, modeling of the whole body relation between anatomy and physiology is not simple. So far, conventional brain study defines the functional map on the surface of brain. Therefore, the authors propose self surgery game for learning the basis of brain by stimulation and reaction. The self surgery game provides an experience to treat oneself by oneself. The game system would support the subject to imagine the relation between actual behavior and brain function map by touching one's own head.

## 2 Game System

The game is designed with two stages; pseudo analysis of one's brain and treatment by the pseudo radiation device. At the first stage, the disease in one's brain is visualized with spheres which are called target. The spheres are presented in three dimensional brain images by superimposition. At the treatment stage, user aims the target by using a pseudo radiation device putting on user's own head. The device called pointer can adjust the depth from the surface of the head to inside. Then, user points the target with the device by direction and depth. Targeting and pushing a button will eliminate the pseudo disease. During the targeting, reactions which are generated by stimulation according to the brain functional map are expressed with symbolized visual and audio effects. Then, the user recognizes the mapping


R. Shumaker (Ed.): Virtual Reality, HCII 2007, LNCS 4563, pp. 670–672, 2007.

between the region and functions by touching the user's own head. Finally, the score of operation are marked by the distance between the target and the targeted point.

## 3 Method

The system consists of four components. The first is position measurement system for head and the pointer tracking. The second is the pointer which is a pseudo radiation device for pointing the target with depth and direction. The third is simulation system for volume visualization and brain deformation. And the fourth is visual and audio effect generation system for symbolized reaction.

Position measurement system is constructed by centering on Polaris sensor. The markers which are coated by retro reflective material are settled on a head gear and the pointer. The direction of insertion is calculated by the position of the head gear and the pointer relatively. Because the sensor system works by infrared ray method, the head gear equips redundant makers to avoid tracking failure caused by intercepting the direct path between the sensor and the makers. The pointer consists of Polaris marker and depth measurement mechanism. Polaris markers are lined for detecting the direction. User pushes head by the pointer, the top of pointer is stored inside the body pursuant to the depth. The pointer gets the length by rotary encoder. The simulation realizes finite element method based soft tissue deformation for simulating puncture of brain. Before pseudo puncture of the brain surface, visualized brain volume image is deformed by the pointer. The target is rendered during deformation and puncture. Physical head surface and virtual brain volume image are calibrated before the puncture simulation.

The visual and audio effect generator is the key component for teaching material. The target which is set by randomized pattern on each game procedure is related to the actual brain function by the position. Prepared mapping list of brain function and the effects is loaded by pointing or target elimination. Pointing adds the effects on the front display and the surround audio. On the other hand, target elimination removes the effects which mean the cure of disease. More than twenty effects are prepared for represent specific disease or behaviors such as vision problem, memory loss, and auditory hallucination.

## 4 Demonstration

The developed system called "Brain-Touch" was demonstrated at International Virtual Reality Contest 2005. The total number of subjects is about 50. The simulation system was installed on a personal computer (Intel Pentium4 - 3.4GHz dual, 4GB Memory). On the whole, female subjects had a tendency not to be good at recognition of 3D coordinates. In contrast, males are good at recognition and immersed operation extremely. Besides, the system is not only interesting as an entertainment but also good for teaching material of brain functions.

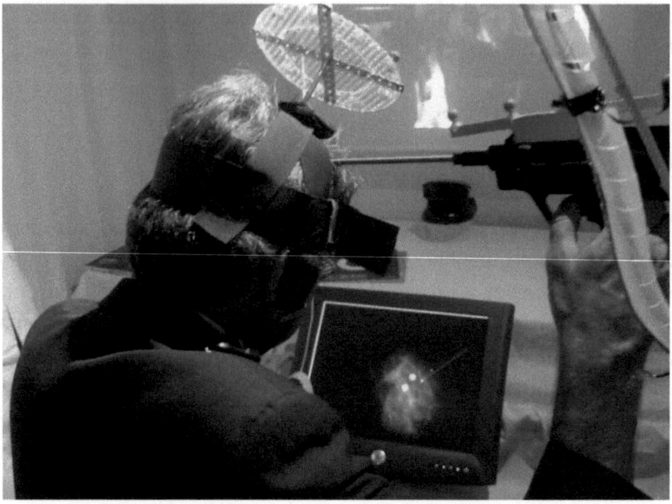

**Fig. 1.** The Proposed "Brain-Touch" system

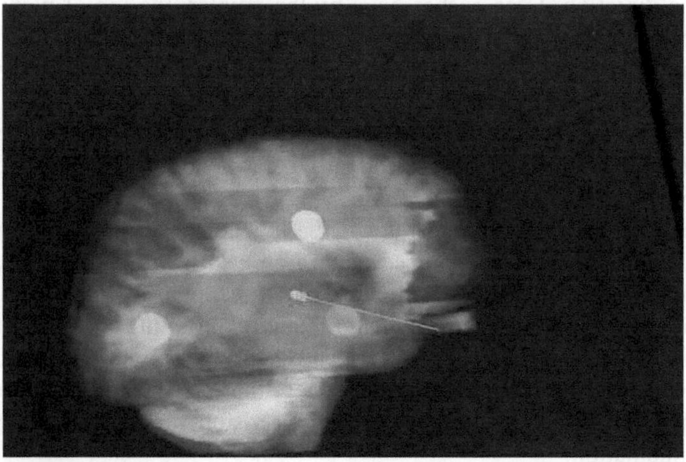

**Fig. 2.** Volume rendered Brain image and the target spheres. The red line is the image of the pointer. Brain volume is deformed before puncture. After the puncture, user targets by adjusting the depth and the direction of the pointer. Viewpoint can be changed interactively.

## 5 Conclusion

The authors proposed a self surgery game system for providing a teaching material of brain function map. The system was developed by an optical sensor and physics-based simulation system. The result of demonstration indicated the effectiveness of teaching material by game system.

# The Value of Re-used the Historic Building by Virtual Preservation: A Case Study of Former British Consulate in Kaohsiung

Zong-Xian Lin[1] and Hong-Sheng Chen[2]

[1] Graduate School of Computational Design, National Yunlin University of Science & Technology, 123 Section 3, University Road, Douliou, Yunlin, 64002, Taiwan, R.O.C
g9434710@yuntech.edu.tw
[2] Ling Tung University, 1, Ling tung Rd., Taichung City, Taiwan, R.O.C., Taiwan
chsh@ntu.edu.tw

**Abstract.** Historic buildings are important to many aspects of human, but most buildings are not protected well. The natural and man-made calamities are major destruction. The destruction of natural and some man-made destruction are unable to avoid. The laws about the preservation of historic building are too passive, because they need a lot of time to establish identity. But before the historic buildings establish identity and between the official documents make a round trip, the buildings are destroyed constantly. To face such problem, we are necessary to suggest new preservation concepts to assist preservation of historic building. Due to development of computer, we can protect the data of historic building by digitization. In this case, I will use virtools to do an interface to help people to build the buildings in the virtual reality. Making everyone can protect the historic buildings by it.

**Keywords:** preservation, virtual reality, virtual preservation.

## 1 Introduction

As time goes on, the buildings are easily destroyed by storm and earthquake. Therefore, the virtual preservation is good to the buildings, historic buildings especially. To face such problems, researchers suggest new preservation concepts for assisting the preservation of historic buildings. In the information era, almost everything is digitalized, including the cities [1]. Due to the development of computer technologies, digitization is helpful to assist data preservation and usage. Furthermore, virtual reality can be applied to simulate any incomplete or fragmentary parts of a building, and even a destroyed environment. There are two methods for virtual preservation in common. One is taking pictures and combining pictures to circular image, and another is to use 3D software to build 3D model. The main advantages of the image-based VR are its photo-quality realism and 3D illusion without any 3D information. Unfortunately, creating content for image-based VR is usually a very tedious process [2]. But the drawback of the first one is the pictures bring deformed images and this way will lose many details. The second one provides

R. Shumaker (Ed.): Virtual Reality, HCII 2007, LNCS 4563, pp. 673–679, 2007.

one or two ways to view the 3D virtual buildings and space, and they always only show the form of the building.

I think the preservation of historic building is should be positive. In this age, the general public also can be one of the members who protect historic buildings. Because there are many drawbacks in the image-based VR at preservation of historic buildings (like the detail of the buildings and the deformed thing in the pictures), I want to protect building by way of making 3D model. But the threshold of technology is too high for the general public that is not good thing for the preservation of historic building. So I want to make an interface for the general public to build the virtual buildings easily.

In this study, I will target the Former British Consulate in Kaohsiung. It is the first building of Western world in Taiwan, and the building materials are come from China. As time goes on, though the building is restored, but it is still possible destroyed in the future. I use this system to build 3D model of Former British Consulate in Kaohsiung and other objects and virtools to interact with users in this system.

## 2 Related Work

### 2.1 Image-Base Virtual Reality

Image-based virtual reality is emerging as a major alternative to the more traditional 3D-based VR. The main advantages of the image-based VR are its photo-quality realism and 3D illusion without any 3D information. [2] But there are some problems in image-based virtual reality like that some things are out of the shape and the viewer can not see some detail in the scene. For example, when I use the software, photovista to make Image-based virtual reality, the viewer will not see the some parts of floor and ceiling and the things at the back of the corner.

### 2.2 The Elements of the Building

There is a frame of the level between the detail of the building and the principal part of the building. If we divide it by physical property, the frame of the level can be divided to “complex – element - component”. [3] The element in this part is meaning like the door, the pillar, etc. The building can be divided to many elements and many elements are used again and again. So we can use characteristic to build some buildings or scene.

### 2.3 Former British Consulate in Kaohsiung

During the last years of Manchu Dynasty, the British make three buildings in Taiwan. The first building is the Former British Consulate at Dagou (this name is the old name of the Kaohsiung.). The consulate was built in 1865 with more than a hundred years of history. It is now the most antique western building preserved in Taiwan, which is listed as the second-class historic spot. [4] When the typhoon “THELMA” pass through Taiwan in1977, the Former British Consulate in Kaohsiung was destroyed serious. Until 1987, government department start to protect the building. We can see many ornaments which represent the characteristic of Renaissance on this building and there are a lot of arched structures on the wall. So there is a lot of important meaning for the Former British Consulate in Kaohsiung.

**Fig. 1.** The pictures of the Former British Consulate in Kaohsiung that happened after the typhoon "THELMA" pass through the Taiwan

# 3 The System

Because there are many elements in the buildings are similar or the same, I think the general public can use this system to build the virtual buildings and make them are the same or similar to original building. In this system, users can draw the element into the main window and control the size of the elements. Using this system to build the buildings or scene is like to play the bricks.

The users can request the amateurs or the experts to make the elements which are the users need with this system. After the users using these elements to build the buildings or scene, users can make a virtual person into the world which is made by

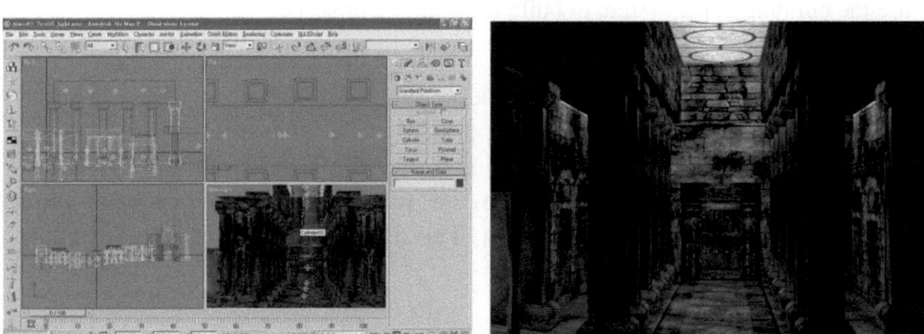

**Fig. 2.** Many Buildings look like very complex, but they may be made up by some elements which are sample shape

users themselves. Then users can look the virtual reality with the viewpoint of the virtual person.

### 3.1 Framework

**System.** In this study, there are two main parts in this system. One part is communication part, and another is building part which is used to build the buildings. This system will combine the two parts with technique is related to website. I will use technique of the website to set up the communication part and make building part with virtools.

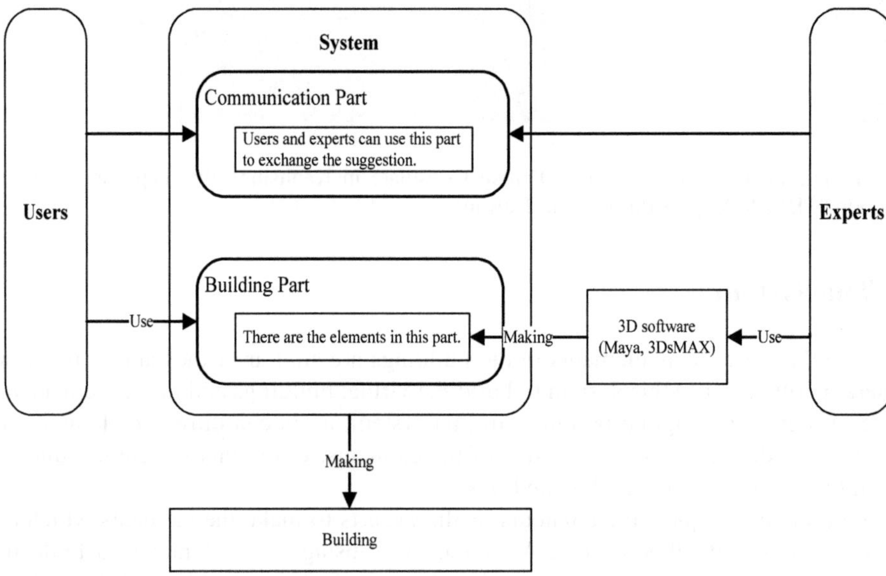


**Fig. 3.** Users and experts can talk with each other by the communication part in the system. Users use the building in the system to build the building or scene.

*Communication Part.* The users and experts can communicate with each other with this part. The users can request the experts to make the elements by leaving the messages and posting the pictures with this part. I think the communication between the users and experts is not limited to the work. They also can talk about the technique and information in 3D domain. The user also can discuss with other user in this part.

*Building Part.* The users are using this part to building. There are many elements for the users to build the buildings in this part. If there are the elements which the users want, the users can use communication part to make the experts know. Then the experts can make the elements for the system. I will set up this part with virtools.

**Users.** In this study, the users are the general public. They can use system to build the buildings or scene and communicate with the experts. The users can use system to build the buildings or scene with the elements in the system. When there are not the elements which the users want to have, the users can request the experts or the amateurs who can use 3D software to make the elements. They also communicate with interests, experts, and amateurs by the system.

**Experts.** In this study, the experts mean people who study in the 3D domain or can use 3D software like 3DsMAX or Maya. They can get the information from the users by the system and update the elements in the system.

### 3.2 Characteristic

**Build the Building yourself.** You can use this system to build the building by yourself. You do not request other people to make it. There are many easy tools and operations to help you to make the building and scene.

**Discussing Become Easier.** You do not need to find the forum in the internet for discussion at random, because the function of the discussion in this system. You can easy to talk to the expert and other users in the communication part of this system. Sometimes the experts do not understand the words which the users say. For this problem, there is the function of posting pictures in the communication. Pictures and words will make you discuss easier.

**Free Viewpoint.** You can see any thing in this system. The viewpoint is free. You can make a virtual person or much virtual people in the scene, and you can see the scene form the viewpoint of the people.

### 3.3 Interface

**Work Area.** There are some functions in this area. Left part is to do base action for the model and middle part is to change the viewpoint by move the camera. Right part is to show the record of the action.

**Action Area.** This part is the main and most important part. Many buildings near us look so commonplace, but they will become invaluable in culture or in architecture in the future. For example,

**Communication Area.** This part includes text area and the tag which can exchange the function of the communication.

### 3.4 Implementation

We can discuss this item from many aspects. Because I want make people easy to use this system for virtual preservation, communication, and others.

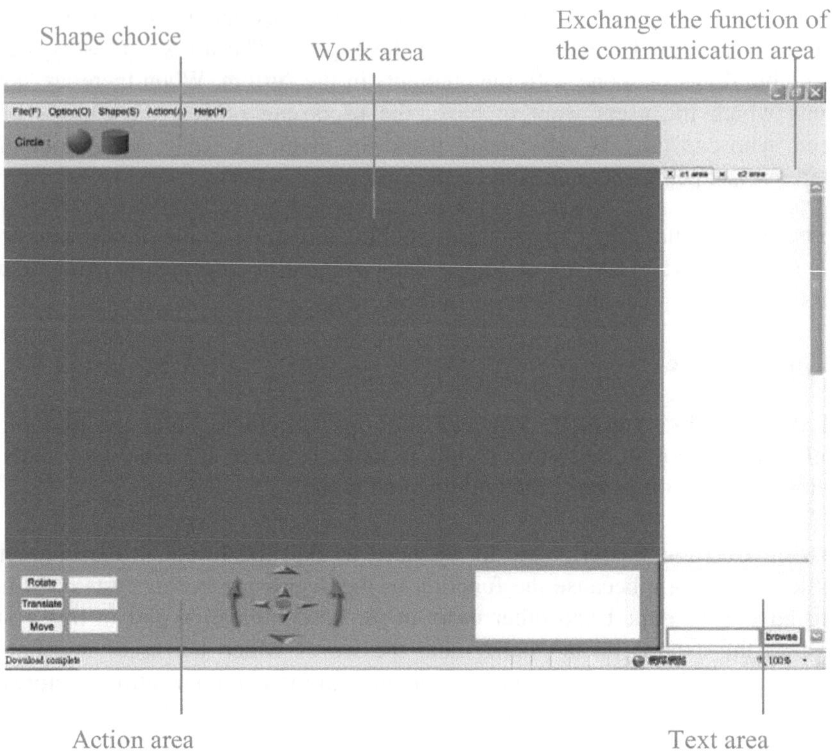


**Fig. 4.** This is the interface of the model of the system. The Right part of the interface is communication part which includes text area and the tag and the left part of the interface is building part which includes work area and action area.

**Virtual Preservation.** This part is the main and most important part. Many buildings near us look so commonplace, but they will become invaluable in culture or in architecture in the future. For example, four-section compound is the building of the masses in the times, but it is the important badge of the culture of the Chinese people now. If we can not protect them now, the meaning and the technique in the building will disappear anytime. Even if the users just make some elements of the building like pillar and can not build the building, it is still important for the preservation of historic buildings.

**Communication.** Besides making the virtual buildings, the communication of the users and the experts is also meaningful. The users can learn some knowledge of 3D domain from the experts with this system. Then the users may interest in the 3D domain and invest in 3D domain. The experts also can know information like history, style, and meaning about the building. I think it is helpful to the experts in architecture and design aspects.

**Others.** You are not just using this system in the preservation of historic buildings. You can also make some things for the model of game scene or just use it like playing games. You can use this to practice the extensity of the students.

## 4 Conclusion

The preservation of buildings is not just implementing by the government. The process is too slow and the government can not do it overall. A natural disaster always happen suddenly that will make buildings destroy all at once. If we can protect the buildings indeed, the later generations will know the buildings by reading books or magazines. Even if we only protect some part of the building, I think it is still helpful to research in the future.

## 5 Future Work

Due to the development of computer technologies, digitization is helpful to assist data preservation and usage. Furthermore, virtual reality can be applied to simulate any incomplete or fragmentary parts of a building, and even a destroyed environment [5]. In addition, the reconstruction process often leads to completely new insights, because it forces the researcher to think about completely new questions, e.g. how everyday life in an ancient building actually was (Where were the doors? Did they have locks?). Virtual reconstructions of ancient sites are an increasing application of computer graphics and virtual reality. [6]

Except preservation, we can combine it with other software (flash, VRML etc.) to do something about interaction like education and tourism. When the buildings become digital information, people can view them anywhere and help people to understand them. For example, The VRML browser reads the file, parses through the file, builds the virtual world and renders the world in a viewpoint of the Web site. The browser provides a user interface for navigation through the virtual world [7].

## References


1. Lin, F.-T.: Prospects of Digital Architecture. CAAD TALKS (2003)
2. Xiong, Y., Turkowski, K.: Creating Image-Based VR Using a Self-Calibrating Fisheye Lens. IEEE (1997)
3. Liu, T.-C.: A Preliminary Study on the Cognitional Behavior of an Architectural Detail, Master's Thesis, Architecture and Urban Design, National Taipei University of Technology, Taipei (2001)
4. Tourism Bureau, Republic of China (Taiwan): (2007) http://202.39.225.132/jsp/Eng/html/attractions/scenic_spots.jsp?id=5279
5. Wang, L.-Y.: A Practicability Study of Virtual Preservation on the Historic Buildings-A Case Study of Re-miao Commercial House in Lukang, Master's Thesis, Graduate of School Industrial Design, National YunLin University of Science and Technology, YunLin (2000)
6. Masuch, M., Strothotte, T.: Visualising Ancient Architecture using Animated Line Drawings. IEEE (1998)
7. The Image Factory: (1999) http://www.imagefact.de/

# Cultural Heritage as Digital Experience: A Singaporean Perspective

Wolfgang Müller-Wittig, Chao Zhu, and Gerrit Voss

Centre for Advanced Media Technology (CAMTech)
Nanyang Technological University (NTU)
50 Nanyang Avenue
Singapore 649812
wmww@camtech.ntu.edu.sg

**Abstract.** Interactive 3D computer graphics technology is now extremely popular, seen in the increasing interest in and use of 3D digitization of cultural heritage contents. This paper introduces a digital interactive cultural heritage system which embeds Virtual-Reality (VR) technology within the Peranakan culture, the Peranakan culture being a Singaporean unique ethnic culture. A prototype has undergone the full developmental process of being implemented, tested, and evaluated. This paper will also discuss the results of the usability test.

## 1 Introduction

In Singapore, CAMTech are the first to implement the use of VR technology as an effective medium of disseminating Peranakan culture. Such work mirrors the use of computer graphics technology to open up new dimensions in varied fields such as archaeology, the arts, tourism, and education. For example, similar efforts are evident in projects ranging from China's Du Huang Cave [1] to DentroTrento in Italy [2].

**Background to the Peranakans.** This community, also known as the StraitsChinese, is descendants of an early Chinese community that settled in what was known as the Malay Archipelago. Their origins date back to at least the 17$^{th}$ century [3], and thus they represent among the oldest historical ethnic communities in Singapore. They possess distinct clothing, cuisine, architecture, and even an individual linguistic system [7]. They combine a Chinese and Malay way of life, and today, with assimilation of certain western cultural elements, form a unique ethnic group, outstanding even against Singapore's multicultural backdrop. In Singapore, Peranakans play the important role of being an influence upon various aspects of Singapore life, for example, its economy, arts, and culture. Intense urbanization and western acculturation has, however, sadly eroded interest in the Peranakans. The young generations in particular, are definitely more interested in technology and its gadgetry rather than history or culture. The question of the preservation and perpetuation of the culture has thus become critical.

R. Shumaker (Ed.): Virtual Reality, HCII 2007, LNCS 4563, pp. 680–688, 2007.

CAMTech is an advanced media technology media provider, so it was inevitable that we respond to the challenge of assisting the Peranakan community with its problem, which has resulted in our project to infuse the Peranakan cultural heritage with VR technology, or *virtual heritage*. Section Two provides the rationale for the choice of VR technology.

## 2 Challenges and Solutions

Three challenges encountered in this domain of Virtual Heritage are:

- 3D documentation
- 3D representation
- 3D dissemination [4].

**3D documentation.** 3D documentation is the process of capturing and managing cultural heritage data, or information about the subject. It is impossible to present all the various manifestations of culture in one frame. Thus the first challenge is selecting what might be the most representative image of that culture. With the Peranakans, we decided to digitally construct Peranakan Shophouses. We made this choice after reviewing the literature, investigating related materials, such as photographs, books, including visits to the local museums, and interviewing Peranakans themselves, as well as experts in their history.

The Peranakan shophouses are typical terrace row houses, normally lengthy and narrow, possessing a distinct five-foot walkway in the front. The architecture is highly artistic, vibrant with color and details which reflect the Chinese and Malay heritage. Combined with an intricate interior design, the shophouses make for an ideal 3D museum.

**3D representation.** The second challenge is to capture and record the 3D data as realistically as possible. This is achieved by using authentic materials, for example, the use of photographs, which are scanned to be used as referencing images or textures for 3D modeling.

The most common method of 3D presentation is 3D modeling and visualization. High quality 3D models are essential to create an impressive and attractive visual. An effective and efficient visualization system is also required to support the rendering of large amounts of 3D modeling.

In this project, we managed to accomplish more than the elaborate modeling of the Peranakan shophouses. We have also established a photo-realistic 3D object library which has around 60 items, including furniture, ceramics, embroidery, silverware and various accessories. These are also accompanied by introductory notes. To enhance and augment the realism of the images, pre-lighting technology is employed to simulate day light effects and shadows.

Figure 1 below shows the rendering images of the 3D models of the interior and façade of the shophouses. The 3D models are visualized using our in-house interactive visualization system. This is which can handle massive 3D data processing.

**Fig. 1.** Interior and façade of the shophouses

**3D dissemination.** 3D dissemination refers to the environment conveyed to users. The most important advantage of a 3D digital culture heritage is that it is an easier, cheaper and safer platform, through which users can access and experience cultural treasures. The growing attention to the importance of culture, be it for education or tourism objectives, has brought about a need for culture to be conveyed in both educational and entertainment formats. It is a widely acknowledged and popular educational principle that learning should be lively achieves all this. It provides immersive experiences as well as real-time interactivity. It can be designed for applications for an individual user or small groups.

Our hardware is back project technology. We have also been researching and exploring for even more avenues to increase interactivity, one of them being the use of a virtual avatar as tour guide, as well as a Chinese calligraphy brush.

## 3 Prototype Development and Implementation

### 3.1 Software System Design

As illustrated in Figure 2 below, the whole system is a layered structure. At the base is the OpenGL library, a mere graphics mechanism which actually knows nothing about the scene structure.

On top of this is the OpenSG library, a scene-graph based real-time rendering system [5]. The advantage of using OpenSG is that it is a Multi-Platform Open Source system which can handle a cluster as well as multithreaded data structures both easily and efficiently, and also capable of being used in various other ways [5]. Our in-house VR system is an extension of the OpenSG library. We call it *VSC Library* because it inherits all the merits of OpenSG but is more application-oriented, and can be customized to different projects.

With this Peranakan project, a *Digital Heritage (DH) Project Library* has been created on the top of the VSC Library. This library includes three main components: scene control nodes, visualization control nodes, and interaction control nodes.

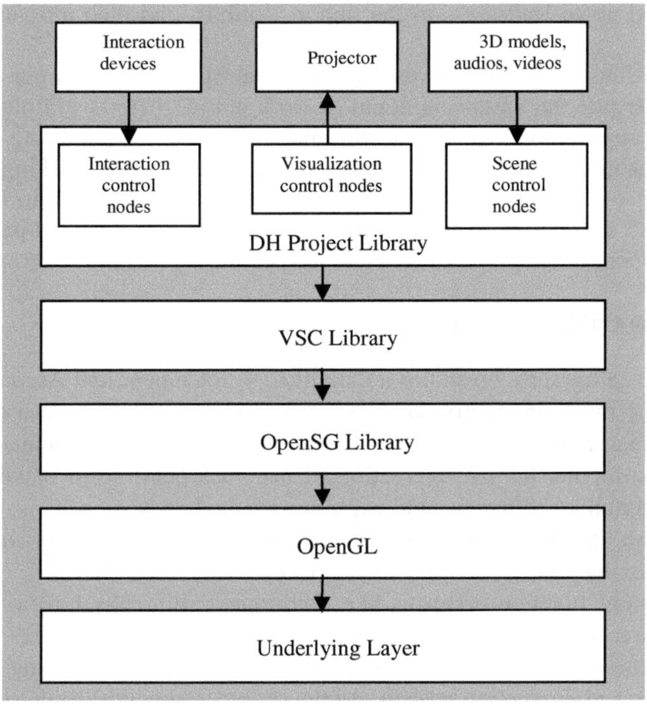


**Fig. 2.** Software system design

The **scene control nodes** load the 3D models and related media files, such as documents, images, audios and videos, into the system. The **visualization control** nodes adjust the visualization hardware, for example, they can control stereoscopic display. The **interaction control** nodes link all the interaction hardware devices. In this project, the device is the Chinese calligraphy brush attached with sensors.

The advantage of this layered structure is its high flexibility and modulation. Especially since the top level controls are designed by using scripting languages, the design of the interaction contents is much easier for programmers and artists who have less knowledge about OpenSG, OpenGL, or other underlying issues. Our paper now focuses on our interaction tools, the *Virtual Tour Guide* and the *Chinese Calligraphy Brush.*

### 3.2 Virtual Tour Guide

Tour guides are commonly used to give information about a heritage or tourism site. Also in use would be information displays or audio broadcasting. Digital heritage sites would thus use virtual tour guides.

Our virtual tour guide is a Chinese-looking male wearing traditional Peranakan clothing as befits the Peranakan background [7]. Besides modeling and texturing by referencing real images, a series of animated body movements and facial expressions is also given him. He can walk, talk, and respond to user requests. For example, he can be called up to lead users to the import exhibits, and then introduce appropriate information.

The modeling and animation uses commercial 3D software, in our case, *Autodesk Maya* [6]. Despite the massive amount of work put in, there is still plenty of room to create even more convincingly realistic images. We are also working on making the avatar appear more natural, fluid in its movements, as well as working on the quality of its responses. One possibility is to add a path-finding function to the virtual tour guide, should users want to visit the house at their leisure, or own pace, rather than having to adhere to the pre-defined avatar-led path.

### 3.3 Chinese Calligraphy Brush

The Chinese calligraphy brush has a long history in Chinese and Asian culture. It was chosen as the major interactive device, being intuitive and easy-to-use, possessing a kind of human-human interface. But when this kind of communication mode is brought to computer-human interaction, it becomes possible to make the computer react to what human beings want to express with the brush.

The "brush" has two functions, one to write commands, another to navigate. It is thus more flexible than traditional writing tools.

The 'writing' function performs like traditional calligraphy brushes. Some simple Chinese characters are chosen as the command words that control the navigation as well as the information display. The brush is connected with tracking sensors. When users imprint any strokes on a blank writing board, the combination of the strokes is recorded and recognized by the underlying pattern recognition algorithm. For example, when a user writes the Chinese character *up*' which is composed of three strokes, the system will guide the user to level two of the shophouse. Non-Chinese speaking users can call the virtual tour guide to help them write the characters. The execution of this function is highly dependent on the accuracy of the pattern recognition algorithm. Our pilot test shows most users, especially non-Chinese speakers, have difficulty writing the characters in a standard way. The difference between handwriting makes the recognition process even harder. However, despites difficulties, most users enjoy this innovative and fun way of learning through experience. Figure 3 below illustrates.

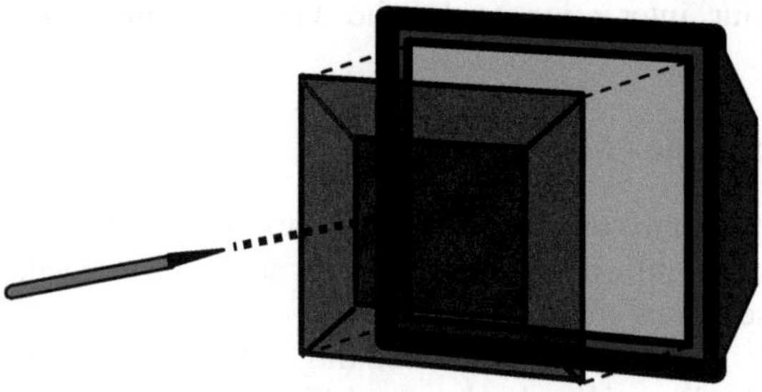

**Fig. 3.** Navigation with brush

To maintain consistency between functions, we also explored how to navigate in the virtual scenario using the calligraphy brush. The position and orientation of the brush is traced by the tracking system, so it is possible to connect the movements of the brush with the Graphics User Interface (GUI) on top of the scenario display. For example, the foreground of the GUI is divided into five zones as shown in Figure 3. When the brush 'points' at the up zone, the user will move forward in the virtual world. Similarly, the bottom, left and right zones activate backward, left and right movements respectively. A touch of the middle zone will stop all navigation and users can then look at the exhibits, 'clicking' with the brush on either menus or information panels for further action. During the implementation stage, a question raised was whether the calligraphy brush really enhanced navigation experiences, more than traditional VR navigation devices. A usability test was conducted to explore this question.

## 4 Usability Test

A test bed was created to study user preferences and adaptability towards different navigational mediums in a virtual environment, in this case, the usage of a Chinese calligraphy brush against the usage of a 3D spacemouse in the virtual shophouse environment.

### 4.1 Setup of the Test bed

The virtual heritage environment was set up with a single double storey shophouse block and a static avatar. A short introduction and instructions on the two navigational tools were given to each tester to better their understanding, after which, they performed short navigation trials on each of the devices to familiarize handling. See Figure 4 below.

**Fig. 4.** Usability test setup

Testers were assigned 3 tasks (in order of ascending difficulty) to undertake during each usability test [7]:

1. Stand in front of the Virtual Tour Guide.
2. Walk around the shophouse and come back to the Virtual Tour Guide and stop.
3. Walk into the shophouse then walk out of the shophouse using the five-foot walkway.

The first task aimed at warming up testers in the virtual environment by instructing them to take a simple one directional route from the default start position to a specific location in front of the avatar. The second task aimed to test the orientation control of each tester with a route that required changes in direction during navigation. This test also studied how reaction varies between usage of the calligraphy brush and spacemouse, in terms of adaptability and ease of movement. The last task aimed to test a more delicate degree of navigational control. Each tester was requested to complete a questionnaire based on their virtual experience.

### 4.2 User Statistics

The study used 26 testers consisting of NTU staff and students (Males: 80%; Females: 20%). Most of them were between 25-30 years of age. It is important to note that a little more than half the group had prior experience navigating in a virtual environment.

## 5 Results

The questionnaire consisted of 16 questions, which every tester had to complete after their entire test round. 80% of the group found usage of the Chinese calligraphy brush as a navigational tool innovating and interesting. It took most testers less than three minutes to become familiar with this interface. Many found the spacemouse interface harder to control, with a longer familiarization period required. Thus testers ranked the 3D spacemouse 'difficult', with many taking three to five minutes getting used to it. 75% testers felt it was easier to navigate with the calligraphy brush. The calligraphy brush enhanced virtual experience for at least 50% of the group. Table 1 lists some of the results after analyzing the questionnaires [7].

The biggest limitation to the current calligraphy brush interaction was the limited degrees of freedom in navigation (i.e. left, right, up, down and centre) and the speed of travel. Many preferred a wider navigation and speed range. But then testers found the 3D spacemouse too sensitive. They reported "spinning" out of their orientation path and getting lost and confused within the environment.

Generally, testers were very positive towards showcasing cultural heritage in a virtual reality environment and the usage of props for interaction. Many felt that VR is a great way to preserve cultural heritage and allows for more information Most also agreed that the introduction of interactive devices was a good idea and served to enhance their VR experience.

**Table 1.** Some questionnaire statistics

| | |
|---|---|
| **What do you think of using a Chinese Calligraphy brush as a writing and navigational tool?** | |
| Quite innovative | 79.2% (19) |
| Not a good idea | 16.7% (4) |
| **Was it easier to navigate with the 3D spacemouse or with the Chinese Calligraphy brush?** | |
| 3D spacemouse | 25.0% (6) |
| Chinese Calligraphy Brush | 75.0% (18) |
| **Do you think the Chinese Calligraphy brush enhances the Virtual Heritage experience compared to a conventional spacemouse?** | |
| Yes | 50.0% (12) |
| No | 41.7% (10) |
| **How long did it take you to get familiar to using the Chinese Calligraphy Brush?** | |
| Less than 3 minutes | 79.2% (19) |
| Less than 5 minutes | 16.7% (4) |
| More than 5 minutes | 4.2% (1) |
| **Do you think props such as flashlights or Chinese Calligraphy Brush should be used according to the specific Virtual Environment?** | |
| Yes, props should be used | 75.0% (18) |
| No, conventional mouse is OK | 20.8% (5) |

## 6 Conclusions and Future Work

We are confident that our idea of educating persons about an unique Singaporean cultural heritage using VR technology with the Virtual Tour Guide and the Chinese calligraphy brush are definitely innovative user interfaces. The usability test indicates that users are generally interested in experiencing traditional cultural contents in a high-tech environment. Innovative interactivity is the key.

To improve the interactivity of our user interface, further work needs to be carried out. More usability tests will be set up to statistically analyze the difficulties of the writing function of the brush interface. We will also work on the Virtual Tour Guide's modeling and animation so that it becomes even more life-like. Adding Artificial Intelligence (AI) or other game elements can also make the interface more user-friendly and entertaining.

## References

1. Lutz, B., Weintke, M.: Virtual Dunhuang Art Cave: A Cave within a CAVE. In: Proceedings of Eurographics, Milan, 1999 (1999)
2. Conti, G., Piffer, S., Girardi, G., Amicis, D.R., Ucelli, G.: Dentrotrento: a Virtual Walk across History, In: Proceeding of the working conference on advanced visual interfaces, Venezia, Italy, 2006, pp. 318–321 (2006)
3. The Peranakan Association in Singapore, http://www.peranakan.org.sg
4. Addison, C.A.: Emerging Trends in Virtual Heritage. IEEE multimedia 7(2), 22–25 (2000)
5. OpenSG system, http://opensg.vrsource.org/trac
6. Autodesk Maya software, http://www.autodesk.com/maya
7. Song, M.: Master Thesis, School of Computer Engineering, Nanyang Technological University, Singapore, Virtual Reality for Cultural Heritage Applications (2006)

# Learning Cooperation in a Tangible Moyangsung

Kyoung Shin Park[1], Hyun-Sang Cho[2], Jaewon Lim[3], Yongjoo Cho[3], Seungmook Kang[4], and Soyon Park[4]

[1] Multimedia Engineering, Dankook University, San 29 Anseo-dong, Cheonan-si, Chungnam, 330-714, Korea
kpark2@hanmail.net
[2] Digital Media Laboratory, Information and Communications University, 517-10 Dogok-dong, Gangnam-gu, Seoul 135-854, Korea
[3] Division of Media Technology, Sangmyung University, 7 Hongji-dong, Jongno-gu, Seoul, 110-743, Korea
[4] Department of Media Art, Jeonju University, 1200 Hyoja-dong, Wansan-gu, Jeonju, 560-759, Korea

**Abstract.** Tangible Moyangsung is a collaborative virtual heritage environment that employs tangible interfaces to encourage group social interaction and cooperation. It is designed for a group of users to play fortification games for reconstructing a Korean war-defensive castle in virtual reality. This paper describes a historical background and cultural meanings of Moyangsung, and details in design, implementation and a user study of the Tangible Moyangsung system. The study results showed that collaborative work using tangible interfaces helped users to be more engaged in the task and learn cooperation to produce better performance.

**Keywords:** Virtual Heritage Environment, Tangible Interface, Collaborative Playing, Game.

## 1 Introduction

Virtual heritage environment is the recreation of cultural heritage using virtual reality technology which allows visitors to experience reconstructing a historical site that no longer exist or travel back in time to experience historical events [1]. In the past, however, most virtual heritage environments are designed for digital preservation focusing on the accurate restoring it to original appearance [2]. Hence, user interactions are typically navigation and passive observation of events in the virtual environment. Recently, interactivity has come into attention in the design of virtual heritage applications. For example, the intelligent tour guide agents, game design approach, and multimodal user interfaces were used to increase a user's cultural learning experience and give innovative ways of storytelling behind the scene [4, 5, 6, 7, 10]. Also, tangible user interfaces are used in the educational applications to strengthen the engagement of children in learning activities [9].

In this paper, we present the Tangible Moyangsung system, a virtual heritage environment designed for a group of users to collaboratively play games using

R. Shumaker (Ed.): Virtual Reality, HCII 2007, LNCS 4563, pp. 689–698, 2007.

tangible interfaces to learn cultural background story of a Korean war-defensive castle, Moyangsung. According to local folklore, this castle was constructed by women. There is a traditional festival held annually on September 9th of the lunar calendar which has been in place for many generations. In this festival, the Dapsungnori ceremony is a highlight event. The ceremony entails women to put stones on top of their heads and parade around the Moyangsung castle where they would leave the stones inside of the castle after the parade. Folklore says anyone who goes around the castle three times can go to the heaven.

The Tangible Moyangsung system consists of three main subsystems: the context server, the virtual environment, and the tangible interfaces. In this system, the tangible interfaces are provided to give a transparency of user interaction with the virtual environment [3]. The tangible interfaces include the Matdol interface (inspired by a Korean traditional stone-made hand mill), the touch-screen interactive map, and the 100-cell based LED board interface for user navigation and interaction with the virtual environment. The board interface allows multiple users to layer bricks by placing tangible transparent acrylic blocks. It is designed to help users engage in the activity which would increase group social interaction and the overall collaborative learning experience.

This paper describes an overview of design and implementation of the Tangible Moyangsung system. It will then discuss the results of a study conducted on six different groups to evaluate whether the Tangible Moyangsung system would bring a group of participants together to complete a given task more efficiently. The comparative study results between collaborative conditions versus individual condition showed that the participants put a lot more effort into collaborative work setting using tangible interfaces. It helped the participants to work cooperatively to enhance group performance. This paper will conclude with a look into the possible direction for future research.

## 2 Tangible Moyangsung

Moyangsung is located in Gochang-gun, Jeollabok-do, South Korea. It is also known as Gochang-Eupsung. The name ‘Moyang’ originates from the ancient geographical name of Gochang in Baekje, one of the three Kingdoms in ancient Korea. Unlike other castles in the same era which were constructed on plain fields as homes for people, Moyangsung was constructed on a hill as a fortress. It also consists of many ‘Ongsung’, a small castle built outside of the main gate to protect against possible enemy attack.

Fig. 1 shows the photograph of Tangible Moyangsung demonstrated at the X-edu studio at Jeonju University, S. Korea. In Tangible Moyangsung, players are first introduced to the historical background of Moyangsung and are given a mission. The mission of the game is to find and repair the damaged walls completely within ten-minute period. The task involves the players to walk around the castle and search for the destroyed parts of the wall. Once they find the damages, they can repair the wall by putting the tangible blocks (i.e., Tetris-pattern blocks made of transparent acrylic plastic) on the pattern appeared on the board interface. As a reward for successfully completing the mission, the players receive an opportunity to experience

**Fig. 1.** The snapshot of users playing an easy (colored-pattern) puzzle on Tangible Moyangsung, installed at the X-edu studio, at Jeonju University, Korea

Dapsungnori. When the players fail the mission, the castle will be destroyed completely.

In Tangible Moyangsung, the game starts with the introduction animation, and then the state is changed to the navigation mode. In the navigation mode, the players walk through the virtual environment using the Matdol interface or the touch-screen interactive map. When the players are close to the collapsed part of castle wall, the state is changed to the repair mode. Then, the same damaged pattern shown in the virtual environment is also displayed on the board interface in color lights. In the repair mode, the players place various shaped blocks on the puzzle pattern shown on the board interface. The state of user interaction with the board interface is periodically checked, and transparently updated in the virtual environment to display bricks filled the broken walls through message passing by the context server. The repair mode ends when the players complete the block placement correctly matched with the pattern, and the state is returned to the navigation mode. Finally, the game ends with the success when the players complete repairing destroyed walls in four different regions in the virtual environment within 10-minutes period. Otherwise, the game will be timed out – i.e., the game is over with the failure.

## 3 System Design

Fig. 2 shows the overall architecture of the Tangible Moyangsung system that displays the event and messages flows among the sub-components of the system. It consists of the context server for managing the main game logic, the virtual environment, and the tangible interfaces for user navigation and interaction. The context server includes the communication manager for the event and message handling among the sub-systems. The virtual environment shows the reconstructed Moyangsung (such as a castle, hills, trees, and buildings) with vivid sounds. It also contains user interaction and event processing modules for state update by the context server and the tangible interfaces.

The tangible interfaces include the Matdol interface and the interactive map for navigation and the board interface for user interaction in the virtual environment. The Matdol interface allows users to rotate its handle to walk through the pre-defined path along with the perimeter of the virtual Moyangsung. The touch-screen interactive map shows the top-down view of the castle and the user's current location in the virtual

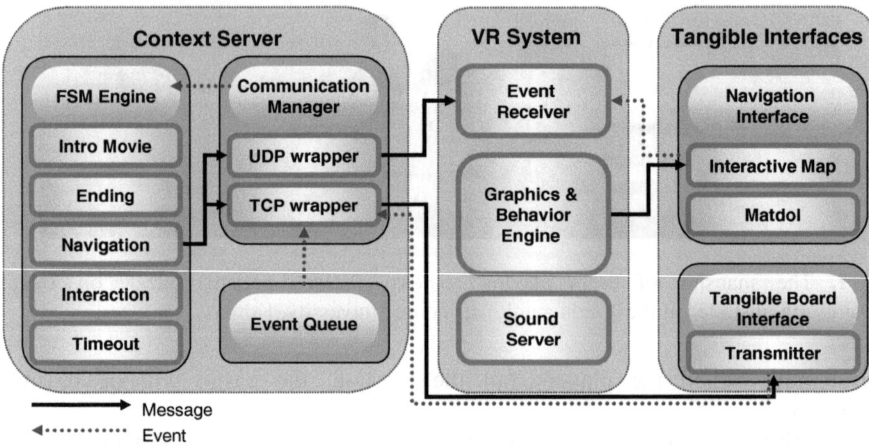


**Fig. 2.** The overall system architecture showing event and message flows among the context server, the virtual environment, and the tangible interfaces

environment. It allows a user to draw a path on the map with his/her finger to navigate in VR. The board interface adopts the Tetris puzzle game metaphor. It allows users to fortify the castle using various tangible blocks. Each block position is detected by 10x10 PIC micro-controller driven switch unit. Each micro-controller cell unit controls LEDs and switches. The board interface is connected to the communication manager by TCP.

### 3.1 Context Server

The context server maintains the game state from the beginning to the end as the players interact with the tangible interfaces in the virtual environment. As shown in Fig. 2, the context server consists of a finite state machine (FSM) controlling the various stages of the game logic and a communication manager employing an event-driven message passing mechanism. The main game logic states are timer, game introduction and ending mode, user navigation mode, and user repairing mode. Events are generated from various sub-components; for example, the virtual environment sends the player's current position events to the context server for checking whether the players are close to the damaged castle region. In addition, when the players put the tangible blocks on the board interface during the repair mode; the board sends the events to the context server that are passed to the virtual environment to display the repairing progress.

In the context server, each module is implemented as an independent thread. The threaded event queue stores the events received from the sub-components through the communication interface. The communication manager has UDP and TCP module for processing the messages and the events. The communication with the board interface is mediated by the transmitter program, sending the messages through the RS485-RS232 converter. The transmitter program also monitors all the cells on the board interface and sends the cell state report messages to the context server.

**Fig. 3.** On the left shows user repairing the damaged wall of the Moyangsung castle in the virtual environment; on the middle shows a pair solving a difficult puzzle (blue color) using tangible blocks; on the right shows a user navigating the virtual environment using the Matdol interface

### 3.2 Virtual Environment

In Fig. 3, the picture on far left shows the progress of user's repairing the Moyangsung damages in the virtual environment. The middle picture shows two users repairing the damaged wall (shown as the difficult puzzle pattern appeared on the board interface) using tangible blocks. The picture on far right shows a user navigating the virtual environment using the Matdol interface. As a new block is placed or removed from the board, a virtual stone is added or removed from the corresponding position of the destroyed wall in the virtual environment. This repair mode ends when the user finishes putting all the blocks in the right places on the board.

The environment is designed for users to participate in the tangible virtual reality experience. It contains the graphics modules (such as model loaders, animation, and navigation and manipulation interaction), the sound modules, and the event receiver module. It is written using the Ygdrasil, a high-level virtual reality authoring toolkit [5]. The current implementation of virtual Moyangsung installed at Jeonju University runs on a large-screen passive stereoscopic virtual reality system, built using the two low-cost DLP projectors, polarization filters and screen, and a Linux PC.

### 3.3 Tangible Interfaces

The tangible interfaces are the Matdol interface and the interactive map for user navigation and the tangible board interface for users when building bricks in the virtual environment. Matdol is a Korean traditional stone hand-mill. Matdol consists of two cylinder-shaped stones overlapped one on top of another, and there is a handle on the side of the upper stone which one can grind the grain using a Matdol by rounding its handle. In Tangible Moyangsung, users can move in the left or right direction along with the pre-defined path facing the exterior of the virtual Moyangsung by moving the Matdol interface as shown in Fig. 3 (on the right). The touch-screen interactive map displays the top-down view of Moyangsung and the user's current location in the virtual environment. Using the interactive map, a user can walk around the virtual environment by drawing a path on the map with their bare finger.

The tangible board interface is designed to ease the virtual Moyangsung repairing. The board consists of 10x10 cells that have uniform squares (40x40 $mm^2$ for each cell). Users can play the puzzle with five different shapes of blocks (i.e., I, L, T, cross, and square shape). As shown in Fig. 3, the damage pattern is displayed on the board during the repair mode. Users' placement or removal of blocks on this board is reflected into the virtual wall. Tangible block turns on the switch embedded on each cell of the board. The LED lights on each cell present the multi-colored pattern to indicate the destroyed pattern. In addition, red, white, and black LED color is used to indicate the state whether the block placement is wrong, correct, or invalid. This tangible board interface is particularly designed for multiple users' simultaneous interaction with the virtual environment to encourage user engagement.

Each cell has its own PIC micro-controller; the controller drives the multi-colored LED lights and the switch turned by a block. Each cell controller has RS485 communication driver which is connected with a single RS485 bus. For each cell, a command can be sent to the controller to illuminate the appropriate LED color. If the board interface status is changed, the cell controller reports the changes to the context server, which then sends a message to change the light color or cell state on the board. As the game progresses, the board interface receives the cell check request message from the transmitter.

## 4 A Case Study

We conducted a case study of twelve persons divided into pairs using the Tangible Moyangsung system to evaluate how the system helped with group collaboration while playing the fortification game. Ten male and two female undergraduate students from Jeonju University volunteered as participants in this study. The range of the participants' age was 22 to 27 years old. They had moderate level computer experience, but most of them had no previous experience with the Tangible Moyangsung system. The game-play was a group to navigate the virtual environment and repair four destroyed areas of the castle. Repairing is done with the placement of all tangible blocks in the right places on the board.

### 4.1 Method

The experiment consisted of three playing conditions: (1) individual, (2) group-together, (3) group with role-division. In the individual condition, each group member worked alone, whereas the group performed the task together in the group-together condition. In the group with role-division condition, one member manipulated I- and cross-shaped blocks while the other manipulated L- and T-shaped blocks and then they shared square-shaped blocks. The participants were given two different levels of task difficulty: easy and hard. In the easy task, the block placement locations are indicated by five different colors (shown in Fig. 1), and the pattern is given by blue color only in the hard task (shown in Fig. 3).

The participants were first given an introduction of the system and the study overview. They were then asked to perform the task (both easy and hard task) under three playing conditions: individual, group-together, or group with role-division.

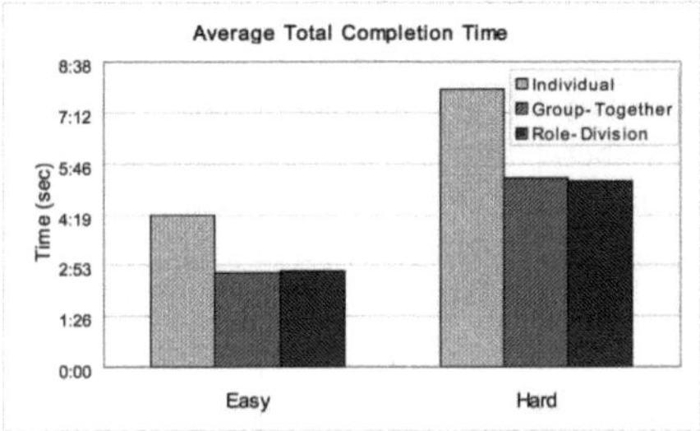


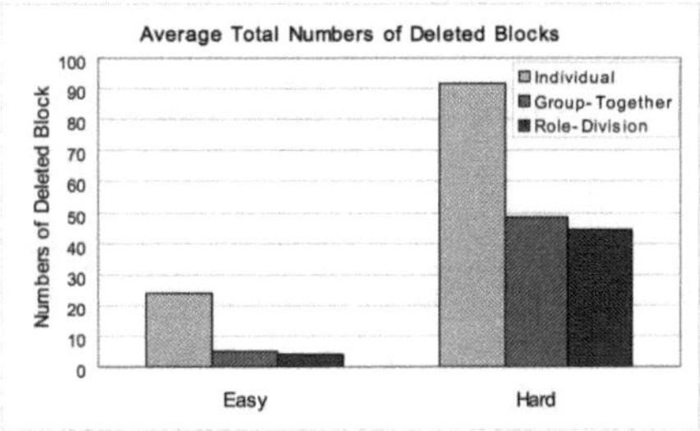


**Fig. 4.** The average total completion time (including navigation) and the average total number of delete blocks (indicating the extra number of trials)

Since the experiment was designed for a within-subject study, the order of condition was randomly given to minimize the participants' learning effect from previous experience with other conditions. Two groups performed the hard and easy task under the group-together condition, followed the role-division condition, and then the individual condition. The next two groups performed the easy and hard task under the individual condition, followed by the group-together condition, and then the role-division condition. The reset of the groups performed the easy and hard task under the role-division condition, followed by the group-together condition, and then the individual condition. A post-test survey was followed at the end of the tasks. The surveys were intended to obtain user feedback regarding the overall system usability and the subjective evaluation on group collaboration and performance efficiency.

All groups in the various test conditions were recorded using a video camera. Their activities were also collected into log data files. These included the total completion time (from the game start to mission completion, including the navigation time), the block completion time for each damage repairing (from the block pattern emergence to the pattern completion), and the number of added or deleted blocks during the repairing mode.

### 4.2 Results

Fig. 4 shows the average total completion time (in minutes and seconds) and the average total number of deleted blocks for easy and hard task on three test conditions. The figure on the right (i.e., the averaged total number of deleted blocks) indicates the number of extra trials than the actual number of block appeared on the pattern. The pattern was easily distinguished by the five distinct LED color lights on the easy task while it was displayed by blue LED light on the hard task. As shown in Fig. 4, users performed significantly better under group-together or role-division than the individual play in both easy and hard task. However, there was no significant overall difference between the group-together and role-division condition although the number of deleted blocks was slightly reduced in the role-division condition.

Table 1 shows the average total completion time and the average total number of deleted blocks (as shown in Fig. 4). It also shows the average block completion time (in minute and seconds) and the average navigation time (in minute and seconds) for each condition. The navigation time was calculated by the difference from the average

**Table 1.** Performance on individual play, group-together, and role-division condition

| Tasks | Conditions | The average total completion time | The average total number of deleted blocks | The average block completion time | The average navigation time |
|---|---|---|---|---|---|
| Easy task | Individual | 4min 17sec | 24 | 48sec | 1min 6sec |
| | Group-together | 2min 41sec | 5 | 25sec | 1min 2sec |
| | Role-division | 2min 44sec | 4 | 28sec | 51sec |
| Hard task | Individual | 7min 52sec | 91.5 | 1min 34sec | 1min 36sec |
| | Group-together | 5min 20sec | 48.3 | 1min 7sec | 54sec |
| | Role-division | 5min 16sec | 44.4 | 1min | 1min 15sec |

total completion time to the average block completion time multiplying by four (blocks). The result shows that the navigation time was also slightly faster in the group-together or role-division condition than the individual condition.

We expected that performance on the easy task was not significantly different among three test conditions because we believed that the only hard task should require help from the other group partner. However, some participants had a hard time finishing the easy task during the individual condition. All group showed that the total completion time was faster when they worked collaboratively (either group-together or role-division) than individually, especially for the hard task.

We also expected that overall performance would be better on the role-division than the group-together condition since the role-division condition forced them to be more cooperative. In our previous experience with group work using Tangible Moyangsung, we found that typically only one group member put blocks while the other members just watched the progress. Sometimes the group members collided putting trying to put the same blocks on the same position on the board. However, unexpectedly in the current study, all group members eagerly collaborated to complete the task as fast as possible regardless of the group-together or role-division condition.

In the pos-test survey, most participants believed that collaborative work helped improve performance by sharing insights between group members. They said that task performance was the most inefficient on the hard task under the individual condition. However, interestingly enough, they insisted that they could concentrate on the task more easily during the individual condition. According to the post-test results, the participants said that they collided with other members the most often on the hard task under the group-together condition and the least often on the easy task under the role-division condition. Interestingly, most participants strongly believed that the role-division condition was better for group cooperation because it helped them increase discourses to complete the task. On the other hand, the participants could still work independently without a conversation since the group-together condition allowed anyone to put any blocks on the board.

The video analysis showed the same result by the post-test survey. We found that the role-division condition (where one member allowed using I- and cross-shaped blocks while the other member allowed using L- and T-shaped blocks only) made the group members to discuss more often. In general they talked to his/her partner a lot to ask for putting the partner's blocks on the board. However, the users seemed to be hindered by this abrupt interrupt as well. Another interesting pattern we observed was that some participants (and groups) heavily utilized the I-shaped blocks to solve the puzzles instead of using other kinds of blocks, especially on the hard task.

## 5 Discussions and Conclusions

This paper presented a collaborative virtual heritage environment designed for a group to play games collaboratively using the tangible interfaces to share cultural experience. While most of virtual heritage applications focus on the reconstruction of cultural objects or places, this system is designed to encourage social interaction among group members which helps them to be more engaged in the cooperative activities.

The user study results showed that all groups performed significantly better during the collaborative condition (either the group-together condition or the role-division condition) since cooperation helped them see the same problem in various perspectives. In addition, when the users played individually, they seemed to be exhausted if the duration time got longer by solving the difficult puzzles. On contrast, the users did not show boredom or fatigue while they played collaboratively. Hence, even though the participants thought that the individual condition was better for concentrating on the task, the result revealed that one's power of concentration was indeed better during the collaborative condition than the individual condition.

In the future, we will also add an intelligent agent to guide users and modify the game story to add more interactive narratives [8]. For example, the tangible board pattern can be adaptively changed according to users' levels, and the scenario or educational contents can be rearranged by user's interests.

## References


1. Gaitatzes, A., Christopoulos, D., Voulgari, A., Roussou, M.: Hellenic Cultural Heritage through Immersive Virtual Archaeology. In: Proc. 6th International Conference on Virtual Systems and Multimedia, Ogaki, Japan, October 3-6, 2000, pp.57–64 (2000)
2. Ikeuchi, K., Nakazawa, A., Hasegawa, K., Ohisi, T.: The Great Buddha Project: Modeling Cultural Heritage for VR Systems through Observation, In: Proc. of IEEE and ACM International Symposium on Mixed Reality and Augmented Reality (ISMAR'03)
3. McNerney, T.: Tangible programming bricks: An approach to making programming accessible to everyone. Masters Thesis, Media Lab, Massachusetts Institute of Technology, Cambridge, MA (1999)
4. Lee, Y., Oh, S., Woo, W.: A Context-Based Storytelling with a Responsive Multimedia System, In: Proc. of Virtual Storytelling 2005, pp.12–21 (2005)
5. Park, K., Leigh, J., Johnson, A.: How Humanities Students Cope with the Technologies of Virtual Harlem, Works and Days 37/38, 19 (1&2), 79–97 (2001)

6. Pape, D., Anstey, J., Carter, B., Leigh, J., Roussou, M., Portlock, T.: Virtual Heritage at iGrid 2000, In: Proc. of INET 2001, Stockholm, Sweden, 5-8 June 2001 (2001)
7. Song, M., Elias, T., Martinovic, I., Mueller-Wittig, W., Chan, T.: 3-2 VRC in edutainment: Digital heritage application as an edutainment tool. In: Procs of the 2004 ACM SIGGRAPH international conference on Virtual Reality continuum and its applications in industry
8. Steiner, K. E., Tomkins, J.: Virtual environments & stories: Narrative event adaptation in virtual environments. In: Proceedings of the 9th international conference on intelligent user interface (2004)
9. Terrenghi, L., Kranz, M., Holleis, P., Schmidt, A.: A cube to learn: a tangible user interface for the design of a learning appliance. Personal and Ubiquitous Computing 10(2) (2006)
10. Watkins, J., Russo, A.: Digital Cultural Communication: Designing Co-Creative New Media Environments. In: Proc. of the 5th conference on Creativity & cognition C&C '05 (2005)

# An Open-Source Virtual Reality Platform for Clinical and Research Applications

Giuseppe Riva[1,2], Andrea Gaggioli[1,2], Daniela Villani[1], Alessandra Preziosa[1], Francesca Morganti[1], Lorenzo Strambi[1], Riccardo Corsi[3], Gianluca Faletti[3], and Luca Vezzadini[3]

[1] Applied Technology for Neuro-Psychology Lab, Istituto Auxologico Italiano, Milan, Italy
[2] Dipartimento di Psicologia, Università Cattolica del Sacro Cuore, Milan, Italy
[3] Virtual Reality & Multi-Media Park, Turin, Italy
giuseppe.riva@unicatt.it

**Abstract.** In recent years, there has been an increasing interest in clinical and research applications of virtual reality (VR). However, the adoption of this approach is still limited by the high costs of software development, lack of technical expertise among end-users, and the difficulty of adapting the contents of the virtual environments (VEs). To address these needs, we have designed and developed NeuroVR, (http://www.neurovr.org), a cost-free virtual reality platform based on open-source software components. NeuroVR allows non-expert users to easily customize a VE by using a set of pre-designed virtual scenes, and to run them in an immersive or non-immersive modality. In this paper, we provide a description of the key functional features of the platform.

**Keywords:** virtual reality, 3D modeling, psychotherapy, neuroscience, open-source software.

## 1 Introduction

Virtual reality is a technology that allows a user to interact in real-time with a simulated three-dimensional space, the virtual environment (VE). A typical VR system consists of a relatively powerful PC for processing data, a fast 3D accelerator graphic card, a set of input devices to allow control of the viewpoint and objects, and a viewing device. VR systems generally fall into two main categories, depending on the technology components that they use. In non-immersive systems, the VE is usually viewed through a standard monitor, and interaction occurs by conventional means such as keyboards and mice. In immersive systems, on the other hand, the user wears an head-mounted display and is provided with tracking systems that allows the views to be changed dynamically according to the movements he makes. The interaction with the virtual scene occurs via a joystick or a glove, and the configuration can include haptic devices that provide the user with force-feedback and can be used to convey a sense of touch, weight, or resistance.

Despite the initial promises, VR has remained for several years an expensive niche application used only in high-end fields such as military, automotive industry,

R. Shumaker (Ed.): Virtual Reality, HCII 2007, LNCS 4563, pp. 699–707, 2007.

medicine and academic research projects. In the last few years, reduction of computer and storage costs has made VR more affordable. However, the wide adoption of this technology requires not only a further fall in the prices of hardware components, but also that software development tools become less expensive and easier to use.

To address this problem, researchers at several universities are developing open-source and low-cost VR platforms for various applications of this technology. Here, we describe of the NeuroVR project, a cost-free software platform based on open-source elements that has been designed to customize and run virtual environments for clinic and research applications.

## 2 VR in Therapy, Research and Education

In recent years, a number of studies have suggested the efficacy of VR in the diagnosis and treatment of various psychological and neurological disorders.

In the field of psychotherapy, most studies have addressed specific phobias, in particular fear of flying, acrophobia, fear of driving, claustrophobia and fear of spiders. In addition, several studies have been published on the use of this approach in eating disorders, social anxiety disorders, sexual disorders, post-traumatic stress disorder and panic disorder with or without agoraphobia [1-4].

Traditional cognitive-behavioral approaches to exposure therapy include *in vivo* exposure and *imaginal* exposure. In the first procedure, patients approach a feared situation step-by-step, supported by therapist's encouragement and skilled advice.

Imaginal exposure consists in having the patient relax, then imagine the stimulus, gradually progressing from the least fearful to the most fearful.

In VR exposure, the patient is immersed in a VE containing the feared stimulus. This procedure has been showed to be at least as effective as these traditional techniques in reducing phobic symptoms [1]. The added-value of this approach consists in the practical advantages offered by the use of VR technology. As stimuli are generated by the computer, the therapist has full control over their intensity and the risk of unpredictable effects is significantly lower than in *in vivo* exposure.

Further, virtual exposure allows to present the patient with realistic three-dimensional visualization of the feared situation. This feature can be very useful when the patient is unable to recreate the scenarios because of pathological avoidance of problematic memories, as it is often the case in post-traumatic stress disorder [3].

Another field where VR has been successfully integrated is physical and neurological rehabilitation [5-9]. The main aim of rehabilitation is to help the disabled person to acquire knowledge and skills in order to gain autonomy, self-reliance, self-worth, and integrate into the community. This process can be broken down in three key areas: a) approaches that decrease disability; b) approaches designed to maximise activity through the acquisition of novel skills and strategies; and c) approaches designed to modify the psycho-social environment, in order to reduce the disadaptive consequences of a specific disability. Research so far conducted suggests that VR-based interventions can improve all these areas. In particular, most clinical rehabilitation studies have addressed the potential role of this technology in improving functional recovery in post-stroke patients [8-9]. In a typical approach, a patient is presented with a virtual task that he/she has to complete by using the dysfunctional arm or leg. The virtual exercise can be performed with the help of a glove that detects finger, wrist and arm motions to manipulate on-screen images, and in some systems haptic/tactile feedback cues are provided. As motor performance improves, the level of difficulty of the exercise can be increased by changing the parameters of the virtual task, and this loop can have beneficial effects on patient's motivation and compliance. In addition, this approach provides the opportunity for ecological validity (as the virtual task can be designed for reproducing real-life situations, i.e. grasping an object), independent practice, and stimulus and response modifications that are contingent on a user's physical abilities.

Another area in which VR has been fruitfully integrated is neuropsychological assessment. Here, the advantage of VR on traditional pen-paper approaches is provided by three key features of this technology: the capacity to deliver interactive 3D stimuli within an immersive environment in a variety of forms and sensory modalities; the possibility of designing of safe testing and training environments, and the provision of "cueing" stimuli or visualization strategies designed to help guide successful performance to support an error-free learning approach [5-7].

VR is being used to similar advantage in many domains outside the clinical field, as in research and education. In particular, this technology has revealed to be a useful tool for cognitive neuroscience [10]. In experimental neuroscience, researchers are faced with the problem of carrying out experiments in an ecologically valid situation, to ensure that results can be generalized. On the other hand, they need to maintain control over all potential intervening variables, and this can be a difficult if not even impossible task when the experiment is carried out outside a scientific laboratory.

Using VR, researchers can model realistic environments in which the subject can interact as in real settings. By using this technology, the experimenter is allowed to measure and monitor a wide variety of responses made by the subject. Further, VR can provide new opportunities and challenges for collaboration and sharing of information, to build increasingly comprehensive models of the brain. Computational neuroscientists need to visualize complex set of data originating from their research.

Using VEs, multimodal data can be simultaneously displayed, enabling different types of data to be merged in a single model. For example, the dynamic processes observed by the electrophysiologist can be combined with the receptor binding studies and histological information obtained by other researchers. This capability provides an opportunity for both enhancing scientific discovery (i.e. detecting new patterns and relationships between data) as well as reducing misinterpretation (observing patterns which are artifacts of the techniques employed).

As concerns learning and training applications, the advantages provided by the use of VR are quite obvious. First of all, there is universal agreement among educators of the value of experiential learning – as Bruner put out, "knowledge begins with enaction" - and VR is the experiential medium *par excellence*. Further, in VR learning environments students can interact with complex information sets in an intuitive, non-symbolic way. For example, the VE MaxwellWorld has been designed to enable the examination of the nature of electrostatic forces and fields, to aid students in understanding the concept of electric flux, and to help them empirically discover Gauss's Law.

Another key feature of VR for learning is involvement and motivation of the student. Research conducted to assess the psychological effects of VR suggests that users can be highly engaged and involved in VEs, at the point that they can perceive that they are acting in a space that is different from that they are physically located – a feeling that has been labeled "sense of presence" [11]. Finally, VR systems can provide safe and controlled training environments, that can be used in those applications in which the practice of technical skills can be dangerous or harmful.

For this reason, VR simulations are becoming the training method of choice in medical schools. For example, within a virtual operating room the trained student is allowed to practice both the surgical procedures and the anatomic-physiological background of operations and diseases [12].

In sum, technical progresses in VR have opened up several new applications in clinic, research and education. Most researchers in these fields agree that VR can help to improve significantly the quality of their work and their productivity, however this approach is still not widespread, and the majority of VR applications are still in the laboratory or investigation stage. If, as we have seen, technology costs are no longer a burden, what are the factors that limit the diffusion of this approach?

## 3 The Need for Easy-to-Use and Open-Source VR Software

Across the last five years, we have conducted an in-depth analysis for understanding the factors that influence the acceptation and adoption of VR technology in both clinic and rehabilitation domains. Results of this investigation allowed us to identify two main factors that limit a wider diffusion of this approach.

A first problem is related to the lack of technical skills among end users. For example, many psychotherapists and rehabilitation professionals are interested in VR, but only a small percentage of them is familiar with the use of computer systems.

Thus, a first challenge that must be faced is to develop VR interfaces that are easily understandable and learnable also for users without technical background.

Strictly connected with this problem is the issue of customization of the content.

The majority of VEs that are available for clinic and research applications are closed-source and cannot be changed, and this prevents the user from the possibility of tailoring the content of the virtual scene according to his needs. This is a significant issue, as often users need to adapt the stimuli to a specific clinical problem. For example, a VE designed treating spider phobia cannot be used for other types of phobia. The same problem applies to research applications. In this case, the need for customization is even more significant, as the stimuli presented to the subject and the experimental parameters that must be controlled can vary notably in accordance to the hypothesis to be tested. In these cases, the researcher is faced with two possibilities.

The first is to create his own virtual application from scratch, asking a software developer company to do the work.

However, this solution can be very expensive. Actually, it has been estimated that the cost of designing and testing a clinical VR application is comprised between 25.000 US$ and 200,000 US$ [13]. The final cost is dependent on many factors, i.e. the need of photorealistic content, the number of virtual scenes, the amount of objects included in the VE, and the complexity of the interaction. Further, optimizing a VE demands significant effort in testing its usability and efficacy, especially if it is designed for clinical applications. Since the option of creating a VE is generally not feasible, the alternative solution available for professionals and researchers who do not have access to large research fundings is to look for commercial computer-gaming platforms. Some of these software applications allow to adapt existing content or create some new games, which can be customized according to the specific needs of the user. A shortcoming of this approach is intellectual property. Because of copyright restrictions, the VEs created by the user cannot be easily distributed or published. As a consequence, the impact of results on the research community is reduced. Further, most of the editors included in gaming platforms are not easily understandable by non-technical users, and require a minimum amount of coding to create a new gaming environment.

The open-source approach holds great promise for achieving enhanced accessibility and fostering the adoption of the VR approach in the clinic and research community. As widely known, the aim of this approach is to make software resources available to the general public without intellectual property restrictions (or with relaxed ones). In recent years, more and more academic and non-academic groups interested in VR are looking towards implementing open-source resources to improve access to this technology, and stimulate a collaborative environment for creating new applications. At present, most application-oriented open-source projects in VR are concentrated in the domains of scientific visualization, architectural design and medical education, while little work has been done so far in the field of therapy and rehabilitation.

Starting from this need, we have designed and developed NeuroVR, a software platform based on open-source components that provides the users with a cost-free VE editor, which allows non-expert users to easily modify a virtual world, to best suit the needs of the clinical or research setting.

## 4 The NeuroVR Project

### 4.1 General Characteristics

NeuroVR is a cost-free virtual reality platform that has been designed to allow non-expert users to easily modify a virtual environment and to run it using an immersive or non-immersive system.

The NeuroVR platform is implemented using open-source components that provide advanced features, including an interactive rendering system based on OpenGL which allows for high quality images. The NeuroVR Editor is created by customizing the User Interface of Blender, an integrated suite of 3D creation tools available on major operating systems, under the GNU General Public License; this implies that the program can be distributed even with the complete source code.

Thanks to these features, clinicians and researchers have the freedom to run, copy, distribute, study, change and improve the NeuroVR Editor software, so that the whole VR community benefits.

### 4.2 The NeuroVR Editor

The majority of existing VEs for psychotherapy are proprietary and have closed source, meaning they cannot be tailored from the ground up to fit specific needs of different clinical applications [11]. NeuroVR addresses these issues by providing the clinical professional with a cost-free VE editor, which allows non-expert users to easily modify a virtual scene, to best suit the needs of the clinical setting.

Using the NeuroVR Editor (see Figure 1), the psychological stimuli/stressors appropriate for any given scenario can be chosen from a rich database of 2D and 3D objects, and easily placed into the pre-designed virtual scenario by using an icon-based interface (no programming skills are required). In addition to static objects, the NeuroVR Editor allows to overlay on the 3D scene video composited with a transparent alpha channel. The editing of the scene is performed in real time, and effects of changes can be checked from different views (frontal, lateral and top).

**Fig. 1.** Screenshot of NeuroVR Editor graphical user interface

The NeuroVR Editor is built using Python scripts that create a custom graphical user interface (GUI) for Blender. The Python-based GUI allows to hide all the richness and complexity of the Blender suite, so to expose only the controls needed to customize existing scenes and to create the proper files to be viewed in the player.

Currently, the NeuroVR library includes 12 different pre-designed virtual scenes, representing typical real-life situations, i.e., the supermarket, the apartment, the park.

These VEs have been designed, developed and assessed in the past ten years by a multidisciplinary research team in several clinical trials, which have involved over 400 patients. On the basis of this experience, only the most effective VEs have been selected for inclusion in the NeuroVR library.

An interesting feature of the NeuroVR Editor is the possibility to add new objects to the database. This feature allows the therapist to enhance the patient's feeling of familiarity and intimacy with the virtual scene, i.e., by using photos of objects/people that are part of the patient's daily life, thereby improving the efficacy of the exposure.

Future releases of the NeuroVR Editor software may also include interactive 3D animations controlled at runtime. A VRML/X3D exporter and a player for PocketPC PDAs are planned Blender features, too.

### 4.3 The NeuroVR Player

The second main component of NeuroVR is the Player, which allows to navigate and interact with the VEs created using the NeuroVR Editor.

NeuroVR Player leverages two major open-source projects in the VR field: Delta3D (http://www.delta3d.org) and OpenSceneGraph (http://www.openscenegraph.org). Both are building components that the NeuroVR player integrates with ad-hoc code to handle the simulations.

The whole player is developed in C++ language, targeted for the Microsoft Windows platform but fully portable to other systems if needed. When running simulation, the system offers a set of standard features that contribute to increase the realism of the simulated scene. These include collision detection to control movements in the environment, realistic walk-style motion, advanced lighting techniques for enhanced image quality, and streaming of video textures using alpha channel for transparency.

The player can be configured for two basic visualization modalities: immersive and non-immersive. The immersive modality allows the scene to be visualized using a head-mounted display, either in stereoscopic or in mono-mode; compatibility with head-tracking sensor is also provided. In the non-immersive modality, the virtual environment can be displayed using a desktop monitor or a wall projector. The user can interact with the virtual environment using either keyboard commands, a mouse or a joypad, depending on the hardware configuration chosen.

### 4.4 The NeuroVR Website

One of the main problems faced by clinicians and researchers who are interested in the use of VR is poor communication. Besides the possibility of disseminating their results on official publications in scientific journals or conferences, they do not have many options to collaborate. Further, most groups are disseminated in different countries and this poses further limitation to the integration of their efforts.

In an attempt to overcome this problem, we have created a website (http://www.neurovr.org) that allows VR researchers to share knowledge and tools generated by their research. The website is designed as a virtual laboratory, where clinical professionals and researchers can interact to foster progresses on their respective application fields. The website contents are in English and provide different types of information and resources. The main section is dedicated to the NeuroVR software. From this section, users can download the latest release of the application, the video tutorials, and the manuals of use. The dissemination section includes an introduction to VR and its various applications. Further, the portal include online usability questionnaires, which NeuroVR end users can fill out to evaluate the system. This feedback is then used by the NeuroVR developers to fix ergonomics problems and bugs. Finally, a scientific section provides users with the latest results and clinical protocols developed by the research community.

## 5 Conclusions

Although VR has finally come of age for clinical and research applications, the majority of them are still in the laboratory or investigation stage. Key limitations to the adoption of this approach include the lack of standardization in VR hardware and software, and the high costs that are required for building and testing a VE from scratch. Actually, the development of a VE requires special software and programming skills that are often unavailable for researchers and clinical professionals. Further, the majority of existing VEs are proprietary and have closed source, meaning that they cannot tailored to fit the needs of a specific clinical or experimental setting.

In this paper, we have described the main features of NeuroVR, a cost-free virtual reality platform used for therapeutic and research applications. NeuroVR allows non-expert users to easily customize a VE, by using a set of pre-designed virtual scenes, and to display them using either an immersive or non-immersive system. A future goal is to provide software compatibility with instruments that allow collection and analysis of behavioral data, such as eye-tracking devices and physiological sensors.

The NeuroVR software is available for download on the NeuroVR project website which has been created to provide researchers and clinical professionals interested with state-of-the art information on VR hardware and software as well as the latest clinical protocols published by the VR community.

**Acknowledgements.** The present work was supported by the Italian MIUR FIRB programme "Neurotiv - Managed care basata su telepresenza immersiva virtuale per l'assessment e riabilitazione in neuro-psicologia e psicologia clinica" - RBNE01W8WH - and Project "Realtà virtuale come strumento di valutazione e trattamento in psicologia clinica: aspetti tecnologici, ergonomici e clinici" - RBAU014JE5.

## References

1. Pull, C.B.: Current status of virtual reality exposure therapy in anxiety disorders: editorial review. Curr. Opin. Psychiatry 18(1), 7–14 (2005)
2. Riva, G., Bacchetta, M., Cesa, G., Conti, S., Molinari, E.: The use of VR in the treatment of eating disorders. Stud Health Technol Inform. 99, 121–163 (2004)
3. Rizzo, A., Pair, J., McNerney, P.J., Eastlund, E., Manson, B., Gratch, J., Hill, R., Swartout, B.: Development of a VR therapy application for Iraq war military personnel with PTSD. Stud Health Technol Inform. 111, 407–413 (2005)
4. Optale, G., Munari, A., Nasta, A., Pianon, C., Baldaro Verde, J., Viggiano, G.: Multimedia and virtual reality techniques in the treatment of male erectile disorders. Int J Impot Res. 9, 197–203 (1997)
5. Morganti, F.: Virtual interaction in cognitive neuropsychology. Stud Health Technol Inform. 99, 55–70 (2004)

6. Rizzo, A.A., Buckwalter, J.J.: Virtual reality and cognitive assessment and rehabilitation: the state of the art. Stud Health Technol Inform. 44, 123–145 (1997)
7. Schultheis, M.T., Himelstein, J., Rizzo, A.A.: Virtual reality and neuropsychology: upgrading the current tools. J Head Trauma Rehabil. 17, 378–394 (2002)
8. Lam, Y.S., Man, D.W., Tam, S.F., Weiss, P.L.: Virtual reality training for stroke rehabilitation. NeuroRehabilitation 21(3), 245–253 (2006)
9. Holden, M.K.: Virtual environments for motor rehabilitation: review. Cyberpsychol Behav. 8(3), 187–211 (2005)
10. Tarr, M.J., Warren, W.H.: Virtual reality in behavioral neuroscience and beyond. Nat. Neurosci 5, 1089–1092 (2002)
11. Mantovani, F., Castelnuovo, G.: The Sense of Presence in Virtual Training: Enhancing Skills Acquisition and Transfer of Knowledge through Learning Experience in Virtual Environments. In: Davide, F., Riva, G. (eds.) Being There: Concepts, Effects and Measurement of User Presence in Synthetic Environments, pp. 167–182. IOS Press, Amsterdam (2003)
12. Ganai, S., Donroe, J.A., St Louis, M.R., Lewis, G.M., Seymour, N.E.: Virtual-reality training improves angled telescope skills in novice laparoscopists. Am J Surg. 193(2), 260–265 (2007)
13. Riva, G.: Virtual reality in psychotherapy: review. Cyberpsychol Behav. 8, 220–230 (2005)

# Colour Correct Digital Museum on the Internet

Janos Schanda and Cecilia Sik Lanyi

University of Pannonia, Hungary
schanda@vision.vein.hu

**Abstract.** Showing pictures of famous artists to students is a fundamental task to teach fine art history. Images found on the Internet are a major resource of such pictures that can replace older albums of fine art collections. The colours reproduced in Internet images are, however, in many instances not correct. Images have been collected both from museums' publications and from the Internet, and some critical areas of the images have been colorimetrically evaluated. Investigations have shown that in some databases the colours of the images are highly distorted. Before using pictures from one or the other database, one should compare the reproductions downloadable from different sources, and select – according to the aesthetic feeling of the user – the artefact that one can assume to come nearest to the original. It is a great pity that the artefacts in the databases are not accompanied with the necessary background information (metadata) that would provide some information on the taking illumination, the spectral sensitivity and gamma of the taking apparatus, and of any transformations the provider has performed. Without this information that is quite common in other areas of image databases, the user is unable to set the reproduction parameters of his or her equipment to get to a reasonable reproduction.

## 1 Introduction

Teaching fine art history without showing the masterpieces of the past centuries is impossible. Unfortunately not every student has the opportunity to see the pictures in their original form. Sometimes the pictures are in a foreign country, in a distant place of the Globe. In the past the only way was to show these pictures by collecting printed copies or photographs, eventually slides. Recently more and more museums get their collections archived in the form of digital artefacts, and eventually provide access to their virtual museum via the Internet.

The pictures of the original images are taken by experts using sophisticated high-end camera systems and illumination equipment to provide artefacts, where the colours come near to the original ones [1]. Colour characterization of high-end digital cameras can yield digital images that hold most of the features of the original [2]. Digital restoration techniques can even help in rejuvenating faded paintings [3]. The recent technique of multi- (or hyper-) spectral image taking provides the possibility to consider the reflectance spectra of the pigments the

R. Shumaker (Ed.): Virtual Reality, HCII 2007, LNCS 4563, pp. 708–717, 2007.

artist used [4], this enables even transformations when looking the pictures under different illuminants.

Despite of all that hard work, the artefacts reproduced on the Internet often show remarkable differences if downloaded from different databases. Regarding these differences the scholar, who would like to display the images, cannot do much. The only way is to look for the picture in several databases and use the artefact based on the personal judgement of the teacher. In the present study our main endeavour was to show the size of the colour differences one has to count with in reality.

To take full advantage of present day colorimetric capabilities the providers of digital museum artefacts should supply more detailed metadata information, as otherwise any further work by the user is only guess-work.

## 2 Some Colorimetric Fundamentals Used in the Present Study

Pictures on the Internet are most often encoded using the IEC recommended sRGB encoding [5], for further details and other encodings see e.g. [6,7]. This encoding assumes standard RGB primaries (standardized RGB phosphors of CRT monitors) and a light intensity – digital value interrelationship, the so called gamma curve.

As every taking camera and every reproducing equipment (monitor, projector, printer) has different encodings, it is usual to transform from the native colour space into a device independent colour space, the CIE recommended *XYZ* or $L^*$, $a^*$, $b^*$ (or CIELAB) space [8,9]. The later one has the advantage that it provides reasonably uniform colour scales in lightness ($L^*$), chroma ($C_{ab}^*$) and gives more or less equidistant scaling along the hue circle ($h_{ab}^*$). Figure 1 shows the co-ordinates of the CIELAB colour space.

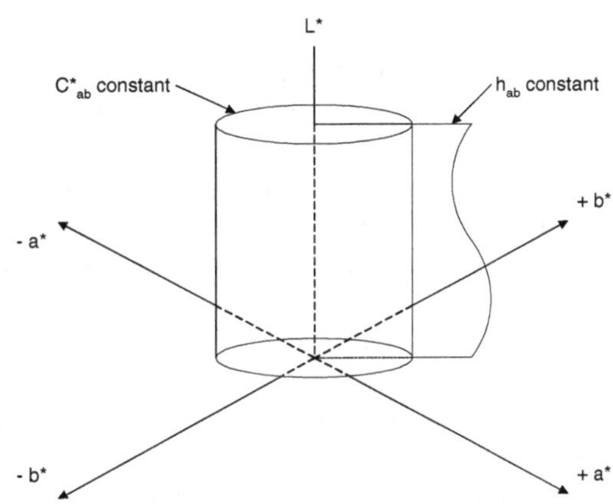


**Fig. 1.** Coordinates of the CIE $L^*$, $a^*$, $b^*$ colour system, called also CIELAB space

The $L^*$ coordinate goes from black ($L^* = 0$) to white ($L^* = 100$), the positive $a^*$ axis shows approximately into the red direction, the negative into the green direction, positive $b^*$ represents yellow, negative $b^*$ blue.

The $h_{ab}^*$ hue angle is constructed as the arcus tangens of $b^*/a^*$. Thus orange colours have arctg($b^*/a^*$) values between 0°and 90°. Colours ranging in hue between yellow and green have hue angles between 90°and 180°, those between green and blue range between 180°and 270°, while purple colours might have hue angles between 270°and 360°.

The $C_{ab}^*$ chroma describes how vivid the colour is, colours with small chroma values are pale, greyish hues; strong, vivid hues have high chroma values.

In the evaluation of the different artefacts we will provide always the $L^*$ lightness value, the $a^*$ and $b^*$ co-ordinates, and also the $h_{ab}^*$ hue-angle and the $C_{ab}^*$ chroma information.

## 3 Some Examples of Images Found in Multiple Databases

The following examples are certainly a non-exhaustive sample of a few pictures where we had access to the database of the museum that kept the original, in some cases to further databases containing an artefact of the picture, and one or even more picture albums of different age. Our intention was to show colour differences of artefacts as might get into the hands of the fine art professor, thus we definitely did not included fresh, un-faded posters recently bought in a museum shop. Further on we have to stress that this investigation was conducted only on digital and printed artefacts, and we had no access to the original paintings, thus we had no information on the colour difference of one or the other artefact compared with the original.

### 3.1 Four Paintings by Leonardo da Vinci

As well known Leonardo made at least two versions of the subject "Madonna/Virgin of the Rocks", the first one is a picture kept in the Louvre, Paris, and the later one in the National Gallery, London. As the subject of both paintings is very similar it seemed to be worth not only investigating how different the coloration of the reproductions of these paintings is as found in different databases (museum albums will from here on be included in the term "database"), but to check how large differences could be found of the same object in the two versions. This can give an insight into the colour constancy memory of the painter, give us some hint how important he thought the colour of a given object was. This can be especially important for human skin tones, as we are often very critical about the reproduction of skin tones, as well as the blue of the robe of the Madonna, as this blue had heraldic information too.

Seven artefacts shown on the Internet of the subject have been analysed, four of them were reproductions of the Louvre version [10-12] three of the National Gallery version [5,12,13]. Further two printed versions of the Louvre and one of the National Gallery versions were included in our investigation.

Figure 2 shows on the example of the Louvre version three areas of skin tone (the forehead of the Madonna and of the angle and the leg of St. John) marked with a white circle. As second hue the blue of the robe of the Madonna was selected, a portion on her shoulder in the Louvre version and on the breast on the National Gallery version. Also these areas are shown in the picture by small circles. These are areas that could be easily identified also on the London version of the picture. From the Louvre version in one of the databases four artefacts were found, two of them showing the same parts of the original but in remarkably different colours (the cause of this is unknown to us).

**Fig. 2.** Black and white reproduction of the Virgin of the Rocks picture, showing the four parts were colour measurement was made

Further versions were selected from museum albums [14-16] where some parts of the of the pictures were enlarged and could be measured with higher accuracy.

Table 1 shows the *L**, *a**, *b** values measured for the three selected skin tones and the portion of the robe, measured on the artefacts from different databases of the Louvre version of the picture, using the following techniques: For the artefacts taken from the Internet the Photoshop Eye-Drop tool was used that provides the data as would be seen if the illumination of the picture was made with CIE illuminant D50 and observation was with the CIE 2 degree observer.

Similar measurements were made on artefacts of the London version of the painting. For this we show in Table 2 data, from different databases, for the forehead of the Madonna, as this is a critical skin tone. As can be seen we got only in one case a pale yellowish colour, in two other cases we got reddish hues.

Both in case of the pictures on the monitor and for the printed pictures a Gretag Magbeth i1 spectrophotometer with a BabelColor software extension[1] was used to obtain also in this case data for CIE illuminant D50 and 2°observer. These data are shown in Table 3 and Table 4.

Similar investigation was made using the famous picture Mona Lisa, taken from[5,6,7,9,10], and the Lady with an Ermine, taken from [5] and [7]. In these artefacts the colour of the forehead was investigated. In this case we show the average results

**Table 1.** Average skin tones, colour of the robe of Maria and their standard deviations (in brackets) for four parts of the Madonna of the Rocks (Louvre) painting using the Photoshop eye-drop tool, based on seven Internet reproductions

| Part of the picture | $L^*$ | $a^*$ | $b^*$ | $h_{ab}^*$ | $C_{ab}^*$ |
|---|---|---|---|---|---|
| A.) Forehead o the Madonna | 81 (±13) | 4 (±2) | 37 (±2) | 84 | 37 |
| Forehead of the angle | 78 (±13) | 13 (±3) | 39 (±9) | 72 | 41 |
| Leg of St.John | 71 (±2) | 19 (±4) | 46 (±5) | 68 | 50 |
| Robe of Mary | 42 (±10) | -12 (±2) | 21 (±7) | 300 | 24 |

[1] Thanks are due to Dr. Danny Pascale for helping our work with this software.

**Table 2.** Skin tones of the forehead of the Madonna, measured with the Photoshop eye-drop tool on artefacts from different databases reproducing the Virgin on the Rocks, National Gallery London version

| $L^*$ | $a^*$ | $b^*$ | $h_{ab^*}$ | $C_{ab}^*$ |
|---|---|---|---|---|
| 96 | -3 | 19 | 279 | 19 |
| 88 | 5 | 9 | 61 | 10 |
| 99 | -5 | 22 | 283 | 23 |

**Table 3.** Average skin tones, colour of the robe of Maria ($L^*$, $a^*$, $b^*$, $h_{ab}^*$, $C_{ab}^*$) and their standard deviations (in brackets) for four parts of the Madonna of the Rocks (Louvre) painting: (A), and of the Virgin of the Rocks (Nat. Gal., London) painting: (B); using the i1 instrument, based on seven Internet reproductions

| Part of the picture | $L^*$ | $a^*$ | $b^*$ | $h_{ab}^*$ | $C_{ab}^*$ |
|---|---|---|---|---|---|
| A.) Forehead o the Madonna | 82 (±11) | 12 (±4) | 39 (±6) | 73 | 41 |
| Forehead of the angle | 80 (±11) | 21(±6) | 45 (±11) | 12 | 221 |
| Leg of St.John | 67 (±11) | 18 (±5) | 36 (±10) | 63 | 40 |
| Robe of Mary | 48 (±7) | 0 (±3) | 2 (±4) | 90 | 2 |
| B.) Forehead o the Madonna | 88 (±13) | 7 (±6) | 23 (+14) | 73 | 24 |
| Forehead of the angle | 90 (±4) | 6 (±5) | 25 (±17) | 77 | 26 |
| Leg of St.John | 87 (±5) | 9 (±4) | 27(±10) | 72 | 28 |
| Robe of Mary | 55(±2) | 3 (±4) | -17 (±5) | 280 | 17 |

**Table 4.** Average skin tones, colour of the robe of Maria ($L^*$, $a^*$, $b^*$, $h_{ab}^*$, $C_{ab}^*$) for four parts of the Madonna of the Rocks (Louvre) painting: (A), and of the Virgin of the Rocks (Nat. Gal., London) painting: (B); using the i1 instrument, based on a printed book image

| Part of the picture | $L^*$ | $a^*$ | $b^*$ | $h_{ab}^*$ | $C_{ab}^*$ |
|---|---|---|---|---|---|
| A.) Forehead o the Madonna | 77 | 3 | 35 | 85 | 35 |
| Forehead of the angle | 72 | 10 | 40 | 76 | 41 |
| Leg of St.John | 72 | 12 | 34 | 71 | 36 |
| B.) Forehead o the Madonna | 74 | 13 | 22 | 59 | 26 |
| Robe of Mary | 45 | -1 | -9 | 264 | 9 |

**Table 5.** Average skin tones and their standard deviations measured on the forehead of the Mona Lisa and the Lady with an Ermine

| Picture and measurement | $L^*$ | $a^*$ | $b^*$ | $h_{ab}^*$ | $C_{ab}^*$ |
|---|---|---|---|---|---|
| A.) Mona Lisa, Photoshop | 84 (±5) | 5 (±5) | 53 (±11) | 85 | 53 |
| Mona Lisa, monitor, i1 | 87 (±3) | 9 (±2) | 49 (±11) | 80 | 50 |
| Mona Lisa, album, i1 | 63 (±3) | 9 (±2) | 30 (±2) | 73 | 31 |
| B.) Lady w. Er., Photoshop | 80 | 14 | 38 | 70 | 40 |
| Lady w. Er., monitor, i1 | 78 | 20 | 41 | 64 | 46 |
| Lady w. Er., album, i1 | 73 | 7 | 24 | 74 | 25 |

obtained when the measurements were taken on the monitor screen by Photoshop and by i1 and from albums by the i1 instrument.

### 3.2 Painting by Vincent van Goagh

As a further example we selected an other masterpiece, Vincent van Gogh's Bedroom (The Art Institute of Chicago, the van Gogh Museum Amsterdam and the Musée d'Orsay versions). The big difference compared with Leonardo's paintings is that while the two Madonna/Virgin on the Rocks paintings are very similar, they radiate the same feeling, the three van Gogh paintings show exactly the same room but painted in very different moods, thus the differences in coloration have to be reproduced exactly to be able to valuate the differences. Three Internet databases [17-19] (in one of them several versions of the painting was found) and two books [20,21] and an art poster [22] have been included in this search.

**Fig. 3.** Vincent van Gogh's The bedroom painting, The Art Institute of Chicago version

Again both the Photoshop eye-drop technique and the i1 instrument were used for the picture displayed on the monitor and the i1 for measuring colours in the printed versions. Figure 3 shows a black-and-white reproduction of the one of the pictures where the five areas, where measurements were taken are shown by white circles.

Number 1 is a part of the bluish green window, 2 represents a part of the blue wall, 3 is a part of the yellow pillow, 4 is a reddish eiderdown, finally 5 is a brown wood colour. Table 6 shows on the example of the van Gogh Museum Amsterdam version the colorimetric values measured on three artefacts downloaded from the Internet, measured with the i1 instrument.

As a next step the results with the three measurement techniques (Monitor picture with Photoshop and i1, printed copy with i1) has been compared. All three Internet versions and a book copy were measured. The average measurement results are seen for the Amsterdam version of "The bedroom"" in Table 7.

Similar measurements were made on three Internet versions of the Artistic Institute, Chicago, picture and on two Internet copies of the d'Orsay version of the "The Bedroom" picture.

**Table 6.** Colorimetric data ($L^*$, $a^*$, $b^*$, $h_{ab}^*$, $C_{ab}^*$) for D50 illumination and 2°observation) of artefacts downloaded from three Internet databases of Vincent van Gogh's Bedroom, van Gogh Museum Amsterdam, version, measured with i1 instrument

| 1.) window | $L^*$ | $a^*$ | $b^*$ | $h_{ab}^*$ | $C_{ab}^*$ |
|---|---|---|---|---|---|
| Database 1 | 59 | -12 | 28 | 293 | 30 |
| Database 2 | 66 | -5 | 41 | 277 | 41 |
| Database 3 | 77 | -13 | 47 | 285 | 49 |
| *Average (AVE)* | *67* | *-10* | *39* | 284 | 40 |
| *Standard deviation (STD)* | *9* | *4* | *10* | | |
| 2.) wall | | | | | |
| Database 1 | 58 | -14 | -6 | 203 | 15 |
| Database 2 | 79 | -7 | -22 | 252 | 23 |
| Database 3 | 86 | -6 | -12 | 243 | 13 |
| *Average (AVE)* | *74* | *-9* | *-13* | 235 | 16 |
| *Standard deviation (STD)* | *14* | *5* | *8* | | |
| 3.) pillow | | | | | |
| Database 1 | 87 | 1 | 53 | 89 | 53 |
| Database 2 | 87 | 11 | 52 | 78 | 53 |
| Database 3 | 85 | -1 | 51 | 271 | 51 |
| *Average (AVE)* | *86* | *4* | *52* | 86 | 52 |
| *Standard deviation (STD)* | *1* | *7* | *1* | | |
| 4.) eiderdown | | | | | |
| Database 1 | 44 | 47 | 23 | 26 | 52 |
| Database 2 | 49 | 55 | 31 | 29 | 63 |
| Database 3 | 39 | 37 | 16 | 23 | 40 |
| *Average (AVE)* | *44* | *46* | *23* | 27 | 51 |
| *Standard deviation (STD)* | *5* | *9* | *7* | | |
| 5.) bed, wood | | | | | |
| Database 1 | 70 | 42 | 54 | 52 | 68 |
| Database 2 | 64 | 44 | 50 | 49 | 67 |
| Database 3 | 77 | 20 | 62 | 72 | 65 |
| *Average (AVE)* | *70* | *35* | *55* | 58 | 65 |
| *Standard deviation (STD)* | *7* | *13* | *6* | | |

## 4 Discussion

As can be seen from the different tables, the colours of the selected objects shows considerable scatter. The CIELAB colour space has been so constructed that the unit

**Table 7.** Colorimetric data ($L^*$, $a^*$, $b^*$, $h_{ab}^*$, $C_{ab}^*$ for D50 illumination and 2°observation) determined on artefacts of Vincent van Gogh's Bedroom, van Gogh Museum Amsterdam version

| 1.) window: | $L^*$ | $a^*$ | $b^*$ | $h_{ab}^*$ | $C_{ab}^*$ |
|---|---|---|---|---|---|
| Internet picture, Photoshop eye-drop | 68 | -15 | 47 | 288 | 49 |
| Internet picture, i1 instrument | 67 | -10 | 39 | 284 | 40 |
| Printed copy, i1 instrument | 81 | -6 | 49 | 277 | 49 |
| AVE | 72 | -10 | 45 | 283 | 46 |
| STD | 8 | 5 | 6 | | |
| 2.) wall | | | | | |
| Internet picture, Photoshop eye-drop | 71 | -12 | -11 | 223 | 16 |
| Internet picture, i1 instrument | 74 | -9 | -13 | 235 | 16 |
| Printed copy, i1 instrument | 72 | -11 | -10 | 222 | 15 |
| AVE | 73 | -11 | -11 | 225 | 16 |
| STD | 2 | 2 | 2 | | |
| 3.) pillow | | | | | |
| Internet picture, Photoshop eye-drop | 83 | 2 | 64 | 88 | 64 |
| Internet picture, i1 instrument | 86 | 4 | 52 | 86 | 52 |
| Printed copy, i1 instrument | 65 | 9 | 40 | 77 | 41 |
| AVE | 78 | 5 | 52 | 85 | 52 |
| STD | 12 | 4 | 12 | | |
| 4.) eiderdown | | | | | |
| Internet picture, Photoshop eye-drop | 37 | 52 | 47 | 42 | 70 |
| Internet picture, i1 instrument | 44 | 46 | 23 | 27 | 51 |
| Printed copy, i1 instrument | 55 | 23 | 33 | 55 | 40 |
| AVE | 45 | 40 | 35 | 41 | 53 |
| STD | 9 | 15 | 12 | | |
| 5.) bed, wood | | | | | |
| Internet picture, Photoshop eye-drop | 69 | 34 | 70 | 64 | 78 |
| Internet picture, i1 instrument | 70 | 35 | 55 | 58 | 65 |
| Printed copy, i1 instrument | 70 | 12 | 54 | 77 | 55 |
| AVE | 70 | 27 | 60 | 66 | 66 |
| STD | 1 | 13 | 9 | | |

Euclidean distance between the coordinates of two colours is just visible if seen side by side. If the two corresponding colours are seen independently from each other then even much larger differences do not disturb. Rich and co-workers [23] reported on the possibility to simulate surface colours on a CRT monitor within a $\Delta E_{ab}^* = 5$ range, although they admit that usual reproduction differences are in the 6 to 12 $\Delta E_{ab}$* units range. As can be seen the differences between the artefacts of the same picture, downloaded from different databases is grossly twice as one would expect from literature data.

If a more detailed analysis is made, some quite unexpected discrepancies can be found: e.g. one of the databases contained four artefacts of the Madonna of the Rocks. In three of them the $L$* value (lightness) of the complexion of the Madonna was within 1.5 %, but the fourth one differed by almost 30 %. Similar differences were found also for the lightness of other parts of the picture, but the hue angles of the objects were quite close to each other.

The Mona Lisa complexion lightness was quite similar in the three Internet databases, the book reproduction differed, however, quite considerably. On the other hand the hue angle differences were within acceptable tolerances.

Analysing the data of the van Gogh paintings one has to state that the artefacts of the same original differ considerably and not systematically in the different databases. This can be seen e.g. on the data as reproduced in Table 6: Comparing the CIE lightness data of the three datasets, we see e.g. that while for the pillow the first two show the same value ($L$* = 87), and the third one is lower ($L$* = 85), for the bed colour the CIE lightness as shown in the third database is 10 % higher then that from database number 1. Also the hue angles show considerable differences, especially for the bed colour: In one case we see an almost orange colour, while in the other case it is a pale yellowish hue. Similar difference can be found also for the blue wall colour, although in that case the lightness of the wall is much higher in the artefact of database 2, compared to database 1, just the opposite is true for the bed colour. In summary we have to state that the three colorations used in the three databases deliver quite different message to the viewer.

## 5 Summary and Conclusions

On the examples shown we have to conclude that the digital artefacts of famous paintings, now available on the Internet – at least partly – poor reproductions of the original. Techniques now available to set the colorimetric characteristics of the different imaging devices (monitors, printers, projectors) provide better agreement between these devices as what one can expect by downloading artefacts from different databases.

First and most important message to the arts teacher is not to rely on one single reproduction, downloaded from one database, but check for more copies of the same painting, and compare their colours, before one is selected to be shown in the class-room.

To the providers of the artefacts one should direct the plea to provide with the reproduction also some information how the reproduction was made: illuminant used to take the picture, encoding, eventual transformations (e.g. lightness scale distortion), etc. This could help in the future to set the necessary transformations to get on the screen the colour impression one would have by looking at the original in the museum.

## Reference


1. Andersen, C.F., Hardeberg, J.Y.: Colorimetric characterization of digital cameras preserving hue plaes. In: Proc. 13 Color Imagiong Conf. Scottsdale, pp. 141–146 (2005)
2. MacDonald, L.W., Ji, W.: Colour characterization of a high-resolution digital camera. In: Proc. First Internat. Conf. on Colour in Graphics. Imaging and Vision, Univ. of Poitiers. pp. 433*–437 (2002)
3. Berns, R.S.: Rejuvenating the appearance of cultural heritage using color and imaging science techniques. In: Proc. AIC Colour 05, Granada, Spain.2005, pp. 369–374 (2005)
4. Mohammadi, M., Berns, R.S.: Diagnosing and correcting systematic errors in spectral-based digital imaging. In: Proc. 13 Color Imaging Conf. Scottsdale, 2005, pp. 25–30 (2005)
5. IEC (1999) IEC 61966–2–1: Multimedia systems and equipment – Colour measurement and management – Part 2–1: Colour management – Default RGB colour space – sRGB, IEC, Switzerland.
6. Morovic, J., Lammens, J.: Colour management in Colorimetry, Understanding the CIE System, Schanda, J. (ed.) CIE Preprint edition (2006)
7. Giorgianni, E.J., Madden, T.E., Spaulding, K.E.: Color managamanet for digital imaging systems, Digital color imaging. In: Sharma, G. (ed.) CRC Press, Boca Raton (2003)
8. CIE 15: 2004 Colorimetry, CIE Central Bureau, Vienna, Austria (2004)
9. Schanda, J.: CIE colorimetry 2004, in Colorimetry, Understanding the CIE System, Schanda, J. (ed.) CIE Preprint edition (2006)
10. Leonardo: Sziklás Madonna, http://www.sk-szeged.hu/kiallitas/leonardo/festmenyei.html#zenesz
11. Atlas Database of the Louvre: http://cartelen.louvre.fr/cartelen/visite?srv=crt_frm_rs&langue=fr&initCritere=true
12. http://en.wikipedia.org/wiki/Leonardo
13. http://www.nationalgallery.co.uk/
14. Pomilio, M.: L'opera completa di Leonardo pittore, Rizzoli Editiore, Milano (1967)
15. Clasen, K.H.: A Louvre képtára, Képzőművészeti Alap Kiadóvállalat
16. Zsámboki, Z.: National Galery, London. Corvina (1988)
17. http://www.artic.edu/artaccess/AA_Impressionist/
18. http://www.3dsrc.com/vangogh/vincent%20vangogh%20-%20La%20chambre%20de%20Van%20Gogh%20a%20Arles.php.
19. http://www.vggallery.com/painting/
20. Hughes, R.: van Gogh, Kopakt, Belser Verl. Stuttgart
21. Metzger, R., Walther, I.F.: Vincent van Gogh, Taschen/Vince Kiadó Budapest2004
22. Art & Image Bestseller Calendar 2006 teNeues Verlag, Kempen (2006)
23. Rich, D.C., Alston, D.L., Allen, L.: Psychophysical verification of the accuracy of color and color-difference simulations of surface samples on a CRT display. Color Res. & Appl. 17, 45–56 (1992)

# 3D Simulation Technology of Cultural Relics in the Digitalized Yin Ruins

Chuangming Shi and Xinyu Duan

Department of Computer Science, Anyang Normal University, Anyang 455000,China
scmscmscm@163.com

**Abstract.** This paper discusses methods of implementing 3D simulation technology of the cultural relics, brings forward 3D simulation technology to implement high-quality, high-precision and vivid texture of the ancient cultural relics by adopting range laser 3D scanner and CCD cameras; suggests the automatic registry methods of 3D laser scanning data, which can make 3D laser scanning data with different viewpoints as well as different resolutions into the same coordinate, so as to achieve the high-precision 3D cultural relic models; proposes to take the reflectivity map of 3D laser scanner as middle reference to realize the accurate mapping of planar images and 3D laser scanning data, so as to obtain simulated cultural relics with vivid texture.

**Keywords:** digitalization, modeling, laser scanning, texture mapping, Yin Ruin's Museum, 3D simulation.

## 1 Introduction

Yin ruins, capital relics in the later stage of Chinese Shang Dynasty (about dated 1300-1046 B.C.), is the key cultural protection unit of P.R.C and the world natural & cultural heritage [1]. Anyang Normal University cooperates with Anyang Yin Ruin's Museum to take research of digital simulation protection and exhibition technology applied by Yin Ruin's Museum. As the subject of Henan key scientific and technological tackling fund project—"Research and implementation of 3D simulation protection technology applied in Yin ruins cultural relics", its objective is to provide the virtual reality interface for browsing cultural relics of Yin Ruin's Museum on the computer platform, offer an all-directional, friendly and convenient browsing tool for clients, supply an appreciation and research platform for archaeologists and artists, and restore some important cultural relics in disrepair.

The digital simulation protection system applied in Yin Ruin's Museum is shown in Fig. 1. The whole system structure can be designed as five levels. The first level is the digitalized input of cultural relics, which can be regarded as the most important part with highest cost. The second one is VRML mould design. The third level is multi-media information database (MDB), including 3D model data, sound, video and other information of Yin ruins cultural relics, which can provide the system data resource and data I/O interface. The fourth one is virtual scene maker, including two

R. Shumaker (Ed.): Virtual Reality, HCII 2007, LNCS 4563, pp. 718–727, 2007.

submodules, 3D model expression and simulation multi-media information expression of cultural relics. The last one is user interface, which is in charge of managing all display scene windows, and receiving all input information of users.

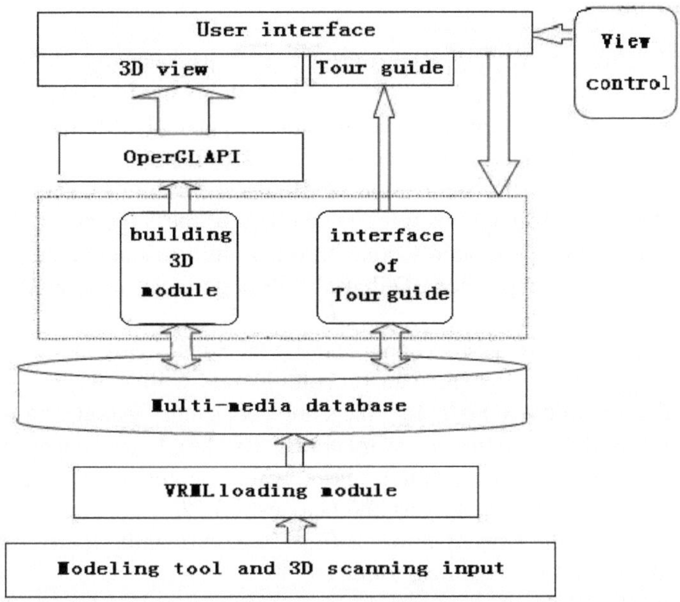


**Fig. 1.** Digitalized model of Yin Ruin's Museum

For this system, the key technology is the first step—the digitalized information collection and processing of Yin ruins cultural relics. Digitalized cultural relics are the basis of cultural relics protection assisted by the computer. According to the features of cultural relics, the research of digitalized cultural relics can be divided into planar and 3D cultural relics digitalized acquisition. The planar cultural relics digitalized acquisition object generally includes the plane design, color, textbook, etc. of cultural relics, the present common digitalized method is to adopt digital photograph technology to take a picture of cultural relics, or use scanners to record as digital image after shooting with a common camera.

For example, the collected scriptures and silk paintings in the British Museum are shot by camera to keep forever. Generally, the digitalized 3D cultural relics presently have three methods, namely the methods based on measurement, computer vision and 3D scanners, in which, the third method is the main stream of present digitalized method. The typical work is: digitalized Michelangelo plan, cooperated and accomplished by American Stanford University, Washington University and Cyberware Company jointly, adopts 3D scanner to record down 10 large-size statues built by Michelangelo, including the well-known David stature [2], etc. In this paper, we mainly discuss the 3D information acquisition technology applied in Yin ruins cultural relics on the basis of 3D scanner methods.

## 2 Implementing of the 3D Digital Simulation Protection Applied in Yin Ruins

### 2.1 3D Digital Information Collection Applied in the Large-Size Cultural Relics of Yin Ruins

The cultural relics of Anyang Yin ruins are various, such as magnificent palace architectures and mausoleums of the emperors in Shang Dynasty, as well as the largest bronze tripod caldron all over the country, namely Simuwu square vessel, there are all kinds of bronze wares, jadeware, inscriptions on bones or tortoise shells, pottery, etc. In terms of the acquisition of 3D data, we adopt Cyrax 2500 3D laser scanning technology and CCD imaging technology to the large-size cultural relics as main acquisition means. We mainly break through multi-resource data comprehensive processing technology to provide 3D digitalized model with accurate dimensions and vivid texture.

Firstly, we shall use 3D laser scanner and digital camera with high resolving power to collect the space and texture data of cultural relics, then make 3D network by collecting all viewpoints' 3D data into the same coordinate system, and build up high-quality digital model through texture mapping. The large-size representative of Yin ruins cultural relics is Si Muwu square vessel, whose height is 1.33m, length is 1.10m and weight for 875kg, it is the largest and heaviest bronze ware that we had unearthed so far, also is rare in the world (shown as Fig. 2). Additionally, there are carriage and horse's pit (shown as Fig. 3), Fuhao tomb, etc.

While we take 3D laser scanning for the large-size cultural relics of Yin ruins, other objects surrounding cultural relics also can be involved in. It requires eliminating useless information from 3D laser scanning data. Therefore, the data blanks may be produced due to sheltering from scanning cultural relics. So we need to eliminate noise during data processing course to pick up scanning cultural relics and fill up data blanks.

It is supposed that the Z-axis of scanner is always vertical to the ground level during scanning process; we adopt the main object scanning distribution method on the basis of statistic distribution [3]. Firstly we will give two definitions: namely the vertical and horizontal scanning sections. The laser scans along with vertical direction, then the plane formed by scanning lines is called as vertical scanning section. Otherwise, if the laser scans along with horizontal direction, then the plane formed by scanning lines is called as horizontal scanning section. The projection distance on horizontal plane between points on the same vertical scanning section is (1):

$$d_{(i,j)}=\sqrt{x_{(i,j)^2}+y_{(i,j)^2}}\ . \tag{1}$$

To the same measured planes and the planes with smaller curvature, horizontal projection distance of the sample points shall be equal. Taking advantage of this feature, according to statistical distribution of horizontal projection distance of the

**Fig. 2.** carriage and horse's pit

**Fig. 3.** Si Muwu square vessel

sample points, we could bring forward main scanning objects. Blank data filling adopts two methods; we adopt linear interpolation method to fill blank data when blanks appear in the plane region, contrarily, we adopt conicoid interpolation method.

Acquisition of 3D models of ancient cultural relics in Yin ruins sometimes needs to set scores or hundreds of viewpoints. 3D data got from each viewpoint is part coordinate system to the viewpoint itself, only coalescing 3D data got from all the viewpoints into the same coordinate system, we could get the whole data description of the ancient cultural relics. The most typical registry schemes are ICP [4] algorithm and registry method [5] based on features. ICP algorithm requires overlap of 3D data point set of all viewpoints and point as registry unit. Registry method based on features requires that firstly extracting computation features among 3D point set. If there are no computation features or no enough features, registry could be taken exactly. Generally speaking, cultural relics get very complex geometry, so we adopt a modified ICP algorithm [6], and gradually realize 3D data quick registry [7] of large-scale cultural relics.

ICP algorithm with point as registry unit needs to find the nearest point in the other point set to the point in the given point set, and calculate the distance from its nearest point. 3D data points got from each viewpoint by 3D laser scanner shall be arranged according to scanning sequence, if making the distance between scanning point and laser scanner take the place of gray level in gray level image, we could get a distance picture. In a similar manner, transform 3D data in a viewpoint into coordinate system of another viewpoint, calculate again the distance between scanning point and new position, and then a projected picture shall be formed. By mosaicing projected picture and distance picture point and combining computation of corresponding points in space two point sets, the best mosaic matrix of the two viewpoints could be got after several adjustments.

In terms of registry strategy, we adopt gradual registry strategy from initial to precise to improve registry speed. 3D laser scanners belong to time-of-flight method laser distance sensor, which only could output 3D coordinate and its reflectance value of synchronously corresponding sample points, with reflectance ratios of all the sample points in each viewpoint construct a reflectivity map, which gets all the features of common images. We utilize reflectivity map to extract 3D edge of cultural relics, registry shall begin from 3D edge points.

Firstly, we shall divide reflectivity maps of two neighbor viewpoints into M and N subgraphs, supposing that there are same pixels in the subgraphs of the two reflectivity maps, and then calculate conformity degree of the two reflectivity maps. Choose three subgraphs with the largest conformity degree, calculate the centroids of their subgraphs, and then initial estimated matrixes of two viewpoints' coordinate transformation could be decided by the three centroids. Secondly, transform the 3D edge points of the two viewpoints into the same coordinate system by the initial estimated matrixes, now make use of modified ICP algorithm to take registry of all the 3D edge points, and accordingly further optimize transformation matrix. Thirdly, make use of optimized transformation matrix to transform all the 3D data points of the two viewpoints into the same coordinate system, take modified ICP algorithm in the range of all the 3D data points, and accordingly further optimize transformation matrix. Finally, make use of most optimized transformation matrix to mosaic 3D data of the two viewpoints into the same

**Fig. 4.** 3D Digital model of Si Muwu square vessel

**Fig. 5.** 3D Digital model of Fuhao tomb pit

coordinate system. The followings are Si Muwu square vessel (Fig. 4) and Fuhao tomb pit (Fig. 5) digital model got in this way.

## 2.2 3D Digital Information Acquisition of Medium and Small-Scale Cultural Relics in Yin Ruins

Anyang Yin Ruin's Museum preserves abundant cultural relics including bronze vessels, jadewares, inscriptions on bones or shells and pottery with small volume. Due to complex shapes, it's hard to get 3D data; due to abundant shapes, colors and textures, it's also hard to get texture Fig.let. For example Fig. 6 is Bronze vessel Fuhao owl statue, Fig. 7 is one jadeware unearthed in Yin ruins.

In the course of obtaining specific data, we adopt the basic same procedure with the scanning operation of large-scale ancient cultural relics, namely using 3D range scanner (Cyrax 2500), with some differences in their operation methods. Firstly, calibration: in the course of scanning, the system coordinate is decided by hardware of the apparatus together with ambient environment, so an unified coordinate system shall be fixed in advance. Calibration work is essential to get precise 3D data. While scanning large-scale ancient cultural relics, we need to change viewpoint, and label each part coordinate system by putting special marker on the fixed position. While scanning small-scale ancient cultural relics, we shall fix scanner, put the cultural relics on the table, and get relationship among each part coordinate system by recording the rotation angle of the table. Secondly, scanning: cultural relics surface shall be sampled from one viewpoint and got a closepacked range image. The sample image of the whole cultural relics could only be got by several times of scanning. Due to some medium and small-scale cultural relics get a lot of surface patches, the scanning time shall be increased properly. Thirdly, registry: sample images got from scanning shall be in respective part coordinate system, and be calibrated in the same global coordinate system. Registry shall be realized on the basis of coordinate system information fixed in the calibration procedure. Medium and small-scale cultural relics get relatively precise calibration, so it is easy to do the registry work.

**Fig. 6.** Bronze vessel Fuhao owl statue

**Fig. 7.** Jadeware unearthed in Yin ruins

### 2.3 Texture Mapping in 3D Cultural Relic Model

Texture mapping is mapping pixel value in planar image bitmap on the corresponding vertexes in 3D solid model to strengthen presence of solid model. Essentially, it is a mapping [8] from a planar texture plan to 3D scene surface, which could be described by the following formula: (u,v)=F(x,y,z)

Including (u,v) and (x,y,z) are the points in texture space and object space respectively. For example: if making a texture mapping on the cylindrical face with h as its height and r as its semidiameter, we could use the following parameter form to express it: $x=r\cos\theta$, $y=r\sin\theta$, $z=h\,\Phi$. Among which $0<=\theta<=2\pi$, $0<=\Phi<=1$.

Through the following linear transformation, make the texture space $[0, 1]\times[0, 1]$ equal with the parameter space $[0, 2\pi]\times[0, 1]$: $u=\theta/2\pi$, $v=\Phi$

Then we could get the texture expression from object space to the texture space.

Making use of the above-mentioned relationship between parameterization and texture mapping, we take texture sample of parameterized plane, and form planar texture pictures of cultural relic grid. As to each point on the planar parameterized plane, from the corresponding relationship of parameterization, simplify texture of cultural relic into only corresponding vertex on the grid of meshes(2):

$$(x, y, z) = f^{-1}(u, v) . \tag{2}$$

As to the vertex on the grid of meshes, from the texture mapping relationship of perspective projection, planar cultural relics image gets its corresponding pixel, which will been added by the color, namely to form planar pictures of 3D cultural relics. Mapping this planar image on the grid of 3D cultural relics through parameterization relationship namely to form 3D cultural relics texture model [9] with independent viewpoint(3).

$$(m, n) = g^{-1}(x, y, z) . \tag{3}$$

Some laser scanners could synchronously and automatically output the corresponding distance value and color value in the course of scanning, finish mosaic between geometric things and surface color texture, output color scanning model. Cyrax2500 3D laser scanner used by us belongs to time-of-flight method laser distance sensor, which could output gray scale model, namely only could output 3D coordinate and its reflectance value of synchronously corresponding sample points. Furthermore, we need additional digital camera with high resolution to obtain color texture information. Namely we need two relatively independent sensors (3D laser scanner and digital camera) to obtain geometry and texture data of cultural relics respectively. The position of 3D laser scanner is relatively stable, while the position of digital camera is relatively flexible.

The geometric data and reflectance data got by 3D laser scanner belong to the same laser pulse signal, which has the same space resolution. Therefore, we take the laser reflectivity map as neutral medium between planar texture data and 3D geometric data. Such laser reflectivity map reflects changes of different colors or different materials. Different materials are expressed by different tones or colors, so we also could find the corresponding edges in the color texture image. Furthermore due to the geometric data and reflectance data are got from the same laser pulse, some geometric capers may be reflected in the corresponding edges; at the same time some geometric capers gets small shades, so there also are corresponding edges in the color texture image. Only simply using Sobel operator could detect the edge points of 3D reflectance and those of planar color texture.

How to mosaic planar color texture data exactly with the corresponding 3D geometric data? Firstly, try our best to detect the edge points of 3D reflectance and those of planar color texture; Secondly, make 3D reflectance edge points project on planar color texture image to find the corresponding points; Thirdly, according to the corresponding points, establish corresponding relation between planar texture data and 3D geometric data in the way of iteration.

We use Tsai calibration method [10] to calculate inside and outside parameter of camera, and then fix the projection relation between 3D geometric point and planar texture point. Initial calibration is the corresponding point got by art, then optimalize calibration result of camera in the way of iteration, finally mapping 3D texture on the 3D grid to get 3D cultural relic model with vivid texture.

## 3 Conclusion

Yin ruins digitalization is a system engineering. This paper mainly discusses methods of realizing 3D simulation technology of the cultural relics, brings forward 3D simulation technology to realize high-quality, high-precision and vivid texture of the ancient cultural relics by adopting range laser 3D scanner; suggests the automatic registry methods of 3D laser scanning data, which can mosaic 3D laser scanning data with different viewpoints as well as different resolution into the same coordinate, so as to achieve the high-precision 3D cultural relic models; proposes to take the reflectivity map of 3D laser scanner as middle reference to realize the accurate mapping of planar images and 3D laser scanning images, so as to obtain simulated cultural relics with vivid texture. With regard to other technologies in digitalized Yin ruins, we will discuss them in the following meetings or exchange opinions with all of you through other media.

**Acknowledgments.** This work is supported in part by Henan Province Natural Science Fund (No. 0624480025)(China). We also thank Prof. Zhigeng Pan for giving us valuable guidance and kindly support.

## References

1. http:// www.ayyx.com
2. Levoy, M., Pulli, K., Curless, B.: The Digital Michelangelo Project: 3D Scanning of Large Statues [CD]. In: Siggraph'2000, ACM Press, New York (2000)
3. Shao-xing, H., Hong-bin, Z.: Modeling Method for Large-Scale Cultural Heritage Sites and Objects Using Real Geometric Data and Real Texture Data[J]. Journal of System Simulation 18(4), 953–954 (2006)
4. Johnson, A.: Spin-Images: A represesmation for 3D surface matching [D]. phD thesis,Robotics Instiue, Carnegie Mellon University, Pittsburgh, PA, August 1997 (1997)
5. Stamos, I., Leordeanu, M.: Automated feature-based range registration of urban scenes of large scale[C]// In: Inter.Conf.Computer Vision and Pattern Recognition, Madison,WI, June 2003 (2003)
6. Sun-Weidong, Z.-A.: Fast Global Registration of Multiple 3D Data Sets from Outdoor Large Scenes[J]. High Technology Letters 14(6), 6–10 (2004)
7. Sequeira, V., Ng, K., Wolfart, E., Gonc alves, G.M, Hogg, D.: Automated reconstruction of 3D models from real environments[C]// ISPRS. Journal of Photogrammetry & Remote Sensing54, 1-22 (1999)

8. Ma-Songde, Zhang-zhengyou.: computer vision—compute theory and arithmetic elements, Beijing science & technology press (1998)
9. Burt, P.J., Andelson, E.H.: A Multiresolution Spline With Application to Image Mosaics[C] // ACM Transactions on Graphics, pp. 217–236. ACM Press, New York (1983)
10. Tsai, R.Y.: A versatile camera calibration technique for high-accuracy 3D machine vision metrology using off-the-shelf TV cameras and lenses[J]. IEEE Journal of Robotics and Automation (S0882-4967) 3(4), 323–344 (1987)

# Mixed Reality Systems for Learning: A Pilot Study Understanding User Perceptions and Acceptance

Yin-Leng Theng[1], Charissa Lim Mei-Ling[1], Wei Liu[2], and Adrian David Cheok[2]

[1] School of Communication and Information
Nanyang Technological University
Division of Information Studies, Singapore
[2] Mixed Reality Lab
National University of Singapore
Department of Electrical and Computer Engineering, Singapore

**Abstract.** This paper describes a pilot study to investigate participants' perceptions of usefulness and usability of our developed Plant Mixed Reality System (PMRS), designed for primary school children (11-12 years old). Preliminary results seemed to indicate participants' intention to use PMRS for learning. The paper concludes with a discussion on how the findings were used to formulate a second study based on the Technology Acceptance Model, and discuss implications on intention to use and acceptance of mixed reality systems for education.

## 1 Introduction

Mixed reality (MXR) is one of the newest technologies explored in edutainment that promises the potential to revolutionise learning and teaching, making learners' experience more "engaging", either through the incorporation of virtual objects into a real three-dimensional scene, or alternatively through the inclusion of real world elements into a virtual environment" [1].

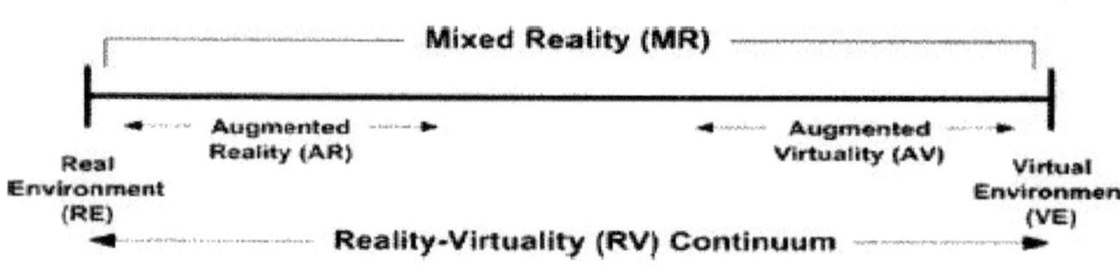


**Fig. 1.** Reality-Virtuality Continuum (Taken from [24])

MXR is a technology that falls under the wider set of technologies known as virtual reality (VR) or virtual environments (VE). A reality-virtuality continuum proposed by [13], illustrates real environment on one end and virtual environment on the other. In between, there may appear flavours of integration such as augmented

R. Shumaker (Ed.): Virtual Reality, HCII 2007, LNCS 4563, pp. 728–737, 2007.

reality (AR) and augmented virtuality (AV), depending on whether reality or virtuality was being enhanced (Figure 1).

## 2 Mixed Reality Projects in Education

In recent years, many MXR applications have been constructed for the learning of astronomy [2], oceanography [4], mathematics [26] and other topics [20]. These technologies are challenging conventional delivery modes in education.

In education, studies on the use of virtual reality (VR) or VEs have been conducted as early as in the 1990s. For example, Bricken and Byrne [3] carried out a summer camp where students aged 10 – 15 years used VR tools to construct and explore virtual worlds. The potential for such virtual technologies is high. Areas that they can be applied to are: formal education, informal education (such as museums), distance learning, vocational training and special needs education. Pan, Cheok, Yang, Zhu and Shi [16] document a number of VE learning projects such as a Magic story cube for storytelling and an interactive mixed reality Kyoto garden. These could be used in formal or informal education.

Woods et al (2004) set up several educational exhibits for Science centers, Museums etc. [25]. Stanton et al [21] collaborate with children and teachers together, design a tangible interface for storytelling. Education Arcade project [17], persons from MIT proposed a new concept "Games to Teach" and they developed three prototypes for electromagnetic, environment and history education. FlatWorld [15] created in USC can be used for education and training goals. Shelton et al [18] developed a system to teach Earth-Sun relationships to undergraduate geography students. It focuses on earth and sun related knowledge such as equinox, solstice to give students an AR experience.

Mathematics is another subject that could benefit from the use of VEs, as proposed by studies such as Pasqualotti and Freitas [17]. Three-dimensional environments enable users to explore spatial relationships, a key aspect in the teaching of geometry. Within the local context, Leow's [11] dissertation study was conducted to explore the relationship between spatial ability and the learning of 3-D geometric objects using an AR prototype. The study seemed to suggest that AR could potentially be useful for students with lower spatial ability to learn 3D objects.

## 3 Case Study: Plant Mixed Reality System (PMRS)

MXR systems are expensive to design and develop. History has shown that as new technologies evolve before maturing and succeeding in penetration and acceptance in our daily lives, there is a need to carry out user studies to understand users' perceptions of usability and usefulness of such technologies as early as possible to avoid expensive remedial work later.

However, to our knowledge, there is no well-accepted evaluation framework to understand students' acceptance of the MXR technologies for learning. This paper attempts to use a well-established Technology Acceptance Model (TAM) [6] to investigate users' intention to use. In this paper, we describe a pilot study, a precursor to a larger study using a modified TAM, in which a small group of participants gave feedback on perceptions of usefulness and usability of our developed Plant Mixed Reality System (PMRS).

PMRS, developed by the Mixed Reality Lab of the National University of Singapore (NUS), is selected as a case study to understand users' perceptions of MXR systems because this system is one of the first known educational MXR programs designed according to the local school syllabus and deployed in a local primary school (School X) in Singapore [14]. It was designed for Primary Five students (11-12 years old), who are taught seed germination, plant reproduction, seed dispersion and photosynthesis in their science lessons.

Most AR education prototypes are being developed to complement/enhance traditional teaching method and are not really classroom-based educational tools. John Dewey's theory [9] of education shows that children soak up knowledge and retain it for use when they are spontaneously induced to look into matters of compelling interest to themselves. As a science module, the experiment and direct experience are very important for students to grasp the knowledge. Many phenomena such as seed germination, photosynthesis, either need long times to happen or difficult to observe using naked eyes. For this reason, the mixed reality (MXR) technology was selected to develop an educational tool for the Plant System. We worked with a group of teachers from School X in Singapore to develop PMRS.

Based on the content from teachers and the real experiment, a system structure was designed. Physical objects were used in this project to give pupils the real experience.

As a classroom-based system, PMRS must be suitable for the classroom environment and at same time also suitable for self-learning. By projecting the display on a big screen, a teacher can use this system as a general teaching tool. For self-learning, texts and sounds were added in this system to help students to better comprehend the contents. In addition, the MXR technology also aims to bring the entertainment elements to the learning process, allowing pupils to learn in a more interesting way.

Unlike immersive VR, the PMRS interfaces allow users to see the real world at the same time as virtual imagery attached to real locations and objects. In a PMRS interface, the user views the world through a hand-held or head-mounted display (HMD), that is, either see-through or overlays of graphics on video of the surrounding environment. The most unique character of PMRS is that the interface allows students to interact with the real world in a tangible way. PMRS aims to provide a totally different learners' experience in education by:

- Supporting seamless interaction between real and virtual environments;
- Using a tangible interface metaphor for object manipulation; and
- Switching smoothly between reality and virtuality.

As shown in Figure 2, using physical spade, pupils can add virtual seed real flowerpots. They can also add virtual seeds using spade as well as add virtual water using watering can. By pressing a button, pupils can observe the seed germination process under different conditions.

Figure 3 shows germination and growth of a healthy bud with enough water, suitable temperature and light. Through observing and using PMRS, students can gain

**Fig. 2.** Adding virtual soil in the flower pot

**Fig. 3.** A healthy bud germinated

knowledge about seed germination from their own experience under the teacher's instruction.

# 4 The Pilot Study

## 4.1 Aim

The pilot study, part of a bigger study to understand perceptions of users based on TAM, was carried out in June 7, 2006, over approximately two hours, in a laboratory. This study focused on a small group of student volunteers. It is difficult to bring children into the design process due to the assumptions and power structure imposed on them by adults [7]. The concept of children as design partners has been applied to cases such as Theng et al [22, 23]. In light of this, the involvement of primary school students in an informal and non-intimidating setting was used to gather the responses of this user group towards the PMRS.

## 4.2 Profiles of Subjects

A group of seven primary school students comprising three boys and four girls were recruited from another local primary school (School Y). These participants were in Primary Six (aged 11 – 12 years old), and had gone through the Primary Five science syllabus the previous year. They were put into 3 groups – Group A (2 girls named A-1 and A-2), Group B (2 girls named B-1 and B-2) and Group C (3 boys named C-1, C-2 and C-3). A group setting was used because this would reflect the real-life scenario in a primary school setting where students were required to work and learn together.

The participants interacted with the PMRS. The session was videotaped to capture the participants' reactions to the program, how they used it and how they interacted in a group. The room set-up involved a camera, a monitor, a board of markers (symbols), a keyboard, as well as cylinders and other objects with a marker card on them, as well as speakers.

## 4.3 Protocol

The session started off with a demonstration of the PMRS program by the Research Engineer. She explained the various modules and the use of the keys and cylinders to interact with the PMRS. This was followed by a brief hands-on session during which the students played around with the program in their groups A, B and C in order to get a feel of the program. After this, the actual task-oriented interaction session of the programs began. Each group was given some questions on the worksheet to answer in order to guide their interaction with the program, and then they were asked to complete a task. Upon completion of the interaction session, the students were asked to fill in the form to obtain their feedback on the PMRS.

Help was available during the session to answer questions or assist on the use of the system. After the interaction session, a brief focus group was conducted to discuss the participants' perceived usefulness and perceived ease of use of the PMRS. The focus group session was also videotaped. Two forms were used to collect data from the students. The first form was for gathering their responses that were specific to PMRS, namely their intention to use it, perceived usefulness and perceived ease of use, as well as the innovation factors and their attitude towards that particular science topic. The second form was for gathering information pertaining to the students themselves and their preferences on the accessibility and ability to collaborate.

## 5 Findings and Analysis

In this section, we begin with interaction summaries of participants with PMRS to understand usability and usefulness issues faced by the participants. The interaction summaries, transcribed from the video-taped accounts, are also coded, with negative comment or problem faced as [N#], and positive comment/observation as [P#].

### 5.1 Interaction Summaries

**Group A.** A-1 and A-2 took turns using the camera [P#1]. They had to observe the difference between a bisexual and a unisexual flower. Initially, they were unsure of what to look out for [N#1], but managed to obtain the answer after some prompting by the researcher. Next, they had to describe the cross-pollination process. With some guidance from the Research Engineer, A-1 used the cylinder to move the bee in the program to make it interact with the flowers.

Both A-1 and A-2 gave positive responses on their intention to use the program. A-1 commented that it would be more interesting to have this program [P#2] in her school and A-2 said, "I think my friends would like it [P#3]". Perceived usefulness was positive on all counts for both students. A-1 overall found the program easy to use [P#4] and said that she would need only some help with using it. In contrast, A-2 did not feel that it was easy to use and remarked, "Cannot see clearly and very difficult to operate [N#2]". Both students liked the program and the graphics [P#5]. A-2 found the bee cute [P#6]. A-1 liked this science topic [P#7], but A-2 did not [N#3].

**Group B.** The students observed from the program what happened when a plant did not disperse its seeds. They then had to interact with the cylinders to find out how different plants dispersed their seeds. B-2 was manipulating the camera and cylinders. B-2 also manipulated the plush monkey that represented the animated monkey in the program. She expressed the answers aloud as she interacted with the program, for example, "Wind", "Splitting", "That's animal". B-1's interaction was more limited. During this Plant program session, she took down some of the answers and used the keys to move to other stages in the program. At the end, B-2 handed the camera to B-1 and completed the worksheet.

Intention to use and perceived usefulness were found to be positive by both students [P#8]. They both did not find the program easy to use [N#4], however, with B-2 citing that it was "hard to focus". Although both liked the graphics [P#9], only B-2 said that she enjoyed using the program [P#10] while B-1 answered "Maybe" to that question. Both gave a "Maybe" to the question on whether they enjoyed being able to pick things up in the program and move them around. They both indicated that they liked this science topic [P#11]. B-2 remarked that the topic was very interesting [P#12]. Table 2 shows the positive and negative comments.

**Group C.** For their task, the students were required to experiment with "growing" a seedling. They began with C-2 holding a small physical plastic "watering can", C-3 holding the camera and C-1 holding a physical plastic "spade". C-2 then took over the camera. With guidance from the Research Engineer, C-2 and C-1 took turns in "scooping" the virtual seeds into the virtual pot with the spade and watering it. C-3 took over the camera again. They "added" sunlight and water to the pot and observed the germination of the seeds. The three participants took turns to use the PMRS and helped each other with the system [P#13]

Intention to use and perceived usefulness of the program were positive for all three students [P#14]. With respect to perceived usefulness, C-2 commented, "The ability to interact with the program and its 3D graphics make using this program fun [P#15]". Perceived ease of use was overall positive, although C-1 and C-2 said that the use of the cylinders was not easy [N#5]. Regarding this point, C-2 found that "the camera was too sensitive [N#6]". The three students enjoyed the program [P#16]. They also liked the graphics, with the exception of C-2, who noted, "Sometimes, part of the graphics disappear [N#7]". C-3 commented that the graphics were "almost better than my computer". All three students liked this science topic.

### 5.2 Focus Group Feedback

The focus group session was held after the participants used the PMRS. The comments made during the focus group concurred with the comments and observations made (see Table 1's summary of the positive comments/observations and negative comments made).

When asked to express what they liked about the program, several students mentioned the monkey. They felt that it was cute. There was also a comment that they liked the program because it was 3D. A student from Group A opined that the Plant program was more fun and less complex. With regard to usefulness, the students said that it could help them recall what they had learnt in their lessons and that it was useful for revision. There was a general preference towards independent exploration, rather than having a teacher using it for demonstration purposes.

In terms of usability, issues were raised regarding the manipulation of the various devices, that is, the camera, the cylinder and the keys. Students brought up the difficulty of positioning the camera properly, citing it as being "hard to focus". They also mentioned that graphics would "disappear", referring to the times during the interaction session when the graphic displayed on the monitor would keep flashing (vanish momentarily) due to hardware and software rendering issues. The graphics would vanish very briefly, perhaps for milliseconds, however, this was perceptible and disrupted continuity. With regard to the issue of the cylinder, there was some perceived lack of sensitivity in obtaining the response from the program. For the keys, they were not intuitive to the students, who experienced difficulty in the navigation. When asked to suggest improvements, one student offered the idea of having a fixed camera to enable a wider field of view. There was also a suggestion to use bigger and clearer fonts for the text, as well as to have the text face the camera.

Overall, it was seen that usability was a major issue for the students. However, they perceived the program to be useful and could conceive of other topics that the program could be useful for, such as Maths/Chemistry/Biology. They also showed a preference for independent exploration, which could indicate high self-efficacy and personal innovativeness.

**Table 1.** Positive and Negative Observations and Feedback on PMRS

| *Activities* | *Positive Comments* | *Negative Comments* |
|---|---|---|
| Observation | 1. Cooperation among students in using the program – took turns in using camera [P#1, 13] | 2. Unsure of what to observe in the program [N#1]. |
| *Feedback* | 1. More interesting than the traditional classroom lesson [P#2, 7, 11, 12]<br>2. Perceived usefulness and positive intention to use program [P#4, 8, 13, 14]<br>3. Perception of peer acceptance of program [P#3]<br>4. "Cute" graphics [P#5, 6, 9]<br>5. Enjoyed using the PMRS [P#10]<br>6. Enjoyed using PMRS because of interactivity and 3-D graphics [P#10, 16].<br>7. Fun to use [P#15]. | 8. Experienced difficulty in use [N#2, 4].<br>9. Did not like the topic selected [N#3]<br>10. Cylinder was not easy to use [N#5].<br>11. Camera was too sensitive [N#6].<br>12. Disliked the momentary "disappearances" of the graphics [N#7] |

## 6 Factors Affecting Perceptions and Acceptance

In this pilot study, we observed comments made by the participants indicating important factors leading to intention to use the PMRS. It would seem that the innovation factors explored might have to be compatibility with needs, values and past experiences, perceived enjoyment, perceived system quality and interactivity. For individual factors, perhaps gender, personal innovativeness and self-efficacy need to be selected. Another factor such as the environmental factor, that is the ability to collaborate, could also used. Some studies have suggested that children like to work and learn together and that group dynamics may play a role in their attitude towards the activity (e.g. [5], [8], etc.), thus, their attitude towards the ability to collaborate when using the programs could also be explored.

To get statistically-evidenced findings, we require a bigger sample of participants to investigate students' perception and acceptance of MXR systems for learning. To design the second study, we examined a number of theories developed to understand the adoption and diffusion of IT-based innovations. Among the key theories, the Technology Acceptance Model [6] has "emerged as the theory of choice", with many studies (424 journal articles as at January 2000) citing the original TAM research paper [6]. It has been proven to be a simple and yet powerful model in predicting acceptance.

Based on findings (that is, feedback given as shown in Table 1) from the pilot study and other studies (e.g. [1], etc.), the following factors selected for the second study were:

- *Perceived enjoyment:* This is defined as the "extent to which the activity of using a specific system is perceived to be enjoyable in its own right, aside from any performance consequences" (see Table 1, Feedback #5-7).
- *Cognitive absorption:* This construct is defined as "a state of deep involvement with software" that consists of five dimensions, namely temporal dissociation, focused immersion, heightened enjoyment, control and curiosity " (see Table 1, Feedback #4-6).
- *System quality:* This is known as "perception on how well the system performs tasks that match with job goals", thus quality can refer to quality of output or information produced by the system " (see Table 1, Feedback #8-12).
- *Personal innovativeness:* This refers to "the willingness of an individual to try out any new information technology" " (see Table 1, Feedback #1).
- *Compatibility:* This is the "degree to which an innovation is perceived as being consistent with the existing values, needs, and past experiences of potential adopters" " (see Table 1, Feedback #1).
- *Self-efficacy:* This is "the belief that one has the capability to perform a particular behaviour". " (see Table 1, Feedback #2).
- *Social influence:* This is a "person's perception that most people who are important to him think he should or should not perform the behaviour in question". " (see Table 1, Feedback #3).

## 7 Conclusion and Future Work

In recent years, more user studies were being carried out on MXR systems. For example, Mikropoulos, Chalkidis, Katsikis, and Emvalotis (1998) [12] investigated the attitudes of students towards educational virtual environments and the peripheral devices. In a more recent example, Shin [19] conducted a user study for an educational VR system for earth science. It was very specific to the system and did not employ any formal evaluation model.

This paper describes a pilot study in an attempt to investigate participants' perceptions of usefulness and usability of our developed PMRS, designed for primary school children (11-12 years old). Preliminary results seemed to indicate participants' intention to use PMRS for learning. However, it is possible that overall positive impression of anything high-tech could affect users' responses. Hence, long-term effects should be investigated, that is, whether experience can affect people's attitudes and behavioural intention towards such systems. Users' criteria for evaluation could evolve as they become more familiar with such technology. For example, they may demand more sophisticated graphics and more novel and varied ways of interacting with the system.

Based on findings from this pilot study, we formulated a second study based on the Technology Acceptance Model, and discuss the probable constructs/factors that are important to investigate intention to use and acceptance of MXR systems for education.

Future work includes carrying out the second study on the PMRS using a modified TAM, with more students and teachers performing different tasks.

**Acknowledgements.** We would like to thank the participants for taking in the study, and Ministry of Education for funding the development of the Plant Mixed Reality System, and NTU's AcRF grant (RG8/03) for funding the pilot study.

## References

1. Agarwal, R., Karahanna, E.: Time flies when you're having fun: Cognitive absorption and beliefs about information technology. MIS Quarterly 24(4), 665–694 (2000)
2. Bakas, C., Mikropoulos, T. A.: Design of virtual environments for the comprehension of planetary phenomena based on students' ideas. In: International Journal of Science Education, vol. 25(8)
3. Bricken, M., Byrne, C.M.: Summer students in virtual reality: A pilot study on educational applications of virtual reality technology. http://www.hitl.washington.edu/publications/r-92-1/.
4. Campbell, B., Collins, P., Hadaway, H., Hedley, N., Stoermer, M.: Web3D in ocean science learning environments: Virtual big beef creek. In: Proc. 3D Web technology (2002)
5. Chin, C., Kayalvizhi, G.: What do pupils think of open science investigations? A study of Singaporean primary 6 pupils. Educational Research, vol. 47(1) (2005) (Retrieved May 10, 2006, from Ebscohost)
6. Davis, F.D.: Perceived usefulness, perceived ease of use, and user acceptance of information technology. MIS Quarterly, vol. 13(3) (1989) (Retrieved May, 10, 2006, from Ebscohost)
7. Druin, A.: The role of children in the design of new technology. (2002) (Retrieved May 10, 2006) from ftp://ftp.cs.umd.edu/pub/hcil/Reports-Abstracts-Bibliography/99-23html/ 99-23.html
8. Gillies, R.M.: The behaviors, interactions, and perceptions of junior high school students during small-group learning. Journal of Educational Psychology, vol. 95(1). (2003) Retrieved May 10, 2006, from Ebscohost.
9. Dewey's, J.: Theories of Education http://www.marxists.org/archive/novack/works/1960/x03.htm
10. Jenkins, H., Klopfer, E., Aquire, K., Tan, P.: Entering the Education Arcade. Computers in Entertainment 1, 1(17) (2003)

11. Leow, M.C.L.: Exploring effectiveness of augmented reality for learning geometry in primary schools: A case study. Unpublished masters thesis, Nanyang Technological University, Singapore (2005)
12. Mikropoulos, T.A., Chalkidis, A., Katsikis, A., Emvalotis, A.: Students' attitudes towards educational virtual environments. Education and Information Technologies 3, 137–148 (1998)
13. Milgram, P., Kishino, F.: A taxonomy of mixed reality virtual displays. IEICE Transactions on Information and Systems E77-D 9 (1994)
14. Ministry of Education. Primary Science Syllabus. (2001) (Retrieved March 10, 2006) from http://www.moe.gov.sg/cpdd/doc/Science_Pri.pdf.
15. Pair, J., Piepol, D.: FlatWorld: A Mixed Reality Environment for Education and Training, Invited presentation at SCI2002 session on Gaming and role play in VR and Augmented Reality (2002)
16. Pan, Z., Cheok, A.D., Yang, H., Zhu, J., Shi, J.: Virtual reality and mixed reality for virtual learning environments. Computers & Graphics 30, 20–28 (2006)
17. Pasqualotti, A., Freitas, C.M.: MAT3D: a virtual reality modeling language environment for the teaching and learning of mathematics. CyberPsychology & Behavior 5(5), 409–422 (2002)
18. Shelton, B.E., Hedley, N.R.: Using augmented reality for teaching Earth-Sun relationships to undergraduate geography students, Augmented Reality Toolkit. In: The First IEEE International Workshop 2002 (2002)
19. Shin, Y. S.: Virtual experiment environments design for science education. In: Proc. Int'l Conference on Cyberworlds 2003, IEEE Computer Society, pp. 388–395 (2003)
20. Slator, B.M., Clark, J.T., Daniels, L.M., Hill, C., McClean, P., Saini-Eidukat, B., Schwert, D.P., White, A.R.: Use of virtual worlds to teach the sciences. In Series on Innovative Intelligence. In: Virtual Environments for Teaching and Learning, vol. 1, pp. 1–35. World Scientific Publishing, Singapore (2002)
21. Stanton, D., et al.: Classroom collaboration in the Design of Tangible Interfaces for Storytelling. In: Proc. CHI 2001, pp. 482–489. ACM Press, New York (2001)
22. Theng, Y.L., Goh, D., Lim, E.P., Liu, Z.H., Ming, Y., Pang, L.S., Wong, B.B.: Applying Scenario-Based Design and Claims Analysis on the Design of a Digital Library of Geography Examination Resources. Information Processing and Management Journal 41, 23–40 (2005)
23. Theng, Y.L., Mohd-Nasir, N., Buchanan, G., Fields, B., Thimbleby, H.: Dynamic digital libraries for children. In: Proceedings of the 1st ACM/IEEE-CS Joint Conference on Digital Libraries. Retrieved May 15, 2006, from ACM Digital Library (2000)
24. Venkatesh, V.: Creation of favorable user perceptions: Exploring the role of intrinsic motivation. MIS Quarterly 23(2), 239–260 (1999)
25. Woods, E., et al.: Augmenting the Science Centre and Museum Experience. In: Proc. of the 2nd international conference on computer graphics and interactive techniques in Australasia and South East Asia, 2004, pp. 230–236 (2004)
26. Yeo, K.K.J., Goh, S.K.E., Koh, E.Z.F.: Exploring plan and elevation geometry with ProDesktop. Journal of Science and Mathematics Education in Southeast Asia. 28(1), 125–136 (2005)

# User Studies of a Multiplayer First Person Shooting Game with Tangible and Physical Interaction

ZhiYing Zhou, Jefry Tedjokusumo, Stefan Winkler, and Bingbing Ni

Interactive Multimedia Lab
Department of Electrical and Computer Engineering
National University of Singapore (NUS)
Singapore 117576
{elezzy,elejt,winkler,g0501096}@nus.edu.sg

**Abstract.** In this paper, we present a new immersive first-person shooting (FPS) game. Our system provides an intuitive way for the users to interact with the virtual world by physically moving around the real world and aiming freely with tangible objects. This encourages physical interaction between the players as they compete or collaborate with each other.

**Keywords:** First Person Shooter, Virtual Reality, Augmented Reality, Physical Interaction, Tangible User Interface.

## 1 Introduction

First Person Shooting (FPS) games are a popular computer game genre. FPS games require a high accuracy of aiming, which is currently provided by the mouse [1]. This traditional method lacks physical and social interaction.

In this paper we present a new implementation of multiplayer FPS games. In our system, the players wear a Head Mounted Display (HMD) with head tracking, and carry a wand in their hand that is also tracked (see Figure 1). With these tracking devices we change the way multiplayer FPS games are played. The player's position and viewing direction are tracked by the head tracker. The wand's orientation corresponds to the gun aiming orientation in the game. As a result, shooting and viewing directions can be different in our system.

The game is played in a rectangular room without obstacles (see Figure 1). We place game items (health, armor, weapon, bullets) in the corners of the room. The player must physically walk to these locations to collect the items. The game style is "death match", which means the players shoot each other until their opponent's health reaches zero. The winner is the one with the most kills. The game style can be easily changed to support more than two players, so there can also be a collaboration component, e.g. battle between two groups.

The paper is structured as follows. In Section 2 we introduce previous related work on FPS games. Section 3 describes our system setup. Section 4 discusses

R. Shumaker (Ed.): Virtual Reality, HCII 2007, LNCS 4563, pp. 738–747, 2007.

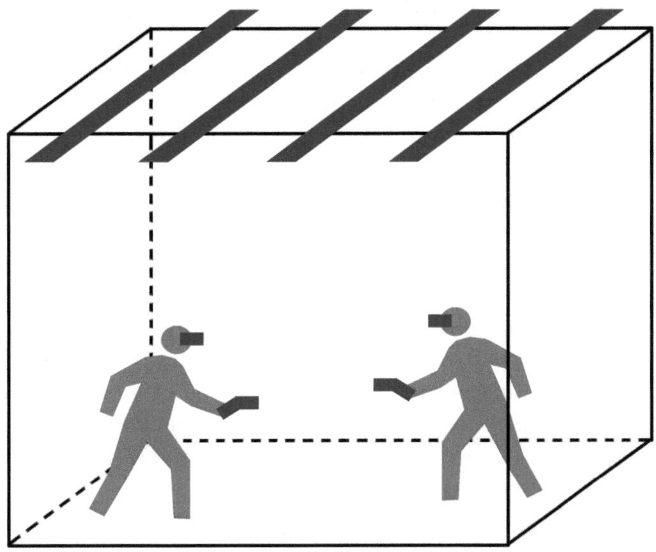

**Fig. 1.** Game environment

the implementation of our system. In Section 5 we evaluate our system by means of a user study. In section 6 we conclude our paper and discuss possible future work.

## 2 Related Work

CAVE Quake [2] provided a great tangible user interface for FPS. CAVE is a 10x10x10 foot "cube" with images projected onto 3 walls and the floor. The player stands in the center, and the CAVE renders the virtual world in front, left, right, and bottom of the player. The player aims the gun using his hand as in the real world. The player typically uses a joystick to move around the virtual world. CaveUT [3] is a similar system; however, it is built using low-priced hardware equipment (around US$ 25.000) compared to CAVE Quake which requires million dollar equipment. Our system differs in the way virtual world is presented. Instead of using projection on walls, we attach a tracking device to the HMD so that the user receives updated first-person views whenever he moves.

ARQuake [4] is a single-player mixed-reality FPS. The player in ARQuake has the freedom to move around the world, but the gun aiming is limited to the center of the view of the Head Mounted Display (HMD), which means the aiming is done by the player's head rather than the player's hand. This is unintuitive, and it is difficult to aim accurately using the head while evading enemies. The game was initially designed as a single player game, so it has no interactivity with other human player. Though this game can be extended to support multiple players, the tracking systems that are used (GPS and markers) are meant for outdoors. Therefore, ARQuake may have accuracy problems to determine whether a bullet shot from one player has actually hit another player. Human Pacman [5] is another example of an outdoor augmented reality game. However, as it is also using GPS for tracking, it suffers from the same accuracy problem as ARQuake. Our system (InterSense IS900) is an indoor system with much higher tracking precision, which is essential for FPS games.

Touch-Space [6] is an indoor mixed-reality game that is situated in a room-size space, using a high accuracy ultrasonic tracking system from InterSense similar to ours. It has 3 stages: physical land exploration, virtual land exploration, and virtual castle exploration. The stages range from augmented reality to virtual reality. Our system differs from Touch-Space in that we add more physical interaction components, for example, collecting armor by moving close to virtual armor boxes, or jumping to avoid bullets. Furthermore, we implement a popular FPS game which involves intensive competition between users, while the tasks in Touch-Space require collaboration.

Beckhaus et al. [1] proposed ChairIO and a Game Gun as new control devices for FPS games. The ChairIO is basically a chair that tilts. The tilt is used to control the movement of the virtual character in the game (forward, backward, left, and right). The ChairIO also support jumping (by bouncing from the chair). However, the user is constrained to sitting on the chair; hence physical movements are very limited. Our system offers free body movements by using wireless trackers. Users can move freely within the room and even jump to avoid bullets. In Beckhaus' work, the gun aiming is done by the Game Gun, which is also limited to the center of the screen, i.e. the game view will always follow the gun's orientation. A similar game controller concept is used in GameRunner [7]. However, in physical life, the user's viewpoint does not necessarily follow the gun. Our solution of separating the views offers a new approach for FPS games.

Table 1 summarizes the comparison between our system and the others. Our system provides an intuitive and tangible controller in the virtual world and at the same time maintains collaborative/competitive physical interaction between

**Table 1.** Feature comparison of immersive game systems

| System Name | Weapon Aiming Method | Virtual Character's Movement | Accuracy | Ability to Shoot Outside the View Range | Physical Interaction between Players |
|---|---|---|---|---|---|
| CAVEQUAKE | Hand | Joystick | High | None | None |
| CAVEUT | Hand | Joystick | High | None | None |
| ARQUAKE | Head | Player's Movement | Low | None | None |
| ChairIO + Gun | Hand | Tilting the chair | High | None | None |
| Game Runner | Handlebar | Treadmill | High | None | None |
| Human Pacman | Not Applicable | Player's Movement | Low | Not Applicable | Yes |
| Touch Space | Hand | Player's Movement | High | None | Yes |
| ***Our System*** | ***Hand*** | ***Player's Movement*** | ***High*** | ***Yes*** | ***Yes*** |

the players. The novelty lies in the ability to aim and shoot other players outside the field of view.

## 3 System

Our system consists of a game engine and an ultrasonic tracking system (InterSense IS900) with a high accuracy (2-3 mm for position and 0.25 deg −0.4 deg for orientation). Its coverage is limited to the space below the sensors, but it can easily be extended by adding more sensors. The tracking system covers a space of $2 \times 4\text{m}^2$ (see Figure 1). The tracking system is connected to a computer (the tracking server), which sends UDP packets containing tracking data (position and orientation) to the tracking clients at a rate of 90 Hz (see Figure 2).

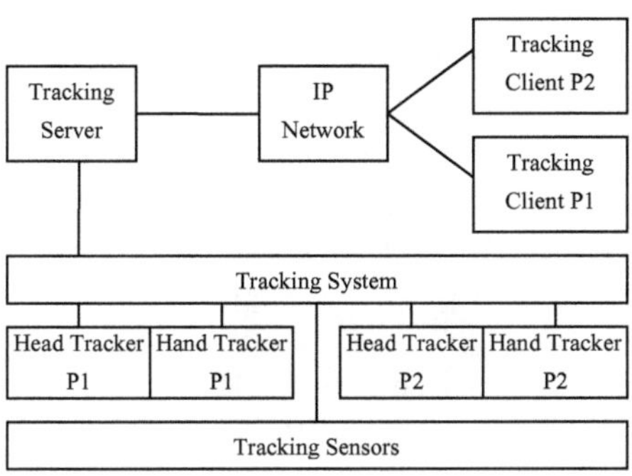


**Fig. 2.** Tracking system

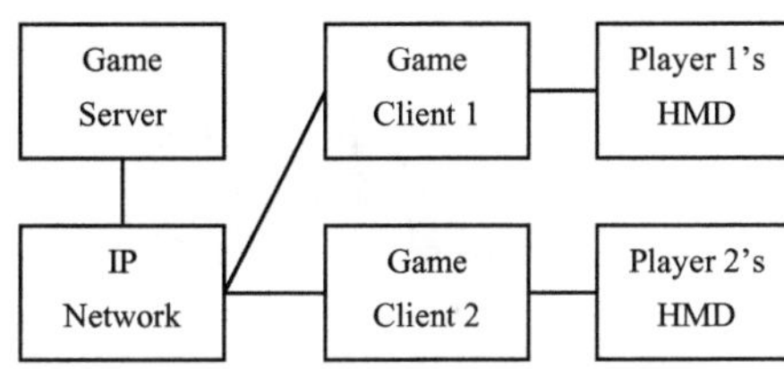


**Fig. 3.** Game system

We use the Cube engine [8], an open source game engine written in C++. The Cube engine has a built-in world editor and supports .md2 models. It supports multiple clients through a client-server architecture. In our implementation we use one server and two clients. Each client does the rendering and sends the result into the player's HMD. The server only receives the information of the client's position, orientation, and action. Then the server broadcasts the information to all other clients (see Figure 3).

We implement the system with 4 trackers for 2 players, as each player needs 2 tracking devices (1 head tracker and 1 wand tracker). The head tracker is mounted on the Head Mounted Display (HMD) to track the player's head position and orientation. The game engine renders the virtual environment based on this information. The wand tracker acts as a gun and is used by the player to aim the weapon in game. The player's HMD displays the image as shown in Figure 4. The small window in the bottom right is the gun radar that shows the gun view. With this gun radar, the player can aim and shoot in any direction inside or outside his own field of view. This adds an element of excitement, as the player can aim and shoot the enemy at his back. The white dot

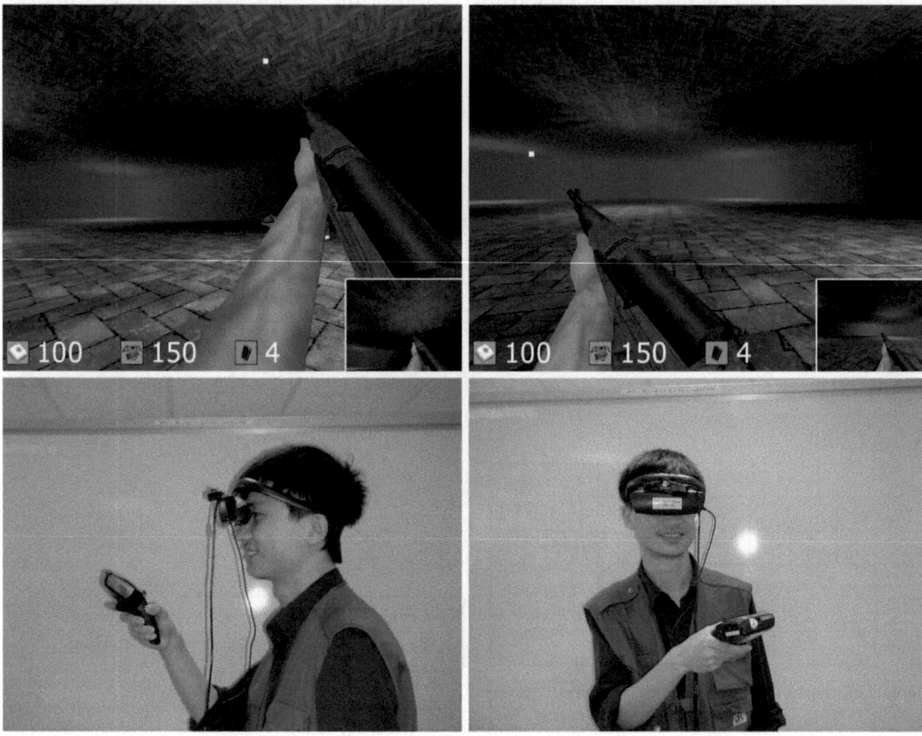


(a) (b)

**Fig. 4.** In-game screenshots and corresponding player poses

in Figure 4 is the weapon pointer. The weapon pointer helps the player aim accurately.

# 4 Implementation

## 4.1 Calibration

The first step to integrate the tracking system and the game engine is calibration. Figure 5(a) shows the real-world coordinate system of the tracking system (where the players move), Figure 5(b) shows the coordinate system of the wand tracker, and Figure 5(c) shows the virtual-world coordinate system of the game engine (where the virtual characters move). The z-axis in the real world points in the opposite direction of the z-axis in the virtual world. The game engine defines yaw as rotation around the z-axis, pitch as rotation around the y-axis, and roll as rotation around the x-axis.

We calibrate the hand tracker to give yaw, pitch, and roll values of 0 when the axes align as in Figure 5(a) and 5(b). Calibrating the position is simple. Because

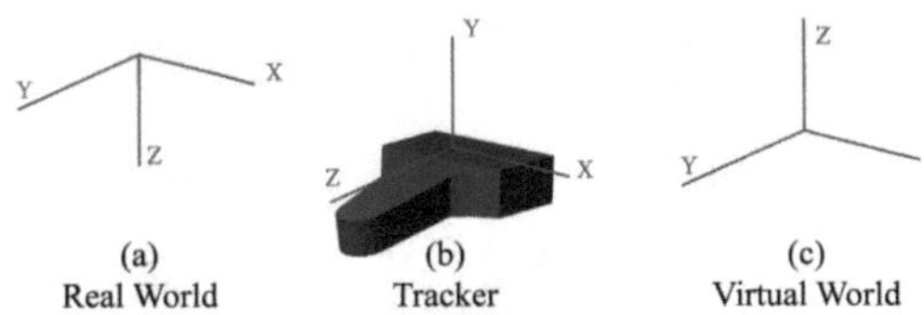


**Fig. 5.** Coordinate systems

the x-axes and the y-axes of the real and the virtual world are aligned, we only need to adjust the scaling.

### 4.2 Weapon Orientation

Like most game engines, the Cube engine's weapon orientation is pointing to the center of the screen and is tied to the player's view. To make the weapon orientation independent of the player's view, we add new variables for yaw, pitch, and roll of the weapon. We render the weapon's orientation according to the data that we get from the wand tracker. This feature is illustrated in Figure 4. Note that we assume the weapon's position to be the same as the head position.

### 4.3 Gun Radar

The Gun Radar (a small window that shows the weapon's point of view) is one of the important features of our system (cf. Figure 4). This radar makes it possible to aim and shoot accurately in an arbitrary direction (even if it is out of the player's view). To render this Gun Radar we create a new view port. In this view port we align the player's position and orientation to the gun's position and orientation. Then we render the virtual world in the view port. After that we restore the orientation and the position of the player. Note that the center view of the gun radar becomes the target point.

### 4.4 Weapon Pointer

The weapon pointer is designed like a laser pointer. It shows the position where the bullet will hit the target. This feature facilitates aiming in the virtual world. It is dependent on the gun radar. We need the z-value of the pixel in the center of the Gun Radar (the target point), which can be read from the z-buffer. Then we have the x, y, and z coordinates of the target point in the frustum. We multiply this point with the inverse projection matrix to get the target point in the game engine's world coordinates. We draw a transparent red dot to mark this area.

### 4.5 Jumping

If the player jumps in the real world, the virtual character in the virtual world will also jump. To achieve this, we detect the delta-z from the head tracker; if it is

**Fig. 6.** Jumping

greater than a certain threshold, we make the player's avatar jump. This feature can be useful to dodge enemy bullets. It also encourages physical movement. Figure 6 illustrates this feature.

## 5 Evaluation

We conducted an informal user study with 30 students (25 males and 5 females). Their age ranged from 19 to 29 years. We conducted 15 sessions of 3 minutes each, in which 2 persons played against each other in a death match battle. For comparison, we also asked them to try the traditional version of the game using keyboard and mouse. After they had tried both interfaces, we asked them to answer the questionnaire. Most of the questions are comparisons between our system and the traditional FPS computer interface. The respondents have to answer on a scale from 1 (prefer traditional implementation) to 7 (prefer immersive system).

We also included some introductory questions to find out about their experience with computers and FPS games. 11 of them had been using computers for more than 10 years, and 23 of them had played FPS games before. The first question was "How would you categorize your self as an FPS gamer?" They have to answer on a scale from 1 (beginner) to 7 (expert). The results are shown in Figure 7. The mean is 3.04. Then we asked how often they play FPS games. The results are shown in Figure 8. Most of them answered "several times" (14 persons).

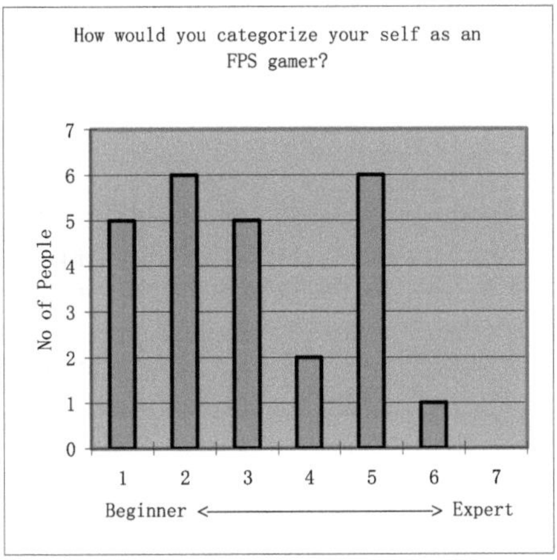


**Fig. 7.** Skill in playing FPS games

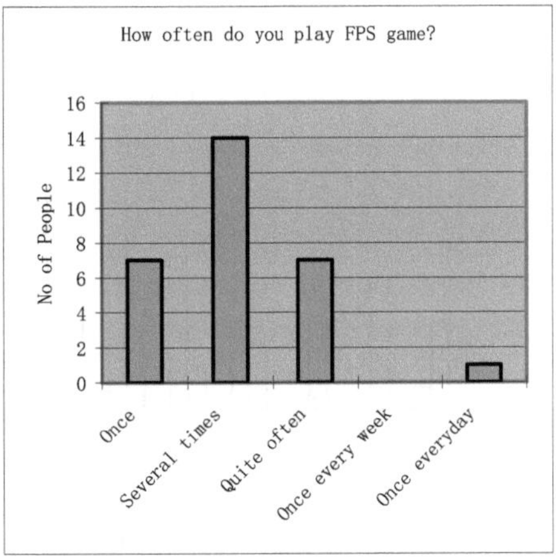


**Fig. 8.** Frequency of playing FPS games

HMD's are not suitable for long-term use. Playing games with an HMD for more than 15 minutes can cause dizziness in some people. A computer screen is generally better for long continuous game play. We wanted to evaluate how comfortable the HMD was for short-term use (3 minutes). The results on a scale from 1 (computer screen preferred) to 7 (HMD preferred) are shown in Figure 9. The mean is 4.43, indicating that our participants are quite comfortable with the HMD.

We also asked the participants to compare the mouse and the wand in terms of accuracy as well as excitement on a scale from 1 (mouse better) to 7 (wand better). The results are shown in Figure 10. The mean is 3.93 for accuracy and

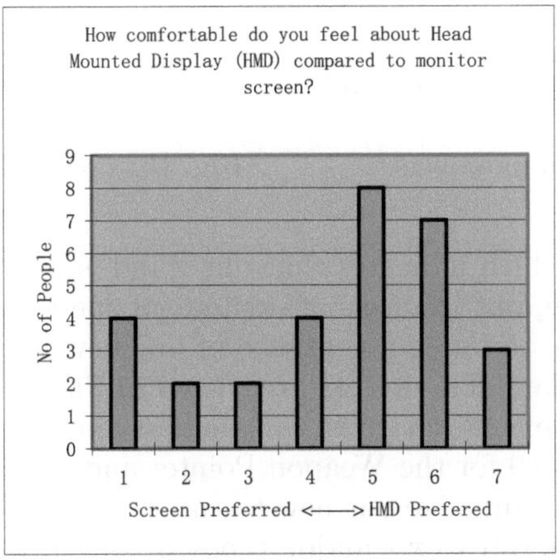


**Fig. 9.** Comfort of HMD

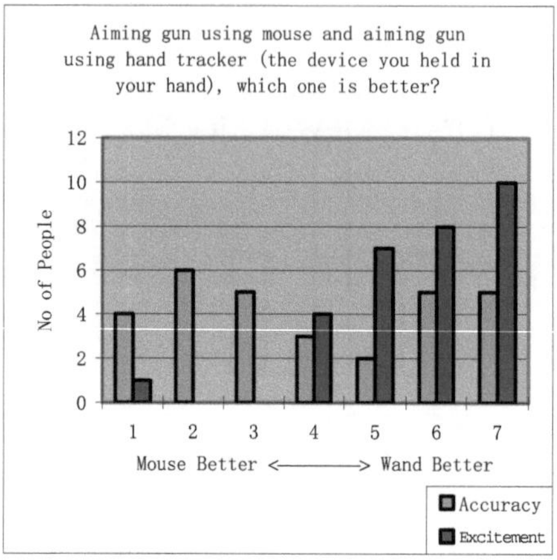


**Fig. 10.** Mouse vs. hand tracker

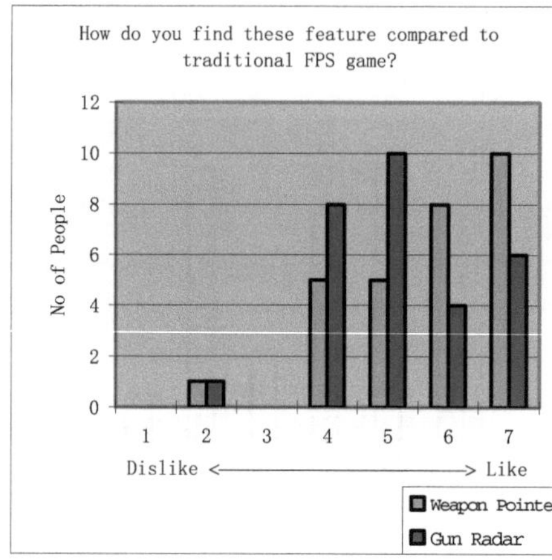


**Fig. 11.** Weapon Pointer and Gun Radar features

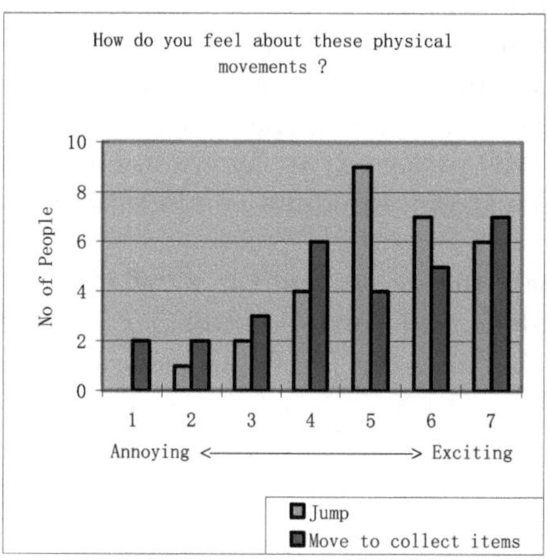


**Fig. 12.** Physical movement

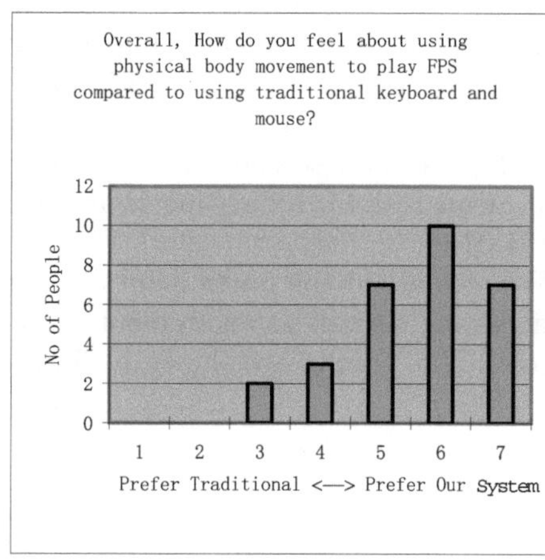


**Fig. 13.** Comparison of interactions

5.66 for excitement, which indicates that our wand is perceived to be about as accurate as the mouse, but in terms of excitement the wand is preferred.

We also investigate the user acceptance of our new game features (Weapon Pointer and Gun Radar). The results are shown in Figure 11 on a scale from 1 (dislike) to 7 (like). From the chart we can see that most answers are 4 or higher. The mean answer is 5.69 for the Weapon Pointer and 5.17 for Gun Radar. This shows that the participants like our new features.

Our system incorporates two major types of physical movements, namely jumping to dodge bullets, and moving to a particular location to collect certain items (health, armor, bullets, etc). We wanted to know how users feel about these physical movements. Figure 12 shows the results on a scale from 1 (very annoying) to 7 (very exciting). The mean answer is 5.28 for jumping and 4.76 for moving to collect items. This shows that physical movements are well liked by the users. Jumping gives more excitement than just moving around by walking.

In the last question we asked "Overall, How do you feel about using physical body movement to play FPS compared to using traditional keyboard and mouse?" The results are shown in Figure 13 on a scale from 1 (prefer traditional interface) to 7 (prefer our system). The mean answer for this question is 5.59, which shows that our system is significantly more attractive than the traditional keyboard and mouse interface for FPS gaming.

## 6 Conclusion and Future Work

We have built an immersive system for FPS games using an ultrasonic tracking system. The system encourages tangible and physical interactions between players, especially in a tense competitive situation. It allows users to move about and look around freely while aiming at targets using a gun-like handheld device. We use a novel way to present the user's view and the gun's view separately. Jumping is also tracked so that the user has more options to avoid the bullets. Our user study shows that people enjoy our system more than the traditional computer-based FPS interface on many levels.

## References


1. Beckhaus, S., Blom, K.J., Haringer, M.: A new gaming device and interaction method for a first-person-shooter. In: Proc. Computer Science and Magic, Leipzig, Germany 2005 (2005)
2. Rajlich, P.: CAVE Quake II. `http://brighton.ncsa.uiuc.edu/~prajlich/caveQuake/`
3. Jacobson, J., Lewis, M.: Game engine virtual reality with CaveUT. Computer 38(4), 79–82 (2005)
4. Thomas, B., Close, B., Donoghue, J., Squires, J., Bondi, P.D., Piekarski, W.: First person indoor/outdoor augmented reality application: ARQuake. Personal Ubiquitous Computing, vol. 6 (2002)
5. Cheok, A.D., Fong, S.W., Goh, K.H., Yang, X., Liu, W., Farzbiz, F.: Human Pacman: A sensing-based mobile entertainment system with ubiquitous computing and tangible interaction. In: Proc. NetGames (Workshop on Network and System Support for Games), Redwood City, CA,2003 pp. 106–117 (2003)
6. Cheok, A.D., Yang, X., Zhou, Z.Y., Billinghurst, M., Kato, H.: Touch-space: Mixed reality game space based on ubiquitous, tangible, and social computing. Personal Ubiquitous Computing 6(5-6), 430–442 (2002)
7. GameRunner. `http://www.gamerunner.us/`
8. Cube Engine. `http://www.cubeengine.com/`

# Plant Modeling and Its Application in Digital Agriculture Museum

Tonglin Zhu[1], Yan Zhou[1], Hock Soon Seah[3], Feng Tian[3], and Xiaolong Yan[2]

[1] College of Information, South China Agicultureal Univ.,
[2] Root Biology Center, South China Agriculture Univ.,
[3] School of Computer Engineering, Nanyang Technological Univ.
{tlzhu}@scau.edu.cn

**Abstract.** This paper presents a 3D plant morpha modeling method based on projection image, and analyzes the influence calibration error on the precision of reconstruction. Mini-section algorithm and Ball B-spline are used to extract the skeleton of the reconstructed image and to fit the meshes respectively. The experiment shows that this method is high-speed and robust, and the reconstructed root, branch, haulm that are columnar is very vivid,. So it indicates that we can achieve a simple and practical plant modeling method that transforms image of entities to surface meshes of plant. And it is helpful for plant morpha digitization and visualization in agriculture digital museum.

**Keywords:** Plant modeling, Geometric modeling, Digital museum.

## 1 Introduction

Digital museum, which is different from traditional museum, carries out exhibition, preservation, education, research and so on, through network in forms of multimedia objects such as WebPages, animation, and video clips. This multimedia information is obtained by digitizing all kinds of entities through high-resolution scanner, digital shoot, and 3-demention (3D) modeling and so on, while it has no entitative exhibition space. Digital museum plays an important role in the fields of resource management, sharing, preservation, education, and scientific research.

Internationally, the digitization of museum has developed remarkably so far. Several museum institutes in P.R.China's main-land and Taiwan have done some excellent work [1], [2]. Most of the digital museums described above emphasize particularly on antique, archaeology, geology and geography etc, and few of them are in terms of agriculture or biology. The digitization of agriculture museum is important for resource sharing, data preservation of agriculture research. Digital agricultural museum of China and digital museum of biology developed by Sun Yat-Sen University [3] have done a lot of pioneering work for digitization of agriculture and biology museum, which provides researchers with abundant network resource and promotes the development of agriculture and biology research. Whereas there is still a lot of work to do about agriculture museum and there are some shortcomings of the existing digital museums. For example, digital museums opened in internet didn't

R. Shumaker (Ed.): Virtual Reality, HCII 2007, LNCS 4563, pp. 748–757, 2007.

make best use of multimedia technology, and there were only static images besides letters, which made the website look bald and unattractive; the small capacity of information of the museum website, and lack of deep level knowledge of multimedia information can't meet the requirement of teaching and research; not use the advanced data compression, transmission and decompression technology and so on.

3D laser scanning technology is the basis of digitization of entities model, so applying 3D modeling technology into museum digitization is a good idea as well. Now, we mainly do research and experiment on 3D modeling of plant root morpha, expecting to apply this technology to museum digitization as well as to various plant growth modeling to construct dynamic model of plants. 3D modeling of plant can compress the data through parameterizing the model and only storing a few mopha parameters, which makes the result more vivid by rendering, texture processing technology and so on. So plant morphological modeling technology plays an important role in the digitization of museums. On the other hand, plant shape is intricate and the plant branches shelter from each other, so the modeling is very difficult and it's a challenge to do it. This paper is organized as follows. Section 2 discusses the principle of 3D modeling based on images and analysis of the precision of the algorithm. Section 3 introduces the mini-section based on skeleton extraction algorithm and Ball B-spline based on mesh generation algorithm. Section 4 shows part of the results and some related images. Section 5 gives conclusions and future works.

## 2 A Fast 3D Reconstruction Algorithm and Precision Analysis

### 2.1 Algorithm Review

Main facilities of the 3D reconstruction system are showed in Fig.1, including two CCD cameras with synchronous image capture card, two electric rotary tables with digital control, a PC, corresponding self-design software and some assistant tools such as equipments for calibration. Before reconstruction, some preparative should be done first, such as the calibration of internal and external parameters of the CCD camera, obtaining of images through the CCD camera rotating around the object, at last the binary conversion of the images, while these steps are introduced in detail in [4]and [5].This paper mainly gives the principle of the 3D reconstruction algorithm in detail. Considering that the plant mainly consists of columnar organs such as root, branch, haulm, we take a segment of root for example to analyze the reconstruction process and the principle. As shown in Fig2, the projections are approximate rectangle, while their inverse-image are cube-like sheets, thus the intrinsic of the algorithm is to work out the common cross part of the inverse-images. We can quantify common cross part to per centum, taking all common part as p=100%, and voting algorithm can also be used, which makes it easier to achieve the algorithm through programming, and makes the reconstructed result better and the algorithm more robust. The algorithm is the combo of working out the cross part and the voting algorithm, and we call it "Space Voting". It is reported that this reconstruction algorithm is about 10 times faster than the 'Space Carving [6]' in a common computer [5].

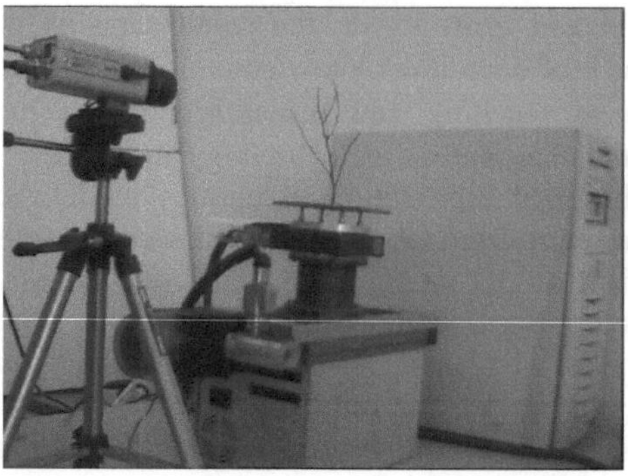

**Fig. 1.** The basic equipment of 3D reconstruction

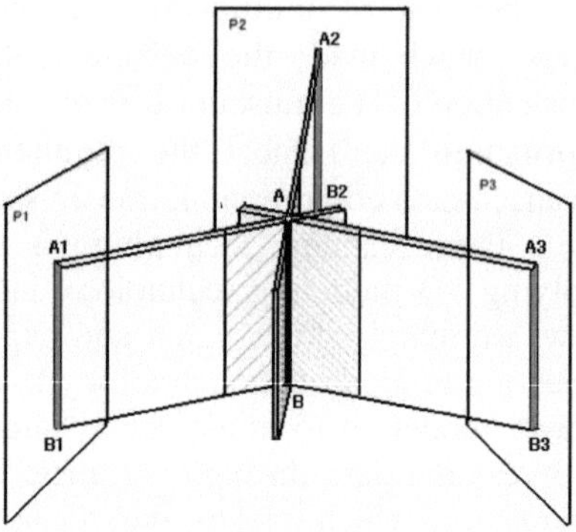


**Fig. 2.** The sketch map of 'Space Voting' principle

## 2.2 Precision Analysis

### 2.2.1 Hypothesis

In the calibration process, the foci ($f_x$, $f_y$) of the camera have been estimated. For convenience, the rotation platform coordinate system serves as the world coordinate system, with the Z direction towards the optical axis of the camera in the initial phase (see Fig.1). If the 3 planes of the camera coordinate system (XY plane, YZ plane, ZX plane) are not parallel with the corresponding planes of the rotation platform coordinate system, 3 spatial angles ($A_{XY}$, $A_{YZ}$ , $A_{ZX}$) should be calibrated. The coordinates of the origin of the camera coordinate system (before rotating) in the rotary stage coordinate system is($X_0$, $Y_0$). The distance between the optical center and the rotation axis is $Z_0$. The concrete research of camera calibration is beyond the scope of this paper.

Reconstruction accuracy of a small object is sensitive to calibration error, especially the error of external calibrated parameters of shift value ($X_0$,$Y_0$, $Z_0$)and rotating value($A_{XY}$, $A_{YZ}$ , $A_{ZX}$), so we have to estimate the error range correctly. Here, we use a plant figure whose root, branch and stem are columnar, and take a single little column for example to analyze the error. For the sake of simplicity, we don't consider the noise disturbance or uneven illumination. It is supposed that the radius of the little column is r while the height is h. Moreover, it is placed at the standard position that is placed vertically at the center of the rotation platform. Its central axis is superposed with the axis of the rotation platform. It is also supposed that the ratio v of reconstructed object volume to original object volume is regarded as its estimating accuracy. It is easy for us to imagine that when the camera rotates around the object in a circle and captures a series of images, the figure in the images are all rectangles, whose sizes are almost the same but only their positions are different. So their original images are some cubes, which are very much like "planks", placed at different positions. Strictly speaking, they are not exactly cubes as the front sides are slightly bigger than the back sides. These planks are of about 2r width, h height and 2L length. Their intersection near the rotating axis of the platform is the reconstructed result based on the matriculated voting ratio. The two kinds of error will be discussed in the following respectively. We assumed that the calibrated error is very small, because if the error is too big, the reconstructed result is very bad and has no significance.

### 2.2.2 Effect by Shift Error

It is assumed that all the calibrated errors of the above 8 parameters are 0 except $X_0$ which is equal to $\Delta x$ . It is also assumed we incorrectly consider that $X_0$ is zero, then when we reconstruct an object, intersect the planks in different directions, the thickness difference of each plank from left to right (according to the rotating axis) is $2\Delta x$ . One side is $(r+\Delta x)$ and the other is $(r-\Delta x)$ . The cross section is as showed in Fig. 3. In circle DCD, O is the rotation platform axis center while $O'$ is the axis center what we think mistakenly, $|OO'| = \Delta x$ . Thus when the camera rotates the platform along a circle, the binary image gained is always a rectangle, however, its central line has $\Delta x$ unit error comparing to y axis of the camera coordinate. When 'matriculated threshold' p is less than 100%, to any point X in the column, AMBN is the circumference whose center is O' and the one that passes X. As $|XO| = r_x$ , $\angle AO'B = 2\alpha$ , the vote ratio is:

$$p_x = \frac{arc(AMB)}{arc(AMBN)} = \frac{2\pi - 2\alpha}{2\pi} \tag{1}$$

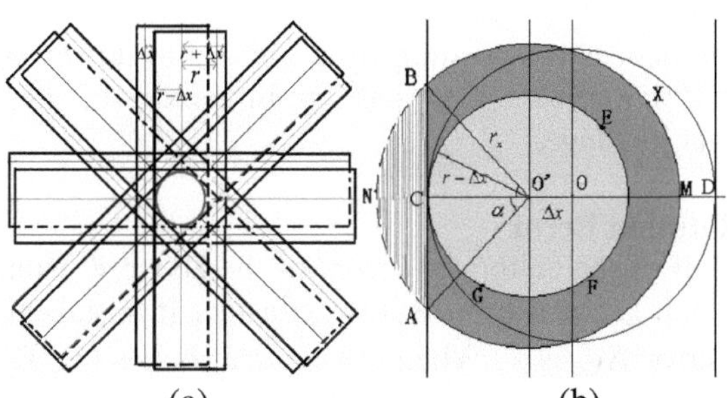

(a) (b)

**Fig. 3.** Sketch map of accuracy analyzing for shift error. (a) the cross section of intersection process of original images. (b) the cross section of the intersecting result.

The necessary condition of that Point X belongs to the reconstructed scenery pixel point set is $p_x \geq p$ , while the extreme case is that $p_x = p$ (or $\pi - \alpha = \pi p$ ) when the dotted line circle AMBN is the base circumference of the reconstructed column in Fig. 3. b. It can be seen from the figure that whose radius is:

$$r_x = \frac{r-\Delta x}{\cos\alpha} = \frac{r-\Delta x}{\cos(\pi - \pi p)} = \frac{r-\Delta x}{|\cos(\pi p)|} \tag{2}$$

Thus the accuracy of the volume is as the following:

$$v = \frac{(r-\Delta x)^2 \cdot h}{r^2 \cos^2(\pi p) \cdot h} = \frac{(r-\Delta x)^2}{r^2 \cos^2(\pi p)} \tag{3}$$

Specifically, when the 'matriculated threshold' $p$ is equal to 100%, after camera rotating round the object in a circle to intersect the original images, there is a little column left whose radius is $r-\Delta x$, as the circumference $EFG$ is showed as in Fig. 3b. Therefore, the accuracy of volume is as the following:

$$v = \frac{(r-\Delta x)^2 h}{r^2 h} = \frac{(r-\Delta x)^2}{r^2} \tag{4}$$

When $(r-\Delta x)^2 = r^2 \cos^2 \pi p$, that is

$$p = \arccos\left(\frac{r-\Delta x}{r}\right) \Big/ \pi \tag{5}$$

v is equal to 1, in this case, the column image reconstructed is as big as the original object. When $r-\Delta x < r \mid \cos \pi p \mid$, the column reconstructed becomes smaller until the radius is $r-\Delta x$ while $r-\Delta x > r \mid \cos \pi p \mid$, the column becomes bigger until the radius is $r+\Delta x$.

Obviously, the shift error $\Delta y$ of Y coordinate has no effect on reconstruction accuracy but just influences the position from upward to downward. Meanwhile, the shift error $\Delta z$ of Z coordinate also has no influence on the accuracy as it is reconstructed all over its range.

### 2.2.3 Effect by Rotation Error

It is supposed that all of the calibrated errors of the above 8 parameters are equal to zero except $A_{YZ}$ which is equal to $\gamma$. But we consider it mistakenly to be equal to 0. That is to say, the error $A_{YZ}$ is $\gamma$. When the camera rotates the object in a circle, the binary projected image is always a vertical rectangle whose base boundary is not horizontal but intersects with the horizontal in r angle, as is shown in Fig. 4. So when

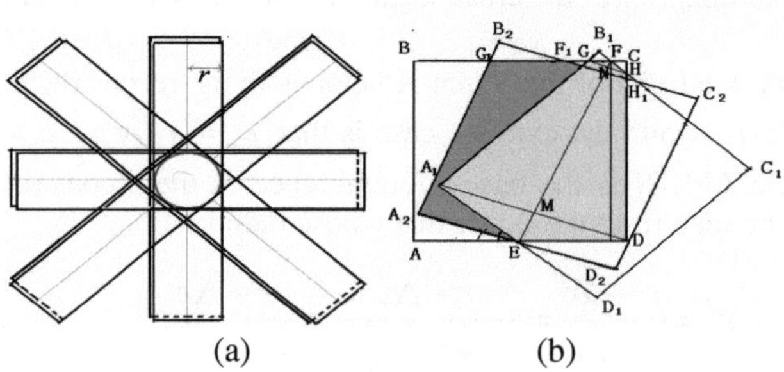


**Fig. 4.** This is the ketch map of accuracy analysis of rotation error. (a) is the cross section of the original images intersection. (b) is the vertical section of the intersecting result.

p is equal to 100%, we rotate the original images along a circle to intersect and the reconstructed images have two cones, one on the top of and the other at the bottom of a truncated cone.

The maximum vertical crossing section is the intersecting part of two rectangles ABCD and$A_1B_1C_1D_1$. That is graphic $A_1EDHFG$ in Fig. 4. And it is not difficult to analyze its radii in upper base and lower base, height. Then the volume of the whole solid of revolution is calculated. But its expression formula is quite complex. In fact, when r is very small, we use the volume of the circular truncated cone whose upper plane diameter is GH, lower plane diameter is $A_1D$ and height is h to replace the volume of the solid of revolution. Thus the error becomes very small.

$$V_1 \approx \frac{1}{2} h\pi[(\frac{r}{2}\cos\frac{\gamma}{2})^2 + (\frac{r}{2}\cos\frac{\gamma}{2} - h\sin\frac{\gamma}{2})^2 \Big/ \cos^2\gamma] \tag{6}$$

Because of the original column volume $V = r^2\pi h$ , according to Equation (6) we can get the reconstructed accuracy as the following formula:

$$V_1 = \frac{1}{2}(\cos^2\frac{\gamma}{2} + ((\cos\frac{\gamma}{2} - \frac{h}{r}\sin\frac{\gamma}{2}) / \cos\gamma)^2) \tag{7}$$

When $p$ is less than 100%, the reconstructed images are determined by the case of intersection of a series of planks that leaned in $\gamma$ angle. Suppose that the threshold of voting ratio is $p$ , then the intersection part of the projected images whose errors are not more than $p\gamma$ are matriculated as the scenery pixel points. Similar with the case when $p$ is equal to 100%, the reconstructed images are also two circular cones and a circular truncated cone whose maximum vertical plane is $A_2EDH_1F_1G_1$ as showed in Fig. 4. Its volume formula and accuracy formula are listed as following:

$$V \approx \frac{1}{2} h\pi(\frac{r}{2}\cos\frac{p\gamma}{2})^2 + \frac{1}{2} h\pi(\frac{r}{2}\cos\frac{p\gamma}{2} - h\sin\frac{p\gamma}{2}) / \cos^2 p\gamma \tag{8}$$

$$V_1 = \frac{1}{2}(\cos^2\frac{p\gamma}{2} + ((\cos\frac{p\gamma}{2} - \frac{h}{r}\sin\frac{p\gamma}{2}) / \cos(p\gamma))^2) \tag{9}$$

Obviously, the rotation error $\Delta A_{XY}$ in $XY$ plane, in practice, can be considered as the initial angle error $\Delta A_{XY}$ , which has no effect on reconstruction accuracy. But if there is error $\Delta A_{ZX}$ in plane $ZX$ , the planks should intersect with the same angle by leaning in every direction. Thus the reconstructed result is also not influenced but just moved in the vertical direction.

### 2.3 An Experiment for Calibrated Errors Effect

To test the above discussion, we select a simple but representative tree branch to do experiments repeatedly to see the effect of the calibrated error. Fig. 5 is the result of the effect of calibrated errors $\Delta x$ and $\Delta A_{YZ}$ on reconstruction accuracy.

**Fig. 5.** Comparing the effects of Calibration errors on reconstructed result of 'Space Voting'. (a) Original object image. (b) - (d) Less error $\Delta \approx 0$, p=60%, 80%, 100 %. (e) - (g) Shift error $\Delta X = 3mm$, p=60%, 80%, 100%. (h)- (j) Rotating error $\Delta A_{YZ} = 6^{\circ} c$. p=60%, 80%, 100%.

p is respectively equal to 60%, 80% and 100%. The diameter of the real branch is 8mm. We also carried out many similar tests for $\Delta y$ , $\Delta z$ , $\Delta A_{XY}$ and $\Delta A_{ZX}$ . The results are the same as the second group in Fig. 5. In the second group, the heights of the branches are the same and the size becomes smaller with the increasing 'matriculated threshold', which may be caused by a calibrated error. This indicates that the 'matriculated threshold' doesn't influence the accuracy under accurate calibration. The third group indicates that shift error, $\Delta x$ doesn't influence the column height and the column radius becomes smaller with the increasing matriculated threshold. We can, nevertheless, use a suitable 'matriculated threshold' to identify the diameter of a reconstructed column with that of a real object. The fourth group shows that despite of the rotating error $\Delta A_{YZ}$ , the reconstructed object looks like a shortened column with two cones on the top and at the bottom. The column radius becomes smaller with increasing matriculated threshold. Appropriate 'matriculated threshold' can keep the column shape and reduce errors. These experimental results confirm our previous theoretical conclusion that the shape of a reconstructed column remains unchanged while its diameter becomes smaller, when we only observe shift errors, that a reconstructed object is a shortened column with one cone on top and the other cone at the bottom, when we only observe rotating errors.

## 3 Skeleton Extraction and the Generation of Surface Meshes

Based on the 3D images reconstructed above, we can extract the skeleton of the plant; use the Ball B-spline to interpolate series of circles on the skeleton curve, then the points used to generate the meshes are sampled on the circles.

### 3.1 Review of Method for Skeleton Extraction

The reconstructed image is a set of unorganized points, so some special points that represent the topology of the plant must be distinguished, such as the base and tip of the plant. We consider the tip of the trunk branch as the Reference-Point (RP), the end of lateral branch as End-Point (EP), and other points on the trunk and lateral branch as Branch-Points (BP). RP and Bp determine the topology of the trunk branch, and EP and BP determine the topology of the lateral branch. For every branch, either trunk branch or lateral branch, we select a point as detecting point every certain length; determine a minimum cross-section of the branch passing through the detecting point by mini cross section algorithm [5]; the central point and the radius of the section is selected as skeleton point and the radius of the branch at this skeleton point respectively. Using this method the skeleton points and the corresponding radii of the whole plant can be extracted. This 'Minimum Cross Section' skeletonization algorithm is more effective to our 3D image than all traditional algorithms [7].

### 3.2 Review of Ball B-Spline for Meshes Generation

After the process described above, the skeleton points and their radius are extracted, and then the interpolation method can be used to generate the curve to indicate the skeleton curve and plant surface. In our experiment, the Multi-Knot Spline [8], [9] interpolation is used to get the skeleton curve. On the other hand, the Ball B-spline model [10], [11] can be used in Ball Multi-Knot Spline algorithm. Ball B-spline is extended from B spline, and it has good application in modeling of objects with arbitrary topology, like plants. The formulas of the Ball B-spline and Multi-knot Spline can be seen in [9].Using these formulas, the skeleton curve can be interpolated, based on which we can use Multi-knot Spline to interpolate series of circles, sample some mesh points uniformly on the circles, at last construct the surface meshes using the mesh points. The algorithm is discussed in detail in [12].

## 4 Experiment Result

Some models of different soybean root systems have been constructed, and experiment shows that both the skeletons and mesh models generated from our modeling method keep the topology of the original root perfectly. Original images and the result are shown in the Fig.6 and Fig7.

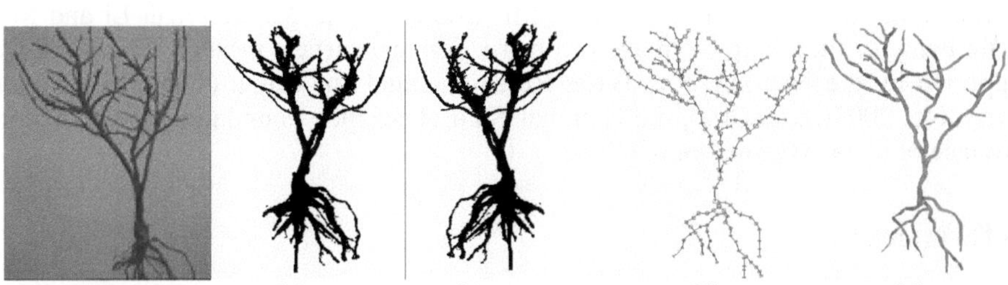

(a) (b) (c) (d) (e)

**Fig. 6.** Result of a privet seedling by 'Space Voting'. (a) the original image ; (b)-(c) two projections of reconstructed result with p=80%; (d)the skeleton model. (e) the surface meshes model.

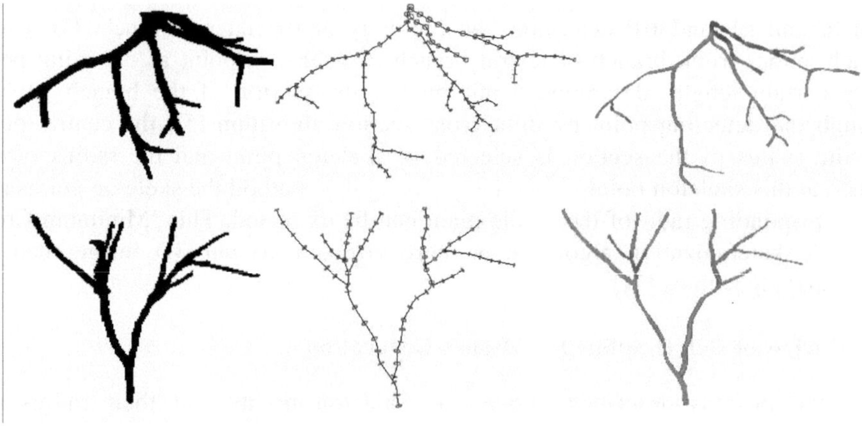

**Fig.7** The 3d reconstruction, skeleton, surface meshes of tree branches

## 5 Conclusion

This paper presents a key technology: a quick plant morphological modeling method based on images obtained through rotating the object. This modeling method consists of three key techniques, including 3D reconstruction, 3D skeleton extraction and surface meshes construction, which are based on columnar characteristics of the plant body. The principle of 3D reconstruction algorithm named "space voting" is to determine the common part of the inverse-images, while the skeleton extraction is based on Mini-cross section algorithm, and the surface meshes construction is based on Ball B-spline. These three algorithms are of lower calculation, higher-speed and strong maneuverability, as well as robust, so they are a set of effective and realistic modeling method, and can be applied to plant morphological digitization and parametric measurement with large-scale samples. Now, the camera calibration is not solved so well, though it influences the reconstructed result remarkably, thereby it influences the precision of skeleton extraction, and surface meshes generation. Thus the future work is to enhance the calibration precision or replace the reconstructed data with laser scan data, so that we can obtain better skeleton points and surface meshes.

**Acknowledgments.** The authors thank Mr. Zhongke Wu, Mr. Zhiyuan Li and Miss Suqin Fang for their help on image reconstruction and surface meshes. This work was supported by the National Key Basic Research Funds of China (The 973 program) (Grant No. 2005CB120902), the National Natural Science Foundation of Guangdong province of China (Grant No. 05006621).

## References

1. Chen, X., Qu, H., Luo, X., Chen, M., Zhang, Y., Hao, K., Mi, S.: The Progress of University Digital Museum Grid. In: Proceedings of the Fifth International Conference on Grid and Cooperative Computing Workshops 2006, pp. 78–85 (2006)
2. Tang, M.-C: Representational Practices in Digital Museums: A Case Study of the National Digital Museum Project of Taiwan. The. International Information & Library Review, 37(1), 51-60 (2005)

3. University Digital Museums. http://www.gzsums.edu.cn/2004/museum/
4. Zhu, T.L., Fang,S.Q., Li, Z.Y, et al.: A Generalized Hough Transform Theory and Its Applications in Computer Vision. Journal of Computational Information System 1(3), 601–607 (2005)
5. Zhu, T.L., Fang, S.Q., Li, Z.Y., et al.: Quantitative Analysis of 3-dimensional Root Architecture Based on Image Reconstruction and Its Application to Research on Phosphorus Uptake in Soybean. Chinese Science Bulletin 51(19), 2351–2361 (2006)
6. Kutulakos, K.N., Seitz, S.M.A: Theory of Shape by Space Carving. International Journal of Computer Vision 38(3), 3199–3218 (2000)
7. Tian, X., Han, G.Q, Li, Z.Y, et al.: 3D Skeletonization and Its Application in Plant Root Image Analysis [J]. Journal of Computational Information System 1(2), 2241–2246 (2005)
8. Qi, D.X., Ding, W., Li, H.S.: A new image Transformation Scheme and Digital Approximation between Different Pictures. Advances in Computational Mathematics, Lecture Notes in Pure and Applied Mathematics, Marcel Dekker Inc, pp. 465–469 (1999)
9. Huang, H., Qi, D.X., Tang, Z.S., et al.: Level of Details for Digital Image Based on Many-Knot Spline. Journal of information of computational science 1(1), 53–56 (2004)
10. Seah, H.S., Wu, Z.K., Tian, F., Xie, X.X., Lu, Y.X., Xiao, X.: Modeling and Visualization of Plants with Ball B-Spline. In: The International Workshop on Advanced Image Technology (IWAIT) 2007, Bangkok, Thailand January 8-9 2007 (2007)
11. Seah, H.S., Wu, Z.K.: Ball B-Spline Based Geometric Models in Distributed Virtual Environments. In Workshop towards Semantic Virtual Environments. SVE, Villars, Switzerland March 2005 (2005)
12. Zhu, T.L., Seah, H.S., Li, Z.Y., et al.: A Method for Modeling Plant Root Morphology Based on Ball Spline (to be appeared).

# Author Index

# Lecture Notes in Computer Science

For information about Vols. 1–4489

please contact your bookseller or Springer

Vol. 4537: K.C.-C. Chang, W. Wang, L. Chen, C.A. Ellis, C.-H. Hsu, A.C. Tsoi, H. Wang (Eds.), Advances in Web and Network Technologies, and Information Management. XXIII, 707 pages. 2007.

Vol. 4536: G. Concas, E. Damiani, M. Scotto, G. Succi (Eds.), Agile Processes in Software Engineering and Extreme Programming. XV, 276 pages. 2007.

Vol. 4534: I. Tomkos, F. Neri, J. Solé Pareta, X. Masip Bruin, S. Sánchez Lopez (Eds.), Optical Network Design and Modeling. XI, 460 pages. 2007.

Vol. 4531: J. Indulska, K. Raymond (Eds.), Distributed Applications and Interoperable Systems. XI, 337 pages. 2007.

Vol. 4530: D.H. Akehurst, R. Vogel, R.F. Paige (Eds.), Model Driven Architecture- Foundations and Applications. X, 219 pages. 2007.

Vol. 4529: P. Melin, O. Castillo, L.T. Aguilar, J. Kacprzyk, W. Pedrycz (Eds.), Foundations of Fuzzy Logic and Soft Computing. XIX, 830 pages. 2007. (Sublibrary LNAI).

Vol. 4528: J. Mira, J.R. Álvarez (Eds.), Nature Inspired Problem-Solving Methods in Knowledge Engineering, Part II. XXII, 650 pages. 2007.

Vol. 4527: J. Mira, J.R. Álvarez (Eds.), Bio-inspired Modeling of Cognitive Tasks, Part I. XXII, 630 pages. 2007.

Vol. 4526: M. Malek, M. Reitenspieß, A. van Moorsel (Eds.), Service Availability. X, 155 pages. 2007.

Vol. 4525: C. Demetrescu (Ed.), Experimental Algorithms. XIII, 448 pages. 2007.

Vol. 4524: M. Marchiori, J.Z. Pan, C.d.S. Marie (Eds.), Web Reasoning and Rule Systems. XI, 382 pages. 2007.

Vol. 4523: Y.-H. Lee, H.-N. Kim, J. Kim, Y. Park, L.T. Yang, S.W. Kim (Eds.), Embedded Software and Systems. XIX, 829 pages. 2007.

Vol. 4522: B.K. Ersbøll, K.S. Pedersen (Eds.), Image Analysis. XVIII, 989 pages. 2007.

Vol. 4521: J. Katz, M. Yung (Eds.), Applied Cryptography and Network Security. XIII, 498 pages. 2007.

Vol. 4519: E. Franconi, M. Kifer, W. May (Eds.), The Semantic Web: Research and Applications. XVIII, 830 pages. 2007.

Vol. 4517: F. Boavida, E. Monteiro, S. Mascolo, Y. Koucheryavy (Eds.), Wired/Wireless Internet Communications. XIV, 382 pages. 2007.

Vol. 4516: L. Mason, T. Drwiega, J. Yan (Eds.), Managing Traffic Performance in Converged Networks. XXIII, 1191 pages. 2007.

Vol. 4515: M. Naor (Ed.), Advances in Cryptology - EUROCRYPT 2007. XIII, 591 pages. 2007.

Vol. 4514: S.N. Artemov, A. Nerode (Eds.), Logical Foundations of Computer Science. XI, 513 pages. 2007.

Vol. 4513: M. Fischetti, D.P. Williamson (Eds.), Integer Programming and Combinatorial Optimization. IX, 500 pages. 2007.

Vol. 4511: C. Conati, K. McCoy, G. Paliouras (Eds.), User Modeling 2007. XVI, 487 pages. 2007. (Sublibrary LNAI).

Vol. 4510: P. Van Hentenryck, L. Wolsey (Eds.), Integration of AI and OR Techniques in Constraint Programming for Combinatorial Optimization Problems. X, 391 pages. 2007.

Vol. 4509: Z. Kobti, D. Wu (Eds.), Advances in Artificial Intelligence. XII, 552 pages. 2007. (Sublibrary LNAI).

Vol. 4508: M.-Y. Kao, X.-Y. Li (Eds.), Algorithmic Aspects in Information and Management. VIII, 428 pages. 2007.

Vol. 4507: F. Sandoval, A. Prieto, J. Cabestany, M. Graña (Eds.), Computational and Ambient Intelligence. XXVI, 1167 pages. 2007.

Vol. 4506: D. Zeng, I. Gotham, K. Komatsu, C. Lynch, M. Thurmond, D. Madigan, B. Lober, J. Kvach, H. Chen (Eds.), Intelligence and Security Informatics: Biosurveillance. XI, 234 pages. 2007.

Vol. 4505: G. Dong, X. Lin, W. Wang, Y. Yang, J.X. Yu (Eds.), Advances in Data and Web Management. XXII, 896 pages. 2007.

Vol. 4504: J. Huang, R. Kowalczyk, Z. Maamar, D. Martin, I. Müller, S. Stoutenburg, K.P. Sycara (Eds.), Service-Oriented Computing: Agents, Semantics, and Engineering. X, 175 pages. 2007.

Vol. 4501: J. Marques-Silva, K.A. Sakallah (Eds.), Theory and Applications of Satisfiability Testing – SAT 2007. XI, 384 pages. 2007.

Vol. 4500: N. Streitz, A. Kameas, I. Mavrommati (Eds.), The Disappearing Computer. XVIII, 304 pages. 2007.

Vol. 4499: Y.Q. Shi (Ed.), Transactions on Data Hiding and Multimedia Security II. IX, 117 pages. 2007.

Vol. 4498: N. Abdennahder, F. Kordon (Eds.), Reliable Software Technologies – Ada Europe 2007. XII, 247 pages. 2007.

Vol. 4497: S.B. Cooper, B. Löwe, A. Sorbi (Eds.), Computation and Logic in the Real World. XVIII, 826 pages. 2007.

Vol. 4496: N.T. Nguyen, A. Grzech, R.J. Howlett, L.C. Jain (Eds.), Agent and Multi-Agent Systems: Technologies and Applications. XXI, 1046 pages. 2007. (Sublibrary LNAI).

Vol. 4495: J. Krogstie, A. Opdahl, G. Sindre (Eds.), Advanced Information Systems Engineering. XVI, 606 pages. 2007.

Vol. 4494: H. Jin, O.F. Rana, Y. Pan, V.K. Prasanna (Eds.), Algorithms and Architectures for Parallel Processing. XIV, 508 pages. 2007.

Vol. 4493: D. Liu, S. Fei, Z. Hou, H. Zhang, C. Sun (Eds.), Advances in Neural Networks – ISNN 2007, Part III. XXVI, 1215 pages. 2007.

Vol. 4492: D. Liu, S. Fei, Z. Hou, H. Zhang, C. Sun (Eds.), Advances in Neural Networks – ISNN 2007, Part II. XXVII, 1321 pages. 2007.

Vol. 4491: D. Liu, S. Fei, Z.-G. Hou, H. Zhang, C. Sun (Eds.), Advances in Neural Networks – ISNN 2007, Part I. LIV, 1365 pages. 2007.

Vol. 4490: Y. Shi, G.D. van Albada, J. Dongarra, P.M.A. Sloot (Eds.), Computational Science – ICCS 2007, Part IV. XXXVII, 1211 pages. 2007.

FSC
www.fsc.org
MIX
Papier aus verantwortungsvollen Quellen
Paper from responsible sources
FSC® C105338

If you have any concerns about our products,
you can contact us on
**ProductSafety@springernature.com**

In case Publisher is established outside the EU,
the EU authorized representative is:
**Springer Nature Customer Service Center GmbH**
**Europaplatz 3, 69115 Heidelberg, Germany**

Printed by Libri Plureos GmbH
in Hamburg, Germany